New American World
A Documentary History of North America to 1612

NEW AMERICAN WORLD

A Documentary History of North America to 1612

IN FIVE VOLUMES

Volume I
America from Concept to Discovery. Early Exploration
of North America.

Volume II
Major Spanish Searches in Eastern North America.
The Franco-Spanish Clash in Florida. The Beginnings
of Spanish Florida.

Volume III
English Plans for North America. The Roanoke Voyages.
New England Ventures.

Volume IV
Newfoundland from Fishery to Colony. Northwest Passage Searches.

Volume V
The Extension of Settlement in Florida, Virginia, and the
Spanish Southwest.

VOLUME V

The Extension of Settlement in Florida, Virginia, and the Spanish Southwest.

Edited, with a Commentary by

DAVID B. QUINN

With the Assistance of

Alison M. Quinn and Susan Hillier

ARNO PRESS
A New York Times Company

and

HECTOR BYE, INC.
New York, 1979

Copyright © David Beers Quinn, Alison Moffat Quinn, 1979

Library of Congress Cataloging in Publication Data
Main entry under title:

The Extension of settlement in Florida, Virginia,
  and the Spanish Southwest.

   (New American world ; v. 5)
    1. Southwest, Old—History—Sources.
2. Florida—History—To 1821—Sources. 3. Virginia
—History—Colonial period, ca. 1600-1775—Sources.
I. Quinn, David Beers. II. Quinn, Alison M.
III. Hillier, Susan.
E101.N47 vol. 5 [F396] 970.01s [976'.01] 78-23466
ISBN 0-405-10764-1

Library of Congress Cataloging in Publication Data
Main entry under title:

New American world.

   Includes bibliographies and indexes.
    1. America—Discovery and exploration—Sources.
2. America—History—To 1810—Sources. I. Quinn,
David Beers. II. Quinn, Alison M. III. Hillier,
Susan.
E101.N47   970.01   77-20483
ISBN 0-405-10759-5

Printed in the United States of America

Contents

Chapter Ninety-two.   Florida, 1586   39

Chapter Ninety-three.   The Emergence of the Franciscan Presence   53

Chapter Ninety-four.   The Search for the English Colony, 1585–1606, and the Exploration of Chesapeake Bay   56

Chapter Ninety-five.   The Uprising of the Guale Indians and Its Suppression, 1597–1598

Chapter Ninety-six.   Plans for Expansion and Proposals for Abandonment of Florida, 1598–1607

Chapter Ninety-seven.   The Spanish Victory over an Anglo-French Expedition

PART XXIII.   THE VIRGINIA COLONY, 1606–1612

Chapter one hundred two.   The Virginia Company: Formal Documents, 1606–1612

Chapter One hundred three.   The Promotional Impulse

Chapter One hundred four.   Early Narratives and Correspondence on Virginia

Chapter One hundred eight.   Juan de Oñate and the Founding of New Mexico, 1595–1609   437

Maps
List of Plates

(Notes on the Maps will precede the plate section in each volume.)

VOLUME V

Preface

FLORIDA, VIRGINIA, and the Spanish Southwest have a certain line of unity running through them. The Florida story (which follows) is one of continuing effort to retain a foothold in the Southeast. True, for a moment, in 1586, only a few groups of soldiers survive Drake's raid and the colony is cut down to two small, struggling garrisons. But it held, always it seemed, the seeds of its own survival (primarily for strategic reasons), even if between 1600 and 1606 the strategic reason seemed less important than it had earlier, when elimination was seriously considered. Florida was saved by the friars and by the English. The former had made enough converts to make it politically embarrassing for the government to retreat so far as to desert Florida altogether. The English came in farther north, just in time to make prestige a reason for holding on. The Virginia story is one of a similar degree of persistence compressed into a much smaller period of time, a mere six years instead of the thirty-eight covered by the Florida story. The mistakes made at Jamestown were legion, and the death roll from natural and unnatural causes was unduly high, but the process of adaptation and readaptation, both in England and in the territory of the colony itself, was so rapid that within the allotted six years the promise was kept. Indeed, after all their mistakes the English might still make effective colonists in America. Finally, in the Southwest, Spain slowly woke up to the need to know at least the contours of the Pacific shore, even if it would not utilize them for any imperial purpose. New Mexico was different. Fray Marcos and Coronado had realized a dream that recurred often enough to lead to a series of New Mexican ventures. The official one, under Oñate, promised too much and produced too little. It was almost as near elimination before 1609 as the Virginia colony was to be at one point in 1610. But coincidentally, just at that time the friars turned the scale there too. The converts could not, in all conscience, be deserted. New Mexico was, after all, to be a continuing Spanish colony: Santa Fe was born in 1610.

San Agustín, Jamestown, Santa Fe, Port Royal, Québec, and Cupids were the six footholds shared equally between the three powers who were to dominate North American history. All were in existence, if not deeply rooted, in 1612.

Introduction

THE THEMES of this concluding volume center on the fact of settlement. The pattern of development is dominated by colonization and attempted colonization rather than discovery and exploration, although both continue. Thus, the emphasis must be on the early attempts of Europeans to settle themselves in the Amerindian's lands, even though this has already appeared as a theme in two preceding volumes. The record is inevitably partial and incomplete. For the point of view of the aboriginal inhabitants of North America, there is no historical documentation whatsoever, and we see the Indian only through white eyes. The invasion of his land and the effrontery of the Europeans in seizing his fishing and hunting grounds and the cleared patches that marked the sites of his recent or current villages—these factors were deeply etched into the consciousness of the indigenous people, but not in ways we can document clearly. Moreover, European missionaries came to change his mental and physical life pattern in new and disruptive ways. We can only attempt to use the creative imagination of the historian to comprehend this in some dim and imperfect manner. We should never forget that this really is the great theme, that the first minor attempts of Europeans to install themselves were, in a very harsh and real sense, the beginning of the end for the Amerindian who had for so long inhabited the great North American continent, and made it his own.

The most striking single development of the later sixteenth century was the endurance of a Spanish colony in Florida, which at times stretched along the modern Georgia coast and into that of South Carolina. Florida, to the Spaniards of the time, was thought of as extending at least to Norumbega (New England) or even to the Bacallaos (Newfoundland). The Spanish colony in Florida in the years 1565 to 1612, in spite of its outstanding significance, is given relatively too small a space in the histories of the beginnings of European enterprise in North America. American history has been read forward from Jamestown or Plymouth or Massachusetts Bay, and has been considered mainly in Anglo-Saxon terms. The period before these seminal place names appear has been thought of primarily as a prelude in which the lines of development that led toward the English settlement could be traced, but where the activity of other Europeans, especially that of the Spaniards, was of minor significance in the broad pattern of historical development that ultimately created the thirteen colonies and the American nation. Since Florida was quiescent for much of the seventeenth century, it impinged to a significant degree on the English colonies only in the eighteenth century. Thus, its existence is scarcely obvious in early Virginia and still less so in early New England.

It was in the sixteenth century that Spanish soldiers, officials, clerics, and a few civilian settlers learned slowly and painfully to come to terms with the conditions of life in North America. Therefore, the history of the Florida colony must form one major theme in several volumes of this collection. It would be easy to fill many volumes with significant material on Florida in this period. The documentation in the Spanish archives, however patchy and incomplete it may be on certain episodes in Florida history, is vastly more extensive than anything we have until the English colonies had been established for many years. Inevitably, much of this material is of a purely routine character. It is concerned with the mechanism of the supply of soldiers and the finding of their means of subsistence from outside Florida; the appointment, inspection, and removal of officials inside the complex network of Spanish imperial administration; routine complaints and reprimands; the special pleadings of officials under consideration for promotion; release from an unrewarding exile in Florida; or recording their quarrels and differences with each other. A multivolume collection might allow a broad spectrum of these materials to be presented. The two installments—all we have been able to give (the first in volume II)—extending to less than half a volume, must be sharply selective. The emphasis tends to be on letters and reports that carry forward the more dramatic episodes in the story, even though they also reveal something of the administrative and supply problems of an isolated and often vulnerable garrison-colony.

It will be clear that the intention in 1565 was to found not merely a chain of garrisons and mission posts in Indian territory, but also to settle substantial civilian populations on North American soil. The failure of the colonization plans within a decade, or little more, is noteworthy. It foreshadows the almost fatally unsuccessful attempts to root Englishmen in Virginia in the early seventeenth century. These episodes raise the complicated question to which we can give no final answer: Why did Europeans take so long to establish themselves, and why did they fail to maintain their cohesion, even their continued existence, when so many of the Spanish colonizing experiments in South and Central America succeeded with (it appeared) little in the way of growing pains or traumatic crises? Part of the answer is that in these parts of the Americas where the Spaniards settled most easily they found indigenous inhabitants who were willing or could be made to work for them. In North America they did not. The Indians proved almost useless as a labor supply. The Spanish settlers were not competent to extend their own efforts sufficiently, so as to supply themselves with enough food for their own needs and to produce something of a surplus for exchange for products they could not grow themselves. Of course, they did not have the advantage of mineral discoveries which, by the aid of slave or semifree labor, had made the Spanish rich in Mexico and Peru. But it is still something of a mystery why so many fell ill, became listless, and were desperately discouraged very soon after they attempted to settle. The documents that follow throw only a few glimpses of light on this major mystery. It is one that will be paid much attention in future by historians who are interested in ecology.

In whatever selection we can make from them, the tales that letters and reports relate are of repeated expansion and repeated contraction. Either military resources fail and missions prove unsuccessful after a period of promise, or colonial communities wither and fade away. This pattern of rise and decay and rebirth is the main theme of Florida history. The second is its functioning as a military and naval listening post for Spain along a coast where its rivals and enemies might (and indeed did) intervene. Sometimes these rivals planned attacks, carried some out, and also experimented (with even less success than Spain itself) in creating colonies well to the north of the effective range of Spanish activity. The final theme is that of the Spanish missions. As we have already seen, the Jesuit story is one of failure and retreat. The Franciscan history is one of slow preparations, a series of advances, dramatic retreats, and then, rather suddenly, an expanding sphere of influence. By the year 1612, this influence has made the Spanish presence one where two garrisons (San Agustín being the only one of any appreciable size, with some of the characteristics of an urban community) are surrounded by a cloud of mission posts that are active, superficially successful at least, in many cases vulnerable. After a longish period of trial and error, they formed an impressive piece of evidence as to Spain's capacity to find some means by which its presence could appear to be justified by its results in altering the indigenous culture and community to conform, at least outwardly, to Christianity, the European religion that Spain regarded as the most prestigious element in its cultural and imperial banner.

Virginia is another story. In one sense the Spanish obsession with Florida is basically military and strategic. In the case of Virginia the keynote was the somewhat utopian theme of a community developing in a territory that had all of the climatic and agricultural advantages of the Mediterranean, thus allowing the cultivation of olives, vines and citrus fruits; in addition it would prove fruitful in pineapples, bananas, and sugar and medicinal plants. The settlers would not have to undergo the fever attacks of the tropics (apart from the more physical threats that a Spanish presence implied). This theme held fast to the imaginations of tough London businessmen, who poured out most of the money to start the first real colony of English settlement outside the British Isles. Virginia grew in the minds of Englishmen out of the accounts of sixteenth-century pioneers, such as Thomas Harriot and Richard Hakluyt, so that it appeared that if Englishmen were to find a place roughly in the same latitude as the Iberian peninsula—or a little farther south—these utopian circumstances would be created if enough effort was brought to bear on their development. Indians there would grow food with which they would feed the settlers until they became established; their native crops could be valuable additions to food crops brought from Europe. A virgin land could supply fine timber; it could contribute equivalents of Baltic-based naval stores; it could even, if stress were laid on profits, start up a timber-based heavy industry, providing products like English glass, pig iron, and potash that would conserve English timber by using American timber instead. Its fish, its wildfowl, and its game would be major assets. That these utopian expectations were not crushed by early misfortunes, were, in fact, even heightened, may be seen by the accounts that William Strachey and John Smith had written by 1612. They stated that the natural resources of Virginia, together with what had been and could be introduced, promised an almost automatic prosperity to any number of Englishmen and Englishwomen who could be brought to face the Atlantic crossing and the unexpectedly high and almost inexplicable death rate, which afflicted the settlement from 1607 onward. Belief in Virginia constituted a main factor in its continuance in the early years. It is in fact a curious hangover, if that is the right word, from the long series of projects displayed in such detail in volume III. Their influence survived and magnified from an era of speculation into a period of action.

In the case of early Virginia, it would be as unwise to ignore this utopianism as it would be to magnify it too greatly. An ideology can sustain a material enterprise only up to a certain point. After all, a settlement was created in Jamestown which produced, quite early, samples of products that appeared to be worth developing and sufficient to justify initial high hopes of prosperity. But in an area of relatively thick Amerindian population, the settlers found that they had less freedom of action than they expected. The Indians were there and could not by any means rapidly be displaced from villages and hunting lands. They helped with corn supplies (although rarely as generously as had been hoped since their economy was not geared to produce a major surplus). They brought in skins, roots, and dyes that were of some potential value. They even succeeded in teaching the Englishmen to grow some corn, although a maize diet does not appear to have suited English stomachs. Nor do they appear to have settled down sufficiently to produce adequate supplies. In the first eighteen months at least, the settlers· could not complain that they were poorly supplied from home, supplies in fact arriving at little more than six-month intervals. What had not been reckoned with was the chronic divisiveness that the governing bodies, which succeeded each other between 1607 and 1610, produced. We shall never have a full story of the extent to which their petty-mindedness and sheer inability to cooperate injured the infant colony. On the other hand, it is difficult for us to appreciate the debilitating effects of the deaths of nearly half of the colonists each year, the wearying task of breaking in newcomers to a harsh routine, and the temptation to sit back and let the more energetic handful get on with the job. What must be conceded, too, is that for well over a year exploration absorbed a good deal of energy. For the first time, explorations upstream into the Piedmont brought a sense of open, unlimited space to Englishmen confronted with an America beyond the coastal plain, but nothing came of proposals to settle there rather than in the river bottoms. Plans to explore and exploit the old Roanoke Island territory also came to very little. What was done well was the slow, careful penetration of each major inlet entering Chesapeake Bay.

This was a major task, and it distracted John Smith and other abler and healthier settlers from constructive work in the immediate vicinity of Jamestown. But it was essential for the settlers to know at least the outlines of the physical context into which they had inserted themselves. Throughout the bay area the great rivers were found to be broken at the Fall Line and to offer, therefore, no long-route travel into the interior except in small boats, or even canoes. Throughout, also, high Amerindian populations were encountered. Densely forested river valleys were broken only by patches of grass or low vegetation where Indian villages had been, or by cornfields and long houses of existing villages. Utopia was clearly not going to have a tabula rasa on which to raise itself.

One striking indication of the fact that even as early as 1608 North American penetration was not at their sole disposal was Smith's encounter with Susquehanna Indians peddling French wares at the head of the bay. Another distracting element was the constant alarms, which reached them from England, of possible Spanish intervention from the south. Even the somewhat farcical comings and goings of Écija and Montijo in 1609 and 1611 caused genuine fear in case they presaged a full-scale Spanish invasion. A result of this was that too much attention was paid to building fortifications against possible Spanish enemies, to the detriment of more productive labor.

For several years the Virginia Company risked the possibility that King James might disavow it in the face of Spanish threats so as to further his own policy of rapprochement with the government of Philip III. In these years, something of the tenacity of the London promoters in keeping the colony supplied went back to their old anti-Spanish sentiments. With Lord Salisbury cautiously keeping the ring between king and merchants, the company held together until Spanish arrogance eventually spurred James into rejecting its claims to monopoly in North America. After 1608 the company could rely on every kind of indirect government aid. The 1609 Virginia Charter mobilized so many different interests behind the colony that it became a truly national venture. Not that this helped it all that much at the receiving end. The new headquarters staff was lost for a year on the way out in 1609 and the colony blundered on (spawning a short-lived new settlement near the falls of the James River), but met such a deadly winter that it almost expired. It seemed that Gates's rescue of the settlers came too late, but Lord De La Warr, with luck as good as that of 1609 had been bad, was able to retrieve the situation. Only during the years 1610–1612 was the colony approaching self-sufficiency in its food supply. However, some contributions from the Indians were still needed. Its produce, too, was largely of low value; timber in general, apart from high quality hardwood, was scarcely worth the carriage. Most of the industrial productions had collapsed; masts, sturgeon, sassafras, deerskins, and the like were scarcely enough to keep the colony going, and were certainly insufficient to enable it to pay its way. However, it was by now a community and was beginning to have some character of its own; Strachey's description of it in 1610 shows it coming to life. But it was still a luxury, not an economic proposition. It might carry on through the contributions of new settlers spending their own capital, or by the profits of sending out indentured laborers, or even by raking in further subscriptions by ever-increasing propaganda campaigns. At the same time, for the sake of prestige it could not be allowed to die. Under the stern Dale regime it was forced to moderate its excesses and get down to producing enough to feed itself and make at least some additional exports. The charter that brought its shareholders into some genuine partnership with the ruling group of merchants in London, and with the colony itself, expressed the expectation that if it did not turn into the utopian money-spinner Smith and Strachey still thought possible, at least it might become a respectable, small offshoot of English influence and territory.

The Spanish Southwest offers a different situation. Here, the coastline was to excite a certain degree of interest once the northern route eastward from the Philippines had been discovered in the 1560s, and the Manila Galleon put into service between Manila and Acapulco in the 1570s. Since eastward-bound vessels often sighted the coast north of Baja California, it was considered, from time to time, that a further survey should be made of the coastline, with some harbors earmarked as possible havens for galleons in distress on the later stages of their long run from the Philippines. But interest was halfhearted. It was not until 1595 that Cermeño was sent up the coast. Little note, however, was taken of his discoveries. The first effective coastal survey, under Vizcaino, was not made until 1602–1603, when charts were constructed and selected harbors particularized. The friars who accompanied the explorers thought the Indians too primitive or too hostile to be worth the effort of conversion. There was no pressure to establish mission colonies.

It was otherwise with New Mexico. As the frontier of New Spain was gradually pushed north, information about the Pueblo Indians continued to trickle south. A few adventurous friars and unscrupulous frontier speculators made illegal forays into the Rio Grande Valley. In the end, alleged missionary prospects and some rumors of precious metals led to the ambitious and official Oñate expedition of 1598. Its formal objective was the conquest, settlement, and missionizing of the Pueblo territories. The land was formally annexed in the name of Spain, and a capital of sorts was set up first in one pueblo and then in another. But Oñate's wide-ranging ambitions, although they led to fresh expeditions to the Plains and even to Coronado's Quivira on the Arkansas River, had little basis on which to found themselves. Only after he finally came back in Mexico in 1607 was the decision made (purely under Franciscan pressure, in the supposed interest of their Pueblo Indian converts) to retrieve the colony and continue it. Nonetheless, the refounding of New Mexico in 1610, along with the establishment of Santa Fe in the same year, was to be definitive. Spain committed itself to maintaining a curious southwestern salient, which retained only rather tenuous links with its parent Mexico.

In comparison, how are we to regard these varied European initiatives? Clearly Spain, claiming as it did the whole of the American continental landmass, could not be wholly unconcerned with the settlement of the territories north and east of its established colonies. Yet, although by 1612 Spain had a long-established colony in Florida through whose mission stations it was reaching out into modern Georgia and the Florida Panhandle, it was committed only to a token presence in eastern North America. After the creation of Jamestown, it was unlikely either to be withdrawn or greatly expanded except under the impetus of some European conflict that had American repercussions. New Mexico was different. It had no strategic or symbolic importance, whatsoever. It was a small luxury conceded to the Franciscan order and was to be supported by a minimal Spanish colony of soldiers and their families. As such it was to last almost unchanged until 1680. Then, after a period of turmoil, it was to be restored before the end of the seventeenth century and was to survive in Spanish hands into the nineteenth century.

England, on the other hand, had every intention of expanding its Virginia colony, although the period after 1610 until 1617 was one of consolidation. Expansion was to begin at an excessive rate in 1618 and was to bring the company down in 1624. Yet, Virginia was a colony of men and women who wished to live in America. All, except indentured servants, had gone voluntarily. If they stayed, company servants became landholders in their own right. Well before the company ended, it could be said that Virginia held within itself (whatever its temporary difficulties) the seeds of ultimate expansion and development as a European community and, moreover, one with a considerable say in its own affairs, not a part of a centralized colonial system like the North American outposts of Spain.

North America's colonies in 1612 were clear intimations that Spain, England, and France had passed the phase of discovery and primary exploration of the coastal lands. All three nations were more or less committed, if on varying bases and strengths, to maintaining groups, or even communities, of their own nationals permanently on North American soil.

Note on Presentation of Materials

SOME INDICATIONS of editorial methods must necessarily be given. We have modernized, except in a very few cases (where explanations are given), usages of "u," "v," "i," and "j." We have kept "yᵉ" although we are well aware that the bastardized thorn it contains annoys linguistic purists. Since we have retained "yt" or "yᵗ" meaning "it," we have expanded on grounds of possible confusion "yᵗ" meaning "that."

From 1582 onward continental dating was ten days ahead of English dating. For French and Spanish documents this must be kept in mind and, also, when relating English documents to continental. Where confusion is likely to arise, double dating has been given.

We have not been afraid to expand contracted words, without indication, in either printed or manuscript sources, except where there is a genuine ambiguity. We have capitalized proper names where we have thought fit to do so. We have added full points to complete sentences and occasionally used either the comma or full point for the slash (/) (where ambiguity might arise from its retention).

Sidenotes are frequent in sixteenth-century published works and less frequently in manuscripts. Usually, they simply form a running index to the contents of the document. Where they do so they have been omitted. But from time to time they either convey additional information or express the point of view of the contemporary editor. In such cases they have been added as footnotes.

Square brackets have been used to fill lacunae conjecturally, although usually with a question mark. They also comprise words or phrases in non-English languages that may not be conveyed clearly in the translation or where the exact words of the document appear important. Occasionally, but only occasionally, they are included to explain a word, or a place name, which otherwise might be wholly unintelligible.

Almost all documents have been printed in full, although where omissions have been made they are indicated in the headnotes. In a few cases where the text was not suitable for transcription in full, abstracts have been made.

For each document or closely associated group of documents bibliographical references have been given. In the case of major sources, of which there have been many editions, this has been expanded in the introduction to the appropriate section. The editors have been generous with their own writing. The introductions to each volume attempt to point to the major characteristics of the selection in that volume and to bring out major comparative points of relationship. Longish introductory passages have been given for main sections where it was felt that headnotes alone might not be sufficient. Subsections have been knit together by brief introductory summaries. Finally, individual headnotes have tried to throw light on the nature of the particular document without trying, however, to summarize its contents in detail. Precise consistency in producing introductory matter of these kinds has not been aimed at or achieved. What assistance appeared to be required for each group of documents was given, rather than attempt to follow a completely consistent plan. Over such a wide range of materials it would be surprising if some discrepancies in treatment, which were not intended, will be observed. A broad measure of uniformity has, it is hoped, been maintained. We believe that, within the terms of our brief, this is the best selection on this scale that we could make. We see many ways in which it could have been improved, but we profoundly believe it will be useful, although it cannot within its scale be definitive. Another generation of editors may perhaps put together on film, after spending unlimited time and money, the complete documentary record of earliest European contacts with America. We hope they do so, but we also wish the users of this present set many interesting and productive hours, reading from a well-printed set of books much of what remains on an endlessly stimulating and engrossing topic.

Abbreviations
Used in the Text

A.G.I., Seville. Archivo General de Indias, Seville

A.G. Simancas. Archivo General de Simancas

B.L. British Library, Reference Division (formerly British Museum Library)

Biggar, H.P. *Precursors of Jacques Cartier*. H.P. Biggar, *The Precursors of Jacques Cartier, 1497–1534*. Publications of the Public Archives of Canada, no. 5. Ottawa, 1911.

Calendar of State Papers, Spanish. (a) *Letters, Despatches and State Papers Relating to the Negotiations Between England and Spain, 1485–1558*. 14 vols., London, 1862–1954; (b) *Letters and State Papers Relating to English Affairs, Preserved Principally in the Archives of Simancas, 1558–1603*. 4 vols. London, 1892–1899.

Colección de documentos inéditos de Indias. *Colección de documentos inéditos relativos al descubrimiento, conquista y colonización de las posesiones Española en América y Oceanía*, edited by Joaquin F. Pacheco, Francisco de Cárdenas, and Luís Torres de Mendoza. 1st series. 42 vols. Madrid, 1864–1889.

Hist. MSS Comm. Historical Manuscripts Commission, *Reports*, London, 1868-.

N.Y.P.L. New York Public Library.

P.R.O. Public Record Office, London.

Quinn, D.B., *Gilbert*. D.B. Quinn, *The Voyages and Colonising Enterprises of Sir Humphrey Gilbert*. 2 vols. London, Hakluyt Society, 1940.

Quinn, D.B., *North American Discovery*. D.B. Quinn, *North American Discovery, c. 1000–1612*. New York, 1971.

Quinn, D.B., *Roanoke Voyages*. D.B. Quinn, *The Roanoke Voyages, 1584–1590*. 2 vols. Cambridge, Eng., Hakluyt Society, 1955.

Taylor, E.G.R., *Hakluyts*. Eva G.R. Taylor, *The Original Writings and Correspondence of the two Richard Hakluyts*. 2 vols. London, Hakluyt Society, 1935.

T.L.S. The Times Literary Supplement. London.

Williamson, J.A., *The Cabot Voyages* (1962). James A. Williamson, *The Cabot Voyages and Bristol Discovery under Henry VII*. Cambridge, Eng., Hakluyt Society, 1962.

Williamson, J.A., *The Voyages of the Cabots* (1929). James A. Williamson, *The Voyages of the Cabots and the English Discovery of North America in the Reigns of Henry VII and Henry VIII*. London, 1929.

VOLUME V

The Extension of Settlement
in Florida, Virginia, and
the Spanish Southwest.

XXI

Spanish Florida II

FLORIDA AS A SPANISH COLONY, 1574–1612

IN MANY RESPECTS, after the death of Pedro Menéndez de Avilés, Florida settled down as a small frontier province. It attracted no new settlers, although in time it lost most of the older ones. Florida was essentially a place where two or three garrisons were maintained, where soldiers were encouraged to bring their wives with them, or to marry Indian girls, so as stabilize the garrison's social basis. But it was subject to crises—either Indian rebellion, or French or English intervention. Moreover, it came to be a testing ground for the Franciscan Order's missionary prowess. Its routine administrative history is thus difficult to illustrate, but its crises stand out and are most sharply illustrated in that which follows.

The years after 1572 indeed were somewhat placid. The supplies brought by the *adelantado* lasted for a time; his newest colonists did not protest against their position at Santa Elena (at least they were not heard to do so) for several years. A series of interim lieutenant governors attempted as far as was possible to maintain stability, and the officials generally tried to divert as much of the *situado* to their own pockets as they could.

With the arrival of Hernando de Miranda as governor in 1576, things began to happen. The settlers and garrison at Santa Elena insisted on being removed, and had to be after the Cusabo Indians almost overran the fort. The last of the genuine colonists drifted off to Cuba or back to

Spain, while the garrison at San Agustín was so dangerously disturbed (it seemed to the governor) that he took what money was in the treasury and returned to Spain. Florida had almost been lost when Menéndez Marqués was sent out to restore the situation. Arriving in July, 1577, with extra troops, he was able to set up a fort again at Santa Elena and restore the morale of the garrisons at San Agustín and San Mateo. Then he learned of a fresh French threat that might have been serious. A French force had built a fort north of Santa Elena, had been driven or tricked out of it by the Indians, but had dispersed in a friendly manner among the tribes, awaiting a chance to attack the Spaniards. An uprising among the Guale Indians held back Spanish counterattacks, but in 1579 Menéndez Marqués took the offensive, using extensive bribery of the Indians as well as force. Most of the French were handed over to him, or captured over a period of time. All but a small handful received the usual reward—death. The years 1577–1580 were marked throughout by fear, energetic response, and final victory for Spain, especially when the bonus of a captured French ship in the St. Johns River in 1580 gave them a fresh batch of prisoners to kill. Florida was living up to its reputation as a graveyard for the French. But the Indians, Cusabo to the north of Santa Elena and the Guale Indians to the south along the coast, were cowed as well. In that atmosphere of repression the first group of Franciscans got their chance. Coming out in 1573 after the Jesuits had left, and being reinforced very gradually, they had something to do with stirring up the Guale Indians in 1577 in reaction to their missionary efforts. When the Indians had been pacified, but not too severely repressed, they began to work to pin the Indians down into villages, to teach them in their own language, to offer them rewards for docility and conformity (at least on the surface) to Christian morality. Thus they began to have their first small successes in conversion.

Menéndez Marqués went in for no new explorations. He was concerned for some years merely to stabilize the position he had established in 1580. Continuing alarms of possible French interventions punctuated the years after 1580, but it was only in 1584 that they began to take concrete form again. It took some time for Menéndez Marqués to discover that it was the English, not the French, who were now becoming active on the coast. The Roanoke voyage of 1584 left some slight repercussions on the Spanish intelligence system. The expedition of 1585, as it loitered in the Caribbean, led to a stream of messages to the Florida governor to guard against an English attack. And although it was known that the English were proposing to colonize, no one knew where they might attempt to do so. Finally, in December, 1585, Menéndez Marqués sent a reconnaissance mission northward but it did not go even as far as Cape Fear, and the whereabouts of the Roanoke colony remained a mystery.

Rumors and news about the Virginia voyage of 1585 were soon overlaid by rumors about Drake. Before Drake reached the Caribbean late in 1585, every post had been warned of possible danger from him. For some five months he sacked and dominated the Caribbean. At the same time Menéndez Marqués planned to defend himself against an English attack and maneuvered to get a field force available with ships to transport it, so that the English colony to the north could be tracked down. At Cartagena, perhaps, Drake heard something of the plans to attack the Roanoke colony. This was one reason why he appeared before San Agustín in May, 1586, wrecked the fort, and forced Menéndez Marqués to withdraw both garrison and populace into the interior to escape total destruction. Had Drake been quicker he might have caught at least part of the Spanish force. As it was, all he could do was destroy San Agustín completely, and leave it a desert for the Spaniards to revive if they could. Surprisingly, the Indians did not massacre the San Agustín inhabitants as the governor had feared. Also surprisingly, Drake allowed San Mateo and Santa Elena to go unscathed so that Menéndez Marqués, helped by timely assistance from Cuba, quickly managed to pull the colony together again. But it was badly shaken, and San Agustín had to be hastily reassembled as a rural camp rather than a as a town.

In 1587 Drake was busy elsewhere, but fresh news came of an English expedition moving through the Caribbean on its way to the settlement to the north. Once again Menéndez Marqués set in motion preparations for a punitive expedition. But, as in 1586, the ship could not make its way into Chesapeake Bay, on the shores of which the governor was convinced the colony was to be found. Only in 1588 was a reconnaissance vessel, under Vicente González, able to explore the Chesapeake. It did so thoroughly, but saw no trace of the English there, although tales of civilized men in the interior, gold, and jewels emerged from conversations and signs with Indian contacts. On the way south, by accident, traces of English occupation were found near what is now Oregon Inlet. At last the location of the English settlement seemed to have been pinned down. By now, however, all Spanish attention was taken up by the great struggle in European waters and by possible diversionary English attacks on the Indies, which could distract the Armada from its task of overpowering England at home. Finally, in 1589 news filtered through of the weak efforts the Roanoke colonies had represented and that the settlers of 1587 were no threat (if they survived at all) to Spanish Florida. In 1590, Menéndez Marqués felt that he had a clear field. With several hundred men he would go north and settle a new Santa Elena (the old had again been abandoned after the Drake raid so that San Agustín could be reinforced) on Chesapeake Bay, thereby denying it to England forever. But permission to do this was countermanded. As his uncle had been in the years 1568–1574, Menéndez Marqués was needed to undertake vital tasks for Spain, to organize the running of the treasure in fast vessels to Europe. This he did with consummate skill and success. When he was asked to go back to Florida in 1593, he said that he could no longer think of doing so.

Florida again seemed to be at a crossroads in the mid-1590s. Franciscans were making a first powerful impact on the Guale Indians and wished to emphasize the missionary prospects of southeastern North America. The direct English threat had receded, so that the garrison remained stable and relatively inactive for years. The question began to be asked whether Spain really needed a foothold in Florida. Wrecks were few; even the English, let alone the French, seemed to think it beneath their notice. From 1595, and for more than a decade, voices were raised to suggest or even to demand that Mexico and the Spanish Crown itself should cease to pay money for a doubtfully useful garrison that had never become the nucleus of an effective colony.

The tenure of the new governor, González Méndez de Canzo, from 1597 to 1602 onward saw the pendulum swing several times. In the first swing, the Indians rebelled against the friars and killed a number of them in islands off the modern Georgia coast; repression, attempted enslavement of the Indians (forbidden by the new king Philip III in 1599), and reinstatement of the missions kept the level of activity high. Méndez de Canzo attempted to raise it higher still by advocating a new policy of expansion. Exciting things were happening in the West where New Mexico was again a center of attention and activity. Why not try to activate the drive to extend Florida? Why not even link it up with New Mexico (at the point when Oñate was talking about a drive to the Atlantic)? These pipe dreams were bolstered by some less fantastic plans. As he understood it, the English were still active on Chesapeake Bay, so he planned to revive the abandoned scheme of 1590 and establish a strong Spanish fort there (which would soon, he thought, make contact with Oñate's men). Then, too, a small expedition had gone into the interior of Georgia and found diamonds or what looked like them, so Tama, as the place was called, became the objective of a new project for the repenetration of the territories behind the coastland. These plans occupied a good part of 1599 and 1600, and Méndez de Canzo remained optimistic that something would come of them. But Philip III was thinking of cutting his commitments in North America, not expanding them. Méndez de Canzo was soon placed on the defensive. The answer came in 1601 that the status quo was to be maintained and there was to be no expansion. The question now turned instead to whether there should be further or total retraction. Memoranda had been accumulating, suggesting that Florida was an unnecessary luxury in the Spanish establishment. Finally, a commission of inquiry arrived to hear evidence at San Agustín concerning what people there felt, and what they would propose.

The inquiry of 1602 produced an interesting cross section of information about Florida. Much of Méndez de Canzo's attempted promotion of the colony was seen to be ill-based. On the other hand, a reasonable number of soldiers and officials and all the friars felt that the colony fulfilled useful functions and should be retained. There was, however, some skepticism expressed. Indeed, the question was bandied around for a further four years, and it was only in 1606 that the Council of the Indies gave a firm opinion in favor of retaining the establishment. By that time the international situation had changed. Peace in Europe had brought no relaxation of tension in North America, but, in fact, the contrary. Pedro de Ibarra, who succeeded Méndez de Canzo in 1603, was an astute and able soldier. He received repeated warnings of renewed French and English initiatives. In 1605 he was successful in destroying an Anglo-French trading and spying expedition at St. Helena Sound, partly because of the unexpected opportunity that gave him the naval forces that could do the principal part of the job for him. Thus, when news reached Florida of English plans to colonize the territory north of Florida (which led to the creation of the Virginia Company in 1606), Ibarra was confirmed in his charge and even given some additional resources. In 1605 Écija failed to find the Lost Colony, hints of which had been given by the crew of the captured ship earlier in the year. Once the news came of the establishment of Jamestown in 1607, however, the Spaniards were in a dilemma. Ibarra and others behind him in Spain were in favor of wiping out the English as soon as possible. Administrative delays and diplomatic complexities in Europe held back decisions, and Ibarra concluded his term of office in 1609 without being able to take any action. His successor, Oliviera, was almost equally inhibited, although he did send out a reconnaissance to the Chesapeake in 1609 (and another was sent directly from Europe in 1611), with little or no effect on the colony. By 1612, Spain had decided to live with the English colonies to the north, even if it would not so admit, just as it was unable to prevent the French from establishing settlements in Canada. The Spanish claim to monopoly in North America, whatever its statesmen might continue to say, was broken at last. This very fact, however, insured the continuance of the Florida colony as a token statement of the Spanish position and as a potential base for a re-advance if circumstances ever favored such a step.

Another transformation was also overtaking Florida. Before 1598, missions formed only a small and not very effective part of Spanish activity. Between 1598 and 1612, especially after 1602, they became a major industry. Every friar who came out took up one of the 300 *plazas* on the establishment, normally available to soldiers and officials only. The soldiers did not like this, and the friars were arrogant about demanding other privileges also. But they were on the winning side, since more and more Indian villages came under their influence on the coast and in the interior of Georgia and even, as a beginning, on the northern base of the western part of the peninsula. In 1606 the visit of the Bishop of Cuba to confirm and baptize marked the new preponderance of the religious over the secular and military elements. Henceforward, the government of Florida was to be a continuing contest between these two forces. Missionary techniques, whatever their limitations in the long run, were at last forming a screen around the residual garrisons at San Agustín and San Mateo (since no attempt was made to revive Santa Elena). In 1612 Florida was still a thinly held outpost of the Spanish empire, but it had a sphere of territorial influence, a small number of garrisons, and an emerging town at San Agustín. Thus it justified its continuance as North America's first and most enduring colonial establishment.

Chapter Ninety-one
Florida, 1574–1586

THIS REALLY falls into two parts; the first is from 1574 to 1577 and the second is from 1577 to 1586. The first is dominated, if it can be said to be dominated, by weak men, typified by Miranda who ran away from his responsibilities. He left a handful of soldiers behind, absconding with the rest and with the civilian settlers of Santa Elena, not to mention a year's pay (the *situado*) amounting to 6,000 ducats. The second period sees the situation retrieved by Menéndez Marqués. Not only does he restore Santa Elena, but he confronts a series of French and Indian challenges and emerges victorious, while at the same time strengthening San Agustín as a place, building up the fort and developing the town. At the end his house, in turn, is brought down by the destructive but not, as it chanced, fatal raid by Sir Francis Drake.

710. [*Circa* 1575]. Memorial of Hernando de Escalante Fontaneda on the Florida Indians.

Fontaneda had served in Florida under Pedro Menéndez de Avilés since the early days of the colony when he was rescued from the Carlos (Calusa) Indians by the adelantado. *The precise circumstances under which he prepared his survey of Florida, or for whom, are not known, but it forms a useful introduction to the period.*

It contains valuable information on the Indians of the southern part of the Florida peninsula, which he knew well, and is less informative on those of the San Agustín and more northerly parts of Florida. Although written after the death of Pedro Menéndez de Avilés, Fontaneda wished to implement his policy of enslaving and deporting the Indians of southern Florida, whom he believed could not be tamed.

First translated by T. Buckingham Smith in A Letter of Hernando de Soto and Memoir of Hernando de Escalante Fontaneda *(Washington, D.C., 1854); here reprinted.*

Very Powerful Lord.

Memoir of the things, the shore, and the Indians of Florida, to describe which, none of the many persons who have coasted that country know how to describe it.

The Islands of Yucayo and of Ahite fall on one side of the Channel of the Vahama. There are no Indians on them, and they lie between Havana and Florida.

There are yet other islands, nearer to the mainland, stretching between the west and east, called the Martires; for the reason that many men have suffered on them, and also because certain rocks rise there from beneath the sea, which, at a distance, look like men in distress. Indians are on these islands, who are of a large size: the women are well proportioned, and have good countenances. There are two Indian towns; in one of them the one town is called Guarugunve, which in Spanish is *pueblo de Llanto*, the town of weeping; the name of the other little town, Cuchiyaga, means the place where there has been suffering.

These Indians have no gold, less silver, and less clothing. They go naked, except only some breech-cloths woven of palm, with which the men cover themselves; the women do the like with certain weeds that grow on trees. These appear like wool, although they are different from it.

The common food is fish, turtle, and snails (all of which are alike fish), and tunny and whale; which is according to what I saw while I was among these Indians. Some eat sea-wolves; not all of them, for there is a distinction between the higher and the lower classes, but the principal persons eat them. There is another fish which we here call *langosta* (lobster), and one like unto a *chapin* (trunk-fish), of which they consume not less than of the former.

On these islands are many deer, and a certain animal that looks like a fox, yet is not, but a different thing from it. It is fat and good to eat. On other islands are very large bears; and, as the islands run from west to east, and the land of Florida passes eastwardly towards these islands, that must be the reason of bears being on them; for the main is near, and they can cross from island to island. But what was a great wonder to the captives who were there, and to those of us in other places, was the existence of deer on the Islands of Cuchiyaga, up to the very town of which I have spoken. Much more would I relate of each of the animals, but that I have other objects which call my attention, and I leave them.

On these islands is likewise a tree we call here *el palo para muchas cosas* [the wood for many uses], well known to physicians; also much fruit of many sorts, which I will not enumerate, as, were I to attempt to do so, I should never be done writing.

To the west of these islands is a great channel, which no pilot dares go through with a large vessel; because, as I have said, of some islands that are on the opposite side towards the sunset, which are without trees, and formed of sand. At some time they have been the foundations of cays, and must have been eaten away by the currents of the sea, which have left them thus bare, smooth and sandy. They are seven leagues in round about, and are called the Islands of the Tortugas; for turtle are there, and many which come at night to lay their eggs in the sand. The animal is of the size of a shield, and has as much flesh as a cow; it is like all kinds of meat, and yet is fish.

Running from south to north between Havana and Florida, the distance to the Tortugas and the Martires there are forty leagues in distance; twenty leagues to the Martires, and thence other twenty to Florida—to the territory of Carlos, a province of Indians, in the language of which signifies a fierce people, as they are called for being brave and skillful, as in truth they are. They are masters of a large district of country, as far as a town they call Guacata, on the Lake of Mayaimi, which is called Mayaimi because it is very large. On the margins are many little villages, which I will name over hereafter. The distance in going from Havana to the farthest islands, which are beyond the Cape of the Martires and almost adjoin Florida, is sixty leagues; because those islands are near seventy leagues in extent, and lie from west to east.

This channel has a variety of passages, and many different outlets and branches. The principal channel is very wide; across it are the Islands of Vermuda, of which I have some idea from what the Indians say; but not wishing to extend this account in that direction, I return to the part of it which treats of the termination of the islands on the north.

The Martires end near a village of Indians called Tequesta, situate on the bank of a river which comes from the interior of the country the distance of fifteen leagues, and issues from another lake of fresh water, which is said by some Indians who have traversed it more than I, to be an arm of the Lake of Mayaimi. On this lake, which lies in the midst of the country, are many towns, although of not more than thirty or forty souls each; and as many more places there are in which people are not so numerous. The inhabitants make bread of roots, which is their common food the greater part of the year; and because of the lake, which rises in some seasons so high that the roots cannot be reached in consequence of the water, they are for some time without eating this bread. Fish is plenty and very good. There is another root, like the truffle of this country, which is sweet; and there are other different roots of many kinds; but when there is game, either deer or birds, they prefer to eat flesh or fowl. I will also mention, that in the rivers of fresh water are infinity of eels, of very high flavor, and enormous trout nearly the size of a man. The eels are the thickness of a thigh, and some of them are smaller. The Indians also eat *lagantos* (alligator), and snakes, and an animal like a rat, which live in the lake, fresh-water tortoises, and many more wild animals which, if we were to continue enumerating, we should never be through.

These Indians occupy a very rocky and a very marshy country. They have no product of mines, or thing that we have in this part of the world. The men go naked, and the women in a short cloak made of a kind of palm-leaf, split and woven. They are subjects of Carlos, and pay him tribute of all the things I have before mentioned, food and roots, the skins of deer, and other articles.

The Auditor Lucas Vasquez, a resident of Santo Domingo, and six others, townsmen of his, I think, left there with vessels, (of which some Indians of the Island of Yeaga, at the end of the Lucayo Islands, give account,) to see the river and land of Santa Elena. Seven leagues to the north of these is a town, which, instead of pronouncing it Orizta, they who went there called it Chicora; and as to the other town, for Guale, they said Gualdape. The Spaniards saw no more towns; for they explored no farther, and did not enter nor examine the coast in earnest, for fear of striking their vessels and getting them lost. Thus they accomplished no more; although it is true that neither gold nor silver is to be got there, as they are to be found only at places remote. It is said, that sixty leagues inland towards the north there are regions of gold and copper; and along the banks of a river, and by lakes, are towns, Otapali, Olagatano, and many others. The inhabitants are neither Chichimecas nor the people of the Jordan. The king is called *mayor y gran Señor* [chief and great lord] in our language; and in that of the Indians of Carlos, it is Zertepe. The cacique is the greatest of the kings, having the renown of Montezuma.

The natives are poor at the place to which Lucas Vasquez and other Spaniards went, although some seed pearls are found there in certain conchs. They eat fish, oysters (roasted or raw), deer, roebuck, and other animals. While they kill these, the women bring wood to roast or to boil with and water in clay pots. If the Spaniards found any gold, it must have come a long way, from the mountains, and from that king of whom I just spoke. The Jordan that is talked of, is a superstition of the Indians of Cuba, which they hold to because it is their creed, not because there is such a river.

Juan Ponz de Leon, giving heed to the tale of the Indians of Cuba and Santo Domingo, went to Florida in search of the River Jordan, that he might have some enterprise on foot, or that he might earn greater fame than he already possessed and close his life,—which is the most probable supposition; or, if not for these objects, then that he might become young from bathing in such a stream. This thought was of itself proof that all must have been fiction that was told by the Indians of Cuba and its whole neighborhood, who, to satisfy their tradition, said that the Jordan was in Florida; to which at least I can say, that while I was a captive there, I bathed in many streams, but to my misfortune I never came upon the river. Anciently, many Indians from Cuba entered the ports of the Province of Carlos in search of it; and the father of King Carlos, whose name was Senquene, stopped those persons, and made a settlement of them, the descendants of whom remain to this day. And the same objects that they who left their country came in quest of in the River Jordan, the kings and caciques of Florida, although savages, took information of and sought after, as though they had been a more polite people, that they might see what river that could be which did such good work, even to the turning of aged men and women back to their youth. So earnestly did they engage in the pursuit, that there remained not a river nor a brook in all Florida, not even lakes and ponds, in which they did not bathe; and to this day they persist in seeking that water, and never are satisfied. In the attainment of the promises of their faith, those of Cuba determined, for such was their vow, to venture their lives on that sea; and it ended in all that numerous people who went over to Carlos forming a settlement: but to this day youth and age find alike that they are mocked, and many have destroyed themselves. It is cause for merriment, that Juan Ponz de Leon went to Florida to find the River Jordan.

We will speak of the country towards Abalachi, which is in the direction of Pánuco, where resounds the fame of its abundance of pearls; and it is certain that they do exist. Between Havalachi and Olagale is a river the Indians call Guasacaesgui, which means in our language, *Rio de Cañas* [river of canes]. On this river, arm of the sea, and coast, are the pearls, which are got in certain oysters and conchs. They are carried to all the provinces and villages of Florida, but principally to

Tocobaja, the nearest town; because in it resides the king, who is chief cacique of the region lying on the right-hand side coming to Havana. He is called Toco-vagachile, has many vassals, and is an independent king. He lives inland on the last cape of the river. There are more than forty leagues of distance, following up the stream, to where Hernando de Soto thought to colonize; but he did not do so, in consequence of his death. When that took place, the intention was abandoned, and the soldiers marched on. The Spaniards, on their way, hung the cacique of Abalachi, because he would not give them provision of maize for the journey; or, as the Indians of the town of Abalachi say, because their cacique had around his neck some large pearls, and in the middle of them a very big one, about the size of an egg of the turtledove—which there are in that country, and have nests in their season on trees—and this is what the Indians state. There are no lands there having either silver or gold, at least the natives do not know of any. Their food is maize and fish; and there is a very great deal of both. They kill a great many deer, antelopes, and other animals, that they eat; but their usual food is fish. They make bread from certain roots, such as I have described before as growing in swamps; and they have fruits of different kinds, which to mention would be endless.

These Indians do not wear clothing, not even the women. They go naked, except some dressed deer-skins made into breech-cloths, with which they only conceal their shame. The females cover themselves about the waist with the straw that grows on trees. This weed is like tow, or wool, but is brown, instead of white.

We will now leave Tocobaga, Abalachi, Olagale, and Mogoso, which are separate kingdoms; and I will name over the villages and towns of the deceased cacique Carlos, who was put to death by sentence of the Captain Reynoso. First, a place called Tampa, a large town, and another town, which is called Tomo; another, Tuchi; and another Soco; another, by the name Ño which signifies town beloved; another, Sinapa; and another, Sinaesta; and another, Metamapo; and another, Sacaspada; and another, Calaobe; and another, Estame; another, Yagua; another, Guevu; another, Muspa; another, Casitoa; another, Tatesta; another, Cayovea; and another, Jutun; another, Tequemapo; and another, with the name of Comachica; also, Quisiyove, and two

other towns of that territory, the names of which I do not recollect, for it has been six years since I came from there. Besides, there are others inland, on the Lake of Mayaimi; and another town, and the first is Cutespa; another, Tavaguemue; another, Tomsobe; another, Enempa, and other twenty towns there are, of which I do not remember the names. There are also two towns more, which are on the Islands of the Yucayos, subject to Carlos, the Indian before mentioned; the one is called Guarungunve, and the other, Cuchiyaga. Carlos, after his father, was lord of these fifty towns, until the time of his execution, as I have said; and now Don Pedro reigns, the son of Sebastián. These two were brought to Havana by Pedro Melendez, that he might gratify them, and he directed that they should be so named; but they became worse than they were before he made them gifts, and still worse would matters have stood had they been christened; but, as I did not wish that they should be, they were not; for, by their conversation, I discovered that baptism was not lawful for them—they were heretics; and since then it appears they have returned to their old ways, and are more wicked than they were formerly.

That people understand the greater part of our strategy, and are archers and men of strength. No one knows that country so well as I know it, who write this; for I was a captive among its inhabitants, from a child the age of thirteen years until I was thirty years old. I speak four languages, but not the language of Ais and Jeaga, which is a country I never travelled into. I wish only to say this more of Carlos,—it has a large population, is rich in pearls, and possesses little gold. The mineral regions of Onagatano are distant on the snowy mountains of Onagatano, who is the farthest vassal of Havalachi and Olagatano, and is far from Olagale, Mogoso, and the people of Cañegacola. These last, the Indians say, are numerous, and are great warriors; they go naked, although some of them are clothed in skins; and they know how to draw, and whatever they see, they paint. They are called Cañogacola, which means a crafty people, skillful with the bow. Notwithstanding these qualities that they have the good arms of the Spaniards will overcome them—good crossbows, firelocks, and shields, swords broad and thick, good horses and escaupiles, with one or two persons who understand their ways, the interpreters being true and trustworthy, not like the Biscayan, who would have sold Pedro Melendez to the Indians had it not been for us, myself and a mulatto, who discovered the treason, otherwise every one must have been slain, and I among the rest.

Pedro Melendez would not then have died in Santander, but in Florida, in the province of Carlos. There is no river nor bay there that can be hidden from me; and had I received the consideration I merit, the Indians at this day would be the vassals of our powerful king Don Felipe, whom God preserve many years! I have already said that the cacique is lord of the River of Canes, where the pearls and lands of lapis lazuli are, and that the gold is afar off in the last dependency and town of Olagale.

One Don Pedro Vizcaíno, whom His Majesty made Keeper of the Swans, was a captive in this province. If he on whom this gift was graciously conferred had been more of a man, the Indians of Ais, Guacata, Jeaga, and their vassals, would already have been subjugated, and even many of them made Christians; but he was a man of little ambition and capacity, so it is useless to have vain regrets. He understands well the language of Ais, and the languages of the other places mentioned, which are spoken as far as Mayaca and Mayajuaca, parts over against them toward the north; but I think that because of the order of Pedro Melendez to hang him, in consequence of a falsehood that he raised against him and Domingo Ruiz, his companion, he was frightened, and came to Spain with the news about Florida, and would not go back again. If he did go back, it must have been to bring with him a son he had among the Indians, as he brought him here and never went there more. And because of the unjust treatment to the interpreters, he desired not to go back, as others of us have not, remaining as we are without pay to this time; for, as we came destitute, it gave us little wish of returning to Florida to serve without any recompense.

The King of Ais and the King of Jeaga are poor Indians, as respects the earth; for there are no lands of silver or of gold where they are; and, in short, they are rich only by the sea, from the many vessels that have been lost well laden with these metals, as was the case with the transport in which Farfan and the mulatto owner were; with the vessel of the Vizcaíno, in which came Anton Granado, who was a passenger, and was captured; and with the vessel of which Juan Christóval was master and captain, lost in the year 1551, when the Indians murdered Don Martin de Guzmán, the Captain Hernando de Andino, Procurador of the Province of Popayán, and Juan Ortiz de Zárate, Distributor of Santa Martha; and there came in her also two sons of Alonzo de Mena, with an uncle, all of them rich. He that brought least was I, but with all I brought twenty-five thousand dollars in pure gold; for my father and mother remained in Carthagena, where they were *comenderos*, and served His Majesty in those parts of Peru, and afterwards in the city of Carthagena, where they settled, and I and a brother were born. Thence they sent us to Spain to be educated; when we were wrecked on Florida, as I have stated.

Other vessels have been lost, among them the armada of New Spain, of which it was said the son of Pedro Melendez was General, for the Indians took a Spaniard that reached the shore whom they found famishing, and I afterwards saw him; also one Juan Rodriguez, a native of Nicaragua. He told us that he came from New Spain, and was going to Castile; that the General was a son of Pedro Melendez, the Asturian; that he came as a sailor in another vessel; and that the people of neither knew any thing of what had befallen the other, until the Indians armed themselves to go to the coast of Ais, when he saw them go and return with great wealth, in bars of silver and gold, and bags of reals, and much clothing. As he was newly captured, or found, and understood not the Indians, I and Juan Rodriguez were the interpreters for this man, and others, as we already knew the language. It was a consolation, though a sad one, for those who were lost after us to find on shore Christian companions who could share their trials and help them to understand those brutes. Many Spaniards have saved their lives by finding before them those associates. For the natives who took them would order them to dance and sing; and as they were not understood, and the Indians themselves are very artful, (for the most so of any are the people of Florida,) they thought the Christians were obstinate, and unwilling to do so. And so they would kill them, and report to their cacique that for their craft and disobedience they had been slain, because they would not do as they were told; which was the answer, as I have said, made to the cacique when he would ask why they had killed them. One day, I, a negro, and two others, Spaniards recently made captives, being present, the cacique, in conversation with his vassals and the great chiefs of his train about what I have just mentioned, asked me, I being *mas ladino* (better acquainted with the language than any one), saying: "Escalante, tell us the truth, for you well know that I like you much: When we require these, your companions, to dance and sing, and do other things, why are they so dissembling and obstinate that they will not? or is it that they do not fear death, or will not yield to a people unlike them in their customs? Answer me; and if you do not know the reason, ask it of those newly taken, who for their own fault are prisoners now, a people whom once we held to be gods come down from the sky." And I, answering my lord and master, told him the truth: "Sir, as I understand it, they are not contrary, nor do they behave badly on purpose but it is because they cannot comprehend you, which they earnestly strive to do." He said it was not true; that often he would command them to do things, and sometimes they would obey him, and at others they would not, however much they might be told. I said to him: "With all that, my lord, they do not intentionally behave amiss, nor for perversity, but from not understanding. Speak to them, that I may be a witness, and likewise this your freedman." And the cacique, laughing, said: "Se-le-te-ga," to the new comers; and they asked what it was he said to them. The negro, who was near to them, laughed, and said to the cacique: "Master, I will tell you the truth; they have not understood, and they ask Escalante what it is you say, and he does not wish to tell them until you command him." Then the cacique believed the truth, and said to me: "Declare it to them, Escalante; for now do I really believe you." I made known to them the meaning of Se-le-tega, which is, "Run to the look-out, see if there be any people coming;" they of Florida abbreviate their words more than we. The cacique, discovering the truth, said to his vassals, that when they should find Christians thus cast away, and take them, they must require them to do nothing without giving notice, that one might go to them who should understand their language. And so it happened, that the man just spoken of, who was called Pijiguini, was the first found after that. In our tongue his name was Martinez, a sailor, as before stated, who came from Mexico in the flota that was lost.

Leaving this matter aside, I desire to speak of the riches found by the Indians of Ais, which perhaps were as much as a million dollars, or over, in bars of silver, in gold, and in articles of jewelry made by the hands of Mexican Indians, which the passengers were bringing with them. These things Carlos divided with the caciques of Ais, Jeaga, Guacata, Mayajuaci, and Mayaca, and he took what appeared to him well, or the best part. These vessels, and the wreck of the others mentioned, and of caravels, with the substance of the Indians of Cuba and Honduras who were lost while in search of the River Jordan, and who came well off, were taken by Carlos, and by the chiefs of Ais and Jeaga. The Indians of the Islands of Guarumgunve are rich; but, in the way that I have stated, from the sea, not from the land. From Tocovaja to Santa Elena, which may comprise a shore of six hundred leagues, there is neither gold nor silver native to the country, and only that of which I have spoken as coming by the sea. The land is abundant in pasturage; but it is not worthwhile for me to say whether there is any fit for settlement or not, since the Indians can live on it; nor yet for the planting of sugar-cane, as I do not know it positively, although some stalks were set out which grew; but as I was not afterwards present, I did not see the result.

In all these provinces which I have named, from Tocovaja-chile to Santa Elena, the people are great anglers, and at no time lack fresh fish. They are great bowmen, and very faithless. I hold it certain they never will be at peace, and less will they become Christians. I will sign this assertion with my name as a very sure thing, for I know what I say. If my counsel be not heeded, there will be trouble, and matters be worse than they were beforetime. Let the Indians be taken in hand gently, inviting them to peace; then putting them under deck, husbands and wives together, sell them among the Islands, and even upon Terra-Firma for money, as some old nobles of Spain buy vassals of the king. In this way, there could be management of them, and their number become thinned. This I say would be true policy; and the Spaniards might then make some stock-farms for the breeding of cattle, and be there to assist the many vessels that are wrecked all the way along from Carlos to the Province of Sotoriva, in which is the port of San Agustin, and river of San Mateo. There the Lutherans of France had made a fort, and found a nook whence to plunder as many ships as should come from Terra-Firma, whether from Mexico, or Peru, or from other parts; which they did, and retired to that river of San Mateo, where resides the perfidious cacique of Sotoriva, Alimacani, and of other places, his dependencies. Midway up the river San Mateo, sixty leagues inland, is another cacique, having an independent sovereignty, and being seignor of his land, whose name is Utina; and Saravay, and Moloa, and many others are his vassals, until coming to Nayaguaca, in the land of Ais, which lies towards Cañaveral, so called by our pilots who sail thither. With these two caciques Pedro Melendez made treaties of friendship. They have no gold, silver, or pearls; their people are poor, very cunning and false, and great archers. They go naked, like the rest of whom I have spoken before.

By way of this River San Mateo, one may go to Tocobaga, on the other side of Florida, to the west; I do not mean all the way by the river, but in this manner: Enter over the bar of the San Mateo, and arrive at Zaravay, which is fifty or sixty leagues in the interior up the river, or at the Province of Utina, and there disembark, keeping a westerly course from town to town, until coming upon the people of Cañogacola, subjects of Tocovaja; and thence upon the country of Tocovaja itself, which lies within on another large river, where Soto was, and where he died.

With this I will end, and say no more; for, if the conquest of that country were about to be undertaken, I would give no further account of it than I have rendered. Its subjugation is befitting His Majesty, for the security of his armadas that go to Peru, New Spain, and other parts of the Indies, which pass, of necessity, along that shore and channel of the Vahama, where many vessels are wrecked, and many persons killed; for the Indians are powerful archers, and oppose them: and because of this, I say, it is well to have a small fort for the protection of that channel, with some income for its repair, and the maintenance of soldiers as a garrison in it, that might be drawn from Mexico, Peru, the Island of Cuba, and all the rest of the Indies. Thus much should be done; and another thing also—to go in search of pearls, for there is no other wealth in that country. So, I conclude, and as this account may become important, I sign it.

Hernando Descalante Fontaneda.

Appendix of notes by Escalante

[a] Columbus discovered the Islands of Yucayo and Achiti; a part of Florida was discovered by other persons, residents of Santo Domingo.

The islands of the Lucayos are made up of three groups, in this wise: First, the islands of the Bahama; second, the islands of the Organos; third, the islands of the Martires, which are adjacent on the west to certain cayos (keys), the Tortugas, formed of sand, and for this reason are not to be seen from a distance, so that many vessels are lost all along the coasts of the Bahama Channel and on the islands of the Tortugas and the Martires.

Havana is towards the south; Florida is towards the north; and in going from the shore of Havana, Island of Cuba, to the mainland, are these islands of the Bahama and the Organos, and the islands of the Martires and the Tertugas. There is a wide channel at the narrowest part, of twenty leagues, between the Havana and the Martires; and thence to Florida there are fourteen leagues; between the islands that lie towards Spain, or rather towards the east, and by the widest part of this passage from them towards the west, there are forty leagues of distance. Many shoals and deep channels exist among them; but there is no passage for ships, or even for brigs, although they are smaller; there are passage-ways for nothing larger than canoes, and those are to the east and northeast. To the westward, to come from Havana and go to Florida, there is a passage; but none to come to Spain, except by the principal channel of Bahama, which is between the Martires and the Havana, the islands of the Yucayos and the Point of Cañaberal; and no other way can be found to make the distance shorter. To bring the course more direct, it might be made through the middle of Florida; but not with vessels only, but by sea and land, through the wide River of Tocobaga to the River San Mateo, the vessels relieving each other on one and the other side to come to Spain.

[b] I will next state generally some things of Florida, and of a river that is called Jordan, in its northern part. We will also speak of that portion of it to the west, where Hernando de Soto died, and Captain Salinas, and also Francisco de Reinoso, and where certain friars were lost, and others made prisoners, some of whom I afterwards saw alive and in captivity. We will then go on to describe the habits, food, and clothes of the Indians of Abalachi, and Mogoso, and other places below it, which are Tocobaga, Osiquevede, Carlos, Ais, and Sonsobe; and of many others will I speak, though not of all. Of each subject I will treat apart, under a separate head; and to begin, I will put forth the foregoing heading concerning the islands of the Lucayos and the Martires, dwelling-places of the Indians.

[c] The men of Abalachi go naked, and the women have waistbands of the straw that grows from trees, which is like wool, of which I shall give some account later on; and they eat deer, foxes, woolly cattle, and many other animals. They collect certain tributes of base gold, mixed with fine, and many colored buckskins. In a river belonging to this people are pearls, which have been noticed. They are archers; but by sending cloth to them, by an experienced and capable linguist, their friendship may be easily won. They are the best Indians in Florida; superior to those of Tocobaga, Carlos, Ais, Tegesta, and the other countries I have spoken of in their succession, as far as the river called Jordan, and of which I have hereinbefore correctly set forth every thing concerning them.

The people of Abalachi are subject to those of Olagale and Mogoso, and others towards the region of the ridge of Aite, who are the most wealthy Indians, and the places they occupy are of the most value. I was two years among them, in search of base gold mixed with fine; but on all the coast of which I shall speak hereafter in this memorial, there is no base gold to be found, much less any pure; for that which the natives have is from the vessels which are wrecked in passing from New Spain and Peru, when storms overtake them in the Channel of the Bahama, and drive them on Cañaberal, or on the Martires—of which the *Cabo de Martires* is called Chichijaga—as far down as the Tertugas, which are opposite to them, and the Havana is also on the south.

[d] And the character of every thing, and the substance of all, I have herein set forth: but I have not mentioned all the places; for they have a variety of names, which I cannot remember. And with so much I pause.

FLORIDA, 1574–1577

DIEGO DE VELASCO, who was lieutenant governor (1574–1576), left few records. Florida, if not settled, was at least fairly quiet, even though sores were festering beneath the surface.

When finally it was decided that there should be a new governor and that he should be Hernando de Miranda, son-in-law of Pedro Menéndez de Avilés, a poor choice was made. Miranda arrived at San Agustín early in 1576. By that time, complaints were coming thick and fast from Santa Elena. In 1573, the settlers had already made known their plight in Spain (353), but nothing had been done for them. Now, when Miranda visited Santa Elena in late February, 1576, they were in a state bordering on revolt. Miranda listened and went away (711). Before he left he set an Indian uprising in motion by proposing that the garrison put pressure on the Indians to cease attacks on the settlers' cattle and force the Indians to supply the garrison with corn. An attempt to do this resulted in the killing of a Spanish force and an Indian uprising. This spread and soon settlers were cooped up in the fort under siege. But Miranda came in time to rescue them nearly 300 in all. This represented a complete abandonment not only of a military outpost but of the only sustained attempt at agricultural settlement by Spaniards in North America so far. The settlers were brought to San Agustín and then to Havana, where most of them settled. At the *presidio* the situation was also uneasy. There were no means of quelling the Indian rebellion which was spreading southward. Miranda could not inspire his men at San Agustín; he could only steal from them. At the end of 1576 he took the annual *situado* of 6,000 ducats and returned to Spain, where he soon found himself treated as the weak criminal he was.

711. February 27, 1576. Santa Elena settlers complain of their condition.

A.G.I., Seville, Santo Domingo 231; 54/5/16; 12; printed and translated in J. T. Connor, Colonial Records, *I 146–151.*

[a] In the city of Santa Elena, on the twenty-seventh day of the month of February, in the year seventy-six, the very Illustrious Señor Hernando de Miranda, Governor and Captain-General of these provinces of Florida for his Majesty, and Adelantado thereof, said—the other settlers being assembled in the *cabildo* of this said city—that he wished to know which of the colonists wanted to remain to settle these provinces of Florida: wherefore he ordered us to assemble, and those who wished to depart from this land of Florida were to say so, and put it in writing, the name of each one being mentioned so that he could give a report and information thereof to his Majesty, in order to see how many were those who wished to go, and how many were those who wished to remain. Wherefore we came together, and a general *cabildo* took place of the *justicia* and *regimiento*, with all the other settlers who at present reside in this city: Diego Hernandes, the *Alcalde Ordinario;* Gonzalo Sanches, Gonzalo Martin, *Regidores;* Francisco Ruyz, a settler; Juan Serrano, Alonso del Olmo Sequeda, for settling the land; Gonzalo Domingues, Sebastian Rodriguez, Diego Dias, Bernabe de Olivares, Francisco Martin Cunplido, Diego Garçia, Pedro Dias, Diego Martin, Juan Biexo, Alonso Garçia, Cristóval Gordillo, Alonso Martin, *Procurador;* Andres Gonsales, Pedro Gomes, Juan Sanches, soldier and married; Francisco Ruyz, soldier and married; Domingo de León, Rodrigo Menea, Juan Mordasso, Blas Hernandes, soldier and married; Maria Estevan, a widow; Guiteria Gonçales. I, the said notary, certify that all the aforesaid assembled at the *cabildo* which took place, in order to see which of them wanted to go to Spain, or wherever his Majesty might command.

Before me, Gonzalo Lopes, notary.

[b] We, assembled and met together, the *cabildo, justicia* and *regimiento*, say that we, with the others mentioned above, were enlisted in Spain before Blas de Merlo, Doctor Sayas and Gonzalo de la Rocha, captains appointed by the Adelantado, Pedro Menéndez de Avillés, by virtue of a royal ordinance, wherein many perquisites were promised to all those who should come to settle these provinces, as is set forth more at length in the said ordinance: giving us all manner of cattle, twelve head with the bull; establishing us on good soil, and giving us allotments of lands for farming and raising cattle. And nothing of all this has been fulfilled to us, unless it be to keep us on an island surrounded by sea water, which is one league long and half a league wide, more or less; the larger part of which island, at every period of spring tides, is overflowed by the sea; and the land is of the kind aforesaid, and we have no other assistance save our own arms, although by doing some hoeing we have broken up a little land which we sow with maize to sustain our children; because the soil is not of the quality for sowing any other sort of [grain for] bread, as a little wheat and barley has been planted here by hoeing and after having headed badly, there is nothing to it but the husk. Besides which, even if the soil were rich and fertile, it has not the [right] climate nor is the earth ever dry, unless it be with the frosts and extreme cold caused therein by the winter, which comes in December and January; for in the months of April and May, when the [grain for] bread ripens in this island, it does nothing but rain all that time, which is when we are sowing and gathering the maize; and so we have suffered and do suffer great hardships, as the harvest is small which we gather therefrom

with excessive labor; because the agreement with us has not been carried out, as has been said. Therefore we have wasted all our means, with which, and with other things, we came well supplied, having been farmers in Spain, where we had all manner of cattle wherewith to work; and so here we feel ourselves lost, and old, and weary, and full of sickness. Even though some of the settlers themselves have brought cattle, it has not been possible to increase or preserve it save at great cost, in feeding them from the little maize we gather; and because of all the aforesaid, we say, as we have said, that we have grown useless, old, tired and sick, and have been ill-treated and insulted by the governors who have governed, and so we say that we, on account of the reasons already given, are not for settling [here]. We therefore beg and request your Honor, one, two and three times, and all the [times] that by law we must, to order permission given to us and a ship to depart from this land, whither his Majesty shall best see opportunity and be most pleased [to send us], outside these provinces, where we can make up for our past losses and hardships; on which petition we submit to your Honor, we are ready to give your Honor evidence; and so we beg that it be produced and given by soldiers and settlers, and that once the said evidence has been given, you order that a copy thereof be given to us, in order that we may show it and appeal before his Majesty, or before his Royal Council of the Indies, or before whomsoever legally shall know our right; wherefore, etc. We likewise request this as an attestation from the present notary, and let the persons present be witnesses.

[Signed:] Alonso Martin.

[c] When his Honor saw this wish and desire of the said settlers not to remain in the country, he said that he charged them on their conscience that they should, in all Christianity and rectitude, and not in untruth and deceit, make their report as best they could before the *alcaldes ordinarios*, as to what they have seen of this country and what they know by experience thereof, in order that the said report be taken to his Majesty. Likewise his Honor wished to make another report through people of credit and reliability, who have been inland, to give a relation to his Majesty as to what the land is, and whether one can till and cultivate it; and his Honor asks that all Christianity be

observed in this, and consideration for what touches the service of God Our Lord and of his Majesty, and the good and conversion of the Indians.

Before me, Gonzalo Lopes, notary.

In this city of Santa Elena, on the ninth day of the month of March of the year seventy-six, Alonso Martin, Procurador General, presented this petition before the very Illustrious Señor Hernando de Miranda, Governor and Captain-General of these provinces of Florida, in the presence of me, the notary, and of witnesses.

[d]   Very Illustrious Señor.

I, Alonso Martin, *Procurador General* of the city of Santa Elena, appear before your Honor, and say that inasmuch as it befits my right to make a report so as to present it before his Majesty or his Royal Council, for the making whereof I asked your Honor's permission, and your Honor ordered that the said report should be made before the *Alcalde Ordinario* of this city; and [inasmuch as] the notary who fills at present the office of notary public is very young, and not accustomed to the office aforesaid, nor of the age the law directs: I ask therefore that your Honor name a notary public in order that all the depositions and necessary writs may pass before him, so that they may be binding and effective; and this I beg and entreat of your Honor, and if need be, I require it. If you should not appoint him, I shall ask the *cabildo* of this city to name him: wherefore, etc.; and I ask for justice and attestation.

When the said petition had been put into writing, he said that he had declared and asked for what was therein contained. His Honor, the Señor Governor, having examined that which was asked by the said Alonso Martin, *Procurador*, said that he was ordering and did order to appear before him the said Domingo de León, who has been notary in this said city, whom the said Governor ordered to accept and fill the office of assistant notary to me, the said notary; from whom he took and received an oath in due form of law, that he will be present when the witnesses are sworn, and will help in administering the oath to them, without having therein any deception or fraud; and he so ordered and provided, and signed it with his signature: witnesses, Diego Enriques, notary, and Francisco Ruys; and then the said Domingo Gonçalez de León, who was present, said that he accepted what his Honor commanded: witnesses, the aforesaid.

This petition was presented before the Señor Alcalde, Diego Hernandes, Alcalde Ordinario, on the ninth day of the month of March of the year seventy-six, in the presence of me, Gonzalo Lopes, notary, and of witnesses.

712. January 10, 1577. Report of the Indian uprising which led to the loss of Santa Elena.

A.G.I., Seville, Santo Domingo 224; printed and translated in J. T. Connor, Colonial Records, *I, 192–203.*

[a] This is a copy, well and faithfully taken, of a report which the very Illustrious Señor, Don Cristóval de Erraso, Knight of the Order of Santiago, Captain-General for his Majesty of the royal armada for the protection of the Indies, caused to be made concerning the uprising of the Indians of the province of Florida, and the capture of the fort of Santa Elena; the tenor whereof is as follows:

In the town of La Yaguana, of the island of Hispaniola, on the nineteenth day of the month of January, in the year one thousand five hundred and seventy-seven, the very Illustrious Señor, Don Cristóval de Erasso, Knight of the Order of Santiago, Captain-General for his Majesty of the royal armada for the protection of the Indies, said that inasmuch as he received tidings, by a letter which the President of the Royal Audiencia of Santo Domingo wrote to his lordship, that the Indians of the province of Florida had risen in rebellion, and seized and burned the fort of Santa Elena and killed thirty or more persons who were therein; and inasmuch as there has now arrived in this town a boat from Havana, wherein have come persons who have been in the said Florida, and know the manner in which the said uprising took place, the death of the said soldiers and the capture of the said fort: therefore, as he wishes to investigate this, to give notice thereof to his Majesty: before me, the aforesaid notary, he made the following report.

[Signed:] Don XPoual Erasso.

[b] And immediately thereupon, on the said day, in the aforesaid month and year, for the investigation of the aforesaid, his lordship commanded to appear before him Pedro Gomes, a sailor of the boat named *Nuestro Señor de la Ayuda,* whereof Juan Diz is master; and he said that he is a native of Villa de Conde, in Portugal; from whom was taken and received an oath in the name of God Our Lord, and he made the sign of the cross with his right hand in due form, which he did thoroughly, and promised to tell the truth. And being questioned in conformity with the heading of this report, he said that he has tidings of the province of Florida, and that what he knows and what has happened is that it is about four months since this witness came on the said boat from the said province, where he had been another four months, more or less; that when, about eight months ago, the said boat arrived in Florida, near the fort of Santa Elena, where they anchored, they learned how Ensign Moyano, with twenty-one soldiers, had gone to a pueblo of Indians they call Oristan, to seek food; and within two or three days of the arrival of the said boat, this witness saw how a soldier whom they call Calderon, of those who had gone with the said Ensign Moyano, came to the said fort and told the people therein, who might have numbered thirty men, without counting the women and children, how the said Ensign Moyano had asked Cacique Oristan and other caciques, who were in [the midst of] a certain feast they hold, that they give him some food for his soldiers. They answered that they had none to give him, and then the said Ensign had drawn his sword, and gone to where the said Indians had their kettles and victuals, and had taken them from them; seeing which, the said Indians had gathered their women and children and gone to the woods; and when the soldiers warned the Ensign that they should return to the fort, that it did not appear safe to them that the said Indians had gone to the woods, the said Ensign replied that they should be silent; that he had to remain there; he jeered at them, and stayed there with the said soldiers, with the fuses of their arquebuses lighted. After this came an old cacique who spoke with the said Ensign, asking him what he did there, whether he wished to make war on the Indians, and for what reason he had made them go to the woods; and the said Ensign had answered him that he did not come to

make war, but to lodge himself with them and ask them for food: that they themselves had chosen to go to the woods; and the said cacique had replied to him: "Then, why dost thou keep the fuses lighted, [if] thou wishest them to return? Put out the fuses!" So the said Ensign had ordered that the fuses should be extinguished; and when the said cacique saw that they were out, he gave a shout, and then the said Indians came forth and slew them all, and that he [Calderon] had fled out of the way. Two or three days after this occurred, this witness saw them come to attack the island; and when a soldier went to attend to some hogs, he never came back again.

At that time, when Governor [=Treasurer] Pero Menéndez [the Younger], Factor Otalora, and Ensign Moreno, the [Assistant] Accountant, and three or four others who were soldiers, for there were nine altogether, had distributed the pay to the people at the fort of San Agustín, and were going in a shallop to the said fort of Santa Elena to pay the people there, carrying his Majesty's money on another vessel, a large one, they travelled by the inland waterway, and near a village they call Guale they stopped to talk with the Indians. One of them, who was the cacique, told them that they should land, and eat and rest themselves... and they did so: and the moment they landed, the Indians of the said village killed them all, for of the said nine persons not one was left alive; and his Majesty's silver remained in the ship without receiving any harm. And after this the said Indians slew nine others, soldiers from the said fort of Santa Elena.

And then the next day after they had killed these soldiers, more than five hundred Indians came to attack the fort, to take by surprise those who were therein; whereupon the General of the said Florida, whom they call Hernando de Miranda, who had been to Havana to arrange for the pay for the people of the said forts, and was [then] in the said fort of Santa Elena, ordered the master of the boat on which was this witness to go to the said fort of San Agustín, to give news of what was happening. And so he went, and gave tidings of what had occurred at Santa Elena, and afterward they returned to the said fort of Santa Elena, which they found up in arms because of the attacks that the said Indians had made upon it. And thereupon the said General, seeing that the said fort was propped up, ready to fall, and that the soldiers had no munitions, ordered that they abandon it, and that all his company should get into three boats which were there, with the vessel which had brought the money; and so immediately all their belongings were put on board, and after them all the people of the said fort embarked, likewise the said General, and they went to the fort of San Agustín. Four pieces of bronze artillery remained in the said fort of Santa Elena, and two others which the Spaniards had buried at the old fort. As soon as the said General and the people from the said fort had embarked, and crossed the bar, they were delayed two or three days, awaiting favorable weather; and they saw many Indians set upon the said fort, and burn all the houses thereof, and they saw them burning. And thereupon, when they had good weather they went to the said fort of San Agustín, where the said General remained, [and] Gutierre de Miranda, with two other captains, of whom they call one De Junco, and the other, Quiros. This is what he knows and what occurred in this case, under the oath he has taken; and [he said] that he is twenty years of age, and he did not sign because he knows not how.

[Signed:] Don X Poual de Eraso.
Before me, Pedro de Rada, notary.

[c] Witness. On the said day, in the aforesaid year, his lordship caused to appear before him, for the investigation of the aforesaid, Domingo Martin, a sailor of the boat called *Nuestra Señora de la Luz;* Captain, Juan Guillen; and he said that he is a native of the town of Avero, in Portugal; from whom was taken and received an oath in legal form, according to the aforesaid. And being questioned in conformity with the heading of this report, he said that he has knowledge of the province of Florida and the forts of Santa Elena and San Agustín, which are therein, because he has seen them and been there; and that what he knows, and what is occuring, is that this witness having gone in a boat from Havana to the said Florida, with meat and other supplies from his Majesty for the people of the said forts; and having arrived in the said boat at the said fort of Santa Elena, and anchored there, as it seems to him in the month of July or August; when this witness arrived, he found the men of the said fort

and the women all gathered therein and in arms, because the Indians one month previous had slain Ensign Moyano and twenty soldiers with him; and that the occasion of their killing them, as those of the said fort declared, was that the said Ensign with the others had gone to a pueblo they call Oristan, where they had found Cacique Oristan and other caciques who were holding a certain feast, whom they asked to give them something to eat. That the said caciques or Indians had answered, [inquiring] how it was that they came in that manner, with their fuses lighted: they must extinguish them if they wished to be given what they asked; that the said Ensign had told the said soldiers to do this: that he alone was sufficient for those Indians; and that as soon as they had extinguished them, the Indians had sprung upon them and killed them all, except one sailor who had escaped through the forest, and come to the fort to give notice thereof. That within a month of the arrival of this witness at the said fort of Santa Elena, there came news of how the Indians had slain Pero Menéndez [the Younger], Governor [sic] of the said forts, likewise his Majesty's Factor and Treasurer, who were on their way from the fort of San Agustín to pay the men who were in the said fort of Santa Elena. And it was said that the manner in which they killed them was that the aforesaid were coming in a shallop by the inland waterway, with five or six other persons, nine altogether, it was said, to the said fort of Santa Elena, for the aforesaid purpose, bringing the King's money on board a vessel; that on arriving at a village they call Guale, they had stopped to speak with the Indians, and a cacique had told them they should land, and eat, and rest themselves; and that when they landed, the Indians killed all nine of them, not one remaining. At the same time that this happened, this witness being at the said fort of Santa Elena, the son of a resident of the fort they called Rodrigo Menca, was missing, for his father had sent him to look after some hogs, and he never returned. The General of the said Florida, whom they called Hernando de Miranda, ordered a captain they called Diego de Solis, to set out with nine soldiers to learn about the said youth, [and] ascertain if there were Indians on the island. He went forth in the morning, before sunrise, and within two or three hours the men at the said fort heard ar-quebuse shots, and they at once said and suspected that the said Captain and those who went with him had been slain by Indians, and the said suspicion was confirmed, because it afterward appeared that they had all been killed, not one being left alive. Then the next day, this witness being in the said fort, a great number of Indians came upon it, and began to shoot many arrows at those within, to which they replied with the artillery and arquebuses. This may have lasted about two hours or more, and because the Indians' arrows gave out, they fled. Two or three days after this happened, the women at the said fort pestered the said General with great weeping and wailing, telling him that they were left alone, that their husbands had been killed, that he must take them away from there; and as the said General would not do so, they seized him, took him by force, and put him on board [one of] two boats and one vessel which were there. When the said General saw this, and that in the said fort there were no more than fifteen or twenty soldiers, all young boys, he commanded that they should embark with their belongings, in the said ship and two boats, and so they all did; and while they awaited good weather, having crossed the bar, they saw how a great number of Indians attacked the said fort, and set fire thereto, and from the ships they saw the houses burning. This witness does not recollect what artillery remained in the said fort, further than that he knows they were bronze pieces, which the Spaniards buried before they departed, and this witness saw that: and so they went to the said fort of San Agustín, wherein all the said people remained, likewise the said General Hernando de Miranda. He presently went to Spain in a vessel which was there, which had come with supplies; and he left there in his place as general, another whom they call Gutierre de Miranda, with two captains: one they call Rodrigo de Junco, and the other, Quiros, with sixty or seventy soldiers; without counting the settlers, who may number fifteen or twenty more. This, which he has said, is what he knows, and the truth, under the oath he took; [he said] that he is twenty years of age, more or less, and did not sign because he knows not how.

[Signed:] Don Xpoual de Eraso.
Before me, Pedro de Rada, notary.

FLORIDA, 1577–1585

PEDRO MENÉNDEZ MARQUÉS, probably the ablest member of his family, was hurriedly sent to Florida with men and equipment to restore the fort at Santa Elena, if not its colony. He managed (from August, 1577, on) to build a new fort, San Marcos, on Parris Island without opposition and to install a garrison there. Unknown to him there was a considerable French presence in the area. The privateer *Le Prince* had gone aground near Santa Elena, and its commander Nicolas Strozzi (a relative of the Queen Mother of France) built a fort for his 180 men. Relations with the Indians were so good that their treachery, the sudden overrunning of the fort, was unexpected. But the French were distributed among the villages as privileged prisoners, encouraged to help the Indians in war. Why they did not combine to attack Menéndez Marqués is not known. Gradually, he learned something of the situation, but was preoccupied with getting San Agustín on its feet again and bolstering the morale of his newly strengthened garrison (increased from 150 to 300).

Apart from a foray in Guale, it was only early in 1579 that he was able to move against the disaffected Guale Indians, whom he repressed savagely, and then moved on to the tribes of the Cusabo group in the vicinity of Santa Elena. In August he was attacked by an Indian force, assisted by some forty Frenchmen. When the Spaniards won, the Frenchmen lost their value in the eyes of the Indians. The Indians soon began sueing for peace and bringing in their French companions to seal their peace with the governor. In this way Menéndez was able to execute them singly and in groups and, as he caught them, any other Frenchmen he could trace. Strozzi himself was taken and, in spite of his birth and the offer of ransom, executed with the rest. Menéndez Marqués even managed to purchase Frenchmen who had gone to live far away to the west (as he did a Captain Rocque of Rouen). Between August, 1579, and the spring of 1580 his victory over the Indians and French was complete. A bonus came with the grounding of a large French ship on the bar at the mouth of the St. Johns River in July, 1580. After a battle, the French captain Gilberto Gil and all his men were killed in battle or captured. Those taken prisoner were killed. Menéndez Marqués's ruthless action, paralleled only by that of his uncle in 1565, showed the virulence of Spanish feeling about any French association whatsoever with North America. Meanwhile, the garrisons were in good shape; San Agustín was growing. Only the news in 1585 of English vessels carrying alleged colonists past Florida to the north caused the governor any serious misgivings.

713. October 21, 1577. Pedro Menéndez Marqués reports on the situation in Florida at his arrival.

A.G.I., Seville, Santo Domingo 231, 54/5/16; printed and translated in J. T. Connor, Colonial Records, *I, 262–277.*

Royal Catholic Majesty
From Havana I reported to your Majesty on what had happened to me up to then during the expedition. I shall now tell what has occurred since. I departed from Havana the day that the fleets and the armada sailed, and in eight days I arrived at the fort of San Agustín, where I found Captain Gutierre de Miranda greatly in need of supplies, for he had but one month's stock of flour at the rate of one pound for each person, and nothing else; and if I had not arrived at that instant, I hold it as my opinion that all would have been lost, as all the coast Indians are in rebellion, and allied with those of Santa Elena and Guale;

there are now in that fort but eighty men, counting soldiers and laborers, and the Indians are always trying to burn the pueblo. So I found it all destroyed, the houses torn down, and men, women and children gathered in the fort; because besides the war with the Indians, in the month of December last past, there appeared off that same fort a French galleon and, as the wind was contrary, she remained four days at anchor outside the bar, without being able to enter; then there came a gust of wind which sent her away from there, and she came to this harbor of Santa Elena, where God was pleased that on crossing the bar, she should be wrecked. All the men escaped, with their arms and munitions, and they came to land at this fort, which was burned and ruined, where they found your Majesty's artillery that was here, and threw it into the sea. When they first arrived, the Indians, thinking they were Spaniards, made very pitiless war upon them, in such wise that there were deaths on the one side and the other; but as soon as they understood that they were strangers, Frenchmen, and friends of theirs, they took them in and showed them much friendliness, and so they remain among them. When I heard all these things in San Agustín, I was in much doubt as to what I should do: whether I should fortify myself with all the men in that fort or whether I should come here; for I found myself with no more than one hundred and thirty-nine men, soldiers and laborers, and having the news of corsairs which I had, it seemed to me a thing against reason to divide them in half for two forts; but on looking your Majesty's cédula carefully over, I saw that your Majesty leaves me therein no open door whatever, whereby to enable me to act according to circumstances: on the contrary, your Majesty expressly commands that with thirty or forty of those I had brought with me from Spain, and with those that were here, I should strengthen this fort of Santa Elena and the others there may be in these provinces, because it so befits your Majesty's service and the safety of the rest of the Indies. On seeing this, and that your Majesty so willed it, I decided on an expedient for building this fort without danger. It was this: I placed an embargo on the two vessels which brought the supplies, and at San Agustín I had all the timber cut and sawed which was necessary for the building of this fort, and when it was cut and sawed, I loaded it on the ships. When I was

ready to set sail with them and the patache from the armada, one of the vessels caught fire, and eighteen quintals of powder were burned therein, and the whole of the ship's poop was hurled into the water; nor has it been found out up to this day how, and in what manner, she was set on fire. In spite of all this, I again prepared her as best I could; and when I was about to set out another time, there suddenly came up a hurricane which lasted an hour and a half, and as San Agustín is a closed harbor, all the ships were stranded without one being left, in such wise that one of them was flooded. I unloaded them once more, beached and repaired them as well as I could, and loaded them again. I sailed from San Agustín, leaving there as much order as I could; sixty men in the fort, and all the women and children collected therein, for I have more fear of the enemies who may come against San Agustín than here, as they will think that here I have my main forces, and that there nobody remains. And so, as I say, I left the sixty men and with them Captain Jhoan de Junco, who is a very good soldier, and experienced, as he has lived there twelve years. I came to this fort with seventy-nine men, and fourteen soldiers the patache brought, which makes eighty-three [recte ninety-three]; and on the way I ran into a storm, so that one of the ships was forced to throw much of the lumber overboard. At last, in spite of all these troubles, I arrived here with all the men well: where, on the same day, I started to build the fort, one hundred and fifty paces away from the nearest woods, because [against] Indians there is no greater protection than the open country. When the Indians saw us coming, they surrounded us from all the forests, as was apparent from the smoke they made, in order to see where we would go to cut timber for the fort; but they were deceived, for within six days of my arrival here, I had all the curtains done. When the enemy saw this, and a blockhouse at a distance, and in such a short time, they tried through spies to learn how many people there were; and so I know not whether they were Frenchmen, or Indians, who came during three nights to reconnoitre us; but up to now they have never been able to ascertain or find out the number I had, for I have seven outposts beyond the fort, every twenty-five or fifty paces, which prevent them from knowing anything. May it please God that they learn nothing henceforth. I hold it as my opinion that, with the aid of the French, they will not fail to come here or to San Agustín, to see if they can get in, although we are so much on the lookout that we shall not give them that opportunity. There is only one thing about it: if the Frenchmen have powder, they can do us much harm, and we shall even be in danger; but if they have none, I fear them not, even though they are many, for their vessel was large, whereof I found the poop here; according to its dimensions, she was a ship of five hundred *toneles*, and I even suspect that she was English, and not French. And I know likewise that she was a ship they called *El Principe*, which fled from the armada at the cape of Tiguron, for after she fled she came to Matanças, a harbor twenty leagues from Havana, where she took on meat and wood, which was given her there by Alonso Xuarez de Toledo: and she took on water: and those who were on board the vessel said that she brought one hundred and eighty men. This was at the beginning of December, and presently, at the end thereof, that ship appeared off San Agustín. I sent Captain Biçente Gonçalez in a launch to Guale, to see if he could obtain information as to what was happening, and not once could he do so, although he spoke with Indians, and with a French or English man; not one of them would ever come to the launch: on the contrary, from the shore they insulted Captain Viçente Gonçalez, telling him that the Spaniards were worth nothing, and were hens, and that they [the Indians] had with them many friends, who would aid them. On hearing this, I ordered Captain Viçente Gonçalez to remain with me, also twelve soldiers who were on that patache, because he is a very diligent and experienced man, and a very good soldier; he serves your Majesty with the greatest love and care, and deserves to be rewarded, since he shows such zeal. Likewise, I burned a ship, one of those that came hither, to avail myself of ten men she had, who although they are sailors, serve for everything, and are arquebusiers. All these tasks I found it necessary to do, because of the few people I have. I also took from the patache two small pieces of field artillery, each of which weighs as much as six quintals, for although your Majesty's ordnance was raised, which the French cast into the sea, it is all large, and I found it needful to take this. I am sending in the patache Captain Rodrigo de Junco, so that, as

he is a man who was present at all this, he may give your Majesty a detailed account of all that has occurred. He came to Havana in my company, as captain of the caravel which brought the hundred soldiers, and with orders from the Council that he should come to serve in the armada. On seeing in Havana the few men I was bringing, he came with me to these provinces. In everything he has helped me as much as he could, and as a man of experience who understands these things so well, I am sending him in order that your Majesty may inform yourself from him. He has been serving your Majesty many years; whatever is entrusted to him, he will know how to do very well, on land as well as on sea.

In conformity with this, it appears to me that your Majesty has need of sending some succor to these provinces, and within a short time, for if this corsair came to colonize it is to be believed that he may have a partner, and it would be a bad thing if they should come and capture a fort, which they can do very easily because of the few people there are. And let your Majesty realize that these two forts cannot exist with less than three hundred men, by any means whatever, one hundred and fifty in each, in order to be able to defend oneself from enemies.

It may be that [against] Indians only, one hundred and fifty are sufficient, although it is to be said to your Majesty that if the one hundred and fifty shall happen to lack supplies they will die, for there are not people [enough] to remain in the forts, and to go and seek food; and let not your Majesty count on the farmers, for at two hundred paces they dare not do any ploughing, and all they cultivate is but a little air in comparison with what they eat and what they exact. The laborers here are all youths, who are soldiers married to daughters of the older farmers; they serve in soldiers' *plazas* because there are no other [men], and they have forty-four women, sixty-two children and eleven pregnant women, about to be confined: which makes in all, one hundred and six persons who perforce must eat, and each day they beg me to give them level land where they can do their sowing, or to turn them out of the country. Let your Majesty consider what I shall do with one hundred and six persons who beg me to feed them, and I with no order therefore from your Majesty. I brought to this fort five women only, with their husbands; they are married to five sawyers. [I brought them] because of the need there was of them, although against their will, as they did not wish to come, saying that there was nothing to eat. So I have given and now give them rations as I do their husbands; and to the others I give nothing until I hear what your Majesty commands. God knows what this costs me from my poverty. I beseech your Majesty to order that there be speedy provision made in this.

I again say to your Majesty that if this presidio is to have but one hundred and fifty soldiers, I think that what I have always told your Majesty would be better: that there be two galleys and one galliot which should guard these presidios and the Windward Islands, for with little more money than the subsidy, from here the one and the other can be protected, so that we shall not be guarding two wooden houses which any corsair who may come could seize with his fingernails, and much reputation would be lost; and galleys are of much more power and strength. But if [the presidios] are to be settled, not less than the three hundred are required, and with them the blockhouses will be strong, and the land can be ploughed and cultivated. Your Majesty will order that which may best please you, for, in God and in my conscience, I know nothing else.

It is likewise an indispensable need, and I certify to your Majesty that it is expedient, that if this country is to be settled, he who has it should have the governorship of Cuba, for under any other arrangement the settlers will perish every day. It is now eleven months since any news has been known in Havana of these presidios, and, your Majesty, over thirteen months will go by before anything may be known. Whereas if the Governor of Cuba were governor of this country, a frigate would come every two months, and what is occurring would be known; there would be trading and trafficking, and the land would be better colonized; and [if this had been so] when the news was learned of the loss of this fort, there would have been no necessity for your Majesty to take measures from Spain. And I, even lately, when I departed from Havana, could have gathered more than fifty persons who remained from the armada and the fleets; but as I had no authority, I came without sailors and without soldiers. And, in God and in my conscience, I

know that this is what is fitting if this [region] is to be settled; and your Majesty may believe that if this be not done, great will be the pity of what happens in this land.

The expenses of these presidios at this time have been excessive, for besides this fort which has cost your Majesty four thousand ducats, more or less, in New Spain there remain another four thousand which were not paid because of the people who were lacking, so that at this time there will be wanting six months' supplies, for there is not enough of the subsidy wherewith to buy them. I sent to Havana about ten days ago, to seek to buy them on trust, and I commended myself to my friends. May it please God to give them the grace to do this. At the present hour I have in the two forts a supply of flour for three months, and of wine for one at most, one pint to a ration; without any other kind of ration or food, because with the loss of the ships we had some damage to the supplies. It would be needful, if your Majesty so please, that you should order at once that a hooker be secured, being a ship drawing little water, and that she be laden with wines and flour, and sent immediately and directly to these provinces; for it will cost your Majesty one half less, and even more than one half, and we shall be relieved promptly. It is a pity what the supplies from New Spain cost landed here; for at this time, in Havana, each cask of flour costs forty-eight or fifty ducats, and the wines, sixty-three or sixty-four ducats a cask; without the freightage, which is high; so that it cost your Majesty this present year, to bring the supplies and munitions to San Agustín and here, about two thousand ducats. And therefore, if this [colony] is to remain on its feet, it is expedient that a couple of frigates be built in Havana, for that which they might cost would be nearly saved the first year; and afterward, they would remain to be used for many years, and there would be no paying out in freight at least one thousand five hundred ducats. Likewise, the money for the cost of the supplies, which your Majesty may order to be sent on that ship, could be taken from the subsidy, and directed to the Casa de la Contratación, or to whomsoever your Majesty may command. It will also be necessary to send one hundred and fifty *escaupiles*, and if more people should come, there should be one for each; two hundred blankets; six hundred shirts, three hundred thereof made of *Ruan,* and three hundred of *crea,* with collars of *olanda;* one thousand pairs of shoes, five hundred thereof made of *vaqueta* and five hundred of Cordovan leather, all with two soles; ten pieces of cloth of London, two hundred doublets of *crea,* fifty of *olanda,* some hats and sword-belts, one quintal of sewing thread of all colors, some pieces of fustian for linings, and buttons. And your Majesty will order that the amounts of all this be sent, so that the proportion which falls to the share of each soldier may be deducted from his salary.

It will likewise be needful that your Majesty command that there be provided fifty quintals of lead, for it costs your Majesty more than six ducats per quintal to bring it hither from New Spain, and in Spain it is at the rate of twenty reals. It will also be necessary to send thirty quintals of wicks, for it is an extraordinary thing how much is used thereof; since I have been here there has not been a night that we have not consumed about twenty pounds, because we dare not extinguish them until we are well fortified. As to powder, it is preferable to provide it from New Spain, for it is much better, and at a reasonable price. And if a ship is to come, let your Majesty order that she shall come directly to Florida, without entering any harbor; and if peradventure there should be no pilot of experience to dare take the risk, let her go straight to Havana: I shall have a person there who will bring her: but if your Majesty does not command that this be speedily provided, we shall have trouble. I have nothing of which to give your Majesty an account, further than the aforesaid. Let your Majesty be pleased to command that there be decreed therein what best befits your Majesty's service, and within a short time. May Our Lord preserve your Royal Catholic Person, and prosper you for many and happy years, with an increase of larger kingdoms, as Christendom has need thereof, and we, your Majesty's servants, desire it.

In Santa Elena, on the twenty-first of October, in the year one thousand five hundred and seventy-seven.

Royal Catholic Majesty,
your Royal Catholic Majesty's humble servant, who kisses your royal hands.

[Signed:] P⁰ Menéndez Marqués.

714. December 12, 1577. Iñigo Ruíz de Castresana reports from Havana on Florida affairs.

A.G.I., Seville (reference uncertain); printed and translated in J. T. Connor, Colonial Records, *II, 27-29.*

Royal Catholic Majesty

On the twenty-third of June last past, General Pedro Melendez Marques sailed from this harbor, with two ships laden with supplies, and a patache from your Majesty's armada—one of those I had brought from New Spain with a vessel of my own, wherewith I went in your Majesty's service, in the said general's company. And because I was present at all that occurred on that voyage, it appeared to me the right thing to give your Majesty an account of such good news, as I know that thereby I serve your Majesty. He set out with the said vessels from the fort of San Agustín, whence he took all the wood needed to build and restore the fort of Santa Elena, in the bay whereof we found the poop of a French ship they call *El Principe.* We had tidings that she had carried two hundred and eighty men, and that two hundred of them died at the hands of the Indians; they say the others are prisoners. It has been attempted with much diligence to seize some Indian of that province, or some Frenchman, to learn the truth about everything. It was not possible to capture any. The general dispatched me with my vessel to this port for supplies, and he remained in great anxiety, to finish building and strengthening the said fort. All the artillery was taken out that had been in the fort of San Felipe, which consisted of three pieces, and two others, large cannon, which were being taken out; concerning all of which I think that General Pedro Melendes [Marqués] will have given your Majesty a long relation; but I believe that this will arrive first, wherefore it appears to me that I am serving your Majesty. May our Lord, whose defender your Majesty is, preserve your very Catholic and royal person, with an increase of kingdoms and dominions, to exalt the holy Catholic faith. From Havana, on the 12th of December, in the year 1577.

Royal Catholic Majesty,
Your royal Catholic hands are kissed by the least of your vassals,

[Signed:] Iñigo Ruiz de Castresana

715. February 12, 1577. Francisco de Carreño, governor of Cuba, reports to Philip II on news from Florida about *Le Prince*.

A.G.I., Seville, Santo Domingo 99, 54/1/15, extract; printed and translated in J. T. Connor, Colonial Records, II, 332–333.

....Today Captain Gutierres de Miranda arrived at this port in a boat from Florida. I had a letter from Governor Pedro Melendez Marques. He advised me that he has built his fort in Santa Elena and that he has begun to treat for peace with the Indians and has had word of some Frenchmen of the ship *El Principe* which was wrecked on the shoals of Santa Elena who are living among the Indians. Likewise, the said Gutierre de Miranda brought an Indian from Los Martires, which are those islands lying off the coast of Florida twenty-five leagues from this fort. The Indian went out in a canoe to talk with him. He knew him and took him and put him in his ship and brought him here to give news of certain ships which those Indians said had been wrecked. That Indian reported that at the end of August two ships were wrecked in Los Martires, and a part of their crews drowned. Those who escaped were killed by the Indians. Those two persons were held alive. These ships are, as we understand it, one belonging to Hernan Lopez, an inhabitant of Teneriffe, which was on its way from New Spain, and in which Doctor Portillo, provisor and schoolmaster of Mexico, was coming under arrest, having been exiled by the audiencia. The other ship belongs to one Escamilla and put in here from Santo Domingo. They did not know how to navigate and at night they were driven by a heavy wind thither, where they had been wrecked. If a town were to be settled there with people from Florida who could go there with fifty men, those Indians would become pacified and if the Spaniards were settled in one of those keys or small islands, they could save the crews of the ships which are wrecked there. And only by having peace with those Indians, each year a boat would go from here to ransom the captive Christians, if they did not kill them. Your Majesty will please provide in this what is according to your pleasure. ...

716. June 15, 1578. Pedro Menéndez Marqués reports on his dealings with the Indians in Florida.

A.G.I., Seville, Santo Domingo 231, 54/5/16; printed and translated in J. T. Connor, Colonial Records, II, 78–91, extracts.

Royal Catholic Majesty

Since I have come to these provinces, I have given your Majesty, by three routes, an account of what has happened during my voyage; and I believe that one of the letters will have reached your Majesty's hands, although I am anxious because the patache I dispatched to Spain, on board of which went Captain Rodrigo de Junco, had not arrived in those kingdoms in the month of January; as by it I wrote at length to your Majesty, and gave a report of what was needed for these provinces. Seeing this, I decided to dispatch this frigate, so that your Majesty may learn what is occurring on this side; and I am sending with this, the duplicate of what I wrote from Santa Helena. I beseech your Majesty to be pleased to order that it [the frigate] be sent back shortly, so that I may know what must be done. By the dispatch boat from New Spain, I wrote to your Majesty that which has happened since I built the fort of Santa Helena... [The said boat] was captured from me by the French, and for this reason I cannot refrain from giving your Majesty an account of what I said in that letter, and from writing somewhat at length in this. When I heard in Santa Helena that the Frenchmen were alive among the Indians, and I knew it likewise by some arquebus shots which I heard one night, I came to this fort, [so that] they should not attack it while I was repairing the other; and here I found that all was well, and the Indians of this province were peaceful, and are more so today than ever. I repaired this fort as best I could, but since it is on the point of falling, it is now indispensable to build another, in such manner that it be in good condition for defense, and they do not find us unwary.

After I arrived here, the Indians advised me that those of Guale and Santa Helena had come to treat with them so that they might all attack this fort; that it would be an easy thing for them to take it with the help of the French. And the

Indians here were not willing to consent to this, saying that they had peace and quietude with us and did not want any strife; and, although they are barbarians, there are, notwithstanding some among them who inform me of that which is happening. I sent a relative of mine to where this meeting was taking place, that he might negotiate with the Indians of Guale to deliver to me the Frenchmen they had, and I would make peace with them. At the beginning they were inclined to do this, and [said] likewise that they would deliver to me the cacique who had harmed the Spaniards, and would make war on his subjects; and in accordance with this, they went and slew the cacique and some few Indians, but they did nothing more, and delivered no Frenchman to me. I went to Guale with two launches, and twenty men therein, and tried by friendly means to enter into an agreement with them, but I could accomplish nothing. By hostile methods it is impossible, because of the few men I have; for in case I wished to take as many as fifty men, there would not be left over forty or so in either fort, as there are always sick people, priests, and friars. On this I went to Santa Helena, and on the way I spoke with an Indian who is my friend. He told me that there are a few more than one hundred Frenchmen, that they are divided among the caciques, that the principal cacique has forty of them, and that they tell and advise the Indians not to trust us; that they will help them, and die among them. I sent to tell those same Frenchmen that they should escape, that I would send to get them, but they answer that they do not want to, because the Indians would hang them at once. This has troubled me, owing to the evil seed they will sow among those Indians; for as to the rest, they will grow weary of going among savages, and will come in search of me; and even the very Indians will not trust them and will kill them. I should much like to break the spirit of those Indians, because, although they have greatly felt the strength of Santa Helena, yet they are much on their mettle, as they see that I have not enough men to go and hunt for them in their houses. And even though it be but for one year, I intend to drive them from their lands, burn their villages, and teach them that we are going after them; this would put a curb on them for their entire lives. Your Majesty will order to be done that which may most please you.

Arrived at Santa Elena, I remained there a few days, for, as it was already summer time, [when] they are in the habit of coming forth to lie in ambush, they came many times to the island; but, although I set some ambushes and [one word illegible], never did they dare show themselves. At last a few showed themselves. When I went after them, however, they took to the woods, for they are like deer. While I was there, one evening a ship arrived off the harbor, and as it was night it cast anchor; and that night God was pleased to send such a storm that it disappeared the next day, and I have seen it no more up to now. I suspect that it was French, and had news of the people who were lost at Santa Helena. I waited there some days, and as I saw that there were no tidings of it, I came hither, where, a week after I arrived, two vessels appeared off this port, one large and the other small; but when they saw the good artillery there was here, and that they could have no advantage, they departed. It was well known that these were corsairs, for the ships showed it. This was on the twelfth of May; never more have they appeared. I speedily sent two launches to run along the coast as far as Santa Helena, but there was no news of them. I know that their whole object was to get those people from Santa Helena. I earnestly wish that I had men to prevent it, for there are people among them who have much knowledge of these provinces, and if they should leave the country alive, some trouble might result in the future; but may it please God that they do not escape. . . .

I have asked the governor of Cuba many times for the farmers from here who are in Havana, and he has been unwilling to send them, saying that he holds no order of your Majesty therefor.[1] And likewise in the matter of supplies for these provinces, he does not behave as well as he should, and as your Majesty commands him by your royal cédula; for it happened that there was nothing to eat here, and we sent to seek food, and he would not allow it to be taken from the country. I entreat your Majesty to order that he be written to about this and reprimanded because, for these provinces, there is much need of aid from Havana.

Last year, in the collection of the subsidy [*situado*] made in New Spain, the royal officials

---

1. Sidenote: "Let the governor of Cuba be written to in conformity with this."

kept for themselves three thousand ducats on account of the vacancies left by the people who had died; Baltasar del Castillo took as his salary five hundred and fifty thousand maravedis, and the fort of Santa Helena cost a great deal, in such wise that there was very little money and I could not collect the six thousand ducats your Majesty allows me to pay the soldiers and what is necessary (for in this I understood that I was serving your Majesty) so that they should not complain that they were not paid. I beseech your Majesty to be pleased to order that a cédula be sent me so that those three thousand ducats shall be returned from New Spain to Florida, for they will supply a great deal.[2] And if your Majesty would be pleased to command that the officials of Vera Cruz should send the subsidy for these provinces to Havana every year, much money would be saved, as it costs a great deal each year to send to collect it, and there are always controversies. It can be brought to Havana, without any risk, in the flagship and admiral's ship of the trading fleet; and what goes to Spain can be sent from there, and the rest can be brought here.

I wrote to your Majesty in another letter that, when I arrived here, there was an order which allowed the soldiers two reals and a half each day for their ration, and that they suffered because the supplies which are brought here cost so much that with one pint of wine and a pound and a half of bread, the two reals and a half are used up, and there is great need; and this even appears to me a case of conscience. It shall be done so this year, until your Majesty commands what may please you; but henceforth, if the supplies and oil and other things are brought from Spain, the full ration can be given them. And if that is not possible, I entreat your Majesty to command to be provided in this matter that which may best please you.

I have here two very estimable friars, and one is a most excellent and learned theologian of the order of St. Francis, by name Fray Alonso Caveças.[3] The guardian in Havana has sent hither a certain commission which they sent to him from Mexico, and so these friars wished to go. I put them off in the best way I could, telling them that

I would entreat your Majesty to command that an order be sent them to the effect that this province shall be exempt from Havana. I beg your Majesty to favor him whenever opportunity migh offer, for he deserves it; and abundant is the need that we have here of a theologian, so that he may give us a good example.

I learned here that the council had sent to Seville a certain cédula ordering me to be detained and the galleon to be delivered to Francisco Carreño. As it is my ambition to attend with much promptness to whatever your Majesty commands me, I did not wait for the time fixed, but set sail when I could, and came here to do this with the greatest speed possible to me, and I accomplished it in the manner which I have written to your Majesty. I greatly desire to know what has been the cause thereof, for I certify to your Majesty that when I stop to think of what it can be, I cannot guess, unless it be some one who dislikes me and has brought some false accusation against me, for I serve your Majesty very faithfully and with much care. And if I wrote to your Majesty from Seville that this province could not well be governed apart from that of Cuba, it is certain that I reaffirm it, and I have never understood that as well as I do now. In order to exonerate myself from any fault they may have imputed to me, and to inform your Majesty of certain things which are fitting for your royal service, there would be need of my going to those kingdoms. [torn] that your Majesty give me permission to [torn] for I shall leave this country in such good condition that your Majesty will be served. And in case I see that, because of something which may happen meantime, my departure would not be opportune, I shall not sail, even though I hold your Majesty's leave therefor; but [if], arrived at that court, your Majesty is satisfied as to any fault of mine, if I be in fault, I will return to these provinces, or wherever your Majesty may order. And if I shall deserve punishment, it is just that your Majesty order it to be given me, for I cannot complain that your Majesty has not always remembered to order that favors be bestowed on me.

This last time I went to Santa Helena, I did my utmost to learn where the French had fortified themselves after they were shipwrecked, and at last I found it, in a wood near a river. According to the plan thereof, there were more people than I

2. Minute: "Cédula that he be aided with the three thousand ducats, because people are going now."
3. Minute: "Let the secretary discuss this with the commissioner of St. Francis".

thought, because it was shaped in a triangle, with three cavaliers, all made of sod and fagots, with its curtain largely of wood, and it had from cavalier to cavalier sixty-six paces. I found five houses within, one piece of bronze artillery of about twelve quintals, one man who was hanged, and many bones of dead people. I burned and destroyed the whole fort; then I came to this fort. I learned afterward that the man who was hanged was a Spaniard.

It is likewise necessary that your Majesty grant me the favor of ordering that your royal cédula be given me to the effect that I may obtain in the town of Havana the supplies and things needed in these provinces, at the same price as they would be sold there by those who bring them from outside; for the governor is somewhat hard in this, and says that he wants to keep that land supplied. But there they never can be in need, and here, we suffer.[4]

There is much need that your Majesty command that one hundred and fifty suits of Mexican armor [escopiles] be provided, similar to those which were made for these provinces in Seville the other time; and the cost thereof shall be sent next year by the trading fleet, to whomsoever your Majesty may direct. And if any greater number of men should come, let your Majesty order that one suit of armor be brought for each of them.[5] May our Lord preserve and prosper your Majesty's Royal Catholic person, with an increase of kingdoms, as Christendom has need thereof, and as we, your Majesty's servants, desire. At San Agustín, on the fifteenth of June, in the year one thousand five hundred and seventy-eight.

Royal Catholic Majesty,

Your royal Catholic Majesty's humble servant, who kisses your royal hands,

[Signed:] Pedro Menéndez Marqués.

717. October 9, 1578. Diego de la Rivera reports on collecting the subsidy for Florida.

A.G.I., Seville, Santo Domingo 115; 54/1/31;

---

4. Minute: "Cédula to the governor ordering him to accommodate him in this, so that they may be provided with supplies."
5. Minute: "Cédula to Señor Licentiate Gamboa in order that he shall provide this, taking into consideration that which Rodrigo de Junco is to carry".

printed and translated in J. T. Connor, Colonial Records, *II, 112–115.*

Sacred Royal Catholic Majesty

Inasmuch as the contador, Martin Dubieta, is writing, he will inform your Majesty of the result of my voyage after leaving the Canary Islands until we reached Domenica. In Domenica it seemed best to General Don Cristobal de Erasso that I should go to collect the subsidy which this armada has in the provinces of New Spain. Accordingly, on August twenty-four, we set out in the frigate of Guadalupe in which Don Gregorio de Erasso comes as captain—the said Don Cristobal going to Cartagena and I with the said frigate going from this port of Havana to escort the Florida ships which are going to take the relief [to Florida]. So we came to the region of the north of Isla Española and the old channel. On the thirteenth of the past month, Rodrigo de Junco with the said relief set out for Florida taking the route of Cruz del Padre which is forty leagues to the windward from this port. The rest of us came to this port of Havana whither by reason of the many sick men who came in the said frigate and who are still sick at present, we were detained because I had fallen sick so that I have been at the point of death and have not been able to embark thus far.

When we entered this port, a ship from Florida entered bringing as news that the people there are well; that the governor, Pedro Melendez Marques, has made friendship with many of the caciques, and that they had brought to him a Frenchman—one of those who were among the Indians—with whom he had spoken of the Frenchmen who were there, among whom is one called Felix, one of those who were captured in the time of Juan Ribau [Jean Ribault], a very good pilot who had escaped, he and others, with a boat in the year sixty-nine; and that the governor was in need of men. Therefore, the relief which your Majesty ordered sent them had arrived at a very good time. Whatever happens I shall always report it to your Majesty. May our Lord guard the royal Catholic person of your Majesty and give you increase in greater kingdoms as Christianity has need and as I [and] your servants desire. Given in Havana, October 9, 1578.

Sacred Royal Catholic Majesty,

Your vassal and servant kisses your Majesty's royal feet,

[Signed:] Diego de Rivera.

718. October 20, 1578. The Council of the Indies recommends that the subsidy to Florida be increased.

A.G.I., Seville, Indiferente General 739; 140/7/ 33; printed and translated in J. T. Connor, Colonial Records, *II, 115–117.*

Sacred Royal Catholic Majesty

Your Majesty has been petitioned on behalf of Pero Menendez Marques, Governor of Florida, that, inasmuch as one hundred and fifty men have been lately sent to succor those forts, and place them in a state of defense; and inasmuch as the 8 million, 788 thousand and odd maravedis of the subsidy for those forts are not even sufficient for the maintenance of the men who were there previously: it be ordered and decreed in such wise that those by whom [the forts] have been thus increased may be able to sustain themselves. And it appears to the council that, inasmuch as the men have been doubled [in number] they should now be given in the subsidy four millions more than what they had, and that for these, they may for the present apply to the governor of Havana, with an order that he inform himself of the [number of] men there are, and of what they need for their maintenance. And if the whole of the four millions be necessary, he shall aid them with them; and if less be sufficient, he shall aid them with that much less; and advise of that which shall be needed, either more or less, so that in accordance therewith agreement may be made as to what may appear fitting to assign for the future. Your Majesty will order what may please you. At Madrid, on the XX. of October, in the year MDLXXVIII.

Sacred Royal Catholic Majesty,

Your Majesty's humble servants, who kiss your royal hands,

> [Signed:] Doctor Gomez de Santillan.
> Licentiate Alonso Martinez Espadero.
> Licentiate Don Diego de Çuniga
> Licentiate Lopez de Sarria.
> Licentiate Henao.

[Minuted:] Let this be done.

[On the back is read:]

1578.   October 20.

Concerning what must be decreed for the maintenance of the men who have been added in the forts of Florida.

719. April 2, 1579. Pedro Menéndez Marqués reports on his suppression of the Guale Indians.

A.G.I., Seville, Santo Domingo 168; 54/3/19; printed and translated in J. T. Connor, Colonial Records, *II, 224–227.*

Very Powerful Sir

I have not given your Highness an account of what has happened in these provinces since I came to them, because there has not been any ship by which I could do so up to now, when I am sending this frigate to one of the ports of that island of Hispaniola, to be laden with horses, mares, and other cattle in order the better to succeed in carrying out what his Majesty has commanded me; and for the brief and efficient dispatch thereof, I am sending Captain Viçente Gonzales therein. I beseech your Highness to have the *alcaldes* of the port where he may arrive ordered to dispatch him with much speed, giving him what he may ask for his money according to its ordinary value among them, without their occasioning any delay whatever; wherein your Highness will be doing me much favor, besides being very useful to his Majesty's service.

After his Majesty sent me the succor which I had entreated him to send, I set about overrunning the country of the enemy who had done the damage in these provinces, and in forty-five leagues of their land which I overran, I burned nineteen villages, and some Indians were killed, without my receiving any injury beyond two soldiers being slightly wounded. Great was the harm I did them in their food stores, for I burned a great quantity of maize and other supplies, and I finally learned the secret of the Frenchmen who were among them in the land. I find that there are twenty-four, not more, whom I desire extremely to get into my power, so that they shall not sow their evil teaching among these people; and for this I have need of the horses for which I am asking, because to think of overtaking these Indians on foot is impossible; and if I have horses they can be caught, and the French can be had. In this province of San Agustín the people are peaceful, and although they were so previously, they are much more so now since they have seen the war I made on the other Indians. May it please our Lord that they may some time become good and Christian, for at present there is no discussing that.

They say flatly that they do not wish to become so, especially the adult men and women, who say that their fathers and ancestors had that religion; that they must preserve it; that if the young people wish to become Christians, they may; that they will not give up their faith. But if we come to ask them for their children in order to teach them the doctrine, they will not give them, and so there will be no fruitful results whatever in this land until our Lord takes a hand in this, for great is the pity that there should be lost so many souls as are lost here.

When I arrived here when I came from Spain two years ago, I found all the people in revolt, for if they had had the opportunity, they would have abandoned the country; but when I came, and built the fort of Santa Helena, and divided them up, they quieted down; particularly when I told them his Majesty's wish, namely, to keep this land on a firm footing. And last year I made them sow much maize, for at this fort alone, over one thousand *fanegas* were gathered, and this season they will gather many more. There are beginning to be many of the fruits of Spain, such as figs, pomegranates, oranges, grapes in great quantity; there are many mulberries from the mulberry trees produced in this same soil, vegetables and greens in large quantities, such as beans, kidney-beans, melons, pumpkins, lettuce, cardoons, onions, and garlic; all of this in abundance, in such manner that I assure your Highness that if there were those who would farm the land, it is ready for it. If, by chance, when this letter shall arrive, there should be some vessel about to sail from that city [of Santo Domingo] for the kingdoms of Spain, I beseech your Highness to advise the council how good and peaceful this country is, and of the news I am here telling of the Frenchmen, and the rest I say to your Highness herein, for I shall not be able to do so until the trading fleet comes to Havana, and it is well that his Majesty should hear this from many sources. May our Lord preserve your most powerful person, and increase [your welfare] for many years, as we, the servants of your Highness, desire. In San Agustín, on the second of April, in the year 1579.

Very powerful Sir,

Your Highness's hands are kissed by your servant,

[Signed:] Pedro Menéndez Marqués.

720. November 8, 1579. Antonio Martínez Carvajal reports the suppression of the Cusabo Indians.

A.G.I. Seville, Santo Domingo 51/2/3 (reference uncertain); printed and translated in J. T. Connor, Colonial Records, *II, 246-251.*

Royal Catholic Majesty

I set forth from Florida and the fort of San Agustín on the tenth of October, and I arrived in this port on the 21st. Today I am sailing for the said Florida, and as it appears to me that your Majesty would be served [thereby], I am sending in this letter a relation of the events which have occurred in the said Florida during the pacification of the Indians, the capture and the killing of some Frenchmen, and other deeds performed by your general, Pedro Menendez Marques.

At the end of the month of July of this year, Pedro Menendez Marques set out from the fort of San Agustín to go to the fort of Santa Elena in order to pay the soldiers of the garrison, and this he did on the eighth of August. Then he set out with about 65 soldiers against the province of Oristan, which had risen in rebellion, to treat of peace and friendship; and while he was doing it, the Indians of the said province, with as many as 300 bowmen, fell upon Pedro Menendez. They wounded about ten Spaniards, but at the end they were routed by Pedro Menendez, and some Indians were slain. And seeing that the said Indians in no way wished for peace, the said Pedro Menendez returned to the fort.

On the 26th of August, Pedro Menendez went forth from the said fort of Santa Elena against a village of Indians about 20 leagues from the said fort, the cacique of which is called Coçapoy, who never had had peaceful or friendly relations with the Spaniards. The said general received tidings from him that he had, in the said village, 40 Frenchmen as a protection, and as friends. That village had about 400 Indians. The said Pedro Menendez, on seeing that this cacique never had a desire to be obedient, nor give up the said Frenchmen, attacked the village on the 29th of the said month, at daybreak, with 200 men he had, who were arquebusiers; and he burned the village, and slew some of the Indians who defended it, and a number of the French, who let themselves be burned, sooner than surrender. He captured and holds prisoners the said cacique, his mother, and other Indian women, likewise 17 Frenchmen whom he holds in custody in the said forts.

Having accomplished this, he went back from the fort of Santa Elena to that of San Agustín, and on the way he passed through the province of Guale, on which the said Pedro Menendez had made war the year previous. Through his skilful management he pacified the said province, and reduced to your Majesty's service all the caciques, including the head cacique. They delivered to the said Pedro Menendez a Frenchman from the ship called *El Principe* [*Le Prince*], which was wrecked at the bar of Santa Elena in the year 1575. The said Frenchmen came from it, and this French captain is called Nicolas Astroço [Nicolas Strozzi]. This done in Guale, we set out from its bar for San Agustín, and by reason of a tempest, which came upon us, one of the two frigates we had was lost, the one on board of which came the general, and I, as being the chief pilot of the said Florida (where I have served your Majesty without failing for one day, since Juan Ribao [Jean Ribault] was destroyed by Adelantado Pedro Menendez). The general and the rest of the people were saved from the wreck of the said frigate, whence he went by land to the fort of San Agustín, where I left him. He and the others are well and happy, and he sent me to this town for certain nails to finish the fort he is building in San Agustín. I am giving this relation as an eyewitness who was present on the said occasions, and on all the others which have arisen since the said time of Juan Ribao.

Inasmuch as I am married, and the adelantado brought about my marriage in the said Florida, and I have a wife and three daughters, and my salary is no more than two hundred ducats, with which I cannot support myself: I beseech your Majesty, as a reward for my services, that your Majesty be pleased to grant me the favor to command that my said salary be increased to the amount you may wish.

May our Lord protect many years your Majesty's royal Catholic person, with an increase of many other kingdoms and dominions. Written from Havana, on the 3d of November, 1579.

Royal Catholic Majesty,

Your Majesty's feet are kissed by your vassal,

[Signed:] Antonio Martinez Carvajal.

721. January 6, 1580. Pedro Menéndez Marqués reports his execution of the French captives.

A.G.I., Seville, Santo Domingo 224, 54/5/9; printed and translated in J. T. Connor, Colonial Records, *II, 252–257.*

Royal Catholic Majesty

After I gave your Majesty an account, through Captain Rodrigo de Junco, of what had occurred in these provinces, certain things happened which all turned out well, our Lord be thanked. I went to Santa Helena to distribute the pay to the soldiers who live there, and, as the Indians would not come to talk with me, I sent a boat with twelve men to seek information from them. The men spoke to them from the boat, and the Indians answered that they did not desire friendship, and began to shoot arrows at them. The boat returned, and when I heard this, I sent a boat a second time, with twenty men, notifying them to make peace; and they were so rebellious that the soldiers grew angry, and [the Indians] wounded five men. When I heard this, I went there with sixty men, and landed; and they waited with great courage, so much so that I marvelled, and they wounded fourteen of my men, but no one was killed. I worked a trick on them as well as I knew how, in such wise that many Indians were slain, and they all fled, and quit the country. I returned to the fort, which was fifteen leagues from there, and before they could spread the news to other villages, I went back and attacked a large village called Coçapoy, which was very well fortified and in the midst of a swamp. I fell upon it at midnight, and did much damage, and I captured a son of the cacique, his wife, a sister, and his mother. More than forty Indians were burned to death, and I seized two Frenchmen, and thereupon I returned to the fort. I learned from the Frenchmen that there were twelve other Frenchmen in that village, and that they did not wish to come to us. Among them was the pilot who, on another occasion, about seven years ago, escaped from here. I sent word to the Indians to give me the Frenchmen and I would give them the women, and they did so although they took their time. I kept the cacique's son as a hostage. They are in such a mood that I have little hope concerning them. I went to the province of Guale and they behaved well, for they delivered to me at once the captain who called himself Nicolao Estroçi, and the others they had, except two boys and one soldier who were far away; and all the caciques came to see me, and renewed their allegiance to your Majesty. To all appearance they are friendly, although one cannot much rely on them. Thence I came to this fort, which I am finishing; it is a good piece, although it has been built with much difficulty. I did not at once work justice [=execute] upon the Frenchmen; not until now. I sent a boat to Santa Helena for some of them, and then justice was worked upon the rest there. I added those who were brought to those who were here, so that those on whom I worked justice, here and at Santa Helena, numbered twenty-three altogether. There remain three boys, one barber and one gunner, who are needed in these provinces as interpreters. From what has been heard, only two men and one boy are now left among the Indians. They have agreed to surrender them. According to their confession, they well deserved death, for they admitted having sacked and burned Margarita Island, Cumana, Guadinilla and other villages, and captured many ships. The captain was rich, because he offered me three thousand ducats as ransom, if I would grant him his life. It did not appear to me expedient for Your Majesty's service that a man like him should get back to France. He was of the Florentine nation, and of good lineage.

I learned from those same Frenchmen and from the Indians, that the French had told the Indians that they would try to give them the fort; and in accordance with the agreement they had made, the Indians came to help. But they came late, and even if they had come earlier, that would have been of little advantage to them, because of the strength of the fort.

Your Majesty's officials for these provinces arrived here about three months ago, and I hope to God that they will serve your Majesty very well. I have much satisfaction with them, for I am freed from papers, which for me is a thing that I desire very much; and so I handed over to them those there were here for accounting and report.

Greatly do I wish that Rodrigo de Junco might return, so that the frigate could go to New Spain and likewise for that which concerns the subsidy for these people; as they have eaten at the cost of those who were here [before them], and if your Majesty has not commanded that aid be sent, I have great fear of some disturbance. For the love of our Lord, let your Majesty order this to be remedied as may best please you, in such wise that we shall not suffer; and as we have been obliged to wait for supplies until now we are short thereof, and if they do not come promptly, we shall have hardship. May our Lord provide in this as may best please him. Amen. May our Lord protect and prosper your Majesty's royal Catholic person for many and happy years, with an increase of more kingdoms, as Christendom has need thereof, and we, your Majesty's servants, desire it. San Agustín, on the 3d of January, in the year 1580.

Royal Catholic Majesty,

Your Royal Catholic Majesty's humble servant, who kisses your royal hands,

[Signed:] Pº Menéndez Marqués.

[Endorsed:] Florida.   To his Majesty.   1580. From Governor Pedro Menendez Marques. Dated 3d of January. Examined. Let him be written to that his Majesty considers that he has been served by him, and let his services be remembered.

722. March 25, 1580. Pedro Menéndez Marqués on his building of Santa Elena.

A.G.I., Seville, Santo Domingo 224, 54/5/9; printed and translated in J. T. Connor, Colonial Records, *II, 225-232.*

Royal Catholic Majesty

After I had given your Majesty an account, in the month of January last past, of what news there was, and how I had worked justice on the French, I came later to this province, as I heard that there remained alive among the Indians, a captain and other Frenchmen; and here I learned from the Indians that there were more Frenchmen, and so I tried by all the ways possible to me to get them into my power. The Indians, because of the fear they have, offered to deliver them to me, and so they went to seek them, and brought me the captain, who was on the other side of the mountain ridge, one hundred and twenty leagues from here, with three other Frenchmen, young boys. The captain was a young man of twenty-eight years, but in my opinion very warlike, and of very fine appearance. He was a native of Rouen and was called Captain Roque. I worked justice upon [=executed] him, and the three I left for the last. I have news that there remain three others, whom the Indians say they will deliver to me within a very brief space. I suspect that there must be more. I shall do my utmost so that none shall remain.

All the Indians are peaceful, those of this province as well as those of the others, as far as San Agustín. I hope in our Lord that satisfactory results will be obtained among them.

This village is being very well built, and because of the method which is being followed, any of the houses appears fortified to Indians, for they are all constructed of wood and mud, covered with lime inside and out, and with their flat roofs of lime. And as we have begun to make lime from oyster-shells, we are building the houses in such manner that the Indians have lost their mettle. There are more than sixty houses here, whereof thirty are of the sort I am telling your Majesty. As this letter is going on the chance of its overtaking some dispatch boat in Havana, I do not give your Majesty a longer account of other things. May our Lord protect and prosper your Majesty's royal Catholic person for many and happy years, with an increase of greater kingdoms, as Christendom has need thereof, and we, your Majesty's servants, desire it. From Santa Elena, on the 25th of March, in the year 1580.

Royal Catholic Majesty,

Your Royal Catholic Majesty's humble servant who kisses your hands

[Signed:] Pº Menéndez Marqués.

723. May 15, 1580. Pedro Menéndez Marqués discusses the administrative problems of Florida.

A.G.I., Seville, Santo Domingo 224, 54/5/9; printed and translated in J. T. Connor, Colonial Records, *II, 296–307.*

Royal Catholic Majesty

On the fifth of January, from San Agustín, I gave your Majesty an account of what had happened up to then, and of the justice I had worked on the French; and afterward on the twenty-fifth of March, from Santa Elena, I reported to your Majesty concerning what had occurred and of my working justice on another French captain, and on my keeping three other boys prisoners. Now I shall tell that which has happened since then.

I left Santa Elena on Holy Thursday for San Agustín, and when I arrived there, I had notice through certain Indians that there were two Christian captives on the coast, thirty leagues from there. Having heard this, and in order to learn what there was, I embarked with thirty men in two launches, and came running along the coast trying to find out about it. Finally it appeared that inland there are two men who are captives, and who, when they were boys and interpreters, had been placed by the adelantado—may he be in heaven—with two friendly caciques, to teach them the [Christian] doctrine; and these caciques afterward rose in rebellion, and made them prisoners. I believe that, with the aid of our Lord, I shall soon get them. I went on all the way down the coast as far as Los Martires, reassuring the Indians; and all along it I left the Indians very peaceful, so that I know that, even if any ship be wrecked, they will slay no one. And I think for this reason that my coming has been of great use, as I promised them that I would ransom from them any Christian whom they might capture there, and if they did not let me do so, I should punish them. When I found myself at Los Martires, twenty-five leagues from this port, I came here because I had received a letter from the governor whom the audiencia sent hither, whereby he advised me that he had received from your Majesty two royal cédulas, one for him and the other for the officials of Vera Cruz, to the effect that they should give and pay him each year four millions of maravedis for the support of the soldiers who came as reinforcements; and he did not write me what method he intends to follow in paying it. Your Majesty's royal officials and I met in San Agustín, and we were agreed that the treasurer, empowered by all, should come to this town to collect it, because the governor had sent to New Spain to collect it. I arrived here on the fourteenth of April, and at once discussed the affair with the governor, in order to return immediately; and he answered me in a manner very unpromising for delivering the money or any part thereof. And when I made plain to him the need there was that those people should be paid, as they had not been for two years; and that it was expedient for your Majesty's service that they should be paid, so that there should not be any mutiny, he replied to me that even if seven Floridas were to be lost, he would not give the money without taking certain measures very foreign to what your Majesty commands by your royal cédula. When I saw this, and that the trading fleet was hourly expected, I decided to wait for it so that Don Bartolomé de Villaviçençio, the general thereof, might set before him the ill service which was being done your Majesty in withholding their pay from those people, as it is so long since they have been paid; and they escaped by swimming, and are naked and abused. The trading fleet arrived here on the third of May, and as the viceroy knew what might happen to that money, he had ordered it to be registered and consigned to the governor and officials of this island, so that they should aid with it as your Majesty commands; but when the money arrived here, the governor took it and put it in his house, and would not let it be placed in your Majesty's chest. Don Bartolomé spoke to him, but nothing was of any avail, for he said that your Majesty ordered that he should make investigations in Florida, but the contrary is true, for your Majesty only orders that he ask for information. The necessary steps are being taken with him to make him deliver the money. I believe that this will not be sufficient, and that there will be the greatest harm done to Florida, for the new people have eaten at the expense of the old, and I have bought supplies for a year ahead, in such wise that there will not be left one real to pay either the new or the old men; and with this money which is here, everything could have been remedied. I do not send your Majesty the solution thereof, because this vessel is sailing before one is made. If perchance he should not give the money, he should be asked to send it to your Majesty registered, by the flagship or the vice-admiral's ship; for it is rather better than it should go over yonder, and your Majesty should have the benefit thereof, than to have it stay here, as I feel that there would not be any lasting advantage from its remaining. And so, if the men are not to be paid, it

is well that the money should go to Spain, for, as always, your Majesty will have a care to grant us grace; and I shall try, in the interval before your Majesty can order that relief be provided, to keep the men in good spirits as best I can, although I fear them. I shall therefore depart for Florida within three days, and shall leave in writing for your Majesty what has happened in this matter, and what more there may be to say. I beseech your Majesty that for this coming year I may have charge of the subsidy for these people, for I doubt whether they can be appeased unless they are paid. If it had not been that I succored them from my means so that they could be clothed—as they had escaped by swimming—they would have suffered very great hardship; and so I shall now be compelled again to seek the wherewithal to clothe them, since the governor will not give the money. I shall do all I can, in this and in all the rest, in such manner that your Majesty may be served in everything.

In Florida I hold ten Frenchmen: one is a surgeon, of whom there was much need; another is a German gunner, and the others are boys and interpreters. As I had ascertained that they had brought the German by force and had taken him from a ship, I had him placed in your Majesty's royal books, so that he should draw a ration and a salary. I condemned the others to be your Majesty's slaves, who should be employed in your Majesty's service in those provinces, and [arranged] that they should be fed from the war stores. I entreat your Majesty to be pleased to do me the favor to command that your royal cédula be sent me, so that these rations may be approved, or let your Majesty order what must be done with those people.

I have had advices that your Majesty has done me the favor to order that a salary of two thousand ducats be given me, one thousand from the subsidy and one thousand from the products of the country. This has been a great benefit to me, but I beseech your Majesty to take into consideration that I am in Florida, always spending, without having one real of profit; that for the present there are no products of the country whereof I can avail myself; and that your Majesty gives and grants to a governor in any part of the Indies, five hundred thousand maravedis, and with them he has the greatest profits, in such wise that in three years he comes out wealthy. I care not so much for the money as I do for the opinion of those who know me; that they should see me in a dangerous post like Florida, and that, after so many hardships, your Majesty shows no more favor to me than to another, when I am serving with so much willingness in a country from which every one flees. I beseech your Majesty to be pleased to order that the two thousand ducats be given me from the subsidy, or from wherever your Majesty may command, for I assure your Majesty as a Christian, that I need the thousand in Florida each year for food, as the prices are excessive at which everything there is retailed. Then, besides that, let your Majesty consider what I shall need to support my wife and household in Seville.

When I kissed your Majesty's hands in El Pardo, and came away to Florida, I besought your Majesty to grant me the habit of Santiago. Since then I have wished that your Majesty should understand the care with which I was serving here, and so I did not treat of this further in the things that your Majesty commanded me; and in the others which have occurred, I have served with the care and diligence that were possible to me. I beseech your Majesty that, if there be occasion, this grace may be bestowed on me, so that henceforth I may serve your Majesty with greater spirit.

I have a great desire to go to those kingdoms to kiss the hands of your Majesty, and give your Majesty an account of many things which are fitting for your royal service, concerning Florida as well as other regions; for, when your Majesty shall have heard them, it may be that your Majesty will feel satisfied as to them or the greater part of them. And likewise, in order to finish rendering my accounts for the time that I was treasurer in your Majesty's armada, for they are ready to be rendered, and I should not wish to die without rendering them, I beseech your Majesty to be pleased to grant me the favor to give me permission to sail in the trading fleet of this coming year, for I shall leave in Florida a person competent for your Majesty's service. And when I return I shall be able to bring my wife and household, and I shall come fittingly, without as much expense as I have since your Majesty is pleased to have me present in Florida and serve your Majesty there; wherein I shall be receiving a very particular favor from your Majesty.

Two years ago a misfortune occurred. Bartolomé Martin[ez], who filled the office of accoun-

tant in Florida, killed an ensign; and it is certain that he was not as much at fault as the dead man, as is apparent from the process. He was sentenced to the galleys, provided that beforehand he was to come to this town of Havana to report to the *visitador*, Baltasar del Castillo, on your Majesty's treasury, which he had had under his charge. He appealed to the royal council of the Indies, and I granted him the appeal, on condition that, before anything else, he should go to render an accounting. He went to do this, and gave it very well; and is a prisoner in the Casa de la Contratación of Seville, under the process against him, while his wife is in Florida, with one child they have, and it is the greatest pity in the world. I beseech your Majesty to be pleased to order that his process be examined; and if he must go to the galleys, or to other parts, let your Majesty command that he be sent to Florida, because that will be enough prison and galleys for him. He will be much use for Florida, being a man of a very ready pen, and [well versed] in accounts, for there is a lack of this; and he will relieve his wife and children as best he may be able.

Here in this town I hear that five English vessels had entered the South Sea by the strait of Magellan. Many years ago, the adelantado, Pedro Menedez, and I suspected this, and I even understand that he discussed it with your Majesty in the royal council of the Indies. I hold it as my opinion that they aimed at a mark in that direction, and are about to hit another, which is at the back of Florida; although their having run along the whole coast, from the strait of Magellan as far as New Spain, is an indication that they wish to have a thorough knowledge of it in order to enter that way. But I hold it for certain that the way out will be in this direction, for the cold regions are equal in altitude; and so I believe that they will come out there, owing to the voyage being very much shorter; for the English have been trying for a long while to enter that way, and if this is not remedied in time by cutting them off from the passages, it will be a difficult thing to do it later on.

The governor made very great efforts here in the matter of verifying the [number of] people there are in Florida, whereat I was much pleased, and let your Majesty trust me that I am not telling your Majesty a thing which is not the truth. And he found that what I said was true, and that the soldiers could not be paid with a much larger sum of money; so he delivered the funds, which, although I said before that they amounted to fourteen thousand ducats, were no more than four millions of maravedis, out of which the governor deducted six hundred ducats, more or less, for the expenses he had had. May our Lord protect and prosper your Majesty's royal Catholic person for many and happy years, with an increase of more kingdoms, as Christendom has need thereof, and we, your Majesty's servants, desire it. In Havana, on the 15th of May, in the year 1580.

Royal Catholic Majesty,

Your Royal Catholic Majesty's humble servant, who kisses your royal hands,

[Signed:] pº Menéndez Marqués.

[Minuted on his French prisoners:] Let him at the first opportunity send all the Frenchmen to these kingdoms, for the galleys of Spain. And in that which concerns the German, he has done well.

724. June 4, 1580. The Council of the Indies recommends to Philip II that Florida should be developed.

The royal officials urged that slaves be sent from Havana to help with the reconstruction of the fort, that cattle were needed (the officials could bring in the cattle themselves), and that a customs house was needed to attract merchants. The Council of the Indies recommended to the king that he grant these requests. These are signs that San Agustín was beginning to develop under Pedro Menéndez Marqués.

A.G.I., Seville, Indiferente General 739; 140/ 7/33; transcript in Division of Manuscripts, Library of Congress, newly translated.

Your Sacred Royal Catholic Majesty.

The Officers of the Royal Exchequer of the Provinces of Florida, in a letter to Your Majesty of last 5th January, say that the fort of San Agustín was already defensible, and that although the defences would soon be finished, since they are made of wood there will always be things needing doing to it, and the men were exhausted from the construction of it and in carrying the wood from the forest on their shoulders: and in addition a great deal of money was spent on sawyers, which expense would end if there were ordered to be sent there some of the slaves which Your Majesty has at Havana: as regards their food they would do their best to try and find it there on the land, with no expense on the Royal Exchequer; in view of this, it seems to the Council that a Cédula could be issued to the effect that the Governor of Havana should send straightaway to the Governor and Officers of Florida, unless they are needed for the work of that town, thirty of the slaves that belong to His Majesty there, for the purpose for which they have been asked, charging them to take care of them and treat them well, and that they should not incur expense on the Royal Exchequer, and should advise about whatever is done and when they should no longer be needed there, so that orders and instructions can be sent to them concerning whatever may have to be done.

They also write that they have no kind of domestic livestock, so that in those forts they never eat fresh meat, and they believe they could be raised very well there; they do not take them there because very few people have the necessary money, and if anyone could do so it would be the Officers themselves; and since in their instructions this, among other things, is forbidden, they request that they be granted permission to raise livestock there, and cultivate the land; and in view of the need they are in, and that there is no particular problem about granting this dispensation to the Officers of those provinces, it seems to the Council that they could be given permission for this, providing that if any problem does arise from this a different decision can be made.

They also write that they have great need to construct a Customs House to attract some merchants to come there, and they ask that permission be granted to do this. It seems to the Council that this could be granted provided that they do not spend on this more than two or three hundred ducats, and that these should come out of the money allotted for the sustenance of those forts.

Your Majesty will instruct as he pleases.

[Signed by the members of the Council of the Indies]

Madrid, 4th June 1580.

[The document is minuted, but the minute is largely illegible: it states that the Royal Officials might have licence to maintain dairy farms for cattle on their own account for four years, but the rest could not be read.]

725. [*Circa* September, 1580]. Report on the fight with the French ship in the St. Johns River.

A.G.I., Seville, Santo Domingo 168, 54/3/19; printed and translated in J. T. Connor, Colonial Records, II, 318–323.

On the eighteenth of July of this year, General Pero Menendez Marques being in this guard house, speaking with the soldiers, at three o'clock in the afternoon there arrived an Indian, perspiring and very tired, who said to the general that he brought him a piece of news; that Contreras, the interpreter, should be called to him at once. The general, seeing this, ordered him to be called immediately, and when he had come, the Indian said: "Sir General, inside the harbor of San Mateo there are a French vessel and a launch, with many people." The general, on hearing this news, asked the Indian when it had entered, if he had spoken with the Frenchmen, and how many of them there were. He said that they had entered the day before, which was the seventeenth of July, during the night, and that he had not counted the men because he could not; but that he had spoken with them, and been aboard their ship, and that the French asked him how many people there were in this fort, and if there were any vessels in the fort [*i.e.*, harbor]. And the Indian said that he answered them that there were no ships whatever in the harbor, except two launches, and that there were few people in the harbor [*i.e.*, fort], and those were sick. The general asked the Indian why he had told them that the people were few and sick, since he knew that there were many, and that there were two large frigates in the harbor. The Indian replied that he and the others thought they would deceive the French, so that they would land, and there they would kill and despoil them. The general, hearing this, ordered a man who is known as Manuel Alvarez, to go on horseback that night to San Mateo, a distance of twelve leagues, arriving there at dawn, when he

could look and see if there were more than that ship, of what size it was, and how many men in his opinion; and he was to endeavor that they should not see either him or his horse, and he was to return here early the next day. The said Manuel Alvarez went, and returned next day, the nineteenth of the said month, at the time of the Ave Maria; and he said that the vessel was a new and small galleas of two sails, of about eighty or ninety tons burden; and that during the morning he saw a crowd of people on deck, but he could not count them; that it seemed to him there were about fifty men, more or less, and a small launch. Hearing this, it appeared to the general that it would be well to go in search of it with two frigates he had, and he ordered the masters and pilots thereof to mast them and put them in readiness that night, for they were dismasted and not equipped. And thus that night they worked, and on the twentieth of the said month, when the day broke, they were ready, and at eight o'clock in the morning they already had the artillery and munitions on board, and they set sail.

The general went in person, with fifty soldiers, ten sailors and three pieces of artillery in the two frigates; and he arrived that very day, the twentieth of the said month, at the bar of San Mateo, three hours before dark, and found the French vessel in danger of foundering at the bar, amid the shoals, that it was trying to get out of. The general decided to close with it, so that it might not get away that night, and so he attacked it with the two frigates. With the first discharge they [*i.e.*, the French] killed three soldiers and wounded eight on the flagship, and on the other frigate they killed Captain Hernando de Quiros and two others. From the flagship at the first discharge they struck down twenty-six Frenchmen, nine killed and seventeen wounded; from the other frigate they struck down three Frenchmen killed and six wounded. The French vessel was boarded for a long hour, until little by little we went on reducing the Frenchmen, only six of whom remained; and they, on seeing this, and that already there was no help for them, and the tide was running out, loosened the cable whereby they were anchored, and let themselves go on the shoals, so that we might all be lost. The general, seeing this, and that now all the vessels were running aground, disengaged himself from the French ship after it had already surrendered and [those aboard] were begging for mercy; placed himself in the channel, anchored near it with one anchor, and later, as the tide rose, the French ship and the other frigate were shattered to a thousand pieces. The general saved the men with three boats he had, and he cut off the heads of the Frenchmen although there was little to cut, for they were in a thousand pieces from their wounds. This done, the general returned to this fort on the next day, the twenty-first of the said month. On our side, the slain numbered eighteen, among them Captain Hernando de Quiros, and the wounded fourteen. The French lost fifty-four, including two negroes they brought, one of whom fought very well. There only remained alive a surgeon and three boys. This, in truth, is what happened, for I was present at all of it.

The captain, who died at San Mateo, was called Captain Gil. He was a native of Corsica, married in Marseilles. He was cased from head to foot in armor which was arquebus proof, and he died of an arquebus shot which struck him through the visor in the temple, for in any other manner it was impossible to kill him.

The rest [of the story] is that with that vessel came another, which remained outside [the bar]. We know not where it went. Two other ships entered a harbor they call Gualequeni, and they made a great show of friendship with the Indians, and took soundings on the bars. On the twenty-eighth of the said month of July, five ships ap-peared at the bar of Guale and tried to cross the bar. The sea was rough and they could not enter. On the seventh of August, three others appeared at the bar of one crossed it, the other two remained outside. On the twenty-eighth day of the said month of August, two other ships appeared at the same bar of Çapala, which is the best there is on this coast. One of them, a patache, crossed it and took soundings at the bar, and on the rivers within it, and returned outside without speaking to the Indians. Two days after the skirmish at San Mateo, another vessel appeared at the bar of San Pedro. In such wise, there are, of corsair ships that arrived in these provinces in the months of July and August of this year 1580, fifteen ships. This is known to be a fact, because the general sent Anton Martin[ez], a pilot, to range along the coast in a launch. And he knew it for certain in the district of Guale, for a Spaniard was there who saw them; because when the first vessels were seen in Guale by the Indians, they immediately gave notice to the captain at Santa Elena, and the captain sent that Spaniard so that he should re-main there and see what happened, and keep the general advised of everything by land, through the Indians, since they were all friendly. We cannot understand the corsairs' designs. May God provide in this as He may best be pleased.

[Endorsed:] News of Florida, in the year MDLXXX.

Chapter Ninety-two
Florida, 1586

THE DESTRUCTION OF SAN AGUSTÍN BY SIR FRANCIS DRAKE, 1586

IN HIS DEVASTATING raid on the West Indies, Drake had intended to attack Havana in May but failed to do so, as he thought his force was not strong enough. He picked up information (probably at Cartagena) that Pedro Menéndez Marqués was intending to destroy the Roanoke Colony established under the auspices of Ralegh and Grenville (446). This led him to divert his attention to San Agustín. Consequently, on May 27/June 7, Drake's fleet appeared outside the bar of Anastasia Island. He landed on the island and mounted a battery opposite the fort. In the morning he landed 300 men and commenced an attack on the fort. Pedro Menéndez Marqués killed several Englishmen, including Sergeant Major Powell, but when heavy guns were landed he abandoned the fort and took to the woods, where he had already sent all the civilian inhabitants of San Agustín. Drake demolished the fort, took its guns, and razed the town, cutting down all its fruit trees. From the houses he carried off furnishings, doors, locks, and tools. He was joined by a number of Negro slaves to whom he offered freedom. One Frenchman and one Spaniard managed to make their escape to him.

From the English side Walter Bigges, *A summarie and true discourse of Sir Frances Drake's West Indian voyage* (London, 1589, for which see D. B. Quinn, *Roanoke Voyages*, and Mary F. Keeler, ed., *Sir Francis Drake's West Indian Voyage* [London, Hakluyt Society, 1977]), and also (445). The principal Spanish sources are translated in Irene A. Wright, ed., *Further English Voyages to Spanish America, 1583-1594* (London, Hakluyt Society, 1951). Those selected are (726) June 17, 1586, Pedro Menéndez Marqués to the Casa de Contratación, giving a brief account of his shattering experience, A.G.I., Santo Domingo 128, translated in Wright, pp. 163-164; (727) the royal officials when they wrote to the king on the same day were more composed, A.G.I., Seville, Contratación 5108, Wright, pp. 164-165; (728) June 30, 1586, a number of the members of the garrison were brought to Havana to be examined, depositions of five of them being given, A.G.I., Seville, Contratación 4802, Wright, pp. 180-184; (729) July 1, 1586, Gabriel de Luxan and Diego Fernández transmit Florida news reaching Havana, A.G.I., Seville, Santo Domingo 126, Wright, pp. 184-186; (730) July 1, 1586, Juan Bautista de Rojas to the king, indicating the help sent from Havana, A.G.I., Seville, Santo Domingo 118, 54/1/34, transcript Library of Congress, Division of Manuscripts, translated in D. B. Quinn, *Roanoke Voyages*, II, 754-756; (731) July 3, 1586, Alonso Suarez de Toledo to the king, an ironic outsider's view, stating boldly that Florida was useless, A.G.I., Seville, Santo Domingo 126, Wright, pp. 186-187; (732) July 4, 1586, Pedro de Araña to the Casa de Contratación, commenting on the strange loot Drake took from San Agustín, A.G.I., Seville, Contratación

5108, Wright, pp. 188–189; (733) July 12, 1586, Alonso Sancho Saez to the king, an accountant's response to Drake's destruction—he believed Drake had gone on to destroy the fort at Santa Elena (he had not been able to cross the bar), A.G.I., Seville, Santo Domingo 231, Wright, pp. 190–191; (734) July 17, 1586, Pedro Menéndez Marqués, now calmer, learns with relief that Santa Elena has been spared and has received some help from there, A.G.I., Seville, Indiferente General 1887, Wright, pp. 190–191; (735) August 12, 1586, further depositions, taken in San Agustín before Pedro de Valdés, clear up many details, A.G.I., Seville, Santo Domingo 229, Wright, pp. 198–202; (736) August 30, 1586, Pedro Menéndez Marqués reports he had sent Captain Vicente González directly to Spain with dispatches, A.G.I., Seville, Contratación 5708, Wright, pp. 202–203; (737) a September letter from Diego Fernández de Quiñones to the king, indicated how Drake had missed Santa Elena and gave details of negroes Drake intended to leave at Jacan [Chesapeake Bay], where it was now known the English were settled, A.G.I., Seville, Santo Domingo 126, Wright, p. 204; (738) September 2, 1586, Juan de Posada from San Agustín added further details of Santa Elena's escape, A.G.I., Seville, Santa Fé 89, Wright, pp. 205–206; finally (739) on September 5, the Casa de Contratación was able to pass the news on to Philip II, A.G.I., Seville, Contratación 5108, Wright, p. 206.

San Agustín had had its moment of fame following its destruction. At a more prosaic level Menéndez Marqués had to take in hand the reconstruction of his fort and town. To do so effectively he withdrew the garrison of Fort San Marcos, which he had established as recently as 1577, from Santa Elena, and it was never replaced. But even if conditions were primitive for a time the plight of the garrison and civilians brought effective assistance from Cuba and from Spain.

726. June 17, 1586. Pedro Menéndez Marqués to the president of the Casa de Contratación.

Very Illustrious Sir

I am reduced to such a situation that I do not know where to begin to relate the hardship and misery which have befallen this land. Therefore this communication will not be long, as will be observed.

On the 6th instant Francis Drake arrived at this port with 42 sail, 23 being large vessels and nineteen pinnaces, frigates and shallops. At dawn on the 7th he landed 500 men and with seven large pinnaces sought me forthwith in the fort. With 80 men I had in the fort I resisted him until nearly midday. In view of my resistance he sent to the ships which lay outside the bar for reinforcements, and in nine vessels landed some 2000 men and planted four pieces of artillery among certain sand dunes near the fort, with which he began to batter it. I retired as best I could, to protect my women and children (more than 200 persons).

Having occupied the fort, the enemy took and sacked the town and burned the church with its images and crosses, and cut down the fruit trees, which were numerous and good. He burned the fort and carried off the artillery and munitions and food supplies.

We are all left with the clothes we stood in, and in the open country with a little munition which was hidden. We are without food of any sort except six hogsheads of flour which will last twenty days at half a pound per head.

I am reporting to His Majesty in full in the accompanying despatch and entreat your lordship to forward it immediately, and to favour me as far and as speedily as possible, since help for Florida must come from your lordship's hands.

Our Lord, etc.

[Signed:] Pedro Menéndez Marqués
San Agustín, June 17, 1586.

727. June 17, 1586. The royal officials of Florida to the Crown.

Sacred Catholic Royal Majesty

As soon as news was received here of the damage which the English corsair had done in Santo Domingo, desiring to prepare as best he could (after consulting the persons best able to advise and after having reached an agreement with us to that effect), General Pedro Menéndez Marquéz built a new fort at the harbour mouth, at the bar, at the end of the channel, to protect the entrance. There he placed all the artillery and munitions. Considering how quickly it was done and by how few people, and with what scanty materials, the fort was very effective and well situated.

Therefore we removed thither the royal strong-box and all the books and papers of the accountant's office and others in addition which seemed important, together with our own valuables, even our clothing. And so did the general and the other soldiers who were there when the enemy arrived and assaulted with such vigor that we were compelled to withdraw under such stress of risk and danger that we could save nothing but the garments on our backs, and our arms and munitions. The enemy took everything. The royal strong-box contained little money because, payments due on account of these two forts being made, there is never much over, most years nothing.

Concerning the enemy's approach and the strength with which he attacked us, the general will report to Your Majesty, in whose compassion we confide, trusting that Your Majesty will decide to order that we be favored and provided for in such great affliction and calamity as this in which we remain, and so do we humbly entreat Your Majesty, whose sacred Catholic royal person Our Lord preserve many and happy years with increase of greater realms and lordships as Christianity has needed. San Agustín, June 17, 1586.

Sacred Catholic Royal Majesty,

Your Majesty's humblest servants and vassals kiss Your Majesty's royal feet.

[Signed:] Alonso Sancho Saez
Rodrigo de Junco
Bartólome de Arguelles

728. June 30, 1586. Depositions of five members of the San Agustín garrison about Drake's taking of the fort and town; taken at Havana.

In the city of San Cristóbal de la Habana,... Cuba,... on the thirtieth day of June in the year one thousand five hundred and eighty-six....

[a] Juan de Lepe, seaman,... being duly sworn... stated that about twenty days ago deponent being in the fort at San Agustin... from said fort twenty sails were descried, and these vessels anchored off the port and landed men from pinnaces. Deponent thinks about 1000 men came ashore. They landed artillery and began to batter the fort of San Agustín. The fight continued through two days, and through two nights they were under arms.

While this attack was going on deponent was putting the women and children on board his bark, in order to convey them to safety in the interior among the peaceable Indians.

Deponent heard that in view of the Englishman's strength and the damage he was doing, the garrison withdrew to the bush.

While deponent was in the bush with the women and children, Pedro Menéndez Marquéz arrived there with the troops, which were retiring.

Later deponent returned and saw that the fort, where Pedro Menéndez Marquéz was, had been burned. The English had burned it and the town and the old fort. They razed the maize fields and carried off everything in the town, and His Majesty's strong-box together with what was in it, which deponent heard was five thousand ducats.

The English remained there seven days, careening a vessel. At the end of that time they left, and three negroes who escaped from them (of those the English had seized in Santo Domingo) said that the Englishman was going to Santa Elena to take that place, and that from there he would proceed to Newfoundland; and this is the truth.

Further, the English carried off all the artillery and subsistence. The general had buried certain pieces but three of ours, who deserted, informed of this and they found these and carried them off...

This is the truth, on the oath he took. He did not sign because he does not know how to write; and he is about 24 years old...

[b] Bartólome Cordoriel... being duly sworn... stated that... he was in the fort of San Agustín on Friday after Corpus Christi when from the fort fifteen sail were sighted.

These being sighted, that night General Pedro Menéndez Marquéz ordered deponent to go with his bark to convey the women and children up the river from the fort into the bush, and so deponent did, making two trips. He also carried up six barrels of flour. Therefore deponent did not see the fight, but he heard the artillery fire exchanged between the fort and the English fleet. They fired and fought two days and two nights.

What deponent did see was nine English dead on the ground, and he heard it said that two of the enemy's pinnaces had been sunk. Three negroes who deserted from the English said that some English had been killed. No Spaniards were killed; but three soldiers deserted to the enemy, one of whom was French, one Flemish, and one Spanish.

After the two days and two nights that the siege lasted, the general withdrew to where deponent was with the women. Sixty men accompanied him.

The English held the port seven days. They careened a ship and at the end of that period burned the town and the fort and destroyed the estates and trees and razed the maize fields, felling and demolishing everything.

Deponent saw His Majesty's chest taken into the fort and later saw that it was not saved, because the English ruined and burned everything...

He signed his name and is about 28 years old...

[c] Francisco Hernández, ensign of the fort at San Agustin... being duly sworn... stated that on Friday after Corpus Christi, on the sixth of the present month of June, certain vessels appeared at sea off the port. They anchored at the entrance at the bar, and, according to persons who counted them, and to three negroes who deserted from the English, these were 23 large ships and many pinnaces and boats, to a total of more than 50 sail in all. Deponent could not count them because he was in the fort, which is more than a league from where they anchored.

Saturday morning at dawn boats and frigates and pinnaces put in, to land men. Twenty pinnaces and boats landed troops which deponent estimates at a thousand men.

They marched in formation with six flags flying, all red, without any other colour whatsoever. As they advanced a piece was fired from the fort, at which they paused and took shelter behind certain sand dunes. Other pieces were fired, which sank two pinnaces which were off the coast with seamen aboard.

As soon as the English discovered the fort, its position, and where they could plant artillery, they informed the English commander, who was on board the ships outside the bar. Thereupon, with twenty additional boatloads of men, the English commander came ashore with all his music. He brought four pieces of artillery and these were set up on land and began to batter the fort. The enemy so busied himself until nightfall on Saturday. The exchange of artillery fire continued until night fell.

At nightfall they took down the masts of all the pinnaces, boats and skiffs preparatory to reembarking therein, for they could not reach the fort except in skiffs, because there was a river between.

Next day in the morning watch without being observed they crossed the river in skiffs at a point where a launch belonging to the fort is stationed. The men there sounded the alarm and those on board this launch fled to the fort. Similarly, laden pinnaces crossed at another place and the fort was surrounded.

Seeing which, and that it was impossible to resist such numbers, since he had only 70 effectives and the fort was made of timber, General Pedro Menéndez Marquéz withdrew to where the women and children were to a total number of 200 souls. Had he delayed he and all his men must certainly have perished; and had they perished it was certain that the hostile Indians would have attacked the women and children and all would have been killed. Therefore the general took this measure to protect them.

The English held the fort seven days, at the end of which period they burned the town and forts, razed everything, even the trees and plantings, carried off all chattels, so that nobody saved anything at all. They took His Majesty's chest. The general had buried certain pieces of artillery, but three soldiers, who deserted to the Englishmen told him where and he carried them away...

He signed his name and is about 40 years old...

[d] Juan Alvarez, soldier of the Florida garrison, being duly sworn... stated that deponent was in the said fort on the sixth of the current month of June when off the port, at sea, appeared 23 large vessels and pinnaces, as many as ten of them with sails, and so many more boats and barges that deponent could not count them.

The same day, Friday, they came to anchor off the bar and Saturday morning in boats and barges and pinnaces sent men to shore and landed a party, the size of which deponent does not know. Once landed, in formation they marched on the fort, in squadrons with their flags flying, and halted behind certain sand dunes and from there withdrew toward the coast, and returned to report to their general. He came ashore with reinforcements and they brought up four pieces of artillery and planted them behind the sand dunes and from there opened fire on the fort. From the fort an answering fire was kept up Saturday afternoon, until nightfall. The fire from the fort sank two pinnaces in which certain men were killed, and later more were killed, to a total of over twenty English casualties. The Englishman killed nobody.

Saturday afternoon the English took down the masts of their pinnaces and boats; on observing which the general summoned a council to determine what to do, of which council deponent knows nothing except that he heard that in view of the enemy's very great strength and since the general had only 80 effectives and could not defend the fort because it was weak, made of timbers, and since if these men died the Indians would kill the women and children, the general [was of the opinion that the garrison should withdraw] and so they retired to where the women were.

The English held the fort seven days and burned the town and razed everything, even the maizefields, at the end of which time they withdrew.

... He signed his name and is about 30 years

old; and he heard that the English carried off the artillery and the contents of the royal chest...

729. July 1, 1586. Gabriel de Luxan and Diego Fernández de Quiñones report from Havana on the news from Florida.

Sacred Catholic Royal Majesty

Monday, the last of June, at one o'clock in the day, a small launch entered this harbour which Pedro Menéndez Marquéz, Your Majesty's governor and captain general of the provinces of Florida, sent with news that on June 6 the corsair Francis Drake appeared off San Agustín with all his fleet. Observing his strength and realizing his own inability to resist the enemy, after the English began to batter the fort and he had done his duty, Pedro Menéndez Marquéz was compelled to retire with all his garrison, and so he did, in order to go to the relief of what was left of San Agustín. For as soon as the English came down upon the fort, the Indians began to burn the town, according to what Pedro Menéndez Marquéz reports at length to Your Majesty in the enclosed despatch.

At the end of seven days, after he had completely razed the fort and destroyed what the Indians had left, and had spoiled the plantations and carried off everything, even to trifles and hardware and the furniture of the houses, leaving nothing whatsoever, according to what Pedro Menéndez Marquéz writes, the Englishman departed on a course for Santa Elena where we are certain nothing will have remained, given the corsair's purpose which, they said, originally was to proceed direct to Santa Elena, paying no attention to San Agustín. However, the Portuguese pilot he carried along, paid as expert and guide solely for the Florida coast and navigation of it, told him, when they reached the neighbourhood of San Agustín that there was the fort wherein the general resided and that it could very easily be taken since in all the forts there were only 300 men, and so to take San Agustín would not delay him. Therefore he carried out the attack.

All the people found safety in the bush. No

subsistence whatever or anything else was left, and by this launch Pedro Menéndez Marquéz sent to ask help in food supplies and equipment, nails, iron, augers, axes, saws, smithy, in order to reestablish the settlement and fortify it. He saved only his harquebuses and a barrel and a demijohn of powder...

We feel certain that nothing will remain of Santa Elena because the aborigines there have never been truly pacified or friendly. If our people escape from the Englishmen, the Indians will fall upon them or both will attack together. Our Lord guide all by His Divine hand!

Because the corsair carried off so many small things of all sorts, leaving nothing, nor any craft, large or small, that he could take along, we certainly believe it to be his intention to make a settlement at some point on the Florida coast so situated as to serve as a base from which to over-run all the Indies and attack the fleets. He has taken with him everything required, by land or sea, to establish a settlement, including even negroes which he seized at Santo Domingo and Cartagena.

Three of these fled from him and remained with Pedro Menéndez Marquéz, and they relate certain things concerning which he will report at greater length to Your Majesty. Pedro Menéndez Marquéz was not without his traitors, for they say that one or two of his Spanish soldiers deserted and went over to the enemy and furnished him full information, advising him not to fear, for the garrison was small and short of munitions. So also a foreign fifer deserted. This encouraged the enemy to attack with greater spirit....

If in passing the corsair called at Santa Elena, as we suppose to be most likely, everything will have been burned and lost, even if the enemy does not remain in occupation. Hereafter, if those forts are to be maintained, they cannot be of timber only and scantily garrisoned. It will be necessary for Your Majesty to take measures so to fortify that they can resist both the Indians and outside enemies; for when the crisis arrives both are foes to the death and our establishments cannot survive unless Your Majesty order the country settled and fortified once for all...

... from Your Majesty's fortress [Havana], July 1, 1586.

Sacred Catholic Royal Majesty

Your Majesty's most loyal and faithful vassals and servitors kiss Your Majesty's royal feet.
  [Signed:] Gabriel de Luxan
  Diego Fernández de Quiñones

730. July 1, 1586. Juan Bautista de Rojas to Philip II.

Sacred Catholic royal majesty: After having sent ahead two packet-boats to Spain in which I forwarded in duplicate [the report?] which will go with this, a small vessel arrived from Florida, despatched hence by the governor of that place, to ask for assistance in the form of men, food, gun-powder and other military stores and equipment with which he could rebuild the fortifications, since the English corsairs had landed on that coast and, he said, overpowered the garrison, captured and burnt the fortress, and, after seven days, they departed and went to Santa Elena, where we understand that all who were there have perished. God grant they may have had a better fate, and that these Lutherans may be confounded, and may he help your majesty to chastise their arrogance in the manner it deserves.

It appears that the corsairs left no artillery in the place, nor anything of iron or metal, but carried all away. The governor withdrew with his men to a place to which they had already sent the women and children. I took statements from four witnesses, selected from those who arrived here, so that your majesty might be fully informed of what happened and of the decisions taken here by the governor, the commander of the fortress and the officials, all of which is being sent to your majesty as evidence about this disaster.

We suspect that this corsair [Drake] wishes to settle near here. If this is so, it will be necessary to be very much, and unceasingly, on our guard. May your majesty, therefore, be pleased to send us in good time, the arms, stores and other things we have already asked for, not omitting anything, because if anything is left out and the enemy should come and find us ill-equipped, your majesty will realise the unfortunate results that will follow.

All that they asked us for from Florida we quickly despatched. Immediately, within four hours, we sent a small vessel with seven *arrobas* of gunpowder and thirteen of lead, biscuits, some oil and other necessities. We are now preparing in great haste a larger ship in which will be sent a number of casks of wine, flour, meat and the military equipment they have requested, as well as four small pieces of artillery, left here by the paymaster, Cevadilla, when he went to New Spain to collect his annual rents. We expect him back in the *flota*, and out of the amounts he has collected the cost of these stores will be paid. The ship will leave here within ten hours.

May God keep and prosper the sacred Catholic royal person of your majesty. May he increase your majesty's kingdoms and dominions, of which Christendom stands in such need, and as I, your majesty's humble servant, desire. Havana, 1 July 1586.

From your majesty's humble servant and vassal.

[Signed:] Juan Baptista de Rojas

731. July 3, 1586. Alonso Suarez de Toledo to Philip II.

Catholic Royal Majesty

On June 30, on the eve of the clearance of this advice-boat which Pilot Pedro Bernal is taking over, there came into this harbour a bark from San Agustín in Florida with news that on the 12th of that month the English corsair's fleet arrived off that fort. From ten pinnaces he landed 300 harquebusiers at San Agustín, where the fort is, and at the mouth of the channel in a swamp, where it was never foreseen that he would land, he set ashore 200 men and five heavy siege guns.

Pedro Menéndez Marquéz was in the fort with 80 men, and all the morning (until the siege guns came up) he defended it and killed some of the enemy, including a captain who was much esteemed by the English commander.

The friendly Indians came down upon a certain estate at a distance from the fort, where the women and children had taken refuge; in view of which, and finding himself surrounded by the enemy and Indians, Pedro Menéndez Marquéz withdrew and abandoned the fort.

The English carried off everything from the houses and from the fort and burned and razed and took away all the artillery.

From there they are proceeding to Fort Santa Elena with which they will deal in the same manner even more easily because it is less defensible and the Indians hostile.

To maintain Florida is merely to incur expense because it is and has been entirely unprofitable nor can it sustain its own population. Everything must be brought from outside. If, although Your Majesty possess Santo Domingo, Puerto Rico, Cuba, Yucatan and New Spain, the garrison of Florida has nevertheless suffered actual hunger, what would happen to foreigners there who must bring their subsistence from a great distance to an inhospitable coast? The land itself would wage war upon them! To say that they can maintain a base there from which to damage the fleets is idle talk because from Cape Cañaveral (which is the end of the Bahama channel) to San Agustín is a bay of 50 leagues and dangerous coast. Let Your Majesty improve this harbor instead, and fortify it, and send the galleons and the armada on this course—that is what is needed, and plain speaking.

Havana, July 3, 1586.

Our Lord preserve the Catholic royal person of Your Majesty in health and life and prosperity as the holy faith and these realms have need.

Catholic Royal Majesty

[I kiss] Your Majesty's royal feet.

[Signed:] Alonzo Suarez de Toledo

732. July 4, 1586. Pedro de Araña to the Casa de Contratación.

Very Illustrious Sir

Just as the two advice-boats were about to sail, Pedro Bernal and Blas González masters, there entered a little open launch from San Agustín in Florida, despatched by Governor Pedro Menéndez Marquéz. He reports that the corsair Francis

Drake with his fleet was sighted from the forts at San Agustín on the 6th of ultimo. He landed men and set up artillery on a hill which commanded the position in which Pedro Menéndez Marquéz had fortified himself because it was a stronger position than San Agustín itself. And after he had used his artillery, events developed as your lordship will see by the enclosed depositions...

The corsair took about 6000 ducats from His Majesty's strong-box and as much more belonging to private individuals who had buried it. He carried off the artillery and food supplies. The total he obtained must be over 8000 ducats. He did more than 40,000 ducats damage in burning the town and razing all its plantations. After he had done this the enemy sailed away on June 13 saying that he was going to Santa Elena.

He will have taken that place as easily and Gutierre de Miranda will have run even greater risk. It is considered that it will have been difficult for him to escape from the Englishman; and if he does, it will be only to encounter worse enemies in the Indians...

Of His Majesty's armada there is no news here, nor has the fleet arrived yet...

Persons coming in from Florida state that the enemy is stronger in ships and men than we were informed... He could come out to meet the fleet from Santa Elena and that coast where unquestionably there is an English settlement.

If there were not, and Francis Drake did not intend to proceed thither after disembogueing, there would be no sense in his taking the pains he took to carry off launches and frigates, implements, locks and all sorts of hardware and negro laborers who in his country are free....

Havana, July 4, 1586.
Very Illustrious Sir
Your lordship's faithful servant who kisses your lordship's hand.
     [Signed:] Pedro de Araña

733. July 12, 1586. Alonso Sancho Saez to Philip II.

Sacred Catholic Royal Majesty
The advent of the English corsair, Francis Drake, has brought this city and fort, civilians, soldiers and civil servants of Your Majesty, to the danger, want, calamity and ruin which may be imagined, to which he and his followers were pleased to reduce us. From this follow the damage, loss, hardship and confusion which our general indicates to Your Majesty in his latter, to which I refer. When the fury of his attack had passed, learning that the enemy had sailed away, apparently on a course for Fort San Marcos at Santa Elena, which is 60 leagues from this fort, we returned to this city from the bush whither we had retired, according to the general's wise provision. Here, naturally, we found our misery and labor doubled by the irreparable damage which had been done.

For, although this land was so newly occupied and cultivated, it was one of the best and most populous to be found in all the Indies, and well supplied with fine fruits because, although we did not know whether it were Your Majesty's intention to carry this establishment on, we who live here had been so much inspired by the harvest obtained in the conversion of the natives to God's service that we were encouraged to build houses which, although made of wood, were expensive because so good. All this, by Your Majesty's most Christian favour, enjoyed for so long, had laid the good commencement and foundation which was to be anticipated—the first fruits and reward which God prepared for him who is accustomed to labor for the exaltation of His holy faith. And if perchance because of our sins (I mean the sins of us who live here) this disaster has occurred, it is not to be supposed that in Your Majesty's most Christian breast there will be lacking the warmth which is expected in order that so holy a work may proceed; just as courage and valor were not lacking in our general's heart to enable him to make the most of the juncture which presented itself, when in an instant he had to make a decision upon which hung the fate of all, whereby may be judged his great astuteness and prudence. Had he acted otherwise than he did, it would have been the greatest temerity, since he was eye to eye with death, as the saying goes. It would be a lengthy and tiresome business to seek to furnish Your Majesty with a detailed account of matters which without such are usually inferred, and I will conclude by saying that having in Fort San Juan lost the papers of the accountant's office and the funds from the deceased persons' estates which were in my charge, this represented nothing more or less than the culmination of my poverty and other persons fared as badly, having trusted solely in that fort. In truth, there was no other place as strong. The royal officials, my colleagues, and I have resumed the work of our offices...

... San Agustín in Florida, July 12, 1586.
Sacred Catholic Royal Majesty
Your Majesty's most humble servant and vassal kisses Your Majesty's royal feet.
[Signed:] Alonso Sancho Saez

734. July 17, 1586. Pedro Menéndez Marqués to Philip II.

Sacred Catholic Royal Majesty
... As reported to Your Majesty in my other despatch, copy enclosed, the corsair left here on June 12 and on the 17th entered Cruz bay with his small vessels, leaving the larger ships outside. He supposed he was at Santa Elena, but Cruz harbour is seven leagues this side. So he departed thence and passed by Santa Elena bay in the night and arrived at Oristan, which is three leagues beyond it. There also he entered in the same order.

God was pleased that he should not find Santa Elena harbour, for it has many shoals and he kept well to sea. He fired his artillery many times expecting to be answered, but he was not.

At Oristan he took on plenty of water and firewood, and a mast for a vessel which was badly in need of repair; and disappeared from there on June 26 with all his fleet.

This was learned from the lookouts which Gutierre de Miranda had among the natives there; further, the warning I sent by sea and land had just reached Santa Elena, from where, in a launch, they immediately sent me eight barrels of flour and a little munition. God be praised for all! The fact that that fort stands is a great help. The corsair cannot have departed out of love with this land, since he found it in such good order, and fruitful and cultivated, although he ruined everything and ordered it to be burned and razed,

showing himself especially severe with my property, against which it seemed he wished to show his greatest rigour. It is to be feared that he, or others whom he will encourage, will not forget that they fared well and will endeavour to damage Your Majesty further; wherefore it will be advisable to be prepared for eventualities since this retreat is suited to their purposes, for it lies on the course by which the fleets and all shipping disembogue. . . .

The three negroes who remained here (of those with the corsair) say that they belong to Your Majesty and are part of the lot working on the fort in charge of Bachiller Tostado in Santo Domingo...
San Agustín, July 17, 1586.
Sacred Catholic Royal Majesty
Your sacred Catholic Royal Majesty's least servant kisses Your Majesty's royal hands.
[Signed:] Pedro Menéndez Marqués

735. August 12, 1586. Further depositions taken before Pedro de Valdés at San Agustín provide additional details of Drake's activities.

In the city of San Agustín, provinces of Florida, on the twelfth day of the month of August in the year one thousand five hundred and eighty-six, before me, the undersigned notary public.

[a] Alonso Sanchez de Mercado, accountant of these provinces, being duly sworn... stated that... on the sixth of last June in the current year, about two or three in the afternoon, sails were sighted which were steering straight towards the bar of this fort. When they had come nearer, eighteen large ships were counted and five smaller ones, a number of pinnaces, frigates and barges, which all stood off along the bar.

The next day, which was Saturday, before daybreak, being with General Pedro Menéndez Marquéz and other soldiers he had selected for the purpose, in the fort of San Juan, newly constructed to repel the enemy, deponent saw that the enemy sent to land large pinnaces to attack the fort. They advanced as day broke, sounding the bar. When they were discovered and the artillery could be directed upon them, fire was opened and the resistance possible was offered.

In view of this, the corsair ordered his pinnaces back to the fleet and, since the large ships could not come up because of the bar and the fort was resisting, they returned to the fleet; and in these pinnaces and in the frigates and barges which had remained with the fleet, they sent to shore a large number of men. Deponent believes that these numbered eight hundred.

Behind certain sand dunes they drew up in formation, flags flying and drums beating; and deponent saw how the pinnaces and frigates and barges withdrew to the ships, and nineteen of them returned a second time and landed about four hundred men.

With these troops they again attacked the fort, which met them with such fire from its artillery that they again withdrew with the loss of one pinnace which was sunk. It was publicly said that the men aboard it were killed.

At this the officer in command of these craft sent a boat to the flagship and deponent observed that two large and nine small frigates came to shore in which apparently they brought large reinforcements and four pieces of heavy brass artillery. They planted these in four positions within an harquebus shot of the fort, which they began to batter. At the same time a large number of men landed from the frigates, pinnaces and barges. Deponent estimates the total number at a thousand men. It was understood that Francis Drake, corsair, was among them because where they set up the artillery in the afternoon there was music of cornets, sackbuts and flageolets.

The exchange of artillery and musketry fire continued all that afternoon. Some English were killed, as appeared later when the corpses were found.

That afternoon the general ordered Juan de Contreras, Indian interpreter for the district around the city, to make a night attack. Since he could not find Indians to accompany him, with only ten of them he attacked the enemy that night and they say that they killed four Englishmen but could not do more because of the enemy's much superior force.

Observing that his assault had had little effect, as soon as night fell the corsair removed the masts from his pinnaces and frigates and in the darkness reconnoitred the position of the fort, so making ready to land his forces. They came up to a launch belonging to His Majesty, and took it, although momentarily it was defended against them.

When the moon rose, observing that all the enemy's pinnaces had come up close to the fort, and that he had landed men on both sides of it, realizing that he was lost beyond earthly help and that it would be a great temerity with so few men to await the attack of so many, and that he could not fire his artillery against the enemy's batteries, appreciating that if the garrison were lost, it meant also the loss of the non-combatants, women and children, who by his order had withdrawn to the bush to the number of about two hundred and fifty persons, the general held a council of the most experienced persons present with him to decide what should be done. As a result they all retired, withdrawing through a swamp, since there was no other way they could go without falling into the enemy's hands. They retired to the place where the rest were, without bringing out of the fort anything except the flag and their arms. As the soldiers left they cast two bronze falcons into the moat, which was not completed.

So also deponent knows and saw that while the general was in the fort, fighting, and the civilians were in retreat, the Indians sacked this city and stole everything there was in the houses. From this may be inferred the evil intention they entertained, and if the general had not taken the wise measure of withdrawing at the moment when he did, these people would certainly have perished at the hands of the Indians, as was obvious.

Next day the corsair occupied the fort and sacked it. He took possession of the town, where he remained six or seven days. At the end of this period he burned and razed it, and carried off everything portable. On retiring he did the same by the fort and withdrew to his fleet and sailed straight for the fort of Santa Elena where it was supposed that he would conduct himself in like manner, since he was strong.

All which has brought great damage and loss on the royal exchequer and private individuals, and devastation on this city, which was well populated, comfortable, fruitful and abounding in many things. Everybody was left naked, stripped of everything, in the open country, and without recourse.

Deponent observed that the general fulfilled his duty, doing everything he possibly could do.

This is the truth on the oath he took and he stated that he was about thirty-six years old; and signed his name.—Alonso Sancho Saez.

[b] Miguel de Valdés, soldier of the garrison, being duly sworn... stated that on Friday last, June sixth of this current year, General Pedro Menéndez Marquéz being in Fort San Juan with a part of the people who were to assemble when the enemy should appear, the look-out made signals that ships were approaching. Thereupon from the fort the signal was given for the rest to report, although the first signal was that a launch was arriving from the fort at Santa Elena. Then the look-out gave the warning signal that many ships were approaching, and accordingly the corsair Francis Drake came up with a fleet of vessels and stood off, along the bar. Deponent estimates (as nearly as he could count) that there were 23 large ships and a great number of smaller craft.

On Saturday following, before dawn, nine large pinnaces entered and sought the fort. As soon as they were seen and the artillery could be fired, the defence opened by sinking one of these pinnaces. They retired and withdrew towards the beach and landed their troops to the number of six hundred men, it was estimated. They drew up in formation behind certain sand dunes there and the pinnaces returned to the fleet. Nineteen pinnaces and frigates and barges came back to land with reinforcements which seemed to be about two thousand men. They again attacked the fort. They met with resistance and again withdrew with the loss of another pinnace which was knocked to pieces.

In view of this the corsair landed heavy artillery which he planted in four different positions at about an harquebus shot from the fort, among the sand dunes. With these he began to batter the fort. The artillery and musketry fire continued until nightfall and some English were killed.

The general ordered Juan de Contreras, interpreter for the Indians of this vicinity, to make a night attack on the enemy. They say that they killed six Englishmen. Because the enemy was numerous they found it convenient to withdraw.

That night the corsair removed the masts from his pinnaces and in the darkness reconnoitred the position of the fort, preparatory to landing the rest of his men. He carried off a launch belonging to His Majesty which was in a bayou near the fort. It offered some resistance. When the moon came up the enemy's pinnaces were discovered near the fort and his troops on shore on both sides of it.

Observing this and in view of the fact that he was lost beyond earthly help and that it would be temerity for so few men to await the attack of so many and in such force, because the fort was built of timbers and not completely finished, and since if he and the men with him were lost it meant nothing more nor less than the loss of the non-combatants who, by his order, had retired to the bush, women and children, to the number of about two hundred and fifty persons, the general summoned a council of the persons of most weight who were present to determine what should de done. They resolved to withdraw through a swamp, at great risk because they were surrounded by the enemy. They removed from the fort nothing but their persons, the flag and their arms because there was no opportunity to do more.

They withdrew to the place where the rest of the people were in retreat. The only thing they could do before they left was to throw two bronze falcons into the moat, which was being built.

Deponent knows, and it was obvious, that had not the general taken this measure, not only the men with him in the fort but also those who had withdrawn to the bush, must have perished because of the evil intention which the Indians demonstrated in that, when they saw the soldiers in the fort fighting and the rest of the people in retreat, they sacked and looted the city, entering its houses and carrying off everything, leaving nothing.

The day after the garrison evacuated it became known that the corsair took possession of the fort and sacked it. Immediately he entered the town, where he remained about six days. At the end of this time he burned everything and carried off what food supplies there were and the artillery. Similarly he burned Fort San Juan and made sail on a course for Santa Elena. They said that although the corsair made every endeavour to converse with soldiers of the fort, the general was vigilant to prevent this.

This is the truth on the oath he took, and he signed his name. He affirmed and ratified this deposition and said that he was about thirty-six years old.

[Signed:] Pedro Miguel de Valdés

736. August 30, 1586. Pedro Menéndez Marqués to the Casa de Contratación.

Very Illustrious Sir

By way of Havana I have twice reported to your lordship on events here, and so also I reported by Captain Vicente González who left here on July 17 with dispatches. Therefore in this communication I will not repeat nor say more than that two days later, on the 19th of July, Captain Juan de Posada arrived with the reinforcements and relief he brought, which came very opportunely.

According to what he says and what we have learned here from the Indians I think that this corsair has an establishment in this country and not far from here, for some of his ships entered a harbor beyond Santa Elena and told the Indians that they were going to their village, which was nearby.

If this is true he will not fail to return this spring to raid this coast and if he returns he will reduce it to utter ruin. I am writing to His Majesty in the matter, entreating him to send relief quickly or, at least, to combine the forts in one, which will then be reasonably strong, although the corsair is so powerful that everything is puny in comparison. Unless this relief arrives, or promise of it, during the month of December, or the middle of January at latest, we shall be completely lost.

I beg your lordship to favor me in so far as may be possible to your lordship, whose very illustrious persons and houses Our Lord preserve and increase through many years as we servitors of your lordship desire.

San Agustín, August 30, 1586.
Illustrious Sir
Your lordship's servant kisses your lordship's hands.

[Signed:] Pedro Menéndez Marquéz

As I was closing this letter an Indian came in from Santa Elena to say that as he left there, which must have been on the 18th of this month, eight sail appeared off Santa Elena, five being large ships and the other three, small; and these three entered and sounded the bar, and went out again, after which they all disappeared. When this Indian was asked why he brought no letter from Gutierre de Miranda he said that he was busied with his men in defence of the place and could not write but bade him relate what he saw, adding that if anything further occurred Gutierre de Miranda would advise. This may be a fabrication of the natives. Nevertheless I immediately sent an ensign in a small bark which I had here, to learn the truth. He will be back in fifteen days at latest. If it is anything important I will inform your lordship by a ship I have here.

Very Illustrious Sir
Your Lordship's servant kisses your lordship's hands.

[Signed:] Pedro Menéndez Marquéz

737. September, 1586. Diego Fernández de Quiñones to Philip II.

Sacred Catholic Royal Majesty

On the 18th [of August] . . . at four in the afternoon a launch from Florida entered this harbour . . . It brought news that the corsair Francis Drake had not found the harbor of Santa Elena. Seeking it, he entered another seven leagues this side. Since he did not see the fort he made sail and passed by Santa Elena in the night. He put off pinnaces to locate the entrance to the port and fired artillery, to see if the fort would reply. Gutierre de Miranda recognized that this was the corsair, for Pedro Menéndez Marquéz had previously warned him, and ordered that no piece of artillery or harquebus be discharged nor any light shown. Since he could discover nothing, the corsair sailed by and entered another port four leagues beyond Santa Elena and there again fired his artillery. Since he found no fort there he took in water and firewood, felled masts for his ships, and from there proceeded on his course toward the Newfoundland Banks.

Pedro Menéndez Marquéz writes me that he took the depositions of three negroes who speak Spanish and remained behind when the corsair left. They say he meant to leave all the negroes he had in a fort and settlement established at Jacan by the English who went there a year ago. There he intended to leave the 250 blacks and all the small craft he had, and cross to England with only the larger vessels with which he threatened these forts and this city, to which he says he will return when it shall be less ready to receive him.

This settlement and fort of theirs at Jacan are directly west of Bermuda, 250 leagues from Santa Elena, from which position they can readily attack the fleets at any season. . . .

San Cristóbal de la Habana, September—, 1586.

Sacred Catholic Royal Majesty

Your Majesty's most loyal, faithful vassal and servant kisses Your Majesty's royal feet.

[Signed:] Diego Fernández de Quiñones

738. September 2, 1586. Juan de Posada to Philip II.

Sacred Catholic Royal Majesty

Fifty days after I left those realms I arrived in these provinces, having called at no intermediate port, a thing no man before me has accomplished. I sailed on a course different from that taken by other pilots who have come hither. And certainly I believe this was ordained by God for, although my arrival was late with respect to the corsair

himself, because the damage was already done and he had gone, I came in time to avoid that which our people feared from the aborigines since ours had no fort, artillery, food supplies, or munitions, and, what was the worst, the natives were plotting to kill them all—soldiers, women and children—as has been ascertained within the last eight days. The reinforcement I brought in men and supplies put an end to this danger, and to want, and to the audacity of these savages. Had I arrived fifteen days later I do truly believe that all would have perished. . . .

The Englishman left happy, it seems, to fall upon Santa Elena, but because there are shoals along the shore he kept well out and when he sighted the coast again he found that he had passed by. He had a fair wind, so that he could not turn back. Therefore he entered a bay there, where he landed a party and greatly flattered the Indians of that district, assuring them that in the spring the English would return and that they had a settlement on the coast near.

All this was learned in consequence of measures the general took and gifts which he gave those Indians. The Indians say that from there he sailed coasting the land toward the northwest.

What confirms the supposition and assures his return, in addition to what was learned of the Indians, is that although he had burned this city and fort he did no damage at all to an Indian village which is a cannon's shot from here. On the contrary, he sent persons there to flatter these natives, just as he did with those yonder; but they found the village deserted because in addition to being Catholics and such close neighbours, they had withdrawn to the bush with their women and children.

The corsair carried off with him a great many negroes and Turks from the galleys, according to the three negroes belonging to Your Majesty who ran away from him and are here. They understand certainly that the enemy has a settlement near these provinces and that these slaves are for use there . . .

San Agustín, September 2, 1586.

Your sacred Catholic Royal Majesty's humble servant who kisses Your Majesty's royal feet.

[Signed:] Juan de Posada

739. September 5, 1586. Casa de Contratación to Philip II.

Sacred Catholic Royal Majesty

On the 3rd of the present month the caravel of which Pedro Bernal Cermeño is master entered the port of San Lucar de Barrameda. He was dispatched by the governor and royal officials and warden of the city of San Cristóbal de la Havana with news that Francis Drake with his fleet appeared within sight of that city on May 29 and disappeared on the 31st without landing men or doing any damage there.

On June 6 he arrived at the port of San Agustín in Florida and on the 7th landed troops and artillery and battered the fort for two days and two nights. Although Pedro Menéndez defended himself, because he could no longer defend himself against the enemy he decided to evacuate the fort and the town and to retire to the bush, whither he had sent the women and the children and his invalids. Francis Drake burned the fort and houses of the town and remained there until the 12th, careening a ship. He steered thence for Santa Elena but because he could not make the port he could do nothing and continued on his course.

Being informed of the loss of San Agustín, the governor and officials of Havana sent the relief in food supplies and artillery and other things for which Pedro Mendéndez Marquéz asked, as shown by lists and writs which they sent us, of which accurate copies are enclosed herewith, and by the deposition which Pedro Bernal Cermeño made at San Lúcar (also enclosed) to which we refer. . . .

We also enclose another relation furnished by the governor and officials of Havana of a deposition they received from Pedro Sanchez, seaman, native of Zaragoza, who escaped from Francis Drake's fleet at Cape San Antonio where the Englishman lay five days, taking on water and firewood. From this Your Majesty will see, in brief, what Francis Drake did at Cartagena and the intentions he had of going to Rio de la Hacha and Honduras and other parts, and the reason why he did not do so. According to this account and to advices so far received it does not appear that he has done more than take Santo Domingo and Cartagena and San Agustín.

Pedro Menéndez Marquéz sent Captain Vicente González in another caravel with news of the loss of San Agustín and events there and to report to Your Majesty on all that happened. From the accompanying deposition Your Majesty will understand what a crossing he made and the corsairs he saw and the adventures he encountered.

Blas González, master of another advice-caravel, has also arrived, sent by the governor and royal officials of Cartagena to report Francis Drake's departure with his fleet from that port, and from the deposition which he has made (enclosed herewith) Your Majesty will see that this fleet was in that harbor 64 days, and what it did there. . . .

From Havana and from Florida and from everywhere else they ask for artillery and arms and munitions and equipment, in order to be prepared, for Francis Drake has threatened those coasts. We entreat Your Majesty to order this looked to in season and to provide them with what they ask, inasmuch as there are many corsairs and they cannot defend themselves without these things. . . .

Chapter Ninety-three
The Emergence of the Franciscan Presence

ALTHOUGH THERE had been Franciscan friars at work since 1573, it was only in the 1590s that they began to make their presence felt. The arrival of Avendaño as governor in 1594 marked a new scale of activity on their part. Fray Francisco de Marrón's letter of July 6, 1594 (740) marks their new confidence in the significance of the missionaries in the colony, and his subsequent letter of January 23, 1596 (741) records the arrival of twelve more missionaries in September, 1595, and confirms and strengthens this trend.

740. July 6, 1594. Fray Francisco de Marrón to Philip II.

A.G.I, Seville, Santo Domingo, 235, 54/5/20; printed in Luis Gerónimo de Oré, Relación histórica de la Florida, edited by Atanasio López, II (1933), 5-6, translated.

Very Excellent Sir:

I was at Havana on behalf of my monastery of St. Francis when Captain Avendaño arrived as governor of the provinces of Florida, and since I had been for some years past in that land at the mandate and commission of Father Friar Francisco de Guzmán, who sent me from the Spanish court, the said Governor Avendaño asked the prelate of Havana for me, saying it was for the service of Your Majesty: and so they sent me as mission head and prelate of the men of religion who live in these provinces, where we arrived on the sixteenth of June of this year, 1594. The Governor sent by Your Majesty was received peacefully and willingly by the garrison: and with matters continuing in this way, without any preceding act of severity by the Governor, six days after his arrival, there was a new disturbance by ten soldiers, who must have been afraid about what had happened, after there had been rumors of their plot to take control of the fort and set fire to the Governor's house, which caused the town great worry and anxiety. I was told about this, and in some confusion I informed the Governor, who with all speed found out who they were, arrested them with great secrecy and put them on a ship, and his great prudence and wisdom has left the whole garrison and the town very quiet and calm.

So that Your Majesty should be best served, and the divine offices in the town church and this monastery should be performed with solemnity and devotion, as they are at present, thanks to the great Christianity and sense of the Governor, both in this respect and in everything else that concerns his rule, the Indian chiefs have been glad to come and give him obedience again, in the name of Your Majesty, demonstrating great love and friendship both to him and to all those in the garrison; so I expect in the Lord that their conversions to Christianity will increase greatly, as many of them already are Christian, because of the great diligence put into this by the few ministers that there are in this land at the moment: here there fit well the words of the Holy Gospels, Mesis quidem multa, operarii autem pauci. With the blessing of God and Your Majesty the preaching of the Holy Gospels will be extended, because apart from the good that results to the souls of these poor natives, it will be most useful to the calm and peace of the whole land. May Our Lord keep the catholic and royal person of Your Majesty, etc.

From this garrison of San Agustín of Florida, 6th July 1594.

There kisses the feet and hands of Your Majesty his obedient vassal and chaplain,

[Signed:] Friar Francisco de Marrón

741. January 23, 1596. Fray Francisco de Marrón to Philip II.

A.G.I., Seville, Santo Domingo 235, 54/5/20; printed in Luis Gerónimo de Oré, Relación histórica de la Florida, *edited by Atanasio López, II (1933), 68, translated.*

Sir:

With the grace and favor which Your Majesty shows to this garrison and the provinces of Florida, the men of religion who are living and staying here, with the closest bond as vassals and chaplains of Your Majesty, attend to what concerns the royal service, and are particularly grateful for the new favor of having sent the twelve men of religion for the conversion and instruction of the natives here. They arrived on the 23rd September last year. They have been distributed to their posts, both in towns and in the provinces of Timuca and Guales and of fresh water, with great enthusiasm in the honour of God and the service of Your Majesty: happy to employ themselves in the improvement of souls, they are learning the languages of the lands they are in, and thus the natives are coming to like them, and gladly come to the mission and ask for Holy Baptism. And since the men of religion are among them, they are peaceful among themselves, and without the wars in which those of one town used to kill those of another at the least excuse; and also they are glad to lend obedience to Your governors, and friendship to the military who are sent to their lands, and this year they have been glad to pay the tribute to Your Majesty, and wish to pay it always.

Since I have gone to visit the men of religion in those parts, as I am the one placed here by the Order for this ministry, I have seen the great distances there are between one town and another, and that the men of religion cannot send the vestments one to another: so they are stopping celebrating and even hearing Mass on Sundays and feastdays. The land and the natives are so lacking that they cannot provide vestments, cups and bells, missals and manuals of the sacraments, and so all the men of religion request Your Majesty to order that we be provided with this which is so necessary to fill this lack, for it is so important. And so that the present necessity should be clear, I am sending with this letter a report concerning ecclesiastical matters.

On the 24th November last year, Our God was pleased to take Governor Domingo Martínez de Avendaño, who had arrived on general visit with great enthusiasm for your royal service. It was decided as the surest and most suitable measure, for the sake of calm and good rule, both in the towns and the armed forces, that there should govern Your Royal Officals Bartolomé de Arguellez, Accountant, Juan Menéndez, Treasurer, and Alonso de las Alas, Crown Agent. The two who were present when the governor died, that is, the treasurer and the crown agent, have been in disagreement, and at times have had lengthy public arguments with words that do not become the gravity of their office, not caring if this should lead to factions and warring opinions, in which some people might wish one of them to govern them rather than the other, and all because they could not agree about sending the advice to Your Majesty for the provision of government, which we need so badly. Juan Menéndez Marquéz, the treasurer, is particularly held to be to blame for this, since he has made most noise. It all stopped with the arrival of Bartolomé de Arguellez, the accountant, who came from New Spain, and brought the pay ship, which arrived on the twelfth of January this year, and with his arrival it was all smoothed out, for he is a man of good ways and a good Christian, who has long experience of the land and so knows how to carry things off with tact, and so he has sent off the advice and many things that had been held up with great pleasure and speed, to the agreement of all. And thus, as such a loyal vassal, he deserves that Your Majesty should give him the favor of the governorship, because I sincerely believe that he has the surest touch in matters over here. And Your

Majesty will be well served with the peace and content of the land: the natives have a particular liking for him, and so, as this is a matter of great importance, the service of Your Majesty, and that this land should have a ruler that governs it perceptively. We, men of religion, your servants, are continually asking God to look after and cause to prosper the catholic royal person of Your Majesty as Christianity needs.

From this city and garrison of San Agustín, 23rd January 1596.

In this garrison of Your Majesty remain Juan de Avendaño, who holds the office of Sergeant Major, and Company Captain Sebastián de Malleda, who both came with the dead governor. They carry out their duties gladly, confident that Your Majesty will order that they should have the favour of being confirmed in their posts, for they are certainly well-deserving men in the service of Your Majesty. And the Sergeant Major, Juan de Avendaño, who is the nephew of the dead governor, since his post is one in which no greater salary is provided for him than that of an ordinary soldier, and he is living in hardship, needs Your Majesty to decree for him some salary with which he can decently get by.

The chaplain and servant of Your Majesty,
[Signed:] Friar Francisco de Marrón

Chapter Ninety-four
The Search for the English Colony,
1585–1606, and the Exploration
of Chesapeake Bay

PEDRO MENÉNDEZ MARQUÉS was naturally concerned to follow up his earlier attempts to locate the English colony when, in 1586, he discovered that Drake intended to visit and reinforce it that same year. At Christmas, 1585, the first reconnaissance had gone no farther than the southern limit of the Carolina Outer Banks. By July, 1586, he was sufficiently far advanced in the reconstruction of San Agustín to dispatch his Portuguese shipmaster and pilot, Vicente González, to bring firsthand news of the Drake raid to Spain and to land along the coast on his way home to see whether he might locate the English port. González reported that he had entered a bay some five miles wide and eighty miles long, leading to the interior. Possibly, this might have been Chesapeake Bay and the James River (although it is more likely to have been the Cape Fear River). There the Indians told him that the English colony was farther north. On November 27, Philip II instructed Pedro Menéndez Marqués himself to go to find the site as soon as he could (742). This letter finally reached Florida on May 2. Taking the vessels that had brought the dispatch, the governor went north, believing that the English were in the Bahía de Santa María, Chesapeake Bay, which his uncle had discovered in 1561 and had visited again in 1572. He appears to have reached the entrance to the bay, but was driven off by a violent storm. Eventually, he put in at Havana. From there he wrote to Spain to admit his defeat (743). He said that he would attempt entry again in 1588, but during a later part of the year. Earlier, officials at Florida had found nothing further on English intentions (744).

Early in 1588 Menéndez Marqués was preoccupied with the removal of the garrison from Santa Elena and the building of a bigger and better fort at San Agustín, but he reported on July 17 that he had sent Captain Vicente González north early in July to make a thorough search of Chesapeake Bay (745). González's own report of that mission has not been found, but a copy of the journal of Juan Menéndez Marqués passed into the possession of Fray Luis Gerónimo de Oré, who printed much later what may well be a complete version of it. This is the first detailed and full account of the bay in existence, but it produced no evidence of English settlement. However, on the Carolina Outer Banks (on the way south), evidence in the form of a slipway and barrels sunk in the sand to catch water indicated the near presence of the English (746). He was back in San Agustín before the end of July. Oré then went on to relate later history regarding the search for the English. In July Pedro de Araña reported that a Spanish sailor had been taken by Captain William Irish into what he believed to be Chesapeake Bay in 1587. There he took in water only and did not encounter any English colonists, but he did see a stray mule (747). Finally, in March, 1589, the same Pedro de Araña was able to obtain in Havana a full deposition from Pedro Diaz, who had been captured by the English, had made several voyages with them to Roanoke Island, had escaped in 1588, and therefore was able to give a precise location for the colony site (454). From this there followed royal instructions for Menéndez Marqués to go to Spain, which he did, arriving in mid-July, 1589 (749). After discussions in the Council of the Indies, a decision was made not to allow the English to maintain a colony on the Outer Banks, or in Chesapeake Bay. Menéndez Marqués was to prepare a major expedition, destroy whatever remained on Roanoke Island, and establish a 300-strong garrison on Chesapeake Bay. But the expedition was postponed: Menéndez Marqués was needed for other purposes, and the scheme had not been revived before he finally retired in 1593.

The question of English settlement lay in a kind of limbo between 1590 and 1598. By then a new governor, Méndez de Canzo, wishing to launch an expansion program, found some evidence of the continued English presence from the Irish soldier David Glavin, who had actually been a Roanoke colonist (755). He also found that some of his officials (notably its commander, Vicente González [748], and his treasurer, Juan Menéndez Marqués) remembered a little about the 1588 voyage, but their recollections showed that neither had a journal to present and their memories were patchy and ineffective. Long after, between 1606 and 1608, when English activity was once more a live issue, Juan Menéndez Marqués was induced to dredge up some further recollections of the 1588 voyage, but they were not of very substantial value either (749). But the revived interest, between 1598 and 1608, in the González voyage is not so important in itself as is the evidence it presents of continued Spanish interest in Chesapeake Bay down to and into the time of its occupation by an English colony.

742. November 27, 1586. Philip II instructs Pedro Menéndez Marqués to investigate the location of the English colony.

AA.G.I., Seville, Indiferente General 541, fol. 7v., translated.

(That he should advise concerning a report that by a river near Newfoundland the Atlantic communicates with the Pacific, and that some Englishmen have settled near.)

The King
Pedro Menéndez, marqués, My Governor and Captain General of the Provinces of Florida. Captain Vicente González has reported that as he was going under your orders along the coast near Newfoundland to find out if, as has been said, there were some pirates based there, he went investigating the whole coast and going into all the bays: and among the many others he went into, he came across one that is two leagues wide at the mouth and extends thirty leagues inland; he talked with an Indian chief whom many of the others respected, and among other pieces of information concerning the fertility and richness of the land, he gathered that to the North of that place there was a river that went through to the other ocean, and that near to it there were some English settlers, as is explained in more detail in the report he made, a copy of which accompanies this letter. It is important to find out in detail what there is in this, so I instruct you with great diligence and care to try and find out if it is true that there is in that area the river which is said to go from one ocean to the other, and how far north it is, and if by any chance it could be found out whether these pirates have tried to sail along it, and where they have settled, and what their plans are; and everything that you can discover either for certain or by hearsay you will send me an account of as quickly as possible.

From Madrid, 27th November 1586.
    [Signed:] I the King
Countersigned and signed by the aforementioned.

743. June 22, 1587. Pedro Menéndez Marqués reports that he has failed to enter Chesapeake Bay.

This letter was probably written to the president of the Council of the Indies, but it has no address.
A.G.I., Seville, Contratación 5108; translated in I. A. Wright, Further English Voyages, pp. 232–233, and also in C. M. Lewis and A. J. Loomie, Spanish Jesuit Mission in Virginia (1953), p. 167. The former is reprinted here.

In Florida on the 2nd of last May I received a dispatch from His Majesty in which he orders me to discover whether any corsairs have settled on that coast, and whether there is a passage, as they say there is, to the other sea. Within five days after I had received it I sailed from San Agustín in the same frigate which brought the dispatch and with two small boats to execute His Majesty's command.

First leaving munitions and reinforcements at Santa Elena, I coasted to latitude 37°, very near Jacan, which is Santa Maria bay. Before one arrives there are three bad shoals which extend far to sea; elsewhere the coast is much better, both the bottom and the shore, than it is between Santa Elena and Cape Cañaveral, for there are very good ports.

Along all the shore that I coasted there is no knowledge of any corsair. I did not go further because the day that I was to enter at Jacan a tremendous storm blew which drove me from the coast and damaged my sail. It drove me to the Lucayos, off this island. Of my two small boats I there lost one, with all its equipment. Luck enabled me to save the crew.

I reached this town three days ago and will leave within four. Next year I will go better prepared and start a little later. The month of May is too early for that coast.

I am reporting fully to His Majesty and also requesting him to give me leave to reconnoiter all that coast as far as the island of San Juan, in order that once for all we may learn its secret; and thence to go in person to report in the matter, that His Majesty may issue orders according to his pleasure, since there will be time for everything because I will not leave San Agustín till the end of May.

Really, it is imperative to explore all that coast, for what I saw of it is very different from what the chart shows. Your lordship can do me favour by recommending this matter to His Majesty.

Meanwhile, God preserve your lordship.

Havana, June 22, 1587.

[Signed:] Pedro Menéndez Marqués

744. March 22, 1587. Diego Fernández de Quiñones to the president of the Casa de Contratación.

A.G.I., Seville, Contratación 5108, translated in I. A. Wright, Further English Voyages, p. 230.

Very Illustrious Sir

Your lordship bids me report whether the English have made any settlement on the Florida coast, which extends towards the Newfoundland Banks. In this matter I have already reported to your lordship, as I have to His Majesty, on what I was able to learn by way of Florida. This was that Pedro Menéndez Marquéz wrote me in reply to my inquiries, addressed to him and to Gutierre de Miranda, saying that 150 leagues beyond Santa Elena, in Jacan, there was a settlement of the English who in September, two years ago, passed by those ports of Florida. Previously they had been in the island of Puerto Rico and in La Española, where they took all kinds of livestock. The English viscount who in the neighbourhood of Bermuda took Corniele out of the Santo Domingo fleet was going to establish this settlement. Corniele will have informed your lordship of that matter, for he went to Seville afterwards.

I have been unable to learn anything further or more definite since, except from certain negroes who ran away from Francis Drake. In Saint Augustine they deposed that all the negroes, male and female, the enemy had with him and certain other equipment which he had taken in Santo Domingo and at Cartagena, were to be left in the fort and settlement which they say exists on that coast.

Later I have tried by every means to learn the facts of the matter. I have written to Pedro Menéndez Marquéz and to Gutierre de Miranda, bidding them in every possible way, by land or sea, to try to learn the truth about this settlement, where and what it is, in order to report upon it to His Majesty and to your lordship. They answer that they have no ship equal to the undertaking but will endeavour shortly to investigate, and will make a reconnaissance of the whole coast, until satisfactory information be obtained as to what is going on or may exist there.

Up to the present nothing more is known nor have I been able to learn anything further, but I am certain that the enemy has an establishment there because it is so suitable a position from which to sally upon these Indies whenever they may desire, for they say they are settled directly west of Bermuda and so, because this would make them such close neighbours, I am as worried as though I knew certainly that they were there. Even if they are not, nothing is lost by being vigilant, for I have no other business in which to occupy myself.

Since Francis Drake left no other corsairs have appeared here, except some ordinary pirates who seek to trade....

Havana, March 22, 1587.

Very Illustrious Sir

Your lordship's truest servant kisses your lordship's very illustrious hands.

[Signed:] Diego Fernández de Quiñones

745. July 17, 1588. Pedro Menéndez Marqués to Philip II.

A.G.I., Seville, Santo Domingo 224, 54/5/9; copy in Woodbury Lowery Transcripts, Division of Manuscripts, Library of Congress; translated in D. B. Quinn, Roanoke Voyages, II, 778–781, here reprinted.

Sire,

In the month of February last I gave your majesty an account of how I had removed the people, the artillery and the military stores from Santa Elena to San Agustín, and had gone on to erect the great fort there. After that, while it was being completed, I sent Captain Bicente Goncalez and a nephew of mine in a bark, very fast of sail

and oar, to run along the coast to 39° which is beyond the bay of Santa Maria. He took thirty competent men with him so that if the English were settling there, he might find out what was happening. He set out at a good time at the beginning of June. I took this precaution because the duke of Medina Sidonia had written to me to be ready by May 15 to undertake the journey in person and to go along the shore as far as the island of San Juan so that we should know once and for all what is on the coast: and I was to go from thence to give an account to your majesty of what should be done. I got ready accordingly, awaiting the order to leave, until June 7, and then, seeing that it did not arrive and time was passing, I decided to send one of the vessels which I had intended to take. This was the one in which Bicente Goncalez set sail, under orders to go as far as 39° to find out what was to be discovered, and I believe it should have returned by now to San Agustín. On my return to Florida I will give an account to your majesty at the first opportunity of what occurred, sending a packet boat if the matter appears to be important.

In Florida there is a sailor, Carlos Morera, who says that it is certain that, in the island of San Juan, close to the Bacallaos, there is an English settlement, for two years ago, this sailor, being in London, there came a ship from that settlement in which was a friend of this sailor who told him positively that they were settling on this island at 43°, that there were a great many Indians there, and that it was only eight leagues from the mainland. And of this he is certain. Of all this I will give an account to your majesty as I have said.

I being about to set out, on July 10, there arrived at Harcos, about twelve leagues from this port, four ships and a pinnace belonging to the English who, landing, seized some meat and took two men from whom they learnt what was going on. Our galleys tried to put to sea, but there was such a strong north-easterly wind that they could not do anything, even leave the harbor. Meantime, two ships from the Islands, laden with wines, making for here were chased by them [the English]. One got away but the other was forced to run ashore a league from this port. She was boarded from the pinnace and some small boats and was being despoiled when Captain Tomas Bernaldo, with 100 men, came to her assistance by land, having left the fortress and headland protected. He forced them to quit the prize from which only a few things of little importance had been taken. The rest of her cargo he had brought in here. The English cleared off after four days and have not reappeared, but it is suspected that they are lying in wait at the mouth of the channel for our ships. . . .

I have a strong suspicion that these ships are from the Florida settlement because I cannot believe that they would be allowed to leave England at this season. Besides they are small ships and are not taking hides but money. It will be necessary to find out their secret next year, since your majesty's instructions have not arrived up to now, July 17, and on the Florida coast winter begins in August. I will procure the necessary knowledge and give an account of it to your majesty. Our Lord guard and prosper the royal catholic person of your majesty for many and happy years as Christendom requires.

From La Habana, 17 July 1588,

[Signed:] Pedro Menéndez Marqués

746. May to July, 1588. The voyage of Vicente González to Chesapeake Bay in 1588.

The only detailed version that exists of the journal of the voyage is that of Juan Menéndez Marqués, in Luis Gerónimo de Oré, Relación de los martires que a avido en las provincias de la Florida *(no place, no date, no printer), which is thought to have been published about 1617 in Madrid. Its value was recognized only in the present century. As* Relación histórica de la Florida en el siglo XVII, *it was edited in 2 volumes by Atanásio López (Madrid, 1931–1933), and was subsequently translated and edited by Maynard Geiger as* The Martyrs of Florida *(Franciscan Studies no. 18, New York, 1936). His translation was modified in the reprint in D. B. Quinn,* Roanoke Voyages, *II, 802–816, and is reprinted here. The journal is preceded in this extract by material on Florida, 1577–1585 and 1588–1593, in which Oré is not always very accurate, but provides us nonetheless with a continuous context for his treatment of the voyage.*

In the year 1577 his majesty ordered Pedro Menéndez Marqués, nephew of the *adelantado*, with the title of governor of Florida and its provinces, to take a force of infantry and rebuild the fort of Santa Elena. He was then admiral of the *galeones* and comptroller of Florida. When the general arrived he put in hand the restoration of the fort of Santa Elena. Taking 100 soldiers with him, they had many encounters with the Indians until the fort was built. From Santa Elena as a center they went forth to burn the Indian villages and to inflict whatever damage they could. In one such attack they killed and captured 120 persons, while in the province of Guale they burned all the towns so that when the Indians saw themselves thus persecuted and their people dead or in captivity they submitted, made peace, and asked for clergy to instruct them in the things necessary for receiving baptism and embracing Christianity. Thus the Indians became more acquiescent and subjected themselves to the Spaniards. The first Christian towns were Nombre de Dios and San Sebastián, for so they named those towns which are near San Agustín.

In the year 1585 it became known that the English had come to settle on the coast of Jacan and, on receiving orders from his majesty, General Pedro Menéndez left San Agustín in a frigate on an expedition to Jacan to reconnoiter and to locate the settlers. So, in the year 1587, coming near to the place, he encountered a storm so fierce that he was forced to put into harbor at great risk to himself. He came to Havana and thence set out for San Agustín where he arrived in July. There, he and Juan de Texeda, the campmaster, agreed that the fort of Santa Elena should be evacuated in order to strengthen that of San Agustín. On his return he soon carried this out.

This was done in view of the fact that the previous year (1586) the corsair, Francis Drake, had burned the fort of San Agustín with the aid of a great force of infantry and artillery which he put on land, and also on account of the small size of the garrison and the meagre defences of the fortress. Concerning the latter, a trumpeter, who went over to him, gave him information. During the time he was in the port, however, considerable damage was inflicted on him, boats being sunk and a number of Englishmen killed. One, in particular, was a person of note who was killed by a soldier, Luís Fernández (who at this time is very old and poor, and has children), with a single shot. For him Drake had so much feeling that he ordered a gun to be fired as a signal to depart. Drake departed and returned to his piratical course. Much more damage would have been inflicted on him and a greater resistance offered, had it not been necessary to take precautions against the Indians of Icaste and Caçacolo who had planned to rebel and to seize the women and children who were in safe keeping in the woods. These the Indians had intended to take for themselves and in their councils had already agreed to apportion out the women among them according to the status of the women and the Indians alike.

His majesty considered it would be well to look to the matter [of subduing the Indians], and to the damage and cost which would result if the Spaniards had to start that task afresh. Moreover, the garrison of the fort was very small and it was impossible to resist the greater strength of the enemy [the English] in a fort constructed of wood and sand, and without hope of succor. . . .

In the following year (1588), towards the end of the month of May, Captain Vicente Gonzáles departed from the port and fortress of San Agustín. With Gonzáles went the sergeant-major, Juan Menéndez Marqués and thirty soldiers and sailors in a bark of San Lúcar which had come to Havana the year before as a packet-boat. This boat was purchased for the voyage, the purpose of the expedition being to run along the coast up to the bay of Madre de Dios del Jacán in order to obtain knowledge of and to reconnoiter the English settlement and fort. After they had made the journey along the coast the party came to Santa Elena and found the Indians at peace, the same being true of Cayagua, which they judged to be a good harbor. Then following the coast, having passed the cape of San Román, they spoke with the Indians, but the interpreters they had with them did not understand the language. They continued their journey, passing the cape of Trafalgar and that of San Juan, likewise two further harbors. Finally, they arrived at the bay of Madre de Dios del Jacán in the month of June in the year 1588.

The mouth of this bay is about three leagues wide, without shoals or reefs and is more than eight fathoms deep at its entrance. It runs N.W.-S.E. and forms a large circular gulf. Between the entrance and the place where one reaches the mainland it extends westward and north-westward for about three leagues. On the mainland, and in an east-west direction with the mouth, is a good harbor which has at its entrance a depth of three fathoms. Rather less than two leagues from there and to the north-west is another harbor where Captain Vicente González declared he had landed when he brought the religious of the *Compañia* [Jesuits], whom Don Luis put to death as has already been told.

Captain Gonzáles said that on a plain which is beyond a bluff where there was a group of pine-trees, an altar had been erected and mass had been said. From there he returned towards the east to where the *adelantado* had been on the mainland, but within the bay and near some small islands and an inlet. There the *adelantado* had finished the upper works of two frigates with which he had sailed to Castile from that place. Thereupon they departed from the said harbor, coasting along the mainland shore towards the north where they discovered another haven which seemed to be a good one and of great depth. On shore there was abundance of large stones while the cape of land to the north formed a high headland. These three harbors can be seen at one glance from the mouth of the bay, the last, however, only faintly.

As they continued to sail northwards the land from the east jutted into the bay. It narrowed so much that at one point, from the western shore towards the eastern side, it was only two leagues wide. After that they discovered coves and inlets, as well as rivers, along the western shore. Then they came upon a large fresh-water river, which, where it entered the bay, was more than six fathoms deep. To the north of it there was very high land, with ravines, but without trees, cleared and like a green field and pleasant to behold. On the southern shore of this river the beach is very calm and it is covered with tiny pebbles. Farther up on the south bank of the same river appeared a delightful valley, wooded, with pleasant land, apparently fertile and suitable for stock-breeding and husbandry. This river was located in latitude 38 degrees. They named it San Pedro.

They continued to sail north along the western shore and passed the night in a small inlet under the protection of high and well-shaded land. The next day many Indians came down to the beach and the one among them who appeared to have the highest standing wore a string of beads round his neck which appeared to be of fine gold. There they seized an Indian youth of about fifteen years of age.

Advancing further, they discovered many other harbors and rivers carrying much water which entered the bay from the western shore until they came to latitude 35°, where they saw mountain ridges, very high, running S.W.-N.E. Still more rivers were found and soon, in the middle of the bay, a small island. Along the western shore the depth began to diminish so much that they could go no further, so they turned eastwards. Opposite the island the land was high, broken and well-wooded, while nearby on the eastern side there were shoals of greater or lesser depth. Sailing closer to the mainland on the east they found a channel of great depth. Still further north they found that the hills began to close in the view.

In different places they found mouths of rivers and coves, while, where this bay ends in a semicircle, it is about as wide as Cádiz harbour. More than two or three leagues before they reached the head of the bay they found the water was fresh. That evening they were on the point of entering a river, west-north-west between some high hills and crags. At high tide the mouth was more than three fathoms deep, but because night was falling they anchored about a quarter of a league inside. At dawn there was low tide, and it was almost a miracle that the bark avoided the great rocks by which the river was enclosed from one side to the other. At great risk, and with shouts of 'Boat here!' and 'Be on your guard there!', she sailed out as far as the mouth of the river which was clear. There they saw a small shad floating on the water, dead and of no use. In a rivulet which came down between the rocks some small trout were seen. This was the eve of the feast of St John the Baptist and out of devotion they called the river San Juan de las Peñas.

They went up on the ridge at a level place and saw on the other side another river and with it ranges of hills and rolling land. Below, in the fold of this range there was a fair valley with trees and with fertile and pleasing land. From latitude 38° up to the end of the bay there is to be found a great quantity of chestnuts and large walnuts, as well as wild vines with swollen grapes. And the same day they left the river and went some distance from the coast and the shore towards the east for a good while. There they discovered a very agreeable inlet, with thick woods where many deer appeared. They entered it towards the north, and sailed as far as its extremity.

There they landed on a pleasant beach, below some small gullies. At that end of the little bay there was a quiet and pleasant valley, with trees but without any craggy places. In it they found many deer. They killed one of these and made a feast of it on the day of the grace-giving St John the Baptist.

Captain Vicente González and the pilot Ginés Pinzón took the latitude which they found to be a little over 40°. They had taken it also at the first harbor after they had entered the bay on the mainland and there they found it to be 37° 37'. On that same day, the feast of St John, they left the end of the bay and sailed southwards along the western shore. In view of the fact that one of the Indians had been captured there (as mentioned before) no Indian appeared on the western shore until the feast of the apostles Peter and Paul. On the morning of that day they crossed to the eastern shore and came to some small islands which are within sight of the mouth of the bay. There they landed.

From that place to a spot further on, and in sight of the inlets where the *adelantado* had been, they steered for the shore, but because the water had so little depth they could not bring the bark to land. Many Indians, of both sexes, came down to the beach. When the Indians waded into the water up to their knees the Spaniards seized one of them and sailed away. When they left the bay it was evening. All that night they worked their way south with the aid of a strong west wind. The same was true of the whole of the next day until sunset. The wind then freshening so much they were forced to dismast the ship and to bring her to the shore by means of oars. They entered on a bar of very little depth, and inside found a large cove, the southern part of which at low tide was almost dry. The view towards the north gave on to a great part of the bay and revealed a large arm in the north-west curve which was heavily wooded. And along the shore towards the north there was another opening which appeared to be better than that by which they had entered, this part of the coast for about a league, between one bar and another, being low and free of sand. And on the inside of the little bay they had entered there were signs of a slipway for small vessels, and on land a number of wells made with English casks, and other debris indicating that a considerable number of people had been here.

The next day they again departed, finding the latitude to be 35½°. Continuing towards the south they passed the three capes previously mentioned. Then in turn they passed the ports of Cayagua, Santa Elena and all the land known as Guale until they arrived at the island of San Pedro which was at that time thickly populated by the Indians. There they found Fray Baltasar López who was beginning to gather abundant fruit in that mission and had already baptized many as Christians. By these the navigators were well received and provided with what they asked for, they having arrived in great need of supplies.

After they passed the bar of this island, they returned to San Agustín in the month of July in the same year 1588. This expedition of exploration and discovery, from start to finish, they made in a little less than a month and a half, according to the report, as exact as it is detailed, made by the said sergeant-major, Juan Menéndez, who is now the royal treasurer in the city of San Agustín.

Because the description of the bay of Madre de Dios and of the harbours, with the observations and bearings of their course, is so trustworthy and so necessary for the time when your majesty may be pleased to command that the bay be cleared of the robbers who have occupied and fortified it for thirty years, it seemed well that I should dwell on it at some length.

The same information was obtained from what was learnt at la Habana from a pilot, Pero Díaz Franco, namely that the harbor which was referred to above as being at 35½°, where the lees in the English barrels were seen, was the site of the English settlement. He said further that he had been taken on two voyages to that place and that at that time there were some 320 men and as many women there.

To the question why they had not seen the settlement from the bark, although they had reached the place where the wells were, he answered that it was not possible to see it since it was ten leagues away on the arm of the sea bearing away from the northern opening into the harbour. Further, they were trying to conceal even having discovered good land until they could settle and fortify it.

The same things were said by David Glavid, who was brought to the city of San Agustín from la Habana, where he had been forced to serve in the galleys. He said that the English had brought him thither by force. But he said further that they had penetrated the interior up a river for many leagues and that they had obtained a quantity of gold dust. This David Glavid who gave this information said that he was an Irishman.

Having obtained accounts of this voyage from the captain, Vicente González, and the sergeant-major, as well as the information the pilot, Pedro Díaz Franco, gave, General Pedro Menéndez desired to go to Castille, leaving in his place his brother-in-law, Juan de Posadas, and taking with him his first cousin, the sergeant-major Juan Menéndez. But he encountered adverse weather and suffered a torn sail. This brought him in sight of Bermuda, Puerto Rico and Santo Domingo, and, being unable to make another port, he arrived at La Yeguana in great distress. Attempting to continue his voyage and to disembogue by Cape San Nicolas, he was prevented by lack of sufficient wind. Consequently, he was forced to double the point of Mayci and take the old channel to la Habana. From there he went to San Agustín, whence he left again for Castille on 18 May 1589. He arrived at the port of San Lúcar on July 5 in the same year, accompanied by Fr. Alonso de Reinoso and the sergeant-major. He then went to court and gave an account of the discovery, previously described, to his majesty.

He was told to return to Havana with four supply ships containing infantry, stores and munitions and from there to take such galleys and merchant ships as seemed fitting and go to San Agustín. There he was to post the new troops and take the seasoned ones with him to 35½°. He was to enter San Agustín with the galleys alone, since the bar has little depth, and to send on the supply ships to the bay. There, after reconnoitering the lie of the land, he was to erect a fort in the place which appeared most suitable to him. He was to leave there the best equipment he could afford with 300 infantrymen. Moreover, he was to give instructions to the commander in charge there that, at the most opportune time, either he or his lieutenant was to explore the interior in order to discover the land, familiarize themselves with its topography, and find out whether there were any mines there.

Such was the understanding. Nevertheless, these orders were not carried out because soon after others were issued, instructing General Pedro Menéndez to go to the Main with two *galizabras* in which he was to bring back to Castille the silver, gold and pearls belonging to his majesty. This he did, leaving the bay of Cádiz on 16 May 1590 and returning with the treasure to the port of Viana de Camiña on September 4 in the same year. The sergeant-major, Juan Menéndez, took the news of his arrival to his majesty of glorious memory at the Escorial, while the treasure was brought to the mint at Segovia.

In the year 1591 Pedro Menéndez was placed in charge of the frigates belonging to the Indies fleet as well as of the transport of the silver from the Main and from New Spain. Having gone to Nombre de Dios he returned to San Lúcar de Barrameda in the month of January 1592.

In the following year, 1593, his majesty was informed that in the *presidio* of San Agustín the people were refusing obedience to the governor, Gutierre de Miranda, who had charge of the government in virtue of a royal warrant. Likewise, Captain Juan de Posadas, who had come to take the treasurer's place on the death of Juan de Cebadilla, was drowned. When the king received this news he ordered General Pedro Menéndez to go to the *presidio* of San Agustín and put down the uprising against the governor. But he had scarcely gone before sickness overtook him and he was forced to ask the king to send over another suitable person in his place. So there were provided for Florida a governor and captain-general, Domingo Martínez de Avendaño; a treasurer, Bartolome de Argüelles; and a comptroller, Juan Menéndez Marqués, the sergeant-major.

The Indian who had been apprehended on the eastern side of the bay died in the harbour of San Pedro of rage and melancholy. The one who had been seized first went to Castille. He accompanied the general on a *gallizabra*, but after the return voyage he died at Viana of the small-pox. Being already a Christian they buried him in the convent of Santo Domingo. He was a clever fellow and spoke much about the excellence and fertility of his land and about the gold that was in it. This, in his native tongue, he called *tapisco*. . . .

747. March 26, 1589. Pedro de Araña to Juan de Ibarra.

The revelations of Alonso Ruiz in July, 1588 (453), and of Pedro Diaz in March, 1589 (454), altered Spanish perceptions of where the English settlement was, and it might appear that here Araña is anticipating the formal relation that Pedro Diaz was shortly to make.

A.G.I., Seville, 54/1/54; copy in Division of Manuscripts, Library of Congress. Translated and reprinted from D. B. Quinn, Roanoke Voyages, *II, 781–782.*

To Joan de Ybarra of the council of the king our master, and his secretary for works, forests and the Indies.

Through Father Andrés de Ubilla who, on the twelfth of this month, left this port for Spain in a small packet-boat, I have written to you, and I will, therefore, now be brief, merely referring to the relation and letter that I am sending with this to his majesty, the contents of which are concerned with occurrences after the date of my letter, being matters which his majesty has desired to know, and concerning which he has given instructions to the general in Florida. With the unfailing desire in which I live to succeed in serving his majesty, I have made a relation of the place where the English are settling on the Florida coast. From my report the truth will be learnt, very different, indeed, from the reports which have already been sent to his majesty, all of which have been intended to serve the ends of certain individuals without involving them in risks of any kind.

As I am writing this, I should wish to be in your presence to declare my regret at what is happening. Truly, one of the things which most distresses me is this thought, which makes me long to be away from the Indies, if only to attend personally to that which I have reported to you.

May our Lord keep you many years. From Havana, 26 March 1589.

Father Andrés has sailed in good weather. God grant that he arrive safely, since his arrival is such importance to the service of his sacred majesty, whose hands I kiss.

[Signed:] Pedro de Araña

748. [1602?] Vicente González's own recollections of the 1588 voyage.

These are clearly very muddled and imprecise and must belong to a period well past 1588, either during the inquiries of the 1598–1602 period or those of 1606–1608. The former is the more probable.

A.G.I., Seville, Mexico 92; M. F. de Navarrete, Colección, XIV (1971), fol. 383; translated in C. M. Lewis and A. J. Loomie, Spanish Jesuit Mission to Virginia, *pp. 193–199, and in D. B. Quinn,* Roanoke Voyages, *from the latter of which it is taken.*

The relation which Captain Vizente González gave of what he observed on the voyage which he made, under orders from Pedro Menéndez Marqués, governor of Florida, in two pinnaces with fifty men to reconnoiter the fort which it was understood the French had made on the Santa Elena coast, with a succinct discourse at the end on the fortification of the said coast and the forts which his majesty holds there.

Captain Vizente González says that Pero Melendez Marques, governor of Florida, had news from the Indians of the Santa Elena coast that the French had a fort there, whither he ordered him to proceed, taking with him fifty soldiers and two pinnaces, with all caution that could be in order to prevent the coast from falling into the hands of the enemy, and thus he did, coasting along the shore towards the Bacallaos. He entered into all the harbors he discovered, which were many, and one of them was two leagues wide at the mouth and extended thirty leagues into the interior. It was five or six leagues across at its widest part and four at the narrowest, until it reached the foot of the mountain range, where there was a powerful chieftain with many subjects who had under him all the chiefs of the territory. They found one chief who went about with four or five rings of gold in his ears, and on his head one piece a palm and a half long and six fingers broad. The rest of the Indians wore copper in a similar manner. He asked the chief where they got what they were wearing. To which he replied that it was three days' journey away from the foot of that range for a laden Indian, which would be twenty-five or thirty leagues, There there was a mountain which contained nothing else. He [González] said to him that indeed he had a great quantity of it, because in his country there was likewise much and it was worth little. The Indian said that it was the same with him and that over there it was esteemed little, while that which the Indians wore, which was copper, they esteemed very much. Captain Vizente González answered that we esteemed it [copper] greatly, in order that he might give the Indian to understand that we were not anxious to find out about the gold, because González realised that if he appeared to desire it, the Indian would bring the gold, a course which did not seem wise, since he did not wish to excite the Indians or [the cupidity of his own followers] since many persons who were with him, saw what he had seen. They have many pearls, and very large ones, except that they are of a purple colour.

Behind this mountain range is Nueva Mexico, as it is called, which, from the foot of the range, over it, to the other side was a five day journey. Here they have a large house with four or five rooms above, and covered externally with plaster. They have many small cows and much silver, as the Indians themselves admit. From this land towards the south there are many silver-mines and mines of crystal. There is also a small ridge containing diamonds, from which the soldiers have taken some to Florida and brought them to Spain, not knowing their value, one of them worth 500 ducats, and another a hundred doubloons, and because they did not know what they were worth they lost heavily on them. In Florida there were soldiers who had been at the silver mines and at the diamond-hill who had a great desire to go there. A Franciscan friar, provincial of the order in Florida, could give information about this, as he knew about it, and also another soldier who is here. In this land they have much maize and beans for food, which are the principal articles in their diet. They have also plenty of cherries, plums, grapes, dried chestnuts, which last all the year round. They have, too, apples, medlars, walnuts, much hunting of all kinds just as in Spain, while the climate of that land is also similar.

The English colony, according to what the Indians have said, is established from this village northwards on a river from which, the said Captain Vicente González is certain, there is a passage to the South Sea, because, in discussion with the Indians as to whether there was any river that went through to the other sea, they replied that, further up from where they were, there was one such river which passed through to the other sea, and so he holds it as certain that the Englishmen are there. To get to this harbor he did not think it was necessary to go to any part of the Indies [first] but to make this voyage direct [from Spain]. He did not think they needed to enter a channel or go out through the Ba[h]ama Channel, and the same was true of their return voyage. They could come within a month, and a month and a half was the most that they need take. It appears to the said Captain Vicente González that the fort of Santa Elena must be linked up with that of San Agustín. Then with part of the forces there and some from here [San Agustín] it would be possible to set out on a journey to make the discovery without incurring any loss, as the soldiers now in Florida would be very willing to go on account of the news they have had of the riches of that place through some of them having seen its wealth with their own eyes.

[Signed:] Vicente González

749. June 7, 1606. Juan Menéndez Marqués's recollections of the 1588 voyage.

Juan Menéndez Marqués settled down after the 1588 voyage into a long career, much of which he spent as treasurer in Florida. He must have lost the precise journal that Oré preserved, because his later versions of the voyage are all rather vague and unspecific. The longest (a) is that of June 7, from A.G.I., Seville, Patronato 1/1/1/19, printed in E. Ruídiaz y Caravia, La Florida, 2 vols. (Madrid, 1893), II, 495–509, from which extracts are given; (b) September 20, 1602, from

A.G.I., Seville, Santo Domingo 224, 54/5/9, copy in Woodbury Lowery Transcripts, IV, Division of Manuscripts, Library of Congress, from which a short extract is given.

There are other papers also: a letter of November 21, 1605, given below in connection with the events of 1605, and a letter of January 5, 1608, translated in Abbie M. Brooks and Annie Averette, The Unwritten History of Old St. Augustine (Saint Augustine, 1909), pp. 77–78; the latter did not add anything further. Items (a) and (b) are reprinted from D. B. Quinn, Roanoke Voyages, II, 816–821.

[a]   If I remember aright, during the year 1589 my first cousin, General Pero Menéndez Marqués, came to Spain with his majesty's leave, after having been for more than fourteen years governor of this fortress. He arrived in Madrid at the end of July of that year and gave an account to his majesty, the members of his royal council of the Indies and, particularly to Señor Don Juan de Diaguez and Señor Juan de Ibarra of various matters, amongst others of the discovery of the Bay of Madre de Dios del Jacan and the information he had of an English settlement on that coast. I, myself, had given a verbal account of the discovery to the last two gentlemen as I had taken part in the expedition in the capacity of sergeant-major of the fortress. The following year, 1590, General Pedro Menéndez Marqués having been ordered by his majesty to go to the Mainland to bring back the silver, gold and pearls which, as crown property, were to have been brought by the *flota*, the general arrived at San Lucár, accompanied by his nephew, Captain Pedro Mendez. I was already at San Lúcar, by the instructions of the duke of Medina Sidonia, awaiting their arrival. The general told me that the council of the Indies had decided that he should set out with four storeships in which there would be infantry, arms, munitions, stores and provisions. On reaching Havana he was to pick up some galleys and frigates which appeared to him suitable for entering the enemy's harbour, the entrance to which was shallow. He was then to put in at this fortress and embark those experienced soldiers who had proved satisfactory, leaving an equal number in their place. He was to proceed from there to attempt the destruction of

the enemy's fort and settlement. The storeships were to be sent ahead to the Bay of Madre de Dios del Jacan, with the surplus provisions and stores, and after he had achieved his objective, he was, with the galleys and the squadron, to go to the Bay, to explore it, to take note of its situation, harbour and entrance and head. He was then to establish in the place which appeared to him most suitable a fort capable of holding 300 infantrymen as a garrison, under a governor, with orders that, when an opportunity arose, he or his lieutenant should penetrate into the interior with half the infantry to try to find out the nature and lie of the land and whether it contained any kinds of precious metals or stones. When that fortress was as well established as this, and was under the captain's control, as this is, I, if I remember aright what the general told me, was to be named governor of the fort and presidency.

We made the voyage to the Main with the two *galizabras* which carried his majesty's silver, gold and pearls that year and with them we entered Brava, Portugal. It was I who carried the news of their arrival to his majesty. Thereafter, I heard nothing more, nor do I know of any discussions about the voyage to Jacan. I, myself, stated my opinion of the country and its mineral resources in an account I wrote at the request of Don Fernando de Baldés who had been instructed by the governor of Cuba, Senor Don Pedro de Baldés, to visit this fortress and report whether, in his opinion, it should be abandoned. This account I transcribe as follows:

So far as the conversion of the native Indians of these provinces is concerned, it seems that no one is better qualified to give a more accurate and dispassionate account than the members of the Franciscan order who, on the behalf and cost of the crown, were engaged in this task, apart, that is, from what I, myself have seen during the fifteen years I have been serving his majesty in this land in company with my cousin General Pedro Menéndez Marqués. During that time there have been Christian Indians in the town of Nombre de Dios and in San Sebastian, both near here. Towards the end of 1587 Fray Alonso de Raynoso arrived from Spain to take up his duties as a missionary. I noted that the Franciscans and General Pedro Menéndez arranged for the missionaries to be distributed to all the villages from the island of San Pedro up to this fortress; also in

San Sebastian and an extensive area of the Rio Dulce under the control of the chieftain Pedro Marqués. I noted also that the work of these missionaries quickly bore fruit. I especially remember how Fray Baltasar Lopez, who was and still is vicar on the island of San Pedro and the missionary then in charge at San Juan brought with them to this fortress a number of Indian chieftains to be converted, and how they were baptized in the cathedral, amongst them Cazacolo, one of the most famous and most feared chieftains in this territory, with whom came his wife and children. In the course of 1588, at the general's command, I went with Captain Vicente González to explore the Bay of Madre de Dios del Jacan and to obtain information about the English settlement. On my return, at San Pedro, I found a number of Indian converts who, with manifest signs of goodwill and devotion, attended mass and listened to the gospel. . . .

Besides the abovementioned, I proposed to indicate, if necessary, harbors from the Bay of Santa Elena up to the Bay of Madre de Dios del Jacan the entrance to which is at 37°. These harbors could be used by vessels of up to 500 tons, and could accommodate such vessels for repair. This is especially true of the harbour at the Bay of Madre de Dios, the entrance to which runs north-west-south-east, there being neither reef nor sand bank along the whole of the entrance nor yet outside it on the seaward side. It has a depth of eight fathoms and a width at the entrance of more than two leagues. When the bay is entered the expanse of water is so great that the land on all sides almost disappears from view. On reaching the mainland after sailing inside for about three leagues in a north-westerly direction there is to be found another large harbor, the depth at the entrance being three fathoms. Coasting along the mainland shore of the bay in a northerly direction excellent harbors and abundant fresh-water rivers are to be found, also well-wooded valleys and what appears to be fertile land, particularly from the 38th parallel northwards as far as 40°, where the bay and its harbors come to an end at the foot of lofty mountain ranges, the lower slopes of which and the valleys amongst them appear fertile and well suited to the cultivation of crops and cattle-breeding. Such is the force of the great rivers that flow down the mountains that they form at this furthestmost point of the bay a large fresh-water pool, and from the narrowest point of the bay to this extremity would, it appears to me, be at least two leagues.

At latitude 38° I saw myself an Indian with rings of gold round his neck. Another Indian was brought from those parts to this fortress, who, when I showed him a chain of gold, said that in his country there was an abundance of that metal, which was called *tapisco*. When he was shown a brass candlestick he said that there was also much brass and that it was called *guapaçina*. On being shown copper he said likewise that there was much of it, but it was of no value and the Indians were not interested in it: they called it *oçoco*. When he was asked where these metals were to be found and how the Indians obtained them, he said that if he left his village at daybreak he would reach by mid-day the foot of a tall mountain, down which fell a great torrent of water which, at ground-level, formed a large pool. The Indians, diving into this pool, emerged with their hands full,

sometimes of pebbles and sand, other times of grains of ore as big as chickpeas, some larger, others smaller, of the three metals mentioned above. On being asked how they treated the ores to make rings, he replied that they melted them over a candle and then beat them into shape.

[b]   On October 28 in the same year General Menéndez Marqués, accompanied by myself, left this port to go to Spain. We sailed northwards and passed within sight of Bermuda to the north. We then made the island of Puerto Rico, but could not enter the harbour that day because of the force of the wind. Putting about, and under stress of weather, we kept a look-out for Santo Domingo which port, however, we were unable to enter, and so went on to Yaguana. From there we set out with the intention of doubling Cape San Nicolás and, making the promontory of Cuba, we reached Havana by the Old Channel from whence we returned to this place.

Chapter Ninety-five
The Uprising of the Guale Indians and
Its Suppression, 1597–1598

THE VERY ACTIVITY and apparent success of the Franciscans soon brought their downfall. The Indians of St. Catherine Island (Guale), one of their strongest centers, rose against them for their interference with native custom and usage. The Indians killed all but one of the missionaries and all of a small group of Spanish soldiers, who were expected to give them protection. Other Indians became restive, and it appeared that a general movement against the Spaniards might develop. The new governor, Méndez de Canzo, moved rapidly up the Georgia coast and attacked and destroyed the offending villages, killing most of their inhabitants, but giving able-bodied men and women to his soldiers as slaves. He also attempted, successfully, the intimidation of other restless tribes. To the Franciscans, it was both a glorious moment of martyrdom and an opportunity to show that they could resume the mission as soon as the civil authorities had established some degree of order. With considerable bravery they went back to their posts (although in devastated Guale there was nothing they could do until some of the scattered population came back). They also stood up against the governor. They believed that his corn tax was too high and was one cause of the revolt (it was fairly soon reduced under their pressure), and that the slavery of the prisoners was wrong (orders came from the government in Spain, in 1599, that all should be released). The missionaries returned to their work of subverting native society in the interests of Christianity with a sense of having surmounted their greatest obstacles, the lack of sufficient martyrs to inspire them and the sense that they could push the governor into following their policies toward the Indians rather than his own.

750. 1597. A general account of the Indian uprising in Guale in 1597.

A. G. de Barcia's Ensayo cronológico de la Florida *(Madrid, 1723) is a very uneven work, but it contains portions of documentary material not otherwise readily available. This account was clearly based on a contemporary Franciscan source. It is translated from pp. 170–172, in J. R. Swanton,* The Early History of the Creek Indians *(Bureau of American Ethnology, Bulletin 73 [1922], pp. 85–87), from which the following is taken. There is a modern translation by Anthony Kerrigan,* Barcia's Chronological History of Florida *(Gainesville, 1951).*

The friars of San Francisco busied themselves for two years in preaching to the Indians of Florida, separated into various provinces. In the town of Tolemaro or Tolemato lived the friar Pedro de Corpa, a notable preacher, and deputy of that doctrina, against whom rose the elder son and heir of the chief of the island of Guale, who was exceedingly vexed at the reproaches which Father Corpa made to him, because although a Christian, he lived worse than a Gentile, and he fled from the town because he was not able to endure them. He returned to it within a few days, at the end of September [1597], bringing many Indian warriors, with bows and arrows, their heads ornamented with great plumes, and entering in the night, in profound silence, they went to the house where the father lived; they broke down the feeble doors, found him on his knees, and killed him with an axe. This unheard-of atrocity was proclaimed in the town; and although some showed signs of regret, most, who were as little disturbed, apparently, as the son of the chief, joined him, and he said to them the day following: "Although the friar is dead he would not have been if he had not prevented us from living as before we were Christians: let us return to our ancient customs, and let us prepare to defend ourselves against the punishment which the governor of Florida will attempt to inflict upon us, and if this happens it will be as rigorous for this friar alone as if we had finished all; because he will pursue us in the same manner on account of the friar whom we have killed as for all."

Those who followed him in the newly executed deed approved; and they said that it could not be doubted that he would want to take vengeance for one as he would take it for all. Then the barbarian continued: "Since the punishment on account of one is not going to be greater than for all, let us restore the liberty of which these friars have robbed us, with promises of benefits which we have not seen, in hope of which they wish that those of us who call ourselves Christians experience at once the losses and discomforts: they take from us women, leaving us only one and that in perpetuity, prohibiting us from changing her: they obstruct our dances, banquets, feasts, celebrations, fires, and wars, so that by failing to use them we lose the ancient valor and dexterity inherited from our ancestors: they persecute our old people calling them witches; even our labor disturbs them, since they want to command us to avoid it on some days, and be prepared to execute all that they say, although they are not satisfied; they always reprimand us, injure us, oppress us, preach to us, call us bad Christians, and deprive us of all happiness, which our ancestors enjoyed, with the hope that they will give us heaven. These are deceptions in order to subject us, in holding us disposed after their manner; already what can we expect, except to be slaves? If now we kill all of them, we will remove such a heavy yoke immediately, and our valor will make the governor treat us well, if it happens that he does not come

out badly." The multitude was convinced by his speech; and as a sign of their victory, they cut off Father Corpa's head, and they put it in the port on a lance, as a trophy of their victory, and the body they threw into a forest, where it was never found.

They passed to the town of Topiqui, where lived Fr. Blàs Rodriguez (Torquemada gives him the appelation of de Montes), they went in suddenly, telling him they came to kill him. Fr. Blàs asked them to let him say mass first, and they suspended their ferocity for that brief time; but as soon as he had finished saying it, they gave him so many blows, that they finished him, and they threw his body outside, so that the birds and beasts might eat it, but none came to it except a dog, which ventured to touch it, and fell dead. An old Christian Indian took it up and gave it burial in the woods.

From there they went to the town of Assopo, in the island of Guale, where were Fray Miguél de Auñon, and Fray Antonio Badajoz; they knew beforehand of their coming, and seeing that flight was impossible, Fray Miguél began to say mass, and administered the sacrament to Fray Antonio, and both began to pray. Four hours afterward the Indians entered, killed friar Antonio instantly with a club [*macana*]; and afterward gave friar Miguél two blows with it, and, leaving the bodies in the same place, some Christian Indians buried them at the foot of a very high cross, which the same friar Miguél had set up in the country.

The Indians, continuing their cruelty, set out with great speed for the town of Asao where lived friar Francisco de Velascola, native of Castro-Urdiales, a very poor and humble monk, but with such forcefulness that he caused the Indians great fear: he was at that time in the city of San Agustín. Great was the disappointment of the Indians, because it appeared to them that they had done nothing if they left the friar Francisco alive. They learned in the town the day when he would return to it, went to the place where he was to disembark, and some awaited him hidden in a clump of rushes, near the bank. Fray Francisco arrived in a canoe, and, dissimulating, they surrounded him and took him by the shoulders, giving him many blows, with clubs (*macanas*) and axes, until his soul was restored to God.

They passed to the town of Ospo, where lived

friar Francisco Davila, who as soon as he heard the noise at the doors was able under cover of night to go out into the country; the Indians followed him, and although he had hidden himself in some rushes, by the light of the moon they pierced his shoulders with three arrows; and wishing to continue until they had finished him, an Indian interposed, in order to possess himself of his poor clothing, which he had to do in order that they might leave him, who took him bare and well bound, and he was carried to a town of infidel Indians to serve as a slave. These cruelties did not fail to receive the punishment of God; for many of those who were concerned in these martyrdoms hung themselves with their bowstrings, and others died wretchedly; and upon that province God sent a great famine of which many perished, as will be related.

The good success of these Indians caused others to unite with them, and they undertook to attack the island of San Pedro with more than 40 canoes, in order to put an end to the monks who were there, and destroy the chief, who was their enemy. They embarked, provided with bows, arrows, and clubs; and, considering the victory theirs, they discovered, near the island, a brigantine, which was in the harbor where they were to disembark, and they assumed that it had many people and began to debate about returning. The brigantine had arrived within sight of the island 30 days before with succor of bread and other things, which the monks needed; but they had not been able to reach the port, although those who came in it tried it many times, nor to pass beyond, on account of a bar (caño) which formed itself from the mainland (?) a thing which had never happened before in that sea. It carried only one soldier, and the other people were sailors, and even less than the number needed for navigation.

Finding the Indian rebels in this confusion the chief of the island went out to defend himself with a great number of canoes. He attacked them with great resolution; and although they tried to defend themselves, their attempt was in vain, they fled, and those who were unable to jumped ashore; and the chief, collecting some of his enemies' canoes, returned triumphantly to his island, and the friars gave him many presents, with which he remained as satisfied as with his victory.

Of the others who had sprung to land none escaped, because they had no canoes in which they might return; some hung themselves with their bowstrings, and others died of hunger in the woods.

Nor were those exempt who escaped, because the governor of Florida, learning of the atrocities of the Indians, went forth to punish the evildoers; but he was only able to burn the cornfields, because the aggressors retired to the marshes, and the highlands prevented him from punishing them, except with the famine which followed immediately the burning of the harvests, of which many Indians died. . . .

The Indians kept the friar Francisco de Avila in strict confinement, ill-treating him much; afterwards they left him more liberty in order to bring water and wood, and watch the fields. They turned him over to the boys so that they might shoot arrows at him; and although the wounds were small, they drained him of blood, because he was not able to stop the blood; this apostolic man suffering these outrages with great patience and serenity. . . .

Wearied of the sufferings of Father Avila the Indians determined to burn him alive. They tied him to a post, and put much wood under him. When about to burn him, there came to the chief one of the principal Indian women, whose son the Spaniards held captive in the city of San Agustín without her having been able to find any way to rescue him although she had tried it. This moved her to beg the chief earnestly that he should give friar Francisco to her to exchange him for her son. Other Indians, who desired to see him free, begged the same thing; and although it cost them much urging to appease the hatred of the chief for the father, he granted what the Indian woman asked, giving him to her so badly treated, that he arrived at San Agustín in such a condition that they did not recognize him: he had endured such great and such continuous labors. He accomplished the exchange, and the people of the city expressed a great deal of sympathy for friar Francisco.

God wished to give a greater punishment to the Indians of Florida, who killed the missionaries so unjustly; and, refusing water to the earth, upon the burning of the crops, there began such a great famine in Florida that the conspirators died miserably themselves, confessing the cause of their misfortune to have been the barbarity, which they exercised against the Franciscan monks.

751. October 4, 1597. Fray Pedro Fernández de Choças to Gonzálo Méndez de Canzo.

This conveyed the first news of the Indian uprising in Guale.

A.G.I., Seville, Santo Domingo 224, 54/5/9; it is contained in the governor's report of January 12, 1598, translated by Jeanette T. Connor from the transcript in the Woodbury Lowery Collection, Library of Congress, both copy and translation in Division of Manuscripts, Library of Congress.

Let Him through whose virtues hell is rendered powerless, give me strength to endure the hardships which confront us at each moment. To-day Saturday, in the morning, twenty-three canoes filled with Indians from all the land and province of Guale appeared in this river of Puturiba; they were going to Guale. After the men of the two of the canoes had disembarked at the village of San Pedro, the principal village of this province, and shot arrows at an Indian who came out of his house when the dogs made a noise and barked, their presence was immediately made known through the whole village from the cries of the wounded man, who is not dead yet. Don Juan and his Indians went in two canoes after the two canoes of the enemy, who drew over to the other side of the river, and landed, leaving in the canoes everything they were carrying. Our Christian Indians went in pursuit of them into the forest until they overtook one, and according to the custom of Indians, they slew him and took his scalp, although his hair was short, as he was a Christian. I censured this, for if they had bound him, as I had told them to do, the cause and reason of the war could have been learned from him. Another canoe was also found adrift, and leaving it at the landing-place, the enemy fled into the forest without the men of this village being able to overtake them. The rest went to Bejesse, which is beyond this island; and there, through an *arequi*,

my fiscal, spoke with the Cacique of Asao and censured him, and he went to his district and begged him to land. He would not do so; rather did he shamelessly show the hat of the Father Vicar of Asao, Fray Francisco de Berascula, saying: "See, hero, [what belonged] to that Father. Come, you others, and bring him *tortas*." He also showed the arquebue with which the said father used to call for a canoe by the streams he had to pass when he went to visit his villages. And [the cacique] said, in a loud voice, that there no longer was any Christianity since Our Lord had permitted this, and the enemy of our Catholic faith had ordained it thus, for the condemnation of so many souls. It is much to be deplored that with the said Father they killed the Father of Guale, Fray Miguel de Auñon; him of Tolomato, Fray Pedro de Corpa; him of Tupiqui, Fray Blas Rodriguez; him of Talapuz, Fray Francisco de Avila, priests all of them; and that they had only kept alive as a prisoner and slave the Father, Fray Antonio de Badajoz, a lay-brother; and they took him to Tulufina with all the martyred religious, as is proved to be the truth by all the spoils which are taken away from them here[1]: cowls and shreds of garments which the Indians divided among themselves. For that is what they did with such inhumanity to the most innocent Lamb [of all]. How they must have felt, Señor General, those little lambs, on receiving martyrdom all alone as they were! The thought of this so moves me that I cannot go on farther. I envy them the crowns of glory which they bear before us; and I await in this desert, by saintly obedience, that which Our Lord in His mercy may have in store for me; for the enemy Indians are already threatening those of this land, telling them to wander away from it and go to Timucua, because there they will not be warred upon again. The number of all the Indians who came might have been upwards of four hundred. May that religious whom they say they have spared from death and are keeping in Tulufina be favored by the one only God; and may they give decent burial to the bodies of the blessed dead; and may it be possible that the dead are not so many. There may be peril in any delay in assistance, although it is not my purpose that they be avenged by fire and sword rather should

---

1. It was Antonio de Badajoz who was killed and Francisco de Avila saved.

the remedy be gentleness and forbearance, as is your Honor's custom and intent, for they should be taken and treated like children. But I beg in mercy that the religious who have been saved may be visited, and taken from the hands of their foes; and if this cannot be shortly provided for our defence, and for the assistance of these Christian natives, it would be well to send six or more veteran soldiers, who could be divided meantime between Bezesi, here and San Pedro, doing the duty of sentinels with the Indians, if they can content themselves with *tortas, gacha,* and fish whenever there is any for here there is nothing else; and even this could not be furnished unless it be for a short time. But they, being honorable men, God will not fail them, for the love of Whom we subject ourselves to these perils; and may He inspire your Honor for the good task, and defend us from our enemies. From Puturiba, the fourth day of October, 1597. The altar-furnishings I used when I said mass in this mission, which his Majesty gave us with the corporal cloths, and a silver chalice from the convent which I had borrowed, were left in Tolomato when I made the journey to the mountains in safety [to Tama?], glory be to God. If it be right, may another be supplied me from his Majesty's funds. Well does your Honor see how necessary this is for my consolation and that of the Indians, and the good and benefit of the souls of purgatory, which has its part in the sacrifice. I supplicate your Honor to provide [in these matters], since therein God our Lord will be served, etc.

[Signed:] Fray Pedro Fernandez de Choças

752. October 7, 1597 to January 12, 1598. Inquiry by Gonzálo Méndez de Canzo into the Indian uprising of 1597 and his actions in regard to the Indians who took part in it.

Méndez de Canzo did not believe in half-measures. He began at once to investigate the uprising, to interrogate all who knew or might have known about it, and, in a personal tour of the area, he began repressive measures to avenge the five Franciscans who were killed. This included de-stroying villages and rounding up Indians as slaves.

A.G.I., Seville, Santo Domingo 224, 54/5/9. Jeanette T. Connor described this as "a remarkable document" and so it is. She translated it from the transcript in the Woodbury Lowery Collection, both copy and translation being in Division of Manuscripts, Library of Congress.

Report on that which happened in the Land of Guale during the Voyage made by Gonçalo Méndez de Canço, Governor and Captain-General of the Provinces of Florida, to investigate and punish the Death of the Religious whom the Indians killed in that Land.

In the city of St. Augustine, in the provinces of Florida, on the 7th of the month of October, 1597, before me, a notary, Gonçalo Méndez de Canço, Governor and Captain-General of these provinces for the King our master, said that to-day, Tuesday, at about ten o'clock in the morning, while he was in his house, despatching the business of his Majesty's service, Martin Gudines arrived, a soldier of this fort, who had gone in a brigantine to take food to the Fathers in the land of San Pedro; and he brought a packet containing letters from the Father, Fray Pedro de Choças, who was on that island, in the mission of Puturiba. And in a letter that the said Father wrote to the said Señor Governor, he related how Indians to the number of four hundred, in twenty-six canoes, had come down from the land of Guale, with the intention of killing the Indians of that island and the Fathers who were on it; and two other canoes, with Indians of the Cacique Don Juan, having gone in pursuit of them, these Indians killed one [of the enemy], and heard from the rest how the Salchiche Indians and others who joined them, had killed the Father Preacher Fray Miguel de Auñon, who lived in the mission of Guale; the Father, Fray Pedro de Corpa, who lived in the mission of Tolomato; the Father, Fray Blas Rodriguez, who lived in Tupiqui; the Father, Fray Francisco de Berascula, who lived in Asao; the Father, Fray Francisco Davila, who lived in Talapo [or Talapuz], priests who said mass; and how they held captive the Father, Fray Antonio de Badajoz, a lay-brother. And as proofs of the above, they brought some pieces of the cowls and garments of the said Fathers, as it all appeared and was evident from the said letter, which, he asked, might be added to this declaration. And in order that measures might be taken for the punishment and remedy of the above, in the manner most suitable to the service of God and of his Majesty, and that the subject might be discussed in the way and form most fitting, the said Governor went at once to the Convent of San Francisco of this city, and conferred with the Father Custodian, Fray Francisco de Marón, where, the royal officials of these provinces being in his company Bartolomé de Arguelles, the Royal Accountant, Juan Menéndez Marqués, the Treasurer, Juan Lopez de Avilés, the Factor and Inspector; and Captains Vicente Gonçales and Pedro de Portierra the said Governor held a council, and ordered the said letter to be read, and the abovesaid having read it, he asked the said Father Custodian and royal officals and captains of infantry, to give him their opinions, as to the most suitable punishment and remedy for the abovesaid crime and the said Governor and royal officials and captains of infantry having treated of and conferred on this affair, they resolved and agreed that in the shortest time possible, they should leave this town with the necessary men and supplies; and this they agreed to and signed with their names. Date *ut supra*. Gonçalo Méndez de Canço; Fray Francisco Marón, Custodian; Bartolomé de Arguelles; Juan Menéndez Marqués; Juan Lopez de Avilés; Captain Vicente Gonçales; Pedro Portierra. Before me, Alonso Garcia de la Vera, Notary.

[a] I, Alonso Garcia de la Vera, chief notary public and of the government in these provinces of Florida and this city of St. Augustine, certify and give truthful testimony to those who may see these presents, as to how Gonçalo Méndez de Canço, Governor and Captain-General of these provinces for his Majesty, having received [the above letter] on the 7th, with the information in it contained after having held a council in the Convent of San Francisco, of this city of Agustín, with the Fathers who were there, and the royal officials and captains, immediately despatched to the land of San Pedro, for the guarding and defence of the Fathers, Fray Pedro Fernandez de Choças, Fray Francisco de Pareja

and the said Don Juan, a cacique, and his Indians, Sergeant Juan de Santiago with six soldiers in his company; and he likewise ordered that with all haste his Majesty's launch should be put in readiness, and the shallop, and a frigate of Diego Franco, a pilot, to go on his voyage; and he ordered that supplies and munitions and other necessary things for the said voyage [be placed in them]; and he made ready the infantry; and with the greatest speed he could, the said Governor left San Agustín, although he was in ill health, on the journey to the province of Guale, on the 17th of October, 1597; and in order that there might be evidence of this, by request of the said Governor, I gave these presents, signed with my name. Done on the shore of San Mateo, October 17th, 1597. Witnesses to what is said: Ensign Alonso Dias, Ensign Rodrigo Vasques, and many other persons and soldiers. Alonso Garcia de la Vera, notary.

[b] In the town of San Pedro, of which Don Juan is the cacique, on the 18th of the month of October, 1597, Gonçalo Méndez de Canço, Governor and Captain-General of these provinces for the King, our master, said that he had come to this said town with one hundred and fifty infantry, whom he then had with him, to investigate the report he had received of the death of the religious who were in the province of Guale, and punish it; and that this was the place where the said Indians came and made an attack, and two Indians of those of the said province of Guale were killed [by those of Don Juan], who took from them a [friar's] robe, which by persons who recognized it, was said to be that of the Father, Fray Francisco de Berascula, of the mission of Asao. The said Indians said that they killed all the religious, except the Father, Fray Antonio de Badajoz, a lay-brother. In order that such a crime might be punished with the severity it called for, and that an investigation might be made of the above; and as before then the said Indians of the province of Guale had killed other religious, captains of infantry and officials of his Majesty's Royal Exchequer, and a great number of infantry; all this in time of peace, as will be declared by witnesses who know it and saw, and heard it said; and as they had shot arrows at the crosses, like apostates of the faith, and had refused obedience to his

Majesty as his vassals in order to hold an inquiry into the above, I, the Governor, made the following official report in this manner Date *ut supra*.

Before me, Alonso Garcia de la Vera, notary.

[Signed:] Gonçalo Méndez de Canço.

[c] And for the said inquiry, the said Governor ordered Don Juan, Cacique, to appear before him, from whom he took and received an oath in due form of law. And being questioned according to the tenor of the above decree, this witness said that on the day of San Francisco last past of this said year, on the 4th of this said month, at dawn, being in his town of San Pedro, in his house, twenty-six canoes arrived, filled with Indians of the province of Guale, all with arrows and *macanas*, which are the weapons with which they fight; and two of the canoes came to the house of Antonio Lopez, an Indian, a subject of this witness. The men in them landed, surrounded the house of the said Antonio Lopez and kept it surrounded until morning, in order that most of the canoes which remained behind might arrive. In the river there was a brigantine belonging to his Majesty which had come from St. Agustín, and the [men of the two] canoes, hearing [sounds from] the brigantine, the twenty-four canoes which remained behind did not dare to attack the town. And at this point, day dawned, and a Christian Indian, called Jusepe, came out of Antonio Lopez's house; and the Guale Indians who were surrounding it shot five arrows at him and knocked him down; and the wounded Indian cried out, giving the alarm, and then this witness heard him, and issued from his house and mustered his Indians. He went down the river after the said Guale Indians, and as he was coming upon them, they left the canoes and landed, and this witness took the two canoes from them, and his men disembarked and pursued the said Guale Indians; and in some thorn-bushes they captured and killed the *mandador* of Guale, and took from him a friar's gown and cowl, which this witness and his Indians knew to belong to the Father, Fray Francisco de Berascula, who was in Asao; and this witness's men returning and retiring to their town, this witness embarked in a canoe and returned by another way to the pursuit of the Indians, and he caught another canoe, and the Indians fled on land, and this witness charged [the men of] his villages that if they could catch any Indian they were to bring him from there the next day. They brought from the village of Ayacamode [Ayacamale?] the scalp of a Guale Indian whom they had caught and killed; and as the Guale canoes were returning to their land, they stopped in the river near a village called Bejesi, which is ruled by this witness, and they spoke with the Indians who were there, and told them that they had slain the five friars who were in Guale; and that Fray Antonio, a lay-brother, they had taken to Tulufina, where they kept him alive; and immediately that very night, this witness despatched advices of what was happening to the Señor Governor. He was asked if he knew whether before now they had killed in Guale other friars and soldiers, or the royal officials. He said he did not remember hearing of other friars or soldiers being killed in Guale, but that he knew that in Guale in the village of Ospogue [Espogue?], they slew Captain Otalora, who was a factor; together with the other royal officials of these provinces, who were carrying the pay from San Agustín to Santa Elena, and some other men with them, who were mostly retired ensigns and sergeants. He was asked if he knows that the Guale Indians are vassals of his Majesty and have pledged him obedience; he said he knows that the Guale Indians are vassals of his Majesty and friends of the Spaniards, and that in the *buhío* of Tolomato the royal Spanish Arms are hung up, fixed on a shield; and this is what he knows, and nothing more, under penalty of the oath he took; and he signed it with his name; and his testimony being read to him, he said he heard it, and confirmed and ratified it, and he said he was about twenty-six years of age.

Before me, Alonso Garcia de la Vera, notary.

[Signed:] Don Juan

[d] And for the investigation of the above, the said Governor ordered to appear before him Antonio Lopez, a principal Indian of San Pedro, a subject of the said Don Juan, Cacique; and through Gaspar de Salas, a soldier and the interpreter of the Indians of San Pedro, the said Antonio Lopez was questioned, according to the tenor of the above decree. And he said that on the

day of San Francisco last past, the said Antonio Lopez being in his house at night, his father-in-law went out, to drive away a barking dog, and as he was going out, the Guale Indians who were surrounding the house shot five arrows at him; and at the outcries of his father-in-law, who said they were coming to make war on him, the said Antonio Lopez ran out of his house, and remained in his *sabana* [field], and then day dawned. And knowing that the Guale Indians were making war on them, he took his bow and quiver of arrows, and went to find Don Juan, his cacique. He found him and the Father, Fray Francisco Pareja, on the shore, where they were launching some canoes with the Spaniards of a brigantine from San Agustín; and the Cacique Don Juan embarked in the canoes with the said Antonio Lopez and other principal Indians, and they went after the two Guale canoes which were crossing the river. Nearing land on the other side, the Guale Indians leaped on shore, fleeing, and Don Juan intercepted them by going up the river, and killed and scalped two of their Indians, and brought the scalps back with two canoes left by those of Guale. They also brought the gown and cowl of a friar; the said Antonio Lopez did not know whose gown it was; and this is all that passed, and that the said Antonio Lopez saw and did know. On being asked if he knew or saw or had heard it said that the Guale Indians had killed before now some religious or friars or other Spaniards or royal officials- he said that he had heard it said that in Espogue, a village of Guale, they killed the royal officials of these provinces, who were going to Santa Elena with the pay, and many other soldiers. On being asked if he knew that the Guale Indians were subjects of the King Don Felipe, our master, and friends of the Spaniards, and had friendly intercourse with them; and that a coat-of-arms of his Majesty had been set up in Tolomato he said he knew that the Guale Indians were subjects of his Majesty and friends of the Spaniards, and that in the *buhío* of Tolomato there was a shield set up, painted with the royal arms: and this he said in answer to that question, and the said Antonio Lopez declared this through the said Gaspar de Salas; and his testimony being read to him, he said he confirmed it; and he did not sign because he did not know how. And he said he was twenty-eight years of age, and the said An-

tonio Lopez, from the appearance of his face, was and appeared to be about forty years old. They did not sign because they did not know how.

[Signed:] Gonçalo Méndez de Canço.

Before me, Alonso Garcia de la Vera, notary.

[e] And after the abovesaid, the said Governor, for the investigation of this affair and clearing up of the truth, took the testimony of Jusepe, a Christian Indian, who was lying wounded in bed, through the said Gaspar de Salas, an interpreter. On being questioned by the said interpreter, according to the above decree, the said Jusepe, an Indian, said that, being in bed at daybreak on the day of San Francisco, he heard a dog of his bark, and thinking he was barking at a horse of Don Juan, the Cacique, he went out of his house; and as he went toward the *sabana*, he said to the dog: "Come here!" - and then they shot five arrows at him, four in the shoulders and one in the arm; and the said Indian, Jusepe, when he felt himself wounded, entered his house to get his bow; again he went forth to the *sabana*, and on trying to arch his bow, he could not do so because he was wounded. He re-entered the house, shouting: "They are going to make war"! and at his shouts, other neighboring Indians came. The said Jusepe heard it said afterward that the enemy were Indians from Guale, and they brought twenty-six canoes; and that Don Juan, the Cacique, pursued them, took two of their canoes, killed two of their Indians and found the gown of a friar; and this is what he knows of this affair. On being asked if he knows or has heard it said that in the province of Guale they had killed before then some friars or royal officials or other Spaniards, the said Jusepe, an Indian, said through the said interpreter, that he knows that in the past, when the said royal officials with soldiers, were on their way from the fort of San Agustín with the pay for Santa Elena, they were all slain in the province of Guale, in the village of Hespogue; and likewise at Tolomato, another time, they killed Aguilar, an interpreter, and other Spaniards; and this he answered to this question.

On being asked if he knows that the Guale Indians are vassals of his Majesty and friends of the Spaniards, the said Jusepe said through the said interpreter, that he knows that in the province of Guale the Indians are vassals of his

Majesty and pay him tribute; are friends of the Spaniards, and as such, had friars in the missions; and in Tolomato, in the *buhío*, there was a shield with the royal arms. And this is what the said interpreter said that the said Jusepe, an Indian, said; and what he knows, and swore to before God, in due form, as being the truth; and he did not sign because he did not know how. And the said Gaspar de Salas said he was twenty-eight years of age; and the said Indian Jusepe, to all appearances, was a man of about fifty.

[Signed:] Gonçalo Méndez de Canço

Before me, Alonso Garcia de la Vera, notary.

[f]   And immediately, for the said investigation, the said Governor and Captain-General ordered to appear before him Vicente Gonçales, Captain of Infantry of the fort of San Agustín, from whom he took and received an oath as prescribed by law. And on being questioned according to the tenor of the above decree, this witness said that having been twenty-three years in these parts, he knows that the Indians had slain interpreters and Franciscan friars in the province of Guale, and that they likewise killed fourteen or fifteen soldiers with Aguilar, an interpreter; whom, because he was an interpreter, they roasted in the fire. And that nineteen years before, when Captain Otalora, the Factor, Pedro Menéndez, the Treasurer, and Miguel Moreno, the Royal Accountant, royal officials of these provinces, went in a launch with sailors and soldiers to carry the pay to Santa Elena- in Espogue, in the province of Guale, they killed them all, in time of peace; and afterward, in the said province, they killed Gaspar Avias. And lately, while this witness was serving in San Agustín with his company, there came news that in the said province of Guale, from Aluste to Asao, the said Indians of Guale had slain all the friars who were in the missions; and this witness saw a friar's robe, which was brought by him who brought the news. And he [the captain] was summoned by the said Governor and Captain-General to a meeting with the royal officials at the Convent of San Francisco, at which were present the Father Custodian and other religious; and where he, as a captain, gave his opinion that it was necessary to come and inquire into and punish the crime; and thus, he had come

in the company of the said Governor to the said town of San Pedro, where all the San Pedro Indians said that the Indians from Guale came to make war on them. And this is what he knows since he has been in these provinces, and it is the truth, under penalty of the oath he took, and he signed it with his name; and he said he was about fifty-five years of age.

[Signed:] Captain Vicente Gonçales

Before me, Alonso Garcia de la Vera, notary.

[g]   And immediately thereupon, the said Governor ordered to appear before him Andres Lopez de Simancas, a soldier from whom was taken and received an oath, as prescribed by law. And on being questioned, according to the tenor of the above decree, he said that since he has been in these provinces he knows that in Guale the Indians had killed soldiers, and Aguilar and Pedro Masduerme, interpreters; and in Guale they roasted the said Aguilar in the fire. Afterward, when Pedro Menéndez the one-eyed, a nephew of the Adelantado Pedro Menéndez de Avilés, who at that time was Treasurer and Lieutenant-Governor in these provinces; Captain Otalora, who was Factor, and Ensign Miguel Moreno, who was Royal Accountant (royal officials of these provinces, all of them) were on their way with the pay of Santa Elena, in a launch with soldiers and sailors; in the said province of Guale, the Indians [pretending to be] friendly and peaceful in the village of Espogue, killed them all and took the bark from them; and since then, in the said province, they slew Gaspar Avias, a corporal. And this witness, having gone with another soldier from Santa Elena to the said province of Guale, the said Indians, in time of peace, wanted to kill him in the principal village of Tolomato; and owing to his quickness they did not kill him and the other man, for they fled in a canoe. And lately, when the said caciques of the province of Guale were friendly and very peaceful [with the Spaniards], and a large part of them were Christians, this witness had heard it said that the said Indians of Guale slew the fathers, religious of the Order of San Francisco, who were teaching them in the missions; and this is what he knows and it is the truth under penalty of the oath he took. And his testimony being read to him, he said he heard it and confirmed it, and

did not sign because he did not know how; and he said he was about sixty years of age.

[Signed:] Gonçalo Méndez de Canço.

Before me, Alonso Garcia de la Vera, notary.

[h] Testimony of Juan de la Cruz, corporal of the fort of San Agustín omitted.

[i] I, Fray Pedro Fernandez de Choças, a preacher of the Order of our Father San Francisco, in Puturiba, a village of Indians of these provinces of Florida- [certify that] on Saturday, the 4th of October, soon after sunrise, the Indians of our mission called me. They were much disturbed and alarmed, and on coming forth from my house I saw and counted eleven canoes of Indian enemies, natives of Ybaha, which among the Spaniards is called Guale. And as I had no other weapons, I invested myself with those of the Church, and began to celebrate the mass of my glorious and seraphic father San Francisco, for it was his day. And at the end of it there came a messenger from the village of San Pedro, who told how the Indians of Guale had made war on them, and had shot arrows at and badly wounded, an Indian named Jusepe; and furthermore, that on a little sandy beach they had shot five arrows at the cross and standard of Our Lord Jesus Christ; and after having plundered a house of the said village, and shot arrows at another, they re-embarked in their canoes, and departed. Thereupon, the Cacique of Bejesi arrived, with the fiscal of the said mission, and three other Indians, messengers and interpreters from the province of Guale; and they certified to me with truth that they had counted twenty-three canoes belonging to the enemy from Guale, at the point of this same island, and in them three or four hundred Indian warriors; and that the Cacique of Asao, with shamelessness, and little fear of God and less understanding of that which he had professed at his baptism, rose at the front of the canoe, saying: "What do you think! We have killed five friars, and one shaven head only, who was a lay-brother, are we keeping in Tulufina alive. See, here, the hat of my friar!" And lifting it aloft as a great trophy, they mocked and jeered at it and the Christian law, like apostates and excommunicates of the Catholic faith. On that same day, when night had come, our Indians entered the *buhío*, while all the rest were assembled at the

mission, with the oars of a canoe they had taken from the enemy, and some canoes and other spoils they found there; and I learned how the Indians of San Pedro had taken two other canoes, and pursued one of the Indian enemies and slain another, after these had killed a boy [of our friendly Indians]. Among the spoils found by those of San Pedro, were the gown and cowl of the Father, Fray Francisco de Berascula; and by this, therefore, as well as by his hat which they held before us in Bejesi, as also because his cacique came by there; together this with [the fact that] this said religious did not come from his mission to mine, having promised me to come within a fortnight to bring me the altar-cloths, chalice and other things which, when I went to teach in the mountains of Ocute, I left in Tolomato—by all this I gathered and inferred that they had given him martyrdom, and to the other blessed religious likewise; as the enemies themselves said, and gloried in their deed. Or, at the very least, they held them captive, and closely imprisoned, for since then, no Indian or canoe or any other thing had come from that land to this, although they had promised to return and make war on all these Christians; for whose defence and protection I wrote to the Señor General Gonçalo Méndez de Canço, residing in San Agustín, and begged him to send six or more veteran soldiers wearing *escaupiles*, to this island, with the greatest speed with which it could be done. They travelled night and day, by land, by streams and through swamps, until they arrived here at San Pedro, where, with a guard and sentinel, were the Father, Fray Francisco Pareja and I, with our Christians, awaiting the Señor General and his army, who arrived at this village on October 17, 1597. By request of the said Señor General, I say and certify that all that is written above is the truth, on account of which I signed it with my name.

Fray Pedro

[Signed:] Fernandez de Choças

[j] On the 4th day of the month of October of the year 1597, the day of our Father San Francisco, I, Fray Francisco de Pareja, being in San Pedro, a village of Indians of these provinces of Florida, certify that on that day, at twilight, while I stood at the church door, I heard the Indians of this village shouting: "War! War!" And every one, much alarmed, ran to where the Indians were

shouting; and the Guale Indians, seeing that they were coming after them, embarked in two canoes they brought, and started to flee, rowing with great haste. I went forth with other Spaniards whom the Señor General had sent here in a brigantine, and we saw those in the canoes fleeing. At this, we sent a messenger to the village of Puturiba, in order that they might run to see what was happening there; and the cacique of that land, Don Juan, set out to intercept the foe with two canoes; and they, seeing themselves surrounded and intercepted, fled along a little stream toward the woods. Upon being overtaken, one of their men was killed, not far from there, and I was informed by the *atequi* that they had surrounded the house of an Indian named Jusepe, who, they say, was badly wounded by arrows. I hastened to his house to hear his confession, and when I returned to the church, I was told how twenty-seven other canoes had arrived near the village from up the river, and that with little fear of God they had landed on a bit of beach there is there; and [the Indians] having discovered a cross ✠ they shot five arrows at it. When I asked them what they meant by this, they told me that they had killed five Fathers whom they had had among them; and this appeared to be the truth, because afterward, as they fled from the brigantine which was here, they spoke with the Cacique of Bejesi, the fiscal of Puturiba and others who were there at the end of the island, where they had to pass, as they went by in their canoes in the middle of the bay; and the Cacique of Asao, at the end of the canoe, said shamelessly and with little fear of God, like an apostate of the Catholic faith: "What do you think, you others! Five friars have we slain, and one only is left with a shaven head because he was a lay-brother. What are you others doing? Come to our land!" And with an air of great satisfaction and victory, he held a hat aloft, saying it belonged to Father Berascula, who was in the mission of his land and village of Asao. Those others replied: "Come here, and you shall take away food and bows and arrows for your land!" And thus they went. That same day the said cacique [of Bejesi] returned in another canoe, and Spaniards in another, and they went toward Talaje, and found another canoe moored [to the river bank], and in it many *macanas*. The men had fled, and in pursuing them, they killed another enemy Indian, and the enemy killed a

boy. At night all the Indians assembled who had gone forth from this village, and among the spoils they brought a robe and cowl of one of the Fathers, which I sent that night to San Agustín, by a messenger dispatched by Don Juan, the Cacique of this village of San Pedro. He was to notify the Señor General of what was occurring, asking him to send six Spaniards for the defence of this church which is here, and these Christians, whom may God keep. He did this the very night the messenger arrived, and they came with much speed, travelling night and day, by land, streams and swamps, until they arrived here, at San Pedro; where, with a sentinel and guard, by order of the said Señor Governor and Captain-General of these provinces, were the Father, Fray Pedro de Choças, and myself, with the other Christians and twelve Spaniards, awaiting the Señor General and his army. He arrived at this said place, in very contrary weather, on the 17th of the said month of October, 1597. All of which I certify to be the truth, and so signed it with my name, by request of the Señor General.

[Signed:] Fray Francisco Pareja.

[k] Gonçalo Méndez de Canço, Governor and Captain-General of these provinces of Florida for the King our master, etc. Inasmuch as to-day, the said day October 7th, 1597, tidings have come from the province of Guale that the Indians there had killed the Franciscan Fathers, the religious who were in the missions, teaching and enlightening them in the holy Catholic faith; and as, until I can leave with the necessary infantry to punish such a crime, it is proper to send a dozen soldiers to the village of San Pedro, where Don Juan, who is friendly, is the cacique; and likewise for the guarding of the Fathers who are there, Fray Pedro de Choças and Fray Francisco Pareja; and as it is proper that with these said soldiers a man should go to command them, that they may obey his orders as though they were mine I hereby appoint Sergeant Santiago to do so, that he may go with the said soldiers with the greatest speed possible, travelling by day and by night, until he arrives at San Pedro; and there he is to mount guard day and night with his men, and if there should be any attack by Indian enemies, the sergeant and soldiers are to protect the Fathers there until they place them in safety. And likewise, in every way they can, they are to help

Don Juan because he is a friend; on all occasions he has shown himself a faithful subject of his Majesty; but they must bear in mind that under no circumstances must they go out of the village of San Pedro, or consent to Don Juan's doing so; and if anything should arise, they are to communicate with the Father, Fray Pedro de Choças, and Father Pareja. Likewise, the Sergeant must not allow the soldiers to do any injury to the Indians, because I am writing to Don Juan to give food to the soldiers, and they are to be contented with that which Don Juan may give them, for I feel sure he will do this very well. And in every way let this order be observed, for thus it befits his Majesty's service. Done in San Agustín, October 7, 1597.

[Signed:] Gonçalo Méndez de Canço.

[l] In compliance with the said Governor's and Captain-General's order above-written, I, the said cacique, Don Juan, and his village, until the infantry, with the greatest speed possible, at the town of San Pedro, where Don Juan is cacique, on Thursday morning, the 10th of the said month of October, where I guarded all that was committed to my charge, and fulfilled [orders]; and I took particular care to watch over the Fathers, the said cacique, Don Juan, and his village, until the said Governor arrived on the 17th of the said month. And in order that there may be a record of my having carried out exactly the said order which was given me, I hereby give the present affidavit, and sign my name to it, before the present notary.

Done in the town of San Pedro, the 22d of October, 1597.

[Signed:] Juan de Santiago

Before me, Alonso Garcia de la Vera, notary.

[m] Gonçalo Méndez de Canço, Governor and Captain-General of these provinces of Florida for the King our master, etc. The order and instructions which Captain Vicente Gonçales must follow in this voyage to Guale in the shallop of his Majesty, are the following: Inasmuch as I have received news that the Indians of Guale have killed the religious who were there, and although it is two days since I arrived in this town of San Pedro and I have tried to investigate and learn [the facts of the case], I have not found a truthful relation of what happened; and that I may make a

decision in order to punish and make war on them with just cause, in the manner most proper to the service of his Majesty, the said Captain will set out in the said shallop. And of the infantry I have here he is to choose as many as twenty-two men wearing *escaupiles*, [and] with the necessary arms, munitions and food he will leave this harbor at once, with all the silence and caution fitting for such an occasion, and go to Tolomato, in the province of Guale. Under no circumstances is he to proceed farther; and he will try to give them to understand that he comes in peace, as though he were bringing supplies to the Fathers, and coming to see how they are. And if any Indian should appear to talk with them, the Captain is to inquire after the Fathers, and ask that they come to see him to receive their gifts, because he wishes to go on farther; and [he is to tell him] that I have been informed by Don Juan, the Cacique of San Pedro, that they came to make war on him; that they are to notify me of what has happened, and if the Salchiches or those of Tulufina have caused [the trouble]. That I well understand that if they should dare to pass through San Pedro, I would be warned of it, and for this reason I send him to learn the truth; and he is to endeavor by every way and means he can to bring me some Indian man or woman from whom I may learn the truth. In case he cannot succeed in obtaining information of what has occurred, and the cause thereof, and he should in no way be able to seize any man, he must try to come here by Thursday in the evening or Friday at dawn, because I have summoned the friendly Indians at that time, and if he be not here no decision can be taken. And anything more that might take place there I leave to his judgment, and the faith I have in his prudence.

Done in San Pedro, on the 19th of October, 1597.

[Signed:] Gonçalo Méndez de Canço

By order of the Señor General, Alonso Garcia de la Vera, notary.

[n] And immediately thereupon I, the said Captain Vicente Gonçales, in fulfilment of the above order of the said Governor and Captain-General, departed in the said launch with the infantry on board; and with all the speed possible I arrived in the province of Guale, two leagues from Tolomato, about sixteen leagues from this town of

San Pedro, where I found a canoe, and an Indian in it. And although I caught sight of him very far off, I chased him, and on the Indian's throwing himself into the water to reach the land, I called him many times in his language. Seeing that he would not return, I ordered several arquebuse shots to be fired at him, from which he received some wounds. Having taken him, I ordered, through the interpreter I had with me, that he be asked how were the Fathers in the missions, because we were bringing them food and presents. He replied to me that they were all dead; and on being asked who had killed them, and the cause of this, he said that all the caciques of the said province had done it, each cacique killing his own friar; that the Indians of Cosahue, the Salchiches, and those of Tulufina and Santa Elena had told them to kill them; and that therefore they themselves slew them, each cacique his own friar. Seeing this, and that there was found in the said Indian's possession a friar's serge frock, we returned with the Indian to the said town of San Pedro with all the haste possible, to report to the said Governor and Captain-General, who was in the said town of San Pedro. And that there may be a record of the above, I gave these presents signed with my name; and on arriving at the said town of San Pedro, I presented the said Indian, with the said serge frock, to the said Governor; which is the truth, and I signed it with my name before the said notary. Done in San Pedro, October 22, 1597.

[Signed:] Captain Vicente Gonçales
Before me, Alonso Garcia de la Vera, notary.

And the said Governor immediately thereupon, ordered me, a notary, to add the said order to the papers in the case he is preparing officially for the investigation into the death of the said Fathers; and this he provided, and signed with his name.

[Signed:] Gonçalo Méndez de Canço.
Before me, Alonso Garcia de la Vera, notary.

[o] In the town of San Pedro, on the 22d of the month of October, 1597, the said Governor, having seen that the said Captain, Vicente Gonçales, brought the said Indian in compliance with the said order, as appeared in the Captain's testimony; the said Governor took the said Indian's declaration, and admonished him, through Andres Lopez, an Indian, to tell the truth as to what had occurred in Guale, and which caciques had killed the Fathers, and how many Fathers were killed; and the said Indian, through the said Andres Lopez, an Indian of Puturiba and a Guale interpreter, replied and said that in the province of Guale, the former caciques and the others slew five friars, who were there, all the caciques assembling to do this, and each mission slaying its own friar. One only was spared, who did not say mass; and the said Andres Lopez, in the language of San Pedro, through Juan de Junco, who repeated his words in Spanish, declared what the said Indian said; Juan de la Torre, a Spaniard, being present, who understood the language of Guale.

On being asked if he knew for what reason the said Indians killed the Fathers, he said that he knew nothing except that all the Guale Indians assembled one night and killed the said Fathers, as he had said above.

On being asked of which cacique he was the subject, he said of him of Cascangue, who was dead.

On being asked if he was present at the death of any friar, or saw any friar killed, he said no.

On being asked who gave him the serge frock he wore, he said he got it by barter from an Indian of Espo, called Tacobiega.

On being asked if he knew where the bodies of the friars were buried, he said he knew that they buried him of Asao in the mission church of Asao; that the friar who was in Guale begged the Indians to bury him at the entrance of the church, and thus he had heard it said that there they buried him; and he did not know where they buried the other Fathers.

On being asked if he knew where were the chalices, the altar furnishings and the books, he said that those of the Father at Asao were held by the cacique there; of the others he knew nothing.

The abovesaid facts, and others, were declared by the said Indian through the said Juan de Junco and Andres Lopez de Simancas, Indian interpreters; the said Andres Lopez declaring them in the Indian language and the said Juan de Junco, in the Spanish, in the presence of the said Governor and of myself, a notary. Present: Juan de la Torre, a Guale interpreter, Ensign Hernando de Mestas and Alonso Diaz; Christoval de Verlanga and Toribio, caciques

[Signed:] Gonçalo Méndez de Canço
Before me, Alonso Garcia de la Vera, notary.

[p]   The Friars' Petition.

In the town of San Pedro, on the 22d of the month of October, 1597, Fray Blas de Montes, Vicar of Nombre de Dios, said: I have come to make an investigation in virtue of a commission from our Father, Fray Francisco de Marrón, Custodian of this *custodia* of Santa Elena and Vicar-General of these provinces of Florida, into the death of the religious whom the Indians killed in the province of Guale, as appeared from the relation made by Father Fray Pedro de Choças, Vicar and preacher of Puturiba, to the said Father Custodian; and from a robe sent to him which had belonged to one of the said dead religious, and from the Indians' searching for and wearing all the things pertaining to their use and that of divine worship. And because, for the above, the opinions and declarations of some Spaniards are necessary, whom I cannot compel to testify without the permission and authority of the said Señor Governor and Captain-General of the abovesaid provinces, who has come here now to punish the culprits, I pray and supplicate him to grant the said permission, that the truth may not remain hidden in such an important case. And of the contrary, etc.

Date *ut supra*.

[Signed:] Fray Blas de Montes.

[q]   On the above day, in the town of San Pedro, I, a notary, read the above paper to Gonçalo Méndez de Canço, Governor and Captain-General of these provinces for his Majesty; and having seen and understood it, he said that on the 7th of this said month of October, 1597, he received tidings that the Indians of Guale had killed the Fathers who were in the missions there, which he learned from a letter of the Father, Fray Pedro Fernandez de Choças. [He at once proceeded to] prepare the infantry, munitions and stores necessary to investigate and punish such a crime; and Our Lord has been pleased to bring him, with all his men, munitions and supplies, to this town of San Pedro, where he is at present. Since his arrival, he has found out how, in the said province of Guale, the Indians killed the said religious, from an Indian captured by the launch which the said Governor sent under the command of Captain Vicente Gonçales, as appears from the order and the Captain's testimony, which are in the proceedings; the In-dian confessed all that the said Father, Fray Pedro Fernandez de Choças, had written in his letter. On account of that, and of the fact that it does not suit the Governor and Captain-General of these provinces for his Majesty, who administers his royal justice, that the said Father, Fray Blas, should interfere by making an investigation in these said provinces, inasmuch as the powers with which the said Father Custodian has invested him are not, nor can be [anything more] than the authority to collect the altar-furnishings and other things pertaining to the religious; for this purpose his Honor, the said Governor, begs the said Father, Fray Blas, and if it be necessary, requests him, to embark with the said Governor for the province of Guale, where he is going with his army of infantry; and on the said voyage he will give more consideration to the person of the said Fray Blas than to his own, and will entertain him and give him a guard in such manner that he will run no risk. And once arrived in the said country and missions where were the said Fathers, he will endeavor, by means of the soldiers with him, [to get possession of] all the chalices, altar-furnishings and other things pertaining to the said church, as well as the wardrobes and personal belongings of the said friars, all that he will deliver, and order to be delivered, to the said Father, Fray Blas, without holding back anything. And he likewise ordered to be given and delivered to him the frock of a religious, which on the said day, yesterday, the said Captain Vicente Gonçales brought him; the Indian the Captain captured had worn it; and likewise he will see to it that the bodies of the said religious be entrusted to his care those that may be recovered in order that by agreement with the said Father, Fray Blas, those that may be found may be conveyed with all possible propriety to the said Convent of San Francisco in San Agustín. And if it suits the said Father, Fray Blas, to make any investigation, or take any steps concerning the abovesaid, let him do so before his Honor, the said Governor, for he on his side is ready to co-operate in every way where the matter is brought under his authority and judicial decree; and if it be necessary, after the said investigation he is conducting at present, is closed, and if the said Father, Fray Blas, or the Father Custodian, should desire it very much, he will order a certified copy to be given him. As for what he asks of

the Governor, the latter requests him if it be necessary not to interfere with the royal jurisdiction, or wield the authority mentioned in his petition, to which he is not entitled; for that would seem as if he wished to usurp the royal jurisdiction, and the said Governor does not give him, or admit or recognize that he has any more authority than that to which he may have the right. And he orders me, a notary, under penalty of [a fine of] 10,000 maravedis, applied by the *Cámara* of his Majesty, not to prepare any legal declaration for the said Father, Fray Blas, or any other friar of his Order; and he commanded this paper to be filed with the Report; and if the said Father Custodian, or the said Father, Fray Blas, should want a copy of this petition it is to be given him, because the giving of the power and royal jurisdiction in this manner so by the service and authority of his Majesty. And this he provided, ordered, and signed with his name.

[Signed:] Gonçalo Méndez de Canço.

Before me, Alonso Garcia de la Vera, notary.

And I, the notary, immediately thereupon read the above declaration to the said Father, Fray Blas de Montes, and delivered to him a serge frock worn by an Indian who was captured in the province of Guale; which declaration was heard by the said Father, Fray Blas de Montes, and he received it and signed it with his name, which I certify, and he asked for a copy of all this.

[Signed:] Fray Blas de Montes

Before me, Alonso Garcia de la Vera, notary.

[s] On the 24th of the month of October, 1597, the said Governor set out with the men, vessels and launches he was conveying to the villages of Guale, to investigate and punish the crime committed by the said Indians, and the death of the said religious, taking in his company the Father, Fray Blas de Montes, to give and deliver to him the belongings of the said religious that may be found, as the above declaration sets forth.

Alonso Garcia de la Vera, notary.

[t] On the 27th of the said month and year, the said Governor, again speaking through an *atequi* interpreter, "en la mata redonda" [meaning?] with the Indian that the said Captain Vicente Gonçales had taken [and questioning him again as to whether] the said Indians were assembled at Ospo, the said Indian reiterated that they were at

Ospo; and the said Governor, hearing the above, ordered his officers to follow him that night and go to Ospo, to surprise the said Indians at dawn; and understanding that they would follow his orders and accompany him, he set forth with the shallops and canoes. On arriving about a league and a half from the said village of Ospo, he found four canoes of Indians missing, and Spaniards among them, to the number of seventy-two persons all told. And seeing the great lack of soldiers, he consulted with the Sergeant-Major, Alonso Dias, and other veteran soldiers, who had had experience in these provinces, like the present notary, Alonso Garcia de la Vera, Sergeant Santiago and Sergeant Verlanga and Simancas; and when they were asked if the soldiers the said Governor had gathered there were sufficient to enable him to land and attack the Indians—the Governor reminding them of the notice they had had to the effect that all the Indians of the province were holding a meeting in Ospo— they answered with one voice that they had enough men to carry out his intention and land and attack the Indians. And hearing the opinion of the abovesaid, the said Governor ordered them to increase their speed in rowing and go to the said village, where, on account of a fog and heavy shower which came at daybreak, they did not at all recognize the land. They asked the said Indian the said Captain had captured, to tell them where were the village and the stream by which they were to reach it, and the said Indian did not tell the truth; he denied that the stream they were on was the right one, and said it was the stream of Tolomato. And the said Governor, realizing that he did this in order to delay till daybreak, that we might be seen by the Indians of the said land, and thus it would be impossible to accomplish what had been planned, commanded that he be delivered to some Indians in a canoe, to be garroted by them, over and above the fact that the said Indian had four or five wounds from the arquebuse shots he had received at the time he was taken. And the said Governor continued his journey and arrived at the said village of Ospo at dawn, and landed with his men, where he was received with many arrows from the Indians, and they wounded several of his soldiers. Notwithstanding, he entered the village with his men, and burned the village and the principal houses and the storehouses for corn, without sparing anything except the church, which he ordered should not be burned; and as they lit the fires while they went on, the Indians would come running and shoot arrows at them, and they were received with arquebue shots. [The Spaniards] found in the said village a mass-book, a breviary, a hat, a chalice cloth and a friar's scalp, which as they were things pertaining to a religious, the said Governor ordered me, the notary, to deliver to the said Father, Fray Blas, as was done. And seeing that he could do them no more harm than he had already, as the said Indians had fled to the forest and gathered there, the said Governor returned to the large launches, to reinforce himself with supplies and munitions in the forest of Asao, and hear about the men and canoes he had lost. And finding the said canoes two leagues from there, he collected them and took them with him till he arrived where were the vessels with the food and munitions. There he reprimanded them for the injury they had done him, and deprived of their command, for the said carelessness, two captains of the guard in the said canoes; he gave them no greater punishment.

[Signed:] Gonçalo Méndez de Canço
Before me, Alonso Garcia de la Vera, notary.

[u] On the 2d of the month of November, the said General, with the men, vessels and launches, left the forest of Asao for Guale; and that day the village of Sapala was burned, and the storehouses and the food it contained. Thence the General departed for Tolomato, where, on landing with all his soldiers, he found the church burned, as well as the principal *buhíos* and the houses of the religious who served there. And as that was the principal town of the land, the said General remained there two days, and despatched *atequi* [interpreters] to climb the trees and call to the Indians to come and speak with the said Governor, [saying] that he would hear them in order to know what had prompted them to kill the religious. None of them came, except a few who came in treachery and killed two friendly Indians.

[Signed:] Gonçalo Méndez de Canço
Before me, Alonso Garcia de la Vera, notary.

[v] On the 4th of the said month, when the said Governor saw that the said Indians did not come, he ordered all the houses in the town to be burned, and in some bushes were found an altar

and an image of Saint Anthony of Padua, which were delivered to the said Father, Fray Blas. The said day he despatched the Sergeant Major, Alonso Dias, with a number of infantry, to the island and village of Guale, to see what was happening there, and whether he could capture some Indians alive; and to do them all the damage they could, in case they could not be taken, and burn the said village and island. That said day, at nightfall, the said Sergeant returned from the said expedition, and related to the said Governor before me, the notary, how in the said village and island he did not find one Indian, but found the church and the friars' house burned. And he burned the large *buhío* [the village council house?] and the house of the cacique, and whatever else he found to burn; and he discovered two graves, and in them, two bodies were buried, which, in his opinion, and that of the men with him, they knew to be those of two religious, Fray Miguel and Fray Antonio, from the marks on their bodies. And they found their arms and legs broken in four places, and their feet tied; and near one of the graves was a head which in his opinion was that of Fray Miguel, because it was found not very far from the body; and they disinterred him with a hoe, to identify him, and buried him again. And they likewise covered the body of the other Father, because it was not properly covered; and on account of the condition of the bodies, the Sergeant could not take them with him, as he had been ordered to do by the said Governor; and he marked the graves, for the time when the Governor might wish to remove the bodies. He brought the head of the Father, Fray Miguel, and small bones [*quesesitos, huesitos*] of the said Fray Miguel's body, and the said Governor delivered them to the said Father, Fray Blas; which declaration the said Sergeant Major made before me, a notary, and signed it with his name.

[Signed:] Gonçalo Méndez de Canço
Alonso Dias
Before me, Alonso Garcia de la Vera, notary.

[w] On the 5th of the month of November, the said Governor despatched the Sergeant Major with infantry to burn the town of Tupiqui, and that day the said Sergeant Major returned and said he had not found one Indian. The church, the friar's house, the principal *buhío* and the cacique's

house were burned, and he found a buried corpse which appeared to him to be that of the Father, Fray Blas Rodriguez, whose head was split into three or four parts. He disinterred it but did not bring it, on account of the condition in which it was, and he again covered it with earth.

On the 6th of the said month, the said Governor sent the said Sergeant Major to the towns of Asao and Talaxe [Talaje], with orders that if he could catch an Indian, to catch him alive, and if not, to do them all the harm he could. That same night the said Sergeant Major returned to where the said Governor was, and said he had found no Indians, but that all the town and houses and food supplies and storehouses for corn, were intact; and the same conditions existed in the town of Talaxe. They burned and destroyed everything, and he made the said declaration before the said Governor, and in presence of me, the notary

[Signed:] Gonçalo Méndez de Canço
Alonso Dias
Before me, Alonso Garcia de la Vera, notary.

[x] And the said Governor, seeing that the said Indians could not be punished farther, because they were very much on the alert, retired on the way to San. Agustín, and arrived at the town of San Pedro on the 8th of this month.

On the 11th of this said month, in the said town of San Pedro, the said Governor, in presence of me, the notary, ordered the cacique of the said town and its land, called Don Juan, and some of his relatives and principal Indians, to assemble in the large church of the said town of San Pedro; whom he notified that they could not remain in the said place without running great risk from the Guale Indians; besides which, the Fathers who were there and in Puturiba were retiring and going to San Agustín, and thus it suited the service of his Majesty that the said Don Juan and his people should retire to Socochuno and San Juan del Puerto and other towns of his country, where the religious could come to teach them without fear, and administer the sacraments to them. And the said Don Juan and his Indians who were there, his relatives and principal men, said through Juan de Junco, an Indian, that it was well. And as they were loyal subjects of his Majesty, and the said Governor saw that the said Don Juan and his Indians obeyed so faithfully the

many of his men had gone in his company to the said province of Guale—he told them that in his orders given them, and the said Don Juan and Majesty's name, he relieved and freed them from the tribute they paid his Majesty, which was one *arroba* of corn each year from each married Indian; and that he did not wish any of them to pay more than six ears of corn as an acknowledgment, as long as his Majesty and his Royal Council of the Indies did not command anything else, taking the above into consideration, and that they were in utter poverty, and sustained themselves the greater part of the year on acorns and shellfish and roots of herbs. And they must not believe, nor think it a fact, as they did, that his Majesty did not love them; the said natives must understand, from the interest he took in them, that he did love them, and longed for nothing more than to have them come into the acceptance of the holy Catholic faith and the law of the Gospel, and hold him for their King and master. And the said Don Juan said that he did so, said so and loved him much; and in place of thanks they gave their salute to the said Governor, according to their custom.

And that said day the said Governor had a talk with the Caciques of Puturiba and Tocohaya, in order that they might retire [from that district]; and he granted them the favor, in his Majesty's name, of freeing them from the tribute, like the others, and left the Sergeant Major, Alonso Diaz, with twenty-four soldiers, to help them to withdraw.

On the 16th of November of this said year, [the Governor] departed from the said town of San Pedro for San Agustín.

[Signed:] Gonçalo Méndez de Canço
Before me, Alonso Garcia de la Vera, notary.

[y] And immediately thereupon, on the said day, month and year, the said Governor and Captain-General said that inasmuch as he was going to the city of San Agustín, and could not be present at the retribution and punishment that the said Indians of Guale deserved, who killed the said religious, not only because he must go and despatch the fortunate vessel which had to bring the pay for these provinces, but also because he must forward to his Majesty notice of these said deaths of the religious, sending to his Royal Council a

report of the abovesaid; the Governor ordered me, the present notary, to give him a certified copy of all that had been accomplished, so that his Majesty and his Royal Council might know and understand how he planned the punishment of the said Indians. And the said Governor said likewise that in the interval before a Report could be given to his Majesty and his Royal Council, he vowed he would punish or investigate the death of the said religious, by force of arms as well as by other methods and artifices of war. And until his Majesty and his Royal Council ordered and commanded what in this case he must do, he would immediately give over all the Indian men and women who might be captured alive in the said province and missions of Guale, where the said religious had been, to serve as slaves to the soldiers who might capture them; inasmuch as the crime committed by the said Indians was so grave, and deserving of an equally heavy penalty and punishment; and this he ordered, provided and signed with his name

[Signed:] Gonçalo Méndez de Canço
Before me, Alonso Garcia de la Vera, notary.

[z]   And I, Alonso Garcia de la Vera, chief notary public of the government in these provinces of Florida and this city of San Agustín, by order of the said Governor, Gonçalo Méndez de Canço, had this transcript taken from the original which I retain, and to which I refer, and I corrected and compared it, and I sign it in testimony of the truth. [Rubric].

Alonso Garcia de la Vera, notary.

We, the royal officials of the royal treasury of these provinces of Florida, who reside in this city of San Agustín, attest and certify to those who may see these presents, how the above Alonso Garcia de la Vera is chief notary public of the government of these provinces of Florida and this city of San Agustín, and is loyal and true; and how entire faith and credit is to be given to such a notary, and to the written proceedings, declarations and other matters which have passed and are passing through his hands, in law and out of court. Done in San Agustín, Florida, on the 12th of January of the year 1598.

[Signed:] Bartolomé de Arguëlles
Juan Menéndez Marqués
Juan Lopes de Avilés

753. July 1, 1598. Gonzálo Méndez de Canzo to Philip II on the recent uprising in Guale.

A.G.I., Seville, Patronato 1/1/1/19; printed in Luis Gerónimo de Oré, Relación histórica de la Florida, *II (1933), 13–16, extract, translated.*

In the city of San Agustín, in the provinces of Florida, on the first day of the month of July in the year fifteen ninety eight, Gonzalo Méndez de Canzo, Governor and Captain General of the Provinces for the King Our Lord, said that whereas in the month of October last, 1597, he had heard how the Indians of the tribal area of Guale had rebelled and renounced obedience to His Majesty, and killed the men of religion of the Order of St Francis who were there for the conversion and instruction of this tribal area and the Indians in it, and although he went in person as quickly as he could with infantry, supplies and boats to the said tribal area of Guale, to investigate and find out and set right the circumstances and chance which the said Indians had had to commit a crime of this kind. and although in the said tribal area and its towns he caused considerable devastation with the infantry he took, in burning their said towns and the food he found, since they were so well forewarned he was unable at that time to carry out any greater punishment nor to take any Indian alive except one, from whom, through the interpreters, no more could be discovered than that the men of religion were dead, as can be seen at greater length from his account, to which he refers. And having seen how very important it was to get to the root of the occurrence and the death of these men of religion, and find out if any of them is alive, and the chance which they had to kill them, as also for having renounced obedience to His Majesty: to which purpose he has used the best means and subterfuges he could, which was by way of La Tama and the neighbouring chiefs, sending them gifts and presents to oblige them to investigate and find out if any man of religion was alive so that they could ransom him, sending them a prize to be offered for that: and he also sent a launch with infantry to the port of Santa Elena, more than fifty leagues from this garrison, to make use of the chief of the Camacu, because of the information which has come to him that he is a chief who has been friendly with the Spaniards, and has Indian soldiers, and being so close he could do a great deal of damage in the area of Guale: and when they had brought to him the ensign Ecija, who went as leader in the said launch, he negotiated with the said chief that he should make war and do as much damage as he could in the said area of Guale, and that he should try to find out if any of the men of religion that had been there was alive, giving him, so that he should undertake all this, many gifts, both on the account of His Majesty and out of his own pocket and resources: and he agreed with this chief that within sixty days he would go and meet him to see the act of war which the said chief would then have done: and in compliance with this, and as it was something of such great importance to His Majesty, on the 23rd of the month of May of this same year, when there were only four days left for the agreement and pact which he had made with this chief, he left this port with two launches, infantry and supplies, to this purpose and to fulfil the agreement which he had made with this chief: and on the twentyfourth, which was one day after he had left this port, when he had reached as far as Havana de Asao, thirty leagues from this port, he ran into a storm and hurricane which forced him to come into land, ruining much of the food and supplies he was carrying, so that he had to run ashore in the launch in which he was going, on the beach at San Mateo: yet despite all this, he continued this voyage to the said port of Santa Elena, transferring to the other launch, which had suffered less and was more fit for sailing, leaving his own aground and damaged on this beach: and when he had arrived at the said port of Santa Elena, and seen and talked to this chief of Camacu, the chief gave him four heads of hair which he said he had taken off four Indians of the said area of Guale, because he had gone to make war on them, and that the chief of Zayaque had taken another three, for he had gone along with him on this raid, and he also assured him that they were holding alive, near Tolofina, in the said area of Guale, one of those six men of religion, called Friar Francisco de Ávila. Once he had been informed of all this, he went along the coast and the ports of this area of Guale, and the quays, to see if any Indian would come out and talk to them: and none came out to them anywhere except one in Tolomato: simply by means of gifts and promises and good argu-

ments he got him to come out and talk: from him too he discovered that the said man of religion was alive: he gave this Indian a reward to take him a letter, and he took it: and when he had a reply he waited at the quayside at Tolomato until various high chiefs and chiefs arrived: he asked them to show him the said man of religion, so that he could be better assured that he was alive, and negotiate with them for his ransom: they did not want to give him up or hand him over then, although he gave them many gifts and many presents, unless he gave to them various boys, sons and heirs of chiefs, that the Governor Domingo Martínez de Avendaño had taken as hostages, for the greater security of the said area: he offered these to the said chiefs and high chiefs, saying that he would bring them to them within thirty days as a ransom for the said man of religion, and also a quantity of axes and hoes and blankets which they asked for in the same ransom: he went back to this port of Tolomato within fifteen days, and negotiated and conferred with the same chiefs and high chiefs for the ransom of this man of religion: he gave presents very generously both to the said high chiefs and chiefs and to the Indians that were gathered there, which were many; but these gifts and presents made no impression on them, being warlike, treacherous and unreliable people, all of whose dealings were based on treachery and trickery: once he had realized this, and that they were not keeping or complying with the word they had given, nor were they prepared to hand over to him the said man of religion, he had to try another way, and acted very angry, saying that if they did not give him this man of religion at once, he would send at once for three hundred soldiers, and put them to the sword, and cut down all their maize and food, and follow them as far as La Tama: and these remarks were enough for them to send him at once this man of religion: when he had taken him and had him in his own control, he kept hold of the Indian hostages he was bringing them, and another seven Indians which he had carefully kept in the launches until he saw what happened: four of them are the most important sons and brothers of chiefs: he brought all of them to this city, where he is now holding them: with these he says he intends to be investigating, and taking their remarks and statements, so they should talk about the deaths they gave and were suffered by the men of religion, and where it was, and how, and why, and if he finds that any of them was participator in these crimes, the deaths, he intends to punish and carry out justice on them, since that is what is best for the service of His Majesty: so that this should be a punishment for them and an example to others, since on other occasions they have committed other treacherous acts and have killed captains and officers, men of religion and other people. And he saw to this and ordered it and signed it with his name. Gonzalo Méndez de Canzo.

At the order of the Lord Governor and Captain General,

[Signed:] Juan Ximénez, scribe.

754. August 3, 1598. Bartolomé de Argüelles reports to the king and to the Council of the Indies on the situation in Florida.

This astringent report by one of the royal officials acts as a counterweight to many of Méndez de Canzo's attempts at self-promotion, and throws much light on the actual situation in Florida in 1598. The fact that it was not considered in the Council of the Indies until July 13, 1601, may in part be due to delays in reaching Spain, or to Spanish bureaucratic lethargy, or even to its own length (some considerable cuts have been made in the translation). It should be remembered that it was addressed to Philip II, whose death in November, 1598, may have interrupted the work of the council for some time.

A.G.I., Seville, Santo Domingo 229, 54/5/14; typescript in Division of Manuscripts, Library of Congress, newly translated.

To the King Our Lord, in his Royal Council of the Indies

Sir,

With a small frigate that left here for Spain on the 2nd of March this year I sent a letter reporting to Your Majesty on the most important things that were happening here, and if it arrived safely, this way, and from the people who went, Your Majesty will have been informed later, that here things have been going so badly that we have no hope of help unless it comes from Your Majesty. For this Governor is acting contrary to the manner and style which has always been followed by the Governors in the past, who, as men of experience, were accommodating both to the needs of the Indians and of the others who are here serving Your Majesty according to their talent and ability, and in matters concerning the distribution of Your Royal Exchequer followed the order that accompanied it; and as matters are now they are based on greed, with greater hardship than the land and the people who work it are able to bear, and the allotted money which Your Majesty has for the maintenance of this garrison is in large part being spent on things other than those for which it was meant, and we, the Royal Officers, who have this in our charge, are powerless to prevent this; so we are compelled to ask humbly for Your Majesty to order this to be put right.

In the letter which, as I said, I wrote to You before, I reported how the land and the Indians were quiet and calm, with great signs that all was going well as regards their conversion, and that they attended diligently to what the Governor ordered, and were paying as tribute one *arroba* of maize which they offered to Governor Avendaño; then this Governor Gonzalo Méndez de Canço arrived, who had never been in this land and did not know how it worked; he could have asked for advice from those who had been here many years in order to govern effectively; not only did he fail to do that, but when some servants of Your Majesty and people concerned about the Royal Service came to talk to him, he rebuffed us so roughly that he told us not to come back; and so at once things started to go wrong: such as the death of Juan Ramírez de Contreras, who was sent by this Governor with an Indian chief and two other Christians near to Cape Canaveral with goods to barter for amber, which is usually there, and then when they came to the Chief of Ais, they killed them; and then in September there occurred the rising of the Indians of Guale, and the martyrdom of the five Franciscan friars who were preaching there and teaching them: there were six working in that province, and we were informed that they had all died, but afterwards it was found out that one had survived who had been left for dead, and after he had suffered greatly as a captive for nine months, the Governor ransomed him; when he went for this purpose, he took the most important chiefs with him in his boats, and since they still had not brought the friar they turned back again, taking with them about six young men, among

THE UPRISING OF THE GUALE INDIANS, 1597–1598

them being one who was found to have helped in the killing of one of the friars: the Governor brought them to this garrison, interrogated them about who had been responsible, and they confessed that the chief of Tolomato had been the instigator and all the others had helped him, and every one who had a friar in his town killed him; this Indian who was captured (the son of a chief called Don Felipe) out of those responsible was ordered to be hung by the Governor: and although the punishment seems to have been well justified, it has been most inconvenient and counterproductive to the intention claimed, for they used to come in with their boats when there was an expedition there, and a fort could have been built which would have been ideal, but now they have been so alienated that it is hard to get hold of any at all of them.

When the frigate left here which I have already mentioned, this Governor had sent a lieutenant with twenty soldiers in a boat to Santa Elena with secret orders, and afterwards, because of the expense incurred on our allotted money this order has been looked at; he ordered them to go to the island of Santa Elena and try to talk to the chief of Escamacu, and give him a number of tools, axes, hoes and other things, and to tell him to try and make war with his Indians on those of Guale and kill and capture as many as he could; and when this lieutenant came close to where this chief is, he found him hunting in a nearby forest; for they are very poor people, and have no other sustenance than a little maize, which lasts them no more than a week when they harvest it, and then the rest of the year they live by hunting, deer, bears, wolves, and shellfish: he came to the boat, and they brought him to this port, which is fifty leagues distance, and the Governor told him personally what I have said, and he said he would do this and start within a couple of months, and with this agreement they took him back to his land in the same boat.

This kind of diplomatic strategy may have the results the Governor wants, but it seems to me and to those of us who know these Indians that this was an outrageous idea, to treat seriously and ask favours from some Indians who a few years ago, Your Majesty's garrison then being on Santa Elena, treacherously killed in their town a lieutenant who had gone peacefully with twenty-five soldiers to visit them and look for some food among them: the Indians got them to douse the wicks of their arquebuses, pretending to be offended that they trusted them so little that they felt it necessary to keep them lit, and then when they had done so these Indians attacked the Spaniards with their arrows and clubs, and only one of the Spaniards escaped, who came back and said what had happened, and they killed others afterwards on different occasions in ambushes and tricks and proclaimed war against them: and now, being as big-headed as they are, that they have gathered that we have had to ask for their help in avenging the wrongs done to us by the Indians of Guale in rebelling and killing the friars, this seems to be quite unworthy of our nation, particularly since all these Indians are native inhabitants, and it must not be generally thought that they should make serious attacks on each other in case by complying they should show some sign of it for the gain they have got out of this and the gain they hope to get later.

From the experience I have had of these people and of the way they live, the way in which we could harm and damage them was for a couple of boats and forty experienced men to go along all the many rivers and channels which there are there and take all the canoes in which they sail from one island to another to hunt and sow, and break them into pieces, and at the time when they have their corn and the other grain called *frijol* and the pumpkins, which is their normal food, without which they will die, when it is flowering, to make a voyage there in eight or ten days and cut it all down; and also to leave them quiet at one of their bases somewhere, and, finding out where it is (as can be done if one tries to find it out) to turn up secretly one day at dawn at that settlement where they are, as we did in 1584 at another town in this region called Potano, which had done a lot of damage to this garrison, and all the responsible Indians were collected there separate from the friendly chiefs, and we went like this, and none of those in the town escaped from paying: I was there then, with Gutierre de Miranda, who at the time was commander of Santa Elena, and General Pero Menéndez Marqués, who ordered this to be done: the same thing should have been done in this matter that has turned up now if we are to get satisfactory recompense from them for the great crime they have committed.

The friars of the Order of St. Francis who were left alive, of those who are working at the conversion and teaching of the natives at Your Majesty's

Orders, are continuing to comply with their duty with great determination among the Indians who have not rebelled, but they are very demoralised to see how little progress they are making; they say this is because the Indians realize how this Governor despises them and lowers their standing in the Indians' eyes, and does ot want them among these Indians and gives them no assurances about them; formerly in the beginning and up to a short time ago they could see how we used to kneel before the friars and kiss their hands to give the Indians a good example, but now they see something different occurring, and the harm this has done has been perfectly obvious, and if Your Majesty does not order this to be set right it will be pointless for the friars to waste their time there. Father Friar Baltasar López, who is acting as priest on the island of San Pedro and has been there with chief Don Juan for ten years now, has written me a letter, and from this Your Majesty will see what is happening there; I thought I would send You the original so that it can be seen clearly, and because the preaching Friar Father Pedro Fernández de Chozas went off in the messenger-frigate on behalf of his superior and the other friars to report on what needs to be done here, he will now have done so and I shall not now expand on this. . . .

The tribute which I said the subject Indians offered to Governor Avendaño was collected until the arrival of this Governor; in the disturbance there was with those of Guale it stopped being collected from them, and on the others of this region and the islands of San Pedro and Pinales this governor increased the tribute, and although it was not very much it seems to have been some kind of gambit for winning the respect of those further inland who judge others according to the level of the tribute levied on each one. Your Majesty will instruct to discover whatever is best so that it can be done.

There are forty of Your Majesty's negro slaves here in this garrison to maintain it; the last twenty of them came here last year, 1597, at the order of Your Majesty, so that with those who were already here they could work on building the fort of stone which Your Majesty ordered to be newly built; since this Governor has come he has kept both groups working on something different from the building of the fort, sawing wood for boats and private individuals, incurring great expense on our allotted money, and although they could have brought a lot of stone for this fort, which has to be brought from three and from five leagues away, this has not been done, nor any other kind of fortification; instead he has taken down part of the trenches which had been made for the protection and defence of the settlement, from behind which it was possible to stop an enemy landing, and a stone bulwark which we had made on top of the wall of the fort, and which in the opinion of all the old soldiers was the best thing that had been made for the defence of the people in the fort, from behind which it was possible to attack an enemy; he had this dismantled entirely, but nobody could find out what possible purpose that was to serve; he has said that he is sure that enemies will not come along there for a long time.

These slaves used to have their lodgings on one side of the settlement, where Governor Avendaño, with the agreement of the Royal Officers, had had some huts made for them of wood and straw behind the trenches; and now this Governor has taken them to live away from the settlement and the trenches to a plain where he ordered them to build their own huts, and there they are right out of the way, and at great risk if an enemy should come or the Indians should betray us: it will be best for Your Majesty to instruct that these negroes should move and come back to the settlement and the fort behind the trenches and that their lodgings should be made there, so that if there is any trouble of any kind they will be there safe and at hand near the fort to go there, as is normally done where there are slaves of Your Majesty, and although there are at the moment four huts of soldiers on the site they could be given some help from the expenses of our allotted money to move them somewhere else, which they could easily do since they are made of wood and palm-leaves, and to help pay the expenses the site and plain where these negroes are now could be sold. This is a matter of importance which it is best for Your Majesty to instruct should be dealt with. . . .

In the other letter I sent I reported how in the company of this Governor there came seven foreigners; one of them English, who himself admits it, and has declared in the agreement in the pay book, that he is from London: the others they say come from Higher Germany, uncommunicative men who cannot speak Spanish: this Governor passed off all these as such in San Lúcar de Barrameda when he set out, and declared under oath when the boat was officially inspected that they were not among those who are prohibited from going to the Indies, as can be seen in the Register of the Treasury in my own office; but this is not so, and besides there are Royal orders that prevent him having any private authority from Your Majesty permitting foreigners being sent to Spain. This governor gave all of these men posts, six of them as artillery men and one as fife-player and bugler: this could turn out to be very harmful on occasions such as the one that arose in an earlier year [1586]. I was present and know by experience when the pirate Francis Drake came into this harbour, and one lone foreigner, who served as fife-player and bugler, signalled with the bugle to the enemy, telling him how few men there were there, and went over to him at night and went off with that expedition. It will be very much to the better service of Your Majesty if these foreigners leave here and do not hold these posts as artillery men, and they should be taken by experienced Spaniards, because artillery is the main strength of the garrisons.

I also informed You how in the company of this Governor there came a nephew of his called Juan García de Navia, in whose name there came over a quantity of goods, both registered and not, and although there was an edict from Your Majesty that an agreement should be made and published in Sevilla that any merchant who should wish to take necessary goods at suitable prices should come to an agreement concerning it on the account of the money allotted to this garrison, as is normal, this was not done; and afterwards, once he had got here, he fixed whatever prices he wished, and in addition the quantity of wine and oil was not of a kind that the soldiers could afford, and it was taken on the account of the allotted money at very inflated prices, and much of the smaller merchandise he has sold and is still selling to these people with the sole authority of this Governor, without fixing the selling price jointly with the Royal Officers, as is normal. This has caused and is still causing great problems for the poor men who serve here: they are made to pay up most rigorously, and they are in pawn for most of the salary owing to them, and the married inhabitants who had given them their holdings and have nothing else to live on, were unable to get any money on pay day because there was Juan García himself next to this Governor at the very table where the pay was being given out, and he collected it all. So the poor inhabitants have all been ruined: in addition, all the means whereby they could work out some kind of a deal here to keep them alive have been pre-empted by this Juan García, for to this purpose there is a small frigate that belongs to this Governor that keeps going back and forth to Cuba and to New Spain with goods: in this way has been broken the normal commercial practice previously followed by other ships that brought needed goods from elsewhere at reasonable prices and payed the Royal Excise Dues; and since this Governor has come, no one has come here from there, and nor will they as long as this goes on, because it is already known out there what is going on here; we have received no letters from anyone, nor can we take the chance to write, because when this frigate sets out is when we are most helpless, and we are told it is going somewhere different from where it is actually going. Things have got so bad that a pound of salt that normally costs here six or seven maravedís can now be sold at a price of one *real*, or two *reales*, and other things likewise: the land and the people who serve Your Majesty on it are kept in great need and subjection; normally when the settlers are suffering needs they cannot remedy they send a request to the Governor for some extra provisions in addition to their rations to feed their wives and children: this used to be done before, and they were sold things at cost price from the allotted money; but the present Governor is not only failing to use this agreement to help them, but when someone approaches him in this kind of need he says there is no chance of giving him provisions, and if he wants something he should approach this Juan García, thereby forcing them to take it at excessive prices, and then they have to sell it again cheaply to stay alive.

The serving military officers, who were experienced men, have been replaced, by this Governor, with raw recruits, which has greatly upset the former; what has upset them most is to find that they are under the command now of this merchant Juan García, whom this Governor has appointed as infantry captain of one of the two companies in this garrison, when the previous captain Vicente González was so experienced, as everyone knows, particularly here, and when this Juan García has never been a soldier nor had any personal experience of it; and now that this Governor has left here at the end of May taking thirty-three men with him in two boats, he left as acting Governor and Captain General this Juan García during the time of his absence and should he die. A copy of that instruction accompanies this letter. A nephew of his, an unprepossessing lad who used to help him treat hides, was made a Lieutenant by this Governor; that has caused a wide scandal: another Captain there was there called Pedro de Portierra, who has served Your Majesty very well as Military Officer, was told to leave, and this Governor brought one of his sons, aged ten, which he had left in Havana: as soon as he arrived he took off him the habit of Saint James that he was wearing and made him put on a sword and dagger on St. James's Day this year: he made an Irish cleric, that he has here as priest, put the sword and the dagger on the altar at the time of the mass and hand them over to the young boy, with extraordinary ceremonies, and this is widely taken to imply that he wants to give him the Company, for he at once appointed him as soldier: and it is not a good idea that in a garrison like this on which Your Majesty spends 480 ducats a year in defence positions as important as this should be filled by people like this, for it makes them useless and dead appointments.

Since all the people who live in this garrison are soldiers, and they have no more possessions than some poor wooden huts in which they live and their salary, it has always been the custom that the debts they incur in mid-year on food and clothes were repaid when they were paid, and if they could not do it one time they waited for the next: and now, as well as receiving nothing from their pay that does not go straight into the hands of this Juan García, he is collecting all the debts left over on behalf of the Law and it can be stated certainly that everything belongs to this Governor before whom the collection is claimed, and the poor houses of these men are being sold and he takes the tithes and costs: this has not been the custom before in this land, and the land cannot bear it until it has more growth and farms, and it will be best for Your Majesty to order this to be set right, and everything else, as seems best. . . .

3rd August 1598

[Signed:] Bartolomé de Argüelles

[The Letter is minuted: "Florida, to his Majesty 1598. Bartolomé de Argüelles, 3rd August. Seen on 13th July 1601."]

Chapter Ninety-six
Plans for Expansion and Proposals for
Abandonment of Florida, 1598–1607

PLANS FOR EXPANSION BY GONZÁLO MÉNDEZ DE CANZO

FROM THE TIME he believed that he had finally put down the Indian insurgency in Guale, Méndez de Canzo concerned himself primarily with promoting plans to bring questions about Florida into a broader setting. The questions included a re-expansion into the interior and a new attempt to establish a colony on Chesapeake Bay. For the former he had Gaspar de Salas's evidence (755) on how he had conducted two friars into the interior of what is now Georgia and there found very fertile land in the Indian territory of Tama, where settlement prospects appeared to be very good and where there were diamonds and other stones (clear quartz was indeed brought from there). This was one direction of possible expansion. Chesapeake Bay was another. David Glavin, an Irish member of the garrison, testified to his experiences as a colonist in Roanoke in 1585–1586 and expressed the view that the English were still there (755). Méndez de Canzo wanted to root them out and plant Spaniards. In 1598 he sent over reports on these matters to Philip II, one of whose last acts (on November 9, 1598) was to invite further details from the governor. He, in turn, proved ready to do so. On February 28, 1600, in glowing terms he wrote to the new King Philip III of his plans to invade both Tama and the Chesapeake and establish a Spanish presence in both areas. He received no encouragement whatever from the new administration which was, in fact, beginning to think of Florida as an unnecessary appendage to an overextended Spanish empire. Moreover, reports sent from Florida, that of December 12, 1599, by Fray Báltasar López (757), and that of the common soldier on February 19, 1600 (758), were by no means favorable to his administration.

755. [1598]. Gaspar de Salas reports on the discovery of the rich territory of Tama, and David Glavin reports on his recollections of Jacan.

A.G.I., *Santo Domingo 224; 54/5/9; printed in Manuel Serrano y Sanz*, Documentos históricos de la Florida y la Luisiana siglos XVI al XVII *(Madrid, 1913), pp. 141–159, extracts; the Salas (a), newly translated, the Glavin (b), reprinted from D. B. Quinn*, Roanoke Voyages, II, *834–838.*

[a]   Witness Gaspar de Salas, soldier.

And then straightway the said Governor and Captain General made appear before him Gaspar de Salas, soldier of this garrison, from whom was taken and received the oath in legal form, under which he promised to speak truly on anything he should be asked about; and he was asked to speak and declare to the effect of the said chapter of the letter: and as to what he knows of the disposition of the land and the plants of the said Tama and the town of Ocute, since he has been and stayed there, this witness said that for more than twenty years he has been serving His Majesty in this garrison and in that of Santa Elena, and that since he knows the language of the province of Guale and of San Pedro, the said Señor General ordered him last year (1597) to go with two friars of the order of St. Francis, Brother Pedro Fernández de Chosas and Brother Francisco de Veras; so they went together at the order of their prelate and the said Governor to discover inland; and he arrived in the company of the said priests at the town they call La Tama, which he thinks must be about fifty leagues from this garrison; and although they left Guale for this Tama and spent eight days on the journey, seven of them through uninhabited country, they did not find in all this way any good land until they arrived at Tama, where there was a large quantity of food, corn, kidney beans, and much game, deer, wild turkeys with fleshy necks (*gallinas de papada*), and many other wild game birds, and a large quantity of fish and sturgeon, called royal in Spain, and similarly fruit, such as very fat grapes in large bunches which taste as good as those of Spain, and white plums rather like the large green Spanish ones, and cherries and watermelons and other fruit. For all round the said town of La Tama and its borders there is very good grey-brown land, which sticks to the feet like clay when it rains: in some areas there are a number of treeless hills where he has seen kinds of metallic stone: in some places, he and the priests, of those stones which seemed metallic they took from what was above ground, since they had nothing to dig with: this witness took some of those stones, and bringing back fragments of them he gave some of them to the said Governor, and others to a jeweller who was in this city at that time (who died recently): the said jeweller had never in his life encountered them before, and said to him that there was silver where those stones had been brought from, because he had got silver out of them, and that he had got the said silver from the said fragments because they came from the slag and surface waste of the said mine; and that if they looked for the vein there, they would be very rich mines: and this the said Señor Governor will be able to know better because he also has the information and had dealings with the said jeweller. Also, next to the said mines there grows a herb which the Indians value highly for medicines they use to heal themselves, and for wounds, which they call "guitamo real": also this witness and the said priests collected some stones which grow like crystal in the said hills and next to large rivers, and others like fine glass. From there, La Tama, they came after a day's journey to Ocute, where they were very well received by the chief, who gave them many presents, and the women brought there their textiles, which he calls overalls, like painted tablecloths, which some of those who have been in New Spain say are rather like the clothes worn there. They wanted to go on further, but the chief of the said town of Ocute tried to stop them, becoming very insistent and weeping to them, saying that if they went ahead the Indians were bound to kill them: for a long time earlier (it must be when Soto went there) they had killed some men, despite his taking many people, and on horseback too, and that they would find it easier to kill them since there were few of them: and this is why they did not go ahead, but returned from there. Also they heard the Indians of that town, and the Salchiches, say that beyond a very high range which there was four days' march away, a kind of fire used to shine when the sun was out, and that on the other side of it there were some people who wore their hair short, and that they had found the pine trees cut down with axes, and he thinks that these can only be signs of Spanish men: and he thinks the said land to be very apt for producing any kind of grain, even wheat, with many fertile river plains and flocks, and rivers with drinkable water in places: he thinks that anyone who knows how to wash for gold should go to those rivers: and they came back by a different route from the one they went out, much better, through more populated country, for there were only two days through unpopulated areas and on the other route there were seven, and the horse which the two priests took found the going easier as far as Yufera and Cascangu, towns of friendly Indians, where they were made welcome, until they came back to San Pedro from the chief Don Juan: and he said this that he knows from having seen it and heard it, as it is said: and he said he was approximately thirty-eight years of age, and did not sign for he does not know how, and the said Governor signed it.

[Signed:] Gonçalo Méndez de Canço
Before me, Joan Ximénez, Clerk.

[b] Deposition of David Glavin, Irish soldier.

'On the aforementioned day, month and year, the governor and captain-general, Gonçalo Méndez de Canço ordered David Glavin, an Irishman and a soldier of this garrison, to appear before him, who took the oath in due form, making the sign of the cross with his right hand. Having heard the governor's instructions and the paragraph from his majesty's letter, he said that he had never been in Tama, or knew the land. What he knows of these provinces is through living in them, and in this garrison of San Agustín, for more than five years. In 1584 the English stole a ship, laden with wine and merchandise, from him coming from Nantes in the province of Brittany as she was rounding the cape of Surlinga, and brought him with them to the Indies. Richarte de Canpoverde [Grenville] was general in command of nine sail, large and small, and brought him with them to Jacan, which is on the coast in a latitude of 36 degrees. There Canpoverde put into port and set on shore up to 150 settlers, amongst whom your witness remained as they did not give him a passage back. There, as soon as they had disembarked, they began to make brick and tiles for a fort and houses. He remained with them a year and a half until Francis Drake, who sacked some harbors in the Indies, amongst them this one, San Agustín, arrived with his fleet. Drake then carried away the English from Jacan in his ships—this witness amongst them—and took them to England. In London the witness understood that he fell out of favor with the queen for having brought the settlers from Jacan. And later he saw two ships being fitted out with 200 men, many settlers and their wives to return again to settle Jacan. They again seized this witness and brought him with them towards Jacan. Thus he came with them to the island of Puerto Rico, where, in a harbor on the southern side, they took in water and provisions. The witness was told to make his escape which he did. He warned Puerto Rico that they were making ready five ships in England to come to capture and sack Puerto Rico, and that they might be there by Whit Sunday. He warned the said Diego Menéndez, who then was governor of Puerto Rico. Because he had had warning the galleons did no harm, although they came at the time anticipated. They came also with the intention, after making their attack, of carrying more settlers to Jacan, and following the ships with which this witness came. Thus he considers it certain that the English are in Jacan. For additional proof he said that last year, 1599, being in Havana, Don Beltran de la Cueva was bringing certain Englishmen from Lima belonging to an English ship which he had taken from the son of Juan Acaes [Hawkins]. Among them was a young man who declared that, at the same time as they left Plemua for the Straits of Magellan, two ships had sailed in their company carrying supplies of people, ammunition, clothes, implements, axes and spades for the settlers of Jacan, which confirmed his opinion that they are still there.

When he was asked his views on Jacan at the time he was there, whether there was gold and silver to be found, and what it produced, he said that when he was there they sowed wheat and barley which grew in great abundance. The land produced many and good things. Thus there were grapes, plums, apples, cherries and chestnuts in great quantity, and also nuts, corn, beans and gourds, as well as very many kinds of fish so that each month had its special kind. There was also much gold and pearls for he saw Richarte de Canpoverde bargain for more than an *arroba* of gold. His opinion was that the gold was not very fine, as he heard it said that it must be between sixteen and eighteen carats. This was because it was crude since the Indians did not know the way to refine it. He noticed that all the chiefs wore rings of gold. They had also amongst them a great quantity of pearls, some of them very large, many of which Richarte de Canpoverde carried away. This witness bartered for one the shape of an acorn and even larger, very transparent and beautiful, but when Richarte de Canpoverde heard of it he took it away from him. Moreover, the English had word that some forty leagues from there, upstream, at the head of a mountain from which the river sprang, there were gold mines, but because they fell short of food they did not reach the mines, having to return when they had gone half-way. As he has already said, the English are in Jacan. It does not seem likely that they would abandon so fertile a land where there was so much gold and so many pearls.

This witness has given this account to the said general in order that it may be sent to his majesty. This is what he knows and has seen, according to the oath he has taken, and, having heard it read over, he signed it with his name. He said he was about forty years of age.

David Glavid signed this in my presence
Juan Ximenes, scribe

756. February 28, 1600. Gonzálo Méndez de Canzo to Philip III, recommending the expansion of Florida.

A.G.I., Seville, Santo Domingo 224; 54/5/9; translated in D. B. Quinn, Roanoke Voyages, *II, 826–833.*

Sire,

Your majesty's letter of 9 November 1598 I received on 18 January 1600 in reply to two of mine setting out the situation of these provinces in relation to your royal service. [Your majesty's letter I had] through ensign Hernando de Mestas, but it has been delayed in reaching me as you will perceive from this acknowledgement, inasmuch as the said ensign had informed me that a French ship captured him off Puerto Rico. While he managed to send the packet ashore they held him for more than five months as he had been wounded by two arquebus shots. Although they managed to send the packet on from Puerto Rico to Havana a certain person called Licona kept it hidden from the governor Don Juan Maldonado, and if the said ensign had not come there himself it seems that it would not have reached me at all, seeing that the French had him for five months and that it took him five days to trace the packet once he reached Havana. . . .

Furthermore, your majesty requests from me a very detailed account, derived from the nearest Indians and their chieftains, of Tama and its territory so that inland discoveries can be continued. Having conferred with the most experienced persons in this fortress and the chieftains I am to send a full report of all I learn together with, if possible, the plan and description of the country it is considered desirable to enter.

In complying with your majesty's orders I would recall that in a paragraph of the letter which I sent to your majesty on 23 February 1598, by Ensign Hernando de Mestas, I advised your majesty that it was of the utmost importance for the advancement of the gospel and for the increase of your majesty's possessions that a town should be established inland at a place called Tama. From there exploration could be carried on until New Mexico should be reached, or at least until the Spaniards, making expeditions from there, should be encountered. This is set out at greater length in the paragraph to which I refer. I gave this advice at the time without knowledge or experience of other harbors and territories, however, as I shall inform your majesty in this letter. Nor can I send to your majesty the plan or description of the aforementioned Tama on account of there being no friendly chieftain who has been there, nor any sensible Spaniard except a soldier of this garrison named Gaspar de Salas. When I arrived here on your majesty's service I sent the said soldier in the company of two monks who reached Tama, and what I learned from him, I advised you in the previous letter. Although I now have endeavoured to make the said Gaspar de Salas give me the description and plan of Tama, he could do no more than make a deposition, which I had him make formally in my presence and which your majesty will find enclosed in this letter. Likewise, in the said testimony there are depositions of certain persons long resident in these provinces who have made excursions inland in the company of Captain Juan Pardo and Ensign Moyano, with whom there came back two native Indian girls from the farthest point inland at which the captain and ensign arrived. One of these girls is married to Juan de Ribas, a soldier of this garrison, one of those making a deposition, and the other Teresa Martin, widow of another soldier of San Agustín, likewise, a declaration of Ensign Francisco Fernandez de Ec[ija], one of the oldest soldiers in the garrison at present, and also the declaration of David Glavid an Irishman who was in Jacan in the town which Richarte de Campoverde, the Englishman, first founded; all of which may your majesty be pleased to see and consider because they seem to me to be of great importance.

In view of the said deposition, and the information which I tried to compile most carefully, I am obliged to change my opinion concerning the advice contained in the aforementioned letter. I now say that the discovery and settlement which ought to be made is in virtue of a plan which accompanies this letter and which your majesty ought to look at. This plan was made by the Irishman, David Glavid and contains in it the first discovery which the English made, as well as the other discoveries of rivers and inland territory. This can be seen from the lettering in each part of the sketch, and although it is not perfect, the defects are due to the fact that there is not anyone in this garrison who knows how to draw. David made it as he saw and remembered it. In it the places can clearly be seen where the English established their fort and settlement, and also where he believes they are at present, that is, northwards from this garrison at a latitude of 37 degrees, while they entered for the first time at 35½ degrees according to the plan. Your majesty may be able to gain information about this settlement from England. In case that is not possible, it would be well to order a thorough investigation to be made here. I myself shall do all in my power to inquire about this settlement if I am not prevented by the duties of your service or illness and, indeed, to this end, I have already begun to make investigations through the chief of the Escamacu of Santa Elena, whom I summoned to come here and who has arrived today. Of what he knows, I shall fully inform your majesty immediately. In case the English have such a settlement, my opinion is that your majesty should order them to be driven out and made to leave the land which they have usurped and settled, in spite of the fact that it is yours, and great inconvenience, expense and bloodshed may result therefrom if a remedy is not sought in time. Another consideration is this: the year that Francis Drake destroyed this fortress, he dismantled the settlement and carried off the settlers to England, for which he fell out of favor with the queen. She immediately went to great trouble to send out new settlers and much valuable aid, as is clear from David's deposition. David asserts that the land is very extensive, that there is much gold and many pearls in addition to fertile land and its fruits. There are also good harbors for ships and farther up still better ones, while the fort is at the latitude which those coming down from New Mexico to this coast must pass. If the settlement is really there, it seems fitting to me that your majesty should deal with the problem by supplying us with 1000 men, not counting the sailors who man the ships carrying supplies and arms necessary for such an undertaking. Among these arms there should be 300 *escupiles* because it is clear that where one has

many native Indians as allies the *escupil* is necessary for them also. They should enter with ammunition and rations for a year from the day they land in order that they should not go short of these things. That this be done with due circumspection, and that it be not known in England, the infantry should come as the usual quota sent each year to the Indies for your treasure. In regard to the bread, flour, beans and other vegetables, they can be provided by New Spain, since the ships will be very full and such supplies would spoil coming from Spain. From there we should get only wines, oil, vinegar, and powder, lead, ammunition, arquebuses, some muskets and the *escupiles*. Since I suspect that at present, your majesty is short of heavy artillery, the two or three pieces which will have to be carried this fortress could supply. The men must be the best and most capable technicians that can be found. In addition to the larger seagoing vessels, which should be up to 100, or at most 150 tons burden, capable of entering shallow water, there should be a dozen shallow-draft pinnaces made specially to land troops and to enter the channels and rivers. These can very well be made here. We should have, moreover, two priests, a dozen sawyers with saws to make any necessary repairs to the ships or other equipment; likewise carpenters and a complete assortment of nails, a blacksmith and armorer. In case these English are not settled where it is supposed that they are and this project is abandoned, your majesty will order what seems fitting to you to be done.

I repeat that the true correct exploration and penetration inland in order to learn its secrets fully, and to discover those of New Mexico, must be by the same way that Captain Juan Pardo and Ensign Moyano entered. We should make special investigations in regard to the mine and to the stones which they say are diamonds, since the said Ensign Moyano resolved to return from Spain solely because of the said stones and pearls. This affair seems to me to be worthy of consideration and today the business would have been much further advanced if the Ensign and your governor, Pedro Menéndez, had not died. Furthermore we should make inquiries concerning the many mines of silver and gold which they say there are, pushing forward and exploring everything until we come upon the people from New Mexico. For this discovery I believe that 300 infantrymen will be necessary, all of them arquebusiers and well protected with the *escupil* as for war with the Indians no other armour except this is of any value. As for the coat of mail, the arrow could go through it and the splinters of it would be very dangerous; the buffalo-leather coat is pierced very easily; and the corselet is very heavy armour and, moreover, if the arrow hits it it will rebound and injure the next person; so that it is clear that the *escupil* is the best armor because the arrow is stopped by it and sticks. These should be made particularly carefully and of cotton—they are not made of wool. I understand that the best *escupiles* are made in Spain by the friars of Our Lady of *los Remedios* of Triana. Furthermore, it will be necessary to bring an alchemist, a silversmith and a lapidary.

In regard to supplies for these 300 soldiers, I am informed that once they are in the interior, there is food in great abundance, so that, providing the ammunition does not fail, there will be enough to eat, as can be seen from the information accompanying this letter. Likewise, there will be necessary for the expedition 400 axes and 400 spades, 100 sets of Flemish butchers' knives, 1500 *reales* worth of heavy blue glass beads, 200 ordinary mirrors, 100 pairs of scissors—all to be given to the chieftains and Indians in the country through which we shall pass. And they will also be useful as barter for food, which trade they make gladly. We shall also need 18 bolts of canvas to make light suits for the soldiers to be worn under the *escupiles*, for tents, for the repair of the supplies; 1500 pairs of leather shoes—sizes 11, 12 and 13, 1000 shirts of medium fine linen, 300 coloured felt hats. In addition to the swords which each soldier shall carry, we shall need 150 dress and short swords, because on such occasions many are usually broken; 300 saddlebags to serve as knapsacks; a good surgeon, a couple of barbers, about 10 horses, which can be brought from Havana, to carry supplies and for the use of the officers and of the sick, of which there are usually some, so that they may have a little alleviation of their condition.

If this expedition can be made with the desired success and if New Mexico can be reached, your majesty will be pleased to give the necessary orders; and since the commander from there must agree with the one from here in choosing a harbor, fort site, etc., it would be well, your majesty being willing, to leave this matter to the discretion of the leader of the expedition from these provinces. And, as I have high hopes for the success of this business, I would, though a mere soldier, be pleased, if I were a wealthy man, to spend that wealth in your majesty's service in bringing to light and exploring that territory, increasing your majesty's realms and becoming an instrument for the saving of so many souls for heaven, as I trust will take place if your majesty should be pleased to put this plan into effect. The zeal I have for your service obliges me to make my report in great detail and to hope that the enterprise will be successful.

As for my private affairs, I cannot refrain from recalling to your majesty that for more than thirty years I have been continuously in your service, twenty of them in positions of trust as a captain of infantry, commander of your fleet of frigates at Puerto Rico, and, more recently, here, where I am now serving with the care and conscientiousness which are well-known to your majesty and with such cost to myself that, despite the favor your majesty has shown me regarding my salary, I am still unable to meet expenses and support myself. In other letters I have requested your majesty to be pleased to order me to be paid a reasonable allowance, and your majesty's letter of 9 November 1598, now to hand, asks me to remind you, as I am now doing, to order the payment to me of my full arrears of salary from the pay-chest here, according to the favor of your majesty's warrant, for the two years ending on 23 September 1598.

May our Lord keep your majesty, of whom all Christendom hath need. San Agustín, Florida, 28 February 1600.

[Signed:] Gonzálo Méndez de Canço

757. December 12, 1599. Fray Báltasar López to Philip III.

Printed in Luis Gerónimo de Oré, Relación histórica de la Florida, *edited by Atanasio López, II (1933), 10–13, translated.*

Sir:

Although the men of religion of the Order of my father St Francis who at the order of Your

Majesty come to these parts of the Indies to work in the conversion of the natives here in general have the obligation to account to Your Majesty for what is going on here, and in particular I and those of us that chance has sent to live in these provinces of Florida, being kept and maintained by Your Royal Exchequer, ought to write by means of our Commissar General and prelate, so that he should come here to see to the fulfilling and setting right of what crops up, since this land lacks among other things the necessary passage and equipment, I decided to write this letter to Your Majesty with the intention that under my own signature it should go more safely, informing and advising of things of great weight and importance to your royal service concerning the increase of this land.

On other occasions which have occurred for a ship to leave this port, going by way of Havana, for the reasons referred to, I have written to Your Majesty giving advice and account of the state which the conversion of the natives here had reached, and of the little progress it was making, in view of the slight favor and assistance which is shown to the men of religion who come to this land for this purpose, particularly since there came to govern here Gonzalo Méndez de Canzo, and although I could right now concerning this and other aspects of his behaviour write and say new things, I will not, trusting that Your Majesty, as such a Christian King and Lord, will have already seen to setting things right, and referring back to what I have written.

It is about thirteen years now since I came to this land, and I have gone from one part of it to another, although being based with the chief Don Juan on the island of San Pedro, who I have brought up and baptized with all his Indians. And I have seen and pondered and come to the conclusion that the instructions of Your Majesty to keep three hundred Spaniards paid at such cost in such a bad position as this place San Agustín can only have been due to lack of accurate information, because although I do not wish to quarrel with the aims and purposes which have led Your Majesty to keep a garrison and settlement in this land, it is quite obvious that the same intention and purpose could have been fulfilled by settling one of the ports further up, for there are lots of them better than this one, with land which can be cultivated and provide food for the poor inhabitants, who are

here suffering hardship with their wives and children with just one soldier's pay and rations, because they are hemmed in within the perimeter, surrounded by salt water marshes, and the land inland is of the same kind, useless, which leads out to the other sea at Tocobaga, and there is a distance of forty leagues, most of which I have gone, with considerable difficulty: and the port is one of the worst on this coast; it is only small frigates that can come into it, and just so that nobody could possibly fail to admit the damage there could be in hanging onto a place like this it happened on the 22nd September last, this year, that with the strong wind there was the sea came into the whole town and demolished many of its houses, and that of the guard corps, and part of the fort, leaving behind great damage, ruining the fruit trees that there were, knocking down some defences which the land itself had from before, and since the sea flattened everything it is now likely to flood the whole town with just a slight wind and running water; and despite all this I see that since the previous governors, not being sufficiently well informed of the nature of the land, or for other purposes, could not be bothered to try and look for another better site and account for it to Your Majesty, the present governor is not doing that even now, nor is trying to do what it is so vital that he should; instead he is selling sites again from his exchequer to rebuild houses, without realizing that this is costing Your Majesty more, for having to move the settlement it is necessary to pay the inhabitants for the value of their houses, as Your Majesty ordered it to be paid to the people of Santa Elena when you ordered that garrison to be pulled down, but as in all the time since he came here there have been so many problems and he knows that he cannot remain in power, he is trying harder than ever to get money to go home rich, and that makes the need for remedy even greater, and for Your Majesty to be informed of this disappointment. And although the chance arose last year, [15]93, for Bartolomé de Argüelles, Accountant of Your Royal Exchequer, to go to Your Court at the agreement of the governor to explain to Your Majesty what was going on out here, and we men of religion that were here insisted that he should explain the nature of this place, and the deception involved in keeping it occupied with so many people and at such cost, and we discovered that he did so, and Your Majesty ordered information to be given on what was best to be done in this, it was to no avail, because the man from whom they would presumably try to get the information probably would not have said what was required in this matter in order not to be involved in any complaint that might be made against him for not having explained this situation before: and somebody who is here at the moment, Mateo Luis, chief pilot of these provinces, told me that when he was in the Casa de la Contratación in Sevilla, somebody had come to him to find out if it would be a good idea to move this garrison to the province of Guale, and he said that it would be of the greatest importance since there were better ports and land there, and it could achieve the same and better results than this fort, but they never came back again to ask him to make a statement in the enquiry that was being carried out. And in view of these matters and the damage done by lack of correct information, and what I know for certain and have seen with my own eyes, it is essential to point out as I am here pointing out to Your Majesty that to get the information on what is happening in this matter and on what is best for your royal service it would be best for you to order as soon as possible that Bartolomé de Argüelles should come in person to your court and give information about everything, as he is someone who has been serving Your Majesty in this land for more than twenty years: when I came here I heard excellent reports about him which later fitted with his actions, and when he was present in the fort of Santa Elena as ensign and lieutenant to the governor, he kept that garrison in excellent order, and he was the first to send men of religion among the Indians, accompanied by guard soldiers, and he had them held in great respect, so that the Indians themselves and their chiefs were so well affected by the way that he treated them that they feel deep love and goodwill towards him, and apart from this the enthusiasm which he obviously brings to bear to the affairs of your royal service and the good of the people who serve here promises that he will not fail to give a very good account, from which God and Your Majesty will be well served, and that for the execution of this task nobody will do it better: for I have always heard particularly from Father Friar Francisco de Marrón, who was mission head here, who was for more than forty years in these Indies, as monastery superior in Perú and the provinces of Guatemala and New Spain, that he had always seen the great damage done by the people sent out to govern here not having experience of the land. This is something that with our own eyes we have seen and realized here in Florida, and time has made it completely obvious, and it will always be damaging: for although I and the other men of religion keep on writing to this Accountant from our missions, saying that on every occasion that arises he should explain to Your Majesty everything that needs to be done, and we insist on this to him, and he tells us that he does so, and that reassures us, it is very different to hear him live and in person, and as long as this is not done we do not believe that the good result we wish for will be achieved. For although Your Majesty has here other royal officials, the treasurer and the crown agent, we do not deal with this sort of matter through them, for we see they have different behaviour and inclinations, very close to this governor concerning other matters to their advantage: and the matters I deal with here and am talking about are of such great importance, and delay could cause such great damage and problems, that I humbly beg Your Majesty to pardon the insistence with which I speak, and be pleased to order it to be considered and undertaken with the necessary speed. And we the poor religious chaplains of Your Majesty are trusting in this, and I, in my humble prayers that everything should be successful will ask God to preserve the catholic and royal person of Your Majesty for long and very successful years, as Christianity needs.

From this monastery of St Francis, in the city and garrison of San Agustín, on the 12th December 1599.

Minor chaplin of Your Majesty,
[Signed:] Friar Bálthasar López

758. February 19, 1600. Juan Núñez de los Rios complains to Philip III and the Council of the Indies about the treatment of the married soldiers in Florida.

A rank-and-file plea that Méndez de Canzo, by his monopolizing tendencies, was making life impossible for married members of the San Agustín garrison is a significant item to be placed against his own self-aggrandizing reports. The precise accuracy of its statements cannot be checked.

A.G.I., Seville, Santo Domingo 231, 54/5/16; typescript in Division of Manuscripts, Library of Congress, newly translated.

Sir,

As a last resort and compelled by the great necessity and hardship being suffered by the poor inhabitants of the town and fort of San Agustín in Florida since the arrival as Governor of Gonzalo Méndez de Canço, appealing to the protection of Your Majesty, that as Most Christian King and Lord should not allow his poor subjects and vassals to be mistreated and exploited by those who govern them, to whom Your Majesty always sends orders to the contrary, and since there is here no magistrates' court as there is in other cities to give information about this kind of behaviour and ask for redress, I have dared to do this myself: and if I and others have not done so before, it is because we have been suffering it and bearing it as best we could, and we assumed that Your Majesty would be informed of everything by other means and would by now have ordered this to be set right by sending out someone else who would act differently, and the poor inhabitants would be better treated and the service of Your Majesty promoted; for instead, since this Governor came, much of the land that had already been gained, and the Indians pacified, has been lost. I came here in 1578, twenty-two years ago now, as reinforcements from Spain with several others whom Your Majesty ordered to be brought to these provinces, and have served and worked for Your Majesty on every matter that has arisen in the fort of Santa Elena and this one of San Agustín: I married the daughter of one of the early settlers who were here and had come before with the warm encouragement given by former Governors: we got by, and farmed enough to support the settlers, their wives and children: they had permission to leave here to look for whatever they needed. But now the Governor has not only forbidden us from going out for this purpose but he has taken over the market in the settlement, both wholesale and retail, under the hands and order of

a cousin of his called Juan García, who was brought from Spain in his company with a large quantity of goods, which he has been and still is selling at outrageous prices, and in this way he gets all the money: and he has not been prepared to have the settlers paid any of the money that was owing to them before he came; the Governor says himself that he will not order anything to be paid except in the following way, that a lieutenant from his company enquires at his command of the soldiers who wish for some goods, and draws up a list of what they want from the person who is selling it to them under the orders of this Juan García, even though he himself measures it and administers it, and then the Governor signs that himself, and this money is collected from the table on pay-day, and no other debts are allowed: if some soldier is hard up or ill and asks for some help from the provisions on account from Your Majesty's stores to help him, as used to be done before according to what he had, this Governor does not do this even if they are dying, and he says that if they want some of these goods that he will give the document for it to be given them, and they have to take it (and then they sell it at half of what it cost them); and all the disputes that arise here are judged by this Captain Juan García before his cousin the Governor, and it is generally thought all to be the same pockets that are concerned in the disputes because he is the only one who gets paid whatever is owed, as I said: and just a few days back it happened to me, my house was burnt down with more than ten thousand ducats' worth of my own belongings; and on some things worth just a few *reales* that I recovered from the burnt ruins out of my belongings this Juan García made a demand in the name of someone from Havana who is a great friend of his and from the same place, saying that on a certain number of shirts that he had given me to sell for him I ought to pay him back their value; and they had been burnt, as everyone in the settlement could see quite obviously; and since I was able to give such an indisputable account of it, but afraid that my just case would lose because this Juan García is the cousin of the Governor and is in charge of his Exchequer, I asked him with the due respect that he should act in company with one of the Royal Officers and Regidores, since there was no other judge or magistrate: for this he fined me fifty thousand maravedís and six months of exile and he had me arrested and kept me in the fort for many days and since harmed me in other ways: and in this way, and because the poor settlers have lost the means of making a living and feeding our wives and children, and not being allowed to appeal except before the Royal Council in Spain, when Your Majesty has granted a decree that they can be allowed for Mexico, our just case goes by default since we cannot and are not allowed to go in pursuit of it and it is such a long way: this can only be remedied if Your Majesty takes pity on us, being so far and cut off, where this Governor has no superior, and sends someone else in his place to act differently and right the wrongs and allow those who live here to make a living—meanwhile, we beseech Your Majesty to be pleased to instruct him to offer us the chance to sail from here to some other place where we can make a better living: for if everyone here does not write the same, that is only because they do not dare to, from the danger they would be in if the Governor captured their letters; I am at great risk in doing so: there were many other things I had to say, but I leave them because I understand that one of the Officers of Your Royal Exchequer whose business it is to send You this kind of information will have sent it to you: but we are all agreed that Your Majesty must send to put everything right soon. So may God guard the Royal Catholic Person of Your Majesty for many prosperous years, as Christianity needs. From this town and fort of San Agustín, 19th February 1600.

[Signed:] Juan Núñez de los Ríos

To the King Our Lord in His Royal Council of the Indies.

[Minuted:] "Florida. To His Majesty. 1600. Juan Núñez de los Ríos, 19th February."

759. February 20, 1600. Doña María, chief of Nombre de Dios, to Philip III.

The village of Nombre de Dios lay just outside San Agustín itself and became virtually its Indian barrio. *The placing of power in the hands of women chiefs opened the way to the Christianizing of the tribe. María had followed her mother,*

who had remained loyal during Drake's raid in 1586. Her letter is part of a campaign Méndez de Canzo was building up to show that he was needed in Florida and that he had the support of the local population. It contrasts with the complaints against him in the previous document.
Archivo de Indias, Seville, Santo Domingo 231; 54/5/16; copy in Division of Manuscripts, Library of Congress, translated.

To the King Our Lord In His Royal Council of the Indies.

Although I am unworthy that my letters should go to the Royal hands of Your Majesty, so as not to seem ungrateful for the favours I receive from them I have dared to do this. Lieutenant Hernando de Mestas gave me a letter from Your Majesty: may Our Lord God repay you for the favour shown to me therein, and prosper and increase his Royal crown. Although it may seem that I am of a people newly converted to the Christian faith, I have been since childhood, and my mother was the closest chief to this garrison of San Agustín, the first to become Christian, who served and treated well the Spaniards, without faltering in her purpose, and giving signs of good faith and friendship at the time when the English pirate came to this garrison: since I have taken her place I have done as much as I can, and will do even more gladly from now on, being all the more sure that I am serving a very Christian and good King and Lord.

To the General Gonzalo Méndez de Canço, who governs these provinces in the name of Your Majesty, all the natives of these provinces owe a great deal, for the kindness and good things he is doing for us, helping us in our needs and administering us in justice and peace: and now in particular he has just helped me with a number of tools, axes and/hoes, and flour and clothing, up to the value of a hundred and fifty ducats, which he said he was kind enough to send asking for from Your Majesty: so I humbly kiss Your Royal hands in thanks for that, for as well as having been of great assistance to me it has also been an example, so that the other Indians further inland should realize the liberal hand with which Your Majesty favours his subjects and be more willing subjects themselves, and come and receive Holy Baptism, and become Christians. May Our Lord keep Your Majesty as he is powerful, and grant You long life so that hereby You can support and protect Christian doctrine in these provinces.

Drawn up in the town of Nombre de Dios, Florida, on the 20th of February, 1600.
[Signed:] Doña María chief.
[Endorsed:] Florida to his Majesty 1600. Doña María, chief. 20th February. Seen 13th July 1601. No need to reply.

THE PROPOSED ABANDONMENT OF FLORIDA, 1600–1607

THE SKEPTICAL RECEPTION that Méndez de Canzo's expansionist plans received at the hands of Philip III's administration from 1600 onward prepared the way for the investigation of an alternative, the possible abandonment of Florida as a military outpost and its retention only as a missionary enterprise, or its complete liquidation, missionaries and all. Philip III wrote to Pedro de Valdés, governor of Cuba, on November 5, 1600, to suggest that the recent Indian uprising against the missionaries might mean that they were unwilling to be Christianized. Therefore, the question also arose as to whether the military post served any vital function. The upshot of this was the holding of formal *visita* at San Agustín in August and September, 1602, in which Fernando de Valdés, son of the governor of Cuba, interrogated everyone on the question, from the governor downward. Charles W. Andrade has summarized these inquiries in his *Florida on Trial, 1593–1602* (Coral Gables, 1959).

Canzo continued to favor expansion rather than contraction, but retracted somewhat his more elaborate earlier plans. A number of statements were made to the effect that neither English nor French had found the Southeast of much use to them, and it was questionable if the area was of much more value to the Spanish. The officials could not agree about the Indians. They were incorrigible; they might be kept under control better in the future; they might perhaps someday be an asset to the colony. The friars argued that the fact that so few had joined the Guale revolt outside its own area suggested that the missionary tide was turning and they had new successes to report. Some thought the fortress might be better located on St. Catherine Island (Guale) rather than at San Agustín. Cuban official opinion still favored developing the west and Gulf coasts and abandoning the east, although all through the proceedings the shipwreck-rescue function of the colony was seen to be of value. The friars thought the civil authorities should be brought under the control of the religious, in which case Florida could well be maintained. We have no final reports, but the mass of data collected was duly sent to Spain and perhaps, over a period, read and digested.

The possibility of cutting down the Florida garrison rumbled on through the correspondence of 1603 and 1604, but no decision was made. Juan de Ibarra, governor from 1603–1609, did not press for one. But his practicality and skill (and no doubt his success in the 1605 operation against the *Castor and Pollux*) led to his being left alone. The friars made their point by pushing more clergy into Florida and vastly extending the range of their operations. It might seem that their *doutrinas*, teaching centers where Christian doctrine and a little reading and writing were taught in the vernacular, together with the development of catechisms and other devotional works in Timucua (largely the work of Fray Francisco de Pareja, who later had them printed in Mexico), were something of a turning point. Finally, in 1606, the missionaries could stage their great demonstration, a visitation by their bishop, Juan Cabeza Altamirano, of Cuba. He confirmed some 350 white and Indian Christians at San Agustín and then went on to confirm older Indian converts and to baptize many new ones. In all it was claimed that 2,074 persons came under his ministrations.

This made it much more difficult to argue that the missions were a failure or that withdrawal was desirable from the religious aspect. It also heightened the struggle between the civil and missionary authorities for places on the establishment. Ibarra became alarmed at the incursion of the friars, because every missionary put on the strength reduced his garrison by one soldier. A tense situation developed between arrogant clerics and obstinate laymen, which grew steadily worse between 1606 and 1609. Meanwhile, however, events were working toward a strengthening of the garrison's status. News of the Virginia Company's charter in April, 1606, led immediately to the recommendation of the Junta de Guerra, a Committee of the Council of the Indies, that Florida should be maintained to counter English plans (764). This was confirmed in January, 1607 (765): If the English were to come to Virginia, Florida must remain, especially if it could be used as a base from which to root them out.

760. September 22, 1602. Gonzálo Méndez de Canzo to Philip III.

A.G.I., Seville, Santo Domingo 224, 54/5/9; copy in Woodbury Lowery Collection, Division of Manuscripts, Library of Congress; extracts translated in Albert C. Manucy, The History of Castillo de San Marcos & Fort Matanzas *(Washington, D.C., National Park Service, 1955), pp. 10–12.*

Señor:

...My opinion is, if it please your majesty, that you should not order the abandonment of this presidio until in the meantime an entry into the interior can be made, and it can be known and understood with certainty whether there are mines of gold and silver, precious stones and pearls. This entry can be made easily and at little cost in this way (your majesty being pleased to consider the said entry favorably), by ordering a number of about sixty or seventy soldiers to be provided besides those who already serve here.

In abandoning this presidio entirely, two difficulties are manifest to me, in my opinion very serious, which your majesty ought to consider. These are: if this fort should be abandoned, it would be obligatory to withdraw the Christian Indians who are protected by it, as well as the religious who teach them, because the said religious might continue to work among them. Their lives would meet with much danger and the said Indians would return to their idolatries as they used to. And the other: since the year of [one thousand] five hundred eighty-nine, many Spaniards (who were shipwrecked on the coast of this province) escaped and were delivered from death, because this presidio was nearby.

The said year [1589] on this coast four battered and dismasted ships under command of the general Martin Perez de Olesabal, more than four hundred persons. One of their ships entered this port and from here it departed for Spain.

The said year [1589] the crew of the frigate in the service of this presidio discovered and rescued another forty persons of another ship from the said flota that was lost on Cape Canaveral.

The year of ninety-two [1592] another ship in distress, which was sailing from Havana to Santo Domingo, put into this port battered and damaged. Here it was repaired in every way that was necessary and continued its voyage....

So then, there are in all five hundred seventy-eight persons who had fled here at times. Consistent with these two considerations, then, your majesty will at once determine and command what might better serve and befit your service and the service of God, our Lord. . . .

[Signed:] Gonçalo Méndez de Canço

761. September 14, 1602. The Franciscan view of Florida's prospects.

Summarized from the Valdés visita of August to September, 1602, in Charles W. Andrade, Florida on Trial, 1593–1602 (Coral Gables, 1959), pp. 60–61.

Fray Pedro Bermejo said that he had lived eight years in Florida and during all that time had been engaged in converting natives to the Christian religion. He was stationed at nearby Nombre de Dios. In his parish were located such villages as Solo, Capuaca and Palica, all within three leagues distance of his headquarters. He said that it was his experience that the Indians were quite willing to be converted and did not oppose being baptized. He thought them to be generally docile. Naturally, just as in any other place, there were some who made trouble. The problem in Florida was. . .that the past governors had not shown the necessary enthusiasm in fulfilling their duties of punishing these rebellious individuals. The governors had never cooperated fully with the Franciscan fathers in insisting that they respect the friars as an integral part of the Spanish authority. If the executive authority in San Augustín had been more cooperative the number of baptisms could have been greater. It was even hard to maintain discipline among the converted natives because of the governors' laxity in enforcing the laws.

He requested that His Majesty inform the governor that:

1. He should cooperate with the Franciscan fathers.
2. He should support the loyal Indian chiefs who were anxious to see that the troublesome characters were duly punished.
3. He should threaten all subversive individuals with severe punishments if they persisted in disturbing the peace.

4. The governor and his assistants should visit the native villages several times during the year and bring justice to those who had misbehaved.
5. There were larger Indian villages which had chiefs, but at the same time there were many little hamlets of three to five houses that had no leader. These hamlets should be abolished and their inhabitants moved to the larger villages. In this way these scattered Indians could be more easily converted. He said that it was his opinion that those Indians thus moved would be happier in the larger communities. From his own experience he knew that it was extremely difficult for any friar to keep in contact with and help the natives who lived in these isolated clusters.
6. It was imperative. . .that the King send more priests to Florida. There were only five Franciscans now in Florida and that was simply not enough. Two of the five were in poor health. It was no longer a matter of new conversions but rather of keeping Christian those who had been baptized, for some large Christian Indian villages had no priest to attend to their spiritual needs.

762. April 12, 1604. Pedro de Ibarra to Philip III.

The new governor was impressed by the demand of the Indians for friars to live among them. He had been visited by some fifty chiefs who declared their allegiance and who asked for missionaries. He considered that at least twelve would be needed (he was later to find that too many friars could be an impediment to civil government). The Crown agreed and twelve additional friars were sent.

A.G.I., Seville, Indiferente General 1420; 145/3/1; transcript in Division of Manuscripts, Library of Congress, extract, translated.

After I had spread the news of my arrival in these provinces, there came to pay me allegiance in the name of Your Majesty more than 50 chiefs from different areas: I entertained and looked after them as well as I could, both because Your Majesty ordered me to and because they are living as Catholics, and are showing very clear signs of the fruit being produced in them by the teaching missions (*doutrinas; doctrinas*); for they have asked me to send them friars, since there are no more than four men of the Church among them. To judge from the areas that lack them, at least another 12 will be needed, and it would be best to have them sent quickly, and that some of them should be preachers and men of letters, according to the great faith with which these people are asking for them. In this way I comply with what Your Majesty has ordered me in Your Royal Charter, where it says that I should tell you what is the situation in this question of the missions.

[Minuted—that a new commissary, Fray Alonso de Nozeda, was to bring 12 additional friars to Florida and that arrangements should be made for their despatch.]

763. March 15, 1604. Pedro de Ibarra to Philip III on rumors of a foreign colony in western Florida.

Pedro de Valdés forwarded to Spain the copy of a letter that he had received from Pedro de Ibarra to send on to the king. It shows Ibarra, at the opening of his governorship, being extremely sensitive to reports of foreign intervention at any place within his jurisdiction. A number of reports came in during the years 1604 to 1606 stating that there were foreigners with the Calusa in western Florida. That there was any systematic contact, such as is here suggested between French or English and the Calusa, is not established and is very unlikely. French privateers may indeed have made a few calls, and it seems likely that there were English and French individuals among the miscellaneous shipwrecked Europeans with the Calusa, but that is all.
A.G.I., Seville, Santo Domingo 224; 54/5/9; translated.

Copy of the letter from Pedro de Ibarra, Governor of Florida.

I am sending this boat to Your Majesty, on the 15th March 1604, to inform you that in Carlos Creek, in the Province of Florida, beyond Tocogava to the South-West, fifty leagues from here, are two large ships and other small ones, with soldiers on land building houses for settlement: they have women with them, and the governor is married. I have not managed to find out what nationality they are. I have been given this news by some friendly Indians, who have been there. And since there is nothing I can do about it from here, I have told the people who brought the news that I do not believe it (although I have been informed from another source); this is what has to be done when forces are as small as the ones I have here. I think it was a sensible decision not to let on that I knew, or else I would just succeed in making the weakness of my forces obvious, and the people in the Provinces would lose respect for me when they saw that I did nothing about it. From here to there there are many rivers, channels and awkward crossings; they have taken that position for the boats that come and go by there from New Spain. I am told by Captain Ecija, who knows that area so well, that Our ships have to come to that area in order to find the channel whose depth is known. In the next boat to come to You in April, I shall inform you of whatever news is brought by another two friendly Indians that I have sent to different places.

[Signed:] Pedro de Ibarra.
[Endorsed:] Don Pedro de Valdés.

764. April 28, 1606. Recommendation that on military grounds Florida be maintained.

A.G., Simancas, Estado 2024, translated.

The enclosed Consulta of the War Council [Junta de Guerra] of the Indies was seen in the Council as Your Majesty ordered it to be sent, and the decisions were as follows.

The Constable of Castille deferred in general to those who know more about matters in Florida; as concerns the first point, he said that careful thought is no less necessary before dismantling a fort than before building it, and so the instructions of the Junta that the fort of San Agustín should not be completely dismantled is essential so that it is not left quite unprotected; since it is very much to the service of Our Lord and the piety of Your Majesty to keep peaceful and in good condition those Indians who have converted to Our Holy Faith, and those who might wish to convert later should find someone to take them in, look after them and teach them, for every soul won is invaluable: but even so, to this purpose it is enough that the fort should remain in the state that seems best to the Junta. Still, it could be that the French, who have already had a foothold there, and were expelled forcibly, or other enemies might be attracted by the ease with which they could take the fort now that it is less strong and without artillery, and kill the 250 soldiers that remained, and might try to do this, so he asks Your Majesty to consider if it will be best to keep it as it now is, for the humiliation that would be suffered if the enemies succeeded.

On the second point he agreed with the decision of the Junta and those who know most about the damage that could be avoided and the benefit that would come from making the fort as seems best to the Junta on one of those islands.

Count Olivares agreed on both points with the decisions of the Junta for the same reasons they put forward.

Your Majesty will order it to be done and carried out as he thinks best, 28th April 1606.

765. January 26, 1607. Confirmation of the recommendation that Florida be retained.

A.G.I., Seville, Indiferente General 1867; 147/5/16; transcript in the Division of Manuscripts, Library of Congress, translated.

Council of War of the Indies, 26th January 1607. Authorizing a decision of the Council of War on certain reports of the intentions of the English.

Sirs:

From the copy of a decision which the Council of War has sent to this Junta, it seems that on the 16th October last year it gave a report to Your Majesty that it had gathered from certain information that a merchant from Plymouth [Plemna] had said that as some ships were going to look for a passage to the north-west to the East Indies and Japan in 1605 they hit the coast of Florida in an area of very good land peopled by Indians who were so civilized and well off that they thought it would be an excellent idea to take some of them to England; they were there in Plymouth, and the talk was that a great fleet was going to be fitted out [for the spring] to take everything that would be needed for Englishmen to go and live in that land with their wives and children; and although the Council was sure that this was wrong, and that the area they call Florida is in fact the land called Virginia, further to the north, they still thought that it was worth investigating this, and now this has happened to review the decisions of this Council dealing with the reformation of the fort of San Agustín in Florida, and to consider whether it would be a good idea to change any of the decisions that had been taken; a copy of these decisions was looked at in the Junta and the replies given by Your Majesty (who ordered that the decisions of the Council of War should be put into effect at once), and discussing everything with great care it has decided to explain to Your Majesty that the reformation that has been ordered to be done of the fort of San Agustín was carried out with great care and the advice of experienced intelligent and reliable men, and so, as far as this is concerned, there seems to be no reason that compels us to add to the decisions already taken, and the plans of the enemy are not thought to involve going to set foot in Florida, for this is a land where they could not stay.

Madrid, 26th January 1607.

[Signed:] The Count of Lemos
The Count of Puñonrostro
Don Bernardo de Velasco
The Marqués de San German
Estéban de Ibarra
The Licenciado Villagutierre
Don Francisco Duarte

[Minute on the verso:] Everywhere people should be on the watch, for the enemy will not just have one plan in mind.

Chapter Ninety-seven
The Spanish Victory over an
Anglo-French Expedition

THE CAPTURE OF THE *CASTOR AND POLLUX*

IN MARCH, 1605, Pedro de Ibarra had the greatest success of his period as governor of Florida. He captured a ship, with an Anglo-French crew, which was trading in a bay some five leagues north of Santa Elena in what is now St. Helena Sound.

In 1603, a ship, which was later found to have had a mixed French and English crew, worked its way up the Florida coast, trading, it was said, with the Indians. Later it emerged that the men had taken back a Guale Indian and trained him as an interpreter.

In February, 1605, a small vessel was seen to be sounding the waters near San Agustín and moving north. It was later set upon by the Indians of Guale, who killed Captain John Jerome of Plymouth and his pilot Samuel; the rest of its men, however, got away. They were said to have been following a greater ship. Ibarra kept contact with it as far as he could by coast patrols. Then, fortunately for him, a small vessel came in, which he sent up the coast to make contact with the foot patrols. With its aid, he learned that the English were probably to be found in the vicinity of Santa Elena. Then the frigate *San Josephe* came in from Havana and was promptly sent north. Finally another frigate, the *Asunçión*, was sent around by Pedro de Valdés from Cuba, specifically to deal with the intruders about whom he had information. The result was that the three vessels caught the large English ship *Castor and Pollux* unprepared. It was attacked, set on fire (although the fire was put out), and surrendered, while the remainder of the foreigners came out from the shore in their other boats and were taken prisoner. It would appear that most of the prisoners (some seventeen or eighteen) were handed over to the Guale Indians, as a change from the usual practice of killing them off at once), and the three leading persons on board were taken to San Agustín and interrogated.

A strange story emerged. Henry IV had issued a commission in January, 1604, to Guillaume de la Mothe (attached to the French ambassador's household in London) and Bertrand Rocque of St Malo to make a voyage to America in the ship *Castor and Pollux*, an English vessel. They were to trade and explore the coasts from the West Indies to Acadia. Their main backer in London was a Channel Islander called Peter de Beauvoir, and he had close contacts with both La Mothe and Rocque. The expedition was under La Mothe's orders although Rocque was to accompany it. The ship was apparently prepared at Plymouth, under Captain John Jerome, and had a mixed French and English crew. With it was to go the pinnace *Pollux and Castor*. They were to buy tobacco and maize in the West Indies, then go along the Florida coast, north of where the Spanish were, and trade these things with the Indians and also sell them the assorted tools and weapons that made up their main cargo. This is what they were doing when they were taken. They were exchanging goods for sassafras and china root, with a few skins, for their cargo though they had also a substantial amount of tobacco left. What was more surprising was that they were to go on to call at "Crotuan" [Croatoan] and buy silk grass from the supposedly surviving Lost Colonists; then they were to go to the Penobscot (Río de Gamas) to look for Cartier's "Anneda" (the anti-scorbutic), large beasts, and metals, finally ending up at the Bay of Fundy, where a gold mine (actually a copper lode) had been found in 1603. On board was a doctor-herbalist, whose name in Spanish, Dr. Juan de Bona Semana, clearly concealed something like Bonnesemaine (or even Goodwick).

The prisoners, Rocque as part-owner and victualer, Bonnesemaine as an educated man, and Bodran as the purser, were interrogated and proved to be well-informed about the voyage. What became of them afterward is not known. The ship, eventually disposed of, was inventoried and provided a most valuable indication of a cargo for Indian trade. Ibarra sent the whole dossier to Spain. He then sent the *Asunçión* up the coast, under Captain Francisco Éçija (the victor of the St. Helena Sound battle) to look for the English colony. His voyage, in August and September, 1605, produced interesting information about the coast north of Santa Elena, led him to a few Frenchmen captured by the Indians, but took him not much farther than Cape Romain before he returned (A.G.I., Seville, patronato 1/1/1/19, ramo 29).

The story of the capture reached England (it is not clear precisely how), and there were diplomatic repercussions, but the Spanish Court refused to discuss it with the English ambassador. A complaint was made directly by some English merchants (a draft in bad Spanish being in PRO, SP 94/12, fols. 202–211), which declares that "Peter de Beauvoir and other merchants following put to sea a ship called the *Castor and Pollux* with a pinnace [the *Pollux and Castor*], manned by 35 men, with divers sorts of merchandise of great value, to discover the coasts of Virginia, Norumbega and Acadia in the parts of America. The said ship and pinnace, entering the Bahama Channel and sailing along the coast of Florida in order to accomplish their intended voyage, were forced to enter the river called St. Helena to obtain water and to refresh themselves, being there for a certain time trading with the savages, the which bay is not part of the Bay of the Governor of Spain or any minister of Spain." They were there set on by three ships of the governor of Havana, Pedro de Valdés, the vessels captured, the crews killed or taken prisoners, and the survivors sent ultimately (it was believed) to work as slaves on the fortifications of the Indies. No response came to this complaint. Later, it was understood that some of the men had been dispersed among the Indians of the interior. The Spaniards maintained that they were merely dealing, as usual, with piratical intruders, but in virtue of the recent peace they did not put them to the sword at once. The main dossier of the case was sent to the French ambassador in Paris to enable him to make representations there since the original commission was issued by Henry IV, but he appears to have obtained little satisfaction. The dossier remained in the ambassador's papers. The proposals of the Council of the Indies for disposing of the affair, made on February 27, 1606, were probably accepted by Philip III (265).

The matter has been discussed in D. B. Quinn, "An Anglo-French 'Voyage of Discovery' to the North America in 1604–1605, and its sequel," *Miscellanea Charles Verlinden* (Gent, 1974), 513–534, and in "James I and the Beginnings of Empire in America," *Journal of British Commonwealth History*, II (1974), 135–152.

766. April, 1605. Proceedings in the case of the *Castor and Pollux*.

A. G., Simancas, Estado Francia, B 89 (K.1607/ 10), fols. 1–17; newly translated in full except for a few formal passages.

[a] In the city of Santo Agustín, provinces of La Florida, on the tenth day of the month of April, in the year one thousand, six hundred and five, Señor Pedro de Ibarra, governor and captain-general of these provinces for our master the king, declares the following before the aforementioned clerk: on the third day of the month of February last a pinnace [*lancha*] began to sound the bar of this city. On the first day his grace believed it to be a friendly vessel, but on the second, when it repeated its actions, he realised that it was in enemy hands, for, although it had time to enter, it failed to do so, continuing on both days to sound the bar from north to south, and then returning northwards. Since at the time there was no vessel in this port that might be sent after it, he despatched overland, under a corporal, a force of infantrymen, all of whom knew the language to enable them to join up with the Indians and enquire along the coast if the said boat had entered any harbour. They had some success and after three days it was learned that the said vessel had entered San Pedro, eighteen leagues to the north of this port, where it sounded inside the bar; the Indians, not recognizing it, spoke with the men on board—they saw that there were up to twelve persons—who said that they were Frenchmen, returning from Santa Elena in search of their large ship. When the boat continued along the Guale shore, sounding and surveying the bars right along the coast, the friendly Indians of this island killed two [of its crew], the captain and the pilot, and captured ten others, whom they brought to this garrison. His grace was also informed that a large ship, with nine pieces of artillery and up to twenty-seven persons, was in the Bay of Shoals [Baya de los Baxos], fifty leagues from this port and five from Santa Elena, trading with the Indians for sassafras and China-root. Since an advice-boat [*patax*] in the service of this garrison had just reached this city, and in the conviction that it was a great disservice to his majesty for such enemy ships to come to this coast to sound the bars, survey the harbors and trade with the Indians, he put some twenty soldiers on the advice-boat, under the command of Captain Francisco Fernandes de Ecixa, and had it made ready to go in pursuit of the enemy vessel, with orders not to lose it in the event of a fight. And with the arrival at this garrison of the frigate *San Josephe*, of the service of these provinces, following the departure of the said captain, he ordered it with all possible speed to make ready and take on another thirty persons, and then to go in search of the said captain and, having joined with him, to seek the said enemy. And at this time a frigate from la Havana, sent by Don Pedro de Valdés, governor and captain-general of the island of Cuba, arrived in this port with up to fifteen persons, soldiers and sailors, under the command of lieutenant Pedro Toste, who had been sent to report on why there were enemies along this coast, committing robberies, and to see what was the reward that they had come in search of; he [Ibarra] similarly ordered this frigate to leave with the frigate *San Josephe*, which was commanded by lieutenant Ferdinourdo Min de Bayona, so that they might search together for the said captain Francisco Fernandes de Ecixa, whom they would find in San Pedro or along the Guale shore, and under whose command they would place themselves; the said captain ordered lieutenant Toste to fly the admiral's flag belonging to his Grace, which he had in his possession, and all three ships went in search of the said enemy. They entered the Bay of Shoals and, finding it there, executed the orders that they carried to engage it in combat: the flagship *San Josephe*, which was carrying the said captain, boarded and grappled with the enemy, while the other two ships, unable to do the same, went in front; while the said flagship was fighting with the enemy he cut his cables and headed for the beach, and seeing he was already beaten and overcome, set fire to his ship; the other ships, picking up men in small boats, came to put out the said fire. Up to twenty-one live and wounded French and English were taken, apart from those who lost their lives on the occasion; there were three men killed on the *San Josephe*, and a number of others, including the said captain, were wounded. They have now brought the ship back to this city with the said twenty-one French and Englishmen. When his grace tried to discover

if the captain and pilot of the said enemy ship were alive, he discovered that they had died on the occasion of the fight, and that the only leaders still alive were one of the victuallers [*armadores*] of the said ship, and a herbalist-doctor and the clerk [purser] of the said ship: the *armador* has been brought to his Grace wounded and burnt, and the clerk wounded, together with some papers and instructions, written in the French language, carried by the said enemy, and since it is fitting to inform his majesty all about the said event his Grace orders that a sworn declaration be taken from the said captain Francisco Fernandes de Ecixa, for which he declares this decree, and similarly that a declaration be taken from the said *armador*, doctor and clerk of the said ship, who are to be interrogated along the lines of the following questions and articles:

[b]   First. They shall be asked if you are a Christian, and if they are [what about] the other people who came in the said ship, and of what nationality they are, and what employment they have, and where you learnt to speak the Spanish language?

Item: if they know that it has been learnt that passports have been issued [or peaces made] between Spain and France and England?

Item: from which port did they leave with the said ship for these parts, and who sent them, and what people do they bring and from which nations, and what artillery do they bring, and what was the captain and the pilot of the said ship called and whose is it?

Item: if more ships set out and where they headed, and which ports of the Indies they have visited, and which ships they have robbed, and if they have sent any prisoners to France or to England, and where they robbed a small frigate [*fragatilla*] which was going from this garrison to La Havana, where Gonzalo Juan was going, and in which part they found it, and if they have come on other occasions to the Indies to rob this coast and trade, and which Indians they traded with, and what was it that they traded?

Item: if the instructions and patents that are shown to them are those that they bring in the said ship and if the *armador* is the one referred to in one of the instructions?

Item: what the ship is called and whose is it, and what did the pinnace [*patache*] that came with it do, and if the boat that came sounding the bars of

this coast belonged to it, and why it was sounding them, and where did they leave the other ship mentioned in the instruction?

Item: what place is that called Crotuan contained in the instruction, and which Englishmen are settled there, and in what latitude of this coast is it, and how long has it been settled and on what authority?

Item: if they know in what latitude is the great river Lagama along this coast, where they were ordered to winter with the ship, and if they know that there are mines along this coast, and for which metals, and if they are known and who discovered them, and when, and if they know that the mine is above forty degrees?

Item: what herb is that called Oyssan or Bissanque, and where was it discovered, and by whom, and what is it good for?

Item: what tree is that called Aneda or Gumedan, and what is it good for, and what is the place where the large beasts are, and which beasts are they and who discovered them, and which latitudes are they in?

Item: for what purpose, being in the Bay of Shoals [Baya de los Baxos], a harbor of this coast, which belongs to the king Don Felipe our lord, when the ships of this garrison arrived, and Captain Francisco Fernandes de Ecixa, who was in command of them, sent to tell them to surrender and yield themselves, they refused to do so before offering resistance and fighting, killing and wounding some soldiers of this garrison, and rather than surrender (their ship) set fire to it so that it would burn?

The Señor general orders that these questions and articles be put to the said Englishmen and Frenchmen contained in this decree, and that the said information be dated and decreed according to justice, and this I decree and sign.

[Signed:] Pedro de Ibarra.

Before me Alonso Garcia de la Vera, clerk

[c]   Deposition of the captain

In the city of Santo Agustín de la Florida, on the twelfth day of the month of April in the year one thousand, six hundred and five, the señor governor and captain-general Pedro de Ybarra in the presence of myself, the aforementioned clerk, summoned before him Captain Francisco Fernandes de Ecixa, who is captain of one of the two companies that serve his majesty in this garrison, from whom he took and received the oath in due legal form, and he did it well and fully, swearing by God and Holy Mary on the sign of the cross, and he promised to answer truthfully whatever was asked of him, and he was questioned according to the tenor of the decree [*auto de oficio*]. He said that it is true that on the third day of February this year a boat arrived at the bar of this harbor and anchored there; the sentinel at the mouth of the bar sounded the signal for a ship, as is customary, and the said boat, did not enter this harbor, but continued sounding the bar from one part to another; and although it was believed on that day that it was friendly, it was then made clear on another that it was in enemy hands, for, returning to sound the bar, it failed to enter and returned to the north. This witness immediately learnt and saw that, since at that time there was no vessel in this garrison to send after the said boat by sea, the señor general was despatching men in its pursuit overland, under a corporal, (with orders) to issue warnings all along the coast, having joined up with the Indians, and, if the boat entered any port, to try a successful maneuver against it; and this witness knows that three days after the said boat left the bar of this harbor news came to the señor general that it had entered the bar of San Pedro, eighteen leagues from this garrison, where it was sounding and reconnoitring the bar, and that the men on board had told the Indians that they were French and English, returning to Santa Elena in search of their large ship which was there. And since the patache *Asunción*, which serves this garrison, had entered port on the eighth day of the said month of February the señor general commanded that it make ready and ordered this witness to embark in it with supplies, munitions, and up to twenty soldiers from this garrison, and to lead it in search of the enemy, with instructions, in the event of finding him, to maneuver against him and to engage him in combat, without any thought of shrinking from it, with a view to making him yield. And so this witness embarked on the said patache *La Asunción*, left the bar of this harbor on the ninth day of the said month of February and reached the bar of San Matheo, where he was informed by the Indians and the priest of the curacy, Father Quetana, that the boat that had entered San Pedro had already gone, and this witness returned through the bar of San Juan and

went in search of the harbor where the said boat had been, and learned that it had left the bar for Santa Elena in search of its ship. Returning past Guale, in search of the said boat, he reached the village of Assao, which is on the Guale shore, and learned that the English boat had entered the bar of Cofunufe, which is in the island of Guale, and that the Indians there had killed two and captured two of the eight men on board her; and he went ahead with a canoe to the island of Guale, leaving the vessel there, and brought back the two Frenchmen who were alive, and he obtained news that the large ship was in the Bay of Shoals, trading with the Indians for sassafras and china-root; and with this news he returned to his vessel, which he had left at Assao, bringing with him the said Frenchmen, and went back to San Pedro, where he found an order from the señor general instructing him to wait there because the frigate *San Josephe* had been sent with all speed to join him, and telling him that on the next day another frigate, which had come from La Havana with lieutenant Atoste, would be sent in search of him; and then the next day the said frigate *San Josephe* and the frigate from La Havana arrived in the said harbor of San Pedro, bringing an order for this witness to embark in the *San Josephe* and, with the other two vessels in support, go after the enemy ship to the Bay of Shoals, where he should try to come alongside it and overcome it. In accordance with the said order this witness set out in search of the said enemy, ordering the flagship standard to be hoisted on the *San Josephe*, and, entering the Bay of Shoals, next to Santa Elena, on the third day of the month of March, found the said enemy ship there, trading with the Indians for wood sticks of sassafras and china-root; he sent a soldier and an interpreter [*lengua*] to tell the enemy to surrender according to the rules of war [*a buena guerra*], and the captain of the ship sent him back to report that they did not want to surrender or yield; in view of this reply this witness decided on the fifth day of the said month, when he had wind, and seeing that the said enemy ship was equipped [*pavesado?*] and laden [*jareteado?*] with much artillery and in a position ready to fight, that the *San Josephe* should grapple with it, ordering the frigate from La Havana and lieutenant Atoste, who was on board it, and the patache *Asuncion* to follow him; seeing that the said two vessels were not with him, this witness and his men took the frigate *San Josephe* in to grapple with the enemy and fought with him, and the other two ships did not grapple with him; and in the midst of the struggle the enemy set fire (to the ship) and the men of the frigate *San Josephe* and this witness, going on board to try to put out the fire, overcame it and captured it; both the other ships had made for the shore, and the rest of the men from the friendly frigates managed to assist from the land and from a little boat with the quenching of the fire. The captain of the enemy ship, the pilot, and five other persons died in the fight on board the said ship, and another twenty-one were wounded and captured, including the merchant and *cargador* of the said ship; two of the soldiers of this garrison died on the frigate *San Josephe*, and this witness and other soldiers were wounded. After the capture of the enemy [ship] this witness came with it to this city, rigging it as best he could, and thus he brought it back, with the prisoners and the unloaded goods that he collected, and which have been inventoried. This is the truth, and what happened on the occasion of the said voyage, and, having had his statement read to him, he declares that he sees it, and he affirms, ratifies it, and signs his name to it, and declares he is sixty years old, more or less. Señor general Pedro de Ybarra.

[Signed:] Fran'co F'z

Before me Alonso Garcia de la Vera, clerk.

[d]   Declaration of the armador

In the city of Santo Agustín of La Florida, on the thirteenth day of the month of April in the year one thousand, six hundred and five, the señor governor and captain-general Pedro de Ybarra to obtain the said information summoned before him the merchant [*cargador*] of the said ship, who, since he said he was a Christian, received and gave the oath in due legal form with a sign of the cross, swearing on God and Holy Mary and promising to answer truthfully whatever was asked of him, and under the said oath his confession was taken and the following questions were put to him: he was asked if he is a Christian and if the other people who came in the said ship are, and what he is called and of what nation is he, and what is his age and occupation, and where he learnt to speak the Spanish language - he said that he was called Beltran Rrogues [Rocque?] and that he is of French nationality from the city of St Malo

[Ssamalo] in Brittany, and that he is Christian and that he regards the rest of the people who came in the ship as Christians, on account of having heard them say so, and that some of them are English and some French, and that he is thirty-three years old, more or less, and that he has no other occupation apart from that of being a merchant, and that he learned to speak the Spanish language in Catexena de Lebante.

Asked if he knows, or has heard it said, or if it has come to his notice that passports have been issued between France and Spain and England—he said that when he left England, which was a year ago, he knows that the king of France had twice ordered it to be publicly proclaimed that no Frenchman should go to Spain, on pain of [losing] his life, and that he does not know if any permits have been declared in England.

Asked from which port they sailed for these parts, and who sent them, and which people came and of what nations, and what artillery, and what the captain and the pilot of the said ship were called, he said that they left from the port of Plymouth [Plemua] in England, and that they were sent by Guillermo de la Mota a native of St Malo, and that when they set out there were thirty-six persons, French and English, and that they brought nine pieces [of artillery], six of them bronze falcons and three of cast iron, and that the master and pilot of the ship, who was in charge of everything was not known by the name of captain, and he was called Juan Xeronimo [John Jerome], that he was of English nationality, and that the ship belonged to Guillermo de la Motay, and that he does not know [the names of] his partners, and this he replied to this question.

Asked when they set out from Plymouth he said that it was in the month of May in the year one thousand, six hundred and four.

Asked if they set out in the company of the other ships he said that the only ones to leave were themselves with their pinnace [lancha]. Asked what route they took, and which ports in the Indies they visited, and which ships they robbed, and what the people on board did, and if they sent any prisoners to France or England— he said that they first put in to land at the Island of Trinidad, and there exchanged linens and other goods for some four or five hundred pounds of tobacco with the inhabitants, and from there went Punta Araya [Punta de Rrey], where the Flemings take salt, and they took a little salt; they encountered two caravels, on their way towards La Havana and from one of them, which was at anchor, they took sixty or seventy sacks of flour, which they were told came from Caracas, but did it no other harm, leaving it with its crew, sails, gear and other cargo and taking only that which they needed for their sustenance, and the other caravel set sail and they did not catch it; from there they went on to Los Jardines, twenty leagues to the east of the Isla de Pinos, where, finding a large ship aground and abandoned, they went to it in their boat and saw that it was loaded with pipes of wine, and they took some forty or fifty pipes of wine and went with them to Guanaibez in the island of Hispaniola and sold them in exchange for money to other English, French and Dutch ships which were trading there for other goods; and from there they continued towards La Havana by way of Cape Santo Anton, and alongside La Cruz del Padre they encountered a large fishing boat and went towards it, and its crew fled to land and they took it and found only a number of bannikins [*benequines*] of salt on board, and since their own boat was foundering for lack of caulking and had just been beached they offered it to the crew of the fishing boat in exchange for theirs, but the latter would not take it, saying that Don Pedro de Valdéz would hang them if he knew that they had talked to them, and so they left their boat behind and took the fishing boat; and then they encountered another vessel [*fragata*] carrying hides and tallow and they took them without harming either the people on board or the ship and its gear; leaving it behind they came out of the Bahama Channel at Xega or Santa Lucia, where they spent the night at sea and the day on land, and at night in severe weather they lost sight of their boat and when in the morning, on their return to land, they saw one sailing by, which had just passed this witness's ship, they attacked it, believing it to be their boat, and they reached it and made it lower sail by firing a piece of artillery and muskets; and they went on board and said they were going from this garrison to La Havana, and they asked for the merchant and he was pointed out to them, and from the aft mast the merchant, whose name they did not see, opened a chest and they took some four pounds of amber, and a gold chain, and some two thousand *pesos* in *reales* and some clothes, which the sailors

immediately carried away, and then they set them free with their vessel, tackle and sails without harming them any further and set out in search of Santa Elena; and he said that they have not sent any prisoners to England or France or captured any ship other than those referred to, and this was his reply to this question.

He was asked if he had come on previous occasions to the Indies to steal or trade and he said that this was the only time that he had come.

Asked with which Indians of this coast he has traded and what they traded, he said that they entered the Bay of Shoals, next to Santa Elena, with his ship, and traded with the Indians there for sassafras sticks in exchange for axes and knives and things made of beads and dug up china-root with their own hands, and that they went with the boat for the sassafras to the water's edge, where the Indians loaded it—an Indian of Guale called Anga served them as interpreter—and they were there when they were found by the men of this garrison.

Asked if the boat that arrived to sound the bar of this harbor was his, he said that he does not know what his boat did, for, after losing it on coming out of the Channel, he did not see it again until he arrived in this city, although he found two men from the boat who told him that they had moved along this coast and two men had been captured and two killed in Guale, and this was his answer.

Asked what merchandise he brought from England and France in the ship, he said that all that they brought consisted of tools and cauldrons and beads, and other things for trade with the Indians, and this was his answer.

He was shown a patent written on parchment, with a seal with three fleur-de-lis and a signature saying "EN RY" and another saying "PAR LE ROY DE NOBILES," and an instruction on a piece of paper with a signature saying "Guillermo de la Mota," both written in French. Asked if this is the licence that he brought, if the patent is from the king of France, and the instruction from Guillermo de la Mota, he said that the parchment patent is the very same one that he brought in his ship, and the seal is that of the king of France, and that he was given it in England by Guillermo de la Mota, that the instruction is that given to him by Guillermo de la Mota for his voyage, and that it is the same Beltran Rrogues referred to in the patent and the instruction, and this was what he said to this question.

Asked if he knows the location of the place called Crotuan, referred to in the instruction, and in which latitude it lies, and which Englishmen are settled there, and when they settled it, and on what instructions—he said that he does not know where the said place is, but he understands that its latitude is thirty-six and a half degrees, and they were to go in search of it along the coast, and that he does not know how many Englishmen are settled there, but that he believes that they came to settle fifteen years ago, and he does not know with what authority except that they were sent by an Englishman called GUATER RRALE [Walter Ralegh], who himself brought them and left them the first time, and now they had to go and search for them, and this was what he said to this question.

Asked if he knows the latitude of the great DE LA GAMA river, along this coast, where he is ordered to winter, he said that it is on this coast at latitude forty-three degrees—asked if he knows the latitude of the mine, and which metal it is for, he said that he knows that the mine is at forty-four and a half degrees on this coast, and that it is a gold mine.

Asked if he is aware that it is known and who discovered it and when, he said that two years ago some ships came to this coast from St Malo to trade with the Indians and fish, and, when they reached the Canada river, the Indians gave the crews of the ships samples from the gold mine, and took them to it in canoes and showed it to them, and the soldiers took some rocks from the mine to France to report it, and he understands that it is at forty-four and a half degrees, which is where he was to look for it with his ship.

Asked if he knows what grass is that called OYSAN or BISSANQUE, he says that he has not seen it, but he knows that when the Englishman Walter Ralegh [Guatarrale] came to settle some Englishmen they took some of the said grass to England and announced that the Indians spun it to make cloth, and they worked it in England and saw that it was silk, like that from China, and for this reason he was to seek it along this coast and take back what he could, and he believes that it is to be found where the English are settled, and this was what he said.

Asked if he knows what tree is that called ADOANEDA or HUMEDAY, in which latitude it is, and what it is good for, he said that he does not know in what latitude is the said tree, but he has been told that it is to be found along this coast and that he had to look for it, and that according to what he has heard it is good for labour pains [enfermedades de dolores] and buboes, and so he was to look for it and take it away, and this was what he said.

Asked why, when he was in the Bay of Shoals, a harbor of this coast belonging to the king don Felipe, our lord, and the ships of this garrison arrived under the command of Captain Ecixa and they were ordered to surrender, they refused to do so and fought until they were defeated, and killed some men from this garrison and wounded others, and set fire to themselves—he said that when the ships of this garrison arrived in the Bay of Shoals this deponent was not in the ship, having gone with the canoe to the river up the coast for sassafras, and that he did not know then of the message from the captain. When he returned that night they told him that the ships of the garrison of San Agustín had arrived there and that the governor of San Agustín, who was on board, had sent to tell them to surrender under the rules of war, and that if they resisted they would all be put to the knife. They defended themselves and their ship and fought to see if they could escape capture, and they were taken and overcome. He said that the fire broke out in the main-topsail of the ship and the ship began to burn, and he heard it said that a Fleming had set fire to a barrel of powder. And thus they were captured and brought to this garrison as prisoners, and this is the truth and what has occurred in the course of his voyage since they left Plymouth until they were taken, and that which they stole was in the ship, together with some tools and cauldrons which they brought with them, and this is the truth, under the oath that he took, and, having had his statement read to him, he said that he hears it, and he confirms and ratifies it, and signs his name.

Likewise he was shown another patent, written on parchment, showing that it was dated in Lyon on the fourteenth of July of the year one thousand and six hundred, with a seal of three fleur-de-lis and a signature saying Henry [Enrii], with "por EL REY pitener" beneath, and a printed document containing a proclamation.

Asked if he knows them, he said that he knows them and brought them with him in his ship, and the seal is that of the king of France, and that the patent is a licence for a voyage that he made to the Levant in the year one thousand and six hundred, and the proclamation states that nobody should trade along the coast of Canada in La Florida without licence from Senor de MOS [Sieur de Monts], gentleman-in-ordinary of his chamber. And this is the truth and he signed it, and the señor governor signed it, noting that Crotuan is a harbour in the provinces which the English call La Virginia, which is where they are settled and where they went.

[Signed:] Pedro de Ybarra. Bertran Rregues.

Before me Alonso Garcia de la Bera, clerk.

[e]   Declaration of the doctor

In the city of Santo Agustín de la Florida, on the fourteenth day of the month of April in the year one thousand, six hundred and five, the said señor governor and captain-general Pedro de Ybarra, before me the aforementioned clerk, had brought before him the doctor who was brought from the said English ship, and since he did not know how to speak Spanish his confession was taken through the interpreter Pedro Chico de Haxo, who asked him what he was supposed to and answered what the doctor said, and the said confession was taken in the following form:

An oath was sworn by the said Pedro Chico de Haxo, and he did it well and properly, under which he was warned that he should put the questions that he was ordered, without adding or omitting anything, and that he should answer what the doctor answered. He promised to do this under the said oath and, accordingly, he was ordered to ask the said doctor the following in this form:

The said Pedro Chico was instructed to ask the said doctor if he is a Christian. He said that he is. Asked of what nation, he said that he is French, of the Burgundian nation. Asked what is his age and occupation, he said that he is thirty years old and a doctor by profession, and this he answered. Asked what he is called, he said that he was called Juan de Bona Ssemana.

Asked if he knows, or whether it has come to his notice, that passports have been issued between Spain, France and England, he said that he understands that before they came to these parts passports had been issued between France, Spain and England, but he does not know for certain, and this he answered.

Asked from which port they departed with the said ship, and who sent them, and what men they brought and of what nationality, and what artillery they brought, and what was the name of the captain of the said ship, and if the other men who came in the said ship are Christians, he said that they departed from the port of Plymouth in England, and that they told him that they came with a licence from the king of France, and that thirty-four persons came in the ship, and that he understands that they brought nine or seven pieces, and that the captain and master of the ship was called John Jerome [Juanes Xironimo], and that he does not know what the pilot was called, but both were English, and that he knows that the Frenchmen who came in the ship were Christians, but he does not know if any of the Englishmen were.

Asked if he knows what the ship was called and whose it is, he said that he has heard it said that it is called Castor Polus [*Castor and Pollux*], and that he has heard it said that it belongs to Guillermo de la Mota, a Frenchman who lives in England, and this he answered.

Asked if he knows that some heretical books came in the ship, he said that the French books that came were Catholic, and that many English books came, but he does not know if any of them were Catholic, since he does not understand the English language, and this he answered to this question.

Asked how they came to bring him and why they brought him, he said that they told him to come in the ship and that they were going near to Spain, and he said that they assured him that they were not coming to harm anybody, but only to trade for sassafras, and a wood [palo] that they call Aloes, and china-root, and some tobacco, and thus he went on board the ship, and this he answered to this question.

Asked if other ships left with them, he said that another small patache left, and this he answered.

Asked which ports in the Indies they have visited, and which ships they have robbed, and if they have sent any prisoners to England or France, and what the crews of the ships that they captured did—he said that they came to the port of La Trinidad, the first port that they saw in the Indies, and were trading tobacco there for a fortnight in exchange for wine and other things, and from there they went to a port called Punta del Rey to take on salt, and there they encountered two ships like caravels, and they captured one of them, which was loaded with flour, and took about a third of the flour, which it was carrying in sacks, to eat, and they left the caravel and its crew without doing it any further harm; and from there they came towards the Ysla de Pinos, where, on some sand-banks, they found a large ship, beached and abandoned, and they went on board and took off some forty-three or forty-four pipes of wine, and from there they went to Guanaybes and sold them for money to English ships that were there; and from there they returned past Jamaica and were waiting to come out and they came towards La Havana, and they encountered a fishing boat alongside La Cruz del Padre and they captured it—it was carrying only a little salt, and the crew fled to shore, and they took it in exchange for their patache, because their own was sinking and was not as good [as the fishing boat] and they left it behind. Two days after leaving there they captured another small ship which was carrying cowhides and tallow, and they took them and left the crew and the vessel without harming them; and from there they came out [of the Florida Channel] and some sixty leagues from this harbour encountered a small packet-boat which, they were told was travelling from this garrison, and they captured it: this witness did not go on board it, but he saw that they brought amber, money and a gold chain from it, and he does not know how much they took, and they left it without doing further harm to the people on board; and from there they came back to Santa Elena and entered the Bay of Shoals, and were obtaining sassafras from the Indians in exchange for tools and beads, and gathering china-root—they had to stay there until the ship was full—and they have not sent any prisoners to France or England, for they brought with them everything that they had stolen, and this he answered to this question.

Asked what cargo the ship brought from England, he said that they brought tools and cauldrons to exchange with the Indians for sassafras and china-root, and this he answered.

Asked if he has come on previous occasions to the Indies to steal or trade along this coast, he said that this was the first time in his life that he had left his own land, but he does not know if any of the others have come before, and this he answered.

He was shown two patents on parchment and asked if they are those that they brought in the ship, and if they are from the king of France, and if the seal and arms on them is the royal seal—both are in the French language, and one contains a signature which says "en RY" and another which says "PAR LE ROY DE NOBILES," and the other has another signature which says "en RY" and another which says "Per le ROY Potier"; he said that it is true that they are the patents and licence that came in the said ship, and he knows the signatures on them, and the seal and arms, to be those of the king of France, and that he has seen them previously on the ship, and this he declared in reply to this question.

An instruction on a piece of paper and another like a printed proclamation were shown to him and he was asked if he had seen them previously—he said that he had previously seen the printed proclamation in France, and that he has not seen the instruction, but it seems to him that the signature which is at the bottom of it is that of Guillermo de la Mota, and this he answered.

Asked if a *fragatilla* or boat that was engaged in sounding this bar was that which came with their ship, he said that they brought with them as a pinnace [patache] the boat that they captured, but it was separated from the ship during a storm at the mouth of the Channel, and came to this coast looking for the ship, and that later he has learned here from men on her who were captured how they sounded this bar, and entered the bar of San Pedro and went along the Guale shore, where two of them were killed and two more captured, and this he said.

Asked if he knows that the *armador* of the ship and the person referred to in the patents is the Beltran Rrogues who is held prisoner here, he said that yes he is, and this he answered.

Asked if he knows what place is that called CROTUAN referred to in the instruction, and in which latitude it lies on this coast, and which Englishmen are settled there, and how long they have been settled, and on what authority, he said that he knows nothing of such a place and has heard nothing of it other than having heard it said that there is an English settlement along this coast, that he does not know where it is nor when they settled, and this he said to this question.

Asked if he knows in what latitude on this coast is the river that they call de Lagama, and if he knows or has heard it said that there are some mines on this coast, and for which metals, and who discovered them and when, he said that he understands absolutely nothing of things of the sea, but he has heard it said that there are gold mines on this coast, and this he answered to this question.

Asked if he knows what grass is called OYSAN or BISANQUE, what it is good for, and who discovered it, he said that he neither knows nor has seen such grass, nor does he know what it is good for, and this he answered.

Asked if he knows what tree is that called ANEDA or GUEMEDA, and what it is good for, and which is the place where they say are the large beasts, and what beasts are they, and who discovered them, he said that he does not know such a tree and has not heard it spoken of, and the same with reference to the beasts, for they only told him that they were coming to look for sassafras, and china-root, and wood [palos] of aloes, and this he answered to this question.

Asked why, when he was with his ship in the Bay of Shoals, a harbor of this coast belonging to the king Don Felipe, our lord, and the ships of this garrison arrived with captain Francisco Fernandez de Ecixa, who was in command of them, and he sent a soldier to tell them to give themselves up according to the rules of war, they did not want to comply, but first fought and killed some men from this garrison, and set fire to themselves when they saw that they were beaten—he said that, although it is true that, when they were in the Bay of Shoals and the ships of this garrison arrived, they sent to them a soldier who spoke with the captain of the ship, this witness does not know what they discussed, and that the merchant of the ship was not in the ship, having gone ashore for sassafras; when the merchant returned that night he was in his bed and does not know what they did, and when the ships of this garrison went to grapple with them he was below deck. And he said that it is true that he heard artillery- and musket-fire, but he does not know from which ships they were firing, although he does know and saw that the Spanish men came on board his ship and overcame it and

captured it, and seized this witness and the others whom they brought, having killed the captain of the ship and four others, and wounded others—and he heard it said that the ship's pilot had been killed in the patache—and thus they were brought here with the ship and delivered to the señor general, and this is the truth and what the said Pedro Chico declared him to have declared.

The said Juan de Bona Ssemana to the questions that have been put to him contained in this declaration, and they signed it with their names, and, the said confession being read and related to him by the said Pedro Chico, he said that he affirmed and ratified it. And the señor general signed.

[Signed:] Pedro de Ybarra
Juan de Bona Ssemana
Pedro Chico de Haro
Before me, Alonso Garcia de la Vera, clerk.

[f] Declaration of the clerk [escribano]

After the aforesaid, in the said city of Santo Agustín de la Florida, on the day, month and year referred to above, the said governor and captain-general for the said inquiry had brought before him the clerk of the said English ship, who said he was called Julian Bodian, to take down his declaration, which, since he knows how to speak Spanish, was taken from him before me, the clerk, in the following form: He was asked of what nation he is, and if he is a Christian, and what is his age and occupation, and he said that he is of French nationality, a native of the city of St Malo in Brittany, and that his age will be twenty-three years, and that his occupation is that of merchant, and that he is a Christian by the grace of God, and this he answered. After the aforesaid declaration that he was a Christian an oath was administered to him on a sign of the cross, and he did it well and properly, and he promised to reply truthfully to whatever was asked of him, and, under the said oath, the following questions were put to him in this manner.

He was asked which people came in the said ship, and of what nation were they, and from which port did they depart with the ship, and if the people who come in it are all Christians, and who sent them—he said that they set out with the ship from the port of Plymouth in England eleven months ago, and that thirty-four persons, Englishmen and Frenchmen came in it, and that he knows that the Frenchmen are Christians but does not know if the Englishmen are, and that the ship belongs to Guillermo de la Mota [Guillaume de la Mothe], a Frenchman, and that the person who sent them was Guillermo de la Mota himself, who lives in England.

Asked if when they left Plymouth with the ship he knew or had heard it said that passports had been issued between Spain and France or England, and where he learned to speak the Spanish language, and what the ship is called, he said that when they left England the king of France had ordered that no French ship was to go to Spain on pain of [loss of] life, and that ships were crossing from England to Spain, and that he learned to speak the Spanish language in Spain—in Sevilla, and Cadiz, and Cartaxena, and Alicante, and other parts where he has been many times, and that the ship is called Castor Polus, and this he answered.

Asked what artillery they brought in the ship, and what the captain of the said ship was called, he said that they brought nine pieces, six of them bronze bases and three pieces of cast iron, and that the captain of the ship is called Jeronimo [Jerome] and the pilot was called Samuel, and this he answered. Asked if other ships set out with them, and which ports of the Indies they have visited, and what prisoners they have taken, and what they did to the crews of the ships they have captured, and which prisoners they have sent to France or England, and where they robbed a small ship going from this port to La Havana, whose merchant was Gonzalo Juan, and what they stole from him and what they did—he said that the first port of the Indies that they found was the island of La Trinidad, and that there they obtained a little tobacco from the local people in exchange for tools and shirts, and from there they came to Punta de Rey, where the Flemish take on salt and took a little salt. There they ran into two caravels and captured the one that was at anchor, and, finding it loaded with sacks of flour, which, they were told, came from Caracas, they took from it for food up to seventy sacks, and left behind the rest of the cargo, the gear, and the crew, without touching them or doing them any further harm, and the other caravel fled and they did not catch it. From there they turned towards the Isla de Pinos, and there found a Flemish ship of three hundred tons or more beached and abandoned on some sand banks, and loaded with pipes of wine, and they took up to forty pipes of the wine

and carried them to Guanaybes, in the island of Hispaniola, and sold them for money to some English and Flemish ships that were there trading for hides, and then they took the Havana route to come through and next to La Cruz de Padre they captured two small ships: one of them had nobody on board, its crew having gone, and they took it for their pinnace, since their patache was letting in much water, and the other was carrying hides and tallow, which they took, leaving the vessel and the crew without doing them any further harm. Coming out of the Channel, in sight of the coast of La Florida, they ran into a storm and lost [contact with] the craft that they had brought as their pinnace, and the following day, seeing a vessel with a poop sail coming and about to pass them, and believing it to be the boat that they had lost, they went towards it—it was a small vessel and made it lower its sails by firing artillery and muskets; they captured it and the men on board said that they were going from this port to La Havana, and they robbed it of money and amber, although he does not know how much it would be, and a gold chain, which they took to their ship, and they let the boat and its crew go on their way without doing them any further harm. They then continued towards Santa Elena and entered the Bay of Shoals, where they began to trade with the Indians for sassafras roots, in exchange for tools, and to collect china-root until they were found there by the ships that came from this garrison, and this he answered.

Asked what cargo they carried in their ship when they set out from England, he said that the ship brought axes, knives, and other tools, and cauldrons to trade on these coasts for sassafras, china-root and marten skins, and this he said.

Asked if they brought many Lutheran or heretic books in the said ship, he said that the Frenchmen brought some Catholic books and the Englishmen many Lutheran books written in English, and this he answered.

Asked about and shown two patents written on parchment, one with a signature saying "en RY" and another saying "PAR LE ROY DE NOBILE," and the other with a signature saying "EN RY—PAR LE ROY POTIER," and with two seals with a shield and three fleur-de-lis on each, and asked if he knows them, and if they brought them in their ship, and if the signatures and the seal are those of the king of France, he said that he has seen the said patents in his ship and he knows that the signatures and seals on them are the arms of the king of France and his signatures, because he has seen many others which were written in the French language, and this he answered.

He was shown another instruction, written by hand on a piece of paper with a signature saying Guillermo de la Mota, and another like a printed proclamation, and asked if he knows them—he said that he knows that the instruction is written in French and that the signature at the bottom is that of Guillermo de la Mota, which he recognizes on account of having seen it elsewhere, but that he has not seen the document before now, and that he has seen the printed proclamation many times, both on the ship and in Plymouth and France, and that, by command of the king of France, it orders that no person should go to the coast of Canada without licence from Monsur de Mos [Monsieur de Monts], on pain of [losing his] life, and this he answered to this question.

Asked if the merchant held captive here is the Beltran Rrogues referred to in the patent and instruction, he said that he is the very one referred to in the patents and instructions, and this he answered.

Asked if he knows which place is that called Crotuan, where Englishmen are settled on this coast, and if he knows in which latitude it is situated, and which Englishmen are settled there, he said that he has heard it said that there are Englishmen settled on this coast, but he does not know where, and this he answered to this question. Asked if he knows the latitude in which the great La Gama river is situated on this coast, and if he knows whether any gold mine has been discovered on this coast—he said that he does not know the latitude in which the La Gamas river is situated, but he had heard it said that he was to go there to winter, and that he does not know whether there is a gold mine on this coast, except that he heard it said to some Indians in the Bay of Shoals, next to Santa Elena that there were gold mines inland, but he does not know the latitude of the mine, and this he answered.

Asked if he knows which grass is one that is called Oysan or Bissanque, who discovered it, and what it is good for, and where it is, he said that he does not know of such a grass, nor has he seen it or heard it spoken of, and this he answered.

Asked if he knows a tree that is called ANEDA or GUMEDA, or has heard it referred to, and what it is good for, and where it is on this coast, he said that he does not know it and has not heard it referred to except on this occasion.

Asked if he knows where is the place of the breat beasts, he said that he does not know.

Asked if he, or any other of the persons who came in the ship, had come to this coast or to the Indies on previous occasions to trade or plunder, he said that he has not come before to the Indies or to this coast, and, apart from two Englishmen, a gunner and a sailor, who came two years ago to the very Bay of Shoals on this coast, where they loaded a ship with sassafras and china-root and then returned to England, he does not know if any others who came with them on the ship have been before to this coast or to the Indies, and this he answered.

He was asked why, when they were in the Bay of Shoals, trading, it being a harbor on this coast of the king Don Felipe, our lord, and, with the arrival of the ships of this garrison under the command of Captain Ecixa, they were sent a message that they should surrender and give themselves up according to the rules of war, they did so only after offering resistance and fighting, and killing some soldiers from this garrison and wounding others, and why, seeing themselves beaten, they started a fire to burn themselves with gunpowder—he said that the captain of the ship was unwilling to surrender without a fight, in which they were boarded, the captain and six other persons were killed, others were wounded, and they were overcome and captured, and that he does not know who started the fire—he only saw the ship burning; and so they were killed and captured, and this witness, and others were brought as prisoners, with their ship, to this city and handed over to the señor general, and this is what happened on the voyage from their departure from England until they were captured, and this is the truth on the oath that he swore. His statement being read to him, he said that he hears it, and he confirmed and ratified it and signed it with his name.

[Signed:] P'o de Ybarra
Julian Bodran
Before me, Alonso Garcia de la Vera, clerk.

[g]   Auto [decree]

In the city of Santo Agustín de la Florida, on the fifteenth day of the month of April in the year one thousand, six hundred and five. Seeing the above declarations and statements, from which it is evident and it seems that they were sent by Guillermo de la Mota, and that the ship is his, the señor governor and captain-general orders that the said merchant, clerk and doctor be asked to declare what person is the said Guillermo de la Mota, and what is his occupation, and where does he live, and similarly, that the doctor be asked what sassafras and china-root are good for. When the said statements have been taken everything shall be brought to him as evidence for the judicial proceedings, and this he provides and signs.

[Signed:] Pedro de Ybarra
Before me, Alonso Garcia de la Vera, clerk.

[h] Immediately the said clerk [purser] of the ship, Julian Bodran was brought before the said governor and captain-general in the presence of myself, the clerk, and, after swearing an oath and being questioned according to the above decree, he said that Guillermo de la Mota, the person who sent them and to whom the ship belongs, is a Frenchman by nationality, a native of the city of St Malo, and a merchant by occupation, who lives in England, in London, in the house of the French ambassador who is in England, and he is always in the company of the ambassador, and this is the truth under the oath that he swore, and he signed it with his name.

[Signed:] Pedro de Ybarra
Julian Bodran
Before me, Alonso Garcia de la Vera, clerk.

[i] In like manner the señor governor and captain-general had brought before him the said Beltran Rrogues, merchant, who took and received the oath in due legal form, and having done it well and properly, was asked what man is the said Guillermo de la Mota, and of what nationality, and what is his occupation and business, and where does he live—he said that Guillermo de la Mota is a Frenchman, as he has already stated, a native of the city of St Malo, the son of a merchant, who usually resides at the court of England with the ambassadors of France, because he was brought up in England and understands the language, and they send him on business to the king of France, and he serves as secretary to ambassadors; he said that when he sent them the said Guillermo de la Mota was asked by the sailors whether, if they encountered any Spanish ship on their return from the Indies, they could capture it

only by virtue of the patent, and he told them orally that they could indeed take it, and this he declared and signed and declared to be true.

Declared before the said Pedro de Ybarra.
Beltran Rrogues
Before me, Alonso Garcia de la Vera, clerk.

[j] Immediately the said doctor, Juan de Bona Ssemana, appeared before the said señor governor and captain-general. He swore on oath and under it was asked what man is Guillermo de la Mota, he who sent them, and what is his occupation, and of what nation is he, and where does he live—he said the Guillermo de la Mota is a Frenchman, a native of St Malo, the son of a nobleman, and that he lives in England on account of knowing the language of the kingdom, and always attends the ambassadors of France who are in England, and goes to Paris on business; he has heard it said that he talks very regularly with the kings of England and France.

Asked what sassafras and china-root are good for in his country, and what value they possess—he said that the sassafras that is sold in St Malo is worth eight *reales* a pound and that good china-root from China is worth two ducats a pound, and that china-root and sassafras are good for making drugs and medicines, and this is the truth and what he knows under the oath that he took, and he signed his name. And he said he was of the age (stated) in his said statement.

[Signed:] Pedro de Ybarra.
Juan de Bona Ssemana.
Before me, Alonso Garcia de la Vera, clerk.

[k]   Auto

In the city of Santo Agustín de la Florida on the seventeenth day of the month of April in the year one thousand, six hundred and five, señor Pedro de Ybarra, governor and captain-general of these provinces for the king our lord, having seen the statements of the said captain Francisco Fernandez de Ecixa, and Beltran Rrogues, and Juan de Bona Ssemana, and Julian Bodran, Frenchmen, and the patents and instructions taken from them, written in the French language, two of them on parchment, and one hand-written, and the other printed, which, at the order of his grace were translated from French into Castilian by the Frenchmen master Antonio Jeruxano, who came from La Havana, and the said Beltran Rrogues, in the presence of myself: the clerk orders that both the said patents that are translated into Castilian and the instruction and the proclamation be added to these declarations, and a transcript with two or more seals be prepared in public form and manner for despatch to his majesty in the Royal Council of the Indies... and this he provides, orders and signs with his name.

[Signed:] Pedro de Ybarra
Before me, Alonso Garcia de la Vera, clerk.

[l] This is an exact copy of both a decree, written in French, on parchment, with a seal and three fleur-de-lis, and a signature that says "EN RREY" and another that says "PER LE ROY DE NOBILES," and of an instruction written by hand on a piece of paper in the said French language, with a signature at the bottom saying Guillermo de la Mota, which are those taken from Beltran Rrogues and which contain the order for the voyage he was to make to these provinces of La Florida, and of another instruction, likewise written on parchment with a seal with three fleur-de-lis and signature saying "en RY PAR LE RROY POTIER," and of a printed proclamation, all of which likewise were taken from the said Beltran Rrogues, and, by order of señor Pedro de Ybarra, governor and captain-general of these provinces, translated from the French into the Castilian language by master Antonio Jeruxano, a Frenchman, who came from La Havana, and Juan de Bona Ssemana, before myself, the clerk, and this I testify. By order and command of the said señor governor and captain general, I, the clerk, extract the said decrees and instructions and proclamation from those that were translated into Castilian, and they are as follows.

[m]   Patent. By Command of The King

To all the lieutenant-general governors in our provinces, marshals of France, admirals, vice-admirals, bailiffs, captains of their country [capitanes de campaña], judges or their deputies, captain-governors of our fortresses, ports and bays, captain-commanders and leaders of our fighting men, both at sea and on land, and all other justices, officers and subjects who will see this patent, greetings: our dearly-beloved Guillermo de la Mota and Beltran Rrogues, of our city of St Malo in Brittany, at our own command have armed two ships named the Castor Polux and the

Polus Castor to undertake the voyage, as captains of the said ships, to mainlands and islands of America from the river Marañon to Cape Breton which is at the end of the southern land of the said America, both to trade and to discover lands and places for our benefit. We have given them our letters of permission for these motives, and desiring the profit and growth of commerce for our benefit and advantage, and that of our friends and allies of our lands and vassals, we have granted permission to the said de la Mota and Rrogues, and we permit and resolve by these present orders, to pursue the said voyage with the said ships and their crews, and to lade them with all sorts of merchandise and commodities that seem to them fitting and necessary for the success of the said voyage, with the obligation to pay the duties that are due and to reload with other merchandise which is to be brought back to our kingdoms and the lands of our friends. If the trade and discovery should be prevented or impeded by any of our vassals, friends, neighbours, or others, we permit and grant authority to the said de la Mota and Rrogues, their ships and crews, both by sea and land to take and acquire the persons and fortunes of all those who prevent and impede, or attempt to prevent and impede, the aforementioned de la Mota and Rrogues in their trade and discoveries, as enemies of our kingdom and crown. We desire and order that you have permitted what is contained in this our permission, and allow the said de la Mota and Rrogues, together with their ships and crew, to enjoy and use it fully, without doing them or allowing to be done to them any harm or injury, instead giving them all the favour and aid and assistance that might be necessary. Since this is our will we ask and require all kings, princes, potentates and republics, our friends and allies, their officers and vassals to endeavour to do what is fitting with the said men, their ships and the crews on them, so that they might freely conclude their said voyage, promising where appropriate our gratitude to those whom they might commend to us. Given in Paris on the tenth of January, in the year one thousand, six hundred and four. Henry. By command of the king, de Neville.

[n]   Instructions
Memorial of what should be done on the voyage intended, by the grace of god, in the ship named

Castro Polus and her Pinnace Polus Castro in the parts of the Western Indies and their islands in the year one thousand, six hundred and four. First, god granting good weather, you are to use it and take advantage of it to sail together, you and your pinnace. If, because of a change of weather or some other accident, you are separated, you are to have arranged the instructions and signals necessary for the one to recognise the other.

You are to make your way directly to the island of La Trinidad, remembering above all not to go leeward of it, for if you go to leeward you will not be able to reach it, if this happens go to the other islands and attempt to trade above all for tobacco; whether in the said island or in any other place, you are to try to trade for as much tobacco as you can get in exchange for your merchandise and take it away.

You are to try to trade for all the maize that you can get, and, this done, go directly on your way to La Florida, either to Santa Elena or some other harbor that you choose, where you will try to exchange your maize and tobacco for the things that they have. You are to cut sassafras, china-root, Tus bark, and other things, and load them onto your ship and pinnace. And when you have finished loading your cargo you are to go along the coast and try to reach a place called CROTUAN, concentrating upon discovering the harbors with your pinnace and long-boat, trying to trade all your maize, and learning what happened to the Englishmen who were left there. And from there you are to continue along the coast and anchor in the great river called the Rio de Gama, where you will spend the winter, and there you will try to discover if there are any mines. After wintering there, you will continue your journey in the spring for the purpose of trading along the coast of Acadia. Above all you will try to discover the mine, which, some people have assured me, is situated at forty-four and a quarter degrees; you are not to accept this yet, but instead are to look everywhere for it. When your voyage is over you are to return to this place, Plymouth, where you will find a message from me, and if by chance you arrive at Conques [Conquet?] you will find letters from me there in the house of señor Jaques Prebost or in the house of captain Jiraldo—and if on your return there is war between the French and the Spaniards, and peace has been made between the English and the Spaniards, you will arrive at the island of Guernsey [Jernesse], and there you will find letters in the house of Señor Jaymes Beaboir [James Beauvoir] or in the house of señor Belian, the merchant. You will govern yourself in everything according to the weather and the circumstances, and I leave the execution of the voyage to your discretion, I will pray to God to give you his blessing. In Plymouth on the seventeenth of May in the year one thousand, six hundred and four.

[Signed:] Guillermo de la Mota.

Throughout, whether in La Florida, Virginia, Moranbexo [Norumbega], or Acadia, you will remember to look for the grass called Oyssanc or Bissanque, which are the trees that produce silk, and also the tree called Aneda or Gumeda; and you will take care to scrutinise all the drugs, fruits, and grasses, roots, wood, dyes, flowers and minerals, and other rocks, and you will bring samples of them and mark the places where each thing is found. If you succeed in discovering the place where the beasts with the great teeth are to be found, you are only to look for them and examine the place where they are to be found. . . .

[Patent of July 14, 1600, for the Mediterranean voyage, not translated]

[o]   Proclamation

Henry, by the grace of god king of France and of Navarre, to our friends and loyal counsellors, the officers of our admiralty of Normandy, Brittany, Huyena [Guienne] and Picardy, to each of them in their own right and in the extension of their jurisdictions and districts, greetings.

We have for many important reasons ordered, charged, and constituted the Señor de Monsts [Sieur de Monts], gentleman-in-ordinary of our chamber and our lieutenant-general, to people and settle lands, coasts and mainlands, of Acadia and other adjacent areas between forty and forty-six degrees, and there to establish our authority, and henceforth to somehow ensure somewhat that our subjects be protected and assisted to frequent and settle in the said places and trade there with the savage inhabitants, as we have already declared more plainly by our letters patent issued and delivered for this purpose to the said Señor de Monts on the eighth of

November last [1603]; and in accordance with the conditions and articles under which he shall be charged with the conduct and execution of this enterprise, to help it and those who may be joined and associated with him, and to give them some profit and help to support the dispensation, it has been agreeable to us and we have promised and assured that it will not be permitted to any of our subjects, other than those who enter in association with the said person for the implementation of the said dispensation, for the space of ten years to trade in marten goods and other merchandise in the lands, harbours, rivers and approaches in the extension of his command, and this we wish for the reasons and other considerations that move us; and we instruct and order each of you in the extension of your said powers, jurisdictions and districts, for your part since we, using our full royal power and authority have expressly provided and instructed all merchants, masters and captains of ships, other of our subjects, whatever their quality and condition, and others that for the space of ten years none but those who have entered into association with the said Señor de Monsts for the said enterprise, under the articles and conventions agreed by us, are to arm ships and go in them or send them to trade for marten goods and other merchandise with the savages, frequent, trade, or communicate with the area from Cape Rase as far as forty degrees, which contains all the coast Acadia, the land of and Cape Breton, the Bays of Cencler and Calor, Isla Oradada, Gaspei and Gigigue, Desmetanles, Quimin, Tadusac, and the river of Canada, both from one shore [costa] to the other, and all the bays and rivers along the said coasts, on pain of disobedience, confiscation of all their vessels, victuals, arms and merchandise in favour of the said señor de Monts and his associates, a fine of thirty thousand livres as security, and punishment and penalty for their disobediences—and we permit you, just as we have permitted and permit the said señor de Monts and his said associates, to take, aprehend and detain the persons, ships, merchandise, arms and victuals of those who contravene this our present safeguard and ordinance, in order to bring and deliver them into the hands of the justices, who will proceed as appropriate against the persons and property of the said transgressors. This is our will, and we order and instruct you to immediately have this published and read in all the places and public squares where you deem it necessary in your said dominions and jurisdictions, so that none of our said subjects can claim to be ignorant of it, but instead will obey and comply with this our will, and to enable you to do this we have given and we give you authority, comission, and special command. Given in Paris on the eighteen of December in the year of grace one thousand, six hundred and three, and, of our reign fifteen.

    [Signed:] Henry. And lower down "por el rrey potier."

These said patents, instruction, and proclamation were taken and translated from those written in the Castilian language by the said master Antonio and Juan de Bona Ssemana, Frenchmen, and I, the clerk, extracted them. I sign with my name. Alonso Garcia de la Vera, clerk....

Ff. 13–14 are largely formal except for Pedro de Ibarra's order of 21 March 1605 that an inventory be made by various treasury officials of the captured ship's guns, etc., gear, and contents.

[p]   Inventory

Firstly the hull of the ship captured from the English, which was given the name Nuestra Señora del Rosario, its rudder, and two pumps, one at the poop and the other at the prow.

A foremast with its yard and helm gear.

A sprit-sail yard with its tackle and rigging.

A great lower sail, old and torn.

A worthless wheel.

Two old lower sails from the foremast.

An old sprit-sail.

Two iron anchors, one large the other smaller, in boxes.

An old streaming cable with three splices, with which the ship supported itself, measuring seventy-one fathoms and weighing twenty-three *arrobas*.

Three new pieces of hemp cable, measuring a hundred and seven fathoms and weighing fifty-seven *arrobas*.

Four *arrobas* and fifteen *libras* of new hemp.

Forty-seven *arrobas* of old, used hemp rigging and cordage in pieces.

Eighteen *arrobas* of hemp rigging and cordage in burnt pieces.

A used hemp sail weighing nine *arrobas*.

A small copper cauldron.

A chain and a half of iron for the nettings of the said ship, with eight iron awning-stanchions.

An iron two-pronged lever.

A boat and a tender, both small and old, belonging to the ship.

An iron marlin spike.

Four water casks.

One iron flag-staff.

Two windlass drills.

One three-footed iron stewpot.

Twenty-one muskets with cases and keys.

Five musket-barrels without cases and keys.

An old iron morion.

Three and a half *arrobas* of gunpowder.

Half an *arroba* of hemp cord.

One hundred and thirty round balls of cast iron for all types of artillery, and chain shot.

Four old iron backplates.

Six small copper ladles for the artillery, three snatch-blocks, a wad-hook, and two ferrules.

Artillery

Two bronze stone-mortars with iron ends, with four chambers—two of bronze and two of iron—one of them number two hundred and fifty-four, the other number two hundred and nineteen.

A bronze falcon with two iron covers, number two hundred and twenty-six.

Another bronze falcon like that above, with two iron chambers, two marks like zeros, and a two.

Another bronze falcon, with an iron cover and two numbers, one of them sixteen, the other twenty-nine.

Another bronze falcon with another iron cover and two numbers, one eleven and the other fifteen.

A cast-iron piece, breech number one thousand and thirty.

Another piece like that above of cast iron, number one thousand, three hundred and ten, of cast iron.

Another piece of cast iron, breech number one thousand, four hundred and thirty.

A box with various medicines.

All the things listed above were adjudged to belong to his majesty by order of the señor governor. The inventory continued for the rest of the things that came in the said ship, as follows:

Twenty-seven *arrobas* of biscuit in poor condition.

One hundred and seventy-three *arrobas* of flour in sacks.

Twenty-two and a half *arrobas* of salt.

Five barrels of pork.

Fifty-four hairy skins.

Forty tanned hides of shoe-leather.

Forty-four *varas* of small cotton cloth.

Thirty-nine rusty iron frying pans.

Twenty copper cauldrons, large and small, most of them broken.

One hundred and forty-three iron handaxes.

Twelve iron pickaxes.

Six iron chains.

Two hundred iron pruning-knives.

Two hundred and six boxes of butcher's knives.

One hundred and sixteen boxes of small knives.

Sixty-three wooden-handled knives.

Sixty-three iron points like daggers.

Twenty-seven large water coolers.

Twenty-four large, wooden-handled knives.

Eighteen iron rasps with wooden handles.

Twenty-one iron hinges [*bisarnias*, meaning doubtful]

Thirty iron hand saws with wooden handles.

One hundred and twenty-eight tools like small tongs.

Twenty-three iron bills.

Four hammer heads.

Twenty-one iron reaping hooks.

Four iron harpoons.

Two hundred and fifty long iron lances like javelins.

A small box with a quantity of small harpoons and iron points.

Twelve large iron swords.

Four wooden scoops with iron handles.

A quarter set of nails weighing sixteen *arrobas*.

A grindstone.

Three barrels full of tobacco, amounting to sixty-five bundles.

Seven thirds of tallow weighing sixteen *arrobas*.

A barrel full of pitch.

Forty-three bundles of sarsaparilla.

A cask and two barrels containing white flour.

Another with a little beer.

A pile of china-root.

Two hundred and sixteen *arrobas* of sassafras wood. . . .

[The remaining material is formal, indicating what was done with these items. Some were publicly sold—the proceeds going to the treasury. The proceeds in all amounted to 9,247 reales.]

767. November 21, 1605. Juan Menéndez Marqués to an unknown religious in Spain about the seizure of the *Castor and Pollux*.

Juan Menéndez Marqués, treasurer of Florida, attempted to link up the recent capture of the Castor and Pollux *and the documents obtained with it, with his earlier experience in the expedition of 1588 (749 and see 746), and the depositions of Pedro Diaz in 1589 (454) and of David Glavin in 1600 (755). His description of the entrance through the Carolina Outer Banks to Roanoke Island is accurate (although we know of no Spaniards having gone there after 1588), as is his description of the entrance to Chesapeake Bay (the shores of which he describes briefly). He did not think of the "Gran Río de la Gama" as being Gomes's Penobscot but considered it rather to be Chesapeake Bay.*

A.G.I., Seville, Santo Domingo 224, 54/5/9; copies in J. T. Connor Papers, Division of Manuscripts, Library of Congress, and in J. G. Shea MS 29/3, Georgetown University Library (the latter without a precise source reference). The latter seems to have been from the original letter; the former is from an unsigned and unattributed copy. Translation (using both copies).

News reached here of an enemy ship which was loading sassafras on this coast in the province of Guale near Santa Elena in the Bay of Shoals. The Señor governor sent a small squadron in search of it, and God deigned to grant them such good fortune that, with the loss of only two men killed, they overcame it and brought it to this garrison. They bring papers, instructions and patents of the King of France, concerning trade, commerce and discovery of mines on this coast, and a settlement which it is known the English had a long time ago [literally "many days ago"]. I believe that the Señor governor is informing His Majesty of all this, and that it must cause some concern.

Keep on the look-out, Your Paternity, and understand that no Spaniard can talk about or has actually seen this coast between latitudes 33 and 40 degrees other than captain Vicente Gonçales and the pilot Gines Pinçon, who in the company of the said captain and myself—when I was sergeant-major here—went by order of the general who is in heaven [Pedro Menéndez Marqués] to learn and seek information about this settlement—and comparing the indications and signs that we found with the *Relaçion* of Pero Diaz Pimienta [Pedro Diaz, March 21, 1589], pilot and resident of Garachico, and David Glavid [or Glavin, February 8, 1600], Irishman, who were in the said settlement, we found that it was in a spot just above latitude thirty-five degrees, and that it is marked by three large sand-dunes on the beach; it has two entrances—that on the northern side is the good one and small ships can enter through it; inside there is a large bay, and, going from east-north-east to west-south-west, mountainous, well-wooded land can be seen: they say it is an island and that there was the settlement and fort of the Englishman.

The Bay of Mother of God of Jacan, at latitude 37 degrees, is entered from north-west south-east or, to put it better, from south-east north-west, for its transverse position is south-east. It has a mouth of about three leagues, without any sort of shoal or reef in the mouth, and from its middle to the southern side is seven or eight fathoms deep. About three leagues round to the north-west, and all around, there is a large bay, from which the land becomes almost invisible [literally "which is almost lost sight of from land"]. And then, coasting to the north, many fine harbours and fresh-water rivers—the narrowest is at least two leagues wide—are seen on the coast of the western side, until at latitude forty degrees it ends in a large gulf of fresh-water, surrounded by hills from which powerful rivers descend, with valleys and land well-shaded and apparently fertile for (livestock) breeding and cultivation. And inside the said bay at latitude 38 degrees we saw Indians wearing gold *chagalas* [gorgets?] around their necks. This bay, I suspect, must be where the English and French put the so-called Gran Rio de la Gama [literally "where the English and French call..."], and if it seems convenient to Your Paternity to report this to the lords of the council, you may do so with the satisfaction that this account is correct and true, and I ask God to confound the wicked designs of the enemies of our

Holy Catholic Faith and to always give victory over them to His Majesty. Amen.

I gave a very full, written report of the council a long time ago of what happened on the aforementioned voyage, and of the discovery of the said harbour and bay

[Signed:] Juan Menéndez Marqués

768. February 27, 1606. The Council of the Indies to Philip III on the disposition of the *Castor and Pollux* and her men.

This tells us all that exists about the subsequent history of the men (left to the Indians so long as they cared to keep them alive), the ship Castor and Pollux *(reequipped for the Spanish West Indies squadron), and the rewarding of Pedro de Ibarra (one fifth of the assessed value of the ship and 1,500 ducats as well), while the utmost secrecy was to be maintained about the affair itself. This was the advice of the Council of the Indies to the king, and it may probably be assumed that it was adopted.*

A.G.I., Seville, Indiferente General 1867; 147/5/16; transcript in Division of Manuscripts, Library of Congress, translated.

Sire: In an opinion of 14 October last year the council informed Your Majesty of a certain capture made by Pedro de Ybarra, governor and captain general of the provinces of La Florida, of a ship with nine pieces of artillery and 21 French and English prisoners, who went to trade with the Indians of those coasts; and that, although from the gravity of the case they deserved to be punished with rigour, it was not decided to do this until a report had been made to Your Majesty, on account of the inconveniences which might increase with respect to the peaces with France and England; and that to avoid expense to the exchequer of Your Majesty he had meanwhile sent them inland, in charge of the chiefs, with an order that they should not allow them to communicate with each other or to see the sea; and that [the matter] having been considered by the Council, together with the patents and instructions which they carried (copies of which, translated, into Castilian, were sent to Your Majesty with the declarations of some of the prisoners), which

show that they went with the intention of trading in those parts, and that they traded where they could, and robbed on the sea many of the vassals of Your Majesty, it had seemed appropriate that, for having contravened what is established by laws and *cédulas* of Your Majesty, and on account of the great information and knowledge that these prisoners have of those provinces and their coasts, and the harm that could result from this, they should be punished, doing justice to them.

Likewise it was reported to Your Majesty in the said opinion that the said governor, Pedro de Ibarra, had requested Your Majesty that, in consideration of the 20 years that he has served in Flanders, and of the difficulties and losses, to both health and pocket, that he suffered in the voyage that he undertook to La Florida, to do him the favour [of granting him] the said ship with its gear [*adreços*], or the sum at which it would seem it has been valued by the senior shipmaster de Rivera and Your Majesty's pilot there, and the fifth part of the said prize which belongs to Your Majesty, as it is customary to do for those who have served and serve in similar posts and circumstances; and that it had seemed to the council that, on account of the care and good diligence that he had displayed on this occasion, and that he displayed in all things in his charge, and in order to encourage him to continue to do so, he might be granted the said fifth share, and a sum of one thousand five hundred ducats, paid from the subsidy of the said garrison, rather than the ship, and its gear and artillery, these being reserved, as they have to be, for Your Majesty, since it seemed that the ship was suitable for the Armada of Barlovento.

And since Your Majesty so far has not ruled on this opinion, and on account of the fact that the delay in putting into execution the punishment of these pirates could produce greater inconveniences, for the Indians are a people which is easily aroused, as well as on account of the continuing cost to the royal exchequer of the residence [in this court] of the person who brought this report and awaits its resolution before leaving, it has seemed appropriate to the Council to send this reminder to Your Majesty on both points, and to entreat you to condescend to order that all be resolved with brevity, so that, with the same, the governor might be informed of what decision Your Majesty has deigned to take. In Valladolid, 27 February 1606.

Chapter Ninety-eight
The Victory of the Friars, 1606–1612

769. May 19, 1606. Spanish activity on the Gulf coast.

What precisely was the role of Antonio Matheos, who is described as Lieutenant of Apalache, is not clear. Pedro de Ibarra had clearly sent a party to set up a base (called San Luis) for reconnoitering along the coast from Apalache Bay and Apalachicola Bay to Pensacola Bay, Mobile Bay, and beyond. Matheos was in contact with the Apalache Indians and through them with the Indians of Tama (central Georgia). Christian Indians (Timucua from the east?) are also mentioned. There is a rather vague hunt for some unidentified "English" going on, but it is not clear that there were any English in the area (although there may have been a few shipwrecked French). The extension of the range of the Florida colony into this area was a novel development, but no permanent posts were maintained there and Matheos must shortly have returned to San Agustín.

A.G.I., Seville, Santo Domingo 224, 54/5/9; copy in Library of Congress, Division of Manuscripts, translated.

A letter from the Lieutenant of Apalache, Antonio Matheos, to the Señor Governor and Captain General of Florida, about the return of the English to the province of Apalachicoli.
San Luis, 19th May 1606.

Señor Governor and Captain General. I received your lordship's letter, dated the 23rd of last month, which went from hand to hand and arrived in mine on the 30th of the same month; I have also received another from your lordship, of the 27th of the same month, which was brought by Rodrigo Ximénes, and came into my hands on the 15th day of this month. I did not reply straight-way and at once to this second letter, as you ordered me to, because none of the Indians which I had sent to Apalachicoli had come back until today, when two of them have arrived: another two stayed in the said province, for reasons which your lordship will see herein. The news they bring is this: they went, as I had ordered them, to all the places in the said province, and everywhere they were made welcome except in the places Casista and Caveta: for they had sent them two messages before they arrived at the said two towns, in which they told them that they did not want them to go there, for they were from Apalache and hence their enemies; thus, they should try not to go there, for they would not be able to go peacefully; but despite this, the scouts decided to go there and risk what might happen to them, sending them with the second messenger the message that they were not from Apalache but from Thama [sino es Thamas], and that all they were coming for was to see their relations and buy something, so they should not take offence. And when the said two scouts arrived between the said two places, they were playing a ball game [*pelota*]: they waited there until the game ended, and in all this interval of time nobody came to speak to them, even though one of the scouts did have some relations there. And coming to the place of Casista, before they went into it the chief of the said town came up to them and asked them where they were going, and hadn't he sent them a message not to enter his town? For apart from not getting anything to eat there, nobody was going to talk to them, for he knew that they had been sent on some reconnaissance mission, and since they were enemies of theirs they were not to enter his town. So he gave them a canoe to cross the river in, and they went on to Tasquique: here and in Colome they were made very welcome, and they were told that although the Christians had burnt their towns, they were prepared to put up with it, for it had been their fault, although on the whole the chiefs of Casista and Caveta were to blame, who had deceived and entangled the others by bringing in the English and forcing them to take them in, and they had fled to the mountains, which was why they had burnt their places: but that if another such time came they would not flee, for they knew now how the Spanish acted. In Caveta they gave them the same reception as in Casista, giving them to understand that although they were sowing, they did not intend to remain there; so also the said scouts say that in these two places nothing has been done nor begun to be done, and in the other two, that is Colome and Tasquique, there are many things, both finished and begun. The said scouts also say that the chief of Apalachicoli told them to come at top speed to warn me that when five men of his place had been hunting in the Chicara area of Calossa [*la chicara of Calossa*], which is five days journey distant from the said province, they had heard a number of shots and seen from far away very many people who were coming towards the river Pedernales; they had not worked out what people they were, for they had seen them from far away, and one of the five who were hunting left at once to give this news to the said chief, and for this reason, and to find out who the people are, the said two scouts remained there. They also say the said chief said that he would be careful about posting sentinels, and when he knew who the people were, whether they were English, Chichimecos or Chiscas, whether they had come to that province or to this, he would tell us with all speed; and they also say that the English who were there went to the province of Ticopache to talk to the chiefs and leaders, and when they returned to Caveta they went off to San Jorge, telling them that within two months they would be back to see them with many more men. This news seems to me to have little foundation, because it was only the said chief and another man from another place who said this, for although the men from Thama have brothers and relations there, they say that they said nothing to them; I judge the scouts to be as honest as all of them. Regarding the people they say are approaching, I think this is invention too, for if it were true, I reckon that they would not have told us; even so, I shall send word to the Lieutenant at Timucua that he should be on his guard, which is always necessary in those parts.

They say that the said chief of Apalachicoli is going to come to this province next month, and I reckon that he will come with another plot in mind like the last one; they also say that he was wanting to go for the royal weapons [to steal guns?] and bring them to his town. He has not replied to the note I sent him, for the Indian who took it has not returned. Chestnuts, the said chief says he has been unable to find; he sent a little yellow and white earth which Juan de Florencia will bring to your Lordship: he will leave here the day after tomorrow. Blue stones or earth are not found over there. They say there is some very good earth in Timucua; I shall send to find out where the yellow earth is from: it is very good, and goes red when you burn it with a candle.

The chief from Tavasa came and brought twenty-four Christians, men and women; I did not give him the axe, nor the beads which your Lordship ordered me to in your letter, because he had already gone, and it would have been a pity to have given it to him, for he is the greatest of ruffians: for in his presence there came out to the road when they were coming two of his vassals, and one of those who had carried my note they wanted to kill, but the Chacatos turned on them and gave him a thorough beating, and one wanted to finish him off with a hatchet; if the one who was carrying the note had not told him not to do such a thing, for I never order them to mistreat anyone, and if things had not been the way they are, the chief would not have gone until the other Christians had come and taken the arrogant brute bound; but we must dissimulate until the proper time comes for him to pay for it all. I think they are all getting the impression that we Christians are not men, and it is very necessary, when occasion arises, to show them what's what. The Chicaras, according to the said chief of Tabara, came to his town saying that they were coming to this province, but they have not turned up; it could be they thought better of it. The Ticopaches had also done so, if it is true that the English went there; and as regards the presents which your Lordship says has to be made to them, it seems to me that it will be better not to give them anything unless they have given signs of deserving it.

As regards the report which your Lordship requires me to make of the way to the shore of Espíritu Santo, I am not neglecting this; recently I have made several investigations, but not as many as I think are necessary for what your Lordship wishes, because some of the Indians are at war with others of them, and not knowing the land, although of the news I have received I have had a written account for more than six months, as the man who writes this will tell your Lordship, in which I have indicated the rivers and the places and the distance there is from one to another, and the reason for my not sending it on to your Lordship is that I don't think it's very good, although I can understand it well enough since it was me that made it. From here to the place of Panzacola [on Pensacola Bay] you can go by canoe from San Marcos, taking experienced Indians, which there are in this province in the place of the Chines, and from there it is necessary to get in touch with the Indians of La Mobila [Mobile Bay], who will be about twelve leagues away from Panzacola; for these Mobilas, since they are at war with the Panzacolas, have never come to this province, and it would not be difficult, if we could talk to them, to find out about the said bay. Beyond the Mobilas and the river of that name is that of Estanani, four days' journey away. Although the main place of this province, which is called Ducascaxi, is, according to the Indians there, seven days distant from the sea, travelling by the said river, and so it looks to me from the navigation chart that this river is not fifty leagues from the said bay, if this business over Apalachicoli wasn't in the state it is, with the permission of your Lordship, as I asked for it last year, in less than a month I would go and come to Panzacola and Estanani and I would give news to your Lordship, but certain news, about the said bay, and I reckon that if this reconnaissance trip is not made first the journey will not be very safe, or at least its success will not be assured: your Lordship will decide in this as you think best.

I sent the maize to the Lieutenant of Timucua. I think, according to the news I have, it is already in Santa Fee; four Indians were needed for the canoe: Alonso de Morales paid one of them because he was carrying 230 kilos of maize for himself; the canoe cost nothing, being a service of His Majesty; I paid the other three Indians with the ten knives that had come from the stores, and two more which I added to suit their work; the Portuguese and the smith are staying in this garrison, and Francisco Vélez is going back as your Lordship orders, and the reason for his not being the bearer of this letter is that he is not very expert in the paths; Lorenço Guerrero is taking it, who has promised me to put it into your hands in six days. May God keep your Lordship many years. San Luis, May 19th, 1606. The servant of your Lordship, I kiss your hand.

[Signed:] Antonio Matheos.

770. March to June, 1606. The triumphal visitation of the Bishop of Cuba.

As has been seen, the friars were in some difficulty with the civil authorities, but they were also making such spectacular progress in the conversion of the Indians that they persuaded the Bishop of Cuba, Juan Cabezas Altamirano, whose diocese included Florida, to come to Florida. He could settle quarrels between them and the governor in their favor (he did not), and give a convincing demonstration that Florida was now a Christian country that deserved every consideration as such (which he did). The bishop did his ecclesiastical work well, confirming all the Spaniards, half-breeds, and older Indian converts in the San Agustín area to the number of 350, and then going (often at some risk to himself) to confirm the older Indian converts and to baptize new ones in outlying missions. Altogether, he ministered in his visitation to well over 2,000 persons. The episcopal visitation was very much a turning point in Florida history. It is clear that the movement to abandon Florida for secular reasons was waning in 1606. Now a convincing demonstration had been given as to why it would not be possible to withdraw for ecclesiastical reasons. Whether the Christian Indian population was as large and stable as the visitation appeared to disclose was another matter.

A.G.I., Seville, Santo Domingo 235, 54/5/20; printed in Luis Gerónimo de Oré, Relación histórica de la Florida, edited by A. López, I (1931), 37–43, newly translated.

His Excellency Friar Don Juan Cabezas Altamirano set out from the city of Santiago de Cuba on the 10th October 1605, and arrived at the town of San Salvador de Bayamo on the thirteenth of that month. While he was there, Captain Alonso Díaz Mejía arrived from the provinces of Florida, who informed the prelate that between Governor Pedro de Ibarra and the men of religion who were in the city of San Agustín and the Indian towns there was great disagreement, and that it would be as well if he went there himself to patch them up. "And also, in view of the many conversions there were of native Indians brought into our holy catholic faith, and as they had baptized them in conformity with it, in order that he should confirm them, together with the necessity which the neighbours and inhabitants of the said city of San Agustín had of the said Sacrament of Confirmation, since no prelate from among his predecessors had gone to those provinces since they had been discovered and settled, as is well known." These arguments persuaded the Bishop to go to the provinces of Florida, and he told Alonso Díaz that he would set off with him: but as they were making preparations for the voyage, a fierce storm came on them, which put out of action the boat that His Excellency was to use: he had to leave Bayamo for Puerto del Príncipe, and waited a long time to see if a boat could be prepared to take him to Florida. After many difficulties which there were in the way of undertaking the journey, he arrived at the city of San Agustín on the 15th March 1606, "where they gave him the best reception they could: he visited the said holy church, and ordered to be published a general edict of visitation, and then in succession another of general ordination: and having on Holy Thursday blessed the Holy Oil and Chrism, as is normal on such days, and with the ceremonies that the law prescribes, he performed the ceremony on Holy Saturday, the 25th of that month and year, and celebrated the aforesaid general ordination, in which were brought into the Orders, of both natives of this city and children of natives of it (with the correct ceremonies for all orders preceding) a number of more than twenty ordinands, with the helpers that came with His Excellency. And having published the banns for a general confirmation, His Excellency celebrated this Sacrament in the same holy church on Easter Sunday, where it seems that there were confirmed, of all people, adult and younger, several children of local inhabitants (according to the census that was taken of it) three hundred and fifty people, with

the accustomed solemnity, His Excellency publicly declaring to them the said Sacrament of Confirmation and the circumstances thereof.

Continuing with the said confirmations, His Excellency went to a town which is near this city, a quarter of a league away, called Nombre de Dios, on the 2nd April of the same year. Its chief is Doña María: she is married to a Spaniard, a soldier of this garrison. It is said that this chief has more than three thousand Indians in her district: although they are not all Christian, they are friendly: they are divided among many other towns. It is said that Doña María takes a very real interest in the affairs of this garrison and the Spaniards in it. She was confirmed, and two legitimate children of hers, and also two hundred and thirteen natives and a few Spaniards, probably as many as twenty. In charge of this teaching center [dotrina] is Father Romero, of the Order of St Francis.

His Excellency left this city of San Agustín on a visit to the native Indians, and for their confirmation, on the 11th of the said month of April, in a boat: this was given to him by the governor of these provinces, for this purpose, and to carry some guard soldiers on deck. His Excellency arrived at San Pedro, which is twenty leagues distant, on the twelfth of the same month. This parish is in the charge of Father Friar Juan Bautista de Capilla, of the same Order. This town is the head of the district whose chief is the aforementioned Doña María. They say she very often lives there; at the moment it is situated on a small islet, because there are a few narrow channels of salt water that separate it from the mainland. There was confirmed in this parish one legitimate son of the said Doña María. They say he is the heir, for he is older than the others she has. Also confirmed were Juan Quevedo, chief of San Juan: Don Antonio, chief of San Antonio: Gáspar, chief of Santo Domingo: Pedro López, chief of Tocoyo: Andrés López, chief of Putumba. They are also subjects of the said Doña María. Of the other natives there were also confirmed three hundred and eight people, of all ages, on the thirteenth and fourteenth of that April as appears on the census that was taken thereof.

On the 18th April of the same year, His Excellency left the said parish of San Pedro in the same boat, sailing inland from there by some channels of salt water. He was unable to leave earlier from this parish of San Pedro, because of very strong contrary winds that prevented sailing. He arrived at the parish of Talaje on the 22nd of April. It is ten leagues from the said parish of San Pedro. This parish is held by Friar Diego Delgado, of the Order of St Francis. He visited the church, as elsewhere. This town is on the mainland, on the banks of a full river of fresh water. At the order of the chief, who is called Don Diego, the natives received His Excellency with the best celebrations they could and great cheer. This Don Diego is a greater chief than any nearby: the others all obey him, despite each being chief of their own town. There were confirmed himself, his son in law Don Marco, and the chief of Asao, and that of Fasque, and the chief of Alaje, and that of Ofulo, and that of Cascangue and of Luque, towns in the surrounding area: and from them came to the Confirmation two hundred and seventy two people, in two Confirmation ceremonies, for they waited for the people to collect together from their farms.

On the same day, the 24th April, His Excellency left Talaje, continuing his voyage, visit, and confirmation journey in the same boat. On the 26th of April he arrived at Espogache. This town is subject to the said Don Diego. It is on the mainland. There is no friar in the parish. The said Friar Don Delgado sometimes comes here, for it is no more than six leagues from his parish of Talaje. His Excellency visited the church, as usual. On the 26th April were confirmed the chief of this town and that of Falquiches, and that of Capala, and that of Espogache. In this parish His Excellency baptized the chief of Tuquepi, and confirmed him with the catechism, because it was and is understood that his conversion is of great significance since he is chief of a nation of Indians called the Salchiches. They are warlike people, and not Christian, as is known. With the conversion of the chief is understood their conversion also, and so that they should not change their mind the Bishop speeded up proceedings, with the baptism and confirmation in the said manner: His Excellency baptized and confirmed him himself, and the wife of this chief also, who wanted to become Christian too. There were also confirmed two hundred and eight people, as appears on the census. In this parish it happened that His Excellency went with the treasurer Juan Menéndez,

who was going as leader of the soldiers who were with His Excellency to the community house of the said natives, where, on Sundays, they used to receive him in their way, because that is where they were given the talk which is customary on the arrival of His Excellency, and he proposed, through interpreters, to the Indians that he would take what they were owing to His Majesty, since he was spending so much on their behalf without any interest at all, simply for the sake of showing them the way to Heaven, and that His Majesty was sending His Excellency and the Fathers for that purpose: and the said Father, Friar Diego Delgado, was there, and said that they were not coming on behalf of His Majesty, and that if they had come it was at the command of their prelate, and that His Excellency should not say that in the other parishes, because they would not let him. To which His Excellency replied that he was more honest than them, and he was proud of it, and so he ordered the same thing to be said in the other parishes, where the other Fathers made no objection.

On the 29th of April of the same year, His Excellency went continuing his visits and confirmations, to which purpose he left the said parish of Espogache in the same boat. He arrived at the parish of Guale on the 30th April. It is a distance of six leagues. It is in the charge of Father Friar Pedro Ruiz. He visited the church, as usual. The Indians welcomed him with great cheer. He carried out confirmation on the first day of May of that year. The following chiefs were confirmed: the head chief [el mico], the chief of Aluste, that of Otafe, that of Oculeya and of Unelcapa, and that of Culopala, and that of Talapo, and that of Chatufo. All these chiefs are subjects of the said Don Diego. There were also confirmed two hundred and eighty six people. Guale is a small island.

Continuing the said visits and confirmations, His Excellency left the said parish of Guale on the fourth of May the same year in the same boat, arriving on his visit on his way to this said city of San Agustín and other towns, where there were some of the said natives still to be confirmed: he arrived at the parish of San Pedro the seventh of the same month, and going through the same confirmations again, there were some confirmed who missed it the first time, and they are now incorporated with the others who were confirmed in the same parish: and continuing this visit, he came to the parish of San Juan on the eighth of the same month and year, where were four Fathers (and with them there happened to them what is described in the report that accompanies this one). This parish is apparently in the charge of Father Friar Francisco Pareja. His Excellency visited the church, and said mass there as in all the other parishes he visited. On the nineteenth of May His Excellency confirmed, in the church of this parish, Doña María and Don Alonso, chief of Vera Cruz, and Doña Francisca, chief of San Mateo, and the chief of San Pablo, and the chief of Vera Cruz, and the chief of Chinica. They are all subjects of the said Doña María, chief of San Pedro. There were also confirmed four hundred and eighty two people, both from the said towns of the chiefs and from the said parish of San Juan. All these said natives of this parish and of the others which His Excellency visited are such poor people, in such poverty that they go with their bodies naked, except that the women wear a little grass for decency, so it was necessary for His Excellency to give them and provide them with wax and bandages for these confirmations at his own expense, which he took for this purpose from this city of San Agustín, as is well known. With this His Excellency finished these visits and confirmations in those districts, and he came back to this city of San Agustín on the 12th of May that same year: here he is waiting for suitable weather to go and visit the other natives that live inland in what is called the province of Potano, for since there has been a great deal of rain he has not yet gone.

And when the weather got better here, so it appeared, it seems that His Very Reverend Excellency left this city of San Agustín for the purpose of the said visits and confirmations in the said province of Potano, on the 12th June of the same year: by land, although there was a great deal of water on the paths, as the ground is marshy and easily flooded. He arrived the same day at the town of Tocoy, and having visited the church, as usual, he confirmed in the said town, on the thirteenth of this month and year, ninety people. There was confirmed the chief of Ais. They are very poor people, like the others. It was necessary for this Confirmation for His Excel-

lency to provide them with wax and bandages, because they had none and could not buy them, they were so poor. This is agreed in the census that was taken of it.

On the 15th June of the same year, His Excellency left the same town of Tocoy in furtherance of his visits and confirmations. He came to a town which they call Antonico. It is twenty leagues distant from the town of Tocoy, and the town of Tocoy is five leagues distant from this city here. He went by boat, for he could not go by land, because of some very large lakes, which the natives go over, for they go by canoe, on the fifteenth of the same month and year. Some Indians from some towns that are in the neighbourhood were summoned, and when they had arrived His Excellency confirmed on the sixteenth and seventeenth of that month, two hundred and twenty five people, of all ages. The chief of that town was confirmed, and also the chief of Filcoche, and that of Elanogue, and that of Calvay, and that of Yaocay, which are nearby towns. The people, like the rest, are very poor and needy. These parishes are held by Friars of St. Francis. From there His Excellency came back to this city, not having any more towns to visit nor confirm, on the 19th of June of the same year, where His Excellency is staying, to see if in the payship that is expected to arrive on the first of July next a prelate from Nueva España is coming to bring together these Fathers and leave them in peace with the said governor Pedro de Ibarra. In the meanwhile, His Majesty should provide and send what His Excellency asks him for by letter, and also set up constitutions and statutes by which in spiritual matters the churchmen and laymen can be regulated and governed, until the provincial synod determines completely what is best for the reform of the customs of the whole diocese . . .

771. November 1, 1609. Fray Juan Baptista de Capilla to Philip III.

The bitter animosity of the friars to Ibarra's attempt to keep some check on their activities in the interests of the civil and military population is well illustrated in this letter.

A.G.I., Seville, Santo Domingo 235; 54/5/20; printed in Luis Gerónimo de Oré, Relación histórica de la Florida, *edited by A. López, II (1933), 36–37, translated.*

Sire

On other occasions those men of religion who are here in these provinces for the conversion of the natives have written and explained to Your Majesty the great trouble which we have had and still have, caused by what we have suffered, and still suffer, for some time at the hands of Pedro de Ibarra, Your Majesty's Governor in these provinces, spreading false stories about some of us and exiling others; he has done this to the preachers of the Holy Gospels because they criticize some vices and scandalous incidents and advised him to love virtues and reward them, and to those servants of Your Majesty who have been and still are unwilling to go along with his wishes and bless his actions and behavior, although they are acting in defence of the Royal Exchequer: he has been and is persecuting them in such a way that it has been and is a great trouble and annoyance both to the Spaniards and men of religion, and to the native Indians themselves: for his actions and words can only be held in check by God and by Your Majesty, whose representative he is in the government and protection of your kingdoms. And in this great area of Florida it would be possible to win over many more minds and extend our territory if the men of religion were helped with a bit more enthusiasm and ministers, who with only evangelical words and the alms which Your Majesty orders to be given to them for sustenance would be able to win over much more, since people turn up every day asking for baptism and conversion: and since there are not the ministers this is not dealt with: as more than 28 chiefs are asking in the province of Timucua and Great Apalache, and there is no one to go and help them: even if six men of religion were requested, twelve more would be needed.

And since Pedro de Ibarra fulfilled his time of six years on the 20th October, which was when he took up his post here in the name of Your Majesty, with the humility which we owe to Our Lord and King as faithful vassals and chaplains we beseech and beg Your Majesty that, with the speed the case needs, You should be pleased to provide and send us in his place someone to govern us with enthusiasm for Christianity and good intentions, to help and encourage this work of the conversion of minds which we have in hand: and that he should not be gripped by ambition and unreasonable greed, but be content with reason and moderation; that he should respect priests and treat them with the honour due to the priestly order, reward virtues and hate vices. And really, so that this work of conversion can advance, it seems best that Your Majesty should name one of the servants that he has here who have served him for many years, who would be very acceptable to the Spanish men of religion and to the natives, because for these lands it is very much to the point to have experience of its affairs, unlike some of those who come who lose a lot of time before they can govern properly. If Your Majesty orders it in this way, we are sure that it will turn out to be greatly to the service of God and of Your Majesty, whom may God preserve for many years for the defence of the faith, as Christianity needs, and so that with the necessary speed this garrison and these provinces are reassured with the remedy for which we ask and beg Your Majesty, as it is most necessary.

From San Agustín, Florida, November the 1st 1609.

[Signed:] Fray Juan Baptista de Capilla.

772.   May 5, 1609. Francisco Pareja and Alonso Serrano to Philip III on the need of the missionaries.

Although Father Pareja and Fray Serrano claimed to have settled some of their differences with the governor, Pedro de Ibarra (who was about to give up his post), they remained insistent that additional missionaries who had arrived should be paid out of the establishment, and that still further friars were needed.

A.G.I., Seville, Santo Domingo 232, 54/5/17; J. T. Connor Collection, Division of Manuscripts, Library of Congress, translated.

My Lord,

In every matter that has arisen concerning the

Court of Your Majesty we have written giving an account of some things and asking for others of which we found ourselves in need: and what was most urgently requested so far was an end to the many altercations there were in these provinces between the Governors of Your Majesty and the men of the Church: Thank God, these are over now after the measures taken to deal with them, and we live in harmony, and Pedro de Ibarra, Governor of Your Majesty in these provinces, despite these altercations, has helped us charitably, providing us with what has been asked of him, particularly in matters concerning the faith, the spread of it among the Indians, or new mission areas, as he has done in the new ones recently established, giving what was needed for them together with his goodwill, which is not the least important thing. The only matter in which he seems to us to have acted with some meanness has been in not being prepared to give us payment for the new ministers, of which we dealt at greater length last year, 1608, and again last March, 1609, wherein he says that he has not forwarded it for lack of an order from Your Majesty.

There have also been made to Your Majesty on our behalf some representations concerning things that need to be done: such as providing men of the Church, who are badly needed, for the harvests are great and the harvesters are few, and some of them worn out with the daily hardship suffered in this work of conversion, for every day, God be praised, there are coming to us countless souls to whom we are hoping to teach the doctrine, with many others, if God grants us His favour and Your Majesty yours (as You do), and it is true that after the grace of God, which touches these heathens, the Governor of Your Majesty has known how to attract them, who it seems has seen the present increase of Our Holy Catholic Faith and what was necessary to avoid disappointing those who are asking for the water of baptism, taking men of the Church away from other missions to give them to these, so that more men of the Church are needed: we raised this with the Governor, who saw how necessary they are and gave us his word that with this report he will ask Your Majesty for them. May Our Lord God be pleased to give Your Majesty life and health so that as so Catholic a King he may raise and spread the Faith in these new kingdoms, since on the part of the Chaplains and the Governors of Your

Majesty the will for such a Holy Work will not be lacking. May Heaven prosper the Royal Person of Your Majesty.

From this Convent of the Conception, San Agustín, Florida, 5th May 1609.

Humble chaplains and vassals of Your Majesty.

[Signed:] Friar Francisco Pareja,
Superior
Friar Alonso Serrano, Councillor

[Addressed:] Catholic Royal Majesty the King Our Lord in His Kingdoms of Spain, May Our Lord God keep him.

773. June 20, 1615. Pedro de Ibarra explains the nature of his controversy with the friars, 1603–1609.

A.G.I., Seville, Santo Domingo 235; 54/5/20; printed in Luis Gerónimo Oré, Relación histórica de la Florida, *edited by A. López, II (1933), 38–44, extract.*

Sir:

In the year 1602, Your Majesty ordered me to go and govern the provinces of Florida. I found there five friars of the order of St Francis, and as afterwards the land was increasing, these men of religion and some chiefs asked me to ask Your Majesty to send them more friars, because of the great need they had of them, as I did: and You were pleased to send some, not as many as there were after I came, and they wrote during my time as governor that they were all needed for the missions. The expense which each one incurs each year from Your Majesty is one thousand five hundred and thirty five reales. The argument I had with them was this: when I saw that the prelate was asking me for so many friars that he said he needed, and that many of them were not present in their missions, but were there in the city of San Agustín, where they were not needed, nor was there a post there for any more than their prelate and one companion (and for those who were unwell to go there to recover), who received every four months the food for the others who were in their missions, and that others were going outside these provinces somewhere else, I told their prelate to tell them to attend to their duties, that the holy zeal of Your Majesty should be fulfilled in that task of conversion, and that he should give them this order because I knew that there were dying in their missions many children without baptism and other people without confession; when I saw that this was getting me nowhere, I told the crown agent, who was in charge of the provisions, that he should send none to any friar that was not in his mission, or legitimately held up within the provinces: and that put things right. The same can be done now, if Your Majesty orders that pay should only be given to those who are present at their posts, except for the prelate and his companion; and if they want to be there where they are not needed, or to go outside the provinces, that should not be at the expense of Your Majesty: in this way either a large part of the Exchequer will be saved, or they will go and do the job Your Majesty sends them there to do there, present at their missions....

Madrid, 20 June 1615.

[Signed:] Pedro de Ibarra.

FLORIDA IN 1612

THE TWO FOLLOWING letters, one from Juan Fernández de Olivera, written on October 13, 1612, shortly before his death (774), and the other from the Governing Body of the Franciscan Custodianship in Florida, October 16, 1612 (775), sum up very well the situation of the secular and missionary elements at this time. The Franciscans look back to a time not far distant when their Christianity was opposed and derided, where now it is accepted and called for by chiefs far beyond their borders (at least so they say). They admit the difficulties that the governor has in obtaining sufficient soldiers to give them protection in, for example, the new mission they wish to establish at Apalache. At the same time, they clearly regard their work as more important than that of the civil officials who are there, in their view, to serve them as far as possible. Olivera, on the other hand, does not complain about the additional twenty-one friars who have just arrived, but he does point out that there are now fifty friars occupying fifty of the 300 places in the garrison, that he is short of some fifty soldiers and that, of his remaining 200, not all are able-bodied. He does, however, report progress in the western part of the peninsula, where a mission has been received in a friendly manner by the Carlos [Calusa] Indians of Tampa Bay. He hears no news and has no contact with Virginia, which clearly he does not regard as a menace to the continuance of a Spanish Florida.

774. October 13, 1612. Juan Fernández de Olivera to Philip III.

A.G.I., Seville, Santo Domingo 232; 54/5/17, no.73; copy in J. T. Connor Collection, Division of Manuscripts, Library of Congress, extracts, translated.

Sire,

The ships that I sent to Seville for arms and other provisions arrived here with them on the 24th of July with twenty-one friars that Your Majesty sent for the conversion of the natives here: both they and I were particularly pleased about this, giving great thanks to the Lord for the eagerness and enthusiasm they have brought to help them in their holy work; for my part and from these provinces I also give thanks to Your Majesty, praying to the Lord that he repays you and increases it as is wished.

On this ship I received a letter from Your Majesty dated the 1st March, in which it says that the Council of War of the Indies saw another letter of mine dated 15th December last year, 1611; this Council instructs me that on everything that turns up around Virginia I should always write back to the Council. I have written several times to say that from this fort nothing can be found out by land, for the Indians on this coast have no communications with those near Virginia, and they speak different languages and are usually at war with each other, and there are many marshes and rivers in between: to find out I have tried many means: as regards everything else that has occurred in reply to the letters of Your Majesty that I received from the hands of Don Diego de Molina, I also wrote at length, sending the orders and instructions that I had with it, for I had stayed behind, thinking that they should not take it with them: it all went together with the letter of 15th December: and since that letter will have been seen by now, I shall not say more in this one than that in that one I recounted the route that would best be taken by any fleet that were to come to this coast, and told of a sandbank and port that there is on the route called Ballenas at 31 degrees or more north, which is the most suitable for large ships, and which could be set up if necessary as a place to take on water and other things.

And since concerning the other matters I mentioned in this letter Your Majesty told me to keep looking and decisions would be taken, I thought I should point out again that for matters here to go better it is necessary that they should be as I requested in my letter of the 12th May of the same year, or else otherwise I am unable to help the friars or protect them in the missions that have asked for them, and in many of which I keep pointing out why I fail to send them for fear of some disaster, particularly in Apalache where there are very many people and the chiefs are not much respected, which has caused the friars to be withdrawn on two occasions; and if I do not have the infantrymen that I have asked for to go to all problems and to act as the protection that I have offered to these chiefs in the name of Your Majesty, the advantage that we aim for cannot be won: for after the arrival of these twenty-one friars, some chiefs have come to ask for them and pay obedience from more than a hundred and fifty leagues from here (the distance of the cape of Apalache) and further, and also from the northern frontier, and it is essential in whatever we offer them that they should either be protected or we

should not send them. For they will be in danger, and it would cause great anxiety and little peace, but if there were soldiers here every problem could be dealt with, for I cannot do this with the ones I have here now, leaving this post unguarded, reasonably, for there are only one hundred and fifty active soldiers to see to everything: the other posts are filled by sailors and artillery men and fifty friars who also serve as soldiers, and we are another fifty short of the three-hundred strength we ought to have; when the garrison was set up the money allotted was just for infantry and those who keep the place running and two chaplains; now there are here many unfit soldiers which it would be as well for Your Majesty to instruct what is to be done with them, for although there are some to whom I have wanted to give permission to go, they say they have spent out their lives and have nowhere to go and nothing to live on, which is why I have not ended their positions even though I think they are holding posts that others could serve in: there are also some I have stationed on the missions who work all year at taking food to the friars; which is why it is not possible to go ahead with this new plan for conversion which the Lord has been pleased should go ahead: and these are very badly needed for the ordinary guard of this garrison, and those who are doing it now suffer great hardship and illness: which is why I beseech Your Majesty to order that this should be seen to.

Also Your Majesty instructed me to tell him what is happening about the path and river that was discovered for going to the coast of Apalache and Carlos bay, which I wrote that I would have reconnoitred this summer with the launch and the canoes that I had made on this river to punish the chiefs of Pooy and Tocopaca. I made arrangements for it and sent word to the heirs of these chiefs that from now on they should do no damage to the Christian settlements, for that punishment was dealt out for the damage done by their predecessors. I also sent them some gifts, offering them peace and friendship on behalf of Your Majesty: and with this, and their fear of what had happened before, they willingly offered it on their own behalf; and by this route I sent to say the same to the Chief of Carlos, who is the most powerful on all that coast, sending him too some gifts: he replied that he did not want any more war with the Christians and that he wanted peace and friendship with them, and that to check this I should send this launch to his land: and since it looked propitious I had it sent, and it left this river in the middle of June, and in it Lieutenant Juan Rodríguez de Cartaya, a reliable person for these matters, with twenty soldiers and a pilot, to go reconnoitring everything: they came to a large bay belonging to the chief of Pooy, at twenty seven and a third degrees north, and confirmed their friendship, and gave him other gifts that they were carrying for this purpose, with which the chief was left happy and secure; then they left for Carlos, and went into a large river called Tampa, at twenty-six and a sixth degrees north: here and all along the coast there were large settlements of Indians subject to Carlos, and according to the orders they had been given they came out to welcome the launch with gifts for the soldiers of fish, and other things: they arrived at Carlos' own settlement, which is inside a large river and sandbank at twenty-six degrees north. As soon as they were seen, more than sixty canoes came out with a large number of unarmed Indians, bringing many women with them, which among these people is the greatest sign of friendship, and they welcomed the lieutenant on behalf of their chief: he sent word to him through the interpreter he had with him that to confirm the friendship they were concerned with he should come to the launch: to which he replied two or three times that he had never been in a boat, and that the lieutenant should come on land, where they would meet, but the lieutenant said he would not, because of the few people he had and the orders he had been given, and made the chief come out on a large canoe with more than forty Indians, and many other canoes with people in, and when they arrived at the launch he embraced the lieutenant saying that he was doing so in my name and as a sign of the friendship that from then on he wished to have with the Spaniards, and he for his part would do nothing else. He and his people made great signs of rejoicing, and had brought out two golden nose-rings of the size of the palm of a hand, and smaller ones weighing about two ounces which they normally wear on their foreheads, which they gave to the lieutenant saying that he should give them to me as a sign of the friendship they had, and also handed over a negro from Havana that he had, who had got lost in a canoe and landed up on that coast, saying that if he ever had any other Christian people he would

hand them over with the same willingness, and that from then on any Spanish people or ships who should put into that coast in bad weather, he would give them a good journey and if necessary put them on the right route for this garrison in security, because this chief is so much feared by the others that even those round here pay him tribute. The lieutenant thanked him for this and assured him of the same friendship, and gave him some gifts that he was carrying for this purpose, and similarly to other chiefs and Indians who were with him: with which they were left very content, and so am I with the good way it turned out, and I trust in God that within a short time friars can be placed there in safety, to bring in great benefit, because this chief has more than sixty settlements under him, not counting the very many others that pay him tribute, as I said....

13 October 1612.

[Signed:] Juan Fernández de Olivera

775. October 16, 1612. The Franciscans of Florida to Philip III.

A.G.I., Seville, Santo Domingo 232; 54/5/17, no. 73; copy in J. T. Connor Collection, Division of Manuscripts, Library of Congress; extracts translated.

Sire,

The Governing Body, [*el difinitorino*] in the name all the friars in this custodian [*custodia*] in Florida, wish Your Majesty good health, and urgently pray to God that he should keep and preserve from harm such a good and catholic Lord.

The conversion of the natives in these provinces has been going so well that it is as we could wish it to be. We are sure that God's time has now come when they all want to be good Christians, and so they come from very far off to ask for baptism and to give obedience to Your Majesty; which is wonderful for those of us who have been here in this land as friars for eighteen or twenty years, calming and civilizing the Indians with so little expectation of seeing this that all our mission seemed to be turning into hatred and detestation against us, against the service of Your Majesty and against all manner of Spaniards, and against the herds we tried to bring into the land, when they killed them and exterminated them as if they were vermin and did the same to our trees and seeds trying to get rid of all trace and smell of us; in addition they set up a thousand ambushes in the forests and roads and fisheries to kill them, as indeed they did, obliging those who formed the garrison on Santa Elena to leave their garrison unguarded, as indeed they did, not being able to escape from the attacks of the Indians: they did the same to the friars, making fun of them, turning Christian more as a gesture than because they were Christian, and so then at the start we went through many hardships and many fatal setbacks, for they tried to kill us on many occasions, as indeed they succeeded in the Province of Guale, where they martyred five friars and captured others, and although they did not martyr them for their faith, they really martyred them for the law of God that they were teaching them, and our commandments, which were most opposed to their way of life and customs, and in particular with those who were both Christian and married, for we did not let them have more than one wife each, and John the Baptist was killed for nothing more than criticizing Herod for this. This is the reason which was and still is given now by those Indians who admit their sin, for their martyring them. It is established fact in this land that after the death of these blessed friars these people have been getting calmer and more tractable until the point we are at now, when it can be assumed faithfully that the saints in Heaven are asking God for the conversion of the natives in this land. This has been greatly helped by the Governor who Your Majesty at present has in this land: for he is very friendly, kind, Christian and generous to the natives, which is what they were wanting: hearing of this chiefs have come forward for baptism and to give obedience to Your Majesty from over a hundred leagues away; the Governor has received them well, giving them gifts, and food, and clothing, and other things that they consider most valuable, sending them back to their lands so content that some were saying that they would act as heralds of his great friendship, and that they would persuade those who live beyond them to come and meet him and make friends with him

and give obedience to Your Majesty, with the result that every day he has Indians and Chiefs from different areas, when they had not dared come before because previous Governors ignored them. We who have gone as friars to their lands have been received very kindly, and they ask us to stay among them, and we reply that there are not enough friars and that we could not leave the settlements we have in our charge: they ask us earnestly that we put up a cross for them and establish a site where they can make churches of their own for whenever there might be someone to teach them.

At this point the friars whom Your Majesty sent arrived, and were welcomed both by the Spaniards and by these Indians; the friars are now shared out among the Indians and working with great spirit. There are about fifty of us now and we live off the 300 posts that Your Majesty has established here, and in our place there are as many posts for soldiers again, less as many in the boats where there are usually as many veteran and ill officers. The Governor is unhappy at finding himself with so few soldiers and so many obligations to meet with them; for this reason he has decided not to appoint missions nor to send friars to Apalache, for it is so far away, and it would be necessary in that land to establish a settlement or a fortress with soldiers as defence, and so that they should have provisions for the friars by sea, because from this garrison by land it is impossible to carry provisions, or to help them, or defend them when they need it, and for this reason the friars who have gone out to look at the land have come back again. In addition, some of the Indians are not obedient to their chiefs, and the chiefs would like, with the favour and protection of Your Majesty, to control their Indians: for the Governor sent to many of us asking us what he should do in this matter, and we agreed that for the moment he should not appoint missions and the friars should not go until he has sent a report to Your Majesty, and that in the meanwhile he should keep them happy with good hopes for the future and presents. In addition to this, there are friars fairly close to Apalache, on the frontier of that province, with the intention of learning and knowing that language: we said they could go there and the friars would instruct them in matters of faith; we are extending the protection of this garrison and its soldiers among the Indians inland, and if anything should go wrong among them the Governor has not the men with which to set it right; and if it is not set right, the Indians might be encouraged to dare to harm and attack the Christian Indians; to remedy this, we refer to the report and request made by the Governor of Your Majesty, his request that for the increase and preservation of this land and the service of Your Majesty he now has nothing to give to the Indians if Your Majesty does not now allot it to him, and that everything he gives to them peacefully to please and pacify them to the good of the service of God and of Your Majesty is nothing compared with what would have to be spent in a war against them—just on wicks for the arquebuses more would have to be spent—and besides, it does no good to make war on them for in their settlements they have no buildings nor belongings to lose, and they think nothing of moving camp from one place ten leagues or so to another place, and as they move freely and the land is mountainous they would harm us more than we would harm them, for they can act as wild animals and would kill our people in all the passes. Willingly with the word of the gospel, and with one of the works of piety, clothing the naked, they come with their hands crossed, offering us their land, their will and their poor food for when we go there, wanting Your Majesty to send settlers to their land to teach them to plough it and everything else suitable; we think this very important, who have known these people in times past: so we give thanks to God who has arranged it so and to Your Majesty who has undertaken and still undertakes such a good work, even with great

expense on his Royal Exchequer: and if Your Majesty should send men to settle here, let them be Castilians of the kind who are good and simple men without any land of their own to work and cannot support themselves however hard they work, because in this land they will find very good forests and pastures in which to raise herds, as good as those of Medellín in Extremadura: fine forests of oaks, holm-oaks, walnut-trees, so clear of undergrowth that horses can be run beneath the trees. Great pinetrees, mulberry trees for silk, much land good for bread. Rivers for mills and so good that this land is only known as bad land for lack of people, and for the resistance encountered among the Indians. We friars have seen to these Indians in spiritual matters, and have tried out the land, and sown corn, and it grows as abundantly and well as in the Vega of Morata: and once it got under way, Your Majesty would get so much benefit from this land, with less expense, because we could live off alms, without expense to Your Majesty, and this land could support Havana, the fleets and navies with flour and other things, and there would be so much activity there of treaties and contracts that it would not be as unknown to people as it is now....

16th October 1612

The Religious of the custodianship of the *Custodia* of Santa Elena of Florida, Chaplains to your Majesty.

[Signed:] Father Pedro Ruiz, Father Pedro Bermejo, Fray Francisco Martinez, Fray Estevan de Sant Andrés

Chapter Ninety-nine
Spain and Virginia, 1609–1611

NOTHING ILLUSTRATES more clearly the gap between Spanish pretensions to dominate the whole of North America, and to have indefeasible rights to do so, than its inaction in regard to Virginia. Repeatedly, plans had been made to find and root out the supposedly continuing Lost Colonists. Similarly, resolution after resolution was passed from 1606 onward to destroy the fledgling Virginia. None of these was acted on. There were two very minor reconnaissances only. The first (in 1609) saw the Spaniards turn tail at the first sight of an English ship. The second (in 1611) involved the loss of the two leading members of the expedition, the only gain being an English pilot. They were completely without results. Spain reconciled itself, if with a continuing bad grace, to the English presence in Virginia.

776. September, 1609 (after the 24th, with a postscript of November 28).
Journal of Francisco Fernández de Écija on his Virginia voyage.

The failure of the Spanish government to do anything more than fulminate against English intervention in Virginia during the years 1606–1608 has been attributed [in D. B. Quinn, "James I and the Beginnings of Empire in America," Journal of British Commonwealth History, II *(1974), 1–17] to lethargy combined with the belief (which ultimately proved to be mistaken) that James I could be bullied, cajoled, and blackmailed into repudiating the Virginia Company. When Pedro de Ibarra was instructed to send a reconnaissance vessel northward from San Agustín in the early summer of 1609, the English were wholly committed to the maintenance of the colony, as the charter of that year fully indicated. Ecija had tried to find the Lost Colonists in 1605, but had turned back before he came within range of where they might possibly be. Ibarra then said that he would send him in the summer of 1606 on a more extended reconnaissance, but so far as is known no English-seeking expeditions were mounted between 1605 and 1609. Écija reached Chesapeake Bay on July 24 and sighted an English ship there: The vessel belonged to Samuel Argall, who was there to fish for sturgeon. Écija, seeing that it was larger than his own, took evasive action and made for home. He had identified the James River as the seat of the English occupation and that was all. His long report is mainly of interest for his description of the coast northward from Santa Elena, which his 1605 report had also covered in great detail.*

A.G.I., Seville, Patronato 261, ramo 2; translated by Victor Tyler, "A Spanish Expedition to Chesapeake Bay in 1609," American Neptune, *XVII (1957), 181–194; it was retranslated by P. L. Barbour and some two thirds of it (since it is very wordy) was printed in his* The Jamestown Voyages, *II, 292–319, from which it is reprinted, with one or two corrections suggested by Dr. Barbour.*

Sunday, which was the 21st of June [1609], after hearing mass and coming out of the principal church of this city of San Agustín in Florida, Captain Francisco Fernández de Écija, with all those who had been notified and signalized for this adventure—they were, the said Captain, and Ensign [*alférez*] Juan Rodríguez de Cartaya, the said Captain's second-in-command [*alférez*], and Juan de Santiago, an ensign off duty and named third in command under the said Captain, and other soldiers and officers off duty to the number of twenty-five persons, and [also] María de Miranda, a native of Santa Elena and interpreter for that country, wife of Juan de Espinosa, a soldier of this garrison—he, the Captain went with the other ranks named to the residence of General Pedro de Ybarra, and when the said Captain and others mentioned were before him he made an address, and after he had embraced all of them, one by one, the said Captain went aboard the zabra named *La Asunción de Cristo*, which for this occasion was fitted out and provided with supplies and munitions and stores such as were needed, and two pieces of artillery, one of bronze and the other of cast iron.

And after we had gone aboard the said zabra and were settled and at ease, the said captain called all those mentioned above, and when they were assembled gave another talk.

And at midday the said captain asked the pilot if we could put out to sea, and the said pilot said yes, that the tide was beginning to ebb: and when the anchor was weighed, the sails were spread to cries of *buen viaje* ['bon voyage!'], and we left in high spirits. And so we sailed on until four o'clock in the afternoon, when the wind was dead ahead, and we anchored two leagues out to sea; and as night closed in such a storm blew up that we were at the mercy of God all night, with the sea breaking over the prow. And so we remained until daybreak, when we weighed anchor with much difficulty, since the storm was increasing and the sea very heavy, and we all but ran onto the [coastal] sandbank, and we anchored again until high tide, and when it was time we weighed anchor again, and we came up against the sandbank at San Agustín once more (where we had sailed from), at eleven o'clock on Monday the 22nd of the said month of June.

Here we waited until Friday, 26 June, for the weather [to change], when with very little wind, and what there was of it veering, between sailing and being towed we got away from the sandbank.

And Saturday the 27th of the said month we entered the Bay of Whales [*en abra de ballenas*]

and continued therein as far as Gualaquini, which we reached on the said day, and then the next day, since the weather did not permit putting to sea we went on by [inland] channels to the Bay of Zapala.

On Thursday the 2nd of July we crossed the sandbank of Zapala out to sea.

And Friday the 3rd of the said month we reached the sandbank of Santa Elena which we crossed at nine o'clock on that day, and we went to anchor by San Felipe Channel. Here the said captain had two muskets fired [as a signal] for some Indians to come to hear about certain matters.

And Saturday the fourth the cacique of Escamaque came and talked with the said captain, who regaled him, and then he related how some ships had passed not long before, within sight of land, toward the north, and said that he knew nothing further, and after taking leave that same Saturday night he went home.

And Sunday the 5th of the said month of July we crossed the said sandbank of Santa Elena, beating to windward.

And Monday the 6th of the said month we reached the sandbank of Cayagua which we passed over, with a man always in the crow's-nest to observe the bay and rivers for any ship [*baxel*] which might be there, going always under a good guard and with caution. And when the said captain had dropped anchor he ordered two musket-shots [to be fired] for the Indians to come to hear about some matters concerning the said voyage. And since it was already late and no Indian had come because the towns were scattered, the said captain ordered the corporal Diego de Cárdenas to take the ship's boat with another soldier, with their arms, and four sailors, toward the shore, and go along it, shouting and calling to the Indians to reassure them. And the said corporal went and carried out the order given him, and he neither saw nor heard a single Indian, and with that he returned to the zabra to report to the said captain what had occurred. And now that it was night the said captain had two more musket-shots fired, and after two hours, more or less, the sentries saw a fire toward the north-west, on a hilltop between two rivers, and reported this to the said captain. And he then ordered two more musket-shots, and when they heard these, the Indians who had made the fire replied with shouts, and since it was not a good time to go for them, the said captain gave orders to reassure the Indians.

And on Tuesday the 7th, the captain ordered the corporal Cárdenas to go ashore in the ship's boat with three other soldiers and four sailors, and talk with the Indians, and if they wanted, to bring some of them. This was done and he brought an Indian named Alonso ever since there had been a garrison at Santa Elena. Alonso spoke the language of Río Jordán, and he [was] talking with María de Miranda, who was one of his people who had welcomed him in her house along with the *mandador mayor* [ruling chief] of the Río Jordán [district] when the said Captain Écija brought them [back] in 1605 when he went exploring up to Cape San Román. And the said captain got information about some things which the said Alonso knew. When he had this information, the said captain regaled him and six Indians who had come with him with food and drink and beads and other things, and upon suggesting to him that he go along in the zabra, he freely offered to go. So then the said captain sent the Indians away in a canoe, and ordered the anchor weighed and the sails spread, with the sea-breeze setting in [*llegando la viraçon la descaveçante*], we got away at midday, beating to windward.

Reaching the Jordán, we passed the sandbank on Wednesday the 8th of the said month of July, always with a lookout in the crow's-nest watching the river and coves for some stray enemy. Landwards from the two headlands there is a great river, which we sailed up until we got to some small houses and plots of ground sown with corn where the Indian chief lived whom we call the Mandador ['Commander'] of the Jordán, [and] who is the one whom the said captain brought to Saint Augustine some time before. And after he had anchored, the said captain ordered Ensign Juan Rodríguez, his assistant, to go ashore in the ship's boat and take the Indian Alonso to talk to the Indians and manage to bring one of them or, even better, the Mandador himself. And upon receipt of this order the said ensign boarded the boat with two soldiers and four sailors, with their arms, and when he had landed with due prudence, the said Mandador came to the beach, and the said ensign welcomed him affectionately and brought him to the ship, with a canoe following with two sons of his and another Indian. And the said captain regaled him with food and drink, and gave

the Mandador a hoe and a few beads, and beads to the others too, and after going into public matters publicly he took him to the stern cabin and through the Indian Alonso, who interpreted with the help of María de Miranda, asked him if he knew anything about our voyage [i.e., why it was made]. And he said that thirteen days before a ship had been over the sandbank of San Cristóbal, which is two leagues south of this River Jordán, and that it was anchored and had a boat astern, and he said that a brother of his understood that it had been to the village or fort of the English. But when the said captain inquired for him, the said Mandador said he was not there, but in a village called Xoye, up the river, near his own. And so with promises and flattery the said captain got him to bring the brother, and also tried to get hold of the Frenchman who the Mandador said was in the interior, in the village of his cacique named Sati, and to this end the said captain offered him as ransom for the said Frenchman two hatchets and two hoes, and a box of knives and twenty strings of beads. And when all of the foregoing had been discussed, an Indian came from his two sons who was to go as messenger to where the Frenchman was, and the said captain showed him the said ransom which he had promised for the said Frenchman, telling him to tell the cacique of Sati that he had come for the Frenchman who was his captive, and that the said captain was his friend, and that everything he had showed him would be given to him [the cacique] as ransom and gift for [giving over] the said Frenchman, and so that he would not think it was all idle words he would get a bunch of beads, which the said captain did to bind him more. And so also another messenger was sent to the Mandador's brother, offering him many gifts. And so the said Indians left, and the Mandador went ashore with them since it was late, strongly urging the messengers to be speedy.

And the morning of Saturday the 11th of the said month the Mandador's brother arrived, and the captain regaled him, and alone with María de Miranda and the Indian Alonso the said captain began to ask the said Indian if he knew where the settlement of the English, or French, was, and what he knew about it. To this he answered that he had started from his village, which would be four or five leagues northwards from the Jordán, and that he had left there and gone to a village called Daxe. And when he was asked how far it was from his village there, he said it was four days' journey, and that in the said village of Daxe he had had word that near there, in a village called Guandape on a river that runs to the sea, the English had settled on an island surrounded by water but for a strip which unites it to the mainland, that in the said port there were usually [some] ships, and that it was three months since seven ships sailed from this port, and that six of them sailed north, and one south, and that this one carried colours and beat a war-drum, and that there were spare ships remaining in the port, and that he himself had not seen this, but the Indians of the said village of Guandape had told him, because they usually came and went where the English were. And furthermore he said that usually ships came and went every day from the north to the said settlement. And when he was asked if we could see the said English, he said that he thought we could, because judging by what they told him they were near the salt water, and that they would see us because the island where they are settled is near the sandbank. And when he was asked if they knew if they [the English] had a fort, he said yes, and that they had told him it was of wood, and he likewise said that the said enemy had made an alliance with the neighbouring caciques, and that seven of them were friends, and that they [the English] regaled them greatly, and gave them clothes [and] tools, and that they had them sow, for they did not bother with sowing but with fortifying. And as he was being informed of all this, the said captain ordered me to note down, letter by letter, all that the interpreters were telling him. And likewise, so that the said captain would understand where the said English were, a sketch of the coast was drawn for him as far as the Cape of San Román, along with the sandbanks there, and the said Indian said that it was beyond the Cape, and with this it was concluded, and the said Indian was given some cases of knives, and some beads, and something to eat and drink. And he went ashore with his brother the said Mandador, who had been present throughout.

And Sunday the 12th of the said month, in the morning, the Indian Alonso, who was brought as interpreter, who was on land waiting for the messenger to come (who had gone for the Frenchman), came and brought a string with five knots, and said through the said interpreter María de Miranda that the Indian who had gone to Sati had come back and said that he brought those five knots and that five days from then he would have the cacique of Sati [with him], and he [the cacique] would bring the Frenchman. And when the said captain saw that there would be much delay and that considerable damage would result in that he would not be able to carry out his objectives because of the loss of time, he ordered us to weigh anchor and go to the entrance of the sandbank, leaving the said Indian Alonso in the village, asking him urgently, if he could take the Frenchman to Saint Augustine, for him to do so, promising him many gifts, both for himself and for whomever brought him. And at this time he gave him a hoe and a case of knives and some strings of beads. And the said captain left him and all of them very grateful and pleased.

When we arrived with all due speed at the entrance of the sandbank that day, since we could not get out, the said captain ordered wood cut, and the ensign, his assistant, went ashore with the guard, and in short order the sailors got two boatloads of wood, and when they were all back on board we set the bronze piece on a low mounting designed for it in the prow, and then we dressed ship. And the said captain showed each one his post, and when everything was in order he spoke to everybody, explaining what they were to do in any event.

And two hours after nightfall [10.00 to 10.30 p.m.] we heard shouts and [saw] lights on shore, and when we answered the voice it seemed to be the Mandador of the said River Jordán, and the said captain ordered the corporal Cárdenas and five other men to go ashore in the ship's boat, with orders for them not to land until they recognized who it was, and to bring the one who shouted [after] they had [learned] what he wanted. And when they had reached the shore and recognized the Indian as the Mandador they cautiously took him aboard. And when they reached the zabra, the said captain talked with him through the said María de Miranda, for the said Indian knew something of the language of Escamaqu [which María de Miranda spoke], because the Indian we brought [apparently the same one] had been in her land as an interpreter, [and] had seen that we had already arrived. And furthermore he said he wanted to tell the said captain that the heir of the cacique of Sati had come to his village and had brought the Frenchman. And when he had heard this the said captain regaled him in fine fashion, and the said Indian slept aboard and was very grateful for the present the said captain had given him.

And at midnight at high tide the said captain ordered anchor weighed, and we went to the said Mandador's village. And Monday morning the 13th of the said month a great number of Indians arrived, and the heir of Sati, who brought the Frenchman, and other chief caciques, whom the said captain received with much love and happiness. And he presented the promised ransom, and they turned the Frenchman over to him, who said his name was Juan [Jean] Corbe [Corbet?], a native of Le Havre (de Grace), and then he began to give many tools, such as hatchets and hoes, and knives and beads, and food and drink. And when they were all very happy, and had talked to them with only the said María de Miranda, interpreter, so far as the said Indian, the Mandador, understood the language of Escamaqu, and after he had got such information as he could, the said caciques and Indians took their leave and went ashore very happy. And here we remained until Tuesday afternoon [14 July], with rain-storms and bad weather. And the afternoon of that day we sailed down to the sandbar and Wednesday morning the 15th of the said month of July we sailed out to sea to continue our voyage.

And at four in the afternoon of this day the said captain called the ensign, his assistant, and Juan Rodríguez, master artillery gunner, and with them discussed a number of things which ought to be done or prepared in advance, which he brought up as follows: [discussion omitted.]

And after rounding the Cape of San Román Friday the 17th of the said month of July, as we passed there were great smoke-signals along the coast at two or three leagues from one another, and so the captain ordered that a man be put on regular sentry duty in the crow's-nest, to reconnoitre and descry anything that might be on the sea or land or the sandbanks and coves and everywhere.

The night of the same day it was necessary to cast off the ship's boat because we could not sail nor beat to windward with it. Furthermore, in case we ran across some ship, there would be no chance of their obliging us to go to them, and also

because if we reached the enemy's port, they would see that we had no boat, and would send a lighter out. So we opened a scuttle and it sank.

And Saturday morning the 18th of the said month the said captain ordered the zabra dressed, and the men to their posts, ready for anything that might happen, for we were descrying and inspecting sandbanks and it seemed to him that we were getting to a place where we could catch sight of the enemy when we did not expect it. And when everything was in order and inspected, the said captain called all the soldiers and harangued them as follows: [omission].

And thus we arrived at the Cape of Trafalgar. We passed it the same day, and on Sunday afternoon, the 19th of the said month we rounded Cape Engaño, and after we rounded it we discovered an inlet [or passage] to the north-east of the said cape, which we reached. And we dropped anchor and stayed there until Monday morning, the 20th.

That day we explored a sandbank where we understood the English had settled, and where they had stayed some time before, and they [i.e., Indians] made a big smoke-signal on a hill inside [the inlet]. And so we sailed along the shallows, under orders given by the said captain in accordance with the opinions he had been given, examining closely everything he could. And each man did the same thing from his post, arms in hand, and the artillery ready to fire, and two men in the crow's-nest on the look-out, who said that there was nothing in the bay [Pamlico Sound] but the smoke which all of us saw. And since the passage was troublesome, as it appeared, and there was no sign of anything, and finding nothing after a second look, the said captain decided to go on with our voyage.

And when there was one more hour of sun left that day, seven Indians came to the shore and began to wave at us, and shout, and because we had a land-wind we were going so close to shore that we heard them, and the captain ordered sails furled. And when we were as close as a stone's throw from the surf, we called them, but they seemed timid, and climbed a hillock and began to play on pipes. And since we were so near, the captain ordered the anchor dropped, and we kept calling them, but they did not make a move of any sort to come down to the beach. And seeing that they were not coming, and that we could not talk with them, and that it was getting night, the said captain ordered the anchor weighed, and we went a little out to sea, and dropped anchor again.

And during the dawn watch, Tuesday the 21st of the said month there was a great rain-storm with a land-wind, and we stayed until it was calm enough for us to weigh anchor and proceed with our voyage. But when we had gone about two leagues the wind got so strong that we had to drop anchor, and we rode there all day Tuesday.

And during the dawn watch, Wednesday the 22nd of the said month, the wind veered to the north and by daybreak wind and sea had increased so that we had to get behind the sandbank. And since that day was [the feast of] la Magdalena [St Mary Magdalen], we called it Magdalena Bank. And getting as far as the sandbank and wanting to find some way to enter, [the sea] broke over everything and no channel offered safety, and right over the shoals we had to furl sail and get out, and so we went out to sea, staying until about nightfall we put about toward land, and when we were near we anchored, since the weather had cleared up. And we remained anchored there, two leagues south of the sandbank, until the next day.

And Thursday the 22nd of the said month, when the *virazón* [afternoon sea-breeze] came at ten o'clock from the south-east, we weighed anchor and pursued our route. And all that time they did not stop doing the same thing they had been doing to us on the said hill, [for] in the bay, three leagues north of this sandbank, they began making a lot of smoke, inland from north to south, with more smoke which they made behind us in the said bay of la Magdalena.

And arriving at the place where I said the Indians had come out, they made another great smoke-signal on the coast, and as we got where that was six Indians came out to us, waving at us as before, and shouting. And when he saw them, the said captain ordered a landing-party, but we could not talk with them because they slipped away and clambered up the hillocks, while we were anchored, watching. And when the captain saw that we could not communicate with them at all, he ordered us to sail on. And as we left them behind, out from the hillocks where they had hidden, came a huge number of them, with their bows and quivers, and six of them came running after us as fast as they could along the beach for a long time until we left them behind. And even then they kept whistling with their pipes and shouting. And we got the idea from what we heard that they were playing on those pipes in some harmony, and judging by the sound they were pipes made by foreigners. Hence we inferred that it was a signal they had for ships that passed, they were so diligent. Then, since it was night, we anchored.

And Friday the 24th of the said month we weighed anchor and continued our route with a good guard, and when we had gone until midday we saw a sandbank of good size, and here, after we had reconnoitred and coasted along the shallows in accordance with the orders already mentioned, we drew lots to see which we should call it, San Cristóbal or Santiago, and it fell out Santiago.

And arriving this same day at the Bay of Jacán [Chesapeake Bay], at five o'clock in the afternoon, a very short bit before reaching the tip of the southern shore, the sentinel in the crow's-nest spotted a ship anchored in the bay. And because it was already late, the said captain ordered the anchor dropped, for we would not enter until the next day. And then he ordered all necessary preparations made, and the artillery put in order, each man taking his post, and dividing the infantry into three watches, so that all of them would stand guard that night, the captain himself and the two ensigns taking part, one in each watch.

And in view of the situation, the said captain summoned the said ensign, his assistant, and the ensign Juan de Santiago, and the sergeant Millán, and the sergeant Miguel de las Alas, and the corporal Diego de Cárdenas, and the corporal Antón García, and Francisco de Salazar y Zúñiga [the chronicler], and Andrés González the pilot, and Juan Rodríguez the master gunner, and Domingo Rodríguez the master, and when they were all assembled before him, he began to speak as follows: [speach omitted; silence was commanded, and they waited to see if the ship in question came out into the ocean.]

And Saturday the 25th of the said month of July, at dawn, a sailor climbed into the crow's-nest and found that the said ship was just as it was the day before, and the conclusion was then reached that it was an enemy acting as a guard and sentinel, and because they had a land-wind, a moon [past last quarter], and a tide [presumably, all unfavourable], had not sailed out nor come looking for us. And so we put everything in order, and weighed anchor because the tide was going out and there was no wind until nine o'clock, when the tide began to come in and the *virazón* [veering wind] began to blow from the north-east. At this juncture we set sail, keeping a look-out in the crow's-nest all the time, who observed that the said ship was also setting sail, coming in our direction, while we managed always to keep to windward, in which we had the advantage because we set sail from outside [the bay] and the incoming tide threw him [the enemy] off his course as much as it did us. And so he could not get to the windward of us, and we sailed right for him, coming up close. But at the same time that the said ship set sail, a great smoke-signal reached us from the north shore, which was immediately answered by another on the west-northwest, which is where there is a river of great volume according to Juan de Santiago and others who had sailed with Captain Vicente González some time back. And from this it was inferred and recognized that the said ship was a sentinel, for the reasons mentioned before; because when it sailed they started the smoke, and immediately it was answered from where they have the garrison, as the Indians said, for these clouds of smoke were neither more nor less signals than those they made along the coast. Indeed, as we continued on our way we had to admit that it was a ship incomparably greater in burden than ourselves, because we saw that it carried two topsails and a great flag at the masthead, and because the ship was very long and flush-decked [*largo y raso*]. And as we got closer, the said ship was coming toward us, each one trying to get to the windward. And the said captain and all the rest recognized [who had] the advantage, and that at that time the wind was light and scant and was carrying us into a cove, and the said enemy was deceiving us with the topsails on the gunwale [waiting] for the current to carry us into the cove, just where he wanted us.

The said captain [then] summoned the ensign, his assistant, and the ensign Juan de Santiago, and the said pilot, and Juan Rodríguez the master gunner, and asked their opinion, saying that this enemy was trying to shut us up in the bay where he could be our lord and master, because he had lowered his topsails and was letting himself drift with the tide, as they saw, and what did they think, and be quick about it. [Exchange of opinions omitted.]

And at this time the enemy, who was already very close to us, since he could not get to the windward of us, began to fall off to leeward, and so we veered in the other direction, and the said ship tacked toward west-north-west stern-on to us, and revealed a stern which was like a castle, And we, since we could neither go ahead nor land [*multiplicar tierra!*], anchored in the middle of the bay, rather toward the south side than the north, and we were [there] more than two hours, while the said ship with wind and tide astern sailed more than three leagues in the said direction of west-north-west, apparently always toward the interior, and after two hours, or three, it appeared to be turning back in our direction.

And the reason was, in our opinion, that after warning had been given there in the interior to their settlers, the wind changed suddenly to north-west, and it [the ship] bore down on us again, and while we were observing it, the wind which brought the said ship came upon us.

And the said captain ordered the anchor weighed, and the sails spread, and our course set to the south, not sparing a rag of canvas, for that seemed to all of us and to the captain the right thing to do, since, as has been said, the enemy had notified their garrison, which we knew was there, and the whole countryside was notified. Because, if the said enemy was not a patrol, the smoke-signals would not have been made, the ones answering the others, nor would he [the enemy] have tried to show us the mouth of the river [i.e., the route to the settlement], which led us to infer that the enemy took into consideration that if we were friends we would enter, and if not he would put us where we were not our own masters, and when he saw that we dropped anchor and did not follow him, he returned to bear down on us.

Furthermore it was inferred that if [the ship in question] were not at home, knowing, as it knew, its advantage over us, there was no reason for it to enter [the bay] as it did, but to try to get to the windward of us, or to stand still until it saw what we were going to do; and in case it was not at home there but was a corsair [privateer] that came looking for booty, he would have observed that we had more advantage over him than he over us [and] would have gone back out to sea in time, for he had room, wind and tide [in which to do so].

But after the captain had considered these and other possibilities, he ordered the pilot to continue on the southern tack until nightfall.

And the said enemy kept on following the course we were taking, and pursuing us until sunset, and at that time we sailed out of the bay into the sea, and the said ship reached the place where we had found it where it dropped anchor, as it seemed to us.

And since the night was dark, the said captain ordered the pilot to steer to the east so as to be swallowed up and [thus] hide our route from him, in case he were to follow us, as we understood he would with boats, according to word the said captain had from the Indians who had communication with us.

And at this same time, when we were three or four leagues out to sea, the said captain was obliged on certain grounds, which will be explained, to summon the pilot Andrés González, and the master Domingo Rodríguez, and the ensign, his assistant, and Juan Rodríguez the master gunner, and when they were all there he said the following: [He told the officers that he was supposed to go as far as 44½ degrees, but asked their opinions. All of them being against such a trip, largely because of the lateness of the season, he decided to return to the south.]

And Sunday morning the 26th of the said month of July, after posting a man in the crow's-nest and scanning the sea, in accordance with the said decision the said pilot ordered to steer southwards with the wind west.

This day the said captain summoned Juan Rodríguez, the master gunner, and the Frenchman, and in French (which the said Juan Rodríguez understood) asked the said Frenchman what had not been possible before, for the said Frenchman had forgotten his own language and talked Indian, and when they asked him something he answered in Indian, and could not be understood, but after the said Juan Rodríguez kept on talking to him he got his own tongue back. And when the said captain asked him if he had word of any people, either French or English, who had settled on this coast, the said Frenchman answered that when he was in the village of the chief who kept him prisoner, which was called Sati, he saw three Indians who the Frenchman knew came from where there was an English settlement, and [he learned] that they had made a fort of wood, and their village was built of wood, and that he had seen the hatchets and knives and biscuit, which were little cakes of wheat flour, and he said that they had two large ships mounted like castles on guard at the fort, and two more on guard as senti-

nels by the sandbank [at the entrance of the bay], without counting others that went and came, and he likewise said a ship came from England every year laden with supplies and munition. And when he was asked where the Indians were who had told him this, he said that one Indian was from a village called Guamuihurta, and the other two from another village, which is called Quixis. And likewise he was asked if he knew the distance by land from the village of Sati to the English settlement, [but] he said that he did not know, because the Indians covered part of it in canoes, and dawdled, a great deal on the way, and he added that the said Indians and his master wanted to take him to the said English village for ransom, and for fear that they would take him there he ran away, and was a fugitive in the forest for two days. And when they asked him if he would recognize any of the said Indians, he said yes, any of them. And he also said that one of the said Indians was interpreter for the same English, and that the others told him that he was, and served as, [their] executioner, and that this same Indian twice more wanted to take him to the said English. And the said captain said that he should watch and see if by chance this Indian or either of the other two came to the boat, and if he came, for him [the Frenchman] to tell the said captain secretly. And the said Frenchman said he would, and here this conversation and examination came to an end.

[In summary: They got back safely to 33° 30′ on or about 4 August 1609. The next day a bad storm drove them back to 35° 30′ on 6 August. On Sunday 9 August, at 10 a.m. they sighted land, at four leagues to the north of Cape San Román. They had bad weather again about 15 August. On Friday, 21 August, they saw the Mandador of Jordán once more, and asked how far it might be from there to the English settlement by land. They learned it was fifty leagues; and that it was a hundred leagues to Saint Augustine. Another explanation was that it was a four-day trip from the Jordán River to Daxe, and from Daxe to Guandape a day and a half, 'and that is where the English are.' On Thursday, 25 August, they went up the river for water, and met many Indians, including three caciques, Sati, Gaandul, and Guatari. Thursday the 27th they set sail for the Bay of Cayagua.]

And the morning of Friday the 28th of the said

month we entered the Bay of Cayagua, and went to anchor at the mouth of two big rivers, one of which enters from the north and the other from the north-west. And here on this day came eight or nine canoes, and among these came one by the northern river with eight Indians. And when they came up to the zabra an Indian came aboard with an old hat on his head. And as soon as he came aboard the Frenchman recognized him, and informed the said captain that the Indian was one of the ones who he said had gone to the English settlement. And when he was informed of this, the said captain summoned the ensign his assistant, and ordered him to bring the Indian to talk with him [the captain], and this he did. And taking him into the cabin along with the said Frenchman and Juan Rodríguez the master gunner to interpret for the Frenchman, he [the captain] began to ask through the Frenchman if he had been in the said English settlement, and he said he had. And he was asked what people and fortifications there were, and he answered that there was a lot of people and one fort. And understanding that he understood, as he did, the language spoken at Santa Elena, the said captain ordered the said María de Miranda to talk with him. And when she asked the same questions asked by the said Frenchman in the language of Sati, he said that he did not know anything about the matter and that he did not understand the Frenchman, showing that he was sorry for what he had said. And when the said María de Miranda repeated to him what he had previously said to the Frenchman that he did know, he answered that the Frenchman had lied, and that he had not said that. And whether they insisted or wheedled, he still denied [everything]. And when he saw this, the said captain ordered him manacled and put under custody until he had made an investigation. And thus we had him with us until Saturday, the 29th of the said month, when a canoe arrived with the cacique *descamaqu* [of Escamaqu] who was in a gathering in Cayagua, and the cacique of Ostano, and the same of Cayagua and two heads of tribes and the Indian Alonso whom we had brought as interpreter, and when we inquired whether they knew if the Indian who was in irons knew anything about the Englishmen, they all said no. And when he had finished, he regaled them with a hatchet and other things, [and] they took their leave and left, the said Indian Alonso remaining with us, whom

the said captain asked what he knew about the shackled Indian. And he said that he knew nothing with regard to that matter. And so neither from the cacique nor from any other Indian could anything more be extracted than what Alonso said: that he was from the interior, from a village named Ypaguano, and if the prisoner knew anything it had not come to his attention.

And this same day the said captain called the Frenchman and through Juan Rodríguez told him to watch what he said; that he did not want to accuse the Indian, for all the caciques and Indians denied it. And the said Frenchman replied that he was not mistaken, and that the Indian who was in irons was one of the three whom he had seen in the village of Sati, who had come from the settlement of the said Englishmen. And when he had been told once more to consider well what he was saying, the said Frenchman said that he had already considered it well, and that if it were not true, for them to hang or burn him. And when he saw this, the said captain ordered the said Indian summoned again, and with many kind words and promises he once again used the said María de Miranda to ask what he had asked before, and between coercion and persuasion, with crafty and astute words, the said captain got out of him that it was true that he had gone to a village named Daxe and that there he had heard from the people of that village that there was an English settlement near there, somewhat farther north, as he pointed out, and from this said village of Daxe to that of the Englishmen there was a river by which the Indians communicated with the said English. And when he was asked if ships could enter that river, he said that he did not know, and he was also asked if it [the settlement] had many people. He answered that the said Indians said yes. And when he was asked if they had a fort, he said that there was a very large house where the English cacique lived. And when he [the captain] said, why did he not confess right away, and say what he knew, he answered, for fear of both of them [English and Spanish alike], for he understood that they were asking about other people about whom there was a report [*noticia*], in Guatari, which is in the interior. And when he was asked what people this was, he said they were Spaniards, and that they had Negroes with them. And when they went on asking questions about this and all the rest, he said for them not to ask any more for the time being, that he would run over it all in his memory and would tell what he knew, for we had to take [him] with us. And in view of this, he was not questioned any further, and the said Captain and María de Miranda were diligent in rewarding him as they did, the one for what he had solicited [and obtained], and the other because he [the Indian] seemed to be very important, for all the time we were in this port, Indians of both sexes visited him continuously, especially five or six brothers of his, and one of them asked permission to come and be with him, and the said captain gave it. And the prisoner and he were somewhat consoled, although the said María de Miranda, as interpreter, consoled them in the name of the captain, and gave them many promises, and [said] that taking them along was not to do them harm.

And that same day, Friday the 4th of the said month [September], the said captain discussed with the Indian Alonso the interpreter and the cacique of a village in the same harbour, through the said María de Miranda, whether they would venture to go and reconnoitre by land where the said English were settled, and the said Indian offered to go gladly, and also two brothers of the two captive Indians offered to go with him. And the said captain was very grateful, and promised to reward them when they came with the information [he wanted]. And the said captain gave orders to the said Indian Alonso that they should go as far as the village of Daxe, taking with them the brother of the Mandador of the Jordán, who had been there four or five times, and if any Indians from Daxe should go where the Englishmen were, they were to go with them, and not to let it be known that they were sent by the Spaniards, and that they had not seen them or known them, and that they should go as simple Indians, observing everything, such as the strength they had in men and ships and artillery, and what entry [to the settlement] there was over the strip of land, and if the fortress was large, and if they were bringing stone [to strengthen it]. And the said Indian promised the said captain to bring a report of everything, without missing a thing, and that he would come back shortly. A great deal of faith can be placed in all this, and hope [of success], for the said Indian Alonso will do it because he is a Christian Indian and has 'rank' in Saint Augustine on two counts, first from

when the said captain brought him there as has been said, and then because he came back of his own volition, for he had offered to, and he was always very much regaled, and loaded with ransom money and bits of jewelry, and was very friendly with the Spaniards. Furthermore we can be certain that they will come back because the said Indians who volunteered to go with him to the said English settlement are brothers of the two Indians whom the said captain is taking with him, and all three of them gave their word that they would be back in Saint Augustine within forty or fifty days.

And Saturday the 5th of September we sailed from this port for Santa Elena, and Sunday the 6th of the said month we entered the said Bay of Santa Elena, with not an Indian or cacique there to speak to us.

Tuesday the 8th of the said month we sailed out to sea for the Bay of Shoals, and entered it the same day, and here we stayed for eight days with a storm [blown in] from the north-east.

And Tuesday the 15th of the said month we sailed out to sea for the Cofonufo sandbank, and we entered behind it on Wednesday the 16th of the said month, and the said captain ordered us to go to the village of Yoa while the weather permitted, and Wednesday [?] the 17th we reached the said village of Yoa, and remained here until Sunday the 20th of the said month. And after hearing mass from Father Juan de Guadalupe, who the day before had gone from his sermon to see the said captain, we weighed anchor and sailed for the said sandbank of Cofonufo. And since we could not get out we went by the inner channels to the Bay of Zapala, and from there to the Bay of Espogue [? - *despogue*].

And Wednesday the 23rd of the said month of September we sailed out to sea through the said Bay of Espogue, headed for the sandbank of Saint Augustine.

And Thursday the 24th of the said month of September at five in the afternoon we entered [the port of] this garrison of San Agustín, Florida, in the year of 1609. Infinite thanks to God for ever and ever, Amen. Jesus.

[Signed:] Francisco de Salazar y Zúñiga

[Addendum:] And Thursday the 15th of October following there reached me in this city of San Agustín, Florida, Alonso the Christian and a son of his and three brothers of the Indians whom Captain Écija took with him, and the Mandador of the Jordán, and after I had received them well, and regaled them, I asked them through the interpreter María de Miranda [for their report, saying] that I was pleased that they had lived up to their word so well in coming, and that they tell me what news they brought. The said Alonso, the Indian, answered that he left his land promptly to carry out what he had promised the said captain, and took with him the brother of the Mandador of the Jordán, who knew about the settlement, and when they had reached Guaño, five days from Alonso's village, the Indians there quarrelled with them a great deal because they had told the Spaniards that there was an English settlement near there, and this ended in a great fracas. And when it was a little quieter they [the people there] told them that they did not need to go any farther, that there was nothing to see, and for them to go back for they were afraid for their lives, and that this had happened without their saying anything [about the Spaniards], from which it is inferred that the English have won the Indians over as far as there. I kept all eight of them here for several days, during which I rewarded them, and when they wanted to go back to their homes I gave all of them tools and beads, and I dressed up the first two because they offered their services to me and gave their word to come back to see me in as many days as they gave me knots in a string, which were seventy-three, and they will do what they can to get to the village of Guandape itself, and bring me a complete report of everything, and with this they left very happy, after I had given them provisions for their journey, and people to accompany them as far as Santa Elena, on the 20th of October. And the Indian Alonso remained here, where he said he wanted to be for a month, amusing himself. And so the rewards were for him alone, for he ordered his son to go home.

[Added, in a different, smaller hand:] Which Indian Alonso asked my permission to go home on the 15th of November, and I gave it to him, and many gifts and ransom money and supplies for the trip and a corporal who was an interpreter to accompany him nearly to his village, which Indian [Alonso] promised to return with any information which is certain [i.e., 'firm'], and who will give all proper provision and assistance to the two Indi-

ans whom I am keeping here until Christmas in accordance with the declaration [or obligation?] they left with me in the form of knots [in a string], that they would return at that time, which I hold for sure.

[Signed:] Pedro de Ybarra

28 November 1609

777. May 5, 1611. Recommendations to Philip III that the English colony in Virginia should be destroyed.

Écija's report of his 1609 voyage was not finally considered until May, 1611, when the Junta de Guerra, *the war subcommittee of the Council of the Indies, recommended that Virginia should be attacked and destroyed. A further reconnaissance was, however, necessary. This led to the sending from Lisbon of a caravel under Diego de Molina, as captain, Marco Antonio Perez as master, and Francis Lymbry, an Englishman who had already done some espionage for Spain in Virginia, as pilot. Their cover story was to be that they were looking for the wreck of a Spanish ship so that they could recover its cannon.*

A.G.I., Seville, Indiferente General 1868; 147/5/17; printed and translated in I. A. Wright, "Spanish Policy Toward Virginia, 1606–1612," American Historical Review, XXV (1920), 463–467.

Council for War in the Indies, March 5, 1611; with what is offered concerning Virginia, which the English are occupying.

My Lord:

Your Majesty, by *cédula* of November 8, 1608, transmitted through this council for war, commanded Pedro de Ybarra, at that time governor and captain general of Florida, to order Captain Francisco Fernandez de Écija, or some other that he found satisfactory, to go along the coast northward, and, passing Cape San Roman, to reconnoitre all that relates to Virginia and the ports, bays, and reefs along its coast in the places that can be fortified, and see whether the English, or other nations, have gone to these regions, and whether they have set foot and fortified themselves in any, and where and how and with what people and forces, or whether they have settled any place, and by what route they have gone, and of what quality that land is, and what these nations can obtain from it, and with what Indians they communicate, and what is the distance from Florida to Virginia or to that place where they have settled, and with what measures and forces they can be driven from there and frustrated of their designs and punished. In pursuance of which the governor despatched the said captain Écija in a pinnace with twenty-five sailors and soldiers and an Indian woman, a native of those provinces and having their language, married to a Spanish soldier, and some hoes and other things of iron which he gave him to obtain the good-will of the Indians and to rescue a Frenchman whom a cacique of those regions had for many years held captive, in order that he also might serve them as interpreter; and by the instructions that he gave him he ordered that he should use the diligence which Your Majesty commanded, until he should come to the latitude of 37½ degrees which is the place where he understood that the settlement of the English was, and that if he did not find them there he should go on to the goldmine that is in 44½ degrees, examining the great Rio de Gama which is in 43 degrees; and the said Captain Écija went out from the port of San Agustín de la Florida to carry out this undertaking on June 26, 1609, and went along reconnoitring and sounding all the ports and bays that he found along the coast, and having come to the river which they call Jordan on July 8 he there obtained information from an Indian chieftain and others, and was told that at four days' journey, having traversed the plain of San Roman, they were at the settlement of the English in a village which is called Guandape, lying beside a river which runs into the sea, and it is on an island surrounded by water, which on one side is joined to the mainland, and that ordinarily there are ships in that port, and three months ago seven departed from it, and six of them took the course to the north and the other to the south, and in the harbor there remained always some on guard, and every day many others came and went, up the coast to the northward, and that they had made a fort but that it was of wood, and they had made a league with the neighboring caciques, and that

with eight of them they associated as friends, and they entertained them much and gave them clothes and tools and ordered them to sow grain, although the English themselves did not occupy themselves with this but with their fortification, and in the place where information was had of all this Captain Écija rescued the Frenchman, called Juan Corbe, a native of Harve de Gracia, and with him they set sail, on July 15, pursuing their voyage, and on the 25th, having come to the Bay of Jacán (which by another name they call Virginia) he perceived a ship anchored in it, and since it was of much greater tonnage than that in which they were, for it carried two topsails and a great banner at its masthead, and since he had perceived that it desired to entrap them in the bay where it could be master, because it withdrew before them, they did not venture to follow it nor to close with it, so they went thence to 35½ degrees, whence, because of storms and because the season was advanced for those seas, they returned to the Jordan, and there they again sought information respecting the English, and the Indians confirmed what they had said before and added that alongside the wooden fort they had cast much stone into the water, mid-leg deep, and that they brought it in boats, and that there were many women and children who went about through the fields and houses of the neighboring Indians, and that from the Rio Jordan to the settlement by a straight path overland it was little more than fifty leagues, and to Sant Agustín de la Florida one hundred, so that from there to the place where the English are fortifying themselves it is 150 leagues; and the Frenchman whom they rescued declared that from the Indians of the town in which he was kept captive, who frequently went and came to the settlement of the English, he had learned that they had built a wooden fort and a town made of the same and had two large ships with guns, guarding the fortlike castles, and two others as guards and sentinels of the bar, in addition to those that went and came, and that every year a ship came from England laden with provisions and munitions; and with this relation the governor Pedro de Yvarra sent a pilot-book of the voyage, which the said Captain Écija caused to be made by the pilot that was with him, stating the sea-marks and the character of the harbors and bays that there are from Florida to the place to which they went, and the governor says in his letter that it appears to him that the plan the English entertain, as far as he has been able to learn, is to fortify themselves in the said bay of Jacán (the mouth of which is four leagues and more across, and a stone's throw off from its entrance you have twenty fathoms at least), and to make an expedition into the land, taking for that purpose sufficient people, until they shall come to Nueva Mexico, Nueva Galicia, and Vizcaya, and Çacatecas, which are in the same latitude, and to go across the land to the other sea at the west, since from that part of Florida great rivers go up into the land and from the other sea also it is known that others go up, not smaller, and that there is little distance from the one set of rivers to the other, and the enemy could go up through those of the east coast and go down through those of the west, and fortify themselves in the ports of that sea and there make ships and fleets and overrun the whole coast of New Spain, Tierra Firme, Peru, and China, to the great damage of the crown and subjects of Your Majesty, and that before more of the land is seized upon it would be expedient to manage to drive him from it, since as to the natives they do not deprive them of any of their religious ceremonies, which is what they most cherish, and at the same time they appease and entertain them, though with things of little value, and keep them very pleased and contented and are attaching them all to themselves, and on that northward coast they will be able to settle at the bar of Cayagua, which is a good position, seventy leagues from the garrison of Florida, in 33½ degrees, to which they can come by land from their settlement, and there there are many Indians very well provided with the fruits of the earth and other supplies.

And having examined all this in the council (*junta*) for war, together with other papers which were brought to it incidentally, though of little credit, and seeing that Your Majesty, in response to a *consulta* of March 23 of this year (to the effect that one should suspend the execution of the project which had been sent out by the council (*consejo*) of war to consider a reconnaissance of Virginia, and that this should be in the hands of this council (*junta*) because it concerned it and was matter that had been introduced in it) commanded that that which had been resolved upon by the said council (*consejo*) of war should be done, and that if to this council any other thing

occurred which ought to be prepared toward the carrying out of what is to be done it should be consulted, and considering the damages and great inconveniences which are to be expected from the neighborhood of these English and the anxiety to which they would put all the West Indies and their trade, especially if they plant in those regions the religion which they profess, our opinion has been that it would be greatly to the service of God and of Your Majesty and the universal good of your subjects to break up their plans at once, driving them from there before they take more root and possess themselves of more land and fortify themselves, have greater forces and extend through other regions, as they will go on to do, since none other is their design, and if this is not done in time it will afterward be very difficult.

But that it may be done successfully, because the information now possessed is not thought sufficient, it will be well to obtain certain and complete information of all there is in Virginia, and for this purpose in addition to the means which the council (*consejo*) of war has taken and ordered to be taken, another method is suggested, which is that if Your Majesty would be pleased to send two religious of the English Seminary, that more satisfaction may be obtained, by their going to England and embarking on the first occasion that any ships are going from there to Virginia, and having informed themselves of the inhabitants, settlement, and fortifications, and the character and form of the harbor or harbors where they are fortifying themselves they should return to England in the same trading ships and from there to Spain, with greater and more complete knowledge of all that is possible, in order that, having obtained whatever information is necessary through both channels, a plan may be put into execution to go in sufficient forces to drive them away.

Don Diego Ybarra and Don Fernando Xiron, inasmuch as it is highly important that no time should be lost in a matter of such consequence, are of the opinion that while these measures are being taken we should proceed to bring together (giving out that they are for some other purpose of the service of Your Majesty) some four or five thousand men and the ships necessary for them, which should be good and proper for this purpose, with sailors experienced in that navigation, that, taking into view the experience, knowledge, and adaptedness that are suitable for such an enterprise, they should think to be sufficient forces to carry out what is desired; moreover that if the new information obtained should require that these forces should be larger they may be rapidly increased, so that, all being ready, the fleet may put to sea by the end of March of the coming year 1612, which is the season most suitable for the voyage they have to make, since when the summer begins contrary winds are customary in those seas, and so they would go at great hazard, and at least the costs incurred would be wasted because they would not be able to have any good effect. Your majesty will order inquiry and the providing of what is most pleasing to him. Madrid May 5, 1611.

[Signed:] Don Diego de Ybarra, Don Diego Brochero, Don Fernando Giron, Licenciado Don Francisco Arias Maldonado, Doctor Bernardo de Olmedilla, Licenciado Don Francisco de Tejeda

778. Examination of John Clark about events in Virginia in 1611.

The appearance of the Spanish vessel at Point Comfort led in the end to the seizure of Don Diego de Molina (who was not repatriated until 1616) and of Marco Antonio Perez (he died in Virginia), along with the English pilot Francis Lymbry (also retained in Virginia until 1616, but hanged for a crime committed on shipboard when being repatriated), and the hurried departure of the Spanish vessel with the English pilot, John Clark, as a hostage. Clark was taken to Havana and took part in inquiries about Virginia, making a deposition about the events of 1611 and the state of the colony at that time. He, too, was ultimately repatriated.

A.G.I., Seville, Indiferente General 1867; 147/5/16; printed and translated in I. A. Wright, "Spanish policy toward Virginia, 1606–1612," American Historical Review, XXV (1920), 470–474.

Declaration of the Englishman from Virginia.

That he is called Juan Clerg and is a native of London, a pilot, thirty-five years of age, and that he is of the religion of his king, and in the month of March of this year sailed from the port of the said city for Virginia with three ships, the one of 300 tons, another of 150, and another of 90, and that the course they took was for Dominica and Niebes, where they took in water, and from there, sighting Porto Rico, they took their course to the north, and the first land they discovered was twelve leagues to the west of the port of Virginia, and that at other times they are not accustomed to go to Dominica, to get water, but sail for 22 degrees, steering to the west [and] west-northwest without sighting land or making the Windward Islands, and that the coast is clear, and at forty leagues, running from the southeast to the west-southwest, there are sixty fathoms, at thirty leagues fifty, at twenty leagues thirty-six, at ten leagues eighteen, and at five leagues fifteen fathoms, and five leagues off the land the least water there is is from five to four fathoms, and in the mouth itself of the bay there are from twelve to fourteen fathoms, and along the south shore of the harbor is a shoal which has not more than one fathom to a fathom and a half of water, and on the north side of it, in the mouth itself of the bay alongside the harbor, there are ten or twelve fathoms of water, and from one point of the harbor to the other there are from eight to five fathoms of water, and within there is a good roadstead for ships, well sheltered from all winds, and within the bay itself there are five rivers, flowing in different directions, and of four of these he has no knowledge as to what kind they are.

That at the mouth of the said harbor, in one of these rivers, there are four fortifications on the north side, all on one bank, and that the first fort is at the mouth of the river, where there are fifty persons settled, men and women, of whom forty are fit to bear arms, and that the fort is of palisades and timber, without stone or brick, and has seven pieces of artillery, two of them of about thirty-five hundredweight and the rest of thirty, twenty, and eighteen, and all cast-iron, and that the second fort is two-thirds of a league from there, and another at a distance of one musket-shot, and the fourth at another musket-shot, each having one cast-iron piece for defense against the Indians, and the principal settlement, where there is another fortification, is twenty leagues up the river from the first fort, and in it there are sixteen pieces, and it is also surrounded by palisades, and the houses of the settlement are all wood and the cannon of cast-iron like the rest, and ships of deep draft go up to the said settlement.

That where there is least water in the channel of the river there are three fathoms and one half of water, but that this changes sometimes with the freshes, although the difference between flood and ebb is not more than half a fathom, and that barges go thirty leagues farther up from the town, that is, fifty from the mouth of the harbor.

That it is not possible to journey by land along the river bank, and that from the uppermost part of the river to the South Sea would be sixteen or eighteen days' journey, as they have understood from the native Indians, and that he does not know that pirates or ships from any region gather in the said port and river, and that in all the settlements and fortifications there are about 1000 persons, 600 of them fit to bear arms and the rest women, boys, and old men.

That he does not know that there is any further trade with England than that some provisions and clothing and other things have been brought for the people that are settled there, and on the return voyage they go back laden with wood for hogsheads and for ships, and sassafras wood, and that also they have brought over 100 cows, 200 pigs, 100 goats, and 17 mares and horses, and that he understands that there is a certain gold-mine which is the cause why his king gives permission to sail from England to those parts, although up to the present time they have not found any gold or silver, though they have sought for it, nor do the Indians bring any of it, and he denied that he had confessed to the master that pieces of gold were found.

That that land has been governed by a brother of the Conde Nontonborlan, named Perse, who brought his government to an end at the coming of a knight who is called Don Tomas, who was in the three ships in which the deponent made his voyage, and who governs by the order of the king of England.

That in August of this year they expect four ships with some people and a quantity of cattle, under command of Don Tomas Guies, and that those who sail to these regions and gather there are abandoned people, who are accustomed to live by piracy.

That he has been only once in Virginia, and that at present there were six ships there, and the three that went with him, and of the other three, two were made in Bermuda, where one from England came ashore in a storm, with more than 150 persons, and among them some officials, and taking the iron, pitch, and what else was necessary, they made them two years ago, the one of seventy tons and the other of twenty-five, and that the last of the said vessels was a barge of about twelve or thirteen tons, made in the said Virginia, where they were also making a galley of twenty-five benches, but that it would not be finished very soon, because of having little that is prepared and not having the necessary men, and that it is five years since they began to settle that land, and that all those who are there or go to it are English.

That the Indians of that land are sometimes at peace and other times at war, and go clothed in deer skins and with their bows and arrows, which are *gusamar* [?], and that the produce they gather is maize and walnuts, and up in the land there are many deer and the cattle that they have taken from England, and as to fisheries at times there is abundance and at others very little.

And as to the manner in which they took him, he declares that a caravel having come to the said harbor of Virginia a boat came ashore from it with some men, of whom three landed, two Spaniards and an Englishman, the last of whom this deponent knew, because two years ago he saw him in the city of Malaga serving as a pilot in the armada of Don Luis Faxardo, and that the soldiers who went down to the shore with the captain of the fort who is called David, took all three, and they all ate together, and then they ordered the deponent with three or four others to go and bring the caravel into the port, and he went to the shallop, and one of the mariners put him into the boat, carrying him on his shoulders, and when they saw him in it they would not let him go, but carried him on board the caravel, where they kept him all night, and in the morning they set him in a boat together with the master of the caravel and other men and went to the land to speak with the English and to ask them for their three men, which they did, saying that they would give them the deponent in return for these, to which they replied that until they should have given account to the governor of that land, who was at the settlement, they could not do anything, and the master and the people of the caravel, seeing this, feared that the ships which were in the port might do them some harm, and being unwilling to wait longer went away to Havana taking him with them.

Declaration of the master, pilot, and mariner.

That when they sailed from the port of Havana, which was one day after Corpus Christi, Don Diego de Molina, who had command of the caravel, told them that they were going to seek the artillery of a ship which had been lost on the coast of Florida, and that they should sail in that direction, which they did, and came to the port of San Agustín of those provinces, where they remained with the governor five days, and from there they sailed on the 15th or 16th of June and took their course up along the said coast, sounding, until they came to 37 degrees, where they found a great bay, and that Don Diego de Molina said that this was the place which they were to seek, and that having entered and sounded the bay up to the middle of it they found that at the entrance it has fifteen fathoms and then from ten to four, and that they saw that there was a ship anchored near a point where there was a fort like an intrenchment, and near it they went ashore in a shallop, and Don Diego de Molina and the ensign Marco Antonio Perez and the English pilot they had taken with them, a spy [confidente] married in Lisbon, jumped ashore, having their muskets, and Don Diego ordered the master, this deponent, to put to sea with all the people, and that they should not come to land nor disembark in any manner unless they should so signal to them, and that being in sight of what went on they saw some fifty men, English or Flemish as it appeared to them, come out in three or four squads from a cove, and they seized them and took away their arms and took them to a fort, and an hour later twenty Englishmen returned in three squads and called to the master, this deponent, and requested him to come to land, and he said to them to first bring back his captain, and the English replied that it was not possible, and while this was going on others came with the English spy whom they had taken, and seeing that the master would not come to land they told the latter that he should call him, assuring him that they would not do him damage, but that he should be regaled, but that although to comply with their orders he did it, yet by some signs and by his sad countenance he gave

him to understand that he was taken prisoner, and that consequently he should go away and thereupon [this deponent] ordered a sailor to swim ashore and try to learn something concerning the captain, but they would not let him speak with the English spy, and then eight others came, and one of them said he wished to speak to the master, and the sailor undertook to carry him out upon his shoulders, and did so, and when they had come to the caravel he tried to persuade the master to come to land, and he not only would not do it but, seeing that they would not bring back his captain and the other two companions, he put out to sea with the Englishman, and although the latter tried to escape from the caravel they detained him and brought him to Havana, and on the voyage they asked him certain things, and among other things he said that a hundred leagues up into the land there was a mountain from which they obtained pieces of gold.

779.   February 18, 1613. Reexamination of John Clark in Spain about Virginia.

After his ordeal before the Havana board of inquiry, John Clark was taken to Spain and reexamined there, in Madrid, on February 13, 1613, on behalf of the Council of the Indies.

Although Spain continued to take a hostile line toward English intervention in Virginia, there was not, subsequently, any attempt at interference there, but Molina, while a prisoner, managed to send out some reports of what was going on.

A.G.I., Seville, Indiferente General 1868; 147/5/17; printed and translated in I. A. Wright, "Spanish policy toward Virginia, 1606–1612," American Historical Review, XXV (1920), 476–479.

Confession of the English Pilot of Virginia.

In the city of Madrid on the 18th day of the month of February of 1613 the Señor Licenciado Don Francisco de Texada, of His Majesty's Royal Council of the Indies and of his council for war in the Indies, for certain purposes touching the service of His Majesty caused to be brought before him a man, English by nation, who was in the custody of Captain Don Alonso Flores by order of the said war-council, and in the presence of me the present scribe his Worship took and received this man's oath in form of law, and he gave it well and completely, and having been sworn the following questions were asked him.

Being asked how he was called, he said that he is called Juan Clarque.

Being asked of what place he was an inhabitant and native, he said that he is an inhabitant of the city of London in England.

Being asked if he is a Roman Catholic, he said yes.

Being asked what office and profession he has, he said a pilot and that for four years he has followed that office, though before this he was in a way of knowing it, because for four years he had sailed in different parts of the world.

Being asked when he made the voyage to Virginia and with whom and for what purposes and how he was brought to the city of Havana, he said that in the previous year of 1611 at the beginning of March he set sail from the port of London in a ship of 300 tons in which he went as pilot, together with two other ships, the one of 150 tons and the other of 90, in which went 300 men of war in addition to the mariners and 600 barrels of flour and 50 of powder and some boxes of arquebusses, the whole despatched on account of the merchants of London for Virginia, as general of which went Don Thomas Diel, who was to live there, as in fact he remained, as governor of Virginia; and they spent upon that voyage two months and one half, and the course they took was that from England they were sailing to the southwest until they came into the latitude of the Canary Islands, which was at 28 degrees, and from there they sailed west-southwest to the latitude of Dominica in 14½ degrees, where they took in water and stayed two days, and from there they sailed north-northwest to the island of Niebes, where they remained four days refreshing the people, because they had some men sick, and from there northwest-quarter-north to the Passage, up which they went until they made the coast of Virginia between the Cape of Deception and Cape Henry and that the reason for steering northwest-quarter-north and north-northwest several times was because of the currents which pushed them to the northeast and the variation of the needle which they warned him to be 7 and 8

degrees, and from there they sailed north-north-west until they were off Cape Henry, which is one of the capes between which one enters into the bay, into which they entered, and proceeded to go up within the river to a point which in English they call Punt Confort, which in Castilian means Point of Consolation; and there they put the people ashore, and the mariners took the three ships up the river to the principal place, which they call Jacobus, where they anchored, because the ships could not go up beyond the said port, though ships of 40 or 50 tons, which draw two yards and one half of water, can go up 30 leagues, and that this deponent being in company with the English, because he had come from that principal place to bring a barge with flour of that which he brought in the ships, for the provision of the English who garrison the forts at Point Comfort, there came a long-boat in which were twelve or thirteen men, of whom three landed, and the captain of the fort having gone to them with a squad of soldiers asked the three men (one of whom this deponent knew, that he was an Englishman and a pilot, because of having seen him in a house when Don Luis Faxardo went to burn the galleons of Tunis) why they came there and they replied, to seek a ship of the king of Spain which had been lost on that coast, and the captain told him that he would have to give account to his governor of their coming, who was then at the principal place, called Jacobus, twenty leagues from there, and so he did in a barge. And he said to one of the three that in order that the caravel should not be lost in the bay where it had anchored, they should bring it up into the river and to Point Comfort, where it would be safe, and he having replied that whoever was left in her would not know how to do it and that they should give him a pilot for that purpose, the captain ordered this deponent to take the same long-boat in which the three had come and go on board the said caravel, and so he did, and on his coming to her the master said that he would not sail in unless they brought back to her those who were missing and as [the English captain] would not give them up, though on another day the long-boat returned for them, the said caravel, without waiting longer, sailed away with this deponent to Havana, leaving the three in the power of the English.

Being asked what roadsteads and of what quality and what forts and of what sort there are from the bay up to the said city of Jacobus, he said that the bay is seven or eight leagues wide and with good soundings, although ships have not security or shelter in it, and so go in until they shelter themselves behind Point Comfort, as he did, where there is room for thirty ships up to 800 tons to anchor, for although when the wind is north some sea is felt in there, it is not a matter of much importance; and on that same point there is a fort beside the shore where seven pieces of artillery are mounted, each of about thirty hundredweight, placed alongside the water in such a way that, since the entrance is narrow and the channel is not more than a musket-shot broad, ships cannot enter or anchor without the artillery doing them damage, and in that fort there are fifty soldiers of ordinary garrison, and half a league from it there are two other small fortifications each having one piece of artillery of ten or twelve hundredweight, to guard the cornfields from the Indians, and that these forts and the first one, on the point, are fortified with stout palisades well joined together.

Being asked how many houses there were in the said place called Jacobus and of what sort and what soldiers and what artillery, he said that there are about 100 wooden houses and in them and in the other places that he has mentioned about a thousand men capable of bearing arms, what with traders and soldiers and laborers, and thirty women, and that the place is fortified with palisades in the form mentioned and probably has about sixteen pieces of artillery, ten heavy and the other smaller, the heavy pieces of about forty or fifty hundredweight, and the others of about sixteen or seventeen, and that he does not know that there is any other settlement besides that, and that of the Indians some are friendly and some are not, and that it appears to him that there is no great number of either sort; and that what up to the present time he has seen taken from that region to England by way of merchandise is timber for making different things, and sassafras, and what they bring from England are provisions of flour and other things and munitions and cattle of different sorts, which do well.

Being asked if he knows that they have found any mines of silver he said that he does not know.

Being asked if he knows the reasons why the English have settled that country and for how long at that place, he said that he understands that they have been settled at that place for six years and that the reasons are to acquire land and build ships and that he does not know the result, beyond the fact that they are in such a situation that in fifteen days at most they can reach the Windward Islands.

Being asked how long it takes to sail from Virginia to England, he said a month, and that he has understood that the voyage is good, and that sometimes they sail east-quarter-northeast until they make the islands of Flores, but that it is possible for them not to make them on their way to England, though it is better and safer navigation to make the islands, and that for Spain, sailing east, they make the islands of Fayal or Tercera, whence the ordinary course is taken.

Being asked how many times he has been in Virginia, and for how long, and what ships he found there [beside] that in which he was, he said that he has made no other voyage than that which he has mentioned, and that he was there forty days before he was taken, and that he found there a ship of 150 tons about to sail for England with timber and sassafras.

Being asked what he believes the English will have done to the three persons who were left in their power, he says that he considers it certain that they will not be ill-treated, because the English do not ill-treat prisoners.

Being asked if he has learned subsequently that there is in this court any news respecting them, he said that an Englishman who lives in the Calle Mayor of this town told this deponent that an acquaintance of his told him that he had talked in England with the English pilot who went with Don Diego Molina, and he was one of the three who was left in Virginia.

Being asked his age, he said that he was forty years old. And he signed this with his name and declared that what he has said in this his answer and declaration is the truth, under obligation of the said oath which he has taken. And his Worship has added his rubric.

[Signed:] John Clark. I, Damian de Carrion y Bricuela, was present.

XXII

England and Virginia, 1599–1606

THE WAR WITH SPAIN and its commitment of so many ships to the royal service and of so many more to licensed and profitable privateering in the Caribbean and elsewhere sufficiently explains the length of the gap between the Virginia voyages of 1584–1590 and those which preceded the foundation of the Virginia Company in 1606. The crucial figure in the 1590s and for the opening years of the seventeenth century was Sir Walter Ralegh, and the essential factor in his importance was the presumed survival of the Lost Colony of 1587 in North America. If there was a colony, then his monopoly powers, entitling him to control all English voyages to the North American mainland, continued to exist. So long as the colony was not found to have been destroyed, he need not worry, and he certainly maintained the supposition that it was alive and that his monopoly power continued intact down to the loss of his patent in the summer of 1603 at the hands of the new monarch James I. He is found, for example, actively asserting his patent in 1602. So it was essential to him to find out, as discreetly as possible, what the evidence was which would justify him in reviving colonization in Virginia at his own time and on his own terms. He was preoccupied by the presumed gold of Guyana between 1593 and 1598. Although he contemplated, so he said at least, calling in to look for the colony in 1595 on his return voyage from the Orinoco, he was unable to do so. Towards the end of the decade, he began to send out discreet probing voyages in small trading vessels that were directed to the area between Cape Fear and the mouth of the Chesapeake Bay. But, if such voyages began about 1599, we do not know that he picked up any information about the English survivors—or alternatively, about the destruction of the remnant of the colony—before his disgrace and imprisonment in July,

1603. The evidence we have is minimal and is largely confined to the years of 1602 and 1603. If a ship, arriving in the Thames in September, 1603, brought Indians from the Chesapeake Bay (as seems possible, though it is not certain that they did not come for elsewhere), some trickle of information on the colonists may have reached London then, but it was too late to be of importance to Ralegh, as he was a prisoner in the Tower of London. Such information, if it indeed reached England either in 1603 or in 1605, could have played a significant part behind the scenes in leading to the mobilizing of widespread support at Court and in the City of London, as well as in the outports of Plymouth and Bristol, thereby leading to the issue of the Virginia Company charter in April, 1606.

We know nothing for certain about the Lost Colonists. Some circumstantial evidence indicates fairly strongly that a substantial party of them survived in the territory of the Chesapeake Indians until some time between 1605 and 1607, when they and their hosts were massacred by Powhatan. A smaller party may have remained at Roanoke Island for a time and then moved away to take refuge with Manteo near Cape Hatteras. Nothing is known of their fate, though it is not impossible that they joined their comrades near the Chesapeake. Unless more concrete evidence is found in the future, the precise circumstances of their survival and eventual fate will remain unknown. An attempt is made to survey the evidence and to offer some very tentative conclusions in D. B. Quinn, *England and the Discovery of America* (1974), pp. 432–481.

Chapter One hundred
Prelude to the Virginia Company

THE REVIVAL OF THE SOUTH VIRGINIA VOYAGES, 1599–1605, AND THE EMERGENCE OF THE VIRGINIA COMPANY IN 1606

IN 1602 SIR WALTER RALEGH was said to have sent out no less than five fruitless expeditions to find the Lost Colonists of 1587. Two were presumably those of 1588 (452) and 1590 (457). Others, of which nothing is known, appear to have taken place in 1599, 1600, and 1601. Samuel Mace was sent to search south of Cape Hatteras in 1602, to trade with the Indians, and to bring home some products he could obtain for himself. This he did, well to the south of Roanoke Island in the vicinity of modern Cape Lookout, without getting any news of them (780). In 1603 Bartholomew Gilbert was sent out in the *Elizabeth* to search for them in Chesapeake Bay. He failed to find the entrance, went ashore elsewhere, was killed by the Indians, and his ship returned home about the end of September (782). Mace was scheduled to go again in 1603. If he did, he may have brought with him the Virginia Indians, who gave a demonstration of the handling of one of their canoes in the Thames near Lord Cecil's house on September 2 (783). If these Indians were from the Chesapeake Bay area and had survived in England, later they may have given information of value. If they were not brought by Mace, they were the result of a voyage of which we are not aware. Ralegh had now gone to the Tower and had no more power to influence American voyages. The *Castor and Pollux* and the *Pollux and Castor*, when they set out in 1604, were expected to call and purchase silk grass from the lost colonists at Croatoan (that is well south of Roanoke Island), but were captured in 1605 by the Spaniards at St. Helena Sound (766). It is just possible that Captain Christopher Newport, on his way back from the Caribbean, entered Chesapeake Bay in 1605, but there is no evidence, except his skill in entering it in 1607, that he did, although he presented an alligator or crocodile to King James in that year. Nonetheless, a joint plan to send colonists both to North Virginia (Mawooshen) (489) and to South Virginia (Chesapeake Bay) emerged at the opening of 1606.

The initiative taken by Sir John Popham, Lord Chief Justice of the King's Bench, to embark on the sponsorship of a major Virginia enterprise was communicated to Lord Salisbury by Sir Walter Cope about January, 1606 (784). Popham wished Salisbury, or the Privy Council, to extend to him some formal invitation to call together the gentlemen and merchants who had an interest in combining to form a colonizing company, so that they might work out a practical scheme for a unified development. Presumably through his interest in the Plymouth area, Popham himself was mainly interested in north Virginia (as has been shown in volume III), but he was anxious to combine a venture to this area by adventurers from the southwest with a venture to south Virginia backed by the Court and London merchants. It was presumably after such a meeting or meetings and, we suspect, the private advice of Lord Salisbury on what would and would not be acceptable to King James, as well as the good offices of Sir Walter Cope, that a draft charter emerged and eventually passed the great seal on April 10 (797). It would be helpful to penetrate further the negotiations behind the issue of the charter but so far sufficient evidence to do so has not yet emerged. The names of the nominees for the London division of the enterprise in the charter itself help a little, but not very much. The Reverend Richard Hakluyt, Prebendary of Westminster, was certainly a long-time supporter of Virginian colonization and had, clearly, been consulted; Sir George Somers had been identified in some measure with overseas ventures (as, for example, in the Roanoke voyages of 1585), but neither Sir Thomas Gates nor Edward Maria Wingfield is so far known to have earlier overseas interests. The nominees for the southwestern division—Raleigh Gilbert, William Parker, and George Popham—are more obvious choices, primarily representing the influence of Sir John Popham, who regarded this part of the venture as virtually his own affair. The charter was to say nothing clearly about finance, but several private promoters warned that Parliament might need to be brought in to give the venture sufficient financial backing (785–786).

780. 1602. Samuel Mace's voyage to the coast south of Cape Hatteras.

All that is known of the voyage is that it was sponsored by Sir Walter Ralegh and that the note we have of it was included in John Brereton's Briefe and true relation *(459), not long after Mace returned in August, 1602. It was reprinted in S. Purchas,* Pilgrimes, *IV (1625), 1654 (XVIII [1906], 321.*

A briefe Note of the sending another Barque this present yeere 1602. by Sir Walter Raleigh, for the searching out of his Colonie in Virginia.

Samuel Mace of Weimouth, a very sufficient Mariner, an honest sober man, who had beene at Virginia twice before, was employed thither by Sir Walter Raleigh, to finde those people which were left there in the yeere 1587. To whose succour he hath sent five severall times at his owne charges. The parties by him set forth, performed nothing; some of them following their owne profit elsewhere; others returning with frivolous allegations. At this last time, to avoide all excuse, hee bought a Barke, and hired all the companie for wages by the moneth: who departing from Weimouth in March last, 1602. fell fortie leagues to the South-westward of Hataraske, in 34. degrees or therabout; and having there spent a moneth; when they came along the coast to seeke the people, they did it not, pretending that the extremitie of weather, and losse of some principall ground-tackle, forced and feared them from searching the Port of Hataraske, to which they were sent. From that place where they abode, they brought Sassafras, Radix Chinæ, or the China Root, Benjamin, Cassia lignea and a rind of a tree more strong than any Spice as yet unknowne, with divers other commodities, which hereafter in a larger discourse may come to light.

781. 1602. Thomas Harriot and Mace's voyage.

The eminent mathematician, Thomas Harriot, whose Briefe and true report *(1588) (365) had revealed the first Virginia to Englishmen, provided a list of articles to be taken on Mace's voyage. They are in B.L., Additional MS 6788, fol. 417 (first printed in D. B. Quinn, "Thomas Harriot and the Virginia Voyages of 1602,"* William and Mary Quarterly, *3rd. series, XXVIII (1970),*

273. The inclusion of an Algonquian phrase suggests that he may have provided the expedition with a word list for this language.

Whether compasses or diales.
Copper not brasse 20 or 30 pound in plates.
some as thin as paper and small and great.

Hatchetes. 5. doz.	Mattockes. 20
Kniues. 50. doz.	Iron shouelles 20.
lead and powder.	Sheres.
powder and shot.	Sawes.
clothes for men.	
Booke of voyages.	

What is this.   Kecow hit tamen.   What is your
   name.

Ianuary .29♀ .

$$\frac{1601}{1602}$$

Copper in plates.
delyfer theym

at 16d the pound. ⎱
276 pieces.   ⎰   + 42s + 8d

a payne of glass   ⎱
and punches—   ⎰   + 3s + 4d

                              46s + 0d

videlicet.

of 7 inches. square.	10.
round.	05.
6 inches. square.	20.
round.	10.
4 inches. square	40.
round.	20.
3 inches. square	100.
of a smaller.	
size and iblonge	71.
and different begnesses.	
	276.

782. 1603. Thomas Canner's account of Bartholomew Gilbert's voyage in search of Chesapeake Bay.

Bartholomew Gilbert, the London goldsmith who accompanied Bartholomew Gosnold to north Virginia (New England) in 1602 (458), was commissioned by Sir Walter Ralegh in August, 1602, to go in 1603 (accompanied by another ship under Samuel Mace) to search for the lost colonists and to trade with the Indians. This time it is clear the search was to take place well to the north of Cape Hatteras, in Chesapeake Bay if it could be found. After a voyage through the West Indies, the Elizabeth was blown up the North American coast, too far out to sea to sight land. They took a sight on June 23 and found that they were a little north of 40° (between the mouths of the Delaware and the Hudson). Turning south, they made slow progress; by July 25 they were near the mouth of Chesapeake Bay, but were blown away. On July 29 (whether they were north or south of 37° is not known), Gilbert went ashore with a party at a point where there appeared to be a river entrance. They were quickly set upon by Indians; Gilbert and three other men were killed. The remaining eleven men set out for England, arriving in London about the end of September.

S. Purchas, Pilgrimes, IV (1625), 657–658 (XVIII [1906], 329–335).

A Relation of the Voyage made to Virginia, in the Elizabeth of London, a Barke of fiftie tunnes by Captaine Bartholomew Gilbert, in the yeere 1603. Written by Master Thomas Canner a Gentleman of Bernards Inne his companion in the same Voyage.

Upon Wednesday in Easter weeke, the seventeenth of Aprill, after I had taken my leave of some few of my loving and deere friends in Bernards Inne, I rode toward Southampton, there to bespeake Bisket and some other provision for our Barke, wherein Master Bartholomew Gilbert went as Captaine, which had beene in Virginia the yeere before with Captaine Bartholomew Gosnold. After our businesse was dispatched here, wee came into Plimmouth, from whence wee put forth the tenth of May. And the six and twentieth of the same, we were in the latitude of 32. degrees, hoping to have had sight of the Ile of Madera, whereof we missed, in which course we met with two or three English men of warre.

The first of June, we were in the latitude of 27. degrees, and haled over toward the Ilands of the West Indies, and the fifteenth of this moneth toward night wee saw Land. Master Gilbert and the Master Henrie Suite dwelling within the Iron Gate of the Towre of London, tooke it to be the

Bermudas: being very neere the shore they sounded many times and had no ground, at the last they found good ground in fourteene or fifteene fathomes. There wee cast Anchor. In the morning we weighed, and sounded still as we trended by the shoare: but after wee were past a Cables length from our Road, we had no Land againe in forty or fifty fathomes: we kept still by the shore not yet being certaine what Iland it was. The sixteenth in the morning, wee spied the people comming from the shore, who when they came neere, cried out for barter or trade: when they came close aboord, they made signes and cried out to see our colours, which we presently put forth in the maine top, and told them we were Ingleses, Amigos, and Hermanos, that is, Englishmen, their friends and brothers. Assoone as they understood we were Englishmen, they were bolder to come neere: we threw them a Rope, and one came aboord us: wee traded with them for some Tobacco, Pine-apples, Plantanes, Pompions and such things as they had: wee gave them Bugles, Knives, Whistles, and such toyes. Here we kept close by the shore. When this Canoa had traded with us, and uttered all they had and drunke of our Beere, beeing kindly used they departed: and then presently after divers Canoas came, we traded and used them as the first. One of them told us that Iland was Santa Lucia. We bestowed all that forenoone shaking in the wind (for we had no ground to Anchor) neere the shore to trade with them. Then wee set our course for Saint Vincent, but finding a current against us and the wind very scant, we doubted we should not fetch it, and that if we did, peradventure we might bee put to the leeward of Dominica, and so consequently of Mevis or Nieves; for which Iland we were specially bound for to cut Lignum vitæ, in the same. Therefore Master Gilbert thought good to let Saint Vincent alone, although in it is the best Tobacco of all the Ilands, yet in the end hee put roomer for Dominica, whereof we had sight the seventeenth of June, and came close to the shore; and presently one Canoa came aboord, as at Santa Lucia, being sent with two men belike to discover us, and to see what entertainment they should have, we used them kindly and so dismissed them. There came more full of men, with divers of their commodities.

The nineteenth in the morning being Sunday, we anchored in a good Road at Mevis [Nevis], and after went on shore to seeke Lignum vitæ, Master Gilbert, with the Master and divers of the company sought farre into the Woods, but found none but one little Tree, and here and there where one had bin cut: so we were in doubt to find enough heere to load our ship, a just plague unto us for prophaning the Sabbath in travelling about our worldly businesse, when there was no necessitie. This day in the Evening some went out with the Boate unto the shore, and brought on boord a Tortoyse so big that foure men could not get her into the Boate but tied her fast by one legge unto the Boat, and so towed her to the ship, when they had her by the ship, it was no easie matter to get her on boord.

The next day we went on shore againe to search another part of the wood for Lignum vitæ: and then God be thanked we found enough. This day at night we opened our Tortoyse, which had in her about 500. Egges, excellent sweet meate, and so is all the whole fish. Upon Tuesday in the morning we went all on shore saving the Carpenter and Thomas, and Master Gilberts man to fell wood, and this day we felled good store. All the rest of this moneth and three dayes more we continued here every day labouring sore, first in sawing downe the great trees, and sawing them againe into logs, portable out of the thicke wood to the Sea-shoare, so in the Boates, and so to the ship: where M. Gilbert his paines profited double as well in example as in worke, for hee was never idle, but either searching out more trees, or fetching drinke for the Labourers, or doing one thing or other: so that in this just fortnight that wee stayed here, wee had gotten on boord some twenty tuns. Within a few dayes after the Tortoyse was eaten God sent us another. One of these fishes were sufficient meat for twentie men for three or foure dayes if it could bee preserved, but in that Climate no salting can preserve it above two dayes, hardly so long. Now the wood growing thinne, and hardly to be found on this Iland, he thought it best to stay no longer here, but to goe for Virginia, to search for better store. And so upon Sunday the third of July in the afternoone we weighed Anchor, and sailed North-west and by North, and that night passed by Saint Christopher, and another little Iland Munday the fourth in the morning we had sight of the Iland, we went into the Woods to search for Lignum vitæ, but found none but one tree, which he cut and went on boord, we sought also for fresh water, but found none: At Evening went on shore into the bottome of the Bay to dray the Net; and there we gat good store of fine fresh fish, and much more, enough to have laden our Boat we should have gotten, if at every draught we had not had in the Net a Tortoyse, which stil brak through and so carried away the fish with them. At one draught among the rest we had two in the Net, a yong one and an old one: the Net held the young one.

Wee weighed and went through betweene the two Ilands into the mayne Ocean, toward our long desired Countrey Virginia, distant three hundred and fiftie leagues from us. Wee sayled North North-west.

The seventh, we ran still North-west and North and by West. The eight, wee kept the same course. The ninth, we kept still the same course. The winde beganne to vere some thing to the Southward, which had beene constant still, from the Ilands of the Canaries, unto the Ilands of the West Indies. And now began the winde to draw towards the West, and then is it as constant there. The reason I deferre to longer consideration. The current setteth out of the Gulfe of Mexico, and from the mayne shore.

Sunday the tenth, we kept still the same course, and had now but a small gale almost becalmed. The eleventh, we continued the same course with the same small gale we went North. Tuesday the twelfth we kept the same course, if any at all, for, for the most part we were becalmed.

Wednesday the thirteenth, the calme continued, the Sunne being extremely hot in the calme. Thursday the fourteenth, the calme continued as hot as before. These dayes we ayred our Newland fish called Poore John, which proved ill done. For after it was ayred, it rotted the sooner, being burnt in the same. On Friday the fifteenth, God sent us a reasonable gale. The sixteenth and seventeenth, the calme came againe. Munday, we had a good gale, and went North and by West, and North North-west. The nineteenth, twentieth, and one and twentieth, we had an excellent gale, and ranne North North-west. Then we cast out the Lead and looked out for land, but found no ground nor saw no land, and therefore we much doubted that the current had set us very farre to the leeward of the place which wee were bound for, being the Chesepian Bay; but that could not

be knowne till it pleased God to bring us to land. In the afternoone about six of the clocke we cast out the Lead againe, and had ground in thirtie fathomes, whereof we were glad and thanked God, knowing we could not be farre from land.

Saturday the three and twentieth in the morning, about eight of the clocke wee saw land in the height of 40. degrees and odde minutes, very fine low land, appearing farre off to bee full of tall Trees, and a fine sandie shoare, but a great siege: we saw no Harbour, and therefore coasted along to seeke one to the Northward, the wind being at West.

Sunday the foure and twentieth, the wind being about the North-east we beat hard to fetch an Head-land, where we thought we saw an Harbour: but when we came up with it, wee perceived it was none, and all our labour lost. And therefore the wind beeing now more full in our teeth at the North-east, wee considered it were better to put roome, so that if the winde should stand, then we should fetch the Bay of Chesepian, which Master Gilbert so much thirsted after, to seeke out the people for Sir Walter Raleigh left neere those parts in the yeere 1587. if not, perhaps we might find some Road or Harbour in the way to take in some fresh water: for now wee had none aboord.

On Munday the five and twentieth of July at night wee came neere the mouth of the Bay[1]: but the wind blew so sore, and the Sea was so high, that the Master durst not put in that night into the Sea: and so continued next day.

On Wednesday the seven and twentieth, at night the winde came faire againe, and wee bare againe for it all night, and the wind presently turned againe. Thursday the eight and twentieth, considering our extremitie for water and wood, victuals and beere likewise consuming very fast, we could no longer beate for it, and therefore ran roomer, determining for this time to seeke it no more[2].

Friday the nine and twentieth, being not farre from the shoare, which appeared unto us exceeding pleasant and full of goodly Trees, and with some shew of the entrance of a River[3], our Captaine Bartholomew Gilbert accompanied with Master Thomas Canner a Gentleman of Bernards

1. Sidenote: "The mouth of the Chesepian Bay."
2. Sidenote: "They departed Eastward from the mouth of the Chesepian Bay."
3. Sidenote: "A shew of entrance of a river."

Inne, Richard Harison the Masters Mate, Henry Kenton our Chirurgion, and one Derricke a Dutchman, went on shore in the Boate from the ship which lay above a mile from the land, and with their weapons marched up into the Countrey, leaving two youths to keepe the Boate: but shortly after the Indians set upon them, and one or two of them fell downe wounded in sight of our yong men that kept the Boat, which had much a doe to save themselves and it. For some of the Indians roming downe to them, would have haled it on shore, which notwithstanding they saved, and with heavie hearts gat unto the ship with the losse of their Captain and foure of their principall men. Thus being but eleven men and Boyes in all in the ship, though our want of water and wood were great, yet wee durst not adventure the losse of any more of our small company in this place; Therefore our Master Henry Sute tooke his course home for England by the Iles of the Acores, and fell first with the Pike, and afterward entring into our Chanell, had first sight of Portland, and thence came up the River of Thames unto Ratcliffe, about the end of September 1603. finding the Citie most grievously infected with a terrible plague.

783. September 2, 1603. Virginia Indians in the Thames.

It is suggested (D. B. Quinn, England and the Discovery of America [1974], pp. 419–431) that the "Virginians" who demonstrated a canoe on the Thames near Robert Cecil's house in the Strand (he was then Lord Cecil) may have been brought by Samuel Mace from Chesapeake Bay in 1603 (780–781). If not, another expedition of which nothing is known went to North America in this year also. It is indicated that Sir Walter Cope (784) was present.

The documentary entries are in a list of rewards given for or by Lord Cecil from July 20 to September 6, 1603. The list is at Hatfield House, Cecil Family and Estate Papers, Accounts 6/31, and is partly printed in D. B. Quinn, England and the Discovery of America (1974), pp. 430–431.

2 Septembre

geven by Myles to ij watermen that brought the cannowe to my Lords howse   v[s]

geven by my Lord to the virginians   iiij[s]

geven by Sir Walter Cope to the keeper of the House   x[s]

geven by him to Sir Baptist Hickes his servantes for my Lord   v[s]

geven to the virginians   v[s]

geven to a payre of ores that waited on the Virginians when they rowed with ther Cannow   xij[d]

784. [*Circa* January, 1606]. Sir Walter Cope to the Earl of Salisbury.

Early in 1606 Sir John Popham's preliminary discussions about the formation of a Virginia Company were so far advanced that he was able to have Sir Walter Cope write to Lord Salisbury asking him, as Principal Secretary of State, or the Privy Council collectively, to send Popham authority to call together the gentlemen and merchants who were interested in the plan in order to draft a suitable scheme. Privy Council records are missing so it is not known what response Popham obtained, except that the Virginia Charter duly followed.

Hatfield House, Cecil MS 191/120 (Hist. MSS Comm., Calendar of Hatfield Manuscripts, XVIII [London, 1940], 84).

Sir my Lorde cheffe Justyce, foreseeynge in thexperyence of hys place The infynite numbers of Cashiered Captaines & Soldyers, of pore artezans that woulde, & cannot worke, & of Idell vagrantes that maye & will not worke, whose Encrease threateneth the state, ys affectionately bent to the plantation of Virginia, in the which he hathe allredye taken greate paynes, & meaneth to dysburse 500[li.] per annum for fyve yeares. If the action prosper he desyreth for hys better expedicion two Lynes from your Lordship in particular / or from the Lordes [of the Privy Council] in generall / by vertue wherof he maye cawle the undertakers gentlemen merchantes &c unto him /

& by ther advyse to sett downe the best manner of project, which beyng agreed upon, shalbe spedely Retourned to your Lordshipps, because the best Season for the Jorney aprocheth; & after Receave such further dyrection as to your wysedomes maye be thought fytt.

Your honours most humbly
    [Signed:] Walter Cope

[Addressed:] To the Right honorable the Earle of Salisbury hys Majestes Princypall Secretary at the Courte

[Endorsed:] 1605 Sir Walter Cope to my Lorde

785. [Between March 25 and April 9, 1606]. Edward and Thomas Hayes to the Earl of Salisbury.

Edward Hayes, well known for his writings on North America for over twenty years (362–364), and his relative, Thomas Hayes, approached Lord Salisbury with a plan for the public financing of a Virginia venture at some point before the Virginia Charter of April 10 was issued. The details of their plan are not now attached to the letter, but they intended to circulate copies amongst members of the House of Commons, whose support would be essential. One of the copies, which is stylistically clearly a Hayes document and which embodies their scheme, was revived and presented as his own by one T. Gerolyn to Sir Julius Caesar on January 5, 1607/1608, and followed the letter as if it was of 1606 (786).

The letter is Hatfield House, Cecil MS 119/6 (calendared in Hist. MSS Comm., Calendar of Hatfield Manuscripts, *XVIII [London, 1940], 407–408), printed in Alexander Brown,* The First Republic in America *(New York, 1898), pp. 3–5.*

Pardon us (Right honorable) that we presume to move this project presented herewith unto you. so remote from the course of your great Affayres as America is from Englande wherin our presumpcion (we confess) may be taxed of unadvised rashnes. Bicause the waight of this our home state hath already so much upon you, that to presse private more may be thought importunate, or rather in us a want of judgemente/.

But the propertie of virtue and true honour is to putt no limittes unto ye doing of good, in which the farther that mortall men can procede, the nearer they approache unto God. And you whom God hathe extraordinarily indued and made Cumpleat in all abilities which may extend to thadvauncement of most high & honest Causis, will not (we are perswaded) take any such mocion to be impertinent to you, but well deserving to be patronised by one so honorable a personage as your self: the same reaching and aspiring to the Chiefest good that man Can prepound./

But For as much as so great a business for planting of Christianitie amongst heathens can never be duly effected by private meanes, in which Course som of us have many yeares past ventred both life and substance without Fruite: We have devised another waye without offence to publike or private, Wherby the Cause may be compleatly set forward, supported and Seconded untill it be grown to such perfeccion as yt may stand of it self and give large Recompence to all Coasistauntes./

Whiche meanes requyreth the Consent of Parliament, Whereunto a mocion is drawn by us, and a brieff discourse of inducementes allso, for satisfaction of sondry objections which have ben made heretofore. Seming fytt to leave as little scruple as may be in mens myndes and Consciences, whose furtheraunces must be requyred in the house, somme Coppies whereof we intend to deliver amongst diverse of our Frendes memberes of the same./

Neverthles, before we procede, we thought it our duties fyrst to acquaynt your lordship therwith, without whose grace and honorable advice we desyre not to doo any thing. For which Consideracion we hombly present your Honour with the Fyrst view of our project which we hope after your accustomed maner you will voutsafe to accept, Being in this and all services devoted unto you: and so rest attending your Honoures pleasure as we shall understand by this Deliverer.
Your Honoures most bounden.
    Tho: Hayes./ Edward: Hayes

[Addressed:] To the Right honorable the Earle of Salisbury of his Majestes privie Councell.

[Endorsed (other hand):] 1606. Master Hayes to my Lord

786. 1606. "Reasons to move the High Court of Parlament to raise a stocke for the maintaining of a Collonie in Virgenia."

Alexander Brown, The Genesis of the United States, 2 vols. (Boston, 1890), I, 36–38, printed this document as if it belonged to 1606, which it must since it clearly precedes the charter of April 10, 1606. Such a scheme for public support was presented to Lord Salisbury in later March or early April, 1606 by Thomas and Edward Hayes. Brown did not appreciate that this particular version (which he did not always read correctly) was addressed by one T. Gerolyn to Sir Julius Caesar (apparently as if it were his own) on January 5, 1607/1608. It appears, by both content and style, that it was one of the copies which the Hayes partners proposed in 1606 to distribute to members of Parliament, and it is here assigned, conjecturally but with considerable confidence, to 1606 and to Thomas and Edward Hayes, even though T. Gerolyn appears to have presented it as his own.

B.L., Lansdowne MS 160, fols. 356–357.

Reasons or motives for the raising of a publique stocke to be imploied for the peopling and discovering of such Countries as maye be fownde most convenient for the supplie of those defects which this Realme of Englande most requireth.

1. All Kingdomes are maintained by Rents or traficque, but especially by the latter, which in maritaine places most florisheth by means of Navigation.

2. The Realme of Englande is an Ilande impossible to be otherwise fortified then by stronge shippes and able mariners and is secluded from all corners with those of the maine continent, therefore fit abundance of vesselles be prepared to exporte and importe merchandize.

3. The furniture of shipping consist in Mastes, Cordage, Pich, Tar, Rossen &c. of which Englande is by nature unprovided and at this presente injoyeth them only by favor of forraigne Potentes [=Potentates].

4. The life of shipping resteth in number of able Mariners and worthey Chieftaines, which cannot be maintained without assurance of rewarde of honorable meanes to be imployed and sufficient seconde of their adventures.

5. Private purces are cowld Coumpfortes to adventurers and have ever ben fownde fatall to all interprices hetherto undertaken by the English, by reason of delaies, Jeloces and unwillingnes to backe that project which succeeded not at the first attempt.

6. The Example of Hoillinders is verie pregnante by a maine ba[r]cke or stocke have effected marvelous matters in traficque and navigacion in fewe years.

7. It is honorable for a state rather to backe an exploite by a publique consent, then by a private monopoly.

8. Where Collonies are fownded for a publique-well [being? they?] maye continewe in better obedience, and become more industrious, then where private men are absolute signors of a voiage, for as much as better men of haviour and qualitie will ingage themselves in a publique service, which carrieth more reputacion with it, then a private, which is for the most parte ignominious in the end, as being presumed to ayme at a lucre and is subject to emulacon, fraude and invie, and when it is at the greatest hight of fortune, can hardly be tollerated, by reason of the Jelosie of state.

9. The manifest decaye of shipping and mariners and of manie Borowe and Porte townes and Havens cannot be releaved by private increase, nor amended otherwise than by a voluntary consent of manie purces of the Well-publique.

10. It is publicly knowne that trafique with our neighbor Countries begin to be of small request, the game seldom answering the merchantes adventure and forraigne states either are already or at this presente are preparing to inrich them selves with woole and cloth of their owne which heertofore they borrowed of us, which purpose of theirs being achived in Fraunce and it hath been already in Spaine and Italy, which purpose of theirs therefore we must of necessigty forgoe our greate showing if we doe not wish [to] prepare a place fit for the vent of our wares and to set out Marriners on worke, who dayly runn to serve forraigne nacions for wante of imployment, and cannot be restrained by anie Lawe when necessatie inforseth them to serve and hire of a stranger rather than to serve at home.

11. That Realme is most compleet and wealthie which either hath sufficient to serve it selfe or can

finde the meanes to exporte of the naturall comodites then it hath occason necessarily to importe, consequently it muste insue that by a publique consent, a Collony transported into a good and plentiful climate able to furnish our wantes, our monies and wares, that nowe run into the handes of our adversaries, or cowld frendes, shall passe unto our frendes and naturall kinsmen, and from them likewise, we shall receive such things as shalbe most available to our necessaties, Rich intercourse of trade maye rather be called a home bread trafique, than a forraigne exchange.

12. Forraigne nacions yearly attempt discoveries in strange coastes moved thereunto by the Jolosy of state which affecteth that gaine most which is gotten either without anie tuck of their neighbors, or at best by smalest advantage that maye turne unto them by their trafique.

13. Experience teacheth us that it is dangerous to our state to interprice a discovery and not to procead therein even to the verie sifting it to the uttermost for not only disreputacon groweth thereby, disability and power weake to proceed or bewraiing our owne Idelnes and want of Counsell to mannage our enterprices, as if the glorious state of ours, rather broched by the vertue of our Ancesters, then of our owne worthines.

14. The want of our fresh and presente supplie of our discoveries hath in manner taken awaye the title which the Lawe of nacions giveth us unto the Coast first fownde out by our industrie, forasmuch as whatsoever a man relinquiseth mayebe claymed by the next findor as his just property, neither is it sufficient to set foot in a Countrie but to possesse and howld it, in defence of an invading force (for wante whereof) the King of Denmarke intendeth into northwest passage (as it is reported) and it is also reported that the French intendeth to inhabit Virgenia, which they may safely achieve, if their second prove stronge and ours languishe for want of sufficient and tymly supplie, which cannot be had but by the meanes of multitude contributorys.

The circumstances necessarily to backe a Collony sent owt are these:

1. Reputacion and opinion of thinterprice.

2. A competent some of monie raised aforehande to supplie all accidentes that distrust, heerby maye be wrought in forraigne states to attempt anie thing in prejudice of our Collonies, becawse they maye be well asured that where there is not a publique purse, and a Comon consent to prosecute an accion, it is but botlesse to hope of advantage to be gotten with out revenge.

3. As fewe are most apt to make a conquest, so are publique weales fitter to howld what is gotton and skilfullor by industrie to inrich it.

4. It is probable that if the whole state be ingaged in theise adventures, yt wil be no hearde matter when aparant grownde of profit is laied to perswade every County according to the proportion of bignes and abelitie to builde barkes and shippes of a Compotent size and to maintaine them, when Gentlemens yongest sons and other men of quality may be imployed.

5. Also it importeth much that no man be suffered to venture more than he may maye be deamed able to spare owt of his owne superfluity, or if he go in person, he would Idely spende at home lest such men entring into a rage of repentance, and thereby discorage others and scandilize the interprice.

The monie to be raised to the use and purposes aforesaid following:

1. Ought not to be levied of those things which maye hinder the Comon wealth to injoye the necessaries of victualls and aparell, but shall rather advance them to the neady.

2. It shall not be raised without moderacon, and ease to the payer, neither shall anie thinge be demanded from anie man without presente aparence of gaine and hope of fwtwre profit.

3. It shall not be raised upon the sweat of the poore, or industrie of the husbandman Artificer, or tradisman.

4. It is not to be levied to a privats intent.

But it is to be raised:-

1. Upon the emoderate gaines of those that contrary to lawe abuse the poore, but in such sorte that the payer shall for every ij^d paied gaine iiij^d.

2. That they upon whom the maine chardge of payment shall lye maye be greater gainers than the merchant adventuors.

3. That the whole state shalbe interested in the benifit of it.

4. That the superflous wastes maye be avoyded of which the poore most want.

5. The Merchandize increasing thereby, the Realme shalbe inriched yearly manie thousandes

powndes, and the Kings impostes and Customes increased.

6. That at the least CC thowsande powndes yearly maye be saved in the Realme which nowe is consumed to the displeasure of God and hurte of the people.

Also it is reason that the Kings Majestie have as well parte of the monie so raised, either to adventure or otherwise dispose at his Highnes good pleasure.

1. In respect of his roiall assent to be given to an Act of Parlament enabling Commissioners to gather the monies aforesaid.

2. Privileges and lysence to transporte a Collonie or Collonies are to be obtained at the Kinges handes, neither is it reason that his Highnes prerogative showld be valued at no thinge.

3. The the Kings Majestie will be engaged in honor the rather to asist and protect the project.

4. It would savior to much of affectacion of a populor State to levie monies without imparting some convenient porcion to his Majestie.

5. That porcion ought not to be so smale, that it showld seame to undervalue the kings greatnes and favour.

[Endorsed:] Reasons to move the High Court of Parlament to raise a stocke for the maintaining of a Collonie in Virgenia and many other good uses in such manner, that the payer shall gaine 2^s for every xii^d disburshed, with the good of the whole kingdom and ten thousande powndes yearly brought to his Majestes receiptes.

5 Januarii. 1607.

[Signed:] T. Gerolyn

Chapter One hundred one
A Case in the High Court of Admiralty Concerning the *Susan Constant* Prior to Her Departure for Virginia

T HE *Susan Constant*, 120 tons, was a new ship only one year in commission and had made one voyage to Spain before being chartered for the voyage to Virginia under the command of Christopher Newport. Her owners were Colthurst, Dapper, Wheatley and Company, Wheatley presumably being the merchant who sold masts and deal boards (795), commodities which Virginia was expected to provide in quantity. She was loaded in the Pool of London and, about the middle of November, 1606, was piloted by John Davis of Dartmouth to a berth at Ratcliff Cross farther downstream. She was anchored alongside a partly laden ship, the *Philip and Francis*, 100 tons, owned by Philip Bernard (or Barnard) and John Francisco Soprani. The *Philip and Francis* had been at this berth for some time (as long as ten weeks according to one deposition). On November 23, at the turning of the tide, the two ships collided, causing damage to both of them. Philip Bernard then brought a case against Colthurst and Company, alleging negligence on the part of the men left in charge, before the High Court of Admiralty.

For Bernard it was said that the *Susan Constant* was moored too close to the *Philip and Francis*. Consequently, those in charge of Bernard's ship had warned the *Susan Constant* to adjust her anchor cables to avoid damage when the ship swung with the tide. Henry Ravens, master of the *Philip and Francis*, had also gone to Christopher Newport's house to ask him to see that this was done. For the *Susan Constant* it was claimed that her men urged the *Philip and Francis* to use a cable to hold their ship off and that some of the crew of the *Susan Constant* had gone on board to help them to do this but found there was no cable available for this purpose. In an attempt to hold the *Susan Constant* clear, a cable was thrown to a passing caravel (also the *Susan*), which was unable to take the strain and cut the cable. The resulting collision damaged three ports on the *Susan Constant* and broke the beak head and bowsprit of the *Philip and Francis*, as well as dislodging her sheet anchor. The *Philip and Francis* was removed for repairs, costing £5 13s 3d. The *Susan Constant* remained at her berth.

The libel and answer of each party have not been found but undated interrogatories for each party are given below. The examination of witnesses began on December 13 and continued until December 16. Depositions by Henry Ravens, Thomas Daniell, John Cox, William Paramore, and William Warner, all members of the company of the *Philip and Francis*, and by John Coursey, John Harvie, and Jeremias Deane for the *Susan Constant*, follow the relevant interrogatory. The Court's decision has not been found. On December 20, the *Susan Constant* raised anchor and set out on her long voyage to Virginia.

Alison Quinn found the original depositions and gave those of Ravens and Coursey to P. L. Barbour to print in *The Jamestown Voyages*, I, 55–60. The other depositions (and the interrogatories found by Susan Hillier) are printed for the first time.

171

787. [December, 1606]. Interrogatories on behalf of Philip Bernard (or Barnard) in the case of the *Susan Constant.*

P.R.O., HCA 23/6, part I, fol. 314, without date.
(Interrogatories administered on the part of Philip Bernard and his associates against the depositions sworn to on the part of Robert Colthurst and his associates. The first interrogatory merely warns the person being examined that he is in danger of punishment if he answers falsely.)

f. 314r

2. Item interrogetur quilibet testis presentis whether they or any of them are servantes to the party producent or to any of his company owners or officers of the ship the Susan Constant. Et interrogetur ut supra.

3. Item interrogetur at what tyme of the day or night and upon what day of the moneth or weeke the said ship the Suzan Constant came first to moore and reside at anker in the place where she did the harme to the ship the Phillip and Francis libellate. Et interrogetur ut supra.

4. Item who brought the said ship the Suzan Constant to moore there And how long had the said ship the Phillip and Francis byn tied and moored there before the said ship the Suzan Constant came thither. Et interrogetur ut supra.

5. Item whether did the said ship the Phillip and Francis come to the aforesaid ship the Suzan Constant from Ratcliff where she lay at anckor into the Poole or the said ship the Suzan Constant to her the said Phillip and Francis riding at a peere Ratcliffe aforesaid at such tyme as the harmes libellate were donne. Et interrogetur ut supra.

6. Item in case any of the purposed witnesses shall endever to depose of any purposed negligence of any of the company of the Phillip and Francis aforesaid. Tunc interrogetur whether at the first comying of the said ship the Suzan Constant did not they of the Phillip and Fraunces that were then in her at the same tyme and at diverse other tymes after geve warning to them of the said Suzan Constant to loke to their mooring and willed them to ryde clere of the said Phillip and Fraunces. Et interrogetur ut supra.

7. Item whether did not the said ship the Suzan Constant after such tyme as she had donne the harmes to the Phillip and Fraunces aforesaid new

moore their said ship the Suzan Constant the next day following. Et interrogetur ut supra.

8. Item in case the said Suzan Constant had ben moored as she ought to have byn why was she new moored the next day after she had donne the harmes aforesaid. Et interrogetur ut supra.

9. Item whether did they or any of them see the said ship the Phillip and Fraunces after such tyme as she was hurt by the Suzan Constant remove out of her mooring and for what cause did she soe remove as they or any of them knowe or have heard. And whether yt was not for feare she the said ship the Phillip and Fraunces soe removed least by her tarrying there she had receyved further hurt of the said Suzan Constant. Et interrogetur ut supra.

10. Item how long did the said ship the Phillip and Francis lye at anckor in the place where the harmes aforesaid were don into her before the Suzan Constant came thither as they know or have credibly heard. Et interrogetur ut supra.

11. Item in case the said Suzan Constant had not come downe to the said Phillip and Frauncis while she lay at anchor as aforesaid whether had she byn hurt by the said Suzan Constant or her bolt spritt and sheat ancker broken as by the said Suzan the Constant they were. Et interrogetur ut supra.

12. Item interrogetur how many of them of the Suzan Constant were drunke or had drunke well as such tyme as the said ship the Suzan Constant feel foule upon the Phillip and Frauncis aforesaid. Et interrogetur et specificet the names and surnames of them that were soe drunke or that were well whittled with drinke as aforesaid. Et interrogetur.

788. December 13, 1606. Examination of Henry Ravens in the case of the *Susan Constant.*

P.R.O., HCA 13/38, December 13, 1606.

Philippus Barnardo et navem the Susan Constant

Henricus Ravens de Ratcliff nauta ubi per xvj annos moram fecit annos natus quadraginta duos vel circa testis in hac parte productus juratus et examinatus Dicit quod Philippum Barnardo per octo annos Christoferum Newporte per xvj annos et Robertum Colthurst ex visu respective noverit.

Ad primum articulatum libelli affirmat that the articulate shipp the Phillipp and Francys is victualled furnished and sett to sea by Phillipp Barnardo and John Francisco Soprani and by them this examinate and the mariners are paide theire wages And therefore he thinketh they are owners of the said shipp. Ad aliter nescit.

Ad secundum dicit he knoweth that the Phillipp and Francys lay at anker in the River of Thames within the jurisdiction of the Admiraltie over against Ratcliff betwixte vj and vjj weekes and had ankers cables buoy and all other thinges fitt for such a shipp of his knowledge who is master of the same shipp.

Ad tertium et quartum affirmat verum esse that the Susan Constant articulate came to an anker and cast her ankers so nere unto the Phillipp and Francys that she could not ride cleare but that the Phillipp and Francys brake downe two of the portes of the said shipp the Susan Constant and thereuppon this examinate wente to the house of Christopher Newporte beinge Captaine or master of the said shipp the Susan Constant and lefte worde that his shipp was mored to nere to this examinates shipp and that he should take order to more her cleare and warninge was afterwards given by the mariners beinge in the said shippe the Phillipp and Francys of his knowledge.

Ad quintum affirmat verum esse that the Phillipp and Francys lay at anker vj or vij weekes in the place aforesaid before the Susan Constant came to anker by her of his knowledge.

Ad sextum et scedulam affirmat verum esse that the said shipp the Susan Constant on the xxiij^{th} of November last came uppon the Phillipp and Francys in the night tyme uppon the eb at highe water by the necligence of the company of the said shipp the Susan Constant and brake the beake heade the bowspritt and the sheate anker of the same shipp of this examinates certaine knowledge who came on borde as the said shippes were foule one of the other and sawe that the company of the Susan Constant sate tiplinge and drinkinge and never looked out or endevored to cleare the ships. And he knoweth that the said owners have repayred the said damadge and the timber employed in the mendinge of said beake

head cost xvij^s viij^d and foure carpenters wrought thre dayes in mendinge the same and had ij^s a day for theire worcke which came to xxiij^s and the paintinge of the said beake heade cost v^s vij^d. And he also knoweth that the bowe spritt cost newe makinge xxxiij^s and the sheate anker cost xxxiij^s in repayringe the same which he knoweth to be true for that he disbursed the moneye for the carpenters worcke and the bowespritt and sheate anker mendinge and the owners had a bill for paymente of the rest. Whereby he knoweth the premisses to be true.

Ad septimum referet se ad registrum huius curie et ad juram.

Ad octavum affirmat eundem esse verum Reddendo rationem ut supra.

Ad nonum affirmat the owners have susteyned damadge by reason of the said hurtes for that the shipp hath byn stayed from her viadge longer tyme then she would to be repayred and in that tyme the mariners were paid their wages. Ac aliter nescit.

Ad decimum affirmat eundem esse verum ut ex actis huius curie apparent.

Ad ultimum dicit predeposita per eum esse vera.

Ad Interrogatoria

Ad primum responsum est supra.

Ad secundum respondet he is appointed to goe master of the said shippe the Phillipp and Francys by the said owners. Ac aliter respondet negative.

Ad tertium respondet negative.

Ad quartum respondet he is worth xx^{li} his debte paide. Ac aliter respondet negative.

Ad quintum respondet he is master of the said shipp the Phillipp and Francys and came on borde as the ships were foule one of the other fearinge the ships would have byn belyed on same ankers. And sayth there were thre of the ships company on borde when the hurte was don and as yt was endeinge the respondent with others came on borde.

Ad sextum respondet the Susan Constant and the Phillipp and Francys are nere of one burthen in his judgement and the Susan Constant was laden and the Phillipp and Francys was thre partes laden. And sayth that a shipp deepest laden is surest turned with the tide because she hath most hold of the water.

Ad septimum respondet the Phillipp and Francys was mored as she oughte to be nether to slack nor to toghte and did no hurte to the Susan Constant to his knowledge.

Ad octavum respondet negative.

Ad nonum respondet there was as much cable vered in the Phillipp and Francys as might be without doinge greate hurte to other ships. Ac aliter respondet se nescire.

Ad decimum respondet verum esse that the company of the Susan Constant when yt was to late did fasten a haulster uppon a carvell that rode there but if they had don yt in tyme the hurte might have byn prevented. And he hearde that the company of the said Carvell cutt the said haulster. Ac aliter respondet negative.

Ad xj respondet there was rome enoughe for a haulf dozen shipps to have layne belowe the said shippes but as the Susan Constant was mored there was not roome enoughe for her and the Phillipp and Francys to ride there cleare.

[Signed:] per me Henrie Ravns

789. December 14, 1606. Examination of Thomas Daniell in the case of the *Susan Constant*.

P.R.O., HCA 13/38, December 14, 1606.

Phillippus Barnardo contra navem the Susan Constant Primus testis supra parte

Thomas Daniell Civitatis Bristollum nauta ubi natus erat iam apud Wappinge moram trahens annos natus xxij vel circa Testis in hac parte productus iuratus et examinatus dicit quod Phillippum Barnardo per duas septimanis noverit partes respondens non novit.

Ad primum articulum libelli in hac causa dicti affirmat that Phillipp Barnardo came yesterday on borde the Phillipp & Francys and paid this examinate and the rest of the mariners of the same shipp theire haulf wages and therefore he thinketh he is owner or parte owner of the said shipp. Ac aliter nescit.

Ad secundum affirmat eundem nauta esse se veritatem For this examinate is a mariner of the said shipp & knoweth the same to be true.

Ad tertium et quartum affirmat verum esse that the articulate shipp the Susan Constant came to an anker right against Ratcliffe crosse and cast

her anker within the moringes of the Phillipp and Francys which rode then there and longe before this examinate was hired to serve in the said shipp the Phillipp and Francys And after the said shipp the Susan Constant was in her moringes this examinate did many tymes forwarne them of the Susan Constant to look to their shipp and have care that she came not foule of the Phillipp and Francys by reason she was layd so neere that uppon the turninge of every tide the ships were ready to come foule one of the other. Ac aliter nescit.

Ad quintum affirmat verum esse that this examinate beinge lefte in the Phillipp and Francys with some others to kepe the same did many times and sondry dayes before the hurte was don forwarne them in the Susan Constant to forsee that they came not foule of the Phillipp & Francys, and did her hurte and asked them to tripp theire anker to that ende and they answered that then they should lye foule of other ships belowe them. Ut dicit, Ac aliter nescit.

Ad sextum et scedulam affirmat verum esse that the said shipp the Susan Constant on the 23th of november last beinge before warned by this examinate and others to looke to theire moringes came foule of the said shipp the Phillipp & Francys lyeinge quietly at anker as aforesaid, and brake her beake heade and her bowespritt and the flooke of her sheate anker which lay uppon the bowe and by the faulte and necligence of the company of the Susan Constant not well moringe theire shipp in the said place which hurtes were repayred by the owners of the said shipp the Phillipp and Francys but what the same cost he knoweth not.

Ad septimum nescit deponere.

Ad octavum et scedulum nescit plura dicere prius dictum est.

Ad nonum decimum et undecimum referet se ad prius dicit et ad iuram.

Ad xij dicit predeposita prout esse verum.
[Signed:] Thome Daniell

790. December 14, 1606. Examination of John Coxe in the case of the *Susan Constant*.

P.R.O., HCA 13/38, fols. 163v.–164, December 14, 1606.

Phillipus Barnardo et navem the Susan Constant

Johannes Coxe de Ratcliff famulus viduc Harris ibidem qua cum per quinque annos moram fecit annos natus xxiij vel circa Testis in hac parte productus iuratus et examinatus Dicit quod Phillipum Barnardo per annum noverit Christoferum Newporte per idem tempus et Robertum Colthurst non novit.

Ad primum articulatum libelli predicti affirmat that Phillip Barnardo payeth the mariners of the articulate shipp the Phillipp and Francys theire wages and by him & his partners the said shipp is victualed and sett forth And therefore he thinketh is owner or parte owner thereof.

Ad secundum affirmat he hath byn a mariner of the Phillipp and Francys aboute a monethes space, and knoweth that she was mored at her ankers in the River of Thames within the jurisdiction of the Admiralty of England over against Ratcliffe crosse and there lay having ankers cables buoys and all other thinges befittinge such a shipp of his knowledge.

Ad tertium et quartum affirmat verum esse that after the Phillipp and Francys had remayned at anker many dayes & nights in the place aforesaid, there came thither the articulate ship the Susan Constant and cast anker verey nere to the Phillipp and Francys for so much that the company of the Phillipp and Francys fearinge the Susan Constant would come foule of them gave them warninge to looke to theire moorings and shortly after the ships came foule one of the other and were cleared, & then they were warned againe to looke unto yt that they did no hurte to the Phillipp & Francys as of this examinates certaine knowledge. Ac aliter nescit.

Ad quintum articulam he knoweth that the Phillipp and Francys lay quietly at anker sundrye weekes in the place aforesaid before the Susan Constant came to anker there. Ac alia qui prius dictum est nescit deponere.

Ad sextum et scedulam attestatus verum est that about thre weekes past on a Sonday nighte the said shipp the Susan Constant came foule of the said shipp the Phillipp & Francys lyeing quietly at anker as aforesaid, and by the fault & negligence of the company thereof not well moringe the same brake the beake head, bowespritt and sheate anker of the Phillipp and Francys, which the owners of the Phillipp and Francys

have since repaired, but what the same cost he knoweth not. Ac aliter nescit.

Ad reliquos articulos nescit plura dicere quam prius dictum est.

[Signed:] John Coxe

791. December 14, 1606. Examination of William Paramore in the case of the *Susan Constant*.

P.R.O., HCA 13/38, December 14, 1606.

Philippus Barnardo contra navem the Susan Constant

Willelmus Paramore de Sandwiche nauta ubi natus erat annos agens viginti vel circa Testis in hac parte productus iuratus et examinatus dicit se Philippum Barnardo per acte hebdomadus Christopherus Newporte ex visu noverit Robertum Colthurst non nossit.

Ad primum articulum libelli affirmat eundem continere in se veritatem For this examinate hath byn paide haulf wages by the said Phillipe Barnardo since the tyme he was hired to saile therein and he understandeth that he and Francisco Sopricin have victualed and sett furthe the said shipp for this intented viadge.

Ad secundum dicit he knoweth that the said shipp the Phillipp and Francys hath remayned at anker in the River of Thames within the Jurisdiction of the Admiraltie over against Ratcliffe crosse aboute ten weekes space for so long this examinate hath belonged to the said shipp and knoweth that she had cables buoyes ankers and all other thinges fitt for such a shipp.

Ad tertium et quartum affirmat verum esse that the articulate shipp the Susan Constant came to an anker nere the Phillipp & Francys and mored so nere that they lay twart the haulse of the Phillipp and Francys, and sondry of the company of the Phillipp and Francys forwarned them of the Susan Constant thereof, and uppon that warninge they removed theire anker further of, and sayd that the anker of the Phillipp and Francys was come home which was not, of his knowledge. Ac aliter nescit.

Ad quartum affirmat eundem verum esse ut penes dictum est.

Ad sextum et scedulam affirmat verum esse That the said shipp the Susan Constant in the night tyme on this day thre weekes as he remembreth came uppon the Phillipp and Francys lyenge at anker as aforesaid and by theire necligence brake the beake heade and as he hearde the sheate anker also which he knoweth to be true For that he was then on bord and sawe the beake heade and bowspritt broken as aforesaid. Ac aliter nescit saving that the owners have since repayred the said hurtes.

Ad reliquos articulos nescit plura dicere quam prius dictum est.

[Signed:] William Paramore

792. December 15, 1606. Examination of William Warner in the case of the *Susan Constant*.

P.R.O., HCA 13/38, December 15, 1606.

Philippus Barnardo contra navem the Susan Constant

Willelmus Warner de Ratcliff nauta ubi per septimum habitaverit annos agens xxxj vel circa Testis in hac parte productus iuratus et examinatus dicit quod Philippus Barnardo per tres annos Christoferum Newporte per idem tempus et Richard Colthurst ex visu respective novirit.

Ad primum articulum libelli in hac causa dati dicit that Phillipp Barnardo & John Francisco Sopcuni beare the name to be owners of the articulate shipp the Phillipp & Francys and as owners they have furnished and victualed to sea the said shipp and doe pay the mariners there wages and therefore he thinketh they are owners of the said shipp. Ac aliter nescit.

Ad secundum he this examinate hath belonged to the said shipp the Phillipp and Francys two monethes and upwardes and duringe that tyme he knoweth the said shipp hath layne at ankor in the River of Thames within the Jurisdiction of the Admiralty over againste Ratcliff and had ankers cables buoyes and other necessaries fitt for such a shippe of his knowledge.

Ad tertium et quartum dicit he knoweth that the articulate shipp the Susan Constant came to

an anker nere the place where the Phillipp & Francys was mored and there lay of his knowledge. Ac aliter nescit.

Ad quintum affirmat he knoweth that the Phillipp & Francys lay at anker in the said place at the least fyve weekes space before the Susan Constant came to an anker by her For that she was one of the company of the Phillipp & Francys and knoweth yt to be true.

Ad sextum et scedulam affirmat verum esse that the said shipp the Susan Constant on Sonday was this weekes last in the nighte tyme come uppon the Phillipp & Francys lyenge at anker in the Thames in maner aforesaid uppon the ebbe at high water and brake her beake head bowespritt and sheate anker of this examinates knowledge who came on borde as the said ships were foule one of the other and did his endevor to cleare them but could not by reason of other shipps that rid asterne so as they could not vire the cable but should have don more harme to the other shippes but by whose defalte the same hapened he knoweth not. Howe be it he sayth that when this examinate came on borde the Phillipp & Francys he founde sondry persons in the Susan Constant tiplinge and singinge and he blamed them for that they did not in tyme cleare the ships and they answered that yf they had don eany harme they must answer yt. Ac aliter nescit Savinge he knoweth the owners of the Phillipp and Francys have made a newe beake heade and sett a newe bowespritt and have mended the anker but what the same cost he knoweth not. Ac aliter nescit.

Ad reliquos articulos nescit plura dicere quam prius dictum est.

[Signed:] William Warner

793. [December, 1606]. Interrogatories on behalf of Robert Colthurst in the case of the *Susan Constant*.

P.R.O., HCA 23/6, part I, fols. 316v.–318, without date.

Interrogatories administered on the part of Robert Colthurst and his associates against the depositions sworn on the part of Philip Bernard.

1. Warn the deponent against the penalties of making false statements.

2. Ask whether the deponent has any place in

the household of the parties for whom he has testified or has any stipend as such.

3. Ask whether the deponent has payments due him from or debt outstanding with the parties.

4. Ask what are his means, what is he worth in his own goods and is he rated for the royal subsidy.]

5. Item interrogetur eorum quilibet whither were one of the Companie of the said shipp the Philip & Francis what place had he in the said shipp, whither was he on bord the said shipp at the time of the paste hurte libellate or was he in shore, yf on shore upon what occasion went he on shore & how manie of his Companie were on bord their said shipp at the time of the pased hurt aforesaid. Et fiat ut supra.

6. Item interrogetur eorum quilibet whither he knowe beleeve or have heard that the shippe the Susan Constance was a shipp of a greater burthen & deeply laden & prepared for her vioage & whither was the shipp the Philipp & Francis empty & unladen or how manie tonne of goods were on bord her & whither could the said shipp the Susan Constance be carried or turne aboute with the tyde as soone as the Philipp & Francis. Et fiat ut supra.

7. Item interrogetur eorum quilibet whither he or anie of Couteste or anie of the Companie of the Philipp & Francis had left their cables somewhat over longe & whither did the tide or fload came the said shipp the Philipp & Francis against the Susan Constance & did breake & hurte her in divers places. Et specificet what places were she broken or hurt & to what value did the said damage extend. Et fiat ut supra.

8. Item interrogetur eorum quilibet whither he knowe beleeve or have heard said that the Company of the Susan Constance did desire the Company of the Philippe & Francis aforesaid to veere their Cable or else their said shippes were in daunger of greate hurte and did also proffer themselves to goe aboarde the said shipp the Philipp & Francis to helpe to cleare & to save her from the paste hurt or damage. Et fiat ut supra.

9. Item interrogetur eorum quilibet whether did the Companie of the Philipp & Francis at the entreaty of the Companie of the Susan Constance aforesaid for the safety of their shippe veere their cable or what diligence or meanes did they use for the safety of their shippe, & whither did they suffer the Companie of the Susan Constance or anie of them to come on bord the Philipp & Francis to helpe to cleare her as he knoweth beleeveth or hath heard said. Et fiat ut supra.

10. Item interrogetur eorum quilibet whither the Companie of the shipp the Susan Constance did also fasten their Cable or halster to another carvell beinge nere unto them, & whither did the master or some or one of the Companie of that Carvell Cut their said cable or halster, & whither the said shipps the Philipp & Francis & the Susan Constance beene cleared by fastening the said cable or halster in the said Carvell yf it had not beene cutt as aforesaid as he knoweth beleeveth or hath heard said. Et fiat ut supra.

11. Item interrogetur eorum quilibet whither the place where the said shippes the Philipp & Francis & the Susan Constance laie at anchor as aforesaid was able & fitt to receave and containe two or 3 shippes of the bignes of the two shippes aforesaid & how manie hath he ever knowne to lie at one time in that place as he knoweth beleeveth or have heard said. Et fiat ut supra.

794. December 13, 1606. Examination of John Coursey in the case of the *Susan Constant*.

P.R.O., HCA 13/38, December 13, 1606.

Die sabbato xiij Decembris 1606
Philippus Barnardo et navem the Susan Constant et Christoferum Newport respondet

Primus testis Newporte

Johannes Coursey de Limehouse nauta ubi per decem annos moram fecit annos natus xxviij vel circa. Testis in hac parte productus juratus et examinatus dicit quod Christoferum Newporte per quatuor annos noverit. Philippus Barnardo non novit.

Ad primum articulum allegationis in hac causa date affirmat he knoweth that Master Dapper Master wheatley and Robert Colthurst and others theire partners are owners of the articulate shipp the Susan Constant of the porte of London and the tacle and apparell thereof and so have byn ever since the buildinge thereof which ys aboute a yeare past. For they builte the same shipp furnished rigged victualed and manned her and sett her to sea on a viadge for Spaine of this examinates certaine knowledge from this porte of London.

Ad secundum dicit verum esse that the Susan Constant is of the burthen of one hundreth and twenty tonnes or thereaboutes and was fully laden with victualls and other necessaries for the viadge intended and the articulate shipp the Phillipp and Francys is aboute one hundreth tonnes in burthen and had nothinge in her but some parte of her victualls to his knowledge when the dammadge in question hapned and they both then lay in the River of Thames over against Ratcliff Crosse att an anker of this examinates knowledge who was then one of the company of the said shipp the Susan Constant.

Ad tertium quartum et quintum affirmat verum esse that the Susan Constant beinge of greater burthen and deeper laden then the Phillipp and Frances could not be turned or caried aboute by the tide uppon the ebbe so soon as the said shipp the Phillip Frances as also for that the Phillipp Frances was mored to longe and so havinge much cable out was quickly turned aboute uppon the ebbe and came uppon the said shipp the Susan Constant before she was turned with the tide and brake of thre of her portes and did her dammadge. And as the shippes were borde and bord one uppon the other this examinate and company of the Susan Constant spake to them in the Phillipp and Francys and preyed them to vere theire cable or else the one shipp would hurte thother and offered to goe on borde the Phillipp and Francys to helpe to cleare the shippes and save them from hurte. Notwithstandinge he sayth that the company then on borde the Phillipp and Francys beinge thre or foure youthes could not vere theire cable but used these speeches or the like in effecte viz. our barke is as stronge as your sides and therofe we will not vere. Where uppon two of this examinates company seeinge theire wilfulnes wente on borde the Phillipp and Frances to vere the cable and cleare the shipp and comminge on borde founde the cables ende at the butts so as there was no more cable to vere out and then they called for a haulster to make fast to the cable so to lengthen yt out and havinge none the company of the Susan Constant would have brought a haulster to make fast to the

cable and they of the Phillipp and Frances would not suffer it to be brought on borde and so by theire owne wilfulnes they receaved such hurte as hapned unto them for if they had vered the cable or suffered the company of the Susan Constant to doe yt theire had no hurte hapned to the said ships or eyther of them of this examinates knowledge who was then in the Susan Constant and sawe what hapned concerninge the said dammadge.

Ad sextum affirmat verum esse that this examinate and company of the Susan Constant seeinge the obstinacy and necgligence of the said company of the Phillipp and Francys did cast and fasten a halster uppon a Carvell that lay thereby at anker so to cleare the shipps and in his judgement by that meanes had cleared them but that the company of the Carvell cutt the halster which was fastened unto them ut dicit.

Ad septimum affirmat eundem continere in se veritatem for within these two dayes there rode two ships in the same birthes where the said ships the Susan Constant and Phillipp and Francys rode at anker and the one never hurte the other.

Ad octavum affirmat eundem continere in se veritatem for this examinate was in the Susan Constant when the said ships were foule one of the other and knoweth the hurte which hapned to the Phillipp and Francys hapned by the faulte negligence and wilfulnes of them that were in the Phillipp and Francys Reddendo rationem ut supra. For that this examinate and company did their uttermost endever to cleare the said shipps and could not be suffered by them of the Phillipp and Francys ubi prius dictum est.

Ad ultimum dicit predeposita per eum esse vera.

[Signed:] John Coursey his X marke

Ad Interrogatoria in folio sequente.
Responsa Johannes Coursey ad Interrogatoria.
Ad primum responsum est supra.
Ad secundum respondet negative. Savinge that he is hired by the moneth to serve in the Susan Constant.
Ad tertium respondet that the Susan Constant came to an anker about x or xj of the clock as he remembreth at the place where she yet rideth about a moneth past otherwise the tyme he remembreth not.
Ad quartum respondet that one Master Davis brought the said shipp to her mooringes at the place aforesaid where the Phillipp and Francys

was then at an anker and had byn by the space of thre weekes before as he thinketh.

Ad quintum respondet that the Susan Constant rode first aloft in the poole and came downe to Ratcliffe where the Phillipp and Francys lay about a weeke before hurte hapned as he remembreth.

Ad sextum respondet he never knewe or hearde that eany of the company of the Phillipp and Francys ever warned them to loose theire moorings or to ride cleare of the Philipp and Francys.

Ad septimum respondet that the nexte day after the hurte they tript theire anker aboute haulfe a boates length further out from the chanell because the Phillipp and Francys lienge twart of the said anker had hawled yt some what into the chanell. Ac aliter respondet negative.

Ad octavum responsum est supra.

Ad nonum respondet he sawe the Phillipp and Francys the nexte tide after the said hurte remove on borde an other shipp because she should not come foule of the Susan Constant eany more as he thinketh. Ac aliter respondet se nescire.

Ad decimum respondet the Phillipp and Francys was at anker in the said place before the Susan Constant came thither but howe longe she had layne there he knoweth not.

Ad undecimum respondet that if the Susan Constant had continued still in the poole there could not hurte have hapned betwixte her and the Phillipp and Francys as he believeth. Ac aliter nescit.

Ad xij^um respondet there was not eany of them drunck nether had byn that day drinkinge to his knowledge.

[Signed:] Johannes X Coursey

795. December 13, 1606. Examination of John Harvie in the case of the *Susan Constant*.

P.R.O., HCA 13/38, fols. 161–161v., December 13, 1606.

Phillipus Barnardo 2

Johannes Harvie de Gosporte in Comitatu Southampton ubi per quartum habitaverat annos natus xix vel circa Testis in hac parte productus iuratus et examinatus Dicit quod Christoferum Newport et Robertum Colthurst per parte hebdomodus noverit Phillipum Barnardo non novit.

Ad primum articulum affirmat that the shipp articulate called the Susan Constant belongeth to Master Dapper and Robert Colthurst and is victualed furnished & sett to sea by them as he understandeth. Ad aliter nescit.

Ad secundum affirmat verum esse that the articulate ships the Phillipp and Francys and the Susan Constant lay at anker over against Ratcliffe crosse, and the Susan Constant is a greater shipp and was deeper laden than the said Phillipp & Frances at the said tyme when the ships lay there of his sight & Knowledge beinge one of the company of the said shipp the Susan Constant.

Ad tertium affirmat eundem continere in se veritatem et reddat rationem ascentur that he was in the Susan Constant, and since that the other shipp the Phillipp & Francys beinge the lesser shipp and lighter laden was first turned with the tide and came uppon the Susan Constant & brake downe her portes sheeringe alongst by her side as the Susan Constant rode uppon the flood and before she was turned with the ebbe.

Ad quartum et quintum affirmat verum esse that this examinate and companye of the Susan Constant seeinge the Phillipp & Francys come uppon them, desired them of the Phillipp & Francys to vere their cable to avoide the danger that might ensue, they answered theire backes were as harde as our bellyes, or to that effecte, and would not vere theire cable, whereuppon this examinate and companye seinge theire wilfulnes offered to goe on borde to helpe them, and this examinate and Francys Thompson wente on borde the said shippe the Phillipp & Francys to vere the cable & found the cables ende att the butts that yt could not be further vired, and then asked them for a haulser to bende to the cables end & they answered they had none then this examinate and others of his company would have broughte a haulser from theire shipp to bende to the cable and they of the Phillipp & Frances would not suffer them to bringe any on borde or helpe to cleare the shipp but utterly forbad them of this examinates sight & knowledge.

Ad sextum attestatas verum esse that as regarde of the wilfulnes of the company of the said shipp the Phillipp & Francys beinge but two then on bord, this examinate & company to cleare the shipp made fast a haulser on a carvell which then rode by, and thus he thinketh had by that meanes cleared the ships, but that they in the Carvell cutt the haulser so fastened on them of this examinates certaine knowledge.

Ad septimum affirmat eundem continere in se veritatem For as he saide the Lion and the Dragon have since layne in the same berth where the Phillip & Francys lay without doinge any hurte to the said shipp the Susan Constant.

Ad octavum verum esse that the damadge which happened to the said shipp the Phillip and Francys hapned by faulte wilfulnes and negligence of the company of the said shipp the Phillip and Francys and not by any faulte of this examinate and company of the Susan Constant reddenda rationem ut supra.

Ad ultimum predeposita per eum esse vera.

Ad Interrogatoria

Ad primum respondet he is a mariner and liveth by the sea. Ac aliter non ut supra.

Ad secundum respondet he is only a mariner hired to saile in the Susan Constant. Ac aliter respondet negative.

Ad tertium respondet that the Susan Constant came to anker about xij of the clocke in the day tyme at the place where the hurte libellate hapened aboute a weeke as he thinketh before the same chanced. Ac aliter non recolit.

Ad quartum respondet Master Davis brought the Susan Constant to and mored her at the place aforesaid And he knoweth that the Phillip and Francys was there at anker when the Susan Constant came thither but howe longe before he knoweth not.

Ad quintum respondet that the Susan Constant rode in the Poole before and came downe to Ratcliff crosse where the Phillipp and Francys lay at anker.

Ad sextum respondet negative pro parte suo.

Ad septimum respondet that this respondent and company of the Susan Constant did not newe moore theire said shipp after the hurte don but only they removed theire anker aboute a quarters of a boates length but nether vired or heved out or haled in eany cable in doinge the same.

Ad octavum respondet the anker aforesaid was removed because they feared the boy rope had byn foule or lost.

Ad nonum respondet he sawe the Phillipp & Francys remove the nexte tyde after the hurt don from her moringes on bord an other shipp because her mooringes came home as he thinketh. Ac aliter nescit.

Ad decimum respondet the Phillipp & Francys was at an anker at the place aforesaid before the Susan Constant came thither, but howe longe before he knoweth not.

Ad undecimum referit se ad prius dicti. Ac aliter nescit.

Ad xij respondet that none of the company of the Susan Constant were drunck or had drunck hard to his knowledge when the said hurte hapned For as he sayth there was no other beare but four shillinges beere on borde at that tyme.

[Signed:] John harvey his X mark

796. December 14, 1606. Examination of Jeremias Deane in the case of the *Susan Constant*.

P.R.O., HCA 13/38, December 14, 1606.

Philippus Barnardo contra navem the Susan Constant 3

Die dominico 14 Decembris 1606 Jeremias Deane natus in Insula Vectis [Isle of Wight] nauta iam in Civitate London commorans annos natus xxij vel circa Testis in hac parte productus iuratus et examinatus dicit quod Robertum Colthurst per mensem noverit Philippum Barnardo non novit.

Ad primum articulum allegationis in hac causa affirmat he hath understood that Master Dupper Robert Colthurst and one that selleth mastes & deale bordes are owners of the articulate shipp the Susan Constant and the tacle and apparell thereof and that the same shipp is sett out by them for this viadge intended. Ac aliter nescit.

Ad secundum affirmat that the Susan Constant is of the burthen of one hundreth and twenty tonnes and had in her provision and ladinge at such tyme as she rode nere the Phillip and Francys over against Ratcliffe crosse and the said shipp the Phillip & Francys is a lesser shipp and had little or noe ladinge to his knowledge when she lay there. Ac aliter nescit.

Ad tertium affirmat verum esse that the said shipp the Phillip & Francys beinge unladen as he thinketh and slakly mored quickly turned about and sponed upp uppon the Susan Constant at a full sea before the Susan Constant beinge deeper laden felte the turninge of the tide, and brake downe two of the portes of the Susan Constant of this examinates knowledge then beinge in the Susan Constant and one of the company thereof.

Ad quartum et quintum affirmat verum esse that as the said shipp the Phillipp and Francys came foule of the Susan Constant this examinate and others of the company called to them that were in the Phillipp & Francys and desired them to veere theire cable or else our shipp would indaunger the other and they answered they were mored there before the Susan Constant and they had no cable to veere, and one Francys Thompson the owners servant of the Susan Constant seeinge their wilfulnes wente on bord the Phillipp & Francys to helpe to vere the cable and found the cables ende at the bittes as he sayd so as the cable could not be veered. Ac aliter nescit.

Ad sextum affirmat verum esse that this examinate and company of the Susan Constant to cleare them selves from the Phillippe and Francys did cast a haulser uppon a carvell which rode by and made the same fast to the same Carvell called the Susan and by reason of the strength of the tide and for that they of the Phillipp and Francys would not veere theire cable the ships could not be cleared but the one wronged the other of this examinates knowledge & the company of the Carvell cutt the haulser which was fastened to them.

Ad septimum dicit eundem esse verum that this examinate hath seene that since the said hurte don there hath two ships rid in the same birth without wronginge one the other.

Ad octavum affirmat eundem continere in se veritatem Reddendo rationem ut supra that the company of the said shipp the Phillipp and Francys would use no diligence to save them selves or vere the cable but answered when they were requested to vere theire cables that they would not sayeinge our barke is as stronge as yourselves whereas this examinate and company of the Susan Constant did theire uttermost endevor to avoide the said dammadge.

Ad ultimum dicit predeposita per idem esse verum.

Ad Interrogatoria

Ad primum respondet he is a mariner and getteth his livinge by his labor at sea.

Ad secundum respondet negative.

Ad tertium respondet the Susan Constant on a monday came downe from the poole and ankered over against Ratcliffe crosse. Ac aliter non recolit.

Ad quartum respondet that John Davis of Dartmouth brought the Susan Constant to her said moringes at Ratcliffe crosse near where the Phillip & Francys rode then and before but howe longe he knoweth not.

Ad quintum responsum ut supra that the Susan Constant came to the place aforesaid where the Phillipp & Francys lay at anker.

Ad sextum respondet se nescire.

Ad septimum respondet verum esse that after the hurte don and departure of the Phillipp & Francys from her place where she lay this respondent and company wayed theire sothermost anker & removed yt further out of their chaines about haulfe a boates length but nether vered nor hauled eany cable to doe yt.

Ad octavum respondet the said anker was removed for that yt was brought home by the Philipp & Francys in the nighte tyme by lyenge twarte the saide anker as he thinketh.

Ad nonum respondet he sawe the Phillip & Francys remove from her moringes after the hurte don because her ankers were come home as he thinketh. Ac aliter nescit.

Ad decimum respondet he thinketh the Phillipp & Francys lay a weeke in the saide place where the hurte hapened before the Susan Constant came thither. Ac aliter respondet se nescire.

Ad undecimum respondet yt is true the Susan Constant and Phillip & Francys had not come foule one of the other if the Susan Constant had remained in the poole where she ridd before. Ac aliter respondet se nescire.

Ad xij respondet there were not eany droncke in the Susan Constant at the tyme aforesaid nether had dronck furder to his knowledge.

[Signed:] Jeremy Deane I D his marke

XXIII

The Virginia Colony, 1606–1612

THE VIRGINIA COMPANY AND ITS COLONY AT JAMESTOWN, 1606–1612

THE VIRGINIA COMPANY, which was responsible for sending out the first colonists to Jamestown and therefore has a position of priority in the annals of English settlement, was established by royal charter on April 10, 1606. The two divisions of the company, one based in Plymouth to deal with north Virginia (38° to 45° N), and the other based in London for south Virginia (34° to 41° N), allowing a gap of 100 miles between the colonies, were to be controlled by a Royal Council for Virginia. This was to nominate councils inside each colony, which in turn were to select their own presidents (and turn them out by majority vote if they wished to do so). The activities of the Plymouth division, which was hopelessly undercapitalized, and its failure in 1608 have already been dealt with in volume III.

In December, 1606, three ships left England under the London Company's auspices, traveling by way of the West Indies (where they picked up specimens of plants and some livestock to be tried out in the colony) to the Chesapeake where, after some controversy, they chose Jamestown as the site which most nearly met the requirements of their instructions. After discovering who were to be their rulers (a sealed box contained the councillors' names), the colonists proceeded to divide themselves into three groups, as instructed, one for construction and fortification; one to sow and develop the terrain, while acting as guards for the settlement; and a third to explore the area. There were problems. Many of the colonists were ill-suited for pioneer conditions and unwilling to work at construction. There was continued uncertainty as to the ultimate objectives—were the settlers to concentrate on finding mineral wealth (false hopes of gold early in their experience had a disturbing effect), or were they to concentrate on agriculture? Finally, how much energy was to be spent in exploration? Christopher Newport took a party to the Falls of the James River in 1608, while attempts were made to trace Ralegh's Lost Colonists, but the hard fact that discovery principally meant finding where corn could be bought from the Indians was only gradually revealed to them. A final question mark that had to be tested by time and experiment was whether Virginia could provide outlets for fuel-consuming industry transferred from England—potash, glass, and iron production.

Indiscipline and uncertainty were fostered by lack of strong and continuous control in the colony, a state of affairs that had been virtually assured by the lax provisions of the arrangement for the carrying on of government. According to Wesley Frank Craven (*The Southern Colonies in the Seventeenth Century* [1949], p. 71), the colony was "cursed with a plethora of leaders," almost none of whom, it may be added, could lead. Council members elected the governor but could dismiss him when he ceased to please them, as they did with the first governor, Edward Maria Wingfield. The quarrels inside the governing group and its lack of a coherent policy meant that individual settlers could behave almost as they wished, and after the first spurt of activity, there was little attempt to settle down to experimental and practical agriculture and horticulture. Too much emphasis was placed on potential mineral discoveries and the possibilities of a passage to the South Sea. Some attempts were made to find a staple food crop, but many of the seeds and roots brought by the colonists failed to flourish. It was some time before Indian help was sought and obtained in instructing them in the cultivation and harvesting of indigenous food crops. The rapid toll of disease and death, together with the long, hot, and humid summer, was an unnerving and sweltering shock in 1607. The cold and ice storms of the winter of 1607–1608 were equally unexpected. The fact that the climate was quite different from what had been expected clearly had, and continued to have, an unsettling effect, even though subsequent winters in the main appear to have been mild.

The arrival of several new batches of colonists in 1608 added to the problems of the much reduced initial nucleus. No preparations had been made, either in January, April, or October, to receive and house additional settlers. After a long and unhealthy sea crossing these newcomers—including the first two women—initially were unable to settle down and make homes for themselves, plant crops, and take an energetic part in the development of a pioneer outpost. The only ray of comfort was that the burning of the greater part of the first settlement, in January, 1608, led to its vigorous reconstruction on a larger scale through the energy and skill of Christopher Newport. But Newport was a temporary visitor only. In the latter part of 1607, the initial weight of the exploration of neighboring Indian tribes had fallen on Captain John Smith. His capture by the Pamunkey Indians toward the end of the year and his subsequent release by Powhatan gave him, and through him the settlers, valuable insights into the surrounding Amerindian society, with which they began, in some small measure, to come to terms. Later in 1608 Smith emerged as the one man who had an effective degree of initiative. He carried his boat's crew far up Chesapeake Bay to its head (where he made contact with the Iroquoian Susquehanna) and explored not only the creeks of the eastern shore but the major rivers paralleling the James River on the western side of the bay. He made significant penetrations of all the major rivers and was especially impressed by the mighty Potomac (whose Indian population was outside the range of Powhatan's influence). He found that it too, like the James River, was barred by falls and so was clearly not a passage to the Pacific. When at last Smith was selected as governor and he had induced the settlers to take their coats off and clear ground of trees so that an effective planting area could be established, it may be argued that he had already spent too much time and effort in expanding the topographical knowledge of the area for the colonists, instead of concentrating all his efforts on the provision of a firmer agricultural base. Neither did his temporary accommodations with the Powhatan Indians and the other Algonkian tribes with whom he was in contact establish a stable trading base between the two communities, nor did they bring to an end the intermittent hostility and mutual raiding of settlements. It is also clear that not enough effort was put into the industrial experiments: German and Polish "experts" in the industrial arts, such as iron production and glassmaking, were not kept closely to their tasks. When they were seen to be making little progress, they preferred to take shelter with Powhatan rather than risk Smith's reprimands or sterner measures.

The colony might have run down gradually if it had not been that the company at home made an exceptional effort to keep it supplied and did not, after October, 1608, inundate it with new settlers. Moreover, the obvious failure of the type of administration arranged for in 1606 led to the launching of what was, in effect, a new public corporation to replace the old closed circle of adventurers, which had been loosely supervised by a royal council that remained incapable of understanding the colony's needs or providing for them. The 1609 charter was an ambitious document. It endeavored to involve statesmen, courtiers, gentlemen, merchants, and even small craftsmen-adventurers in the running of a major overseas venture. The new council was visibly related in the hundreds of men and corporations named as subscribers in the new charter. It was decided, further, to give the colony a unified and effective government. Hereafter there was to be a governor (who could appoint a deputy) and a council, but the latter was to be purely advisory. Within the limits of his instructions from the Council of the Company, the governor was to make all major decisions. The colonists were to be much more numerous than hitherto, and, although they would be the company's servants for seven years, they were offered some chances for individual initiative (gardens to their homes, for example) while they held this status. At the end of the period they were to be provided with free land which could make them substantial landowners within a foreseeable time (however, few were able to survive long enough to benefit).

With Sir Thomas Gates as deputy to the new governor Lord De La Warr, who was to follow later, the principal expedition in 1609 offered considerable prospects of creating a major settlement. The prestige of king and country alike was involved in the prosperity of the colony. The plan went awry through a strange accident. The vessels were scattered on the way out and the *Sea Adventure*, unwisely carrying the whole command structure—governor, marshal, and secretary, with all the documents required to put the colony on a formal basis—went aground on Bermuda. Gates was to retrieve his reputation by emerging unscathed with two newly made pinnaces and most of his 180 men in 1610, but this was too late to avoid the mishaps and tragedy of the year 1609 and its following winter and spring in Virginia itself. The new arrivals wanted to upset the old order of things—although each was a vital partner of the other—new and old settlers quarreled. Francis West set up a new settlement at the Falls, but it did not flourish and was soon abandoned. John Smith was eased, none too gently, from his old-style governorship, and one of the original settlers, George Percy, was put in charge. In fact, few of the new arrivals was ever hardened to the life of a settlement. They came too late to plant crops. Their stores, which had seemed ample, rapidly diminished. Indian supplies were intermittent after Smith's departure since no one but he could work the intricate barter system he had devised, and the Indians were alarmed by the arrival of more white men than they had ever expected to see. Powhatan had seemed certain that Jamestown would remain only a small outpost. The result was gradual deterioration as disease began to affect the colonists, and, in any event, a considerable number of the new settlers proved unwilling to do any useful work, while the administration failed to coax or cajole them into taking part in any effective corporate efforts. The result was the "starving time," which passed into myth and legend but which reduced the hundreds to a starving handful. By May, 1610, only seventy persons remained alive, and Jamestown was declining as neglect and decay developed in this death-ridden outpost.

When Sir Thomas Gates arrived from Bermuda with Sir George Somers and William Strachey (the new secretary), the pigmeat he brought with him scarcely provided more than very short-term sustenance for the despairing remnant. As an experienced soldier Gates realized the situation was hopeless. He decided to evacuate, hoping against hope that he could get enough supplies in Newfoundland to bring back a revived group of colonists late in the year (though he might well have had to take them back to England). As he sailed downstream he was intercepted by Lord De La Warr's expedition that appeared at last, barely in time to restore the position. Supplies were again available, but plans were made to supplement them from Bermuda and by a fishery expedition to the cod banks off New England. In addition, De La Warr brought order. Moreover, Gates's seasoned men provided, after a year's self-help in Bermuda, a valuable leaven for the miserable older colonists and the raw unseasoned newcomers. At the same time it was clear that the outpouring from England of settlers in 1609, and even in 1610, was too large to be absorbed. Further internal reform and additional rethinking at home had to take place so that a degree of permanence could be achieved.

As a result of Gates's visit to England in 1610, the situation was explained to the company's council and a more rigorous policy was decided on. More adequate stores were to be sent until it was certain the colony could provide for itself. It was encouraged, even compelled, to do so by being placed in a legal straight jacket. The dominance of the company's officers over its servants was to be made clear. Sir Thomas Dale, as marshal and second in command to the governor, was concerned to make military service for guard duty and punitive expeditions a requirement for the able-bodied. When under orders for this type of service, he put the men under very severe discipline. Since Spanish raids were known to be a possibility following Écija's reconnaissance in 1609, new forts had been erected, or were in advanced stages of construction, at Cape Comfort, Cape Henry, and Cape Charles. The ships Sir Thomas Dale and Sir Thomas Gates brought out late in 1610 contained skilled craftsmen and much in the way of household goods and tools so that the material structure of the new society could be underpinned, but it is clear they were not put to very good use. Gradually, a body of laws was built up and was based on the governor (or his lieutenant governor), the marshal, and an organizing secretary. Dale began to enforce the laws in 1610; they were elaborated by Lord De La Warr under the instructions he carried. They were finally codified in the late summer of 1611 and brought to England by Strachey where they received the company's approval. Much has been made of their severity, and rightly so, since the settlers were to be under more rigorous control than if they had remained in England. Nonetheless, it has been recently pointed out that they did not make excessive demands on the colonists for labor and may have been very selectively enforced.

The rules had little and only short-term effect on the shiftless men who were still coming to Virginia. E. D. Morgan points out (*American Slavery, American Freedom* [1975], p. 73) that early in 1611 when Lord De La Warr, for health reasons left the colony for England and control was put back in the hands of the old colonist George Percy, no corn was sown. In May Dale came to find "nothing planted except 'some seeds put into a private garden or two,'" while the settlers amused themselves by bowling in the streets. They relied on the Indians or the company to supply them with food. It is also clear that they no longer attempted to treat the Indians with any degree of fairness. Raiding their towns and villages and stealing their corn became commonplace. It is no wonder that Jamestown and the new town of Henrico upstream became, for several years, little more than military outposts, which were beleaguered from time to time, disciplined but scarcely productive centers. A new phase was to emerge when a *modus vivendi* with the Indians was established in 1614. This lasted at least a few years; finally, tobacco was to bring to the colony its long desired and easily raised profitable export crop, which soon led it away from its squalid beginnings to something of an economic boom.

The first colony has been termed by E. D. Morgan "a fiasco"; it was and it was not. Certainly Englishmen had yet to show either statesmanship or organized ferocity in dealing with Indian society, nor had they learned how to gain a subsistence in the new land, fertile as it was, but a few men had learned a great deal about America. Strachey and Smith had returned laden with experience and knowledge. From this base, and with a further reorganization of the company in 1612, which made its governors more responsive to the shareholders, a bridgehead, at least, had been established by the end of that year, from which a Virginia colony, with its own special problems ranging from Indian relations to Black slavery, would grow and eventually flourish.

The early history of Virginia has long attracted the attention of historians on both sides of the Atlantic, and because of their concern many of the manuscripts relating to the years 1606 to 1612 have survived and have been published, often in several separate editions. The documents themselves fall into several distinct groups. First, there are the official records of the Virginia Company. Unfortunately, the first court book of the company has not survived, but many papers, including the three charters and instructions to the first leaders, are extant. These reveal the intentions behind the earliest settlement and the attempts to amend the regulations and organization in both England and America to fit the conditions in Virginia. Many of these documents were first published by William Stith in *The History of the First Discovery and Settlement of Virginia* (Williamsburg, 1747), and later by William W. Hening in *The Statutes at Large*, vol. I (Richmond, 1823), and by Alexander Brown in *The Genesis of the United States*, 2 vols. (Boston, 1890). The surviving court records, with many additional formal documents, were edited by Susan M. Kingsbury, *The Records of the Virginia Company of London*, 4 vols. (Washington, D.C., 1906–1935), and a useful brief collection, including the charters and instructions, was edited by Samuel H. Bemiss as *The Three Charters of the Virginia Company* (Williamsburg, 1957). Narratives and extracts of official documents relating to the period up to the granting of the second charter in 1609 can be found in Philip L. Barbour, ed., *The Jamestown Voyages under the First Charter*, 2 vols. (Cambridge, Eng., Hakluyt Society, 1969). The strict laws for the conduct of the colony, compiled between 1609 and 1611 by Sir

Thomas Gates, Sir Thomas Dale, and Lord De La Warr in accordance with their instructions, were brought to England late in 1611 by William Strachey, secretary of the colony, and were published as *For the Colony in Virginea Britannia. Lawes divine, morall, martiall etc.* (London, 1612). They are the first printed impression of the earliest code compiled specifically for the American experience. Although they were harsh compared with the prevailing laws in England (for example the death penalty was laid down for any attempt to steal a boat, an object vital to life in the colony), they reflect rather the conditions in the colony that made such laws necessary. A reprint of the first edition of the *Lawes* was made by Peter Force in *Tracts and Other Papers*, 4 vols. (Washington, D.C., 1836–1846). The *Lawes* were also more recently edited by David Flaherty (Charlottesville, 1969).

The propaganda campaign of the Virginia Company is one of the first on record to be sustained for a number of years. The company was very successful in preventing unofficial accounts from appearing in print (though it did not prevent John Smith's first tract being printed in London in 1608 or his book in 1612 in Oxford). Robert Gray's *A good speed to Virginia* (London, 1609) had little effective content, but Robert Johnson's *Nova Britannia* (London, 1609) held some information as well as pure propaganda. A great advance was made in the pair of tracts, *A true declaration of the estate of the colonie in Virginia* (London, 1610) and *A true and summarie declaration of the purpose and end of the plantation begun in Virginia* (London, 1610). These made a clear appeal to an intelligent and literate audience. *The relation of the right honourable the Lord De-la-Warre . . . of the colonie planted in Virginia* (London, 1611) was a gallant attempt to retrieve the situation caused by the unexpected return of the governor from his charge in Virginia. The propaganda effect of Strachey's collection *For the Colony in Virginea Britannia. Lawes* (1612) is more difficult to judge. People of substance could be assured that the colony would be under effective control (so that they might get their investment back); persons attracted to the colony might regard the severity of the code as a disincentive. These secular tracts were backed up by sermons that were probably as influential, if not more so, than those put out in a less elevated context. The practice of the company of having sermons made and published on its behalf continued for some years. In addition, a great deal of propaganda was verbal (as with the City of London Companies) and by letter. No systematic collection of all the Virginia Company propaganda material has so far been attempted.

A few items from manuscript sources in this collection show that it is still possible to find minor additions to the well-known documentation. A suit in the High Court of Admiralty shows that the *Susan Constant* was involved in a collision in the Thames in November, 1606; all so far known from the resulting case is given, as some light is thrown on the history, ownership, and manning of this celebrated vessel. A few extracts from the London City Company records indicate the types of relationship that prevailed between it and the Virginia Company. There is evidence of the stopping of the *Hercules* by pirates off the Lizard in 1611; they ignored the cargo she was bringing from Virginia as not worth their seizing (819). There is also a sidelight on a ship the *Discovery*, which deserted the colony, when she was sent to fish for the colonists and came home instead (821).

For Virginia it is possible to give only a very small and not wholly representative case of samples in this collection. Fortunately, her outstanding documentation is well known. For the period down to the second charter, Philip L. Barbour, *The Jamestown Voyages* (1969) is virtually definitive. Other collections cited for the 1609–1612 period are somewhat dated. Barbour's forthcoming edition of the *Works of John Smith*, under the auspices of the Institute of Early American History and Culture, will continue to provide editions of the quality now demanded. Systematic editing of the Virginia material in S. Purchas, *Pilgrimes*, would be a valuable project.

Chapter One hundred two
The Virginia Company: Formal Documents, 1606–1612

Between The First charter of April, 1606, and the third charter of 1612 the essential basis for a colonizing company had been worked out. The Royal Council for Virginia, a prototype for an English Council of the Indies, was a clumsy device. Its second-level officials and leading merchants were not really capable of directing the affairs of what was, by necessity, mainly a joint-stock commercial venture. The experience of the period 1607–1609, when the Royal Council for Virginia was active, brought its method of appointing the council in the colony into complete disrepute: the quarrels and weaknesses that resulted from this type of council became all too painfully obvious. On the other hand, the Council for Virginia was kept very much in the background during the period of severe controversy with the Spaniards from 1606 to 1608 and was not even mentioned in the diplomatic correspondence of this period. The desire to hide its existence from the Spaniards rendered it less effective than it might have been in 1608, so that it almost seems to have gone out of practical existence before the end of the year. The Virginia colony was carried on solely by a group of London merchants headed by Sir Thomas Smith. The failure of the Plymouth Company to establish a settlement in north Virginia simplified the task of eliminating the Council for Virginia. Now there was only the London Company in the field. Thus in 1609, not only was the opportunity taken of drawing a vast number of new individuals and groups into the London Company but the ruling council, the King's Council for Virginia, was incorporated in and became the Council of the Company itself. Thereafter the company was able to operate on a larger scale, though mishaps of 1609 and 1610 held it back, but the establishment of an authoritarian government in Virginia, with a governor advised but not controlled by his local council, paved the way for further reform. The charter of 1612 enabled the shareholders, at last, to have some effective voice in appointing the officials and the council, as well as making their opinion felt in the quarterly meetings of the Court. In 1612 the Virginia Company was fully equipped, at a formal level, to run a colony.

797. April 10, 1606. The charter that created the Virginia companies.

The first Virginia Charter of April 10, 1606, which created the Virginia companies, was a shell into which substance could gradually be put. The nominees for the First (or London) colony, which was to plant south Virginia, and for the Second (or Plymouth) colony, which was to plant north Virginia, were no doubt representative of the unofficial body of adventurers that had been assembled in each place. The formal matrix to bind them was a royal council that was to have jurisdiction over all colonies subsequently created, but specifically over the First and Second colonies. Outside the rules it made, the adventurers were free to make their own arrangements about actually creating the colonies.

Substance gradually filled out this framework, but the charter tells virtually nothing about the actual organization of the two groups of adventurers who did the work.

The warrant under the Privy Seal was issued on April 5, 1606 (P.R.O., C82/1729, m. 1) and the patent sealed on April 10 (P.R.O., 4 James I, part 19, memb. 1-4, C66/1709). The original patent probably perished in the destruction of the Virginia Company's early records. Copies were printed by William Stith, The History of the First Discovery and Settlement of Virginia *(Williamsburg, 1747), App. I, pp. 1-8, William W. Hening,* The Statutes at Large, being a Collection of All the Laws of Virginia from the First Session of the Legislature in the Year 1619 *(Philadelphia, 1823), I, 57-66, and Alexander Brown,* The Genesis of the United States, *2 vols. (Boston, 1890), I, 52-63. There is a good text in P. L. Barbour,* The Jamestown Voyages, *2 vols. (Cambridge, Eng., Hakluyt Soc., 1969), I, 24-34, and a convenient one in Samuel T. Bemiss (ed.),* The Three Charters of the Virginia Company *(Williamsburg, 1957), pp. 1-12, both from the Patent Roll entry. Bemiss's division of the charter into paragraphs has been maintained.*

James, by the grace of God etc. Whereas our loving and weldisposed subjects, Sir Thomas Gates and Sir George Somers, Knightes; Richarde Hackluit, Clarke, Prebendarie of Westminster; and Edwarde Maria Winghfeilde, Thomas Hannam and Raleighe Gilberde, Esquiers; William Parker and George Popham, Gentlemen; and divers others of our loving subjects, have been humble sutors unto us that wee woulde vouchsafe unto them our licence to make habitacion, plantacion and to deduce a Colonie of sondrie of our people into that parte of America commonly called Virginia, and other parts and territories in America either appartaining unto us or which are not nowe actuallie possessed by anie Christian prince or people, scituate, lying and being all along the sea coastes between fower and thirtie degrees of northerly latitude from the equinoctiall line and five and fortie degrees of the same latitude and in the maine lande betweene the same fower and thirtie and five and fourtie degrees, and the ilandes thereunto adjacente or within one hundred miles of the coaste thereof;

And to that ende, and for the more speedy accomplishemente of theire saide intended plantacion and habitacion there, are desirous to devide themselves into two severall colonies and companies, the one consisting of certaine Knightes, gentlemen, merchauntes and other adventurers of our cittie of London, and elsewhere, which are and from time to time shalbe joined unto them which doe desire to begin theire plantacions and habitacions in some fitt and conveniente place between fower and thirtie and one and fortie degrees of the said latitude all alongest the coaste of Virginia and coastes of America aforesaide; and the other consisting of sondrie Knightes, gentlemen, merchauntes, and other adventurers of our citties of Bristoll and Exeter, and of our towne of Plymouthe, and of other places which doe joine themselves unto that colonie which doe desire to beginn theire plantacions and habitacions in some fitt and convenient place betweene eighte and thirtie degrees and five and fortie degrees of the saide latitude all alongst the saide coaste of Virginia and America as that coaste lyeth;

Wee, greatly commending and graciously accepting of theire desires to the furtherance of soe noble a worke which may, by the providence of Almightie God, hereafter tende to the glorie of His Divine Majestie in propagating of Christian religion to suche people as yet live in darkenesse and miserable ignorance of the true knowledge and worshippe of God and may in tyme bring the infidels and salvages living in those parts to humane civilitie and to a setled and quiet governemente, doe by theise our lettres patents graciously accepte of and agree to theire humble and well intended desires;

And doe, therefore, for us, our heires and successors, graunte and agree that the saide Sir Thomas Gates, Sir George Sumers, Richarde Hackluit and Edwarde Maria Winghfeilde, adventurers of and for our cittie of London, and all suche others as are or shalbe joined unto them of that Colonie, shalbe called the Firste Colonie, and they shall and may beginne theire saide firste plantacion and seate of theire firste aboade and habitacion at anie place upon the saide coaste of Virginia or America where they shall thincke fitt and conveniente betweene the saide fower and thirtie and one and fortie degrees of the saide latitude; and that they shall have all the landes, woods, soile, groundes, havens, ports, rivers, mines, mineralls, marshes, waters, fishinges, commodities and hereditamentes whatsoever, from the said first seate of theire plantacion and habitacion by the space of fiftie miles of Englishe statute measure all alongest the saide coaste of Virginia and America towardes the weste and southe weste as the coaste lieth, with all the islandes within one hundred miles directlie over againste the same sea coaste; and alsoe all the landes, soile, groundes, havens, ports, rivers, mines, mineralls, woods, marrishes, waters, fishinges, commodities and hereditamentes whatsoever, from the saide place of theire firste plantacion and habitacion for the space of fiftie like Englishe miles, all alongest the saide coaste of Virginia and America towardes the easte and northeaste as the coaste lieth, together with all the islandes within one hundred miles directlie over againste the same sea coaste; and alsoe all the landes, woodes, soile, groundes, havens, portes, rivers, mines, mineralls, marrishes, waters, fishinges, commodities and hereditamentes whatsoever, from the same fiftie miles everie waie on the sea coaste directly into the maine lande by the space of one hundred like Englishe miles; and shall and may inhabit and remaine there; and shall and may alsoe builde and fortifie within anie the same for theire better safegarde and defence, according to theire best discrecions and the direction of the Counsell of that Colonie; and that noe other of our subjectes shalbe permitted or suffered to plante or inhabit behinde or on the backside of them towardes the maine lande, without the expresse licence or consente of the Counsell of that Colonie thereunto in writing firste had or obtained.

And wee doe likewise for us, our heires and successors, by theise presentes graunte and agree that the saide Thomas Hannam and Raleighe Gilberde, William Parker and George Popham, and all others of the towne of Plymouthe in the countie of Devon, or elsewhere, which are or shalbe joined unto them of that Colonie, shalbe called the Seconde colonie; and that they shall and may beginne theire saide firste plantacion and seate of theire first aboade and habitacion at anie place upon the saide coaste of Virginia and America, where they shall thincke fitt and conveniente, betweene eighte and thirtie degrees of the said latitude and five and fortie degrees of the

same latitude; and that they shall have all the landes, soile, groundes, havens, ports, rivers, mines, mineralls, woods, marishes, waters, fishinges, commodities and hereditaments whatsoever, from the firste seate of theire plantacion and habitacion by the space of fiftie like Englishe miles, as is aforesaide, all alongeste the saide coaste of Virginia and America towardes the weste and southwest, or towardes the southe, as the coaste lieth, and all the islandes within one hundred miles directlie over againste the saide sea coaste; and alsoe all the landes, soile, groundes, havens, portes, rivers, mines, mineralls, woods, marishes, waters, fishinges, commodities and hereditamentes whatsoever, from the saide place of theire firste plantacion and habitacion for the space of fiftie like miles all alongest the saide coaste of Virginia and America towardes the easte and northeaste or towardes the northe, as the coaste liethe, and all the islandes alsoe within one hundred miles directly over againste the same sea coaste; and alsoe all the landes, soile, groundes, havens, ports, rivers, woodes, mines, mineralls, marishes, waters, fishings, commodities and hereditaments whatsoever, from the same fiftie miles everie waie on the sea coaste, directlie into the maine lande by the space of one hundred like Englishe miles; and shall and may inhabit and remaine there; and shall and may alsoe builde and fortifie within anie the same for theire better saufegarde according to theire beste discrecions and the direction of the Counsell of that Colonie; and that none of our subjectes shalbe permitted or suffered to plante or inhabit behinde or on the backe of them towardes the maine lande without the expresse licence or consente of the Counsell of that Colonie, in writing thereunto, firste had and obtained.

Provided alwaies, and our will and pleasure herein is, that the plantacion and habitacion of suche of the saide Colonies as shall laste plante themselves, as aforesaid, shall not be made within one hundred like Englishe miles of the other of them that firste beganne to make theire plantacion, as aforesaide.

And wee doe alsoe ordaine, establishe and agree for us, our heires and successors, that eache of the saide Colonies shall have a Counsell which shall governe and order all matters and causes which shall arise, growe, or happen to or within the same severall Colonies, according to such lawes, ordinannces and instructions as shalbe in that behalfe, given and signed with our hande or signe manuell and passe under the Privie Seale of our realme of Englande; eache of which Counsells shall consist of thirteene parsons and to be ordained, made and removed from time to time according as shalbe directed and comprised in the same instructions; and shall have a severall seale for all matters that shall passe or concerne the same severall Counsells, eache of which seales shall have the Kinges armes engraven on the one side there of and his pourtraiture on the other; and that the seale for the Counsell of the saide Firste Colonie shall have engraven rounde about on the one side theise wordes: Sigillum Regis Magne Britanie, Francie et Hibernie; on the other side this inscripture rounde about: Pro Consillio Prime Colonie Virginie. And the seale for the Counsell of the saide Seconde Colonie shall alsoe have engraven rounde about the one side thereof the foresaide wordes: Sigillum Regis Magne Britanie, Francie et Hibernie; and on the other side: Pro Consilio Secunde Colonie Virginie.

And that alsoe ther shalbe a Counsell established here in Englande which shall in like manner consist of thirteen parsons to be, for that purpose, appointed by us, our heires and successors, which shalbe called our Counsell of Virginia; and shall from time to time have the superior managing and direction onelie of and for all matters that shall or may concerne the govermente, as well of the said severall Colonies as of and for anie other parte or place within the aforesaide precinctes of fower and thirtie and five and fortie degrees abovementioned; which Counsell shal in like manner have a seale for matters concerning the Counsell with the like armes and purtraiture as aforesaide, with this inscription engraven rounde about the one side: Sigillum Regis Magne Britanie, Francie et Hibernie; and rounde about the other side: Pro Consilio Suo Virginie.

And more over wee doe graunte and agree for us, our heires and successors, that the saide severall Counsells of and for the saide severall Colonies shall and lawfully may by vertue hereof, from time to time, without interuption of us, our heires or successors, give and take order to digg, mine and searche for all manner of mines of goulde, silver and copper, as well within anie parte of theire saide severall Colonies as of the saide maine landes on the backside of the same

Colonies; and to have and enjoy the goulde, silver and copper to be gotten there of to the use and behoofe of the same Colonies and the plantacions thereof; yeilding therefore yerelie to us, our heires and successors, the fifte parte onelie of all the same goulde and silver and the fifteenth parte of all the same copper soe to be gotten or had, as is aforesaid, and without anie other manner of profitt or accompte to be given or yeilded to us, our heires or successors, for or in respecte of the same.

And that they shall or lawfullie may establishe and cawse to be made a coine, to passe currant there betwene the people of those severall Colonies for the more ease of traffique and bargaining betweene and amongest them and the natives there, of such mettall and in such manner and forme as the same severall Counsells there shall limitt and appointe. And wee doe likewise for us, our heires and successors, by theise presents give full power and auctoritie to the said Sir Thomas Gates, Sir George Sumers, Richarde Hackluit, Edwarde Maria Winghfeilde, Thomas Hannam, Raleighe Gilberde, William Parker and George Popham, and to everie of them, and to the saide severall Companies, plantacions and Colonies, that they and everie of them shall and may at all and everie time and times hereafter have, take and leade in the saide voyage, and for and towardes the saide severall plantacions and Colonies, and to travell thitherwarde and to abide and inhabit there in everie of the saide Colonies and plantacions, such and somanie of our subjectes as shall willinglie accompanie them, or anie of them, in the saide voyages and plantacions, with sufficiente shipping and furniture of armour, weapon, ordonnance, powder, victall, and all other thinges necessarie for the saide plantacions and for theire use and defence there: provided alwaies that none of the said parsons be such as hereafter shalbe speciallie restrained by us, our heires or successors.

Moreover, wee doe by theise presents, for us, our heires and successors, give and graunte licence unto the said Sir Thomas Gates, Sir George Summers, Richarde Hackluite, Edwarde Maria Winghfeilde, Thomas Hannam, Raleighe Gilberde, William Parker and George Popham, and to everie of the said Colonies, that they and everie of them shall and may, from time to time and at all times for ever hereafter, for theire severall defences, incounter or expulse, repell and resist, aswell by sea as by lande, by all waies and meanes whatsoever, all and everie suche parson and parsons as without espiciall licence of the said severall Colonies and plantacions shall attempte to inhabit within the saide severall precincts and limitts of the saide severall Colonies and plantacions, or anie of them, or that shall enterprise or attempt at anie time hereafter the hurte, detrimente or annoyance of the saide severall Colonies or plantacions.

Giving and graunting by theise presents unto the saide Sir Thomas Gates, Sir George Somers, Richarde Hackluite, and Edwarde Maria Winghfeilde, and theire associates of the said Firste Colonie, and unto the said Thomas Hannam, Raleighe Gilberde, William Parker and George Popham, and theire associates of the saide Second Colonie, and to everie of them from time to time and at all times for ever hereafter, power and auctoritie to take and surprize by all waies and meanes whatsoever all and everie parson and parsons with theire shipps, vessels, goods and other furniture, which shalbe founde traffiqueing into anie harbor or harbors, creeke, creekes or place within the limitts or precincts of the saide severall Colonies and plantacions, not being of the same Colonie, untill such time as they, being of anie realmes or dominions under our obedience, shall paie or agree to paie to the handes of the Tresorer of the Colonie, within whose limitts and precincts theie shall soe traffique, twoe and a halfe upon anie hundred of anie thing soe by them traffiqued, boughte or soulde; and being straungers and not subjects under our obeysannce, untill they shall paie five upon everie hundred of suche wares and commoditie as theie shall traffique, buy or sell within the precincts of the saide severall Colonies wherein theie shall soe traffique, buy or sell, as aforesaide; which sommes of money or benefitt, as aforesaide, for and during the space of one and twentie yeres nexte ensuing the date hereof shalbe whollie imploied to the use, benefitt and behoofe of the saide severall plantacions where such trafficque shalbe made; and after the saide one and twentie yeres ended the same shalbe taken to the use of us, our heires and successors by such officer and minister as by us, our heires and successors shalbe thereunto assigned or appointed.

And wee doe further, by theise presentes, for us, our heires and successors, give and graunte unto the said Sir Thomas Gates, Sir George Sumers, Richarde Hackluit, and Edwarde Maria Winghfeilde, and to theire associates of the saide Firste Colonie and plantacion, and to the saide Thomas Hannam, Raleighe Gilberde, William Parker and George Popham, and theire associates of the saide Seconde Colonie and plantacion, that theie and everie of them by theire deputies, ministers and factors may transport the goods, chattells, armor, munition and furniture, needfull to be used by them for theire saide apparrell, defence or otherwise in respecte of the saide plantacions, out of our realmes of Englande and Irelande and all other our dominions from time to time, for and during the time of seaven yeres nexte ensuing the date hereof for the better releife of the said severall Colonies and plantacions, without anie custome, subsidie or other dutie unto us, our heires or successors to be yeilded or paide for the same.

Alsoe wee doe, for us, our heires and successors, declare by theise presentes that all and everie the parsons being our subjects which shall dwell and inhabit within everie or anie of the saide severall Colonies and plantacions and everie of theire children which shall happen to be borne within the limitts and precincts of the said severall Colonies and plantacions shall have and enjoy all liberties, franchises and immunities within anie of our other dominions to all intents and purposes as if they had been abiding and borne within this our realme of Englande or anie other of our saide dominions.

Moreover our gracious will and pleasure is, and wee doe by theise presents, for us, our heires and successors, declare and sett forthe, that if anie parson or parsons which shalbe of anie of the said Colonies and plantacions or anie other, which shall trafficque to the saide Colonies and plantacions or anie of them, shall at anie time or times hereafter transporte anie wares, marchandize or commodities out of any our dominions with a pretence and purpose to lande, sell or otherwise dispose the same within anie the limitts and precincts of anie of the saide Colonies and plantacions, and yet nevertheles being at the sea or after he hath landed the same within anie of the said Colonies and plantacions, shall carrie the same into any other forraine countrie with a purpose there to sell or dispose of the same without the licence of us, our heires or successors in that behalfe first had or obtained, that then all the goods and chattels of the saide parson or parsons soe offending and transporting, together with the said shippe or vessell wherein suche transportacion was made, shall be forfeited to us, our heires and successors.

Provided alwaies, and our will and pleasure is and wee doe hereby declare to all Christian kinges, princes and estates, that if anie parson or parsons which shall hereafter be of anie of the said severall Colonies and plantacions, or anie other, by his, theire, or anie of theire licence or appointment, shall at anie time or times hereafter robb or spoile by sea or by lande or doe anie acte of unjust and unlawfull hostilitie to anie the subjects of us, our heires or successors, or anie of the subjects of anie king, prince, ruler, governor or state being then in league or amitie with us, our heires or successors, and that upon suche injurie or upon juste complainte of such prince, ruler, governor or state or their subjects, wee, our heires or successors, shall make open proclamation within anie the ports of our realme of Englande, commodious for that purpose, that the saide parson or parsons having committed anie such robberie or spoile shall, within the terme to be limitted by suche proclamations, make full restitucion or satisfaction of all suche injuries done, soe as the saide princes or others soe complained may houlde themselves fully satisfied and contented; and that if the saide parson or parsons having committed such robberie or spoile shall not make or cause to be made satisfaction accordingly within such time soe to be limitted, that then it shalbe lawfull to us, our heires and successors to put the saide parson or parsons having committed such robberie or spoile and theire procurers, abbettors or comfortors out of our allegeaunce and protection; and that it shalbe lawefull and free for all princes and others to pursue with hostilitie the saide offenders and everie of them and theire and everie of theire procurors, aiders, abbettors and comforters in that behalfe.

And finallie wee doe, for us, our heires and successors, graunte and agree, to and with the saide Sir Thomas Gates, Sir George Sumers, Richarde Hackluit and Edwarde Maria Winghfeilde, and all other of the saide Firste Colonie, that wee, our heires or successors, upon peticion in that behalfe to be made, shall, by lettres pa-

tents under the Greate Seale of Englande, give and graunte unto such parsons, theire heires and assignees, as the Counsell of that Colonie or the most part of them shall for that purpose nomminate and assigne, all the landes, tenements and hereditaments which shalbe within the precincts limitted for that Colonie, as is aforesaid, to be houlden of us, our heires and successors as of our mannor of Eastgreenwiche in the countie of Kente, in free and common soccage onelie and not in capite.

And doe, in like manner, graunte and agree, for us, our heires and successors, to and with the saide Thomas Hannam, Raleighe Gilberd, William Parker and George Popham, and all others of the saide Seconde Colonie, that wee, our heires and successors, upon petition in that behalfe to be made, shall, by lettres patentes under the Great Seale of Englande, give and graunte unto such parsons, theire heires and assignees, as the Counsell of that Colonie or the most parte of them shall for that purpose nomminate and assigne, all the landes, tenementes and hereditaments which shalbe within the precinctes limitted for that Colonie as is afore said, to be houlden of us, our heires and successors as of our mannor of Eastgreenwich in the countie of Kente, in free and common soccage onelie and not in capite.

All which landes, tenements and hereditaments soe to be passed by the saide severall lettres patents, shalbe, by sufficient assurances from the same patentees, soe distributed and devided amongest the undertakers for the plantacion of the said severall Colonies, and such as shall make theire plantacion in either of the said severall Colonies, in such manner and forme and for such estates as shall [be] ordered and sett downe by the Counsell of the same Colonie, or the most part of them, respectively, within which the same lands, tenements and hereditaments shall ly or be. Althoughe expresse mencion [of the true yearly value or certainty of the premises, or any of them, or of any other gifts or grants, by us or any our progenitors or predecessors, to the aforesaid Sir Thomas Gates, Knt. Sir George Somers, Knt. Richard Hackluit, Edward Maria Wingfield, Thomas Hanham, Ralegh Gilbert, William Parker, and George Popham, or any of them, heretofore made, in these presents, is not made; or any statute, act, ordnance, or provision, proclamation, or restraint, to the contrary hereof had, made, ordained, or any other thing, cause, or matter whatsoever, in any wise notwithstanding. In witnesse wherof we have caused these our letters to be made patents; witnesse our selfe at Westminster the xth day of Aprill 1606, in the fourth year of our reign of England, France, and Ireland, and of Scotland the nine and thirtieth. Per breve de privato sigillo

798. December 10, 1606. Instructions for the council in Virginia.

The instructions actually sent with Newport in December, 1606, and forming the foundation for the administration of the colony from 1607 to 1609 survive only in a late manuscript. This has been frequently used by Virginia historians. The absurd formality of the instructions combined with the looseness of the authority of the governor over his council do not reflect much credit on the King's Council for Virginia which compiled them.

Library of Congress, Division of Manuscripts; the best edition is that in P. L. Barbour, The Jamestown Voyages, *I (1969), 45–48.*

Certain Orders and Directions Conceived and Set Down the tenth Day of December in the Year of the Reign of Our Soverain Lord King James of England France & Ireland the fourth and of Scotland the fortieth by his majesties Counsel for Virginia for the better Government of his Majesties Subjects both Captains Soldiers Marriners and Others that are now bound for that Coast to Settle his Majesties first Colony in Virginia there to be by them Observed as Well in their passages thether by Sea as after their arrival and Landing there.

Whereas Our said Soverain Lord the king by Certain Articles Signed by his Majestie and Sealed with his highness privy Seal hath appointed us whose names are Underwritten with Some Others to be his Majesties Counsel for Virginia Giving unto us by his Majesties Warrant under the said Privy Seal full power and authority in his Majesties name to nominate the first several Councellors of the Several Colonies which are to be planted in Virginia and to Give Directions unto the Several Councellors for their better Government there we having Such Due respect as is requisite to a Service of Such importance being assembled together for the better Ordering and Directing of the Same Do by this Our Writing Sealed With his Majesties Seal appointed for this Coun[s]el Ordain Direct & Appoint in manner and form following.

First whereas the Good Ship Called the Sarah [*sic* for Susan] Constant and the Ship Called the Godspeed with a pinnace called the Discovery are now ready Victualed riged and furnished for the said Voyage We think it fit and So Do Ordain and Appoint that Captain Christopher Newport Shall have the Sole Charge to appoint Such Captains Soldiers and Marriners as Shall Either Command or be Shiped to pass in the said Ships or pinnace and Shall also have the Charge and Oversight of all Such munitions victuals and Other provisions as are Or Shall be Shiped at the publick Charge of the Adventurers in them or any of them And further that the said Captain Neweport shall have the Sole charge and Command of all the Captains Soldiers and marriners and Other persons that Shall Go in any the Said Ships and pinnace in the said Voyage from the Day of the Date hereof until Such time as they Shall fortune to Land upon the Said Coast of Virginia and if the said Captain Newport should happen to Dye at Sea then the Masters of the said Ships and pinnace Shall Carry them to the Coast of Virginia aforesaid.

And whereas We have Caused to be Delivered unto the said Captain Newport Captain Barthol-[omew] Gosnold and Captain John Ratcliffe Several instruments Close Sealed with the Counsels Seal aforesaid Containing the names of Such Persons as we have appointed to be of his Majesties Counsel in the said Country of Virginia we Do Ordain and Direct that the said Captain Christopher Newport Captain Bartholomew Gosnold and Captain John Ratcliffe or the Survivor Or Survivors of them Shall Within four and twenty hours next after the said Ships Shall arrive upon the said Coast of Virginia and not before Open and Unseal the said Instrument and Declare and publish unto all the Company the names therein Set down and that the persons by Us therein named are and Shall be known and taken to be his Majesties Counsel of his first Colony in Virginia aforesaid. And further that the said Counsel So by us nominated Shall upon the publishing of the said Instrument proceed to the Election and nomination of a President of the said Counsel and the said President in all matters of Controversy and Question that Shall arise During the Continuance of his Authority where there shall fall Out to be Equality of Voices shall have two Voices and Shall have full power and Authority with the advice of the Rest of the said Counsel or the Greatest part of them to Govern Rule and Command all the Captains and Soldiers and all Other his Majesties Subjects of his Colony according to the true meaning of the Orders and Directions Set Down in the articles Signed by his Majestie and of these presents And that immediately upon the Election and nomination of the Said President the President himself Shall in the presence of the said Counsel and Some twenty of the Principal Persons adventurers in the said Voyage to be by the Said President and Counsel Called thereunto take his Corporal Oath upon the holy Evangelists of Alleageance to Our Soverain Lord the king and for performance of this Duty in his Place in manner and form following.

I, N Elected President for his Majesties Counsel for the first Colony to Virginia Do Swear that I Shall be a true and faithfull Servant unto the Kings majestie as A Councellor & President of his Majesties Counsel for the first Colony planted or to be Planted in any the territories of America between the Degrees of 34 and 41 from the Equinoctial Line Northward and the trades thereof and that I Shall faithfully and truely Declare my mind and Opinion according to my heart and Conscience in all things treated of in that Counsel and Shall keep Secreet all matters Committed and Revealed unto me Concerning the same Or that Shall be treated of Secreetly in that Counsel until [such] time as by the Consent of his Majesties Privy Counsel or the Counsel of Virginia or the more part of them publication Shall be made thereof and of all matters of Great importance or Difficulty I Shall make his Majesties General Counsel for Virginia acquainted therewith and follow their Directions therein I Shall to the best of my Skill and Knowledge uprightly and Duely Execute all things committed to my Care and Charge according to Such Directions as are or Shall be Given unto me by or from his Majestie his heirs or Successors or his or

their Privy Counsel or his or their Councel for Virginia according to the tenour Effect and true meaning of his Majesties Letters Patents and of Such articles and instructions as are Set Down by his highness under his Majesties Privy Seal for and Concerning the Government of the said Colony and my uttermost bear faith and alleageance unto the kings Majesty his heirs and Lawful Successors as Shall assist and Defend all Jurisdictions Preheminences and Authorities Granted unto his Majesty and annexed unto the Crown as against forrain Princes Persons & Potentates whatsoever be it by Act of Parliament or Otherwise And Generally in all things I Shall Do as a true and faithfull Servant and Subjects Ought to Do to his Majesty So help me God And after the Oath So by him taken the said President Shall Minister the Like Oath to Every One particularly of the said Counsell Leaving out the name of President only.

And Finally that after the arrival of the said Ship upon the Coast of Virginia the Counsell names published the said Captain Newport Shall with Such Number of Men as Shall be Assigned him by the President and Counsel of the said Colony Spend and Bestow two Months in Discovery of Such ports and Rivers as Can be found in that Country and Shall Give Order for the present Laiding and furnishing of the two Ships abovenamed with all Such principal Comodities and Merchandize as Can there be had and found in Such Sort as he may Return with the said Ships full Laden with Goods and Merchandizes bringing With him full Relation of all that he hath passed in the said Voyage by the end of May next if God Permit.

799. March 9, 1607. Enlargement of the royal council for Virginia.

By March 9, 1607, both companies had taken shape in London and Plymouth, and expeditions had been sent out to establish Jamestown and Fort St. George, respectively. By Letters under the Privy Seal of that date to the fourteen men originally nominated to the royal council on November 20, 1606, were added fifteen men to represent the London Company (or indeed to constitute it) and ten to represent the Plymouth

Company. It is clear that these men formed the working executive under which the respective colonies were being dispatched, and they were to have considerable influence in the royal council in respect to the particular colonies with which they were concerned. With the original grantees of the 1606 charter they, in fact, made up the London and Plymouth Companies, respectively, although the adventurers in those companies had presumably some say also in the administration of the money collected to dispatch and maintain the colonies. Thereafter the royal council (so far as we are aware) ceased to function, its work being done severally in the two companies whose leaders were by this document given de facto authority to represent the council in their respective companies.

Again, no authoritative text survives. Though the later P.R.O., CO 5/1354, fol. 49–53, copy was apparently used in W. W. Hening, Statutes, I (1823), 76–79, with Virginia State Library, "Patents, No., 1543–1651." Good editions collating both are again contained in P. L. Barbour, The Jamestown Voyages, I (1972), 71–76, and S. T. Bemiss, Three Charters, pp. 13–22.

An ordinance and constitution enlarging the number of our Councel for the two several Colonies and plantations in Virginia and America between 34 and 45 degrees of northerly latitude, and augmenting their authority for the better directing and ordering of such things as shall concerne the said Colonies.

James, by the grace of God, &c. Whereas wee, by our letters patents under our Great Seale of England bearing date the tenth day of April last past, have given licence to sundry our loving subjects named in the said letters patents and to their associates to deduce and conduct two several Colonies or plantations of sundry our loving people willing to abide and inhabit in certaine parts of Virginia and America with divers preheminences, priviledges, authorities and other things, as in and by the said letters patents more particularly it appeareth; and whereas wee, according to the effects and true meaning of the said letters patents, have by a former instrument, signed with our hand and signe manuel and sealed with our Privy Seal of our realme of England,

established and ordained that our trusty and welbeloved Sir William Wade, Knight, our Lieutenant of our Tower of London; Sir Thomas Smith, Knight; Sir Walter Cope, Knight; Sir George Moor, Knight; Sir Francis Popham, Knight; Sir Ferdinando Gorges, Knight; Sir John Trevor, Knight; Sir Henry Montague, Knight, Recorder of our citty of London; Sir William Rumney, Knight; John Dodderidge, Esqr., our Solicitor General; Thomas Warr, Esq.; John Eldred, of our city of London, merchant; Thomas James, of our citty of Bristol, merchant; and James Bagge, of Plymouth in our county of Devon, merchant; should be our Councel for all matters which should happen in Virginia or any the territories of America aforesaid, or any actions, businesse or causes for and concerning the same, which Councel is from time to time to be encreased, altered or changed att the nomination of us, our heires and successors, and att our and their will and pleasure; & whereas our said Councel have found by experience their number being but fourteen in all and most of them dispersed by reason of their several habitations far and remote the one from the other, and many of them in like manner far remote from our citty of London where, if need require, they may receive directions from us and our Privy Councel and from whence instructions and directions may be by them left and more readily given for the said Colonies; that when very needful occasion requireth there cannot be any competent number of them by any meanes be drawne together for consultation; for remedy whereof our said loving subjects of the several Colonies aforesaid have been humble suitors unto us and have to that purpose offered to our Royal consideration the names of certaine sage and discreet persons, & having with like humility entreated us that the said persons, or soe many of them as to us should seem good, might be added unto them and might (during our pleasure) be of our Councel for the foresaid Colonies of Virginia; wee therefore for the better establishing, disposing, orderring and directing of the said several Colonies within the degrees aforesaid, and of all such affaires, matters and things as shall touch and concerne the same, doe, by these presents signed with our hand and signe manuel and sealed with our Privy Seale of our realme of England, establish and ordaine that our trusty and welbeloved Sir Thomas Challonor, Knight; Sir Henry

Nevil, Knight; Sir Fulke Grevil, Knight; Sir John Scot, Knight; Sir Robert Mansfield, Knight; Sir Oliver Cromwel, Knight; Sir Morrice Berkeley, Knight; Sir Edward Michelbourne, Knight; Sir Thomas Holcroft, Knight; Sir Thomas Smith, Knight, Clerk of our Privy Councel; Sir Robert Kelligrew, Knight; Sir Herbert Croft, Knight; Sir George Copping, Knight; Sir Edwyn Sandys, Knight; Sir Thomas Row, Knight; and Sir Anthony Palmer, Knight; nominated unto us by and on the behalfe of the said First Colony; Sir Edward Hungerford, Knight; Sir John Mallet, Knight; Sir John Gilbert, Knight; Sir Thomas Freale [Freake], Knight; Sir Richard Hawkings, Knight; Sir Bartholomew Mitchel, Knight; Edward Seamour, Esq.; Bernard Greenville, Esq.; Edward Rogers, Esq.; and Matthew Sutcliffe, Doctor of Divinity; nominated to us by and on the behalfe of the said Second Colony, shall together with the persons formerly named, be our Councel for all matters which shall or may conduct to the aforesaid plantations or which shall happen in Virginia or any the territories of America between 34 & 45 degrees of northerly latitude from the aequinoctial line and the islands to the several Colonies limited and assigned, that is to say, the First Colony from 34 to 41 degrees of the said latitude, and the Second Colony between 38 and 45 degrees of the said latitude.

And our further will and pleasure is, and by these presents for us, our heires and successors wee doe grant unto our said Councel of Virginia, that they or any twelve of them att the least, for the time being, whereof six att the least to be members of one of the said Colonies, and six more att the least to be members of the other Colony, shall have full power and authority to ordaine, nominate, elect and choose any other person or persons att their discretion to be and to serve as officer or officers to all offices and places that shall by them be thought fitt and requisite for the businesse and affaires of our said Councel and concerning the plantation or plantations aforesaid, and for the summoning, calling and assembling of the said Councel together when need shall require, or for summoning and calling before the said Councel any of the adventurors or others which shall passe on unto the said several Colonies to inhabit or to traffick there, or any other such like offices or officers which in time shall or may be found of use, behoofe or impor-

tance unto the Councel aforesaid. And the said Council or any twelve of them as is aforesaid shall have full power and authority from time to time to continue or to alter or change the said officers and to elect and appoint others in their roomes and places, to make and ordain acts and ordinances for the better ordering, disposing and marshalling of the said several Colonies and the several adventurers or persons going to inhabit in the same several Colonies, or of any provision or provisions for the same, or for the direction of the officers aforesaid, or for the making of them to be subordinate or under jurisdiction one of another, and to do and execute all and every of their act and things which by any our grants or letters patents heretofore made. they are warranted or authorised to do or execute so as always none of the said acts and ordinances or other things be contrary or repugnant to the true intent and meaning of our said letters patents granted for the plantation of the said several Colonies in Virginia and territories of America as aforesaid, or contrary to the laws and statutes in this our realm of England, or in derogation of our prerogative royal. Witness ourself at Westminster the ninth day of March in the year of our reign of England, France and Ireland the fourth, and of Scotland the fortieth.

800. November 20, 1606. Instructions for the Virginia Company.

The charter of April 10 provided only a skeletal structure for the three bodies that were to supervise the colonies from England and to operate in London and Plymouth to create the colonies in south and north Virginia, respectively. Letters under the Privy Seal, dated November 20, gave these bodies substance. The royal council ("the kings Councel of Virginia") was named and authorized to give directions to the various colonies to be established in North America, and was instructed on what to do in this respect. Nothing was said on how the colony-organizing bodies were to operate, but the presidents and councils that were to be established in the colonies they created were given defined authority under the royal council.

No authoritative text survives. W. W. Hening,
Statutes, I (1823), 67–75, supported by Virginia
State Library, Richmond MS "Patents, No. 2,
1643–1651," provided unofficial texts. Good edi-
tions of these are in P. L. Barbour, The James-
town Voyages, I (1969), 34–44, and S. T. Bemiss,
Three Charters (1957), pp. 23–26.

Articles, instructions and orders made, sett
down and established by us the twentieth day of
November, in the year of our raigne of England,
France and Ireland the fourth and of Scotland the
fortieth, for the good order and government of the
two several Colonies and plantations to be made
by our loving subjects in the country commonly
called Virginia and America, between 34 and 45
degrees from the aequinoctial line.

Wheras wee, by our letters pattents under our
Great Seale of England bearing date att
Westminster the tenth day of Aprill in the year of
our raigne of England, France and Ireland the
fourth and of Scotland the 39th, have given lycence to sundry our loving subjects named in the
said letters pattents, and to their associates, to
deduce and conduct two several Collonies or plantations of sundry our loving people willing to
abide and inhabit in certaine parts of Virginia
and America, with divers preheminences,
priviledges, authorities and other things, as in
and by the same letters pattents more particularly it appeareth; wee, according to the effect
and true meaning of the same letters pattents,
doe by these presents, signed with our hand,
signe manuel and sealed with our Privy Seale of
our realme of England, establish and ordaine that
our trusty and welbeloved Sir William Wade,
Knight, our Lieutenant of our Tower of London;
Sir Thomas Smith, Knight; Sir Walter Cope,
Knight; Sir George Moor, Knight; Sir Francis
Popeham, Knight; Sir Ferdinando Gorges,
Knight; Sir John Trevor, Knight; Sir Henry
Montague, Knight, Recorder of the citty of London; Sir William Rumney, Knight; John Dodderidge, Esq., Sollicitor General; Thomas la
Warr, Esq.; John Eldred, of the citty of London,
merchant; Thomas James, of the citty of Bristol,
merchant; and James Bagge, of Plymouth, in the
county of Devonshire, merchant; shall be our
Councel for all matters which shall happen in
Virginia or any the territories of America between 34 and 45 degrees from the aequinoctial
line northward and the islands to the several
Collonies limitted and assigned; and that they
shal be called the King's Councel of Virginia,
which Councel or the most part of them shal have
full power and authority att our pleasure, in our
name and under us, our heires and successors, to
give directions to the Councels of the several
Colonies which shal be within any part of the said
country of Virginia and America within the degrees first above mentioned, with the islands
aforesaid, for the good government of the people
to be planted in those parts and for the good
ordering and disposing of all causes happening
within the same (and the same to be done for the
substance thereof as neer to the common lawes of
England and the equity thereof as may be) and to
passe under our seale app[ointed] for that Councel, which Councel and every or any of them shall
from time to [time] be increased, altered or
changed and others put in their places att the
[nomi]nation of us, our heires and successors and
att our and their will and plea[sure]; and the same
Councel of Virginia or the more part of them, for
the time bei[ng], shall nominate and appoint the
first several Councellours of those several Councells which are to be appointed for those two
several Colonies whi[ch are] to be made plantations in Virginia and America between the degrees [before] mentioned, according to our said
letters pattents in that behalfe made; and that
each of the same Councels of the same several
Colonies shal, by the major part of them, choose
one of the same Councel, not being the minister of
God's word, to be President of the same Councel
and to continue in that office by the space of one
whole year, unlesse he shall in the mean time dye
or be removed from that office; and wee doe
further hereby establish & ordaine that it shal be
lawful for the major part of either of the said
Councells, upon any just cause, either absence or
otherwise, to remove the President or any other
of that Councel from being either President or
any of that Councel, and upon the deathes or
removal of any of the Presidents or Councel it shal
be lawfull for the major part of that Councel to
elect another in the place of the party soe dying or
removed, soo alwaies as they shal not be above
thirteen of either of the said Councellours; and
wee doe establish & ordaine that the President

shal not continue in his office of Presidentship above the space of one year; and wee doe especially ordaine, charge and require the said Presidents and Councells and the ministers of the said several Colonies respectively, within their several limits and precincts, that they with all diligence, care and respect doe provide that the true word and service of God and Christian faith be preached, planted and used, not only within every of the said several Colonies and plantations but alsoe as much as they may amongst the salvage people which doe or shall adjoine unto them or border upon them, according to the doctrine, rights and religion now professed and established within our realme of England; and that they shall not suffer any person or persons to withdrawe any of the subjects or people inhabiting or which shall inhabit within any of the said several Colonies and plantations from the same or from their due allegiance unto us, our heires and successors, as their immediate soveraigne under God; and if they shall find within any of the said Colonies and plantations any person or persons soe seeking to withdrawe any of the subjects of us, our heires or successors, or any of the people of those lands or territories within the precincts aforesaid, they shall with all diligence him or them soe offending cause to be apprehended, arrested and imprisoned until he shall fully and throughly reforme himselfe, or otherwise, when the cause soe requireth, that he shall withall convenient speed be sent into our realme of England, here to receive condigne punishment for his or their said offence or offences; and moreover wee doe hereby ordaine and establish for us, our heires and successors that all the lands, tenements and hereditaments to be had and enjoyed by any of our subjects with the precincts aforesaid shal be had and inherited and injoyed according as in the like estates they be had & enjoyed by the lawes within this realme of England; and that the offences of tumults, rebellion, conspiracies, mutiny and seditions in those parts which maybe dangerous to the estates there, together with murther, manslaughter, incest, rapes and adulteries committed in those parts within the precincts of any the degrees above mentioned (and noe other offences) shal be punished by death, and that without the benefit of the clergy except in case of manslaughter, in which clergie is to be allowed; and that the said several Presidents and Councells and the

greater number of them within every of the several limits and precincts shall have full power and authority to hear and determine all and every the offences aforesaid within the precinct of their several Colonies, in manner and forme following, that is to say, by twelve honest and indifferent persons sworne upon the Evangelists, to be returned by such ministers and officers, as every of the said Presidents and Councells, or the most part of them respectively, shall assigne; and the twelve persons soe returned and sworne shall, according to their evidence to be given unto them upon oath and according to the truth in their consciences, either convict or acquit every of the said persons soe to be accused & tried by them; and that all and every person or persons which shall voluntarily confesse any of the said offences to be committed by him shall, upon such his confession thereof, be convicted of the same as if he had been found guilty of the same by the verdict of any such twelve jurors, as is aforesaid; and that every person and persons which shall be accused of any of the said offences and which shall stand mute or refusing to make direct answer thereunto, shall be and be held convicted of the said offence as if he had been found guilty by the verdict of such twelve jurors, as aforesaid; and that every person and persons soe convicted either by verdict, his own confession or by standing mute or by refusing directly to answer as aforesaid of any of the offences before mentioned, the said Presidents or Councells, or the greatest number of them within their several precincts and limitts where such conviction shall be had and made, as aforesaid, shall have full power and authority by these presents to give judgment of death upon every such offended without the benefit of the clergy, except only in cause of manslaughter, and noe person soe adjudged, attainted or condemned shall be reprived from the execution of the said judgment without the consent of the said President and Councel, or the most part of them by whom such judgment shall be given; and that noe person shal receive any pardon or be absolutely discharged of any the said offences for which he shall be condemned to death, as aforesaid, but by pardon of us, our heires and successors, under the Great Seale of England; and wee doe in like manner establish and ordaine if any either of the said Collonies shall offend in any of the offences before mentioned, within any part between the degrees aforesaid, out of the precincts of his or their Collony, that then every such offender or offenders shall be tried and punished as aforesaid within his or their proper Colony; and that every the said Presidents and Councells, within their several limits and precincts and the more part of them, shall have power and authority by these presents to hear and determine all and every other wrongs, trespasses, offences and misdemeanors whatsoever, other than those before mentioned, upon accusation of any person and proofe thereof made by sufficient witnesse upon oath; and that in all those cases the said President and Councel, and the greater number of them, shall have power and authority by these presents respectively, as is aforesaid, to punish the offender or offenders, either by reasonable corporal punishment and imprisonment or else by a convenient fine, awarding damages, or other satisfaction to the party grieved, as to the said President & Councel or to the more part of them shall be thought fitt and convenient, having regard to the quality of the offence or state of the cause; and that alsoe the said President & Councel shall have power and authority by virtue of these presents to punish all manner of excesse, through drunkennesse or otherwaies, and all idle, loytering and vagrant persons which shall be found within their several limits and precincts, according to their best discretions and with such convenient punishment as they or the most part of them shall think fitt; alsoe our will and pleasure [is], concerning the judicial proceedings aforesaid, that the same shall be made and done summarily and verbally without writing until it come to the judgment or sentence, and yet, nevertheless, our will and pleasure is that every judgment and sentence hereafter to be given in any of the causes aforesaid, or in any other of the said several Presidents and Councells or the greater number of them within their several limits and precincts, shall be breifely and summarily registred into a book to be kept for that purpose, together with the cause for which the said judgment or sentence was given; and that the said judgment and sentence soe registered and written shall be subscribed with the hands or names of the said President and Councel or such of them as gave the judgment or sentence; alsoe our will and pleasure is and wee doe hereby establish and ordaine that the said several Col-

lonies and plantations, and every person and persons of the same, severally and respectively, shall within every of their several precincts for the space of five years next after their first landing upon the said coast of Virginia and America, trade together all in one stocke, or devideably but in two or three stocks att the most, and bring not only all the fruits of their labours there but alsoe all such other goods and commodities which shall be brought out of England or any other place into the same Collonies, into severall magazines or storehouses for that purpose to be made and erected there, and that in such order, manner and form as the Councel of that Collony or the more part of them shall sett downe and direct; and our will and pleasure is and wee doe in like manner ordaine that in every of the said Collonies and plantations there shall be chosen three, elected yearely by the President and Councell of every of the said several Colonies and plantations or the more part of them: one person of the same Colony and plantation to be Treasurer or Cape-merchant of the same Colony and plantation to take the charge and mannageinge of all such goods, wares and commodities which shall be brought into or taken out of the several magazines or storehouses, the same Treasurer or Cape-merchant to continue in his office by the space of one whole year next after his said election, unless he shall happen to dye within the said year or voluntarily give over the same or be removed for any just or reasonable cause; and that thereupon the same President and Councell or the most part of them shall have power and authority to elect him again or any other or others in his room or stead to continue in the same office as aforesaid; and that alsoe there shall be two or more persons of good discretion within every of the said Colonies and plantations elected and chosen yearely, during the said terme of five years, by the President and Councel of the same Collony or the most part of them respectively within their several limits and precincts, the one or more of them to keep a book in which shall be registred and entred all such goods, wares and merchandizes as shall be received into the several magazines or storehouses within that Colony, being appointed for that purpose, and the other to keep a like book wherein shall be registred all goods, wares and merchandizes which shall issue or be taken out of any the several magazines or storehouses of that

Collony, which clarks shall continue in their said places but att the will of the President and Councel of that Colony whereof he is, or of the major part of them; and that every person of every the said several Colonies and plantations shall be furnished with all necessaries out of those several magazines or storehouses which shall belong to the said Colony and plantation in which that person is, for and during the terme and time of five yeares by the appointment, direction and order of the President and Councell there, or of the said Cape-merchant and two clerks or of the most part of them within the said several limits and precincts of the said Colonies and plantations; alsoe our will and pleasure is and wee doe hereby ordain that the adventurers of the said First Colony and plantation shall and may during the said terme of five years elect and choose out of themselves one or more Companies, each Company consisting of three persons att the least who shall be resident att or neer London, or such other place and places as the Councel of the Colony for the time being, or the most part of them, during the said five years shall think fitt, who shall there from time to time take charge of the trade and accompt of all such goods, wares, merchandizes and other things which shall be sent from thence to the Company of the same Colony or plantation in Virginia, and likewise of all such wares, goods and merchandizes as shall be brought from the said Colony or plantation unto that place within our realme of England, and of all things concerning the mannaging of the affaires and profits concerning the adventurors of that Company which shall soe passe out of or come into that place or port; and likewise our will and pleasure is that the adventurors in the said Second Colony and plantation shall and may, during the said terme of five years, elect out of themselves one or more Companies, each Company consisting of three persons att the least who shall be resident att or near Plymouth in our county of Devon within our realme of England, and att such one, two or three other places or ports as the Councel of that Colony or the most part of them shall think fitt, who shall there from time to time take care and charge of the trade & accompt of all such goods, wares, merchandizes and other things which shall be sent from thence to the same Colony and plantation in Virginia, and likewise of all such goods, wares and merchandizes as shall be brought from the said Colony and

plantation in Virginia into our realme of England, and of all things concerning the mannaging of the affaires and profits of the adventurors of that Company; alsoe our will and pleasure is that noe person or persons shall be admitted into any of the said Colonies and plantations, there to abide and remaine, but such as shall take not only the usual oath of obedience to us, our heires and successors; but alsoe the oath which is limitted in the last session of Parliament, holden at Westminster in the fourth year of our raigne, for their due obedience unto us, our heires and successors, that the trade to and from any the Colonies aforesaid may be mannaged to and from such ports & places within our realme of England as is before in these articles intended, any thing set down heretofore to the contrary notwithstanding; and that the said President and Councel of each of the said Colonies, and the more part of them respectively, shall and may lawfully from time to time constitute, make and ordaine such constitutions, ordinances and officers for the better order, government and peace of the people of their several Collonies, soe alwaies as the same ordinances and constitutions doe not touch any party in life or member, which constitutions & ordinances shall stand and continue in full force untill the same shall be otherwise altered or made void by us, our heires or successors, or our or their Councel of Virginia, soe alwaies as the same alterations be such as may stand with and be in substance consonant unto the lawes of England or the equity thereof; furthermore, our will and pleasure is and wee doe hereby determine and ordaine that every person and persons being our subjects of every the said Collonies and plantations shall from time to time well entreate those salvages in those parts and use all good meanes to draw the salvages and heathen people of the same several places and of the territories and countries adjoining to the true service and knowledge of God, and that all just, kind and charitable courses shall be holden with such of them as shall conforme themselves to any good and sociable traffique and dealing with the subjects of us, our heires and successors which shall be planted there, whereby they may be the sooner drawne to the true knowledge of God and the obedience of us, our heires and successors under such severe paines and punishments as shal be inflicted by the same several Presidents and Councells of the said several Colonies, or the most part of them, within their several limits and precincts, on such as shall offend therein or doe the contrary; and that as the said territories and countries of Virginia and America within the degrees aforesaid shall from time to time increase in plantation by our subjects, wee, our heires and successors will, ordaine and give such order and further instructions, lawes, constitutions and ordinances for the better rule, order and government of such as soe shall make plantations there as to us, our heires and successors shall from time to time be thought fitt & convenient, which alwaies shall be such as may stand with or be in substance consonant unto the lawes of England or the equity thereof; and lastly wee doe ordaine and establish for us, our heires and successors that such oath shall be taken by each of our Councellors here for Virginia, concerning their place and office of Councell, as by the Privy Councell of us, our heires and successors of this our realme of England shall be in that behalf limited & appointed; and that each Councellor of the said Colonies shall take such oath for the execution of their place and office of Councel as by the Councel of us, our heires and successors here in England, for Virginia, shall in that behalfe be limited and appointed; and aswell those several articles and instructions herein mentioned and contained as alsoe all such as by virtue hereof shall hereafter be made and ordained, shall as need shall require, by the advice of our Councel here for Virginia be transcripted over unto the said several Councells of the said several Colonies under the seale to be ordained for our said Councell here for Virginia; In witnesses &c.

801. May 23, 1609. The second Virginia Charter, the first to the London Company alone.

The efforts of 1607–1609 to establish a colony at Jamestown were on a small scale but were conducted from England with skill and celerity. The fact that they produced promise not performance made it essential to expand or abandon. Partly for political motives, the members of James I's government led by Lord Salisbury determined to mobilize such a major effort behind the Virginia enterprise that it would be evident to Spain that it was now an English national commitment. The mobilization of courtiers, lords, gentlemen, merchants, and London City Companies in 1609 was embodied in the charter of 1609, which constituted a great corporation to run a major colonial venture. The charter of May 23, 1609, embodied these intentions. The Council of the Company was now constituted as the Royal Council for the Virginia Company, the separate royal council being eliminated. With its treasurer as its executive head, it was empowered to run the whole enterprise under such powers, generous ones, as were set out in the charter, and, above all, to constitute an effective individual governor in the colony and to lay down laws for the colonists. One restriction placed on the colony was that it should not admit Catholics so that the oath of supremacy (repudiating the temporal authority of the Pope) must be taken by all emigrants. The charter, however, gave no power to the mass of the adventurers and created an oligarchy, the council, to rule them as well as the colony.

The original charter has not survived. It was printed from later copies in W. Stith, History of Virginia (1747), App. 80–98 pp. 8–22 by W. W. Hening, Statues, I (1823), and by A. Brown, Genesis, I (1890), 208–237. The entry in P.R.O., Patent Roll, 7 James I, part 8, memb. 21–29, C66/1796, was edited by S. T. Bemiss, Three Charters, pp. 27–54. The names of the subscribers are omitted although those of the council are retained.

James, by the grace of God, etc. To all etc.

Whereas, at the humble suite and request of sondrie oure lovinge and well disposed subjects intendinge to deduce a colonie and to make habitacion and plantacion of sondrie of oure people in that parte of America comonlie called Virginia, and other part and territories in America either apperteyninge unto us or which are not actually possessed of anie Christian prince or people within certaine bound and regions, wee have formerly, by oure lettres patents bearinge date the tenth of Aprill in the fourth yeare of oure raigne of England, Fraunce, and Ireland, and the nine and thirtieth of Scotland, graunted to Sir Thomas Gates, Sir George Somers and others, for the more speedie accomplishment of the said plantacion and habitacion, that they shoulde devide themselves into twoe collonies—the one consistinge of divers Knights, gentlemen, merchaunts and others of our cittie of London, called the First Collonie; and the other of sondrie Knights, gentlemen and others of the citties of Bristoll, Exeter, the towne of Plymouth, and other places, called the Second Collonie—and have yielded and graunted maine and sondrie priviledges and liberties to each Collonie for their quiet setlinge and good government therein, as by the said lettres patents more at large appeareth.

Nowe, forasmuch as divers and sondrie of oure lovinge subjects, as well adventurers as planters, of the said First Collonie (which have alreadie engaged them selves in furtheringe the businesse of the said plantacion and doe further intende by the assistance of Almightie God to prosecute the same to a happie ende) have of late ben humble suiters unto us that, in respect of their great chardeges and the adventure of manie of their lives which they have hazarded in the said discoverie and plantacion of the said countrie, wee woulde be pleased to graunt them a further enlargement and explanacion of the said graunte, priviledge and liberties, and that suche counsellors and other officers maie be appointed amonngest them to manage and direct their affaires [as] are willinge and readie to adventure with them; as also whose dwellings are not so farr remote from the cittye of London but that they maie at convenient tymes be readie at hande to give advice and assistance upon all occacions requisite.

We, greatlie affecting the effectual prosecucion and happie successe of the said plantacion and comendinge their good desires theirin, for their further encouragement in accomplishinge so excellent a worke, much pleasinge to God and profitable to oure Kingdomes, doe, of oure speciall grace and certeine knowledge and meere motion, for us, oure heires and successors, give graunt and confirme to oure trustie and welbeloved subjects, Robert, Earle of Salisburie . . . [and 618 individuals]. The companie of mercers . . . [and 54 London city companies].

And to such and so manie as they doe or shall hereafter admitt to be joyned with them, in forme hereafter in theis presentes expressed, whether they goe in their persons to be planters there in the said plantacion, or whether they goe not, but doe adventure their monyes, goods or chattels, that they shalbe one bodie or communaltie perpetuall and shall have perpetual succession and one common seale to serve for the saide bodie or communaltie; and that they and their successors shalbe knowne, called and incorporated by the name of The Tresorer and Companie of Adventurers and Planters of the Citty of London for the Firste Collonie in Virginia.

And that they and their successors shalbe from hensforth, forever enabled to take, acquire and purchase, by the name aforesaid (licens for the same from us, oure heires or successors first had and obtained) anie manner of lands, tenements and hereditaments, goods and chattels, within oure realme of England and dominion of Wales; and that they and their successors shalbe likewise enabled, by the name aforesaid, to pleade and to be impleaded before anie of oure judges or justices, in anie oure courts, and in anie accions or suits whatsoever.

And wee doe also, of oure said speciall grace, certaine knowledge and mere mocion, give, grannte and confirme unto the said Tresorer and Companie, and their successors, under the reservacions limittacions and declaracions hereafter expressed, all those lands, countries and territories scituat, lieinge and beinge in that place of America called Virginia, from the pointe of lande called Cape or Pointe Comfort all alonge the seacoste to the northward twoe hundred miles and from the said pointe of Cape Comfort all alonge the sea coast to the southward twoe hundred miles; and all that space and circuit of lande lieinge from the sea coaste of the precinct aforesaid upp unto the lande, throughoute, from sea to sea, west and northwest; and also all the island[s] beinge within one hundred miles alonge the coaste of bothe seas of the precincte aforesaid; togeather with all the soiles groundes, havens and portes, mynes, aswell royall mynes of golde and silver as other mineralls, pearles and precious stones, quarries, woods, rivers, waters, fishings, comodities, jurisdictions, royalties, priviledges, franchisies and preheminences within the said territorie and the precincts there of whatsoever; and thereto or there abouts, both by sea and lande, beinge or in anie sorte belonginge or appertayninge, and which wee by oure lettres patents maie or cann graunte; and in as ample manner and sorte as wee or anie oure noble progenitors have heretofore graunted to anie companie, bodie pollitique or corporate, or to anie adventurer or adventurers, undertaker or undertakers, of anie discoveries, plantacions or traffique of, in, or into anie forraine parts whatsoever; and in as large and ample manner as if the same were herin particulerly mentioned and expressed: to have, houlde, possesse and enjoye all and singuler the said landes, countries and territories with all and singuler other the premisses heretofore by theis [presents] graunted or mencioned to be grannted, to them, the said Tresorer and Companie, their successors and assignes, forever; to the sole and proper use of them, the said Tresorer and Companie, their successors and assignes [forever], to be holden of us, oure heires and successors, as of oure mannour of Estgreenewich, in free and common socage and not in capite; yeldinge and payinge, therefore, to us, oure heires and successors, the fiftie parte onlie of all oare of gould and silver that from tyme to time, and at all times hereafter, shalbe there gotton, had and obtained, for all manner of service.

And, nevertheles, oure will and pleasure is, and wee doe by theis presentes chardge, commannde, warrant and auctorize, that the said Tresorer and Companie and their successors, or the major parte of them which shall be present and assembled for that purpose, shall from time to time under their common seale distribute, convey, assigne and set over such particuler porcions of lands, tenements and hereditaments, by theise presents formerly graunted, unto such oure lovinge subjects naturallie borne of denizens, or others, aswell adventurers as planters, as by the said Companie, upon a commission of survey and distribucion executed and retourned for that purpose, shalbe named, appointed and allowed, wherein oure will and pleasure is, that respect be had as well of the proporcion of the adventure as to the speciall service, hazarde, exploite or meritt of anie person so as to be recompenced, advannced or rewarded.

And for as muche as the good and prosperous successe of the said plantacion cannot but cheiflie depende, next under the blessinge of God and the supporte of oure royall auctoritie, upon the provident and good direccion of the whole enterprise by a carefull and understandinge Counsell, and that it is not convenient that all the adventurers shalbe so often drawne to meete and assemble as shalbe requisite for them to have metings and conference aboute theire affaires, therefore we doe ordaine, establishe and confirme that there shalbe perpetually one Counsell here resident, accordinge to the tenor of oure former lettres patents, which Counsell shall have a seale for the better governement and administracion of the said plantacion besides the legall seale of the Companie or Corporacion, as in oure former lettres patents is also expressed.

And further wee establishe and ordaine that

Henrie, Earl of Southampton
William, Earl of Pembrooke
Henrie, Earl of Lincoln
Thomas, Earl of Exeter
Roberte, Lord Viscounte Lisle
Lord Theophilus Howard
James, Lord Bishopp of Bathe and Wells
Edward, Lord Zouche
Thomas, Lord Laware
William, Lord Mounteagle
Edmunde, Lord Sheffielde
Grey, Lord Shanndoys
John, Lord Stanhope
George, Lord Carew
Sir Humfrey Welde, Lord Mayor of London
Sir Edward Cecil
Sir William Waad
Sir Henrie Nevill
Sir Thomas Smith
Sir Oliver Cromwell
Sir Peter Manwood
Sir Thomas Challoner
Sir Henrie Hovarte
Sir Frauncis Bacon
Sir George Coppin
Sir John Scott
Sir Henrie Carey
Sir Roberte Drurie
Sir Horatio Vere
Sir Eward Conwaye
Sir Maurice Berkeley
Sir Thomas Gates
Sir Michaele Sands
Sir Roberte Mansfeild
Sir John Trevor
Sir Amyas Preston
Sir William Godolphin
Sir Walter Cope
Sir Robert Killigrewe
Sir Henrie Fanshawe
Sir Edwyn Sandes
Sir John Watts
Sir Henrie Montague

Sir William Romney
Sir Thomas Roe
Sir Baptiste Hicks
Sir Richard Williamson
Sir Stephen Powle
Sir Dudley Digges
Christopher Brooke
John Eldred and
John Wolstenholme
shalbe oure Counsell for the said Companie of
Adventurers and Planters in Virginia.

And the said Sir Thomas Smith wee ordaine to be Tresorer of the said Companie, which Tresorer shall have aucthoritie to give order for the waninge of the Counsell and sommoninge the Companie to their courts and meetings.

And the said Counsell and Tresorer or anie of them shalbe from henceforth nominated, chosen, contynued, displaced, chaunged, altered and supplied, as death or other severall occasions shall require, out of the Companie of the said adventurers by the voice of the greater parte of the said Counsell and adventurers in their assemblie for that purpose; provided alwaies that everie Councellor so newlie elected shalbe presented to the Lord Chauncellor of England, or to the Lord Highe Treasurer of England, or the Lord Chambleyne of the housholde of us, oure heires and successors, for the tyme beinge to take his oathe of a Counsellor to us, oure heires and successors, for the said Companie and Collonie in Virginia.

And wee doe by theis presents, of oure especiall grace, certaine knowledge and meere motion, for us, oure heires and successors, grannte unto the said Tresorer and Companie and their successors, that if it happen at anie time or times the Tresorer for the tyme beinge to be sick, or to have anie such cause of absente from the cittie of London as shalbe allowed by the said Counsell or the greater parte of them assembled to be the deputie Tresorer for the said Companie; which Deputie shall it shall and maie be lawfull for such Tresorer for the tyme beinge to assigne, constitute and appointe one of the Counsell for Companie to be likewise allowed by the Counsell or the greater parte of them assembled to be the deputie Tresorer for the said Companie; which Deputie shall have power to doe and execute all things which belonge to the said Tresorer duringe such tyme as such Tresorer shalbe sick or otherwise absent, upon cause allowed of by the said Counsell or the major parte of them as aforesaid, so fullie and wholie and in as large and ample manner and forme and to all intents and purposes as the said Tresorer if he were present himselfe maie or might doe and execute the same.

And further of oure especiall grace, certaine knowledge and meere mocion, for us, oure heires and successors, wee doe by theis presents give and grannt full power and aucthoritie to oure said Counsell here resident aswell at this present tyme as hereafter, from time to time, to nominate, make, constitute, ordaine and confirme by such name or names, stile or stiles as to them shall seeme good, and likewise to revoke, dischardge, channge and alter aswell all and singuler governors, oficers and ministers which alreadie hath ben made, as also which hereafter shalbe by them thought fitt and meedefull to be made or used for the government of the said Colonie and plantacion.

And also to make, ordaine and establishe all manner of orders, lawes, directions, instructions, formes and ceremonies of government and magistracie, fitt and necessarie, for and concerninge the government of the said Colonie and plantacion; and the same att all tymes hereafter to abrogate, revoke or chaunge, not onely within the precincts of the said Colonie but also upon the seas in goeing and cominge to and from the said Collonie, as they in their good discrecions shall thinke to be fittest for [the] good of the adventurers and inhabiters there.

And we doe also declare that for divers reasons and consideracions us thereunto especiallie moving, oure will and pleasure is and wee doe hereby ordaine that imediatlie from and after such time as anie such governour or principall officer so to be nominated and appointed by oure said Counsell for the governement of the said Colonie, as aforesaid, shall arive in Virginia and give notice unto the Collonie there resident of oure pleasure in this behalfe, the government, power and aucthority of the President and Counsell, heretofore by oure former lettres patents there established, and all lawes and constitucions by them formerlie made, shall utterly cease and determined; and all officers, governours and ministers formerly constituted or appointed shalbe dischardged, anie things in oure said former lettres patents conserninge the said plantacion contayned in aniewise to the contrarie notwithstandinge; streightlie chardginge and commaundinge the President and Counsell nowe resident in the said Collonie upon their alleadgiance after knowledge given unto them of oure will and pleasure by theis presentes signified and declared, that they forth with be obedient to such governor or governers as by oure said Counsell here resident shalbe named and appointed as aforesaid; and to all direccions, orders and commandements which they shall receive from them, aswell in the present resigninge and giveinge upp of their aucthoritie, offices, chardg and places, as in all other attendannce as shalbe by them from time to time required.

And wee doe further by theis presentes ordaine and establishe that the said Tresorer and Counsell here resident, and their successors or anie fower of them assembled (the Tresorer beinge one), shall from time to time have full power and aucthoritie to admitt and receive anie other person into their companie, corporacion and freedome; and further, in a generall assemblie of the adventurers, with the consent of the greater parte upon good cause, to disfranchise and putt oute anie person or persons oute of the said fredome and Companie.

And wee doe also graunt and confirme for us, oure heires and successors that it shalbe lawfull for the said Tresorer and Companie and their successors, by direccion of the Governors there, to digg and to serche for all manner of mynes of goulde, silver, copper, iron, leade, tinne and other mineralls aswell within the precincts aforesaid as within anie parte of the maine lande not formerly graunted to anie other; and to have and enjoye the gould, silver, copper, iron, leade, and tinn, and all other mineralls to be gotten thereby, to the use and behoofe of the said Companie of Planters and Adventurers, yeldinge therefore and payinge yerelie unto us, oure heires and successors, as aforesaid.

And wee doe further of oure speciall grace, certaine knowledge and meere motion, for us, oure heires and successors, grannt, by theis presents to and withe the said Tresorer and Companie and their successors, that it shalbe lawfull and free for them and their assignes at all and everie time and times here after, oute of oure realme of England and oute of all other [our] dominions, to take and leade into the said voyage, and for and towards the said plantacion, and to travell thitherwards and to abide and inhabite therein the said Colonie and plantacion, all such and so manie of oure lovinge subjects, or anie other straungers that wilbecomme oure lovinge subjects and live under oure allegiance, as shall willinglie accompanie them in the said voyadge and plantation with sufficient shippinge, armour, weapons, ordinannce, municion, powder, shott, victualls, and such merchaundize or wares as are esteemed by the wilde people in those parts, clothinge, implements, furnitures, catle, horses and mares, and all other thinges necessarie for the said plantation and for their use and defence and trade with the people there, and in passinge and retourninge to and from without yeldinge or payinge subsedie, custome, imposicion, or anie other taxe or duties to us, oure heires or successors, for the space of seaven yeares from the date of theis presents; provided, that none of the said persons be such as shalbe hereafter by speciall name restrained by us, oure heires or successors.

And for their further encouragement, of oure speciall grace and favour, wee doe by theis present for us, oure heires and successors, yeild and graunte to and with the said Tresorer and Companie and their successors and everie of them, their factors and assignes, that they and every of them shalbe free and quiett of all subsedies and customes in Virginia for the space of one and twentie yeres, and from all taxes and imposicions for ever, upon anie goods or merchaundizes at anie time or times hereafter, either upon importation thither or exportation from thence into oure realme of England or into anie other of oure [realms or] dominions, by the said Tresorer and Companie and their successors, their deputies, factors [or] assignes or anie of them, except onlie the five pound per centum due for custome upon all such good and merchanndizes as shalbe brought or imported into oure realme of England or anie other of theis oure dominions according to the auncient trade of merchannts, which five poundes per centum onely beinge paid, it shalbe thensforth lawfull and free for the said Adventurers the same goods [and] merchaundizes to export and carrie oute of oure said dominions into forraine partes without anie custome, taxe or other duty to be paide to us, oure heires or successors or to anie other oure officers or deputies; provided, that the saide goods and merchaundizes be shipped out within thirteene monethes after their first landinge within anie parte of those dominions.

And wee doe also confirme and grannt to the said Tresorer and Companie, and their successors, as also to all and everie such governer or other officers and ministers as by oure said Counsell shalbe appointed, to have power and aucthoritie of governement and commannd in or over the said Colonie or plantacion; that they and everie of them shall and lawfullie maie from tyme to tyme and at all tymes forever hereafter, for their severall defence and safetie, enconnter, expulse, repell and resist by force and armes, aswell by sea as by land, and all waies and meanes whatsoever, all and everie such person and persons whatsoever as without the speciall licens of the said Tresorer and Companie and their successors shall attempte to inhabite within the said severall precincts and lymitts of the said Colonie and plantacion; and also, all and everie such person and persons whatsoever as shall enterprise, or attempte at anie time hereafter, destruccion, invasion, hurte, detriment or annoyannce to the said Collonye and plantacion, as is likewise specified in the said former graunte.

And that it shalbe lawful for the said Tresorer and Companie, and their successors and everie of them, from time to time and at all times hereafter, and they shall have full power and aucthoritie, to take and surprise by all waies and meanes whatsoever all and everie person and persons whatsoever, with their shippes, goods and other furniture, traffiquinge in anie harbor, creeke or place within the limitts or precincts of the said Colonie and plantacion, beinge allowed by the said Companie to be adventurers or planters of the said Colonie, until such time as they beinge of anie realmes or dominions under oure obedience shall paie or agree to paie, to the hands of the Tresorer or [of] some other officer deputed by the said governors in Virginia (over and above such subsedie and custome as the said Companie is or here after shalbe to paie) five poundes per centum upon all goods and merchaundizes soe brought in thither, and also five per centum upon all goods by them shipped oute from thence; and being straungers and not under oure obedience untill they have payed (over and above such subsedie and custome as the same Tresorer and Companie and their successors is or hereafter shalbe to paie) tenn pounds per centum upon all such goods, likewise carried in and oute, any thinge in the former lettres patents to the contrarie not withstandinge; and the same sommes of monie and benefitt as aforesaid for and duringe the space of one and twentie yeares shalbe wholie imploied to the benefitt and behoof of the said Colonie and plantacion; and after the saide one and twentie yeares ended, the same shalbe taken to the use of us, oure heires or successors, by such officer and minister as by us, oure heires or successors, shalbe thereunto assigned and appointed, as is specified in the said former lettres patents.

Also wee doe, for us, oure heires and successors, declare by theis presents, that all and everie the persons beinge oure subjects which shall goe and inhabit within the said Colonye and plantacion, and everie of their children and posteritie which shall happen to be borne within [any] the lymitts thereof, shall have [and] enjoye all liberties, franchesies and immunities of free denizens and naturall subjects within anie of oure other dominions to all intents and purposes as if they had bine abidinge and borne within this oure kingdome of England or in anie other of oure dominions.

And forasmuch as it shalbe necessarie for all such our lovinge subjects as shall inhabitt within the said precincts of Virginia aforesaid to determine to live togither in the feare and true woorshipp of Almightie God, Christian peace and civill quietnes, each with other, whereby everie one maie with more safety, pleasure and profitt enjoye that where unto they shall attaine with great paine and perill, wee, for us, oure heires and successors, are likewise pleased and contented and by theis presents doe give and graunte unto the said Tresorer and Companie and their successors and to such governors, officers and ministers as shalbe, by oure said Councell, constituted and appointed, according to the natures and lymitts of their offices and places respectively, that they shall and maie from time to time for ever hereafter, within the said precincts of Virginia or in the waie by the seas thither and from thence, have full and absolute power and aucthority to correct, punishe, pardon, governe and rule all such the subjects of us, oure heires and successors as shall from time to time adventure themselves in anie voiadge thither or that shall at anie tyme hereafter inhabitt in the precincts and territorie of the said Colonie as aforesaid, according to such order, ordinaunces, constitution, directions and instruccions as by oure said Counsell, as aforesaid, shalbe established; and in defect thereof, in case of necessitie according to the good discretions of the said governours and officers respectively, aswell in cases capitall and criminall as civill, both marine and other, so alwaies as the said status, ordinaunces and proceedinges as neere as convenientlie maie be, be agreable to the lawes, statutes, government and pollicie of this oure realme of England.

And we doe further of oure speciall grace, certeine knowledge and mere mocion, grant, declare and ordaine that such principall governour as from time to time shall dulie and lawfullie be aucthorised and appointed, in manner and forme in theis presents heretofore expressed, shall [have] full power and aucthoritie to use and exercise marshall lawe in cases of rebellion or mutiny in as large and ample manner as oure lieutenant in oure counties within oure realme of England have or ought to have by force of their comissions of lieutenancy.

And furthermore, if anie person or persons, adventurers or planters, of the said Colonie, or anie other at anie time or times hereafter, shall transporte anie monyes, goods or marchaundizes oute of anie [of] oure kingdomes with a pretence or purpose to lande, sell or otherwise dispose the same within the lymitts and bounds of the said Collonie, and yet nevertheles beinge at sea or after he hath landed within anie part of the said Colonie shall carrie the same into anie other forraine Countrie, with a purpose there to sell and dispose there of that, then all the goods and chattels of the said person or persons so offendinge and transported, together with the shipp or vessell wherein such transportacion was made, shalbe forfeited to us, oure heires and successors.

And further, oure will and pleasure is, that in all questions and doubts that shall arrise upon anie difficultie of construccion or interpretacion of anie thinge contained either in this or in oure said former lettres patents, the same shalbe taken and interpreted in most ample and beneficiall manner for the said Tresorer and Companie and their successors and everie member there of.

And further, wee doe by theis presents ratifie and confirme unto the said Tresorer and Companie and their successors all privuleges, franchesies, liberties and immunties graunted in oure said former lettres patents and not in theis oure lettres patents revoked, altered, chaunged or abridged.

And finallie, oure will and pleasure is and wee doe further hereby for us, oure heires and successors graunte and agree, to and with the said Tresorer and Companie and their successors, that all and singuler person and persons which shall at anie time or times hereafter adventure anie somme or sommes of money in and towards the said plantacion of the said Colonie in Virginia and shalbe admitted by the said Counsell and Companie as adventurers of the said Colonie, in forme aforesaid, and shalbe enrolled in the booke or record of the adventurers of the said Companye, shall and maie be accompted, accepted, taken, helde and reputed Adventurers of the said Collonie and shall and maie enjoye all and singuler graunts, priviledges, liberties, benefitts, profitts, commodities [and immunities], advantages and emoluments whatsoever as fullie, largely, amplie and absolutely as if they and everie of them had ben precisely, plainely, singulerly and distinctly named and inserted in theis oure lettres patents.

And lastly, because the principall effect which wee cann desier or expect of this action is the conversion and reduccion of the people in those partes unto the true worshipp of God and Christian religion, in which respect wee would be lothe that anie person should be permitted to passe that wee suspected to affect the superstitions of the Churche of Rome, wee doe hereby declare that it is oure will and pleasure that none be permitted to passe in anie voiadge from time to time to be made into the saide countrie but such as firste shall have taken the oath of supremacie, for which purpose wee doe by theise presents give full power and aucthoritie to the Tresorer for the time beinge, and anie three of the Counsell, to tender and exhibite the said oath to all such persons as shall at anie time be sent and imploied in the said voiadge.

Although expresse mention of the true yearly value or certainty of the premises, or any of them, or of any other gifts or grants, by us or any of our progenitors or predecessors, to the aforesaid Treasurer and Company heretofore made, in these presents is not made; or any act, statute, ordinance, provision, proclamation, or restraint, to the contrary hereof had, made, ordained, or provided, or any other thing, cause, or matter, whatsoever, in any wise notwithstanding. In witnes whereof we have caused these our letters to be made patent. Witness ourself at Westminster, the 23d day of May in the seventh year of our reign of England, France, and Ireland, and of Scotland the forty second.

802. [May, 1609]. Instructions for Sir Thomas Gates for the government of Virginia.

Under the authority of the second charter, Sir Thomas Gates was constituted the first governor of Virginia by the Council of the Virginia Company. His council in the colony was named (though it was to be advisory only), and he was given extensive powers for the government of the colony. Much of the instructions is taken up with matters of detail that arise out of the previous history of the colony over the past two years and cannot be fully understood without reference to correspondence with the officials there, not all of which has survived. These instructions did not become operative because Gates was shipwrecked and remained in Bermuda until his arrival in Virginia in May, 1610. He promulgated the public parts of his instructions on May 24, 1610. They were largely superseded by instructions given to Lord De La Warr, who replaced him as governor, when De La Warr was leaving England in June, 1610. De La Warr promulgated the public parts of his instructions and confirmed the relevant parts of Gates's on June 10, 1610.

The original commission has not survived. A draft in the Bodleian Library (how far representative of the final version is not known), Ashmole MS 1147, fols. 175–190, was first printed in contracted form in Records of the Virginia Company of London, *edited by S. M. Kingsbury, 4 vols. (Washington, D.C., 1906–1935), III, 12–24, and, with expansions, in S. T. Bemiss,* Three Charters, *pp. 55–69.*

Instruccions, orders and constitucions by way of advise sett downe, declared and propounded to Sir Thomas Gates, Knight, Governor of Virginia and of the Colony there planted and to be planted and of all the inhabitants thereof, by us His Majesties Counsell for the direction of the affaires of that countrey for his better disposinge and proceedinge in the government thereof accord-

inge to the authority and power given unto us by virtue of His Majesties lettres patents.

1. Havinge considered the greate sufficiency and zealous affeccion which you, Sir Thomas Gates, have many waies manifested unto us, and havinge therefore by our Commission under our hands and seales constituted and ordained you to be the Governor of Virginia, wee His Majesties Counsell for that plantacion, have consulted and advised uppon divers instruccions for your safer and more deliberate proceedinge therein; and therefore doe requier and charge you, accordinge to the Comission in that behalf directed unto you, presently with all convenient speede to take the charge and of our fleete consistinge of eight good shippes and one pinnace and of six hundred land men to be transported under your commaund, and with the first winde to sett saile for Virginia. And in your passage thither you shall not land nor touch any of the Kinge of Spaines his Dominions quetly possessed, without the leave or licence of the governor of such place as you shal by accident or contrary windes be forced into. You shall also hold counsell with the masters and pilots and men of the best experience what way is safest and fittest for you to take, because we hold it daungerous that you should keepe the old course of Dominico and Meuis [= Nevis] lest you fall into the hand of the Spaniard, who may attend in that roade ready to intercept you:

2. When it shall please God that you have safely attained the Kings River, and our porte and seate of James Towne in Virginia, wee advise you to call by proclamacion into some publique place, all the governors, officers, and other His Majesties subjects aswell already seated there as transported with you, to whom you shall cause your Commission to be directly reade, whereby significacion may be had of His Majesties pleasure in establishinge you the Governor of that countrey and plantacion, and the President, Councell and Colony there may take notice of the revocacion of that fourme of governement by the first lettres patents constituted and confirmed, and accordingly yeald due obedience unto you, their Governor.

3. You shall demaund then and resume into your hands the former lettres pattents and all instruccions & publique instruments given or sent unto them and all bookes and records whatsoever of the generall proceedings untill this time, and

dispose of them in the future according to your discrecion.

4. Beinge setled in your government, you shall call unto you, for your further advise and graver proceedinge, their principall officers and gentlemen whom we do ordaine and appointe to be of the Councell and who for earliness of their undertakings and their greate paines and merits doe well deserve this honor & respect from us: Sir George Summers, Knight, and Admirall of Virginia; Captaine John Smith, nowe President; Captaine John Radclif; Captaine Peter Winne, Seirjant Major of the fort; Master Mathewe Scrivenor, whom out of our good experience of his abilities in that kinde we doe name and appointe to be Secretary of that Councell; Captaine John Martine; Captaine Richard Waldoe, master of the workes; Captaine Woode; and Master Fleetwoode, whom we assure ourselves you will use with all good respecte in their places and to whome wee expecte that you shall give such other preferrements as their former paines have deserved, and in all matters of importance we require you to call them to consultacion and to proceede therein with their advice; and wee doe give further power and authority to you, to give the oathe of Counsellor to such as are now named, or any other oathe in the like case, according to your direccion. Provided that they shall not have, single nor together, anie bindinge or negative voice or power uppon your conclusions but doe give you full authority, uppon just occasion to sequester any of them from the execucion of any place whatsoever, and to depute another thereunto untill significacion unto us be here made:

5. You shall have power and authority to dispose and graunte any other officer or commaunds whatsoever, either of governement or warr, except such as are already disposed of by us to any persons of rancke or merite (adventurers beings first regarded), according to your discrecion and so discharge or revoke the same or to sequester any so made or constituted by us.

6. You shall take principall order and care for the true and reverent worship of God that his worde be duely preached and his holy sacraments administred according to the constitucions of the Church of England in all fundamentall pointes, and his ministers had in due observance and respecte agreeable to the dignity of their callinge. And that all atheisme, prophanes, popery, or schisme be

exemplarily punished to the horror of God and to the peace and safety of his Church, over which, in this tendernes and infancy, you must be especially solicitous & watchefull.

7. You shall, with all propensenes and diligence, endeavour the conversion of the natives to the knowledge and worship of the true God and their redeemer Christ Jesus, as the most pious and noble end of this plantacion, which the better to effect you must procure from them some convenient nomber of their children to be brought up in your language and manners, and if you finde it convenient, we thinke it reasonable you first remove from them their Iniocasockes or Priestes by a surprise of them all and detaininge them prisoners, for they are so wrapped up in the fogge and miserie of their iniquity and so tirrified with their continuall tirrany, chained under the bond of deathe unto the divell that while they live amounge them to poison and infecte them their mindes, you shall never make any great progres into this glorious worke, nor have any civill peace or concurre with them. And in case of necessity or conveniency, we pronounce it not crueltie nor breache of charity to deale more sharply with them and to proceede even to dache [=death] with these murtherers of soules and sacrificers of God's images to the divill, referringe the consideracion of this as a waighty matter of important consequence to the circumstances of the busines and place in your discrecion.

8. You shall for capitall and criminal justice in case of rebellion and mutiny and in all such cases of [proved?] necessity, proceede by martiall lawe according to your comission as of most dispatch and terror and fittest for this governement; and in all other causes of that nature as also in all matters of civill justice, you shall finde it properest and usefullest for your governement to proceede rather as a chauncelor than as a judge, rather uppon the naturall right and equity then uppon the nicenes and lettre of the lawe which perplexeth in this tender body, rather then dispatcheth all causes so that a summary and arbitrary way of justice discreetely mingled with those gravities and fourmes of magistracy as shall in your discrecion seeme aptest for you and that place, wilbe of most use both for expedicion and for example:

9. You shall for the more regard and respect of your place, to begett reverence to your authority

and to refresh their mindes that obey the gravity of those lawes under which they were borne; at your discrecion use such fourmes and ensignes of governement as by our lettres pattents wee are enabled to grant unto you; as also the attendance of a guarde uppon your person, and in all such like cases you shall have power to make, adde or distinguishe any lawes or ordinances at your discrecion accordinge to the authority limited in your comission.

10. You shall, for the choice of plantacions observe two generall rulles: that you rather seeke to the sun then from it, which is under God the first cause both of health and riches; and that such places which you resolve to build and inhabite uppon have at the leaste one good outlett into the sea & fresh water to the land; that it be a dry and wholesome earth and as free from woode as possiblie you may, whereby you may have roome to discover about you and unshady ground to plant nere you.

11. You must in every plantacion principally provide of your owne a common graunge and storehowse of corne, besides that which you will obtaine by tribute or trade with the natives.

12. In the distribucion of your men accordinge to these advises and relacions which wee have receaved, we advise you to continue the plantacion at James Towne with a convenient number of men, but not as your situacion or citty, because the place is unwholsome and but in the marish of Virginia, and to keepe it onely as a fitt porte for your shippes to ride before to arive and unlade att; butt neither shall you make it your principall storehowse or magazin either of armes, victualls or goods, but because it is so accessable with shipping that an enemy may be easily uppon you with all the provision of ordinance and municion and it is not to be expected that anie fortificacion there can endure an enemy that hath the leasure to sitt downe before it.

13. The place you chose for your principall residence and seate to have your catle, provisions of corne, foode, and magazin of other municion in, as your greatest strength, trust and retraite, must be removed some good distance from any navigable river, except with small boates, by which no enemy shall dare to seeke your habitacion; and if in this place some good fortificacion be made to which no ordinance can be brought by water, if you be provided of victuall, you may dispute possession till a straunger be wearied and starved.

14. Above the over falles of the Kinges River it is likely you shall finde some convenient place to this purpose whither no enemy with ease can approache nor with ordinance at all but by land, with at howe great disadvauntage he shall seeke when he must discover and fight at once uppon straightes, in woodes, at foordes, and places of all inconveniency, is easy to be considered; besides, you shall have the commodity of the braunche of the river to bringe downe your provisions from within the land in canooes and smalle boates in the River of Chechehounnack, neere unto you and not farre of another navagable outlett into the sea by the River of Pamaouke.

15. Foure dayes journey from your forte southewards is a towne called Ohonahorn seated where the River of Choanocki divideth it self into three braunches and falleth into the Sea of Rawnocke in thirtie five degrees; this place, if you seeke by Indian guides from James forte to Winocke by water, from thence to Manqueocke, some twenty miles from thence to Caththega, as much and from thence to Oconahoen, you shall finde a brave and fruiteful seate every way unaccessable by a straunger enemy, much more abundant in pochon and in the grasse silke called Cour del Cherva and in vines, then any parte of this land knowne unto us. Here we suppose, if you make your principall and cheife seate, you shall doe most safely and richely because you are in the part of the land inclined to the southe, and two of the best rivers will supply you; besides you are neere to riche copper mines of Ritanoc and may passe them by one braunche of this river, and by another, Peccarecamicke, where you shall finde foure of the Englishe alive, left by Sir Walter Rawely, which escaped from the slaughter of Powhaton of Roanocke, upon the first arrivall of our Colonie, and live under the proteccion of a wiroane called Gepanocon, enemy to Powhaton by whose consent you shall never recover them; one of these were worth much labour, and if you finde them not, yet sea[r]ch into this countrey, it is more probable then towards the north.

16. These three habitacions seeme enoughe for the nomber of the people nowe transported, over every one of which you must appointe a discreete commaunder that shall sett your men to severall workes accordinge to their undertakings in the

bookes by which they were receaved; in every one of these there must be builte a church and a storehowse and a parte of land sett out for corne for the publique and some allotted to the care of manuringe and preparinge thereof. In buildinge your towns you shall as easily keepe decorous and order as confusion; and so you shall prepare for ornament and safety at once, for every streete may answere one another and all of them the markett place or storehowse in the midle which at the leaste must be paved and made firme and dry.

17. Your enemies can be but of two sortes, straungers and natives; for the first, your defence must be uppon advauntage of the place and way unto it, for fortes have no other use but that a fewe men may defend and dispute their footinge with them against a greater nomber and to winne time which, if you can do, a stranger cannot longe abide where he must bringe all his releis [relief?] with him, and he shall have no way to beseidge you but by blockinge you in and plantinge betwene you and the sea, to which if you have two outeletts he must be very able and powerfull that can do it; to prevent this you shall build some small forte that may discry the sea neere Cape Comforte, and there hold a reasonable garrison and keepe alwaies watch and longe boate that may be ready to take the alarum and able to cary away our men, and munition if you shall not be able to defend it. Besides it is not safe to lett any of the savages dwell betwene you and the sea least they be made guides to your enemies. To this commaunde wee desire Captaine Smith may be allotted aswell for his earnest desire as the greate confidence & trust that we have in his care & diligence.

18. The second enemy is the natives who can no way hurte you but by fire or by destroyinge your catle, or hinderinge your workes by stealth or your passages in small nombers; and in this sorte of warr there is most perill-if you be not very carefull, for if they may destroy but one harvest or burne your townes in the night they will leave you naked and exposed to famine and cold, and convey themselves into wodes where revenge wilbe as difficult as unnecessary; to prevent that you must keepe good watches in the fielde and suffer none of them to come nere your corne in those daungerous seasons; and continuall centinells without the walles or uttermost defences in the night; and you must give order that your catle

be kept in heards waited and attended on by some small watch or so enclosed by them selves that they destroy not your corne and other seed provisions.

19. For Powhaton and his Weroances it is clere even to reason beside our experience that he loved not our neighbourhood and therefore you may no way trust him, but if you finde it not best to make him your prisoner yet you must make him your tributary, and all other his weroances about him first to acknowledge no other lord but Kinge James, and so we shall free them all from the tirrany of Powhaton . . . upon them. Every lord of a province shall pay you and send you into your forte where you make your cheif residence so many measures of corne at every harvest, soe many basketts of dye, so many dozens of skins, so many of his people to worke weekely, and of every thinge somewhat, accordinge to his proporcion in greatenes of territory and men; by which meanes you shall quietly drawe to your selves an annuall revenue of every commodity growinge in that countrey and this tribute payd to you, for which you shall deliver them from the exeacions of Powhaton which are now burdensome, and protect and defend them from all their enemies; shall also be a meanes of clearinge much ground of wood and of reducing them to laboure and trade seinge for this rent onely they shall enjoye their howses, and the rest of their travell quietly and many other commodities and blessings of which they are yet insensible.

20. If you hope to winne them and to provide for your selves by trade you wilbe deceaved, for already your copper is embased by your abundance and neglect of prisinge it and they will never feede you but for feare. Wherefore, if you perceave that they, uppon your landinge, fly up into the countrey and forsake their habitacion, you must seise into your custody half there corne and harvest and their Weroances and all other their knowne successors at once whom, if you intreat well and educate those which are younge and to succeede in the governement in your manners and religion, their people will easily obey you and become in time civill and Christian.

21. If you make friendship with any of these nations, as you must doe, choose to doe it with those that are farthest from you and enemies unto those amonge whom you dwell, for you shall have least occasion to have differences with them and

by that meanes a suerer league of amity, and you shalbe suer of their trade partely for covetousnes and to serve their owne ends, where the copper is yett in his primary estimacion which Powhaton hath hitherto engrossed and partely for feare of constrainte. Monocon, to the east and head of our river, Powhatons enemy; and the Manahockes, to the northeast to the head of the River of Moyompo in the necke of the land to the west betweene our bay and the sea; Cathcatapeius, a greater Weroance then he is, also his enemy to the Southeast and South—he hath no freinde to the north; the Massawoymekes make continuall incursions uppon him and uppon all those that inhabite the Rivers of Bolus and Myomps and to the northwest; Pocoughtuwonough infecteth him with a terrible warr. With those you may hold trade and freindeship good cheape for their [r]emotenes will prevent all offence which must needes happen betweene us and them which we are mingled with to the North. At the head bay is a large towne where is store of copper and furres called Cataaneon that trade and discovery wilbe to great purpose, if it may be setled yearely.

22. Such trade as you shall finde necessary or profitable for you with the Indians you shall endeavour to drawe them to seeke of you and to bringe their commodities into your forte, which will greatly ease the imployment of many men, and this you may bringe to passe by seeminge to make litle estimacion of trade with them and by pretendinge to be so able to consist within your selves as that you neede care for nothinge of theires, but rather that you doe them a curtesy to spare such necessaries as they want as leetle iron tooles, or copper, or the like such as are convenient for traffique; and so one officer or two in every forte, whom you must onely appointe to be truncmasters, may dispatch the whole busines of trade which els will cost you many mens laboures if you seeke it far from home. And besides these you must, by proclamacion or edicte publiquely affixed, prohibite and forbidd uppon paine or punishement of your discrecion all other persons to trade or exchange for anything but such as shalbe necessarie for foode or clothinge; and uppon all such commodities of yours as shall passe away from you whatsoever, you must sett prises and values under which the trunckemaster must not trade, and so you shalbe such to uphold the reputacion of your commodity and to make your traffique rich, desired and certaine; over this

truncemaster there must be appointed a cape merchant or officer belonginge to the store or provision house that must deliver by booke all such things as shalbe allowed for trade and receave and take an accounte of whatsoever is retourned, accordinge to the prises therein sett, and so beinge booked must store them up, to the publique use of the colony.

23. You must constitute and declare some sharpe lawe with a penaltie thereon to restraine the trade of any prohibited goods, especially of swordes, pikeheads, gunnes, daggers, or any thinge of iron that may be turned against you, and in case of such offence punishe severely; have also especially regard that no arte or trade tendinge to armes in any wise, as smithey, carpentry, of or such like, be taught the savages or used in their presence, as they may learne therein.

24. Havinge deduced your colony into severall seates and plantacions that may commodiously answere and receive one another, you must devide your people into tennes, twenties, & so upwards, to every necessary worke a competent nomber, over every one of which you must appointe some man of care and [skill] in that worke to oversee them and to take daily accounte of their laboures; and you must ordaine that every overseer of such a nomber of workemen deliver once a weeke an accounte of the wholle committed to his charge [to] the cheife governor or captaine of the fourte; and that they also once a moneth make the like accounte to you or your officer and that such goodes or provisions as are advanced or gotten above expence may be receaved and entred into the capemarchantes booke and so stored and preserved to the publique use of the colony. And thus you shall both knowe howe your men are imployed, what they gett & where it is, as also the measure of your provision and wealth.

25. For such of your men as shall attend any worke in or nere aboute every towne, you shall doe best to lett them eate together at seasonable howers in some publique place, beinge messed by sixe or five to a messe, in which you must see there bee equality and sufficient that so they may come and retourne to their worke without any delay and have no cause to complaine of measure or to excuse their idlenes upon the dressinge or want of diett. You may well allowe them three howers in a somers day and two in the winter, and shall call them together by ringinge of a bell and by the same worne them againe to worke; for such

as attend any labouer so farre from the forte, as they cannot returne at seasonable times, there must be a steward appointed that shall oversee there diett and provision, els thoughe you give every one a reasonalbe allowance for many dayes some will eate two meales at one & soe:

26. You shall give especiall order to the cheif commaunder of every forte that the armes, powder and munition be well stored and looked into and that the men be disposed into severall companies for warr and captaines appointed over every fifty to traine them at convenient times and to teache them the use of their armes and weapons and they may knowe whether uppon all occasions and sudden attempts they shall repaire to find them in a readines.

27. You must take especiall care what relacions come into England and what lettres are written and that all thinges of that nature may be boxed up and sealed and sent to first to the Councell here, according to a former instruccion unto the late president in that behalf directed; and that at the arivall and retourne of every shipping you endeavour to knowe all the particuler passages and informacions given on both sides and to advertise us accordingly.

28. Whensoever you consult of any busines of importance, wee advise you to consider and deliberate all thinges patiently & willingly and to heare every man his oppinion and objeccion, but the resultants out of them or your owne determinacion what you intend to doe not to imparte to any whatsoever, but to such onely as shall execute it, and to them also under the sealle of your commaundement and but at the instant of their partinge from you or the execucion of your will.

29. Next after buildinge, husbandry and manuringe the countrey for the provision of life and conveniency, wee comend unto your care foure principall waies of enrichinge the colonies and providinge returne of commodity, of which you must be very solicitouse that our fleetes come not home empty nor laden with useles marchandize. The first is discovery either of the southe seas or royall mines, in the search of both which we must referre you to the circumstances of your peace and your owne discrecion; the second is trade whereby you recover all the commodities of those countreys that ly far of and yet are accessable by water; the third is tribute, by which you shall advaunce parte of what soever the next lande can provide you can produce; the fourth is labour of

your owne men in makinge wines, pitche, tarre, sope, ashes, steele, iron, pipestaves, in sowinge of hempe and flaxe, in gatheringe silke of the grasse, and providinge the worme and in fishinge for pearle, codd, sturgion, and such like.

30. Wee require you to call before you Captaine John Radcliffe and one . . . Webbe who hath complained by peticion delivered unto you of divers injuries and insolences done unto him in the governement of the said Captaine Radcliffe, and accordingly to heare the cause and doe justice in it as you shall finde reason in it your owne discrecion.

31. Whereas suite hath bine made unto us as for the retourne of Richard Potts, David Wiffin and Post Ginnet, and sufficient reasons declared to move us to graunte the same which hath bine agreed unto by the Councell assembled, wee require you to give them their licence to come backe by the next shipping with such condicions or limitacions of retorne or otherwise as you shall thinke good.

32. Whereas peticion hath bine made by the friends of John Tavernor, capemarchant of the forte and store in Virginia, for his retorne uppon some urgent occasion and for some time into England, we require you to licence him so to do if it be his desire when you arive there; and we doe nominate and appointe Thomas Wittingham into his roome and office, beinge one in whose sufficiency and honesty we have greate confidence.

33. There beinge one George Liste, servant to John Woodall and sent over by him with a chest of che[r]urgery sufficiently furnished, we require you to give your licence to William Wilson, his fellowe, if the said George Liste doe stay with you, to come backe in this passage, the better to enfourme us what medicines and drugges are fittest to be provided for the use of the colonie against the next supply.

34. You shall be very wary of grantinge freedomes and of givinge your sealle to any but uppon good consideracion and greate merite, least you make cheape the best way of our recompence; and in those you doe you shall give with such limitacions of retorne in reasonable time as in your discrecion shall seeme good.

35. If it shall please God that you should dy either in your way or in your government (which his mercy forbid) before other order be taken by us therein, wee requier and commaund that the Councell there established open a blacke boxe,

marked with the figure of one and sealed with our sealle, wherein they shall finde our determinacion concerninge the successor to the governement; and do, in His Majesties name, charge and commaund every person within the precincte of the Colony to give and yeild due obedience to him so named and appointed accordinge unto his commission unto him, directed as they will aunswere to the contrary at their uttermost perill.

36. Wee also requier you, the present Governor & all your successors, to keepe secret to your selves, unsealed and unbroken up, all such lettres, schedules and instruments and whatsoever wee shall deliver you soe under our sealle, especially two blacke boxes with divers markes wherein are our commissions in cases of death or other vacacion of the Governor untill such time as you shall find your self unlikely to live or determined to returne, uppon which occasions wee requier you that they be delivered before all the Councell to be opened successively after such death or departure out of Virginia of any Governor.

Provided that in all thinges herein contained, except onely the succession, wee doe by these our lettres instruccions binde you to nothinge so strictly but that uppon due consideracion and good reason, and uppon divers circumstances of time and place wherein we cannot here conclude, you may in your discrecion departe and dissent from them and change, alter or establishe, execute and doe all ordinances or acts whatsoever that may best conducte to the glory of God, the honor of our Kinge and nation to the good and perfect establishment of our Colony. Geven under our hands and Councell sealle the [ ] day of May[1], in the seaventh yeare of His Majesties ragne of England, Fraunce & Ireland and Scotland the two and fortithe.

803. 1610. Instructions to Thomas West, Lord De La Warr, governor of Virginia.

The disappearance of Gates and his instructions left the colony in a constitutional limbo during

1. Before May 15.

the summer of 1609 to May, 1610, when Gates at last arrived to take up his governorship. In the meantime Lord De La Warr, constitutd governor of Virginia, was given fresh instructions for the government of the colony, which represented a more limited program of activity, but he was also furnished with a copy of Gates's instructions, certain articles of which he was told he should implement. De La Warr arrived at Jamestown in June, 1610, just in time to prevent Gates from abandoning the settlement. He promulgated the public parts of his instructions and the relevant parts of Gates's on June 10, 1610.

An undated copy survives in the Bodleian Library, Ashmole MS 1147, fols. 191-205. It was first printed by S. H. Kingsbury, Records, III, 24-29, in a contracted form, and in an expanded form in S. T. Bemiss, Three Charters (1957), pp. 70-75.

Instructions, orders and constitucions by way of advise sett downe, declared, propounded and delivered to the Right Honourable Sir Thomas West, Knight, Lord La Warr, Lord Governor and Capten Generall of Virginea and of the Colonies there planted and to be planted and of all other the inhabitants thereof, by us, His Majesties Counsell for the Companie of Adventurers and Planters in Virginea resident in England under the hands of some of us for the direccion of the affares of that countrey for his better disposinge and proceedinge in the government thereof, accordinge to the authoritie and power given unto us by His Majesties lettres patents in that behalf, together with a copie of certaine of the cheifest instruccions which have bene formerlie given to Sir Thomas Gates, Knight, for his direccion, which coppie we have given to his Lordship to peruse and looke into but leave it to his discretion to use and put them in execution or to beare to be advised or directed by them further then in his owne discretion he shall thinke meete.

We, the said Councell, havinge considered the great & zealous affeccion which you, Sir Thomas West, Knight, Lord Lawarr, have many wayes manifested unto us and for the furtherance and advaunceinge of the plantacion of Virginea have therefore by our commission under the handes of some of us, constituted you to be Lord Governor and Captaine Generall of Virginea and for your more safe and deliberate proceedinge in your goverment there, have advised, constituted & agreed uppon divers instructions followinge, vizt:

1. First, we require your Lordship to take into your charge our fleete consistinge of three good shippes with the masters, mariners, sailors and one hundred and fiftie landmen goinge in them to be transported under your commaund with what speed conveniently you maye unto Virginea and with the first winde to sett saile for that place and in your passage thither not to lande or touche uppon anye of the Kinge of Spaine his dominions by him quietly possessed without the licence of the governour of such place first obtained, unles by necessitie of winde and weather you shalbe forced thereunto; in which passage you shall holde councell with the masters, pilates and men of best experience what way is safest and fitt for you to take for your arrivinge in Virginea.

2. Your Lordships beinge landed there, we wishe you should (with what convenientcy you may by proclamacion made) call into some publique place all the governors, officers, and other His Majesties subjects, aswell already seated there as transported with you, to whom you shall manifest your commission and cause it to be publiquely read to them, to the end His Majesties pleasure may be knowne as alsoe our choise in establishinge your Lordship Governor of Virginea and of the plantacion of there: and that the President, Counsell and Colony there may take notice of our revocacion of all former kindes and formes of goverment, constituted or confirmed, and that they accordingely may yeild due obedience unto you, theire Lord Governor and Captaine Generall, at which time we holde it fitt you tender unto every of them the oath of supremacy to be by them taken whereby they shall manifest theire obedience and loyaltie to His Majestie and you thereby the better assured of theire fidelities as alsoe to be the rather encouraged to comitt matter of counsell and charge unto them; att which time alsoe your Lordship shall, in our opinions, doe well to give generall commaundement that all former private or publique quarels, greivances or grudgs be from thenceforth from amongest them utterly abbandoned and forgotten and they willingly embrace peace and love as becommeth Christians without discention or hindrance to the common good or quiet.

3. Moreover, your Lordship shall demaunde and resume into your hands all former commissions and all instructions and publique instruments given or sent unto them and all bookes and records whatsoever of all the proceedings untill this time and dispose of all theire offices and places in the future according to your discretion; except the office of Leiuetennante Governor, which your Lordship is by your commission to bestowe upon Sir Thomas Gates, if he shalbe there to execute the same, and office of Marshall uppon Sir Thomas Dale, at this cominge thither, and the office of Admirall upon Sir George Sumers, if he shalbe there, and the office of Viceadmirall upon Capten Newport, he beinge there to supplye the said place.

4. Your shippes beinge discharged of theire provision, we wishe that they, the seamen and soe manie others as shalbe needfull for that worke, be, with what convenient speed you may, employed to theire fishinge for sturgeons and other fish; which done we desier your Lordship should make up the residue of theire fraight with divers of the best severall patterns of the land, commodities that you can gett there havinge regarde more to the goodnes and qualitie of them then to the quantity; and to retorne the said shippes for England with as quick dispatch as you may for easinge of the Companie of Adventurers of the charge both of wages of the said shippes seamen and victualls which they must be att untill they retorne.

5. After your Lordship is settled in your governement, we thinke it very behofefull that you employ soe many of your people as shalbe needfull in sowing, setting and plantinge of corne and such rootes for foode as you for your better provision, sustentacion and maintennance shall thinke meete to be planted.

6. As touching your landmen, we thinke fitt your Lordship should reduce them all into severall bandes and companies of fifties or more when you thinke good and to committ the charge of them to severall officers and captaines to be exercised and trained up in martiall manner and warlike discipline.

7. Your Lordship is to take principall order and care for the true worship and service of God as by havinge the Gospell preched, frequent prayers and the sacraments often administred as becommeth Christians. And that such your ministers

and preachers as shalbe with you be had in due respect agreable to theire dignitie and callinge and that your Lordship, with the counsell of your said prechers and ministers, doe, as occasion shall be offered, proceede in punishinge of all atheisme, prophanisme, popery and scisme by exemplary punishment to the honor of God and to the peace and safety of his church over which in this tenderness and infancy your Lordship must be especially solicitous and watchfull.

8. It is very expedient that your Lordship with all diligence indeavor the conversion of the natives and savages to the knowledge and worship of the true God and theire redemer Christ Jesus as the most pious and noble end of this plantacion; which the better to effecte you are to procure from them some of theire children to be brought up in our language and manners and, if you finde it convenient, we thinke it necesserie you first remove from them the iniococks or priests by a surprise of them and detaninge them prisoners and in case they shalbe willfull and obstinate then to send over some three or foure of them into England, we may endevor theire conversion here.

9. We holde it requisite that your Lordship in causes of civill justice, proceede rather as a counsellor then as a judge; that is to saie, rather uppon the right and equitie of the thinge in demaunde then uppon the nicenes and letter of the lawe, which perplexeth in this tender body rather then dispatcheth causes. Soe that a summary and arbitrary way of justice, mingled with discreet formes of magistracy as shall in your discretion seeme aptest for your Lordship to exercise in that place, wilbe of most use both for expedicion and example and for criminall causes, you are to deale therein according to your comission and good discretion;

10. That your Lordship doe not permitt any shippe or vessell to trade or traffique within your precincte to carrie from thence any commodities or marchandizes without warrant brought you or sent to your Lordship from the Councell for the Company of Adventurers under the Councell seale.

11. We doe require your Lordship that with what possible speed and conveniency you may, after you are setled, you appointe a convenient number with guides and some discreete commaunder to discover northwest, south and southwest, beyonde the faulls ten or twelve dayes journey, and that assone as may be your Lordship send unto us the narracion of that voyage what rivers, lakes or seas they finde or here of with the circumstanc there unto belonginge.

12. If Sir Thomas Gates be there arrived and Sir George Sommers and Capten Newport, or any of them, that your Lordship doe give unto Sir Thomas Gates the place or office of Leiuetennant Governor to your Lordship duringe the time of your Lordship and his abode there together, and in your Lordships absence he beinge there to be your deputy and cheif generall and commaunder of the whole Colonye and Companie, and to rule and governe according to suche instructions as your Lordship shall limitt and appointe him; and that Sir George Sommers may have the office of Cheif Admirall under your Lordship and that Sir Ferdinando Weyneman may have the office of Master of the ordinance, and that Capten Newport may have the office of Viceadmirall unto your Lordship.

13. Your Lordship must take especiall care what relacions come into England and what lettres are written & that all things of that nature may be boxed up and sealed and sent first to the Counsell here, accordinge to a former instruction unto the late Governor in that behalf directed; and that att the arrival and retorne of every shipping you endeavor to knowe all the particuler passages and informacions given on both sides and to advertise us accordingly.

14. Last of all, for temporall government & particuler proceedinge in your planacion, in respect of the shortnes of time, we commende unto your Lordship the copie of some of the cheifest of the old instruccions before mencioned to have bene formerly delivered to Sir Thomas Gates, to be used or refused as you shall in your wisdome thinke fitt, neither is or meanes to tie your Lordship to the stricte perfourmance of theis newe instructions but as occasion of time, place or necessetie shall requir your Lordship may doe therein as shall seeme best in your owne discretion.

[Signed by the following members of the Council of the Company:] Southampton, Pembroke, Philip Mountgomery, Edward Cecill, Walter Cope, Dudly Diggs, William Rumney, Thomas Smith, Robert Drewrye, Robert Maunsell, Baptist Hicks, Christofer Brooke.

The copie of the old instruccions which were formerly with others delivered to Sir Thomas Gates, Knight, att his goinge to Virginea for his direccion in his goverment there, and noew are by us, His Majesties Councill for the Companie of Adventurers for Virginea, given to the Right Honourable, the Lord La Warr to looke into and advise on and at his discretion to use [or] forbeare to put them in execucion.

Such of the old instructions which were formerly given to Sir Thomas Gates, Knight, and nowe delivered to the Lord La Warre, beginne att the ninth instruccion in the articles in thi booke which by waye of advise were sett down to the said Sir Thomas Gates and soe are written ontill you come to the thirtith instruccion which 30th, 31, 32 & 33 instructions are not given his Lordship but the 34th is given him, but not the 25 nor 36, but the effect of the provisoe followinge is given.

804. June 22, 1611. "Lawes divine, morall and martiall" promulgated for the colony of Virginia by Sir Thomas Dale, marshal and deputy governor of Virginia.

William Strachey served as secretary to Sir Thomas Gates (mainly in Bermuda but latterly in Virginia), to Lord De La Warr, June, 1610 to [March], 1611, and briefly to Sir Thomas Dale. Gradually, on the basis of the instructions of 1609 and 1610 and the existing practices of 1607–1609, a body of law and of public and private observance had grown up. On taking over when De La Warr left early in 1611, Dale developed these into a comprehensive system of regulations, which he promulgated on June 22, 1611. A copy was given to Strachey when he left the colony so that they could be publicized in England. Strachey arrived in England in September, 1611, and evidently found these laws to meet the approval of the Council of the Company, since they were printed under his editorship. The preface was a complimentary sonnet to the Council of the Company in which he outlined their background. For the colony in Virginea Britannia. Lawes divine, morall, and martiall, etc. (London, Walter Burre, 1612) was a lengthy pamphlet, calculated to make any person who read it wary of setting foot in

Virginia as a soldier or settler, unless he was determined to behave himself with the utmost probity and obedience (or else hope that such severe laws would not be enforced). It was reprinted in P. Force, Tracts, III, 9–68; and edited by David Flaherty (Richmond, 1969).

The following extracts only are given. (a) the preamble and items 1–22 of the general civil code, and (b) the preamble and items 1–4 for the martial laws, which will give a sufficient indication of their character. They were operative until the arrival of Sir Francis Yeardley as governor in 1618.

[a] Articles, Lawes, and Orders, Divine, Politique, and Martiall for the Colony in Virginea: first established by Sir Thomas Gates Knight, Lieutenant Generall, the 24th of May 1610. exemplified and approved by the Right Honourable Sir Thomas West Knight, Lord Lawair, Lord Governour and Captaine Generall the 12th of June 1610. Againe exemplified and enlarged by Sir Thomas Dale Knight, Marshall, and Deputie Governour, the 22nd of June. 1611.

Whereas his Majestie like himselfe a most zealous Prince hath in his owne Realmes a principall care of true Religion, and reverence to God, and hath alwaies strictly commaunded his Generals and Governours, with all his forces wheresoever, to let their waies be like his ends, for the glorie of God.

And forasmuch as no good service can be performed, or warre well managed, where militarie discipline is not observed, and militarie discipline cannot be kept, where the rules or chiefe parts thereof, be not certainely set downe, and generally knowne, I have (with the advise and counsell of Sir Thomas Gates Knight, Lieutenant Generall) adhered unto the lawes divine, and orders politique, and martiall of his Lordship (the same exemplified) an addition of such others, as I have found either the necessitie of the present State of the Colonie to require, or the infancie, and weaknesse of the body thereof, as yet able to digest, and doe now publish them to all persons in the Colonie, that they may as well take knowledge of the Lawes themselves, as of the penaltie and punishment, which without partialitie shall be inflicted upon the breakers of the same.

1. First since we owe our highest and supreme duty, our greatest, and all our allegeance to him, from whom all power and authoritie is derived, and flowes as from the first, and onely fountaine, and being especiall souldiers emprest in this sacred cause, we must alone expect our successe from him, who is onely the blesser of all good attempts, the King of kings, the commaunder of commaunders, and Lord of Hostes, I do strictly commaund and charge all Captaines and Officers, of what qualitie or nature soever, whether commanders in the field, or in towne, or townes, forts or fortresses, to have a care that the Almightie God bee duly and daily served, and that they call upon their people to heare Sermons, as that also they diligently frequent Morning and Evening praier themselves by their owne exemplar and daily life, and dutie herein, encouraging others thereunto, and that such, who shall often and wilfully absent themselves, be duly punished according to the martiall law in that case provided.

2. That no man speake impiously or maliciously, against the holy and blessed Trinitie, or any of the three persons, that is to say, against God the Father, God the Son, and God the holy Ghost, or against the knowne Articles of the Christian faith, upon paine of death.

3. That no man blaspheme Gods holy name upon paine of death, or use unlawful oathes, taking the name of God in vaine, curse, or banne, upon paine of severe punishment for the first offence so committed, and for the second, to have a bodkin thrust through his tongue, and if he continue the blaspheming of Gods holy name, for the third time so offending, he shall be brought to a martiall court, and there receive censure of death for his offence.

4. No man shall use any traiterous words against his Majesties Person, or royall authority upon paine of death.

5. No man shall speake any word, or do any act, which may tend to the derision, or despight of Gods holy word upon paine of death: Nor shall any man unworthily demeane himselfe unto any Preacher, or Minister of the same, but generally hold them in all reverent regard, and dutiful intreatie, otherwise he the offender shall openly be whipt three times, and ask publike forgivenesse in the assembly of the congregation three several Saboth daies.

6. Everie man and woman duly twice a day upon the first towling of the Bell shall upon the working daies repaire unto the church, to hear divine Service upon pain of losing his or her dayes allowance for the first omission, for the second to be whipt, and for the third to be condemned to the Gallies for six Moneths. Likewise no man or woman shall dare to violate or breake the Sabboth by any gaming, publique, or private abroad, or at home, but duly sanctifie and observe the same, both himselfe and his familie, by preparing themselves at home with private prayer, that they may be the better fitted for the publique, according to the commandements of God, and the orders of our Church, as also every man and woman shall repaire in the morning to the divine service, and Sermons preached upon the Saboth day, and in the afternoon to divine service, and Catechising, upon paine for the first fault to lose their provision, and allowance for the whole weeke following, for the second to lose the said allowance, and also to be whipt, and for the third to suffer death.

7. All Preachers or Ministers within this our Colonie, or Colonies, shall in the Forts, where they are resident, after divine Service, duly preach every Sabbath day in the forenoone, and Catechise in the afternoone, and weekely say the divine service, twice every day, and preach every Wednesday, likewise every Minister where he is resident, within the same Fort, or Fortresse, Townes or Towne, shall chuse unto him, foure of the most religious and better disposed as well to informe of the abuses and neglects of the people in their duties, and service to God, as also to the due reparation, and keeping of the church handsome, and fitted with all reverent observances thereunto belonging: likewise every Minister shall keepe a faithful and true Record, or Church Booke, of all Christnings, Marriages, and deaths of such our people, as shall happen within their Fort, or Fortresses, Townes or Towne at any time, upon the burthen of a neglectfull conscience, and upon paine of losing their Entertainement.

8. He that upon pretended malice, shall murther or take away the life of any man, shall bee punished with death.

9. No man shal commit the horrible, and detestable sins of Sodomie upon pain of death; and he or she that can be lawfully convict of Adultery shall be punished with death. No man shall ravish or force any woman, maid or Indian, or other,

upon pain of death, and know the that he or shee, that shall commit fornication, and evident proofe made thereof, for their first fault shall be whipt, for their second they shall be whipt, and for their third they shall be whipt three times a weeke for one month, and aske publique forgivenesse in the Assembly of the Congregation.

10. No man shall bee found guilty of Sacriledge, which is a Trespasse as well committed in violating and abusing any sacred ministry, duty or office of the Church, irreverently, or prophanely, as by beeing a Church robber, to filch, steale or carry away any thing out of the Church appertaining thereunto, or unto any holy, and consecrated place, to the divine Service of God, which no man should doe upon paine of death: likewise he that shall rob the store of any commodities therein, of what quality soever, whether provisions of victuals, or of Arms, Trucking stuffe, Apparrell, Linnen, or Wollen, Hose or Shooes, Hats or Caps, Instruments or Tooles of Steele, Iron, etc. or shall rob from his fellow souldier, or neighbour, any thing that is his, victuals, apparell, household stuffe, toole, or what necessary else soever, by water or land, out of boate, house, or knapsack, shall bee punished with death.

11. Hee that shall take an oath untruly, or beare false witnesse in any cause, or against any man whatsoever, shall be punished with death.

12. No manner of person whatsoever, shall dare to detract, slaunder, calumniate, or utter unseemely, and unfitting speeches, either against his Majesties Honourable Councell for this Colony, resident in England, or against the Commitees, Assistants unto the said Councell, or against the zealous indeavors, and intentions of the whole body of Adventurers for this pious and Christian Plantation, or against any publique booke, or bookes, which by their mature advise, and grave wisdomes, shall be thought fit, to be set foorth and publisht, for the advancement of the good of this Colony, and the felicity thereof, upon paine for the first time so offending, to bee whipt three severall times, and upon his knees to acknowledge his offence and to aske forgivenesse upon the Saboth day in the assembly of the congregation, and for the second time so offending to be condemned to the Galley for three yeares, and for the third time so offending to be punished with death.

13. No manner of Person whatsoever, con-

trarie to the word of God (which tyes every particular and private man, for conscience sake to obedience, and duty of the Magistrate, and such as shall be placed in authoritie over them), shall detract, slaunder, calumniate, murmur, mutenie, resist, disobey, or neglect the commaundments, either of the Lord Governour, and Captaine Generall, the Lieutenant Generall, the Martiall, the Councell, or any authorised Captaine, Commaunder or publike Officer, upon paine for the first time so offending to be whipt three severall times, and upon his knees to acknowledge his offence, with asking forgivenesse upon the Saboth day in the assembly of the congregation, and for the second time so offending to be condemned to the Gally for three yeares: and for the third time so offending to be punished with death.

14. No man shall give any disgracefull words, or commit any act to the disgrace of any person in this Colonie, or any part thereof, upon paine of being tied head and feete together, upon the guard everie night for the space of one moneth, besides to bee publikely disgraced himselfe, and be made uncapable ever after to possesse any place, or execute any office in this imployment.

15. No man of what condition soever shall barter, trucke, or trade with the Indians, except he be thereunto appointed by lawful authority, upon paine of death.

16. No man shall rifle or dispoile, by force or violence, take away any thing from any Indian comming to trade, or otherwise, upon paine of death.

17. No Cape Marchant, or Provant Master, or Munition Master, or Truck Master, or keeper of any store, shall at any time imbezell, sell, or give away any thing under his Charge to any Favorite, of his, more then unto any other, whome necessity shall require in that case to have extraordinary allowance of Provisions, nor shall they give a false accompt unto the Lord Governour, and Captaine Generall, unto the Lieuetenant Generall, unto the Marshall, or any deputed Governor, at any time having the commaund of the Colony, with intent to defraud the said Colony, upon paine of death.

18. No man shall imbezel or take away the goods of any man that dyeth, or is imployed from the town or Fort where he dwelleth in any other occasioned remote service, for the time, upon pain of whipping three severall times, and res-

titution of the said goods againe, and in danger of incurring the penalty of the tenth Article, if so it may come under the construction of theft. And if any man die and make a will, his goods shall be accordingly disposed; if hee die intestate, his goods shall bee put into the store, and being valued by two sufficient praisers, his next of kinne (according to the common Lawes of England),shall from the Company, Committies, or adventurers, receive due satisfaction in monyes, according as they were praised, by which meanes the Colonie shall be the better furnished; and the goods more carefully preserved, for the right heire, and the right heire receive content for the same in England.

19. There shall be no Capttain, Master, Marriner, saylor, or any else of what quality or condition soever, belonging to any Ship or Ships, at this time remaining, or which shall hereafter arrive within this our River, bargaine, buy, truck, or trade with any one member in this Colony, man, woman, or child, for any toole or instrument of iron, steel or what else, whether appertaining to Smith Carpenter, Joyner, Shipwright, or any manuall occupation, or handicraft man whatsoever, resident within our Colonie, nor shall they buy or bargaine, for any apparell, linnen, or wollen, householdstuffe, bedde, bedding, sheete towels, napkins, brasse, pewter, or such like, eyther for ready money, or provisions, nor shall they exchange their provisions, of what quality soever, whether Butter, Cheese, Bisket, meal, Oatmele, Aquavite, oyle, Bacon, any kind of Spice, or such like, for any such aforesaid instruments, or tooles, Apparell, or householdstuffe, at any time, or so long as they shall here remain, from the date of these presents upon paine of losse of their wages in England, confiscation and forfeiture of such their monies and provisions, and upon peril beside of such corporall punishment as shall be inflicted upon them by verdict and censure of a martiall Court: Nor shall any officer, souldier, or Trades man, or any else of what sort soever, members of this Colony, dare to sell any such Toole, or instruments, necessary and usefull, for the businesse of the Colonie, or trucke, sell, exchange, or give away his apparell, or household stuffe of what sort soever, unto any such Seaman, either for mony, or any such foresaid provisions, upon paine of 3 times severall whipping, for the

one offender, and the other upon perill of incurring censure, whether of disgrace, or addition of such punishment, as shall bee thought fit by a Court martiall.

20. Whereas sometimes heeretofore the covetous and wide affections of some greedy and ill disposed Seamen, Saylers, and Marriners, laying hold upon the advantage of the present necessity, under which the Colony sometimes suffered, have sold unto our people, provisions of Meale, Oatmeale, Bisket, Butter, Cheese etc., at unreasonable rates, and prises unconscionable: for avoiding the like to bee now put in practise, there shall no Captain, Master, Marriner, or Saylor, or what Officer else belonging to any ship, or shippes, now within our river, or heereafter which shall arrive, shall dare to bargaine, exchange, barter, truck, trade, or sell, upon paine of death, unto any one Landman member of this present Colony, any provisions of what kind soever, above the determined valuations, and prises, set downe and proclaimed, and sent therefore unto each of your severall ships, to bee fixed uppon your Maine mast, to the intent that want of due notice, and ignorance in this case, be no excuse, or plea, for any one offender herein.

21. Sithence we are not to bee a little carefull, and our young Cattell, and Breeders may be cherished, that by the preservation, and increase of them, the Colony heere may receive in due time assured and great benefite, and the adventurers at home may be eased of so great a burthen, by sending unto us yeerely supplies of this kinde, which now heere for a while, carefully attended, may turne their supplies unto us into provisions of other qualities, when of these wee shall be able to subsist our selves, and which wee may in short time, be powerful enough to doe, if we wil according to our owne knowledge of what is good for our selves, forbeare to work into our own wants, againe, by over hasty destroying, and devouring the stocks, and authors of so profitable succeeding a Commodity, as increase of Cattel, Kine, Hogges, Goates, Poultrie etc. must of necessity bee granted, in every common mans judgement, to render unto us: Now know thee therefore, these promises carefully considered, that it is our will and pleasure, that every one, of what quality or condition soever hee bee, in this present Colony, to take due notice of this our Edict, whereby

wee do strictly charge and command, that no man shall dare to kill, or destroy any Bull, Cow, Calfe, Mare, Horse, Colt, Goate, Swine, Cocke, Henne, Chicken, Dogge, Turkie, or any tame Cattel, or Poultry, of what condition soever; whether his owne, or appertaining to another man, without leave from the Generall, upon paine of death in the Principall, and in the accessary, burning in the Hand, and losse of his eares, and unto the concealer of the same foure and twenty houres whipping, with addition of further punishment, as shall be thought fitte by the censure, and verdict of a Martiall Court.

22. There shall no man or woman, Launderer or Launderesse, dare to wash any uncleane Linnen, drive bucks, or throw out the water or suds of fowle cloathes, in the open streete, within the Pallizadoes, or within forty foote of the same, nor rench, and make cleane, any kettle, pot, or pan, or such like vessell within twenty foote of the olde well, or new Pumpe: nor shall any one aforesaid, within lesse then a quarter of one mile from the Pallizadoes, dare to doe the necessities of nature, since by these unmanly, slothfull, and loathsome immodesties, the whole Fort may bee choaked, and poisoned with ill aires, and so corrupt (as in all reason cannot but much infect the same) and this shall they take notice of, and avoide, upon paine of whipping and further punishment, as shall be thought meete, by the censure of a martiall Court.

[b]   The Summarie of the Marshall Lawes.

Thee are now further to understand, that all these prohibited, and forefended trespasses and misdemenors, with the injoyned observance of all these thus repeated, Civill and Politique Lawes, provided, and declared against what Crimes soever, whether against the divine Majesty of God, or our soveraigne, and Liege Lord, King James, the detestable crime of Sodomie, Incest, Blasphemie, Treason against the person of the principall Generals, and Commaunders of this Colonie, and their designs, against detracting, murmuring, calumniating, or slaundering of the Right Honourable the Councell resident in England, and the Committies there, the general Councell, and chiefe Commaunders heere, as also against intemperate raylings, and base unmanly speeches, uttered in the disgrace one of another

by the worser sort, by the most impudent, ignorant, and prophane, such as have neither touch of humanitie, nor of conscience amongst ourselves, against Adultery, Fornication, Rape, Murther, Theft, false witnessing in any cause, and other the rest of the Civill, and Politique Lawes and Orders, necessarily appertaining, and properly belonging to the Government of the State and Condition of the present Colony, as it now subsisteth: I say thee are to know, that all these thus joyned, with their due punishments, and perils heere declared, and published, are no lesse subject to the Martiall law, then unto the Civill Magistrate, and where the Alarum, Tumult, and practise of arms, are not exercised, and where these now following Lawes, appertaining only to Martiall discipline, are diligently to be observed, and shall be severely executed.

1. No man shall willingly absent himself, when hee is summoned to take the oath of Supremacy, upon paine of death.

2. Every Souldier comming into this Colonie, shall willingly take his oath to serve the King and the Colonie, and to bee faithfull, and obedient to such Officers, and Commaunders, as shall be appointed over him, during the time of his aboad therein, according to the Tenor of the oath in that case provided, upon paine of being committed to the Gallies.

3. If any Souldier, or what maner of man else soever, of what quality or condition soever he be, shal tacitely compact, with any Sea-man, Captain, Master, or Marriner, to convay himselfe a Board any shippe, with intent to depart from, and abandon the Colony, without a lawful Passe from the Generall, or chiefe commander of the Colonie, at that time, and shall happen to bee prevented, and taken therwith, before the shippe shall depart out of our Bay, that Captaine, Maister or mariner, that shall so receive him, shall lose his wages, and be condemned to the Gallies for three yeeres, and he the sworne servant of the Colony, Souldier, or what else, shall bee put to death with the Armes which he carrieth.

4. When any select, and appointed Forces, for the execution and performance of any intended service, shall bee drawne into the field, and shall dislodge from one place unto another, that Souldier that shall quit, or forsake his Colors, shall be punished with death.

805. March 12, 1612. The third charter of the Virginia Company.

The principal object of the third charter, apart from certain alterations in boundaries, was to modify the oligarchical character of the company by making its council elective and its laws and regulations authorized at the great quarterly meetings of its subscribers under which the body of adventurers (greatly enlarged in number in the charter) could influence the policy of the company while still leaving much power in the hands of its council. The charter also authorized the holding of a lottery to supplement lagging subscriptions and tardy returns from the colony. Until the dissolution of the company in 1624 it governed relations between Crown and company and between company and colony. Through its operation, major changes could be made in the running of company and colony as they were felt to be necessary. In its emancipated form the company created a lasting colony but did not solve either its administrative or economic problems.

The original charter does not survive. Copies were printed by W. Stith, History of Virginia (1747), app. 23–32; W. W. Hening, Statutes (1823), I, 98–110; A. Brown, Genesis, II, 540–553. The entry on P.R.O., Patent Roll, 9 James I, part 14, memb. 28–34, C66/1709 is printed by S. T. Bemiss, Three Charters, pp. 76–94. Names of additional subscribers (659 individuals and 56 corporate bodies) are omitted.

James, by the grace of God King of England, Scotland, France and Ireland, Defender of the Faith; to all to whom [these presents shall come,] greeting. Whereas at the humble suite of divers and sundry our lovinge subjects, aswell adventurers as planters of the First Colonie in Virginia, and for the propagacion of Christian religion and reclayminge of people barbarous to civilitie and humanitie, we have by our lettres patent bearing date at Westminster the three and twentieth daie of May in the seaventh yeare of our raigne of England, Frannce and Ireland, and the twoe and fortieth of Scotland, given and graunted unto them, that they and all suche and soe manie of our loving subjects as shold from time to time for ever after be joyned with them as planters or adven-

turers in the said plantacion, and their successors for ever, shold be one body politique incorporated by the name of The Treasorer and Planters of the Cittie of London for the First Colonie in Virginia;

And whereas allsoe for the greater good and benefitt of the said Companie and for the better furnishing and establishing of the said plantacion we did further graunte and confirme by our said lettres patent unto the said Treasorer and Companie and their successors for ever, all those landes, contries and territories scituate, lyeing and being in that part of America called Virginia, from the point of land called Cape Pointe Comfort all along the seacoste to the northward twoe hundred miles, and from the said point of Cape Comfort all along the seacoste to the sowthward twoe hundred miles, and all the space and circuit of land lying from the sea coste of the precinct aforesaid up or into the land throughout from sea to sea, west and northwest, and allso all the islandes lying within one hundred miles along the coast of both the seas of the precinct aforsaid, with diverse other grannts, liberties, franchises, preheminences, privileges, proffitts, benefitts, and commodities, grannted in and by our said lettres patent to the said Tresorer and Companie, and their successors, for ever:

Now for asmuchas we are given to undestande that in these seas adjoyning to the said coast of Virginia and without the compasse of those twoe hundred miles by us soe grannted unto the said Treasurer and Companie as aforesaid, and yet not farr distant from the said Colony in Virginia, there are or may be divers islandes lying desolate and uninhabited, some of which are already made knowne and discovered by the industry, travell, and expences of the said Company, and others allsoe are supposed to be and remaine as yet unknowen and undiscovered, all and every of which itt maie importe the said Colony both in safety and pollecy of trade to populate and plant, in regard where of, aswell for the preventing of perill as for the better comodity and prosperity of the said Colony, they have bin humble suitors unto us that we wold be pleased to grannt unto them an inlardgement of our said former lettres patent, aswell for a more ample extent of their limitts and territories into the seas adjoyning to and uppon the coast of Virginia as allsoe for some other matters and articles concerning the better government of the said Company and Collony, in which point our said former lettres patents doe not extende soe farre as time and experience hath found to be needfull and convenient:

We, therefore, tendring the good and happy successe of the said plantacion both in respect of the generall weale of humane society as in respect of the good of our owne estate and kingedomes, and being willing to give furtherannt untoall good meanes that may advannce the benefitt of the said Company and which maie secure the safety of our loving subjects, planted in our said Colony under the favour and proteccion of God Almighty and of our royall power and authority, have therefore of our especiall grace, certein knowledge and mere mocion, given, grannted and confirmed, and for us, our heires and successors we doe by theis presents, give, graunt and confirme unto the said Treasurer and Company of Adventurers and Planters of the said Citty of London for the First Colony in Virginia, and to their heires and successors for ever, all and singuler the said iselandes scituat and being in anie part of the said ocean bordering upon the coast of our said First Colony in Virginia and being within three hundred leagues of anie the partes hertofore graunted to the said Treasorer and Company in our said former lettres patents as aforesaid, and being within or betweene the one and fortie and thirty degrees of Northerly latitude, together with all and singuler landes, groundes, havens, ports, rivers, waters, fishinges, mines and mineralls, aswell royal mines of gold and silver as other mines and mineralls, perles, precious stones, quarries, and all and singuler other commodities, jurisdiccions, royalties, priviledges, franchises and preheminences, both within the said tract of lande uppon the maine and allso within the said iselandes and seas adjoyning, whatsoever, and thereunto or there abouts both by sea and land being or scituat; and which, by our lettres patents, we maie or cann graunt and in as ample manner and sort as we or anie our noble progenitors have hertofore graunted to anie person or persons or to anie Companie, bodie politique or corporate or to any adventurer or adventurers, undertaker or undertakers of anie discoveries, plantacions or traffique, of, in, or into anie foreigne parts whatsoever, and in as lardge and ample manner as if the same were herein particularly named, mencioned and expressed: provided allwaies that the said iselandes or anie the pre-

misses herein mencioned and by theis presents intended and meant to be grannted be not already actually possessed or inhabited by anie other Christian prince or estate, nor be within the bounds, limitts or territories of the Northerne Colonie, hertofore by us graunted to be planted by divers of our loving subjects in the northpartes of Virginia. To have and to hold, possesse and injoie all and singuler the said iselandes in the said ocean seas soe lying and bordering uppon the coast or coasts of the territories of the said First Colony in Virginia as aforesaid, with all and singuler the said soiles, landes and groundes and all and singular other the premisses heretofore by theis presents graunted, or mencioned to be grannted, to them, the said Treasurer and Companie of Adventurers and Planters of the Cittie of London for the First Colonie in Virginia, and to their heires, successors and assignes for ever, to the sole and proper use and behoove of them, the said Treasurer and Companie and their heires, successores and assignes for ever; to be holden of us, our heires and successors as of our mannor of Eastgreenwich, in free and common soccage and not in capite, yealding and paying therefore to us, our heires and successors, the fifte part of the oare of all gold and silver which shalbe there gotten, had or obteined for all manner of services, whatsoever.

And further our will and pleasure is, and we doe by theis presents grannt and confirme for the good and welfare of the said plantacion, and that posterity maie hereafter knowe whoe have adventured and not bin sparing of their purses in such a noble and generous accion for the generall good of theire cuntrie, and at the request and with the consent of the Companie aforesaid, that our trusty and welbeloved subjects.

George, Lord Archbishopp of Canterbury... [names omitted] whoe since our said last lettres patent are become adventurers and have joined themselves with the former adventurers and planters of the said Companie and societie, shall from henceforth be reputed, deemed and taken to be and shalbe brethren and free members of the Companie and shall and maie, respectively, and according to the proportion and value of their severall adventures, have, hold and enjoie all suche interest, right, title, priviledges, preheminences, liberties, franchises, immunities, profitts and commodities whatsoever, in as lardge, ample and beneficiall manner to all intents, construccions and purposes as anie other adventures nominated and expressed in anie our former lettres patent, or anie of them have or maie have by force and vertue of theis presents, or anie our former lettres patent: whatsoever.

And we are further pleased and we doe by theis presents grant: and confirm that

Phillip, Earle of Montgomery
William, Lord Paget
Sir John Harrington, Knight
Sir William Cavendish, Knight
Sir John Sammes, Knight
Sir Samuell Sandys, Knight
Sir Thomas Freke, Knight
Sir William St. John, Knight
Sir Richard Grobham, Knight
Sir Thomas Dale, Knight
Sir Cavalliero Maycott, Knight
Richard Martin, Esquier
John Bingley, Esquier
Thomas Watson, Esquier, and
Arthure Ingram, Esquier,

whome the said Treasurer and Companie have, since the said [last] lettres patent, nominated and sett downe as worthy and discreete persons fitt to serve us as Counsellors, to be of our Counsell for the said plantacion, shalbe reputed, deemed and taken as persons of our said Councell for the said First Colonie in such manner and sort to all intents and purposes as those whae have bin formerly ellected and nominated as our Counsellors for that Colonie and whose names have bin or are incerted and expressed in our said former lettres patent.

And we doe hereby ordaine and grannt by theis presents that the said Treasurer and Companie of Adventurers and Planters, aforesaid, shall and maie, once everie weeke or oftener at their pleasure, hold and keepe a court and assembly for the better ordering and government of the said plantacion and such thinges as shall concerne the same; and that anie five persons of the said Counsell for the said First Collonie in Virginia, for the time being, of which Companie the Treasurer or his deputie allwaies to be one, and the nomber of fifteene others as the least of the generality of the said Companie assembled together in such court or assembly in such manner as is and hath bin heretofore used and accustomed, shalbe said, taken, held and reputed to be and shalbe a full and

sufficient court of the said Companie for the handling, ordring and dispatching of all such casuall and particuler occurrences and accidentall matters of lesse consequence and waight, as shall from time to time happen, touching and concerning the said plantacion.

And that, nevertheles, for the handling, ordring and disposing of matters and affaires of great waight and importance and such as shall or maie in anie sort concerne the weale publike and generall good of the said Companie and plantacion as namely, the manner of government from time to time to be used, the ordring and disposing of the said possessions and the setling and establishing of a trade there, or such like, there shalbe held and kept everie yeare uppon the last Wednesdaie save one of Hillary, Easter, Trinity and Michaelmas termes, for ever, one great, generall and solemne assembly, which fower severall assemblies shalbe stiled and called The Fower Great and Generall Courts of the Counsells and Companie of Adventurers for Virginia; in all and every of which said great and generall Courts soe assembled our will and pleasure is and we doe, for us, our heires and successors forever, give and graunt to the said Treasurer and Companie and their successors for ever by theis presents, that they, the said Treasurer and Companie or the greater number of them soe assembled, shall and maie have full power and authoritie from time to time and att all times hereafter to ellect and choose discreet persons to be of our [said] Counsell for the said First Colonie in Virginia and to nominate and appoint such officers as theie shall thinke fitt and requisit for the government managing, ordring and dispatching of the affaires of the said Companie; and shall likewise have full power and authority to ordaine and make such lawes and ordinances for the good and wellfare of the said plantacion as to them from time to time shallbe thought requisite and meete: soe allwaies as the same be not contrary to the lawes and statutes of this our realme of England; and shall in like manner have power and authority to expulse, disfranchise and putt out of and from their said Companie and societie for ever all and everie such person and persons as having either promised or subscribed their names to become adventurers to the said plantacion of the said First Colonie in Virginia, or having bin nominated for adventurers in theis or anie our lettres patent or having bin otherwise admitted and nominated to be of the said Companie, have nevertheles either not putt in anie adventure [at] all for and towards the said plantacion or els have refused and neglected, or shall refuse and neglect, to bringe in his or their adventure by word or writing promised within six monthes after the same shalbe soe payable and due.

And wheras the failing and nonpaiment of such monies as have bin promised in adventure for the advanncement of the said plantacion hath bin often by experience found to be danngerous and prejudiciall to the same and much to have hindred the progresse and proceeding of the said planta-cion; and for that itt seemeth to us a thing reason-able that such persons as by their handwriting have engaged themselves for the payment of their adventures, and afterwards neglecting their faith and promise, shold be compellable to make good and kepe the same; therefore our will and plea-sure is that in anie suite or suites comenced or to be comenced in anie of our courts att Westmins-ter, or elswhere, by the said Treasurer and Com-panie or otherwise against anie such persons, that our judges for the time being both in our Court of Channcerie and at the common lawe doe favour and further the said suits soe farre forth as law and equitie will in anie wise suffer and permitt. anie wise suffer and permitt.

And we doe, for us, our heires and successors, further give and graunt to the said Tresorer and Companie, and their successors for ever, that theie, the said Tresorer and Companie or the greater part of them for the time being, so in a full and generall court assembled as aforesaid shall and maie, from time to time and att all times hereafter, for ever, ellect, choose and permitt into their Company and society anie person or persons, as well straungers and aliens borne in anie part beyond the seas wheresoever, being in amity with us, as our naturall liedge subjects borne in anie our realmes and dominions; and that all such persons soe elected, chosen and admitted to be of the said Companie as aforesaid shall thereuppon be taken, reputed and held and shalbe free members of the said Companie and shall have, hold and enjoie all and singuler freedoms, liberties, franchises, priviledges, immunities, benefitts, profitts and commodities, whatsoever, to the said Companie in anie sort belonging or apperteining as fully, freely [and] amplie as anie

other adventurer or adventurers now being, or which hereafter att anie time shalbe, of the said Companie, hath, have, shall, maie, might or ought to have or enjoy the same to all intents and purposes whatsoever.

And we doe further of our speciall grace, cer-taine knowledge and mere mocion, for us, our heires and successors, give and grantt to the said Tresorer and Companie and their successors, for ever by theis present that itt shalbe lawfull and free for them and their assignes att all and everie time and times hereafter, out of anie our realmes and dominions whatsoever, to take, lead, carry and transport in and into the said voyage and for and towards the said plantacion of our said First Collonie in Virginia, all such and soe manie of our loving subjects or anie other straungers that will become our loving subjects and live under our allegiance as shall willingly accompanie them in the said voyage and plantacion; with shipping, armour, weapons, ordinannce, munition, powder, shott, victualls, and all manner of merchandizes and wares, and all manner of clothing, implement, furniture, beasts, cattell, horses, mares, and all other thinges necessarie for the said plantacion and for their use and defence, and for trade with the people there and in passing and retourning to and froe, without paying or yealding anie sub-sedie, custome or imposicion, either inward or outward, or anie other dutie to us, our heires or successors, for the same, for the space of seven yeares from the date of theis present.

And we doe further, for us, our heires and successors, give and grannt to the said Treasurer and Companie and their successors for ever, by theis present, that the said Treasurer of the said Companie, or his deputie for the time being or anie twoe others of our said Counsell for the said First Colonie in Virginia for the time being, shall and maie attall times hereafter and from time to time, have full power and authoritie to minister and give the oath and oathes of supremacie and allegiannce, or either of them, to all and every person and persons which shall, at anie time and times hereafter, goe or passe to the said Colonie in Virginia:

And further, that itt shalbe likewise lawfull for the said Tresorer, or his deputy for the time, or anie twoe others of our said Counsell for the said First Colonie in Virginia, for the time being, from time to time and att all times hereafter, to minister such a formall oathe as by their discrescion shalbe reasonably devised, aswell unto anie person or persons imployed or to be imployed in, for, or touching the said plantacion for their honest, faithfull and just dischardge of their service in all such matters as shalbe committed unto them for the good and benefitt of the said Company, Colonie and plantacion; as alsoe unto such other person or persons as the said Treasurer or his deputie, with twoe others of the said Counsell, shall thinke meete for the examinacion or clearing of the truith in anie cause whatsoever concerninge the said plantacion or anie business from thence proceeding or there unto proceeding or thereunto belonging.

And, furthermore, whereas we have ben certefied that diverse lewde and ill disposed persons, both sailors, souldiers, artificers, husbandmen, laborers, and others, having received wages, apparrell or other entertainment from the said Company or having contracted and agreed with the said Companie to goe, to serve, or to be imployed in the said plantacion of the said First Colonie in Virginia, have afterwards either withdrawen, hid or concealed themselves, or have refused to goe thither after they have bin soe entertained and agreed withall; and that divers and sundry persons allso which have bin sent and imployed in the said plantacion of the said First Colonie in Virginia at and upon the chardge of the said Companie, and having there misbehaved themselves by mutinies, sedition, and other notorious misdemeanors, or having bin employed or sent abroad by the governor of Virginia or his deputie with some ship or pinnace for provisions for the said Colonie, or for some discoverie or other buisines and affaires concerning the same, have from thence most trecherouslie either come back againe and retorned into our realme of England by stelth or without licence of our Governor of our said Colonie in Virginia for the time being, or have bin sent hither as misdoers and offenders; and that manie allsoe of those persons after their retourne from thence, having bin questioned by our said Counsell here for such their misbehaviors and offences, by their insolent and contemptuous carriage in the presence of our said Counsaile, have shewed little respect and reverence, either to the place or authoritie in which we have placed and appointed them; and others, for the colouring of their lewdnes and misdemeanors committed in

Virginia, have endeavored them by most vile and slanndrous reports made and divulged, aswell of the cuntrie of Virginia as alsoe of the government and estate of the said plantacion and Colonie, as much as in them laie, to bring the said voyage and plantacion into disgrace and contempt; by meanes where of not only the adventures and planters alreadie ingaged in the said plantacion have bin exceedingly abused and hindred, and a greate nomber of other our loving and welldisposed subjects otherwise well affected and inclyning to joine and adventure insoe noble, Christian and worthie an action have bin discouraged from the same, but allsoe the utter overthrow and ruine of the said enterprise hath bin greatlie indanngered which cannott miscarrie without some dishonor to us and our kingdome;

Now, for asmuch as it appeareth unto us that theis insolences, misdemeanors and abuses, not to be tollerated in anie civill government, have for the most part growne and proceeded inregard of our Counsaile have not anie direct power and authoritie by anie expresse wordes in our former lettres patent to correct and chastise such offenders, we therefore, for the more speedy reformacion of soe greate and enormous abuses and misdemeanors heretofore practised and committed, and for the preventing of the like hereafter, doe by theis present for us, our heires and successors, give and grannt to the said Treasurer and Companie, and their successors for ever, that itt shall and maie be lawfull for our said Councell for the said First Colonie in Virginia or anie twoe of them, whereof the said Tresorer or his deputie for the time being to be allwaies one, by warrant under their handes to send for, or cause to be apprehended, all and every such person and persons who shalbe noted or accused or found, att anie time or times here after, to offend or misbehave themselves in anie the offences before mencioned and expressed; and uppon the examinacion of anie such offender or offendors and just proofe made by oath taken before the Counsaile of anie such notorious misdemeanors by them committed as aforesaid; and allsoe uppon anie insolent, contemptuous or unreverent carriage and misbehavior to or against our said Counsell shewed or used by anie such person or persons soe called, convented and apearing before them as aforesaid; that in all such cases theie, our said Counsell or anie twoe of them for the time being, shall and maie have full power and authoritie either here to binde them over with good suerties for their good behaviour and further therein to proceed to all intents and purposes, as itt is used in other like cases within our realme of England; or ells att their discrescion to remannd and send back the said offenders or anie of them unto the said Colonie in Virginia, there to be proceeded against and punished as the Governor, deputie and Counsell there for the time being shall thinke meete; or otherwise, according to such lawes and ordinannces as are or shalbe in use there for the well ordring and good governement of the said Colonie.

And, for the more effectuall advauncing of the said plantacion, we doe further, for us, our heires and successors, of our especiall grace and favour, by vertue of our prorogative royall and by the assent and consent of the Lordes and others of our Privie Counsalle, give and grannte unto the said Tresorer and Companie full power and authoritie, free leave, libertie and licence to sett forth, errect and publishe one or more lotterie or lotteries to have continuance and to [endure] and be held for the space of one whole yeare next after the opening of the same, and after the end and expiracion of the said terme the said lotterie or lotteries to continue and be further kept, during our will and pleasure onely and not otherwise. And yet, nevertheles, we are contented and pleased, for the good and wellfare of the said plantacion, that the said Tresorer and Companie shall, for the dispatch and finishing of the said lotterie or lotteries, have six months warninge after the said yeare ended before our will and pleasure shall, for and on that behalfe, be construed, deemed and adjudged to be in anie wise altered and determined.

And our further will and pleasure is that the said lottery or lottaries shall and maie be opened and held within our cittie of London or in anie other cittie or citties, or ellswheare within this our realme of England, with such prises, articles, condicions and limitacions as to them, the said Tresorer and Companie, in their discreascions shall seeme convenient.

And that itt shall and may be lawfull to and for the said Tresorer and Companie to ellect and choose receivors, auditors, surveyors, comissioners, or anie other officers whatsoever, att their will and pleasure for the better marshalling and guiding and governing of the said lottarie or lottaryes; and that itt shalbe likewise lawfull to and for the said Tresorer and anie twoe of the said Counsell to minister unto all and everie such persons soe ellected and chosen for officers as aforesaid one or more oathes for their good behaviour, just and true dealing in and about the lottarie or lottaries to the intent and purpose that none of our loving subjects, putting in their monies or otherwise adventuring in the said generall lotterie or lottaries, maie be in anie wise defrauded and deceived of their said monies or evill and indirectlie dealt withall in their said adventures.

And we further graunt in manner and forme aforesaid, that itt shall and maie be lawfull to and for the said Treasurer and Companie, under the seale of our Counsell for the plantacion, to publishe or to cause and procure to be published by proclamacion or otherwise, the said proclamacion to be made in their name by vertue of theise present, the said lottarie or lotteries in all citties, townes, boroughts, throughfaires and other places within our said realme of England; and we will and commande all mayors, justices of peace, sheriffs, bayliffs, constables and other our officers and loving subjects whatsoever, that in noe wise theie hinder or delaie the progresse and proceeding of the said lottarie or lottaries but be therein and, touching the premisses, aiding and assisting by all honest, good and lawfull meanes and endevours.

And further our will and pleasure is that in all questions and dobts that shall arise uppon anie difficultie of construccion or interpretacion of anie thing conteined in theis or anie other our former lettres patent the same shalbe taken and interpreted in most ample and beneficiall manner for the said Tresorer and Companie and their successors and everie member there of.

And lastly we doe by theis present retifie and confirme unto the said Treasorer and Companie, and their successors for ever, all and all manner of priviledges, franchises, liberties, immunities, preheminences, profitts and commodities whatsoever graunted unto them in anie our [former] lettres patent and not in theis present revoked, altered, channged or abridged. Although expresse mencion [of the true yearly value or certainty of the premises, or any of them, or of any other gift or grant, by us or any of our progenitors or predecessors, to the aforesaid Tresurer and Company hertofore made, in these Presents is not made; or any statute, act, ordinance, provisions, proclamation, or restraint, to the contrary thereof heretofore made, ordained, or provided, or any other matter, cause, or thing, whatsoever, to the contrary, in any wise, notwithstanding.]

In witnes whereof we have caused these our letters to be made patents. Wittnes our selfe att Westminster, the twelveth daie of March in the ninth year of our reign of England, France, and Ireland, and of Scotland the five and fortieth.

Chapter One hundred three
The Promotional Impulse

F ROM ITS EARLIEST days the Virginia Company rarely lacked ingenuity and enterprise in seeking to accumulate capital for its ventures or to raise the morale of potential subscribers and adventurers. Some examples are given of approaches to companies or individuals who might provide money. Other examples are given of the pamphlets of an official character that boosted Virginia or sought other means to advertise her merits. No examples (they are long-winded and in content only of intermittent interest) of the sermons preached to potential subscribers are given. There the theme that the company was set up largely to save the souls of the heathen could be pressed and the missionary impulse stirred in Protestant audiences who might not care to let all the credit for conversions go to the papists even if, during the years 1606–1612 at least, the company made no attempt to implement its pious promises. Yet, over the whole spectrum of its publicity campaign, the company must be regarded as highly successful. Seeing that in these years no really valuable cargoes came to England and that each expedition cost more than the last with less return, the bringing in of money by fair and not so fair means must be regarded as an outstanding achievement in promotion.

806. 1609–1610. Reactions of some London livery companies to requests to support the Virginia Company.

The livery companies of the City of London were drawn in as participants in the Virginia venture in the second charter of 1609. A few examples, drawn from the company records in the Guildhall Library, London, may throw some light on how some of the companies participated. They are (a) MS 5570/1, Fishmongers Company, Ledger I (1592–1610), fol. 547, a precept for Virginia; (b) MS 11588/2, Orders of the Court of Assistants of the Grocers Company, 1591–1616, p. 528, a letter from the Council of Virginia, March 1, 1610; (c) p. 582, an order for payment on April 25, 1610; (d) MS 11571/9, fol. 356v, Wardens Accounts of the Grocers Company, 1601–1611, payment for Virginia, April 25, 1610.

[a] Fishmongers Company, 20 March 1608 [-1609].

A precept for Virginia

At the same Court Master Warden Boyntell did bring in a precept from the Lord maiour directed to this Companye to call all the Company together & verrye effectually to exhort them to venture moneys to Virginia for plantation thereof and most of the lyverye having before ben spoken withall and the generaltye of the Companye nowe being warned and particularly or mostly perswaded to adventure not on of them will consent to adventure any thinge wherefore it is agreed that aunswere shalbe made to the precept accordingly.

[b]   Grocers Company,
1 March 1609–1610.

A lettre from the Counsell of Virginia/A precept from the Lord maior

This daye in the afternoone the Call of the generallitie & the readinge of the ordinaunces, was spared in respect of extraordinarie busynes nowe in hand namelie the readinge as well of a letter sent from the Counsell & Companie of the honorable plantacion of Virginia. As alsoe of a precept sent from the Right honourable the Lord Maior unto this companie, the chiefe scope & purporte whereof is to rayse some voluntary contribution out of the best disposed & most hable of the Companie towardes the sayd plantacion, And further as by the sayde letter & precept more playnelie maie appeare a true coppie whereof are here under wrytten. After the readinge of which sayde latter & precepte yt pleased the Right honourable the Lord maior to make a most worthie & pithie exortacion unto the generallitie concerninge the premisses, requiringe everie of them in his particular person to come upp to the Clarke & to sett downe what & how much he will contribute for soe honourable a service, which was done accordinglie, & also notice taken & theire names sett downe, aswell those which weare contributours as those which denyed & refused to make any such contribucion/

[c]   Grocers Company,
25 April 1610.

Plantacion in Virginia 100^{li.} to be payed to Sir Thomas Smythe

It is agreed and ordred by the Courte that the moneys which have been collected of divers Brothers of this Companye for and towardes the plantacion of his Majesties subjects in Virginia and remayning uppon accompte in the handes of Master Wardens which the rest promised to be Collected shalbe by Master Wardens encreased to an C^{li.} of the Comon goodes of this house and by them payd over to Sir Thomas Smythe knighte Treasorer of his Majestes Colonyes in Virginia. And to take a Bill of adventure for the same use of this Companye.

[d]   Grocers Company,
25 April 1610.

Payd more to Sir Thomas Smythe Knighte ye Treasorer of Virginia according to an order of Courte of the xxv daye of Aprill 1610 the Some of one hundred poundes. For the which a Bill of adventure is taken to th'use of this Companye.

807. [April to May], 1609. Robert Johnson's *Nova Britannia*.

During the latter months of 1608 and the early ones of 1609, every effort was being made by Sir Thomas Smith and his associates in the London division of the Virginia Company to prepare the way for a further, and it was hoped, final expansion of their enterprise. One instrument was the propaganda pamphlet. Robert Johnson's Nova Britannia: offering most excellent fruites by planting in Virginia. Exciting all such as are well affected to further the same *(London, printed for Samuel Macham, 1609), was an ambitious effort to supplement oral propaganda by printed. The specious device of dedicating it to Sir Thomas Smith, as if it did not emanate from him and his associates to begin with, is transparent. Apart from long lists of products that can be grown there, Johnson gives very little concrete information on Virginia. What is interesting is that he does make an open challenge to the Spanish view that they hold unreserved rights to the whole of America, and he excludes the Catholics from any share in the enterprise. He attacks persons who might have scruples about invading and stealing the lands of the Indians (compare 485) with rather specious pleas about the peaceful intentions of the company and the desire of the settlers to civilize and Christianize the people. He indicates that the people welcomed the English intruders. His main emphasis is to make clear that unlimited land will be taken, that settlements twenty miles apart will gradually take up all the land between them, and that investors will be well treated. After seven years' employment of the common stock, they will be given land generously. This, of course, does not fit at all with the "protection" of the Indians. The pamphlet is spec-*

ifically a trailer for the new charter that had already been promised and that was to be finally granted on May 23, one incentive being that immediate subscribers would have their named inscribed in it. Its appeal to greed is its main strength.

The precise date of the publication is not known. It cannot be earlier than the last few days in March or later than the middle of May. It was reprinted in P. Force, Tracts, I (1836), no. 6.

To the Right Worshipfull Sir Thomas Smith, of London, Knight of one of his Majesties Councell for Virginia, and Treasurer for the Colonie, and Governour of the Companies of the Moscovia and East India Merchants, Peace, health, and happiness in Christ.

Right worshipfull Sir,
Forasmuch as I have alwayes observed your honest zeale to God, accompanied with so excellent carriage and resolution, in actions of best consequence, I cannot but discover unto you for your further encouragement, the summe of a private speech or discourse, touching our plantation in Virginia, uttered not long since in London, where some few adventurers (well affecting the enterprise) being met together touching their intended project, one among the rest stood up and began to relate (in effect) as followeth.
R. J.

Nova Britannia.
Offering most excellent fruites by Planting in Virginia.

Whereas in our last meeting and conference the other day, observing your sufficient reasons answering all objections, and your constant resolution to go on in our Plantation, they gave me so good content and satisfaction, that I am driven against my selfe, to confesse mine own error in standing out so long, whereby many of you (my friends) were engaged in the business before mee, at whose often instigations I was but little moved, and lightly esteemed of it till being in place, where observing the wise and prudent speech, of a worthy Gentleman, (well knowne to you all) a most painful mannager of such publike affayres within this Cittie, which moved so effectually, touching the publike utilitie of this noble enter-

prise, that withholding no longer, I yielded my money and endeavours as others did to advance the same, and now upon more advised consideration, I must needes say I neuer accompted my poore meanes employed to better purpose, then (by Gods helpe) the successe of this may bee, and therefore I cannot but deliver (if you please to heare) what I rudely conceive of a suddaine.

There are divers monuments already publisht in Print to the world, manifesting and shewing, that the Coasts and parts of Virginia have beene long since discovered, peopled and possessed by many English, both men, women, and children, the naturall subjects of our late Queene Elizabeth, of famous memorie, conducted and left there at sundrie times. And that the same footing and possession is there kept and possessed by the same English, or by their seede and of-spring, without any interruption or invasion, either of the Savages (the natives of the countrie) or of any other Prince or people (for ought wee heare or know) to this day, which argueth sufficiently to us (and it is true) that over those English and Indian people, no Christian King or Prince (other then James our Soveraigne Lord and King) ought to have rule or Dominion, or can by possession, conquest or inheritance, truely claime or make just title to those Territories, or to any part thereof, except it bee (as wee heare of late) that a challenge is laid to all, by vertue of a Donation from Alexander the first Pope of Rome, wherein (they say) is given all the West Indies, including Florida and Virginia, with all America, and whatsoever Ilands adjacent.

But what is this to us? they are blind indeede that stumble here; it is much like that great donation of Constantine whereby the Pope himselfe doeth hold and claime the Cittie of Rome, and all the Westerne Empire, a thing that so crosseth all Histories of truth, and sound Antiquitie, that by the apt resemblance of those two Donations, the whole West Empire, from a temporall Prince to the Pope, and the whole West Indies, from the Pope to a temporall Prince. I doe verily gesse they be neere of kinne, they are so like each other, the one an olde tale vaine and fabulous, the other a new toy most idle and ridiculous.

When the flatterers of Cambises King of Persia, could find no law to warrant his immoderate lust and incestuous marriage with his owne daughter, yet they told him of another law which they had found, whereby the Kings of Persia might doe what they listed: if in these cases likewise there be a law that the Pope may doe what he list, let them that list obey him, for we beleeve not in him.

Letting goe (therefore) these legendarie fables, which howsoever some men holde authenticke as their Creede, yet are they in the judgement of wise men, things of no value, nor doe import to us, any cause of doubt or feare, but that we goe on in our honest enterprise, and lawfull purpose now in hand, that (as wee hope) his Majestie mindeth not the relinquishing his estate and enterest, derived to him by right of succession, from his immediate predecessor, but for the further planting and succouring our old Colony, hath given us leave to make new supplies, which wee lately sent thither under the conduct of Christopher Newport Captaine: And hath granted many gratious priviledges, under the great Seale, to us and to our Heirs for ever, that will adventure or plant in the said plantation: So I wish and intreat all well affected subjects, some in their persons, others in their purses, cheerefully to adventure, and joyntly take in hand this high and acceptable worke, tending to advance and spread the kingdome of God, and the knowledge of the truth, among so many millions of men and women, Sauage and blind, that never yet saw the true light shine before their eyes, to enlighten their minds and comfort their soules, as also for the honor of our King, and enlarging of his kingdome, and for preservation and defence of that small number of our friends and countrymen already planted, least for want of more supplies we become a scorne to the world subjecting our former adventures to apparent spoile and hazard, and our people (as a prey) to be sackt and puld out of possession, as were the French out of Nova Francia, not many yeares ago, and which is the lest and last respect (yet usuallie preferred) for the singular good and benefite that will undoubtedly arise to this whole nation, and to everie one of us in particular, that will adventure therein, as by true relation (God willing) I shall make it manifestly appeare to all.

It is knowne to the world, and cannot bee forgotten, that the dayes and raigne of Queene Elizabeth, brought forth the highest degree of wealth, happinesse and honour, that ever England had before her time, whereof to let passe the particular praises, as impertinent to my purpose, I doe onely call to minde our Royall Fleetes and Marchants Shippes, (the Jewels of our land) our excellent navigators, and admirable voyages, as into all parts and round about the Globe with good successe, to the high fame and glorie of our Nation, so especially their aime and course was most directed to the new found world, to the maine land and infinite Ilands of the West Indies, intending to discover with what convenience to Plant and settle English Colonies, in places not already possessed and inhabited by subjects of other Christian Princes, wherein after many tedious and perilous adventures, howsoever strange seas and miserable famine, had devoured and distressed shipps and men of inestimable value, yet were not the remnant escaping, swallowed up of despaire, nor their hart and spirits daunted with feare, but daily armed afresh with invincible courage, and greater resolution (scorning to sit downe by their losses) made newe attempts, not induring to looke on whilst so huge and spacious countries (the fourth part of the world) and the greatest and wealthiest part of all the rest, should remain a wilderness, subject (for the most part) but to wild beasts and fowles of the ayre, and to savage people, which have no Christian, nor civill use of any thing, and that the subjects onely of one Prince Christian, which but within the memorie of man began first to creepe upon the face of those Territories, and now by meanes of their remnants settled here and there, do therefore imagine the world to be theirs, shouldring out all other nations, accounting themselves Kings and Commanders, not onely in townes and places where they have planted, but over all other partes of America, which containe sundrie vast and barbarous Regions, many of which (to this day) they never knew, nor did ever setle foote therein: which notwithstanding, if it were yeelded them as due, yet their strength and meanes farre inferiour to their aspires, will never stretch to compasse or replenish the hundredth part thereof: and this we proved true not many yeares agoe, our Prince and theirs being then at open hostilitie, their best and chiefest residences were scattered with so poore and slender troups, that with handfuls of men (at sundry times) we ran thorow all, surprizing and sacking their strongest forts and townes in those parts, and might long since with ease, following and seconding our forces, have set them to their stint.

But seeing we so passed by their dwellings,

that in seating our selves, wee sought not to unsettle them, but by Gods mercy, after many stormes, were brought to the Coast of another countrie, farre distant and remote from their habitations: why should any frowne or envie at it, or if they doe, why should wee (neglecting so faire an opportunitie) faint or feare to enlarge our selves. Where is our force and aunctient vigour? Doth our late reputation sleepe in the dust? No, no, let not the world deceive it selfe, we still remaine the same, and upon just occasion given, we shall quickly shew it too: having now by Gods blessing, more meanes then ever heretofore, beeing strongly fenced where wee wonted to lie open: Our plant, we trust, is firmely rooted, our armes and limmes are strong, our branches faire, and much desire to spread themselves abroad.

But before I come to discribe this earthly Paradice, or to prove the points of my proposition mentioned before, you shall knowe, that the first discovery and actuall possession taken thereof was in the raigne and by the subjects of Henry the seventh of England, at which time did Spaine also discover, and by that right of discovery, doth retaine and holde their Nova Hispania, and all other their limmits upon that Coast: But that we now intend to ground upon is a more late Discoverie and actuall possession, taken in the name and right of Queene Elizabeth, in Anno 1584, the 13 of July, as it is truely set downe in the Booke of English Voyages, by sundry English Captaines and Gentlemen in that Voyage, whose names are recorded in that discourse (and many of which are yet living) whereof when her Majestie had true information, shee named the Countrey Virginia, and did assigne to Walter Raleigh (then a Gentleman of worth) power and Authoritie to Plant forces and Colonies there, at his pleasure, who transported thither in Anno 1587, by the conduct of John White chiefe Leader, above an hundred Men, Women, and Children at one time, and left them there to inhabite to this day: Notwithstanding, it is true indeede (as some may object.) It is now above twentie yeeres agoe since these things were done, and yet ever since in all this time, we never sawe or heard of any good that hath come from thence, nor of any hope, that might encourage us anew to engage our selves therein.

But let us rightly weigh the reasons of it, and then judge: Those hundred and upwards, conducted thither by John White and whose particular Names you may see Recorded in the same Booke of Voyages, were left there, with intent and promise, to be supplied from England, with more companies and all necessaries, the next yeere following: in the meane time, they were to Plant and fortifie themselves in best manner they could, and to make a discoverie of such Minerals, and other merchandize, as the countrey should yeeld by nature. But as all good Actions have their Crosses and their Bane attending on them, so had this: for that those which had the Managing of a new supply, being the next yeere sufficiently furnished to Sea for that ende, yet most unnaturally, being Tainted with that common corruption of time, turned their head another way, and with greedie minds, betooke themselves wholly to hunt after Pillage upon the Spanish Coast where spending their men, their time and provisions, they were not able (beeing come and arrived at the port) to make up into the land to visite and relieve their friends, but were forced to retire for England againe, whereby the edge of those adventurers that set them foorth was so abated, that this most honourable enterprise so happily begunne, was by this last occasion most unhappily ended, neither had our poore countri-men left there, any meanes from thence to visite us, nor in all this time to give us any light of their owne estate: whereas then, if those beginnings had beene followed as they ought, and as by Gods helpe wee now entend, that countrey had long since become a most royall addition to the Crowne of England, and a very nursery and fountaine of much wealth and strength to this kingdome.

When Christopher Columbus (the first bewrayer of this new world) was to make his proffer where he liked best, hee chose Henry the seventh of England, as in those dayes the most worthy, and best furnished for Navigations, of all the Kings in Christendome: offering to invest his Majestie with the most pretious and richest vaines of the whole earth, never knowne before, as he did also the like to the Kings of Portugale and Spaine, who (as the story saith) for his poore apparell and simple lookes, and for the noveltie of his proposition, was of most men accounted a vaine foole, and utterly rejected: save that the Spanish better conceiving then some others, beganne to entertaine and make use of his skill, which within these hundred yeares, hath brought foorth those apparent fruits to the world as cannot be hidde. Their Territories enlarged, their Navigations encreased, their subjects enricht, and their superfluitie of coyne over-spreading all parts of the world, procures their Crowne to flourish, and highly commendeth the wisedome of Spaine: whose quicke apprehension and speedy addresse, prevented all other Princes: albeit (as you know) their greatness of minde arising together with their money and meanes, hath turmoiled all Christendome these fourtie yeares and more.

And this I but mention, to note the blind diffidence of our English natures, which laugh to scorne the name of Virginia, and all other new projects, bee they never so probable, and will not beleeve till wee see the effects: as also to shew how capable men ought to bee, in things of great importance, advisedly to take the first occasions. We reade of Haniball, when chasing home the Romanes to the gates of Rome, and neglecting then to scale the walles, could never after with all his strength and policies come neere the like advantage: yet I must briefely tell you now, what I conceive with joy, that howsoever the businesse of this plantation hath beene formerly miscarried, yet it is now going on in better way, not enterprised by one or two private subjects, who in their greatnesse of minde, sought to compasse that, which rather beseemed a mighty Prince, (such as ours) or the whole State to take in hand: for it is not unknowen to you all, how many Noble men of Honourable mindes, how many worthy Knights, Merchants, and others of the best disposition, are now joyned together in one Charter, to receive equall priviledges, according to their several adventures: every man engaging his purse, and some Noble-men, Knights and Gentlemen, intending to goe in their owne persons, which I did heare to protest and vow, against anie people, whomsoever shall any way seeke to entrappe or impeach our proceedings, an utter revenge upon their bodies or goods, if they be to bee found upon Sea or land: whereby we have assured hope (God assisting us) to be effectually able to make good against all, and in short time to bring to a most happy event the thing we take in hand.

And now in discribing the naturall seate and disposition of the countrie it selfe: if I should say no more but with Caleb and Joshua, The land which we have searched out is a very good land, if the Lord love us, he will bring our people to it, and

will give it us for a possession. This were enough to you that are willing, but yet a little more in particular observed, by the best Mappes and Printed discourses, and by conference of such as have beene lately there and seene it, I thinke good to deliver to satisfie others: First the Voyage is not long nor tedious, sixe Weekes at ease will send us thither, whereas sixe Moneths suffice not to some other places, where wee Trade: our course and passage is thorow the great Ocean, where is no feare of Rockes or Flattes, nor subject to the streights and restraint of forraine Princes, most Winds that blow, are apt and fit for us, and none can hinder us: when wee come to the Coast, there is continuall depth enough, with good Bottome for Anchor hold, and the Land is faire to fall with all, full of excellent good Harbours: the world affoords no better for Shippes of all burdens, many pleasant Ilands great and small affronting the Coast: Two goodly Rivers are discovered winding farre into the Maine, the one in the North part of the Land by our Westerne Colonie, Knights and Gentlemen of Excester, Plymouth and others: The other in the South part thereof by our Colonie of London: Upon which River, being both broad, deepe and pleasant, abounding with store of fish, our Colony have begun to fortify themselves, and have built a towne, and named it (in honor of our King) James towne, fourescore miles within land, upon the North side of the River (as is London upon the River of Thames) from whence we have discovered the same River, one hundred myles further into the mayne Land, in the searching whereof, they were so ravisht with the admirable sweetnesse of the streame, and with the pleasant land trending along on either side, that their joy exceeded and with great admiration they praised God.

The country it selfe is large and great assuredly, though as yet, no exact discovery can bee made of all. It is also commendable and hopefull every way, the ayre and clymate most sweete and wholsome, much warmer then England, and very agreeable to our Natures: It is inhabited with wild and savage people, that live and lie up and downe in troupes like heards of Deare in a Forrest: they have no law but nature, their apparell skinnes of beasts, but most goe naked: the better sort have houses, but poore ones, they have no Arts nor Science, yet they live under superior command such as it is, they are generally very loving and gentle, and doe entertaine and relieve our people with great kindnesse: they are easy to be brought to good, and would fayne embrace a better condition: the land yeeldeth naturallie for the sustentation of man, aboundance of fish, both scale and shell: of land and water fowles, infinite store: of Deere, Kaine and Fallow, Stags, Coneys, and Hares, with many fruits and rootes good for meate.

There are valleyes and plaines streaming with sweete Springs, like veynes in a naturall bodie: there are hills and mountaines making a sensible proffer of hidden treasure, never yet searched: the land is full of mineralles, plentie of woods (the wants of England) there are growing goodly Okes and Elmes, Beech and Birch, Spruce, Walnut, Cedar and Firre trees, in great aboundance, the soile is strong and lustie of its owne nature, and sendeth out naturally fruitfull Vines running upon trees, and shrubbes: it yeeldeth also Rosin, Turpentine, Pitch and Tarre, Sassafras, Mulbery-trees and Silke-wormes, many Skinnes and rich furres, many sweete woodes, and Dyers woodes, and other costly dyes: plenty of Sturgion, Timber for Shipping, Mast, Plancke and Deale, Sope ashes, Caviare, and what else we know not yet, because our daies are young. But of this that I have said, if bare nature be so amiable in its naked kind, what may we hope, when Arte and Nature both shall joyne, and strive together, to give best content to man and beast? as now in handling the severall parts propounded, I shall shew in order as they lie.

For the first (if I forget not my selfe) how it may tend to advance the kingdome of God, by reducing savage people from their blind superstition to the light of Religion, when some object, wee seeke nothing lesse then the cause of God, beeing led on by our owne private ends, and secondly how we can warrant a supplantation of those Indians, or an invasion into their right and possessions.

To the first we say, as many actions both good in themselves, and in their successe, have beene performed with badde intents: so in this case, howsoever our naughtines of minde may sway very much, yet God may have the honor, and his kingdome advanced in the action done: but yet by the way, me thinks this objection comes in due time, and doth well admonish us, how to rectifie our hearts and ground our meditations before we

begin: we doe generally applaud, and highly commend the goodness of the cause, and that it is such a profitable plough, as every honest man ought to set his hand unto, both in respect of God and the publike good, this is our generall voice, and we say truth, for so it is.

But wee must beware that under this pretence that bitter root of greedy gaine be not so settled in our harts, that beeing in a golden dreame, if it fall not out presently to our expectation, we slinke away with discontent, and draw our purses from the charge. If any shew this affection, I would wish his baseness of minde to be noted. What must be our direction then, no more but this: if thou dost once approve the worke, lay thy hand to it cheerfully, and withdraw it not till thy taske bee done, at all assayes and new supplies of money be not lagge, nor like a dull horse thats alwaies in the lash, for heere lies the poison of all good attempts, when as men without halling and pulling, will not be drawne to performance, for by this, others are discouraged, the action lies undone, and the first expence is lost: But are wee to looke for no gaine in the lewe of all adventures? yes undoubtedly, there is assured hope of gaine, as I will shew anon in due place, but look it be not chiefe in your thoughts, God that hath said by Solomon: Cast thy bread upon the waters, and after many daies thou shalt find it; he will give the blessing: And as for supplanting the savages, we have no such intent: Our intrusion into their possession shall tend to their great good, and no way to their hurt, unlesse as unbridled beastes, they procure it to themselves: Wee purpose to proclaime and make it knowne to them all, by some publike interpretation that our comming thither is to plant our selves in their countrie: yet not to supplant and roote them out, but to bring them from their base condition to a farre better: First, in regard of God the Creator, and of Jesus Christ their Redeemer, if they will beleeve in him. And secondly, in respect of earthly blessings, whereof they have now no comfortable use, but in beastly brutish manner, with promise to defend them against all publike and private enemies. Wee can remember since Don Jon Daquila with his forces invading Ireland, a noble civill kingdome, where all (except a few runagates) were setled in the truth of Religion, and lived by wholsome laws, under the milde government of Christian Kings and Princes, long before his grandsiers cradle: yet hee thought it no robberie to proclaime and publish to the world, that his comming thither, was to none other end, but to free their Nation from their bondage, and tyrannous subjection, and to bring the blind soules to Catholike religion: a plausible pretence, the least end of his thought.

But if this were coyned in those dayes by the Printers themselves, to passe for currant thorow the world, howsoever base it was indeede, wee hope they will be as favourable to our case, and give as free passage and allowance to our invasion, much more currant, and so farre different, as not to bring a people (according to our proverbe) out of the frying panne into the fire, but to make their condition truely more happy, by a mutuall enterchange and commerce in this sort: That as to our great expence and charge, wee make adventures, to impart our divine riches, to their inestimable gaine, and to cover their naked miserie with civill use of foode, and clothing, and to traine them by gentle meanes to those manuall artes and skill, which they so much affect, and doe admire to see in us: so in lewe of this, wee require nothing at their hands, but a quiet residence to us and ours, that by our owne labour and toyle, we may worke this goode unto them and recompence our owne adventures, costs and traveils in the ende: wherein, they shall be most friendly welcome to conjoyne their labours with ours, and shall enjoy equall priviledges with us, in whatsoever good successe, time or meanes may bring to passe. To which purpose, wee may verily beleeve, that God hath reserved in this last age of the world, an infinite number of those lost and scattered sheepe, to be won and recovered by our meanes, of whom so many as obstinately refuse to unite themselves unto us, or shall maligne or disturbe our plantation, our chattel, or whatsoever belonging to us: they shall be held and reputed recusant, withstanding their owne good: and shall be dealt with as enemies of the Common-wealth of their countrie: whereby how much good we shall performe to those that be good, and how little injury to any, will easily appeare, by comparing our present happinesse with our former ancient miseries, wherein wee had continued brutish, poore and naked Britanes to this day, if Julius Cæsar with his Romane Legions (or some other) had not laid the ground to make us tame and civill.

But for my second point propounded, the honour of our King, by enlarging his kingdomes, to prove how this may tend to that: no argument of mine can make it so manifest, as the same is cleere in it selfe: Divine testimonies shew, that the honour of a king consisteth in the multitude of subjects, and certainly the state of the Jewes was farre more glorious, by the conquests of David, and under the ample raigne of Solomon, then ever before or after: The twelve Tribes were then all subject: the bordering Nations tributarie, no doubt a happie subjection to many of them: whereby they had the better meanes to beleeve and know God the Creator of heaven and earth: Honourable I graunt is just Conquest by sword, and Hercules is fained to have had all his felicity, in subduing and rooting out the Tyrants of the world, but unfainedly it is most honourable indeede, to subdue the tyranny of the roaring Lion, that devoures those poore soules in their ignorance, and leads them to hell for want of light, when our Dominions shall be enlarged, and the subjects multiplied of a people so bought and ransomed, not by stormes of raging cruelties (as West India was converted) with rapiers point and Musket shot, murdering so many millions of naked Indians, as their stories doe relate, but by faire and loving meanes, suiting to our English natures, like that soft and gentle voice, wherein the Lord appeared to Elias: How honourable will this be, in the sight of men and of ages to come? but much more glorious in the sight of God, when our King shall come to make his triumph in heaven. The prophet Daniel doth assure, that for this conquest of turning manie unto righteousnesse, hee shall shine as the starres for ever and ever.

And yet this is not all that may be saide, the auncient law, the law of Moses settes it downe, as a blessed thing, when the Prince and people of God, shall bee able to lend to all, and neede to borrow of none, and it added very much to the fame and wisedome of king Solomon, which the world came farre and neere to wonder at, in that his kingdomes were replenished with golde and silver in aboundance, and with riches brought in by shippes sent yearely forth in ample trade of Merchandize, whereof wee reade not the like among all the kings of Israel. And upon good warrant I speake it here in private, what by these new discoveries into the Westerne partes, and our hopefull settling in chiefest places of the East, with our former knowne trades in other parts of the world, I doe not doubt (by the helpe of God) but I may live to see the dayes (if Marchants have their due encouragement) that the wisedome, Majestie, and Honour of our King, shall be spread and enlarged to the ends of the world, our Navigations mightily encreased, and his Majesties customes more then trebled.

And as for the third part, the releeving our men already planted, to preserve both them and our former adventures, I shall not neede to say much, the necessitie is so apparent, that I hope no Adventurer will be wanting therein.

Our Saviour Christ resembles them that give over in their best duties, to foolish builders, that having laid the foundation, doe gravell themselves in the midde way and so become ridiculous: It had beene extreame madness in the Jewes (when having sent to spy the land that flowed with milke and honey, and ten for two returned backe with tydings of impossibilitie to enter and prevaile,) if then they had retyred and lost the land of promise: No doubt, the Devill that envied then that enterprise of theirs, doth now the like in ours, and we must make accompt, and look to bee encountered with many discouragements, partly by our friends and neighbours, (such as we use to say) will neither goe to Church nor tarrie at home, as also (which is no new thing) even by such as have been sent to spy the land, one while objecting the charge will be great, the businesse long, and the gaines nothing, and besides the Anakimes that dwell in the mountaines, will come and pull us out by the eares, with such like fooleries I know not what.

But wee must be prepared with Caleb and Josua (so highly commended) to oppose an extraordinarie zeale against the detractings of such, to rescue our enterprize from malicious ignorance, and to still their murmurings with reproofe, for though in ordinarie and common occasions, it be our duetie to be carried with ordinarie patience, meekness and humilitie, yet to shew an excellent spirit, when the cause is worth it, and in such a case as this, requiring passing resolution: It is but our weaknesse to stumble at strawes, and a basenesse to gnaw upon every bone that is cast in our way, which wee may observe by those noble dogges of Albania presented to king Alexander, whose natures contemned to encounter or prey upon seely beasts of no valour, but with an overflowing courage flying upon the Lion and the Tyger, did then declare their vertue.

And now it followes, how it can be good for this Commonwealth: which is likewise most apparant many waies. First, if we consider what strength of shipping may be raysed and maintained thence, in furnishing our owne wants of sundrie kindes, and the wants of other Nations too, in such needfull things arising thence which can hardly now be obtained from any other part of the world, as planck and tymber for shipping, with Deale and Wainscot, pipestaves and clabbord, with store of Sope ashes, whereof there grow the best woods to make them in great aboundance, all which we may there have, the wood for the cutting, and the Ashes for the burning, which though they be grosse commodities, yet no Marchandize is better requested, nor will sooner yeelde golde or silver in any our bordering Nations. England and Holland alone, spend in these about three hundreth thousand poundes sterling every yeare. we may transport hether or unto Hamborough, Holland, or other places, fiftie per centum better cheape, then from Prusia or Polonia, from whence they are onely now to be had, where also the woods are so spent and wasted, that from the place where the wood is cut and the ashes burnt, they are brought by land at least two hundred miles to ship. And from thence we may have Iron and Copper also in great quantitie, about which the expence and waste of woode, as also for building of Shippes, will be no hurt, but great service to that countrey; the great superfluity whereof, the continuall cutting downe, in manie hundred yeares, will not be able to overcome, whereby will likewise grow a greater benefite to this land, in preserving our woodes and tymber at home, so infinitely and without measure, upon these occasions cutte downe, and falne to such a sicknesse and wasting consumption, as all the physick in England cannot cure.

We doubt not but to make there in few yeares store of good wines, as any from the Canaries, by replanting and making tame the Vines that naturally grow there in great abundance, onely send men of skill to doe it, and Coopers to make caskes, and hoopes for that and all other uses, for which there is woode enough at hand.

There are Silke-wormes, and plenty of Mulberie-trees, whereby Ladies, Gentlewomen and little children, (beeing set in the way to doe it) may bee all imploied with pleasure, in making Silke, comparable to that of Persia, Turkey, or any other. We may bring from thence Sturgion, Caviare, and new land-fish of the best. There grows hempe for Cordage, an excellent commoditie, and flaxe for linnen cloth; which beeing sowen and well manured, in such a clymate and fertile soyle, will make great benefite, and will put downe that of other countries.

And for the making of Pitch, Tarre, Turpentine, Sope-ashes, Deale, Wainscott, and such like, wee have alreadie provided and sent thither skillfull workemen from forraine parts, which may teach and set ours in the way, whereby we may set many thousands a worke, in these such like services.

For as I tolde you before, there must be Art and industry with our helps and means extended, with a little pacience to bring these things to passe, wee must not looke to reape with joy, except we sow in tears: The aboundance of King Solomons golde and silver, did not raine from heaven upon the heads of his subjects: but heavenly providence blessed his Navigations and publike affayres, the chiefe meanes of their wealth.

Experience hath lately taught us by some of our neighbour Provinces, how exceedingly it mounts the State of a Commonwealth, to put forth Navigation (if it were possible) into all parts and corners of the world, to furnish our owne wants, and also to supply from one kingdome to another, such severall needfull things, as for want of shipping and other meanes they cannot furnish of themselves, for this will raise experience, and men of skill, as also strength at Sea and land, with honour, wealth, and riches, returning still to the heads and fountaines, from whence their first occasions grew.

Wee may but looke a little backe, and wee shall see what a novice our nation was within these sixscore yeeres, in case of forraine trade, not knowing whence to fetch, nor which way to transport, but onely to some marte or staple towne, within two daies sailing, and that was counted so great a matter then, that therefore they were called Marchant adventurers, and the great Hulkes of Italy, which in those daies brought spices Corants and such like, and landes at Southampton, (the Storehouse then for Marchandize) are Chronicled for wonders in our English Stories

for indeede we knew no better then, but were content (as babes) with Easterlings on the one hand and Lumbards on the other, which were continuall Liegers in Loundon, and fed us as they listed.

And take this ever as a rule, that Domesticke Marchandizing brings forth but poore effects in a Commonwealth, whereof I needed not have shewed example further then our owne doores.

What was the case of England before the golden daies of Queene Elizabeth at whose comming to the crowne, the state of Marchants was so poore and meane, that renting out her customes in wardes, but at a very lowe rate, yet it brought the farmer upon his knees.

A man that markes the difference, and shall compare those times and these together, shall thinke it were impossible, (unlesse his knowledge taught him otherwise) that the dayes and raigne of one Elizabeth, whose hand was ever lending to distressed neighbour Princes, and her sword unsheathed continually, repulsing forraine enemies, should yet releeve and raise the state of her customes, the strength of her Navie, and the condition of her people, every way seven fold to that they were before, onely by encouraging the royall trade of Marchandize, as wee see it this day apparant: Let God have the honour, and blessed be her memory, and the memoriall of those managers of State in her daies, for their worthy counsells, many of which though they now sleepe, and rest with their Soveraigne in peace, yet some doe still remaine, and doe succeede in place, where long may they stand and their seede after them, like the Pillars and Worthies of King David, to shielde the head and honour of our Solomon, and still to uphold and enlarge our happinesse for ever: and this I am driven to speake and mention by the way, where I meant it not in regard of some which upon a disaster beginne to waxe weary of all, discouraging themselves and others, from this and all other forraine adventures: to let them know, that each thing hath encrease, from whence it had beginning: and to put our selves in mind, that wee faile not in furthering those causes that bring forth such effects.

Another instance might be shewed in one particular, which taxeth very much our English Nation, and all the subjects of our soveraigne King, that enjoying such plentie of woodlands, and fruitfull soiles, within England, Scotland, Ireland

and Wales: yet our want of industry to bee such, that Netherlanders which have not a stick of wood growing nor any land for sowing, should surpasse and goe beyond us in continuall plenty of corne and shipping, me thinks the reformation hereof should find more favour at our hands, that in such points of civil pollicie, no people of lesser meanes should cast us so behinde, and each well minded man should lend his helpe to heale and cure such staines and scarres in the face of our state, as being viewed and wayed well, may very well make us blush.

And now to our present businesse in hand, which so many stumble at, in regard of the continuall charge, I would have them know, that it cannot be great nor long, as the businesse may be handled. Two things are expecially required herein, people to make the plantation, and money to furnish our present provisions and shippings now in hand: For the first wee neede not doubt, our land abounding with swarmes of idle persons, which having no meanes of labour to releeve their misery, doe likewise swarme in lewd and naughtie practises, so that if wee seeke not some waies for their forreine employment, wee must provide shortly more prisons and corrections for their bad conditions, for it fares with populous common weales, as with plants and trees that bee too frolicke, which not able to sustaine and feede their multitude of branches, doe admit an engrafting of their buds and sciences into some other soile, accounting it a benefite for preservation of their kind, and a disburdening their stocke of those superfluous twigs that suck away their nourishment. And we shall find that hence it was, the Gothes and Vandalles with other barbarous nations, seeing an overflowing of their multitudes at home, did therefore send their Armies out as raging floods at sundrie times, to cover the faces of Spain, Italy and other Provinces, to free their owne from pestering: so that you see it no new thing, but most profitable for our State, to rid our multitudes of such as lie at home, pestering the land with pestilence and penury, and infecting one another wich vice and villanie, worse then the plague it selfe: whose very miseries drives many of them, by meanes to be cutte off, as bad and wicked members, or else both them and theirs to be releeved at the common charge of others.

Yet I doe not meane, that none but such unsound members, and such poore as want their bread, are fittest for this imployment: for we intend to have of every trade and profession, both honest, wise and painefull men, whereof our land and Citie is able to spare, and furnish many (as we had experience in our last sending thither) which will be glad to goe, and plant themselves so happily, and their children after them, to holde and keepe conformitie, with the lawes, language and religion of England for ever.

Touching which, I doe earnestly admonish you to beware and shunne three kindes of people: the first, a most vile minded sort, and for the most part badde members of this Citie, by some meanes shaken out of their honest courses, and now shifting by their wittes, will be allwaies devising some unhappines to wrong the plantation: such as daily beate their braines, and seeke by lying suggestions, under colour of good pretence to the Common-wealth to infringe our auncient liberties, and would (if they were not mette withall and curbed by authoritie) make a monopoly to themselves, of each thing after other, belonging to the freedome of every mans profession, the very wrack of Merchandizing.

The second sort are papists, professed or Recusant of which I would not one, seasoned with the least taint of that leaven, to be setled in our plantation, nor in any part of that country, but if once perceived, such a one, weede him out, and ship him home for England, for they will ever be plotting and conspiring, to root you out if they can, howsoever they sweare, flatter, and equivocate, beleeve them not: keepe onely these two examples in minde.

Watson the Seminarie priest in his printed Quodlibets: he, of all other men protesteth the greatest truth and fidelity to his Prince and countrey; objecting all the bloudy plottes and treasons, to have come from the combination of Jesuits, and from Parsons, that Arch-Atheist in chiefe, but as for himselfe, hee wished no longer to live and breath, then the thoughts of his hart should be true and upright to his Prince and Countrey: Notwithstanding, this Watson was the very first wretch of all other, that had his hand in treason against our King, and reapt his reward according to his wish.

The other example is a Popish Pamphlet, called the Lay Catholikes Petition, offered to his Majestie for tolleration of Popery, protesting likewise their fidelitie and unfained love to his Majestie, offering to be bound life for life with good suerties for their loyail behaviour: happy men had we been to have taken their bonds, (no doubt) for even at that instant, when this petition was exhibiting, the chiefe heads of those lay Catholikes, were then labouring with all their might to undermine the Parliament house, to shake the Pillers, and the whole frame of the Kingdome to shivers.

And which is more, there is newly dispersed an idle discourse against an honorable peasonage of this Land, by a Papist, that termes himselfe a Catholike Divine, defending Garnet the Popish Priest; saying, there was nothing against him at his arraignement, but onely his acquaintance with the Powder-plotte: which (saith hee) beeing revealed unto him in auricular confession, hee might not therefore by the lawe and righte of Catholike religion, disclose nor make it knowne.

How like you these Catholikes and this divinitie? If they grow so bold and desperate in a mighty settled State, howe much more dangerous in the birth and infancie of yours? Therefore if you will live and prosper, harbor not this viperous broode in your bosome, which will eat out and consume the wombe of their mother.

The third sort to avoide, are evill affected Magistrates, a plague that God himselfe complaines of by the Prophet Isaiah: O my people, they that leade thee, cause thee to erre. Touching which, I am no way able to speake enough, for herein lies the very life of all: let no partialitie preferre them, unless they be werthy men; if they be Papists or Popishly minded; if prophane Atheists, contemning God and his word, turning religion to policy, unchaste, idle, ambitious, proud and tyrannous, forgetting their allegiance to their King, and duety to their countrey, neglecting their commission of imployment, advancing vilde and vitious persons like themselves, and basely using those that are vertuous, godly, and well affected: then looke for no blessing nor assistance of God, but misery, crosses, and confusions in all wee take in hand: but in men of knowledge, and religious education, there is ever found true humilite, temperance and justice, joyned with confidence, valour and noble courage, such as was in Moses the man of God; whose justice exceeded, and courage was incomparable, and yet the meekest man that went upon the earth: tenne of such will chase an hundred: no adversitie can make them despayre, their provident care will

ever be to repulse injuries, and represse the insolent, to encourage the paineful and best minded, to employ the sole to some honest labours, and to releeve with mercy and commiseration, the most feeble, weakest and meanest member.

And as for the generall sort that shall goe to bee planters, bee they never so poore, so they be honest, and painefull, the place will make them rich: all kinde of Artificers wee must first imploy, are Carpenters, Ship-wrights, Masons, Sawyers, Brickemakers, Bricklayers, Plowmen, Sowers, Planters, Fishermen, Coopers, Smiths, Mettelmen, Taylers, Turners, and such like, to make and fitte all necessaries, for comfort and use of the Colony, and for such as are of no trades (if they bee industrious) they shall have there imployment enough, for there is a world of means to set many thousands a worke, partly in such things as I mentioned before, and many other profitable workes, for no man must live idle there.

And by this imploiment, we may happily stop the course of those Irregular youths of no religion, that daily run from us to Rome and Rhemes for exhibition, which after a little hammering and trayning there by Parsons and his Impes, they become pliable for the impression of any villany whatsoever, as appeares by their positions and practises at home and abroad.

And hereby our Marriners shall not lie idle, nor our Owners sell their ships for want of freight: you know how many good ships are daily solde, and made away to forreine nations: how many men for want of imploiment, betake themselves to Tunis, Spaine and Florence, and to serve in courses not warrantable, which would better beseeme, our owne walles and borders to bee spread with such branches, that their native countrey, and not forreine Princes, might reape their fruit, as being both exquisite Navigators, and resolute men for service, as any the world affords.

Wee intend to plant there (God willing) great plentie of Sugar Canes, for which the soyle and clymate is very apt and fit; also Linseed, and Rapeseeds to make Oiles, which because the soyle is strong and cheape, may there be sowed and the oyle made to great benefite: wee must plant also Orenges, Limons, Almonds, Anniseeds, Rice, Cummin, Cotton wool, Carowey seeds, Ginger, Madder, Olives, Oris, Sumacke, and many such like, which I cannot now name, all very good

Marchandize, and will there grow and increase, as well as in Italy or any other part of the streights, whence we fetch them now. And in searching the land there is undoubted hope of finding Cochinell, the plant of rich Indico, Graine-berries, Beaver Hydes, Pearles, rich Treasure, and the South sea, leading to China, with many other benefites which our day-light will discover.

But of all other things, that God hath denied that countrie, there is want of Sheepe to make woollen cloth, and this want of cloth, must alwaies bee supplied from England, whereby when the Colony is thorowly increased, and the Indians brought to our Civilitie (as they will in short time) it will cause a mighty vent of English clothes, a great benefit to our Nation, and raising againe of that auncient trade of clothing, so much decayed in England: whose lifting up againe (me thinkes I see apparantly approaching,) by the good disposi-tions of our best sort of Citizens, who willingly engage themselves to undertake all new discov-eries, as into this of the West, and by the North West to find out China. And unto the East beyond the Cape, into the Red Sea, the gulfe of Persia, the streights of Sunda, and among all the Kings of India, for the good and honour of our Nation: Which calles to minde, a blind Prophesie in one of the Sibells, that before the ende of the world there shall be a discoverie of all Nations: which shall come to bee knowne and acquainted to-gether, as one neighbour with another, which since the confusion of tongues have lyen obscure and hid.

But however that bee, yet these good mindes and resolutions, doe serve for imitation to others, and doe deserve assuredly the best encourage-ment, whereby wee shall not still betake our selves to small and little Shipping (as we dayly do beginne,) but shall reare againe such Marchants Shippes both tall and stout, as no forreine Sayle that swimmes shall make them vaile or stoope: whereby to make this little Northerne corner of the world, to be in short time the richest Store-house and Staple for marchandize in all Europe.

The second thing to make this Plantation is money, to be raised among the adventurers, wherein the sooner and more deeply men engage themselves, their charge will be the shorter, and their gaine the greater, as in this last point which I have to speake for the good of each particular Adventurer, I will make it plaine.

First you shall understand, that his Majestie hath granted us an enlargement of our Charter, with many ample priviledges, wherein we have Knights and Gentlemen of good place: Named for the Kings counsell of Virginia to governe us: As also every Planter and Adventurer shall be in-serted in the Patent by mane. This ground being laide, wee purpose presently to make supply of Men, Women and Children (so many as we can) to make the Plantation. Wee call those Planters that goe in their persons to dwell there: And those Adventurers that adventure their money and go not in person, and both doe make the members of one Colonie. We do account twelve pound ten shillings to be a single share adventured. Every ordinary man or woman, if they will goe and dwell there, and every childe above tenne yeares, that shall be carried thither to remaine, shall be allowed for each of their persons a single share, as if they had adventured twelve pound ten shillings in money. Everie extraordinarie man, as Divines, Governors, Ministers of State and Justice, Knights, Gentlemen, Physitions, and such as be men of worth for special services, are all to goe as planters, and to execute their several functions in the Colonie, and are to be maintained at the common charge, and are to receive their Divident (as others doe) at seven yeares end, and they are to be agreed with all before they goe, and to be rated by the Councell, according to the value of their persons: which shall be set downe and Reg-istred in a booke, that it may alwaies appeare what people have gone to the Plantaion, at what time they went and how their persons were valued: And likewise, if any that goe to bee planters will lay downe money to the Treasurer, it shall be also registred and their shares inlarged accord-ingly be it for more or lesse. All charges of setling and maintaining the Plantation, and of making supplies, shall be borne in a joint stock of the adventurers for seven yeares after the date of our new enlargement: during which time there shall be no adventure, nor goods returned in private from thence, neytheir by Master, Marriner, Planter, nor Passenger, they shall be restrained by bond and search, that as we supplie from hence to the Planters at our owne charge all necessaries for food and apparel, for fortifying and building of houses in a joynt stock, so they are also to returne from thence the encrease and fruits of their labours, for the use and advancement of the same joynt stocke, till the end of seven yeares: at which time wee purpose (God willing) to make a division by Commissioners appointed, of all the lands granted unto us by his Majestie, to every of the Colonie, according to each mans severall adventure, agreeing with our Register booke, which wee doubt not will bee for every share of twelve pound tenne shillings, five hundred acres at least. Now if any thinke that wee shall bee tyed to a continuall charge, of making new supplies for seven yeares, let them conceive thus much, that if we doe it thorowly at the first, by engaging our selves at once, in furnishing many men and other meanes: assuredly after the second yeare, the returnes from thence will be able with an over-plus, to make supplies at large, so that our purses shall be freed, and the over-plus of stock will also grow to greatness, which stock is also (as the land) to be divided equally at seven yeares end or sooner, or so often as the company shall thinke fit for the greatness of it, to make a Divident.

And as by this wee shall be soone freed from charge and expence, so there grows a greater benefit to the planters (by bestowing their labours cheerfully) to make returne of stocke, for hereby the sooner they freeing us from disbursements, the more our shares and portions will be lessened in the Divident of Stocke and land at seven yeeres end, whereby the lesse comming to us, the more will be to them, so that heere is no discouragement any way, if men will be capable to doe themselves good. But if we will be so wise to linger, and lie in the winde, to heare what newes, to bring in our stocke next yeare, and when we are behinde for foure or five Adventures, we come dropping in with one or two and still runne in arrerages for twice so much: (For I know many that would bring in stocke amongst us, but they lie out to see what successe first: and upon such like termes.) Is this Gentleman-like, or Marchant-like, in truth it is paultry, and such as would bring all to naught, if we should bee so minded too, and I tell you true, our single shares will make but a hungry plantation, if we doe not at the least double them now: and therefore I urge it the more, for that the very life of all is now in the beginning by making our supplies thoroughly, and thence will our gaines arise both sooner and certain. Yet I grant that others may come in hereafter at any time, eyther to adventure his person or money, or both, but if there be spent

one yeere of the seven before he comes in, or hee that comes in with the first shall notwithstanding bee a yeare behinde in supplies, they shall be both alike shortened in a seventh part of the Divident both of stocke and lands, and if two yeeres behinde, then shortened two sevenths, and if but six moneths, yet a fourteenth part, for every man is Registred according to the time, his money or person beganne to adventure, or made supply, so that they which come late, get not the start of those that bore the first brunt of the business, and this will neither advantage him that withholds, nor hinder him that is forward, for whatsoever falles from him that is slack, will be found of him that supplies in due time. But every man that comes in now in the first of these seven yeeres and shall afterwards upon all occasions perform in due time, every twelve pound tenne shillings so brought in shall bee accounted an entire single share, and shall receive accordingly without a-bridgement, as it had beene brought in, when the enterprise first beganne and not otherwise.

And as for the divisions of landes at seven yeeres ende which (some may object) will be little worth, and unequally divided: let them understand, that no man shall have his lot entirely in one place, to be all of the best, or all of the worst, but each man shall have proportionably to his adventures, in three or foure distinct differences, that may bee made in the goodnesse or badnesse of the groundes by Commissioners equally chosen by the Adventurers heere, and the Planters there; and as for the value and little worth now, of those grounds in Virginia, we know that in England within these thirty or fortie yeeres, the yeerely rent of those grounds (in many places) were not worth five shillings, that now do goe for fourtie and more.

And howsoever those grounds in Virginia are now but little worth indeede, yet time and meanes will make them better, considering how they passe our grounds in England, both in regard of the soile and clymate, fitte for many precious uses: And also in how many severall places we purpose to plant our Colony, and not to bestow our costs upon James-towne onely, and upon the grounds lying thereabout, and to let all the rest lie barren: for seeing his Majestie hath graunted to our Colony as much circuite of ground as all England almost, we purpose (God willing) if wee may be supplied with sufficient meanes, to settle out of hand, sixe or seven plantations more, all upon, or neare our main-river, as capitall townes, twenty myles each from other, and every plantation shall manure and husband the lands and grounds lying neere unto it, and allotted for the circuite thereof, and shall all endevour for a joynt stocke, and shall be still supplied from hence with more money and provisions, and against any publike injury shall be ready to unite, and joyne themselves together. And by this meanes wee shall come to have our Divident in landes of worth and well manured, which will be eyther bought or rented of us at a good value by the planters, or by such as intend hereafter to inhabite there, as also by these several plantations (which happily one place better fitting then another) wee shall bring forth more severall sorts of Marchandize, and be also better fortified: and besides the Planters will be in such hope to have their owne shares and habitations in those lands, which they have so husbanded, that it will cause contending and emulation among them, which shall bring foorth the most profitable and beneficiall fruites for the joynt stocke.

Whereby undoubtedly, wee shall be soone freed from further expence, our gaines will grow, and our stocke encrease, we shall fell our tymber, saw our planck, and quickly make good shipping there, and shall returne from thence with good imployment, an hundred saile of good shippes yearely, all which good and much more, wee shall withstand and bring our selves into a laborinth, if wee pinch and spare our purses now: therefore not to holde you longer with many wordes, (being neere Exchange time as I take it) remember what I have said in proving my proposition, and take my conclusion in a word or two.

Seeing our provocations are so many, our cause and title good, avaunt all idle oracles that seeke to bar us: The wisedome of the wisest saith in these cases. Whatsoever thy hand shall find to doe, do it with all thy might.

Our forefathers not looking out in time, lost the prime and fairest proffer of the greatest wealth in the world, and wee taxe their omission for it, yet now it falles out, that wee their children are tryed in the like, there being yet an excellent portion left, and by Divine providence offered to our choice, which (seeing we have armes to embrace,) let it not be accounted hereafter, As a prize in the hands of fooles, that had no hearts to use it.

The honour of our nation is now very great by his Majesties meanes, and wee his subjects cannot enlarge and uphold it by gazing on, and talking what hath beene done, but by doing that good, which may bee commended hereafter, if we sitte still and let slip occasions, we shall gather rust, and doe unfeather our owne wings, committing the folly of the wise Romanes heerein, that in time of their glory, flowing with the conquestes and spoiles of the world, and having gotten the Goddesse Victoria to Rome, they clipt her wings, and set her up among their Gods, that shee might take her flight no more, as she had formerly done from the Gretians and others, and so effeminating their valour with idlenesse and security, it brought confusion and ruine to their state.

Let not such a prize of hopefull events, so lately purchased by the hazard of our valiant men, in the deepe Seas of forreine dangers, now perish in the Haven by our neglect, the lives of our friends already planted, and of those noble Knights and Gentlemen that entend to goe shortly, must lie at our mercy to be releeved and supplied by us, or to be made a prey unto others, (though wee feare not the subjects of any Prince in amity, that they will offer wrong unto us:) And howsoever wee heare tales and rumours of this and that, yet be not dismaid, for I tell you, if we finde that any miscreants have wronged, or goe about to hurt our few hundreds there, we shall be ready to right it againe with many thousands, like the giant Anteus, whose often foiles renued his strength the more.

And consider well that great worke of freeing the poore Indians from the devourer, a compassion that every good man (but passing by) would shew unto a beast: their children when they come to be saved, will blesse the day when first their fathers saw your faces.

If those undaunted English and Scottish Captaines that so often ventured their lives, and spilt their blood, to re-conquer Palestina from the Turks and Sarazens, had seen the gappe so open in their daies, and the way leading to so many goodly purchases, certainely it had not now beene left for us to doe. How strange a thing is this that all the States of Europe have beene a sleepe so long? That for an hundred yeares and more, the wealth and riches of the East and West should runne no other current but into one coffer, so long till the running over, spread it selfe abundantly among a factious crew of new created Friers, and that to no more speciall end, then with instigating bloody plots to pierce the heart of a Christian State and true Religion.

It is long since I read in a little treatise, made by Frith, an English Martyre, an excellent foretelling touching the happinesse of these Northerne Ilands, and of great wonders that should be wrought by Scots and English, before the comming of Christ, but I have almost forgotten, and cannot readily call it to minde as I would, and therefore I omitte it now, Protesting unto you, it would be my griefe and sorrow, to be exempted from the company of so many honourable minded men, and from this enterprise, tending to so many good endes, and then which, I truely thinke this day, there is not a worke of more excellent hope under the Sun, and farre excelling (all circumstances wayed) those Noble deedes of Alexander, Hercules, and those heathen Monarks, for which they were deemed Gods among their posterity.

And so I leave it to your consideration, with a memorable note of Thomas Lord Howard, Earle of Surry, when K. Henry the eight, with his Nobles at Dover tooke shipping for Turwin and Turney, and bidding the said Earle farewell, whom he made Governour in his absence; the Story sayth the Nobleman wept, and tooke his leave with teares, an admirable good nature in a valiant minde, greeving to be left behinde his Prince and Peeres in such an honourble service.

808. 1610. *A true declaration of the state of Virginia.*

The official printed propaganda of the Virginia Company in 1609 had not been of a very high quality, but when reports of disaster grew over the years 1609–1610, the company considered that it must make a more literate, informed, and impassioned plea to the community not to abandon the colony. Above all it did this in the longish tract, A true declaration of the estate of the colonie in Virginia, with a confutation of such scandalous reports as have tended to the disgrace of so worthy an enterprise. Published by advise and direction of the Councell of Virginia *(London,*

for William Barret, 1610). The tract met many of their requirements, even if its academic wrappings must have been rather too heavy for some. However, it is the most distinguished piece of propaganda for the colony and its best apologia. It is, therefore, given as an example. Closely linked with it in time and content, although the form was simpler and the length less, was A true and summarie declaration of the purpose and end of the plantation begun in Virginia *(London, 1610).*

A true declaration *was reprinted from the original edition in P. Force,* Tracts, *4 vols., III (Washington, 1836–1840), no. 1.*

There is a great distance, betwixt the vulgar opinion of men, and the judicious apprehension of wise men. Opinion is as blind Ordipus, who could see nothing, but would heare all things, Hinc aucupari verba rumoris vagi, to hawke after the winged report of a vagabond rumor. But judgement, is as Salomon in his throne, able by the spirit of wisedome, to discerne betwixt contesting truth, and falshood: neither depending on the popular breath of fame, which is ever partiall, nor upon the event of good designes, which are ever casuall. These two commanders of our affections, have divided the universall spirits of our land, whilst (in the honorable enterprise for plantation in Virginia) some, are carried away with the tide of vulgar opinion, and others, are encouraged, by the principles of religion, and reason. But because, it is for hawkes and not for men, to build their nests in aires, and because the honor and prosperity of this so noble an action, is eclipsed by the interposition of clamorous & tragicall narrations: the compiler of this relation endevoureth to wash away those spots, which foule mouths (to justifie their owne disloialty) have cast upon so fruitfull, so fertile, and so excellent a country. Wherein he professeth, that he will relate nothing (concerning Virginia) but what he hath from the secrets of the judiciall councell of Virginia, from the letters of the Lord La Ware, from the mouth of Sir Thomas Gates, whose wisdomes (he conceiveth) are not so shallow, as easily to be deceived of others, nor consciences so wretched, as by pretences to deceive others.

But when a matter of such consequence, is not to be shufled over with supine negligence, and when no man raiseth a faire building, that laith not a firme foundation, it will not be impertinent, to dig a little deeper, that we may build a great deale higher: and from the universall policie of all civill states (in replenishing the world with colonies of domesticall subjects) to derive this wisedome to our populous state and country.

Colonies.

That which Origen said of Christs actions in vertues morall, holdeth proportion with Gods actions in government politicall, Dei facta, sunt nostra præcepta, Gods actions, are our instructions: who (in the eleventh of Genesis) turned the greatest cursing, into the greatest blessing, and by confusion of tongues, kept them from confusion of states; scattering those cloven people, into as many colonies over the face of the earth, as there are diversities of languages in the earth. Now if Tertullians rule be true, Omne genus ab origine censendum that every action is most beutifull in the originall. Can there be a better beginning then from God, whose wisedome is not questioned, and whose footsteps in all succeeding ages have beene followed. Search the records of divine truth, and humane monuments of state, you shall find, Salmanasar transporting the Babilonians, and other Gentiles, to Samaria: and replenishing with the captives of Israell, the dispeopled confines of Media.

You shall find that 140. yeeres after the destruction of Troy, the Ionian colony, was carried from Greece, to Asia: by which that famous City of Ephesus was first builded, and inhabited. You shall find the Egiptians, planted Babilon, Argos, and Athens. The Phenicians first inhabiting Carthage, Utica, and Thebes. That Timolcon and the city of Corinth, at one time repeopled Sicilie, with 10000. soules. That the Romans deduced 53. colonies out of the City of Rome into the wombe of Italy. That Bremius an Englishman by birth, but sonne in law to the King of France, with an equall third part of the kingdome, entred into the hart of Italy, gave the prime sacke to the City of Rome, and diverted from thence to Gallogræcia, whose offspring possesse that land unto this day.

That the Admirall of France, among all the feares and discouragements of civill wars, never gave over the project of plantation in Florida.

Which heroicall actions, have not beene undertaken by so mighty states and Princes, upon triviall and vulgar motives, when by these courses that first blessing (of crescite and multiplicamini, increase and multiplie) hath beene sanctified: the meaner sorte have beene provided: the matter of plagues, famine and sedition, hath beene exhausted: the fennes of a state politique were drained: the enemies of their peace were bridled: the revenues of their treasury were augmented: and the limites of their dominions were enlarged.

Which divine, humane, externall, and domesticall, examples, doe shine before us, as a Pharaoes towre, that wee should not make shipwracke of our intentions, concerning Virginia.

Blacke envie, and pale feare, being not able to produce any arguments, why that should bee lawfull for France, which is (in us) unlawfull: that which to Rome was possible, (to us) is impossible: that which to others is honourable, and profitable, (in us) should bee traduced, as incommodious, base, and contemptible: wherefore under these three heads of lawfulnesse, possibility, and commoditie, will I marshall all those reasons, which may resolve the religious, encourage the personall, confirme the noble, and satisfie the timorous adventurer.

Three Heads, Lawfull, Possible, Profitable.

First, if it bee unlawfull: it must be so, either in respect of the law of God, or in regard of the lawe of man. If in respect of Gods lawe, (considering our primarie end is to plant religion, our secondarie and subalternate ends are for the honour and profit of our nation) I demand a resolution of this plaine question: whether it bee not a determinated truth, that the Gospell should bee preached, to all the world, before the end of the world? If, it must bee preached, (as heaven and earth must passe awaie, but Gods word shall not pass awaie) then must it bee preached, one of these three waies: Either meerly Apostolically, without the helpe of man, (without so much as a staffe) or meerely imperiallie, when a Prince, hath conquered their bodies, that the Preachers may feede their soules; Or mixtly, by discoverie, and trade or marchants; where all temporall meanes are used for defence, and security, but none for offence, or crueltie. For the first (to preach Apostolicallie) it is simplie impossible: except wee had the gift of tongues, that everie nation might heare the word of God in their owne language; or the guift of miracles, that it might be confirmed, with wonders from heaven; which two beeing ceased, questionlesse the identicall commission of the Apostles is expired: Or if yet the matter bee urged, that God by fishers did convert Emperors and therefore that wee must adventure our lives without humane helpe; yet must it bee remembred, that there is no Apostolicall preaching, but where wee may expect either their conversion, or our martyrdome. But we can expect neither, not their conversion who cannot understand us, nor our martyrdome, when the people of Florida, did devoure the Preachers of the word, without speaking any word. Non quia Christiani, sed quia homines, not because they were christian men, but because they were men, wee cannot be said to be martyrs, when wee are not killed because wee are christians. And therefore the Jesuite Acosta confesseth (notwithstanding Bellarmines relation of Indian miracles) that they have no tongues, they have no signes from heaven, and they can have no martyrdome, and by consequent there is no means left of Apostolicall preaching.

For the second, to preach the Gospell to a nation conquered, and to set their soules at liberty, when we have brought their bodies to slaverie; It may be a matter sacred in the Preachers, but I know not how justifiable in the rulers. Who for their meere ambition, doe set upon it, the glosse of religion. Let the divines of Salamanca, discusse that question, how the possessor of the west Indies, first destroied, and then instructed.

The third, belongs to us, who by way of marchandizing and trade, doe buy of them the pearles of earth, and sell to them the pearles of heaven; which action, if it be unlawfull, it must proceede from one of these three grounds, either because we come to them, or trade with them, or tarrie and dwell and possesse part of their country amongst them.

Is it unlawfull because wee come to them? why is it not a dutie of christianitie, to behold the imprinted footsteps of Gods glorie, in every region under heaven? Is it not against the lawe of nations, to violate a peaceable stranger, or to denie him harbour. The Ethiopians, Egyptians, and men of China, are branded with a foule marke of sanguinarie and barbarous inhumanity, for blessing their Idols, with the bloud of strangers.

It is not unlawfull to trade with them, except Salomon shall bee condemned for sending for gold to Ophir, Abraham for making a league with Abimilech, and all christendome shall bee traduced, for having comerce with Turks and miscreants.

Finallie, it is not unlawfull, that wee possesse part of their land and dwell with them, and defend our selves from them. Partlie because there is no other, moderate, and mixt course, to bring them to conversion, but by dailie conversation, where they may see the life, and learne the language each of other.

Partlie, because there is no trust to the fidelitie of humane beasts, except a man will make a league, with Lions, Beares, and Crocodiles.

Partlie because there is roome sufficient in the land (as Sichem sometime said) for them, and us: the extent of an hundred miles, being scarce peopled with 2000. inhabitants.

Partlie, because they have violated the lawe of nations, and used our Ambassadors as Ammon did the servants of David: If in him it were a just cause to warre against the Ammonites, it is lawfull, in us, to secure our selves, against the infidels.

But chieflie because Paspehay, one of their Kings, sold unto us for copper, land to inherit and inhabite. Powhatan, their chiefe King, received voluntarilie a crown and a scepter, with a full acknowledgment of dutie and submission.

Principallie when Captaine Newport was with Powhatan at Warow a comaco hee desired him to come from James towne as a place unholesome, and to take possession of an other whole kingdome which he gave unto him. If any man alleadge, that this was done in subtlety, not that they ever meant we should possesse them, but that they might first gaine by us, and then destroy us. This makes our cause, much the juster, when God turned their subteltie, to our utilitie: giving unto us a lawfull possession, (as Pharaoe gave Goshen to Israell; or Ephron sold his cave to Abraham) and freeing us, from all impious and sinister construction. If anie man alleadge, that yet wee can possesse no farther limits, than was allotted by composition, and that fortitudo sine justitia, est iniquitatis Materia, fortitude without justice, is but the firebrand of iniquitie. Let him know that Plato defineth it, to bee no injustice, to take a sword out of the hand of a mad man; That

Austen hath allowed it, for a lawfull offensive warre, quod ulcisitur injurias that revengeth bloudie injuries. So that if just offences shall arise, it can bee no more injustice to warre against infidells, than it is when upon just occasions wee warre against Christians. And therefore I cannot see, but that these truths, will fanne away all those chaffie imputations, which anie Romish boasters (that challenge a monopolie of all conversions) will cast upon it, or any scrupulous conscience can impute unto it. Certainlie the Church of Geneva in the yeere 1555. determined in a Synode, whereof (Calvine) was president, to send Peter Richier, and William Quadrigarius, under a French Captaine to Brasilia, who although they were supplanted, by the comming of the Cardinall of Loraine, and the trecherie of their double hearted leader, yet would not the Church of Geneva, (after a Synodicall consultation) have sent their ministers to such an adventure, had not all scruples, (in their judgement) beene cleared by the light of Scripture.

When therefore, it is a sweete smelling sacrifice, to propagate the name of Jesus Christ, when the Babylonish Inchantresse (if her owne Calenders, are to bee credited) hath compassed sea, and land, to make, sixe, eight, or ten millions, of Romish proselites. When there is no other, mixt, moderate, course, to transport the Virginian soules to heaven. When there hath beene a reall concession from their rurall Emperour, that hath licensed us to negociate among them, and to possesse their countrie with them. When there is more unpeopled continent of earth, than wee and they (before the dissolution of the pillars of heaven) can overburden with multitude. When we never intend to play the Rehoboams, and to scourge them with scorpions. It is not good, to create more sinnes, then God ever censured: nor to brand that action with impietie, which God hath begun for promulgating of his glorie Nunquid ideo deforme est, quia figura mentitur? is the action therefore deformed, because a false glasse doth slander it?

Concerning the other braunch of this discourse, wherein some slie whisperers would seeme to cast an aspersion of injustice upon the action, supposing some forraine Prince to have a former interest.

Certainlie hee is but a rotten subject that quarrells the actions of his countrie, descrying a serpentine stinge under the faire leaves of pietie. And though it bee not for a theoreticall Schollar, to circumscribe the dominions of Princes, yet a few proofes from antiquitie, shall suffice to controwle ignorant or presumptuous follie.

In the yeare 1170. Madocke the sonne of Owen Guyneth Prince of Northwales (leaving the land in contention betwixt his two brethren Howell and David) sailed into the West Indies, and after a second, and a third returne, and supplie, setled himselfe in those dominions.

In the yeere 1495. John Cabot a Venetian, but the indenized subject of King Henrie the seaventh discovered the North parts of America, to Meta incognita, and so it was annexed to the Crowne of England.

As for the donation of Alexander the sixt; it is but a reciprocall clawing, when Emperors create their servants Bishops universall, and shavelings create their Lords, Emperors generall.

If the donation of Constantine were not more virtuall for Saint Peters partrimonie, wee should have neede of more purgatories, to maintaine fuell in the Popes kitchen: for if the kingdome of Christ was not on earth, what a transubstantiated power, doth the pretended Vicar of Christ claime, to dispose all the kingdomes of the earth. Petrarch recordeth a memorable historie, of Sautius brother to the King of Spaine, who was elected generall against the Saracens of Egypt, and comming to Rome for that purpose, the Bishop of Rome, made it to bee proclaimed in the Consistorie that hee bestowed the kingdome of Egypt upon Sautius. Sautius understanding this favour, (by his interpreter) commanded to proclaime the Pope, great Caleph of Baldacho: perfuming the sonne of pride, with his owne smoke.

The Pope having no more power, to make Sautius a King, then Sautius had power to make the Pope a Caleph. Let such retailers of Crownes remember, who it was that sometime saide, all these will I give thee if thou wilt fall downe, and worship me, And yet with this item that the divell pretended to give no more than he saw.

These points beeing thus defined, I come to the possibility. Against which three maine impediments are objected. First the daungerous passage by sea, secondlie the barrennesse of the countrie, thirdly the unholesomnesse of the climate: the storme that seperated the admirall from the fleete prooving the first, the famine amongst our men importing the second, the sicknesse of our men arguing the third. All which discouragements doe astonish our men with feare, as though our expences were unprofitable, when our ends are impossible.

But before I shall enter into this discourse I must crave leave to make a necessarie digression, and to justifie his reputation whose worth is of speciall regard in this plantation.

Sir Thomas Gates supposeth himselfe accused publiquelie and in print of a treeble defect.

First that hee ranne so farre Southerlie and into the Tropique, that the heat caused the infection in the ships.

Secondlie that hee gave a sealed direction, that if they were seperated by anie storme, that they should make for the Barvada in the West Indies, which direction himselfe following, it caused his shipwracke, but the other shippes, (upon better judgement) declining these instructions, arived safelie in Virginia.

Thirdlie that hee caried in one bottome all the principall Commissioners who should successivelie have governed the Colonie. Against all which imputations, hee maketh this just Apologie.

First hee confesseth that a little before they came unto the Canaries, that hee entred into consultation with Sir George Summers, Captaine Newport, and the other of chiefe regarde in the fleete, wherein it was resolved by an uniformitie of consent, to runne southerlie into the Tropique, which they did, till they came to the height of foure and twentie, but hee denieth that this course was anie cause of infection. For in the *Faulcon*, the *Blessing*, the *Lyon*, (and in the *Admirall* wherein were one hundred and fiftie soules) there was not one sicke of the pestilence nor other disease; In the other two ships the infection was somewhat hote, but they shipped the same from London; To the second hee affirmeth, that hee first gave them sealed instructions (not to bee opened till a time of storme) which directed them to the Barvada, But after when they came to the height of foure and twentie, hee countermaunded those directions by word of mouth, and assigned them, (that if they were scattered) that they should make with all speede for Virginia. Which himselfe (esteeming the price of time unvaluable) woulde have executed, had not the violent leake of the shippe hindred him, So

that the other ships safe arivall in Virginia, proceeded originallie from his advise and authoritie.

To the third, he briefly signifieth, that no other Commissioners were in his Ship, but such, (as for especiall reasons) were precisely and peremptorily appointed, by the Councell of Virginia. And thus you see, that Tacitus wisely observed two great enemies of great actions, Ignorantiam veri, & Invidiam, the ignorance of Truth, and the emulation of Vertue.

To returne therefore unto the maine channell of this discourse, and to dispell the clouds of feare, that threaten shipwracks, and sea-dangers: For we are not to extenuate the seas tempestuous violence, nor yet therefore to dispaire of Gods assisting providence. For true it is, that when Sir Thomas Gates, Sir George Summers, and Captaine Newport, were in the height of 27. and the 24. of July 1609. there arose such a storme, as if Ionas had been flying unto Tarshish: the heavens were obscured, and made an Egyptian night of three daies perpetuall horror; the women lamented; the hearts of the passengers failed; the experience of the sea Captaines was amased: the skill of the marriners was confounded: the Ship most violently leaked, and though two thousand tunne of water by pumping from Tuesday noone till Fryday noone was discharged, notwithstanding the Ship was halfe filled with water, and those which laboured to keepe others from drowning were halfe drowned themselves in labouring. But God that heard Ionas crying out of the belly of hell, he pittied the distresses of his servants; For behold, in the last period of necessitie, Sir George Summers descryed land, which was by so much the more joyfull, by how much their danger was despairefull. The Islands on which they fell were the Bermudos, a place hardly accessable, through the environing rocks and dangers: notwithstanding they were forced to runne their Ship on shoare, which through Gods providence fell betwixt two rockes, that caused her to stande firme and not immediately to be broken, God continuing his mercie unto them, that with their long Boats they transported to land before night, all their company, men, women, and children, to the number of one hundred and fiftie, they carryed to shoare all the provision of unspent and unspoyled victuals, all their furniture and tackling of the Ship, leaving nothing but bared ribs, as a pray unto the Ocean.

These Islands of the Bermudos, have ever beene accounted as an inchaunted pile of rockes, and a desert inhabitation for Divels; but all the Fairies of the rocks were but flocks of birds, and all the Divels that haunted the woods, were but heards of swine. Yea and when Acosta in his first booke of the hystories of the *Indies*, averreth, that though in the continent there were diverse beasts, and cattell, yet in the Islands of Hispaniola, Jamaica, Marguarita, and Dominica, there was not one hoofe, it increaseth the wonder, how our people in the Bermudos found such abundance of Hogs, that for nine moneths space they plentifully sufficed: and yet the number seemed not much diminished. Again, as in the great famine of Israell, God commanded Elias to flie to the brooke Cedron, and there fed him by Ravens; so God provided for our disconsolate people in the midst of the Sea by foules: but with an admirable difference: unto Elias the Ravens brought meat, unto our men the foules brought (themselves) for meate: for when they whisteled, or made any strange noyse, the foules would come and sit on their shoulders, they would suffer themselves to be taken and weighed by our men, who would make choise of the fattest and fairest, and let flie the leane and lightest. An accident, I take it, that cannot be paralleld by any Hystorie, except when God sent abundance of Quayles to feed his Israel in the barren wildernesse. Lastly they found the berries of Cedar, the Palmeto tree, the prickle peare, sufficient fish, plentie of Tortoises, and divers other kinds, which sufficed to sustaine nature. They found diversity of woods, which ministred materials for the building of two Pinaces, acoording to the direction of the three provident Governours.

Consider all these things together. At the instant of neede, they descryed land, halfe an hower more, had buried their memorial in the Sea. If they had fel by night, what expectation of light, from an uninhabited desart? they fell betwixt a laberinth of rockes, which they conceive are mouldred into the Sea, by thunder and lightning. This was not Ariadnes threed, but the direct line of Gods providence. If it had not beene so neere land, their companie or provision had perished by water: if they had not found Hogs, and foule, and fish, they had perished by famine: if there had not beene fuell, they had perished by want of fire: if there had not beene timber they could not have transported themselves to Virginia, but must have beene forgotten forever. Nimium timet qui Deo non credit, he is too impiously fearefull, that will not trust in God so powerfull.

What is there in all this tragicall Comædie that should discourage us with impossibilitie of the enterprise? when of all the Fleete, one onely Ship, by a secret leake was indangered, and yet in the gulfe of Despair, was so graciously preserved. Quæ videtur pæna, est medicina, that which we accompt a punishment of evill, is but a medicine against evill.

After nine Moneths aboarde in these Islands, on the 10th of May 1610. they imbarqued themselves in their two new built Pinaces, and after some eleven daies saile, they arrived neere point Comfort upon the coast of Virginia: where they had intelligence of so wofull miserie, as if God had onely preserved them, to communicate in an new extremitie.

From which calamitie, the other arguments of impossibilitie are framed; for if the Countrie bee barren, or the scituation contagious; as famine, and sicknesse, destroy our Nation: wee strive against the streame of reason, and make ourselves the subjects of scorne and derision. Therefore in this maine point of consequence, I will propound this plaine and simple methode; First to demonstrate that there is, and may be in Virginia a sufficient meanes (in all abundance) to sustaine the life of man; Next that the Climate is wholesome and temperate, agreeing with the constitutions of our men; Thirdly, that those extremities proceeded from accidentall and not inherent evils. Lastly, I will delineate the state of the Colony, as Sir Thomas Gates left it under the government of the honorable L. Laware: whereby it shall appeare, that all difficulties are amended, and that the State of that Countrie is sufficiently mannaged.

Corne.

To begin, with the staffe of bread. It is avowed unto mee, in writing, in the words of the Author. that hath been there, as followeth. They use to put their wheat into the ground, five cornes in one spit of earth, and two beanes with them: which wheat cornes multiplying into divers stalks, grow up twelve, or fourteene foote high: yeelding some foure, five, or six eares, on every stalke; and in every eare, some five hundred, some six hundred, some seaven hundred cornes: the two beanes, runne upon the stalkes of the wheat, as our garden pease upon stickes, which multiplie to a wonderous increase. I cannot let slip a great secret, (saith the Author) whereof I will avouch no more, then with my hands and eyes I have handled and seene, and whereof to my great comfort, I have often tasted: The wheate beeing sowen thicke, some stalkes beare eares of corne, and some (like siences in trees) beare none: but in those barren stalkes, there is as much juice as in some sugar cane, of so delicate a tast, as no fruit in England, is comparable to it; out of which Sir Ralph Lane conceived, that wee may extract sugar, in great quantity. But Sir Thomas Gates affirmeth that our men doe make cordiall drinke thereof, to their great comfort.

Pease. Fruits. Hearbs.

Besides, the naturall Pease of the Countrie returne an increase innumerable, our garden fruits, both roots, hearbes, and flowers, doe spring up speedily, all things committed to the earth, do multiply with an incredible usurie.

Beasts.

The beasts of the Countrie, as Deere, red, and fallow, do answere in multitude (people for people considered) to our proportion of Oxen, which appeareth by these experiences. First the people of the Countrie are apparelled in the skinnes of these beasts; Next, hard by the fort, two hundred in one heard have been usually observed: Further, our men have seene 4000. of these skins pyled up in one wardroabe of Powhaton; Lastly, infinite store have been presented to Captaine Newport upon sundry occurrents: such a plentie of Cattell, as all the Spaniards found not in the whole kingdome of Mexico, when all their presents were but hennes, and ginycocks, and the bread of Maize, and Cently.

There are Arocouns, and Apossouns, in shape like to pigges, shrowded in hollow roots of trees; There are Hares and Conies, and other beasts proper to the Countrie in plentifull manner.

Wildfoule.

Our transported Cattell, as Horses, Kine, Hogs, and Goats, do thrive most happily: which is confirmed by a double experiment; one, of Sir Ralph Lane, who brought Kine from the West Indian Island; the other of our Colony, who need take no other care of them, but least they should straie too farre, or be stolne from them. The Turkyes of that Countrie are great, and fat, and exceeding in plentie. The rivers from August, or September, till February, are covered with flocks of Wildfoule: as swannes, geese, ducke, mallard, teal, wigeons, hearons, bitters, curlewes, godwights, plovers, snights, dottrels, cormerants, (to use the words of Sir Thomas Gates) in such abundance as are not in all the world to be equalled.

Fruits.

The Fruits: as apples, running on the ground, in bignesse and shape of a small lemmon, in colour and tast like to a preserved Apricock: grapes and walnuts innumerable; the vines being as common as brambles, the walnut trees as the elmes in England. What should I speake of cucumbers, muske melons, pompions, potatoes, parsneps, carrets, turnups, which our gardens yeelded with little art and labour. God in this place is ever concurring with his gracious influence, if man strangle not his blessings, with carelesse negligence. It shall suffice to conclude in the words and phrase of that noble Governour, the Lo. Laware, as it is warranted to mee by the copie of his Letters sent to the Virginian Councell.

Howsoever, men have belyed both it and themselves, heretofore, yet let no rumor of the Countrie (as if in the wombe thereof lay not these elementall seeds of plenty and increase) wave any mans faire purposes, or wrest them to a declyning and falling off from the businesse.

Temperature.

For the healthinesse and temperatenesse of the Clymate, agreeing to our constitutions, much neede not be related, since in all the former written Treatises, it is expressly observed.

No man ought to judge of any Countrie by the fennes and marshes (such as is the place where James towne standeth) except we will condemne all England, for the Wilds and Hundreds of Kent and Essex. In our particular, wee have an infallible proofe of the temper of the Countrie: for of an hundred and odd, which were seated at the Falles, under the government of Captaine Francis West, and of an hundred to the Sea-Ward on the South side of the river, (in the Countrie of the Nansamunds) under the charge of Captaine John Martin; of all these two hundred, there did not so much as one man miscarrie: when in James Towne, at the same time, and in the same moneths, 100. sickned, and halfe the number died.

The like experiment was long since in the regiment of Sir Raph Lane, where, in the space of one whole yeare, not two of one hundred perished. Adde unto this the discourse of philosophie; when in that Countrie flesh will receive salt, and continue unputrified (which it will not in the West Indies) when the most delicate of all flowers, grow there as familiarly, as in the fields of Portingale, where the woods are replenished with more sweet barks, and odors, then they are in the plesantest places of Florida. How is it possible that such a virgin and temperat aire, should work such contrarie effects, but because our fort (that lyeth as a semy-Iland) is most part invironed with an ebbing and flowing salt water, the owze of which sendeth forth an unwholsome & contagious vapour? To close up this part with Sir Thomas Gates his experiment: he professeth, that in a fortnights space he recovered the health of most of them by moderat labour, whose sicknesse was bred in them by intemperate idlenes.

If any man shall accuse these reports of partiall falshood, supposing them to be but Utopian, and legendarie fables, because he cannot conceive, that plentie and famine, a temperate climate, and distempered bodies, felicities, and miseries can be reconciled together, let him now reade with judgement, but let him not judge before he hath read.

The ground of all those miseries, was the permissive providence of God, who, in the forementioned violent storme, seperated the head from the bodie, all the vitall powers of regiment being exiled with Sir Thomas Gates in those infortunate (yet fortunate) Ilands. The broken remainder of those supplies made a greater shipwrack in the continent of Virginia, by the tempest of dissention: every man overvaluing his own worth, would be a Commander: every man underprising an others value, denied to be commanded. The emulation of Cæsar and Pompey, watered the plains of Pharsaly with bloud, and distracted the sinewes of the Romane Monarchy. The dissentions of the three besieged Captains

betraied the Citie of Hierusalem to Vespasian: how much more easily might ambitious discord teare in peeces an infant Colony, where no eminent and respected magistrats had authoritie to punish presumptuous disobedience. Tacitus hath observed, that when Nero sent his old trained souldiers to Tarantum and Autium, (but without their Captains and Centurians) that they rather made a number, then a Colony: every souldier secretly glided into some neighbour Province, and forsooke their appointed places: which hatched this consequent mischiefe; the Cities were uninhabited, and the emperour was frustrated: when therefore licence, sedition, and furie, are the fruits of a headie, daring, and unruly multitude, it is no wonder that so many in our colony perished: it is a wonder, that all were not devoured. Omnis inordinatus animus sibi ipsi fit pæna, every indordinate soule becomes his owne punishment.

The next fountaine of woes was secure negligence, and improvidence, when every man sharked for his present bootie, but was altogether carelesse of succeeding penurie. Now, I demand whether Sicilia, or Sardinia (sometimes the barnes of Rome) could hope for increase without manuring? A Colony is therefore denominated, because they should be Coloni, the tillers of the earth, and stewards of fertilitie: our mutinous loiterers would not sow with providence, and therefore they reaped the fruits of too dearebought repentance. An incredible example of their idlenes, is the report of Sir Thomas Gates, who affirmeth, that after his first comming thither, he hath seen some of them eat their fish raw, rather than they would go a stones cast to fetch wood and dresse it. Dij laboribus omnia vendunt, God sels us all things for our labour, when Adam himselfe might not live in paridice without dressing the garden.

Unto idlenesse, you may joyne treasons, wrought by those unhallowed creatures that forsooke the Colony, and exposed their desolate brethren to extreame miserie. You shall know that 28. or 30. of the companie, were appointed (in the Ship called the *Swallow*) to truck for Corne with the Indians, and having obtained a great quantitie by trading, the most seditious of them, conspired together, persuaded some, & enforced others, to this barbarous project. They stole away the Ship, they made a league amongst themselves to be professed pirates, with dreames of mountaines of gold, and happy robberies: thus at one instant, they wronged the hopes, and subverted the cares of the Colony, who depending upon their returne, fore-slowed to looke out for further provision: they created the Indians our implacable enemies by some violence they had offered: they carried away the best Ship (which should have been a refuge, in extremites:) they weakned our forces, by substraction of their armes, and succours. These are that scum of men that fayling in their priacy, that beeing pinched with famine and penurie, after their wilde roving upon the Sea, when all their lawlesse hopes failed, some remained with other pirates, they met upon the Sea, the others resolved to return for England, bound themselves by mutuall oath, to agree all in one report, to discredit the land, to deplore the famyne, and to protest that this their comming awaie, proceeded from desperate necessitie: These are they, that roared out the tragicall historie of the man eating of his dead wife in Virginia; when the master of this Ship willingly confessed before 40 witnesses, that at their comming awaie, they left three moneths victuals, and all the cattell living in the Fort: sometimes they reported that they saw this horrible action, sometimes that Captaine Davies sayd so, sometimes that one Beadle the Lieutenant of Captaine Davies did relate it, varying this report into diversitie of false colours, which hold no likenesse and proportion: But to cleare all doubts, Sir Thomas Gates thus relateth the tragedie.

There was one of the companie who mortally hated his wife, and therefore secretly killed her, then cut her in pieces and hid her in divers parts of his house: when the woman was missing, the man suspected, his house searched, and parts of her mangled body were discovered, to excuse himselfe he said that his wife died, that he hid her to satisfie his hunger, and that he fed daily upon her. Upon this, his house was againe searched, where they found a good quantitie of meale, oatmeale, beanes and pease. Hee thereupon was araigned, confessed the murder, and was burned for his horrible villany.

Now shall the scandalous reports of a viperous generation, preponderate the testimonies of so worthie leaders? shall their venemous tongues, blast the reputation of an auncient & worthy Peere, who upon the ocular certainty of future blessings, hath protested in his Letters, that he will sacrifice himselfe for his Countrie in this service, if he may be seconded; and if the company doe give it over he will yet lay all his fortunes upon the prosecution of the plantation? shall sworne lyes, and combined oathes, so far priviledge trechery, and piracy as to rob us of our hopes, & to quell our noble resolutions? God forbid: Qui in mendacio confidit, cito diffidit, a lyers confidence, is but a blazing diffidence.

Unto Treasons, you may joyne covetousnesse in the Mariners, who for their private lucre partly imbezled the provisions, partly prevented our trade with the Indians, making the matches in the night, and forestalling our market in the day: whereby the Virginians were glutted with our trifles, and inhaunced the prices of their Corne and Victuall. That Copper which before would have provided a bushell, would not now obtaine so much as a pottle: Non habet eventus sordida præda bonos, the consequent of sordid gaine is untimely wretchednesse.

Joyne unto these an other evill: there is great store of Fish in the river, especially of Sturgeon; but our men provided no more of them, then for present necessitie, not barrelling up any store against that season the Sturgeon returned to the sea. And not to dissemble their folly, they suffered fourteene nets (which was all they had) to rot and spoile, which by orderly drying and mending might have been preserved: but being lost, all help of fishing perished. Quanto majora timentur dispendia, tanto promptior debet esse cautela, fundamentall losses that cannot be repealed, ought with the greatest caution to be prevented.

The state of the Colony, by these accidents began to find a sensible declyning: which Powhatan (as a greedy Vulture) observing, and boyling with a desire of revenge, he invited Captaine Ratclife, and about thirty others to trade for Corne, and under the colour of fairest friendship, he brought them within the compasse of his ambush, whereby they were cruelly murthered, and massacred. For upon confidence of his fidelitie, they went one and one into severall houses, which caused their severall destructions, when if but any sixe had remained together, they would have been a bulwarke for the generall preservation. After this, Powhatan in the night cut off some of our boats, he drave away all the Deere into the farther part of the Countrie, hee and his people destroyed our Hogs, (to the number of about sixe hundred) he sent none of his Indians to trade with us, but laicd secret ambushes in the woods, that if one or two dropped out of the fort alone, they were indaungered.

Cast up this reckoning together: want of government, store of idlenesse, their expectations frustrated by the Traitors, their market spoyled by the Mariners, our nets broken, the deere chased, our boats lost, our hogs killed, our trade with the Indians forbidden, some of our men fled, some murthered, and most by drinking of the brackish water of James fort weakened, and indaungered, famyne and sicknesse by all these meanes increased, here at home the monies came in so slowly, that the Lo. Laware could not be dispatched, till the Colony was worne and spent with difficulties: Above all, having neither Ruler, nor Preacher, they neither feared God nor man, which provoked the wrath of the Lord of Hosts, and pulled downe his judgements upon them. Discite justitiam moniti. Now, (whether it were that God in mercie to us would weede out these ranke hemlockes; or whether in judgement to them he would scourge their impieties; or whether in wisedome he would trie our patience, Ut magna magnè desideremus, that wee may beg great blessings earnestly) our hope is that our Sunne shall not set in a cloude, since this violent storme is dispersed, since all necessarie things are provided, an absolute and powerfull government is setled, as by this insuing relation shall be described.

When Sir Thomas Gates arrived in Virginia, the strange and unexpected condition wherein he found the Colony, gave him to understand, how never was there more neede of all the powers of judgement, then at this present; it being now his charge, both to save such as he found so forlorne and wretched, as to reddeme himselfe and his from falling into the like calamities. All which considered, he entred into consultation with Sir George Summers, and Captaine Newport, and the Gentlemen and councell of the former government. They examined first their store, which after two cakes a day to a man, would hold out but sixteene dayes, (it being five moneths betwixt the stealing away of the *Swallow*, and his landing) the Corne of the Indians but newly sowed, not an eye of Sturgeon, as yet appeared in the river: And therefore at the same consultation it was con-

cluded by a generall approbation, That they should abandon the Countrie, and in the foure Pinaces (which remained in the river) they should make for the New found land, where (it beeing fishing time) they might meete with many English Ships, into which they hoped to disperse the most of the Company.

This conclusion taking effect, upon the seventh of June Sir Thomas Gates (having appointed every ship her complement and number, and delivered likewise to each a proportionable weight of provision) caused every man to repaire aboord; his company (and of his company himselfe) remained last on shore, to keepe the towne from being burned, which some of our owne company maliciously threatned. About noone they fell downe with the tyde to the Iland of Hogges, and the next morning to the Mulbury Iland: at what time, they discovered the long Boate of the Lord Laware, which his Lordship (hearing of this resolution by the Captaine of the Fort, which standeth at the mouth of the river) suddenly dispatched with letters to Sir Thomas Gates, which informed him of his Lordships arrivall. Upon receite of these letters, Sir Thomas Gates bore up the Helme, and that night with a favourable winde relanded all our men at the Fort. Before which, the tenth of June (being Sunday) his Lordship came with all his Fleete, went ashore in the afternoone, heard a Sermon, read his Commission, and entred into consultation for the good of the Colony.

In which secret counsell, I will a little leave his Lordship, that wee may duly observe the revealed counsell of God. He that shal but turne up his eye, and behold the spangled Canopie of heaven, shall but cast down his eye, and consider the imbroidered Carpet of the earth, and withall shall marke, how the heavens heare the earth, the earth heare the corne and oyle, and they relieve the necessities of man, that man wil acknowledge Gods infinite providence. But hee that shall further observe, how God inclineth all casuall events, to worke the necessary helpe of his Saints, must needs adore the Lords infinite goodnesse. Never had any people more just cause to cast themselves at the foot-stoole of God, and to reverence his mercy, then our distressed Colony: for if God had not sent Sir Thomas Gates from the Bermudos within foure daies, they had all beene famished: if God had not directed the heart of that worthy Knight, to save the Fort from fire at their shipping, they had been destitute of a present harbor, and succor; if they had abandoned the Fort any longer time, and had not so soone returned, questionlesse the Indians would have destroied the Fort, which had beene the meanes of our safety among them, and a terrour unto them. If they had set Saile sooner, and had lanched into the vast Ocean, who could have promised, that they should have encountered the Fleet of the Lo. La-ware? especially when they made for the New-found land, a course contrary to our Navies approaching. If the Lord La-ware had not brought with him a yeares provision, what comfort could those soules have received, to have beene relanded to a second destruction? Brachium Domini, this was the arme of the Lord of Hosts, who would have his people to passe the redde Sea and Wildernesse, and then to possesse the land of Canaan: It was divinely spoken of heathen Socrates, Si Deus sit solicitus pro te, cur tu tibi sis solicitus? If God for man be carefull, why should man be over distrustfull?

The noble Lord governor, after mature deliberation, delivered some few words to the company, laying just blame upon them for their haughty vanities, and sluggish idlenesse; earnestly entreating them to amend those desperate follies, lest he should be compelled to draw the sword of Justice, and to cut off such delinquents, which he had rather draw (even to the shedding of his vital blood) to protect them from injuries; heartning them with relation of that store hee had brought with him; constituting officers of all conditions to rule over them, allotting every man his particular place to watch vigilantly and worke painefully. This Oration and direction being received with a generall applause, you might shortly behold the idle and restie diseases of a divided multitude, by the unity and authority of this government, to be substantially cured. Those that knew not the way to goodnes before, but cherished singularity and faction, can now chalke out the path of all respective duetie and service: every man endeavouring to out-strip each other in diligence: the French preparing to plant the Vines, the English labouring in the woods and groundes: every man knoweth his charge, and dischargeth the same with alacrity. Neither let any man be discouraged, by the relation of their daily labor, (as though the sappe of their bodies should be spent for other mens profite) the setled times of working (to effect all themselves, or the Adventurers neede desire) requiring no more pains then from sixe of clocke in the morning untill ten, and from two of the clocke in the afternoone till foure: at both which times they are provided of spiritual and corporall reliefe. First, they enter into the Church, and make their prayers unto God; next, they returne to their houses, and receive their proportion of foode. Nor should it be conceived, that this busines excludeth Gentlemen, whose breeding never knew what a daies labour meant; for though they cannot digge, use the square, nor practise the axe and chizell; yet may the stayde spirits of any condition finde how to employ the force of knowledge, the exercise of counsell, the operation and power of their best breeding and qualities. The houses which are built are as warme and defensible against winde and weather, as if they were tiled and slated; being covered above with strong boordes, and matted round within, according to the fashion of the Indians. Our forces are now such as are able to tame the fury and treachery of the Savages: our Forts assure the Inhabitants, and frustrate all assailants. And to leave no discouragement in the heart of any, who personally shall enter into this great action, I will communicate a double comfort: first, Sir George Summers (that worthy Admiral) hath undertaken a dangerous adventure, for the good of the Colony.

Upon the fifteenth of June (accompanied with Captaine Samuel Argoll) he returned in two Pinaces unto the Bermudos; promising (if by any meanes God will open a way to that Iland of Rockes) that he would some returne with sixe moneths provision of flesh, and with live Hogges to store againe Virginia. It is but eleven daies saile, and we hope that God will send a pillar of fire to direct his journey. The other comfort is, that the Lord governour hath built two new Forts (the one called Fort Henry, and the other Fort Charles, in honor of our most noble Prince and his hopefull brother) upon a pleasant hill, and neere a little rivelet, which we call Southhampton river. They stand in a wholsome ayre, having plenty of springs of sweete water; they command a great circuit of ground, containing wood, pasture and meadow; with apt places for vines, corne and gardens. In which Forts it is resolved, that all those that come out of England shall be at their first landing quartered; that the wearisomnes of the sea may bee refreshed in this pleasing part of the countrey.

The fertility of the soile, the temperature of the climate, the form of government, the condition of our people, their daily invocating of the name of God, being thus expressed; Why should the successe (by the rules of mortall judgement) be despaired? Why should not the rich harvest of our hopes be seasonably expected? I dare say, that the resolution of Cæsar in Fraunce, the designes of Alexander in Greece, the discoveries of Hernando Cortes in the West, and of Emanuel, King of Portugale in the East, were not incouraged upon so firme grounds of state and possibility. All which I could demonstrate out of their owne Records, were I not prevented with hast, to satisfie their longings, who with an open eare, hearken after the commodities of the countrey: whose appetites I will no longer frustrate, then their eyes can runne over this succinct Narration.

I called it a succinct Narration, because the commodities in former Treatises have beene largely described, which I will here only epitomise, lest any man should change his resolution, when the same grounds remaine, which were the cause of his former adventure.

The Councell of Virginia (finding the smalnesse of that returne, which they hoped should have defraied the charge of a new supply) entred into a deepe consultation, and propounded amongst themselves, whether it were fit to enter into a new contribution, or in time to send for home the Lord La-ware, and to abandon the action. They resolved to send for sir Thomas Gates, who being come, they adjured him to deale plainely with them, and to make a true relation of those things which were presently to be had, or hereafter to be hoped for in Virginia. Sir Thomas Gates with a solemne and sacred oath replied, that all things before reported were true: that the country yeeldeth abundance of wood, as Oake, Wainscot, Walnut trees, Bay trees, Ashe, Sarsafrase, live Oake, greene all the yeare, Cedar and Firre; which are the materials, of soape ashes, and pot ashes, of oyles of walnuts, and bayes, of pitch and tarre, of Clap boards, Pipe-staves, Masts and excellent boardes of forty, fifty and sixtie length, and three foote bredth, when one Firre tree is able to make the maine Mast of the greatest ship in England. He avouched, that there are incredi-

ble variety of sweet woods, especially of the Balsamum tree, which distilleth a pretious gum; that there are innumerable White Mulberry trees, which in so warme a climate may cherish and feede millions of silke wormes, and returne us in a very short time, as great a plenty of silke as is vented into the whole world from al the parts of Italy: that there are divers sorts of Minerals, especially of Iron oare, lying upon the ground for ten miles circuite; (of which we have made triall at home, that it maketh as good Iron as any is in Europe:) that a kinde of hempe or flax, and silke grasse doe grow there naturally, which will affoord stuffe for all manner of excellent Cordage: that the river swarmeth with Sturgeon; the land aboundeth with Vines, the woodes doe harbor exceeding store of Beavers, Foxes and Squirrils, the waters doe nourish a great encrease of Otters; all which are covered with pretious furres: that there are in present discovered dyes and drugs of sundry qualities; that the Orenges which have beene planted did prosper in the winter, which is an infallible argument, that Lymmons, sugar Canes, Almonds, Rice, Anniseede, and all other commodities which we have from the Staights, may be supplied to us in our owne countrey, and by our owne industry: that the corne yeeldeth a trebble encrease more then ours; and lastly, that it is one of the goodliest countries under the sunne; enterveined with five maine Rivers, and promising as rich entrals as any Kingdome of the earth, to whom the sunne is so neerer a neighbour.

What these things will yeelde, the Merchant best knoweth, who findeth by experience, that many hundreth of thousands of pounds are yearly spent in Christendome in these commodities. The Merchant knoweth, that Caveare and Traine which come from Russia, can be brought hither but once in the yeare, in regard of the Ice: and that Sturgeon which is brought from the East countries, can come but twice a yeare; and that not before the end of Aprill, or the beginning of May; which many times in regard of the heat of those moneths, is tainted in the transportation: when from Virginia they may be brought to us in foure and twenty daies, and in al the colde seasons of the yeare. The Merchants know, that the commodity of sope and pot ashes are very scant in Prussia; that they are brought three hundred miles by land, and three hundred miles by rivers, before they come to the Sea; that they pay a custome there, and another in Denmarke, which enhanceth the prices exceedingly: But in Virginia they may have them without carriage by land or custome (because five Navigable Rivers doe lead up five several waies into the bowels of the whole countrey.) As therefore the like Rivers, are the cause of the riches of Holland, so will these be to us a wondrous cause of saving of expences. The merchant knoweth, that through the troubles in Poland & Muscovy, (whose eternall warres are like the Antipathy of the Dragon & Elephants) all their traffique for Mastes, Deales, Pitch, Tarre, Flax, Hempe, and Cordage, are every day more and more indangered, and the woods of those countries are almost exhausted. All which are to be had in Virginia with farre lesse charge, and farre more safety. Lastly, the Merchant knoweth, that for our commodities in the Staights, as sweet wines, orenges, lemmonds, anniseeds, &c. that we stand at the devotion of politique Princes and States, who for their proper utility, devise all courses to grinde our merchants, all pretences to confiscate their goods, and to draw from us al marrow of gaine by their inquisitive inventions: when in Virginia, a few yeares labour by planting and husbandry, will furnish all our defects, with honour and security; especially since the Frenchmen (who are with the Lord Governour) do confidently promise, that within two yeares we may expect a plentifull Vintage.

When therefore this noble enterprise, by the rules of Religion is expressly justified; when the passages by Sea are all open and discovered; when the climate is so fruitfully tempered; when the naturall riches of the soile are so powerfully confirmed: will any man so much betray his owne inconsiderate ignorance, and bewray his rashnesse; that when the same Sunne shineth, he should not have the same eies to beholde it; when the same hope remaines, he should not have the same heart to apprehend it? At the voyage of Sir Thomas Gates, what swarmes of people desired to be transported? what alacrity and cheerefulnesse in the Adventurers by free wil offerings, to build up this new Tabernacle? Shall we now be dejected? Shall we cast downe our heads like Bull rushes? because one storme at sea hath deferred our joyes and comforts! We are too effeminate in our longings, and too impatient of delaies. Gods al-disposing providence, is not compellable by

mans violence: Let any wisedome give a solide reason, why his purpose should be changed, when those grounds which gave life to his first purpose, are not changed. It is but a golden slumber, that dreameth of any humane felicity, which is not sauced with some contingent miserie. Dolor & voluptas, invicem cedunt, Greife and pleasure are the crosse sailes of the worlds ever-turning-windmill. Let no man therefore be over wise, to cast beyond the moone and to multiplie needlesse doubts and questions. Hannibal, by too much wisedome, lost opportunity to have sacked Rome. Charles the eighth of Fraunce, by temporising, lost the Kingdome of Naples, and the governement of Florence: Henry the seventh by too much over-warines, lost the riches of the golden Indies. Occasion is pretious, but when it is occasion. Some of our neighbours would joine in the action, if they might be joynt inheritors in the Plantation; which is an evident proofe, that Virginia shall no sooner be quitted by us, then it will be reinhabited by them. A dishonor of that nature, that will eternally blemish our Nation; as though we were like the furious Pyrrhus, or impetuous Swissers, who in a brunt can conquer any thing, but with wisedome can maintaine nothing. It is time to wipe away such an imputation of Barbarisme, especially since the consequence is so pregnant, that without this or the like, the state cannot subsist without some dangerous and imminent mutation. He is over blinde that doth not see, what an inundation of people doth overflow this little Iland: Shall we vent this deluge, by indirect and unchristian policies? shal we imitate the bloody and heathenish counsell of the Romanes, to leave a Carthage standing, that may exhaust our people by forraine warre? or shall we nourish domesticall faction, that as in the dayes of Vitellius and Vespasian, the sonne may imbrew his hands in the blood of the father? Or shall we follow the barbarous foot-steps of the state of China, to imprison our people in a little circle of the earth, and consume them by pestilence? Or shall we like the beast of Babylon, denie to any sort the honourable estate of mariage, and allow abhominable stewes, that our people may not over increase in multitude? Or shall we take an inhumane example from the Muscovite, in a time of famine to put tenne thousand of the poore under the yce, as the Mice and Rats of a state politique? If all these be diabolicall and hellish projects, what other meanes remaines to us, but by setling so excellent a Plantation, to disimbarke some millions of people upon a land that floweth with all manner of plenty?

To wade a little further, who ever saluted the monuments of antiquity, and doth not finde, that Carthage aspired to be Empresse of the world, by her opportunity of havens and multitude of shipping? What hindereth the great Mahumetane Prince, from seazing upon al the territories of Europe, but onely the want of skilfull marriners? What created the rich and free states of Holland, but their winged Navy? It was a fit embleme that painted death standing upon the shoares of Fraunce, Germany and Spaine, and looking over into England: intymating unto us, that so long as we are Lords of the narrow seas, death stands on the other shoares, and onely can looke upon us: but if our wooden wals were ruinated, death would soone make a bridge to come over, and devoure our Nation. When therefore our mils of Iron, and excesse of building, have already turned our greatest woods into pasture and champion, within these few years; neither the scattered Forrests of England, nor the diminished Groves of Ireland, will supply the defect of our Navy. When in Virginia there is nothing wanting, but onely mens labours, to furnish both Prince, State and merchant, without charge or difficulty. Againe, whither shall wee transport our cloth, and how shall we sustaine our Artisans? Shall we send it into Turkey? Some private and deceitfull avarice hath discredited our merchandize. Into Spaine? it aboundeth with sheepe and wooll. Into Poland and Muscovy? the daunger doth overballance the gaine in times of contention. Into Fraunce and Germany? they are for the most part supplied by their owne peace. When if our Colony were peopled in Virginia, mutabit vellera merces, we shall exchange our store of cloth for other merchandize. Let any man resolve why the Councell of Virginia, doe now most earnestly continue their adventures? why those that were (eye witnesses) of the former supposed miseries, do voluntarily returne with joy and comfort? why those noble and worthy personages, doe offer to make the action good upon the hazard of their lives & fortunes? And why Sir Thomas Gates longeth and hasteneth to go thither again, and the Lord La-ware desireth so earnestly to stay there? Are not all these things as deere to them as to any other of the Adventurers? Have not their hopes the same wings? their feares the

same fetters? their estates the same rockes? their lives and soules greater gulfes of perill and despair? And yet neither the imbracements of their wives, nor indulgence to their babes, nor the neglect of their domesticke fortunes, nor banishment from their native soile, nor any experimented dangers have broken their noble resolution.

And therefore, he that desireth to purchase infallible hope of private utility; hee that aimeth at the honor & wealth of his native country; he that esteemeth his owne repute as deere as his owne eies; he that endeavoureth to enlarge the dominions of his Prince, and the Kingdome of his God: let him remember what hee hath already spent, which is all buried; let him consider the consequences of state, which are all vanished into smoake; let him conceive what a scorne we shall be made to the maligners of our state abroad, and our il affected at home; let him meditate, the external riches of other Kingdoms, able to buy and sell the monarch of the west; let him heare the triumphant boasting of the Beast of Rome, as though God would not suffer our schismaticall and hereticall Religion, to be infused into a new converted Region: O all ye worthies, follow the ever-sounding trumpet of a blessed honour; let Religion be the first aim of your hopes, & cætera adijcientus, and other things shall be cast unto you: your names shall be registred to posterity with a glorious title; These are the men, whom God raised to augment the State of their countrey, and to propagate the Gospell of Jesus Christ. Neyther ought any man to live under Augustus, as if he lived under Domitian, quibus inertia est pro sapientia; to whom sluggishnes & privacy is imputed for wisedome and pollicy. The same God that hath joyned three Kingdomes under one Cæsar, wil not be wanting to adde a fourth, if wee would dissolve that frosty Icinesse which chilleth our zeale, and maketh us so cold in the action. But is a meere Idæa, speculation and fancy, to sow sparingly, and yet expect for to reape plentifully; when a penurious supply is like the casting on of a little water upon a great fire, that quencheth not the heat, but augments it: when procrastinating delayes, and lingring counsels, doe lose the opportunity of flying time; whereby we rather bewray our Colony then releeve them: let no man adore his golde as his God, nor his Mammon as his Maker. If God have scattered his blessings upon you as snow, will you returne no tributary acknowledgement of his goodnesse? If you will, can you select a more excellent subject, then to cast downe the altars of Divels, that you may raise up the Altar of Christ: to forbid the sacrifice of men, that they may offer up the sacrifice of contrite spirites; to reduce Barbarisme and infidelity, to civill government and Christianity? Si frigido loquor, nihil loquor; If I speake to a man void of piety, I speake but the words of winde and vanity; otherwise how doth that man groane under the worlds corruption, that doth not actually or vocally hasten the worldes conversion? Doubt ye not but God hath determined, and demonstrated (by the wondrous preservation of those principal persons which fell upon the Bermudos) that he will raise our state, and build his Church in that excellent climate, if the action be seconded with resolution and Religion.

Nil disperandum Christo Duce, & Auspice Christo.

809. [1611]. Council of the Virginia Company to Sir Ralph Winwood.

How far afield the Council of the Virginia Company was prepared to go for subscribers is shown by this letter to Sir Ralph Winwood, English ambassador to the United Provinces, an old friend of the Virginia enterprise, asking him to solicit subscriptions among English officers serving with the Dutch forces. They enclosed a copy of a pamphlet, most probably A true declaration of the state of Virginia *(808), and gave him evidence of the great preparations being made to follow up Lord De La Warr's initiative by additional reinforcements early in 1611.*

A rough copy, probably sent by Winwood to his wife, is in Buccleugh and Queensberry MSS, Winwood Papers, vol. IX, printed by S. M. Kingsbury, Records, III, 31-32, but here with expansions.

Sir,

Having addressed lately our Letters to the Coronells and other chiefe Commaunders of the Englishe in those Netherland partes for the ad-vauncing of the woor[t]hie enterprise of planting Coloneyes of our Natyon in the fruitfull and rich Countrye of Virginia, and to drawe them into socyetye of that Action, and consequently to contrybucion towardes the charge hereof: We have thought fitt not onelye to offer ourselves to your Lordship in like sorte, but in regard of your place also, and personale woorth and sufficyency, to pray your best assistance in forwarding the same among those Noble and woorthie gentlemen unto whom we have by our Letters or other wise recommended it. And for youre better informacion, we have sent you herewith a true relacion of that business, in a book latelye printed, and published by us concerning it: And fa[r]ther certefie you that this Actyon having receaved heartofore many disasserous impedymentes by the factyousnes and insufficyencye of sundrye the Governours and others in Virginia, is now [at] length settled in so good order and forwardnes by the industryous and prudent Goverment of the Lord La Warre, that we have resolved to second his Lordship with three important Supplies, Whearof the first we send presentelye one [under] the conduct of Sir Thomas Gates Lieuttennaunt generall, and Sir Thomas Dale, Marshall of Virginia, and the rest arre to followe in the two years next ensuing.

And according hereunto the Adventurours have also resolved to furnishe out this Charge with three yearlye Supplyes of Moneye, Som with 12^{li} [10]^s a year many other with doble, and some also with [tre]ble that

Our desire and hope is that youre Lordship will in all occasions be ayding to this woorthy Actyon tending so much to the honoure and happynes of our Natyon: And so praying your answear to be returned to Sir Thomas Smith oure Treasurour, We rest

your Lordships verie loving friendes
H. Southampton, Montgomery, Tho. Smythe, Tho. Howard, R. Lisle, Robert Mansell, Walter Cope, Edwin Sandys, Sir Raphe Winwood Knight.

[Addressed:] To oure honorable friend Sir Raphe Winwood Knight Lord Ambassadour from his Majestye with the States of the United Provinces.

[Endorsed, in another hand:] For my Lady Winwood. The recommendation of the plantation in Virginia.

810. June, 1611. Lord De La Warr's *Relation*, an apology for his return.

Lord De La Warr's unexpected appearance in England in June, 1611, was a considerable shock to the Council of the Virginia Company, as it was speculated, and soon found to be the case, that neither Sir Thomas Dale nor Sir Thomas Gates had reached Jamestown before De La Warr left, and that, therefore, one of the more prominent old settlers, George Percy, who by this time was not well-trusted, had been left as acting lieutenant governor. De La Warr maintained that ill health had driven him to try to make a visit to Nevis to recuperate but that his ship was unable to make its way there and so came to England instead. The governor reassured the council that all was well, and they, in turn, attempted to reassure the public by publishing as soon as possible a small pamphlet, The relation of the right honourable the Lord De-La-Warre ... of the colonie planted in Virginia *(London, 1611). It was reprinted by S. Purchas,* Pilgrimes, *IV (1625), 1762–1764 (XIX [1906], 85–90), from which it is given here.*

A short Relation made by the Lord De-La-Warre, to the Lords and others of the Counsell of Virginia, touching his unexpected returne home, and afterwards delivered to the generall Assembly of the said Company, at a Court holden the twentie five of June, 1611. Published by authoritie of the said Counsell.

My Lords, &c.

Being now by accident returned from my Charge at Virginia, contrary either to my owne desire or other mens expectations, who spare not to censure mee, in point of dutie, and to discourse and question the reason, though they apprehend not the true cause of my returne, I am forced (out of a willingnesse to satisfie every man) to deliver unto your Lordships, and the rest of this Assembly, briefly (but truly) in what state I have lived, ever since my arrivall to the Colonie; what hath beene the just occasion of my sudden departure thence; and in what termes I have left the same: The rather because I perceive, that since my comming into England, such a coldnesse and irresolution is bred in many of the Adventurers, that some of them seeke to withdraw those payments, which they have subscribed towards the Charge of the Plantation, and by which that Action must be supported and mayntained, making this my returne, the colour of their needlesse backwardnesse and unjust protraction. Which, that you may the better understand, I must informe your Lordships, that presently after my arrivall in James Towne, I was welcommed by a hot and violent Ague, which held me a time, till by the advice of my Physition, Doctour Lawrence Bohun (by bloud letting) I was recovered as in my first Letters by Sir Thomas Gates, I have informed you. That Disease had not long left me, till (within three weekes after I had gotten a little strength) I began to be distempered with other grievous sicknesses, which successively and severally assailed mee: for besides a relapse into the former Disease, which with much more violence held me more then a moneth, and brought me to great weaknesse, the Flux surprized mee, and kept me many dayes; then the Crampe assaulted my weake bodie, with strong paines; and afterwards the Gout (with which I had heretofore beene sometime troubled) afflicted me in such sort, that making my bodie through weaknesse unable to stirre, or to use any manner of exercise, drew upon me the Disease called the Scurvy; which though in others it be a sicknesse of slothfulnesse, yet was in me an effect of weaknesse, which never left mee, till I was upon the point to leave the World.

These severall Maladies and Calamities, I am the more desirous to particularise unto your Lordshippes (although they were too notorious to the whole Colonie) lest any man should misdeeme that under the generall name and common excuse of sicknesse, I went about to cloke either sloth, or feare, or any other base apprehension, unworthy the high and Honorable Charge, which you had entrusted to my Fidelitie.

In these extremities I resolved to consult my friends, Who finding Nature spent in mee, and my body almost consumed, my paines likewise daily encreasing, gave me advise to prefer a hopefull recovery, before an assured ruine, which must necessarily have ensued, had I lived but twentie dayes longer in Virginia: wanting at that instant, both food and Physicke, fit to remedy such extraordinary Diseases, and restore that strength so desperately decayed.

Whereupon, after a long consultation held, I resolved by generall consent and perswasion, to ship my selfe for Mevis [= Nevis], an Island in the West Indies, famous for wholsesome Bathes, there to try what helpe the Heavenly Providence would affoord mee, by the benefit of the hot Bath: but God, who guideth all things, according to his good will and pleasure, so provided, that after we had sayled an hundred Leagues, we met with Southerly windes which forced mee to change my purpose (my bodie being altogether unable to endure the tediousnesse of a long Voyage) and so steere my course for the Westerne Ilands, which I no sooner recovered, then I found helpe for my health, and my sicknesse asswaged, by meanes of fresh Diet, and especially of Orenges and Lemons, an undoubted remedy and medicine for that Disease, which lastly, and so long, had afflicted me: which ease as soone as I found, I resolved (although my body remayned still feeble and weake) to returne backe to my charge in Virginia againe, but I was advised not to hazard my selfe before I had perfectly recovered my strength, which by counsell I was perswaded to seeke in the naturall Ayre of my Countrey, and so I came for England. In which Accident, I doubt not but men of reason, and of judgement will imagine, there would more danger and prejudice have happened by my death there, then I hope can doe by my returne.

In the next place, I am to give account in what estate I left the Colonie for government in my absence. It may please your Lordships therefore to understand, that upon my departure thence, I made choice of Captaine George Percie (a Gentleman of honour and resolution, and of no small experience in that place) to remayne Deputie Governour, untill the comming of the Marshall Sir Thomas Dale, whose Commission was likewise to be determined, upon the arrivall of Sir Thomas Gates, according to the intent and order of your Lordships, and the Councell here.

The number of men I left there, were upward of two hundred, the most in health, and provided of a least ten moneths victuals, in their Store-house (which is daily issued unto them) besides other helps in the Countrey, lately found out by Captaine Argoll by trading with pettie Kings in those parts, who for a small returne of a piece of Iron, Copper, &c. have consented to trucke great quantities of Corne, and willingly imbrace the intercourse of Traffique, shewing unto our people certaine signes of amitie and affection.

And for the better strengthening and securing of the Colonie, in the time of my weaknesse there, I tooke order for the building of three severall Forts, two of which are seated neere Point Comfort, to which adjoyneth a large circuit of ground, open, and fit for Corne: the third Fort is at the Falls, upon an Iland invironed also with Corne ground. These are not all manned, for I wanted the commoditie of Boats, having but two, and one Barge, in all the Countrey, which hath beene cause that our fishing hath beene (in some sort) hindered for want of those provisions, which easily will be remedied when we can gaine sufficient men to bee imployed about those businesses, which in Virginia I found not: but since meeting with Sir Thomas Gates at the Cowes neere Portsmouth, (to whom I gave a particular account of all my proceedings, and of the present estate of the Colonie as I left it) I understood those wants are supplyed in his Fleet.

The Country is wonderfull fertile and very rich, and makes good whatsoever heretofore hath beene reported of it, the Cattell alreadie there, are much encreased, and thrive exceedingly with the pasture of that Countrie: The Kine all this last Winter, though the ground was covered most with Snow, and the Season sharpe, lived without other feeding then the grasse they found, with which they prospered well, and many of them readie to fall with Calve: Milke beeing a great nourishment and refreshing to our people, serving also (in occasion) as well for Physicke as for food, so that it is in no way to be doubted, but when it shall please God that Sir Thomas Dale, and Sir Thomas Gates, shall arrive in Virginia, with their extraordinary supply of one hundred Kine, and two hundred Swine, besides store of all manner of other provisions for the sustenance and maintenance of the Colonie, there will appeare that success in the Action as shall give no man cause of distrust that hath alreadie adventured, but encourage every good minde to further so worthy a worke, as will redound both to the glory of God, to the credit of our Nation, and to the comfort of all those that have beene Instruments in the furthering of it.

The last Discovery, during my continuall sicknesse, was by Captaine Argoll, who hath found a Trade with Patamack (a King as great as Powhatan, who still remaynes our Enemie, though not able to doe us hurt.) This is in a goodly

River called Patomack, upon the borders whereof there are growne the goodliest Trees for Masts, that may bee found else-where in the World: Hempe better then English: growing wild in abundance: Mynes of Antimonie and Lead.

There is also found without our Bay to the Northward an excellent fishing Banke for Cod and Ling, as good as can be eaten, and of a kind that will keepe a whole yeere in ships hold, with little care; a triall whereof I now have brought over with me. Other Ilands there are upon our Coasts, that doe promise rich Merchandize, and will further exceedingly the establishing of the Plantation, by supply of many helpes, and will speedily affoord a returne of many worthy commodities.

I have left much ground in part manured to receive Corne, having caused it the last Winter to be sowed for Roots, with which our people were greatly releeved. There are many Vines planted in divers places, and doe prosper well, there is no want of any thing, if the action can be upheld with constancie and resolution.

Lastly, concerning my selfe and my course, though the World may imagine that this Countrie and Climate, will (by that which I have suffered beyond any other of that Plantation) ill agree with the state of my bodie, yet I am so farre from shrinking or giving over this honourable Enterprize, as that I am willing and readie to lay all that I am worth upon the adventure of the Action, rather then so Honourable a Worke should faile, and to returne with all the convenient expedition I may, beseeching your Lordships and the rest, not onely to excuse my former wants, happened by the Almightie Hand: but to second my Resolutions with your friendly indevours: that both the State may receive Honour, your selves Profit, and I future Comfort, by beeing imployed (though but as a weake Instrument) in so great an Action.

And thus having plainly, truly, and briefly delivered the cause of my returne, with the state of our affaires, as we now stand, I hope every worthy and indifferent hearer, will by comparing my present resolution of returne, with the necessitie of my comming home, rest satisfied with this true and short Declaration.

Chapter One hundred four
Early Narratives and Correspondence
on Virginia

THE NUMBER of diaries kept by the earliest settlers of Virginia must have been large. Those that survive, however, represent only a very small proportion of the original total. The records of George Percy (811) and Gabriel Archer (812) of the early days of the 1607 settlement were particularly detailed. Even so it can be seen that after the first flush of interest in the new land the diary form tends to decline. The newcomer may still be impressed by the novelty of his surroundings, but to his companions who have been there for some time, the ordinariness of being in a new land begins to assert itself. Later settlers tend to compose long documents about their experiences only if they have grievances to present in detail—Edward Maria Wingfield was probably the first to do so (813)—or else because they were intending to write what was, in effect, more a history than a journal. The short diary entries tend to give place to letters as communications improved. In a changing situation newcomers still wished to communicate with friends, sponsors, or even with the Virginia Company at home. Lord Salisbury was the recipient of a number of letters from Virginia because settlers felt he was the most important single representative of government concerned with the colony (816). Peter Wynne's chatty letter to Sir John Egerton (814) is precisely the sort of which fewest have survived, though George Yeardley's to Sir Henry Peyton is another (818). William Strachey, however, used the opportunity of writing to a lady (whose name we do not know) to give a virtual history of the Bermuda episode and of his subsequent sojourn in Virginia (817). Letters of humble people in Virginia to their families in England are very unlikely to survive; for the letter to be extant, the recipient is much more likely to have been a gentleman or nobleman. There must have been a very large body of correspondence piling up in the hands of the company, kept in its Treasurer's house it seems, at least in the early days. Only a few letters that happened to be copied for some purpose and given to others have survived from this archive. Where there are legal cases, such as those in the High Court of Admiralty, the depositions of witnesses are often as vivid and immediate as those of persons actually writing of actions at sea or in the colony (821). But it is diaries, letters, and depositions that give best the flavor of life in the new setting.

811. December 20, 1606 to September, 1607. George Percy's "A Discourse of the Plantation of the Southern Colonie in Virginia."

In many ways George Percy's account of the founding of Jamestown and of the early months of the colony is the most interesting and lively, even though it later marks the dark deaths of so many of the colonists from early August, 1607, onward. It represents Samuel Purchas's selection from what may have been a longer document, but there is no reason to believe that the portion printed has been tampered with.

S. Purchas, Pilgrimes, *IV (1625) (XVIII* [*1906*], *403–419); P. L. Barbour*, The Jamestown Voyages, *I, 129 146; D. B. Quinn, ed., George Percy*, Observations Gathered out of A Discourse of the Southern Colony in Virginia by the English, 1606 *(Charlottesville, 1967).*

Observations gathered out of a Discourse of the Plantation of the Southerne Colonie in Virginia by the English, 1606. Written by that Honorable Gentleman Master Goerge Percy.

On Saturday the twentieth of December in the yeere 1606. the fleet fell from London, and the fift of January we anchored in the Downes; but the winds continued contrarie so long, that we were forced to stay there some time, where wee suffered great stormes, but by the skilfulnesse of the Captaine wee suffered no great losse or danger.

The twelfth day of February at night we saw a blazing Starre, and presently a storme. The three and twentieth day we fell with the Iland of Mattanenio in the West Indies. The foure and twentieth day we anchored at Dominico, within fourteene degrees of the Line, a very faire Iland, the Trees full of sweet and good smels inhabited by many Savage Indians, they were at first very scrupulous to come aboord us. Wee learned of them afterwards that the Spaniards had given them a great overthrow on this Ile, but when they knew what we were, there came many to our ships with their Canoas, bringing us many kindes of sundry fruites, as Pines, Potatoes, Plantons, Tobacco, and other fruits, and Roane Cloth abundance, which they had gotten out of certaine Spanish ships that were cast away upon that Iland. We gave them Knives, Hatchets for exchange which they esteeme much, wee also gave them Beades, Copper Jewels which they hang through their nosthrils, eares, and lips, very strange to behold, their bodies are all painted red to keepe away the biting of Muscetos, they goe all naked without covering: the haire of their head is a yard long, all of a length pleated in three plats hanging downe to their wastes, they suffer no haire to grow on their faces, they cut their skinnes in divers workes, they are continually in warres, and will eate their enemies when they kill them, or any stranger if they take them. They will lap up mans spittle, whilst one spits in their mouthes in a barbarous fashion like Dogges. These people and the rest of the Ilands in the West Indies, and Brasill, are called by the names of Canibals, that will eate mans flesh, these people doe poyson their Arrow heads, which are made of a fishes bone: they worship the Devill for their God, and have no other beliefe. Whilest we remayned at this Iland we saw a Whale chased by a Thresher and a Swordfish: they fought for the space of two houres, we might see the Thresher with his flayle lay on the monstrous blowes which was strange to behold: in the end these two fishes brought the Whale to her end.

The sixe and twentieth day, we had sight of Marigalanta, and the next day wee sailed with a slacke saile alongst the Ile of Guadulupa, where we went ashore, and found a Bath which was so hot, that no man was able to stand long by it, our Admirall Captaine Newport caused a piece of Porke to be put in it: which boyled it so in the space of halfe an houre, as no fire could mend it. Then we went aboord and sailed by many Ilands, as Mounserot and an Iland called Saint Christopher, both uninhabited about; about two a clocke in the afternoone wee anchored at the Ile of Mevis. There the Captaine landed all his men being well fitted with Muskets and other convenient Armes, marched a mile into the Woods; being commanded to stand upon their guard, fearing the treacherie of the Indians, which is an ordinary use amongst them and all other Savages on this Ile, we came to a Bath standing in a Valley betwixt two Hils; where wee bathed our selves and found it to be of the nature of the Bathes in England, some places hot and some colder: and men may refresh themselves as they please, finding this place to be so convenient for our men to avoid diseases, which will breed in so long a Voyage, wee incamped our selves on this Ile sixe dayes, and spent none of our ships victuall, by reason our men some went a hunting, some a fouling, and some a fishing, where we got great store of Conies, sundry kinds of fowles, and great plentie of fish. We kept Centinels and Courts de gard at every Captaines quarter, fearing wee should be assaulted by the Indians, that were on the other side of the Iland: wee saw none nor were molested by any: but some few we saw as we were a hunting on the Iland. They would not come to us by any meanes, but ranne swiftly through the Woods to the Mountaine tops; so we lost the sight of them: whereupon we made all the haste wee could to our quarter, thinking there had beene a great ambush of Indians there abouts. We past into the thickest of the Woods where we had almost lost our selves, we had not gone above halfe a mile amongst the thicke, but we came into a most pleasant Garden, being a hundred paces square on every side, having many Cotton-trees growing in it with abundance of Cotton-wooll, and many Guiacum trees: wee saw the goodliest tall trees growing so thicke about the Garden, as though they had beene set by Art, which made us marvell very much to see it.

The third day, wee set saile from Mevis: the fourth day we sailed along by Castutia and by Saba: This day we anchored at the Ile of Virgines, in an excellent Bay able to harbour a hundred Ships: if this Bay stood in England, it would be a great profit and commoditie to the Land. On this Iland wee caught great store of Fresh-fish, and abundance of Sea Tortoises, which served all our Fleet three daies, which were in number eight score persons. We also killed great store of wilde Fowle, wee cut the Barkes of certaine Trees which tasted much like Cinnamon, and very hot in the mouth. This Iland in some places hath very good ground, straight and tall Timber. But the greatest discommoditie that wee have seene on this Iland is that it hath no Fresh-water, which makes the place void of any Inhabitants.

Upon the sixt day, we set saile and passed by Becam, and by Saint John de Porto Rico. The seventh day, we arrived at Mona: where wee watered, which we stood in great need of, seeing that our water did smell so vildly that none of our men were able to indure it. Whilst some of the Saylers were a filling the Caskes with water, the Captaine, and the rest of the Gentlemen, and other Soldiers marched up in the Ile six myles, thinking to find some other provision to maintaine our victualling; as wee marched we killed two wild Bores, and saw a huge wild Bull, his hornes was an ell betweene the two tops. Wee also killed Guanas, in fashion of a Serpent, and speckled like a Toade under the belly. These wayes that wee went, being so troublesome and vilde going upon the sharpe Rockes, that many of our men fainted in the march, but by good fortune wee lost none but one Edward Brookes Gentleman, whose fat melted within him by the great heate and drought of the Countrey: we were not able to relieve him

nor our selves, so he died in that great extreamitie.

The ninth day in the afternoone, we went off with our Boat to the Ile of Moneta, some three leagues from Mona, where we had a terrible landing, and a troublesome getting up to the top of the Mountaine or Ile, being a high firme Rocke step, with many terrible sharpe stones: After wee got to the top of the Ile, we found it to bee a fertill and a plaine ground, full of goodly grasse, and abundance of Fowles of all kindes, they flew over our heads as thicke as drops of Hale; besides they made such a noise, that wee were not able to heare one another speake. Furthermore, wee were not able to set our feet on the ground, but either on Fowles or Egges which lay so thicke in the grasse: Wee laded two Boats full in the space of three houres, to our great refreshing.

The tenth day we set saile, and disimboged out of the West Indies, and bare our course Northerly. The fourteenth day we passed the Tropicke of Cancer. The one and twentieth day, about five a clocke at night there began a vehement tempest, which lasted all the night, with winds, raine, and thunders in a terrible manner. Wee were forced to lie at Hull that night, because we thought wee had beene neerer land then wee were. The next morning, being the two and twentieth day wee sounded; and the three and twentieth and foure and twentieth day, but we could find no ground.[1] The five and twentieth day we sounded, and had no ground at an hundred fathom. The six and twentieth day of Aprill, about foure a clocke in the morning, wee descried the Land of Virginia: the same day wee entred into the Bay of Chesupioc directly, without any let or hinderance; there wee landed and discovered a little way, but wee could find nothing worth the speaking of, but faire meddowes and goodly tall Trees, with such Fresh-waters running through the woods, as I was almost ravished at the first sight thereof.

At night, when wee were going aboard, there came the Savages creeping upon all foure, from the Hills like Beares, with their Bowes in their mouthes, charged us very desperately in the faces, hurt Captaine Gabrill Archer in both his hands, and a sayler in two places of the body very

---

1. Sidenote: "We were driven to try that night, and by the storme were forced neere the shoare, not knowing where we were."

dangerous. After they had spent their Arrowes, and felt the sharpnesse of our shot, they retired into the Woods with a great noise, and so left us.

The seven and twentieth day we began to build up our Shallop: the Gentlemen and Souldiers marched eight miles up into the Land, we could not see a Savage in all that march, we came to a place where they had made a great fire, and had beene newly a rosting Oysters: when they perceived our comming, they fled away to the Mountaines, and left many of the Oysters in the fire: we eat some of the Oysters, which were very large and delicate in taste.

The eighteenth day we lanched our Shallop, the Captaine and some Gentlemen went in her, and discovered up the Bay, we found a River on the Southside running into the Maine; we entered it and found it very shoald water, not for any Boats to swim: Wee went further into the Bay, and saw a plaine plot of ground where we went on Land, and found the place five mile in compasse, without either Bush or Tree, we saw nothing there but a Cannow, which was made out of the whole tree, which was five and fortie foot long by the Rule. Upon this plot of ground we got good store of Mussels and Oysters, which lay on the ground as thicke as stones: wee opened some, and found in many of them Pearles. Wee marched some three or foure miles further into the Woods, where we saw great smoakes of fire. Wee marched to those smoakes and found that the Savages had beene there burning downe the grasse, as wee thought either to make their plantation there, or else to give signes to bring their forces together, and so to give us battell. We past through excellent ground full of Flowers of divers kinds and colours, and as goodly trees as I have seene, as Cedar, Cipresse, and other kindes: going a little further we came into a little plat of ground full of fine and beautifull Strawberries, foure times bigger and better then ours in England. All this march we could neither see Savage nor Towne. When it grew to be towards night we stood backe to our Ships, we sounded and found it shallow water for a great way, which put us out of all hopes for getting any higher with our Ships, which road at the mouth of the River. Wee rowed over to a point of Land, where wee found a channell, and sounded six, eight, ten, or twelve fathom: which put us in good comfort. Therefore wee named that point of Land, Cape Comfort.

The nine and twentieth day we set up a Crosse at Chesupioc Bay, and named that place Cape Henry. Thirtieth day, we came with our ships to Cape Comfort; where wee saw five Savages running on the shoare; presently the Captaine caused the shallop to be manned, so rowing to the shoare, the Captaine called to them in signe of friendship, but they were at first very timersome, until they saw the Captain lay his hand on his heart: upon that they laid down their Bowes and Arrowes, and came very boldly to us, making signes to come a shoare to their Towne, which is called by the Savages Kecoughtan. Wee coasted to their Towne, rowing over a River running into the Maine, where these Savages swam over with their Bowes and Arrowes in their mouthes.

When we came over to the other side, there was a many of other Savages which directed us to their Towne, where we were entertained by them very kindly. When we came first a Land they made a dolefull noise, laying their faces to the ground, scratching the earth with their nailes. We did thinke that they had beene at their Idolatry. When they had ended their Ceremonies, they went into their houses and brought out mats and laid upon the ground, the chiefest of them sate all in a rank: the meanest sort brought us such dainties as they had, & of their bread which they make of their Maiz or Gennea wheat, they would not suffer us to eat unlesse we sate down, which we did on a Mat right against them. After we were well satisfied they gave us of their Tabacco, which they tooke in a pipe made artificially of earth as ours are, but far bigger, with the bowle fashioned together with a piece of fine copper. After they had feasted us, they shewed us, in welcome, their manner of dancing, which was in this fashion: one of the Savages standing in the midst singing, beating one hand against another, all the rest dancing about him, shouting, howling, and stamping against the ground, with many Anticke tricks and faces, making noise like so many Wolves or Devils. One thing of them I observed; when they were in their dance they kept stroke with their feet just one with another, but with their hands, heads, faces, and bodies, every one of them had a severall gesture: so they continued for the space of halfe an houre. When they had ended their dance, the Captaine gave them Beades and other trifling Jewells. They hang through their eares Fowles legs: they shave the right side of their heads with a shell, the left side they weare of an ell long tied up with an artificiall knot, with a many of Foules feathers sticking in it. They goe altogether naked, but their privities are covered with Beasts skinnes beset commonly with little bones, or beasts teeth: some paint their bodies blacke, some red, with artificiall knots of sundry lively colours, very beautifull and pleasing to the eye, in a braver fashion then they in the West Indies.

The fourth day of May, we came to the King of Werowance of Paspihe: where they entertained us with much welcome; an old Savage made a long Oration, making a foule noise, uttering his speech with a vehement action, but we knew little what they meant. Whilst we were in company with the Paspihes, the Werowance of Rapahanna came from the other side of the River in his Cannoa: he seemed to take displeasure of our being with the Paspihes: he would faine have had us come to his Towne, the Captaine was unwilling; seeing that the day was so far spent he returned backe to his ships for that night.

The next day, being the fift of May, the Werowance of Rapahanna sent a Messenger to have us come to him. We entertained the said Messenger, and gave him trifles which pleased him: Wee manned our shallop with Muskets and Targatiers sufficiently: this said Messenger guided us where our determination was to goe. When wee landed, the Werowance of Rapahanna came downe to the water side with all his traine, as goodly men as any I have seene of Savages or Christians: the Werowance comming before them playing on a Flute made of a Reed, with a Crown of Deares haire colloured red, in fashion of a Rose fastened about his knot of haire, and a great Plate of Copper on the other side of his head, with two long Feathers in fashion of a paire of Hornes placed in the midst of his Crowne. His body was painted all with Crimson, with a Chaine of Beads about his necke, his face painted blew, besprinkled with silver Ore as wee thought, his eares all behung with Braslets of Pearle, and in either eare a Birds Claw through it beset with fine Copper or Gold, he entertained us in so modest a proud fashion, as though he had beene a Prince of civill government, holding his countenance without laughter or any such ill behaviour; he caused his Mat to be spred on the ground, where hee sate downe with a great Majestie, taking a pipe of

Tabacco: the rest of his company standing about him. After he had rested a while he rose, and made signes to us to come to his Towne: Hee went formost, and all the rest of his people and our selves followed him up a steepe Hill where his Palace was settled. Wee passed through the Woods in fine paths, having most pleasant Springs which issued from the Mountaines: Wee also went through the goodliest Corne fieldes that ever was seene in any Countrey. When wee came to Rapahannos Towne, hee entertained us in good humanitie.

The eight day of May we discovered up the River. We landed in the Countrey of Apamatica, at our landing, there came many stout and able Savages to resist us with their Bowes and Arrowes, in a most warlike manner, with the swords at their backes beset with sharpe stones, and pieces of yron able to cleave a man in sunder. Amongst the rest one of the chiefest standing before them crosse-legged, with his Arrow readie in his Bow in one hand, and taking a Pipe of Tobacco in the other, with a bold uttering of his speech, demanded of us our being there, willing us to bee gone. Wee made signes of peace, which they perceived in the end, and let us land in quietnesse.

The twelfth day we went backe to our ships, and discovered a point of Land, called Archers Hope, which was sufficient with a little labour to defend our selves against any Enemy. The soile was good and fruitfull, with excellent good Timber. There are also great store of Vines in bignesse of a mans thigh, running up to the tops of the Trees in great abundance. We also did see many Squirels, Conies, Black Birds with crimson wings, and divers other Fowles and Birds of divers and sundrie collours of Crimson, Watchet, Yellow, Greene, Murry, and of divers other hewes naturally without any art using.

We found store of Turkie nests and many Egges, if it had not beene disliked, because the ship could not ride neere the shoare, we had setled there to all the Collonies contentment.

The thirteenth day, we came to our seating place in Paspihas Countrey, some eight miles from the point of Land, which I made mention before: where our shippes doe lie so neere the shoare that they are moored to the Trees in six fathom water.

The fourteenth day we landed all our men

which were set to worke about the fortification, and others some to watch and ward as it was convenient.[2] The first night of our landing, about midnight, there came some Savages sayling close to our quarter: presently there was an alarum given; upon that the Savages ran away, and we not troubled any more by them that night. Not long after there came two Savages that seemed to be Commanders, bravely drest, with Crownes of coloured haire upon their heads, which came as Messengers from the Werowance of Paspihæ; telling us that their Werowance was comming and would be merry with us with a fat Deare.

The eighteenth day, the Werowance of Paspihæ came himselfe to our quarter, with one hundred Savages armed, which garded him in a very warlike manner with Bowes and Arrowes, thinking at that time to execute their villany. Paspihæ made great signes to us to lay our Armes away. But we would not trust him so far: he seeing he could not have convenient time to worke his will, at length made signes that he would give us as much land as we would desire to take.[3] As the Savages were in a throng in the Fort, one of them stole a Hatchet from one of our company, which spied him doing the deed: whereupon he tooke it from him by force, and also strooke him over the arme: presently another Savage seeing that, came fiercely at our man with a wooden sword, thinking to beat out his braines. The Werowance of Paspiha saw us take to our Armes, went suddenly away with all his company in great anger.

The nineteenth day, my selfe and three or foure more walking into the Woods by chance wee espied a path-way like to an Irish pace: wee were desirous to knowe whither it would bring us; wee traced along some foure miles, all the way as wee went, having the pleasantest Suckles, the ground all flowing over with faire flowers of sundry colours and kindes, as though it had beene in any Garden or Orchard in England. There be many Strawberries, and other fruits unknowne: wee saw the Woods full of Cedar and Cypresse trees, with other trees, which issues out sweet Gummes like to Balsam: wee kept on our way in this Paradise, at length wee came to a Savage Towne, where wee found but few people, they told us the rest were gone a hunting with the Werowance of Paspiha: we stayed there a while, and had of them Strawberries, and other things; in the meane time one of the Savages came running out of his house with a Bowe and Arrowes and ranne mainly through the Woods: then I beganne to mistrust some villanie, that he went to call some companie, and so betray us, wee made all the haste away wee could: one of the Savages brought us on the way to the Wood side, where there was a Garden of Tobacco, and other fruits and herbes, he gathered Tobacco, and distributed to every one of us, so wee departed.

The twentieth day the Werowance of Paspiha sent fortie of his men with a Deere, to our quarter: but they came more in villanie than any love they bare us: they faine would have layne in our Fort all night, but wee would not suffer them for feare of their treachery. One of our Gentlemen having a Target which hee trusted in, thinking it would beare out a slight shot, hee set it up against a tree, willing one of the Savages to shoot; who tooke from his backe an Arrow of an elle long, drew it strongly in his Bowe, shoots the Target a foote thorow, or better: which was strange, being that a Pistoll could not pierce it. Wee seeing the force of his Bowe, afterwards set him up a steele Target; he shot again, and burst his arrow all to pieces, he presently pulled out another Arrow, and bit it in his teeth, and seemed to bee in a great rage, so hee went away in great anger. Their Bowes are made of tough Hasell, their strings of Leather, their Arrowes of Canes or Hasell, headed with very sharpe stones, and are made artificially like a broad Arrow: other some of their Arrowes are headed with the ends of Deeres hornes, and are feathered very artificially. Pasphia was as good as his word; for hee sent Venison, but the Sawse came within few dayes after.

At Port Cotage in our Voyage up the River, we saw a Savage Boy about the age of ten yeeres, which had a head of haire of a perfect yellow and a reasonable white skinne,[4] which is a Miracle amongst all Savages.

This River[5] which wee have discovered is one of the famousest Rivers that ever was found by any Christian, it ebbes and flowes a hundred and threescore miles where ships of great burthen

---

2. Sidenote: "Their Plantation at James Towne."
3. Sidenote: "Land given."

4. Sidenote: "Yellow haired Virginian."
5. Sidenote: "River of Pohatan."

may harbour in safetie. Wheresoever we landed upon this River, wee saw the goodliest Woods as Beech, Oke, Cedar, Cypresse, Wal-nuts, Sassafras and Vines in great abundance, which hang in great clusters on many Trees, and other Trees unknowne, and all the grounds bespred with many sweet and delicate flowres of divers colours and kindes. There are also many fruites as Strawberries, Mulberries, Rasberries and Fruits unknowne, there are many branches of this River, which runne flowing through the Woods with great plentie of fish of all kindes, as for Sturgeon all the World cannot be compared to it. In this Countrey I have seene many great and large Medowes[6] having excellent good pasture for any Cattle. There is also great store of Deere both Red and Fallow. There are Beares, Foxes, Otters, Bevers, Muskats, and wild beasts unknowne.

The foure and twentieth day wee set up a Crosse at the head of this River, naming it Kings River, where we proclaimed James King of England to have the most right unto it. When wee had finished and set up our Crosse, we shipt our men and made for James Fort. By the way wee came to Pohatans Towre where the Captaine went on shore suffering none to goe with him, hee presented the Commander of this place with a Hatchet which hee tooke joyfully, and was well pleased.

But yet the Savages murmured at our planting in the Countrie, whereupon this Werowance made answere againe very wisely of a Savage, Why should you bee offended with them as long as they hurt you not, nor take any thing away by force, they take but a litle waste ground, which doth you nor any of us any good.

I saw Bread made by their women which doe all their drugerie. The men takes their pleasure in hunting and their warres, which they are in continually one Kingdome against another. The manner of baking of bread is thus, after they pound their wheat into flowre with hote water, they make it into paste, and worke it into round balls and Cakes, then they put it into a pot of seething water, when it is sod throughly, they lay it on a smooth stone, there they harden it as well as in an Oven.

There is notice to be taken to know married women from Maids, the Maids you shall alwayes see the fore part of their head and sides shaven close, the hinder part very long, which they tie in a pleate hanging downe to their hips. The married women weares their haire all of a length, and is tied of that fashion that the Maids are. The women kinde in this Countrey doth pounce and race their bodies, legges, thighes, armes and faces with a sharpe Iron, which makes a stampe in curious knots, and drawes the proportion of Fowles, Fish, or Beasts, then with paintings of sundry lively colours, they rub it into the stampe which will never be taken away, because it is dried into the flesh where it is sered.

The Savages beare their yeeres well, for when wee were at Pamonkies, wee saw a Savage by their report was above eight score yeeres of age. His eyes were sunke into his head, having never a tooth in his mouth, his haire all gray with a reasonable bigge beard, which was as white as any snow. It is a Miracle to see a Savage have any haire on their faces, I never saw, read, nor heard, any have the like before. This Savage was as lustie and went as fast as any of us, which was strange to behold.

The fifteenth day of June, we had built and finished our Fort which was triangle wise, having three Bulwarkes at every corner like a halfe Moone, and foure or five pieces of Artillerie mounted in them we had made our selves sufficiently strong for these Savages, we had also sowne most of our Corne on two Mountaines, it sprang a mans height from the ground, this Countrey is a fruitfull soile, bearing many goodly and fruitfull Trees, as Mulberries, Cherries, Walnuts, Ceders, Cypresse, Sassafras, and Vines in great abundance.

Munday the two and twentieth of June, in the morning Captaine Newport in the Admirall departed from James Port for England.

Captaine Newport being gone for England, leaving us (one hundred and foure persons) verie bare and scantie of victualls, furthermore in wares and in danger of the Savages. We hoped after a supply which Captaine Newport promised within twentie weekes. But if the beginners of this action doe carefully further us, the Country being so fruitfull, it would be as great a profit to the Realme of England, as the Indies to the King of Spaine, if this River which wee have found had beene discovered in the time of warre with

6. Sidenote: "Low Marshes."

Spaine, it would have beene a commoditie to our Realme, and a great annoyance to our enemies. The seven and twentieth of July the King of Rapahanna, demanded a Canoa which was restored, lifted up his hand to the Sunne, which they worship as their God, besides he laid his hand on his heart, that he would be our speciall friend. It is a generall rule of these people when they swere by their God which is the Sunne, no Christian will keepe their Oath better upon this promise. These people have a great reverence to the Sunne above all other things at the rising and setting of the same, they sit downe lifting up their hands and eyes to the Sunne making a round Circle on the ground with dried Tobacco,[7] then they began to pray making many Devillish gestures with a Hellish noise foming at the mouth, staring with their eyes, wagging their heads and hands in such a fashion and deformitie as it was monstrous to behold.

The sixt of August there died John Asbie of the bloudie Fluxe. The ninth day died George Flowre of the swelling. The tenth day died William Bruster Gentleman, of a wound given by the Savages, and was buried the eleventh day.

The fourteenth day, Jerome Alikock Ancient, died of a wound, the same day Francis Midwinter, Edward Moris Corporall died suddenly.

The fifteenth day, there died Edward Browne and Stephen Galthrope. The sixteenth day, there died Thomas Gower Gentleman. The seventeenth day, there died Thomas Mounslic. The eighteenth day, there died Robert Pennington, and John Martine Gentleman. The nineteenth day, died Drue Piggase Gentleman. The two and twentieth day of August, there died Captaine Bartholomew Gosnold one of our Councell, he was honourably buried, having all the Ordnance in the Fort shot off with many vollies of small shot.

After Captaine Gosnols death, the Councell could hardly agree by the dissention of Captaine Kendall, which afterward was committed about hainous matters which was proved against him.

The foure and twentieth day, died Edward Harington and George Walker, and were buried the same day. The sixe and twentieth day, died Kenelme Throgmortine. The seven and twentieth day died William Roods. The eight and twentieth day died Thomas Stoodie, Cape Merchant.

The fourth day of September died Thomas Jacob Sergeant. The fift day, there died Benjamin Beast. Our men were destroyed with cruell diseases as Swellings, Fluxes, Burning Fevers, and by warres, and some departed suddenly, but for the most part they died of meere famine.[8] There were never Englishmen left in a forreigne Countrey in such miserie as wee were in this new discovered Virginia. Wee watched every three nights lying on the bare cold ground what weather soever came warded all the next day, which brought our men to bee most feeble wretches, our food was but a small Can of Barlie sod in water to five men a day, our drinke cold water taken out of the River, which was at a floud verie salt, at a low tide full of slime and filth, which was the destruction of many of our men. Thus we lived for the space of five moneths in this miserable distresse, not having five able men to man our Bulwarkes upon any occasion. If it had not pleased God to have put a terrour in the Savages hearts, we had all perished by those vild and cruell Pagans, being in that weake estate as we were; our men night and day groaning in every corner of the Fort most pittifull to heare, if there were any conscience in men, it would make their harts to bleed to heare the pittiful murmurings & out-cries of our sick men without reliefe every night and day for the space of six weekes, some departing out of the World, many times three or foure in a night, in the morning their bodies trailed out of their Cabines like Dogges to be buried: in this sort did I see the mortalitie of divers of our people.

It pleased God, after a while, to send those people which were our mortall enemies to releeve us with victuals, as Bread, Corne, Fish, and Flesh in great plentie, which was the setting up of our feeble men, otherwise wee had all perished. Also we were frequented by divers Kings in the Countrie, bringing us store of provision to our great comfort.

The eleventh day, there was certaine Articles laid against Master Wingfield which was then President, thereupon he was not only displaced out of his President ship, but also from being of the Councell. Afterwards Captaine John Ratcliffe was chosen President.

The eighteenth day, died one Ellis Kinistone

---

7. Sidenote: "The Savages use to sacrifice to the Sunne."

8. Sidenote: "Miserable famine."

which was starved to death with cold. The same day at night, died one Richard Simmons. The nineteenth day, there died one Thomas Mouton.

William White[9] (having lived with the Natives) reported to us of their customes in the morning by breake of day, before they eate or drinke both men, women and children, that be above tenne yeeres of age runnes into the water, there washes themselves a good while till the Sunne riseth, then offer Sacrifice to it, strewing Tobacco on the water or Land, honouring the Sunne as their God, likewise they doe at the setting of the Sunne.[10]

812. May 21 to June 21, 1607. Gabriel Archer gives the earliest description of the country and the people encountered in Virginia.

On grounds of style and by internal evidence, Gabriel Archer is generally accredited as the author of the anonymous "A relatyon of the Discovery of our River, from James Forte into the Maine." It overlaps to some extent with Percy.

This is printed from P.R.O., State Papers, Colonial, CO 1/1, fols. 46–52, in P. L. Barbour, The Jamestown Voyages, I, 80–98, but is not given here. It is followed (ibid., I, 98–104) by two brief memoranda (a) "The Discription of the now discovered River and Country of Virginia" (fols. 53–55); and (b) "A Brief discription of the People" (fols. 55–56v.). Although not in an identical hand, both of these have been attributed to Archer on good internal indications of authorship. They parallel very well his description of New England in 1602 (460) to which, indeed, he refers.

The Discription of the now discovered River and Country of Virginia; with the Liklyhood of ensuing ritches, by Englands ayd and industry.

This River (we have named our kinges River) extends it self 160 myles into the mayne land

9. Sidenote: "He was a made man." This has not been satisfactorily explained.
10. Sidenote by Purchas: "The rest is omitted, being more fully set downe in Cap. Smiths Relations."

betwene two fertile and fragrant bankes, two miles, a mile, & where it is least a quarter of a myle broad, navigable for shipping of 300 tunn 150 miles: the rest deep enough for small vessells of six foot draught; it ebbs and flowes 4 foote, even to the skirt of an overfall, where the water falls downe from huge great Rockes: making in the fall five or six severall Ilettes, very fitt for the buylding of water milnes thereon, beyond this not two dayes journey, it hath two branches which come through a high stoney Country from certaine huge mountaines called Quirank, beyond which needes no relacion (this from the overfall was the report and discription of a faithfull fellow, who I dare well trust upon good reasons) from these mountaines Quirank come two lesse rivers which runn into this great one, but whether deep enough for shipps or noe I yet understand not, here be many small Rivers of brookes which unlade them selves into this mayne river at severall mouthes, which veynes devide the salvage kingdomes in many places, and yeeld pleasant seates, in all the Country over by moystening the frutefull mould. The mayne river aboundes with Sturgeon very large and excellent good: having also at the mouth of every brook and in every creek both store and exceeding good fish of divers kindes, and in y[e] large soundes neere the sea are multitudes of fish, bankes of oysters, and many great crabbs rather better in tast then ours, one able to suffice 4 men: And within sight of land into the sea we expect at tyme of yeare to have a good fishing for codd: as both at our first entring we might perceive by palpable conjecture seeing the codd follow the shipp yea bite at the [ ] as also out of my owne experience not farre of to the northward, the fishing I found in my first voyage to Virginia.

This land lyeth low at the mouth of the River & is sandy ground, all over besett with fayre pyne trees: but a litle up the river it is reasonable high; and the further we goe (till we come to the overfall) it still ryseth increasing. It is generally replenisht with wood of all kindes and that the fayrest yea and best that ever any of us (traveller or workman) ever sawe, being fitt for any use whatsoever, as shipps, howses, plankes, pales boordes mastes, waynscott, Clappboord, for pikes or elswhat.

The soyle is more fertill then canbe wel exprest it is altogether Aromaticall giving a spicy tast to the rootes of all trees plantes and hearbs: of it self a black fatt sandy mould, somewhat slymy in touch and sweet in savour: under which about a yard is in most places a redd clay fitt for brick, in other marle, in some, signification of mynnerall, in other gravell stones and rockes, it hath in diverse places fullers earth, and such as comes out of Turky called terra sigillata. It produceth of one corne of that Country wheate sometymes two or three stemnes or stalkes on which grow eares above a spann longe. besett with cornes at the least 300 upon an eare for the most part 5, 6, & 700. the beanes and peaz of this Country have a great increase also: It yeelds two cropps a yeare. Being tempered and tyme taken I hould it natures nurse to all vegetables, for I assure myself no knowne continent bringes forth any vendible necessaryes which this by planting will not afford: for testemony in part, this we fynd by proof: from the west Indies we brought a certeine delicious fruite called a pina, which the Spanyard by all art possible could never procure to grow in any place, but in his naturall site, this we rudely and carelessly sett in our mould, which fostereth it and keepes it greene, and to what Issue it may come I know not, our west Indy plantes of orenges & Cotten trees thrive well, likewise the potatoes pumpions & mellions: All our garden seedes, that were carefully sowne prosper well, yet we only digged the ground half a [foot?] deep threw in the seedes at randome carelessly and scarce rakt it. It naturally yeeldes mulbery trees, Cherry trees, vines aboundance, goosberyes, strawberyes, hurtleberryes, Respesses, ground nuttes, scarrettes, the roote called sigilla Christi, certaine sweet thynn shelled nuttes, certaine ground aples, a pleasant fruite and many other unknowne.[1] So the thing we crave is some skillfull man to husband sett plant and dresse vynes, suger canes, olives rapes hemp flax, lycoris pruyns, currantes raysons, and all such thinges, as the North Tropick of the world affordes; also saffran woad hoppes and such like.[2]

The Comodityes of this Country, what they are in Esse, is not much to be regarded, the inhabitantes having no comerce with any nation, no respect of profitt, neither is there scarce that we call meum et tuum among them save only the kinges know their owne territoryes, & the people their severall gardens yet this for the present by the consent of all our Seaman, meerly our fishing for Sturgeon cannot be lesse worth then 1000li a yeare, leaving hering and codd as possibilityes.

Our Clapboord and waynscott (if shipps will but fetch it) we may make as much as England can vent: we can send (if we be frendes with the salvages or be able to force them) 2 3 4 or 5000li a yeare of the earth called terra Sigillata. Saxafrage what store we please. Tobacco after a yeare or two 5000li a yeare. we have (as we suppose) ritch dyes, if they prove vendible, worth more then yet is nominated; we have excellent furrs in some places of the Country great store, we can make pitch Rozen and Turpentyne; there is a gumme which bleedeth from a kind of maple (the bark being cutt) not much vnlike a Balsome both in sent and vertue. Apothecary drugges of diverse sortes, some knowne to be of good estimacion, some strange of whose vertue the salvages report wonders[3]—we can by our industry and plantacion of comodious marchandize make oyles wynes soape ashes, wood ashes, extract from minerall earth Iron copper &c: we have a good fishing for muskles, which resemble mother of pearle. & if the pearle we have seene in the kinges eares & about their neckes come from these shells, we know the bankes. To conclude I know not what can be expected from a common wealth that either this land affordes not or may soone yeeld.

[b]   A Breif discription of the People.

There is a king in this land called great Pawatah, vnder whose dominions are at least 20ty severall kingdomes, yet each king potent as a prince in his owne territory. these have their Subjectes at so quick Comaund, as a beck bringes obedience, even to the resticucion of stolne goodes which by their naturall inclinacon they are loth to leave. They goe all naked save their privityes, yet in coole weather they weare deare skinns, with the hayre on loose: some have leather stockinges up to their twistes, & sandalls on their feet, their hayre is black generally, which they weare long on the left side, tyed up on a knott, about which knott the kinges and best among them have a kind

1. Sidenote: "The Rubish this land naturaly bringeth forth."
2. Sidenote: "The liklyhood of profitt by Industry."

3. Sidenote: "Furres Pitch Rosen Turpentine A maple gumme Wisacan or Virginia bloud wort which heales poysoned woundes."

of Coronett of deares hayre coloured redd, some have chaines of long linckt copper about their neckes, and some chaines of pearle, the common sort stick long fethers in this knott, I found not a grey eye among them all. their skynn is tawny not so borne, but with dying and paynting them selves, in which they delight greatly. The wemen are like the men, onely this difference; their hayre groweth long al over their heades save clipt somewhat short afore, these do all the labour and the men hunt and goe at their plesure. They live comonly by the water side in litle cottages made of canes and reedes, covered with the barke of trees; they dwell as I guesse by families of kindred & allyance some 40^tie or 50^ti in a Hatto or small village; which townes are not past a myle or half a myle asunder in most places. They live upon sodden wheat beanes & peaze for the most part, also they kill deare take fish in their weares, & kill fowle aboundance, they eate often and that liberally; they are proper lusty streight men very strong runn exceeding swiftly, their feight is alway in the wood with bow & arrowes, & a short wodden sword, the clerity they use in skirmish is admirable. the king directes the batle & is alwayes in front. Their manner of entertainment is upon mattes on the ground under some tree, where they sitt themselves alone in the midest of the matt, & two mattes on each side, on which they[r] people sitt, then right against him (making a square forme) satt we alwayes. when they came to their matt they have an usher goes before them, & the rest as he sittes downe give a long showt. The people steale any thing comes neare them, yea are so practized in this art that lookeing in our face they would with their foot betwene their toes convey a chizell knife, percer or any indifferent light thing: which having once conveyed they hold it an injury to take the same from them; They are naturally given to trechery, howbeit we could not finde it in our travell up the river, but rather a most kind and loving people. They sacrifice Tobacco to the Sunn fayre picture or a harmefull thing, as a sword or peece also; they strincle some into the water in the morning before they wash. they have many wives, to whome as neare as I could perceive they keep constant. the great king Pawatah had most wives: These they abide not to be toucht before their face. the great diseaze reignes in the men gener-

ally, full fraught with noodes botches and pulpable apparances in their forheades, we found above a hundred. The wemen are very cleanly in making their bread and prepareing meat. I found they account after death to goe into an other world pointing eastward to the Element, and when they saw us at prayer they observed us with great silence and respect especially those to whome I had imparted the meaning of our reverence. To conclude they are a very witty and ingenious people, apt both to understand and speake our language, so that I hope in god as he hath miraculously preserved us hither from all dangers both of sea and land & their fury so he will make us authors of his holy will in converting them to our true Christian faith by his owne inspireing grace and knowledge of his deity.

813. May, 1607 to May, 1608. Edward Maria Wingfield's replies to the charges made against him in Virginia.

The first governor, who was named in the instructions opened when the first expedition reached Virginia, was clearly unfit for his task. He was petty-minded and had no capacity to control men, especially the litigious, quarrelsome, and greedy crew by which Jamestown was founded. Deposed from his governorship, he was imprisoned and insulted. When Christopher Newport arrived in January, 1608, he rescued Wingfield and brought him back to England with him. The pathetic document we have from Wingfield's hands is clearly a draft of the case that he proposed to make to the King's Council for Virginia in explanation of what had happened in Virginia. The opening draft letter is dignified enough, and the early stages of his narrative, where he gives an account (though he refers to an earlier journal not now extant) of the establishment of the settlement, is coherent and useful, though scarcely as clear a one as was given by either Percy or Archer. After his deposition as governor on September 10, 1607, his narrative degenerates into a scandalous chronicle of the behavior of the ruling group in the colony, from which he emerges as a person of some dignity but very poor judgment and also as a man who has a basic contempt for his fellow colonists unless they were by birth gentlemen (Bartholomew Gosnold and George Percy were among the few who thus qualified). Intermittently, he provides interesting information and also a means of checking some of John Smith's assertions. The narrative continues until his return to the Thames on May 21, 1608. He then adds a string of answers to real (or supposed) charges to be made against him, Whether or not he ever submitted a document based on this draft to the Council for Virginia is unknown, nor is anything known of penal or other proceedings against him. The permission given to Archer (who came to England to accuse him) to return to Virginia in 1609 suggests, at least, that his statements against Archer were not accepted.

Lambeth Palace, Lambeth MS 250, fols. 382-396.; printed in P. L. Barbour, The Jamestown Voyages, *I (1969), 213-229.*

[a] Right worshipfull: and more worthy

My due respect to your selves, my allegiance (if I may so terme it) to the Virginean action, my good heede to my poore reputacion thrust a penne into my handes, so jealous am I to bee missing to any of them; if it wandereth in extravagantes, yet shall they not bee idle to those Phisitions, whose loves have undertaken the saftie and advancement of Virginia.

It is no small comfort that I speake before such gravitie, whose judgement no forrunner can forestall with any opprobrious untruths whose wisedomes can easily disroabe malice out of her painted garments from the ever reverenced truth.

I did so faithfully betroth my best indeavors to this noble enterprize as my carriage might endure no suspition: I never turned my face from daunger, or hidd my handes from labour, so watchfull a Sentinel stood my self to my self.

I know wel a troope of errors continually beseege mens actions, some of them ceased on by malice, some by ignorance: I doo not hoodwinck my carriage in my self love, but freely and humblie submit it to your grave censures.

I do freely and truely Anatomize the governement and governours that your experience may applie medicines accordinglie, and upon the truth

of this journall do pledge my faith, and life, and so do rest.

yours to commaund in all service
    unsigned

[b] Here followeth what happined in James Towne in Virginia after Captayne Newports departure for England.

Captayne Newport haveing allwayes his eyes and eares open to the proceedinges of the Collonye, 3. or 4. dayes before his departure, asked the president how he thought himself setled in the government, whose answere was that no disturbaunce could indaunger him of the Collonye, but it must be wrought eyther by Captayne Gosnold, or Master Archer; for the one was strong with freinds and followers, and could if he would; and the other was troubled with an ambitious spirit, and would if he could: The Captayne gave them both knowledg of this the Presidentes opinion, and mooved them with many intreatyes to be myndefull of their dutyes to his Majestie and the Collonye.

The 22th [June] Captayne Newport retorned for England, for whose good passadge, and safe retorne wee made many prayers to our allmighty god/

June the 25th an Indian Came to us from the great Poughwaton with the worde of peace, that he desired greatly our freindshipp that the wyroaunces, Paspaheigh, and Tapahanagh should be our freindes, that wee should sowe and reape in peace, or els he would make warrs upon them with us; This message fell out true, for both those wyroaunces have ever since remayned in peace, and trade with us: Wee rewarded the messinger, with many tryfles, which were great wonders to him.

This Powatan dwelleth 10 myles from us vpon the River Pamaonche, which lyeth North from us; the Powatan in the former jornall mencioned (a dwellar by Captayn Newports faulls) ys a wyroaunce, and under this great Powaton, which before wee knew not/

The 3 of July 7 or 8 Indians presented the President a Dear from Pamaonke, a wyroaunce desiring our freindshipp, they enquired after our shipping, which the President said was gon to Croatoon; they feare much our shipps; and therefore he would not have them thinck it farr from us;

their wyrounce had a Hatchet sent hym, they wear well Contented with trifles: A litle after this Came a Dear to the President from the great Powatan: he and his messingers were pleased with the like trifles: The President likewise bought divers tymes Dear of the Indyans, beavars and other flesh, which he alwayes caused to be equally devided amongst the Collonye.

About this tyme divers of our men fell sick, wee myssed above Forty before September did see us, amongst whom was the Worthy and Religious gent Captayn Bartholmew Gosnold, upon whose lief stood a great part of the good succes, and fortune of our government and Collony: In his sicknes tyme the president did easily foretell his owne deposing from his Comaund, so much differed the president and the other Councellors on mannaging the government of the Collonye.

The 7th of July Tapahanah a wyroaunce dweller on Salisbery side hayled us with the word of peace, the President with a Shallopp well manned went to him, he found him sytting on the ground Crossed legged as is their Custome, with one attending on him, which did often saie this is the wyroance Tapahanah, which he did likewise confirme with stroaking his brest, he was well enough knowne for the President had sene him diuerse tymes before, his Countynance was nothing cherefull, for wee had not seene him since he was in the feild against us, but the President would take no knowledg thereof, and used him kindely, giving him a red Wascoat, which he did desire; Tapahanah did enquire after our shipping; he receyved answer as before, he said his ould store was spent, that his new was not at full groath by a foote; That as sone as any was ripe he would bring it, which promise he truly performed.

The [   ] of [   ] Master Kendall was put of from beeing of the Counsell, and committed to prison, for that it did manyfestly appeere he did practize to sowe discord betwene the President and Councell.

Sicknes had not now left us vj able men in our Towne, gods onely mercy did now watch and Warde for us, but the President hidd this our weakenes carefully from the salvages, never suffring them in all his tyme to come into our Towne.

The vjth of September Paspaheigh sent us a boy that was run from us, this was the first assurance of his peace with us, besides wee found them no Canyballs: The boye observed the men & women to spend the most part of the night in singing, or howling, and that every morning the Women Carryed all the litle Childrenn to the Rivers sides, but what they did there he did not knowe.

The rest of the wyroances doe likewise send our men runnagates to us home againe, using them well during their beeing with them; so as now they being well rewarded at home at their retorne, they take litle joye to travell abroad without Pasportes.

The Councell demaunded some larger allowaunce for them selves, and for some sick their fauorites, which the President would not yield unto without their Warrantes.

This matter was before propounded by Captayn Martyn, but so nakedly as that he neyther knew the quantity of the stoare to be but for xiij weekes and a half under the Cap[e] Merchauntes hand, he prayed them further to Consider the long tyme before wee expected Captayn Newportes retorne, the incertainty of his retorne, if god did not favour his voyage, the long tyme before our harvest would be ripe, and the doubtfull peace that wee had with the Indyans, which they would keepe no longer then opertunity served to doe us mischeif.

It was then therefore ordered, that every meale of fish or fleshe should excuse the allowance for poridg, both against the sick and hole.

The Counsell therefore sitting againe upon this proposition instructed in the former reasons and order, did not thinke it fit to breake the former order by enlarging their allowance, as will appeere by the most voyces reddy to be shewed under their handes.

Now was the Comon store of oyle, vinigar, sack, & Aquavite all spent saveing twoe Gallons of each; the sack reserved for the Comunion table, the rest for such extreamityes as might fall upon us, which the President had onely made know[n]e to Captayn Gosnold, of which course he liked well, the vessells wear therefore boonged upp: When Master Gosnold was dead the President did acquaint the rest of the Councell with the said Remnant: but lord how they then longed for to supp up that litle remnant for they had now emptied all their owne bottles, and all other that they could smell out.

A litle wile after this the Councell did againe fall

upon the President for some better allowance for themselves and some few the sick their privates: The President protested he would not be partiall, but if one had any thing of him, every man should have his portion according to their places, Nevertheles that upon their Warrantes he would deliver what pleased them to demaund. Yf the President had at that tyme enlarged the proportion according to their request, without doubt in very short tyme he had starved the whole Company, he would not joyne with them therefore in such an ignorant murder without their owne Warrant.

The President well seeing to what end their ympacience would growe, desired them earnestly & often tymes to bestowe the Presidentshipp amonge themselues, that he could obey, a private man, as well as they could Comaund, but they refused to discharge him of the place, sayeing they mought not doe it, for that hee did his Majestie good service in yt.

In this meane tyme the Indians did daily relieve us with Corne and fleshe, that in three weekes the Presidant had reared upp xx men able to worke, for as his stoare increased he mended the Comon pott; hee had laid up besides provision for 3. weekes, wheate beforehand.

By this tyme the Councell had fully plotted to depose Wingfeild the then President, and had drawne certeyne Artycles in Wrighting amongst them selves and toke their oathes upon the Evangelistes to observe them, th'effect whereof was first:

To depose the then President.

To make Master Ratcliff the next President.

Not to depose the one th'other.

Not to take the deposed President into Councell againe.

Not to take Master Archer into the Councell or any other without the Consent of every one of them; To theis they had subscribed, as out of their owne mouthes, at severall tymes it was easily gathered.

Thus had they forsaken his Majesties government sett us downe in the instruccions, & made it a Triumvirat.

It seemeth Master Archer was nothing acquainted with theis artycles, though all the rest crept out of his noates and Comentaryes that were preferred against the President yet it pleased god to Cast him into the same disgrace and pitt that he prepared for an other, as will appeere hereafter.

The 10 of September, Master Ratcliff, Master Smyth, and Master Martynn Came to the Presidentes Tennt with a Warrant subscribed under their handes to depose the President, sayeing they thought him very unworthy to be eyther President or of the Councell, and therefore discharged him of bothe: Hee answered them that they had eased him of a great deale of Care, and trouble; that long since hee had divers tymes profered them the place at an easier rate, and further that the President ought to be removed (as appeereth in his Majesties instruccions for our government) by the greater number of xiij voyces Councellors, that they were but three, and therefore wished them to proceede advisedly, but they told him if they did him wrong, they must answere it; Then said the deposed President I ame at your pleasure, dispose of me as you will without further Garboile.

I will now wright what followeth in my owne name and give the new President his title, I shalbe the briefer being thus discharged, I was Comytted to a Serjeant, and sent to the Pynnasse: but I was answered with if they did me wronge, they must answere it.

The 11th of September I was sent for to Come before the President, and Councell upon their Court daie, they had now made Master Archer Recorder of Virginia; The President made a speeche to the Collony that he thought it fitt to acquaint them whie I was deposed. I ame now forced to stuff my Paper with frivilous trifles, that our grave and worthy Councell may the better strike those vaynes where the Corrupt blould lyeth, and that they may see in what manner of government the hope of the Collony now travayleth.

First Master President said that I had denyed him a penny whitle, a Chickyn, a spoonfull of beere, and served him with foule Corne, and with that pulled some graine out of a bagg shewing it to the Company.

Then start up Master Smyth, and said that I had tould him playnly how he lied, and that I said though wee were equall heere, yet if he were in England he would thinck scorne his man should be my Companyon.

Master Martyn followed with, he reporteth that I doe slack the service in the Collonye, and doe nothing but tend my pott, spitt, and oven, but he hath starved my sonne, and denyed him a spoonefull of beere; I have freindes in England shalbe revenged on him, if ever he Come in London.

I asked master President if I should answere theis Complaintes, and whether he had ought els to charge me with all; with that he pulled out a paper booke, loaded full with Artycles against me, and gave them Master Archar to reade: I tould Master President and the Councell; that by the instruccions for our government, our proceedinges ought to be verball, and I was there ready to answere: but they said they would proceede in that order; I desired a Coppie of the Articles, and tyme given me to answere them likewise by wrighting, but that would not be graunted; I badd them then please themselves; Master Archer then redd some of the Artycles, when on the suddaine Master President said: staie, staie, wee knowe not whether he will abide our Judgment, or whether he will appeale to the King, sayeing to me: how saie you, will you appeale to the King or no. I apprehended presently that gods mercy had opened me a Waie through their ignorance, to escape their malice, for I never knewe howe I might demaunde an appeale, besides I had secret knowledg how they had forejudged me to paie five fould for anything that Came to my handes, whereof I could not discharge my self by wrighting, and that I should lye in prison untill I had paid it.

The Cape Marchant had delivered me our Marchantdize without any noat of the pertycularyties under my hand, for himself had receyved them in grosse; I like wise as occasion mooved me spent them in Trade, or by guift amongst the Indians, so likewise did Captayn Newport take of them; when he went up to discouer the kinges river, what he thought good, without any noate of his hand, mentioning the Certainty, and disposed of them as was fitt for him, of these likewise I could make no accompt, onely I was well assured I had never bestowed the valewe of three penny Whitles to my owne use, nor to the private use of any other, for I never carryed any favorite over with me, or intertayned any thear, I was all one, and one to all.

Upon theis consideracions I answered Master President and the Councell that his Majesties handes were full of mercy and that I did appeale to his Majesties mercy, they then comytted me prisoner againe to the master of ye Pynnasse with theis words: looke to him well he is now the kinges prisoner.

Then Master Archer pulled out of his bosome an other paper booke full of Artycles against me, desiring that he might reade them in the name of the Collony: I said I stood there ready to answere any mans Complaint whome I had wronged, but no one man spoke one word against me, then was he willed to reade his booke, whereof I complayned; but I was still answered if they doe me wrong they must answere it: I have forgotten the most of the Artycles they were so slight (yet he glorieth much in his penn worke) I knowe well the last, and a speeche that he then made savored well of a mutyny; for he desired that by no meanes, I might lye prysoner in the Towne, least boath he, and others of the Collony, should not give such obedience to their Comaund as they ought to doe, which goodly speech of his they easilye swallowed.

But it was usuall, and naturall to this honest gent Master Archer to be allwayes hatching of some mutany, in my tyme, hee might have appeered an author of 3 severall mutynies.

And hee (as Master Pearsie sent me worde) had bought some Witnesses handes against me to divers artycles with Indian Cakes (which was no great matter to doe after my deposall, and considering their hungar) perswations and threates; at an other tyme he feared not to saie openly, and in the presence of one of the Councell, that if they had not deposed me when they did, he hadd gotten twenty others to him self, which should have deposed me, but this speech of his was likewise easily dijested.

Master Croftes feared not to saie that if others would joyne with him, he would pull me out of my seate, and out of my skynn too; others would saie, (whose names I spare) that unlesse I would amend their allowance, they would be their owne Carvers; for these mutinus speeches, I rebuked them openly, and proceeded no further against them, Considering th'end of mens lives in the kinges service there; one of the Councell was very earnest with me to take a guard aboute me, I answered him I would no guard but gods love, and my owne innocencie. in all theis disorders was Master Archer a Ring leader.

When Master President and Master Archer

had made an end of their Artycles above mencioned, I was agine sent prisoner to the Pynnasse, and Master Kendall taken from thence had his liberty, but might not Carry Armes.

All this while the Salvages brought to the Towne such Corne and flesh as they could spare, Paspaheighe by Tapahanaes mediation was taken into freindshipp with us, the Councellors (Master Smyth especially) traded up and downe the River with the Indyans for Corn, which releved the Collony well.

As I understand by report I ame much charged with starving the Collony; I did allwayes give every man his allowance faithfully, both of Corne, oyle, aquivite &c as was by the Counsell proportioned, neyther was it bettered after my tyme, untill towards th'end of March, a Bisket was allowed to every workeing man for his breakefast, by meanes of the provision brought us by Captayn Newport, as will appeere here after: It is further said I did much banquit, and Ryot: I never had but one Squirell roasted, whereof I gave part to Master Ratcliff then sick; yet was that Squirell given me; I did never heate a flesh pott, but when the Comon pot was so used likewise; Yet how often Master Presidentes and the Councellors spittes have night & daie bene endaungered to break their backes so laden with swanns, geese, duckes, &c, how many tymes their flesh pottes have swelled, many hungry eies did behold to their great longing: and what great Theeves, and theeving thear hath bene in the Comon stoare since my tyme, I doubt not but is all ready made knowne to his Majesties Councell for Virginia.

The 17th daie of September I was sent for to the Court to answere a Complaint exhibited against me by Jehu Robinson, for that when I was president, I did saie, hee with others had Consented to runn awaye with the Shallop to newfound land, at an other tyme, I must answere Master Smyth, for that I had said hee did conceale an intended mutany; I tould Master Recorder those wordes would beare no actions, that one of the Causes was done without the lymites mencioned in the Patent graunted to us, and therefore prayed Master President that I mought not be thus lugged with theis disgraces and troubles; but hee did weare no other eies or eares then grew on Master Archers head; The Jury gaue the one of them 100li, and the other twoe hundred pound damages for slaunder, then Master Recorder did very learnedly comfort me, that if I had wrong, I might bring my writ of error in London, whereat I smiled.

I seeing their lawe so speedie and cheape, desired Justice for a Copper Kettle, which Master Crofts did deteyne from me, hee said I had given it him, I did bid him bringe his proofe for that; he Confessed hee had no proofe, Then Master President did aske me if I would be sworne I did not give it him, I said I knew no cause whie to sweare for myne owne, hee asked Master Crofts if he would make oath, I did give it him, which oath hee tooke, and wann my Kettle from me, that was in that place and tyme, worth half his waight in gold; yet I did understand afterwards that he would have given John Capper the one half of the Kettle to have taken the oath for him, but hee would no Copper on that price.

I tould Master President I had not knowne the like lawe and prayed they would be more sparing of law, untill wee had more witt, or wealthe, that lawes were goode spies, in a populous, peaceable, and plentifull Cuntry, whear they did make the good men better, & stayed the badd from being worse ,that wee weare so poore as they did but robb us of tyme that might be better ymployed in service in the Collonye.

The [ ] daie of [ ] the President did beat James Read the Smyth, the Smyth stroake him againe, for this he was condempned to be hanged, but before he was turned of the Lather he desired to speake with the President in private, to whome he accused Master Kendall of a mutiny, and so escaped himself: What Indictment master Recorder framed, against the Smyth I knowe not, but I knowe it is familiar for the President, Counsellors, and other officers to beate men at their pleasures, one lyeth sick till death, an other walketh lame, the third cryeth out of all his boanes, which myseryes they doe take upon their Consciences to Come to them by this their Almes of beating. Wear this whipping, lawing, beating, and hanging in Virginia knowne in England I feare it would drive many well affected myndes from this honorable action of Virginia.

This Smyth Comyng aboord the Pynnasse, with some others, aboute some busines 2 or 3 dayes before his arraignement brought me Comendacions from Master Pearsye, Master Waller, Master Kendall, and some others saieing they would be glad to see me on shoare: I answered him they were honest gentlemen and had carryed themselves very obediently to their gouernors, I prayed god that they did not thinck of any ill thing unworthie themselves; I added further that upon Sundaie if the weathiar were faire, I would be at the sermon, lastly I said that I was so sickly, starved, lame, and did lye so could, and wett in the Pynnasse as I would be dragged thithere before I would goe thither any more, sundaie proved not faire I went not to the Sermon.

The [ ] daie of [ ] Master Kendall was executed being shott to death for a mutiny. In th'arrest of his Judgment he alleaged to Master President that his name was Sicklemore, not Ratcliff: & so had no authority to pronounce Judgment, then Master Martyn pronounced Judgment.

Some what before this tyme the President, and Councell had sent for the keyes of my Coffers, supposing that I had some Wrightinges Concerning the Collony, I requested that the Clearke of the Councell might see what they tooke out of my Coffers, but they would not suffer him or any other, under Cullor heereof they tooke my bookes of Accompt, and all my noates that concerned the expences of the Collony, and instructions under the Cape Marchantes hande of the stoare of provision, diuers other bookes & trifles of my owne proper goodes, which I could neuer recover. Thus was I made good prise on all sides.

The [ ] daie of [ ] the President Comaunded me to Come on shore, which I refused as not rightfully deposed and desired that I mought speake to him and the Councell in the presence of 10 of the best sorte of the gentry, with much intreaty some of them wear sent for, then I tould them, I was determined to goe into England to acquaint our Councell there, with our weaknes; I said further their lawes, and government was such as I had no joye to live under them any longer; that I did much myslike their triumverat, haveing forsaken his Majesties instruccions for our government, and therefore praied there might be more made of the Councell: I said further I desired not to goe into England, if eyther Master President, or Master Archer would goe but was willing to take my fortune with the Collony, and did also proffer to furnish them with 100ᶥⁱ towards the fetching home the Collonye, if the action was given over; They did like of none of my proffers, but made divers shott at mee in the Pynnasse: I seing their resolucions went a shoare

to them, whear after I had staied a while in conference they sent me to the Pynnasse againe.

The 10th of December Master Smyth went up the Ryuer of the Chechohomynaies to trade for Corne, he was desirous to see the heade of that River, and when it was not passible with the Shallop, he hired a Cannow and an Indian to Carry him up further, the river the higher grew worse and worse then hee went on shoare with his guide, and left Robinson & Emmery, twoe of our men in the Cannow, which were presently slayne by the Indians Pamaonkes men; and hee himself taken prysoner, and by the meanes of his guide his lief was saved, and Pamaonche haveing him prisoner Carryed him to his Neybors wyroances to see if any of them knew him for one of those, which had bene some twoe or three yeers before us in a River amongst them Northward, and taken awaie some Indians from them, by force, at last he brought him to the great Powaton (of whome before wee had no knowledg) whoe sent him home to owr Towne the viijth of January.

During Master Smythes absence the President did swear Master Archer, one of the Councell, contrary to his oath taken in the Artycles agreed upon betweene themselues (before spoken of), and contrary to the kinges instruccions, and without Master Martyns consent, whereas there weare no more but the President and Master Martyn then of the Councell.

Master Archer being setled in his authority sought how to Call Master Smyths lief in question, and had indited him upon a Chapter in Leviticus for the death of his twoe men; hee had hadd his tryall the same daie of his retorne, and I believe his hanging the same, or the next daie, so speedie is our lawe thear, but it pleased god to send Captayn Newport unto us the same evening to our unspeakeable comfortes; whose arryvall saved Master Smyths leif, and myne, because hee tooke me out of the Pynnasse, an gave me leave to lye in the Towne: Also by his comyng was prevented a Parliament, which yᵉ newe Counsailor Master Recorder intended thear to summon; Thus error begot error.

Captayne Newport haveing landed, lodged, and refreshed his men, ymploied some of them aboute a faire stoare house, others aboute a stove, and his Maryners aboute a Church, all which workes they finished cherefully and in short tyme.

The 7 of January, our Towne was almost quite

burnt, with all our apparell and provision; but Captayn Newport healed our wants to our great Comforts, out of the great plenty sent us by the provident and loving care of our worthie & most worthie Councell.

This Vigillant Captayne slacking no opertunity that might advaunce the prosperity of the Collony haveing setled the Company uppon the former workes, tooke Master Smyth and Master Scrivener (an other Councellor of Virginia, upon whose discretion liveth a great hope of the action) went to discover the Ryver Pamaonche on the further side, whearof dwelleth the great Powaton, and to trade with him for Corne: This River lyeth North from us, and runneth east and West, I have nothing but by relation, of that matter, and therefore dare not make any discourse thereof least I mought wrong the great desart, which Captayn Newports love to the action hath deserved, especially himself being present, and best able to give satisfaccion thereof, I will hasten therefore to his retorne.

The 9th of Marche he retorned to James Towne, with his Pynnasse well loaden with Corne, Wheat, beanes, and Pease, to our great Comfort & his worthi Comendacions.

By this tyme the Counsell & Captaine haveing intentively looked into the Carryadge bothe of the Councellors, and other officers removed some officers out of the stoare; and Captayn Archer, a Councellor, whose insolency did looke upon that litle in himself with great sighted spectacles, derrogating from others merrites by spueing out his venemous libells, and infamous Cronicles, upon them; as doth appeere in his owne hand wrighting / For which & other worse trickes he had not escaped ye halter, but that Captayn Newport interposed his advise to the Contrarye.

Captayne Newport haveing now dispatched all his busines and sett the Clocke in a true course (if so the Councell will keepe it) prepared himself for England upon the xth of Aprill, and arryved at Blackwall on Sunday the xxjth of Maye 1608.

[c] I humbly crave some patience to answere many scandalus imputacions, which malice, more than malice hath scattered upon my name, and those frivolous greevances objected against me by the President and Councell, and though *nil conscire sibi* be the onely maske that can well cover my blushes; yett doe I not doubt, but this my Appollogie shall easily wipe them awaie.

It is noysed that I Combyned with the Spanniards to the distruccion of the Collony: That I ame an Athiest because I Carryed not a Bible, with me, and because I did forbid the preacher to preache, that I affected a Kindome: That I did hide of the Comon provision in the ground.

I Confesse I have alwayes admyred any noble vertue & prowesse as well in the Spanniards (as in other Nations) but naturally I have alwayes distrusted, and disliked their neighborhoode.

I sorted many bookes in my house to be sent up to me at my goeing to Virginia, a mongst them a bible; They were sent me up in a Trunk to London, with divers fruite, conserves, & preserves, which I did sett in Master Crofts his house in Ratcliff; In my beeing at Virginia I did understand my trunck was thear broken up, much of my sweete meates eaten at his Table, some of my bookes which I missid to be scene in his handes; and whether a mongst them my Bible was so ymbeasiled, or mislayed, by my servauntes; and not sent me I knowe not as yet.

Twoe or three sundayes morninges the Indians gave us allarums at our Towne, by that tymes they wear answered, the place aboute us well discovered, and our devyne service ended, the daie was farr spent: The preacher did aske me if it weare my pleasure to have a sermon, hee said hee was prepared for it: I made answere that our men weare weary, and hungry, and that hee did see the tyme of the daie farr past (for at other tymes hee never made such question but the service finished he began his sermon) & that if it pleased him wee would spare him, till some other tyme: I never failed to take such noates by wrighting out of his doctrine as my Capacity could Comprehend, unlesse some raynie day hindred my indeavour,

My mynde never swelled with such ympossible mountebanck humors, as could make me affect any other Kingdome then the kingdome of heaven.

As truly as god liveth I gave an ould man then the keeper of the private stoure, 2 glasses with sallet oyle which I brought with me out of England for my private stoare, and willed him to bury it in the ground, for that I feared the great heate would spoile it, whatsoever was more I did never Consent unto, or knewe of it: And as truly was it protested unto me, that all the remaynder before mencioned of the oyle, wyne &c which the President receyued of me, when I was deposed, theye themselues poored into their owne bellyes.

To the Presidentes and Councelles objections I saie, that I doe knowe Curtesey and Civility became a governor; no penny whitle was asked me but a kniffe, whereof I had none to spare, the Indyans had long before stoallen my knife, of Chickins, I never did eat but one, and that in my sicknes; Master Ratcliff had before that tyme tasted of 4 or 5: I had by my owne huswiferie bred above 37 and the most part of them of my owne Poultrye, of all which at my Comyng awaye I did not see three liveing: I never denyed him (or any other) beare when I had it, the Corne was of the same which wee all lived upon.

Master Smyth in the tyme of our hungar had spred a Rumor in the Collony that I did feast my self and my servauntes, out of the Comon stoare, with entent (as I gathered) to have stirred the discontented Company against me, I tould him privately in Master Gosnolds Tent, that indeede I had caused half a pinte of pease to be sodden, with a peese of porke of my owne provision for a poore old man, which in a sicknes (whereof he died) he much desired, and said that if out of his malice he had given it out otherwise, that hee did tell a lye. It was proved to his face, that he begged in Ireland like a rogue, without lycence, to such I would not my name should be a Companyon.

Master Martins payns during my Comaund never stirred out of our Towne tenn scoare, and how slack hee was in his watching and other dutyes, it is too well knowne: I never defrauded his sonne of anything of his owne allowance, but gave him above it, I believe their disdainefull usage, and threates which they many tymes gave me, would have pulled some distempered speeches out of farr greater Pacyence then myne; yet shall not any revenging humor in me befoule my penn with their base names and liues here and there, I did visit Master Pearsie, Master Hunt, Master Brewster, Master Pickasse, Master Allicock, ould Short, the Bricklayer and diverse others, at severall tymes, I never miscalled at a gentleman at any time.

Concerning my deposing from my place, I can well proove that Master Ratcliff said if I had used him well in his sicknes (wherein I finde not my self guilty of the contrary) I had never bene deposed.

Master Smith said if it had not bene for Master Archers I hadd never bene deposed: since his being heere in the Towne he hath said that he tould the President, and Councell that they were

frivolous objections they had Collected against me, and that they had not doone well to depose me; Yet in my Conscience I doe believe him the first & onely practizer in theis practises.

Master Archers quarrell to me was, because hee had not the choise of the place for our plantation, because I misliked his leying out of our Towne in the pinnasse, because I would not sware him of the Councell for Virginia, which neyther I could doo or he deserve.

Master Smyths quarrell because his name was mencioned in the entended & Confessed mutiny by Galthropp.

Thomas Wootton the Surieon, because I would not subscribe to a Warrant (which he had gotten drawne) to the Treasurer of Virginia to deliver him mony to furnish him with drugges, and other necessaryes, & because I disallowed his living in the pinnasse, haveing many of our men lyeing sick, & wounded in our Towne to whose dressinges by that meanes he slacked his attendance.

Of the same men also Captayn Gosnold gave me warning misliking much their dispositions, and assured me they would ley hold of me if they could, and peradventure many, because I held them, to watching warding, and workeing, and the Collony generally because I would not give my consent to starve them; I cannot rack one word, or thought from my self, touching my Carryadg in Virginia other then is herein sett downe.

If I may now at the last presume upon Your fauours; I ame an honourable suitor; that your owne love of truth will vouchsafe to cleare me from all false aspersions happining since I embarked me into this affaire of Virginia, for my first worke (which was to make aright choise of a spirituall Pastor) I appeale to the remembraunce of my Lord of Caunterbury his grace; who gave me very gracious audience in my request. And the world knoweth, whome I tooke with me; truly in my opinion a man not any waie to be touched with the rebellious humors of a popish spirit, nor blemished with ye least suspition of a factius scismatick, whereof I had a speciall Care. for other objections if your worthie selves be pleased to sett me free, I have learned to dispise ye populer verdict of ye vulgar. I ever chered up my self with a confidence in ye wisdome of graue judicious Senatours & was never dismayed in all my service by any synister event, though I bethought me of ye hard begininges which in former ages betided those worthy spirites, that planted the greatest Monarches in Asia & Europe, wherein I observed rather yᵉ troubles of Moses & Aron, with other of like History, then that venom in the mutinous brood of Cadmus or that harmony in yᵉ swete consent of Amphion: And when with yᵉ former I had considered that even the b[r]etheren at their plantacion of the Romaine Empire were not free from mortall hatred, & intestine garboile, likewise that both yᵉ Spanish & English Records are guilty of like factions, it made me more vigillant in yᵉ avodying thereof: and I protest my greatest contencion was to prevent contencion, and my chiefest endeavor to preserve the lives of others, though with yᵉ great hazard of my own for I never desired to enamell my name with bloude: I rejoyce that my travells & daungers haue done somewhat for the behoof of Jerusalem in virginia. If it be objected as my oversight to put my self amongst such men, I can saie for my self there wear not any other for our consort. & I could not forsake yᵉ enterprise of opening so glorious a Kingdome unto yᵉ king, wherein I shall ever be most ready to bestow yᵉ poore remainder of my dayes, as in any other his Heighnes disignes according to my bounden duty with yᵉ utmost of my poore Tallent.

[Endorsed:] A Discourse of Virginia
Per Edward Maria Wingfilld

814. November 26, [1608]. Peter Wynne to Sir John Egerton.

From the original in Huntington Library, Ellesmere MS 1683, printed in P. L. Barbour, The Jamestown Voyages, I (1969), 245–246.

Most noble knight

It was not so desirous to come into this Country, as I am now willing here to end my dayes for I fine it a farr more pleasant and plentifull country than any report made mencion of Upon the River which wee are seated I have gote six or seaven score miles, and so farr is navigable afterward I travailed between 50 or 60 myles by land, into a Country Called Monacon who owe no subjection to Powaton; this land is very high ground and

fertill, being very full of delicate springes of sweet water: the ayre more helthfull than the place wher wee are seated, by reason it is not subject to such fogges and mistes as we continually have. The people of Monacon speak a farr differing language from the subjectes of Powaton, theyr pronuciation being very like Welch so that the gentlemen in our Company desired me to be theyr Interpreter. The comodities as yet knowne in this Country whereof there wilbe great store, is Pitch. Tarr. Sope ashes, and some dyes, whereof we have sent examples. As for thinges more precious I omit till tyme (which I hope wilbe shortly) shall make manifest proof of it. As concerning your request of Bloud houndes, I cannot learne that ther is any such in this Country: only the dogges which are here are a Certeyne kind of Currs like our wariners hey dogges in England; and they keepe them to hunt theyr land fowles, as Turkeys and such like, for they keep nothing tame about them. Hereafter I doubt not to give you at large a farther relacion then as yet I am able to doe, and doe therfore desire you to take theis fewe lines in good part and hold me excused for the rest untill Fitter oportunity. Thus Comending my service to your good love with many thankes for all favours and kindnesses received from you I doe ever remayne

Your most devoted in all service

[Signed:] Peter Wyn

James Towne in Virginia this xxvi of November.

[Addressed:] To the honourable Sir John Egerton at Yorke House geve these.

[Endorsed:] Capten Peter Wynne. Virginia.

815. August 31, 1609. Gabriel Archer's account of his voyage with the Virginia fleet.

The fleet of seven vessels that attempted to cross directly from the Canaries in 1609 was scattered by a storm. The flagship, the Sea Adventure, *alone failed to appear (as she had gone aground on Bermuda); the rest arrived fairly close to each other. Archer had been in Virginia before and was an old antagonist of John Smith whom he found presiding as governor and unwilling to surrender authority until Gates arrived. Archer describes to an unknown friend the arrangements made at this time.*

The only text is in S. Purchas, Pilgrimes, IV (1625), 1733–1734 (XIX [1906], 1–4).

From Woolwich the fifteenth of May, 1609, seventh saile weyed anchor, and came to Plimmouth the twentieth day, where Sir George Somers, with two small Vessels, consorted with us. Here we tooke into the Blessing (being the ship wherein I went) sixe Mares and two Horses; and the Fleet layed in some necessaries belonging to the action: In which businesse we spent time till the second of June. And then wee set sayle to Sea, but crost by South-west windes, we put in to Faulenmouth, and there staying till the eight of June, we then gate out. Our Course was commanded to leave the Canaries one hundred leagues to the Eastward at least, and to steere away directly for Virginia, without touching at the West Indies, except the Fleet should chance to be separated, then they were to repaire to the Bermuda, there to stay seven dayes in expectation of the Admirall; and if they found him not, then to take their course to Virginia.

Now thus it happened; about six dayes after we lost the sight of England, one of Sir George Somers Pinnasses left our company, and (as I take it) bare up for England; the rest of the ships, viz. The Sea Adventure Admirall, wherein was Sir Thomas Gates, Sir George Somer, and Captaine Newport: The Diamond Vice-admirall, wherein was Captaine Ratcliffe, and Captaine King. The Falcon Reare-admirall, in which was Captaine Martin, and Master Nellson: The Blessing, wherein I and Captaine Adams went: The Unitie, wherein Captaine Wood, and Master Pett were. The Lion, wherein Captaine Webb remained: And the Swallow of Sir George Somers, in which Captaine Moone, and Master Somer went. In the Catch went one Matthew Fitch Master: and in the Boat of Sir George Somers, called the Virginia, which was built in the North Colony, went one Captaine Davies, and one Master Davies. These were the Captaines and Masters of our Fleet.

We ran a Southerly course from the Tropicke of Cancer, where having the Sun within sixe or seven degrees right over our head in July, we bore away West; so that by the fervent heat and loomes breezes, many of our men fell sicke of the Calenture, and out of two ships was throwne over-boord thirtie two persons. The Viceadmirall was said to have the plague in her; but in the Blessing we had not any sicke, albeit we had twenty women and children.

Upon Saint James day, being about one hundred and fiftie leagues distant from the West Indies, in crossing the Gulfe of Bahoma, there hapned a most terrible and vehement storme, which was a taile of the West Indian Horacano; this temptest seperated all our Fleet one from another, and it was so violent that men could scarce stand upon the Deckes, neither could any man heare another speake, being thus divided, every man steered his owne course, and as it fell out about five or six dayes after the storme ceased (which endure fortie foure houres in extremitie) the Lion first, and after the Falcon and the Unitie, got sight of our Shippe, and so we lay a way directly for Virginia, finding neither current nor winde opposite, as some have reported, to the great charge of our Counsell and Adventurers. The Unity was sore distressed when she came up with us, for of seventy land men, she had not ten sound, and all her Sea men were downe, but onely the Master and his Boy, with one poore sailer, but we relieved them, and we foure consorting, fell into the Kings River haply the eleventh of August. In the unity were borne two children at Sea, but both died, being both Boyes.

When wee came to James Towne, we found a Ship which had bin there in the River a moneth before we came; this was sent out of England by our Counsels leave and authority, to fish for Sturgeon, and to goe the ready way, without tracing through the Torrid Zoan, and shee performed it: her Commander was Captaine Argoll (a good Marriner, and a very civill Gentleman) and her Master one Robert Tindall.

The people of our Colonie were found all in health (for the most part) howbeit when Captaine Argoll came in, they were in such distresse, for many were dispersed in the Savages townes, living upon their almes for an ounce of Copper a day, and fourescore lived twenty miles from the Fort, and fed upon nothing but Oysters eight weekes space, having no other allowance at all, neither were the people of the Country able to relieve them if they would. Whereupon Captaine Newport and others have beene much to blame to informe the Counsell of such plenty of victuall in this Country, by which meanes they have beene slacke in this supply to give convenient content. Upon this, you that be adventurers, must pardon us, if you finde not returne of Commodity so ample as you may expect, because the law of nature bids us seeke sustenance first, and then to labour to content you afterwards. But upon this point I shall be more large in my next Letter.

After our foure Ships had bin in harbour a few dayes, came in the Viceadmirall, having cut her maine Mast over boord, and had many of her men very sicke and weake, but she could tell no newes of our Governour, and some three or foure dayes after her, came in the Swallow with her maine Mast overboord also, and had a shrewd leake, neither did she see our Admirall.

Now did we all lament much the absence of our Governour, for contentions began to grow, and factions, and partakings, &c. Insomuch as the President, to strengthen his authority, accorded with the Mariners, and gave not any due respect to many worthy Gentlemen, that came in our Ships: whereupon they generally (having also my consent) chose Master West, my Lord de la Wars brother, to be their Governour, or president de bene esse, in the absence of Sir Thomas Gates, or if he miscarried by Sea, then to continue till we heard newes from our Counsell in England. This choice of him they made not to disturbe the old President during his time, but as his authority expired, then to take upon him the sole government, with such assistants of the Captaines, as discreetest persons as the Colonie afforded. Perhaps you shall have it blazoned a mutenie by such as retaine old malice; but Master West, Master Percie, and all the respected Gentlemen of worth in Virginia, can and will testifie otherwise upon their oathes. For the Kings Patent we ratified, but refused to be governed by the President that now is, after his time was expired, and onely subjected our selves to Master West, whom we labour to have next President. I cannot certifie you of much more as yet, untill we grow to some certaine stay in this our state, but by the other Ships you shall know more. So with my harty commendations I cease. From James Towne this last of August 1609.

816. October 4, 1609. John Radcliffe to Lord Salisbury.

The summer of 1609 was a difficult one at Jamestown. Many ships arrived but not Lord De La Warr's lieutenant governor, Sir Thomas Gates (shipwrecked on Bermuda). The Radcliffe letter (like that of another preceding it) gives some impression of what was being done, but there is clearly lacking a sense of direction since the whole headquarters staff and all instructions were missing.

P.R.O., CO 1/1, fol. 66; printed in P. L. Barbour, The Jamestown Voyages, *II, 283–284.*

Right Honorable, according to your gratious favour being bound I am bold to write the truth of some late accidentes, be falne his Majesties Virginia collonye. Sir Thomas Gates, and Sir George Summers Captaine Newport and 180 persons or ther about, are not yet arrived and we much feare they are lost, and alsoe a small pinish. The other shipps came all in but not together; we were thus separated by a storme; two shipps had great loss of men by the calenture; and most of them all much weatherbeaten. At our arrivall we found an English shipp, riding at James towne and Captaine Argoll hir commaunder. We heard that all the Counsell were dead but Captaine Smith the President, who reigned sole governor without assistantes and would at first admitt of no councell but himselfe. This man is sent home to answere some misdeamenors whereof I perswade me he can scarcly clear him selfe from great imputation of blame. Master George Pearcye my Lord of Northumberlandes brother is elected our President, and Master West my Lord la wars brother, of the councell with me and Captaine Martine, and some few of the best and worthyest that inhabitie at James towne are assistantes in ther advise unto us. Thus have we planted 100 men at the falls, and some others upon a champion, the President is at James towne, and I am raysing a fortification upon point Comfort, alsoe we have been bold to make stay of a small shipp for discoverye and to procure us victualls wherof we have exceedinge much need four the country people set no more than sufficeth each familye a yeare, and the wood is yet so thice, as the labor to prepare so much ground as would be to any purpose is more then we can afford, our number being soe necessarylie dispersed: soe that if I might be held worthye to advise the directors of this busines: I hold it fitt that ther should be a sufficient supply of victualls for one yeare, and then to be sparinge, it would less hinder the collonye. Thus fearinge to be too offenive in a tedious boldness, I cease, wishinge all hapines to your Honnor yea wear it in the expense of my life and bloud. From James towne this 4th of October, 1609.

Your Honnors in all obedience and most humble dutye

[Signed:] John RadClyeffe./S[o] Comenly Called

[Addressed:] To the Right Honourable the Earle of Salisburye Lord high Treasurer of England deliver these from Virginia

817. 1610. William Strachey's "True Reportory": an extract.

The treatise, which survives only in the version printed by Samuel Purchas, Pilgrimes, *IV (1625), 1735–1758, was written by William Strachey, secretary to the colony in Virginia, to an unnamed lady. It is one of the finest pieces— clear, specific, descriptive, critical—in the literature of the whole period of early seventeenth- century American enterprise. The main part is devoted to the voyage of the* Sea Enterprise, *flag- ship of the seven ships which were to give new life to Virginia, in 1609, to her casting away, virtually intact, on Bermuda, and her resurrec- tion under the energetic rule of Sir Thomas Gates, Sir George Somers, and no doubt, William Strachey, until in two new pinnaces largely made from her, almost all of the 180-man com- plement of the* Sea Adventure *at last reached Virginia on May 21, 1610. Space is too limited to include the whole. The light it throws on Virginia, rather than the tale of adventure on Bermuda, must be the criterion; consequently only that latter portion is included.*

S. Purchas, Pilgrimes, *IV, 1748–1758 (XIX [1906], 41–72).*

Their departure from Bermuda and arrivall in Virginia: miseries there, departure and returne upon the Lord La Warres arriving. James Towne described.

From this time we only awaited a favourable Westerly wind to carrie us forth, which longer then usuall now kept at the East, and South-east, the way which wee were to goe. The tenth of May early, Sir George Summers and Captaine New- port went off with their long Boates, and with two Canoaes boyed the Channell, which wee were to leade it out in, and which was no broader from Shoales on the one side and Rockes on the other, then about three times the length of our Pinnasse. About ten of the clocke, that day being Thursday, we set sayle an easie gale, the wind at South, and by reason no more winde blew, we were faine to towe her with our long Boate, yet neither with the helpe of that, were we able to fit our Bowyes, but even when we came just upon them, we strucke a Rocke on the starboord side, over which the Bowye rid, and had it not beene a soft Rocke, by which meanes she bore it before her, and crushed it to pieces, God knowes we might have beene like enough, to have returned anew, and dwelt there, after tenne monethes of carefulnesse and great labour a longer time: but God was more mercifull unto us. When shee strucke upon the Rocke, the Cock-swayne one Walsingham beeing in the Boate with a quicke spirit (when wee were all amazed, and our hearts failed) and so by Gods goodnesse wee led it out at three fadome, and three fadome and an halfe water. The wind served us easily all that day and the next, when (God be ever praysed for it) to the no little joy of us all, we got cleere of the Ilands. After which holding a Southerly course, for seven dayes wee had the winde sometimes faire, and sometimes scarce and contrarie: in which time we lost Sir George Sum- mers twice, albeit we still spared him our mayne top-sayle, and sometimes our fore course too.

The seventeenth of May we saw change of water, and had much Rubbish swimme by our ship side, whereby wee knew wee were not farre from Land. The eighteenth about midnight wee sounded, with the Dipsing Lead, and found thirtie seven fadome. The nineteenth in the morning we sounded, and had nineteene and an halfe fadome, stonie, and sandie ground. The twentieth about midnight, we had a marvellous sweet smell from the shoare (as from the Coast of Spaine, short of the Straits) strong and pleasant, which did not a little glad us. In the morning by day breake (so soone as one might well see from the fore-top) one of the Saylers descryed Land about an houre after, I went up and might discover two Hummockes to the Southward, from which (Northward all along) lay the Land, which wee were to Coast to Cape Henrie. About seven of the clocke we cast forth an Anchor, because the tyde (by reason of the Freshet that set into the Bay) made a strong Ebbe there, and the winde was but easie, so as not beeing able to stemme the Tyde, we purposed to lye at an Anchor untill the next flood, but the wind comming South-west a loome gale about eleven, we set sayle againe, and having got over the Barre, bore in for the Cape.

This is the famous Chesipiacke Bay, which wee have called (in honour of our young Prince) Cape Henrie over against which within the Bay, lyeth another Headland, which wee called in honour of our Princely Duke of Yorke Cape Charles; and these lye North-east and by East, and South-west and by West, and they may bee distant each from the other in breadth seven leagues, betweene which the Sea runnes in as broad as betweene Queeneburrough and Lee. Indeed it is a goodly Bay and a fairer, not easily to be found.

The one and twentieth, beeing Munday in the morning, wee came up within two miles of Point Comfort, when the Captaine of the Fort discharged a warning Peece at us, whereupon we came to an Anchor, and sent off our long Boat to the Fort, to certifie who we were; by reason of the shoales which lye on the South-side, this Fort easily commands the mouth of the River, albeit it is as broad as betweene Greenwich, and the Ile of Dogges.

True it is, such who talked with our men from the shoare, delivered how safely all our ships the last yeere (excepting only the Admirall, and the little Pinnasse in which one Michael Philes commanded of some twentie tunne, which we towed a sterne till the storme blew) arrived, and how our people (well increased) had therefore builded this Fort; only wee could not learne any thing of our long Boat, sent from the Bermudas, but what wee gathered by the Indians themselves, especially from Powhatan, who would tell our men of such a

Boat landed in one of his Rivers, and would describe the people, and make much scoffing sport thereat: by which wee have gathered, that it is most likely, how it arrived upon our Coast, and not meeting with our River were taken at some time or other, at some advantage by the Savages, and so cut off. When our Skiffe came up againe, the good newes of our ships, and mens arrivall the last yeere, did not a little glad our Governour: who went soone ashoare, and assoone (contrary to all our faire hopes) had new unexpected, uncomfortable, and heavie newes of a worse condition of our people above at James Towne.

Upon Point Comfort our men did the last yeere (as you have heard) rayse a little Fortification, which since hath beene better perfected, and is likely to proove a strong Fort, and is now kept by Captaine James Davies with forty men, and hath to name Algernoone Fort, so called by Captaine George Percy, whom we found at our arrivall President of the Colony, and at this time like-wise in the Fort. When we got into the Point, which was the one and twentieth of May, being Munday about noone; where riding before an Indian Towne called Kecoughton, a mightie storme of Thunder, Lightning, and Raine, gave us a shrewd and fearefull welcome.

From hence in two dayes (only by the helpe of Tydes, no winde stirring) wee plyed it sadly up the River, and the three and twentieth of May we cast Anchor before James Towne, where we landed, and our much grieved Governour first visiting the Church caused the Bell to be rung, at which (all such as were able to come forth of their houses) repayred to Church where our Minister Master Bucke made a zealous and sorrowfull Prayer, finding all things so contrary to our expectations, so full of misery and misgovernment. After Service our Governour caused mee to reade his Commission, and Captaine Percie (then President) delivered up unto him his Commission, the old Patent and the Councell Seale. Viewing the Fort, we found the Pallisadoes torne downe, the Ports open, the Gates from off the hinges, and emptie houses (which Owners death had taken from them) rent up and burnt, rather then the dwellers would step into the Woods a stones cast off from them, to fetch other fire-wood: and it is true, the Indian killed as fast without, if our men stirred but beyond the bounds of their Blockhouse, as Famine and Pestilence did within; with many more particularities of their sufferances (brought upon them by their owne disorders the last yeere) then I have heart to expresse. In this desolation and misery our Governour found the condition and state of the Colonie, and (which added more to his griefe) no hope how to amend it or save his owne Company, and those yet remayning alive, from falling into the like necessities. For we had brought from the Bermudas no greater store of provision (fearing no such accidents possible to befall the Colony here) then might well serve one hundred and fiftie for a Sea Voyage: and it was not possible, at this time of the yeere to amend it, by any helpe from the Indian. For besides that they (at their best) have little more, then from hand to mouth, it was now likewise but their Seed-time, and all their Corne scarce put into the ground: nor was there at the Fort, (as they whom we found related unto us) any meanes to take fish, neither sufficient Seine, nor other convenient Net, and yet if there had, there was not one eye of Sturgeon yet come into the River. All which considered, it pleased our Governour to make a Speech unto the Company, giving them to understand, that what provision he had, they should equally share with him, and if he should find it not possible, and easie to supply them with some thing from the Countrey, by the endevours of his able men, hee would make readie, and transport them all into their Native Countrey (accommodating them the best that he could) at which there was a generall acclamation, and shoute of joy on both sides, for even our owne men began to be disheartened and faint, when they saw this misery amongst the others, and no lesse threatned unto themselves. In the meane while, our Governour published certaine Orders and Instructions, which hee enjoyned them strictly to observe, the time that hee should stay amongst them, which being written out faire, were set up upon a post in the Church for every one to take notice of.

If I should be examined from whence, and by what occasion, all these disasters, and afflictions descended upon our people, I can only referre you (honoured Ladie) to the Booke, which the Adventurers have sent hither intituled, Advertisements unto the Colony in Virginia: wherein the ground and causes are favourably abridged, from whence these miserable effects have beene produced, not excusing likewise the forme of government of some errour, which was not powerfull enough among so headie a multitude, especially, as those who arrived here in the supply sent the last yeere with us: with whom the better authoritie and government now changed into an absolute command, came along, and had beene as happily established, had it pleased God, that we with them had reached our wished Harbour.

Unto such calamity can sloath, riot, and vanity, bring the most setled and plentifull estate. Indeede (right noble Lady) no story can remember unto us, more woes and anguishes, then these people, thus governed, have both suffered and puld upon their owne heads. And yet true it is, some of them, whose voyces and command might not be heard, may easily be absolved from the guilt hereof, as standing untouched, and upright in their innocencies; whilest the privie factionaries shall never find time nor darknesse, to wipe away or cover their ignoble and irreligious practises, who, it may be, lay all the discredits, and imputations the while upon the Countrie. But under pardon, let me speake freely to them: let them remember that if riot and sloth should both meet in any one of their best Families, in a Countrey most stored with abundance and plentie in England, continuall wasting, no Husbandry, the old store still spent on, no order for new provisions, what better could befall unto the Inhabitants, Landlords, and Tenants of that corner, then necessarily following cleannesse of teeth, famine and death? Is it not the sentence and doome of the Wiseman? Yet a little sleepe, a little slumber, and a little folding of the hands to sleepe: so thy poverty commeth, as one that travelleth by the way, and thy necessitie like an armed man. And with this Idlenesse, when some thing was in store, all wastfull courses exercised to the heigth, and the headlesse multitude, (some neither of qualitie nor Religion) not imployed to the end for which they were sent hither, no not compelled (since in themselves unwilling) to sowe Corne for their owne bellies, nor to put a Roote, Herbe, &c. for their owne particular good in their Gardens or elsewhere: I say in this neglect and sensuall Surfet, all things suffered to runne on, to lie sicke and languish; must it be expected, that health, plentie, and all the goodnesse of a well ordered State, of necessitie for all this to flow in this Countrey? You have a right and noble heart (worthy Lady) bee judge of the truth herein. Then suffer it not bee concluded unto you, nor beleeve, I beseech you, that the wants and wretchednesse which they have indured, ascend out of the povertie and vilenesse of the Countrey, whether bee respected the Land or Rivers: the one, and the other, having not only promised, but powred enough in their veines, to convince them in such calumnies, and to quit those common calamities, which (as the shadow accompanies the body) the precedent neglects touched at, if truely followed, and wrought upon. What England may boast of, having the faire hand of husbandry to manure and dresse it, God, and Nature have favourably bestowed upon this Country, and as it hath given unto it, both by situation, height, and soyle, all those (past hopes) assurances which follow our well planted native Countrie, and others, lying under the same influence: if, as ours, the Countrey and soyle might be improved, and drawne forth: so hath it indowed it, as is most certaine, with many more, which England fetcheth farre unto her from elsewhere. For first wee have experience, and even our eyes witnesse (how yong so ever wee are to the Countrie) that no Countrey yeeldeth goodlier Corne, nor more manifold increase: large Fields wee have, as prospects of the same, and not farre from our Pallisado. Besides, wee have thousands of goodly Vines in every hedge, and Boske running along the ground, which yeelde a plentifull Grape in their kinde. Let mee appeale then to knowledge, if these naturall Vines were planted, dressed, and ordered by skillful Vinearoones, whether wee might not make a perfect Grape, and fruitefull Vintage in short time? And we have made triall of our owne English seedes, kitchen Hearbs, and Rootes, and finde them to prosper as speedily as in England.

Onely let me truely acknowledge, they are not an hundred or two of deboist hands, dropt forth by yeare after yeare, with penury, and leisure, ill provided for before they come, and worse to be governed when they are here, men of such distempered bodies, and infected mindes, whom no examples daily before their eyes, either of goodnesse or punishment, can deterre from their habituall impieties, or terrifie from a shamefull death, that must be the Carpenters, and workemen in this so glorious a building.

Then let no rumour of the poverty of the Country (as if in the wombe thereof there lay not those elementall seedes, which could produce as many faire births of plenty, and increase, and better hopes, then any land under the heaven, to which the Sunne is no neerer a neighbour) I say, let no imposture rumour, nor any fame of some one, or a few more changeable actions, interposing by the way, or at home, wave any mans faire purposes hitherward, or wrest them to a declining and falling off from the businesse.

I will acknowledge, deere Lady, I have seene much propensnesse already towards the unity, and generall endeavours: how contentedly doe such as labour with us, goe forth, when men of ranke and quality, assist, and set on their labours? I have seene it, and I protest it, I have heard the inferioor people, with alacrity of spirit professe, that they should never refuse to doe their best in the practise of their sciences and knowledges, when such worthy, and Noble Gentlemen goe in and out before them, and not onely so, but as the occasion shall be offered, no lesse helpe them with their hand, then defend them with the Sword. And it is to be understood, that such as labour, are not yet so taxed, but that easily they performe the same, and ever by tenne of the clocke have done their Mornings worke: at what time, they have their allowances set out ready for them, and untill it be three of the clocke againe, they take their owne pleasure, and afterwards with the Sunne set, their dayes labour is finished. In all which courses, if the businesse be continued, I doubt nothing, with Gods favour towards us, but to see it in time, a Countrie, an Haven, and a Staple, fitted for such a trade, as shall advance assureder increase, both to the Adventurers, and free Burgers thereof, then any Trade in Christendome, or then that (even in her earely dayes, when Michael Cavacco the Greeke, did first discover it to our English Factor in Poland) which extends it selfe now from Calpe and Abila, to the bottome of Sidon, and so wide as Alexandria, and all the Ports and Havens North and South, through the Arches to Cio, Smyrna, Troy, the Hellespont, and up to Pompeys Pillar, which as a Pharos, or watch Tower, stands upon the wondrous opening into the Euxine Sea.

From the three and twentieth of May, unto the seventh of June, our Governour attempted, and made triall of all the wayes, that both his owne judgement could prompe him in, and the advice of Captaine George Percy, and those Gentlemen whom hee found of the Counsell, when hee came in, as of others; whom hee caused to deliver their knowledges, concerning the State and Condition of the Countrey: but after much debating, it could not appeare, how possibly they might preserve themselves (reserving that little which wee brought from the Bermudas in our Shippes, and was upon all occasions to stand good by us) tenne dayes from starving. For besides that the Indians were of themselves poore, they were forbidden likewise (by their subtile King Powhatan) at all to trade with us; and not onely so, but to indanger and assault any Boate upon the River, or stragler out of the Fort by Land, by which (not long before our arrivall) our people had a large Boate cut off, and divers of our men killed, even within command of our Blocke-house; as likewise, they shot two of our people to death, after we had bin foure and five dayes come in: and yet would they dare then to enter our Ports, and trucke with us (as they counterfeited underhand) when indeede, they came but as Spies to discover our strength, trucking with us upon such hard conditions, that our Governour might very well see their subtiltie, and therefore neither could well indure, nor would continue it. And I may truely say beside, so had our men abased, and to such a contempt, had they brought the value of our Copper, that a peece which would have bought a bushell of their Corne in former time, would not now buy a little Cade or Basket of a Pottle. And for this misgovernment, chiefely our Colony is much bound to the Mariners, who never yet in any Voyage hither, but have made a prey of our poore people in want; insomuch, as unlesse they might advance foure or five for one (how assured soever of the payments of their Bils of Exchange) they would not spare them a dust of Corne, nor a pinte of Beere, to give unto them the least comfort or reliefe, although that Beere purloyned, and stolne perhaps, either from some particular supply, or from the generall store: so uncharitable a parcell of people they be, and ill conditioned. I my selfe have heard the Master of a Shippe say (even upon the arrivall of this Fleete, with the Lord Governour and Captaine Generall, when the said Master was treated with for such Commodities as hee brought to sell) that unlesse hee might have an East Indian increase, foure for one, all charges cleered, hee would not part with a Can of Beere. Besides, to doe us more villany and mischiefe, they would send of their long Boates still by night,

and (well guarded) make out to the neighbour Villages, and Townes, and there (contrary to the Articles of the Fort, which now pronounce death for a trespasse of that qualitie) trucke with the Indians, giving for their trifles Otter skinnes, Bevers, Rokoone Furres, Beares skinnes, &c. so large a quantity, and measure of Copper, as when the Trucke-Master for the Colony, in the day time offered trade, the Indians would laugh and scorne the same, telling what bargains they met withall by night, from our Mangot Quintons (so calling our great Shippes) by which meanes, the Market with them forestalled thus by these dishonest men, I may boldly say, they have bin a consequent cause (this last yeare) to the death and starving of many a worthy spirit; but I hope to see a true amendment and reformation, as well of those as of divers other intollerable abuses, thrust upon the Colony by these shamelesse people, as also for the transportation of such provisions and supplies as are sent hither, and come under the charge of pursers (a parcell, fragment, and odde ends of fellowes dependancies to the others) a better course thought upon: of which supplies, never yet came into the Store, or to the Parties, unto whom such supplies were sent, by relation hitherto, a moitie or third part; for the speedy redresse of this, being so soveraigne a point. I understand how the Lord Governour and Captaine Generall, hath advised unto the Counsell, that there may be no more provisions at all delivered unto Pursers, but hath intreated to have the provision thus ordered. He would have a Commissary Generall of the Victuals to be appointed, who (receiving the store for the Colony, by Indenture from the Treasurer, and Victuallers in England) may keepe a just accompt, what the grosse amounteth unto, and what is transported every Voyage, in severall kindes, as of Bread, Meate, Beere, Wine, &c. which said Commissary shall deliver over the same, to the Master of every Ship, and take an Indenture from the said Master, of what he hath in charge, and what he is to deliver to the Treasurer of the store in Virginia: of which, if any be wanting, he the said Master shall make it good, out of his owne intertainment, otherwise the Pursers, Stewards, Coopers, and quarter Masters, will be sure still, not onely to give themselves and their friends double allowances, but thinke it all well gotten that they can purloine and steale away.

Besides that the Indian thus evill intreated us,

the River (which were wont before this time of the yeare to be plentifull of Sturgion) had not now a Fish to be seene in it, and albeit we laboured, and hold our Net twenty times day and night, yet we tooke not so much as would content halfe the Fishermen. Our Governour therefore sent away his long Boate to coast the River downward, as farre as Point Comfort, and from thence to Cape Henry, and Cape Charles, and all within the Bay: which after a seven nights triall and travaile, returned without any fruites of their labours, scarse getting so much Fish as served their owne Company.

And to take any thing from the Indian by force, we never used, nor willingly ever will: and though they had well deserved it, yet it was not now time, for they did (as I said before) but then set their Corne, and at their best, they had but from hand to mouth; so as what now remained? such as we found in the Fort, had wee staid but foure dayes, had doubtlesse bin the most part of them starved, for their best reliefe was onely Mushrums, and some hearbes, which sod together, made but a thin and unsavory broath, and swelled them much. The pitty hereof moved our Governour to draw forth such provision as he had brought, proportioning a measure equally to every one a like. But then our Governor began to examine how long this his store would hold out, and found it (husbanded to the best advantage) not possible to serve longer then sixteene dayes: after which, nothing was to be possibly supposed out of the Countrey (as before remembred) nor remained there then any meanes to transport him elsewhere. Whereupon hee then entred into the consultation with Sir George Summers, and Captaine Newport, calling unto the same the Gentlemen and Counsell of the former Government, intreating both the one and the other to advise with him what was best to be done. The provision which they both had aboord himselfe and Sir George Summers, was examined, and delivered, how it, being rackt to the uttermost, extended not above, as I said, sixteene dayes, after two Cakes a day. The Gentlemen of the Town, who knew better of the Country, could not give him any hope, or wayes, how to improve it from the Indian. It soone then appeared most fit, by a generall approbation, that to preserve and save all from starving, there could be no readier course thought on, then to abandon the Country, and accommodating themselves the best that they

might, in the present Pinnaces then in the road, namely in the Discovery and the Virginia, and in the two, brought from, and builded at the Bermudas, the Deliverance, and the Patience, with all speede convenient to make for the New found Land, where (being the fishing time) they might meete with many English Ships into which happily they might disperse most of the Company.

This Consultation taking effect, our Governor having caused to be carried aboord all the Armes, and all the best things in the store, which might to the Adventurers make some commodity upon the sale thereof at home, and burying our Ordnances before the Fort gate, which looked into the River. The seventh of June having appointed to every Pinnace likewise his complement and number, also delivered thereunto a proportionable rate of provision, hee commanded every man at the beating of the Drum to repaire aboord. And because hee would preserve the Towne (albeit now to be quitted) unburned, which some intemperate and malicious people threatned, his owne Company he caused to be left ashoare, and was himselfe the last of them, when about noone giving a farewell, with a peale of small shot, wee set saile, and that night, with the tide, fell downe to an Iland in the River, which our people have called Hogge Iland; and the morning tide brought us to another Iland, which we have called Mulberry Iland; where lying at an ancor, in the afternoone stemming the tide, wee discovered a long Boate making towards us, from Point Comfort: much descant we made thereof, about an houre it came up; by which, to our no little joyes, we had intelligence of the honorable my Lord La Warr his arrivall before Algarnoone Fort the sixt of June, at what time, true it is, his Lordship having understood of our Governours resolution to depart the Country, with all expedition caused his Skiffe to be manned, and in it dispatched his letters by Captain Edward Bruster (who commandeth his Lordships Company) to our Governour, which preventing us before the aforesaid Mulberry Iland, (the eight of June aforesaid) upon the receipt of his honours letters, our Governour bore up the helme, with the winde comming Easterly, and that night (the winde so favourable) relanded all his men at the Fort againe: before which (the tenth of June, being Sunday) his Lordship had likewise brought his Ships, and in the afternoone, came a shoare with Sir Ferdinando Weinman, and all his Lordships followers.

Here (worthy Lady) let mee have a little your pardon, for having now a better heart, then when I first landed, I will briefely describe unto you, the situation and forme of our Fort. When Captain Newport in his first Voyage, did not like to inhabit upon so open a roade, as Cape Henry, nor Point Comfort he plied it up to the River, still looking out for the most apt and securest place, as well for his Company to sit downe in, as which might give the least cause of offence, or distast in his judgement, to the Inhabitants. At length, after much and weary search (with their Barge coasting still before, as Virgill writeth Æneas did, arriving in the region of Italy called Latium, upon the bankes of the River Tyber) in the Country of a Werowance called Wowinchapuncke (a ditionary to Powhatan) within this faire River of Paspiheigh, which wee have called the Kings River, a Country least inhabited by the Indian, as they all the way observed, and three-score miles & better up the fresh Channell, from Cape Henry they had sight of an extended plaine & spot of earth, which thrust out into the depth, & middest of the channell, making a kinde of Chersonesus or Peninsula, for it was fastened onely to the Land with a slender necke, no broader then a man may well quaite a tile shard, & no inhabitants by seven or six miles neere it. The Trumpets sounding, the Admirall strooke saile, and before the same, the rest of the Fleete came to an ancor, and here (as the best yet offered unto their view, supposed so much the more convenient, by how much with their small Company, they were like inough the better to assure it) to loose no further time, the Colony disimbarked, and every man brought his particular store and furniture, together with the generall provision ashoare: for the safety of which, as likewise for their owne security, ease, and better accommodating, a certaine Canton and quantity of that little halfe Iland of ground, was measured, which they began to fortifie, and thereon in the name of God, to raise a Fortresse, with the ablest and speediest meanes they could: which Fort, growing since to more perfection, is now at this present in this manner.

A low levell of ground about halfe an Acre, or (so much as Queene Dido might buy of King Hyarbas, which she compassed about with the thongs cut out of one Bull hide, and therein built her Castle of Byrza) on the North side of the River, is cast almost into the forme of a Triangle, and to Pallizadoed. The South side next the River (howbeit extended in a line, or Curtaine six score foote more in length, then the other two, by reason the advantage of the ground doth so require) containes one hundred and forty yards: the West and East sides a hundred onely. At every Angle or corner, where the lines meete, a Bulwarke or Watchtower is raised, and in each Bulwarke a peece of Ordnance or two well mounted. To every side, a proportioned distance from the Pallisado, is a setled streete of houses, that runs along, so as each line of the Angle hath his streets. In the middest is a market place, a Store house, and a Corps de guard, as likewise a pretty Chappell, though (at this time when wee came in) as ruined and unfrequented: but the Lord Governour, and Captaine Generall, hath given order for the repairing of it, and at this instant, many hands are about it. It is in length threescore foote, in breadth twenty foure, and shall have a Chancell in it of Cedar, and a Communion Table of the Blake Walnut, and all the Pewes of Cedar, with faire broad windowes, to shut and open, as the weather shall occasion, of the same wood, a Pulpet of the same, with a Font hewen hollow, like a Canoa, with two Bels at the West end. It is so cast, as it be very light within, and the Lord Governour and Captaine Generall doth cause it to be kept passing sweete, and trimmed up with divers flowers, with a Sexton belonging to it, and in it every Sonday wee have sermons twice a day, and every Thursday a Sermon, having true preachers, which take their weekely turnes, and every morning at the ringing of a Bell, about ten of the clocke, each man addresseth himselfe to prayers, and so at foure of the clocke before Supper. Every Sunday, when the Lord Governour, and Captaine Generall goeth to Church, hee is accompanied with all the Counsailers, Captaines, other Officers, and all the Gentlemen, and with a Guard of Holberdiers in his Lordships Livery, faire red cloakes, to the number of fifty, both on each side, and behinde him: and being in the Church, his Lordship hath his seate in the Quier, in a greene Velvet Chaire, with a Cloath, with a Velvet Cushion spread on a Table before him, on which he kneeleth, and on each side sit the Counsell, Captaines, and Officers, each in their place, and when he returneth home againe, he is waited on to his house in the same manner.

And thus inclosed, as I said, round with a

Pallizado of Planckes and strong Posts, foure foote deepe in the ground, of yong Oakes, Walnuts, &c. The Fort is called in honour of his Majesties name, James Towne; the principall Gate from the Towne, through the Pallizado, opens to the River, as at each Bulwarke there is a Gate likewise to goe forth, and at every Gate a Demi-Culverin, and so in the Market Place. The houses first raised, were all burnt by a casualty of fire, the beginning of the second yeare of their seate, and in the second Voyage of Captain Newport, which since have bin better rebuilded, though as yet in no great uniformity, either for the fashion, or beauty of the streete. A delicate wrought fine kinde of Mat the Indians make, with which (as they can be trucked for, or snatched up) our people do dresse their chambers, and inward roomes, which make their houses so much the more handsome. The houses have wide and large Country Chimnies in the which is to be supposed (in such plenty of wood) what fires are maintained; and they have found the way to cover their houses: now (as the Indians) with barkes of Trees, as durable, and as good proofe against stormes, and winter weather, as the best Tyle defending likewise the piercing Sunbeames of Summer, and keeping the inner lodgings coole enough, which before in sultry weather would be like Stoves, whilest they were, as at first, pargetted and plaistered with Bitumen or tough Clay: and thus armed for the injury of changing times, and seasons of the yeare, we hold our selves well apaid, though wanting Arras Hangings, Tapistry, and guilded Venetian Cordovan, or more spruse household garniture, and wanton City ornaments, remembring the old Epigraph:

We dwell not here to build us Bowers,
And Hals for pleasure and god cheere:
But Hals we build for us and ours,
To dwell in them whilst we live here.

True it is, I may not excuse this our Fort, or James Towne, as yet seated in some what an unwholesome and sickly ayre, by reason it is in a marish ground, low, flat to the River, and hath no fresh water Springs serving the Towne, but what wee drew from a Well sixe or seven fathom deepe, fed by the brackish River owzing into it, from whence I verily beleeve, the chiefe causes have proceeded of many diseases and sicknesses which have happened to our people, who are indeede strangely afflicted with Fluxes and Agues; and

every particular season (by the relation of the old inhabitants) hath his particular infirmity too, all which (if it had bin our fortunes, to have seated upon some hill, accommodated with fresh Springs and cleere ayre, as doe the Natives of the Country) we might have, I beleeve, well escaped: and some experience we have to perswade our selves that it may be so, for of foure hundred and odde men, which were seated at the Fals, the last yeere when the Fleete came in with fresh and yong able spirits, under the government of Captain Francis West, and of one hundred to the Seawards (on the South side of our River) in the Country of the Nansamundes, under the charge of Captaine John Martin, there did not so much as one man miscarry, and but very few or none fall sicke, whereas at James Towne, the same time, and the same moneths, one hundred sickned, & halfe the number died: howbeit, as we condemne not Kent in England, for a small Towne called Plumsted, continually assaulting the dwellers there (especially new commers) with Agues and Fevers; no more let us lay scandall, and imputation upon the Country of Virginia, because the little Quarter wherein we are set downe (unadvisedly so chosed) appeares to be unwholesome, and subject to many ill ayres, which accompany the like marish places.

4

The Lord La Warres beginnings and proceedings in James Towne. Sir Thomas Gates sent into England; his and the Companies testimony of Virginia, and cause of the late miseries.

Upon his Lordship's landing at the South gate of the Pallizado (which lookes into the River) our Governour caused his Company in armes to stand in order, and make a Guard: It pleased him, that I should beare his Colours for that time: his Lordship landing, fell upon his knees, and before us all, made a long and silent Prayer to himselfe, and after, marched up into the Towne, where at the Gate, I bowed with the Colours, and let them fall at his Lordship's feete, who passed on into the Chappell, where he heard a Sermon by Master Bucke our Governours Preacher; and after that, caused a Gentleman, one of his owne followers, Master Anthony Scot his Ancient, to read his Commission, which intituled him Lord Governour, and Captaine Generall during his life, of the Colony and Plantation in Virginia (Sir Thomas Gates our Governour hitherto, being now stiled therein Lieutenant Generall.)

After the reading of his Lordships Commission, Sir Thomas Gates rendred up into his Lordship his owne Commission, both Patents, and the Counsell Seale: after which, the Lord Governour, and Captaine Generall, delivered some few words unto the Company, laying many blames upon them for many vanities, and their Idlenesse, earnestly wishing, that he might no more finde it so, least he should be compelled to draw the sword of Justice, to cut off such delinquents, which he had much rather, he protested, draw in their defence, to protect them from injuries; hartening them with the knowledge of what store of provisions he had brought for them, viz. sufficient to serve foure hundred men for one whole yeare.

The twelfth of June, being Tuesday, the Lord Governour and Captaine Generall, did constitute, and give places of Office, and charge to divers Captaines and Gentlemen, and elected unto him a Counsell, unto whom he did administer an Oath, mixed with the oath of Allegiance, and Supremacy to his Majestie: which oath likewise he caused to be administered the next day after to every particular member of the Colony, of Faith, Assistance, and Secrecy. The Counsaile which he elected were. Sir Thomas Gates Knight, Lieutenant Generall. Sir George Summers Knight, Admirall. Captaine Percy Esquire, and in the Fort Captaine of fifty. Sir Ferdinando Weinman Knight, Master of the Ordnance. Captaine Christopher Newport, Vice-admirall. William Strachei Esquire, Secretary, and Recorder.

As likewise the Lord Governour and Captaine Generall, nominated Captaine John Martin, Master of the Battery workes for Steele and Iron: and Captaine George Webb Sergeant Major of the Fort: and especiall Captaines over Companies were these appointed; Captaine Edward Bruster, who hath the command of his Honours owne Company. Captaine Thomas Lawson. Captain Thomas Holecroft. Captaine Samuell Argoll. Captaine George Yardley, who commandeth the Lieutenant Generals Company. Divers other Officers were likewise made, as Master Ralph Hamer, and Master Browne, Clarkes of the Counsell, and Master Daniell Tucker, and Master Robert Wilde, Clarkes of the Store, &c.

The first businesse which the Lord Governour and Captaine Generall (after the setling of these Officers) thought upon, was to advise with his Counsell, for the obtaining of such provisions of victuals for store, and quality, as the Countrey afforded. It did not appeare, that any kinde of Flesh, Deere, or what else, of that kinde, could be recovered from the Indian, or to be sought in the Countrey, by the travaile or search of his people, and the old dwellers in the Fort (together with the Indians not to friend) who had the last winter, destroyed and killed up all the Hogges, insomuch, as of five or sixe hundred (as it is supposed) there was not one left alive; nor an Henne, nor Chicke in the Fort; and our Horses and Mares, they had eaten with the first, and the provision which the Lord Governour, and Captaine Generall had brought, concerning any kinde of flesh, was little or nothing; in respect it was not drempt of by the Adventurers in England, that the Swine were destroyed.

In Counsell therefore the thirteenth of June, it pleased Sir George Summers Knight, Admirall, to propose a Voyage, which for the better reliefe, and good of the Colony, he would performe into the Bermudas, from whence he would fetch six moneths provision of Flesh and Fish, and some live Hogges to store our Colony againe: and had a Commission given unto him the fifteenth of June, 1610. who in his owne Bermuda Pinnace, the Patience, consorted with Captaine Samuell Argoll, in the Discovery (whom the Lord Governour, and Captaine Generall, made of the counsell before his departure) the nineteenth of June, fell with the Tyde from before our Towne, and the twenty two left the Bay, or Cape Henry a sterne.

And likewise, because at the Lord Governour, and Captaine General's first comming, there was found in our owne River no store of Fish; after many trials, the Lord Governour, and Captaine Generall, dispatched in the Virginia, with instructions, the seventeenth of June, 1610. Robert Tyndall, Master of the De la Warre, to fish unto, all along, and betweene Cape Henry, and Cape Charles, within the Bay; who the last of the said moneth returned unto us againe, but as ill speeding as the former, whom our Governour (now Lieutenant Generall) had addressed thither before for the same purpose. Nor was the Lord Governour, and Captaine Generall in the meane while idle at the Fort, but every day and night hee caused the Nets to be hawled, sometimes a dozen times one after another. But it pleased not God so to blesse our labours, that we did at any time take one quarter so much, as would give unto our people one pound at a meale a peece, by which we might have better husbanded our Pease and Oatemeale, notwithstanding the great store we now saw daily in our River: but let the blame of this lye where it is, both upon our Nets, and the unskilfulnesse of our men to lay them.

The sixth of July Sir Thomas Gates Lieutenant Generall, comming downe to Point Comfort, the North wind (blowing rough) he found had forced the long Boate belonging to Algernoone Fort, to the other shoare upon Nansamund side, somewhat short of Weroscoick: which to recover againe, one of the Lieutenant Generals men Humfrey Blunt, in an old Canow made over, but the wind driving him upon the Strand, certaine Indians (watching the occasion) seised the poore fellow, and led him up into the Woods, and sacrificed him. It did not a little trouble the Lieutenant Governour, who since his first landing in the Countrey (how justly soever provoked) would not by any meanes be wrought to a violent proceeding against them, for all the practises of villany, with which they daily indangered our men, thinking it possible, by a more tractable course, to winne them to a better condition: but now being startled by this, he well perceived, how little a faire and noble intreatie workes upon a barbarous disposition, and therefore in some measure purposed to be revenged.

The ninth of July, he prepared his forces, and early in the morning set upon a Towne of theirs, some foure miles from Algernoone Fort, called Kecoughtan, and had soone taken it, without losse or hurt of any of his men. The Governour and his women fled (the young King Powhatans Sonne not being there) but left his poore baggage, and treasure to the spoyle of our Souldiers, which was only a few Baskets of old Wheate, and some other of Pease and Beanes, a little Tobacco, and some few womens Girdles of Silke, of the Grassesilke, not without art, and much neatnesse finely wrought; of which I have sent divers into England, (beeing at the taking of the Towne) and would have sent your Ladiship some of them, had they beene a Present so worthy.

We purposed to set a Frenchman heere a worke to plant Vines, which grew naturally in great plentie. Some few Corne fields it hath, and the Corne in good forwardnesse, and wee despaire not but to bee able (if our men stand in health) to make it good against the Indian.

The continuall practices of the subtle King Powhatan, doth not meanely awaken all the powers and workings of vertue and knowledge, in our Lord Governour and Captaine Generall, how to prevent not only his mischiefes, but to draw him upon some better termes, and acknowledgement of our forces and spirits, both able and daring to quit him in any valiant and martiall course whatsoever, he shall dare to runne with us, which hee doth yet scarsly beleeve. For this therefore, since first, and that so lately, he hath set on his people, to attempt us with private Conspiracies and actuall violence, into the one drawing his Neighbour Confederates and under Princes, and by the other working the losse and death of divers of our men, and by such their losse seising their Armes, Swords, Peeces, &c. of which he hath gathered into his store a great quantitie and number by Intelligence above two hundred Swords, besides Axes, and Pollaxes, Chissels, Howes, to paire and clense their ground, with an infinite treasure of Copper, our Lord Governour and Captaine Generall sent two Gentlemen with an Ambassie unto him, letting him to understand of his practises and outrage, hitherto used toward our people, not only abroad but at our Fort also: yet flattering him withall how the Lord Governour and Captaine Generall did not suppose, that these mischiefes were contrived by him, or with his knowledge, but conceived them rather to be the acts of his worst and unruly people, his Lordship therefore now complayning unto him required, that hee (being so great and wise a King) would give an universall order to his Subjects, that it might bee no more so, lest the Lord Governour and Captaine Generall should be compelled (by defending him and his) to offend him, which he would be loath to do: withall he willed the Messengers to demand of him the said Powhatan, that he would either punish or send unto his Lordship such of his people whom Powhatan knew well not long before, had assaulted our men at the Blockhouse, and but newly killed foure of them, as also to demaund of Powhatan, willing him to returne unto the English Fort, both such men as hee detayned of ours, and such Armes as he had of theirs in his possession, and those conditions performed, hee willed them to assure unto Powhatan that then their great Werowance, the Lord Governour and Captaine Generall would hold faire quarter, and enter friendship with him, as a friend to King James and his Subjects. But refusing to submit to these demands, the Lord Governour and Captaine Generall gave in charge to the Messengers, so sent to signifie unto Powhatan that his Lordship would by all meanes publike and private, seeke to recover from him such of the English as he had, being Subjects to his King and Master, unto whom even Powhatan himselfe had formerly vowed, not only friendship but homage, receiving from his Majestie therefore many gifts, and upon his knees a Crowne and Scepter with other Ornaments, the Symbols of Civill State and Christian Soveraigntie, thereby obliging himselfe to Offices of dutie to his Majestie. Unto all which Powhatan returned no other answere, but that either we should depart his Country, or confine our selves to James Towne only, without searching further up into his Land, or Rivers, or otherwise, hee would give in command to his people to kill us, and doe unto us all the mischiefe, which they at their pleasure could and we feared: withall forewarning the said Messengers, not to returne any more unto him, unlesse they brought him a Coach and three Horses, for hee had understood by the Indians which were in England, how such was the state of great Werowances, and Lords in England, to ride and visit other great men.

After this divers times, and daily hee sent sometimes two, sometimes three, unto our Fort, to understand our strength, and to observe our Watch & Guard, and how our people stood in health, and what numbers were arrived with this new Weroance: which being soone perceived our Lord Governour and Captaine Generall forewarned such his Spies, upon their owne perill, to resort no more unto our Fort. Howbeit, they would daily presse into our Block-house, and come up to our Pallizado gates, supposing the government as well now, as fantasticall and negligent in the former times, the whilest some quarter of a mile short of the Block-house, the greatest number of them would make assault, and lye in ambush about our Glasse-house, whether, divers times indeed our men would make out either to gather Strawberries, or to fetch fresh water; any one of which so stragled, if they could with conveniencie, they would assault and charge with their Bowes and Arrowes, in which manner they killed many of our men: two of which being Paspaheans, who were ever our deadliest enemies, and not to be reconciled; at length being apprehended (and one of them a notable villaine, who had attempted upon many in our Fort) the Lord Governour caused them to be manacled, and convented before him and his Counsell, where it was determined that hee that had done so much mischiefe should have his right hand strooke off, sending him away withall, with a message to Powhatan, that unlesse hee would yet returne such Englishmen as he detayned, together with all such their Armes (as before spoken of) that not only the other (now Prisoner) should die, but all such of his Savages (as the Lord Governour and Captaine Generall, could by any meanes surprize) should runne the same course: as likewise the Lord Governour and Captaine Generall would fire all his Neighbour Corne Fieldes, Townes, and Villages, and that suddenly, if Powhatan sent not to contract with him the sooner.

What this will worke with him, wee know not as yet, for this was but the day before our ships were now falling to Point Comfort, and so to set sayle for England: which ships riding before Weroscoick to take in their fraight of Cedar, Clap-boord, Blacke Wal-nut, and Iron Oare, tooke Prisoners likewise the chiefe King of Weroscoick, called Sasenticum, with his Sonne Kainta, and one of his chiefe men. And the fifteenth day of July, in the Blessing Captaine Adams brought them to Point Comfort, where at that time (as well to take his leave of the Lieutenant Generall Sir Thomas Gates, now bound for England, as to dispatch the ships) the Lord Governour and Captaine Generall had pitched his Tent in Algernoone Fort.

The Kings Sonne Kainta the Lord Governour and Captaine Generall, hath sent now into England, untill the ships arrive here againe the next Spring, dismissing the old Werowance, and the other with all tearmes of kindnesse, and friendship, promising further designes to bee effected by him, to which hee hath bound himselfe, by divers Savage Ceremonies, and admirations.

And thus (right Noble Ladie) once more this famous businesse, as recreated, and dipped a new into life and spirit, hath raysed it (I hope) from infamy, and shall redeeme the staines and losses under which she hath suffered, since her first Conception: your Graces still accompany the least appearance of her, and vouchsafe her to bee limmed out, with the beautie which wee will begge, and borrow from the faire lips: nor feare you, that shee will returne blushes to your cheekes for praysing her, since (more then most excellent Ladie) like your selfe (were all tongues dumbe and envious) shee will prayse her selfe in her most silence: may shee once bee but seene, or but her shadow lively by a skilfull Workman set out indeed, which heere (bungerly as I am) I have presumed (though defacing it) in these Papers to present unto your Ladiship.

After Sir Thomas Gates his arrivall, a Booke called A true Declaration of Virginia, was published by the Company, out of which I have heere inserted this their publike testimonie of the causes of the former evils and Sir Thomas Gates his Report upon Oath of Virginia.

The ground of all those miseries, was the permissive Providence of God, who, in the fore-mentioned violent storme, seperated the head from the bodie, all the vitall powers of Regiment being exiled with Sir Thomas Gates in those infortunate (yet fortunate) Ilands. The broken remainder of those supplyes made a greater shipwracke in the Continent of Virginia, by the tempest of Dissention: every man over-valuing his owne worth, would be a Commander: every man underprizing anothers value, denied to be commanded.

The next Fountaine of woes was secure negligence, and improvidence, when every man sharked for his present bootie, but was altogether carelesse of succeeding penurie. Now, I demand whether Sicilia, or Sardinia (sometimes the Barnes of Rome) could hope for increase without manuring? A Colony is therefore denominated, because they should be Coloni, the Tillers of the Earth, and Stewards of fertilitie: our mutinous Loyterers would not sow with providence, and therefore they reaped the fruits of too deere bought Repentance. An incredible example of their idlenesse, is the report of Sir Thomas Gates, who affirmeth, that after his first comming thither, he hath seene some of them eat their fish raw, rather then they would goe a stones cast to fetch wood and dresse it. Dei laboribus omnia vendunt, God sels us all things for our labour, when Adam himselfe might not live in Paradice without dressing the Garden.

Unto idlenesse, you may joyne Treasons, wrought by those unhallowed creatures that for-sooke the Colonie, and exposed their desolate Brethren to extreame miserie. You shall know that eight and twentie or thirtie of the Company, were appointed (in the ship called the Swallow) to trucke for Corne with the Indians, and having obtained a great quantitie by trading, the most seditious of them, conspired together, perswaded some, and enforced others, to this barbarous project. They stole away the ship, they made a league amongst themselves to be professed Pirats, with dreames of Mountaines of Gold, and happie Robberies: thus at one instant, they wronged the hopes, and subverted the cares of the Colonie, who depending upon their returne, fore-slowed to looke out for further provision: they created the Indians our implacable enemies by some violence they had offered: they carried away the best ship (which should have beene a refuge in extremities:) they weakened our forces, by subtraction of their armes and succours. These are that scumme of men that sayling in their Piracie, that being pinched with famine and penurie, after their wilde roving upon the Sea, when all their lawlesse hopes failed, some remayned with other Pirates, they met upon the Sea, the others resolved to returne for England, bound themselves by mutuall Oath, to agree all in one report to discredit the Land, to deplore the famine, and to protest that this their comming away, proceeded from desperate necessitie: These are they, that roared out the Tragicall Historie of the man eating of his dead Wife in Virginia; when the Master of this ship willingly confessed before fortie witnesses, that at their comming away, they left three monethes victuals, and all the Cattell living in the Fort: sometimes they reported that they saw this horrible action, sometimes that Captaine Davies said so, sometimes that one Beadle the Lieutenant of Captaine Davies did relate it, varying this report into diversitie of false colours, which hold no likenesse and proportion: But to cleere all doubts, Sir Thomas Gates thus relateth the Tragedie.

There was one of the Company who mortally hated his Wife, and therefore secretly killed her, then cut her in pieces and hid her in divers parts of his House: when the woman was missing, the man suspected, his House searched, and parts of her mangled bodie were discovered, to excuse himselfe he said that his Wife died, that he hid her to satisfie his hunger, and that hee fed daily upon her. Upon this, his House was againe searched, where they found a good quantitie of Meale, Oat-meale, Beanes and Pease. He thereupon was arraigned, confessed the Murder, and was burned for his horrible villany.

Now shall the scandalous reports of a viperous generation, preponderate the testimonies of so worthy Leaders? Shall their venemous tongues, blast the reputation of an ancient and worthy Peere, who upon the ocular certainty of future blessings hath protested in his Letters, that he will sacrifice himselfe for his Countrie in this service, if he may be seconded; and if the Company doe give it over, hee will yet lay all his fortunes upon the prosecution of the Plantacion?

Unto Treasons, you may joyne covetousnesse in the Mariners, who for their private lucre partly imbezeled the provisions, partly prevented our Trade with the Indians making the Matches in the night, and forestalling our Market in the day: whereby the Virginians were glutted with our Trifles, and inhaunced the prices of their Corne and Victuall. That Copper which before would have provided a bushell, would not now obtaine so much as a Pottle.

Joyne unto these another evill: there is great store of Fish in the River, especially of Sturgeon; but our men provided no more of them then for present necessitie, not barrelling up any store against that season the Sturgeon returned to the Sea. And not to dissemble their folly, they suffered fourteene nets (which was all they had) to rot and spoyle, which by orderly drying and mending might have beene preserved: but being lost, all helpe of fishing perished.

The state of the Colony, by these accidents began to finde a sensible declining: which Powhatan (as a greedy Vulture) observing, and boyling with desire of revenge, hee invited Captaine Ratcliffe, and about thirty others to trade for Corne, and under the colour of fairest friendship, hee brought them within the compasse of his ambush, whereby they were cruelly murthered and massacred. For upon confidence of his fidelitie, they went one and one into severall houses, which caused their severall destructions, when if but any sixe had remained together, they would have beene a Bulwarke for the generall preservation. After this, Powhatan in the night cut off some of our Boats, he drave away all the Deere into the farther part of the Countrey, hee

and his people destroyed our Hogs (to the number of about six hundred) hee sent one of his Indians to trade with us, but layed secret ambushes in the Woods, that if one or two dropped out of the Fort alone, they were indangered.

Cast up the reckoning together: want of government, store of idlenesse, their expectations frustrated by the Traytors, their market spoyled by the Mariners, our Nets broken, the Deere chased, our Boats lost, our Hogs killed, our trade with the Indians forbidden, some of our men fled, some murthered, and most by drinking of the brackish water of James Fort weakened and indangered, famine and sicknesse by all these meanes increased; here at home the monyes came in so slowly, that the Lord Laware could not bee dispatched till the Colony was worne and spent with difficulties: Above all, having neither Ruler, not Preacher, they neither feared God, nor man, which provoked the wrath of the Lord of Hosts, and pulled downe his judgements upon them. Discite justitiam moniti.

The Councell of Virginia (finding the smalnesse of that returne, which they hoped should have defrayed the charge of a new supply) entred into a deepe consultation, and propounded amongst themselves, whether it were fit to enter into a new contribution, or in time to send for home the Lord La-ware, and to abandon the action. They resolved to send for Sir Thomas Gates, who being come, they adjured him to deale plainly with them, and to make a true relation of those things which were presently to be had, or hereafter to be hoped for in Virginia. Sir Thomas Gates with a solemme and sacred oath replied, that all things before reported were true: that the Countrey yeelded abundance of Wood, as Oake, Wainscot, Walnut Trees, Bay Trees, Ashe, Sarsafrase, live Oake, greene all the yeere, Cedar and Fir; which are the materialls, of Soape ashes, and Pot ashes, of Oyles of Walnuts, and Bayes, of Pitch and Tar, of Clapboards, Pipe-staves, Masts and excellent boards of fortie, fiftie, and sixtie length, and three foot breadth, when one Firre tree is able to make the maine Mast of the greatest Ship in England. He avouched that there are incredible varietie of sweet woods, especially of the Balsamum tree, which distilleth a precious Gumme; that there are innumerable white Mulberry trees, which in so warme a climate may cherish and feede millions of Silke-wormes, and returne us in a very short time, as great a plenty of Silke as is vented into the whole world from all the parts of Italy: that there are divers sorts of Minerals, especially of Iron oare lying upon the ground for ten Miles circuite; (of which wee have made a triall at home, that it maketh as good Iron as any is in Europe:) that a kinde of Hempe or Flaxe, and Silke Grasse doe grow there naturally, which will afford stuffe for all manner of excellent Cordage: That the River swarmeth with all manner of Sturgeon: the Land aboundeth with Vines; the Woods doe harbour exceeding store of Beavers, Foxes, and Squirrels; the Waters doe nourish a great encrease of Otters, all which are covered with precious Furres: that there are in present discovered Dyes and Drugges of sundry qualities; that the Orenges which have beene planted, did prosper in the winter, which is an infallible argument, that Lemmons, Sugar Canes, Almonds, Rice, Anniseede, and all other commodities which wee have from the Straights, may be supplied to us in our owne Countrey, and by our owne industry: that the Corne yeeldeth a terrible encrease more then ours: and lastly, that it is one of the goodliest Countries under the Sunne; enterveined with five maine Rivers, and promising as rich entrals as any Kingdome of the earth, to whom the Sunne is no neerer a neighbour.

818. November 18, 1610. George Yeardley to Sir Henry Peyton.

Bodleian Library, English History MS 29724, fol. 3, printed in S. H. Kingsbury, Records, III, 29–31, contractions expanded.

Honorable Sir upon the returne of the last Fleete of Shipps which brought my Lord La Warr (our Lord Governour & Captaine Generall,) into this Countrie; I did not forbeare to challenge your noble patience With reading unworthy & fruitles Lines, & although at this present I am little or nothing better furnished with any matter of valew, either for discovery of Mynes, or ought els worth your Knowledge, yet when I consider your many and noble favours towards me (which when I forgett to acknowledge, let me for ever be putt out of your remembrance) I thought good to wright something, if but thereby to preserve my humble service in your honoured memory.

For the present state & condicion of this Countrie, it wants only Supportes, round & free supplies, both of men & moneyes, to make good the mayne & profitable endes of a moste happy plantation. Concerning the Countrie & the soile thereof, wee finde it fertile & full of encrease, bringing forth goodly Corne, many kindes of Fruites, naturall Vines & quickly rendring us our owne Countrie seedes, & Rootes which wee bury therein, as prosperous & unchangeable for tast and quantitie as England it selfe For these Commodities of pitch & tarr Soape ashases, Wood Iron etc. most true it is Noble Sir, that there they bee most plentifully to bee returned home, if soe bee it the meanes & skilfull workemen together with fitt provisions for those Labourers (untill the Colour may quitt some of these Charges, by planting their owne Vines, sowing their owne Corne, & broodinge their owne Cattaile, Kine, Swine, Goates etc. which would shortly be, & had bin ere this, had the Government bin carefully & honestly established & carried here these 3 yeres passed) may be provided & sent over to worke in those businesses.

For the opening & finding out of Silver or gold wee have now probable Intelligence to bee brought unto: for which Cause our Lord Governour hath gathered together most of his Choysest men & intendeth a voyadge forthwith up unto a famous fall or Cataract of Waters, where leaving his pinasses & Boates safe riding, he purposeth to Leade us up into the Land called the Monocane 2 or 3 dayes Journey, where at the foote of certaine mountaines hee meaneth to build a Forte, & there to wynter some of his people, who shall every day digg at these mynes, & though they prove not according to our expectation, yet wee have lost nothing but our Labour, with this advantage nevertheless that wee shall have a redoubt & some of our men in it, against the next springe, when his Lordship intendeth to march that way something more southerly for the finding out the South Sea.

Wee have some hope also by a Westerly Trade through a faire & goodly Bay lying in the height of 38° (some 30 leagues from our owne Bay) newly discovered since his Lordships comming heither, from whence wee promise our selves many commodities both of fish from the Bay, for our Colour, and from the tractable Indians of that place (of whome wee have made already some tryall) both Corne, furres etc.

And (Honorable Sir) I have by these few yet troublesome Lines given you the accompt & truth of what wee know and purpose concerning this his Majesty's Countrie & newe Kingdome, as further passages herein (materiall & worthy your Knowledge) shall occure & bee off[e]red unto us, I will presume to addresse them unto you, ever vowing myselfe in the utmost of my endeavoures to doe your service, I kisse your Honoured Hand. In Virginia dated at James Towne the xviii^th of November, 1610,

At your Commandement
       [Signed:] George Yardley

[Addressed:] To the Honourable Sir Henry Peyton. Knight at his House in the Blackfryers or els where Yeave these London

819. July, 1611. The ship *Hercules* from Virginia stopped by pirates near Lands End.

The Hercules, *Robert Adams, captain, sailed from Virginia on May 25 (Brown, Genesis, I [1890], 488). P.R.O., High Court of Admiralty, Oyer and Terminer, HCA 1/47, fols. 217v–218, Examination of Robert Adams, July 22, 1611.*

July 22. Robert Adama of Lymehouse maryner Captayne of the Hercules of London sworne and examined before the right worshipfull Master doctor Concerninge his fate beinge at sea, and what pyratts he mett at sea, and what they tooke from this examinate and Companie Cominge from Virginiea bounde for London with the said shipp the Hercules laden with black wallnuttree and sassafrixa & some sturgion about the sixte of this monethe of July mett with nyne sayle of pyrattes betweene the Landes ende, and the Lizard whereof Peter Eason [Easton] was Commander of their Admirall, and one Bathe a Forriest man was Commander of the rere Admirall, and they have descried this examinate and Companie Comminge, shott at this examinates shipp,

whereuppon this examinate stroke sayle, and then presentlie the pyratte came aboard their shipp, and tooke out all this examinates powder and shott out of their shipp beinge a barrell & halfe of powder, and some five hundred waight of greate shott and allso carried away Certayne pikes swordes and musketts and ladles and springes, and some matches the quantitie thereof he Cannot Certaynelie say and nothinge else and after they had ransacked theie said shipp, and taken what they would, they Commanded this examinate and Companie to come aboarde their Admirall which was the Concord of London whereof the said Peter Eason was Captayne which they had taken some foure dayes before they tooke this examinate and beinge Come aboard their Admirall Captayne Eason tooke away two of this examinates Companie by force as namelie one Charitye Newall borne in Lyme whoe was gonners mate of the Hercules and Robert Atley of Ratcliffe and after they had taken away these two men, they suffered this examinate, and Company to departe to their owne shipp agayne and so lefte them.

Beinge demanded what he or anie of his Companie receaved of the said pyrattes or what else the said pyrattes tooke out of their said shipp or from anie of their Companie sayth by vertue of his oathe that he neither persons examined nor anie of his Companie receaved anie thinge from the said pyrattes at all to his knowledge, nor the said pyrattes tooke anie thinge else from them savinge the Surgions Cheste with his Instrumentes. And more he cannot say.

       [Signed:] Robart Addames

820. June 19 to August 31, 1610. Samuel Argall's fishing voyage off the New England coast.

Lord De La Warr was anxious to exploit all possible food supplies for his colony in June, 1610. Two pinnaces were pressed into service for the transport of pigs and other food from Bermuda, but neither Argall (in his own ship) nor Sir George Somers (in Patience, *one of the Bermuda vessels) could reach the island. So they then ran northward to attempt to catch fish in-*

stead. Argall lost touch with Somers but cruised up the coast as far as Maine, fishing where he could, with moderate success, and arrived back at the mouth of the Chesapeake at the end of August. His meandering course, recorded in his journal, is reminiscent of the course of Hudson's 1609 voyage along the same coast (522). It was the first of several links between the Virginia colony and the Northeast coast in which Argall was the moving spirit.

The sole text is that in S. Purchas, Pilgrimes, IV (1625), 1758–1762 (XIX [1906], 73–84).

The Voyage of Captaine Samuel Argal, from James Towne in Virginia, to seeke the Ile of Bermuda, and missing the same, his putting over toward Sagadahoc and Cape Cod, and so backe againe to James Towne, begun the nineteenth of June, 1610.

Sir George Summers, being bound for the Ile of Bermuda with two Pinnaces, the one called the Patience, wherein he sailed himselfe, set saile from James Towne in Virginia, the nineteenth of June, 1610. The two and twentieth at noone we came to an anchor at Cape Henry, to take more balast. The weather proved very wet: so wee road under the Cape till two of the clocke, the three and twentieth in the morning. Then we weighed and stood off to Sea, the wind at South-west. And till eight of the clocke at night it was all Southerly, and then that shifted to South-west. The Cape then bearing West, about eight leagues off. Then wee stirred away South-east. The foure and twentieth, at noone I observed the Sunne, and found my selfe to bee in thirtie sixe degrees, fortie seven minutes, about twentie leagues off from the Land. From the foure and twentieth at noone, to the five and twentieth at noone, sixe leagues East, the wind Southerly, but for the most part it was calme. From the five and twentieth at noone, to the sixe and twentieth about sixe of the clocke in the morning, the winde was all Southerly, and but little. And then it beganne to blow a fresh gale at West South-west. So by noone I had sailed fourteene leagues East, South-east pricked. From the sixe and twentieth at noone, to the seven and twentieth at noone, twentie leagues East, South-east. The wind shifting from the West, South-west Southerly, and so to the East,

and the weather faire, but close. From the seven and twentieth at noone, to the eight and twentieth at noone, sixe and twentie leagues East, South-east, the wind shifting backe againe from the East to the West. Then by mine observation I found the ship to be in thirtie five degrees fiftie foure minutes. From the eight and twentieth at noone, to the nine and twentieth at noone, thirtie sixe leagues East by South, the wind at West, North-west. Then by my observation I found the ship to be in thirtie five degrees, thirtie minutes pricked. From the nine and twentieth at noone, to the thirtieth at noone, thirtie five leagues East, South-east. The winde shifting betweene West, North-west, and West, South-west, blowing a good fresh gale. Then by my observation I found the ship to be in thirtie foure degrees, fortie nine minutes pricked. From the thirtieth of June at noone, to the first of July at noone, thirtie leagues South-east by East, the winde at west, then I found the ship in thirtie foure degrees pricked.

From the first of July at noone, to the second at noon, twentie leagues East, South-east southerly, the wind West, then I found the ship to bee in thirtie three degrees, thirtie minutes pricked, the weather very faire. From the second at noone, to the third at foure of the clocke in the afternoone it was calme, then it beganne to blow a resonable fresh gale at South-east: so I made account that the ship had driven about sixe leagues in that time East. The sea did set all about the West. From that time to the fourth at noone, seventeene leagues East by North, the wind shifting betweene South-east and South South-west, then I found the ship to bee in thirtie three degrees, fortie minutes, the weather continued very faire. From the fourth at noone, to the fifth at noone, ten leagues South-east, the wind and weather as before, then I found the ship to be in thirtie three degrees, seventeene minutes pricked. From the fift at noone, to the sixt at noone, eight leagues South-west, then I found the ship to be in thirtie two degrees, fiftie seven minutes pricked; the wind and weather continued as before, only we had a small showre or two of raine. From the sixt at noone, to the seventh at noone, seventeene leagues East by North, then I found the ship to be in thirtie three degrees, the wind and weather as before. From the seventh at noon, to the eight at noone, fourteene leagues North-east, then I found the ship to be in thirtie three degrees, thirtie two minutes, the wind and weather continued as before. From the eight at noon to the ninth at noone, five leagues South-east, there I found the ship to be in thirtie three degrees, twentie one minutes, the wind at South-west, the weather very faire. From the ninth at noone, to the tenth at noone, five leagues South, the wind westerly; but for the most part it was calme, and the weather very faire. From the tenth at noone, to the eleventh at noone it was calme, and so continued untill nine of the clocke the same night, then it began to blow a reasonable fresh gale at South-east, and continued all that night betweene South-east and South, and untill the twelfth day at noone: by which time I had sailed fifteene leagues West southerly: then I found the ship in thirtie three degrees, thirtie minutes. From that time to foure of the clocke the twelfth day in the morning twelve leagues West by North, the wind all southerly, and then it shifted betweene South and South-west, then wee tacked about and stood South-east, and South-east by South: so by noone I had sayled five leagues South-east by East; then I found the ship in thirtie three degrees ten minutes. From the thirteenth at noone, to the fourteenth at noone, twenty leagues South-east by East, the wind shifting betweene the South-west, and West South-west, then I found the ship to be in thirtie two degrees, thirtie five minutes. From the fourteenth at noone, to the fifteenth at noone, twentie leagues South-east, then I found the ship to be in thirty two degrees, the wind as before: then we tacked about, and lay Northwest by West. From the fifteenth at noone, to the sixteenth at noone, twelve leagues North by West, the wind shifting betweene South-west and West, and the weather very stormy, with many sudden gusts of wind and rayne.

And about sixe of the clocke in the afternoone, being to windward of our Admirall I bare up under his lee: who when I hayled him, told me that he would tack it up no longer, because hee was not able to keepe the sea any longer, for lacke of a road and water: but that hee would presently steere away North North-west, to see if he could fetch Cape Cod. Which without delay he put in execution. His directions I followed: so from the sixteenth day at noone, to the seventeenth at noone I had sailed thirtie eight leagues North North-west: then I found my ship to be in thirtie

foure degrees, ten minutes. The seventeenth and eighteenth dayes were very wet and stormy, and the winds shifting all points of the Compasse. The nineteenth day, about foure of the clocke in the morning it began to cleere up, and then we had a very stiffe gale betweene East and North-east. From the seventeenth at noone, to the nineteenth at noone, I had sayled fiftie five leagues North North-west, then I found the ship to be thirtie sixe degrees, thirty minutes. From the nineteenth at noone, to the twentieth at noone, thirty five leagues North-west: then I was in thirty seven degrees, fifty two minutes, the weather now was fairer and the wind all easterly. From the twentieth at noone, to the twentie one at noone, we sayled twenty leagues North by West, the wind betweene East and South-east, and the weather very faire: At the sunne setting I observed, and found thirteene degrees, and an halfe of westerly variation, and untill midnight we had a reasonable fresh gale of wind all southerly, and then it fell calme and rained, and so continued very little wind untill the two and twentieth at noone, and shifting all the points of the Compasse: yet by mine observation that I made then, I found that the ship had run twentie five leagues North, for I found her to be in forty degrees, one minute, which maketh me thinke that there was some tide or current that did set Northward. Againe, those that had the second watch did say, That in their watch they did see a race, and that the ship did drive apace to the Northward, when she had not a breath of wind.

From the two and twentieth at noone, untill ten of the clocke at night, we had a fresh gale of wind, betweene East and South-east, and then it shifted all westerly, and so continued untill two of the clocke the twenty three in the morning: and then it began to be very foggy and but little wind, yet shifting all the points of the Compasse, and so continued untill ten of the clocke, and then it began to cleere up. At twelve of the clocke I observed, and then I found the ship to be in fortie degrees fiftie minutes: so from the twenty two at noone, to the twenty three at noone I had sayled twenty leagues Northward. From the twenty three at noone, to the twenty foure, at three of the clocke in the morning it was calme, and then we had a reasonable fresh gale of wind all southerly, and so it continued untill noon southerly, in which time I had sailed twelve leagues North. And about foure of the clocke in the afternoone, we had forty seven fathoms of water, which water we did find to be changed into a grasse green in the morning, yet we would not heave a lead, because our Admirall was so farre on head of us: who about three of the clocke in the afternoone lay by the lee, and fished till I came up to him: and then I fitted my selfe and my boat, and fished untill sixe of the clocke. And then the Admirall fitted his sailes, and stirred away North, whom I followed with all the speed I could. But before seven of the clocke there fell such a myst, that I was faine to shoot off a Peece, which he answered with a Cornet that he had aboord. So with hallowing and making a noyse one to another all the night we kept company. About two of the clocke, the twenty five day in the morning we tooke in all our sailes, and lay at Hull untill five of the clocke: and then finding but small store of fish, we set saile and stirred away North-west, to fetch the mayne land to relieve our selves with wood and water, which we stood in great need of. About two of the clocke in the afternoone we tooke in all our sailes and lay at Hull, at which time I heaved the lead three times together, and had three sundry kindes of soundings. The first a blacke peppery sand, full of peble stones. The second blacke peppery, and no stones: The third blacke peppery, and two or three stones.

From the fourth at noone, to the twentie five, at two of the clocke in the afternoone, I sayled thirteene leagues West North-west: and the weather continuing very foggy, thicke, and rainy, about five of the clocke it began to cease, and then we began to fish, and so continued untill seven of the clocke in betweene thirty and forty fathoms, and then we could fish no longer. So having gotten betweene twentie and thirty Cods, we left for that night: and at five of the clocke, the twenty sixe in the morning we began to fish againe, and so continued untill ten of the clocke, and then it would fish no longer: in which time we had taken neere one hundred Cods, and a couple of Hollybuts. All this while wee had betweene thirty and forty fathoms water: before one of the clocke in the afternoone we found the ship driven into one hundred and twenty fathoms, and soft blacke Ose. Then Sir George Somers sent me word, that he would set saile, and stand in for the River of Sagadahoc; whose directions I followed.

Before two of the clocke we set saile, and stirred away North-west by North, the wind South South-west, and the weather continued very fogy. About eight of the clocke wee tooke in all our sailes, and lay at Hull at that night. The seven and twentieth, about seven of the clocke in the morning we heaved the lead, and had no ground in one hundred and twentie fathoms. Then I shot off a Peece, but could not heare none answere from our Admirall: and the weather was so thicke, that we could not see a Cables length from our ship. Betweene nine and ten of the clock we did thinke that we did heare a Peece of Ordnance to windward: which made me suppose our Admirall had set saile, and that it was a warning piece from him. So I set sayle and stood close by the wind, and kept an hollowing and a noise to try whether I could find him againe: the wind was at South-west, and I stood away West North-west. From the sixe and twentieth, at two of the clocke in the afternoone, to eight of the clocke at night I had sayled nine leagues Northwest. The seven and twentieth at noone I heaved the Lead, in one hundred and twenty fathoms, and had no ground. Then I stirred away Northwest, till foure of the clocke at night: then I heaved the Lead againe one hundred and twenty fathoms, and had no ground. Then I tooke all my sailes and lay at Hull, and I had sayled seven leagues North-west. The eight and twentieth, at seven of the clocke in the morning I did sound in one hundred and twenty fathoms, and had no ground. Then I set sayle againe, and steered away North, and North by West. At noone I heaved in one hundred and twenty fathoms againe, and had no ground. So I steered on my course still, the wind shifted betweene South and South-west, and the fog continued. At foure of the clocke in the afternoone, I heaved one hundred twenty fathoms againe, and had no ground: so I stood on untill eight of the clocke, by which time I had sailed twelve leagues: then I heaved the Lead againe, and had blacke Ose, and one hundred thirty five fathoms water. Then I tooke in all my sayles and lay at hull untill the nine and twentieth, at five of the clocke in the morning. Then I set saile againe, and steered away North, and North by West. At eight of the clocke I heaved the Lead againe, and had blacke Ose in one hundred and thirty fathoms water. Betweene eleven and twelve of the clocke it began to thunder, but the fogge continued not still. About two of the clocke in the afternoone, I went out with my Boat my selfe and heaved the Lead, and had blacke Ose in ninety fathoms water: by which time I had sailed six leagues North by West more. Then I tooke in all my sayles saving my Forecourse and Bonnet, and stood in with those sailes onely. About six of the clocke I sounded againe, and then I had sixty five fathoms water. Assoone as I came aboord it cleered up, and then I saw a small Iland, which bare North about two leagues off; whereupon I stood in untill eight of the clocke: And then I stood off againe untill two of the clocke in the morning the thirtieth day. Then I stood in againe, and about eight of the clocke I was faire aboord the Iland. Then I manned my Boat and went on shoare, where I found great store of Seales: And I killed three Seales with my hanger. This Iland is not halfe a mile about, and nothing but a Rocke, which seemed to be very rich Marble stone. And a South South-west Moon maketh a full Sea. About ten of the clocke I came aboord againe, with some Wood that I had found upon the Iland, for there had beene some folkes that had made fiers there. Then I stood over to another Iland that did beare North off me about three leagues; this small rockie Iland lyeth in forty foure degrees. About seven of the clocke that night I came to an anchor among many Ilands in eight fathoms water: and upon one of these Ilands I fitted my selfe with Wood and Water, and Balast.

The third day of August, being fitted to put to Sea againe, I caused the Master of the ship to open the boxe wherein my Commission was, to see what directions I had, and for what place I was bound to shape my course. Then I tried whether there were any fish there or not, and I found reasonable good store there; so I stayed there fishing till the twelfth of August: and then finding that the fishing did faile, I thought good to returne to the Iland where I had killed the Seales, to see whether I could get any store of them or not; for I did find that they were very nourishing meate, and a great reliefe to my men, and that they would be very well saved with salt to keepe a long time. But when I came thither I could not by any meanes catch any. The fourteenth day at noone I observed the Sun, and found the Iland to lie in forty three degrees, forty minutes. Then I shaped my course for Cape Cod, to see whether I could get any fish there or not: so by the fifteenth

that noone, I had sailed thirty two leagues South-west, the wind for the most part was betweene North-west and North. From the fifteenth at noone, to the sixteenth at noone I ran twenty leagues South, the wind shifting betweene West and South-west. And then I sounded and had ground in eighteene fathoms water, full of shels and peble stones of divers colours, some greene, and some blewish, some like diamants, and some speckled. Then I tooke in all my sayles, and set all my company to fishing, and fished till eight of the clocke that night: and finding but little fish there, I set sayle againe, and by the seventeenth at noone I had sayled ten leagues West by North, the wind shifting betweene South and South-west. From noone, till six of the clocke at night, foure leagues North-west, the wind shifting betweene West and South-West. Then it did blow so hard that I tooke in all my sayles, and lay at hull all that night, untill five of the clock the eighteenth day in the morning: and then I set saile againe, and by noone I had sailed foure leagues North-west, the wind betweene West and South-west. From the eighteenth at noone, to the nineteenth at noone ten leagues West by West, the wind shifting betweene South and South-west, and the weather very thick and foggy.

About seven of the clocke at night the fogge began to breake away, and the wind did shift westerly, and by midnight it was shifted to the North, and there it did blow very hard untill the twenty at noone: but the weather was very cleere, and then by my observation I found the ship to bee in the latitude of forty one degrees, forty foure minutes, and I had sailed twenty leagues South-west by West. From the nineteenth at noone, to the twentieth at noone: about two of the clocke in the afternoone I did see an Hed-land, which did beare off me South-west, about foure leagues: so I steered with it, taking it to bee Cape Cod; and by foure of the clocke I was fallen among so many shoales, that it was five of the clocke the next day in the morning before I could get cleere of them, it is a very dangerous place to fall withall: for the shoales lie at the least ten leagues off from the Land; and I had upon one of them but one fathom and an halfe water, and my Barke did draw seven foot. This Land lyeth South-west, and North-east, and the shoales lie off from it South and South by West, and so along toward the North. At the North-west by West Guards I observed the North-starre, and found the ship to be in the latitude of fortie one degrees, fiftie minutes, being then in the middle of the Sholdes: and I did finde thirteene degrees of westerly variation then likewise. Thus finding the place not to be for my turne, assoon as I was cleere of these dangers, I thought it fit to returne to James Towne in Virginia, to the Lord-Delawarre, my Lord Governour, and there to attend his command: so I shaped my course for that place. And the one and twentieth day by noone I had brought my selfe South South-west thirtie three leagues from this Cape: and I had the wind shifting all this while betweene North and North-west, and the weather very faire and cleere. From the one and twentieth at noone, to the two and twentieth at noone, I ran thirtie leagues South-West by West, and then by mine observation I found the ship to be in thirtie nine degrees, thirtie sixe minutes: and I had twelve degrees westerly variation, and the wind shifting betweene North and North-east, and the weather very faire and cleere. From the two and twentieth at noone, to the three and twentieth at noone, nine leagues South-west by West; and then by observation I did find the ship in thirtie nine degrees, twentie foure minutes, and I had eleven degrees of westerly variation: and there did blow but very little wind, and shifting betweene West and North, and the weather very faire and cleere. From the three and twentieth at noone to the foure and twentieth at noone eighteene leagues South-west, and then I found the shippe to be in thirtie eight degrees fortie two minutes: and I had twelve degrees of Westerly Variation, and the wind shifting betweene North and West, and the weather very faire.

From the foure and twentieth at noone, to the five and twentieth at noone, two and twentie leagues West by South, the wind shifting betweene North and East. And then I found the ship to bee in thirtie eight degrees five and twentie minutes, and the same Variation that I had before, and the weather very faire.

From the five and twentieth at noone, to the six and twentieth at noone, five and twentie leagues Westerly, the wind all shifting betweene South and South-west. And I had thirteene degrees five and twentie minutes of Westerly Variation. About six of the clocke at night the water was

changed, and then I sounded and had red sandie ground in twelve fathomes water about twelve leagues from the shore.

The seven and twentieth by day in the morning, I was faire aboord the shore, and by nine of the clocke I came to an Anchor in nine fathomes in a very great Bay, where I found great store of people which were very kind, and promised me that the next day in the morning they would bring me great store of Corne. But about nine of the clocke that night the winde shifted from South-west to East North-east. So I weighed presently, and shaped my course to Cape Charles. This Bay lyeth in Westerly thirtie leagues. And the Souther Cape of it lyeth South South-east and North North-west, and in thirtie eight degrees twentie minutes of Northerly Latitude.

The eight and twentieth day, about foure of the clocke in the afternoone I fell among a great many of shoales, about twelve leagues to the Southward of Cape La Warre. So there I came to an Anchor in three fathomes water, the winde beeing then all Easterly, and rode there all that Night.

The nine and twentieth in the morning I weighed againe, the wind being all Southerly, and turned untill night, and then I came to an Anchor in seven fathomes water in the offing to Sea.

How the tyde did set there, or whether that there did run any current or not, I cannot say; but I could find neither current nor tyde.

The thirtieth in the morning I weighed againe, the wind still Southerly, and turned all that day, but got very little, so at Evening I stood off to Sea untill midnight, and then stood in againe.

The one and thirtieth, about seven of the clocke at night I came to an Anchor under Cape Charles in foure fathomes, and one third part water, and rode there all that night.

821. 1610–1611. Voyage of the *Discovery* to and from Virginia.

The Discovery, *sent out to get fish for the colonists, deserted them and returned to England.*
    P.R.O., HCA 1/47, fol. 298, examination of James Paine.

James Paine of Yarmouth Mariner aged xxx

yeares or thereaboutes examined before the right Worshipfull Master Doctor Trevor one of the Judges of the Admiralty of his late being in Virginia, and howe he came thence Sayth that this examinate was hired by Sir Thomas Smith knight about xiiij monethes past to goe to Virginea, and to be ymployed there in fisshing, and this examinate wente thither with Sir Thomas Gates and there fisshed, And did such busines as the Generall appointed him to doe And sayth that this examinate and nyne more as namely James Gentleman, Master John Simpson, Edward Primerose, Gotwod [?], Thurtells, Robert England, William Lawson, Edward Turnor [and] Hubbardyn and a boy were by the said Sir Thomas Gates there generall sent to sea a fisshing about the beginning of May last with a Warrantt under his hand in a smale Barck called the Discovery belonginge to the company, and comming to sea they killed some fishe and by reason the Weather was foule and thicke, and that they were nere the shore, the Master stood to seaward / and in the morning the Master willed them as his company to prepare them selves for Fisshinge and they all exceptinge this examinate aggreeinge togeather with the Master, they would not come any more in Virginia, but would for England, and so informed the Master to sett his course for England, which he did, and they arived at Dartmouth first and from thence came to Dover Roade and [arived] there the Master sente this examinate with a lettre to Sir Thomas Smith, which he delivered him in Tuesday night last.

Being asked what shipp or shipps they mett with at sea & what goodes they had from them Sayth they mett with a shipp of Colchester laden with oade comming from the Islandes but none of them wente on bord the said shipp, or any other, or had any thing from any shipp in there whole viadge Savinge that they mett with a French man and wantinge breade, they gott a hogshead of breade & haulf a dozen peeces of beefe of him, and gave him a murderor in lue thereof.

Beinge asked what goodes they have brought home in the said shipp Sayth they haue not brought anye saving a little salte, and savinge that one called master Joseph Sleave came passenger with them from Dartmouth and there putt a packe or two on bord the said shipp to be brought to London by cocquett which is yet on borde as he thinketh.

[Signed:] James Payne

Chapter One hundred five
John Smith and William Strachey on
the Early Virginia Settlement

THESE TWO MEN differed from their Virginia contemporaries. They had the idea of systematically recording their experiences in the new colony. Their objectives were to be its historians. Smith's *A true relation* (1608) was a crude but vigorous attempt to chronicle the founding phase of the colony. In 1612 he purported (to what extent is not clear) to have based his narrative on the diaries of associates in the colony, and it does seem probable that he impounded other men's diaries in order to provide material for his own narrative, *The proceedings*. When Smith wished to assert that his picture of the colony was not his personal view alone, he generously reattributed some of the material to the authors, after he had altered the substance to suit his own point of view. There is no doubt that the mass of observations which he put into his *Map of Virginia* was largely his own. These involved considerable note-taking and emerged largely during the preparation of his map. No doubt much of the material was gathered by his companions, but it was selected and developed by him in the systematic treatment both of the resources of the country and the character of its people. The combination of analysis and narrative made *A map of Virginia . . . the proceedings* (1612) the outstanding work on early Virginia.

William Strachey, as secretary of the colony for more than a year, had at his disposal such records as had accumulated since the burning of Jamestown early in 1608 and which had not been destroyed subsequently, before Gates's colonists attempted to leave Virginia in 1610 (when they were intercepted by Lord De La Warr). He clearly aimed to write a literary work. A university-trained man, he intended to fit the new society, its peoples and products, into a setting of general history. That he did so using a draft of Smith's material, made available to him when he was still in Virginia, is suggested though not yet established. Whatever his method, he added much from his own observation and that of his associates (notably Dr. Lawrence Bohun) in Virginia. His picture of barbarian society—the Amerindians as he saw them—is a mature one, and his observations on natural resources are often shrewd and colorful when he has something to add to Smith. That he never finished his "Historie of Travaile" was partly because he lacked a patron and partly because he found that Smith had written about so many things before him. The two, however, make a fascinating pair of books and ought to be read closely together. The narrative of Smith (822) and the topographical and natural history sections of Strachey (823) are all we can include here.

822. 1607-1612. John Smith, "The Proceedings of the English colony in Virginia."

In 1612, some time after his final break with the Virginia Company, John Smith had published in Oxford his two-part book, A map of Virginia... written by Captaine Smith... whereunto is annexed the proceedings of these colonies. *The latter was said to have been taken faithfully from the writings of Dr. [John?]Russell, Thomas Studley, Anas Todkill, Jeffra Abot, Richard Wiefin, William Phettiplace, Nathaniel Powel, and Richard Pots by W[illiam] S[ymonds]. These men, no doubt, kept journals that were usable, and it is probable that the whole was revised somewhat by the Reverend William Symonds. But there is no doubt that on every page the personality and viewpoint of John Smith were impressed. The* Proceedings *is the most important single contemporary work on the Virginia colony from 1607 to 1612. It plays lightly on its early troubles (many covered in Smith's earlier* A true relation of such occurances and accidents of noate as hath hapned in Virginia since the first planting of that collony [1608]), *but it carried forward the story through the glorious days of his own governorship and the sad decline which the colony suffered after he was first challenged and then obliged to leave Virginia in 1609. If it is taken as Smith's account of his stewardship as seen through his own and other sympathetic eyes, it is a most valuable document, full of insights as well as information on Virginia, but it is not objective history. It is a chapter in Smith's autobiography, which, it seems, he always managed to get other persons to write for him, while its rhetorical speeches to Powhatan and others have little more fictional reality than those placed in the mouth of Hernando de Soto by Garcilaso de la Vega, the Inca, in* La Florida de la Inca *in 1605. But the mainstream of the story, so long as it is remembered that it is Smith's story and not that of a detached observer, is a major document that cannot be omitted from any selection such as this. The* Map *is vital for its map and its description of the topography and for its information on Indian society and natural resources, but there is not room for it.*

W. S., A map of Virginia *(Oxford, Joseph Barnes, 1612), was included in John Smith,* Works, *edited by E. Arber (Birmingham, 1884), reissued with an introduction by R. B. Bradley, 2 vols. (London, 1910). The first modern edition was in P. L. Barbour,* The Jamestown Voyages, *2 vols. (1969), II, 327-464; it is included in Barbour's definitive edition of* The Works, *3 vols., to be published by the University of North Carolina Press for the Institute of Early American History and Culture.*

The Proceedings of the English Colony in Virginia, taken faithfully out of the writings of Thomas Studly Cape-marchant, Anas Todkill, Doctor Russell, Nathaniel Powell, William Phetiplace, and Richard Pot, with the laboures of other discreet observers, during their residences.

1

It might wel be thought, a countrie so faire (as Virginia is) and a people so tractable, would long ere this have beene quietly possessed, to the satisfaction of the adventurers, and the eternizing of the memorie of those that affected it. But because all the world doe see a defailement; this following Treatise shall give satisfaction to all indifferent readers, how the businesse hath beene carried, where no doubt they will easily understand and answer to their question, howe it came to passe there was no better speed and successe in those proceedings.

Captaine Bartholomew Gosnold, the first mover of this plantation, having many yeares solicited many of his friends, but found small assistants; at last prevailed with some Gentlemen, as Master Edward Maria Wingfield, Captaine John Smith, and diverse others who depended a yeare upon his projects, but nothing could be effected, till by their great charge and industrie it came to be apprehended by certaine of the Nobilitie, Gentrie, and Marchants, so that his Majestie by his letters patents, gave commission for establishing Councels, to direct here, and to governe, and to execute there; to effect this, was spent another yeare, and by that time, three ships were provided, one of 100 Tonns, another of 40. and a Pinnace of 20. The transportation of the company was committed to Captaine Christopher Newport, a Marriner well practised for the westerne parts of America. But their orders for governement were put in a box, not to be opened, nor the governours knowne untill they arived in Virginia.

On the 19 of December, 1606. we set saile, but by unprosperous winds, were kept six weekes in the sight of England; all which time, Master Hunt our Preacher, was so weake and sicke, that few expected his recoverie. Yet although he were but 10 or 12 miles from his habitation (the time we were in the Downes) and notwithstanding the stormie weather, nor the scandalous imputations (of some few, little better then Atheists, of the greatest ranke amongst us) suggested against him, all this could never force from him so much as a seeming desire to leave the busines, but preferred the service of God, in so good a voyage, before any affection to contest with his godlesse foes, whose disasterous designes (could they have prevailed) had even then overthrowne the businesse, so many discontents did then arise, had he not with the water of patience, and his godly exhortations (but chiefly by his true devoted examples) quenched those flames of envie, and dissention.

Wee watred at the Canaries, wee traded with the Salvages at Dominica; three weekes we spent in refreshing ourselves amongst these West-India Iles; in Gwardalupa we found a bath so hot, as in it we boiled porck as well as over the fire. And at a little Ile called Monica, we tooke from the bushes with our hands, neare 2 hogshheads full of birds in 3 or 4 houres. In Mevis, Mona, and the Virgin Iles, we spent some time, where with a lothsome beast like a Crocadil, called a Gwayn, Tortoses, Pellicans, Parrots & fishes, we daily feasted. Gone from thence in search of Virginia, the company was not a little discomforted, seeing the Marriners had three daies passed their reckoning and found no land, so that Captaine Ratcliffe (Captaine of the Pinnace) rather desired to beare up the helme to returne for England, then make further search. But God the guider of all good actions, forcing them by an extream storme to hul all night, did drive them by his providence to their desired port, beyond all their expectations, for never any of them had seene that coast. The first land they made they called Cape Henry, where anchoring, Master Wingfield, Gosnoll, and Newport, with 30 others, recreating themselves on

shore, were assalted by 5 Salvages, who hurt 2 of the English very dangerously. That night was the box opened, and the orders read, in which Bartholomew Gosnoll, Edward Wingfeild, Christopher Newport, John Smith, John Ratliffe, John Martin, and George Kendall, were named to bee the Councell, and to choose a President amongst them for a yeare, who with the Councell should governe. Matters of moment were to be examined by a Jurie, but determined by the major part of the Councell in which the President had 2 voices. Untill the 13 of May they sought a place to plant in, then the Councell was sworne, Master Wingfeild was chosen Precident, & an oration made, whie Captaine Smith was not admitted of the Councell as the rest.

Now falleth every man to worke, the Councell contrive the Fort, the rest cut downe trees to make place to pitch their Tents; some provide clapboard to relade the ships, some make gardens, some nets, &c. The Salvages often visited us kindly. The Precidents overweening jealousie would admit no exercise at armes, or fortification, but the boughs of trees cast together in the forme of a halfe moone by the extraordinary paines and diligence of Captaine Kendall. Newport, with Smith, and 20 others, were sent to discover the head of the river: by divers smal habitations they passed, in 6 daies they arrived at a towne called Powhatan, consisting of some 12 houses pleasantly seated on a hill; before it 3 fertil Iles, about it many of their cornefields, the place is very pleasant, and strong by nature, of this place the Prince is called Powhatan, and his people Powhatans, to this place the river is navigable, but higher within a mile, by reason of the Rockes, and Iles, there is not passage for a smal boate, this they call the Falles, the people in al parts kindly intreated them, til being returned within 20 miles of James towne, they gave just cause of jealousie, but had God not blessed the discoverers otherwise then those at the fort, there had then beene an end of that plantation; for at the fort, where they arrived the next day, / they found 17 men hurt, and a boy slaine by the Salvages, and had it not chanced a crosse barre shot from the ships strooke down a bough from a tree amongst them that caused them to retire, our men had all been slaine, being securely all at worke, and their armes in drie fats.

Hereupon the President was contented the

Fort should be pallisadoed, the ordinance mounted, his men armed and exercised, for many were the assaults. and Ambuscadoes of the Salvages, and our men by their disorderly stragling were often hurt, when the Salvages by the nimblenesse of their heeles well escaped. What toile wee had, with so smal a power to guard our workmen adaies, watch al night, resist our enimies and effect our businesse, to relade the ships, cut downe trees, and prepare the ground to plant our corne, &c.

I referre to the readers consideration. Six weekes being spent in this manner, Captaine Newport (who was hired only for our transportation) was to return with the ships, now Captaine Smith, who all this time from their departure from the Canaries was restrained as a prisoner upon the scandalous suggestions of some of the chiefe (envying his repute) who fained he intended to usurpe the governement, murder the Councell, and make himselfe king, that his confederats were dispearsed in all the three ships, and that divers of his confederats that revealed it, would affirme it, for this he was committed, 13 weekes he remained thus suspected, and by that time the ships should returne they pretended out of their commisserations, to referre him to the Councell in England, to receave a check, rather then by particulating his designes make him so odious to the world, as to touch his life, or utterly overthrowe his reputation; but he much scorned their charitie, and publikely defied the uttermost of their crueltie, hee wisely prevented their pollicies, though he could not suppresse their envies, yet so wel he demeaned himselfe in this busines, as all the company did see his innocencie, & his adversaries malice, and those suborned to accuse him, accused his accusers of subornation; many untruthes were alleaged against him; but being so apparently disproved begat a generall hatred in the harts of the company against such unjust commanders; many were the mischiefes that daily sprong from their ignorant (yet ambitious) spirits; but the good doctrine and exhortation of our preacher Master Hunt reconciled them, and caused Captaine Smith to be admitted of the Councell; the next day all receaved the Communion, the day following the Salvages voluntarily desired peace, and Captaine Newport returned for England with newes; leaving in Virginia 100. the 15 of June 1607.

The names of them that were the first planters, were these following.

Master Edward Maria Wingfield. ⎫
Captaine Bartholomew Gosnall. |
Captain John Smyth. |
Captain John Ratliffe. ⎬ Councell.
Captain John Martin. |
Captain George Kendall. ⎭
Master Robert Hunt Preacher
Master George Percie. ⎫
Anthony Gosnoll. |
Captain Gabriell Archer. |
Robert Ford. |
William Bruster. |
Dru Pickhouse. |
John Brookes. |
Thomas Sands. |
John Robinson |
Ustis Clovill. |
Kellam Throgmorton. |
Nathaniell Powell. |
Robert Behethland. |
Jeremy Alicock. |
Thomas Studley. ⎬ Gentlemen.
Richard Crofts. |
Nicholas Houlgraue. |
Thomas Webbe: |
John Waler. |
William Tankard. |
Francis Snarsbrough. |
Edward Brookes. |
Richard Dixon. |
John Martin. |
George Martin. |
Anthony Gosnold: |
Thomas Wotton, Siergeant |
Thomas Gore. |
Francis Midwinter. ⎭
William Laxon. ⎫
Edward Pising. |
Thomas Emry. ⎬ Carpenters.
Robert Small. ⎭
Anas Todkill.
John Capper.
James Read, Blacksmith.
Jonas Profit, Sailer.
Thomas Couper, Barber.
John Herd, Bricklayer.
William Garret, Brick layer
Edward Brinto, Mason.
William Love, Taylor.
Nicholas Skot, Drum.
John Laydon. ⎫
William Cassen. ⎬ Labourers.
George Cassen. ⎭

Thomas Cassen.   ⎫
William Rods.   ⎪
William White.   ⎪
Ould Edward.   ⎪
Henry Tavin.   ⎬ Labourers.
George Golding.   ⎪
John Dods.   ⎪
William Johnson.   ⎪
Will Unger.   ⎭

William Wilkinson. Surgeon

Samuell Collier.   ⎫
Nathaniel Pecock. ⎬ Boyes.
James Brumfield.   ⎪
Rich. Mutton.   ⎭

with diverse others to the number of 105.

2

What happened till the first supply.

Being thus left to our fortunes, it fortuned that within tenne daies scarse ten amongst us coulde either goe, or well stand, such extreame weaknes and sicknes opressed us. And thereat none need mervaile, if they consider the cause and reason, which was this; whilest the ships staied, our allowance was somewhat bettered, by a daily proportion of bisket which the sailers would pilfer to sell, give or exchange with us, for mony, saxefras, furres, or love. But when they departed, there remained neither taverne, beere-house nor place of relief but the common kettell. Had we beene as free from all sinnes as gluttony, and drunkennes, we might have bin canonized for Saints; But our President would never have bin admitted, for ingrossing to his privat, Otemeale, sacke, oile, aquavite, beefe egs, or what not, but the kettel; that indeede he allowed equally to be distributed, and that was halfe a pinte of wheat and as much barly boyled with water for a man a day, and this having fryed some 26. weeks in the ships hold, contained as many wormes as graines; so that we might truely call it rather so much bran then corne, our drinke was water, our lodgings castles in aire, with this lodging and diet, our extreame toile and our continuall labour in the extremity of the heate had in bearing and planting pallisadoes, so strained and bruised us, so weakned us, as were cause sufficient to have made us as miserable in our native country, or any other place in the world. From May to September, those that escaped; lived upon Sturgion, and sea-Crabs, 50. in this time we buried, The rest seeing the Presidents projects to escape these miseries in our Pinnas by flight (who all this time had neither felt want nor sicknes) so moved our dead spirits, as we deposed him; and established Ratcliffe in his place, (Gosnoll being dead) Kendall deposed, Smith newly recovered, Martin and Ratliffe was by his care preserved and relieved, but now was all our provision spent, the Sturgeon gone, all helps abandoned each houre expecting the fury of the Salvages; when God the patron of all good indeavours in that desperate extreamity so changed the harts of the Salvages, that they brought such plenty of their fruits, and provision as no man wanted.

And now where some affirmed it was ill done of the Councel to send forth men so badly provided, this incontradictable reason will shew them plainely they are too ill advised to nourish such il conceipts; first the fault of our going was our owne, what coulde bee thought fitting or necessary wee had, but what wee should finde, what we should want, where we should be, we were all ignorant, and supposing to make our passage in two monthes, with victuall to live, and the advantage of the spring to worke; we weare at sea 5. monthes where we both spent our victuall & lost the opportunity of the time, and season to plant.

Such actions have ever since the worlds beginning beene subject to such accidents, and every thing of worth is found full of difficulties, but nothing so difficult as to establish a common wealth so farre remote from men and meanes, and where mens mindes are so untoward as neither do well themselves nor suffer others; but to proceed.

The new President, and Martin, being little beloved; of weake judgement in dangers, and lesse industry in peace, committed the managing of all things abroad to captaine Smith: who by his owne example, good words, and faire promises, set some to mow, others to binde thatch, some to build houses, others to thatch them, himselfe alwaies bearing the greatest taske for his own share, so that in short time, he provided most of them lodgings neglecting any for himselfe. this done, seeing the Salvages superfluity beginne to decrease (with some of his workemen) shipped himselfe in the shallop to search the country for trade, the want of the language, knowledge to mannage his boat without sailers, the want of a sufficient power, (knowing the multitude of the Salvages) apparell for his men, & other necessaries, were infinite impediments, yet no discouragement. Being but 6 or 7 in company he went down the river to Kecoughtan, where at first they scorned him, as a starved man, yet he so dealt with them, that the next day they loaded his boat with corne, & in his returne he discovered & kindly traded with the Weraskoyks, in the meane time those at the fort so glutted the Salvages with their commodities as they became not regarded.

Smith perceiving (notwithstanding their late miserie) not any regarded but from hand to mouth, (the company being well recovered) caused the Pinas to bee provided with things fitting to get provision for the yeare following; but in the interim he made 3. or 4. journies and discovered the people of Chickahamine yet what he carefully provided the rest carelesly spent. Wingfield and Kendall living in disgrace, seeing al things at randome in the absence of Smith, The companies dislike of their Presidents weaknes, & their smal love to Martins never-mending sicknes, strengthened themselves with the sailers, and other confederates to regaine their former credit & authority, or at least such meanes abord the Pinas, (being fitted to saile as Smith had appointed for trade) to alter her course and to go for England. Smith unexpectedly returning had the plot discovered to him, much trouble he had to prevent it till with store of fauken and musket shot he forced them stay or sinke in the river, which action cost the life of captaine Kendall. These brawles are so disgustfull, as some will say they were better forgotten, yet all men of good judgement will conclude, it were better their basenes should be manifest to the world, then the busines beare the scorne and shame of their excused disorders. The President and captaine Archer not long after intended also to have abandoned the country, which project also was curbed, and suppressed by Smith. The Spanyard never more greedily desired gold then he victuall, which finding so plentiful in the river of Chickahamine where hundreds of Salvages in divers places stood with baskets expecting his comming. And now the winter approaching, the rivers became so covered with swans, geese, duckes, & cranes, that we daily feasted with good bread, Virginia pease, pumpions, and putchamins, fish, fowle, and diverse sorts of wild beasts as fat as we could eat them: so that none of our Tuftaffaty humorists desired to goe for England. But our comædies never endured long without a

Tragedie; some idle exceptions being muttered against Captaine Smith, for not discovering the head of Chickahamine river, and taxed by the Councell, to bee too slowe in so worthie an attempt. The next voyage hee proceeded so farre that with much labour by cutting of trees in sunder he made his passage, but when his Barge could passe no farthr, he left her in a broad bay out of danger of shot, commanding none should goe ashore till his returne, himselfe with 2 English & two Salvages went up higher in a Canowe, but hee was not long absent, but his men went ashore, whose want of government, gave both occasion and opportunity to the Salvages to surprise one George Casson, & much failed not to have cut of the boat & all the rest, Smith little dreaming of that accident, being got to the marshes at the rivers head, 20 myles in the desert, had his 2 men slaine (as is supposed) sleeping by the Canowe, whilst himselfe by fowling sought them victuall, who finding he was beset with 200 Salvages, 2 of them hee slew, stil defending himselfe with the aid of a Salvage his guid, (whome hee bound to his arme and used as his buckler,) till at last slipping into a bogmire they tooke him prisoner: when this newes came to the fort much was their sorrow for his losse, fewe expecting what ensued. A month those Barbarians kept him prisoner many strange triumphes and conjurations they made of him, yet hee so demeaned himselfe amongst them, as he not only diverted them from surprising the Fort, but procured his owne liberty, and got himselfe and his company such estimation amongst them, that those Salvages admired him as a demi-God. So returning safe to the Fort once more staied the Pinnas her flight for England, which til his returne, could not set saile, so extreame was the weather, and so great the frost.

His relation of the plentie he had seene, especially at Werowocomoco, where inhabited Powhatan (that till that time was unknowne) so revived againe their dead spirits as all mens feare was abandoned, Powhatan having sent with his Captaine divers of his men loaded with provision, he had conditioned, & so appointed his trustie messengers to bring but 2 or 3 of our great ordenances, but the messengers being satisfied with the sight of one of them discharged, ran away amazed with feare, till meanes was used with guifts to assure them our loves. Thus you may see what difficulties stil crossed any good indeavour, and the good successe of the businesse, and being thus oft brought to the very period of destruction, yet you see by what strange meanes God hath still delivered it. As for the insufficiencie of them admitted in commission, that errour could not be prevented by their electors, there being no other choice, and all were strangers each to others education, quallities, or disposition; & if any deeme it a shame to our nation, to have any mention made of these enormities, let them peruse the histories of the Spanish discoveries and plantations, where they may see how many mutinies, discords, and dissentions, have accompanied them and crossed their attempts, which being knowne to be particular mens offences, doth take away the generall scorne and contempt, mallice, and ignorance might else produce, to the scandall and reproach of those, whose actions and valiant resolution deserve a worthie respect. Now whether it had beene better for Captaine Smith to have concluded with any of their severall projects to have abandoned the Countrie with some 10 or 12 of them we cal the better sort, to have left Master Hunt our preacher, Master Anthony Gosnoll, a most honest, worthie, and industirous gentleman, with some 30 or 40 others his countrie men, to the furie of the Salvages, famin, and all manner of mischiefes and inconveniences, or starved himselfe with them for company, for want of lodging, or but adventuring abroad to make them provision, or by his opposition, to preserve the action, and save all their lives, I leave to the censure of others to consider.

Thomas Studley

3
The arrivall of the first supply with their proceedings and returne.

All this time our cares were not so much to abandon the Conntrie, but the Treasurer & Councell in England were as diligent and carefull to supplie us. Two tall ships they sent us, with neere 100 men, well furnished with all things could be imagined necessarie, both for them and us. The one commanded by Captaine Newport: the other by Captaine Nelson, an honest man and an expert marriner, but such was the leewardness of his ship [the Phenix], (that though he were within sight of Cape Henry) by stormy contrarie windes,

was forced so farre to sea, as the West Indies was the next land for the repaire of his Masts, and reliefe of wood and water. But Captaine Newport got in, and arived at James towne, not long after the redemption of Captaine Smith, to whome the Salvages every other day brought such plentie of bread, fish, turkies, squirrels, deare, & other wild beasts, part they gave him as presents from the king; the rest, hee as their market clarke set the price how they should sell.

So he had inchanted those poore soules (being their prisoner) in demonstrating unto them the roundnesse of the world, the course of the moone and starres, the cause of the day and night the largenes of the seas the quallities of our ships, shot and powder, The devision of the world, with the diversity of people, their complexions, customes and conditions. All which hee fained to be under the command of Captaine Newport, whom he tearmed to them his father; of whose arrival, it chanced he so directly prophecied, as they esteemed him an oracle; by these fictions he not only saved his owne life, and obtained his liberty, but had them at that command, he might command them what he listed. That God that created al these things; they knew he adored for his God, whom they would also tearme in their discourses, the God of captaine Smith. The President and Council so much envied his estimation amongst the Salvages (though wee all in generall equally participated with him of the good therof) that they wrought in into their understandings, by their great bounty in giving 4. times more for their commodities then he appointed, that their greatnesse and authority, as much exceed his, as their bounty, and liberality; Now the arrivall of this first supply, so overjoyed us, that we could not devise too much to please the mariners. We gave them liberty to truck or trade at their pleasures. But in a short time, it followed, that could not be had for a pound of copper, which before was sold for an ounce. Thus ambition, and sufferance, cut the throat of our trade, but confirmed their opinion of Newports greatnes, (wherewith Smith had possessed Powhatan) especially by the great presents Newport often sent him, before he could prepare the Pinas to go and visit him; so that this Salvage also desired to see him. A great bruit there was to set him forwarde: when he went he was accompanied, with captaine Smith, & Master Scrivener a very wise understanding gentleman newly arrived & admitted of the Councell, & 30. or 40. chosen men for that guarde. Arriving at Werowocomo Newports conceipt of this great Salvage, bred many doubts, and suspitions of treacheries; which Smith, to make appeare was needlesse, which 20 men well appointed, undertooke to encounter (with that number) the worst that could happen; there names were.

Nathaniell Powell.
Robert Beheathland.
William Phettiplace.
Richard Wyffin.
Anthony Gosnoll.
John Taverner.
William Dier.
Thomas Coe.
Thomas Hope.
Anas Todkell

with 10. others whose names I have forgotten, These being kindly received a shore, with 2. or 300. Salvages were conducted to their towne: Powhatan strained himselfe to the uttermost of his greatnes to entertain us, with great shouts of Joy, orations of protestations, and the most plenty of victual hee could provide to feast us. Sitting upon his bed of mats, his pillow of leather imbroydred (after their rude manner) with pearle & white beades, his attire a faire Robe of skins as large as an Irish mantle, at his head and feet a handsome young woman; on each side his house sate 20. of his concubines, their heads and shoulders painted red, with a great chaine of white beads about their necks, before those sate his chiefest men in like order in his arbor-like house. With many pretty discourses to renue their olde acquaintaunce; the great kinge and our captaine spent the time till the ebbe left our Barge aground, then renuing their feasts and mirth we quartred that night with Powhatan: the next day Newport came a shore, and received as much content as those people could give him, a boy named Thomas Savage was then given unto Powhatan who Newport called his son, for whom Powhatan gave him Namontacke his trusty servant, and one of a shrewd subtill capacity, 3. or 4. daies were spent in feasting dancing and trading, wherein Powhatan carried himselfe so prowdly, yet discreetly (in his Salvage manner) as made us all admire his natural gifts considering his education, as scorning to trade as his subjects did, he bespake Newport in this manner.

Captain Newport it is not agreeable with my greatnes in this pedling manner to trade for trifles, and I esteeme you a great werowans, Therefore lay me down all your commodities togither, what I like I will take, and in recompence give you that I thinke fitting their value. Captaine Smith being our interpreter, regarding Newport as his father, knowing best the disposition of Powhatan told us his intent was but to cheat us; yet captaine Newport thinking to out brave this Salvage in ostentation of greatnes, & so to bewitch him with his bounty, as to have what he listed, but so it chanced Powhatan having his desire, valued his corne at such a rate, as I thinke it better cheape in Spaine, for we had not 4. bushels for that we expected 20. hogsheads, This bred some unkindnes betweene our two captaines, Newport seeking to please the humor of the unsatiable Salvage; Smith to cause the Salvage to please him, but smothering his distast (to avoide the Salvages suspition) glaunced in the eies of Powhatan many Trifles who fixed his humour upon a few blew beades; A long time he importunatly desired them, but Smith seemed so much the more to affect them, so that ere we departed, for a pound or two of blew beads he brought over my king for 2 or 300 bushels of corne, yet parted good friends. The like entertainement we found of Opechanchynough, king of Pamaunke whom also he in like manner fitted, (at the like rates) with blew beads: and so we returned to the fort. Where this new supply being lodged with the rest, accidently fired the quarters, & so the Towne, which being but thatched with reeds the fire was so fierce as it burnt their pallizadoes (though 10. or 12 yardes distant) with their armes, bedding, apparell, and much private provision. Good Master Hunt our preacher lost all his library, and al that he had (but the cloathes on his backe,) yet none ever see him repine at his losse. This hapned in the winter, in that extreame frost, 1607. Now though we had victuall sufficient, I meane only of Oatemeale, meale, and corne yet the ship staying there 14. weeks when shee might as well have been gone in 14. daies, spent the beefe, porke, oile, aquavite, fish, butter, and cheese, beere and such like; as was provided to be landed us. When they departed, what their discretion could spare us, to make a feast or two with bisket, pork beefe, fish, and oile, to relish our mouths, of each somwhat they left us, yet I must confess those that had either mony, spare clothes, credit to give bils of payment, gold rings, furres, or any such commodities were ever welcome to this removing taverne, such was our patience to obay such vile commanders, and buy our owne provision at 15 times the valew, suffering them feast (we bearing the charge) yet must not repine, but fast; and then leakage, ship-rats, and other casualties occasioned the losse, but the vessell and remnants (for totals) we were glad to receive with all our hearts to make up the account, highly commending their providence for preserving that. For all this plentie our ordinarie was but meale and water, so that this great charge little relieved our wants, whereby with the extreamity of the bitter cold aire more then halfe of us died, and tooke our deathes, in that piercing winter I cannot deny, but both Skrivener and Smith did their best to amend what was amisse, but with the President went the major part, that their hornes were too short. But the worst mischiefe was, our gilded refiners with their golden promises, made all men their slaves in hope of recompence, there was no talke, no hope, no worke, but dig gold, wash gold, refine gold, load gold, such a brute of gold, as one mad fellow desired to bee buried in the sandes, least they should by their art make gold of his bones, little need there was and lesse reason, the ship should stay, their wages run on, our victuall consume, 14 weekes, that the Marriners might say, they built such a golden Church, that we can say, the raine washed neare to nothing in 14 daies. Were it that Captaine Smith would not applaud all those golden inventions, because they admitted him not to the sight of their trials, nor golden consultations I knowe not; but I heard him question with Captaine Martin and tell him, except he would shew him a more substantiall triall, hee was not inamoured with their durtie skill, breathing out these and many other passions, never anything did more torment him, then to see all necessarie businesse neglected, to fraught such a drunken ship with so much gilded durt; till then wee never accounted Captaine Newport a refiner; who being fit to set saile for England, and wee not having any use of Parliaments, plaies, petitions, admirals, recorders, interpreters, chronologers, courts of plea, nor Justices of peace, sent Master Wingfield & Captain Archer with him for England to seeke some place of better imploiment.

4
The arival of the Phoenix, her returne, and other accidents

The authoritie nowe consisting in refining, Captaine Martin and the still sickly President, the sale of the stores commodities maintained their estates as inheritable revenews. The spring approching, and the ship departed, Master Skrivener and Captain Smith divided betwixt them, the rebuilding our towne, the repairing our pallisadoes, the cutting downe trees, preparing our fields, planting our corne, & to rebuild our Church, and recover our store-house; al men thus busie at their severall labours, Master Nelson arived with his lost Phœnix (lost I say, for that al men deemed him lost) landing safely his men: so well hee had mannaged his ill hap, causing the Indian Iles to feed his company that his victuall (to that was left us before) was sufficient for halfe a yeare, he had nothing but he freely imparted it, which honest dealing (being a marriner) caused us admire him, wee would not have wished so much as he did for us. Nowe to relade this ship with some good tidings. The President (yet notwithstanding with his dignitie to leave the fort) gave order to Captaine Smith and Master Skrivener to discover & search the commodities of Monacans countrie beyound the Falles, 60 able men was allotted their number, the which within 6 daies exercise, Smith had so well trained to their armes and orders, that they little feared with whome they should encounter. Yet so unseasonable was the time, and so opposite was Captain Martin to everything, but only to fraught his ship also with his phantasticall gold, as Captaine Smith rather desired to relade her with Cedar, which was a present dispatch; then either with durt, or the reports of an uncertaine discoverie. Whilst their conclusion was resolving, this hapned.

Powhatan to expresse his love to Newport, when he departed, presented him with 20 Turkies, conditionally to returne him 20 Swords, which immediatly were sent him; Now after his departure hee presented Captaine Smith with the like luggage, but not finding his humor, obaied in sending him weapons, he caused his people with 20. devises to obtain them, at last by ambuscadoes at our very ports they would take them per force, surprise us at work, or any way, which was so long permitted that they became so insolent, there was no rule, the command from England was so straight not to offend them, as our authority bearers (keeping their houses) would rather be anything then peace breakers: this charitable humor prevailed, till well it chaunced they medled with captaine Smith, who without farther deliberation gave them such an incounter, as some he so hunted up and downe the Ile, some he so terrified with whipping, beating and imprisonment, as for revenge they surprised two of his forraging disorderly souldiers, and having assembled their forces, boldly threatned at our ports to force Smith to redeliver 7. Salvages which for their villanies he detained prisoners, but to try their furies, in lesse then halfe an houre he so hampered their insolencies, that they brought the 2. prisoners desiring peace without any farther composition for their prisoners, who being threatned and examined their intents and plotters of their villanies confessed they were directed only by Powhatan, to obtaine him our owne weapons to cut our own throats, with the manner how, where, and when, which wee plainely found most true and apparant, yet he sent his messengers & his dearest Daughter Pocahuntas to excuse him, of the injuries done by his subjects, desiring their liberties, with the assuraunce of his love, after Smith had given the prisoners what correction hee thought fit, used them well a day or two after, & then delivered them Pocahuntas, for whose sake only he fained to save their lives and graunt them liberty. The patient councel, that nothing would move to warre with the Salvages, would gladly have wrangled with captaine Smith for his cruelty, yet none was slaine to any mans knowledge but it brought them in such feare & obedience, as his very name wold sufficiently affright them. The fraught of this ship being concluded to be Cedar, by the diligence of the Master, and captaine Smith shee was quickly reladed; Master Scrivener was neither Idle nor slow to follow all things at the fort, the ship falling to the Cedar Ile, captaine Martin having made shift to be sicke neare a yeare, & now, neither pepper, suger, cloves, mace, nor nugmets, ginger nor sweet meates in the country (to injoy the credit of his supposed art) at his earnest request, was most willingly admitted to returne for England, yet having beene there but a yeare, and not past halfe a year since the ague left him (that he might say somewhat he had seene) hee went twice by water to Paspahegh a place neere 7. miles from James towne, but lest the dew should distemper him, was ever forced to returne before night, Thus much I thought fit to expresse, he expresly commanding me to record his journies, I being his man, and he sometimes my master.

Thomas Studly. Anas Todkill.

Their names that were landed in this supply:

Matthew Scriviner, appointed to be of the Councell.

Michaell Phetyplace.
William Phetyplace.
Ralfe Morton.
William Cantrill.
Richard Wyffin.
Robert Barnes.
George Hill.
George Pretty.
John Taverner.
Robert Cutler.
Michaell Sickelmore.
Thomas Coo.
Peter Pory.
Richard Killingbeck.
William Causey.
Doctor Russell.
Richard Worley.
Richard Prodger.
William Bayley.
Richard Molynex.
Richard Pots.
Jefrey Abots.
John Harper.
Timothy Leds.
Edward Gurganay.
George Forest.
John Nickoles.
William Gryvill.

} Gentlemen.

Daniell Stalling Jueller.
William Dawson Refiner.
Abraham Ransacke Refiner.
William Johnson Goldsmith.
Peter Keffer a Gunner.
Robert Alberton a Perfumer.
Richard Belfield Goldsmith.

Ramon Goodyson.
John Speareman.
William Spence.
Richard Brislow.
William Simons.

} Labourers.

John Bouth.
William Burket.
Nicholas Ven.
William Perce.
Francis Perkins.
Francis Perkins.
William Bentley.
Richard Gradon. } Labourers.
Rowland Nelstrop.
Richard Salvage.
Thomas Salvage.
Richard Miler.
William May.
Vere.
Michaell.
Bishop Wyles.

John Powell.
Thomas Hope.
William Beckwith. } Tailers.
William Yonge.
Laurence Towtales.
William Ward.

Christopher Rodes.
James Watkings.
Richard Fetherstone.
James Burne.
Thomas Feld. } Apothecaries.
John Harford.

Post Gittnat a Surgion.
John Lewes a Couper.
Robert Cotten a Tobaco-pipe-maker.
Richard Dole a blacke Smith & divers others to
the number of 120.

5

The accidents that happened in the Discoverie of the bay.

The prodigality of the Presidents state went so deepe in the store that Smith and Scrivener had a while tyed both **Martin** & him to the rules of proportion, but now Smith being to depart, the Presidents authoritie so overswayed Master Scriveners discretion as our store, our time, our strength and labours was idlely consumed to fulfill his phantasies. The second of June 1608. Smith left the fort to performe his discoverie, with this company.

Walter Russell Doctour of Physicke.
Ralph Morton.
Thomas Momford.
William Cantrill. } Gentlemen.
Richard Fetherstone.
James Bourne.
Michael Sicklemore.

Anas Todkill.
Robert Small. } Souldiers.
James Watkins.
John Powell.
James Read blacke smith.
Richard Keale fishmonger.
Jonas Profit fisher.

These being in an open barge of two tunnes burthen leaving the Phenix at Cape-Henry we crossed the bay to the Easterne shore & fell with the Iles called Smiths, Iles the first people we saw were 2. grimme and stout Salvages upon Cape-Charles with long poles like Javelings, headed with bone, they boldly demanded what we were, and what we would, but after many circumstances, they in time seemed very kinde, and directed us to Acawmacke the habitation of the Werowans where we were kindly intreated; this king was the comliest proper civill Salvage wee incountred: his country is a pleasant fertill claysoile. Hee told us of a straunge accident lately happened him, and it was? Two deade children by the extreame passions of their parents, or some dreaming visions, phantasie, or affection moved them againe to revisit their dead carkases, whose benummed bodies reflected to the eies of the beholders such pleasant delightfull countenances, as though they had regained their vital spirits. This as a miracle drew many to behold them, all which, (being a great part of his people) not long after died, and not any one escaped. They spake the language of Powhatan wherein they made such descriptions of the bay, Iles, and rivers that often did us exceeding pleasure. Passing along the coast, searching every inlet, and bay fit for harbours & habitations seeing many Iles in the midst of the bay, we bore up for them, but ere wee could attaine them, such an extreame gust of wind, raine, thunder, and lightning happened, that with great daunger we escaped the unmercifull raging of that ocean-like water. The next day searching those inhabitable Iles (which we called Russels Iles) to provide fresh water, the defect whereof forced us to follow the next Easterne channell, which brought us to the river Wighcocomoco, the people at first with great furie, seemed to assault us, yet at last with songs, daunces, and much mirth, became very tractable, but searching their habitations for water, wee could fill but 3, and that such puddle, that never til then, wee ever knew the want of good water, we digged and searched many places but ere the end of two daies wee would have refused two barricoes of gold for one of that puddle water of Wighcocomoco. Being past these Iles falling with a high land upon the maine wee found a great pond of fresh water, but so exceeding hot, that we supposed it some bath: that place we called Point Ployer, being thus refreshed in crossing over from the maine to other Iles, the wind and waters so much increased with thunder, lightning, and raine, that our fore-mast blew overbord and such mightie waves overwrought us in that smal barge, that with great labour wee kept her from sinking by freeing out the water, 2 daies we were inforced to inhabit these uninhabited Iles, which (for the extremitie of gusts, thunder, raine, stormes, and il weather) we called Limbo. Repairing our fore saile with our shirts, we set saile for the maine & fel with a faire river on the East called Kuskarawaocke, by it inhabit the people of Soraphanigh, Nause, Arsek, and Nautaquake that much extolled a great nation called Massawomekes, in search of whome wee returned by Limbo, but finding this easterne shore shallow broken Iles, & the maine for most part without fresh water, we passed by the straights of Limbo for the weasterne shore So broad is the bay here, that we could scarse perceive the great high Cliffes on the other side; by them wee anchored that night, and called them Richards Cliffes. 30 leagues we sailed more Northwards, not finding any inhabitants, yet the coast well watred, the mountaines very barren, the vallies very fertil, but the woods extreame thicke, full of Woolves, Beares, Deare, and other wild beasts. The first inlet we found, wee called Bolus, for that the clay (in many places) was like (if not) Bole-Armoniacke: when we first set saile, some of our gallants doubted nothing, but that our Captaine would make too much hast home; but having lien not above 12 daies in this smal Barge, oft tired at their oares, their bread spoiled with wet, so much that it was rotten (yet so good were their stomacks that they could digest it) did with continuall complaints so importune him now to returne, as caused him bespeake them in this manner. Gentlemen if you would remember the memorable historie of Sir Ralfe Lane, how his company importuned him to proceed in the discoverie of Morattico, alleaging, they had yet a dog, that being boyled with Saxafras leaves,

would richly feed them in their returnes; what a shame would it be for you (that have beene so suspitious of my tendernesse) to force me returne with a months provision scarce able to say where we have bin, nor yet heard of that wee were sent to seeke; you cannot say, but I have shared with you of the worst is past; and for what is to come of lodging, diet, or whatsoever, I am contented you allot the worst part to my selfe; as for your feares, that I will lose my selfe in these unknowne large waters, or be swallowed up in some stormie gust, abandon those childish feares, for worse then is past cannot happen, and there is as much danger to returne, as to proceed forward. Regaine therefore your old spirits; for return I wil not, (if God assist me) til I have seene the Massawomekes, found Patawomeck, or the head of this great water you conceit to be endlesse. 3 or 4 daies wee expected wind and weather, whose adverse extreamities added such discouragements to our discontents as 3 or 4 fel extreame sicke, whose pittiful complaints caused us to returne, leaving the bay some 10 miles broad at 9 or 10 fadome water.

The 16 of June we fel with the river of Patawomeck: feare being gone, and our men recovered, wee were all contented to take some paines to knowe the name of this 9 mile broad river, we could see no inhabitants for 30 myles saile; then we were conducted by 2 Salvages up a little bayed creeke toward Onawmament where all the woods were laid with Ambuscadoes to the number of 3 or 400 Salvages, but so strangely painted, grimed, and disguised, showting, yelling, and crying, as we rather supposed them so many divels, they made many bravadoes, but to appease their furie, our Captaine prepared with a seeming willingnesse (as they) to encounter them, the grazing of the bullets upon the river, with the ecco of the woods so amazed them, as down went their bowes & arrowes; (and exchanging hostage) James Watkins was sent 6 myles up the woods to their kings habitation: wee were kindly used by these Salvages, of whome we understood, they were commaunded to betray us, by Powhatans direction, and hee so directed from the discontents of James towne. The like incounters we found at Patawomeck Cecocawone & divers other places, but at Moyaones Nacothtant and Taux, the people did their best to content us. The cause of this discovery, was to search a glistering mettal, the Salvages told us they had from Patawomeck, (the which Newport assured that he had tryed to hold halfe silver) also to search what furres, metals, rivers, Rockes, nations, woods, fishings, fruits, victuals and other commodities the land afforded, and whether the bay were endlesse, or how farre it extended. The mine we found 9 or 10 myles up in the country from the river, but it proved of no value: Some Otters, Beavers, Martins, Luswarts, and sables we found, and in diverse places that abundance of fish lying so thicke with their heads above the water, as for want of nets (our barge driving amongst them) we attempted to catch them with a frying pan, but we found it a bad instrument to catch fish with. Neither better fish more plenty or variety had any of us ever seene, in any place swimming in the water, then in the bay of Chesapeack, but there not to be caught with frying-pans. To expresse al our quarrels, treacheries & incounters amongst those Salvages, I should be too tedious; but in briefe at al times we so incountred them & curbed their insolencies, as they concluded with presents to purchase peace, yet wee lost not a man, at our first meeting our captaine ever observed this order to demaunde their bowes and arrowes swords mantles or furres, with some childe for hostage, wherby he could quickly perceive when they intended any villany. Having finished this discovery (though our victuall was neare spent) he intended to have seene his imprisonments acquaintance upon the river of Toppahannock. But our boate (by reason of the ebbe) chansing to ground upon a many shoules lying in the entrance, we spied many fishes lurking amongst the weedes on the sands, our captaine sporting himselfe to catch them by nailing them to the ground with his sword, set us all a fishing in that manner, by this devise, we tooke more in an houre then we all could eat; but it chanced, the captaine taking a fish from his sword (not knowing her condition) being much of the fashion of a Thornebacke with a longer taile, whereon is a most poysoned sting of 2. or 3 inches long, which shee strooke an inch and halfe into the wrist of his arme the which in 4. houres had so extreamly swolne his hand, arme, shoulder, and part of his body, as we al with much sorrow concluded his funerall, and prepared his grave in an Ile hard by (as himselfe appointed) which then wee called Stingeray Ile after the name of the fish. Yet by the helpe of a precious oile Doctour Russell applyed, ere night his tormenting paine was so wel asswaged that he eate the fish to his supper, which gave no less joy and content to us, then ease to himselfe. Having neither Surgeon nor surgerie but that preservative oile, we presently set saile for James Towne; passing the mouth of Pyankatanck, & Pamaunke rivers, the next day we safely arrived at Kecoughtan. The simple Salvages, seeing our captaine hurt, and another bloudy (which came by breaking his shin) our number of bowes, arrowes, swords, targets, mantles and furs; would need imagine we had bin at warres, (the truth of these accidents would not satisfie them) but impaciently they importuned us to know with whom wee fought, finding their aptnes to beleeve, we failed not (as a great secret) to tel them any thing that might affright them what spoile wee had got and made of the Masawomeckes, this rumor went faster up the river then our barge; that arrived at Weraskoyack the 20. of Julie, where trimming her with painted streamers, and such devises we made the fort Jealious of a Spanish frigot; where we all safely arrived the 21. of July, there wee found the last supply, al sicke, the rest, some lame, some bruised, al unable to do any thing, but complain of the pride and unreasonable needlesse cruelty of their sillie President, that had riotously consumed the store, & to fulfill his follies about building him an unnecessarie pallas in the woodes had brought them all to that miserie; That had not we arrived, they had as strangely tormented him with revenge. But the good newes of our discovery, and the good hope we had (by the Salvages relation) our Bay had stretched to the South-sea, appeased their fury; but conditionally that Ratliffe should be deposed, & that captaine Smith would take upon him the government; their request being effected, hee Substituted Master Scrivener his deare friend in the Presidencie, equally distributing those private provisions the other had ingrossed; appointing more honest officers to assist Scrivener, (who then lay extreamelie tormented with a callenture) & in regard of the weaknes of the company, and heat of the yeare they being unable to worke; he left them to live at ease, but imbarked himselfe to finish his discovery.

Written by Walter Russell and Anas Todkill.

6

What happened the second voyage to discover the Bay.

The 20. of July Captaine Smith set forward to finish the discovery with 12. men their names were

Nathaniell Powell.	
Thomas Momford.	
Richard Fetherstone.	Gentlemen.
Michaell Sicklemore.	
James Bourne.	
Anas Todkill.	
Edward Pysing.	
Richard Keale.	Souldiers.
Anthony Bagnall.	
James Watkins.	
William Ward.	
Jonas Profit.	

The winde beeing contrary caused our stay 2. or 3. daies at Kecoughtan the werowans feasting us with much mirth, his people were perswaded we went purposely to be revenged of the Massawomeckes, in the evening we firing 2. or 3. rackets, so terrified the poore Salvages, they supposed nothing impossible wee attempted, and desired to assist us. The first night we ancored at Stingeray Ile, the nexte day crossed Patawomecks river, and hasted for the river Bolus, wee went not much farther before wee might perceive the Bay to devide in 2. heads, and arriving there we founde it devided in 4, all which we searched so far as we could saile them; 2. of them wee found uninhabited, but in crossing the bay to the other, wee incountered 7. or 8. Canowes-full of Massawomecks, we seeing them prepare to assault us, left our oares & made way with our saile to incounter them, yet were we but five (with our captaine) could stand; or within 2. daies after wee left Kecoughtan, the rest (being all of the last supply) were sicke almost to death, (untill they were seasoned to the country) having shut them under our tarpawling, we put their hats upon stickes by the barge side to make us seeme many, and so we thinke the Indians supposed those hats to be men, for they fled withall possible speed to the shoare, and there stayed, staring at the sailing of our barge, till we anchored right against them. Long it was ere we could drawe them to come unto us, at last they sent 2 of their company unarmed in a Canowe, the rest all followed to second them if need required;

These 2. being but each presented with a bell, brought aborde all their fellowes, presenting the captain with venison, beares flesh, fish, bowes, arrows, clubs, targets, and beare-skins; wee understood them nothing at all but by signes, whereby they signified unto us they had been at warres with the Tockwoghs the which they confirmed by shewing their green wounds; but the night parting us, we imagined they appointed the next morning to meete, but after that we never saw them.

Entring the River of Tockwogh the Salvages all armed in a fleete of Boates round invironed us; it chanced one of them could speake the language of Powhatan who perswaded the rest to a friendly parly: but when they see us furnished with the Massawomeckes weapons, and we faining the invention of Kecoughtan to have taken them perforce; they conducted us to their pallizadoed towne, mantelled with the barkes of trees, with Scaffolds like mounts, brested about with Barks very formally, their men, women, and children, with dances, songs, fruits, fish, furres, & what they had kindly entertained us, spreading mats for us to sit on, stretching their best abilities to expresse their loves.

Many hatchets, knives, & peeces of yron, & brasse, we see, which they reported to have from the Sasquesahanockes a mighty people, and mortall enimies with the Massawomeckes; The Sasquesahanockes, inhabit upon the chiefe spring of these 4. two daies journey higher then our Barge could passe for rocks. Yet we prevailed with the interpreter to take with him an other interpreter to perswade the Sasquesahanocks to come to visit us, for their language are different: 3. or 4. daies we expected their returne then 60. of these giantlike-people came downe with presents of venison, Tobacco pipes, Baskets, Targets, Bowes and Arrows, 5 of their Werowances came boldly abord us, to crosse the bay for Tockwogh, leaving their men and Canowes, the winde being so violent that they durst not passe.

Our order was, dayly to have prayer, with a psalm, at which solemnitie the poore Salvages much wondered: our prayers being done, they were long busied with consultation till they had contrived their businesse; then they began in most passionate manner to hold up their hands to the sunne with a most fearfull song, then imbracing the Captaine, they began to adore him in like manner, though he rebuked them, yet they proceeded til their song was finished, which don with a most strange furious action, and a hellish voice began an oration of their loves; that ended, with a great painted beares skin they covered our Captaine, then one ready with a chaine of white beads (waighing at least 6 or 7 pound) hung it about his necke, the others had 18 mantles made of divers sorts of skinnes sowed together, all these with many other toyes, they laid at his feet, stroking their ceremonious handes about his necke for his creation to be their governour, promising their aids, victuals, or what they had to bee his, if he would stay with them to defend and revenge them of the Massawomecks; But wee left them at Tockwogh, they much sorrowing for our departure, yet wee promised the next yeare againe to visit them; many descriptions and discourses they made us of Atquanahucke, Massawomecke, and other people, signifying they inhabit the river of Cannida, and from the French to have their hatchets, and such like tooles by trade, these knowe no more of the territories of Powhatan then his name, and he as little of them.

Thus having sought all the inlets and rivers worth noting, we returned to discover the river of Pawtuxunt, these people we found very tractable, and more civill then any, wee promised them, as also the Patawomecks, the next yeare to revenge them of the Massawomecks. Our purposes were crossed in the discoverie of the river of Toppahannock, for wee had much wrangling with that peevish nation; but at last they became as tractable as the rest. It is an excellent, pleasant, well inhabited, fertill, and a goodly navigable river, toward the head thereof; it pleased God to take one of our sicke (called Master Fetherstone) where in Fetherstons bay we buried him in the night with a volly of shot; the rest (notwithstanding their ill diet, and bad lodging, crowded in so small a barge in so many dangers, never resting, but alwaies tossed to and againe) al well recovered their healthes; then we discovered the river of Payankatank, and set saile for James Towne; but in crossing the bay in a faire calme. such a suddaine gust surprised us in the night with thunder and raine, as wee were halfe imployed in freeing out water, never thinking to escape drowning yet running before the winde, at last we made land by the flashes of fire from heaven, by which light only we kept from the splitting shore,

until it pleased God in that black darknes to preserve us by that light to find Point Comfort, and arived safe at James Towne, the 7 of September, 1608. where wee found Master Skrivener and diverse others well recovered, many dead, some sicke. The late President prisoner for muteny, by the honest diligence of Master Skrivener the harvest gathered, but the stores, provision, much spoiled with raine. Thus was that yeare (when nothing wanted) consumed and spent and nothing done; (such was the government of Captain Ratliffe) but only this discoverie, wherein to expresse all the dangers, accidents, and incounters this small number passed in that small barge, with such watrie diet in these great waters and barbarous Countries (til then to any Christian utterly unknowne) I rather referre their merit to the censure of the courteous and experienced reader, then I would be tedious, or partiall, being a partie;

By Nathaniell Poell, and Anas Todkill.

7

The Presidencie surrendred to Captaine Smith, the arrivall and returne of the second supply: and what happened.

The 10. of September 1608. by the election of the Councel, & request of the company Captaine Smith received the letters patents, and took upon him the place of President, which till then by no meanes he would accept though hee were often importuned thereunto. Now the building of Ratcliffes pallas staide as a thing needlesse; The church was repaired, the store-house recovered; building prepared for the supply we expected. The fort reduced to the forme of this figure, the order of watch renued, the squadrons (each setting of the watch) trained. The whole company every Satturday exercised in a fielde prepared for that purpose; the boates trimmed for trade which in their Journey encountred the second supply, that brought them back to discover the country of Monacan, how, or why, Captaine Newport obtained such a private commission as not to returne without a lumpe of gold, a certainty of the south-sea or one of the lost company of Sir Walter Rawley I know not nor why he brought such a 5 pieced barge, not to beare us to that south sea, till we had borne her over the mountaines: (which how farre they extend is yet unknowne) as for the coronation of Powhatan & his presents of Bason,

Ewer, Bed, Clothes, and such costly novelties, they had bin much better well spared, then so ill spent. For we had his favour much better, onlie for a poore peece of Copper, till this stately kinde of soliciting made him so much overvalue himselfe, that he respected us as much as nothing at all; as for the hiring of the Poles and Dutch to make pitch and tarre, glasse, milles, and sope-ashes, was most necessarie and well. But to send them and seaventy more without victuall to worke, was not so well considered; yet this could not have hurt us, had they bin 200. (though then we were 130 that wanted for our selves.) For we had the Salvages in that Decorum, (their harvest beeing newly gathered) that we feared not to get victuall sufficient had we bin 500. Now was there no way to make us miserable but to neglect that time to make our provision, whilst it was to be had; the which was done to perfourme this strange discovery, but more strange coronation: to loose that time, spend that victuall we had, tire & starve our men, having no means to carry victuall, munition, the hurt or sicke, but their owne backs, how or by whom they were invented I know not; But Captaine Newport we only accounted the author, who to effect these projects had so gilded all our hopes, with great promises, that both company and Councel concluded his resolution. I confesse we little understood then our estates, to conclude his conclusion, against al the inconveniences the foreseeing President alleadged. There was added to the councell one Captaine Waldo, and Captaine Winne two ancient souldiers and valiant gentlemen, but ignorant of the busines (being newly arrived) Ratcliffe was also permitted to have his voice, & Master Scrivener desirous to see strange countries, so that although Smith was President, yet the Councell had the authoritie, and ruled it as they listed; as for cleering Smiths objections, how pitch, and tarre, wanscot, clapbord, glasse, & sope ashes, could be provided to relade the ship; or provision got to live withal, when none was in the Country and that which we had, spent before the ships departed; The answer was, Captaine Newport undertooke to fraught the Pinnace with corne, in going and returning in his discoverie, and to refraught her againe from Werawocomoco; also promising a great proportion of victuall from his ship, inferring that Smiths propositions were only devises to hinder his journey, to effect it himselfe;

and that the crueltie Smith had used to the Salvages, in his absence, might occasion them to hinder his designes; For which, al workes were left; and 120 chosen men were appointed for his guard, and Smith, to make cleere these seeming suspicions, that the Salvages were not so desperat, as was pretended by Captaine Newport, and how willing he was to further them to effect their projects, (because the coronation would consume much time) undertooke their message to Powhatan, to intreat him to come to James Towne to receive his presents, accompanied only with Captaine Waldo, Master Andrew Buckler, Edward Brinton, & Samuell Collier, with these 4 hee went over land against Werawocomoco there passed the river of Pamaunke in the Salvages Canowes, Powhatan being 30 myles of, who, presently was sent for, in the meane time his women entertained Smith in this manner.

In a faire plaine field they made a fire, before which he sitting uppon a mat; suddainly amongst the woods was heard such a hideous noise and shriking, that they betooke them to their armes, supposing Powhatan with all his power came to surprise them; but the beholders which were many, men, women, & children, satisfied the Captaine there was no such matter, being presently presented with this anticke, 30 young women came naked out of the woods (only covered behind and before with a few greene leaves) their bodies al painted, some white, some red, some black, some partie colour, but every one different, their leader had a faire paire of stagge hornes on her head, and an otter skinne at her girdle, another at her arme, a quiver of arrowes at her backe, and bow and arrowes in her hand, the next in her hand a sword, another a club, another a pot-stick, all hornd alike, the rest every one with their severall devises. These feindes with most hellish cries, and shouts rushing from amongst the trees, cast themselves in a ring about the fire, singing, and dauncing with excellent ill varietie, oft falling into their infernall passions, and then solemnely againe to sing, and daunce. Having spent neere an houre, in this maskarado; as they entered; in like manner departed; having reaccommodated themselves, they solemnely invited Smith to their lodging, but no sooner was hee within the house, but all these Nimphes more tormented him then ever, with crowding, and pressing, and hanging upon him, mostly tediously crying, love you not mee. This salutation ended, the feast was set, consisting of fruit in baskets, fish, & flesh in wooden platters, beans and pease there wanted not (for 20 hogges) nor any Salvage daintie their invention could devise: some attending, others singing and dancing about them; this mirth and banquet being ended, with firebrands (instead of torches) they conducted him to his lodging.

The next day came Powhatan; Smith delivered his message of the presents sent him, and redelivered him Namontack, desiring him come to his Father Newport to accept those presents, and conclude their revenge against the Monacans, whereunto the subtile Salvage thus replied.

If your king have sent me presents, I also am a king, and this my land, 8 daies I will stay to receave them, your father is to come to me, not I to him, nor yet to your fort, neither will I bite at such a baite: as for the Monacans, I can revenge my owne injuries, and as for Atquanuchuck, where you say your brother was slain, it is a contrary way from those parts you suppose it. But for any salt water beyond the mountaines, the relations you have had from my people are false, wherupon he began to draw plots upon the ground (according to his discourse) of all those regions; many other discourses they had (yet both desirous to give each other content in Complementall courtesies) and so Captaine Smith returned with this answer.

Upon this Captaine Newport sent his presents by water, which is neare 100 miles, with 50 of the best shot, himselfe went by land which is but 12 miles, where he met with our 3 barges to transport him over. All things being fit for the day of his coronation, the presents were brought, his bason, ewer, bed & furniture set up, his scarlet cloake and apparel (with much adoe) put on him (being perswaded by Namontacke they would doe him no hurt.) But a fowle trouble there was to make him kneele to receave his crowne, he neither knowing the majestie, nor meaning of a Crowne, nor bending of the knee, indured so many perswasions, examples, and instructions, as tired them all. At last by leaning hard on his shoulders, he a little stooped, and Newport put the Crowne on his head. When by the warning of a pistoll, the boates were prepared with such a volly of shot, that the king start up in a horrible feare, till he see all was well, then remembring

himselfe, to congratulate their kindnesse, he gave his old shoes and his mantle to Captain Newport. But perceiving his purpose was to discover the Monacans, hee laboured to divert his resolution, refusing to lend him either men, or guids, more then Namontack, and so (after some complementall kindnesse on both sides) in requitall of his presents, he presented Newport with a heape of wheat eares, that might contain some 7 or 8 bushels, & as much more we bought ready dressed in the towne, wherewith we returned to the fort.

The ship having disburdened her selfe of 70 persons, with the first gentlewoman, and woman servant that arrived in our Colony; Captaine Newport with al the Councell, and 120 chosen men, set forward for the discovery of Monacan, leaving the President at the fort with 80. (such as they were) to relade the shippe. Arriving at the falles, we marched by land some forty myles in 2 daies and a halfe, and so returned downe to the same path we went. Two townes wee discovered of the Monacans, the people neither using us well nor ill, yet for our securitie wee tooke one of their pettie Werowances, and lead him bound, to conduct us the way. And in our returne searched many places wee supposed mynes, about which we spent some time in refining, having one William Callicut a refiner, fitted for that purpose, from that crust of earth wee digged hee perswaded us to beleeve he extracted some smal quantitie of silver (and not unlikely better stuffe might bee had for the digging) with this poore trial being contented to leave this faire, fertill, well watred countrie. Comming to the Falles, the Salvages fained there were diverse ships come into the Bay to kill them at James Towne. Trade they would not, and find their corn we could not, for they had hid it in the woods, and being thus deluded we arrived at James Towne, halfe sicke, all complaining, and tired with toile, famine, and discontent to have only but discovered our gilded hopes, and such fruitlesse certaineties, as the President foretold us.

No sooner were we landed, but the President dispersed many as were able, some for glasse, others for pitch, tarre and sope ashes, leaving them, (with the fort) to the Councels oversight. But 30 of us he conducted 5. myles from the fort to learn to make clapboard, cut downe trees, and ly in woods; amongst the rest he had chosen Gabriell Beadell, & John Russell the only two gallants of this last supply, and both proper gentlemen: strange were these pleasures to their conditions, yet lodging eating, drinking, working, or playing they doing but as the President, all these things were carried so pleasantly, as within a weeke they became Masters, making it their delight to heare the trees thunder as they fell, but the axes so oft blistered there tender fingers, that commonly every third blow had a lowd oath to drowne the eccho; for remedy of which sin the President devised howe to have everie mans oathes numbred, and at night, for every oath to have a can of water powred downe his sleeve, with which every offender was so washed (himselfe & all) that a man should scarce heare an oath in a weeke.

By this, let no man think that the President, or these gentlemen spent their times as common wood-hackers at felling of trees, or such like other labours, or that they were pressed to any thing as hirelings or common slaves, for what they did (being but once a little inured) it seemed, and they conceited it only as a pleasure and a recreation, Yet 30 or 40 of such voluntary Gentlemen would doe more in a day then 100 of the rest that must been prest to it by compulsion. Master Scrivener, Captaine Waldo, and Captaine Winne at the fort, every one in like manner carefully regarded their charge. The President returning from amongst the woodes, seeing the time consumed, and no provision gotten, (and the ship lay Idle, and would do nothing) presently imbarked himselfe in the discovery barge, giving order to the Councell, to send Master Persey after him with the next barge that arrived at the fort; 2. barges, he had himselfe, and 20. men, but arriving at Chickahamina that dogged nation, was too wel acquainted with our wants, refusing to trade, with as much scorne and insolencie as they could expresse. The President perceiving it was Powhatans policy to starve us, told them he came not so much for their corne, as to revenge his imprisonment, and the death of his men murdered by them, & so landing his men, and ready to charge them, they immediatly fled; but then they sent their imbassadours, with corne, fish, fowl, or what they had to make their peace, (their corne being that year bad) they complained extreamly of their owne wants, yet fraughted our boats with 100 bushels of corne, and in like manner Master Persies, that not long after us arrived; they having done the best they could to content us, within 4. or 5. daies we returned to James Towne.

Though this much contented the company (that then feared nothing but starving) yet some so envied his good successe, that they rather desired to starve, then his paines should prove so muchmore effectuall then theirs; some projects there was, not only to have deposed him but to have kept him out of the fort, for that being President, he would leave his place, and the fort without their consents; but their hornes were so much too short to effect it, as they themselves more narrowly escaped a greater mischiefe.

All this time our old taverne, made as much of all them that had either mony or ware as could bee desired; and by this time they were become so perfect on all sides (I mean Souldiers, Sailers, and Salvages,) as there was ten-times more care, to maintaine their damnable and private trade, then to provide for the Colony things that were necessary, neither was it a small pollicy in the mariners, to report in England wee had such plenty and bring us so many men without victuall, when they had so many private factors in the fort, that within 6. or 7. weekes after the ships returne, of 2. or 300. hatchets, chissels, mattocks, and pickaxes scarce 20 could be found, and for pikeheads, knives, shot, powder, or any thing (they could steale from their fellowes) was vendible; They knew as well (and as secretly) how to convay them to trade with the Salvages, for furres, baskets, mussaneekes, young beastes or such like commodities, as exchange them with the sailers, for butter, cheese, biefe, porke, aquavite, beere, bisket and oatmeale; and then faine, all was sent them from their friends. And though Virginia afford no furs for the store, yet one mariner in one voyage hath got so many, as hee hath confessed to haue solde in England for 30.

Those are the Saint-seeming worthies of Virginia, that have notwithstanding all this, meate, drinke, and pay, but now they begin to grow weary, their trade being both perceived and prevented; none hath bin in Virginia (that hath observed any thing) which knowes not this to be true, and yet the scorne, and shame was the poore souldiers, gentlemen and carelesse governours, who were all thus bought and solde, the adventurers cousened, and the action overthrowne by their false excuses, informations, and directions, by this let all the world Judge, how this businesse could prosper, being thus abused by such pilfering occasions.

The proceedings and accidents, with the second supply.

Master Scrivener was sent with the barges and Pinas to Werawocomoco, where he found the Salvages more ready to fight then trade, but his vigilancy was such, as prevented their projectes, and by the meanes of Namontack got 3. or 4. hogsheads of corne, and as much Red paint which (then) was esteemed an excellent die.

Captaine Newport being dispatched with the tryals of pitch, tarre, glasse, frankincense, and sope-ashes, with that clapbord and wainscot could bee provided met with Master Scrivener at Point Comfort, & so returned for England, leaving us in all 200. with those hee brought us.

The names of those in this supply are these.

Captaine Peter Winne.	were appointed to bee of the Councell.
Captaine Richard Waldo.	

Master Francis West.
Thomas Graues.
Rawley Chroshaw.
Gabriell Bedle.
John Russell.
John Bedle.
William Russell.
John Gudderington.
William Sambage.
Henry Collings.
Henry Ley.
Harmon Haryson.
Daniell Tucker.   } Gentlemen.
Hugh Wollystone.
John Hoult.
Thomas Norton.
George Yarington.
George Burton.
Henry Philpot.
Thomas Maxes.
Michaell Lowicke.
Master Hunt.
Thomas Forest.
William Dowman.
John Dauxe.
Thomas Abbay.

Thomas Phelps.
John Part.
John Clarke.   } Tradesmen.
Jefry Shortridge.
Dius Oconor.

Hugh Wynne.
Davi Uphu.
Thomas Bradley.
John Burras.
Thomas Lavander.   } Tradesmen.
Henry Bell.
Master Powell.
Davi Ellys.
Thomas Gipson.

Thomas Dowse.
Thomas Mallard.
William Taler.
Thomas Fox.
Nicholas Hancock.
Walker.   } Laborers.
Williams.
Morrell.
Rose.
Scot.
Hardwin.

Milman.   } Boyes.
Hellyard.

Mistresse Forest and Anne Burras her maide, 8. Dutchmen, and Poles with divers to the number of 70. persons.

Those poore conclusions so affrighted us all with famine; that the President provided for Nansamund, tooke with him Captaine Winne & Master Scrivener (then returning from Captaine Newport), these people also long denied him trade, (excusing themselves to bee so commanded by Powhatan) til we were constrained to begin with them perforce, and then they would rather sell us some, then wee should take all; so loading our boats, with 100. bushels we parted friends, and came to James Towne, at which time, there was a marriage betweene John Laydon and Anna Burrowes, being the first marriage we had in Virginia.

Long he staied not, but fitting himselfe & captaine Waldo with 2. barges, from Chawopo, Weanocke and all parts there, was found neither corne nor Salvage, but all fled (being Jealous of our intents) till we discovered the river and people of Appametuck, where we founde little. that they had, we equally devided, betwixt the Salvages and us (but gave them copper in consideration). Master Persie, and Master Scrivener went also abroad but could finde nothing.

The President seeing this procastinating of time, was no course to live, resolved with Captaine Waldo, (whom he knew to be sure in time of need) to surprise Powhatan, and al his provision, but the unwillingnes of Captaine Winne, and Master Scrivener (for some private respects) did their best to hinder their project: But the President whom no perswasions could perswade to starve, being invited by Powhatan to come unto him, & if he would send him but men to build him a house, bring him a grinstone, 50. swords, some peeces, a cock and a hen, with copper and beads, he would loade his shippe with corne, the President not ignoraunt of his devises, yet unwilling to neglect any opportunity, presently sent 3. Dutch-men and 2. English (having no victuals to imploy them, all for want thereof being idle) knowing there needed no better castel, then that house to surprize Powhatan, to effect this project he took order with Captaine Waldo to second him if need required; Scrivener he left his substitute; and set forth with the Pinnas 2. barges and six and forty men which only were such as volentarily offered themselves for his iourny, the which (by reason of Master Scriveners ill successe) was censured very desperate they all knowing Smith would not returne empty howsoever, caused many of those that he had appointed, to finde excuses to stay behinde.

8

Captaine Smiths journey to Pamaunke.

The 29 of December hee set forward for Werawocomoco, his company were these.

In the Discovery barge, himselfe.

Robert Behethland.
Nathaniell Powell.
John Russell.
Rawly Crashaw.
Michaell Sicklemore.
Richard Worlie. } Gentlemen.

Anas Todkill.
William Love.
William Bentley.
Geoffery Shortridge.
Edward Pising.
William Warde. } Souldiers.

In the Pinnace.

Master George Persie, brother to the Earle of Northumberland,

Master Frauncis West, brother to the Lord Dela-Ware.

William Phetiplace Captaine of the Pinnas.

Jonas Profit Master.

Robert Ford clarcke of the councell.

Michael Phetiplace.
Geoffery Abbot Sergeant.
William Tankard.
George Yarington.
James Bourne.
George Burton.
Thomas Coe. } Gentlemen.

John Dods.
Edward Brinton.
Nathaniel Peacocke.
Henry Powell.
David Ellis.
Thomas Gipson.
John Prat.
George Acrigge.
James Reade.
Nicholas Hancocke,
James Watkins.
Anthony Baggly Sergeant.
Thomas Lambert.
Edward Pising Sergeant. } Souldiers.

4. Dutchmen and Richard Salvage were sent by land, to build the house for Powhatan against our arrivall.

This company being victualled but for 3. or 4. daies lodged the first night at Weraskoyack, where the President tooke sufficient provision; This kind Salvage did his best to divert him from seeing Powhatan, but perceiving he could not prevaile, he advised in this maner Captaine Smith, you shall finde Powhatan to use you kindly, but trust him not, and bee sure hee have no opportunitie to seaze on your armes, for hee hath sent for you only to cut your throats; the Captaine thanked him for his good counsell, yet the better to try his love, desired guides to Chowanoke, for he would send a present to that king to bind him his friend. To performe this iourney, was sent Michael Sicklemore, a very honest, valiant, and painefull souldier, with him two guids, and directions how to search for the lost company of Sir Walter Rawley, and silke grasse: then wee departed thence, the President assuring the king his perpetuall love, and left with him Samuell Collier his page to learne the language.

The next night being lodged at Kecoughtan 6 or 7 daies, the extreame wind, raine, frost, and snowe, caused us to keepe Christmas amongst the Salvages, where wee were never more merrie, nor fedde on more plentie of good oysters, fish, flesh, wildfoule, and good bread, nor never had better fires in England then in the drie warme smokie houses of Kecoughtan, But departing thence, when we found no houses, we were not curious in any weather, to lie 3 or 4 nights together upon any shore under the trees by a good fire. 148 fowles the President, Anthony Bagly, and Edward Pising, did kill at 3 shoots. At Kiskiack the frost forced us 3 or 4 daies also to suppresse the insolencie of those proud Salvages; to quarter in their houses, and guard our barge, and cause them give us what wee wanted, yet were we but 12 with the President, and yet we never wanted harbour where we found any houses. The 12 of Januarie we arrived at Werawocomoco, where the river was frozen neare halfe a mile from the shore; but to neglect no time, the President with his barge, so farre had approached by breaking the Ice as the eb left him amongst those oozie shoules, yet rather then to lie there frozen to death, by his owne example hee taught them to march middle deepe, more then a flight shot through this muddie froye ooze; when the barge floted he appointed 2 or 3 to returne her abord the Pinnace, where for want of water in melting the salt Ice they made fresh water, but in this march Master Russell (whome none could perswade to stay behind) being somewhat ill, and exceeding heavie, so overtoiled him selfe, as the rest had much adoe (ere he got a shore) to regaine life, into his dead benummed spirits, quartering in the next houses we found, we sent to Powhatan for provision, who sent us plentie of bread, Turkies, & Venison. The next day having feasted us after his ordinarie manner, he began to aske, when we would bee gon, faining hee sent not for us, neither had hee any corne, and his people much lesse, yet for 40 swords he would procure us 40 bushels. The President shewing him the men there present, that brought him the message and conditions, asked him how it chaunced he became so forgetful, thereat the king concluded the matter with a merry laughter, asking for our commodities, but none he liked without gunnes and swords, valuing a basket of corne more pretious then a basket of copper, saying he could eate his corne, but not his copper.

Captaine Smith seeing the intent of this subtil Salvage; began to deale with him after this manner, Powhatan, though I had many courses to have made my provision, yet beleeving your promises to supply my wants, I neglected all, to satisfie your desire, and to testifie my love, I sent you my men for your building, neglecting my owne: what your people had you have engrossed, forbidding them our trade, and nowe you thinke by consuming the time, wee shall consume for want, not having to fulfill your strange demandes, as for swords, and gunnes, I told you long agoe, I had none to spare And you shall knowe, those I have, can keepe me from want, yet steale, or wrong you I will not, nor dissolve that friendship, wee have mutually promised, (except you constraine mee by your bad usage.

The king having attentively listned to this discourse; promised, that both hee and his Country would spare him what they could, the which within 2 daies, they should receave, yet Captaine Smith, (saith the king) some doubt I have of your comming hither, that makes me not so kindly seeke to relieve you as I would; for many do informe me, your comming is not for trade, but to invade my people and possesse my Country, who dare not come to bring you corne, seeing you thus armed with your men. To cleere us of this feare, leave abord your weapons, for here they are needlesse we being all friends and for ever Powhatans.

With many such discourses they spent the day, quartring that night in the kings houses, the next day he reviewed his building, which hee little intended should proceed; for the Dutchmen finding his plenty, and knowing our want, and perceived his preparation to surprise us, little thinking wee could escape, both him and famine, (to obtaine his favour revealed to him as much as they knew of our estates and projects, and how to prevent them); one of them being of so good a judgement, spirit, and resolution, & a hireling that was certaine of wages for his labour, and ever well used, both he and his countrimen, that the President knewe not whome better to trust, & not knowing any fitter for that imploiment, had sent him as a spie to discover Powhatans intent, then little doubting his honestie, nor could ever be certaine of his villany, till neare halfe a yeare after.

Whilst we expected the comming in of the countrie, we wrangled out of the king 10 quarters of corne for a copper kettle, the which the President perceived him much to affect, valued it at a much greater rate, but (in regard of his scarcety) hee would accept of as much more the next yeare, or else the country of Monacan, the king exceeding liberall of that hee had not yeelded him

Monacan. Wherewith each seeming well contended; Powhatan began to expostulate the difference betwixt peace and war, after this manner.

Captaine Smith you may understand, that I, having seene the death of all my people thrice, and not one living of those 3 generations, but my selfe, I knowe the difference of peace and warre, better then any in my Countrie. But now I am old, & ere long must die, my brethren, namely Opichapam, Opechankanough, and Kekataugh, my two sisters, and their two daughters, are distinctly each others successours, I wish their experiences no lesse then mine, and your love to them, no lesse then mine to you; but this brute from Nansamund that you are come to destroy my Countrie, so much affrighteth all my people, as they dare not visit you; what will it availe you, to take that perforce, you may quietly have with love, or to destroy them that provide you food? what can you get by war, when we can hide our provision and flie to the woodes, whereby you must famish by wronging us your friends; & whie are you thus jealous of our loves, seeing us unarmed, and both doe, & are willing still to feed you with that you cannot get but by our labours? think you I am so simple not to knowe, it is better to eate good meate, lie well, and sleepe quietly with my women & children, laugh and be merrie with you, have copper, hatchets, or what I want, being your friend: then bee forced to flie from al, to lie cold in the woods, feed upon acorns roots, and such trash, and be so hunted by you, that I can neither rest, eat, nor sleepe; but my tired men must watch, and if a twig but breake, everie one crie there comes Captaine Smith, then must I flie I knowe not whether, and thus with miserable feare end my miserable life; leaving my pleasures to such youths as you, which through your rash unadvisednesse, may quickly as miserably ende, for want of that you never knowe how to find? Let this therefore assure you of our loves and everie yeare our friendly trade shall furnish you with corne, & now also if you would come in friendly manner to see us, and not thus with your gunnes & swords, as to invade your foes. To this subtil discourse the President thus replied.

Seeing you will not rightly conceave of our words, wee strive to make you knowe our thoughts by our deeds. The vow I made you of my love, both my selfe and my men have kept, as for your promise I finde it everie daie violated, by some of your subjects, yet wee finding your love

and kindnesse (our custome is so far from being ungratefull) that for your sake only, wee have curbed our thirsting desire of revenge, else had they knowne as wel the crueltie we use to our enimies as our true love and curtesie to our friendes. And I thinke your judgement sufficient to conceive as well by the adventures we have undertaken, as by the advantage we have by our armes of yours: that had wee intended you anie hurt, long ere this wee could have effected it; your people comming to me at James towne, are entertained with their bowes and arrowes without exception; we esteeming it with you, as it is with us, to weare our armes as our apparell. As for the dangers of our enimies, in such warres consist our chiefest pleasure, for your riches we have no use, as for the hiding your provision, or by your flying to the woods, we shall so unadvisedly starve as you conclude, your friendly care in that behalfe is needlesse; for we have a rule to finde beyond your knowledge.

Manie other discourses they had, til at last they began to trade, but the king seing his will would not bee admitted as a lawe, our gard dispersed, nor our men disarmed, he (sighing) breathed his mind, once more in this manner.

Captaine Smith, I never used anie of Werowances, so kindlie as your selfe; yet from you I receave the least kindnesse of anie. Captaine Newport gave me swords, copper, cloths, a bed, tooles, or what I desired, ever taking what I offered him, and would send awaie his gunnes when I intreated him: none doth denie to laie at my feet (or do) what I desire, but onelie you, of whom I can have nothing, but what you regard not, and yet you wil have whatsoever you demand. Captain Newport you call father, and so you call me, but I see for all us both, you will doe what you list, and wee must both seeke to content you: but if you intend so friendlie as you saie, sende hence your armes that I may beleeve you, for you see the love I beare you, doth cause mee thus nakedlie forget my selfe.

Smith seeing this Salvage but trifled the time to cut his throat: procured the Salvages to breake the ice, (that his boat might come to fetch both him and his corne) and gave order for his men to come ashore, to have surprised the king, with whom also he but trifled the time till his men landed, and to keepe him from suspition, entertained the time with this reply.

Powhatan, you must knowe as I have but one

God, I honour but one king; and I live not here as your subject, but as your friend, to pleasure you with what I can; by the gifts you bestowe on me, you gaine more then by trade; yet would you visite mee as I doe you, you should knowe it is not our customes to sell our curtesie as a vendible commoditie. Bring all your Country with you for your gard, I will not dislike of it as being over jealous. But to content you, to morrow I will leave my armes, and trust to your promise. I call you father indeed, and as a father you shall see I will love you, but the smal care you had of such a child, caused my men perswade me to shift for my selfe.

By this time Powhatan having knowledge, his men were readie: whilst the ice was breaking, his luggage women, and children fledde, and to avoid suspition, left 2 or 3 of his women talking with the Captaine, whilst he secretly fled, and his men as secretlie beset the house, which being at the instant discovered to Captain Smith, with his Pistol, Sword & Target, he made such a passage amongst those naked divels, that they fled before him some one waie some another, so that without hurt he obtained the Corps du guard; when they perceived him so well escaped, and with his 8 men (for he had no more with him). To the uttermost of their skill, they sought by excuses to dissemble the matter, and Powhatan to excuse his flight, and the suddaine comming of this multitude, sent our Captaine a greate bracelet, and a chaine of pearle, by an ancient Orator that bespoke us to this purpose, (perceiving then from our Pinnace, a barge and men departing & comming unto us.) Captaine Smith, our Werowans is fled, fearing your guns, & knowing when the ice was broken there would come more men, sent those of his to guard his corne from the pilfrie, that might happen without your knowledge: now though some bee hurt by your misprision, yet he is your friend, and so wil continue: and since the ice is open hee would have you send awaie your corne. and if you would have his companie send also your armes, which so affrighteth this people, that they dare not come to you, as he hath promiseed they should: nowe having provided baskets for our men to carrie the corne, they kindlie offered their service to gard our armes, that none should steale them. A great manie they were, of goodlie well appointed fellowes as grim as divels; yet the verie sight of cocking our matches against them, and a few words, caused them to leave their bowes & arrowes to our gard, and beare downe our corne

on their own backes; wee needed not importune them to make quick dispatch. But our own barge being left by the ebb, caused us to staie, till the midnight tide carried us safe abord, having spent that halfe night with such mirth, as though we never had suspected or intended any thing, we left the Dutchmen to build, Brinton to kil fowle for Powhatan (as by his messengers he importunately desired) and left directions with our men to give Powhatan all the content they could, that we might injoy his company at our returne from Pamaunke.

9
How we escaped surprising at Pamaunke.

Wee had no sooner set saile, but Powhatan returned, and sent Adam and Francis (2. stout Dutch men) to the fort, who faining to Captaine Winne that al things were well, and that Captaine Smith had use for their armes, wherefore they requested newe (the which were given them) they told him their comming was, for some extraordinary tooles and shift of apparell, by this colourable excuse, they obtained 6. or 7. more to their confederacie, such expert theefes, that presently furnished them with a great many swords, pikeheads, peeces, shot, powder and such like, they had Salvages at hand ready to carry it away, the next day they returned unsuspected, leaving their confederates to follow, and in the interim, to convay them a competencie of all things they could, for which service they should live with Powhatan as his chiefe affected: free from those miseries that would happen the Colony. Samuell their other consort, Powhatan kept for their pledge, whose diligence had provided them, 300. of their kinde of hatchets, the rest. 50. swords, 8. peeces, and 8. pikes: Brinton, & Richard Salvage seeing the Dutch-men so strangly diligent to accommodate the Salvages these weapons attempted to have got to James Towne, but they were apprehended; within 2. or 3. daies we arrived at Pamaunke: the king as many daies, entertained us with feasting and much mirth: & the day he appointed to begin our trade, the President, with Master Persie, Master West, Master Russell, Master Beheathland, Master Powell, Master Crashaw, Master Ford, and some others to the number of 15. went up to Opechancanougs house (near a quarter of a mile from the river,) where we founde nothing, but a lame fellow and a boy, and all the houses about, of all things abandoned; not long we staide ere the king arrived, and after him came divers of his people loaded with bowes and arrowes, but such pinching commodities, and those esteemed at such a value, as our Captaine beganne with him in this manner.

Opechancanough the great love you professe with your tongue, seemes meere deceipt by your actions; last yeare you kindly fraughted our ship, but now you have invited me to starve with hunger. You know my want, and I your plenty of which by some meanes I must have part, remember it is fit for kings to keepe their promise, here are my commodities, where of take your choice; the rest I will proportion, fit bargaines for your people.

The king seemed kindly to accept his offer; and the better to colour his project, sold us what they had to our own content; promising the next day, more company, better provided; (the barges, and Pinnas being committed to the charge of Master Phetiplace) the President with his old 15 marched up to the kings house, where we found 4 or 5 men newly come with great baskets, not long after came the king, who with a strained cheerefulnes held us with discourse, what paines he had taken to keepe his promise; til Master Russell brought us in news that we were all betraied: for at least 6. or 700. of well appointed Indians had invironed the house and beset the fields. The king conjecturing what Russell related, we could wel perceive how the extreamity of his feare bewrayed his intent: whereat some of our companie seeming dismaide with the thought of such a multitude; the Captaine incouraged us after this manner.

Worthy countrymen were the mischiefes of my seeming friends, no more then the danger of these enemies, I little cared, where they as many more, if you dare do, but as I. But this is my torment, that if I escape them, our malicious councell with their open mouthed minions, will make mee such a peace-breaker (in their opinions) in England, as will break my neck; I could wish those here, that make these seeme Saints, and me an oppressor. But this is the worst of all, wherein I pray aide me with your opinions, should wee begin with them and surprize this king, we cannot keep him and defend well our selves, if we should each kill our man and so proceede with al in this house; the rest will all fly, then shall we get no more, then the bodies that are slaine, and then starve for victuall: as for their fury it is the least danger; for well you

know, (being alone assaulted with 2 or 300 of them) I made them compound to save my life, and we are now 16 & they but 700. at the most, and assure your selves God wil so assist us, that if you dare but to stande to discharge your peeces, the very smoake will bee sufficient to affright them; yet howsoever (if there be occasion) let us fight like men, and not die like sheep; but first I will deale with them, to bring it to passe, we may fight for some thing and draw them to it by conditions. If you like this motion, promise me youle be valiant. The time not permitting any argument, all vowed, to execute whatsoever he attempted, or die; whereupon the captaine, approaching the king bespoke him in this manner.

I see Opechancanough your plot to murder me, but I feare it not, as yet your men and mine, have done no harme, but by our directions. Take therefore your arms; you see mine; my body shalbe as naked as yours; the Ile in your river is a fit place, if you be contented: and the conqueror (of us two) shalbe Lord and Master over all our men; otherwaies drawe all your men into the field; if you have not enough take time to fetch more, and bringe what number you will, so everie one bring a basket of corne, against all which I will stake the value in copper; you see I have but 15 men, & our game shalbe the conquerer take all.

The king, being guarded with 50 or 60 of his chiefe men, seemed kindly to appease Smiths suspition of unkindnesse, by a great present at the dore, they intreated him to receive. This was to draw him without the dore where the present was garded with (at the least) 200 men and 30 lying under a greate tree (that lay thwart as a Barricado) each his arrow nocked ready to shoot; some the President commanded to go & see what kinde of deceit this was, and to receive the present, but they refused to do it, yet divers offered whom he would not permit; but commanding Master Persie and Master West to make good the house, tooke Master Poell and Master Beheathland to guard the dore, and in such a rage snatched the king by his vambrace in the midst of his men, with his pistoll ready bent against his brest: thus he led the trembling king, (neare dead with feare) amongst all his people, who delivering the Captaine his bow and arrowes, all his men were easily intreated to cast downe their armes, little dreaming anie durst in that manner have used their king; who then to escape himselfe, bestowed his presents in good sadnesse. And having caused all his multitude to approach disarmed; the President argued with them to this effect.

I see you Pamaunkies the great desire you have to cut my throat; and my long suffering your iniuries, have inboldened you to this presumption. The cause I have forborne your insolencies, is the promise I made you (before the God I serve) to be your friend, till you give me just cause to bee your enimie. If I keepe this vow, my God will keepe me, you cannot hurt me; if I breake it he will destroie me. But if you shoot but one arrow, to shed one drop of blood of any of my men, or steale the least of these beades, or copper, (I spurne before me with my foot) you shall see, I will not cease revenge, (if once I begin) so long as I can heare where to find one of your nation that will not deny the name of Pamaunke; I am not now at Rasseneac (halfe drownd with mire) where you tooke me prisoner, yet then for keeping your promise, and your good usage, & saving my life, I so affect you, that your denials of your treacherie, doth half perswade me to mistake my selfe. But if I be the marke you aime at, here I stand, shoote hee that dare. You promised to fraught my ship ere I departed, and so you shall, or I meane to load her with your dead carkases; yet if as friends you wil come and trade, I once more promise not to trouble you, except you give me the first occasion. Upon this awaie went their bowes and arrowes, and men, women, and children brought in their commodities, but 2 or three houres they so thronged about the President, and so overwearied him, as he retired himself to rest, leaving Master Beheathland and Master Powel to accept their presents; but some Salvage perceiving him fast asleepe, and the guard carelesly dispersed, 40 or 50 of their choice men each with an English sword in his hand, began to enter the house, with 2 or 300 others that pressed to second them. The noise and hast they made in, did so shake the house, as they awoke him from his sleep, & being halfe amazed with this suddaine sight, betooke him straight to his sword and target, Master Crashaw and some other charging in like manner, they thronged faster back, then before forward. The house thus clensed, the king and his ancients, with a long oration came to excuse this intrusion. The rest of the day was spent with much kindnesse, the company againe renuing their pre-

sents of their best provision. And what soever we gave them, they seemed well contented with it.

Now in the meane while since our departure, this hapned at the fort, Master Scrivener willing to crosse the surprizing of Powhatan; 9 daies after the Presidents departure, would needs visit the Ile of Hogges, and took with him Captaine Waldo (though the President had appointed him to bee readie to second his occasions) with Master Anthony Gosnoll and eight others but so violent was the wind (that extreame frozen time) that the boat sunke, but where or how, none doth knowe, for they were all drowned; onlie this was knowne, that the Skiffe was much overloaded, & would scarse have lived in that extreame tempest, had she been emptie; but by no perswasion hee could bee diverted, though both Waldo and 100 others doubted as it hapned. The Salvages were the first that found their bodies, which so much the more encouraged them to effect their projects. To advertise the President of this heavie newes, none could bee found would undertake it, but the journey was often refused of all in the fort, untill Master Wiffin undertooke alone, the performance thereof; wherein he was encountred with many dangers & difficulties, and in all parts as hee passed (as also that night he lodged with Powhatan) perceived such preparation for warre, that assured him, some mischiefe was intended, but with extraordinarie bribes, and much trouble, in three daies travell at length hee found us in the midst of these turmoiles. This unhappie newes, the President swore him to conceale from the rest, & so dissembling his sorrow, with the best countenance he could, when the night approached, went safely abord with all his companie.

Now so extreamely Powhatan had threatned the death of his men, if they did not by some meanes kill Captaine Smith, that the next day they appointed the Countrie should come to trade unarmed: yet unwilling to be treacherous, but that they were constrained hating fighting, almost as ill as hanging, such feare they had of bad successe. The next morning the sunne had not long appeared, but the fieldes appeared covered with people, and baskets to tempt us ashore. The President determined to keepe abord, but nothing was to bee had without his presence, nor they would not indure the sight of a gun; then the President seeing many depart, and being unwilling to lose such a booty, so well contrived the Pinnace, and his barges with Ambuscadoes, as only with Master Persie, Master West, & Master Russell armed, he went ashore, others unarmed he appointed to receive what was brought; the Salvages flocked before him in heapes, and (the bancke serving as a trench for retreat) hee drewe them faire open to his ambuscadoes, for he not being to be perswaded to go to visit their king, the King came to visit him with 2 or 300 men, in the forme of two halfe moons, with some 20 men, and many women loaded with great painted baskets; but when they approached somewhat neare us, their women and children fled; for when they had environed and beset the fieldes in this manner, they thought their purpose sure; yet so trembled with fear as they were scarse able to nock their arrowes; Smith standing with his 3 men readie bent beholding them, till they were within danger of our ambuscado, who, upon the word discovered themselves, and he retiring to the banke; which the Salvages no sooner perceived but away they fled, esteeming their heeles for their best advantage.

That night we sent to the fort Master Crashaw and Master Foard, who (in the mid-way betweene Werawocomoco and the fort) met 4 or 5 of the Dutch mens confederates going to Powhatan, the which (to excuse those gentlemens Suspition of their running to the Salvages) returned to the fort and there continued.

The Salvages hearing our barge depart in the night were so terriblie affraide, that we sent for more men, (we having so much threatned their ruine, and the rasing of their houses, boats, and canowes) that the next day the king, sent our Captaine a chaine of pearle to alter his purpose; and stay his men, promising (though they wanted themselves) to fraught our ship, & bring it abord to avoid suspition, so that 5 or 6 daies after, from al parts of the countrie within 10 or 12 miles in the extreame cold frost, and snow, they brought us provision on their naked backes.

Yet notwithstanding this kindnesse and trade; had their art and poison bin sufficient, the President with Master West and some others had been poysoned; it made them sicke, but expelled it selfe; Wecuttanow a stout yong fellow, knowing hee was suspected for bringing this present of poison, with 40 or 50. of his choice companions (seeing the President but with a few men at Potauncat) so prowdlie braved it, as though he expected to incounter a revenge; which the President perceiving in the midst of his companie did not onlie beat, but spurned him like a dogge, as scorning to doe him anie worse mischiefe; whereupon all of them fled into the woods, thinking they had done a great matter, to have so well escaped; and the townsmen remaining, presentlie fraughted our barge, to bee rid of our companies, framing manie excuses to excuse Wecuttanow (being son to their chiefe king but Powhatan) and told us if we would shew them him that brought the poyson, they would deliver him to us to punish as wee pleased.

Men maie thinke it strange there should be this stir for a little corne, but had it been gold with more ease we might have got it; & had it wanted, the whole collonie had starved. We maie be thought verie patient, to indure all those injuries; yet onlie with fearing them, we got what they had. Whereas if we had taken revenge, then by their losse we should have lost our selvs. We searched also the countries of Youghtanund and Mattapamient, where the people imparted that little they had, with such complaints and tears from women and children; as he had bin too cruell to be a Christian that would not have bin satisfied, and moved with compassion. But had this happened in October, November, and December, when that unhappie discoverie of Monacan was made, we might have fraughted a ship of 40 tuns, and twice as much have bin had; from the rivers of Toppahannock, Patawomeck, & Pawtuxunt. The maine occasion of our temporizing with the Salvages was to part friends, (as we did) to give the lesse cause of suspition to Powhatan to fly; by whom we now returned, with a purpose, to have surprised him & his provision, for effecting whereof, (when we came against the towne) the President sent Master Wiffin and Master Coe, ashore to discover and make waie for his intended project. But they found that those damned Dutch-men had caused Powhatan to abandon his new house, and Werawocomoco, and to carrie awaie all his corne & provision; and the people, they found (by their means) so ill affected that had they not stood well upon their guard, they had hardlie escaped with their lives. So the President finding his intention thus frustrated, & that there was nothing now to be had, and therefore an unfit time to revenge their abuses, helde on his course for James Towne; we having in this Jornie (for 25l of copper 50l of Iron and beads) kept 40 men 6. weekes, and dailie feasted with bread, corne, flesh, fish, and fowle, everie man having for his reward (and in consideration of his commodities) a months provision; (no trade being allowed but for the store,) and we delivered at James Towne to the Cape-Marchant 279 bushels of corne.

Those temporall proceedings to some maie seeme too charitable; to such a dailie daring trecherous people: to others unpleasant that we washed not the ground with their blouds, nor shewed such strange inventions, in mangling, murdering, ransaking, and destroying, (as did the Spaniards) the simple bodies of those ignorant soules; nor delightful because not stuffed with relations of heaps, and mines of gold and silver, nor such rare commodities as the Portugals and Spaniards found in the East & West Indies. The want wherof hath begot us (that were the first undertakers) no lesse scorne and contempt, then their noble conquests & valiant adventures (beautified with it) praise and honor. Too much I confesse the world cannot attribute to their ever memorable merit. And to cleare us from the worlds blind ignorant censure, these fewe words may suffise to any reasonably understanding.

It was the Spaniards good hap to happen in those parts, where were infinite numbers of people, whoe had manured the ground with that providence, that it afforded victuall at all times: and time had brought them to that perfection, they had the use of gold and silver, and the most of such commodities, as their countries afforded, so that what the Spaniard got, was only the spoile and pillage of those countrie people, and not the labours of their owne hands. But had those fruit-full Countries, beene as Salvage as barbarous, as ill peopled, as little planted, laboured and manured as Virginia, their proper labours (it is likely) would have produced as small profit as ours. But had Virginia bin peopled, planted, manured and adorned, with such store of pretious Jewels, & rich commodities, as was the Indies; then had we not gotten, and done as much as by their examples might bee expected from us, the world might then have traduced us and our merits, & have made shame and infamy our recompence and reward.

But we chanced in a lande, even as God made it. Where we found only an idle, improvident, scattered people; ignorant of the knowledge of gold, or silver, or any commodities; & carelesse of any thing but from hand to mouth, but for baubles of no worth; nothing to encourage us, but what accidentally wee found nature afforded. Which ere wee could bring to recompence our paines, defray our charges, and satisfie our adventurers, we were to discover the country, subdue the people, bring them to be tractable, civil, and industrious, and teach them trades, that the fruits of their labours might make us recompence, or plant such colonies of our owne that must first make provision how to live of themselves, ere they can bring to perfection the commodities of the countrie, which doubtles will be as commodious for England, as the West Indies for Spaine, if it be rightly managed; notwithstanding all our homebred opinions, that will argue the contrarie, as formerly such like have done, against the Spaniards and Portugals. But to conclude, against all rumor of opinion, I only say this, for those that the three first yeares began this plantation, notwithstanding al their factions, mutenies, and miseries, so gently corrected, (and well prevented) peruse the Spanish Decades, the relations of Master Hacklut, and tell mee how many ever with such smal meanes, as a barge of 2 Tunnes; sometimes with 7. 8. 9, or but at most 15 men did ever discover so many faire and navigable rivers; subject to many severall kings, people, and nations, to obedience, & contribution with so little bloud shed.

And if in the search of those Countries, wee had hapned where wealth had beene, we had as surely had it, as obedience and contribution, but if wee have overskipped it, we will not envy them that shall chance to finde it. Yet can wee not but lament, it was our ill fortunes to end, when wee had but only learned how to begin, and found the right course how to proceed.

By Rich. Wiffin, William Phettiplace, and Anas Todkill.

10
How the Salvages became subject to the English.

When the shippes departed, al the provision of the store (but that the President had gotten) was so rotten with the last somers rain, and eaten with rats, and wormes, as the hogs would scarcely eat it, yet it was the souldiers diet, till our returnes: so that wee found nothing done, but victuall spent, and the most part of our tooles, and a good part of our armes convayed to the Salvages. But now, casting up the store, & finding sufficient till the next harvest, the feare of starving was abandoned; and the company divided into tennes, fifteenes, or as the businesse required, 4 houres each day was spent in worke, the rest in pastimes and merry exercise; but the untowardnesse of the greatest number, caused the President to make a generall assembly, and then he advised them as followeth.

Countrimen, the long experience of our late miseries, I hope is sufficient to perswade every one to a present correction of himselfe; and thinke not that either my pains, or the adventurers purses, will ever maintaine you in idlenesse and sloth; I speake not this to you all, for diverse of you I know deserve both honor and reward, better then is yet here to bee had: but the greater part must be more industrious, or starve, howsoever you have bin heretofore tolerated by the authoritie of the Councell from that I have often commanded you, yet seeing nowe the authoritie resteth wholly in my selfe; you must obay this for a law, that he that will not worke shall not eate (except by sicknesse he be disabled) for the labours of 30 or 40 honest and industrious men, shall not bee consumed to maintaine 150 idle varlets. Now though you presume the authoritie here is but a shaddow, and that I dare not touch the lives of any, but my own must answer it; the letters patents each week shall be read you, whose contents will tell you the contrary. I would wish you therefore without contempt seeke to observe these orders set downe: for there are nowe, no more Councells to protect you, nor curbe my indeavors. Therefore hee that offendeth let him assuredly expect his due punishment. Hee made also a table as a publike memoriall of every mans deserts, to encourage the good, and with shame to spurne on the rest to amendment. By this many became very industrious, yet more by severe punishment performed their businesse; for all were so tasked, that there was no excuse could prevaile to deceive him, yet the Dutchmens consorts so closely still convaid powder, shot, swords, and tooles, that though we could find the defect, we could not find by whom it was occasioned, till it was too late.

All this time the Dutchmen remaining with Powhatan, received them, instructing the Salvages their use. But their consorts not following them as they expected, (to know the cause, they sent Francis their companion (a stout young fellow) disguised Salvage like) to the glasse-house, (a place in the woods neere a myle from James Towne) where was the randavus for all their unsuspected villany, 40 men they procured of Powhatan to lie in Ambuscadoe for Captaine Smith, who no sooner heard of this Dutchman, but hee sent to apprehend him, who found he was gon, yet to crosse his returne to Powhatan, Captaine Smith presently dispatched 20 shot after him, and then returning but from the glasse-house alone, hee incountred the king of Paspaheigh, a most strong stout Salvage, whose perswasions not being able to perswade him to his ambush, seeing him only armed but with a fauchion, attempted to have shot him; but the President prevented his shot by grapling with him, and the Salvage as well prevented him for drawing his fauchion, and perforce bore him into the river to have drowned him; long they struggled in the water, from whence the king perceiving two of the Poles upon the sandes would have fled; but the President held him by the haire & throat til the Poles came in; then seeing howe pittifully the poore Salvage begged his life, they conducted him prisoner to the fort. The Dutchman ere long was also brought in, whose villany, though all this time it was suspected, yet he fained such a formall excuse, that for want of language, Win had not rightly understood them, and for their dealings with Powhatan, that to save their lives they were constrained to accommodate his armes, of whome he extreamely complained to have detained them perforce; and that hee made this escape with the hazard of his life, and meant not to have returned, but only walked in the woods to gather walenuts: yet for all this faire tale (there was so smal appearance of truth) hee went by the heeles; the king also he put in fetters; purposing to regaine the Dutch-men, by the saving his life; the poore Salvage did his best, by his daily messengers to Powhatan, but all returned that the Dutchmen would not returne, neither did Powhatan stay them, and bring them fiftie myles on their backes they were not able; daily this kings wives children, and people, came to visit him with presents, which hee liberally bestowed to make his peace, much trust they had in the Presidents promise, but the king finding his gard negligent (though fettered) yet escaped; Captaine Win thinking to pursue him, found such troopes of Salvages to hinder his passages, as they exchanged many volies of shot for flights of arrowes. Captaine Smith hearing of this, in returning to the fort tooke two Salvages prisoners, the one called Kemps, the other Kinsock, the two most exact villaines in the countrie; with those, Captaine Win, and 50 chosen men attempted that night to have regained the king, and revenged his injurie (and so had done if he had followed his directions, or bin advised by those two villaines that would have betraied both their king and kindred for a peece of copper), but hee trifling away the night, the Salvages the next morning by the rising of the sunne, braved him come a shore to fight, a good time both sides let flie at other, but wee heard of no hurt, only they tooke two Canows, burnt the kings house and so returned.

The President fearing those bravadoes, would but incourage the Salvages, begun himselfe to trie his conclusions; whereby 6 or 7 Salvages were slaine, as many made prisoners; burnt their houses, tooke their boats with all their fishing weares, and planted them at James Towne for his owne use; and nowe resolved not to cease till he had revenged himselfe upon al that had injured him, but in his journey passing by Paspaheigh towards Chickahamina, the Salvages did their best to draw him to their ambuscadoes; but seeing him regardlesly passe their Countrey, all shewed themselves in their bravest manner, to trie their valours, he could not but let flie, and ere he could land, the Salvages no sooner knewe him, but they threw downe their armes and desired peace; their Orator was a stout young man called Ocanindge, whose worthie discourse deserveth to be remembered; and this it was.

Captaine Smith, my master is here present in this company thinking it Captaine Win, and not you; and of him hee intended to have beene revenged, having never offended him: if hee have offended you in escaping your imprisonment; the fishes swim, the fowles flie, and the very beastes strive to escape the snare and live; then blame not him being a man, hee would entreat you remember, your being a prisoner, what paines he tooke to save your life; if since he hath injured you he was compelled to it, but howsoever, you have revenged it with our too great losse, we perceive & well know you intend to destroy us, that are here to intreat and desire your friendship, and to enjoy our houses and plant our fields, of whose fruit you shall participate, otherwise you will have the worst by our absence, for we can plant any where, though with more labour, and we know you cannot live if you want our harvest, and that reliefe wee bring you; if you promise us peace we will beleeve you, if you proceed in revenge, we will abandon the Countrie. Upon these tearmes the President promised them peace, till they did us injurie, upon condition they should bring in provision, so all departed good friends, & so continued till Smith left the Countrie.

Ariving at James Towne, complaint was made to the President that the Chickahaminos, who al this while continued trade, and seemed our friendes, by colour thereof were the only theeves, and amongst other things, a pistol being stolne, and the theefe fled, there were apprehended 2 proper young fellows that were brothers, knowne to be his confederats. Now to regain this pistoll, the one we imprisoned, the other was sent to returne againe within 12 houres, or his brother to be hanged, yet the President pittying the poore naked Salvage in the dungeon, sent him victuall and some charcole for fire; ere midnight his brother returned with the pistoll, but the poore Salvage in the dungeon was so smothered with the smoke he had made, and so pittiously burnt, that wee found him dead, the other most lamentably bewailed his death, and broke forth in such bitter agonies, that the President (to quiet him) told him that if herafter they would not steal, he wold make him alive againe, but little thought hee could be recovered, yet (we doing our best with aquavitæ & vinegar) it pleased God to restore him againe to life, but so drunke and affrighted that he seemed lunaticke, not understanding any thing he spoke or heard, the which as much grieved and tormented the other, as before to see him dead; of which maladie (upon promise of their good behaviour afterward) the President promised to recover him and so caused him to be laid by a fire to sleepe, who in the morning (having well slept) had recovered his perfect senses; and then being dressed of his burning, and each a peece of copper given them, they went away so well contented, that this was spread amongst all the Salvages for a miracle, that Captaine Smith could make a man alive that is dead; these and many other petty accidents, so amazed and affrighted both Powhatan and all his people that from all parts with presents they desired peace, returning many stolne things which wee neither demaunded nor thought of. And after that, those that were taken stealing (both Powhatan and his people) have sent them backe to James Towne to receive their punishment, and all the countrie became absolutely as free for us, as for themselues.

11

What was done in three monthes having victuall. The store devoured by rats, how we lived 3 monthes of such naturall fruits as the countrie afforded.

Now wee so quietly followed our businesse, that in 3 monthes we made 3 or 4 last of pitch and tarre, and sope ashes, produced a triall of glasse, made a well in the forte of excellent sweete water (which till then was wanting) built some 20 houses, recovered our Church, provided nets and weares for fishing (& to stop the disorders of our disorderly theeves & the Salvages) built a blocke house in the necke of our Ile, kept by a garrison to entertaine the Salvages trade, & none to passe nor repasse, Salvage, nor Christian, without the Presidents order, 30 or 40 acres of ground we digged, and planted; of 3 sowes in one yeare increased 60 and od pigges, and neere 500 chickens brought up themselves (without having any meate given them) but the hogges were transported to Hog Ile, where also we built a blocke house with a garrison, to give us notice of any shipping, and for their exercise they made clapbord, wainscot, and cut downe trees against the ships comming. We built also a fort for a retreat, neare a convenient river upon a high commanding hill, very hard to be assaulted, and easie to be defended; but ere it was half finished this defect caused a stay; in searching our casked corne, wee found it halfe rotten, the rest so consumed with the many thousand rats (increased first from the ships) that we knewe not how to keepe that little wee had. This did drive us all to our wits ende, for there was nothing in the countrie but what nature afforded. Untill this time Kemps and Tassore, were fettered prisoners, and daily wrought, and taught us how to order and plant our fields. Whome now (for want of victuall) we set at libertie, but so wel were they used, that they little desired it; and to express their loves, for 16 daies continuance, the Countrie brought us (when least) 100 a daie of squirrils, Turkies, Deare, and other wild beastes; but this want of corne occasioned the end of all our workes, it being worke sufficient to provide victuall. 60 or 80 with Ensigne Laxon were sent downe the river to live upon oysters, & 20 with leiftenant Percie to trie for fishing at Point-Comfort, but in 6 weekes, they would not agree once to cast out their net. Master West with as many went up to the falles, but nothing could bee found but a fewe berries and acornes; of that in the store every one had their equall proportion. Till this present (by the hazard and endeavour of some 30 or 40) this whole number had ever been fed. Wee had more Sturgeon then could be devoured by dogge and man; of which the industrious, by drying and pownding, mingled with caviare, sorrel, and other wholsome hearbs, would make bread and good meate; others would gather as much Tockwough roots in a day, as would make them bread a weeke, so that of those wilde fruites, fish and berries, these lived very well, (in regard of such a diet) but such was the most strange condition of some 150, that had they not beene forced nolens volens perforce to gather and prepare their victuall they would all have starved, and have eaten one another: of those wild fruites the Salvages often brought us: and for that the President would not fulfill the unreasonable desire of those distracted lubberly gluttons, to sell, not only our kettles, howes, tooles, and Iron, nay swords, peeces, & the very ordenance, and houses, might they have prevailed but to have beene but idle, for those salvage fruits they would have imparted all to the Salvages, especially for one basket of corne they heard of, to bee at Powhatans, 50 myles from our fort, though he bought neere halfe of it to satisfie their humours, yet to have had the other halfe, they would have sold their soules, (though not sufficient to have kept them a weeke) thousands were their exclamations, suggestions, and devises, to force him to those base inventions, to have made it an occasion to abandon the Countrie. Want perforce constrained him to indure their exclaiming follies till he found out the author, one Dyer, a most craftie knave, and his ancient maligner, whom he worthely punished, and with the rest he argued the case in this manner.

Fellow souldiers, I did little thinke any so false to report, or so many so simple to be perswaded, that I either intend to starve you, or that Powhatan (at this present) hath corne for himselfe, much lesse for you; or that I would not have it, if I knewe where it were to be had. Neither did I thinke any so malitious as nowe I see a great many, yet it shall not so much passionate me, but I will doe my best for my worst maligner. But dreame no longer of this vaine hope from Powhatan, nor that I will longer forbeare to force you from your Idlenesse and punish you if you raile, you cannot deny but that by the hazard of my life, many a time I have saved yours, when, might your owne wils have prevailed, you would have starved, and will doe still whether I will or no. But I protest by that God that made me, since necessitie hath not power to force you to gather for your selvs those fruits the earth doth yeeld, you shall not only gather for your selves, but for those that are sicke: as yet I never had more from the store then the worst of you; and all my English extraordinarie provision that I have, you shall see mee devide among the sick. And this Salvage trash, you so scornfully repine at, being put in your mouthes your stomacks can digest it, and therefore I will take a course you shall provide it. The sicke shal not starve, but equally share of all our labours, and every one that gathereth not every day as much as I doe, the next daie shall be set beyond the river, and for ever bee banished from the fort, and live there or starve.

This order many murmured, was very cruell, but it caused the most part so well bestir themselues, that of 200 men (except they were drowned) there died not past 7 or 8. As for Captaine Win, and Master Ley, they died ere this want happened, and the rest died not for want of such as preserved the rest. many were billitted among the Salvages, whereby we knewe all their passages, fieldes, and habitations, howe to gather and use their fruits, as well as themselves.

So well those poore Salvages used us, (that were thus Billited) as divers of the souldiers ran away, to search Kemps our old prisoner. Glad was this salvage to have such an occasion to testifie his love, for insteed of entertaining them, & such things as they had stolne with all the great offers and promises they made them to revenge their injuries upon Captaine Smith, First he made himselfe sport, in shewing his countrymen (by them) how he was used; feeding them with this law who would not worke must not eat, till they were neere starved, continuallie threatning to beate

them to death, neither could they get from him, til perforce he brought them to our Captaine, that so we contented him, and punished them: as manie others that intended also to have followed them, were rather contented to labour at home, then adventure to live Idle among the Salvages, (of whom there was more hope to make better christians and good subjects, then the one halfe of those that counterfeited themselves both.) For so afeard were all those kings and the better sorte of their people, to displease us that some of the baser sort that we have extreamelie hurt and punished for their villanies, would hire us, we should not tell it to their kings or countrymen, who would also repunish them, and yet returne them to James Towne to content the President, by that testimonie of their loves.

Master Sicklemore well returned from Chawonock, but found little hope and lesse certainetie of them were left by Sir Walter Rawley. So that Nathaniell Powell & Anas Todkill, were also, by the Quiyoughquohanocks, conducted to the Mangoages to search them there. But nothing could we learne but they were all dead, this honest, proper, good promis-keeping king, of all the rest did ever best affect us, & though to his false Gods he was yet very zealous, yet he would confesse, our God as much exceeded his, as our guns did his bowe and arrowes, often sending our President manie presents to praie to his God for raine, or his corne would perish, for his Gods were angrie all this time. To reclaime the Dutchmen, and one Bentley an other fugitive, we imploied one William Volda (a Switzer by birth) with pardons and promises to regaine them. Litle we then suspected this double villaine, of anie villanie, who plainlie taught us in the most trust was the greatest treason. For this wicked hypocrit, by the seeming hate he bore to the lewd condition of his cursed countrimen, having this opportunitie by his imploiment to regaine them, conveighed them everie thing they desired to effect their project to destroie the colonie. With much devotion they expected the Spanyard to whom they intended to have done good service. But to begin with the first opportunitie, they seeing necessitie thus inforced us to disperse our selves; importuned Powhatan to lend them but his forces, and they would not onlie destroie our hogs, fire our towne, and betraie our Pinnas; but bring to his service and subjection the most part of our companies.

With this plot they had acquainted manie discontents and manie were agreed to their divelish practise. But one Thomas Dovese & Thomas Mallard, whose christian harts much relenting at such an unchristian act, voluntarily revealed it to Captaine Smith: who did his best it might be concealed, perswading Dovese and Malard to proceed in the confederacie: onlie to bring the irreclamable Dutch men, and inconstant Salvages in such a maner amongst his ambuscadoes, as he had prepared, as not manie of them shoulde ever have returned from out our peni[n]sula. But this brute comming to the ears of the impatient multitude, they so importuned the President to cut of those Dutchmen, as amongst manie that offered to cut their throates before the face of Powhatan. Master Wiffin and Jefra Abot were sent to stab or shoot them; but these Dutch men made such excuses accusing Volday whom they supposed had revealed their project, as Abbot would not, yet Wiffin would, perceiving it but deceipt. The king understanding of this their imploiment, sent presentlie his messengers to Captaine Smith to signifie it was not his fault to detaine them, nor hinder his men from executing his command, nor did he nor would he maintaine them, or anie to occasion his displeasure. But ere this busines was brought to a point, God having seene our misery sufficient, sent in Captaine Argall to fish for Sturgion with a ship well furnished with wine and bisket, which though it was not sent us, such were our occasions we tooke it at a price, but left him sufficient to returne for England, still dissembling Valdo his villany, but certainlie hee had not escaped had the President continued.

By this you may see, for all those crosses, treacheries, and dissentions, howe he wrastled and overcame (without bloud shed) all that hapned. Also what good was done, how few died, what food the country naturally affordeth, what small cause there is men shoulde starve, or be murdered by the Salvages, that have discretion to manage this courage and industry. The 2. first years though by his adventures he had oft brought the Salvages to a tractable trade, yet you see how the envious authority ever crossed him, and frustrated his best endeavours. Yet this wrought in him that experience and estimation among the Salvages, as otherwaies it had bin impossible he had ever effected that he did, though the many miserable yet generous and worthy adventures, he had long, & oft indured as wel in some parts of Africa, and America, as in the most partes of Europe and Asia by land or sea had taught him much, yet in this case he was againe to learne his Lecture by experience. Which with thus much a doe having obtained, it was his ill chance to end, when hee had but onlie learned how to begin. And though hee left these unknowne difficulties, (made easie and familiar) to his unlawfull successors, whoe onlie by living in James Towne, presumed to know more then al the world could direct them though they had all his souldiers with their triple power, and twise triple better meanes, by what they have done in his absence, the world doth see: and what they would have done in his presence, had he not prevented their indiscretions: it doth justlie approve what cause he had to send them for England. But they have made it more plaine since their returne, having his absolute authoritie freely in their power, with all the advantages, and opportunity that his labours had effected. As I am sorry their actions have made it so manifest, so I am unwilling to say what reason doth compell me, to make apparant the truth, least I should seeme partial, reasonlesse, or malitious.

12
The Arivall of the third supply.

To redresse those jarres & ill proceedings, the Councell in England altered the government & devolved the authoritie to the Lord De-la-ware. Who for his deputie, sent Sir Thomas Gales, & Sir George Somers, with 9 ships & 500 persons. they set saile from England in May 1609 a smal catch perished at sea in a Herycano. The Admirall, with 150 men, with the two knights, & their new commission, their bils of loading with all manner of directions, and the most part of their provision arived not. With the other 7 (as Captaines) arived Ratliffe, whose right name was Sickelmore, Martin, and Archer. Who as they had been troublesome at sea, beganne againe to marre all ashore. For though, as is said, they were formerly deposed & sent for England: yet now returning againe, graced by the title of Captaines of the passengers, seeing the admirall wanting, and great probabilitie of her losse, strengthned themselves with those newe companies, so railing and exclaiming against Captaine Smith, that they mortally hated him, ere ever they see him. Who understanding by his scouts, the arivall of such a fleet (little dreaming of any such supply) supposing them Spaniards, hee so determined and ordered his affaires, as wee little feared their arivall, nor the successe of our incounter, nor were the Salvages any way negligent or unwilling, to aide and assist us with their best power, had it so beene, wee had beene happy. For we would not have trusted them but as our foes, whereas receiving those as our countriemen and friends, they did their best to murder our President, to surprise the store, the fort, and our lodgings, to usurp the governement, and make us all their servants, and slaves to our owne merit, to 1000 mischiefes those lewd Captaines led this lewd company, wherein were many unruly gallants packed thether by their friends to escape il destinies, and those would dispose and determine of the government, sometimes one, the next day another, to day the old commission, to morrow the new, the next day by neither. In fine, they would rule all or ruine all; yet in charitie we must endure them thus to destroy us, or by correcting their follies, have brought the worlds censure upon us to have beene guiltie of their bloods. Happy had we bin had they never arrived; and we for ever abandoned, & (as we were) left to our fortunes, for on earth was never more confusion, or miserie, then their factions occasioned.

The President seeing the desire those braves had to rule, seeing how his authoritie was so unexpectedly changed, would willingly have left all and have returned for England, but seeing there was smal hope this newe commission would arive, longer hee would not suffer those factious spirits to proceed. It would bee too tedious, too strange, and almost incredible, should I particularly relate the infinite dangers, plots, & practises, hee daily escaped amongst this factious crue, the chiefe whereof he quickly laid by the heeles, til his leasure better served to doe them justice; & to take away al occasions of further mischiefe. Master Persie had his request granted to returne for England, and Master West with 120 went to plant at the falles. Martin with neare as many to Nansamund, with their due proportions, of all provisions, according to their numbers.

Now the Presidents yeare being neere expired he made Martin President, who knowing his own insufficiencie, and the companies scorne, and conceit of his unworthinesse, within 3 houres re-signed it againe to Captaine Smith, and at Nansamund thus proceeded. The people being contributers used him kindly: yet such was his jealous feare, and cowardize, in the midst of his mirth, hee did surprize this poore naked king, with his monuments, houses, and the Ile he inhabited; and there fortified himselfe, but so apparantly distracted with fear, as imboldned the Salvages to assalt him, kill his men, redeeme their king, gather and carrie away more then 1000 bushels of corne, hee not once daring to intercept them. But sent to the President then at the Falles for 30 good shotte, which from James towne immediately were sent him, but hee so well imploid them, as they did just nothing, but returned, complaining of his childishnesse, that with them fled from his company, and so left them to their fortunes.

Master West having seated his men at the Falles, presently returned to revisit James Towne, the President met him by the way as he followed him to the Falles: where he found this company so inconsiderately seated, in a place not only subject to the rivers inundation, but round invironed with many intollerable inconveniences. For remedy whereof, he sent presently to Powhatan, to sell him the place called Powhatan, promising to defend him against the Monacans, and these should be his conditions (with his people) to resigne him the fort and houses and all that countrie for a proportion of copper: that all stealing offenders should bee sent him, there to receive their punishment: that every house as a custome should pay him a bushell of corne for an inch square of copper, and a proportion of Pocones as a yearely tribute to King James, for their protection as a dutie: what else they could spare to barter at their best discreation.

But both this excellent place and those good conditions did those furies refuse, contemning both him, his kind care and authoritie. the worst they could to shew their spite, they did. I doe more then wonder to thinke how only with 5 men, he either durst, or would adventure as he did, (knowing how greedy they were of his blood) to land amongst them and commit to imprisonment the greatest spirits amongst them, till by their multitudes being 120, they forced him to retire, yet in that retreate hee surprised one of the boates, wherewith hee returned to their shippe, wherein was their provisions, which also hee tooke. And well it chaunced hee found the marriners so tractable and constant, or there had beene small possibility he had ever escaped. Notwithstanding there were many of the best, I meane of the most worthy in Judgement, reason o[r] experience, that from their first landing hearing the general good report of his old souldiers, and seeing with their eies his actions so wel managed with discretion, as Captaine Wood, Captaine Web, Captaine Mone, Captaine Phitz-James, Master Partridge, Master White, Master Powell and divers others. When they perceived the malice and condition of Ratliffe, Martin, and Archer, left their factions; and ever rested his faithfull friends: But the worst was, the poore Salvages that dailie brought in their contribution to the President, that disorderlie company so tormented those poore naked soules, by stealing their corne, robbing their gardens, beating them, breaking their houses, & keeping some prisoners; that they dailie complained to Captaine Smith he had brought them for protectors worse enimies then the Monocans themselves; which though till then, (for his love) they had indured: they desired pardon, if hereafter they defended themselves, since he would not correct them, as they had long expected he would: so much they importuned him to punish their misdemeanores, as they offered (if hee would conduct them) to fight for him against them. But having spent 9. daies in seeking to reclaime them, shewing them how much they did abuse themselves, with their great guilded hopes, of seas, mines, commodities, or victories they so madly conceived. Then (seeing nothing would prevaile with them) he set saile for James Towne: now no sooner was the ship under saile but the Salvages assaulted those 120 in their fort, finding some stragling abroad in the woods they slew manie, and so affrighted the rest, as their prisoners escaped, & they scarse retired, with the swords & cloaks of these they had slaine. But ere we had sailed a league or shippe grounding, gave us once more libertie to summon them to a parlie. Where we found them all so stranglie amazed with this poore simple assault, as they submitted themselves upon anie tearmes to the Presidents mercie. Who presentlie put by the heeles 6 or 7 of the chiefe offenders, the rest he seated gallantlie at Powhatan, in their Salvage fort they built and pretilie fortified with poles and barkes of trees sufficient to have defended them from all the Salvages in Virginia, drie houses for lodgings 300 acres of grounde readie to plant, and no place so strong, so pleasant and delightful in Virginia, for which we called it Nonsuch. the Salvages also he presentlie appeased; redelivering to every one their former losses. Thus al were friends, new officers appointed to command, and the President againe readie to depart. But at that Instant arrived Master West, whose good nature with the perswasions and compassion of those mutinous prisoners was so much abused, that to regaine their old hopes new turboiles arose. For the rest being possessed of al their victuall munition and everie thing, they grow to that height in their former factions, as there the President left them to their fortunes, they returning againe to the open aire at West fort, abandoning Nonsuch, and he to James Towne with his best expedition, but this hapned him in that Journie.

Sleeping in his boat, (for the ship was returned 2 daies before,) accidentallie, one fired his powder bag, which tore his flesh from his bodie and thighes, 9. or 10. inches square in a most pittifull manner; but to quench the tormenting fire, frying him in his cloaths he leaped over bord into the deepe river, where ere they could recover him he was neere drownd. In this estat, without either Chirurgion, or chirurgery he was to go neare 100. miles. Ariving at James Towne causing all things to bee prepared for peace or warres to obtain provision, whilest those things were providing, Martin, Ratliffe, and Archer, being to have their trials their guiltie consciences fearing a just reward for their deserts, seeing the President unable to stand, & neare bereft of his senses by reason of his torment, they had plotted to have murdered him in his bed. But his hart did faile him that should have given fire to that mercilesse pistol. So, not finding that course to be the best they joined togither to usurp the government, thereby to escape their punishment, and excuse themselves by accusing him. The President, had notice of their projects: the which to withstand, though his old souldiers importuned him but permit them to take of their heads that would resist his commaund, yet he would not permit them, But sent for the masters of the ships and tooke order with them for his returne for England. Seeing there was neither chirurgion, nor chirurgery in the fort to cure his hurt, and the ships to depart the next daie, his commission to be suppressed he knew not why, himselfe and souldiers to be re-warded he knew not how, and a new commission graunted they knew not to whom, the which so disabled that authority he had, as made them presume so oft to those mutinies and factions as they did. Besides so grievous were his wounds, & so cruell his torment, few expected he could live, nor was hee able to follow his businesse to regaine what they had lost, suppresse those factions and range the countries for provision as he intended, and well he knew in those affaires his owne actions and presence was as requisit as his experience, and directions, which now could not be, he went presently abord, resolving there to appoint them governours, and to take order for the mutiners and their confederates. Who seeing him gone, perswaded Master Persie (to stay) and be their President, and within lesse then an howre was this mutation begun and concluded. For when the company understood Smith would leave them, & see the rest in Armes called Presidents and councellors, divers began to fawne on those new commanders, that now bent all their wits to get him resigne them his commission, who after many salt and bitter repulses, that their confusion should not be attributed to him for leaving the country without government and authority; having taken order to bee free from danger of their malice; he was not unwilling they should steale it from him, but never consented to deliver it to any. But had that unhappy blast not hapned, he would quickly have quallified the heate of those humors and factions, had the ships but once left them and us to our fortunes, and have made that provision from among the Salvages, as we neither feared Spanyard, Salvage, nor famine: nor would have left Virginia, nor our lawfull authoritie, but at as deare a price as we had bought it, and paid for it. What shall I say? but thus we lost him, that in all his proceedings, made Justice his first guid, and experience his second; ever hating basenesse, sloth, pride, and indignitie, more then any dangers; that never allowed more for himselfe, then his souldiers with him; that upon no danger would send them where he would not lead them himselfe; that would never see us want what he either had, or could by any meanes get us; that would rather want then borrow, or starve then not pay; that loved actions more then wordes, and hated falshood and cousnage worse then death: whose adventures were our lives, and whose losse our

deathes. Leaving us thus with 3 ships, 7 boates, commodities ready to trade, the harvest newly gathered, 10 weekes provision in the store, 490 and odde persons, 24 peeces of ordinances, 300 muskets snaphanches, and fire lockes, shot, powder, and match sufficient, curats, pikes, swords, and moryons more then men: the Salvages their language & habitations wel knowne to 100 well trained and expert souldiers; nets for fishing, tooles of all sortes to worke, apparell to supply our wants, 6 mares and a horse, 5 or 600 swine, as many hens and chicken; some goates, some sheep, what was brought or bread there remained, but they regarded nothing but from hand to mouth, to consume that we had, tooke care for no thing but to perfit some colourable complaints against Captaine Smith, for effecting whereof, 3 weekes longer they stayed the 6 ships til they could produce them. that time and charge might much better have beene spent, but it suted well with the rest of their discreations.

Now all those, Smith had either whipped, punished, or any way disgraced, had free power and liberty to say or sweare any thing, and from a whole armefull of their examinations this was concluded.

The mutiners at the Falles, complained hee caused the Salvages assalt them, for that hee would not revenge their losse, they being but 120, and he 5 men and himselfe, and this they proved by the oath of one hee had oft whipped for perjurie and pilfering. The dutchmen that he had appointed to bee stabd for their treacheries, swore he sent to poison them with rats baine. The prudent Councel, that he would not submit himselfe to their stolne authoritie. Coe & Dyer, that should have murdered him, were highly preferred for swearing, they heard one say, he heard Powhatan say, that he heard a man say: if the king would not send that corne he had, he should not long enjoy his copper crowne, nor those robes he had sent him: yet those also swore hee might have had corne for tooles but would not. The truth was, Smith had no such ingins as the king demanded, nor Powhatan any corne. Yet this argued he would starve them. Others complained hee would not let them rest in the fort (to starve) but forced them to the oyster bankes, to live or starve, as he lived himselfe. For though hee had of his owne private provisions sent from England, sufficient; yet hee gave it all away to the weake and sicke, causing the most untoward (by doing as he did) to gather their food from the unknowne parts of the rivers & woods, that they lived (though hardly) that otherwaies would have starved, ere they would have left their beds, or at most the sight of James Towne to have got their own victuall. Some propheticall spirit calculated hee had the Salvages in such subjection, hee would have made himselfe a king, by marrying Pocahontas, Powhatans daughter. It is true she was the very nomparell of his kingdome, & at most not past 13 or 14 yeares of age. Very oft shee came to our fort, with what shee could get for Captaine Smith, that ever loved and used all the Countrie well, but her especially he ever much respected: & she so well requited it, that when her father intended to have surprized him, shee by stealth in the darke night came through the wild woods and told him of it. But her marriage could no way have intitled him by any right to the kingdome, nor was it ever suspected hee had ever such a thought, or more regarded her, or any of them, then in honest reason, & discretion he might. If he would he might have married her, or have done what him listed. For there was none that could have hindred his determination. Some that knewe not any thing to say, the Councel instructed, and advised what to sweare. So diligent they were in this businesse, that what any could remember, hee had ever done, or said in mirth, or passion, by some circumstantiall oath, it was applied to their fittest use, yet not past 8 or 9 could say much and that nothing but circumstances, which all men did knowe was most false and untrue. Many got their passes by promising in England to say much against him. I have presumed to say this much in his behalfe for that I never heard such foule slaunders, so certainely beleeved, and urged for truthes by many a hundred, that doe still not spare to spread them, say them and sweare them, that I thinke doe scarse know him though they meet him, nor have they ether cause or reason, but their wills, or zeale to rumor or opinion. For the honorable and better sort of our Virginian adventurers I think they understand it as I have writ it. For instead of accusing him, I have never heard any give him a better report, then many of those witnesses themselves that were sent only home to testifie against him. Richard Pots, W[illiam] P[ettiplace].

When the ships departed Captain Davis ar-rived in a smal Pinnace with some 16 proper men more, to those were added a company from James Towne under the command of Captaine Ratliffe to inhabit Point Comfort. Martin and Master West having lost their boates, and neere halfe their men amongst the Salvages, were returned to James Towne, for the Salvages no sooner understood of Captaine Smiths losse, but they all revolted, and did murder & spoile all they could incounter. Now were we all constrained to live only of that which Smith had only for his owne company, for the rest had consumed their proportions. And now have we 20 Presidents with all their appurtenances, for Master Persie was so sicke he could not goe nor stand. But ere all was consumed, Master West and Ratliffe each with a pinnace, and 30 or 40 men wel appointed, sought abroad to trade, how they carried the businesse I know not, but Ratliffe and his men were most slaine by Powhatan, those that escaped returned neare starved in the Pinnace. And Master West finding little better successe, set saile for England. Now wee all found the want of Captaine Smith, yea his greatest maligners could then curse his losse. Now for corne, provision, and contribution from the Salvages; wee had nothing but mortall wounds with clubs and arrowes. As for our hogs, hens, goats, sheep, horse, or what lived, our commanders and officers did daily consume them, some small proportions (sometimes) we tasted till all was devoured, then swords, arrowes, peeces, or any thing we traded to the Salvages, whose bloody fingers were so imbrued in our bloods, that what by their crueltie, our Governours indiscreation, and the losse of our ships; Of 500, within 6 monthes after there remained not many more then 60. most miserable and poore creatures. It were to vild [=too vile] to say what we endured; but the occasion was only our owne, for want of providence, industrie, and governement, and not the barrennesse and defect of the countrie, as is generally supposed, for till then in 3 yeares (for the numbers were landed us) we had never landed sufficient provision for 6 months such a glutton is the sea, and such good fellowes the marriners, wee as little tasted of those great proportions for their provisions, as they of our miseries, that notwithstanding ever swaid and overruled the businesse: though we did live as is said, 3 yeares chiefly of what this good countrie naturally affordeth: yet now had we beene in Paradice it selfe (with those governours) it would not have beene much better with us, yet was there some amongst us, who had they had the governement, would surely have kept us from those extremities of miseries, that in 10 daies more would have supplanted us all by death.

But God that would not it should bee unplanted, sent Sir Thomas Gates, and Sir George Sommers, with a 150 men, most happily preserved by the Bermondoes to preserue us. Strange it is to say how miraculously they were preserved, in a leaking ship, in those extreame stormes and tempests in such over-growne seas 3 daies and 3 nights by bayling out water. And having given themselvs to death, how happily when least expected that worthy Captaine Sir George Somers, having lien all that time cuning the ship before those swalowing waves, discovered those broken Iles, where how plentifully they lived with fish & flesh, what a paradice this is to inhabit, what industrie they used to build their 2 ships, how happily they did transport them to James Towne in Virginia, I refer you to their owne printed relations.

But when those noble knights did see our miseries (being strangers in the country) and could understand no more of the cause but by their conjecture, of our clamors and complaints, of accusing or excusing one an other, they imbarked us with themselves, with the best means they could, and abandoning James Towne set saile for England.

But yet God would not so have it, for ere wee left the river; we met the Lord de-la-ware, then governour for the countrie, with 3 ships exceeding well furnished with al necessaries fitting, who againe returned them to the abandoned James Towne, the 9. of June, 1610, accompanied with Sir Ferdinando Wainman, and divers other gentlemen of sort. Sir George Somers, and Captaine Argall he presentlie dispatcheth to require the Bermondas to furnish them with provision: Sir Thomas Gates for England to helpe forward their supplies: himselfe neglected not the best was in his power for the furtherance of the busines and regaining what was lost. But even in the beginning of his proceedings, his Lordship had such an incounter with a scurvy sickenesse, that made him unable to weld the state of his body, much lesse the affaires of the colonie, so that after 8. monthes sicknesse, he was forced to save his life by his returne for England.

In this time Argall not finding the Bermondas, having lost Sir George Somers at sea, fell on the coast of Sagadahock, where refreshing himselfe, found a convenient fishing for Cod. With a tast whereof hee returned to James towne, from whence the Lord De-la-ware sent him to trade in the river of Patawomecke, where finding an English boy those people had preserved from the furie of Powhatan, by his acquaintance had such good usage of those kind Salvages, that they fraughted his ship with corne, wherewith he returned to James Towne, and so for England with the Lord governour, yet before his returne, the adventurers had sent Sir Tho. Dale with 3 ships, men and cattell, and all other provisions necessarie for a yeare, all which arived the 10 of May, 1611.

Againe, to second him with all possible expedition there was prepared for Sir Tho Gates, 6 tall ships with 300 men, and 100 kyne, with other cattel, with munition and all manner of provision could bee thought needfull, and they arived about the 1 of August next after safely at James towne.

Sir George Somers all this time was supposed lost: but thus it hapned, missing the Bermondas, hee fell also as did Argall with Sagadahock, where being refreshed, would not content himselfe with that repulse, but returned againe in the search; and there safely arived. But overtoiling himselfe on a surfeit died. And in this Cedar ship built by his owne directions, and partly with his owne hands, that had not in her any iron but only one bolt in her keele, yet well endured thus tossed to and againe in this mightie Ocean, til with his dead bo[dy] she arived in England at [=Lyme Regis?] Line, & at Whitchurch in Dorsetshire, his body by his friends was honourably buried, with many volies of shot, and the rights of a souldier. And upon his Tombe was bestowed this Epitaph

Hei mihi Virginia, quod tam cito præterit æstas,
Autumnus sequitur, sæviet inde & hyems.
At ver perpetuum nascetur, & Anglia læta
Decerpit flores, Floryda terra tuos.

Alas Virginia Somer so soone past
Autume succeeds and stormy winters blast,
Yet Englands joyfull spring with Aprill shewres,
O Floryda, shall bring thy sweetest flowers.

Since there was a ship fraughted with provision, and 40 men, and another since then with the like number and provision to stay in the Countrie 12 months with Captaine Argall.

The Lord governour himselfe doth confidently determine to goe with the next, or as presently as hee may in his owne person, with sundry other knights & gentlemen, with ships & men so farre as their meanes will extend to furnish; as for all their particular actions since the returne of Captaine Smith, for that they have beene printed from time to time, and published to the world, I cease farther to trouble you with any repetition of things so well knowne, more then are necessarie.

To conclude the historie, leaving this assurance to all posteritie, howe unprosperously things may succeed, by what changes or chances soever, The action is honorable and worthie to bee approved, the defect whereof hath only beene in the managing the businesse; which I hope now experience hath taught them to amend, or those examples may make others to beware, for the land is as good as this booke doth report it.

WILLIAM STRACHEY'S "HISTORIE OF TRAVAILE INTO VIRGINIA BRITANNIA," 1610–1612

WILLIAM STRACHEY spent from May, 1610, to the late summer of 1611 in Virginia as secretary (first to Sir Thomas Gates and later to Lord De La Warr, later still to George Percy), as acting lieutenant governor, and finally as lieutenant governor to Sir Thomas Dale. During his stewardship of the records of the colony (one of his duties), he began to compose a "History" of English enterprise in North America which he intended to finish on his return to England. He never achieved this, but during 1612 he had completed all he felt inclined to do without finding a patron who would reimburse him for some of his costs and assist in its publication, especially if he had been rejected, as might appear highly probable, by the Virginia Company itself. He applied successively to three patrons (though in what order we do not know) and was turned down, also for reasons unknown, by all of them. Consequently his book lay unfinished: copy 1 was presented to Sir Francis Bacon, now B.L., Sloane MS 1622, edited by R. H. Major as *The Historie of Travaile into Virginia Britannia* (London, Hakluyt Society, 1849); copy 2 went to Henry Percy, Earl of Northumberland, then a prisoner in the Tower of London, whose brother, George Percy, Strachey knew in Virginia, formerly a Petworth MS, now in Princeton University Library, edited by Louis B. Wright and Virginia Freund as *The Historie of Travell into Virginia Britannia* (London, Hakluyt Society, 1953); and copy 3 to Sir Allen Apsley, purveyor to the Royal Navy, now Bodleian Library, Ashmole MS 1622, unedited except for a vocabulary of Indian words which it alone contains.

Strachey had much to say about the topography of the country, about its Indian inhabitants and about its commodities, fauna, flora, and geology. It is evident that much of what he has to say on all these subjects comes from John Smith, although he also has a good deal to add. The parallels to *The map of Virginia* are too close for this to be set aside. It is usually thought that Strachey hastily incorporated Smith material from *The map* when he got a printed copy in 1612. This is untenable. Close study of Strachey's material indicates that he has blended observations of his own on the spot with those of John Smith and added much to them on Indian society, so that he could only have had a manuscript copy of Smith's report on Virginia in his possession while he was in Virginia. There is every reason, therefore, to believe that John Smith, after his return to England, wrote and gave to the Council of the Virginia Company, a report consisting essentially of what he printed in *The map* in 1612, and that this, or a copy of it, was sent to the secretary of the colony in Virginia and used there by him. If this is so, we have no means of knowing whether Strachey knew it was by Smith or not, or whether he considered he was entitled to appropriate a report that emanated from the company as a basis for his own history. It must surely be the case that Strachey's first approach for support for his history would have been made to the Virginia Company itself and was rejected (though we have no evidence for this), and that his successive pleas for patronage came subsequent to this rejection. The appearance in print of Smith's *A map of Virginia* would therefore have been a blow to Strachey, but one he must have believed he could overcome if he got a patron, since he could then rewrite his history as a different book, one very largely independent of Smith. But the very existence of Smith's printed book (which he read and refers specifically to the printed map) may have worked decisively against him. But, since 1849, Strachey's work has been very highly regarded for its own sake, since much of what he put into it (in spite of the plagiarism) is of very considerable value. Two samples only are given here (since the book is too long to reprint): (a) Chapter 2, his topographical description of the rivers falling into Chesapeake Bay (823); and (b) Chapter 10, his description of the commodities of Virginia (824). The Indian material, though invaluable, is impossible to select. The text used is that of the 1849 edition.

823. William Strachey on the rivers flowing into Chesapeake Bay.

2

Description of the five principall rivers within the Chesapeak Bay, together with such by-streames which fall into them; a description of the Sasquesahanougs of Cape La Warre; the falling with our coast; the fitness of Cape Comfort to fortefie at.

On the west side of the bay, we said were five faire and delightfull navigable rivers, of which we will now proceede to report. The first of these rivers, and the next to the mouthe of the bay, hath his course from the west and by north. The name of this river we call the Kings River, they call Powhatan, according to the name of a principall country that lyeth upon the head of yt; the mouthe of this river is neere three myles in breadth, yet doe the shoells force the channell so neere the land, that a sacre will overshoot yt at point blanck. This river hath a channell, for a hundred and forty miles, of depth betwixt seven and fifteen fathome, holding in breadth, for the most parte, two or three miles; and in which are many isles, both great and small. Yt falleth from rocks far west, in a country inhabited by a nation, as aforesaid, that they call Monacan; but where yt cometh into our discovery, yt is Powhatan. In the furthest place that hath been diligently observed, are falls, rocks, showlds, etc., which makes yt past navigation any higher; albeit, forty miles above the said falls, yt hath two branches, or other rivers, that fall into yt: the head of the northermost comes from certaine steepe mountaines, that are said to be impassable; the head of the other comes from high hills afar of, within the land, from the topps of which hills, the people saie they see another sea, and that the water is there salt; and the journey to this sea, from the falls, by their accompt, should be about ten daies, allowing, according to a march, some fourteen or sixteen miles a day. In the runing downeward, the river is enriched with many goodly brooks, which are maynteyned by an infinite number of small rundells and pleasant springs, that disperse themselves for best service, as doe the vaines of a man's body.

From the south side there falls into this river, first, the pleasant river of Appamatuck; next (more to the east) are the two rivers of Quiyoughcohanock; a little further is a bay, wherein falleth three or four pretty brookes and creeks, that half entrench the inhabitants of Warraskoyack; then the river of Nandsamund, and lastly, the brooke of Chesapeak.

From the north side is the river of Chickahamania, the black river of James Towne; another by the Cedar Isle, wherein are great stoore of goodly oysters; then a convenient harbour for crayes, frygatts, or fisher-boates, at Kecoughtan, the which By-Rill so conveniently turneth yt self into baies, coves, and creeks, that the place is made very pleasant thereby to inhabite, the corne fields being circled therein in manner as so many peninsulaes. The most of these by-rivers are inhabited by severall nations, or rather families, taking theire names from those rivers, and wherein a severall governour or weroance comaundeth.

The first, and next the river's mouthe, are the Kecoughtans, then the Paspapeghes, the Arrohatecks, and the place called Powhatan. On the south side of this river are the Appamatucks, the Quiyoughcohanocks, the Warraskoyacks, the Nandsamunds, the Chesapeaks; of this last place, the bay beareth his name.

Fourteene miles norward from the river Powhatan, is the river Pamunck, which we call the Prince's River, navigable sixty or seventy miles with shippes of good burthen; but with catches and small barkes, thirty or forty miles further. At the ordinary flowing of the salt water, yt devideth yt self, at Cinquoteck, into two gallant braunches: on the south braunch enhabite the people of Youghtamund; on the north braunch, Mattapament. On the north syde of this river is Werowocomoco, where theire great kinge inhabited when we came first into the country. Ten or twelve miles lower, on the south side of this river, is Kiskiak; these, as also Appamatuck, Orapaks, Arrohatack, and Powhatan, are their great king's inheritance, chief alliance, and inhabitaunce. Upon Youghtamund is the seat of Powhatan's three brethren, whome, we learne, are successively to govern after Powhatan, in the same dominions which Powhatan, by right of birth, as the elder brother, now holdes. The rest of the countryes under his comand, are (as they report) his conquests.

Before we come to the third river, that falleth from the mountaines, there is another river, which takes not his birth or head so high, but is only some thirty miles navigable, and yssueth from out the riffs and breaches from the inland; the river is called Payankatank, the inhabitants whereof are but few (not now above forty or fifty), and are the remayne of the conquered Kecoughtans, whome he transported thither; for in the yeare 1608, Powhatan surprised the naturall inhabitaunce of Payankatank, his neighbours and subjects. The occasion was to us unknowne; but the manner was thus performed. First, he sent divers of his men to lodge amongst them one night, pretending a generall hunt, who were to give the allarum unto an ambuscado of a greater company within the woodes, who, upon the signe, given at the hower appointed, environed all the howses, and fell to the execution. Twenty-four men they kild outright (the rest escaping by fortune and their swift footmanship); and the long haire of the one side of their heads, with the skin cased off with shells or reedes, they brought away to Powhatan. They surprised also the women and childrene and the Weroance, all whome they presented to Powhatan. The lockes of haire, with their skynnes, they hanged on a lyne betweene two trees; and of these Powhatan made ostentation, as of a greate triumphe, at Werowocomoco, not longe after, shewing them to such the English as came unto him at his appointment, to trade with him for corne, thincking to have terrified them with this spectacle, and, in the midst of their amazement, to have seased them; but, God be praysed, yt wrought not feare but courage in our people, and awaked their discreations to stand upon their guard the more cautulously; and, by that meanes, they came off agayne from him, contrary to his purpose. And let me truly saie, how they never killed man of ours, but by our men's owne folly and indiscretion, suffering themselves to be beguiled and enticed up into their howses, without their armes; when then (indeed) they have fallen uppon them, and knockt out their braynes, or stuck them full of arrowes (no force) for their credulity. But of so many men which the common report, out of ignoraunce, gives out here to have been slayed by those Indians, I would but knowe if they can name me three men that they ever killed of ours in skirmish, fort or field, but by this kind of subtilty in them and weakness in ours; and whome the sword of justice would have cut off (had they escaped the Indians), for adventuring so amongst them, either against discipline and the charge given them, or, indeed, against common sense and duty unto their owne lyves.

The third navigable river by the Naturalls of

old was called Opiscatumeck, of late Top-pahanock, and we the Queen's River; this is navigable some one hundred and thirty miles. At the top of yt inhabite the people called Mannahoacks, amongst the mountaynes, but they are above the place described in Captain Smithe's mappe. Uppon this river, on the north side, are seated a people called Cuttatawomen, with thirty fighting men; higher on the river are the Moraughtacunds, with thirty able men; beyond them Toppahanock, with one hundred men; far above is another Cuttatawomen, with twenty men; on the south, far within the river, is Nandtaughtacund, having one hundred and fifty men; this river also, as the former, hath her burthen extraordinary both of fish and fowle.

The fourth river is called Patawomeck, and we call Elizabeth River, and is six or seven miles in breadth; yt is navigable one hundred and twenty miles, and fed, as the rest, with many sweet rivers and springs, which fall from the bordering hills; many of them are planted, and yeld noe lesse plentye and variety of fruict then the other rivers; yt exceedeth with aboundance of fish, and is inhabited on both sides: first, on the south side, at the very entrance, is Wighcocomoco, and which hath some one hundred and thirty fighting men; beyond that is Cekakawwon, with thirty men; then Onawmanient, with one hundred men; then Satawomeck, with one hundred and sixty able men: here doth the river devide ytself into three or four convenient rivers; the greatest of the least is called Quiyough, tending nor-west, but the river ytself turneth nor-east, and is still a naviga-ble streme. On the westerne side of this bought is Taxenent, with forty able men; somewhat further is Potapoco, with twenty men. In the east parte of the bought of the river is Pamacocack, with sixty men; after Moyoones, with one hundred men; and lastly, Nacothtank, with eighty able men. The river, ten miles above this place, maketh his passage downe a low pleasand valley, over-shadowed in many places with high rocky mountaines, from whence distill innumerable sweet and pleasant springs.

Within this river Captain Samuell Argoll, in a small river which the Indians call Oeniho, anno 1610, trading in a bark called the *Discovery*, for corne, with the great king of Potawomeck, from him obteyned well neere four hundred bushells of wheat, pease, and beanes, beside many kind of furrs, for nyne pounds of copper, four bunches of leads, eight dozen of hatchetts, five dozen of knives, four bunches of bells, one dozen of cizers, all not much more than 40s. English; as also from the said king's brother Iopassous, king of a place called Pastanzo, recovered an English boy, called Henry Spilman, who had lived amongst them one whole yeare, and despayring of ever seeing his native country, his father's howse, (for he was discended of a gentill family), or Christians any more; likewise here Captain Argoll found a myne of antimonye (which seldome goes unaccom-panyed with quicksilver), as also a kind of hevy black sand upon the bancks, which, being washed, weyed massy with lead.

The fifte river is called Pawtuxunt, and is of a lesse proportion then the rest, but the channell is sixteen or eighteen fathome deepe in some places; here are infinite sculls of divers kynds of fish more than elsewhere. Upon this river dwell the people called Acquintanacsuck, Pawtuxunt, and Matta-pament; two hundred men was the greatest strength that could be there perceaved by our discoveries, but they inhabite togither, and not so dispersed as the rest; these, of all other, were found the most civile to give entertainment, and therefore from them we receaved great curtesie and much good cheare.

Thirtye leagues norward is a river not inhab-ited, yet navigable, by reason of the red earth or clay resembling bolearmoniack; the discoverers called yt Bolus. At the end of the bay (where is six or seven miles in breadth) there fall into yt four small rivers, three of them yssuyng from divers boggs, envyroned with divers mountaines. Uppon the river inhabite a people called the Sas-quesahanougs; they are seated two dayes higher then was passage for the discoverers' barge; howbeyt, sixty of the Sasquesahanougs came to the discoverers with skynns, bowes, arrowes, targetts, swords, beades, and tobacco-pipes for presents. Such great and well-proportioned men are seldome seene, for they seemed like giants to the English,—yea, and to the neighbours,—yett seemed of an honest and simple disposicion, with much adoe restrayned from adoring the discov-erers as gods. These are the most straung people of all those countryes, both in language and attire; for their language yt may well beseeme their proportions, sounding from them as yt were a great voice in a vault or cave, as an eccoe; their attire is the skyns of beares and woulves; some have cassocks made of beares' hides and skyns, that a man's neck goeth through the skynn's neck, and the eares of the beare are fastened to his shoulders behind, the nose and teeth hanging downe his brest, and at the end of the nose hangs a bear's paw; the half sleeves cominge to the elboe were the necks of beares, and the armes through the mouth, with pawes hanging in a chaine for a jewell; his tobacco-pipe three quarters of a yard long, prittely carved with a bird, a deare, or with some such devise, at the great end, sufficient to beat out the braynes of an horse. Likewise their bowes, and arrowes, and clubbs, are sutable to their greatnes; these are scarse knowne to Powhatan. They can make well neare 600 able and mightie men, and are pallisadode in their townes to defend them from the Massawomecks, their mortall enemyes. Five of these chief Weroances came abourd the discoverers, and crossed the bay with them in their barge: the picture of the greatest of them is here portrayed the calf of whose leg was three quarters of a yard about, and all the rest of his lymes so answerable to that proportion, that he seemed the goodliest man they ever sawe; his haire the one syde was long, the other shorne close, with a ridge over his crowne like a coxcomb; his arrowes were five quarters long, headed with flints or splinters of stones, in forme like a heart, an ince broad, and an ynch and a half or more long; these he wore in a woolve's skyn on his back for his quiver, his bow in the one hand and his club in the other.

On the east side of the bay, is the river of Tockwough, and uppon yt a people that can make a hundred men, seated some seven miles within the river, where they have a fort very well pallisadode, and mantelled with the bark of trees; next to them are the Ozinies, with sixty men; more to the south of that east side of the bay, is the river of Kuscarawoak, upon which is seated a people with two hundred men; after that, is the river of Wicocomaco, and on it a people with one hundred men. The people of these rivers are of a little stature, and of another language from the rest, and very rude; but they on the river of Accohanock, with forty men, and they on the river of Accomack, with eighty men, doe equallize any of the territories of Powhatan, and speak his language, who, over all those, doth rule as kinge.

Southward, they went to some parts of Chawonock and the Mangoangs, to search them there left by Sir Walter Raleigh; which parts, to

the towne of Chesapeack, hath formerly bene discovered by Master Harriotts and Sir Ralph Lane. Amongst those people, are thus many severall nations, of sondry languages, which environ Powhatan's territories: the Chawonocks, the Mangoangs, the Monacans, the Mannacans, the Mannahocks, the Sasquesahanougs, the Acquanachuks, the Tockwoghes, and the Nuskarawaoks. Of all these, not any one understandeth another, but by interpreters; their severall habitations are more plainly described by the annexed mappe, set forth by Captain Smith, of whose paines taken herein, I leave to the censure of the reader to judge. Sure I am there will not returne from thence, in hast, any one who hath bene more industrious, or who hath had (Captain Geo. Percie excepted) greater experience amongst them, however misconstruction maye traduce here at home, where is not easily seene the mixed sufferaunces, both of body and mynd, which is there daylie, and with no few hazards and hearty griefes undergon.

The mappe will likewise present to the eye the way of the mountaynes, and current of the rivers, with their severall turnings, bayes, shoulders, isles, inletts, and creekes, the breadth of the waters, the distances of places, and such like. In which mappe, observe this, that, as far as you see the little crosses, either rivers, mountaines, or other places, have discovered; the rest was had by informacion of the salvadges, and are set downe accordinge to their instruccions.

Likewise, from the north point of our bay, which (as aforesaid) the Indians call Accowmack, and we Cape Charles, hath the coast all along bene discovered, even to the river of Sachadehoc; for Captain Argoll, in his returne from the search of the Bermudas, anno 1610, after he had lost Sir George Somers, 28 July, in a dangerous fogg, well beaten to and fro, fell with the mayne, standinge for Cape Cod, and made good, from 44 degrees, what Captayne Bartho. Gosnoll and Captayne Waymouth wanted in their discoveries, observing all along the coast, and drawing the plotts thereof, as he steered homewardes, unto our bay; and divers tymes went ashore, offering acquaintaunce and trade unto the people: and in the latitude of 39 discovered another goodly bay, into which fell many tayles of faire and large rivers, and which might make promise of some westerly passage; the cape whereof, in 38½, he called Cape

Lawar, from which, not far off, lay a faier banck into the sea, as upon the Newfoundland, where he hawled excellent fish, both hollibut, cod, and ling, of which he brought an essay and tast of two hundred couple into the colony; an excellent fish, and of such a kind that will keepe a whole yeare in shipp's hold, with little care, a triall whereof his lordshippe likewise brought with him into England; and uppon the shoares, in divers places, he killed great store of seales.

Concerninge the falling with our owne coast, yt is true that there cannot be a bolder shoare to come in, withall, in any country in the world; for, first, before we come in sight of yt thirty leagues, we smell a sweet savour, as is usually from off Cape Vincent, the south cape of Spayne (if the wynd come from the shoare); besides, we have chaunge of water, and sounding at twenty-five fathoms, twenty leagues off.

The coast of South Virginia, from Cape Henry, lieth south and north, next hand some seven leagues, where there goeth in a river (as is neerest gessed by the Chawonocks and Mangoangs), but it is not navigable far; all along this coast, for seven leagues, we have seven and eight fathome of water, within one league of the shoare, one not farre. More to the southward of this in-lett river, is a cape of an island called Croatoan, which cape is that which we call the South Cape of Virginia; beyond which cape, so-ward and no-west of this cape, or Croatoan, lye certayne smale islands (as before remembred), that front the coast of the mayne; but the sea betweene the mayne and them, is not for any shipping to passe. Into this shallow sea, there falls divers rivers from the mayne, which the salvadges have discribed unto us, and plentye of people thereon.

If we come in with the Chesapeak Bay open, our soundings are fifteene fathome to five; but if we hit the channell, we have no lesse than seven or eight fathome; soe yt is all over bold inough, having neither ledges of rocks, no barres, no sandy shelfes, but the bottom even and plaine.

Our two capes, Cape Henry and Cape Charles, doe lye no-east and by east, and so-west; and they be distant each from other, in breadth (where the sea runs in betweene both lands, so making our bay, and only entrance into our country), as broad as may be betweene Quinborowgh and Lee.

When we come in with Cape Henry, we have six, seven, and eight fathome, to the point at the bottome of the bay and mouthe of King's River, into which all shippes that will enter, must borrowe soe much of the shoare, as to come within little lesse then musquett shott of the point, by reason of the showldes lying uppon the sotherne shoare; by which may be observed howe convenient and necessary a pointe that is for a substanciall fortificacion to be raised, to secure all the other forts and townes upon this river from what enemies soever.

824. William Strachey's description of the commodities of Virginia.

10
Of the commodities of the country,—fruicts, trees, beasts, fowle, fish, perle, copper, and mines.

That yt may yet further appeare howe this country is not so naked of commoditie nor wretched of provision fitt for the sustenance of mankind, as some ygnorantly ymagine, and others have falcely reported, I will in this chapter propose (for the testimonie of the truith thereof I may appeale to many hundreds, which may convince), the relation of a discourse only for forme or assentacion delivered; nor lett any man suppose that materialls of so good a navie as maie be there framed for planckes, masts, pitch, and tarre, soapashes, turpentine, iron, cordage, mulberry trees for silke, and another kind of silke of the grasse, saxafras, and other aromaticall druggs, gums, oyle, and dyes are of noe value, or not worthy the exposure of a colonie for secondarie and politique endes to be established there, since Muscovia and Polonia doe yearlie receave manie thowsandes for pitch, tarre, sopeashes, grain, flax, cordage, sturgeon, masts, yardes, waynscot, firrs, glasse, and such like; also Swethland receaves much from us for iron and copper; France, in like manner, for wyne, canvass, and salt; Spayne as much for iron, steele, figgs, raysons, and sacks; Italy for silks and velvetts, consumes our chief commodities; Holland maynteynes yt self by fishing and trading at our own dores. All these temporize with others for necessity, but all as uncertaine as peace and warre; besides the charge, travell, and daunger in transporting them by seas, lands, stormes, and pyratts. Then how much may Virginia have the prerogative for the benefitt of our land, when as within one hundred miles all these are to be had either readie provided by nature, or ells to be prepared, were there but industrious men to labour; so as, then, here is a place, a nurse for soldiers, a practize for marriners, a trade for marchants, a reward for the good, and, that which is most of all, a busines most acceptable to God, to bring poore infidells to his knowledge; and, albeit, our shipps (some will object) now returning from thence yearly, come freighted home only, yet with certaine pretious woods; yt is to be remembered how that from Hispaniola, Cuba, and Portrico the Spaniards, in their yearely daies of possessing the Indies, made returnes a long tyme of the like, as of cassia, fistula, ebony, guacum, lignum vitæ, etc., untill they found out the mynes, as may wee, we doubt nothing, in the heart and bosome of ours when we shalbe enabled truly to dissect yt, fynding such appearances now in the suburbs of yt, as yt were, the which to tyme, the true revealer of great thinges, I submit, or rather to Him from whom, if our unthankfulness deprive us not of the blessing, we may expect a prosperous and assured compensacion and satisfaccion to wipe of all skores, *et in assem satisfacere*, all the chardges and disbursements which have hitherto gone out for yt; albeit, such is the busines, as yt should awake all charitable Christians to follow yt according to the goodness of the cause, and not according to the greatnes of profitt and commodities. Lett Mammon perish with his gold, that hath no other but such stubble meerely to enkindle the flame of his zeale unto so holie a worke.

The natives have here a kinde of wheat which they call poketawes, as the West Indians call the same maiz. The forme of yt is of a man's tooth, somewhat thicker; for the preparing of the ground for which, they use this manner:—they bruise the barke of those trees which they will take awaie neere the roote, then do they scorch the rootes with fier, that they grow no more; the next yeare, with a crooked piece of wood, they beat up those trees by the rootes, and in their mowldes they plant their corne: the manner is

thus, they make a hole in the earth with a stick, and into yt they put three or five graines of wheat, and one or three of beanes: these holes they make four or five foot one from another, for the corne being set close together, one stalke would choakells the growth of another, and so render both unprofitable. Their women and children do contynually keepe the ground with weeding, and when the corne is growne middle high, they hill yt about like a hoppeyard, and the stalke will growe a man's height, or rather more, from the ground, and every stalke commonly beareth twoo eares, some three, manie but one, and some none. Every eare groweth with a great hose or pill about yt and above yt; the stalke being greene hath a sweet juyce in yt, somewhat like a sugar-cane, which is the cause that when they gather the corne greene, they suck the stalkes, for as we gather greene peas, so do they, their corne being greene, which excelleth their old.

Peas they have, which the natives call assentemmens, and are the same which in Italy they call fagioli.

Their beanes are little like a French beane, and are the same which the Turks call garvances, and these kind of pulse they much esteeme for daynties.

By their dwellings are some great mulberrye trees, and these in some parte of the country are found growing naturally in pretty groves: there was an assay made to make silke, and surely the wormes prospered excellently well untill the master workeman fell sick, during which tyme they were eaten with ratts, and this wilbe a commoditie not meanely profitable. Now yt is seriously considered of, and order taken that yt shalbe duly followed.

In some places we fynd chestnutts, whose wild fruict I maie well saie equallize the best in Fraunce, Spaine, Germany, Italy, or those so commended in the Black sea, by Constantinople, of all which I have eaten.

They have a small fruict growing in little trees, husked like a chestnut, but the fruict most like a very small acron, this they call chechniquamins, and these, with chesnutts, they boile four or five houres, of which they make both broth and bread, for their chief men, or at their greatest feasts.

They have cherries much like a damoizin, but for their tast and cullour we called them cherries; and a plomb there is, somwhat fairer then a cherrie, of the same relish, then which are seldome a better eaten.

They have a berry much like our goose-berries in greatness, cullour, and tast, these they call rawcomenes, and they doe eate them rawe or boyled.

In the watry valleis groweth a berry which they call ocoughtanamins, very much like unto capers; these they gather and dry in the heat of the sun, and when they will eate them, they boyle them nere halfe a daie, for otherwise they differ not much from poison.

Nattourne groweth as our bents doe in meadowes, the seed is not much unlike to rie, though much smaller; these they use for a deyntie bread, buttered with deare's suett.

They have a plomb which they call pessemmins, like to a medler, in England, but of a deeper tawnie cullour; they grow on a most high tree. When they are not fully ripe, they are harsh and choakie, and furre in a man's mouth like allam, howbeit, being taken fully ripe, yt is a reasonable pleasant fruict, somewhat lushious. I have seene our people put them into their baked and sodden puddings; there be whose tast allowes them to be as pretious as the English apricock; I confesse it is a good kind of horse plomb.

Here is a cherry-redd fruict both within and without (as I have seene the like in the Bermudas), which wee call the prickle peare; in the Indies they are well knowne to every common marryner; they beare a broad, thick, spungeous leafe, full of kernells; they be like unto the pomegranet; the tast of this peare is verie pleasant, and the juyce cold and fresh, like the water in the West Indian nut called cocus; the juyce is sharpe and penetrable like deale-wyne, prescribed powerfull against the stone.

Here is a fruict by the naturalls called a maracock; this groweth generally low, and creepeth in a manner amongst the corne (albeit I have seene yt, planted in a gardein within our fort, at James Towne, to spred and rise as high as the pale); yt is of the bignes of a queen apple, and hath manie azurine or blew karnells, like as a pomegranet, and yt bloometh a most sweet and delicate flower, and yt is a good sommer cooling fruict, and in every field where the Indians plant their corne be cart-loads of them.

The macokos is of the forme of our pumpeons,—I must confesse, nothing so good,—

'tis of a more waterish tast; the inhabitants seeth a kind of million, which they put into their walnut-milke, and so make a kynd of toothsome meat.

In Aprill, Maie, and June, are great store of strawberries, raspices, hurts, etc., and many hearbs in the spring time are comonly dispersed throughout the woodes, good for broathes and sallotts, as violetts, purselin, sorrell, and roses, in their season, etc., besides many we used whose names we knowe not.

It would easilie raise a well-stayed judgement into wonder (as Sir Thomas Dale hath writt sometimes unto his majesty's counsell here for Virginia to behold the goodly vines burthening every neighbour bush, and clymbing the toppes of highest trees, and those full of clusters of grapes in their kind, however dreeped and shadowed soever from the sun, and though never pruned or manured. I dare saie yt, that we have eaten there, as full and lushious a grape as in the villages betweene Paris and Amiens, and I have drunck often of the rathe wine, which Doctor Bohune and other of our people have made full as good, as your French British wyne.

Twenty gallons at a tyme have bene sometimes made without any other helpe then by crushing the grape with the hand, which letting to settle five or six daies, hath, in the drawing forth, proved strong and headdy. Unto what perfection might not these be brought by the art and industry of manie skilfull *vineroones*, being thus naturally good? And how materiall and principall a commoditie this maie prove, either for the benefitt of such who shall inhabit there, or to be returned over hither (especially where we maie have pipe staves to make our casks of, so cheape, and at hand), I preferre yt to indifferent judgements.

Many rootes the Indians have here likewise for food. The chief they call tockowhough and yt groweth like a flag in low muddy freshes; in one day a salvadge will gather sufficient for a weeke: these rootes are much of the greatnes and tast of potatoes. They use to rake up a great nomber of them in old leaves and ferne, and then cover all with earth or sand, in the manner of a coal-pit; on each side they contynue a great fier a daie and a night before they dare eate yt: rawe, yt is no better then poison, and being roasted (except yt be tender and the heat abated, or sliced and dryed in the sun, mixed with sorrell and meale, or such like), yt will prickle and torment the throat extreamely, and yet in sommer they use this ordinarily for bread.

They have another roote which they call vighsacan; as the other feedeth the bodie, so this cureth their hurts and diseases, yt is a smale roote, which they bruise and applie to the wound.

Pocones is a small roote that groweth in the mountaines, which, being dried and beat into powlder, turneth red, and this they use for swellings, aches, annoynting their joynts, paynting their heads and garments with yt, for which they accompt yt very pretious and of much worth.

Musquaspenne is a root of the bignes of a finger, and as red as blood; in drying, it will wither almost to nothing: with this they use to paynt their matts, targetts, and such like.

There is here great store of tobacco, which the salvages call apooke; howbeit yt is not of the best kynd, yt is but poore and weake, and of a byting tast, yt growes not fully a yard above ground, bearing a little yellowe flower, like to hennebane, the leaves are short and thick, somewhat round at the upper end; whereas the best tobacco of Trynidado and the Oronoque is large, sharpe, and growing two or three yardes from the ground, bearing a flower of the bredth of our bellflowers in England: the salvages here dry the leaves of this apooke over the fier, and sometymes in the sun, and crumble yt into poulder, stalks, leaves, and all, taking the same in pipes of earth, which very ingeniously they can make. We observe that those Indians which have one, twoo, or more women, take much,—but such as yet have no appropriate woman take little or none at all.

Here is also pellitory of Spaine, and divers other symples, which our appothecaries have geathered and found to be good and medicinable.

In the low marishes grow plotts of onions conteyning an acre of ground or more in manie places, but they are small, like the chiballs, or schallions, not past the bignes of the toppe of one's thumb: they eate well sod or otherwise in sallet or in bakt meats. Our people find good and wholsome relish in them; howbeit the inhabitants cannot abyde to eate of them; and these onions doe for the most part appeare in the last season of the yeare, for yt is to be understood how the Indians devide the yeare into five seasons,—the winter, which they call popanow, the spring, cattapeuk, the sommer, cohattayough, the earing of their corne,

nepenough, the harvest and fall of the leafe, taquitock.

They have divers beasts fitt for provision; the chief are deare, both redd and fallow; great store in the country towards the heads of the rivers, though not so many amongst the rivers. In our island, about James Towne, are some few nothing differing from ours in England, but that of some of them the antletts of their hornes are not so manie. Our people have seene two hundred, one hundred, and fifty in a herd.

There is a beast they call arocoune, much like a badger, tayled like a fox, and of a mingle black and grayish cullour, and which useth to live on trees, as squirrels doe. Excellent meate we kill often of them: the greatest nomber yet we obteyne by trade.

Squirrells they have, and those in great plentie; are very good meat; some are as great as our smallest sort of wild rabbitts, some blackish, or black and white, like those which here are called silver hayred; but the most are grey.

A small beast they have which the Indians call assapanick, not passing so big as a ratt, but we call them flying squirrells, because, spreading their leggs, from whence to either shoulder runs a flappe, or fynne, much like a batt's wing, and so stretching the largeness of their skyns, they have bene seene to make a pretty flight from one tree to another, sometymes thirty or forty yardes.

An opussum is a beast as big as a pretty beagle, of grey cullour; yt hath a head like a swyne; eares, feet, and tayle like a ratt; she carries her young ones under her belly, in a piece of her owne skyn, like as in a bagg, which she can open and shutt, to lett them out or take them in, as she pleaseth, and doth therein lodge, carry, and suckle her young, and eates in tast like a pig.

Muscascus is a beast black in cullour, proportioned like a water ratt; he hath a cod within him, which yieldeth a strong sent, like unto musk; yt is a good meat if the cod be taken out, otherwise the flesh will tast most strong and ranck of the musk; so will the broath wherein yt is sod.

Hares they have some few about James Towne; but both in the islands and mayne, up at the falls, and below about Fort Henry and Charles Fort, great store; howbeit they are no bigger than our conies.

Beares there be manie towards the sea-coast, which the Indians hunt most greedily; for indeed they love them above all other their flesh, and therefore hardly sell any of them unto us, unles upon large proffers of copper, beads, and hatchetts. We have eaten of them, and they are very toothsoome sweet venison, as good to be eaten as the flesh of a calfe of two yeares old; howbeit they are very little in comparison of those of Muscovia and Tartaria.

The beaver there is as big as an ordinary water dog, but his leggs exceeding short; his forefeet like a doggs, his hinder like a swannes, his tayle somewhat like the forme of a rackett, bare, without haire, which, to eate, the salvages esteeme a great delicate.

Otters there be manie, which, as the bevers, the Indians take with gynns and snares, and esteeme the skynns great ornaments; and of all these beasts they use to feed when they catch them.

Lyons I will not posetively affirme that the country hath, since our people never yet saw any; howbeit, in their discoveryes to the Mangoagues, they did light once upon twoo skynns, which, by all the judgements in the fort, were supposed to be lyons' skinnes; and this last yeare, myself being at the falls with Sir Thomas Dale, I found in an Indian howse certaine clawes tyed up in a string, which I brought awaie, and into England, and they are assured unto me to be lyons clawes.

There is also a beast, which the Indians call votchumquoyes, in the forme of a wild catt.

Their foxes are like our silver-hayred conies, of a small proporcion, and not smelling so ranck like those in England.

The doggs of the country are like their woulves, and cannot barke, but howle, and are not unlike those auncyent doggs called cracutæ, which were said to be engendred of a wolfe and a bitch, and are like the Turkish jackalls, keeping about the graves of the dead, in the common poliandrium or place of sepulture.

Their woulves are not much bigger then our English foxes.

Martins, polecatts, weesells, and monkeys we knowe they have, because we have seene many of their skynns, though very seldome any of them alive; but one thing is worth the observing,—we could never perceave that their flies, serpents, or other vermyn, were any waie pernitious,—when, in the south part of America, they are alwaies dangerous, and often deadly.

Likewise, as they have fruicts and beasts, so have they fowle, and that great store. Of birdes,

the eagle is the greatest devourer, and many of them there: there be divers sortes of hawkes, sparhawkes, laneretts, goshawkes, falcons, and ospreys; I brought home from thence this yeare myself a falcon, and a tassell, the one sent by Sir Thomas Dale up his highnes the Prince, and the other was presented to the Earle of Salsburye, faire ones. What the prowf of them maie be, I have not learned, they prey most upon fish.

Turkeys there be great store, wild in the woods, like phesents in England, forty in a company, as big as our tame bere, and yt is an excellent fowle, and so passing good meate as I maye well saie, yt is the best of any kind of flesh which I have ever yet eaten there.

Partridges there are little bigger then our quailes! I have knowne of our men to have killed them with their small shott, sometime from off a tree five or six at a shoot.

Cranes, white and grey; herons, both grey and white woosells, or black byrds, with redd showlders; thrushes, and divers sorts of small byrdes, some carnation, some blew, and some other straunge kyndes, to us unknowne by name.

In winter there are great store of swannes, geese, brants, duck, widgeon, dottrell, oxeyes, mallard, teale, sheldrakes, and divers diving fowles, and of all these sortes, that aboundance, as I dare avowe yt, no country in the world may have more.

Parakitoes I have seene manie in the winter, and knowne divers killed, yet be they a fowle most swift of wing, their winges and breasts are of a greenish cullour, with forked tayles, their heades, some crymsen, some yellowe, some orange-tawny, very beautifull. Some of our colonie who have seene of the East Indian parratts, affirme how they are like to that kynd, which hath given us somewhat the more hope of the nerenes of the South Sea, these parratts, by all probability, like enough to come from some of the countryes upon that sea.

A kind of wood-pidgeon we see in the winter time, and of them such nombers, as I should drawe (from our homelings here, such who have seene, peradventure, scarce one more then in the markett) the creditt of my relation concerning all the other in question, yf I should expresse what extended flocks, and how manie thousands in one flock, I have seene in one daie, wondering (I must confesse) at their flight, when, like so many thickned clowdes, they (having fed to the norward in the daye tyme) retourne againe more sowardly towards night to their roust; but there be manie hundred witnesses, who maie convince this my report, yf herein yt testifieth an untruth.

To the naturall commodities which the countrye hath of fruicts, beasts, and fowle, we maie also adde the no meane commoditie of fish, of which, in March and Aprill, are great shoells of herrings.

Sturgeon, great store, commonlie in Maie if the yeare be forward. I have beene at the taking of some before Algernoone fort, and in Southampton river, in the middst of March, and they remaine with us June, July, and August, and in that plenty as before expressed in the chapter.

Shaddes, great store, of a yard long, and for sweetnes and fatnes a reasonable good fish, he is only full of small bones, like our barbells in England.

Grampus, porpois, seales, stingraies, bretts, mulletts, white salmons, troute, soles, playse, comfish, rockfish, eeles, lampreys, cat-fish, perch of three sorts, shrimps, crefishes, cockles, mushells, and more such like, like needles to name, all good fish.

There is the garfish, some of which are a yard long, small and round like an eele, and as big as a man's legg, having a long snout full of sharp teeth.

Oysters there be in whole bancks and bedds, and those of the best: I have seene some thirteen inches long. The salvages use to boyle oysters and mussells togither, and with the broath they make a good spoone meat, thickned with the flower of their wheat; and yt is a great thrift and husbandry with them to hang the oysters upon strings (being shauld and dried) in the smoake, thereby to preserve them all the yeare.

There be twoo sorts of sea crabbs, and the one our people call a king crabb, and they are taken in shoall waters from off the shoare a dozen at a tyme hanging one upon another's taile; they are of a foote in length and half a foote in bredth, havinge manie leggs and a long tayle; the Indians seldome eate of this kind.

There is a kind of shelfish of the proporcion of a cockle, but far greater, yt hath a smooth shell, not ragged as our cockles; 'tis good meat, though somwhat tough.

Tortoyses here (such as in the Bermudas) I have seene about the entrance of our bay, but we have not taken of them, but of the land tortoyses we take and eate dailie; the difference betweene which is nothing in shape, but in cullour and bignes, those of the land are gray with a long tayle, those of the sea have black shells, speckled with yellowe, the bodyes great in compasse like a targett.

But the most straung fish is a small one, so like the picture of St. George's dragon as possible can be, except the leggs and winges, and the toad fish, which will swell till yt be like to burst when yt cometh into the ayre.

Thus yt appeareth, that this country affordeth manie excellent vegitables and living creatures; yet, I must saie true, of grasse, for the present, there is little or none but what groweth in low marshes, for all the country is overshadowed with trees, whose droppings contynually turneth grasse to weedes by reason of the rancknes of the grownd, which would soone be amended by good husbandry.

Howbeit, woodes yt hath, great, beautifull, fruictfull, pleasant, and profitable, the grounds cleane under them, at least passeable both for horse and foote. The oake here, for stature and tymber, may compare with any, being so tall and streight, that they will beare [ ] square of good tymber for twenty yardes long; of this wood there is twoo or three severall kyndes, the acrons of one kind, whose barke is more white then the other, is somewhat sweetish, which, being boyled halfe a daie in severall waters, at last affordes a sweet oyle, which they call monohominy: they keepe yt in gourdes to annoint their heads and joynts; the fruict they eate made in bread or otherwise.

There is also elme and ash, of which are made sopeashes. Yf the trees be very great, the ashes wilbe verry good, and melt to hard lumps being carefully burned; but if they be small, and suffered to partake too much of the smoak, they wilbe but powder, nothing so good as the other, besyde they wilbe very fowle and black.

Of walnutts there be three kindes, the black walnutt which is returned home yearly by all shipping from thence, and yields good profitt, for yt is well bought up to make waynscott tables, cubbardes, chaires, and stooles, of a delicate grayne and cullour like ebonie, and not subject to the worme: the fruict of this is little, yt is thinne shelled, and the karnell bitter. Annother kynd there is, which beares a great fruict, with a hard shell, and the meat very sweet, and of these the

Indians make oyle to droppe their joynts and smeere their bodies with, which do make them supple and nymble. The third sort is, as this last, exceeding hard shelled, and hath a passing sweet karnell; this last kind the Indians beat into pieces with stones, and putting them, shells and all, into morters, mingling water with them, with long woodden pestells pound them so long togither untill they make a kind of mylke, or oylie liquor, which they call powcohicora.

There is a kynd of wood which we call cypres because both the wood, the fruict, and leafe, did most resemble yt; and of these trees there are some neere three fathome about at the root very streight, and fifty, sixty, or eighty foote without a braunch.

The cedars, for savour and cullor, maie compare with those of Lybanon, the clymate of the one and the other differing little.

Of saxafras there is plenty enough, the rootes whereof, not monie yeares since, were sold for twenty shillings per lb. and better, and if order maie yet be taken that overmuch quantety be not returned, and that which shalbe brought be kept in one hand, all Europe maie be served thereof at good rates. The cedars and saxafras yeild a kynd of gomme in a small proporcion of themselves; there have bene conclusions tryed to extract yt out of the wood, but nature affourded greater quantety then art could produce.

There are pines infinite, especially by the sea coast, and manie other sortes, the use of which are commodious for shipping, pipe-staves, clapbourd, yardes and masts for shipping, and those here are so faire and large, as a ship of three-hundred tonne burthen, called the Starre (sent thither the last yeare upon purpose fitted and prepared with scupper-holes to take in masts), was not able to stowe forty of the fower score, unles they should have cut them shorter, which is a commoditie, rightly understood, of such moment for this kingdome (all the easterly countryes from whence we have hitherto had them, so ympoverished and wasted as they are not able to furnish his majesty's navie, witnes how hardly were obteyned those which we had last from thence, and those upon his majesty's private and particular letter to the king of Denmark) as were ynough (yt may be boldly sayd) to make good the whole charge of our plantation.

By the dwellings of the salvages are bay-trees, wild roses, and a kynd of low tree, which beares a cod like to the peas, but nothing so big: we take yt to be locust.

Crabb trees there be, but the fruict small and bitter, howbeit, being graffed upon, soone might we have of our owne apples of any kind, peares, and what ells.

Besides these fruict-trees, there is a white poplar, and another tree like unto yt, that yieldeth a verye cleere and odoriferous gumme like turpentine, which I have heard Doctor Bohune, and some of our surgeons there, saie, maie well be reckoned a kynd of balsome, and will heale any greene wound.

There groweth in the island of James Towne a small tree, of leaves, armes, and fruict, like the mirtle tree, the fruict thereof hath a tast with the mirtle, but much more bynding; these trees growe in great plentie, round about a standing pond of fresh water in the middle of the island, the pill or rind whereof is of a great force against inveterate dissentericall fluxes, of which Doctor Bohune made open experiment in manie of our men labouring with such diseases, and therefore wisheth all such phisitians as shall goe thither to make use thereof.

For mineralls we will promise nothing; but the hope of which, seeing the low grownd, yieldes manie faire shewes; the mountaines cannot be doubted but that in them manie sortes will be found: and our people, in their first discovery into the Monocan country discovered two mynes, the one within six miles of the head of the falls, which takes the name of Namantack, the fynder of yt: which is conceaved wilbe worth the exploring, and with little charge; the other lyes in the mydwaie betweene twoo townes of Monocan, the neerest called Mowhemincke, the furthest, Massinnacock, distant one from another fourteen miles, of whose goodnes there is no doubt, since the sparre only taken no further then two or three foote into the earth affourdes mettall worth the labour. And concerning a silver-myne, not far from the same place, an Helvetian, one William Henrick Faldoe, assured our Lord Generall, and therefore made his provision for the search thereof; and having bene in England, made earnest suit unto our threasourer and his Majestie's counsaile resident for Virginia, with whome he contracted, and entred into condicions for one yeare and a halfe for the full performaunce of this worke; but his lordship being not at that time enabled with sufficient companie to make good that search, by raising forts and planting so far into the country (which only must have secured the workemen), yt hath pleased God, since that tyme, that the said Helvetian hath died of a burning fever, and with him the knowledge of that myne, which, in his life-time, he would not be drawn to reveyle unto any one ells of the colonie: and there is extant an old plott, which his Lordship hath shewed me, wherein, by a Portugall, our seat is layd out, and in the same, two silver mynes pricked downe; and at the head of the said falls, the Indians there inhabiting tip their arrowes with cristall, and we fynd manie pieces scattered in the gritt and sand of the same, where, likewise, on Pembrook side, Sir Thomas Dale hath mentioned, in his lettres to the lordships of the Counsaile, of a goodlie iron myne; and Captain Newport hath brought home of that mettell so sufficient a triall, as there hath bene made sixteen or seventeen tonne of iron so good, as the East Indian marchants bought yt of the Virginian Companie, preferring yt before any other iron of what country soever; and for copper, the hills to the norwest have that store, as the people themselves, remembred in the first chapter, called the Bocootauwanaukes, are said to part the solide mettall from the stone without fire, bellowes, or additamant, and beat it into plates, the like whereof is hardly found in any other parte of the world: likewise Captain Argoll (as his Lordship beares record in his printed narration), in the river Potawomeck, found a myne of antimony, which, as aforesaid, never dwells single, but holds assured legue with quicksilver, as likewise a myne of lead; and we heare the Indians make manie particular discriptions of allam mynes to the southward.

Lastly, that the lakes have perles yt cannot be doubted, for we ourselves have seen manie chaynes and braceletts worne by the people, and wee have found plentie of them in the sepulchres of their kings, though discoloured by burning the oysters in the fier, and deformed by the grosse boring. And thus (to conclude), we maie well saie how these poore people have manie morrall goodes, such as are by accidens plentifull ynough amongst them: and as much (poore sowles) as they come short of those bona moralia which are per se, for the countrie (who sees not by what hath bene sayd?) is not so barren, ill destyned, and wretched, under an unhappy constellation, but that yt hath (even beside necessary helpes and commodities for life) apparent proufes of many naturall riches, and which are all bona fortunæ. Again, they are healthie, which is bonum corporis: nor is nature a stepdame unto them concerninge their aptas membrorum compositiones; only (God wot) I must graunt, that bonum morale, as aforesaid, which is per se, they have not in medio, which is in virtute: and then, how can they ever obtayne yt in ultimo, which is in fælicitate? To teach them both, which is the end of our planting amongst them; to lett them knowe what vertue and goodnes is, and the reward of both; to teach them religion, and the crowne of the righteous; to acquaint them with grace, that they maie participate with glorie; which God graunt in mercye unto them.

XXIV

Spain in the Southwest, 1580–1612

DURING THE THIRTY YEARS between 1580 and 1612 Spain revived her interest both in the coastlands and in the interior which lay to the north of Mexico proper. The results, so far as the coast was concerned, were mainly cartographical: Cermeño and Vizcaíno established not only the general outline of the coast well into the forties of north latitude, but also identified a number of important harbors, notably Monterey (but also San Diego) which could be used in emergency by the returning Manila Galleon. This new knowledge, strangely enough, was not sufficient to prevent the European professional cartographers from turning California into a great island, which comprised Alta as well as Baja California on many maps. This is probably a tribute to the degree of secrecy maintained by Spain about her actual discoveries.

The situation on land was rather different. The expeditions of Chamuscado, Espejo, and Castaña de Sosa were amateur forays into the north from the mining area of north Mexico. Fed on misty tales left over from Marcos de Niza and Coronado, they again brought Spain into New Mexico in spite of official policy to leave it alone. They then inspired an official *entrada* under Juan de Oñate, but nearly a decade of effort on his part achieved few of his anticipations and led to the establishment of no effective colony. After 1605 it appeared that the whole area would again be abandoned, but one new consideration saved it—the existence of a Christian population (exaggerated by the Franciscan friars) in New Mexico. Finally, in 1609 Peralta was given the task of at last turning New Mexico into a mission province with a minimum military presence. This was to be the limit of Spanish enterprise in the West until the end of the seventeenth century. But it was to be a seed from which in the end a widely dispersed Spanish empire in western North America was to grow.

Spanish interest in the lands to the north of Mexico waned during the fifty years after the return of Coronado and Cabrillo (see volume I). The government officials attempted to concentrate the efforts of the settlers into consolidating Spanish power in the lands already colonized. This was coupled with a new attitude toward exploration itself which laid emphasis on the rights and spiritual welfare of the Indians and which forbade by law adventurers from going north in search of fame and fortune. At the same time a new area for exploration and personal glory had been opened up by the discovery of the Philippines in 1542–1543.

However, the adventurous spirit could not be dimmed completely. In 1564 an expedition under Miguel López de Legaspi left Mexico to undertake the subjugation of the Philippines. After this had been achieved, it was realized that the only practical way to supply the new colony was from Mexico, which heralded the beginning of a regular trade by means of the annual Manila Galleon. But contrary winds and currents made the return voyage to America difficult. This led to a discussion as to the most suitable route. The first vessels sent back by Legaspi under the general control of Andrés de Urdaneta, sailed northeast to the Californian coast at about 27° N and then turned south. The agreement that this was the most likely route, coupled with the need to find a safe harbor for returning ships to use for shelter and repairs, revived interest in the shores of California, an interest which was increased by a sudden foreign threat to Spanish dominance in the area. In the summer of 1579 Sir Francis Drake was on the coast repairing the *Golden Hind*, which was leaking badly after his exploits against Spain in South America. The exact location of his landfall has not yet been decided; it could either have been Drakes Bay or San Francisco Bay (see volume I). Encouraged by this event, Viceroy Contreras made plans to explore the northwest coast. In 1584 Francisco Gualle, while en route from Macao to Mexico, sailed along the Californian coast southwards from about 37½° N. Two years later Gualle was commissioned to go to the Philippines, to return by way of California, and to search for a suitable harbor and for two islands in the Pacific which, according to persistent legend, would yield fabulous wealth. Gualle died in Manila and was succeeded by Pedro de Unamuno who brought the ship back to Mexico. Not surprisingly he failed to discover the islands but he did land on the coast at 36½° N in the vicinity of Morro Bay and explored inland, encountering hostile Indians. However, the search for a safe harbor was little advanced by this voyage and under a new viceroy, Villamanrique, who was not in favor of the exploration plans, it was soon forgotten, receiving no mention in the records of the later explorers, although Unamuno's experiences with the Indians were remembered and twenty years later Vizcaíno was ordered not to go inland.

Exploration of the California coast was revived in the next decade by Viceroy Velasco who was deeply worried about the dangers inherent in the return journey from the Philippines since the English threat reappeared in the guise of Thomas Cavendish who attacked and plundered one of the homecoming galleons in 1587. Velasco saw the need for a lengthy reconnaissance to be made from Mexico rather than as an afterthought of the voyage from the Philippines, but he was hampered by lack of money. Such a voyage was not made until 1595 when Sebastian Cermeño, a Portuguese sailor, was sent from Manila. He explored the coast in the vicinity of 40° N and visited Monterey, San Francisco Bay, and Drakes Bay where his vessel was driven ashore and wrecked. The launch was sent back to Acapulco with some of the men while the others made their way back overland through northern Mexico. Simultaneous with the dispatch of Cermeño, Velasco commissioned Sebastián Vizcaino, who had traded for several years between Mexico and the East, to explore the Gulf of California and establish settlements in the peninsula. Although this project failed, the expedition to the Gulf aroused royal interest and resulted in the order of September, 1599, for the exploration of the northern Californian coast from Mexico. Vizcaíno was appointed to lead the venture. He was to examine the coast in detail and to make soundings in the ports. All this information was to be incorporated into a map. Strict curbs were placed on his personal power by a council which he was forced to consult. In 1602 he set out with three ships visiting San Diego Bay, Monterey Bay, and Drakes Bay, although he missed San Francisco Bay. One of the vessels managed to reach as far north as 43° before they were all driven back by bad weather and illness. On their return, the sailors who had gone farthest north, erroneously maintained they had found a great river and bay at 41° N, just south of Cape Mendoçino. It was assumed that this connected with the Strait of Anian and the Gulf of California, and this notion soon appeared on the maps, making California into an island. For Vizcaíno the most important event of the whole expedition was the discovery of Monterey Bay, and he wrote to the king and the viceroy exaggerating its advantages and urging the creation of a settlement there. In January, 1606, the Council in Spain agreed that Monterey was in a convenient position for ships returning from the Philippines and recommended that a voyage under Vizcaíno should be made to the islands in 1607, calling in at Monterey on the way home. However, the new viceroy, Montesclaros, believed that Monterey was too far north and off the route of the returning galleons. He was also worried about possible English interference in such an isolated colony. He turned his attention to the two mythical islands that Unamuno had failed to find in 1587. In 1698 Vizcaíno was ordered to search for them. Once again the possibility of a great fortune in gold and silver turned the Spaniards away from more practical considerations. Opinions on the area, with the exception of Vizcaíno's rapture over Monterey, were generally unfavorable. The Indians were not numerous or well advanced, merely very unfriendly. The coastal areas seemed unsuitable for colonization, and none of the explorers went far enough inland to see the agricultural possibilities of the valleys. The idea of the settlement of California was therefore abandoned and was not achieved for a further 150 years when Monterey did become the capital. However, between 1587 and 1603 a fairly thorough examination of the California coast had been made as far north as Point Reyes, and several notable landmarks had been examined and appeared in European maps for the first time.

The last two decades of the sixteenth century also saw a revival of interest in the exploration of the area discovered by Coronado. Since his return in 1542, much of northern Mexico had been explored, the Indians conquered, and missions and settlements established. In 1567 Santa Bárbara was founded in the Conchos Valley, and by 1580 the settled frontier had reached the head of the river. It was this stream that furnished the new avenue northwards. The military frontier had progressed even further, and the desire to explore the more distant regions was rekindled by new reports of the Pueblo Indians heard by soldiers going north in pursuit of marauding natives. These rumors attracted the attention of Fray Augustín Ruiz (or Rod-ríguez), a Franciscan father working at a convent near Santa Bárbara, who desired to go north to convert the Indians. Apparently, he easily obtained the permission of the viceroy, Mendoza, since the new official policy was to encourage priests and friars in the effort to discover new lands rather than to rely on the dubious motives of the fortune hunters. Thus Father Ruiz became the religious head of an expedition that headed north in June, 1581, completely unaware of the achievements of Coronado. For the protection of the three friars, Ruiz was given a military escort led by Francisco Chamuscado. Although the description of the route taken by the expedition is often vague and confusing, it is certain that the men went along the Conchos-Rio Grande River system into New Mexico and visited most of the pueblos found by Coronado except those to the northwest in Arizona. They also went east across the Pecos River to the Canadian River and the Buffalo Plains. The party returned to Santa Bárbara in April, 1582, but without Chamuscado who had died on the way and the three friars, one of whom had been killed by the Indians. The other two had elected to stay alone to carry out their work of conversion at the mission they had founded on the Rio Grande above the site of Albuquerque. The news brought back by the party, who told of civilized, settled Indians, great herds of buffalo, and hinted at the possibility of great riches, caused great excitement on the frontier and resulted in a scramble for the honor to lead the next expedition. This turned out to be a strictly unofficial venture in the hands of Antonio de Espejo, a cattle rancher, who offered to go north to ascertain the fate of the two friars who, it was rumored, had been killed by the Indians. The small expedition, which included one friar, set out northward in November, 1582, along the Conchos and Rio Grande rivers upstream to the land of the Tigua Indians where it was finally established that the two missionaries had been murdered. However, Espejo pushed on further, going beyond Acoma and Zuñi, to the Moqui towns of western Arizona where he found some mineral deposits. Taking a small party, he retraced his steps eastwards as far as the Pecos River where he was able to confirm the stories of the buffalo herds. On his return in September, 1583, Espejo brought back glowing reports of the area which further strengthened the resolve of the authorities to send out an official expedition. But bureaucracy in Mexico was slow and before Juan de Oñate left in 1598, at least two more unofficial parties visited the pueblo country. The first of these was led by Castaño de Sosa, the lieutenant governor of Nuevo León, who in 1591 marched the whole of the colony at Almadén, his headquarters, into the promised land of the pueblos. They crossed the Rio Grande and then spent several uncomfortable weeks floundering among mountains and canyons in search of a new route to the Pecos River. Turning north, Castaño eventually set up his headquarters on the Rio Grande, about forty miles to the north of Albuquerque. It was here that an official party led by Juan de Morlete caught up with Castaño and ordered him and his followers back to Mexico and to the arms of the authorities. The misfortune of Castaño did not deter others, and three years later another unofficial band of adventurers set out. They were led by Captain Leyva de Bonilla, who had been sent to the frontier to chase hostile Indians. His story was told to Oñate in 1598 by an Indian who had joined the party. Apparently, Leyva explored the Rio Grande and went east to the Buffalo Plains and was on his way north toward Quivira in modern Kansas when he was killed by his second in command, Antonio de Humaña, who did reach Quivira before being murdered, along with most of the party, by Indians.

It took the authorities in New Spain some fifteen years after the return of Espejo to organize and dispatch the official expedition to New Mexico. First, they had to unscramble the numerous claims of frontiersmen to lead the venture. Eventually, in September, 1595, the choice fell on Juan de Oñate who had served in Mexico for many years. The appointment of a new viceroy caused more delays as did the official order for an inventory to be made of everything that was to be taken on the expedition. In 1597 the king finally ordered Viceroy Monterrey to permit Oñate to carry on and in the spring of 1598 the large, well-organized party set out from the Conchos River with the specific purpose of colonizing New Mexico. They soon reached the Rio Grande where Oñate took formal possession of the land in the name of the king of Spain and made his headquarters on the river at San Juan near the present site of Bernalillo. From here he gained the allegiance of all the towns in the vicinity, including Acoma, Zuñi, and the Hopi pueblos, and sent out men to explore the entire area as far east as the Canadian River and into northern Arizona where they found mines that held the possibility of great wealth. Exploration was brought to a temporary halt by the uprising of the Indians at Acoma and by the need for reinforcements, but by 1601 the natives had been quelled by harsh reprisals (the next major uprising occurred in 1680). More men had arrived from Mexico and Oñate was now ready to go in search of Quivira, the land to the northeast visited by Coronado in 1541. Traveling along the Pecos and Canadian rivers, and then overland to the Arkansas River, he arrived at his destination, an extensive settlement probably on the site of Wichita, Kansas. On his return in September, 1601, he found that rebellion among the colonists, which had been brewing for some time, had eventually broken out, and most of them had left for Mexico. Here they spread rumors about the conditions in the north which led to suggestions that Oñate should be replaced as leader. Undeterred, he determined to find the "South Sea" and a harbor where provisions from Mexico could be landed. In 1604 he went westward, following the footsteps of Espejo, and then down the Colorado River to the Gila River and the Gulf of California. He returned to New Mexico in 1605 and ruled for two more years, when complaints about his conduct came to a head and he resigned.

Oñate had achieved much in settling and exploring large areas of New Mexico and Arizona, more than 1,000 miles from Mexico City, although in doing so he had undoubtedly acted harshly against both colonists and Indians, and deserved some of the criticism levelled at him. However, it would have been impossible to lead a successful colonizing venture of this nature without the exercise of strong discipline. The recall and resignation of Oñate owe as much to the attitude of the Spanish officials as to his own conduct. Lengthy discussions had been held in Mexico and New Spain on the future of the colony, and at one point it was decided that it should be abandoned, but it was saved by the need to stand by the many thousands of natives who had been baptized. By 1607 it was agreed by Viceroy Montesclaros and the Council of the Indies that the work of exploration should cease in favor of consolidation of what had been achieved. This was adopted as official policy in January, 1609. It was to remain the official attitude to New Mexico during the whole period of Spanish domination of the region.

Chapter One hundred six
The Interior Reopened by the Spaniards:
The Expedition of 1581–1593

T HE CURBING of northward exploration and exploitation after 1543 and the embodiment, in the New Laws of the Indies of 1573, of elaborate rules for making (or in the great majority of cases not making) new conquests, represented the desire of the viceroyalty officials to retain some hold over what Spaniards were doing at the borders of an amorphous empire. With North America stretching northward into an apparent infinity, something had to be done to retain some sense of order and control at the periphery, in fact to create a border region which would not be needlessly extended. An approximate limit was set at Santa Bárbara and was retained for many years. Two types of pioneers still existed, mining prospectors and missionizing clergy, and when they combined they could sometimes make nonsense of the law.

In 1581–1582 a small and tragic expedition penetrated from Santa Bárbara to the Rio Grande pueblos. In August, 1581, Fray Agustín Rodríguez and his soldier-prospector associate Francisco Chamuscado declared the title of Philip II to San Felipe del Nuevo Mexico on the Rio Grande. Rodríguez remained with another friar to found a mission (and was never seen again), while Chamuscado died on the return march. But one of the survivors, Hernán Gallegos, left a narrative (and we also hear of a map that eventually got to England but was lost there), and so New Mexico emerged as a possible objective for Spanish expansion, forty years after Coronado abandoned it (851).

The expedition of 1581–1582 set in motion another, which was to become much better known. Another soldier-prospector, Antonio de Espejo, with Fray Bernardino Beltrán, made an extensive tour through part of the western and much of the eastern Pueblo territory in 1582–1583 and came back with stories of impressive Indian settlements and a few samples of minerals. This produced a report by Espejo in October, 1583 (827), followed up by a letter to Philip II in April, 1584 (826), which revealed what the expedition had found and asked for help to create a permanent Spanish presence there, although this was premature. By accident the expedition obtained wide publicity in Europe. In his *Historia . . . de la China* (Madrid, 1586), Juan González de Mendoza had incidentally included a reasonably full account of the Espejo expedition, which he had picked up in Mexico. Richard Hakluyt excerpted it in Paris in 1586 as *El viaje de hizo Antonio de Espejo* and from this derived one French and two English publications, while González's own book became very popular and was many times reprinted. New Mexico was a topic for discussion in Europe well before the Spanish government had decided to do anything to occupy it.

The third move was a spontaneous one, the expedition of Gaspar Castaña de Sosa (in reality a Portuguese, Gaspar Castanha de Sousa), in 1590, when he moved the sparse Spanish population of Almadén, where he was lieutenant governor of Nueva León, northward to colonize New Mexico for Spain. This crazy venture succeeded to the point that Sosa established his colonists (women and children as well as men) at a pueblo he named Santo Domingo, in the upper part of the eastern Pueblo area, the Indians proving curious but mainly friendly and helpful. But Sosa was sent for and brought back with his colonists: a small military expedition under Juan Morlete reached Santo Domingo in March, 1591, summarily collected the colonists, and marched them back to Mexico. A report was drawn up by the Viceroy's Council and transmitted to Spain on November 10, 1592, which gave some vivid glimpses of the territory (828). Long afterwards, in 1599, a Mexican Indian called Jusepe, gave an account of a still further illicit expedition, about 1593, under Francisco Leyva de Bonilla, to the Plains northeast of the Pueblo area, but he and his men (except for the Indians) were ultimately all killed (829).

Thus far the ventures of the years 1581 onward were small in scale and unimportant in effect. Cumulatively, they aroused the interest of the Mexican viceroyalty in New Mexico. Friars, prospectors, and soldiers wished to go there: reports had suggested there was good irrigated land, generous and rich Indians, and some hope of mineral wealth. Ultimately, these forces brought about an official attempt to occupy and develop New Mexico as a Spanish province.

The González de Mendoza, *Historia... de la China* (Madrid, 1585, etc.), has a complex bibliography of its own. *El viaje que hizo Antonio de Espejo* (Paris, 1586), gave rise to *Histoire des terres nouvellement descouvertes* (Paris, 1586), *New Mexico* (London, 1587), and to its inclusion in R. Hakluyt, *Principal navigations*, III (1600), 383–406, and subsequent editions. Apart from some incidental material on the Agustín Rodríguez (Ruiz) expedition in the Espejo text, little more appeared in print. An intercepted letter of 1590 led Hakluyt to believe (III [1600], 386) that the Spanish government had committed itself by 1590 to colonize New Mexico, but that was all.

For New Mexico a number of the older collections are valuable: A. F. and F. R. Bandelier, *Historical Documents Relating to New Mexico, Nueva Vizcaya and Approaches Thereto*, 3 vols. (Albuquerque, 1923), C. W. Hackett, *Historical Documents Relating to New Mexico*, 2 vols. (Washington, D.C., 1923–1937), and especially, Herbert E. Bolton, *Spanish Explorations in the Southwest* (New York, 1908, reissued 1963), which has been drawn on here. George P. Hammond and Agapito Rey, *Rediscovery of New Mexico 1580–1594* (Albuquerque, 1966), have translated, often for the first time, the material from the Archivo de Indias and elsewhere. For Castaña de Sosa, Albert H. Schroder and Dan S. Matson, *A Colony on the Move. Gaspar Castaña de Sosa's Journal 1590–1591* (Sante Fe, 1965), is also of value.

825. July 8, 1582. Hernán Gallegos's "Relation" of the Rodríguez-Chamuscado expedition of 1581–1582: extracts.

A.G.I., Seville, Patronato 22; translated in G. P. Hammond and A. Rey, Rediscovery of New Mexico, *pp. 67–114, selections, from which pp. 84–99, 108–110, are taken.*

9

How we left the said frontier and entered the territory of another nation; and of the reception we were accorded.

After we took our leave of this people, the Indians led us to a large pueblo of another nation, where the inhabitants received us by making the sign of the cross with their hands in token of peace, as the others had done before. As the news spread, the procedure in this pueblo was followed in the others.

We entered the settlement, where the inhabitants gave us much corn. They showed us many ollas and other earthenware containers, richly painted, and brought quantities of calabashes and beans for us to eat. We took a little, so that they should not think we were greedy nor yet receive the impression that we did not want it; among themselves they consider it disparaging if one does not accept what is offered. One must take what they give, but after taking it may throw it away wherever he wishes. Should one throw it to the ground, they will not pick it up, though it may be something they can utilize. On the contrary, they will sooner let the thing rot where it is discarded. This is their practice. Thus, since we understood their custom, we took something of what they gave us. Moreover, we did this to get them into the habit of giving freely without being asked. Accordingly, they all brought what they could. The supply of corn tortillas, corn-flour gruel, calabashes, and beans which they brought was such that enough was left over every day to feed five hundred men. Part of this the natives carried for us. The women make tortillas similar to those of New Spain, and tortillas of ground beans, too. In these pueblos there are also houses of three and four stories, similar to the ones we had seen before; but the farther one goes into the interior the larger are the pueblos and the houses, and the more numerous the people.

The way they build their houses, which are in blocks, is as follows: they burn the clay, build narrow walls, and make adobes for the doorways. The lumber used is pine or willow; and many rounded beams, ten and twelve feet long, are built into the houses. The natives have ladders by means of which they climb to their quarters. These are movable wooden ladders, for when the Indians retire at night, they pull them up to protect themselves against enemies since they are at war with one another.

These people, like the others, wear clothing. I have decided to describe their attire here because, for barbarians, it is the best that has been found. It is as follows: [some of] the men cut their hair short and leave on top—I mean, on the crown of their heads—a sort of skull cap formed by their own hair, while others wear their hair long, to the shoulders, as the Indians of New Spain formerly did. Some adorn themselves with pieces of colored cotton cloth three-fourths of a vara in length and two-thirds in width, with which they cover their privy parts. Over this they wear, fastened at the shoulders, a blanket of the same material, decorated with many figures and colors, which reaches to their knees, like the clothes of the Mexicans. Some (in fact, most) wear cotton shirts, hand-painted and embroidered, that are very pleasing. They use shoes. Below the waist the women wear cotton skirts, colored and embroidered; and above, a blanket of the same material, figured and adorned like those used by the men. They adjust it after the fashion of Jewish women, and gird it with embroidered cotton sashes adorned with tassels. They comb their hair, which is worn long.

These people are handsome and fair-skinned. They are very industrious. Only the men attend to the work in the cornfields. The day hardly breaks before they go about with hoes in their hands. The women busy themselves only in the preparation of food, and in making and painting their pottery and *chicubites*, in which they prepare their bread. These vessels are so excellent and delicate that the process of manufacture is worth watching; for they equal, and even surpass, the pottery made in Portugal. The women also make earthen jars for carrying and storing water. These are very large, and are covered with lids of the same material. There are millstones on which the natives grind their corn and other foods. These are similar to the millstones in New Spain, except that they are stationary; and the women, if they have daughters, make them do the grinding.

These Indians are very clean people. The men bear burdens, but not the women. The manner of carrying loads, sleeping, eating, and sitting is the same as that of the Mexicans, for both men and women, except that they carry water in a different way. For this the Indians make and place on their heads a cushion of palm leaves, similar to those used in Old Castile, on top of which they place and carry the water jar. It is all very interesting.

The women part their hair in Spanish style.

Some have light hair, which is surprising. The girls do not leave their rooms except when permitted by their parents. They are very obedient. They marry early; judging by what we saw, the women are given husbands when seventeen years of age. A man has one wife and no more. The women are the ones who spin, sew, weave and paint. Some of the women, like the men, bathe frequently. Their baths are as good as those of New Spain.

In all their valleys and other lands I have seen, there are one hundred pueblos. We named the region the province of San Felipe and took possession of it in the name of his Majesty by commission of his Excellency, Don Lorenzo Suárez de Mendoza, Count of Coruña, viceroy, governor and captain-general of New Spain.

These Indians call corn "cunque"; water "pica"; the turkey "dire"; and a woman "ayu." When they want to drink they say "sesa." They call the cotton blanket... [there is a blank]. Their language is very easy to learn. They are the most domestic and industrious people, and the best craftsmen found in New Spain. Had we brought along interpreters, some of the natives would have become Christians, because they are a very intelligent people and willing to serve.

10

How we learned of the buffalo; and the distance from this province and settlement to the region where they were to be found.

While we were at the pueblo which we named Malpartida—a league from the one already discovered and which we called San Mateo—we asked if there were many minerals in the vicinity, showing the natives the samples we had taken along for that purpose and requesting them to lead us to the place where such riches might be found. They immediately brought us a large quantity of different kinds, including some of a coppery steellike ore. This mineral appeared to be rich and assayed about twenty marcos per hundredweight. The others assayed less. When we asked them where they obtained the ore, they gave us to understand that there were many minerals near the province and pueblo; and they thought that part of what they had shown came from there. We went to investigate and discovered mines of different ores. The natives indicated that the Indians in the region of the buffalo had given them a part of the ore.

Some of these natives paint themselves with stripes. When they told us of the buffalo, we asked them what people lived in that region; whether they had houses and cultivated corn; whether they wore clothes; and how many days it was from their own locality to the buffalo, because we wanted to go and see the animals. We added that we would reconcile them with those other people. They indicated to us that the inhabitants of the buffalo region were not striped; that they lived by hunting and ate nothing but buffalo meat during the winter; that during the rainy season they would go to the areas of the prickly pear and yucca; that they had no houses, but only huts of buffalo hides; that they moved from place to place; that they were enemies of our informants, but nevertheless came to the pueblos of the latter in order to trade such articles as deerskins and buffalo hides for making footwear, and a large amount of meat, in exchange for corn and blankets; and that in this way, by communicating with one another, each nation had come to understand the other's language.

When we heard this and the report on the buffalo, we decided to find the herds and to explore the land in which they lived; for we realized that there must be good grazing in a place where there were as many buffalo as the Indians reported. The region must be fertile and have many grassy plains and plenty of water, to judge by the number of buffalo the natives said there were. Taking up some handfuls of soil, they said that the animals were just as numerous as the grains of sand in their hands, and that there were many rivers, water holes, and marshes where the buffalo ranged. We were much pleased by this news.

In reply to our questions the natives stated that the buffalo were two days' journey away. We asked them why they lived so far from the herds, and they replied that it was on account of their cornfields and cultivated lands, so that the buffalo would not eat the crops; for during certain seasons of the year the buffalo came within eight leagues of the settlement. They also said that the Indians who followed these herds were very brave, fine hunters with bow and arrow who would kill us. But God our Lord inspired us with such courage that we paid no attention to what was said and decided that we would go to see the cattle. We told the natives that some of them should accompany us, inasmuch as the buffalo were so near, and that we would kill game for them. They answered that they did not want to go, because the Indians who followed the buffalo were enemies and very cunning; and that the two peoples would kill each other and start trouble. As we were so few, we did not dare to force these natives to go with us, preferring to travel without a guide by the route they had indicated.

11
How we left the settlement to go in search of the buffalo; and of the route we took.

We left the settlement and province of San Felipe on September 28 of that year to go in search of the buffalo, in view of the reports that the natives had given us. On the first day we traveled six leagues through plains with good pasture for cattle. Accordingly, we thought the Indians had not told the truth, for we noticed that this pasture was untouched by the buffalo, and that the tracks left by them seemed very old. At the end of the day we slept without a drop of water, both men and horses, which occasioned much anxiety, because we feared that under such conditions our animals would become exhausted.

The following day we went through a forest with many pine trees which appeared to be the largest that had been discovered in New Spain. In addition to pines, there were carine and cypress trees. After five leagues we came to an extensive gorge where we found a large pool of rainwater. Here the horses drank, and we stopped at this spot for the night, being fatigued from the previous day.

On the next day we continued to travel across plains, night overtaking us after we had gone seven leagues. We went without water as on the preceding day; and so we thought we were lost, due to the lack of water and because the Indians had told us the buffalo were only a two days' journey from the settlement. Since we had traveled three full days and had failed to locate them, it seemed to us that we must have lost our way. But God our Lord inspired us with great courage and emboldened us to penetrate strange and hostile lands.

The next morning, after we had gone forward another league, God was pleased to lead us to a large pool of brackish water in a plain below a canyon, where we stopped to refresh the animals from the fatigue of the foregoing day. On the following morning we continued our march through this canyon, and all along it we found pools of briny water. We called it San Miguel, because we reached it on the day of the blessed Saint Michael. This valley is suitable for sheep, the best for that purpose ever discovered in New Spain. On the same day we went five leagues down the valley and came to a very large pool of water where we halted for the night. We noticed that numerous people had left this place the preceding day, and we found many buffalo tracks. For this reason we thought the people in question must be those who followed the buffalo and that we were close to the herds. This pleased us very much in view of our desire to see them.

The next morning, after traveling a league, we came to a river with a large volume of water and many trees and we named it Santo Domingo. It contained brackish water suitable for cattle. Accordingly, we thought the buffalo would be found there, because a river as good as this one could not fail to be frequented by cattle and because all along the way we had found their tracks.

Continuing down this same river four leagues we went toward a column of smoke which we had noticed. We wanted to see whether there were people there of whom we could inquire about the buffalo. We came upon a rancheria on this river in which we found fifty huts and tents made of hides with strong white flaps after the fashion of field tents. Here we were met by more than four hundred warlike men armed with bows and arrows who asked us by means of signs what we wanted. We replied that we were coming to visit them and that they were our friends; but they were intent upon fighting us with their arrows. We decided to attack them if necessary but did not actually do so, waiting first to see if they would accept peace. Although on the point of clashing with them, should they provoke us, we restrained ourselves, though there was no fear in us.

So we withdrew our force to see what the outcome would be. Then we made the sign of the cross with our hands in a token of friendship and the Lord was pleased to fill them with fear while inspiring us with renewed courage. When they saw that we made the sign of the cross as an indication of peace, they, too, made the same sign. Moreover, they welcomed us to their land and ranchería. Then Father Fray Agustín Rodríguez dismounted and took a cross from his neck for them to kiss, in order to let them know that we were children of the sun and that we were coming to visit them. They soon began to rejoice and make merry, and to give us of what they had.

We spent the day in this ranchería, where we called together all the Indians, and then discharged an harquebus among them. They were terrified by the loud report and fell to the ground as if stunned. It was God our Lord who put such fear of an harquebus into these Indians, in spite of the fact that they numbered two thousand men. They asked us not to fire any more, because it frightened them greatly. We were very much pleased by this, although we did not let them know it. We asked them where the buffalo were, and they told us that there were large numbers two days farther on, as thick as grass on the plains. They described the entire region where these herds roamed, but not one native wished to come along with us. Thus we saw that we had strayed and had not followed the route suggested by the Indians of the pueblos.

These semi-naked people wear only buffalo hides and deerskins for covering themselves. At this season they live on buffalo meat, but during the rainy season they go in search of prickly pears and yucca. They have dogs which carry loads of two or three arrobas, and they put leather packsaddles on these animals, with poitrels and cruppers. They tie the dogs to one another as in a pack train, using maguey ropes for halters. The packs travel three or four leagues per day. These dogs are medium-sized shaggy animals.

The following morning we went down this same river, and since we found no buffalo after two days, we wandered on bewildered. It was not advisable to travel over plains like these without guides, so we returned to the river by command of our leader. We went back to the ranchería, where we had left the many people, in order to get an Indian guide, either willingly or by force, to take us to the buffalo. This purpose was accomplished; we went to the said ranchería, seized an Indian, bound him, brought him to camp, and handed him over to our leader so that we could start at once and continue our journey to the cattle. Noting that the Indians of the ranchería had become

angry, we decided to prepare ourselves fully for battle, as we were in the habit of doing under such circumstances; and also to maintain a careful vigil, even though we were tired as a result of keeping guard for six months. This was a tremendous strain, for one can well imagine that keeping watch every single night for a whole year was enough to exhaust forty men, to say nothing of our small group of eight.

Then, in the morning, we started off with the guide and journeyed laboriously for three days, during which we had no water, until we reached a place where we found some small pools with hoes, since at first they did not contain enough water for even one of our animals. By God's will, as these pools were opened, so much water flowed from them that it was sufficient for ten thousand horses. We named the pools Ojos Zarcos. Traces of buffalo were found here, and we killed one—the first that we had seen on the trip. This led us to believe that the herds were near by. We remained another day at the pools in order to refresh our horses, which were tired out from the previous day. We had gone without water for more than forty hours, and if we had been without it one more day we should have perished. But God our Lord is merciful. In the time of greatest need, He gives aid, as was especially manifest on this occasion.

We asked the guide whom we took along where the other buffalo were. He said there were many and that we would see them the next day in large numbers at a water hole. So, on the following day, which was October 9, we reached some lagoons of very brackish water. Here we found many such pools in a valley that extends from these lagoons toward the sunrise. We named this valley and its pools Los Llanos de San Francisco and Aguas Zarcas, because they formed such good plains. In these plains there is a spring, the best to be found in New Spain for people afflicted with dropsy.

At the water holes on the plains we found many buffalo, which roamed in great herds or droves of more than five hundred head, both cows and bulls. They are as large as the cattle of New Spain, hump-backed and wooly, with short, black horns and big heads. The bulls have beards like he-goats. They are fairly swift and run like pigs. They are so large that when seen in the midst of a plain they resemble ships at sea or carts on land. According to our estimate and that of the men who discovered them, the bulls must weigh more than forty arrobas each when three years old. Their meat is delicious and to our taste as palatable as that of our beef cattle.

We killed forty head with our harquebuses, to be used as food. It is easy to kill these animals, for as soon as they are wounded they stop moving and, on stopping, they are slain. There are so many buffalo that there were days when we saw upward of three thousand bulls. The reason there are so many males together is that at a certain season of the year they separate from the cows. They have very fine wool, suitable for any purpose, and their hides are the best that have been found on any cattle up to the present time.

Here we learned that this valley and its waters extended to the river where the great bulk of the buffalo ranged; according to the natives the herds cover the fields in astonishing numbers. The leader and the discoverers at first resolved to look for the river described, but later they realized that this was not a good plan because they were running short of supplies. Had it not been for that drawback, we would have gone on to explore the river, so that we could report to his Majesty on what had thus been discovered.

Accordingly, on October 19 of that year [1581], we left the valley of San Francisco, turning back toward the settlement from which we had started. From that point to the location of the buffalo, we traversed forty leagues of difficult road, and were on the point of perishing for lack of water and for our original failure to obtain a guide at the settlement. We learned that from this place to the buffalo there were two days of travel, more or less, following the direct route of which the Indians had told us. We went back over the same route we had followed on our first entry, because we knew of no other.

The Indian we had taken as guide from the ranchería we now sent ahead, well laden with meat and very happy because he had seen us kill the buffalo. Indeed, it seemed as if it was the will of God that not one of us should fire his harquebus at an animal without felling it. This greatly astonished the guide who had led us to the herds. After leaving us he told of what he had seen us do, how we killed the buffalo, and other things. In view of this the whole ranchería which he had left behind, and from which we had taken the guide by force, came to meet us peacefully. The inhabi-

tants said that they wanted to take us to the buffalo and would lead us to a place where there were many herds, as they showed us by signs. We gave part of what we had—that is, some of the meat—to those who seemed to be caciques, for they stand out readily. We told them we would return shortly, which pleased them, and they gave us to understand that they would await us. Thus we left them, though we kept our vigil in order that, under the pretext of friendship and peace, they should not try to avenge the seizure of the guide whom we had taken from them to help find the buffalo. He was one of their own people. We then turned back toward the said settlement, our starting point.

12
Telling how, upon our arrival at the settlement, we gave orders that the inhabitants should provide us with food supplies.

When we arrived at the settlement, a pueblo which we named Piedra Aita, we decided that we would start there to explain how we had run short of provisions, in order that the natives of this and other towns should give us the food necessary for our sustenance. Moreover, if this pueblo gave us provisions, they would be given to us everywhere in the province. Up to that time, the natives had not been asked to supply anything for our maintenance.

We all assembled to consult with our leader and to determine the method which should be used in obtaining the provisions. It was decided first of all to tell the natives by means of signs that we had used up the supplies brought with us, and that since they had plenty they should give us some because we wanted to go on. When they realized this and saw that the supplies we had brought were exhausted, they thought of starving us to death and acted as if deaf. We told our leader that the natives had paid no attention to us and pretended not to understand.

To this he replied that it was not advisable to use force, for we could see plainly that the people in these pueblos were very numerous and that within an hour after their call to arms three thousand men would gather and kill us. When the leader expressed this opinion, the soldiers argued that, inasmuch as he had authority to seize the provisions we needed for men and horses, he should make use of it, because we preferred to die fighting rather than from starvation, especially since we were in a land with ample food. Since our leader was ill, he replied that we could do what we thought best, provided that we did not incite the natives to revolt and that they gave us the provisions willingly.

When our men found that the Indians rebelled at our request for food, our leader, rising from his sick bed, and seven companions armed themselves and went to the pueblo with their horses in readiness for war. When the Indians saw we were armed, they withdrew into their houses and fortified themselves in the pueblo, which was composed of three hundred houses of three and four stories, all of stone. Seeing that the Indians had retired to their houses, we entered the town, and, carrying a cross in our hands, asked them for some corn flour because we had nothing to eat. The natives understood, but held back, not wishing to give it. Confronted with the hostile attitude of the Indians, some of our men fired a few harquebuses, pretending to aim at them in order to intimidate them into giving us the food we needed. We wanted them to understand that they had to give it, either willingly or by force.

In order that no one should complain of having provided much while another gave less, the soldiers decided that each house should contribute a little and that for this purpose a measure should be made which held about half an almud of ground corn flour. Then the natives brought us quantities of ground corn from every house in the pueblo, fearing us and the harquebuses—which roared a great deal and spat fire like lightning—and thinking we were immortal, since we had told them that we were children of the sun and that the sun had given us these weapons for defense. Seeing that we did not ask for anything except food for ourselves, all gave something and told us they were our friends, though the friendship they feigned was due more to fear than to anything else. We remained on our guard lest, being Indians, they should treacherously plan some trick and attack us unawares.

Since this pueblo had contributed nine loads of flour as a present and the news had spread throughout the province, we were given exactly the same amount, no more and no less, at the other pueblos, so that we did not lack food during the entire trip. For all this, and the many favors

He had granted us, insuring that we should never be without provisions, we offered thanks to God. All the pueblos thus gave us supplies as tribute; and as they are now accustomed to it, they will not resent giving such tribute when someone goes to start settlements. Together with the supply of corn and flour, they presented us with large numbers of turkeys, of which they have many flocks and do not value highly. Of the provisions that they offered us we took only what was necessary, and what was left over we returned to them. This pleased them very much, and they told us they were our friends and would give us food and whatever else we might need. They did this due to fear rather than from any desire to befriend us. It was presumably because of that attitude and the fact that we had asked for and taken provisions from them that they attempted to unite the province in order to seize us by force and kill us.

13
Concerning the attempt of the Indians to kill us, the gathering that they held, and how they overcame their fear of us.

After the events related above, and after the natives had given us what we needed for our support, in characteristic Indian fashion, they determined to seize us treacherously by night and kill us if they could. The cause for this was the fact that, after we had seen the settlement (poblazón), with which we were very much pleased, Father Fray Juan de Santa María, one of the friars in our party, decided to return to the land of the Christians in order to give an account and report of what had been discovered to his prelate and to his Excellency, the viceroy.

Everyone condemned the decision as inadvisable, for he would not only endanger his own life, but imperil the soldiers, and in addition would jeopardize further exploration of the land. We urged him to wait until we had inspected everything about which the natives had informed us, and had gone to see the buffalo, in order that a complete report of all this might be taken to the friar's prelate and to his Excellency, as any account that he could give now would be incomplete, since we had not seen the most important things. To this advice Fray Juan de Santa María replied that he was determined to return to Christian territory and report on what he had seen. His departure caused much unrest in the land and trouble for us. Without the permission of his superior, he left the party at vespers on the feast of Our Lady of September.

When the natives saw that the friar was leaving, they became alarmed, believing he was going to bring more Christians in order to put them out of their homes; so they asked us by signs where he was going, all alone. We tried to dissuade them from their wicked thoughts, but, as they were Indians, this did not prevent them from doing evil. They followed the friar and killed him after two or three days of travel. We knew nothing of this until we returned from our trip to the buffalo; and even though the natives told us they had slain the father in the sierra, which we named the Sierra Morena, we pretended not to understand. Seeing that we paid no attention to the death of the friar and that they had killed him so easily, they thought they would kill us just as readily. From then on they knew we were mortal; up to that time they had thought us immortal.

When we learned that the natives had killed the friar and that they intended to slay us also, we decided to withdraw gradually. We stopped at a pueblo which we named Malpartida, and at a distance of one league from that spot we discovered some mineral deposits. While we were at this pueblo, some Indians from another settlement, which we named Malagón, killed three of our horses. We soon missed the animals and learned how the Indians of this district of Malagón had killed them. When the leader and the soldiers realized what had happened, they determined that such a crime should not go unpunished. The leader ordered five of the party—Pedro de Bustamante, Hernán Gallegos, Pedro Sánchez de Chaves, Felipe de Escalante, and Pedro Sánchez de Fuensalida—to go to the pueblo of Malagón, where it was reported the three horses had been killed; to find and bring before him the culprits, either peaceably or by force; and to make some arrests at the pueblo in order to intimidate the natives.

When the five soldiers learned of their leader's orders, they armed themselves, made ready their horses, and proceeded to Malagón, which they found to consist of eighty houses of three and four stories with plazas and streets. Entering the pueblo in fighting order, as men who were angry, they found the Indians keeping watch on the housetops and asked who had killed the three missing horses. In order to protect themselves from the harm that might befall them, the natives replied they had committed no such deed. As soon as we heard this answer, we discharged the harquebuses to make the Indians think we were going to kill them, although we incurred great risk in doing so, for we were only five men facing the task of attacking eighty houses with more than a thousand inhabitants. When we had fired our harquebuses, the natives became frightened, went into their houses, and stayed there. To placate us they threw many dead turkeys down the passageways to us, but we decided not to accept the offering so that they would know we were angry. Then we asked twenty or thirty Indians who appeared on the roofs and who seemed to be the chief men of the pueblo—the cacique among them—to give us either the horses or the culprits who had killed them. To this they replied that their people had not slain the animals; and they asked us not to be angry, declaring that they were our friends.

Since the natives did not surrender those who had killed the horses, Hernán Gallegos, Pedro Sánchez de Fuensalida, and Pedro de Bustamante dismounted and went up to the houses to see if they could find any trace of horseflesh. The other soldiers guarded the pueblo to protect their companions from danger. Hernán Gallegos and Pedro de Bustamante soon found pieces of horseflesh in two houses of the pueblo and came out to notify their comrades of the discovery. We then fired the harquebuses once more, and the Indians, observing our conduct, were more frightened than defiant, since we had expressed our will with such determination. Gallegos and Bustamante then mounted; and all five of us, holding horseflesh in our hands, again asked the Indians who were keeping watch to tell us which men were guilty of killing the horses. We warned them to deliver those men to us, because we wanted to kill them or take them to our leader so that he might have them put to death; and we added that if the natives would not give up the culprits, we would have to kill them all. We challenged them to come out of their pueblo into the open so that we might see how brave they were: but they were very sad and answered that they did not want to fight us, for we were brave men, and that it was the Indians in the next pueblo who had killed our horses, thinking they were animals like the native buffalo.

Then we soldiers attacked the pueblo again in order to capture some Indians. They took refuge in the pueblo, but some hurled themselves from the corridors into the open in an attempt to escape, whereupon Hernán Gallegos and Pedro de Bustamante rushed after them and each seized an Indian by the hair. The natives were very swift, but the horses overtook them. After apprehending them, the soldiers took them to the camp of the leader to be punished, in view of their crime and as an example to the others.

Before this happened and before returning to camp, we decided to set fire to the pueblo so that the inhabitants would not perpetrate such a crime again. Pedro de Bustamante then picked up a bit of hay, started a fire by means of an harquebus, and prepared to burn the pueblo; but his companions would not allow the town to be burned and so many people to perish, lest all should suffer for the guilt of perhaps eight individuals.

Thus we returned to the camp with the prisoners and delivered them to our leader, who ordered that they should be beheaded on the following morning. To this the soldiers replied that he should consider what it meant to imprison these Indians for a day; that it was not good policy; that if they were to be executed it should be done at once, for there were more than a thousand Indians in the camp who might attempt some wickedness on account of the imprisonment of the two Indians. When the leader realized that the soldiers were right, he ordered Pedro de Bustamante, the notary [Gallegos], and the other soldiers to place a block in the middle of the camp's plaza, where the rest of the Indians were watching, and to cut off the heads of the prisoners with an iron machete as punishment for them and as an example to the others. The preparations were carried out as ordered; although, as the friars had decided to remain in that settlement [en aquella poblazón], it was agreed that at the time when the Indians were to be beheaded the friars should rush out to free them—tussle with us, and snatch the victims away from us in order that the Indians might love their rescuers, who were resolved to remain in the land.

All was so done. At the moment when the soldiers were about to cut off the heads of the Indians, the friars came out in flowing robes and saved the captives from their perilous plight. As we pretended that we were going to seize them, the Indians who were watching immediately took hold of the friars and the prisoners and carried all of them off to their houses, mindful of the great support they had found in the priests. Because of what we had done and proposed to do, the natives became so terrified of us that it was surprising how they trembled. This was willed by God on high, for we ourselves were but a small force.

The following morning, many Indians from the pueblo of Malagón came, heavily laden with turkeys and other food for our use, entreating us not to be angry with them, since they would not commit such deeds again. In the future they would watch and round up the horses, so that none would be lost. They assured us that they were our friends. We were very much pleased at this, although we did not show it, in order that they and the other natives might hold us in even greater fear.

A few days later the Indians assembled for the purpose of killing us, but that did not deter us from going to explore the land in order to verify the information that we had been given. When we left, and again after we returned to camp, we realized clearly and definitely that they wanted to kill us, and that the people of the entire region were gathering for this purpose; so we decided to take precautions and to continue keeping careful watch, as we had done up to that time. Since we watched with more zeal than in the past, the natives became aware of it. If they had shown great friendship for us before, they showed even more now.

In spite of their fear, we came to the conclusion from their conduct that they wanted to kill us; wherefore we determined to attack and kill them, and to burn some of their small pueblos even though we should perish in the attempt, in order that they might fear the Spaniards. We challenged them many times so that they might know there was no cowardice in us. But as the friars had decided to remain in the said settlement [en la dicha poblazón], we sometimes—in fact, most of the time—relinquished our rights in order that the fathers might remain in the province and be content. Nevertheless, their decision to stay was against the judgment of all, because the natives had killed the other friar and because they were to remain among such great numbers of idolatrous people.

THE JOURNEY OF ANTONIO DE ESPEJO

AS RELATED ABOVE, the account of the Espejo journey published in González de Mendoza, *Historia... de la China* (1586 and subsequently) became well known. This version in Spanish and English remains in R. Hakluyt, *Principal navigations*, III (1600), 383–406 (X [1904], 169–185). However, during the nineteenth century more significant material made its appearance, namely Espejo's own report sent to Philip II. The report was prepared at Santa Bárbara in October, 1583, and was sent with a letter to the king of Spain in April, 1584. The prefatory letter to the king, April 23, appeared in Spanish in two slightly differing versions in *Colección de documentos inéditos*, XV, 100–101 and 162–163, while versions of the report were published in the same volumes, pp. 101–126 and 163–189.

The letter was translated in H. E. Bolton, *Spanish Explorations in the Southwest*, p. 195 (and also in G. P. Hammond and A. Rey, *The Rediscovery of New Mexico, 1580–1594*, pp. 233–234) and the report in Bolton, pp. 168–192 (and in Hammond and Rey, pp. 213–231). They are reprinted from Bolton (826–827).

826. April 23, 1584. Antonio de Espejo to Philip II.

His Very Catholic Royal Majesty:

Since from the relation which accompanies this letter your Majesty will be informed of the lands and provinces which, by God's favor, and with the desire to serve your Majesty and increase the royal crown, like a loyal and faithful vassal, I have discovered and traversed since the month of November, 1582, when I set out from the government of Nueva Vizcaya with a religious and fourteen soldiers whom I took with me, moved and compelled by a very pious and charitable occasion, I will omit telling of them now; but I beg your Majesty to please be assured of my zeal, so dedicated to the service of your Majesty, and consider it well that I should finish my life in the continuation of these discoveries and settlements; for with the estate, prominence, and friends which I possess, I promise to serve your Majesty with greater advantage than any others who are attempting to make a contract with you regarding this enterprise. I beg your Lordship to please order that it be made with me, your Majesty granting me the mercy, honor, and favor corresponding to my very great desire to increase the realms of your Majesty and the Catholic faith, by the conversion of millions of souls who lack the true knowledge, and to elevate my name and my

memory the better to serve and to merit the favor of your Majesty, whom God our Lord exalt and preserve many years, as the vassals of your Majesty have need. San Salvador, April 23, 1584.—His Very Catholic Royal Majesty.—Your Majesty's most humble vassal,

[Signed:] Antonio Espejo

827. October, 1583. Antonio de Espejo's account of his expedition to New Mexico, 1582–1583.

Account of the Journey which I, Antonio Espejo, Citizen of the City of Mexico, native of the City of Cordoba, made at the close of the year 1582, with Fourteen Soldiers and a Religious of the Order of San Francisco, to the Provinces and Settlements of New Mexico, which I named Nueva Andalucía, in Honor of my Native Land.

In order that this account may be better and more easily understood it should be observed that in the year 1581 a friar of the Order of San Francisco, named Fray Agustin y Ruiz, who resided in the valley of San Bartolomé, having heard through certain Conchos Indians who were communicating with the Pazaguates, that to the north there were certain undiscovered settlements, endeavored to obtain permission to go to them for the purpose of preaching the Gospel to the natives. Having obtained permission from his prelate and from the viceroy, the Count of Coruña, this friar and two others, named Fray Francisco Lopez and Fray Jhoan de Santa Maria, with seven or eight soldiers of whom Francisco Sanchez Chamuscado was leader, went inland in the month of June of 1581, through the said settlements, until they arrived at a province called Tiguas, situated two hundred and fifty leagues north of the mines of Santa Bárbola, of the government of Nueva Vizcaya, where they began their journey. There Fray Jhoan de Santa Maria was killed, and as they saw that there were many people, and that for any purpose either of peace or of war they themselves were too few, the soldiers and their leader returned to the mines of Santa Bárbola, and from there went to Mexico, which is one hundred and sixty leagues distant, to report to the viceroy, in the month of May, 1582.

The two religious who remained, with the desire to save souls, believing that they were safe among the natives, did not wish to come away, but prefered to stay in the said province of the Tiguas, through which Francisco Vasquez Coronado long ago passed on his way to the conquest and discovery of the cities and plains of Cibola. And thus they remained with three Indian boys and a half-breed, whereat the Order of San Francisco was greatly grieved, regarding it as certain that the Indians would kill the two religious and those who remained with them. Entertaining this fear, they wished and endeavored to find someone who would enter the said land and bring them out and succor them. For this purpose another religious of the same order, named Fray Bernaldino Beltran, a resident of the monastery of the Villa of Durango, capital of Nueva Vizcaya, offered to make the journey, with the authority and permission of his superior.

And as at that time it happened that I was in that jurisdiction, and that I heard of the wise and pious desire of the said religious and of the entire order, and knowing that by so doing I would serve our Lord and his Majesty, I offered to accompany this religious and to spend part of my wealth in paying his expenses and in taking some soldiers, both for his protection and defense and for that of the religious whom he was going to succor and

bring back, if the royal justice, in his Majesty's name, would permit or order me to do so. Accordingly, having learned of the holy zeal of the said religious and of my intention, and at the instance of the said Fray Bernardino, Captain Joan de Ontiveros, *alcalde mayor* for his Majesty in the pueblos called the Cuatro Cienegas, which lie within the said jurisdiction of Nueva Vizcaya, seventy leagues east of the mines of Santa Bárbola, gave his order and commission that I, with some soldiers, should enter the new land to succor and bring out the religious and men who had remained in it.

And so, by virtue of said order and commission, I enlisted fourteen soldiers, whose names are Joan Lopez de Ibarra, Bernardo de Luna, Diego Perez de Lujan, Gaspar de Lujan, Francisco Barreto, Gregorio Hernandez, Miguel Sanchez Valenciano, Lazaro Sanchez and Miguel Sanchez Nevado, sons of the said Miguel Sanchez, Alonso de Miranda, Pedro Hernandez de Almansa, Joan Hernandez, Cristóbal Sanchez, and Joan de Frias, all of whom, or the major part of whom, I supplied with arms, horses, munitions, provisions, and other things necessary for so long and unaccustomed a journey. Beginning our journey at Valle de San Bartolomé, which is nine leagues from the mines of Santa Bárbola, on November 10, 1582, with one hundred and fifteen horses and mules, some servants, and a quantity of arms, munitions, and provisions, we set out directly north.

After two days' march of five leagues each we found in some rancherías a large number of Indians of the Conchos nation, many of whom, to the number of more than a thousand, came out to meet us along the road we were travelling. We found that they live on rabbits, hares, and deer, which they hunt and which are abundant, and on some crops of maize, gourds, Castilian melons, and watermelons, like winter melons, which they plant and cultivate, and on fish, *mascales*, which are the leaves of *lechuguilla*, a plant half a *vara* in height, the stalks of which have green leaves. They cook the stocks of this plant and make a preserve like quince jam. It is very sweet, and they call it *mascale*. They go about naked, have grass huts for houses, use bows and arrows for arms, and have caciques whom they obey. We did not find that they have idols, nor that they offer any sacrifices. We assembled as many of them as we could, erected crosses for them in the rancherías, and by interpreters of their own tongue whom we had with us the meaning of the crosses and something about our holy Catholic faith was explained to them. They went with us six days beyond their rancherías, which must have been a journey of twenty-four leagues to the north. All this distance is settled by Indians of the same nation, who came out to receive us in peace, one cacique reporting our coming to another. All of them fondled us and our horses, touching us and the horses with their hands, and with great friendliness giving us some of their food.

At the end of these six days we found another nation of Indians called Pazaguantes, who have rancherías, huts, and food like the Conchos. They were dealt with as had been those of the Conchos nation, and they continued with us four days' march, which must have been fourteen leagues, one cacique informing another, so that they might come out to receive us, which they did. In places during these four days' travel we found many mines of silver which, in the opinion of those who know, were rich.

We left this nation, and on the first day's march we found another people called Jobosos. They were shy, and therefore they fled from all the settlements through which we passed, where they lived in huts, for as it was said some soldiers had been there and carried away some of them as slaves. But we called some of them, making them presents, and some of them came to the camp. We gave some things to the caciques, and through interpreters gave them to understand that we had not come to capture them or to injure them in any manner. Thereupon they were reassured, and we erected crosses for them in their rancherías and explained to them something about God our Lord. They appeared pleased, and being so, some of them went on with us till they had taken us beyond their territory. They live on the same things as the Pazaguates, use bows and arrows, and go about without clothing. We passed through this nation, which seemed to have few Indians, in three days, which must have been a distance of eleven leagues.

Having left this nation we came to another who call themselves the Jumanos, and whom the Spaniards call, for another name, Patarabueyes. This nation appeared to be very numerous, and had large permanent pueblos. In it we saw five pueblos with more than ten thousand Indians, and flat-roofed houses, low and well arranged into pueblos. The people of this nation have their faces streaked, and are large; they have maize, gourds, beans, game of foot and wing, and fish of many kinds from two rivers that carry much water. One of them, which must be about half the size of the Guadalquivir, flows directly from the north and empties into the Conchos River. The Conchos, which must be about the size of the Guadalquivir, flows into the North Sea. They have salines consisting of lagoons of salt water, which at certain times of the year solidifies and forms salt like that of the sea. The first night, when we pitched camp near a small pueblo of this nation, they killed five of our horses with arrows and wounded as many more, notwithstanding the fact that watch was kept. They retired to a mountain range, where six of us went next morning with Pedro, the interpreter, a native of their nation, and found them, quieted them, made peace with them, and took them to their own pueblo. We told them what we had told the others, and that they should inform the people of their nation not to flee nor hide, but to come out to see us. To some of the caciques I gave beads, hats, and other things, so that they would bring them in peace, which they did; and from these pueblos they accompanied us, informing one another that we came as friends and not to injure them; and thus great numbers of them went with us and showed us a river from the north, which has been mentioned above.

On the banks of this river Indians of this nation are settled for a distance of twelve days' journey. Some of them have flat-roofed houses, and others live in grass huts. The caciques came out to receive us, each with his people, without bows or arrows, giving us portions of their food, while some gave us *gamuzas* (buckskins) and buffalo hides, very well tanned. The *gamuzas* they make of the hides of deer; they also are tanned, as it is done in Flanders. The hides are from the humpbacked cows which they call *civola*, and whose hair is like that of cows of Ireland. The natives dress the hides of these cows as hides are dressed in Flanders, and make shoes of them. Others they dress in different ways, some of the natives using them for clothes. These Indians appear to have some knowledge of our holy Catholic faith, because they point to God our Lord, looking up to the heavens. They call him

Apalito in their tongue, and say that it is He whom they recognize as their Lord and who gives them what they have. Many of them, men, women, and children, came to have the religious and us Spaniards bless them, which made them appear very happy. They told us and gave us to understand through interpreters that three Christians and a negro had passed through there, and by the indications they gave they appeared to have been Alonso Nuñez Cabeza de Vaca, Dorantes Castillo Maldonado, and a negro, who had all escaped from the fleet with which Pánfilo Narvaez entered Florida. They were left friendly and very peaceful and satisfied, and some of them went with us up the Río del Norte, serving and accompanying us.

Continuing up that river, always to the north, there came out to receive us a great number of Indians, men, women, and children, dressed or covered with buckskins; but we did not learn of what nation they were, through lack of interpreters. They brought us many things made of feathers of different colors, and some small cotton *mantas*, striped with blue and white, like some of those they bring from China; and they gave us to understand by signs that another nation that adjoined theirs, towards the west, brought those things to barter with them for other goods which these had and which appeared from what they told us by signs to be dressed hides of cows and deer; and showing them shining ores, which in other places usually bear silver, and others of the same kind which we carried, they pointed towards the west five days' journey, saying they were taking us to where there an immense quantity of those metals and many people of that nation. They went forth with us four days' journey, which must have been a distance of twenty-two leagues.

These Indians having stopped, and we having travelled four days more up the said river, we found a great number of people living near some lagoons through the midst of which the Rio del Norte flows. These people, who must have numbered more than a thousand men and women, and who were settled in their rancherías and grass huts, came out to receive us, men, women, and children. Each one brought us his present of *mesquital*, which is made of a fruit like the carob bean, fish of many kinds, which are very plentiful in those lagoons, and other kinds of their food in such quantity that the greater part spoiled because the amount they gave us was so great. During the three days and nights we were there they continually performed *mitotes*, balls, and dances, in their fashion, as well as after the manner of the Mexicans. They gave us to understand that there were many people of this nation at a distance from there, but we did not learn of what nation they were, for lack of interpreters. Among them we found an Indian of the Concho nation who gave us to understand, pointing to the west, that fifteen days' journey from there there was a very large lake, where there were many settlements, with houses of many stories, and that there were Indians of the Concho nation settled there, people wearing clothes and having plentiful supplies of maize and turkeys and other provisions in great quantity, and he offered to take us there. But because our course led us north to give succor to the religious and those who remained with them, we did not go to the lake. In this ranchería and district the land and the climate are very good; and nearby there are cows and native cattle, plentiful game of foot and wing, mines, many forests, pasture lands, water, salines of very rich salt, and other advantages.

Travelling up the same river, we followed it fifteen days from the place of the lagoons mentioned above without finding any people, going through country with mesquite groves, prickly pears, mountains with pine groves having pines and pine-nuts like those of Castile, sabines, and cedars. At the end of this time we found a ranchería, of few people but containing many grass huts, many deer skins, also dressed like those they bring from Flanders, a quantity of very good and white salt, jerked venison, and other kinds of food. These Indians received us and went with us, taking us two days' journey from that place, to the settlements, always following the Río del Norte. From the time when we first came to it we always followed this river up stream, with a mountain chain on each side of it, both of which were without timber throughout the entire distance until we came near the settlements which they call New Mexico, although along the banks of the river there are many groves of white poplars, the groves being in places four leagues wide. We did not leave the river from the time when we came to it up to the time of reaching the said provinces, which they call New Mexico. Along the banks of the river, in many parts of the road, we found thickets of grape vines and Castilian walnut trees.

After we reached the said settlements, continuing up the river, in the course of two days we found ten inhabited pueblos on the banks of this river, close to it and on all sides, besides other pueblos which appeared off the highway, and which in passing seemed to contain more than twelve thousand persons, men, women, and children. As we were going through this province, from each pueblo the people came out to receive us, taking us to their pueblos and giving us a great quantity of turkeys, maize, beans, tortillas, and other kinds of bread, which they make with more nicety than the Mexicans. They grind on very large stones. Five or six women together grind raw corn in a single mill, and from this flour they make many different kinds of bread. They have houses of two, three, and four stories, with many rooms in each house. In many of their houses they have their *estufas* for winter, and in each plaza of the towns they have two *estufas*, which are houses built underground, very well sheltered and closed, with seats of stone against the walls to sit on. Likewise, they have at the door of each *estufa* a ladder on which to descend, and a great quantity of community wood, so that the strangers may gather there.

In this province some of the natives wear cotton, cow hides, and dressed deerskin. The *mantas* they wear after the fashion of the Mexicans, except that over their private parts they wear cloths of colored cotton. Some of them wear shirts. The women wear cotton skirts, many of them being embroidered with colored thread, and on top a *manta* like those worn by the Mexican Indians, tied around the waist with a cloth like an embroidered towel with a tassel. The skirts, lying next to the skin, serve as flaps of the shirts. This costume each one wears as best he can, and all, men as well as women, dress their feet in shoes and boots, the soles being of cowhide and the uppers of dressed deerskin. The women wear their hair carefully combed and nicely kept in place by the moulds that they wear on their heads, one on each side, on which the hair is arranged very neatly, though they wear no headdress. In each pueblo they have their caciques, the number differing according to the number of people. These caciques have under them

caciques, I mean *tequitatos*, who are like *Alguaciles*, and who execute in the pueblo the cacique's orders, just exactly like the Mexican people. And when the Spaniards ask the caciques of the pueblos for anything, they call the *tequitatos*, who cry it through the pueblo in a loud voice, whereupon they bring with great haste what is ordered.

The painting of their houses, and the things which they have for balls and dancing, both as regards the music and the rest, are all very much like those of the Mexicans. They drink toasted *pinole*, which is corn toasted and ground and mixed with water. It is not known that they have any other drink or anything with which to become intoxicated. In each one of these pueblos they have a house to which they carry food for the devil, and they have small stone idols which they worship. Just as the Spaniards have crosses along the roads, they have between the pueblos, in the middle of the road, small caves or grottoes, like shrines, built of stones, where they place painted sticks and feathers, saying that the devil goes there to rest and speak with them.

They have fields of maize, beans, gourds, and *piciete* in large quantities, which they cultivate like the Mexicans. Some of the fields are under irrigation, possessing very good diverting ditches, while others are dependent upon the weather. Each one has in his field a canopy with four stakes and covered on top, where they take him food daily at noon and where he takes his siesta, for ordinarily they are in their fields from morning until night, after the Castilian custom. In this province are many pine forests which bear pine-nuts like those of Castile, and many salines on both sides of the river. On each bank there are sandy flats more than a league wide, of soil naturally well adapted to the raising of corn. Their arms consist of bows and arrowes, *macanas* and *chimales;* the arrows have fire-hardened shafts, the heads being of pointed flint, with which they easily pass through a coat of mail. The *chimales* are made of cowhide, like leather shields; and the *macanas* consist of rods half a vara long, with very thick heads. With them they defend themselves within their houses. It was not learned that they were at war with any other province. They respect their boundaries. Here they told us of another province of the same kind which is farther up the same river.

After a stay of four days in this province we set out, and half a league from its boundary we found another, which is called the province of the Tiguas. It comprises sixteen pueblos, one of which is called Pualas. Here we found that the Indians of this province had killed Fray Francisco Lopez and Fray Augustin Ruiz, three boys, and a half-breed, whom we were going to succor and take back. Here we secured a very correct report that Francisco Vasquez Coronado had been in the province, and that they had killed nine of his soldiers and forty horses, and that because of this he had completely destroyed the people of one pueblo of the province. Of all this the natives of these pueblos informed us by signs which we understood. Believing that we were going there to punish them because they had killed the friars, before we reached the province they fled to a mountain two leagues from the river. We tried to bring them back peacefully, making great efforts to that end, but they refused to return. In their houses we found a large quantity of maize, beans, gourds, many turkeys, and many ores of different colors. Some of the pueblos in this province, as also the houses, were larger than those of the province we had passed, but the fields and character of the land appeared to be just the same. We were unable to ascertain the number of people in this province, for they had fled.

Having arrived at this province of the Tiguas and found that the religious in quest of whom we had come, and the half-breed and the Indians who had remained with them, were dead, we were tempted to return to Nueva Vizcaya, whence we had started. But since while we were there the Indians informed us of another province to the east which they said was near, and as it seemed to me that all that country was well peopled, and that the farther we penetrated into the region the larger the settlements we found, and as they received us peacefully, I deemed this a good opportunity for me to serve his Majesty by visiting and discovering those lands so new and so remote, in order to give a report of them to his Majesty, with no expense to him in their discovery. I therefore determined to proceed as long as my strength would permit. Having communicated my intention to the religious and soldiers, and they having approved my decision, we continued our journey and discovery in the same way as heretofore.

In this place we heard of another province, called Maguas, which lay two days' journey to the east. Leaving the camp in this province I set out with two companions for the place, where I arrived in two days. I found there eleven pueblos, inhabited by a great number of people. It seemed to me they must comprise more than forty thousand souls, between men, women, and children. They have here no running arroyos or springs to use, but they have an abundance of turkeys, provisions, and other things, just as in the foregoing province. This one adjoined the region of the cows called *cibola*. They clothe themselves with the hides of these cows, with cotton *mantas*, and with deerskins. They govern themselves as do the preceding provinces, and like the rest have idols which they worship. They have advantages for mines in the mountains of this province, for as we travelled toward them we found much antimony along the route, and wherever this is found there are usually ores rich in silver. In this province we found ores in the houses of the Indians. We likewise discovered that here they had killed one of the religious, called Fray Jhoan de Santa Maria, who had entered with the other religious, Francisco Chamuscado, and the soldiers. They killed him before the said Francisco Chamuscado went to the pacified country. However, we made friends of them, saying nothing of these murders. They gave us food, and having noted the nature of the country, we departed from it. It is a land of many pine forests, with Castilian pine-nuts and sabines. We returned to the camp and the Río del Norte, whence we had come.

Having reached the camp we heard of another province called Quires up the Río del Norte one day's journey, a distance of about six leagues from where we had our camp. With the entire force we set out for the province of the Quires, and one league before reaching it many Indians came out to greet us peacefully, and begged us to go to their pueblos. We went therefore and they received us very well, and gave us some cotton *mantas* many turkeys, maize, and portions of all else which they had. This province has five pueblos, containing a great number of people, it appearing to us that there were fifteen thousand souls. Their food and clothing were the same as those of the preceding province. They are idolatrous, and have many fields of maize and other things. Here we found a parrot in a cage, just like those of Castile, and sunflowers like those of China, decorated with the sun, moon, and stars. Here the latitude was taken, and we found ourselves to be in exactly 37½° north. We heard of another province two days' journey to the west.

Leaving this province, after two days' march, which is fourteen leagues, we found another, called Los Pumames, consisting of five pueblos, the chief pueblo being called Sia. It is a very large pueblo, and I and my companions went through it; it had eight plazas, and better houses than those previously mentioned, most of them being whitewashed and painted with colors and pictures after the Mexican custom. This pueblo is built near a medium-sized river which comes from the north and flows into the Río del Norte, and near a mountain. In this province there are many people, apparently more than twenty thousand souls. They gave us cotton *mantas*, and much food consisting of maize, hens, and bread made from corn flour, the food being nicely prepared, like everything else. They were a more deft people than those we had seen up to this point, but were dressed and governed like the others. Here we heard of another province to the northwest and arranged to go to it. In this pueblo they told us of mines nearby in the mountains, and they showed us rich ores from them.

Having travelled one day's journey to the northwest, a distance of about six leagues, we found a province, with seven pueblos, called the Province of the Emexes, where there are very many people, apparently about thirty thousand souls. The natives indicated to us that one of the pueblos was very large and in the mountains, but it appeared to Fray Bernardino Beltran and some of the soldiers that our numbers were too small to go to so large a settlement and so we did not visit it, in order not to become divided into two parties. It consists of people like those already passed, with the same provisions, apparel, and government. They have idols, bows and arrows, and other arms, as the provinces heretofore mentioned.

We set out from this province towards the west, and after going three days, or about fifteen leagues, we found a pueblo called Acoma, where it appeared to us there must be more than six thousand souls. It is situated on a high rock more than fifty *estados* in height. In the very rock stairs are built by which they ascend to and descend from the town, which is very strong. They have cisterns of water at the top, and many provisions stored within the pueblo. Here they gave us many *mantas*, deerskins, and strips of buffalo-hide, tanned as they tan them in Flanders, and many provisions, consisting of maize and turkeys. These people have their fields two leagues from the pueblo on a river of medium size, whose water they intercept for irrigating purposes, as they water their fields with many partitions of the water near this river, in a marsh. Near the fields we found many bushes of Castilian roses. We also found Castilian onions, which grow in the country by themselves, without planting or cultivation. The mountains thereabout apparently give promise of mines and other riches, but we did not go to see them as the people from there were many and warlike. The mountain people come to aid those of the settlements, who call the mountain people Querechos. They carry on trade with those of the settlements, taking to them salt, game, such as deer, rabbits, and hares, tanned deerskins, and other things, to trade for cotton *mantas* and other things with which the government pays them.

In other respects they are like those of the other provinces. In our honor they performed a very ceremonious *mitote* and dance, the people coming out in fine array. They performed many juggling feats, some of them very clever, with live snakes. Both of these things were well worth seeing. They gave us liberally of food and of all else which they had. And thus, after three days, we left this province.

We continued our march toward the west four days, or twenty-four leagues, when we found a province comprising six pueblos, which they call Amí, or by another name Cibola. It contains a great many Indians, who appeared to number more than twenty thousand. We learned that Francisco Vazquez Coronado and some of the captains he had with him had been there. In this province near the pueblos we found crosses erected; and here we found three Christian Indians, who said their names were Andrés of Cuyuacan, Gaspar of Mexico, and Anton of Guadalajara, and stated that they had come with the said governor Francisco Vasquez. We instructed them again in the Mexican tongue, which they had almost forgotten. From them we learned that the said Francisco Vazquez Coronado and his captains had been there, and that Don Pedro de Tobar had gone in from there, having heard of a large lake where these natives said there were many settlements. They told us that there was gold in that country, and that the people were clothed and wore bracelets and earrings of gold; that these people were sixty days' march from there; that the men of the said Coronado had gone twelve days beyond this province and then had returned, not being able to find water and the supply of water they had carried being exhausted. They gave us very clear signs regarding that lake and the riches of the Indians who live there. Although I and some of my companions desired to go to that lake, others did not wish to assist.

In this province we found a great quantity of Castilian flax, which appears to grow in the fields without being planted. They gave us extended accounts of what there was in the provinces where the large lake is, and of how here they had given to Francisco Vazquez Coronado and his companions many ores, which they had not smelted for lack of the necessary equipment. In this province of Cibola, in a town they call Aquico, the said Father Fray Bernaldino, Miguel Sanchez Valenciano, his wife Casilda de Amaya, Lázaro Sanchez and Miguel Sanchez Nevado, his sons, Gregorio Hernandez, Cristóbal Sanchez, and Juan de Frias, who were in our company, said that they wished to return to Nueva Vizcaya, whence we had set out, because they had learned that Francisco Vazquez Coronado had found neither gold nor silver and had returned, and that they desired to do likewise, which they did. The customs and rites here are similar to those of the provinces passed. They have much game, and dress in cotton *mantas* and others that resemble coarse linen. Here we heard of other provinces to the west.

We went on to the said provinces toward the west, a four days' journey of seven leagues per day. At the end of this time we found another province called Mohoce, of five pueblos, in which, it seemed to us, there are over fifty thousand souls. Before reaching it they sent us messengers to warn us not to go there, lest they should kill us. I and nine companions who had remained with me, namely: Joan Lopez de Ibarra, Bernardo de Cuna, Diego Perez de Luxan, Francisco Barroto, Gaspar de Luxan, Pedro Fernandez de Almansa, Alonso de Miranda, Gregorio Fernandez, and Joan Hernandex, went to the said province of Mohoce, taking with us one hundred and fifty Indians of the province whence we started and the said three Mexican Indians. A league before we reached the province over two thousand Indians, loaded down with provisions, came forth to meet us. We gave them some presents of little value, which we carried, thereby assuring them that we would not harm them, but told them that the horses which we had with us might kill them because they were very bad, and that they should make a stockade where we could keep the animals, which they did. A great multitude of Indians came out to receive us, accompanied by the chiefs of a pueblo of this province called Aguato. They gave us a great reception, throwing much maize flour where we were to pass, so that we might walk thereon. All being very happy, they begged us to go to see the pueblo of Aguato. There I made presents to the chiefs, giving them some things that I carried for this purpose.

The chiefs of this pueblo immediately sent word to the other pueblos of the province, from which the chiefs came with a great number of people, and begged that we go to see and visit their pueblos, because it would give them much pleasure. We did so, and the chiefs and *tequitatos* of the province, seeing the good treatment and the gifts that I gave, assembled between them more than four thousand cotton *mantas*, some colored and some white, towels with tassels at the ends, blue and green ores, which they use to color the *mantas*, and many other things. In spite of all these gifts they thought that they were doing little for us, and asked if we were satisfied. Their food is similar to that of the other provinces mentioned, except that here we found no turkeys. A chief and some other Indians told us here that they had heard of the lake where the gold treasure is and declared that it was neither greater nor less than what those of the preceding provinces had said. During the six days that we remained there we visited the pueblos of the province.

Thinking that these Indians were friendly toward us, I left five of my companions with them in their pueblos, in order that they might return to the province of Amí with the baggage. With the four others whom I took with me I went directly west for forty-five leagues, in search of some rich mines there of which they told me, with guides whom they furnished me in this province to take me to them. I found them, and with my own hands I extracted ore from them, said by those who know to be very rich and to contain much silver. The region where these mines are is for the most part mountainous, as is also the road leading to them. There are some pueblos of mountain Indians, who came forth to receive us in some places, with small crosses on their heads. They gave us some of their food and I presented them with some gifts. Where the mines are located the country is good, having rivers, marshes, and forests; on the banks of the river are many Castilian grapes, walnuts, flax, blackberries, maguey plants, and prickly pears. The Indians of that region plant fields of maize, and have good houses. They told us by signs that behind those mountains, at a distance we were unable to understand clearly, flowed a very large river which, according to the signs they made, was more than eight leagues in width and flowed towards the north Sea; that on the banks of this river on both sides are large settlements; that the river was crossed in canoes; that in comparison with those provinces and settlements on the river, the province where we were then was nothing; and that in that land were many grapes, nuts, and blackberries. From this place we returned to the one whither I had sent my companions, it being about sixty leagues from the said mines to Amí. We endeavored to return by a different route so as to better observe and understand the nature of the country, and I found a more level road than the one I had followed in going to the mines.

Upon arriving at the province of Amí, I found my five companions whom I had left there, and also Father Fray Bernaldino, who had not yet gone back with his companions. The Indians of that province had supplied them all they needed to eat, and he with all of us greatly rejoiced. The caciques came forth to receive me and my companions and gave us plentiful food, and Indians for guides and to carry the loads. When we bade them adieu they made us many promises, saying that we must return again and bring many "Castillos," as they call the Spaniards, and that with this in view they were planting a great deal of maize that year so that there would be ample food for all. From this province Fray Bernaldino and the oth-

ers who had remained with him returned, and with them Gregorio Hernandez, who had accompanied me as ensign, although I urged them not to leave, but to remain and search for mines and other treasures, in the service of his Majesty.

Fray Bernaldino and his companions having departed, with eight soldiers I returned, determined to go up the Rio del Norte, by which we had entered. After having travelled ten days, or about sixty leagues, to the province of the Quires, we went east from there two days' journey of six leagues each, and reached a province of Indians called the Ubates, having five pueblos. The Indians received us peacefully and gave us much food, turkeys, maize, and other things. From there we went in quest of some mines of which we had heard and found them in two days, travelling from one place to another. We secured shining ore and returned to the settlement from which we had set out. The number of people in these pueblos is great, seeming to us to be about twenty thousand souls. They dress in white and colored *mantas*, and tanned deer and buffalo hides. They govern themselves as do the neighboring provinces. There are no rivers here, but they utilize springs and marshes. They have many forests of pine, cedar, and sabines. Their houses are three, four, and five stories in height.

Learning that at one day's journey from this province there was another, we went to it. It consists of three very large pueblos, which seemed to us to contain more than forty thousand souls. It is called the province of the Tamos. Here they did not wish to give us food or admit us. Because of this, and of the illness of some of my companions, and of the great number of people, and because we were unable to subsist, we decided to leave the country, and, at the beginning of July, 1583, taking an Indian from the said pueblo as a guide, we left by a different route from that by which we had entered. At a distance of half a league from a town of the said province, named Ciquique, we came to a river which I named Rio de las Vacas, for, travelling along its banks for six days, a distance of about thirty leagues, we found a great number of the cows of that country. After travelling along this river one hundred and twenty leagues toward the east we found three Indians hunting. They were of the Jumana nation. From them we learned through an interpreter whom we had that we were twelve days' journey from the Conchas River, a distance which we thought must be a little over forty leagues. We crossed over to this river, passing many watering places in creeks and marshes on the way, and found there many of the Cumano nation, who brought us fish of many kinds, prickly pears and other fruits, and gave us buffalo hides and tanned deerskins. From there we came out to the Valley of San Bartolomé, whence Fray Bernaldino Beltran and I, with the companions named herein, had started. We found that the said Father Fray Bernaldino and his companions had arrived many days before at the province of San Bartolomé, and had gone to the Villa of Guadiana.

Everything narrated herein I saw with my own eyes, and is true, for I was present at everything. Sometimes I set out from the camp with a number of companions, sometimes with but one, to observe the nature of that country, in order to report everything to his Majesty, that he may order what is best for the exploration and pacification of those provinces and for the service of God our Lord and the increase of His holy Catholic faith; and that those barbarians may come to know of it and to enter into it. My companions and I have employed in this narrative, as also in the *autos* and *diligencias* which we drew up on the way, all possible and necessary care, as is shown by testimony as authoritative as we were able to procure there. Not all that occurred could be written, nor can I give an account of it in writing, for it would be too long, for the lands and provinces through which we travelled on this journey were many and large.

By the direct course which we took from the Valley of San Bartolomé until we reached the borders of the provinces we visited, it is over two hundred and fifty leagues, and by the route over which we returned it is more than two hundred leagues. Besides this, we travelled more than three hundred more leagues in the exploration of the said provinces and in going through them from one part to another, over both rough and level lands, over lagoons, marshes, and rivers, with great dangers and many difficulties. We found many different tongues among the natives of those provinces, different modes of dress, and different customs. That which we saw and of which I write gives but an inkling of what actually exists in those provinces, for in travelling through them we heard of large settlements, very fertile lands, silver mines, gold, and better governed peoples.

As we saw, dealt with, and heard of large settlements, and as our numbers were few, and as some of my companions were afraid to continue further, we did not explore more than what I have stated. But even to accomplish this much has required of us great courage, which we mustered because we realized that thereby we were serving God our Lord and his Majesty, and that thereby the Indians might obtain some light, and in order that we might not lose our opportunity. We therefore endeavored by all means at our disposal to see and understand everything, learning the facts through interpreters where there were any, or by signs where there were none, the Indians of those provinces showing us by lines which they made on the ground and by their hands the number of days' journey from one province to another, and the number of pueblos in each province, or by the best means at our command for understanding.

The people of all those provinces are large and more vigorous than the Mexicans, and are healthy, for no illness was heard of among them. The women are whiter skinned than the Mexican women. They are an intelligent and well-governed people, with pueblos well formed and houses well arranged, and from what we could understand from them, anything regarding good government they will learn quickly. In the greater part of those provinces there is much game of foot and wing, rabbits, hares, deer, native cows, ducks, geese, cranes, pheasants, and other birds, good mountains with all kinds of trees, salines and rivers, and many kinds of fish. In the greater portion of this country carts and wagons can be used; there are very good pastures for cattle, lands suitable for fields and gardens, with or without irrigation, and many rich mines, from which I brought ores to assay and ascertain their quality. I also brought an Indian from the province of Tamos and a woman from the province of Mohoce, so that if in the service of his Majesty return were to be made to undertake the exploration and settlement of those provinces they might furnish us with information regarding them and of the route to be travelled, and in order that for this purpose they might learn the Mexican and other tongues. For all of this I refer to the *autos* and *diligencias* which are made in the matter, from which will be seen more clearly the good intentions and good-will with which I and my companions served his Majesty in this journey, and the good opportunity there was for doing so in order to report to his Majesty, in whose service I desire to spend my life and my fortune.

I wrote this narrative at the mines of Santa Bárbola, of the jurisdiction of Nueva Vizcaya, at the end of October, 1583, having arrived at the Valle of San Bartolomé, in the said jurisdiction, on the 20th of September of the said year, the day we arrived from the said journey.

[Signed:] Antonio Despejo

828. November 10, 1592. Journal of Castaño de Sosa, lieutenant governor of Nueva León, on his expedition to New Mexico and attempted colony there, 1590–1591: extracts.

Printed in somewhat differing versions in Colección de documentos de Indias, *IV, 283–354, and XV, 191–261. Translated in A. H. Schroder and D. S. Matson,* A Colony on the Move *(1965), and in G. P. Hammond and A. Rey,* Rediscovery of New Mexico, *pp. 245–295, from which pp. 248–256, 268–274, 290–295, are extracted. The journal was examined by the Audiencia of Mexico on November 10, 1592, before it was forwarded to Spain.*

... We left this place [near the Río de las Salinas] on the twenty-fifth and camped by the Río de los Ratones. The twenty-sixth we journeyed on and halted for the night by the Río del Gato. On the twenty-seventh we camped at Barranca, where Viruega's horse got mired down in some deep pools. The twenty-ninth we left Barranca and spent the night in some hills where we found a large water hole. On the thirtieth we left this place and camped in a gully or ravine where some showers fell, supplying us with water. Otherwise we should have had none; and thus the Lord cared for us.

On September 1 we started out again and passed through a ravine where our big cart broke down and the oxen were sent back. The second we went on to spend the night in another ravine, without water. On September 3 we continued our journey and camped in a walnut grove where we found many nuts. The fourth we went on and spent the night by the Río de Roldán. On the sixth we halted for the night at the Río de Viruega, where there were many nuts and grapes. The eighth we left this place and camped near a large lake where nuts and grapes were plentiful, and where we also caught many fish.

On the ninth we traveled on to spend the night at the Río Bravo, where we tarried many days waiting for Francisco Salgado, Manuel de Mederos, and a number of other men who were expected with the viceroy's answer. The lieutenant governor had told them that he would wait for them at the Bravo to receive the viceroy's orders, for which purpose he had sent them to Mexico city. Seeing that they were so long in coming back, the lieutenant governor commanded that all corn and wheat be measured in order to find out what provisions were left, and we found that there were only one hundred fanegas. This grieved him, for he thought we had more provisions than that. The cause for the scarcity was the fact that the supplies had not been distributed carefully, since the grain was carried in large baskets and no record had been kept, as the food was in the care of Juan Pérez de los Ríos. The lieutenant governor had not failed to tell him days earlier that he should distribute measured rations to everyone; but Pérez countered on several occasions by saying that his people were not going to be put on short rations, and in order to please him our leader did not compel him to ration the grain. Now, when the corn and wheat finally were measured, the lieutenant governor ordered that the grain should be distributed among the wagons in definite amounts and that the various groups should account for the quantities entrusted to them. He also ordered that from then on each person be given one almud per week; and this command was obeyed.

Meanwhile, in view of the delay in the return of Salgado, Mederos, and their men, and mindful of the scanty provisions, the lieutenant governor decided to go ahead with the expedition. In the process of establishing the route that the army would have to follow, many points of view were expressed by the men, who all differed from the leader with the exception of Captain Cristóbal de

Heredia, Francisco López de Ricalde, Martín de Salazar, and Juan de Carvajal. The opinion of this group was that they should look for the Río Salado. In the end the lieutenant governor instructed Captain Cristóbal de Heredia to start the search. In compliance with this command, Juan Pérez de los Ríos and several companions set out in search of the said river, but could not find it because of the difficult nature of the terrain. Pérez came back with news of a different river, saying that it could be followed, though with difficulty because of the ruggedness of the land bordering it. He added that the trail lay at some distance from the river, and that it would be laborious and costly to send the oxen and horses to the stream itself on account of the many rocks.

The lieutenant governor was satisfied with the report of the river and route; but he again sent out a number of soldiers from his company, giving them instructions to explore another river farther on, in case this was the one he should follow. The soldiers reached the river that had been discovered by Juan Pérez de los Ríos and his men and turned back, saying that it was absolutely impossible to go that way. This grieved the lieutenant governor, since he himself thought it was the route he ought to take. Being weak and in poor health, he could not go in person to find out what he was so eager to learn, and therefore he sent Cristóbal de Heredia on a third mission in another search for the Río Salado. The captain accordingly set out to look for it, taking along Juan Rodríguez Nieto, Juan de Contreras and Pedro Flores. He reached the river previously found, discovering a ford not noted before which the wagons could cross. Continuing over the hills that extended to the Río Bravo, he reached this last-named river and then returned to camp, reporting we could follow that same route to the Río Salado. When Heredia realized that he had found a route he was very pleased, although others held different views, as related above.

On October 1 the lieutenant governor ordered the captain to get the entire expedition ready to start out on the journey, which he did. As we were about to set forth, many differences of opinion again arose in regard to the route we should follow. The captain therefore asked the lieutenant governor to decide which route we were to take and was told that he should head for the Río Salado and should act as guide. Captain Cristóbal

de Heredia did as he was ordered, and we went on to spend the night in a ravine where we found some pools of water.

We resumed our journey on the second and camped for the night by the Río de las Laxas, which we crossed with great difficulty. The fourth we started out again and reached a ravine where we found abundant water.

On the fifth we pursued our quest for the Río Salado until we came to another and very deep ravine. The sixth we reached some small oaks where there was plenty of water.

The seventh we continued in search of the Río Salado, the object of our journey; and Captain Cristóbal de Heredia sent out Juan de Carvajal, Martín de Salazar, Domingo de Santiesteban, and Blas Martínez de Mederos for this purpose. They succeeded in finding the river, which pleased them very much. Domingo de Santiesteban came back to convey the good news that he and his companions had at last discovered the Salado, although it was impossible to reach it because of the many high rocks and gullies. We spent the night in a ravine where there was a pool that supplied water for our people; but the oxen and horses were sent back. We tried every means of reaching the stream, but to no avail; and so we turned back to look for the other river, which we had noted before. Captain Cristóbal de Heredia went ahead to see if it was far away and soon found it, about three leagues from the spot where we had halted.

We set out again on the ninth and spent the night a league from the Río de las Laxas. The eleventh we continued on our way and stopped at some huts where there was no water.

The twelfth we left this place and reached some hills where we found a small pool of water; since we looked in vain for the Río de las Laxas, which was no longer visible, we sent the oxen and horses back to that river and continued vigorously to search for the Río Salado. Salazar, Diego Díaz de Berlanga, and Cristóbal Martín went on this mission. In three or four leagues they again caught sight of it and returned to camp saying that we could not get down to it. Nevertheless, we decided to proceed on our way; and, as we started out, God sent a heavy shower for our relief. We trusted that He would provide, for we knew He was merciful to us.

The fourteenth we left this place and moved on,

camping for the night at the place where Cristóbal de Heredia was given his commission as maese de campo. Then the lieutenant governor, realizing that the journey was being drawn out too long, ordered that only one half an almud of wheat or corn should be given to each person per week; as the ration was small, he tried to buy some oxen from Juan Pérez de los Ríos, to be slaughtered and the meat to be distributed among the people in the camp. In the course of the negotiations with Juan Pérez de los Ríos, who could see that the need was great, he replied that he would not sell a single animal, but that if the lieutenant governor needed oxen in this emergency, they were all available and he would make a gift of them in the name of the king our lord. The lieutenant governor accepted the offer and immediately held a roll call of all his people. Finding that there were upward of one hundred and seventy persons, he ordered the distribution of one and a half pounds of meat per day for each person. With this ration and the grain portion above-mentioned, we were able to get along; but we began at that point to roast maguey in order to supplement the shortage.

On the sixteenth we continued as far as the Lexas, where we camped for the night and where a good shower fell, much to our relief, since we could not reach the river. At this place we roasted a quantity of mescal. The seventeenth we went to La Cañada, where Alonso Jaimez and Ponce got lost.

When we set out again on the eighteenth, Cristóbal de Heredia and some soldiers went ahead to see if there was an approach to the Río Salado. In the course of his search we found that it could not be reached because of the bad terrain and complete lack of water; so he sent Francisco López de Ricalde and Jusepe Rodríguez back to camp while he himself rode on with the rest of his men. The two who came back told the lieutenant governor that there was no possible way of going forward, since they could not find the river, which must have turned abruptly to the west, and since the wagons could not travel by that route. This information displeased everyone, particularly Juan López [Pérez] de los Ríos, who feared that his capital would be lost, though he was even more concerned about his wife and children than his possessions. He complained bitterly, blaming the lieutenant governor for leading him astray. This was what grieved him most. As far as he was concerned, if things turned out badly, he could withdraw to a ranchería and end his days there, since the lieutenant governor had chosen a different route from the one he wanted to follow.

The lieutenant governor listened to all the hysterical complaints of Pérez and others. Then, during a lull, he called the people together and asked them what they thought should be done. There were some who expressed the opinion that they ought to go back and pick up the route that a number of the men had wanted to follow in opposition to the choice of the lieutenant governor. The latter, since the other route was the one he favored, encouraged us as kindly as he could, urging us all—men, women, and children, including the Indians—to commend ourselves to God and to have faith that He and His holy Mother would guide and enlighten us, giving wisdom to our leader so that he would not be wanting in anything, for it was his desire to serve God our Lord and his Majesty. Accordingly, he gave orders to leave this place and to go on, which we did.

Immediately afterward, the lieutenant governor sent some men to look for water along the route we were to follow. When we had gone about a quarter of a league, Francisco López de Ricalde came to the governor (who was bringing up the rear, as was his custom) to tell how Juan Pérez de los Ríos, downhearted and weeping, had asked him to intercede with Castaño to turn back, for the love of God. As soon as Ricalde broached the subject, our leader told him angrily that he did not want to have anyone talk to him about the matter; that, if the Spaniards showed fright, it would be taken as a sign of weakness on their part and they would lose their rights; and that Ricalde should tell Juan Pérez to hold his peace and go on with the trip, instead of discouraging the people. For he, the lieutenant governor (as he had already said) trusted in God, who would not let them lack water, but would provide it for them.

The lieutenant governor now withdrew from the army and marched to one side, accompanied only by a servant named Juan López. After going about half a league he came to a very large pool of water, which delighted him, for in that area such a big pond had never before been found. It seemed that the Lord had indeed provided it, as He always makes provision. Our leader hastened to the wagons and halted them so that the oxen and horses could be driven to water, as was done. Here we decided to wait for Cristóbal de Heredia. He arrived the following day, reporting that he had been unable to reach the river. Some thought that it had disappeared from our route, as had the Laxas.

In the midst of this uncertainty, the lieutenant governor sent Alonso Jaimez and some other men, including Diego Díaz de Berlanga, Cristóbal Martín, Juan López and Francisco de Mancha, with orders to follow certain human tracks found there and to procure, with the help of their interpreter, another Indian who might serve as interpreter for that land and furnish information about it. He, the governor, would follow their trail with the wagons. They set out the next day.

We left this place on the nineteenth, intending to follow the route taken by Alonso Jaimez to some water found two leagues from our starting point, according to a report sent by him through an Indian named Juan de Vega, whom he had taken along as a courier. Not being satisfied with this information, the lieutenant governor dispatched Cristóbal de Heredia to go and see the water, which he did. Finding that it was very scanty and that the route was quite different from the one we were supposed to follow, Heredia returned in great haste and said that Jaimez's road was not the one we meant to take. On being informed of this, the lieutenant governor ordered him to abandon that route and to go straight ahead, which he did. We went on to spend the night near some flat rocks and some water found by Cristóbal de Heredia.

On the twentieth we resumed our journey, much troubled by the scarcity of water, since we had not half the amount needed for that day and night. As was customary, the lieutenant governor dispatched many of his men to search for water in rocky pools or arroyos, since there were no springs anywhere in the land. God favored us, and Domingo de Santiesteban came back to report that in a canyon ahead there were large pools of water. We went on joyously, arrived there at eleven in the morning, unyoked the oxen, and remained at the pools for a couple of hours. Then we yoked the animals again and continued on our way, stopping two or three hours at some hills during the night.

We set forth once more on the twenty-first; and while we were traveling along at midday, we found a pool of water in some rocky shallows where all the people and some of the horses drank a little, but without getting enough, since we had run out of water the preceding night. We marched on and spent the next night in a dry ravine, although a half league away we found enough water for the people, and some of the horses also drank there. That night, owing to the scarcity of water, the lieutenant governor instructed Maese de Campo Cristóbal de Heredia to send some men to look for the Río Salado, with orders not to return until they had seen it and to send someone back to report if they found water.

The maese de campo immediately dispatched Juan de Carvajal, Juan Estrada, Martín de Salazar, Juan Rodríguez Nieto, Pedro Flores, and Gonzalo de Lares, who left that very evening to discharge their commission. After marching about two leagues, they rested for a while during the night, but before dawn they were under way again in accordance with their instructions. The men were intent upon their search for the said river and resolved not to return before finding it, a purpose in which they held firm, when God willed that they should come upon some very large pools. This pleased them immensely on account of the severe shortage of water. In compliance with orders, Pedro Flores went back posthaste to report this discovery. It must have taken him less than an hour to reach the army, while the other men went on to look for the river.

At this stage of our journey the goats got lost and Pedro Pinto rushed back to say that the Indians were stealing them. The lieutenant governor and two or three soldiers went in the direction the Negro had indicated as the route of the supposed thieves, and within about a league he overtook the animals. Actually, the goats had not been stolen by Indians, for they were running away of their own accord, driven by thirst. A large number of the oxen also stampeded, goaded by the same need; but Diego de Viruega rounded them up about two leagues from the camp.

On the twenty-third, as we were yoking our oxen and getting ready to leave, Pedro Flores arrived with the report that water had been found. We went back with him to spend the night in the place described, where we rejoiced to find that the water was plentiful. The next day the men who had discovered the river returned to report that the hills and sierras came to an end at this point, and that the river was about four leagues from our location. They were welcomed for their good news, in view of the hardships we had endured thus far, the poverty of the land, the scanty water, and the exhaustion of the horses, which was what we most regretted. For we were all in the depths of despair because of the rocky terrain on the journey in search of the long-sought Río Salado.

Twenty-five dozen horseshoes were worn out on the mountains here, since there was no way to travel save on horseback. Many horses wore out their shoes in two or three days, incredible as it may seem, and a large number of the animals became lame. So great was the hardship endured before we reached water that only those of our people who witnessed the ordeal will believe how much we suffered. If the discovery of this route were to be paid for in money, it would take an enormous sum.

The lieutenant governor expressed thanks to his companions and the fervent hope that God our Lord and his Majesty would reward them. He also assured them that in so far as might be in his power, he would grant, in the name of the king, any favor they might ask. They should not hesitate to speak, because he could never repay with money their many labors or the enthusiasm with which they had helped him; for if they were to be rewarded with cash it would require a great sum. As if with one voice, his followers replied that they would always be ready to withstand such hardships as they might have to endure, since their main interest lay precisely in doing what the lieutenant governor ordered, in the name of his Majesty. For this he thanked them and said that, by God's will and with His favor, he trusted that they would accomplish their purpose, since it was a very worthy one, and that the king would reward them as he does all who serve him. The lieutenant governor was pleased at the sturdy spirit displayed by his men, and they were no less gratified by what he told them. I cannot exaggerate nor even describe here the aforementioned hardships. In short, after finding the river we were seeking, we thought we had been through the worst of the struggle, and so we remained there in great contentment for two days.

We left the place on the twenty-fifth, and after traveling for two leagues we camped for the night. We were without water.

On the twenty-sixth we set out for the river we had sought so eagerly, but could not find a way down to it except by some steep slopes which we descended with great difficulty. These hardships seemed very light to all of us in our eager desire to serve God and the king. In the descent some wagons broke down, among them one containing the coffer for the royal fifths. We all dismounted and the lieutenant governor told us to go down to the river for a rest with the [undamaged] wagons and the people, while he would remain there with some men to watch the royal coffer, which he did. The next day the wagon [holding the coffer] was made ready and taken to the river. . . .

We resumed our journey on the twenty-seventh [of December], traveling over a fine plain, and spent the night at Urraca. A freak accident befell Juan Rodríguez Nieto at this place. While he was trying to start a fire, a spark flew out from somewhere, and the large and small powder flasks hanging from his belt exploded, but without doing any damage.

On the twenty-eighth we left this camp and traveled all day. One of our men, Pedro Flores, had suffered an attack of melancholia the day before, which left him exhausted and somewhat incoherent. Before starting out, the lieutenant governor asked him to go back to the others, who were following us, with instructions from our leader to camp at Urraca and await further orders. He was sure the sick man would be able to return safely and would find the wagons, at a spot four leagues away. Pedro Flores replied that he would never go back; but some insisted that he should be ordered to do so, for they felt he was really sick and so dangerously melancholic that he appeared in a measure to have lost his mind. The lieutenant governor felt sorry for him in his suffering and again asked him to return, saying that a soldier or servant would be sent to accompany him; but he would not consent. At this point the lieutenant governor talked of turning back on account of Pedro Flores, who felt very badly about it and said that there was no reason for such action.

Since he seemed to feel better, we continued our trip and stopped for the night at a place called Caballo, near a small water hole. This place is so named because here, after the experiences above related, the maese de campo had ordered a horse slaughtered for food when there was nothing else to eat. Shortly afterward Pedro Flores, very cheerful, came to the quarters of the lieutenant governor and said he was quite well and free from pain, but very hungry because, from the time he had left the wagons, he had not eaten a thing; nor had he slept for three nights—something unheard of, it seemed to me. The lieutenant governor rejoiced at what Pedro Flores said, as well he might, because he was very fond of the man. He therefore ordered that Flores be given some meat and three tortillas; these tortillas were a real luxury, since we had almost none. The next morning Pedro Flores was missing and the lieutenant governor ordered the maese de campo to search for him, which he did, accompanied by two other men; but they could not find him and returned to camp. Then, as they were rounding up the horses, they discovered that Pedro Flores's horse was missing, as were his saddle, harquebus, and armor, all of which he had taken with him. Believing he had gone back to the wagons that day, the lieutenant governor ordered the party to proceed, and we obeyed.

We left this place on the thirtieth and camped a short league from the pueblo, after marching over a bad trail. We slept on the bank of the river.

On the thirty-first, before daybreak, the lieutenant governor ordered breakfast prepared, telling us all to eat and to feel confident that we should be well received by the Indians of the entire pueblo, because it was his firm intention to cause them no harm at all. Accordingly, he asked us not to make any move save by his orders or those of the maese de campo. Then we headed straight for the pueblo.

In order that the Indians should be aware of our approach before we came in sight, the governor asked the maese de campo to dispatch some men by a hidden route to see if they could find an Indian who might be sent ahead to the pueblo, so that he could explain to the natives that we were coming not to molest them but to place them under the protection and authority of his Majesty. Martín de Salazar undertook this mission, together with Cristóbal [Martín] and Diego de Viruega, while the lieutenant governor and his party continued on their way toward the pueblo, straight over the path which the other men would have to take after finding the Indian spokesman.

Going forward in this manner, his men in formation and with flag unfurled, the governor, as we came in view of the pueblo, ordered the buglers to blow their trumpets. When he reached the town, he noticed that the natives were in battle array, men as well as women standing fully prepared on the terraces and down below. Surveying the situation, he ordered the maese de campo to pitch camp at the distance of an harquebus shot from the pueblo, on the side where it seemed strongest, and this was done. Then he ordered the two bronze pieces set up, asking Juan Rodríguez Nieto to take charge of them and to keep the fuse lighted in order that everything might be in readiness in case the guns should be needed for defense against the Indians and their pueblo; or rather, in case the natives should try some shameless trick like the one played previously. He urged us to be very alert and to conduct ourselves like brave soldiers, as we were accustomed to do.

After making all these arrangements, the lieutenant governor called to the Indians in sign language, but none would leave his dwelling or come out from behind the barricades, trenches, or ramparts which the pueblo maintained for its defense at the most vital points. Although these had all been constructed earlier, we could not understand the present activities of the Indians; but later they explained to us that they were at war with other groups, and that this was the reason for the fortifications, except that the many earthen bulwarks on the terraces of their houses had been newly added to protect the pueblo against us.

All this took place at about eight o'clock in the morning. The lieutenant governor then left his quarters, accompanied by the maese de campo, Martín de Salazar, Juan de Carvajal, and Blas Martínez de Mederos. On nearing the houses of the pueblo, he called to the Indians and told them he would not do them any harm or injury, but this failed to calm them. On the contrary, they hastened to pile up stones on the terraces. The stones were brought by the women, for the men were all armed, at their posts, and shouting lustily at us.

The lieutenant governor and his soldiers circled the entire pueblo in an effort to soothe the natives with kind words and by signs, offering gifts to placate them, but to no avail. Instead of softening, the Indians shot arrows and hurled quantities of stones by means of slings, growing more and more clamorous. These maneuvers lasted about five hours, while the governor's group marched around the pueblo several times and the main body of soldiers remained in camp, as ordered. Then the group returned to camp, where the lieutenant governor ordered us all to remain armed and to round up the horses. Taking a few more articles of the kind he had given the natives before, such as knives and other small items, they went back to the pueblo, circled it once more, and tried again to give the inhabitants some presents in an attempt to find out who was the captain of the pueblo. As a result of this attempt, our men saw and talked with the chieftain. One of the soldiers in the group on this occasion was Diego de Viruega, who dismounted and tried to climb over a crumbling corner of the fortifications in order to give presents to some Indians near there who showed signs of wanting to be friendly; yet they would not allow him to ascend.

At that moment the captain of the pueblo came up and was given a knife and some other trifles; but even this failed to pacify the natives. So the Spaniards returned to their quarters, and the lieutenant governor said to them: "These Indians do not want to be our friends. What do you gentlemen think?" Several responded by asking what he himself wanted to do with the Indians, and he replied that it was his wish to subdue them by peaceful means without injury to either side. The soldiers countered by saying that he should not waste much time in this effort, as it was useless. The lieutenant governor then summoned Andrés Pérez, the secretary, to accompany him, which Pérez did; and when they had gone back to the pueblo and marched around it, the secretary was asked to certify that Castaño had tried to communicate with the natives by signs and had spent considerable time in circling the pueblo in company with the maese de campo, Martín de Salazar, Juan de Carvajal, Blas Martínez de Mederos, and Diego de Viruega. Since he, the secretary, had witnessed the peaceable overtures made to the Indians by the lieutenant governor, both previously and in the company of the said Andrés Pérez, the latter should so certify, drawing up an affidavit to be witnessed by the others.

The governor then returned to camp and once more asked his men what should be done, since the Indians would not listen to reason; and they all answered with one accord that he ought not to waste any more time on those dogs. He replied by inquiring what course they wished to take, and

the men repeated that the natives should be overcome by force, since they refused to accept the friendship we had offered in peace and goodwill. The lieutenant governor objected that he thought it was by then too late to undertake the task suggested, to which his men replied that if God wished to grant them victory, there was time enough and to spare.

It was then about two o'clock in the afternoon, and we all believed that the lieutenant governor was acting as he did in order to allow the Indians more time. In view of the unanimous opinion of the soldiers, he ordered the maese de campo to post two men on a commanding elevation back of the pueblo so that they could see if any of the inhabitants were leaving. The maese sent Juan de Carvajal and Blas Martínez de Mederos to the observation post and they departed on this mission. The governor returned to the pueblo, where he made another appeal to the Indians and attempted to soothe them; but they would not relent. Moreover, an Indian woman came out on a terrace connecting the houses (which are four or five stories) and threw some ashes at him; and as she did so the natives began to shout. He turned back, commanding all of us who bore arms to make ready for battle and mount our horses. Then he ordered Juan Rodríguez Nieto to fire one of the guns over the pueblo, which Nieto did; at the same time the harquebuses were fired in the hope that this would frighten the natives. As we drew close to the pueblo, the Indians hurled showers of stones, by hand or with slings, and shot many arrows. Still the lieutenant governor went on appealing to them, while they derided him. In the meantime the Indian women showed fierce courage and kept on bringing more stones to the terraces.

Thereupon the lieutenant governor ordered the maese de campo to attack the pueblo in earnest. For our greater protection, Castaño and the maese de campo went to an unoccupied section of the pueblo, where they ordered Diego de Viruega, Francisco de Mancha, Diego Díaz de Berlanga, and Juan Rodríguez Nieto to climb to the top with one of the artillery pieces. The men did so, although with much difficulty, because the Indians were harrying them fiercely from behind a parapet and some trenches. To facilitate the ascent, the lieutenant governor attacked the Indians at this point and forced them to withdraw.

When the soldiers reached the top, he told them to fire their harquebuses from there, aiming wherever the attack would be most effective. Then he returned to the maese de campo and the other men, who were facing the main forces of the pueblo. This being the strongest point, we attacked it with a large number of guns; and the Indians, realizing the strength of our onslaught, replied in kind. None of them abandoned his section or trench; on the contrary, each one defended the post entrusted to him, without faltering in the least. Such intelligence among barbarians seemed incredible.

At the time when the Spaniards were fighting near that section, Thomas, one of the lieutenant governor's Indian servants armed with bow and arrow, began to shoot at the inhabitants; and another Indian, named Miguel, did likewise. When the natives noticed that we were shooting arrows, they became alarmed and showed more fear of those weapons than of our harquebuses. The lieutenant governor then ordered us to shoot in every direction, which we did. Thomas, the above-mentioned Indian, together with Domingo Fernández, a Portuguese, entered one of the houses, while the other men remained at their posts, firing their harquebuses. The Indians, finding themselves hard pressed, abandoned some of the dwellings; and the lieutenant governor, sensing that the place could be entered safely on that side, ordered some of the men to climb to the top of the fortified point and take it. After this was accomplished, he went to the section where Viruega, Mancha, Diego Díaz, and Juan Rodríguez were posted and asked them how things were going. They replied that two of their party were wounded, but that most of the natives were abandoning the stronghold we were trying to seize. One Indian displayed great bravery, going about among his people and bringing reinforcements to the stronghold, but Diego Díaz de Berlanga felled him with an harquebus shot—incredible though it may seem, since he was so far away. When the Indians in that section of the pueblo saw that he had fallen, the majority of them abandoned the position, which was the key point we were trying to take.

The lieutenant governor now left this section, since the men were holding their posts like brave soldiers, as they had done on all other occasions; but before leaving he told them not to fire their harquebuses any more, nor to cause any further damage there. Then he took Diego de Viruega to the point where the battle was still in progress; and here he told Captain Alonso Jaimez to climb to the top with some soldiers, while others from below protected their ascent. This was done. There did not seem to be as large a number of Indians at that spot as there were before; but the few who held their posts behind the barricades defended the terraces very bravely, so that no one could climb to the top except by the slender wooden hand ladders, which only one person at a time could ascend. There were no doors leading from one room to another, but only hatchways just large enough for a single person; and therefore our men, in order to get through them and climb to the terraces, had to ascend without sword or shield, after which they passed the weapons to one another as they climbed. The lieutenant governor, perceiving the danger to our soldiers, ordered the maese de campo and many others to train their harquebuses on the enemy, though he had previously given the order that we should not shoot to kill, because he hoped that God would enable us to defeat our foes without killing them.

In obedience to these orders, the maese de campo brought down an Indian with one harquebus shot, as did both Juan de Contreras and Juan López, a servant of the governor, with the result that the natives were forced to abandon the barricade and our men took it. The first to ascend was Diego de Viruega, followed by Francisco López de Ricalde, Juan Rodríguez de Avalos, Captain Alonso Jaimez, Juan de Estrada, Francisco de Bascones, and Cristóbal Martín. Then the lieutenant governor ordered the buglers and Juan de Contreras, standard bearer of the expedition in the absence of his brother, Francisco Salgado, to climb to the top, where the former were to blow their bugles as a sign of joy and victory. When the pueblo realized that we had occupied this block of buildings, not a soul was venturesome enough to come out on the terraces. . . .

On the eighth [ninth?] of the month we left the abandoned pueblo and went on to Santo Domingo, where we were accorded a very friendly reception. Here the lieutenant governor learned that Alonso Jaimez had run away. The next day, the eighth [tenth?]—after the entire expedition with its wagons had settled in this pueblo for a few days in order that we might conduct from here our search for the mines we had heard about—all of the soldiers and other people in the expedition assembled and asked the lieutenant governor, for the love of God, to overlook certain incidents that had occurred in his camp, since he had forgiven many offenses with great clemency. They pointed out that Alonso Jaimez had absented himself from the camp because he was afraid that the lieutenant governor would certainly punish him, which was the reason why he had run away; and he was very repentant for having offended his leader in any manner. Now all the soldiers and the maese de campo in unison entreated the governor to favor them by pardoning Jaimez; and he answered that, in the name of his Majesty, moved by charity and the suffering they had all endured, he would grant a pardon to Jaimez and to all others who had transgressed the law in any way. Nevertheless, Alonso Jaimez was to be relieved of his commission as captain of the party that was to go to the city of Zacatecas, the Río Grande, and other places, on a recruiting mission. In fact, this commission was revoked publicly and without delay at the time when the governor pardoned all the culprits in the name of his Majesty. We do not record here the names of the others who erred on this occasion, since they have now been pardoned.

On the eleventh a man appeared before the lieutenant governor, asking him to grant some of the company permission to leave for Mexico. He ventured to present this request because they had heard the governor say that anyone who wanted to leave could do so. Our leader told them that the statement was true, and that he reaffirmed it. All those who wanted to leave were free to depart; and he gave them permission because he would rather remain there alone to die than give occasion for unworthy acts. In view of this concession, the group did not actually leave, because there were no longer any soldiers who wanted to go. So, even though there were several disgruntled individuals, nevertheless, when it became apparent that the lieutenant governor was right and that those who wanted to leave were wrong, all the men—the former malcontents as well as the others—remained quietly and in agreement with him. They performed such duties as arose, never alluding to the recent incidents.

While we were in this pueblo of Santo Domingo,

the lieutenant governor and a party of twenty men went out to look for mines and a certain pueblo which he had not visited before. As they went along, taking possession of various settlements, they crossed some mountains where they found two pueblos that had been deserted only a few days earlier on account of wars with other pueblos which forced the inhabitants to leave their homes. This was the explanation given by the Indians who accompanied us, and we ourselves could see plainly that it was true, because there were signs of many having been killed. In these towns we found an abundance of corn and beans.

From these two abandoned settlements we went back to the Río Grande where we had established a camp for our army and the wagons. From what we had seen there and were told everywhere in the land, we deduced that these were the pueblos whose people had killed the friars reported to have come this way. When we reached the first of the two pueblos, there were no natives left in it. While we were there, we noticed that the one across the river was being evacuated in part, and in order to prevent its complete abandonment, the lieutenant governor sent the maese de campo with some soldiers to stop the evacuation. Then the governor and all the rest of us crossed the river, although it was in full flood, and forced some of the people who were fleeing to turn back. Many, however, had remained in the pueblo. Our leader reassured the natives, giving them to understand that they were not to desert their homes, and they were very pleased. When we asked why the people of the other pueblo had fled, we were told they had done so from fear, because they had killed the friars. We explained that they need not run away, and the governor sent some Indians from this [second] pueblo to call the others back. We took possession of the pueblo in the name of his Majesty and named a governor, an alcalde, and an alguacil; then we raised a large cross with the same kind of ceremonies already described.

After this the lieutenant governor went to another pueblo, a quarter of a league away, but he found few people there, as most of them had fled in fear. We recrossed the river and spent the night in the deserted pueblo. From this point, fourteen other settlements could be seen along the river. The Indians said that most of them had been abandoned by the inhabitants due to fear and that they had sought refuge in the mountains or in other pueblos.

The next day, when the lieutenant governor perceived the uneasiness among the natives caused by fear of what they had done, he decided to send most of his men back to the main camp, which was five or six leagues from there. He himself remained behind with Martín de Salazar, Juan de Estrada, Diego de Viruega, Juan Sánchez, Diego Díaz, Andrés Pérez de Berlanga, and Juan de Contreras, hoping that with so few soldiers in their midst the Indians would overcome their fear, acquire a sense of security, and remain in their homes. In order that these hopes might be realized, the maese de campo returned to the camp, while the lieutenant governor stayed behind with his five companions.

Traveling with them up the river, he visited four pueblos, but found them all deserted, except one which seemed to contain some fifty people. He reassured the natives with kind words, gave them some small trinkets, and asked them to go and call back all the other Indians. In the meantime, the governor crossed to the opposite side of the river where still more pueblos were situated, some of which he found fully occupied, while some contained only a few people. He treated the natives generously and reassured them so convincingly that he induced large numbers to return to their pueblos. In fact, his attitude was so kind and friendly that they felt very safe, for he gave them to understand that we would not harm them at all. As a result of this treatment, we saw large numbers of Indians returning from the fields to their homes.

We spent the night in a small pueblo located in the midst of the others, although we took the precaution of posting sentries, since we were only six men. To be sure, our scanty numbers proved effective in calming the Indians, since they could see that most of our men had departed and that the lieutenant governor had only the five companions above-mentioned.

The next day we left this pueblo and went to another one, where the lieutenant governor told the people not to be afraid, since he did not intend to stay, and that they should call back the people of the pueblos where the padres were believed to have been killed. Then we traveled on to the last pueblo on this side of the river [the east bank?], a large one with many inhabitants, who received us well. We appointed a governor and an alcalde for it in the name of his Majesty; and we raised a large cross. This done, we continued on our way to the main camp of the expedition. When we reached a pueblo situated a league from the camp we met an Indian captain who lived there, carrying in his bosom the bowl from a silver chalice. Here the Indians said that many other Spaniards had arrived, in addition to our own forces, which pleased us all very much. The lieutenant governor asked a soldier to watch the Indian with the chalice bowl.

Traveling on, we met Juan de Carvajal, Joseph Rodríguez, and Francisco de Mancha, who were coming to notify the lieutenant governor of the arrival of Captain Juan Morlete with fifty men. The governor asked who they were, and the three soldiers named most of them; but there were none in the group from among the many men whom he had sent to Mexico and whom he was awaiting. He was puzzled by the fact that the party included none of the most important people he was expecting, although he did not show his perplexity. In the afternoon he ordered that we travel at a gallop, because he wanted to enter by day the pueblo where Captain Morlete had his entire camp. Those of us who accompanied the lieutenant governor never heard him say a word beyond what has been stated. As he advanced, he was warned not to enter the pueblo, nor even to approach it, because Captain Morlete and his men were coming to arrest him. When our leader realized the situation, he asked that not a word be said, adding that if they wanted to arrest him, they were welcome to do so, although he was serving his Majesty and had ample authorization for what he was doing. If it was the king's will to have him arrested, he would gladly submit.

Accordingly, the governor accelerated his pace in order to reach his destination before dark. When he arrived at the pueblo, he went to one side of the plaza while Captain Juan Morlete was passing through the center, on his way to his quarters; and as they met they greeted each other. After dismounting, the lieutenant governor walked toward Captain Juan Morlete and his men; the captain, seeing him approach, drew near with his men closely grouped about him. They greeted each other again and embraced; and then many of the others who were friends of the governor embraced him also.

When these demonstrations were over, Captain Morlete drew from his pocket a royal decree, saying that he came by order of Viceroy Don Luis de Velasco in the name of his Majesty to carry out a royal command, which he read to him word for word. The lieutenant governor listened to the reading of the decree, and when it was finished, the captain asked him to submit to arrest. Our leader replied that he was quite willing, if that was the wish of his Majesty, for he was entirely subject to his authority. Then all of them walked to the tents, and Captain Juan Morlete gave orders that the lieutenant governor should be shackled, to which he submitted meekly. Other orders were read to him, containing provisions that concerned him, and he replied that he would obey them all since they came from his king and lord. Whereupon he took the papers, placed them on his head, and then kissed them in the presence of Juan Morlete and the men of Morlete's force and his own. All members of both contingents were greatly pleased at the humility and submissiveness shown by the lieutenant governor; and Captain Juan Morlete, observing Gaspar Castaño's meekness, honored him and treated him in the manner due his rank and merits, which gratified the soldiers of both armies.

829. [*Circa* 1593]. Report on the abortive and fatal expedition of Francisco Leyva de Bonilla and Antonio Gutiérres de Hamaña to the Great Plains.

This was picked up by Juan de Oñate, in February in New Mexico, from the Indian Jusepe.

A.G.I., Seville, Patronato 22; translated in C. P. Hammond and A. Rey, Rediscovery of New Mexico, *pp. 323–326 (given here); it also appears in Hammond and Rey,* Oñate, *I, 416–419 (with some slight variations).*

At the pueblo of San Juan Bautista, New Mexico, on February 16, 1599, Don Juan de Oñate, governor and captain general, leader, colonizer, and pacifier of these kingdoms for the king our lord, said that he had received information that Jusepe, an Indian, a former servant of Antonio Gutiérrez

de Humaña, had fled from his service and was now in this pueblo, and therefore he ordered the following inquiry so as to learn from him what he had seen and what places he had visited with Antonio Gutiérrez de Humaña, and also what information he had gathered, in order that all of this could be brought to the attention of the king our lord, his royal councils, and others. DON JUAN DE OÑATE. Before me, JUAN VELARDE, secretary.

Witness. At the pueblo of San Juan Bautista, New Mexico on February 16, 1599, his lordship, the governor, ordered an Indian to appear before him. With the help of Juan de Caso Barahona, interpreter on this expedition, he said that his name was Jusepe Gutiérrez and that he was a native of Culhuacán. He took his oath by God our Lord and a cross in due legal manner and promised to tell the truth.

On being questioned in regard to the above inquiry, he said that approximately six years ago, a Spaniard named Antonio Gutiérrez de Humaña spoke to him at his own pueblo and took him away under an agreement whereby he was to serve him in some entradas that he was going to make. Accordingly he followed Humaña as far as the valley of Santa Bárbara, where some people were recruited. With these forces he entered this land and traveled among the pueblos for about a year, the greater part of his time being spent at the pueblo of San Ildefonso, which lies about three leagues from this pueblo. From there they went inland through the pueblos of the Pecos and Vaquero Indians where, traveling slowly and resting occasionally, they reached the buffalo in a month. Here at various places they came upon herds of buffalo, and Indian rancherías, some of them uninhabited. Along their route they saw also many marshes, springs, and arroyos with abundant water.

Proceeding on their way in a northerly direction, the farther inland they went, the larger was the number of buffalo they saw. After traveling for fifteen days more by short marches, they reached two large rivers, and beyond them many rancherías with a large number of inhabitants. Farther on, in a plain, they came to a very large settlement which must have extended for ten leagues, because they traveled through it for two days, and it must have been two leagues wide, more or less. One of the two rivers they crossed earlier flowed through this pueblo. The houses were built on frames of poles, covered with straw, like *jacales* (huts or tepees?). They were built close together, along narrow streets, like alleys. However, in some places between the houses there were fields of corn, calabashes, and beans. The natives were very numerous but received the Spaniards peacefully and furnished them abundant supplies of food. These Indians obtained their livelihood from the buffalo.

On leaving this pueblo and proceeding in a northerly direction, after three days' travel the soldiers came upon such a multitude of buffalo that the plain—which was level, for there are no mountains of any kind—was so covered with them that they were startled and amazed at the sight. Continuing farther on they could not see any more Indian rancherías, but only the usual number of buffaloes. This witness says that after they left the pueblo of Pecos they found great numbers of plum trees at five or six places and that they resembled the plum trees of Castile. They found also walnut trees with small nuts. Near a large river some ten days' travel from the said Great Pueblo there were numerous plum, walnut, and some white sapodilla trees. The climate here was more temperate. This river was about one-fourth of a league wide, deep and sluggish. They did not dare to cross it.

This deponent saw that after going three days beyond the said Great Pueblo, discord arose between Captain Leyva and Antonio Gutiérrez de Humaña. The latter remained alone in his tent an entire afternoon and morning, writing, and at the end of this time he sent a soldier named Miguel Pérez to call Captain Leyva, who came, dressed in shirt and breeches. Before he reached the tent, Antonio Gutiérrez de Humaña went out to meet him, drew a butcher knife from his pocket, unsheathed it, and stabbed Captain Leyva twice, from which he soon afterward died. He was buried at once. Then Antonio Gutiérrez de Humaña brought out some papers and showed them to the other men. This witness heard that because Captain Leyva had said that he was going to give Antonio Gutiérrez de Humaña a sound beating with a stick, he killed him. When some Indians who were with the soldiers saw this, five of them, together with this witness, ran away when they reached the aforesaid great river and returned to these pueblos of New Mexico. Some

of them became lost on the plains of the buffalo because they got separated from one another. Only this witness and another man found their way to an Indian ranchería, where they killed his companion. This witness escaped, and in another ranchería nearer this place he was taken prisoner and remained there for a year with the Apache and Vaquero Indians. Then he fled and reached a place near a pueblo of the Pecos. There he heard that Spanish people had come to these pueblos, and so he came to this pueblo, where he now resides.

This is what happened, under his oath. He ratified his testimony when it was read to him. The general questions of the law did not apply to him other than that he had been a servant of Antonio Gutiérrez de Humaña. This fact did not prevent him from telling the truth, which he did, nor was he coached by anyone. He did not know his age, but appeared to be twenty-seven years old. He did not sign because he did not know how. This statement was signed by his lordship and the interpreter. DON JUAN DE OÑATE. JUAN DE CASSO. Before me, JUAN VELARDE, Secretary.

Decree: After the aforesaid, Governor Don Juan de Oñate, having examined the account that Vicente de Zaldívar had made for him of his trip to the buffalo country in which he told of finding the stopping places of Leyva and Antonio de Humaña, ordered the sargento mayor and others who made the journey with him to declare how many camp sites of these men they had come across and how far from these headquarters they had found them. So he decreed and signed. JUAN DE OÑATE. Before me, JUAN VELARDE, secretary.

Witness: Then, on February 17, 1599, his lordship, the governor, ordered to appear before him the sargento mayor, Vicente de Zaldívar, Diego de Zubia, purveyor general, the caudillo, Francisco Sánchez, and Hernando de Ynojos, all of whom took an oath by God our Lord and a cross in due legal manner and promised to tell the truth. On being questioned regarding this inquiry, they agreed unanimously that the governor had sent them from these headquarters to the buffalo country in September of the preceding year, 1598; that the first campsite of the said Leyva and Antonio de Humaña which they encountered was some twenty-four leagues beyond, more or less, and that at about thirty-six leagues they came upon another known stopping place. These were thought to be the places used by Captain Leyva and Antonio de Humaña, which they learned by questioning a former servant of the latter, one who had accompanied their party as guide and interpreter, and by finding horse dung and remains of their fires.

This is what they saw and learned, under their oath. They reaffirmed their deposition, and those who knew how affixed their names: DON JUAN DE OÑATE. VICENTE DE ZALDÍVAR. DIEGO DE ZUBIA. Before me, JUAN VELARDE, secretary.

Corrected and compared with the original by order of the governor [who here signed his name]. Copied at the pueblo of San Juan Bautista, New Mexico, on February 20, 1599. Witness: ALONSO NÚÑEZ, CRISTÓBAL DE HERRERA, and CRISTÓBAL GUILLÉN. In testimony of which I affixed my name and the seal of his lordship. JUAN VELARDE, secretary.

Chapter One hundred seven
The Revival of Coastal Discovery in the West, 1565–1603.

THE PHILIPPINES and their exploitation preoccupied Spain, especially the viceroyalty of Mexico, between 1565 and 1572. Urdaneta's successful publicizing of the northern return route from the Philippines to Mexico revolutionized the prospects of Spanish relations with the Far East. After the foundation of Manila in 1571 and the establishment of an annual Manila Galleon from there to Acapulco, the question of the California coast became one at least worth discussion. Would knowledge of the coast contribute to the safety of the vessels should they be driven too far eastward too soon? Would the existence of a safe harbor help such vessels if there was doubt of their being able to reach Acapulco in a direct voyage? These issues were raised and discussed, but no one was prepared to take action since it was found in practice that the Manila Galleons rarely saw land north of the California Peninsula and, if Baja California was well mapped and known, the need for northward ventures was not urgent.

The appearance of Drake in the Pacific changed this and, as it became known that he had used Alta California in 1579 for a refitting base (and even that he had claimed it for England) (222–231), the desire to do something about these coasts became stronger. It was countered by doubts about bringing publicity to this area since this might tempt other English enemies to it. Against this, some Spaniards wished to explore the possibilities, as Drake had done, of a passage (the Strait of Anian) between northwest America and Europe. Earlier voyages had given little firm information on these matters.

Francisco de Gualle had sighted land at 37° when returning from Manila in 1584 and induced the Mexican authorities to allow him to explore the coast on his next return in 1585. A vessel was allocated for this, but he did not live to make the voyage. Instead, the attempt was made from Mexico. Pedro de Unamuno took a small vessel up the coast in 1587 (831), but his discovery of a bay between 35° and 36° created little interest and nothing was done to follow up his discoveries. Cavendish's capture of the Manila Galleon, *Santa Ana*, in November, 1587, created fresh alarm at possible English intervention on the west coast. It was not, indeed, until 1594 that the viceroy of Mexico dispatched an effective mission up the coast. This was the expedition of Sebastian Rodríguez Cermeño (a Portuguese like Cabrilho) which brought about a description of the coast to almost as far as 42° N. The grounding of the *San Agustín* at Drakes Bay and the return of the expedition with difficulty in their *lancha* in January, 1596 (832), did not prevent Cermeño from providing a conspectus of the coast which was of some appreciable value. It was thereupon decided in principle that the coast should be surveyed and that, in particular, a safe harbor or harbors for any Manila Galleon in difficulty should be firmly located and charted. But priorities were low for doing this. Sebastian Vizcaíno made something of a name for himself in his exploration of the pearl fisheries in the Gulf of California in 1596, and he was chosen to make the voyage. But, as usual, there were long bureaucratic delays. It was not until May, 1602, that three vessels under his command left Mexico. His long and careful exploration of the coast, with charting taking place continuously (though not perhaps with as much expertise as one might expect) brought him to 42° N or a little farther (though he had been told to go to 44° at least). He formally annexed Alta California as the Kingdom of California, and the Carmelite friars he had with him scrutinized any Indians they encountered to assess their suitability as converts (as well as helping with journal-keeping and charting) (833).

The long and complex voyage involved the choice of Monterey as the best site for a Manila Galleon refuge (834), and it was recommended that a post and mission be established there. Between March and June, 1603, the very full documentation of the voyage was examined in Mexico and favorable reports were sent to Spain. But there seemed no urgency to follow up Vizcaíno's findings, and further exploration was neglected. In part, its revival depended on the fate of New Mexico. If in 1598 and 1599 it looked as if it might prove to be a base for a Pacific-reaching dominion, this hope faded and died during the following years. By 1603 it was past and so the need to be further informed about the new Kingdom of California ceased to matter.

The texts and translations of all the western voyages are given exhaustively in H. R. Wagner, *Spanish Voyages to the Northwest Coast* (San Francisco, 1929; reissued Amsterdam, 1966). Donald C. Cutter, ed., *The California Coast: Documents from the Sutro Collection* (Norman, 1969), has some useful materials. W. Michael Mathes, *Californiana. Documentos para la historia de la demarcación comercial de California, 1580–1630*, 2 vols. (Madrid, 1965), adds new documents, while his monograph, *Vizcaíno and Spanish Expansion on the Pacific Ocean, 1580–1630* (Los Angeles, 1972), is also valuable.

830. [1584-1585]. Fray Andrés de Aguirre to the Archbishop of Mexico, proposing the continuation of the California voyages.

He also sent a version to the Viceroy.

A.G.I., Seville, Mexico 27; printed in W. M. Mathes, Californiana, *I (1965), 6–10, and M. F. de Navarrete,* Colección, *XVIII (1971), fols. 140–142; translated in H. R. Wagner,* Spanish Voyages *(1929), pp. 136–137, and in* The California Coast: Documents from the Sutro Collection, *edited by Donald C. Cutter (1969), pp. 11–16, the version used here.*

Most Illustrious Lord: May the Holy Spirit ever dwell in the soul of your most illustrious lordship. The voyage of discovery which your lordship orders to be made, as well for the purpose of gaining a knowledge of the coast and harbors, and the quality of the land and condition of its people, to the present time discovered to the westward of this New Spain in the South Sea, as for the further prosecution of the exploration of that coast and region beyond the forty-first degree of latitude, is of great importance and very necessary both in connection with the return voyage of vessels from the Philippines and all parts of the west, and for the purpose of understanding and knowing the lay of the land and its qualities and those of its people and of the islands of great importance which are understood to lie near that coast. Although the ships which come every year from the west to the port of Acapulco make a landfall on that coast and sail within sight of it for more than five hundred leagues, to the present time it is not known what harbors or stopping places it has. It is very important to know this, so that ships which come needing to stop, after reaching that coast from a distance of two thousand leagues, without touching anywhere, may stop and provide for their needs.

Nor is it of less importance that the exploration of that coast be continued beyond forty-one degrees of latitude in order that its secrets may be revealed, for it is held as certain that it is a portion of the coast of China, unless it be that they are separated by a narrow strait called Anian, which, according to notices had, is in that part of the coast of China lately explored, in fifty-two degrees of latitude. In that region, and on that lying between the Japanese islands and that portion of our coast recently discovered, according to the account that Father Andrés de Urdaneta obtained from a Portuguese captain, there are very rich islands very thickly populated by people of urbane customs. This narrative I saw and read while he and I were going to Spain in order to give to His Majesty an account of the outcome of the first voyage we made by his order, during which the Philippine islands were discovered and settled and the manner of navigating thither and of making the return voyage thence to New Spain was determined.

The said father gave this narrative to His Majesty and I made a copy of it, which I kept until, leaving Spain in this fleet, the ship in which I came was lost, and in it the narrative and all I was bringing with me, on which account His Majesty gave me a reward and alms. What in effect the narrative contained is as follows:

"A Portuguese ship sailed from Malacca for the islands of Japan and at the city of Canton took on board Chinese goods. Arriving within sight of Japan she encountered a storm coming from the west, so severe that it was impossible to reach those islands and she ran before it under very little sail for eight days, the weather being very thick and no land having been seen. On the ninth day the weather abated and cleared, and they sighted two large islands. They reached one of these at a good port, well peopled, there being a great city surrounded by a good stone wall. There were many large and medium sized vessels in port. Immediately on their entering the harbor there flocked to the ship a great number of persons of that land, well-dressed and cared for and manifesting much affection for the people of the ship. The lord of that island and city, learning that they were merchants, sent to the captain of the ship to say that he and those of his people he might select should come ashore without any fear that they would do them harm. On the contrary, he assured them, they should be received well, and he requested that they should bring with them the manifest of the goods the ship brought, for they would take them and trade for them to their

content. The captain communicated this to his people, and it was resolved that the notary of the ship should be sent ashore with the manifest of merchandise and two merchants, one a Portuguese and the other an Armenian, residents of Malacca. The lord of the land received them in his house, which was large and well built, and treated them with affection, making them presents, they understanding one another by signs. The land was very rich in silver and other things, silk and clothing. The notary and the Portuguese merchant returned to the ship in order to land merchandise and store it in a building which was assigned to them for that purpose, while the Armenian remained with the lord of the land and was treated very hospitably. The merchandise having been taken ashore, and a vast number of persons coming to purchase it with a great quantity of silver, in some thirty days they sold all the goods, making great gains, so that all became very rich, and they loaded the ship with silver. During the time that they were on the island they learned that the lord was suzerain of the other island also, which was within sight, four leagues away, and of others which were near to these, all being rich in silver and very populous. These people are white and well-formed, well cared for and clothed in silk and fine clothing of cotton; an affectionate and very affable people. The language differs from that of the Chinese as well as that of the Japanese, and is readily learned, for, in less than forty days that the Portuguese passed on the island, they were able to converse with the natives. These islands abound in the means of maintaining life well—rice, which is the bread they use; fowls like ours in great number; tame ducks and many hogs; goats; buffaloes and much game with deer and wild boars in great abundance; various birds and fowls and fishes, both many and good, and a great plenty of many kinds of fruit. The climate of the land is very good and healthful. These islands are in from thirty-five to forty degrees of latitude. The difference in longitude between them and Japan cannot be arrived at, because they had run before the gale and the weather was very thick and obscure. They ran from Japan to the eastward; and, having disposed of their merchandise, they returned to Malacca. They named these islands, out of regard for the Armenian merchant, who was greatly respected by the people of the ship, 'Isles of the Armenian.'"

This is as much of the narrative, as I remember it, as will serve for the discovery of these islands as well as others in that region and corner of the sea. As regards the rest of that coast, it is very important that this exploration should be made; and for this purpose two coasting vessels of the burden and build which Don Juan de Guzmán may determine will serve. With regard to who should take part in the decision of this matter, as well as in all things concerning this exploration, your most illustrious lordship will follow his own judgment. I pray Our Lord that this may be for His great service and that of His Majesty. Most Illustrious Lord: From the least chaplain of your most illustrious lordship.

[Signed:] Andrés de Aguirre

831. December 1, 1587. Pedro de Unamuno to the Marqués de Villamanrique, Viceroy of Mexico.

In spite of Drake's appearance on the California coast in 1579, nothing was done (beyond the abortive plans of Francisco Gualle). The only expedition sent northwards in a small vessel was that under Pedro de Unamuno. He was accompanied by several clergy and from July 12, 1587 onward, worked his way up the coast of Baja California. In stormy weather they ran rapidly up the coast to about 39° but were forced to return as the vessel was in poor condition. They made a landing and formal annexation at Puerto de San Lucas at 35° 30' (Wagner thought it was Morro Bay), observed and fought with the local Indians, and returned to Acapulco. They were fortunate in missing the English privateer Thomas Cavendish, who had been lying off Cape San Lucas before he took the Santa Ana. *The report is a straightforward one, but it brought no new insights and was soon forgotten.*

Text in M. F. de Navarrete, Coleccíon, *XVIII (1971), fols. 231–244, and W. M. Mathes,* Californiana, *I (1965), 18–37; translated in H. R. Wagner,* Spanish Voyages *(1929), pp. 141–151, here reprinted.*

First, I cleared from the Isla Macarera Sunday, July 12, [1587] at about midday, and sailed twelve leagues east-southeast, finding myself at about eleven o'clock at night far forward of the Isla de Leme, the farthermost of the Macan group, in full 22 ½°.

From Leme we stood away for the Babuyanes, steering east a quarter southeast, and after we had sailed ninety-six leagues on this course, Thursday, July 16, about midday we sighted the Islas Babuyanes, and took the sun. They are in scant 20 ½°. We came in sight of them, sailing on this course, because the compass varied a quarter to the northeast. We corrected it according to its variation.

From the Babuyanes we stood away for an island, shown on some sea charts, called Rica de Oro, 450 leagues distant from them and in lat. 29° to full 31°, on an east-northeast course, and steering for the island, with varying winds, I sailed twelve days on various courses. On July 28 I came in sight of two small islands, each about three leagues in circumference, and separated from each other about a league and a half. They lie north-south a quarter northwest, east-southeast, in latitude 25 ½°, where we observed the sun that day. We circumnavigated the islands, examining them, and saw no harbor, trees nor signs of water; rather, from what we could see of them, we judged them to be of no value for any purpose, so we named them "Sin Provecho."

From these islands we stood away that same night for the Isla de Oro, (which in the preceding paragraph has been stated to be 330 leagues from these islands) on an east-west a quarter northeast-southwest course. Its southern part is in 29° and its northern in scant 32 ½°, according to its position shown on some charts. We found ourselves in this latitude Wednesday, August 19, and searched for the island from east to west and in every other requisite direction. As we did everything possible and could not find it, it may be concluded that it does not exist.

From this latitude of 31°, we stood away on an east-northeast course for another island, shown on some charts, named Rica de Plata, sixty leagues distant from the one named Rica de Oro and its latitude. We steered east-northeast, in accordance with its position and direction as shown on the charts, which is lat. 33° to 34° from its southern to its northern part. Here we found ourselves on Saturday, August 22, and although we searched from east to west, making every possible effort, we could not find the island. Doubtless it does not exist, but somebody on hearsay ordered it drawn on his chart.

Sunday, August 23, at nightfall, we stood away for the islands called Armenio, which, as shown on some charts, is twenty leagues from the above-mentioned Rica de Plata, in a northeast direction in lat. 34° and 35° 20′. Here we found ourselves Wednesday, August 26, and carefully endeavored in every possible way to sight the island. It could not be found, and is believed not to exist.

From the latitude of this Isla de Armenio according to those who say it exists, that is, 35° 20′, we stood away east a quarter northeast and east-northeast for the country of New Spain, to make land in as high a latitude as we could and the weather might permit, in order to make from our landfall as extensive an exploration as possible. Keeping on these courses, on Monday, the last of August, we observed the sun in lat. 37° 12′. When we had sailed 140 leagues on these courses, our mainmast broke in two, as well as the foremast and bowsprit. After we had repaired them as best we could, in order to be able to navigate, we continued on these courses and went up to lat. 39°. On Thursday, September 3, an east-northeast wind struck us, so we could not go farther north. The weather would not permit it, the masts were sprung, the vessel was small, and those aboard had little protection, not having come as well prepared to resist the cold and wet as was advisable. Therefore we dropped down to lat. 32 ½°, where we were on Wednesday, September 30. From this latitude, which we observed that day, we endeavored to go farther north, but because the winds were not favorable, it was hard work to gain any latitude.

Sailing on various courses on account of contrary winds, we managed with difficulty to make latitude full 35 ½°, where we were on Saturday, October 17, 1587, and that day land was sighted. As it was not clear, the land being covered with a thick mist, we were not quite certain that it was land which had appeared. That night, during the first watch, sailing east slightly northeast with a south-southeast wind, we came upon two very small islands near the mainland, about half a league to sea. We came so close to them (within an harquebusshot) that had we not been keeping a good watch on account of the fog, we would have

been lost. We stood out to sea until the morning watch.

Sunday, October 18, on the morning watch, we put in toward land and as day dawned we discerned a high land to the south, with some three pine trees on the highest part which serve as a landmark. At the north [of this land] we saw the smoke of numerous fires at the foot of the hill in some pine woods near the sea. To the north of this a point of land extended about northwest-southeast, and within this point there was a large bay toward the east, which seemed to have harbors in it. We consulted those on board, especially Father Fr. Martin Ignacio de Loyola, commissary to China, and found that all were of the opinion that we should put into the bay and see what was there, since it was for this purpose that we came. We therefore stood in for the bay. On reaching it we saw to the east a long sandy beach middling wide, for which we steered, and there the vessel anchored in twenty-seven fathoms, bottom of fine sand mixed with mud. There is much thick grass around and near the ship, growing out of more than fifteen fathoms of water. These plants are thick and have great leaves and stems, and are the same which sailors say they have seen a hundred leagues at sea floating like great rafts. It is this grass, which grows along all this coast to beyond Isla de Zedros, in latitude full 28 ½°. It does not grow in rivers, as some have declared, but along the coast, as just stated. In this port there is an unlimited quantity of fish of different kinds, trees suitable for masts, water, firewood, and abundant shell-fish with all of which a ship in need could supply itself.

As just stated, we anchored in this port October 18, the day of San Lucas, and we therefore named it Puerto de San Lucas. While thus anchored, about two harquebus-shots off the beach, we observed the sun between eleven and twelve o'clock noon, and found the port to be in full 35 ½°. After a little while we saw two Indians on land, on a slope at the base of a hill, whence they looked us over at their pleasure.

On seeing these Indians, a council was held of those on board and, all being assembled, it was considered what should be done, and whether some soldiers should land and explore the neighborhood of the harbor. All were agreed that the Captain with twelve soldiers and some Indians, armed with swords and shields, should land

and look the ground over and make a reconnaissance of the vicinity of the port. Having left orders aboardship as to what was to be done, and having elected *alcaldes* and *regidores*, that there might be some one to take possession of the port and whatever else might be discovered, I landed with twelve soldiers with their coats of mail and harquebuses, Fr. Martin Ignacio in advance carrying a cross in his hands, and with some Luzon Indians with their swords and shields.

When we had landed in the harbor, a consultation was held as to what direction should be taken, whether toward the place where the Indians had been seen shortly before, or toward the pine woods where some fires had been seen that morning, as there were many trails leading in different directions. We decided to go towards the place where the two Indians had been seen, because the trail that way seemed to be the most trodden, and so we began our march in that direction. Having reached the top of the hill toward the east-northeast, we saw a good-sized river in a plain below, and many beaten trails leading in every direction, but saw no sign of the Indians we had previously seen on the slope. Considering the diversity of the trails leading in every direction, it was agreed to follow one of them, which led southeast toward a high hill from whence what lay about could be seen. With Father Martin leading, his cross in his hand, we set off towards it, two of our Indians ahead as scouts. When we had marched a quarter of a league the Indians discovered people, and having reported that they had seen five persons, went after them. At the same time we hastened our pace in order to speak with them, and meanwhile decided to send Diego Vazquez Mexia, the sergeant, and another soldier with the two Indians to entertain them with pleasant words and show them peace and good will, if they could overtake them. The sergeant went ahead with the scouts after the five persons and although he made every effort they could not be overtaken, for they were high up on the hill. They were naked and fleet, and although the rest of the party advanced at a good gait, they had time to get into a pine wood by way of another high hill. We found two bundles like baskets wrapped up in two deerskins on a steep slope along the trail to the hill. We found nothing in them but two deerskins, little pelts, like rabbit skins, cut and fashioned like a chain, and a few

flowers like wild marjoram, which must serve them for food or drink, as no other seed was found. There were two women among the five persons they had seen, according to the report of the Indian scouts, for they carried two children on their backs. We took one of the two deerskins, leaving in its place two handkerchiefs with their other plunder. Our men were not allowed to take anything of theirs. This done, we went up to the top of the hill, where we halted and looked about to see what could be seen.

Viewing what lay around, we saw nearby another higher hill about three harquebus-shots away. I ordered Joanes de Arrajeta and Cristobal Infanson to go with their swords and shields and two Indians and climb the hill, which was on our right hand, and from there to look about to see if there were any settlements or other indications of people, and to find out if there were any minerals in the hill. They went and looked in every direction as far as they could see, and prospected the hill for minerals. They then came down to where the rest of us were and reported that they could see no settlements, people, nor smoke, nor had they been able to find any mineral in the hill, but that there were many trails, among which was one that seemed to be the most trodden leading up river in an easterly direction.

The party having rested, we descended the hill toward the river, and coming to the bank tried the water which we found very good, as it came down between sandy banks. From there we went up a small hill towards the north, where the river formed a great lake. So near was the sea that there seemed to be a bar and a harbor there, but when we reached the place it was seen to be the dammed-up water of the river, the outlet to the sea being blocked by a great quantity of sand. Nevertheless, there must be some discharge under the sand, otherwise the river water would soon cut away the sand. As it was already late, we returned toward the ship and when we came near, we found on and about a little hill a great quantity of very large pearl-oyster shells and others of numerous shell-fish.

When we reached this hill, as it seemed to be a suitable place to take possession in His Majesty's name of the port and the country, seeing that I and the rest of the party had landed and traversed the country round about and the port quietly and pacifically, as in territory belonging to his domain, I did so in the name of King Philip, our master, in due legal form, through Diego Vasquez Mexia (one of the *alcaldes* elected for this purpose) in his capacity of *Justicia*, setting up a cross as a sign of the Christian faith and of the possession taken in His Majesty's name of the port and the country, cutting branches from the trees which grew thereabouts, and performing the other customary ceremonies. We then went aboard the vessel.

Having had supper, we consulted about what, with God's grace, we should do the next day, and whether we should go inland some distance to see if we could find any settlements or minerals, or signs thereof, seeing that there were so many trails leading in different directions. Having discussed together what it would be advantageous to do, Fr. Martin Ignacio and the other friars being present, and all agreeing, it was resolved that, whereas we had set out to make as thorough an exploration as possible and the season would permit, and whereas to-day, Sunday, October 18, the day of San Lucas, we had discovered this port, landed and taken possession of the country in His Majesty's name, and whereas there were so many well-beaten trails leading in different directions, it was advisable for the Captain with twelve soldiers, a friar and some Indians with their swords and shields, to go inland at dawn for four or five leagues by the best trodden trail (the one which led up the river eastward), and further, that it was advisable to see what the country promised, in order to report fully what there might be to His Majesty and to His Excellency, the viceroy of New Spain, by whom we, in his stead, had been sent upon this undertaking in His Majesty's name. The opinions of all having been taken, it was forthwith ordered to make all the necessary preparations so as to set out at any time after midnight.

Monday, the 19th, about two hours before dawn, I set out on the expedition, with Fr. Francisco de Noguera, and twelve soldiers and eight Luzon Indians with their swords and shields. At that hour I landed, having left orders on board as to what was to be done that day. We proceeded towards the river, and the order of march having been there arranged, and two Indians sent ahead as scouts, we followed the trail leading eastward which the day previous had seemed to us the most beaten. Advancing as noiselessly as possible,

when day dawned we had journeyed two leagues without having seen or heard anything of settlement, smoke, or person. We then drew aside towards the slope of a hill under some oaks and live-oaks and other trees which were on a knoll nearby, and lying there in ambush, we watched all that valley as far as we could see until an hour after sunrise. We could not see any settlement or any people, but we did see two smokes up the river in some thick groves of black oaks, live-oaks, willows, and other high trees which are somewhat thick, resembling ash trees. We proceeded thither as secretly as possible, the two Indians in advance as scouts, and when we reached the place where the smoke was we found that it was caused by the burning of two great black oaks. They were about an harquebus-shot apart, and seemed to have been burning about a month.

From here we set out up river towards the east, following the best beaten trail, and found many footprints of large, medium-sized and small persons, passing both up and down stream, all the sands of the stream being full of them. The bed is of coarse sand, below which the water flows; almost everywhere one can cross dry-shod, the water flowing below except in places where it comes up like springs and forms pools of water. The whole length of the river, from one end to the other, is very much shaded by willows and good-sized osiers, and other tall trees which resemble ash trees; there are many fragrant herbs, such as camomile, pennyroyal, and thyme. After marching about two leagues, sometimes along the bed of the river and sometimes outside of it, without seeing a settlement or people, except the trail, we came upon an old Indian camp northeast of the river, in which there were seventeen large and small dugouts, like Biscay charcoal pits, that is, a large round hole in the ground very well covered over with branches of trees. Judging from the size of the dug-outs, each could hold more than a dozen persons. They seemed to have been made about a month and a half before. Nothing was found in them excepting some poles, which seemed to be of elder, out of which they fashioned their javelins which have oak points hardened by fire. A little apart from the river in the other direction a hut was found among some trees, big enough for about two persons, built of sticks and covered with earth, and having only one small opening.

Inside were dried grass and leaves. We supposed that this was for their chief. From these huts we marched half a league up the river, always following the trail, and then halted beside it on the southeast side in the shade of some willows. Here the men ate and rested and on account of the great heat we remained here until about three o'clock in the afternoon.

After the party had eaten and rested, it was resolved to continue up the river about a league towards a great gap which showed to the east in order to see if we could discover in that opening any settlement, and that after having gone that distance, which it appeared would take us to the foot of a high hill, we should turn back towards the ship and spend the night in some convenient spot in order to return to her in the morning. We therefore marched towards the gap, and having shortly arrived at the foot of the high hill, we looked over the country as far as we could see from among some live-oak trees. We could discover nothing more than that the trail led on eastward, for we could clearly see it continuing on along the skirts of some hills to end, together with many others, in some high hills to the east. Finding that from the foot of the hill nothing could be seen, I ordered three soldiers and three Indians with their swords and shields to climb to the top of it and from there to look in every direction to see if they could see any settlement, people or fires, and also to ascertain whether there were any minerals in it. After a short time they came back to us and reported that they had not been able to discover any settlement, smoke or people, nor did the hill apparently have any minerals in it, but that they could see that the river continued eastward among some hills, and the trail and many others led eastward over the slopes of some hills. Seeing that we could discover no settlements nor people, that the men were somewhat tired and that we had supplies for no more than that night, we marched towards the ship, realizing that it would not be wise to advance farther into unknown territory with so few men, without supplies, and that it would be best to return towards the ship. This was the most advisable course in the opinion of all. Having marched about two leagues, we camped an hour before nightfall under three great black oak trees which were alongside the river at a good distance from the trail, and rested there that night with sentries posted in good order.

The next day, Tuesday, October 20, we proceeded down the river in broad daylight, not doing so at dawn lest the Indians, having seen us by chance, and spying at night, might have laid some ambush. Having marched down about a league and a half, we came upon a camp on both sides of the river, where there were more than thirty dug-outs like those found the day before. Nothing was found in these but some little cord bags made like nets, in which there were some rope ends, very well made out of the bark of trees, some old baskets in which they carry their plunder, and a trough made out of a tree trunk, in which we inferred they grind roots or the bark of trees for some drink or food, as, except for a little seed like the flower of wild marjoram such as we found the first day, we did not see a sign of any seed. We also found some poles like those seen in the other dug-outs the day before. Having searched all around over an area in radius of a couple of harquebus-shots and found no sign other than those above described, we continued on our way, sometimes down the river and sometimes away from it. After we had marched about two leagues and crossed to the west side of the river, we halted at about ten o'clock in the forenoon, being then about a half a league distant from the ship, in order to allow the men to rest. Half an hour having passed, we began our march towards the ship and after going about a quarter of a league halted to rest on a hill, as we were near her. After the men had rested, we went on so as to come within sight of the ship. Marching in our order, when the vanguard was in sight of the ship, all the party being in view of each other, and we were descending the hill towards the beach, where we found the ship's boat and Joanes de Uranzu, on looking back towards the rear guard before those in advance had halted, we saw two Indians come running down a pine clad hill towards the other part of the hill where they were coming up to sight the ship. We turned at once to support them but before we could come to their relief some of them were wounded. We fired on the Indians with our harquebuses when we reached them, and made them retreat to the top of the hill.

At this moment, Juan de Aranguren and Juan de Mendoza came up with many arrow and javelin wounds, and immediately after them, Cristobal Ynfanzon with many arrow wounds. They would have been killed except for timely support. As Felipe de Contreras, who was also in the rear guard, had taken off his coat of mail, he was wounded by a javelin which passed entirely through his breast, so that he could not retreat. From this and other wounds, which he received on account of being disarmed, he died immediately, according to the report made by others of his company. With him they killed one of our Indians with a javelin which he failed to ward off with his shield. As many Indians were again descending the hill, an order was given to look to the wounded and for the rest to close ranks. In view of their great number, and seeing that they continued to come down the hill, we endeavored to reach the beach in our order, as that was the best point from which to defend ourselves. Those who had been aboard ship and had landed to support us, together with those who were on land, joined forces in good order, and we had a fight and skirmish with the Indians in which some of them were killed and many wounded, only one of our men being wounded. They now retreated and separated into three bands, and we withdrew to our post, where it was decided that it would be well to be provided with a raft. In this we might all embark together, as, the ship's boat being too small to take us on board except in many trips, we would find ourselves hard pushed and unable to retire if they returned. The raft was made and shortly brought to land to where the ship's boat was. During this time the enemy attacked us on three fronts but withdrew with loss without wounding any of our men. It was about five in the afternoon when the enemy retired toward the hill where they had wounded our men, and set out sentries. Seeing that it was now late and the enemy had retired, we embarked on the raft and the ship's boat.

Monday, October 19, while I and the other soldiers were inland, Fr. Martin Ignacio de Loyola, Fr. Rufino, Alonso Gomez the pilot, Demitre Cardia, Miguel Sanchez, and others who had remained on board ship went ashore. They reported what had happened to them in the harbor with respect to the Indians. After we had left that morning, they landed to see if there was any settlement or people towards the southwest of the port where the night before a great fire had been seen which lasted almost all night, and also to get some wood and water. While Father Mar-

tin, Alonso Gomez, Joanes de Uranzu, and others went in the direction where the fire had been seen to find out what it was, Gerónimo de Vallejeda, the barber, remained at the river with some Indians, in order to wash, and fetch water and firewood. Twenty-three Indians came down from the pine clad hill, and three came half-way down the hill to see what our men were doing. Two came to the river to talk with Vallejeda, who carried only his sword. After some words had passed among those up the hill, he saw that matters were coming to a bad pass, but merely endeavored to get away from them with fair words, making a gesture with his sword, after they had taken some things from him which he gave them in order to pacify them. The other Indians now came down on them, and took from our Indians, who were washing, some clothes and casks they had brought for the water. They went up the hill and having put this plunder in safe keeping, came back to watch what our men did. At this juncture, Father Martin and the others, who had gone to see what there was to the southwest, came up, and when the Indians saw the rest of the people coming, they comprehended that Vallejeda had deceived them by making signs that there were no other people about than he and the Indians and those who were filling water. They tried to carry him off but failed, as they threw themselves into the water and those on board ship fired at them with their harquebuses, until Father Martin and the others reached the place where Vallejeda and the Indians were. When they arrived at the place where the Indians were on the flank of a hill, these began to raise a great outcry, making many gestures and jumping from one place to the other as if they were about to make an attack, our men in the meantime remaining at their posts without creating any disturbance.

As the Indians had previously made signs of peace, Vallejeda and another of our Indians were sent towards them with some biscuit, cloth, and other things which they had. Three Indians came half-way down the slope to them and wished to take them up the hill to where the others were, but our men were unwilling, so the Indians ate the biscuit, or part of it, and returned to their companions to report what had occurred, although all the rest were looking on. Shortly afterwards the Indians separated into three parties and attacked our men, showing every evidence of a wish to kill them, and shot many arrows at them, but without doing any damage. Father Martin would not allow any harquebus to be fired until it appeared that they were getting arrogant, and then they fired at them and wounded some, compelling them to draw back to the top of the hill. As it was now time to return to their respective quarters, the Indians went to their homes and our men to the ship. To the southwest where our men had gone they found a hut like those already described, and around it and farther distant from it many pearl oyster shells, big shells in large quantities, from which it is inferred that there is much good pearl fishing here, and that these Indians come down to the coast to fish for them, the trails from the east being probably those by which they come and go, from and to the interior. The land on the coast is well suited for wheat and maize, better than we found inland.

Having gone aboard a council was held, after the men had had supper, to consider whether the next day we should land to fight the enemy, or continue on our voyage. It was resolved that it was better to continue our voyage, coasting along the land, and not go ashore after the enemy. The powder had burned the day previous while we were refining it, our men were badly wounded and medicine with which to treat them was scanty, and the unwounded men were too few to resist the enemy without powder or munitions; further, we had done in that port what was necessary to be done, and we could search for other harbors along the coast. It was therefore thought better to go and report to His Excellency on what had occurred, and so it was resolved to leave on Wednesday, October 21, before daybreak.

Having cleared at that time, we followed the coast with contrary winds until Friday the 23d, when in the afternoon, a west-northwest wind blew up with such thick weather that we could not see the land for five days, although we were always within two leagues of it, and even less. On account of this thick weather and because the ship was too small to venture in to explore for ports: we could not see whether there was any harbor on that coast. Wednesday, October 28, while coasting along about two leagues from land, we took a sounding in lat. 30° to get samples of the bottom, since we could not see the land by reason of the thick weather and the darkness caused by the fog.

The lead showed ten fathoms and rocky reefs all along for more than half a league. As soon as we had left this vicinity we came into much disturbed white water, which seemed to be river water. We took some soundings and found almost the same depth. Here we tried to see if there was a harbor, although that day and night and part of the following Thursday we could not see the land to inspect the character of it. As we could not land in the ship's boat, on account of its small size and the somewhat heavy sea running, and as the weather did not clear up, but the wind seemed rather to blow harder, it was resolved to come to Acapulco as quickly as possible, not only to report to Your Excellency on what had occurred, but because the wounded men were badly off for lack of medicine. Further, this coast from Isla de Zerros to Acapulco was all explored a long time ago.

We did not visit the Lequios Islands, Japan nor the Pescadores, as these countries had been explored; besides, the ship was small and carried no artillery, the men on board were few in number, and the people of Japan are numerous and warlike, possessing ships and artillery with which to attack and to defend themselves.

From the Babuyanes, in scant 20 ½°, to the Puerto de San Lucas, which has now been discovered in full 35 ½°, we sailed 1890 leagues on various courses as the weather permitted, although on a straight course it would be about 1550 leagues. In this latitude and on this course it is good sailing, healthier and quicker than in lower latitudes. From the Puerto de San Lucas to Cabo de San Lucas in scant 23° it is 290 leagues, the course being south-southeast about half the way and southeast a quarter south the other half. From Cabo de San Lucas to the Puerto de Acapulco it is about 260 leagues, the course half the way being east-southeast and the rest of the way southeast a quarter east.

November 12, at the mouth of the Puerto de Valle de Banderas in lat. 21° full near Cabo de Corrientes, we met a launch out of the port, which by the order of the Audiencia of Guadalajara, was patrolling the coast to warn the ships from China that the English Corsair was on the coast and to advise them of the damage he had done, and that he was then careening his ship in the Puerto de Mazatlan. The instructions were to sail in search of these ships as high as lat. 25°, two degrees farther north than Cabo de San Lucas. That is a good point at which to receive the warning as time is given to avoid the enemy by standing out to sea. I notified the captain of the launch in His Majesty's name in the best legal form possible to proceed on his way with all diligence, since the matter was of such importance to His Majesty, bidding him sail by night with the land breezes and lie just off shore during the day, as he could keep watch for the China ships from land. Besides, if the enemy's launch came along the coast reconnoitering, it would not find him in the daytime, for navigation is then impossible on account of the northwest winds and the currents. He would therefore get along better and would not be found by the enemy if their launch came out on a scouting expedition. A supply of biscuit, rice and other things which we carried was given him, stocking him in this manner for more than a month and a half, not counting the maize and other provisions which he brought for his own provision. We entered the Puerto de Acapulco Sunday, November 22, whence we wrote Your Excellency and reported at length on the events and hardships of our voyage.

832. November 30, 1595. Abstract of the journal of Sebastian Cermeño on his voyage up the California coast.

Sebastian Rodríguez Cermeño (a Portuguese pilot) was sent by the viceroy, Luis de Velasco, in the ship San Agustín, *accompanied by a* lancha *or small pinnace, to follow up the neglected task of Unamuno, namely to find a possible port of refuge for the Manila Galleon on the Alta California coast. From April, 1594, onward he made a safe voyage northward to a cape he named Cape Mendoçino at his estimated latitude of 41° 46'. It was when he was on his way southward that he ran into difficulty.* San Agustín *ran aground and broke up in Drakes Bay. In January, 1596, he and his crew managed to use the* lancha *to return slowly and painfully to Mexico. The viceroy, the Conde de Monterey, enclosed a summary of his journal in a letter of April 19, 1596, to Philip II.*

A.G.I., Seville, formerly 58/3/12, printed in W. M. Mathes, Californiana, *I, 128-ff; translated in*

H. R. Wagner, Spanish Voyages, *pp. 156–163, from which it is reprinted.*

[a]   Abstract

We left the Puerto de Cabite in the Philippine Islands July 5 in the morning, and anchored that night at the foot of the Frayle. The next day we made sail with a southwest wind, and in the afternoon it began to blow so hard that it was necessary to take shelter at the Isla de Marivelez. The next morning we again set sail with the wind off the land, and before nightfall arrived at the Isla de Fortun, and by midnight had rounded the reefs of Tuley. The following day we anchored at the Isla de Mindora, as the ship was leaking badly. Here we remained until the 14th, when we again made sail with the southeast wind, and before night rounded the Islas de Baco. On the 16th we had left all these behind us. On the 17th we were at the Isla de Cibuyan, and on the 19th at that of Ibalon, where we remained until the 27th, when we again made sail. We shortly encountered a southwest wind, passed Cabo Espiritu Santo, and continued in an east-northeast direction until we were in 17° North. Thence the course was north and then northeast to 22°. From this point we had trouble with the currents and made latitude very slowly, so that we finally fell back to 18°. August 13 we encountered a hurricane from the north and a sea on the beam. A few days later, on the 17th, we saw some islands which are called the Volcanoes of Japan, and saw smoke from one of them before we saw the island. From these islands we still continued northeast in a general direction until we were in short 28° on the 26th. Up to the 30th, when we found ourselves in 30½°, we were sailing with a west and southwest wind in a northeast direction. From August 30 to September 6 we sailed in different directions, but generally northeast, and on the 6th were in 34° 10'. On the 10th we were in 36°, on the 12th in 37°, on the 26th in 39½°, and on October 2 we were in 40°. Still continuing in a northeasterly direction we got up to 41°, where on the 16th we encountered a northeast wind, but the wind soon shifted to the northwest and we continued with a favorable wind, and on the 22d were in full 42° with a smooth sea. Sailing still towards the east, we again encountered an east-northeast wind and a sea on the beam until the 25th, when the wind again turned favorable, and we continued our voyage to the east a quarter northeast until the 29th, when we found ourselves again in full 42°.

In the ship, *San Agustin*, which arrived at Cabo Mendocino on the new discovery of the coast of New Spain Saturday morning, November 4, 1595, before me Pedro de Lugo, scrivener of the King, our master, and the witnesses, Sebastian Rodriguez Sermeño, captain and chief pilot of this new discovery for the King, our master, in virtue of a royal provision dispatched for that purpose by Don Luis de Velasco, member of the Order of Santiago, viceroy, governor and captain-general of New Spain, declared: That in compliance with this provision he had been dispatched from the Puerto de Cabite of Manila by Don Luis Perez Dasmariñas, governor and captain-general there, in the ship *San Agustin*, the property of Captain Pedro Sarmiento, who offered it for the purpose of making the discovery, as is recorded in the documents executed in the matter and which he has in his possession and to which he refers. Having set sail from that port, July 4, of this year, he had come prosecuting his voyage and a straight course and had gone up to the greatest latitude which the weather permitted.

Having reached the latitude of 42° on a coast trending north-south and where the end of the land bore north a quarter northeast, the highest latitude reached, he went in pursuit of his voyage until the present day, November 4, when he came in sight of land, the coast of New Spain. Approaching this as much as he could on that day, until he came within two leagues of it, a little more or less, and having cast the lead for the first time, he found seventy fathoms of water. He went on casting the lead in this manner until he found himself in eighteen fathoms of water and about half a league from land. As night was coming on, he ordered the sails taken in and the ship remained beam to the sea until the following morning, the 5th of the month, when he hoisted them and went following along the coast. The night before, when he sighted land, he saw on it some smoke and fire. Proceeding, he saw that the coast was very bold and dangerous because of a heavy surf caused by the many small islands and reefs near land. It was thus impossible for the ship to

approach nearer shore. Coasting along about the same half a league from land a reef was discovered which might be about a league at sea. This which was Cabo Mendocino was rounded, and the ship again approached land as before. Having ordered two men to the tops to look about to see if there were any reefs ahead, a point of land was discovered with two small islands off it. This appeared to be a port as it made a small *ensenada*. While entering this, the men in the tops saw some great dangerous rocks where the ship would have to anchor. Shouting this out, the ship bore away and stood off to sea away from land, as night was coming on. While sailing, a heavy wind and sea came up at about ten o'clock, which made it necessary to lay the ship's beam to the sea. This was done with so much labor in the ship, that in the whole course of the voyage no such great storm was encountered as blew that night and until the following day, the 6th, when sail was made in the direction of land, with only the lower foresail and without the bonnet, both the ship and the men suffering greatly on account of the strong gale and the heavy sea.

In view of the great danger in which the Captain and Chief Pilot was putting the ship and the men, as she was very small and was almost open, making it necessary to devote two out of three watches to the pump, and terrorized at the danger of the day before while entering the port, the pilot, master, and boatswain made a written demand on him to run with the wind and proceed on his voyage to Acapulco as it was impossible to prosecute the discovery by reason of the ship's being in such a badly battered state, as is on record more fully in the said demand which they made before Alonso Gomez, the scrivener of the ship. Notwithstanding this, Captain Sebastian Rodriguez kept on approaching land and the weather kept improving.

Being now near land, like the day before, he went on following the coast. He ordered some men to the tops to look about and see what was ahead. About midday a point of high land was discovered which revealed a great *ensenada*, in which he entered, sounding with the lead from forty fathoms down to five where he anchored with the ship. This can be taken to be the depth of the whole bay, as after doubling the point this depth of five, six and seven fathoms and no more was never lost. The bottom is clean and of fine sand. The ship anchored in the bay and port about a quarter of a league from shore. Along all the coast which the ship followed after discovering land until she anchored, there were many fires near the sea, and many forests of pines inland from which it may be concluded that it is inhabited by people.

. . . On the day on which the ship anchored in the bay, about four o'clock in the afternoon, many Indians appeared on the beach and soon one of them got into a small craft which they employ, like a çacate of the lake of Mexico. He came off to the ship where he remained quite a time talking in his language, no one understanding what he said. Some cotton cloth and silk things were given him and a red cap. He took them and went back to land. Early the next morning, the 7th, four other crafts like the first came out from land to the ship, and in each one was an Indian. They came alongside where they remained some time talking in their language. Captain Sebastian Rodriguez gave each of them some cotton cloth and taffetas and entertained them the best he could. They went ashore and the Captain at once embarked in the ship's boat with twenty-two men, seventeen being harquebusiers with their arms. Accompanying him were Captain Francisco de Chaves and his ensign, the sergeant and the corporal and three men with shields. These went ashore with the Indians and landed on the beach of the port near some of their underground habitations, in which they live, resembling caves and like those of the Chichimecos Indians of New Spain. They are well-made people, robust and more corpulent than the Spaniards in general. They go naked without covering and with their private parts exposed, but the women cover theirs with straw and skins of animals. Their arms are bows and arrows. They wear their hair long and have no beards; any one who has any removes it. They are painted on the breast and on certain parts of the arms, but the paint is not so decorative as with that of the Chichimecos.

On the same day that the Captain went ashore with his men, he asked all to witness that he took possession of the land and port in the name of the King, our master. He gave it the name "La Baya de San Francisco," and the Reverend Father Fray Francisco de la Concepcion of the Order of the barefoot Franciscans, who comes in the ship, baptized it. The Captain, with his ensign, Juan del Rio, carrying the banner, and the sergeant with the men in order went marching to a village which is about a harquebus-shot from the beach. Here all the Indian men and women, perhaps fifty all told without counting children, were looking on with great fright in seeing people they had never seen before. They were all very peaceable and their arms were in their houses, it not being known up to that time that they had any. They produced a seed the shape of an anise seed, only a little thinner, and having the taste of sesame, of which they make the bread they eat. Their food consists of crabs and wild birds, which are in great abundance near where they live, and many deer, as these have been observed going about. They are beyond comparison the largest that have been seen as will be apparent from the horns which were found, of which the Captain carries a sample.

As the Captain with his men was proceeding the same day from the settlement, about half a league distant inland a band of Indians appeared who approached in a warlike manner, for as soon as they saw the Spaniards they performed a caracole and skirmished in a circle, like the Chichimecos, with loud howls. Shortly, one of them who carried a tall banner of black feathers began to advance towards where the Spaniards were, and having looked them over stopped to view the men. Two Indians, of the friendly ones who were being treated well, talked with them and soon they lowered their arms, put them on the ground, and came towards the Spaniards. The one who carried the banner brought and delivered it to the Captain and all the other Indians approached in an humble manner and as if terrorized, and yielded peacefully. He made much of them, embracing them and giving them some of the taffeta sashes which the Spaniards wore. So the Spaniards came up to them, embracing them and they took their bows and arrows and gave them freely to the Spaniards. They all had their faces painted and annointed in black and red. The Captain and the Spaniards went on until they reached a hill from which the Indians had come down, in order to see if there was any other settlement. On arriving at the top they saw coming an Indian man and a woman who was carrying a child. The Indian had some acorns for his food. These, without showing any fear or running away, came up to the Spaniards and the Captain made much of them and entertained them. The Indian treated the Spaniards to his acorns and the Captain declared that no one should do them any harm or take anything away from them. This done, they returned, going around the whole hill and down to the beach with all the men. Here he fixed his camp and made an entrenchment for defense and to put in hand at once the launch which had to be made for the discovery, having journeyed this day about three leagues. Here Indians from nearby kept coming and the chief talked a long time. When he had finished the Captain made much of them, giving to each pieces of cotton cloth and silk. They remained a good while and then went away without doing anything. All were naked like the rest.

November 15, the Captain embarked in the ship's boat with eight armed Spaniards, and I, the scrivener, went with them. He went up an arm of a river, one of three which empty into the bay and port, to discover what was in them. This one makes a bar on which at high tide there were about three fathoms of water, and from the shoal outside to the anchoring place the distance is two harquebus-shots. One of the rivers is large and enters the land about three leagues. The mouth is narrow and near it there is a settlement of Indians of the same class as those above mentioned. A little farther on there is another of a few people near the water and at quite a distance from these there is another of naked Indians who had their dwellings on a hill. They did not appear to have any arms. This river in places may be about a league wide and in others a half a league. On the west side there are two branches of a half a league each, and on the east side one about a quarter of a league from the bar. On entering this, there is on the right side sweet water which comes down from a copious river, at the entrance of which Indians are settled with their women, well-made people and robust as has been stated. Water good for drinking purposes can be found by digging down a little in any place where there are sandbanks near the sea.

November 30, the ship *San Agustin* having been lost with the food supply in her, the Captain left the camp with eleven Spaniards and some Indians and slaves with their arms on an expedition inland to hunt for food to sustain those who had survived the wreck, as there was nothing to eat. Having journeyed three leagues they found three villages of Indians of the same class and character as those above described, who were settled somewhat apart from each other on an arm of a river of sweet water on the banks of which there were many trees bearing acorns, hazelnuts of Castile, and other fruits of the country, madrones, thistles and fragrant herbs. From here they brought that day and on another day, December 2, a quantity of acorns and another round fruit like a hazelnut, and a quantity of thistles with which the men were sustained and which was to be taken in the launch.

Friday morning, December 8, the day of the Limpia Concepcion de Nuestra Señora, Captain Sebastian Rodriguez departed from the Puerto y Bahia de San Francisco which is in 38° 40', the islands outside being in 38 ½°, in the launch which he built for the discovery named the *San Buenaventura*. He passed close to the islands on the mainland side about a league away. This day he sailed about ten leagues, and that night lay to without sailing. The next day, Saturday, December 9, he went sailing along the coast until sundown, when he anchored in order not to pass behind a point after nightfall. All this coast up to here trends northwest-southeast. No observation was made of the sun because it did not appear, as the day was cloudy and there was a strong wind. He sailed a great deal, perhaps twenty-two leagues, without discovering in all this distance anything worth noting down. In going along very close to land, frequently only a musket-shot from it, all that may be seen is bare land near the sea and pine and oak timber in the high country. No smokes or fires appeared. After departing from this port on Sunday morning the 10th, he made sail with favorable weather and discovered a very large *ensenada* which bore to the east and southeast, all a bold coast. This day he observed the sun at midday in 37°. From the mouth of the *ensenada* the land bore to the south. From morning he sailed seven leagues and anchored behind a point in order not to run before the wind. Monday, at dawn, the 11th of the month, he made sail and traveled twenty leagues. All the coast trends northwest-southeast, is bold and high, and of bare ranges all of a kind, without any point or place of shelter where one could stop. This day, in the morning, as the launch was going along very close to shore, only some two harquebus-shots away, some five or six leagues along the coast some small islands were discovered close to land without any shoal. In all this there were no trees, except a very few on the heights. From these, barrancas, water channels and ravines come down.

Tuesday, December 12, having run with the launch all the night before as there was a good moon and no place where he could anchor, he went sailing from point to point across an *ensenada*, of which the whole could be seen, southeast a quarter south to where off the southeast point of the *ensenada* is a small island which bore southeast from inside the point. He ran this coast that day so close to land that many people could be seen on shore on some cliffs where they had their huts. Near sundown he anchored in front of some villages where they had many *balsas* on land. He spoke to them, shouting out from the launch that we were Christians. One of them responded and said "Christianos," and at once came running down to the shore, and taking a *balsa* and getting into it came alongside the launch where he was received by the Captain and given some cotton cloth and taffetas. Shortly many other Indians came out in the same kind of crafts and were asked by signs to bring some food which was lacking. They went ashore and very soon came back bringing a quantity of bitter acorns and some acorn mush in baskets shaped like medium-sized plates. They gave this in exchange for some cotton cloth and pieces of silk for which they asked and which were given to them. With this they were very contented and exclaimed "Mexico, Mexico." In appearance the people are quiet and peaceable, and were not seen to have any arms. No one went ashore, as it was impossible to do so on account of the reefs and the surf. The people who were assembled seemed to number about three hundred. They were naked and not so large or robust as the first ones. Some have long beards and their hair cut round, and some are more painted with stripes on their faces and arms than the Indians first seen. The land appears to be good and fertile, as it shows verdure and has acorn trees near the villages. They are people who asked for something to be given to them. They are fishermen and there is fish and some shell-fish with which they sustain themselves.

Wednesday morning, the 13th, sail was made with much difficulty from this port, where they found themselves short of food. The seamen and passengers were sick and weak, as there was nothing to eat except a small quantity of bitter acorns which to be eaten had to be roasted. All with much feeling piteously asked and demanded of the Captain to give over prosecuting the discovery and to keep on going with the launch without stopping anywhere until a land could be reached where there was a supply of food, in view of their necessities and the risk of all losing their lives. In spite of all this he diverted them all as best he could with words, and as there was nothing more to eat than what has just been mentioned, the men killed a dog on the launch and ate it, and if there had been more the same would have happened, in view of the great hunger from which they suffered. This day he crossed a great *ensenada* with a heavy sea, and steering towards a point which bore south, passed it during the first nightwatch. Then the coast trends northwest-southeast and when morning of the 14th came, two islands were discovered. The wind was from the east and he went running along the outside one to the south-southeast. The island trends northeast-southwest, and has a small island a league northwest of the outside point with a passage between them. Then between one island and the other there is an opening of a league and a half. Anchor was cast at the outside island on the southeast side. A small boat came alongside with two Indians rowing. They came to the launch and brought some twelve fish and a small seal and presented them. They were given in exchange some pieces of woven silk and cotton which they took so that they should bring more. The little boat came back with three Indians and brought nothing. Fishing with lines was resorted to and some thirty fish were caught which were soon eaten in view of the number of men, who numbered more than seventy, and their great hunger. The Captain at midday observed the sun at this place on the outside island and found it to be in 34° 12'.

At midnight of the same day, sail was made, as the land seemed to offer no help of any kind of food, as it was bare and broken and had no port. He ran until ten hours after nightfall, when he reached the other island, as it was a good night with a clear moon. This trends east-northeast to west-southwest. The first island may be about three or four leagues long and one wide, the second may be about seven or eight, and is the last and nearest to the mainland, with about two leagues of channel between. Soon a large *en-*

senada appeared, across which he sailed towards the south-southeast where the point bore, the coast running southeast a quarter south. That night fire appeared on these islands. All are fishermen, the land is broken like the first, and all the coast is clean. There are some small islands close to the shore. The coast is bold and the Indians are well made and robust, of good size and go naked. The crafts in which they sail are like the board boats of the Philippines. From the last island to the point above mentioned across the *ensenada* is about sixteen leagues. It was not reached during daylight, and as the night was good and no port was found in which to anchor, he went running along the coast near land until morning.

Saturday, the 16th, an island was discovered named San Agustin. The wind turned southeast and he anchored at the island, which trends northwest-southeast. A settlement was seen near the sea, and a craft from it came alongside. Some Spaniards went ashore to see if they could find anything to eat and to take water, which was lacking, but on account of the heavy surf breaking on shore this could not be done. Those who went brought back some cakes made of a very yellow root resembling the sweet potato, which are cooked under the sand. This made some of those who ate them very sick. On Sunday, the 17th of December, the wind kept coming from the southeast which made it necessary to go with the launch to the other side of the island, to anchor in the shelter it afforded. In the place where some Spaniards went ashore many wild onions and tunas were found, and near the water among some rocks a very large fish which had been killed with two wounds. On this more than seventy people sustained themselves for eight days, and if it had not been for this fish all the men, in view of their condition, ran much risk of losing their lives from the great hunger from which they suffered. Not having any water to drink, on the night of that day the wind blew so hard that the launch dragged its anchor more than four leagues along the coast. Returning from there the next day and following the coast of the island, a small *ensenada* suitable for fragatas was discovered, from which a very large stream of water was seen coming down a ravine. Here water was taken, and here he remained two days until the wind calmed down. He then went to where there were more than thirty Spaniards who had been left dressing

the fish where it had been found and they were taken on board. The island is of broken land and measures about twelve leagues in circumference. It trends northwest-southeast and is bare and the color of ashes. The northwest point is in 31° 15′. The water found is in the middle of the island, where all which may be necessary can be taken. All around the island the water is very deep, so much so, that you can come close to land, and at a little distance away from it bottom cannot be found.

Friday morning, December 22, having taken on board the men who were on shore, the launch departed from the island and went sailing with a northwest wind along the coast. As there was great want and lack of food, and all the men were sick and thin from not eating, the launch sailed by night, and also with the moon and kept along the coast which trends from northwest to southeast. The wind blew so hard that for this reason and on account of the demands which the passengers and seamen made on the Captain, it was necessary to run before it until the Isla de Cedros was reached. Passing this by on account of the great hunger which the men were suffering, the Captain came to land in the launch on the coast of Compostela, a league from the Puerto de Chacala, where from a ranch some corn and sun-dried beef was brought to aid them, and with which the men relieved their hunger. This was on the 7th of January of this year [1596]. Here the Captain disembarked and the sick who came on board remained there. He despatched the launch from there to Acapulco.

All this, I, the scrivener, certify to, being present as witnesses Don Garcia de Paredes, Andrés de Porras, and Juan del Rio, the ensign.

[Signed:] Sebastian Rodriguez Sermeño, before me Pedro de Lugo, scrivener of the King. For this purpose I here make my sign in testimony of the truth.

[Signed:] Pedro de Lugo, scrivener of the King.

833. May 5, 1602 to March 21, 1603. Fray António de la Ascensión's "Brief report" of the voyage of Sebastian Vizcaíno up the California coast.

Fray António de la Ascensión, a discalced Carmelite friar, was the principal chronicler of the Vizcaíno voyage and its cartographer as well. His lengthy report, with many sketch maps, is "Relación de la Jornada que hizo General Sevastian Vizcayno al descubrimiento de las Californias el año de 1602. Por mandado del Excelentissimo Señor Conde de Monterey, Virrey que era de la Nueva España, Escrita por el R. P. Fray António de la Ascensión de Orden descalzade Nuestra Señora del Carmen, uno de los tres Relijiosos que fueron a dicha Jornada," now in the Ayer Collection (St. Am. 1038), Newberry Library. It was printed and translated by H. R. Wagner, Spanish Voyages (1929), pp. 180–272, and must be regarded as the primary authority. But the friar made a shorter report also and when, in 1620 Don Francisco Ramírez de Arellano wished to revive the memory of the voyage, he sent to Spain for this shorter version, "A brief report."

The text is in Biblioteca Nacional, Madrid, MS 3042, and was printed in Colección de documentos inéditos de Indias, 1st series, VIII, 537–574, and in W. M. Mathes, Californiana, II (1965), 1175–1202. It is translated in H. E. Bolton, Spanish Exploration in the Southwest, pp. 104–134, from which it is reprinted.

A Brief Report in which is given Information of the Discovery which was made in New Spain, in the South Sea, from the Port of Acapulco to a Point beyond Cape Mendocino; containing an Account of the Riches, the Temperate Climate, and the Advantages of the Realm of the Californias, and setting forth how his Majesty will be able at little cost to pacify it and incorporate it into his Royal Crown and cause the Holy Gospel to be preached in it. By Father Fray Antonio de la Ascensión, a Religious of the Discalced Order of Carmelites, who took part in it and as Cosmographer made a map of it.

1

In the past year of 1602, by order of our very Catholic and most Christian King, Philip III., king of Spain, Don Gaspar de Zúñiga y Acevedo, Count of Monterey, may he be in heaven, being viceroy of New Spain, two small ships and a frigate were equipped by his order and command in the port of Acapulco, which is in New Spain, on the coast of the South Sea. They were supplied with all necessary arms and provisions for a voyage of one year, the time it was thought this expedition would last. Sebastian Vizcaino went as captain and commander of the soldiers and vessels and Captain Toribio Gomez de Corban went as admiral. There embarked in these ships and the frigate two hundred persons, more or less, one hundred and fifty of them select and experienced soldiers, who were also very skilful sailors, to assist in whatever might present itself concerning affairs at sea as well as those of war on land, and to escort the general. Several famous captains and the ensign who had done heroic deeds in his Majesty's service in Flanders and Britain and in the cruise of the galleons embarked as counsellors, all well accustomed and experienced in affairs of war and of the sea. They were Captain Pascual de Alarcon, Captain Alonzo Esteban Pequero, Ensign Juan Francisco Sureano, Ensign Juan de Acevedo Tejeda, and Ensign Melendez. And for steering the ships there went select pilots, very vigilant and experienced, two for each vessel. And for spiritual matters and the guidance of souls, three religious, priests of the Discalced Order of Carmelites, were appointed; they were Father Andrés de la Asumpcion, who went as commissary, Father Tomas de Aquino, and I, Father Antonio de Ascension, who writes this report. They were sent in order that in the name of his Majesty the king our Lord, and of his religion, and of the Province of San Alberto of New Spain, immediate possession might be taken of the realm of the Californias which was to be discovered and explored; in order that thenceforward they might take charge of the conversion and instruction of all the heathen Indians of that realm; and in order that on the voyage they might administer the sacraments to those who were in the ships. Besides these, the viceroy appointed two cosmographers, to survey and map all the coasts, with their ports, inlets, rivers, and bays, with their latitudes and longitudes. These were Captain Gerónimo Martin Palacios and I, I having studied this art and science in the University of Salamanca, where I was born and reared, and where I studied until I took the holy habit which I unworthily wear. I have said this and signed here my name so that persons who may read this brief and concise report may be convinced that in all its contents I am telling the truth; and in order not to be prolix I am brief in everything, with a style plain and simple, as will be seen in what follows.

2

This armada sailed from the port of Acapulco the 5th day of the month of May, of the said year, 1602, every one, before embarking, having confessed and received communion, the captains as well as the soldiers and cabin-boys of the two vessels.

The order which the viceroy gave them was to explore all the coast from the above-mentioned port of Acapulco to the Point of California, and everything from there to Cape Mendocino; and on returning, if there should be time and opportunity, to explore the Mediterranean Sea of California. Pursuant to this order, the armada sailed northwest, coasting all along the shore and land of New Spain as far as the islands of Maçatlan and thence crossing over so as to reach the Point of California. It is fifty leagues across the sea from one side to the other.

From the time this armada sailed from the port of Acapulco until it reached Cape Mendocino there were always strong headwinds, because almost continually the northwest wind prevails on all this coast; it was necessary, therefore, to sail with bowlines hauled, which was an incredible hindrance, as there were days when it was not able to gain a league's headway. Tacking to the sea or to the land, one way or the other, the voyage was made, and for this reason the outward trip was very prolonged, and all the ports, bays, rivers, and inlets of the entire coast were examined very minutely. It took us nine months from the time we left Acapulco to reach Cape Mendocino, where we arrived on the 20th day of the month of January, 1603. Cape Mendocino is in latitude 42° north, and we went even farther, to the latitude of 43°, to what was named Cape San Sebastian, where the coast turns to the northeast, and where the entrance to the Strait of Anian seems to begin.

3

This exploration was made with very great care and vigilance and cost a great deal of labor and exertion and tedious illness, and the lives of many who took part in it, because of undergoing so much labor, in continual pain and always struggling against the wild waves which the sea heaved up and against the winds which caused them. Moreover, the provisions became so stale that they finally had no virtue or nutrition. From these

two causes there ensued a sickness like a pest, which affected every one and was extremely painful, so that more than forty-four persons died on the voyage. I made a report of all that happened on this voyage, in which is related at length everything that took place during it and what was seen and discovered on it, and upon which I rely. This armada returned to Acapulco, and the captain's ship, in which I came, entered it March 21 of the said year, 1603. Thus eleven months were spent on the voyage from the time of sailing until port was made. In this short account I will speak briefly of some of the most important things I saw, learned, and observed throughout the land and seacoast which we saw and explored.

4

This realm of California is very large and embraces much territory, nearly all inhabited by numberless people. It has a good climate, is very fertile, and abounds in many and various kinds of trees, the most of them like those in Spain, abundant pastures of good grazing land, and a great number of different kinds of animals and birds. The sea of all this coast is full of a variety of savory and wholesome fish, which I will mention later. All the land of this realm is in the temperate zone, which is situated in the northern division, and the climates 2, 3, 4, 5, 6, and 8 pass over it. It has the exact form and shape of a casket, being broad at the top and narrow at the point. It is this latter which we commonly call Punta de la California. From there it widens out to Cape Mendocino, which we will describe as being the top and breadth of it. The breadth of this land from here to the other sea, where the Mediterranean Sea of California comes and connects with the sea that surrounds and encircles Cape Mendocino, must be about one hundred leagues. In this part this realm has north of it the Kingdom of Anian, and to the east the land which is continuous with the realm of Quivira. Between these two realms extends the strait of Anian, which runs to the North Sea, having joined the Oceanic Sea which surrounds Cape Mendocino and the Mediterranean Sea of California, both of which are united at the entrance of this strait which I call Anian. Toward the west is the realm of China, and toward the south all the realm of Japan. The most modern maps show that from the meridian corresponding to the Point of California to the meridian corresponding to Cape Mendocino there are sixty degrees of longitude; so that if we give sixteen and a half leagues to each degree, according to the reckoning of cosmographers, it is about one thousand leagues long; but if according to the reckoning of mariners, who give twenty-five leagues to each degree, we should say that its coast and shore is more than fifteen hundred leagues long from northwest to southeast, which is the direction all this realm runs and trends. In latitude, or breadth, it extends from the Tropic of Cancer, that is, from the Point of California, called Cape San Lucas, which is under that tropic, to the latitude of 50°, the highest latitude of this realm—which, I said, is where unite the two seas that surround this realm.

Thus it is plain that this realm of California is a land separate and distinct from the lands of New Mexico and the realm of Quivira, which is continuous with the latter, although there is a long distance and much territory between the one realm and the other. The sea between these two realms, which is the one called the Mediterranean Sea of California, since it is between lands so large and extended, must be about fifty leagues wide. In the middle of it there are many islands, some small and others larger; but I cannot say whether they are inhabited or not. The inhabitants of Cape Mendocino are so opposite and remote from the kingdom of Old Castile in our Spain that it is midnight in the noted city and university of Salamanca when it is noon at Cape Mendocino, and *vice versa:* so that they are the antipodes of each other, being opposite each other, and in the same climate, but with different and diametrically opposite meridians. Hence it follows that they must possess the same atmospheric conditions and climate, having the same winter, summer, and autumn. It is possible that they differ in some conditions and temperatures, because of the different influences of the vertical stars which affect their qualities.

Those who are acquainted with and understand the sphere and cosmography will have no doubt of this; but in order to make myself better understood I made for those who do not understand it a geographic map of it all, which I have with me; and I am sending a copy of it to his Majesty and to his Royal Council of the Indies, that they may understand the great size and the situation of this great realm. And I believe it will be indispensable and important, in order that the present maps of the world may be compared with it and corrected,

because many of the things which are depicted in them relating to matters of this realm are very different from what they actually are. This is not to be wondered at, since the land and seacoast of this realm have never been viewed or explored so exactly and designedly as on this expedition, which went solely for this purpose.

5

The Cape of San Lucas, which is at the extremity of California, whence all this realm begins and takes its name, forms in its shelter a bay called San Bernabé, so spacious that it is a good bay and will accommodate many ships, although it is not protected on all sides. This bay, or cape, of San Lucas is under the Tropic of Cancer, and off the islands of Maçatlan, which, on the coast of New Spain, are the frontier and limit on this side of the bishopric of Guadalajara and of the kingdom which they call Nueva Galicia. It is fifty leagues, more or less, across the sea, which is the width of the Mediterranean Sea of California between the realm of California and that of Galicia. This latter joins the kingdom of New Spain and extends to New Mexico, continuing to the kingdom of Quivira, and terminating at the Strait of Anian, as has already been said. Some call it the Mediterranean because it flows between these two large realms; others call it the Vermillion Sea, since in this passage the water looks a bright reddish color, perhaps because the land at the bottom is red, or it may be from the spawn brought here by the river-fish that come to swim in that sea, this color being caused by the blood; for once I saw that the water at the port of Acapulco was of this bright reddish color, and they told me that it was because of the fish spawn. On the old maps it is called the bay, or gulf, of Ballenas, because there, as on all the coast as far as Cape Mendocino, there are so many whales that they cannot be numbered, nor would it be believed by anybody who had not seen them. And because until now it has been understood to be a bay or large gulf, formed there by the sea, and not a regular and continuous sea, which it is, they gave it this name.

In this passage are the islands called the Marías, and another small one called San Andrés; and through all this sea there are many other islands. Among them, facing the port formed by the Tizon River, which flows into this sea from New Mexico in latitude 35°, is the island of Giganta, where lives the queen of the neighboring peoples. In this sea, on both shores, other islands also, as well as the land of California, have many oyster-beds, which produce pearls, many, rich, and large. They are found as far as latitude 36°, as I say in the last chapter of the report which I made of this discovery.

6

I will say that the wealth and abundance of pearls in this sea is very great, a thing which is well known and remarked upon by persons who have coasted along the sea; and they are, indeed, large and beautiful, choice, and very perfect. The oysters are not very deep, for the Indians search for and bring them up. This is not to make use of the pearls, because they do not understand or value them, but only to eat the fish within. In order to open the oysters and more easily extract their contents they put them in the fire, whereupon they open and the pearls are burned or smoked. When found they are thrown away, as if they were stones of no value.

There are many different kinds of fish in this sea, large and small, which are seen to go in shoals or schools. As they are fish known in other seas, I will here name some of those I have caught, had in my hands, and eaten, so that the abundance, excellence, and wealth of that sea may be understood. There are, as I have said, multitudes of very large whales, and a great quantity of sardines, large and small, slender and thick, which are, according to what they say, the common sustenance of the whales, and may be it is for this reason there are so many. There are ruffles, porgy, sea-bass, corrundas, small sharks, or dogfish, sturgeon, *esmirigalas*, skate, salmon, tunny, ray, *chucos*, sea-horse, little bass, striped tunny, gilt-head, sole, mutton-fish, porpoise, newts, *tirgueros*, common oysters, those that bear pearls, and many other never seen and unknown. And there are octopus. One was caught so large that it wrapped itself around the buoy-rope or line by which the buoy was fastened to the anchor; although it was very heavy, as it had a firm hold, the ship raised it and dragged it behind. It had a mouth like a half-moon. I measured it from one point to the other, crosswise, and it was a *vara* and three quarters, and from the head to the end of the tail it was five and one quarter *varas*. It was broad and flat like a mantle. These fish are of fine flavor, palatable, and wholesome. All these varieties were caught every year by

casting the net, or seine. Sometimes the seine was so full that it broke.

7

The country of this Cape San Lucas is very fertile and healthful, with a fine climate and clear sky. It has good level land and is not very mountainous. All of it is perfectly adapted to cultivation and to keeping and raising stock, both cattle and sheep, goats and swine. There is plenty of wild game for hunting and fowling, such as rabbits, hare, deer, lions, tigers, armadillos, ringdoves, quail, and many ducks. Of trees, there are figs, broccoli, agaves, mangroves, mastick, and, near the beach, a grove of plum trees.

In place of gum or resin, they exude in great quantities very good and fragrant incense. The fruit which they produce is very delicious, as I have been told by those who have tried it on other occasions. There is also on the shore of this land which encircles the Bay of San Bernabé, where I saw all the things mentioned, a lagoon of good fresh water, all surrounded and hedged in with brambles. On the other side, near the rocks and the beach, there is a little lagoon of salt water, left by the sea in high winds, which was covered, all around, with very good salt, plentiful, white, and of a good taste. Here also are many robust Indians, of good disposition, who use bows, arrows, and darts for arms. They gave indications of being bellicose and spirited; for, when some natives came to see us at this port, they said that if the soldiers would put away the arquebuses they carried they would also come without arms. Laying them aside, they seated themselves, saying in a loud voice "Vtesi," that is to say, "Seat yourselves" or "be seated," which is the surest and most certain sign of peace in use among them. With this ceremony they came peaceably, and treated us with friendliness and civility, although always with extreme caution and suspicion, and on hearing an arquebus discharged they immediately ran away. When they came, they always brought with them such little things as they had, showing themselves to be a people grateful and thankful for what the soldiers and religious gave them.

8

It is at this port that his Majesty should order the first settlement of Spaniards to be made when he sends people to pacify the country, in order that the pacification of all this realm and the preaching of the Holy Gospel may begin here. It is situated near and convenient for trade and communication with New Spain and Peru, as the ships to New Spain touch at this place when they come from Peru by the new mode of navigation now in use, and they come in one month. Besides these, it has other advantages for sustaining human life, and for enabling the Spaniards to keep their trade and commerce in good and secure communication, because, besides the pearl-fisheries near by, there is, on the south coast, a neighboring land which we call Sierra Pintada or del Enfado. It has many minerals of various kinds; and one can go by land to extract them, and to get the gold and silver which they may contain. Apparently they are very abundant, according to experience and trustworthy information upon which I rely.

It is the best place that could be found in the world for the maintenance and mode of life of the Discalced Carmelite religious (who, by order of the king, our lord, have charge of the conversion of this realm), and for their abstemious and penitent life, because of the good mild climate as well as the great abundance of many kinds of good fish, as is stated above. The heat of the climate is not so excessive as to need linen, nor does it require much protection against the cold, so that one kind of clothing can be worn all the time. Moreover, the proximity of the country to New Spain and the facility of navigation from one realm to the other is very important for providing it with the religious, for governing them by one provincial, and for conveying some and bringing back others, according as the necessity of the religious may require; for, having settlements as far as the port of Navidad where they can embark if they do not wish to go to Acapulco, in a month one can go from Mexico to the Californias with great ease and comfort.

9

After remaining in this port and bay of San Bernabé some days, we set sail for the purpose of making the exploration of Cape Mendocino. As the coast runs from southeast to northwest, and as the wind is continually from that quarter, that is, northwest, we found it so severe and strong that four times against our will it forced us to put back into the port from which we sailed. Finally, at the end of some days, with bowlines hauled, we

made our way and arrived at the port of Magdalena, which was formerly called the port of Santiago. Here the Indians received us peacefully and, as an acknowledgment of submission, offered the Spaniards their bows and arrows, very nicely wrought, and brought some incense like that we had procured in the Bay of San Bernabé, a sign that there are here a great number of these trees which produce it. An arm of the sea enters this port, unless it is some large river which disembogues here and empties into the sea. But it was ascended only about a league, being left for exploration when we should return from Cape Mendocino. Here many Indians came out to us in their canoes and showed themselves friendly and gentle.

This port is very good and spacious, and has two mouths or entrances. By one, small vessels only can enter; by the other large ones can enter, as it has good soundings. Here and all along this coast there are many whales, and, if it is true that amber comes from their filth, as I understand, from what I saw on this voyage, there must be much amber on this coast; for not far from this place, though farther up on the same coast, we found another port, which was named San Bartolomeo, on whose shore was a large quantity of ambergris, in cakes, like soft, whitish pitch. We did not recognize it as such, and for this reason we took no notice of it. Afterward, when giving a description of it to those who are well acquainted with amber, they said that it was very fine ambergris. There was a large quantity of it in this port. Perhaps God our Lord allowed none of those who went there to know this, since it may be that in the interest of going to obtain it his Majesty will send ministers with the design of converting those Indians, for according to the signs which they gave it will be easy to bring them into our Catholic faith.

10

We went forward, making the exploration carefully and slowly, because head winds impeded it. Other ports and islands were discovered along the coast, and all along it there were many Indians, who signalled us with smoke columns and other signs; but, in order to reach Cape Mendocino, everything was left to be examined on our return. Finally, after much labor we reached the port of San Diego, which is very good and capacious and offers many very good advantages for Spanish settlement. Here the ships were cleaned and oiled again, the place being quiet, and there being many friendly and affable Indians there. They use bows and arrows and appear warlike and valiant, since, notwithstanding they came to see us every day, they always treated us with so great a distrust that they never had complete confidence in us. They pronounced so very well in our language what they heard us speak that anyone hearing them and not seeing them would say they were Spaniards. Every day they would come in order that we might give them some of the fish we caught in the net, and they would go away quietly after they had helped to haul it in.

The harbor is large and secure, and has a large beach within, like an island of sand, which the sea covers at high tide. In the sand on this beach there is a great quantity of yellow pyrites, all full of holes, a sure sign that in the neighboring mountains and adjacent to this port there are gold mines; for the water, when it rains, brings it from the mountains, and the whole watershed converges here. On the sandy beach which I said was in this harbor we found some large pieces, like adobe, brown or dark red in color, and very light in weight, like dried cowdung. They had neither a good nor a bad odor, and they are said to be amber. If this is so, there are great riches and an abundance of amber here.

There are many different kinds of fish, of very good taste and flavor, such as ray, sea-horse, lobster, crab, *guitarras*, sardine, turtle, and many other kinds. There is much wild game for hunting and fowling; and there are many large, grassy pastures. The Indians paint themselves white, and black, and dark London blue. This color comes from certain very heavy blue stones, which they grind very fine, and, dissolving the powder in water, make a stain, with which they daub the face and make on it lines which glisten like silver ribbons. These stones seem to be of rich silver ore, and the Indians told us by signs that from similar stones a people living inland, of form and figure like our Spaniards, bearded, and wearing collars and breeches, and other fine garments like ours, secured silver in abundance, and that they had a name for it in their own language. To ascertain whether these Indians knew silver, the general showed them some silver bowls and a plate. They took it in their hands and spun it

around, and, pleased by the sound, said it was good, and was the same as that possessed and valued highly by the people of whom they had told us. Then he put in their hands a pewter bowl, but when they struck it the sound did not please them and, spitting, they wanted to throw it into the sea.

The people of whom the Indians told us might have been foreigners, Hollanders or English, who had made their voyage by the Strait of Anian and might be settled on the other coast of this land, facing the Mediterranean Sea of California. Since the realm is narrow, as has been said, it may be that the other sea is near that place; for the Indians offered to guide and take us to the place where they say the people are settled. If this is so, it is probable they have large interests and profits there, since their voyage is so long and difficult. Still, it is true that by passing through the Strait of Anian and reaching their land by that latitude, their voyage is only half as long as that from the port of San Juan de Ulúa to Spain. This will be clearly seen from evidence furnished by the globe. In this case, it will be to his Majesty's interest to endeavor to assure himself of the fact: first, in order to know the route, and secondly, in order to expel from there such dangerous enemies, lest they contaminate the Indians with their sects and liberty of conscience, by which great harm to their souls will follow, whereby instructing them and leading them in the paths of the true law of God will be made very difficult. Besides this, his Majesty will be able to secure many other advantages, as I shall show later.

11

After we left the Port of San Diego we discovered many islands placed in a line, one behind another. Most of them were inhabited by many friendly Indians, who have trade and commerce with those of the mainland. It may be that they are vassals of a petty king who came with his son from the mainland in a canoe with eight oarsmen, to see us and to invite us to go to his land, saying that he would entertain us and provide us with anything which we needed and he possessed. He said that he came to see us on account of what the inhabitants of these islands had reported to him. There are many people in this land, so many that the petty king, seeing that there were no women on the ships, offered by signs to give to everyone ten women apiece if they would all go to his land, which shows how thickly populated it all is. And besides, all along, day and night, they made many bonfires, the sign in use among them to call people to their land. Since there was no convenient port where the ships could be secure in the country whence this petty king came, the acceptance of his invitation was deferred until the return voyage.

Thereupon we went forward with our voyage, and at the end of some days arrived at a fine port, which was named Monterrey. It is in latitude 37°, in the same climate and latitude as Seville. This is where the ships coming from the Philippines to New Spain come to reconnoitre. It is a good harbor, well sheltered, and supplied with water, wood, and good timber, both for masts and ship building, such as pines, live oaks, and great white oaks, large and frondose, and many black poplars on the banks of a river that near by enters the sea and was named the Carmelo. In climate, in birds and game, in variety of animals and trees, in everything it is essentially like our Old Spain. When the ships from China arrive at this place they have already sailed four months and they come in need of repairs, which in this harbor they can make very well, and with perfect convenience; therefore it would be a very good thing for the Spaniards to settle this port for the assistance of navigators, and to undertake the conversion to our Holy Faith of those Indians, who are numerous, docile, and friendly. And from here they might trade and traffic with the people of China and Japan, opportunity for that being favorable because of propinquity.

The land of this country is very fertile and has good pastures and forests, and fine hunting and fowling. Among the animals there are large, fierce bears, and other animals called elks, from which they make elk-leather jackets, and others of the size of young bulls, shaped and formed like deer, with thick, large horns. There were many Castilian roses here. There are pretty ponds of fresh water. The mountains near this port were covered with snow, and that was on Christmas day. On the beach was a dead whale, and at night some bears came to feed on it.

There are many fish here, and a great variety of mollusks among the rocks; among them there were certain barnacles, or large shells, fastened to the lowest part of the rocks. The Indians hunt for them to extract from them their contents to eat. These shells are very bright, of fine mother-of-pearl. All along this coast, there is a great abundance of sea-wolves or dogs, of the size of a yearling calf. They sleep on the water, and sometimes go ashore to take the sun; and there they place their sentinel in order to be secure from enemies. The Indians clothe themselves in the skins of these animals, which are healthful, fine, beautiful, and convenient. Finally, I will say that this is a good and commodious port, and might be settled, but this should be done in the way which I shall set forth hereafter.

12

We set sail from here after dispatching the admiral's ship to New Spain with the news of what had been discovered and with the sick who were unfit for service. Among them returned Father Tomás de Aquino, one of the three religious who were going in this fleet, because he had been ill many days, and in order that the sick might have someone to confess them should God desire to relieve them of this life. Our departure in quest of Cape Mendocino was made on the first Sunday after Epiphany, of the year 1603. On the coast we noted the port of San Francisco, where in times past there was lost a ship from China which was coming with orders to explore this coast. I believe that much of the wax and porcelain which the vessel carried is there to-day. And we arrived at Cape Mendocino in latitude 42°, which is the highest latitude at which the China ships sight land. Here, because of the severity of winter in this climate, and of the cold, and the stiffness of the rigging, and because almost all the crew were ill, the sails were lowered. The captain's ship got into the trough of the sea, and, as it could not be steered, the currents that run to the Strait of Anian whose entrance begins here, carried it little by little toward land. In eight days we had ascended more than one degree of latitude, which was up to 43°, in sight of a cape that was named San Sebastian. Near it empties a river that was called Santa Inez. No one landed here, as all the crew were very ill, only six persons being able to walk. Here the coast and land turns to the northeast, and here is the head and end of the realm and mainland of California and the entrance to the Strait of Anian. If on this occasion there had been on the captain's ship even fourteen sound men, without any doubt we should have ventured to explore and pass through this Strait of Anian, since all were of good courage to do this. But the general lack of health and of men who could manage the sails and steer the ship obliged us to turn about toward New Spain, to report what had been discovered and seen, and lest the whole crew should die if we remained longer in that latitude.

With this decision and agreement the return voyage was begun. It was made by coasting along shore with favorable winds, exploring all the ports, bays, and inlets that we had sighted on our outward voyage. As the northwest wind is so usual and continual on this coast, one can easily come from Cape Mendocino to the port of Acapulco in one month, if the pilot knows how to choose the correct routes at the proper times, as I set them down in an itinerary which I made for this voyage. The course which we took on our return was along the coast, and so near it that everything on it was seen with great clearness and distinctness. The Indians, as they saw us pass at a distance, sent up columns of smoke and other signals to attract us; and wherever we landed they gave indications of their good natures and intelligence, hence it appeared to us all that they might easily and with very little labor be taught our Holy Catholic faith, and that they would receive it well and lovingly. But this should be done with great prudence and in the manner that our Master and Redeemer, Jesus Christ, taught us in his Holy Gospel.

As to how persons should be sent to new lands for the conversion of the heathen Indians, I wrote a brief treatise, which I sent to the king, our lord, Philip III. In it I discuss what ought to be done that the people may be converted and that his Majesty may with just title become the lawful emperor and lord of their lands; and to this I refer the reader. Nevertheless, as there I have treated of the general instruction for all, here, for the sake of greater clearness, I will set forth briefly what his Majesty can and ought to do for the conversion of the Indians of this great realm of the Californias in particular, and to pacify their lands and become lord over them with good conscience, as will be seen by beginning with number 23 below of this little treatise.

Finally, returning to our voyage, I will say that we returned to the port of Acapulco on March 22, of the year 1603, having passed through great labor and severe illness, of which died the number of people that I mentioned at the beginning; and I made a full report of all that happened on the voyage, and a map of the situation of this realm.

13
The Method to be observed in Subduing and Settling the Realm of Californias.

All this realm of the Californias can be pacified and settled, and by this means and by the preaching of the Holy Gospel its natives can be led to the fold of our Holy Mother, the Roman Catholic Church, and converted to our Holy Catholic Faith. Now, in order that this may become an accomplished fact, and that his Majesty may effect it at a moderate expense, that which must be commanded, ordered, and provided is as follows:

There should be prepared and equipped in the port of Acapulco two small vessels of two hundred tons burden, and a frigate, with boats with skiffs for their service; and they should be abundantly supplied with stores and munitions of war, as well as with food, rigging, canvas, and everything that may seem necessary for settling in infidel and heathen lands.

While these things are being provided and prepared, there should be raised in Mexico as many as two hundred soldiers, care being taken that they should be good seamen, and also that they be old soldiers, expert and experienced as well in arms as in seamanship, in order that all, uniformly and without distinction, may aid in everything as occasion may offer. And let care be taken that they be good and honorable men in order that on the journey both on sea and land there may be peace, union, and brotherhood among all. Plenty of men of these parts and talents will very easily be found in Mexico if his Majesty will increase their pay in proportion as the double service they have to render demands, and if their pay and allowance be given them punctually when due.

The duty of raising this troop should be assigned to one or two captains, good Christians and God-fearing men, and persons of merit, who have served his Majesty faithfully on other occasions, in war on land as well as in the fleets at sea. To them should be entrusted the appointment of officers to accompany them, who should be persons they are satisfied will perform their service in a Christian and careful manner, and men of experience, who know how to fulfill the offices committed to them, for on these officers depend the good order and discipline of the soldiers. This expedition must be entrusted to a person of courage and talents, of long experience, and accustomed to such charges, in order that he may know how to treat all with love and dignity, and each one individually as his character deserves. Let care be taken that such a person be God-fearing, scrupulous in his conscience, and zealous in the service of his Majesty and in the things relating to the conversion of these souls. To a person of these qualities can be given the office of general of the armada, to whom all, both captains and soldiers, will be subject, and whom they will obey in everything, and whose orders they will follow.

To the general, captains, soldiers, and all who go on this expedition, must be given express order and command that they shall hold themselves in strict obedience and subjection to the religious who are in their company, and that without their order, counsel, and advice, war may not be made, or the heathen Indians be otherwise molested, even if they should give occasion, in order that by this means matters may be conducted with peace and Christianity, and with love and quiet, which is the method to be used in the pacification of that realm, and in the preaching of the Holy Gospel, to which end and aim these expenses and preparations are directed. Not to do this, but the contrary, will be to waste everything, to lose time, and to render the expenditure ineffectual, as has been found by experience many times in this New Spain, in other conquests and pacifications of new lands, whereby God our Lord has been more injured than served.

14

The religious who should go on this expedition are the Discalced of Our Lady of Carmel, the ones to whom are intrusted by his Majesty the conversion, instruction, and teaching of the Indians of this realm of the Californias. On this first entrance there should be six religious, four priests and two lay brothers; and it will be requested of the superiors of this order, in the name of his Majesty, that those whom they assign and appoint for this voyage be persons such as the occasion and enterprise demand, holy, affable, full of love and wisdom, that they may know how to counsel, guide and direct these souls, and to deal with such cases as may present themselves comformably with sound Catholic doctrine.

By observing the indulgences and benefits which the Supreme Pontiffs have granted in favor of new conversions, for their greater increase, these holy friars, with their piety, modesty, simplicity, and religious graciousness, will succeed in winning the wills and hearts of both general and captains, as well as of all the soldiers, in order thereby to lead them in the holy path of virtue; and may they with loving arguments persuade and admonish all, before embarking, to confess their sins and receive the most holy sacrament of the Eucharist, with all the devotion and inclination possible, offering their souls and lives to the service of his divine Majesty, asking of him success for their voyage and expedition. By doing this, with the proper spirit and devotion, the religious will make themselves lords over the hearts and wills of all, and will have authority over all to keep them in peace, love, and unity; and if perchance there should be any dissension among them, they will calm it at once with discretion, and thus animosities, vexations, and enmities, and the mutinies, insurrections, and disobedience to superiors which ordinarily occur on such enterprises, will be avoided.

These religious will be provided with everything necessary for their voyage, such as vessels for saying mass and administering the sacraments, books and vestments and, in particular, something in the way of delicacies that they may have wherewith to give to the sick if there should be any. Likewise, there should be taken on board at the cost of his Majesty a quantity of trifles, Flemish trinkets, such as beads of colored glass, artificial garnets, hawks' bells, mirrors, knives, cheap scissors, Parisian tops, and some articles of clothing.

These things should be divided among the religious and soldiers, so that in places where they may go on shore or where they may choose sites for settlements in the lands of the heathen, they may distribute them, with signs of love and good will, in the name of his Majesty, in order that with these pleasing gifts the heathen Indians may come to feel love and affection for the Christians, and may realize that they are coming to their lands to give them of that which they bring, and not to take away their possessions, and may understand that they are seeking the good of their souls. This is a measure of great importance, to the end that the Indians may become quiet, humane, and peaceable, and obey the Spaniards without opposition or repugnance, and receive with pleasure those who go to preach to them the Holy Gospel and the mysteries of our Holy Catholic faith; to the end, moreover, that the Indians may be grateful and thankful, and, in recompense and pay for what is given them, may assist with whatever of value they may have in their land, things to eat as well as other articles, as they did with us.

With this preparation, the soldiers and religious should embark in the ships provided, no woman going or embarking with them, to avoid offenses to God and dissensions between one another. With the ocean currents that run toward the entrance of California, even if winds favorable to navigation should fail, one can within a month at the most succeed in landing in the Bay of San Bernabé, which is at Cape San Lucas and the extremity of California, the point best fitted for the first settlement.

15

After a landing is made in the Bay of San Bernabé, effort should be made at once to establish the camp in the place that seems most convenient; and it should be of such a style and plan as that some of the houses may serve as a guard and protection to the others. First of all a church should be built, in order that there the priests may celebrate mass every day; and it would be very holy and well if immediately on entrance into this realm the general with his captains and all the soldiers should confess and receive the sacrament, for this would be a very good beginning for making the entrance in proper form, and for following out, with the aid and favor of our Redeemer and Lord Jesus Christ, that which is attempted, namely, the pacification of the realm and the conversion of its inhabitants to our holy Catholic faith.

As to the location of a stronghold to serve as a castle and watch-tower and as a defense in adverse chances, it should be a strong location, high and commanding; and if a secure passage could be made from it to the sea it would be very advantageous as a means of receiving aid or of sending for aid by sea in case any necessity should arise. The Portuguese have generally done this way in the places where they have established themselves in India, and the observance of this stratagem and precaution has succeeded very well with them. This castle and stronghold should

be stocked with artillery carried there for that purpose, together with other defenses customary in such fortresses; and in it should be kept the arms and supplies. Above it there should be a watch-tower in which there should be continually a guard or sentinel, in order that all coming and going to the camp may be carefully watched; for when in lands of heathen Indians, although they may have declared themselves friendly and peaceable, they must not be trusted much; rather, one must live with them and among them with great circumspection, vigilance, and watchfulness, and be gracious and kindly, with wisdom and prudence, showing them love and all good treatment, regaling and giving them gratis of the trifles which, at his Majesty's expense, may have been taken for the purpose of coaxing and winning them.

Besides these buildings, a trading house should be erected, whither the Indians may repair to barter with the Spaniards for whatever they may desire, and in order that they may trade and bargain among themselves; for thereby their communication with us will be greatly facilitated and love and friendship thus engendered.

From this place, with the ships, frigate, and other vessels, they can send to the land of Culiacan, which is a settlement of Christians, or to the islands of Macatlan, or to the pueblo of La Navidad, to bring from there whatever may seem necessary both for the settlement of the land and for sustenance, such as cows, sheep, goats, mares, and hogs, which in two or four days at the most can be sent alive from one side to the other, as the sea lying between is about fifty leagues in width, and is safe and smooth. These animals will grow and multiply as well in this land, since it is suitable for that purpose and is fertile. Likewise it will be possible to cultivate fields of wheat and maize, and to plant vines and gardens, in order that sustenance may be had from within and it may not be necessary to carry it from without. The Indians can be taught and instructed to do the same, and will take everything well, seeing it redound to their advantage.

16

Besides what is said above, the Spaniards in this place will be able to establish fisheries for pearls and other fish, of which there is abundance, to send to New Spain, to sell in Mexico. Very good salt-works can be established; likewise they can work mines, of which there are some near by, as I have said in number VIII. These things being settled with the peace, love and good will of the natives, the religious will give their attention to their ministry, and make a beginning and commencement of converting the Indians, in the way which may seem best to them, founding with great prudence and gentleness the new Christian church to be planted there.

And it would be well to bring from New Spain Indian minstrels, with their instruments and trumpets, that the divine services may be celebrated with solemnity and pomp, and to teach the Indians of the land to sing and play. Likewise it would be well and proper to choose from among the Indians some of the brightest, selecting among the young men and boys such as appear the most docile, talented and capable; and they should be taught and instructed in the Christian doctrine and to read the Spanish primers, in order that along with the reading they may learn the Spanish language, and that they may learn to write and sing, and to play all the musical instruments; because a good foundation makes the edifice firm, and according as care is given in this matter to the beginnings, so will the middle parts and the ends be good.

It is a very easy matter, by this method, to teach the children our language, and they, as they grow up, will teach it to their companions and to their children and families, and in a few years all will know the Spanish language, which will be a very great boon; for they will not lack ministers to teach, guide, and direct them in the path leading to heaven and to their salvation. From here they can continue the planting of settlements of Christians and of the Indians who may be scattered through the mountains, drawing them to the settlements with love, suavity, and gentleness; taking care that the Christian soldiers do not disperse themselves so much that the guard will be diminished and impaired, so that, if the Indians, instigated by the evil one, should try to effect some uprising or to rebel against the Spaniards, there may be someone who can make resistance, and hold them in line, and even punish their insolence if the case demands it.

17

In number 8. I told how with very little trouble it would be possible to explore a certain land that is near here, on the coast of the South Sea, called the land of Enfado, or Pintada. I say that I believe that it has very rich silver ores. This can be explored by land, for it is near, and it might be developed if the ores proved to be of high grade and easily worked; and should they be rich and profitable, the expense which may have been entailed by building this fleet and bringing it to this country might be reimbursed from the fifths of the silver and pearls secured belonging to his Majesty. And this, once established, will necessarily bring great profits to his Majesty and to his royal patrimony, and great increase to his estate, with which there can be sent to this realm whatever number of people may seem to be necessary to pacify and settle it, and the ministers necessary for the conversion and instruction of the natives.

Before making the second settlement, it is well that with the two ships all the Mediterranean Sea of California be explored, examining everything on the coast running from Culiacan to Quivira, as far as the Strait of Anian, to see what rivers, ports and inlets there are on it; as well as along the coast encircling the realm of California, until Cape Mendocino is turned, with all the rivers, ports, bays, and straits which there may be in its whole extent; and to learn on the way where and how are settled the strangers which the Indians said were in the realm near there and in their lands, as I have mentioned above in number 10., and, also, to try to acquire knowledge and information of what the country contains.

By making this exploration with proper care and diligence it will be learned at once what there is along the sea and its coasts, and what people and wealth the region contains; and in what places settlements of Spaniards can be made, from which the religious may go to preach the Holy Gospel and convert souls to our holy Catholic faith. It will be learned, likewise, in what place and region is situated the Tizon River, which comes from New Mexico, how it is situated, what advantages it possesses, and what the distance is from there to the Spanish pueblos; for if it is as they say, and as I mentioned in the last chapter of the report which I made of this exploration, his Majesty could order it settled, so that by this route supplies might be taken to the people of that realm. And from the settlements could be brought to them the necessary live stock and supplies, both for settling the coast and for sustenance. For it is said that it is no more than fifty leagues from one place to the other.

Personally, I think it will be very well that the pacification of the realm of New Mexico should begin at the port of Tizon River, since it is said that the best and richest settlements are on that border; for near there are the Lake of Gold, and the pueblos of the Crowned King (Rey Coronado), and many people. For the preservation of the settlement on the Tizon River it will be very important that opposite it, in the realm and on the coast of California, another Spanish settlement be made, that they may communicate and trade one with another, and lend aid in case of need. Thereby each will stimulate the other to discover new lands and riches, and all may enjoy very good pearl fisheries and mineral wealth, those of New Mexico enjoying the wealth from the Lake of Gold, and those of the Californias that from some rich mountains which are on that border or near it and have an abundance of rich silver ore. Both of these God created for the service of man, as lures, I think, so that in the interest of these temporal things the king, our lord might send his vassals to discover and enjoy them, and, in their company, friars and ministers of the Gospel to undertake the conversion of those natives.

18

Of the reports brought back by those who may go on the ships for this exploration, both of what they may have seen and what they may have heard and learned, one may be given to his Majesty and his Royal Council of the Indies, that he may provide and order what is most fitting to his royal service and to the aggrandizement of his royal crown. I think it would be a matter of great importance to all these western nations of his Majesty if the navigation of the Strait of Anian should be discovered for Spain, as well as the rich city of Quivira, and the position of the realm of Anian, which is understood to be continuous with the realms of China. This will be discovering here another new world, to the end that in all of it may be preached the Holy Gospel, and the conversion undertaken of the many souls throughout its whole extent who live without religion or knowledge of the true God or of his most sacred law. Since all have been ransomed by the most precious blood of Our Redeemer and Lord Jesus Christ, it is a very great pity that they should be

condemned for want of this light and the knowledge of the truth. May His most Holy Majesty, for He created them and died for them, grant that to so many and various nations of lands so remote and as yet undiscovered, knowledge be given of His most holy law, that they may receive and believe it, and that by means of holy baptism their souls may be saved, and that they may enjoy it.

As this realm of the Californias becomes pacified and its natives become converted to our holy Catholic faith, the Spaniards can go on settling other districts and places suitable for effecting the conversion of souls, and affording them profits and advantages; for if the Spaniard does not see any advantage he will not be moved to do good, and these souls will perish without remedy if it is understood that no profit will be drawn from going there. But if they are lured by self-interest they will go on discovering new lands every day, so much, indeed, that it will be necessary to keep them in check lest the forces be weakened, as I have already observed above. If it should seem best to his Majesty, he can command that his Spaniards go by land to settle, some at the port of San Diego, of which I have treated in number X., and others at the port of Monterey, of which I have treated in number XI.; for to endeavor to go by sea to settle there will be a very great and difficult task, on account of the headwinds that prevail along that coast, and because of the great difficulty of sailing there, as I have seen and experienced.

19

As time and occasion offer themselves for dealing with the Indians, the Spaniards will have opportunity to learn how to treat them and how to conduct themselves toward them, and on what occasions and for what causes they may make war upon them, or aid the friendly Indians against their enemies and opponents. Of this I treated at length in a tract which I composed in regard to these things, entitled, "Concerning the method to be observed in preaching the Holy Gospel to the heathen Indians," which is in a preceding part of this notebook. There I state that it is not meet that any war should be made upon the Indians without the counsel and consent of the religious whom the general, captains, and soldiers accompany, in order that everything may be done with devotion and a Christian and pious heart, and the gospel preached with peace, suavity, quietude, love, and sweetness, as our Master and Redeemer Jesus Christ commands us, of which I treated in paragraph 7.

It is well founded in reason and justice that, since the king makes this expedition at his own expense, no other than his own Spanish subjects should undertake it, for they are earning their wages, and they run like faithful vassals to fulfill the orders and mandates given them, not departing in the least from them, as is the practice of Spanish soldiery everywhere; and for this and other reasons, which I have set forth in the treatise mentioned, paragraph V., it is well that his Majesty should make these pacifications at his own expense, and that he should commit them to no one else. And in order that the soldiers may go with subjection and obedience to their superiors, the Spaniards who may be sent by his Majesty on this expedition for the pacification and settlement of this region should be warned that they go not to win land or vassals for themselves, but for the monarchs of Castile, who send them; for it is not right that his Majesty should make rewards of pueblos, or of Indians who are being pacified and converted to our holy faith, to any Spaniard, however great services he may have rendered his Majesty in these realms. For his Majesty will not be able to do so with a good conscience, and it will cause the total ruin and destruction of all the Indians, as happened in the beginning, when all these realms of New Spain were conquered, and as was experienced in the Windward Islands and on the Tierra Firme, as the Bishop of Chiapa, Don Fray Bartolomé de las Casas, relates and discusses at very great length in a treatise written in regard to this point, namely, that it is not fitting to give the Indians in *encomienda* to the Spaniards. He proves it with great erudition, and I refer to it in the treatise cited in paragraph 12.

20

Our very Catholic and most Christian King Philip, king of Spain and supreme emperor of the Western Indies, by reason of the sovereign rule he exercises over them, is obliged in conscience and in justice, and by human and divine law, to procure the conversion of all the Indians of the Western Indies, the obligation being the greater toward those realms already known and discovered, as is now this realm of the Californias, which

has been treated of here; since it is already known and discovered, and the people in it are known, and since it is known how apt and inclined they are to receive our holy Catholic faith. And here I have discussed the manner by which his Majesty will be able at very little cost to send people to pacify this realm and to preach the Gospel to the natives, to convert them to our holy faith.

This obligation of his Majesty to hasten to the conversion of these souls, devoting to it all care, solicitude, and diligence, even if it be at a great expense to his royal estate, is treated of by the Bishop of Chiapa, Don Fray Bartolomé de las Casas, in a book entitled "A Treatise proving the sovereign empire and universal principate which the monarchs of Castile and Leon hold over the Indies," to which I refer in the treatise cited, paragraph I. This being granted, I do not know what security his Majesty can have in his conscience for delaying so long to send ministers of the Gospel to this realm of the Californias. By coming to their aid, conscience will be satisfied and obligation fulfilled. It can be done with ease and little cost, and the result will be the winning of so many souls for God, while to his Majesty will follow increased rewards in heaven, and on earth the lordship over a new world and infinite riches. May God our Lord dispose his mind so to lend aid as will please Him best. Amen.

Written in the convent of San Sebastian, of the Order of Discalced Carmelites, in the City of Mexico, on the 12th of October of the year 1620. And to give it greater credence I signed it with my name.

[Signed:] Fray Antonio de la Ascension.

834. October 9 to December 12, 1603. Vizcaíno reports on the discovery of San Diego Bay: extract.

On December 3, 1603, Vizcaíno finished the writing up of his journal of his significant voyage. It closely parallels the accounts given by Fray Antónío de la Ascención, but it is, of course, of great authority. An example of it is given, taken from the leaving of San Francisco Bay on October 9 (now Drakes Bay) and proceeding down the coast to the exciting discovery of San Diego Bay on November 12.

THE REVIVAL OF COASTAL DISCOVERY IN THE WEST 427

A.G.I., Seville, Mexico, 60/4/37; translated in H. E. Bolton, Spanish Exploration in the Southwest, pp. 52–103, from which pp. 72–82 are reprinted.

10
Departure from the Bay of San Francisco and arrival at that of the Eleven Thousand Virgins.

We set sail, as has been said, from the bay of San Francisco on the 9th of October. The next day we arrived at the island of San Gerónimo, which is nine leagues from this bay. We sailed around it and took its bearings but did not cast anchor, as the weather did not permit it for it was rough and fitful. We skirted the coast on the lookout for the island of Senissas, and Saturday, the 12th of the month, we discovered a very large bay and an island toward the northwest. The general directed Ensign Sebastian Melendes and Anton Flores to go ahead in the frigate to take soundings of the bay, instructing them to give a certain sign if it were suitable for the captain's ship to enter and for us to follow.

Having entered it he discovered it to be so large and good that we went in and cast anchor. Immediately there came alongside peacefully more than twenty canoes of Indian fishermen. We gave them some things, which they received with pleasure. They were catching fish with hooks which appeared to be thorns from some tree, and with lines of *maguey*, plaited and better twisted than ours. They caught fish so easily that within two hours they filled their canoes. On the 13th of the month the general, with the members of the council, decided to go ashore to reconnoitre and see the people there and their manner of living, and to search for water, of which we had great need. The cause of this was the quarter pipes which we carried, for as they had been made in Acapulco of old and gaping and worm-eaten staves, when we thought we had water we were without it. This caused the men much labor, and detained us somewhat on land.

When Ensign Juan de Alarcon went with twelve arquebusiers to do this work he found on the beach three rancherías of Indians, with their women and children, as quiet and free from excitement as if we had had dealings with them for many days. He found water in a lagoon a league from the beach and he returned to report it. The general thought this watering place was too far away and that they would have to work very hard; and that since toward the northwest shore an entrance like a river or estuary had been discovered, in order to find out what it was Ensign Melendes should go to reconnoitre it. He did so, and brought back the report that it was an estuary which came from a large lagoon in the interior of the country, and that it had anchorage in it for the captain's ship. We set sail immediately and within two hours cast anchor in it. The general, his son, and Captain Gerónimo Martin went ashore to explore it, together with Ensign Juan Francisco Suriano, Sebastian Melendez, Martin de Aguiar Galeote, and some soldiers, leaving Ensign Alarcon in his place on board the flagship.

We went more than four leagues along the beach in search of water but did not find any. We found in the woods a large number of hares. The chief pilot, Francisco de Bolaños, entered the estuary above-mentioned with the boat. On taking soundings he found a good depth, but the current was so strong by reason of the high tide that it whirled the ships around like a millrace. The chief pilot and the pilots seeing this, and that our vessels were not very secure, we set sail from there, and the general directed that we should return to the place where we were before. There he went ashore with Ensign Alarcon, and with the men and the picks, leaving in his place Captain Gerónimo Martin. They made wells near the beach, in a patch of rushes, and found so much good water that there was enough for a squadron. The men were happy at hearing this news, and the next day the general and the religious went ashore. Mass was said, and some Indians came and listened to it with great attention, as if exalted. They were told by signs, in answer to their questions, that it had to do with heaven; and the said Indians bowed their heads, kissed the cross, and said the prayers and all the words we told them in our language. The general gave food to the Indians at his table, and they said by signs that there were many Indians inland who shot them with arrows, and that we should go with them. They wore in the Mexican fashion *lilmas* made of skins of animals, with a knot on the right shoulder, leather sandals, and strings of cotton fibre. Their food was generally *mascale*, for there are quantities of *maguey*. This place is very pleasant, for it has a large valley surrounded by lagoons in which are many fish, ducks, and heron, and a grove with hares and deer. The climate of the land is the best in the world, for the night dews last until ten o'clock in the forenoon.

We gave orders to take on water, although it was difficult, owing to the heavy surf on the beach, which flooded the boats. Thursday, the 17th of the month, the general embarked at sunset, though with much trouble and with drenchings, the canoe being flooded when leaving. That night a south wind came up, with a heavy sea oblique to the place where we were—which was in a depth of six fathoms—while near us were the breakers. Seeing our great danger, and that if the wind increased it would drive us on the coast, the general consulted with the cosmographer, chief pilot, his assistant, and experienced seamen as to what should be done to escape the peril which we were in and it was agreed that in the morning we should sail, because at present the fog was so thick that we could not see each other. Accordingly at daybreak we set sail, leaving the anchor and cable to be raised by hand, and with no little effort on the part of the chief pilot, his assistant, and the rest of the crew we went outside, leaving on shore Pasqual de Alarcon, the Father Commissary, Father Fray Tomas de Aquino, Ensigns Melendes and Aguilar, the commander of the squadron, Antonio Luis, and more than forty soldiers, leaving them without food or powder and with only a few ropes. This was what gave the general the most anxiety; however, he remedied the situation by directing the pilot, Anton Flores, to go with the frigate into the estuary, and with the canoe into the lagoon, to aid the men. He did so with great care and no little work, and we at sunset found ourselves off the entrance of the bay. The wind went down, and although there was a heavy sea we cast anchor.

The next day at dawn the general ordered the boatswain, Estevan Lopez, to go with ten sailors in the boat, charging him to make every effort to bring back the men, the cable, and the anchor. The anchor was what caused anxiety for it was the best the ship had. He did this so well that at the end of three hours he had removed the anchor and cable and part of the men who were on shore, returning immediately, together with the frigate. All the troops and men embarked; and the same day, at eight o'clock at night, when all were on board, there were many embraces because those who had come from land were with those of us on shipboard, and especially because the ships were safe.

The next day, Sunday, with a sea breeze we set sail in the continuation of our voyage. The name of the Eleven Thousand Virgins was given to this bay.

11
Departure from the Bay of the Eleven Thousand Virgins and arrival at the Port of San Diego.

We sailed, as we have said, on Sunday, the 20th of the said month, from the Bay of the Eleven Thousand Virgins, and at dawn of the following day the general ordered a sailor to the topmast-head, from there to look for the admiral's ship, which was causing much anxiety, lest some misfortune should have happened to her since she had separated from us. The sailor saw a ship about six leagues out at sea, and immediately Ensign Sebastian Melendez was ordered to go in the frigate to inspect her, carrying orders that if she were the admiral's ship she should be told that we were there, and that if she were some other ship she should wait, in order to carry a package of letters to the viceroy. We also approached her, and at two o'clock in the afternoon we were all together. We recognized her to be the admiral's ship, which gave the greatest pleasure.

After we had saluted the general asked the admiral, Father Fray Antonio, and Captain Peguero where they had taken shelter during the past storm, and whether they were in need of anything. They said that they carried eight quarters of water, and that the late tempest obliged them to put into the Bay of Pescado Blanco, but, not being very safe there, they went to Serros Island, where they remained during the storm; and that on the 25th of the past month Ensign Juan de Azevedo Tejeda had died. This news gave great pain to the general, for he was a good soldier. After sailing forty leagues from the mainland they had discovered a large island, but the weather did not permit them to go to it.

Seeing that the weather was so favorable the general ordered us to continue our voyage, and, following along the coast, the next day we discovered an island some two leagues from the mainland; we did not cast anchor at it, in order not to lose time. It was given the name of San Marcos.

We proceeded, tacking back and forth, and on the eve of the feast of San Simon and San Judas, the 27th of the month, we being in latitude 32° scant, a strong northwest wind came up, with a heavy sea, so that the admiral's ship and the frigate could not weather it unaided. Thereupon the general, with the admiral and the members of the council, determined to put in at a bay which was nine leagues to leeward, to take shelter from the storm, and to provide the admiral's ship with water. This was done, and at sunset of the same day we cast anchor in the said bay.

The next day Captain Peguero and Ensign Juan Francisco, with some soldiers, went on shore with orders to search diligently for water and to treat well the Indians who were on the beach. When they arrived on the land they made wells near the sea and found plenty of good water. More than a hundred Indian warriors came to the place with their bows and arrows and with clubs for throwing. These Indians were very insolent, to the extent of drawing their bows and picking up stones to throw at us. Without taking notice of them except to make signs of peace, the captain and ensign embarked, and having come on board reported to the general what had happened.

The next day Captain Peguero, Ensign Pasqual de Alarcon, and the chief pilot, Francisco Bolaños, went ashore to take water. To them the general gave orders to treat the Indians well and to deal with them with great care and prudence, especially in embarking and disembarking. Arriving on land we found a multitude of Indians arrayed for battle, and although, on our part, we gave them to understand that we intended to do them no harm, but to get water, and although we gave them biscuits and other things, the Indians took no notice of what was given them; on the contrary, they tried to prevent the taking of water and to take from us the bottles and barrels. This made it necessary to fire three arquebus shots at them; whereupon, with the noise of the powder and someone's crying at the death of some of the others, they fled with great outcries; but at the end of two hours a multitude of Indians returned, assembling from different rancherías, holding councils among themselves, apparently, as to what they should do, and then, with arms in hand, they came toward us, who to them seemed few, with their women and children, bows and arrows. Ensign Pasqual de Alarcon went out to meet them, telling them by signs that they must

be quiet, and that they should be friends. Thereupon the Indians said they would do so upon condition that we would not fire any more arquebuses at them, which appeared to them many. They gave a female dog as a hostage, and with this they went away to their rancherías very well satisfied, and we took on water. At midnight, the 30th of the month, the general ordered us to set sail. This bay was named San Simon y San Judas.

Skirting along the coast with much difficulty because the wind was at the prow, on November 5 we discovered two small islands at the mouth of a large bay. As we were entering it night came on and the wind went down, and the chief pilot told the general that he did not think it best to enter the bay that night, and so he stood out to sea, leaving it for the next day. At dawn we found ourselves at the mouth of the bay. As we were entering it a light breeze came up from the east and prevented our going in. The general consulted the admiral, captains, ensign, counsellors, and pilots as to what should be done and all were of the opinion that he should go on and not lose this wind, which was in our favor; we therefore continued our voyage. This bay was given the name of Islas de Todos los Santos.

On the 9th of the said month we discovered two other islands and three farallones, in latitude 33° full, a little more than two leagues from the mainland, and a very large bay. The general ordered Ensign Melendes to go ahead in the frigate, the captain's and admiral's ships following him. Then, while the frigate sailed along the coast of the mainland, the captain's ship went up to the islands. There was so much kelp around them in the bottom of the sea, that, although the water was fourteen fathoms deep, the kelp extended more than six fathoms above the water. The captain's ship passed over it as if it were a green meadow. Some of the kelp looked as large as gourds and was very highly colored, with fruit resembling very large capers and with tubes like sackbuts. These islands were given the name San Martin. The Indians made so many columns of smoke on the mainland that at night it looked like a procession and in the daytime the sky was overcast. We did not land here because the coast was wild.

The next day, Sunday, the 10th of the month, we arrived at a port, which must be the best to be found in all the South Sea, for, besides being protected on all sides and having good anchorage, it is in latitude 33 ½°. It has very good wood and water, many fish of all kinds, many of which we caught with seine and hooks. On land there is much game, such as rabbits, hares, deer, very large quail, royal ducks, thrushes, and many other birds.

On the 12th of the said month, which was the day of the glorious San Diego, the general, admiral, religious, captains, ensigns, and almost all the men went on shore. A hut was built and mass was said in celebration of the feast of Señor San Diego. When it was over the general called a council to consider what was to be done in this port, in order to get through quickly. It was decided that the admiral, with the chief pilot, the pilots, the masters, calkers, and seamen should scour the ships, giving them a good cleaning, which they greatly needed, and that Captain Peguero, Ensign Alarcon, and Ensign Martin de Aguilar should each attend to getting water for his ship, while Ensign Juan Francisco, and Sergeant Miguel de Lagar, with the carpenters, should provide wood.

When this had all been agreed upon, a hundred Indians appeared on a hill with bows and arrows and with many feathers on their heads, yelling noisily at us. The general ordered Ensign Juan Francisco to go to them with four arquebusiers, Father Fray Antonio following him in order to win their friendship. The ensign was instructed that if the Indians fled he should let them go, but that if they waited he should regale them. The Indians waited, albeit with some fear. The ensign and soldiers returned, and the general, his son, and the admiral went toward the Indians. The Indians seeing this, two men and two women came down from a hill. They having reached the general, and the Indian women weeping, he cajoled and embraced them, giving them some things. Reassuring the others by signs, they descended peacefully, whereupon they were given presents. The net was cast and fish were given them. Whereupon the Indians became more confident and went to their rancherías and we to our ships to attend to our affairs.

Friday, the 15th of the month, the general went aboard the frigate, taking with him his son, Father Fray Antonio, the chief pilot, and fifteen arquebusiers, to go and take the soundings of a large bay which entered the land. He did not take the cosmographer with him, as he was ill and occupied with the papers of the voyage. That night, rowing with the flood tide, he got under

way and at dawn he was six leagues within the bay, which he found to be the best, large enough for all kinds of vessels, more secure than at the anchorage, and better for careening the ships, for they could be placed high and dry during the flood tide and taken down at the ebb tide, even if they were of a thousand tons.

I do not place in this report the sailing directions, descriptions of the land, or soundings, because the cosmographer and pilots are keeping an itinerary in conformity with the art of navigation.

In this bay the general, with his men, went ashore. After they had gone more than three leagues along it a number of Indians appeared with their bows and arrows, and although signs of peace were made to them, they did not dare to approach, excepting a very old Indian woman who appeared to be more than one hundred and fifty years old and who approached weeping. The general cajoled her and gave her some beads and something to eat. This Indian woman, from extreme age, had wrinkles on her belly which looked like a blacksmith's bellows, and the navel protruded bigger than a gourd. Seeing this kind treatment the Indians came peaceably and took us to their rancherías, where they were gathering their crops and where they had made their *paresos* of seeds like flax. They had pots in which they cooked their food, and the women were dressed in skins of animals. The general would not allow any soldier to enter their rancherías; and, it being already late, he returned to the frigate, many Indians accompanying him to the beach. Saturday night he reached the captain's ship, which was ready; wood, water, and fish were brought on board, and on Wednesday, the 20th of the said month, we set sail. I do not state, lest I should be tiresome, how many times the Indians came to our camps with skins of martens and other things. Until the next day, when we set sail, they remained on the beach shouting. This port was given the name of San Diego.

835. November 11, 1602 to January 13, 1603. Diego de Santiago on Vizcaíno's voyage: extracts.

Diego de Santiago de Las Juntas wrote an important account of the voyage, "Actas Hechas por el

*escribano Diego de Santiago de las Juntas Cele-
brados por los Capitanes, Piloto y Cosmógrafo
durante la Segunda Navigación de Sebastian
Vizcaíno a California," November 8, 1603, from
which selections have been made.*

A.G.I., Seville, *Mexico* 60/4/37; *printed in* W.
M. Mathes, *Californiana*, I, *380–427, of which pp.
380–407, 412–413, 415–419, have been translated.*

i

In the said ship San Diego, leader of the expedition, anchored on the 11th November 1602 in a
port of anchorage just under 34 degrees, General
Sebastian Vizcayno called a Sea Council of War
with Admiral Toribio Gómez de Corbán and Cap
tain Gerónimo Martín, Geographer, and with the
captains, lieutenant, Chief Pilot, pilots and apprentices on this expedition, and made them a
proposal: he said to them that His Honour has
reached this port of anchorage, which seems to be
very good, and of good enough depth for what His
Majesty is aiming for, as a safe port for ships
coming from the Philippines, and for other purposes in the Royal Service: and that the sea
extends inland as rivers or estuaries, and the land
seems to have trees and be inhabited by people:
and so that everything should be known for sure,
and a complete account could be conveyed of
everything, and of the depth of water in these
rivers and creeks, and of the people there are on
the land, and trees, and everything else the land
offers, he proposed that, if it were agreed, they
should go inland and take a look at it all, so that
they could have a clearer idea of it: after confer-
ring and discussing what is best in the service of
His Majesty, they all agreed and decided that in
the launch of the flagship and the canoe of the
frigate the Chief Pilot, Francisco de Bolaños,
should go and take soundings in all the estuaries
and rivers, and see which part is the most convenient and safe for the ships to put in and be cleaned,
for they are covered in muck and dirt that pre-
vents them sailing properly, and to take on provisions of water and firewood and fish, which is
badly needed: and that he should go on shore and
reconnoitre it all and measure the sun there: and
that once this was all done they should continue
the expedition without losing time: and they gave
this as their decision and signed it. Then the
General ordered that this should be done, and

that the Chief Pilot should go off on his mission
without delay, and that when the ships were tied
up he should go on land and look round and find
out everything there, and that the ships should be
provided with water, and firewood, and fish, and
be cleaned, and that all this should be done as
quickly as possible, and he signed it with the
others.

[Signed:] Sebastián Vizcayno, Toribio
Gómez de Corbán, Gerónimo Martín, Pas-
cual de Alarcón Pacheco, Antonio Flores.
Sebastián Meléndez, Alonso Esteban
Peguero, Juan Francisco Suriano, Fran-
cisco de Bolaños, Juan Pascual, Esteban
Rodríguez, Martín de Aguilar.
Before me: Diego de Santiago, Chief Notary.

ii

In the ship San Diego, leader of the expedition,
on the 16th December 1602, General Sebastián
Vizcayno, under whose command go its seamen,
soldiers and ships, called a Council with Admiral
Toribio Gómez de Corbán and Captain Gerónimo
Martín, Georgrapher, and Captain Peguero, and
Lieutenant Alarcón, and Lieutenant Sebastián
Meléndez, petty officer of the frigate, and
Lieutenant Juan Francisco Suriano, and Lieutenant Martín de Aguilar, and the Chief Pilot Francisco de Bolaños, and the pilot Juan Pascual, and
the pilot Antón Flores, and their apprentices and
masters Esteban Rodríguez and Baltasar de Armas, and made them a proposal: he said to them
that His Honour has reached this anchorage in the
ships of the expedition, which according to the
Chief Pilot and the pilots was over 37 degrees
north, and that yesterday he had sent the frigate
and ordered Lieutenant Sebastián Meléndez, its
officer, and the pilot Antón Flores to go and
reconnoitre and take soundings, and see if there
was any port in a large inlet there was on the
mainland side: and they went, and this morning
the pilot Antón Flores came on board with a plan
drawn of this inlet, and in it there was a port that
seemed very good, and he said that there were
many pine trees on the land, and signs of water,
which is badly needed, because the water in the
ships is salty and running short, and people are
getting ill because of it: he proposed that if it were
agreed they should go there and look for water
and see what the land is like, since it was in such a
good anchorage and it was of such importance to
the purpose of His Majesty in sending the expedi-

tion, and in the voyages of ships coming from the Philippines. And when they had all taken this in, they said that they should land at this port and see what the land was like, and look for water; only Lieutenant Pascual de Alarcón thought that they should not go and land there but continue the journey, for it was over five leagues to windward, and the moon had brought calm weather, and with the water they had there would be enough for fifteen days, and given good weather they could reach the bay where Sebastián Rodríguez Cermeño had been lost, for this Chief Pilot had said there was water there: the General heard everyone's opinion and ordered the majority view to be followed, and that the Chief Pilot and the other pilots should land at the port mentioned by the pilot Antón Flores, and there go off in search of water and everything else needed for the service of His Majesty, and everyone signed it with His Honour.

[Signed:] Sebastián Vizcayno, Toribio Gómez de Corbán, Gerónimo Martín, Alonso Esteban Peguero, Pascual de Alarcón y Pacheco, Martín de Aguilar Galeote, Juan Francisco Suriano, Francisco de Bolaños, Esteban Rodríguez.

Before me: Diego de Santiago, Chief Notary.

iii

In the flagship San Diego, anchored in the port of Monterrey, at 37 degrees latitude, on the 18th December 1602, General Sebastián Vizcayno, under whose command is this expedition said that His Honour carries public and secret orders from the Most Illustrious Count of Monterrey, Viceroy and Captain General of New Spain, in which he is given orders to carry out this expedition from the Cape of St Lucas before everything to Cape Mendocino, and further on to another, called Cape Blanco, and if the coast and the weather permitted, to explore and look at everything he could and was most useful to His Majesty, without leaving anything that he thought might be important without looking at it and taking a complete account of what it is, with its passages, signs, depths and bays usable as ports, all drawn up as laid down in the Regulations of the Sea, for some purposes which His Majesty has in mind; and in pursuance of these orders and instructions he has come on this expedition from that Cape St Lucas as far as this anchorage, without failing to investigate any port, bay, inlet or islands that might be

of importance to the purpose intended (as will be clear from the map made by Captain Gerónimo Martín, Geographer): and this has taken almost eight months since leaving Acapulco, since the weather has not been favourable to this voyage, and in order to do the exploration properly, and investigate and take soundings in these ports, some time and distance was necessarily taken up; with the result that in this most of the provisions, munitions and supplies have been used up which the Viceroy ordered to be provided for eleven months: and in order to carry out to the full the instructions of the Viceroy, both for what is left to be explored up to Cape Mendocino and beyond, and under the secret orders, which are that, once the exploration up to Cape Mendocino has been done and completed, on returning to Cape St Lucas he should enter the mouth and inlet of the Californias, exploring everything up to a latitude of 37 degrees (within two either way) keeping also an account of everything there is there, both of the pearl fisheries and of the many people there are in those lands, of which His Majesty and the said Viceroy have heard a great deal—in order to carry out and fulfil his orders as well and thoroughly as befits a loyal vassal of the King Our Lord, and in accordance with the confidence and faith put in His Honour by the Viceroy, there have arisen the following difficulties: that in view of the length of time that has been spent in reaching this anchorage, in which have been consumed almost all the provisions which were carried for all purposes, the munitions and supplies, rigging and other spares, and that in the great hard work the men have undergone some soldiers and sailors have died and fallen ill, for at the moment over 40 men are ill without medicine or a doctor or comforts to cure them, all of whom are clearly in danger of death, in addition to the fact that the pilot, Juan Pascual (of the second ship) and his apprentice are very ill, so that they are unable to do their job, and there are not enough men to operate this ship, being weak and ill and in obvious danger that if bad weather arose everyone on this ship should be lost and drowned, and the General not having pilots or seamen with which to help them, he summoned at once a Sea Council of War and Good Organization with the Captain, Petty Officer, and Admiral Toribio Gómez de Corbán, and with Captain Gerónimo Martín, Geographer, and with the Captains, Lieutenants Alonso Esteban Peguero and Pascual de Alarcón, Sebastián Meléndez, Officer of the Frigate, and Juan Francisco Suriano, and Martín de Aguilar Galcote, and the Chief Pilot Francisco de Bolaños, and with the pilots Juan Pascual and Antonio Flores, and their apprentices Esteban Rodríguez and Baltasar de Armas, and he ordered in the name of His Majesty that each of them should offer his own opinion, whether it would be best for the service of God and His Majesty that the second ship should be sent to inform the Viceroy with a copy of what has been done in this expedition up to today, being the substance of it, and that those who are the most ill and incapacitated from being of use through bad health should return, and that help should be requested from the Viceroy as provisions, munitions and supplies, and some sailors and soldiers, so that they could go into and explore this Inlet of the Californias, specifying the time and place where this help is to be sent, so that they should wait for it there and with it carry out entirely the voyage of exploration: and that the flagship and the frigate should go ahead to Cape Mendocino, and everything else mentioned in the orders: and he asks each of them for their opinion according to the orders he has from His Lordship, without being moved by passion, friendship or interest other than that the service of God and His Majesty should be achieved and promoted, and the success of this expedition; and when they are given he would decide what seems best and fairest, and thus he ordered, and signed.

[Signed:] Sebastián Vizcayno.
Before me: Diego de Santiago, Chief Notary.

iv

On the same day, in the same flagship, in the presence of the Notary, in conformity with the decision taken in the preceding deposition, there came together this Admiral, Captains Lieutenants, Chief Pilot, pilots and apprentices quoted in the deposition, and being all together, as I, the notary, bear witness, I read them the whole deposition word for word as it is written, and the General instructed them that each one should say what is best for the service of His Majesty: and the opinions were each taken individually as follows.

(In the margin: Opinion of the Chief Pilot, Francisco de Bolaños)

The opinion which I, Chief Pilot Francisco de Bolaños, give in conformity with the deposition which has been read to me, and as is my duty as a Christian and loyal vassal of His Majesty, and as a Pilot and Seaman, is that the second ship should go back to New Spain to inform the Lord Count of Monterrey, carrying an account and copy of everything done on the expedition so far as here, since what has been discovered is very important for the ships sailing from the Philippines, as is the intention of His Majesty; and since the pilot and his apprentice on this second ship are so ill that they cannot carry out their duties, and the seamen weak, and if they were to go on ahead in their present great need of a doctor and medicine and comforts, they will all die, as is happening with those now dying, and if there arose some worsening of the weather which forced them to run before the wind and lose sight of land, they could get lost, not knowing where they were for lack of a sea pilot. Besides, in order to continue the expedition into the inlet of the Californias, as the deposition says, this cannot be done without further help, munitions, supplies and reinforcements, so it will be best to send an account to the Viceroy, indicating the time and place that he is to send this assistance to. And he signed this in the presence of the General, and of myself, the Notary, as I bear witness.

[Signed:] Francisco de Bolaños, Sebastián Vizcayno
Before me: Diego de Santiago, Chief Notary.

v

In this flagship San Diego, on the 19th December 1602, General Sebastián Vizcayno took note of the opinions of the Admiral and Captains and Lieutenants and pilots and their apprentices, concerning whether it was best, for the service of God and His Majesty, that a ship should be sent to New Spain to inform the Most Illustrious Count of Monterrey, on account of the reasons and difficulties explained to them in the deposition, and in view of the fact that all or nearly all of them gave it as their opinion that it was best to send the second ship, carrying an account and copy of everything done so far on this expedition, and the men who were ill, and that the flagship and the frigate should go on ahead and finish investigating what is left on this expedition, and that on the way back they should explore the said inlet of California, that they should send a request to the Viceroy for reinforcements of sailors and soldiers, provisions, and supplies, and that they should send an account of everything: agreeing with the majority opinion, as instructed in the orders of the Viceroy, he orders that the second ship should go back with the account, and that the Captain, Petty Officer and Admiral Toribio Gómez de Corbán should go back with it, and that a copy should be taken at once of everything that has been done on this expedition, the map, the itinerary, the log, depositions and agreements that have been made for the success of this voyage, and be conveyed to the Viceroy, so that he could send an account of it to His Majesty, and that those who were most ill, and incapacitated by bad health from being of any use, both on this flagship and on the second ship and the frigate, should go back on this mission to get better, to which purpose he gives them leave to go; and in view of the fact that the pilot Juan Pascual and his apprentice are ill and unable to carry out their duties, he orders that the office of pilot on this second ship as far as Acapulco (or until this pilot or his apprentice should recover) should be taken by Manuel César Cordero, being a good seaman and skilled in the open sea, having come here with this same duty; and since the pilot Antonio Flores is alone on the Frigate and in poor health, he cannot carry out his duties there all by himself, nor stay up all night, the General orders that there should join him as his Pilot Apprentice Esteban López, the boatswain of this ship, being a good seaman, skilled in the open sea, and that there should come to take over his office as boatswain of this flagship Bartolomé de Orozco, boatswain of the second ship: and that at once, without delay or losing time, the Admiral should have his ship supplied with water and wood for as far as Acapulco, this task being entrusted to Captain Alonso Esteban Peguero, and for this flagship to Lieutenant Pascual de Alarcón, and for the frigate to Lieutenant Martín de Aguilar, and that the Chief Pilot and the carpenters should cut some beams that are needed in the flagship, spars, replacement spars, oar handles, and whatever was particularly needed, as quickly as possible without skimping it, and that when this was all done and the copy taken the message should be sent at once, and the flagship and the frigate go on to Cape Mendocino and the area left to be explored: and he orders the Admiral, Captains and Lieutenants, Boatswains and everyone else mentioned here to do what they have been individually ordered without complaining or objecting to

anything, since this is what is best in the service of His Majesty, and if anyone does the General will declare him to be a disloyal vassal of his Lord and King, and he will be punished.

Also he orders Quartermaster Baltasar de Armas to hand over to Esteban Rodríguez, Quartermaster of this flagship, and to Antonio Flores on the Frigate, the provisions, arms, munitions, rigging and supplies, with a bill of exchange for the aforementioned to take which he will use as a receipt, and a sum owed by the quartermasters, only leaving in the second ship such provisions as may be necessary to reach Acapulco, according to how many men it carries: thus he decided and ordered and signed.

[Signed:] Sebastián Vizcayno
Before me: Diego de Santiago, Chief Notary.

vi

In the San Diego, flagship of this expedition, on the 7th January 1603, at 39 degrees on the way to Cape Mendocino, General Sebastián Vizcaíno called a meeting with his Captains and Lieutenants and the Chief Pilot and the pilots and their apprentices on the council and made a proposal: he said that as everyone agreed that yesterday at sunset a very strong North-Easterly wind and heavy sea had arisen, and that all night they have sailed with only the larger sails, struggling to make headway, which has not been possible, since the wind is so directly opposed to them, and besides everyone is very ill and unable to come to work on the rigging through bad health, nor even on the main topsail, which could lead to one of the masts breaking, or even worse damage he ordered them in the name of His Majesty that each of them should give his opinion as to what was best to do for the success and safety of ship and voyage. When they had discussed it they agreed and gave it as their opinion that they should put into a port which was about two leagues to leeward, which the Chief Pilot, Francisco de Bolaños said he had been in in the ship San Agustín when Sebastián Cermeño had come on his expedition up this coast, which is safe in this wind: and that when the weather improved for them to continue they would sail on to Cape Mendocino: and they signed it. When His Honour saw this he ordered this to be done, and that the Chief Pilot should put in to the port they mention, and then anchor in the safest part, and when the weather improved the journey to Cape Mendocino would continue; and he signed it.

[Signed:] Sebastián Vizcayno, Gerónimo Martín, Alonso Esteban Peguero, Pascual de Alarcón y Pacheco, Sebastián Meléndez, Juan Francisco Suriano, Francisco Bolaños, Esteban Rodríguez
Before me: Diego de Santiago, Chief Notary.

vii

In the San Diego, Flagship of His Majesty, on the 13th January 1603, in an anchorage of about 41 and a quarter degrees, according to the sworn testimony of the Chief Pilot Francisco de Bolaños and his Apprentice Esteban Rodríguez, General Sebastián Vizcayno, under whose command is this expedition, called a council with Captain Gerónimo Martín, Geographer, with the captains and lieutenants, Chief Pilot and apprentice, and made a proposal: he said that His Honour carries orders from the Most Illustrious Count of Monterrey in which he instructs him that once he has arrived at this Cape Mendocino, which they say is at 41 degrees, and that if the weather was not so bad that they would be bound to lose rigging or a mast and thus be doomed, he should go on to Cape Blanco, which is said to be at 44 degrees, and if on arriving he found that the land did not run away Southeast but continued North or North-East, he should follow it for another hundred leagues, but no further, then turning round back to Cape St Lucas in order to enter the inlet of the Californias: and in the same orders the Viceroy instructs him that when any difficult decisions have to be made he should ask the advice and opinion of the others mentioned and follow the majority view, and if the votes were equal he should do what he thinks best for the service of His Majesty: and now there is an occasion for these men to give their opinion on what would be the best thing to do, in view of the fact that winter is starting here in this place with very strong winds and rain, and the men very ill, so that there are not three sailors able to climb aloft to hold the topsails, and the others so weakened in health that noone can come to take the tiller: and so that they should choose rightly what is best in the service of His Majesty, in his name he orders them to give their opinions, without considering anything else but that in everything they should act for the best: and, when the opinions have been

given, he will decide fairly, and thus he decided and ordered and signed.

[Signed:] Sebastián Vizcayno
Before me: Diego de Santiago, Chief Notary.

836. May 23, 1603. Sebastian Vizcaíno to Philip III.

Vizcaíno reports briefly in this personal letter to the king on his 1602–1603 voyage, stressing especially the attractions of the harbor of Monterey.

A.G.I., Seville, Mexico 122; printed and translated in The California Coast: Documents from the Sutro Collection, *edited by Donald C. Cutter (1969), pp. 112–117, from which this is taken.*

In the past year of six hundred and two, by order of your Viceroy, the Conde de Monterrey, I set out on the discovery of the coast of the South Sea with two ships, a *lancha*, and a *barcoluengo*, with the requisite sailors and soldiers, armed and provisioned with everything necessary for a year. I sailed from the port of Acapulco, as I advised Your Majesty at the time, on the 5th of May of said year; and, in conformity with the order and instructions I had, I explored very diligently the whole coast, not leaving harbor, bay, island or gulf without sounding and delineating it in accordance with the rules of good cosmography and the art of demarcation; for, as your Viceroy wrote to Your Majesty, I was accompanied by a cosmographer in whom confidence can be reposed and scientific in the matter of geographical computations, in order that he might put down and note in the most complete manner on map and chart the result of the examination Your Majesty should order, which the Viceroy now forwards, together with the delineation and reports concerning the whole. Among the ports of greatest consideration which I discovered was one in thirty-seven degrees of latitude, which I called Monterey. As I wrote to Your Majesty from that port on the 28th of September of said year, it is all that can be desired for commodiousness and as a station for ships making the voyage to the Philippines, sailing whence they make a landfall on this coast. This port is sheltered from all winds, while on the immediate coast there are pines from which masts of any desired size can be obtained, as well as live oaks and white oaks, rosemary, rock roses, the rose of Alexandria, a great variety of game, such as rabbits, hares, partridges, and other sorts and species found in Spain and in greater abundance than in the Sierra Morena, and flying birds of kinds differing from those to be found there. This land has a benign climate, its waters are good, and it is very fertile—judging from the varied and luxuriant growth of trees and plants; for I saw some of the fruits, particularly chestnuts and acorns, which are larger than those of Spain. And it is thickly settled with people whom I found to be of gentle disposition, peaceable and docile, and who can be brought readily within the fold of the holy gospel and into subjection to the crown of Your Majesty. Their food consists of seeds which they have in abundance and variety and of the flesh of game, such as deer which are larger than cows, and bear, and of cattle and bison and many other animals. The Indians are of good stature and fair complexion, the women being somewhat less in size than the men and of pleasing countenance. The clothing of the people of the coast consists of the skins of the sea-wolves abounding there, which they tan and dress better than is done in Castile; they possess also, in great quantity, flax like that of Castile, hemp and cotton, from which they make fishing-lines and nets for rabbits and hares. They have vessels of pine-wood very well made, in which they go to sea with fourteen paddle-men on each side, with great dexterity—even in very stormy weather. I was informed by them, and by many others I met with in great numbers along more than eight hundred leagues of a thickly settled coast, that inland there are great communities, which they invited me to visit with them. They manifested great friendship for us and a desire for trade; were fond of the image of Our Lady which I showed to them and very attentive to the sacrifice of the mass. They worship different idols, for an account of which I refer to said report of your Viceroy, and they are well acquainted with silver and gold, and said that these were found in the interior.

And, as some port or place on this coast is to be occupied, none is so proper for the purpose as this harbor of Monterey. For the reasons given, this port can be made by ships on the return voyage from the Philippines; and if, after putting to sea, a storm be encountered, they need not, as formerly, run for Japan, where so many have been cast away and so much property lost; and, had this port been known previously, Your Majesty would not have been so badly served. The time of the occurrence of the dry seasons being known, from this place the interior can be reached and explored, such exploration promising rich returns; and proceeding along the coast, the remainder of it can be examined, for, although I went as far as the forty-second degree of latitude, this being the limit fixed in my instructions, the coast-line trends onward to near Japan and the coast of Great China, which are but a short run away, and the same is the case with regard to Tartary and the famous city of Quinsay; and, according to the reports I received, there are to be found very numerous peoples akin to those I have referred to—so the door will be opened for the propagation of the faith and the bringing of so many souls to a knowledge of God in order that the seed of the holy gospel may yield a harvest among all these heathen.

Eleven months were spent on the voyage, during which noteworthy hardships were suffered; and, notwithstanding the unhappy experience of my men, who were all sick and of whom forty-two died before our return to the port of Acapulco, I again offer to serve Your Majesty in continuing this exploration, as I did on the voyage to California and on many others, of which I have given account to your royal council in carefully and exactly prepared documents which I have presented there; and I refer, furthermore, to others now forwarded, in which it is shown I have spent the greater part of my fortune and of my health. Yet the little of these remaining to me, as well as my person, is devoted to your royal service with the constancy, love and fidelity of a loyal vassal and servant of Your Majesty, who, I pray, will order the necessities of my men to be considered and that they be rewarded with favors from those powerful royal hands, and that the same be ordered to be done for the naval and military officers who accompanied me, their persons being recommended to your Viceroy of this New Spain. God guard the royal and catholic person of Your Majesty. Mexico, 23d of May, 1603.

[Signed:] Sebastián Vizcaíno

Chapter One hundred eight
Juan de Oñate and the Founding of
New Mexico, 1595–1609

SUCCESSIVE REPORTS from Mexico and pressure from both missionary and mining interests led the government of Philip II, finally, to decide that New Mexico, the whole of the Pueblo area, which we now know to have comprised some 40,000 Indians living in several hundred villages, should be brought under his control, even though it extended as far as 700 miles from the frontier of Mexico. To organize this ambitious scheme, Juan de Oñate, a man with considerable mining interests, was chosen and given the title not only of governor and captain general of New Mexico, but also of *adelantado* (governor-conqueror), by now almost extinct. After long bureaucratic delays, he was commissioned in September, 1595 (838), but it was not until after a further series of delays that he was able to set out in January, 1598, with some 500 persons, including 129 soldiers and 8 friars. He formally claimed his territory on April 20, 1598, and, marching to the Rio Grande valley, took over two pueblos, renamed San Juan and San Gabriel respectively, as headquarters for the colony, using first one and then the other as his capital. Churches were built and land assigned for cultivation while levies, first voluntary, then forced, were made on the Pueblo people. The friars settled at a pueblo a little farther south which they named Santo Domingo. Stoic acceptance of the intruders marked the early reactions of the Indians.

Exploring parties under Juan de Zaldivar (839) and Marcos Farfán (840), to the east and west, respectively, prepared the way for a western expedition by the governor. The character and limits of the Pueblo country and its surrounding plains were assessed and hopes for mineral wealth expressed. Juan de Torquemada, a Franciscan writer of the early seventeenth century, set the stage for this part of the venture but was critical of later developments (837). The early submission of the Acoma pueblo (842) was followed soon by its resistance to Spanish molestation (843), and the savage punishment of their people by killing and enslavement, with amputations for the males. But Oñate's report in March, 1599, (841) was highly self-congratulatory. On the basis of his reports a reinforcement of several hundred persons (including seventy-three soldiers) reached San Gabriel early in 1600. But complaints that subsistence agriculture, tribute from Indians, and the absence of any exploitable mineral resources were insufficient led, in Mexico, to the gradual denigration of the colony, particularly because Oñate's pressures on the Indians were hindering missionary attempts to convert them (though the latter were beginning to show some successes).

In the summer of 1601 Oñate took many men on a large-scale expedition east and northeast but was no more successful than Coronado in finding Quivira. While he was away, the settlers turned against him. The majority convinced the lieutenant governor, Francisco de Sosa Peñalosa, that they saw no point in remaining, whereupon most of the families deserted the settlements and trekked back to Mexico. Returning in November, 1601, Oñate saw most of his plans destroyed by "traitors." The rump of the colony proved viable, however, and he remained impervious to plans to replace him or abandon the colony. His expedition westward to the Hopi pueblos and down the Colorado River to the Gulf of Mexico in 1605 was a considerable achievement and led him to send further glowing reports.

In Mexico only the influence of the friars kept the colony alive, but, despairing of obtaining necessary supplies of Spanish goods, Oñate finally left the colony in August, 1607. His deputies carried on there, and missionary supplies and helpers flowed in to make it difficult for the government to abandon the alleged 7,000 Christian Indians. Finally, in 1609, permanent occupation was decided on: New Mexico was to be a mission colony, with a small garrison of fifty soldiers. Pedro de Peralta was commissioned as governor and established the first Spanish town, the new capital of Santa Fe, in 1610. Within the next two years, he created Santa Fe as the tiny capital of a missionary outpost, which was to survive unchallenged until 1680. But nearly all the earlier bright hopes of New Mexico were dissipated.

The manuscript sources are mainly in the Archivo de Indias in Seville and have been very fully exploited. There are reliable transcripts of some of them in the Woodbury Lowery Collection in the Library of Congress and in the Bancroft Library.

The earliest published account was the poem by Gaspar Perez de Villegra, *Historia de la Nueva Mexico* (Alcalá, 1610) which has some merits. It was translated as *The History of New Mexico* by Gilberto Espinosa (Los Angeles, 1933, reissued Chicago, 1962). Juan de Torquemada, *Monarcquia Indiana* (Seville, 1615), was a somewhat critical account from the missionary angle, the third edition (Madrid, 1743, reissued Mexico City, 1943) having the title *Primera parte de los viente i un libros spirituales i monarchia Indiana, con el origen i guerras de los Indios Ocidentales, de sus poblaciones, descubrimientos, conquesta, conversion i otras cosas maravillosas de la mesma tierra*, chapters 37 to 39, dealing with Oñate in New Mexico (837). The only other contemporary or near-contemporary printed materials are two documents printed by Gaspar de Villegra, presumably for circulation at Court about 1615, in pursuit of his claims against Oñate. Unique copies of these are in the John Carter Brown Library, from one of which *El Capitan Gaspar de Vilagra para justificacion de las muertes, justicias, y castigos que el Adelantado don Juan de Oñate dizen que hizo en la Nueva Mexico* [*Circa* 1612–1615] some extracts are included (851); the other being *Servicios que a su Magestad la hecho el Capitán Gaspar de Villegra, para que V. M. le haga merced.*

There are useful documents in Adolph F. and Fanny Bandelier, *Historical Documents*, 3 vols. (1923), and especially in H. E. Bolton, *Spanish Explorations in the Southwest* (1908), which have been drawn on here. The great bulk of the materials in the Spanish archives has been translated in George B. Hammond and Agapito Rey, *Oñate, Colonizer of New Mexico*, 2 vols. (Albuquerque, 1953), from which many of the following extracts are drawn.

837. Juan de Torquemada's survey of the Oñate venture from the missionary angle, 1598–1608.

Juan de Torquemada, Monarchia Indiana *(1723), pp. 672–681, newly translated.*

37

An account of what went on in the Provinces of New Mexico after our Spaniards went to settle them, under the command as General of Don Juan de Oñate.

Don Juan de Oñate and his men were sent on

the expedition to New Mexico, followed their course on the way to those lands, and when they arrived in those parts they took possession of them for the King: and the town where Don Juan de Oñate, Governor and Captain General of this Force, stopped and set up camp is called San Gabriel; this place is thirty-seven degrees north and situated between two rivers, and with the waters of the smaller river are irrigated the wheat, barley, maize and everything else they sow in the lands, that is, cabbages, onions and other vegetables, which do very well. The other river is large, called the River of the North, and has many very good fish.

In this place they settled and strengthened their camp, and from here the Spaniards began to win over the obedience of other neighbours, sometimes by force, sometimes willingly, bringing all those towns under their sway, and in some of them were stationed the men of religion who had come for conversion there, although they did not start at once to bring those people to the faith; for as they could not understand each other, the men of Religion could not persuade them of their intention: the Spaniards only managed to convey that they were to pay them tribute and serve them, and when the Indians acted as if they didn't understand, they were made to understand by force. Thus this town was started and maintained, to the annoyance of the Indians, who received them very well at first, but later preferred to flee from them because of the bad treatment shown them.

A few days after arriving, the Governor wanted to tell the Viceroy of New Spain here what had been done and found so far, and there was named for this journey, both by him and the men of Religion, the man who had gone as their Comisario, so that with the greater authority of his person more trust should be put in his information. He left there with one companion, called Friar Cristóbal de Salazar, Priest, Lector in Theology, who had been a prudent and virtuous man in this province, and with a lay friar called Friar Pedro de Vergara. The priest died on the journey, in an unpopulated part, and they buried his body at the foot of a tree, so that they should recognize it again and remove his bones some other time and take them to somewhere inhabited. The Comisario arrived at this city with the soldiers he was bringing and told the Count of what was happening, which was well received: for

they had been wanting news of what had been done on the expedition. Don Juan asked for people to help him, both in the conquest of the land already found as in going further inland to discover more land than that already discovered. The Count ordered flags to be hoisted, and named Captains for the reinforcement which Don Juan de Oñate was requesting, and soldiers were gathered and sent. There was appointed as Comisario for the Franciscan friars that were there, and who were going again (for the one who had come from there was ill and stayed here) on this occasion Father Friar Juan de Escalona, an old man, very religious, virtuous and holy, who is at the moment carrying on in those areas, having now renounced his office of Comisario, remaining subject to the one appointed in his place.

Don Juan de Oñate took an expeditionary force inland, taking with him two men of religion, who were Father Friar Francisco de Velasco, and a lay friar, and visited the other people who had settled in these areas: but they were so out of the way and lacking what they needed that they were dying everywhere, and so they decided to abandon the land and come away so as not to end up dead. Some of them carried out this decision, and so when the Governor came and saw what was going on he wanted to redress the situation, so as not to lose any of the credit which he wanted for the expedition and new discovery; and he began to send back reports as he wished, in which many times what is said suits the taste and preference of the man making the report rather than sticking to historical truth in what he says. For it is very easy for someone who wants to please to say Juan for Pedro, particularly if he sees that his own advantage or disadvantage lies in his saying one rather than the other, particularly in lands where there is no King other than one's desires directed at will. And so it can be seen what must have been happening in those remote and distant lands, I shall transcribe here the reliable words which the blessed Father Friar Juan de Escalona, who was prelate there at the time, wrote to the Father General Comisario, to inform him of what was happening. His is the letter that follows.

Letter of report.

May Jesus be in the holy soul of Your Honour and grant the wish of this lesser son of Your Honour. Since the chance has arisen to write from these Provinces of New Mexico, and give a report to the Viceroy and his Audience of what there is in this land and what has happened, it is right that we should give this to Your Honour also, since there is no less obligation for this. The reason for writing and sending messengers to the Viceroy is, Father, to explain to him how all, or nearly all, of the people here in New Mexico are going and leaving, constrained by the great necessity they are in at the moment from lack of food and clothing, for they have harried the Indians so much that they are dying of hunger, because the Governor and his captains have sacked their settlements, and taken all their maize, which they had saved over six years, until they have been left so without food and in such hardship that out of pure hunger they are mixing some kind of seeds from the countryside with charcoal and eating that: and if God had not provided that some private individuals had sown a little corn in irrigated land, we would have all wasted and died.

Well, now, seeing that the year has been so unproductive, and that it did not rain at the right time, which meant that many grainfields were lost, and that in many of these settlements there is no grain harvest, and that the Governor has not been prepared to sow a communal grainfield so that his captains and soldiers could eat, and in order that they should not all die, both Spaniards and Indians have agreed by common consent that those from the camp should go off to the Tierra de Paz and leave for Santa Bárbara and await there for whatever the Viceroy should tell them to do: either that they should go over somewhere else or come back here, with help and supplies from him, or that they should let them go and settle in Indehe, which they say is a paradise, with a lot of silver, or go to the Valle del Águila to discover the Southern Sea, and see if by that route, which is where the ships come from China to reconnoitre this land, supplies can be obtained from what they bring from China.

Well, in view of the departure of all the laymen, because of the hardships I mentioned, I had to permit the men of religion who were here to go away with them: they made this request very strongly indeed, as Your Honour will be able to see from their petition, which they presented to me for this purpose, with so many reasons and pressing causes that they would have convinced anyone who considered it well: and they are only leaving and abandoning this land altogether because they are forced by necessity: because the

laymen are going away to Santa Bárbara to wait for whatever orders come on behalf of His Majesty, and the men of religion also, waiting for further orders: although so as not to leave it all completely barren, I am staying here with the royal Ensign and a few other Spaniards awaiting the decision over what our orders should be: we shall wait for this for four or five months, for the reply could take that long from those who are going for it and to take the messages, for concerning this we are sending to His Lordship and to Your Honour, although we are staying here at great risk to our lives, for we are few and have no fort in which to be protected, nor corn nor maize to eat. And if nothing comes to us within this space of time, we will go where the army is going to wait, in the military post at Santa Bárbara. Accordingly I beg Your Honour to send me advice, and on behalf of all of us here to make this request of His Lordship the Viceroy, since so that it should not seem that the land is being totally left and abandoned by us we are having the courage to stay here, and also to see if in this time we have any news of the Governor, and of those who went with him, and of Father Friar Francisco de Velasco, and of our brother Friar Pedro de Vergara, who went with him, since I was to go on this journey (as I wrote there), but I confess that seeing the state of affairs in this land, so out of the way and far from Christianity, I did not dare make the journey. Because I saw that just as things have turned out in this we have now, so things will be the same there where they have gone, and wherever they go. And I want somebody else to say these things rather than me, because even if there had not been hunger these were enough for the men of religion to turn back, or at least to live in very great hardship.

Fathers Friar Francisco de San Miguel, Friar Francisco de Zamora, Friar Lope Izquierdo and Friar Gastón de Peralta are those who are now leaving, and I am staying, to be the last to leave: they are going as Army Chaplains, accompanying them on the way.

What I beg of Your Honour is that if men of religion are not going to return here, that you should order me whatever God should inspire you to, because up to now hardly anything has been explored of what they say there is, and here is the means and a stage for going straight on Northwards, or Eastwards, or Southwards, for from that city of Mexico to this post where we are was for us a journey of four hundred leagues, and cattle and other things were brought with great difficulty, and it seems a very great pity to leave everything lost now, and contrary to conscience, particularly since we shall leave here some baptized souls, both of adults and children, and in my view to leave this now was not best for the King, or at least for someone else who could maintain it in Justice and Religion, giving him the tenure of these settlements. Your Honour will pardon the length of this letter, for to give information from such distant lands of what there is, particularly in matters of honour and conscience and the salvation of souls, nothing can be said in a few words. May Our Lord God guide things as best serves His Divine Majesty, and keep Your Honour. From this monastery of San Gabriel in New Mexico, October 1st 1601: the lesser son and subject of Your Honour, Friar Juan de Escalona.

38
The account continues, and the journey to the Provinces of New Mexico.

There is no one so alone that as well as having enemies he does not also have supporters to follow his causes and adopt them as their own, the difference is in whether they are more or less: and so it appeared on this occasion, for although it is true that not everyone felt kindly towards Don Juan de Oñate, and that most people left him, even so there remained a few among those who did not leave who were sorry about this departure and would have preferred them to stay, so as not to remove credit from the expedition that had been undertaken so far, and the honour of the Governor could be maintained: and with this feeling of regret, as soon as the General came back from the expedition to the interior on which he had gone and found out what was happening, as well as regretting it he provided for his own good reputation by sending back information on what had happened, blaming the people who had left, saying that they had deserted the Royal Standard in malice and without due cause and left the land as mutineers and giving signs of treachery. Since these are harsh sounding names which oblige great punishments, they took action against the absentees, to the extent of calling them traitors, and they sentenced them to death, and letters went off with this tale, and reports to the Viceroy and the Audience, and with them was sent the Maestre de Campo, who was nephew of the Governor. And the truth is, that as these gentlemen saw themselves in trouble, they cast around for ways of putting the blame on others, so as not to appear to share it; this is what Adam did, who sinned, and blamed his wife, and his wife blamed the serpent, when it was the man's fault: for if he had not agreed, and had not eaten, he would not have had so much to deal with once the deceit had been done. And so that it can be seen that this is how it is, I want to transcribe here the reliable words of the Holy Comisario Friar Juan de Escalona, who was remaining there, in a letter written to the Provincial Father of these Provinces, as follows:

I have gathered here, from reports that are circulating, that the names of those poor Spaniards who left here are going to be published as Traitors to the King, on the accusation of mutiny: I should be very sorry about this, and should any harm be done to them, after they have suffered so many hardships in this land, bare, hungry and oppressed, having spent their money and now are poor, and in Hospital: and on top of all this to call them traitors and punish them. I beg Your Reverence to help them as far as you can, for there are among them very honourable men who were known and liked here, and if His Majesty, the Viceroy and the Audience heard us all, I do not believe that they would allot them as much blame as is being given them here. They went under great constraints of necessity, with no mind to abandon neither the land nor the Royal Standard, but only with the intention of relieving their necessity and escaping with their lives (as they took reports about all this, which are true, rather than the opposing reports which are now going out from the Governor, that they had food and provisions): His Lordship should not take much notice of the Viceroy, for we all know the neediness of the land, and what the Indians are suffering and saying about this matter, for what has happened so far is going to happen from now on, if something is not done about it, for it has now got to such a state, and I omit the complaints of the Indians which are now beginning, that this year less than six hundred fanegas of corn were harvested, and now they have almost nothing to eat, and if they do eat it they will not have any to sow, and time will show all this to be true.

These reasons are completely opposed to the ones for which these poor people are accused, and they should be believed, since they come from a man of the church all his life and from a disinterested party who was suffering there with those that had remained, and wanted to find a means of converting those souls there without hindrances imposed by the Governor: for if he was not one such and was not on good terms with the ministers, they would have all deserted the place, and even this same Holy man would have wanted to excuse himself if his mind was not made up for him by the sight of souls baptized and unprotected by ministers, which he makes clear in this same letter, saying:

I do not say that I would want to leave, for then I would not be here for the conversion of the Indians (as God is my witness), for I would rather die serving God in their conversion, even if I died in these lands, than die in the sickbay in Mexico: I would prefer everything to be according to the rule and order of the Holy Gospels.

And a little before these words he says:

Your Reverence should try and have the conversion of these lands given to other ministers: for we are not going to be able to sustain it, nor is it suited to us: and if we continue in the circumstances in which our cause now is, many Indians are going to die without baptism, because at the moment we are achieving no more here than chaplains to Don Juan, and this could be done very honourably by a priest, because he could live on the tithes given him by the Spaniards, as we are paying now: and Your Reverence should be sure of this, that this land will never be explored, nor go forward, if His Majesty does not take it into His charge, for all the rest is a waste of time, and offensive rather than pleasing to God, because of what there is, has been, and will be here.

Father Friar Francisco, who came back from the expedition inland, which has just been made, although the land suited him well, says that he will not stay here; because in requests and replies and in going to Spain to give accounts of what has been done and bringing back replies much time will be spent, and so long as there is nothing more than there is now, we are no good for anything, just (as I said) chaplains to the Lord Don Juan: and if Father Friar Francisco goes, I shall have to go with him, for I am not going to stay here with the Governor for everything in the world. For he does not suit me and I do not suit him: he goes better through Sierras and difficult passes than I do; and so we will not come near, for hardships,

nor rough lands, nor cold lands, nor Arrows of mine Enemies hurt me nor frighten me. And now I have said enough. This letter is going by way of those that are going to Tepeacac, because for what we want to be known to arrive to Your land, cunning is needed; because it is said they are searching letters, so that those which are not approved do not arrive there, and that is why all that has been going on here in New Mexico has not been generally known.

From this we conclude that not all the reports and information that were sent by interested parties were accurate, but that those were that were made by the poor people who suffer.

39
Continuing the account of New Mexico.

The things that were happening in those extremely remote provinces of New Mexico at this time, both among laymen and men of religion, can be seen from a letter written by Friar Francisco de San Miguel, an old man, very experienced in the lands of the Zacatecas, very virtuous and exemplary man of religion, to Father Friar Diego Muñoz, Provincial father of the province of Mechuacán, who held the office of which he was leader and General Comisario of New Spain here, because of the death of Father Friar Pedro de Pila, who died in that province. That letter is the one that follows:

Letter:

May Jesus give strength and his divine grace to Your Honour, our Father. About a fortnight ago I wrote to Your Honour, giving an account of our arrival at this place of Santa Bárbara, and twelve days after we arrived there came the Maestre de Campo of Don Juan de Oñate, the Governor, in pursuit of the Captains and poor people who are here: the Governor had sentenced them there to be executed and have great cruelty done to them, after the great services which they have done for God and His Majesty in spending their money and serving personally they themselves, their wives, children and servants, for they all did this, and things we are so reversed in this Tragi-comedy that the men were serving as accompanying the Governor, the women by cooking his food, the children by entertaining him, the servants and followers by serving him, and even the Friars by worshipping him; it is getting to the stage where now we would not find place nor time safe in our lives, property and honour. Sometimes he ordered me (being the prelate) to remove some men of religion from the posts and places where they were (for no other reason than his wish), with the admonition that if I did not do it, he would himself. And it is true that those who have been in that land have given great testimony to their religion, and it is true that the land is not in itself very inhabitable, and with the present Governor governing there, it is not possible to live there. And for these and for a million other reasons, not only was it a good idea, it was absolutely essential to leave, and this to the benefit of the Indians, the Governor, and the Spaniards remaining there; for only a very few people can maintain themselves there, with the Ordinano they now have, and the Governor, so as not to diminish his status, is acting with a thousand deceits, tricks and false pretences, throwing thousands of souls to Hell, and doing things which are not fit to be heard by Christians, with trickery and false appearances; so lucky is the man who can escape such treatment, for even if it is not fitting for us to raise these matters in public, that is no reason why Your Honour should not be alerted to them.

The Governor has made a few excursions, all at the expense of the men of religion and the Indians, as a matter of sine qua non, for he could not make any in any other way, being so poor, and in all of them he has killed a large number of Indians, with great slaughter and spilling of human blood, robbery, sacking, and other things. I beg God to give him grace, so that in this life he should do penitence for it all. These poor people are oppressed, and the Maestre de Campo carries in his reports a thousand lies and false oaths. Because those who are in New Mexico are so oppressed that they cannot do anything other than what they are ordered to do by the Governor, or what they know to be his wish, and in the end it will all come out and the truth be known; and because Fathers Zamora and Lugo, who are trustworthy witnesses, have gone there, from whom an account of everything can be taken. I say no more here, etc. From Santa Bárbara, 29th February 1602.

What was happening can be seen from what is said here. But I do not want to condone what was done because of that: for once they had been posted to that place, it would have been much to the credit and glory of all concerned to have persevered until they had informed those who could give them orders, either to stay or to go somewhere else; but as long as we live in mortal flesh, we cannot control our natural passions (unless God, with particular grace, restrains them) and thus we also use them, despite the sorrow that afflicts us. These people, both religious and secular, showed a narrowness of spirit, and even 'So little faith', as Christ said St. Peter had shown when he went into the sea, to come to him, and as Christ walked by Divine Virtue over the waters of the sea, it seemed to Peter that he was sinking and he shouted for help to come, so that he could tell St. Peter that he who gave him the ability to take one step or two over the water (for that was not just a human act, but supernatural) would also have looked after him had he sunk and been covered by the water. God brought these people to New Mexico for the conversion of these lost sheep, and had made them take that step over the waters of tribulation, and he would have looked after them if they had been submerged by them, if they had called on him with living faith, not weak faith; for the Lord says: that he is with the just man in his tribulations, and somewhere else he says that he has never seen a just man abandoned by the hand of God; for if he causes the sun to rise (as Christ says himself) over the wicked, why shall it not rise also over the good? But as men we err, and in some things our errors are essential: for others which are, although contrary, they should have pardon. Since Satan hindered in this way the conversion of those souls, God redressed this later (who is the true Shepherd of all souls) by sending ministers at once to continue what had been begun by those who had been there and died in that same land in that work, and by those who had gone, beset by the hardships and disasters they suffered.

Six men of religion went, and as Comisario to them and those who were already there Father Friar Francisco de Escobar, a man of Authority, Life and Letters, although as a result of events the Commission had belonged to Father Friar Francisco de Velasco, who had been there for a year, and a command went to the new Comisario, who was going from here, that it should be done like that, and with people who were going as help for whatever should turn up, both as garrisons or expeditions inland, it was all done, and the

Viceroy and the Order were calm again after the worry caused by the confusion and bad preparation of that expedition.

Those people were now touched by the powerful hand of God, and began to be baptized, and last year (1608) they held more than eight thousand souls: and pleased with this they, both the ecclesiastical ministers and the laymen, wrote to the Viceroy and to the Order, and men of religion came away with an account of all that was happening and to ask for assistance, both in temporal and spiritual matters: and this request was generously met: and concerning the spiritual, eight or nine men of religion went to help in this work of the Church, and Father Friar Alonso Peinado as their Comisario and that of those who were there, because this office had been given up by Father Friar Francisco de Escobar, who had held it till then with great authority. The Viceroy supplied them, as was just, and appointed as Captain of the men who went back the same man who was going as Governor in the name of the King: because His Majesty has now taken it into his charge, and this Conquest as his own: and so we gather that the conversion work there will be very successful, because for its reparation there was need of a hand as powerful as that of the King our Lord.

838. October 2, 1595. Instructions by Luis de Velasco, Viceroy of Mexico, to Juan de Oñate.

A.G.I., Seville, Mexico 26; translated in G.B. Hammond and A. Rey, Oñate, I, 65–68.

Instructions of what you, Don Juan de Oñate, who have been appointed governor, captain general, and pacifier of the provinces of New Mexico, are to do in the discharge of your commission.

Before anything else, on receiving your commission as governor, captain general, and pacifier of the provinces of New Mexico, you must swear allegiance and render homage to Vicente de Zaldívar, my lieutenant captain general of the Chichimecas, before a royal notary, who must attest the fact with his signature that, as a faithful subject of his majesty and as a caballero, you will keep and fulfill everything contained in the instructions. Your main purpose shall be the service of God our Lord, the spreading of His holy Catholic faith, and the reduction and pacification of the natives of the said provinces. You shall bend all your energies to this object, without any other human interest interfering with this aim. This oath you must take before embarking on the said expedition.

Both during the organization and progress of the expedition and after the people have been reduced and placed under obedience to the royal crown, you must observe all that is contained in the royal order issued at Bosque de Segovia on July 13, 1573, containing the royal ordinances for new colonizations and pacifications in new discoveries in the Indies, as well as the contract made with you by virtue of those ordinances for the expedition, and you shall carry a testimonial of the said royal order and capitulations. You or the person authorized by you shall acknowledge receipt of the testimonials before the aforesaid notary. This should furnish you with sufficient instructions as to what you are to do. You are under obligation to comply exactly with both legal instruments, as we trust you will do.

Since greater success and better results on the expedition depend on taking the people, provisions, and livestock in good order, thereby avoiding the discomforts and troubles which often result from confusion and poor management, you must be extremely careful that the soldiers and settlers go well disciplined, informed, and prepared. Under all circumstances they must treat the Indians well; they must humor and regale them so that they come in peace and not in war. They must not harm or annoy them nor set them a bad example. This is very important for the success of such an important undertaking. You must arrange it so that the provisions and livestock are not lacking when they are needed but that they are carefully preserved, figuring out first the remoteness of the land and the time that the supplies are desired to last.

Since the success of the undertaking depends on the appropriate and effective means which God our Lord may be pleased to dispose, it is just that you labor to avoid giving any public or private offense against Him by members of the expedition, and you must take it upon yourself to prevent them from doing so by admonishing and punishing severely those who do, in order that it may be seen that you are greatly concerned about this matter.

In order that the priests and friars in your company may be treated with the deference and respect due their rank and dignity, and as they are the ones who will preach the gospel and labor immediately in the conversion of the natives and transmit the faith to them, you shall issue orders at once that they be properly respected and revered in order that the natives may accept them as ministers of the gospel and as persons chosen for the divine cult. Experience has demonstrated how beneficial this is among Indians of all nations.

In order that the people in the said provinces may more quickly and easily realize the danger in which they live and the benefits of the conversion that we are trying to communicate to them by the blandest, easiest, and most friendly means, you must endeavor diligently to obtain interpreters before starting on the expedition or during its progress, interpreters of the languages commonly spoken there. With their help the natives will soon understand what our aims are and will come to the fold of the Catholic church through the preaching and persuasion of the ministers of the gospel.

In order that the Indians who submit may realize how beneficial the association and friendship of the Spaniards are to them, you will take special care that those who may want to go to the houses of the Spaniards voluntarily and remain there, may do so. Those who may want to do so must be well treated and regaled and not offended in the least or given occasion to become irritated. In this matter you shall impose the most severe penalties on transgressors. You shall charge the Spaniards to teach the Indians how they may assist and become useful in the colonization of the land and the preservation of the Spanish organization. Do it in such a way that, upon learning the trades, they may apply themselves and attract others to them. This will make it unnecessary to assign them personal services or to force them to work in necessary cases. Let there be no neglect in this matter, for you know how important it is. This must be attended to from the very start, inducing the natives to serve voluntarily without their taking it as an imposition.

Since it is very important that the officials and authorities be competent and have the necessary

qualifications to discharge their duties, and that they have no defects that may interfere with the proper performance of their tasks, for otherwise serious difficulties would result, you must be careful in appointing the officials you need so that they may be persons who will discharge their obligations faithfully and in a Christian manner. They must be individuals who, under no circumstances, will neglect their duty. Give thought to this matter, in order that the appointments may be good and will not require correctives later. By this clause you are authorized to name only the officials allowed you in the terms of the contract, and no others.

If, in the said provinces, any seaports should be found on the North sea which might be utilized without the harmful results that would ensue either by becoming infested with enemies and by opening a gate through which the profits might be lost, as soon as any such harbor is discovered, you shall notify the viceroy of New Spain, telling him the news and giving an accurate report of the configuration of the coast and the capacity of each harbor, in order that he may take suitable measures. Until this is done you are not to make use of these harbors or consent to anyone's doing so.

Since, according to information available, those provinces are densely populated, it is assumed that the Spaniards will attract the Indians, by good treatment and pay, to their homes to help with the indispensable tasks. The natives must not be compelled to serve against their will, as they resent very much the imposition of personal service. From the very beginning you must endeavor, by all the means that seem most suitable to you, to induce the Indians to live in the homes of the Spaniards in order that they may learn trades and help in the necessary labors, both on the farms and in other occupations of the Spaniards. In this manner the Indians will be benefited and will be able to use this knowledge for themselves in farming and building construction, as the Indians in New Spain have learned to do and by which they support themselves and their homes.

Since forcing the Indians to work in the mines results in their running away and abandoning their homes, which is the opposite of what we are trying to do, you must not permit such labor, unless they themselves should want to engage in this work. You shall always keep in mind how important it is to predispose and incline the Indians to live among the Spaniards and to help them with their work, and thus avoid the need of employing negro slaves, who mistreat the Indians and whom they fear for the harm they cause them.

All of this you must fulfill and carry out with fitting care and diligence, as we trust you will, in order that God our Lord may be served and His holy Catholic faith propagated and the patrimony of the royal crown increased.

Done in Mexico, October 21, 1595 DON LUIS DE VELASCO. By order of the viceroy, MARTÍN LÓPEZ DE GAUNA.

839. September to November, 1598.
Vicente de Zaldívar's expedition
into the Great Plains: extract.

Woodbury Lowery Collection, Division of Manuscripts, Library of Congress; translated in H. E. Bolton, Spanish Expeditions in the Southwest, pp. 223–232, from which pp. 223–230 are given here.

The *sargento mayor* Vicente de Saldivar Mendoca, the *proveedor general* Diego de Cubia, Captain Aguilar, and other captains and soldiers, to the number of sixty, set out from camp for the cattle herds on the 15th day of September, well provided with many droves of mares and other supplies. They reached the Pecos River on the 18th and set out from there on the 20th, leaving Father Fray Francisco de San Miguel of the Order of San Francisco as prelate of that province, and Juan de Dios, lay brother and interpreter of that tongue. That province is the one Espejo named Tamas, from which came a certain Indian named Don Pedro Oros, who died in Tlanepantla under control and instruction of the friars of San Francisco.

Having travelled four leagues they reached the place called Las Ciruelas, where there are very great quantities of Castilian plums, Almonacid plums of Cordoba. On the following day they travelled five more leagues, finding water after going three leagues, although they camped for the night without it. Next day they travelled two leagues to a small stream carrying but little water but containing a prodigious quantity of excellent fish, pilchard, sardines, prawn, shrimp, and *matalote*. That night five hundred catfish were caught with only a fishhook, and many more on the following day. At that place four Indian herdsmen came to see him; they ordered that the Indians be given food and presents. One of them arose and with a loud voice called many Indians who were hidden and they all came to where the Spaniards were. They are powerful people and expert bowmen. The *sargento mayor* gave presents to all and won them over. He asked them for a guide to the cattle and they furnished one very willingly.

Next day they travelled six leagues and reached some rain water. There three Indians came out from a mountain, and, being asked where their ranchería was, they said that it was a league from there, and that they were very much excited because of our being in that land. In order that they might not become more excited by many people going, the *sargento mayor* went to their ranchería with but one companion, telling the three Indians to go ahead and quiet the people, and that he wished only to go and see them and to be their friend. He told them by means of an interpreter whom he had with him, named Jusepillo, one of the Indians who had been brought by Humayna and Leyba, and who had gone with them to a very great river to the east, in the direction of Florida. We all understand this to be the famous Rio de la Magdalena which flows into Florida, and that this was the route followed by Dorantes, Cabeça de Vaca, and the negro who came thence to this land and to the rancherías and mountains of the Patarabueyes.

When he was about three-quarters of a league from his camp a great number of people came out to meet him, by fours and sixes. They asked for the Spaniards' friendship, their method of making the request being to extend the palm of the right hand to the sun and then to bring it down on the person whose friendship they desire. He made them presents also, and they importuned him to go to their ranchería, and although evening was approaching he had to comply so that they would not think he was afraid to go. He reached the ranchería and remained with them in great friendliness, returning to his camp very late at night.

Next day as he travelled many Indians and Indian women came out to meet him, bringing *pinole*. Most of the men go naked, but some are clothed with skins of buffalo and some with blankets. The women wear a sort of trousers made of bucksin, and shoes or leggins, after their own fashion. He gave them some presents and told them by means of the interpreter that Governor Don Juan de Oñate had sent him that they might know that he could protect those who were loyal to his Majesty and punish those who were not. All were friendly and very well pleased. They asked him for aid against the Xumanas, as they call a tribe of Indians who are painted after the manner of the Chichimecos. The *sargento mayor* promised them that he would endeavor to insure peace to them, since he had come to this land for that purpose.

Bidding them goodby, he left that place and travelled ten more leagues in three days, at the end of which time he saw the first buffalo bull, which, being rather old, wandered alone and ran but little. This produced much merriment and was regarded as a great joke, for the least one in the company would not be satisfied with less than ten thousand head of cattle in his own corral.

Shortly afterward more than three hundred buffalo were seen in some pools. During the next day they travelled about seven leagues, when they encountered as many as a thousand head of cattle. In that place there were found very good facilities for the construction of a corral with wings. Orders having been given for its construction, the cattle went inland more than eight leagues. Upon seeing this the *sargento mayor* went on ahead with ten of his soldiers to a river six leagues from there, which flows from the province of the Picuries and the snow-covered range where they are, and where the guide had told him that there were great numbers of cattle. But when he reached the river the cattle had left, because just then many Indian herdsmen crossed it, coming from trading with the Picuries and Taos, populous pueblos of this New Mexico, where they sell meat, hides, tallow, suet, and salt in exchange for cotton blankets, pottery, maize, and some small green stones which they use.

He camped for the night at that river, and on the following day, on his way back to the camp, he found a ranchería in which there were fifty tents made of tanned hides, very bright red and white

in color and bell-shaped, with flaps and openings, and built as skilfully as those of Italy and so large that in the most ordinary ones four different mattresses and beds were easily accommodated. The tanning is so fine that although it should rain bucketfuls it will not pass through nor stiffen the hide, but rather upon drying it remains as soft and pliable as before. This being so wonderful, he wanted to experiment, and, cutting off a piece of hide from one of the tents, it was soaked and placed to dry in the sun, but it remained as before, and as pliable as if it had never been wet. The *sargento mayor* bartered for a tent and brought it to this camp, and although it was so very large, as has been stated, it did not weigh over two *arrobas*.

To carry this load, the poles that they use to set it up, and a knapsack of meat and their *pinole*, or maize, the Indians use a medium-sized shaggy dog, which is their substitute for mules. They drive great trains of them. Each, girt round its breast and haunches, and carrying a load of flour of at least one hundred pounds, travels as fast as his master. It is a sight worth seeing and very laughable to see them travelling, the ends of the poles dragging on the ground, nearly all of them snarling in their encounters, travelling one after another on their journey. In order to load them the Indian women seize their heads between their knees and thus load them, or adjust the load, which is seldom required, because they travel along at a steady gait as if they had been trained by means of reins.

Having returned to camp they had a holiday that day and the next, as it was the feast of Señor San Francisco, and on the 5th of October they continued their march so as to reach the main herd of the cattle. In three days they travelled fourteen leagues, at the end of which they found and killed many cattle. Next day they went three more leagues farther in search of a convenient and suitable site for a corral, and upon finding a place they began to construct it out of large pieces of cottonwood. It took them three days to complete it. It was so large and the wings so long that they thought they could corral ten thousand head of cattle, because they had seen so many, during those days, wandering so near to the tents and houses. In view of this and of the further fact that when they run they act as though fettered, they took their capture for granted. It was declared by those who had seen them that in that place alone there were more buffalo than there are cattle in three of the largest ranches in new Spain.

The corral constructed, they went next day to a plain where on the previous afternoon about a hundred thousand cattle had been seen. Giving them the right of way, the cattle started very nicely towards the corral, but soon they turned back in a stampede towards the men, and, rushing through them in a mass, it was impossible to stop them, because they are cattle terribly obstinate, courageous beyond exaggeration, and so cunning that if pursued they run, and that if their pursuers stop or slacken their speed they stop and roll, just like mules, and with this respite renew their run. For several days they tried a thousand ways of shutting them in or of surrounding them, but in no manner was it possible to do so. This was not due to fear, for they are remarkably savage and ferocious, so much so that they killed three of our horses and badly wounded forty, for their horns are very sharp and fairly long, about a span and a half, and bent upward together. They attack from the side, putting the head far down, so that whatever they seize they tear very badly. Nevertheless, some were killed and over eighty *arrebas* of tallow were secured, which without doubt is greatly superior to that from pork; the meat of the bull is superior to that of our cow, and that of the cow equals our most tender veal or mutton.

Seeing therefore that the full grown cattle could not be brought alive, the *sargento mayor* ordered that calves be captured, but they became so enraged that out of the many which were being brought, some dragged by ropes and others upon the horses, not one got a league toward the camp, for they all died within about an hour. Therefore it is believed that unless taken shortly after birth and put under the care of our cows or goats, they cannot be brought until the cattle become tamer than they now are.

Its shape and form are so marvellous and laughable, or frightful, that the more one sees it the more one desires to see it, and no one could be so melancholy that if he were to see it a hundred times a day he could keep from laughing heartily as many times, or could fail to marvel at the sight of so ferocious an animal. Its horns are black, and a third of a *vara* long, as already stated, and resemble those of the *búfalo;* its eyes are small, its face, snout, feet, and hoofs of the same form as

of our cows, with the exception that both the male and female are very much bearded, similar to he-goats. They are so thickly covered with wool that it covers their eyes and face, and the forelock nearly envelops their horns. This wool, which is long and very soft, extends almost to the middle of the body, but from there on the hair is shorter. Over the ribs they have so much wool and the chine is so high that they appear humpbacked, although in reality and in truth they are not greatly so, for the hump easily disappears when the hides are stretched.

In general, they are larger than our cattle. Their tail is like that of a hog, being very short, and having few bristles at the tip, and they twist it upward when they run. At the knee they have natural garters of very long hair. In their haunches, which resemble those of mules, they are hipped and crippled, and they therefore run, as already stated, in leaps, especially down hill. They are all of the same dark color, somewhat tawny, in parts their hair being almost black. Such is their appearance, which at sight is far more ferocious than the pen can depict. As many of these cattle as are desired can be killed and brought to these settlements, which are distant from them thirty or forty leagues, but if they are to be brought alive it will be most difficult unless time and crossing them with those from Spain make them tamer.

In this region and on this road were found some camps and sleeping places made by Leyba and Humaña when they left this land, fleeing from the men who were coming from New Spain to arrest them.

These cattle have their haunts on some very level mesas which extend over many leagues, for, after reaching the top of them by a slight grade, as of low hills, thirty leagues were travelled, continuously covered with an infinite number of cattle, and the end of them was not reached. The mesas have neither mountain, nor tree, nor shrub, and when on them they were guided solely by the sun. To the north in their highest part flows a medium-sized river, which appears to be a marvel, for at that point it is higher than at its source, and seems rather to flow up than down. It contains many fish and crustaceans. At the base of these mesas, in some places where there are glens or valleys, there are many cedars, and an infinite number of springs which issue from these very mesas, and a half league from them there are large cotton groves.

The Indians are numerous in all that land. They live in rancherías in the hide tents hereinbefore mentioned. They always follow the cattle, and in their pursuit they are as well sheltered in their tents as they could be in any house. They eat meat almost raw, and much tallow and suet, which serves them as bread, and with a chunk of meat in one hand and a piece of tallow in the other, they bite first on one and then on the other, and grow up magnificently strong and courageous. Their weapons consist of flint and very large bows, after the manner of the Turks. They saw some arrows with long thick points, although few, for the flint is better than spears to kill cattle. They kill them at the first shot with the greatest skill, while ambushed in brush blinds made at the watering places, as all saw who went there, and who in company with the said *sargento mayor* consumed in the journey fifty-four days and returned to this camp on the 8th of November, 1598, thanks be to God. . . .

840. November, 1598. Marcos Farfán's western expedition: his discovery of minerals and reports of the South Sea: extracts.

Woodbury Lowery Collection, Division of Manuscripts, Library of Congress; translated in H. E. Bolton, Spanish Expeditions in the Southwest, pp. 239–249, from which pp. 239–247 are taken.

In the pueblo of Cíbola, which the natives call Cuni, on the 11th day of the month of December, 1598, Don Juan de Oñate, governor, captain-general, and adelantado of the kingdoms and provinces of this New Mexico, explorer, pacifier, and colonizer of the same for the king our Lord, said that his Lordship sent Marcos Farfan de los Godos, his captain of the guard and of the horses, with eight companions, from the province of Mohoqui, which is twenty leagues distant from this one, to make a certain exploration of settlements and mines, which captain returned to his presence on this day to report his experiences on

the said expedition and journey. And in order that this may be on record forever and a memorandum of it be had he ordered evidence taken, and that the said captain of the guard and his companions should testify under oath and give an account of all that had occurred and of what they had discovered. Thus he provided and ordered, and signed with his name. Don Juan de Oñate. Before me, Juan Velarde, secretary.

And after the foregoing, in the said pueblo of Cíbola, on the 11th day of the month of December, 1598, the said Señor governor caused to appear before him Marcos Farfan de los Godos, captain of the guard, to whom oath was administered in the name of God our Lord and with the sign of the cross, in due form, and in virtue of which he promised to tell the truth. The foregoing order having been read to him, the witness said that he had set out with the said eight companions from the province of Mohoqui at the order of his Lordship in the month of November of this year. They travelled six leagues towards the west through a land of sand dunes without timber, and where they camped for the night they found a small spring of water, where the horses could not drink, although there was plenty of water for the men. Next morning they set out from this place in the same direction, and having travelled about three leagues they found a river which flowed towards the north, of moderate width and carrying considerable water, with many cottonwoods, level banks, and little pasture.

And travelling on in the same direction they reached the slope of a mountain range in time to camp for the night, having gone about another [three] leagues. They camped without water, and the next morning they set out from this place; and after going two leagues they arrived at a grove of small pines, and at a very deep pool, which was ample to water all the horses and more if there had been more. Travelling on for two leagues along the mountain range, which was covered with snow, they camped for the night on a slope where was found a small amount of grass for the horses. They camped without water. After they had unsaddled the horses and placed the sentinels, two of the Indians whom they were taking as guides said that they knew where there was water very near there, and that they wanted to go and bring some in some gourds. But the witness did not give his consent, as he feared they would flee unless accompanied by a trustworthy person, and accordingly Captain Alonso de Quesada went with them.

He took the Indians ahead of him, and after travelling about three arquebus shots from where we were lodged the Indians saw lights and dwellings, and signalled to the captain that there were the Jumana Indians. The captain, finding himself so near, told them to go over there, and having arrived there he found many Indians and Indian women in four or five rancherías, who surrounded them with their bows and arrows. The captain told them that he had a message for them; that he was not coming to do them harm, but, instead, to give them of what he had. Thereupon they were reassured, and two Indian chiefs of the said ranchería came on with the captain and friendly Indians to where the witness and his companions were. The witness treated them very well, showing them marks of friendship, caressing them, giving them beads and other presents. He then sent them back to their own rancherías, telling them by signs that they should reassure the rest of the people, because they were not going to injure them but to be their friends, and to find out where they secured the ore which the witness showed them.

Next morning the witness and his companions went to the said ranchería, which he found deserted, there being in it only the two chiefs and a woman. They received him with signs of gladness, and as a token of peace gave them pulverized ore and a great quantity of ground dates, which is their food, and a few pieces of venison. The witness in return gave them more beads and presents, and begged them to go with him to show him where they got that ore. One of the Indian chiefs complied willingly.

They left their ranchería, going up a smooth hill. They reached a plain and a very large pine grove with many large and tall pines, which is the beginning of the mountain range, all of which, as stated, was covered with snow which reached to their knees. The Indian chief always going ahead as a guide, they travelled about six leagues along the mountain range, and at the end of this distance they found a rather low valley, without snow and with very good grass, water, and wood, where they spent the night. Leaving this place, on the following day they came in sight of another ranchería because they saw the smoke from it.

And when they came near it the witness took with him three companions, leaving the rest of the men and the horses behind, and went to the said ranchería, where he found a petty Indian chief with about thirty Indians, stained with ores of different colors, and as many as eight or ten dwellings in which were women and children. The witness dismounted and embraced the captain and the other Indians, making signs of peace and friendship, giving them beads and presents of what he had with him, as a token of peace, and making a cross with his fingers, which is the sign they make when they desire peace. The Indians gave them powdered ores of different colors and apparently rich. The witness, after reassuring them, and peace having been made, begged the captain to bring the women and children there, as he wanted to see them and give to them of what he had with him. The Indian chief did so, and within about an hour he brought about forty women and as many children, all dressed in the skins of deer, otter, and other animals, with which they clothe themselves.

The Indian who had come as guide, saying that he felt too tired to go on to the exploration upon which they were going, remained in this ranchería, and begged the chief of it to go on with the witness and his two companions. He consented willingly, and after they had given them venison and of what they had in their ranchería, they set out from it, travelling through a land of pine groves, with the finest of pastures, many cattle, very good prickly pears, and many and large maguey patches, where they saw Castilian partridges, a great many deer, hares, and rabbits.

Having travelled about three leagues, they saw the smoke of another ranchería. Taking ahead of them the other chief as a guide, he said that he wished to go ahead to notify the ranchería, so that they would not become excited, and to tell them that we were men who would do them no harm but were friends. The witness permitted the Indian to go. He reached the ranchería, which was about a league beyond, and reassured the people thereof, who came out to meet him. They arrived at the ranchería and received the chief of it and the rest with signs of joy and peace. They found many women and children, to whom they gave of what they had with them, and the Indians gave them powdered ore of different colors, *mescale*, and venison.

As it was late they camped for the night about two arquebus shots from there, on the bank of a river of fair width and much water, with good pasture and a cottonwood grove. The following morning, as the chief whom they had as a guide wished to return, the witness begged the chief of this ranchería to go with him and show him the mine from which they got ores. He consented willingly, and having travelled about four leagues through very fine, fertile land, with extensive pastures, they came to another river, wider than the first, where they spent the night. This river flowed almost from the north. They crossed it, and having travelled about two leagues they came to another river, much larger, which flowed from the north. They crossed it, and having travelled about a league, arrived at the slopes of some hills where the Indian chief said the mines were whence they got the ore.

And arriving at the slope of the said hills, the banks of the said rivers were seen, with deep ravines having the finest of pastures, and extensive plains. As it was late, they camped that night on the slope of these hills, at a spring of water which issued from one of them, very large and carrying much water, almost hot. Here six Indians from different rancherías of those mountains joined him, and next morning they took him up to the said mine, which was at a good height, although one could go up to it on horseback, for these Indians had opened up a road. There they found an old shaft, three *estados* in depth, from which the Indians extracted the ores for their personal adornment and for the coloring of their blankets, because in this mine there are brown, black, water-colored, blue, and green ores. The blue ore is so blue that it is understood that some of it is enamel. The mine had a very large dump, where there were many and apparently very good ores, which are the ones which have been enumerated.

The vein is very wide and rich and of many outcrops, all containing ores. The vein ran along the hill in plain view and crossed over to another hill which was opposite, where they took from twenty-eight to thirty claims for themselves and for the companions who remained at the camp as a guard to the Señor governor. At one side of the said hill they found another vein of more than two arms' length in width, which they named the vein of San Francisco. Here they took fourteen or

fifteen claims. On the other side of the other part of the outcrop they found another vein which they named San Gabriel, wide and rich in ores, where they took fourteen or fifteen more claims; and on the other side, on the hill of the outcrop, they found another vein which they named the vein of Guerfanos, wide and rich in ores, where they took ten or twelve more claims.

As it was late they descended and slept at the said camp and spring of water; and complying with the instructions which he had from his Lordship he assembled all the Indians he could in order to learn about everything else which there was in the country. When everybody from the rancherías and the mountains had come together he asked them through what country the three rivers which they had seen came, and where they went. They said and indicated by signs, joining them on the ground with a rod, that the said three rivers and two others which joined them further on, all united and passed through a gorge which they pointed out to them, and that beyond the gorge the river was extremely wide and copious, and that on the banks on both sides there were immense settlements of people who planted very large fields of maize, beans, and gourds in a very level country of good climate; and (referring to the snow which they showed him on the mountain which they were leaving behind) they said that neither on the mountain of the mines nor in the settlements of the rivers does it ever snow, because the climate is mild and almost hot. Conditions described on this river and settlements were understood to extend to the sea, which they showed to be salty by dissolving a small quantity of salt in water in order to demonstrate the condition of the sea water.

When the witness asked them where they got some shells which they wore suspended from their noses and foreheads, which are pearl-bearing, they said by signs that they got them from this said salt water, which is thirty days' journey from their rancherías, which, according to their rate of travel, must be eighty or ninety leagues. And making signs with the hands, placing one hand over the other in the form of a shell, they opened it on one side. They said that there these shells were to be found, and that they opened them and found some white and round objects as large as grains of maize; and that it is from the shells that they get them; and that in that neighborhood there are many and very large settlements.

After this was over the captain and his companions set about returning to examine and consider with care the qualities of the country and the mines wherein they found, as has been stated, the said veins, besides many other reports which the Indians give. The veins are so long and wide that half of the people of New Spain can have mines there. At a quarter of a league, half a league, or a league, there is a very great quantity of water from the said rivers and spring, where many water mills can be constructed, with excellent water wheels, and water can be taken out with the greatest ease.

Near to the very mines themselves are enormous pines, oaks, mesquites, walnuts, and cottonwoods, and, as has been stated, great pastures and plains and fine lands for cultivation. The maize which the Indians gather gives most excellent evidence of the bounty of the land, because this witness got down to cut off with his own hand a stalk of that which the Indians had planted and had, and although it appeared to have been broken in the middle, yet this half which he brought to his Lordship so that he might see it was two fathoms and three spans long, and as thick as the wrist. In all this land the good pasture lands continue, and there is much game, as deer, hares, and partridges, and although no fish were seen in the river, because of the little we saw of it, they found on it many Indians clothed in the skins of beavers, which were very fine and well tanned. They found two lizards hung in a ranchería to dry. In the groves on the rivers mentioned there are a great number of birds of all kinds, which is an excellent indication of the good climate of the country, and from what this witness saw in it, the said mountains are without doubt the richest in all New Spain, for the witness has been in almost all the mines of New Spain and he has seen that this country has the same qualities, especially the rich mines of San Andrés.

Hereupon the witness and his companions returned to report to his Lordship all that they had seen and explored and all that they had heard of, as he did. He returned to his presence for two reasons: first, because they lacked provisions, and secondly, because the time allotted for the said journey was up. And this which he has stated is what occurred, what he saw and learned, and is the truth by the oath which he has taken. And it being read to him he reaffirmed and ratified it. He said he was about forty years of age, and was a legally qualified witness. And he signed in his own name with his Lordship. Marcos Farfan de los Godos. Don Juan de Oñate. Before me, Juan Velarde, secretary.

841. March 2, 1599. Juan de Oñate to the Conde de Monterey, Viceroy of Mexico.

Oñate gives an account of his journey to New Mexico and of his subsequent actions. He then proceeds to exaggerate the value of the area as very rich in minerals and adjacent to the Pacific Ocean.

Colección de documentos inéditos, *1st series, XVI, 302–313; translated in H. E. Bolton, Spanish Expeditions in the Southwest, pp. 212– 222, from which it is reprinted.*

From Rio de Nombre de Dios I last wrote to you, Illustrious Sir, giving you an account of my departure, and of the discovery of a wagon road to the Rio del Norte, and of my certain hopes of the successful outcome of my journey, which hopes God has been pleased to grant, may He be forever praised; for greatly to His advantage and that of his royal Majesty, they have acquired a possession so good that none other of his Majesty in these Indies excels it, judging it solely by what I have seen, by things told of in reliable reports, and by things almost a matter of experience, from having been seen by people in my camp and known by me at present.

This does not include the vastness of the settlements or the riches of the West which the natives praise, or the certainty of pearls promised by the South Sea from the many shells containing them possessed by these Indians, or the many settlements called the seven caves, which the Indians report at the head of this river, which is the Rio del Norte; but includes only the provinces which I have seen and traversed, the people of this eastern country, the Apaches, the nation of the Cocoyes, and many others which are daily being discovered in this district and neighborhood, as I shall specify in this letter. I wish to begin by giving your Lordship an account of it, because it is the first since I left New Spain.

I departed, Illustrious Sir, from Rio de Nombre de Dios on the sixteenth of March, with the great multitude of wagons, women, and children, which your Lordship very well knows, freed from all my opponents, but with a multitude of evil predictions conforming to their desires and not to the goodness of God. His Majesty was pleased to accede to my desires, and to take pity on my great hardships, afflictions, and expenses, bringing me to these provinces of New Mexico with all his Majesty's army enjoying perfect health.

Although I reached these provinces on the twenty-eighth day of May (going ahead with as many as sixty soldiers to pacify the land and free it from traitors, if in it there should be any, seizing Humaña and his followers, to obtain full information, by seeing with my own eyes, regarding the location and nature of the land, and regarding the nature and customs of the people, so as to order what might be best for the army, which I left about twenty-two leagues from the first pueblos, after having crossed the Rio del Norte, at which river I took possession, in the name of his Majesty, of all these kingdoms and pueblos which I discovered before departing from it with scouts), the army did not overtake me at the place where I established it and where I now have it established, in this province of the Teguas, until the nineteenth day of August of the past year. During that time I travelled through settlements sixty-one leagues in extent toward the north, and thirty-five in width from east to west. All this district is filled with pueblos, large and small, very continuous and close together.

At the end of August I began to prepare the people of my camp for the severe winter with which both the Indians and the nature of the land threatened me; and the devil, who has ever tried to make good his great loss occasioned by our coming, plotted, as is his wont, exciting a rebellion among more than forty-five soldiers and captains, who under pretext of not finding immediately whole plates of silver lying on the ground, and offended because I would not permit them to maltreat these natives, either in their persons or in their goods, became disgusted with the country, or to be more exact, with me, and endeavored to form a gang in order to flee to that

New Spain, as they proclaimed, although judging from what has since come to light their intention was directed more to stealing slaves and clothing and to other acts of effrontery not permitted. I arrested two captains and a soldier, who they said were guilty, in order to garrote them on this charge, but ascertaining that their guilt was not so great, and on account of my situation and of the importunate pleadings of the religious and of the entire army, I was forced to forego the punishment and let bygones be bygones.

Although by the middle of September I succeeded in completely calming and pacifying my camp, from this great conflagration a spark was bound to remain hidden underneath the ashes of the dissembling countenances of four of the soldiers of the said coterie. These fled from me at that time, stealing from me part of the horses, thereby violating not only one but many proclamations which, regarding this matter and others, I had posted for the good of the land in the name of his Majesty.

Since they had violated his royal orders, it appeared to me that they should not go unpunished; therefore I immediately sent posthaste the captain and procurator-general Gaspar Perez de Villagran and the captain of artillery Geronimo Marques, with an express order to follow and overtake them and give them due punishment. They left in the middle of September, as I have said, thinking that they would overtake them at once, but their journey was prolonged more than they or I had anticipated, with the result to two of the offenders which your Lordship already knows from the letter which they tell me they wrote from Sancta Barbara. The other two who fled from them will have received the same at your Lordship's hands, as is just.

I awaited their return and the outcome for some days, during which time I sent my *sargento mayor* to find and utilize the buffalo to the east, where he found an infinite multitude of them, and had the experience which he set forth in a special report. Both he and the others were so long delayed that, in order to lose no time, at the beginning of October, this first church having been founded, wherein the first mass was celebrated on the 8th of September, and the religious having been distributed in various provinces and *doctrinas*, I went in person to the province of Abo and to that of the Xumanas and to the large and famous salines of this country, which must be about twenty leagues east of here.

From there I crossed over to the west through the province of Puaray to discover the South Sea, so that I might be able to report to your Lordship. When Captain Villagran arrived I took him for this purpose.

What more in good time it was possible to accomplish through human efforts is in substance what I shall set forth in the following chapter. For this purpose it shall be day by day, and event by event, especially regarding the death of my nephew and *maese de campo* [*maestre de Campo*], who, as my rear-guard, was following me to the South Sea. His process, along with many other papers, I am sending to your Lordship. To despatch them earlier has been impossible. I have, then, discovered and seen up to the present the following provinces:

The province of the Piguis, which is the one encountered in coming from that New Spain; the province of the Xumanás; the province of the Cheguas, which we Spaniards call Puaray; the province of the Cheres; the province of the Trias; the province of the Emmes; the province of the Teguas; the province of the Picuries; the province of the Taos; the province of the Peccos; the province of Abbo and the salines; the province of Juni; and the province of Mohoce.

These last two are somewhat apart from the rest, towards the west, and are the places where we recently discovered the rich mines, as is attested by the papers which your Lordship will see there. I could not work or improve these mines because of the death of my *maese de campo*, Joan de Zaldivar, and of the rectification of the results of it, which I completed at the end of last month. Nor could I complete my journey to the South Sea, which was the purpose with which I went to the said provinces, leaving my camp in this province of the Teguas, whence I am now writing.

There must be in this province and in the others above-mentioned, to make a conservative estimate, seventy thousand Indians, settled after our custom, house adjoining house, with square plazas. They have no streets, and in the pueblos, which contain many plazas or wards, one goes from one plaza to the other through alleys. They are of two and three stories, of an *estado* [5 to 6 feet] and a half or an *estado* and a third each, which latter is not so common; and some houses

are of four, five, six, and seven stories. Even whole pueblos dress in very highly colored cotton *mantas*, white or black, and some of thread— very good clothes. Others wear buffalo hides, of which there is a great abundance. They have most excellent wool, of whose value I am sending a small example.

It is a land abounding in flesh of buffalo, goats with hideous horns, and turkeys; and in Mohoce there is game of all kinds. There are many wild and ferocious beasts, lions, bears, wolves, tigers, *penicas*, ferrets, porcupines, and other animals, whose hides they tan and use. Towards the west there are bees and very white honey, of which I am sending a sample. Besides, there are vegetables, a great abundance of the best and greatest salines in the world, and a very great many kinds of very rich ores, as I stated above. Some discovered near here do not appear so, although we have hardly begun to see anything of the much there is to be seen. There are very fine grape vines, rivers, forests of many oaks, and some cork trees, fruits, melons, grapes, watermelons, Castilian plums, *capuli*, pine-nuts, acorns, ground-nuts, and *coralejo*, which is a delicious fruit, and other wild fruits. There are many and very good fish in this Rio del Norte, and in others. From the ores here are made all the colors which we use, and they are very fine.

The people are in general very comely; their color is like those of that land, and they are much like them in manner and dress, in their grinding, in their food, dancing, singing, and many other things, except in their languages, which are many, and different from those there. Their religion consists in worshipping idols, of which they have many; and in their temples, after their own manner, they worship them with fire, painted reeds, feathers, and universal offering of almost everything they get, such as small animals, birds, vegetables, etc. In their government they are free, for although they have some petty captains, they obey them badly and in very few things.

We have seen other nations such as the Querechos, or herdsmen, who live in tents of tanned hides, among the buffalo. The Apaches, of whom we have also seen some, are innumerable, and although I heard that they lived in rancherías, a few days ago I ascertained that they live like these in pueblos, one of which, eighteen leagues from here, contains fifteen plazas. They are a people whom I have compelled to render obedience to His Majesty, although not by means of legal instruments like the rest of the provinces. This has caused me much labor, diligence, and care, long journeys, with arms on the shoulders, and not a little watching and circumspection; indeed, because my *maese de campo* was not as cautious as he should have been, they killed him with twelve companions in a great pueblo and fortress called Acóma, which must contain about three thousand Indians. As punishment for its crime and its treason against his Majesty, to whom it had already rendered submission by a public instrument, and as a warning to the rest, I razed and burned it completely, in the way in which your Lordship will see by the process of this cause. All these provinces, pueblos, and peoples, I have seen with my own eyes.

There is another nation, that of the Cocóyes, an innumerable people with huts and agriculture. Of this nation and of the large settlements at the source of the Rio del Norte and of those to the northwest and west and towards the South Sea, I have numberless reports, and pearls of remarkable size from the said sea, and assurance that there is an infinite number of them on the coast of this country. And as to the east, a person in my camp, an Indian who speaks Spanish and is one of those who came with Humaña, has been in the pueblo of the said herdsmen. It is nine continuous leagues in length and two in width, with streets and houses consisting of huts. It is situated in the midst of the multitude of buffalo, which are so numerous that my *sargento mayor*, who hunted them and brought back their hides, meat, tallow, and suet, asserts that in one herd alone he saw more than there are of our cattle in the combined three ranches of Rodrigo del Rio, Salvago, and Jeronimo Lopez, which are famed in those regions.

I should never cease were I to recount individually all of the many things which occur to me. I can only say that with God's help I shall see them all, and give new worlds, new, peaceful, and grand, to his Majesty, greater than the good Marquis gave to him, although he did so much, if you, Illustrious Sir, will give to me the aid, the protection, and the help which I expect from such a hand. And although I confess that I am crushed at having been so out of favor when I left that country, and although a soul frightened by disfa-

vor usually loses hope and despairs of success, it is nevertheless true that I never have and never shall lose hope of receiving many and very great favors at the hand of your Lordship, especially in matters of such importance to his Majesty. And in order that you, Illustrious Sir, may be inclined to render them to me, I beg that you take note of the great increase which the royal crown and the rents of his Majesty have and will have in this land, with so many and such a variety of things, each one of which promises very great treasures. I shall only note these four, omitting the rest as being well known and common:

First, the great wealth which the mines have begun to reveal and the great number of them in this land, whence proceed the royal fifths and profits. Second, the certainty of the proximity of the South Sea, whose trade with Pirú, New Spain, and China is not to be depreciated, for it will give birth in time to advantageous and continuous duties, because of its close proximity, particularly to China and to that land. And what I emphasize in this matter as worthy of esteem is the traffic in pearls, reports of which are so certain, as I have stated, and of which we have had ocular experience from the shells. Third, the increase of vassals and tributes, which will increase not only the rents, but his renown and dominion as well, if it be possible that for our king these can increase. Fourth, the wealth of the abundant salines, and of the mountains of brimstone, of which there is a greater quantity than in any other province. Salt is the universal article of traffic of all these barbarians and their regular food, for they even eat or suck it alone as we do sugar. These four things appear as if dedicated solely to his Majesty. I will not mention the founding of so many republics, the many offices, their quittances, vacancies, provisions, etc., the wealth of the wool and hides of buffalo, and many other things, clearly and well known, or, judging from the general nature of the land, the certainty of wines and oils.

In view, then, Illustrious Sir, of things of such honor, profit, and value, and of the great prudence, magnanimity, and nobility of your Lordship, who in all matters is bound to prosper me and overcome the ill fortune of my disgrace, I humbly beg and supplicate, since it is of such importance to the service of God and of his Majesty, that the greatest aid possible be sent to me, both for settling and pacifying, your Lordship giving your favor, mind, zeal, and life for the conservation, progress, and increase of this land, through the preaching of the holy gospel and the founding of this republic, giving liberty and favor to all, opening wide the door to them, and, if it should be necessary, even ordering them to come to serve their king in so honorable and profitable a matter, in a land so abundant and of such great beginnings of riches. I call them beginnings, for although we have seen much, we have not yet made a beginning in comparison with what there is to see and enjoy. And if the number should exceed five hundred men, they all would be needed, especially married men, who are the solid rock on which new republics are permanently founded; and noble people, of whom there is such a surplus there. Particularly do I beg your Lordship to give a license to my daughter Mariquita, for whom I am sending, and to those of my relatives who may wish so honorably to end their lives.

For my part, I have sunk my ships and have furnished an example to all as to how they ought to spend their wealth and their lives and those of their children and relatives in the service of their king and lord, on whose account and in whose name I beg your Lordship to order sent to me six small cannon and some powder, all of which will always be at the service of his Majesty, as is this and everything else. Although on such occasions the necessities increase, and although under such circumstances as those in which I now find myself others are wont to exaggerate, I prefer to suffer from lack of necessities rather than to be a burden to his Majesty or to your Lordship, feeling assured that I shall provide them for many poor people who may look to me if your Lordship will grant the favor, which I ask, of sending them to me.

To make this request of you, Illustrious Sir, I am sending the best qualified persons whom I have in my camp, for it is but reasonable that such should go on an errand of such importance to the service of God and his Majesty, in which they risk their health and life, looking lightly upon the great hardships which they must suffer and have suffered. Father Fray Alonso Martinez, apostolic commissary of these provinces of New Mexico, is the most meritorious person with whom I have had any dealings, and of the kind needed by such

great kingdoms for their spiritual government. Concerning this I am writing to his Majesty, and I shall be greatly favored if your Lordship will do the same. I believe your Lordship is under a loving obligation to do this, both because the said Father Commissary is your client as well as because of the authority of his person and of the merits of his worthy life, of which I am sending to his Majesty a special report, which your Lordship will see if you desire, and to which I refer. In his company goes my cousin, Father Fray Cristobal de Salazar, concerning whom testimony can be given by his prelate, for in order not to appear an interested witness in my own cause I refrain from saying what I could say with much reason and truth. For all spiritual matters I refer you to the said fathers, whom I beg your Lordship to credit in every respect as you would credit me in person. I say but little to your Lordship as to your crediting them as true priests of my father Saint Francis. With such as these may your Lordship swell these your kingdoms, for there is plenty for them to do.

For temporal matters go such honorable persons as Captain and Procurator-general Gaspar Perez de Villagran, captain of the guard, Marcos Farfan de los Godos, and Captain Joan Pinero, to whom I refer you, as also to the many papers which they carry. In them your Lordship will find authentic information regarding all that you may desire to learn of this country of yours.

I remain as faithful to you, Illustrious Sir, as those who most protest. Your interests will always be mine, for the assurance and confidence which my faithfulness gives me is an evidence that in past undertakings I have found in your Lordship true help and love; for although when I left I did not deserve to receive the cédula from my king dated April 2, I shall deserve to receive it now that I know that I have served him so well.

And in order to satisfy his royal conscience and for the safety of the creatures who were preserved at Acóma, I send them to your Lordship with the holy purpose which the Father Commissary will explain, for I know it is so great a service to God that I consider very well employed the work and expense which I have spent in the matter. And I do not expect a lesser reward for your Lordship on account of the prayers of those few days. Honor it, Illustrious Sir, for it redounds to the service of God. May He prosper and exalt you to greater offices. In His divine service, which is the highest and greatest I can name, I again beg for the aid requested, much, good, and speedy—priests as well as settlers and soldiers.

842.   October 27, 1598. Act of obedience of the pueblo of Acoma.

A group of Spaniards visited the pueblo of Acoma late in October, 1598. They were headed by Cristóbal de Oñate and were well received. By way of an interpreter the people of Acoma were persuaded to accept the authority and vassalage of Juan de Oñate (as was done with other Pueblo tribes). Later, under Spanish provocation, they repudiated their obedience.

A.G.I., Seville, Patronato 22, Colección de documentos inéditos, 1st series, XVI, 127–132; translated in G. B. Hammond and A. Rey, Oñate, I, 354–356, from which this is taken.

In the name of the most holy trinity . . .: Be it known and manifest to all who may see or in any way hear about this instrument of loyalty and vassalage that Don Juan de Oñate . . . at the foot of a very large rock, on top of which is situated the pueblo of Acoma, accompanied by the most reverend father, Fray Alonso Martínez, apostolic commissary of his Holiness, the friars of the order of Saint Francis, and many captains and soldiers, and there being present also numerous natives, including chieftains, leaders, and common people, and among them three Indians named Coomo, Chaamo, and Ancua, who said that they were chiefs of the pueblo of Acoma, all of whom had been assembled there by the governor; in his presence and before me, Juan Velarde, secretary, with the aid of the reverend father, Fray Alonso Martínez, apostolic commissary, and Don Tomás, Indian interpreter, the governor explained to the chieftains and the other Indians the object of his coming and what it was fitting for them to do.

He told them that he had come to their country to bring them to the knowledge of God and the king our lord, on which depended the salvation of their souls and their living securely and undisturbed in their nations, maintained in justice and order, safe in their homes, protected from their enemies, and free from all harm. Wherefore they should know that there is only one true God Almighty, creator of heaven and earth, rewarder of the good and punisher of the wicked, who has a heaven for the bliss of the former, and a hell for the punishment of the latter. This God and master of all had two servants on earth through whom He governed. The one who ruled in spiritual matters was the pope, Roman pontiff, high priest and head of the church, whose representative in this country was the most reverend father commissary, whom they saw in their midst, and they should respect and venerate him and all the priests wearing the habit, as ministers of God and men of His church. The other, who governed the world in temporal matters, was the most Christian king, Don Philip, our lord, sole defender of the church, king of Spain and the Indies, whose representative in this land was his lordship, the governor, and therefore they should respect and obey him in everything. And it was fitting that they render obedience and vassalage to God and the king, and in their places to the reverend father commissary in spiritual matters and to the governor in temporal affairs and in the government of their nations, as they were free people and owed allegiance to no one. It was to their advantage, moreover, to place themselves of their own free will under the authority of the king, Don Philip, our lord, great monarch and ruler, who would maintain them in peace and justice and defend them against their enemies, and employ them in positions and occupations in political and economic affairs, as would be explained to them in more detail later. Therefore, they should consider whether they wished to render obedience to God and the king.

The chieftains, having heard and understood the above and conferred among themselves about the matter, replied with spontaneous signs of pleasure and accord that they wished to become vassals of the most Christian king our lord, and, as his vassals, they desired to render at once obedience and vassalage for themselves and in the name of their nations. The governor reminded them that they should realize that by rendering obedience and vassalage to the king our lord they would become subject to his will and laws, and that if they failed to observe them they would be punished as transgressors of the orders of their king and natural master. Therefore they should consider what they desired to do and what answer to give. To this they replied that they wished to render the said obedience and vassalage, as they had stated before, both in their own name and in the name of the people of their nations.

The governor said that since this was the case, they should rise, as a sign of obedience, for during all this time they had remained seated, and embrace the father commissary and his lordship and kiss their hands. The said three captains rose and did as they had been directed, as a sign of obedience and vassalage.

The governor ordered me to make a record of these proceedings for him and pointed out that as far as was known and could be learned, the governments and nations in this land were all autonomous and free, not subject to any particular monarch or ruler. They, of their own free will, as has been set forth, wished to have Don Philip, our lord, as their king, and to render obedience and vassalage to him voluntarily, without compulsion from anyone. As I recognized that this was the truth, I made a written record of it for the greater peace and comfort of the royal conscience and in order that the governor's zeal and diligence in the royal service might be manifest to everyone. I gave it to him, with my name and seal affixed. It was likewise signed by the governor and stamped with the great seal of his office. Done at the pueblo of Acoma, October 27, 1598....

843. December 29, 1598. Testimony of Gerónimo Márques on the killing of Spaniards by the Acoma Indians.

When a party of thirty-one Spanish soldiers attempted to obtain supplies from Acoma on December 1, 1598, they did not receive all they asked for and began to abuse the Indians. The latter turned on them and killed three of the soldiers and drove off the rest. Oñate, to make an example of the case, destroyed the pueblo, killed many of the Indians, amputated a limb from every male, and took all who were able to work to be slaves at San Gabriel. The testimony is part of the judicial proceedings which preceded the Spanish revenge attack.

A.G.I., Seville, Patronato 22, translated by G. B. Hammond and A. Rey, Oñate, *I, 430–433, from which it is taken.*

At the pueblo of San Juan Bautista, December 29, 1598, the governor, for the purpose of this investigation, ordered Captain Gerónimo Márquez to appear before him and took his oath by God our Lord and the sign of the cross in due legal manner, and he swore to tell the truth. After the subject of the proceedings had been read to him, this witness declared that what he knew was that he went by order of the governor to pacify the country, and that on his return to this pueblo, he found the maese de campo about to set out to join the governor. The maese asked this witness to get ready and accompany him, and so he and the other soldiers left this pueblo with him. This witness knows from observation that in all the pueblos through which they passed, they treated the Indians well and showered them with kind words and presents of hatchets and other articles that the Indians covet. Every day the maese de campo ordered that no one should harm the natives, nor was any done them in any way. In trade for the above articles the Indians furnished us with the provisions we needed.

Traveling in this manner, the maese de campo arrived with thirty-one soldiers at the pueblo of Acoma on December 1. It must have been about four o'clock in the afternoon. A little over a league before reaching the pueblo a large number of Indians came out peacefully to meet the maese de campo, showing much satisfaction and joy at seeing him. When he observed that at the place where they were to camp there was neither water nor wood, he asked for some and sent this witness with seven soldiers to bring what the Indians might give. This witness went up to the pueblo with some of the Indians and when he reached the top he asked them for the things they were to give the maese de campo, but they sent only a small amount of water and wood. This witness thought they gave it unwillingly, so he and his men went down at once and told the maese de campo what had happened, bringing along from Acoma two or three Indian chiefs and suggesting that these Indians should be detained at the camp to make certain that they would furnish the provisions the next day. The maese de campo replied that all he wanted was to assure the Indians that they would not be harmed or abused in any way. He thought that in this manner, as the Indians gained confidence in us, they would furnish the provisions more willingly. So he let the chiefs go. The next morning they came back and brought a few tortillas and three or four fanegas of maize. The maese de campo asked them for some flour for the journey, as he had already given them articles of trade for it, and promised to give them more. The Indians told him to go to a place some two leagues from the pueblo, where there was water, and they would grind the maize and give him the flour he asked for.

With this the maese de campo moved to the said place, and on Friday, the fourth of the month, accompanied by eighteen men, he went up to the pueblo. He had ordered this witness to remain at the camp with the rest of the soldiers. This witness saw that the maese de campo took along hatchets and other articles for trade to induce the Indians to furnish the flour more readily. On that day, while this witness was at the camp (where the maese de campo had left him in his place), about half an hour after sunset, an Indian servant of Juan del Caso, a soldier, arrived with a naked sword in his hand and told this witness how the maese de campo and those with him had been killed, except a few who had escaped by hurling themselves from the rock. Saved also was Bernabé de las Casas, who had been left to guard the horses at the foot of the rock on which the pueblo is built. When the Spaniards reached the top of the pueblo, the Indians rose in large numbers and killed them with arrows, stones, clubs, and sticks.

Later, two or three hours after dark, Bernabé de las Casas arrived at the camp with the wounded soldiers who had escaped and with the horses that had been left in his care. He told this witness that from the place where he was he could see how the Indians fought and killed the soldiers and hurled them down the cliff. In the morning this witness sent seven soldiers to overtake the governor and notify him of what had happened. Taking the rest of the people and the wounded, this witness went back to the pueblo of San Juan. When the governor returned, this witness heard these soldiers say that on their way the Indians of the pueblo of Acoma came out to attack them, killing one horse, wounding another, and defying them to go back to Acoma. These soldiers likewise told this witness that they saw the Indians dig up and carry away a number of iron bars, some mining tools, and quantities of iron for horseshoeing that this witness had buried there, because he lacked the means to transport it to this pueblo.

On his way back this witness everywhere found fresh tracks of Indians that he thought were spies posted to kill us if they found us off guard.

The governor asked Captain Gerónimo Márquez to declare under oath the location, arrangement, and fortification of the pueblo of Acoma. The captain said that, as he has stated, he was at the pueblo and saw that it was so impregnable that the Indians living in it (and those who might seek refuge there) could defend themselves and escape punishment for their misdeeds. This witness is sure that if this pueblo is not leveled and its inhabitants punished, there will be no security in all of New Mexico, nor could it be settled, as the natives of the pueblos are watching what we do at Acoma and whether we punish them. This witness learned from the Indians themselves that if their crime is punished and they are not allowed to reoccupy the pueblo, it is certain that the whole land will be overawed and it could then be settled without further difficulty.

This is the truth of what this witness knows, under his oath; and he ratified his testimony when it was read to him. He said that he was forty-five years of age, a little more or less, and that the general questions of the law did not apply to him.

[Signed:] Don Juan de Oñate. Gerónimo Márquez.

Before me, Juan Gutiérrez Bocanegra, secretary.

844. June to November, 1601. Oñate's expedition to the east and northeast: extract.

Under Oñate's supervision, a report was prepared of his five-month journey to the east and northeast in view of reports comparable with those that had led Coronado to search for Quivira in 1541. His crossing of the Great Plains and into the prairies was facilitated by the use of carts. On the Arkansas River he found conditions similar to those described by Coronado. He believed he could have proceeded as far as the Atlantic without undue hardship.

Woodbury Lowery Collection, Division of Manuscripts, Library of Congress; translated in H. E. Bolton, Spanish Expeditions in the Southwest, pp. 250–267, from which pp. 250–265 are reprinted.

With particular care, I mean with the consent and counsel both of our Father Commissary, Fray Juan Descalona, and the other fathers who resided in these kingdoms occupied in ministering to souls, and of the officers of the royal troops which his Majesty has herein, and after many supplications, suffrages, sacrifices, and prayers to God our Lord, that his Majesty might reveal His divine will, knowing that that of our most Catholic king and lord Philip, God guard him through infinite years, has been and is that the most holy name of God be proclaimed in these his realms, and His holy gospel preached to these barbarous nations, bound by the power of Satan, the enemy of humankind, the governor and adelantado Don Juan de Oñate determined to make an expedition from these first settlements where at the present time this camp of his Majesty is established, to the interior, by a northern route and direction, both because of the splendid reports which the native Indians were giving of this land, and also because of what an Indian named Joseph, who was born and reared in New Spain and who speaks the Mexican tongue, saw while going with Captain Umaña.

The most necessary things having been arranged for the journey, with the supply of provisions, arms, ammunition, and other requisite military stores, with more than seventy picked men for the expedition, all very well equipped, more than seven hundred horses and mules, six mule carts, and two carts drawn by oxen conveying four pieces of artillery, and with servants to carry the necessary baggage, the journey was begun this year of 1601, the said adelantado, Don Juan de Oñate, governor and captain-general, going as commander, with Vicente de Çaldivar Mendoça as his *maese de campo* and *sargento mayor*, and two religious of the order of our father San Francisco, Fray Francisco de Velasco, priest, and Fray Pedro de Vergara, lay brother. For reasons which prevented all the people from setting out together, it was necessary that some should go out ahead of the others to a convenient place where all should unite. The first left this camp of San Gabriel on the 23d of the month of June, eve of the Most Blessed Precursor, San Juan Bautista, and having travelled for four days they reached the post or pueblo which is called Galisteo, which is one of these first settlements.

There the greater part of the men came together in five or six days, and from there they commenced to march toward the east; and although at two leagues from this post there arose the difficulty of a large mountain which it was feared the carts could not ascend, our Lord was pleased to overcome it by opening a road through which they passed very easily. Having travelled five days we all came to a river in an opening, with peaceful waters, covered with shady groves of trees, some bearing fruits, and with very good fish. Having reached the river on the eve of the learned and seraphic San Buenaventura, we named it San Buenaventura River.

Next day we continued through some extensive plains with very abundant pasturage to another river which they call River of the Bagres and justly so, because of the many catfish which it contains. After the horses had rested we continued our journey, always going east, and in three days arrived at another river, which we named Magdalena, having reached it on her day. Although at first it did not appear promising, we having seen it at a point where it flowed sluggishly among some rocks, and as its banks were not inviting at this point, yet next day and on the other days during which we travelled along it we found it to be so verdant, pleasant, and so covered with vines and other fruits on all sides that we clearly saw that it was one of the best rivers which we had seen in all the Indies. Here some Indians of the nation called Apachi came out with signs of peace. The governor and the other men who were with him made them so many presents that they felt compelled, in view of the small number who had come at the first to see us, to return, and in a little while to come back to our camp with men, women and children, who ratified [the actions of the others] by raising their hands to the sun, which is the ceremony they use as a sign of friendship, and brought to us some small black and yellow fruit of the size of small tomatoes, which is plentiful on all that river. It was as healthful as it was pleasant to taste, for although eaten freely it injured no one.

We took joyous leave and, enjoying the great improvement in the land which we saw each day, we travelled on, following the course of this river, although upon entering the plains which they call Cibola or Cebolo we encountered some openings of rocks half detached, which are those which the mountains of this land give off. They caused the carts trouble, but with the great diligence of the good soldiers who were in charge of them they passed this difficult threshold very well and came out at some very extensive and pleasant plains, where scarcely any mountains like those passed could be seen.

Learning from the guide whom we were taking with us that all the country was now level, we began to travel with greater rapdity and with pleasure occasioned by the coming of the *maese de campo* with the rest of the men who remained behind. And like good soldiers, desirous of serving God our Lord and his Majesty, they were undismayed by the absence of four or five cowardly soldiers, who, frightened by military service as by a nightmare, turned their backs, just when the hopes of seeing grander things were becoming brighter. For these the country promised, since each day, as we descended, it seemed warmer, and it doubtless was warmer than the settlements from whence we had started.

At times it became necessary for us to depart from the main river in order to find a road for the carts; and although we feared the lack of watering places for the cattle, there are so many in this country that throughout the journey at distances of three or four leagues there was always sufficient water for the cattle and for the men; and in many places there were springs of very good water and groves of trees.

In some places we came across camps of people of the Apache nation, who are the ones who possess these plains, and who, having neither fixed place nor site of their own, go from place to place with the cattle always following them. We were not disturbed by them at all, although we were in their land, nor did any Indian become impertinent. We therefore passed on, always close to the river, and although on one day we might be delayed in our journey by a very heavy rain, such as are very common in those plains, on the following day and thereafter we journeyed on, sometimes crossing the river at very good fords.

Each day the land through which we were travelling became better, and the luxury of an abundance of fish from the river greatly alleviated the hardships of the journey. And the fruits gave no less pleasure, particularly the plums, of a hundred thousand different kinds, as mellow and good as those which grow in the choicest orchards of our land. They are so good that although eaten by thousands they never injured anybody. The trees were small, but their fruit was more plentiful than their leaves, and they were so abundant that in more than one hundred and fifty leagues, hardly a day passed without seeing groves of them, and also of grapevines such that although they hid the view in many places they produced sweet and delicious grapes. Because of this the people were very quiet and [not] inclined to injure us in any way, a favor granted by our Lord, for which we did not cease to praise Him and to render a thousand thanks, and in acknowledgment of which the majority of the people endeavored to unburden their consciences and their souls; and God being pleased that on the feast of the Porciuncula, which is the 2d of August, we should reach a place which from times past had been called Rio de San Francisco, with very special devotion to the Most Blessed Confessor the greater part of the army confessed and received communion.

Proceeding on the day of the Glorious Levite and Martyr, San Lorenzo, God was pleased that we should begin to see those most monstrous cattle called *cibola*. Although they were very fleet of foot, on this day four or five of the bulls were killed, which caused great rejoicing. On the following day, continuing our journey, we now saw great droves of bulls and cows, and from there on the multitude which we saw was so great that it might be considered a falsehood by one who had not seen them, for, according to the judgment of all of us who were in any army, nearly every day and wherever we went as many cattle came out as are to be found in the largest ranches of New Spain; and they were so tame that nearly always, unless they were chased or frightened, they remained quiet and did not flee. The flesh of these cattle is very good, and very much better than that of our cows. In general they are very fat, especially the cows, and almost all have a great deal of tallow. By experience we noted that they do not become angry like our cattle, and are never dangerous.

All these cattle are of one color, namely brown, and it was a great marvel to see a white bull in such a multitude. Their form is so frightful that one can only infer that they are a mixture of different animals. The bulls and the cows alike are humped, the curvature extending the whole length of the back and even over the shoulders. And although the entire body is covered with wool, on the hump, from the middle of the body to the head, the breast, and the forelegs, to just above the knee, the wool is much thicker, and so fine and soft that it could be spun and woven like that of the Castilian sheep. It is a very savage animal, and is incomparably larger than our cattle, although it looks small because of its short legs. Its hide is of the thickness of that of our cattle, and the native Indians are so expert in dressing the hides that they convert them into clothing. This river is thickly covered on all sides with these cattle and with another not less wonderful, consisting of deer which are as large as large horses. They travel in droves of two and three hundred and their deformity causes one to wonder whether they are deer or some other animal.

Having travelled to reach this place one hundred and eleven leagues, it became necessary to leave the river, as there appeared ahead some sand dunes; and turning from the east to the north, we travelled up a small stream until we discovered the great plains covered with innumerable cattle. We found constantly better roads and better land, such that the carts could travel without hindrance or difficulty, and although we encountered some large ravines and broken hills, nowhere were there any over which the carts had to pass, as the land was in general level and very easy to traverse. We continued in this direction for some days, along two small streams which flowed toward the east, like the one previously mentioned. We wandered from the direction we had been following, though it did not frighten us much, as the land was so level that daily the men became lost in it by separating themselves for but a short distance from us, as a result of which it was necessary to reconnoitre the country from some of the stopping places. Therefore the camp continued its march by the most direct route possible.

In order to further insure our safety, the governor and adelantado decided to send ahead the *maese de campo* with some companions, and, with the lucky star which ever guides him, in a short time he returned, having found many signs of people, and a country full of pasture lands, which was the matter of deepest concern, since they had been lacking for several days, as there had been none for many leagues, for the fields there were covered with flowers of a thousand different kinds, so thick that they choked the pasture. The cattle of this territory must eat these flowers far better than ours are wont to do, because wherever they were there were multitudes of cattle. Great was the joy felt by all at this good news, because it was what they were hoping for. With the forethought and diligence of the *maese de campo*, which, like a good soldier, he always displayed in matters of war, he had his people prepared and ordered for whatever might happen; and all together we continued our journey and route and reached a small river, carrying little water but so grown with timber that its banks resembled thickly wooded mountains. Here we found many walnut trees loaded with nuts which were nearly as good as those of our country, the trees being taller and having more abundant foliage, and the land being so grown with pasture that it could scarcely be seen. Having slept one night in this pleasant spot, we went on next day three leagues from this point to where flowed a river carrying more water than the last one, and with many fish and larger groves, both of walnuts and of oak, and other valuable timbers. The land was better than that which we had hitherto seen, so good indeed that all said that they never had seen any better in their lives. The cattle were innumerable, and of all kinds of game there was a great abundance—Castilian partridges, turkeys, deer, and hares.

From this point the *maese de campo* began again to explore the country, and having travelled three leagues he discovered a large ranchería, with more than five thousand souls; and although the people were warlike, as it later developed, and although at first they began to place themselves in readiness to fight, by signs of peace they were given to understand that we were not warriors, and they became so friendly with us that some of them came that night to our camp and entertained us with wonderful reports of the people further on. Having heard these reports, at daybreak next day the whole camp marched on through this good country, bounded on both sides by the coolest of rivers and by pleasant groves.

At three in the afternoon we arrived within an arquebus shot of this ranchería, and at some pools that were there we stopped with due care and precaution. From there the governor and the religious went with more than thirty armed horsemen to reconnoitre the people and the ranchería, and they, all drawn up in regular order in front of their ranchos, began to raise the palms of their hands towards the sun, which is the sign of peace among them. Assuring them that peace was what we wanted, all the people, women, youths, and small children, came to where we were; and they consented to our visiting their houses, which all consisted of branches an *estado* and a half long, placed in a circle, some of them being so wide that they were ninety feet in diameter. Most of them were covered with tanned hides, which made them resemble tents. They were not a people who sowed or reaped, but they lived solely on the cattle. They were ruled and governed by chiefs, and like communities which are freed from subjection to any lord, they obeyed their chiefs but little. They had large quantities of hides which, wrapped about their bodies, served them as clothing, but the weather being hot, all of the men went about nearly naked, the women being clothed from the waist down. Men and women alike used bows and arrows, with which they were very dexterous.

We learned while here that this nation was at war with the people settled eight leagues distant towards the interior, and they, thinking that we were going to avenge the murder of the Spaniards who had entered with Umaña, of course took the opportunity to throw the blame upon their enemies and to tell us that it was they who had killed them. Thinking that we were going for this purpose only, they were much pleased, and offered to accompany us, and as we were unable to prevent it, lest we should cause them to make trouble, they went.

They guided us to a river seven leagues from this place, with wonderful banks, and, although level, so densely wooded that the trees formed thick and wide groves. Here we found a small fruit the size of the wild pear or yellow sapodilla, of very good flavor. The river contained an abundance of very good fish, and although at some points it had good fords, in other parts it was extremely deep and vessels could sail on it with ease. It flowed due east, and its waters were fresh and pleasant to taste. Here the land was fertile and much better than that which we had passed. The pastures were so good that in many places the grass was high enough to conceal a horse. The Indians who came with us to this place, in a few hours quickly built a ranchería as well established as the one left behind, which caused no little wonder to all, with the intention of there awaiting the result of our journey, or of awaiting us on our return with evil intent, as later developed, when they threw off their disguise and shamefully made war on us.

We set out from this place the next day, and leaving the river and passing through some pleasant plains, after having travelled four leagues we began to see people who appeared upon some elevations of a hill. Although hostile to this nation they came on, inviting us to battle and war, shouting and throwing dirt into the air, which is the sign used in all this region to proclaim cruel war. Three or four hundred people awaited us in peace, and by the signs which one side was able to make to the other we were assured of friendship. Peace being made, some of these people came to us, and throwing among us some beads which they wore about their necks, proclaimed themselves our friends. They invited us to their houses, but as it was already late it was not possible to go that day, and it became necessary to go to the banks of a large river called the Rio de San Francisco, whose banks in these parts were most beautiful to look upon and were covered with mulberry trees and other trees bearing fruit of very fine flavor. Many people constantly came and went to see us, bringing ears of maize, which were the first we had seen in this good country, and some round loaves of bread, as large as shields and three or four fingers thick, made of the same maize.

All that night we took the necessary care and precaution, but at dawn the following day the people who had represented themselves as friendly to us were stationed at our rear in a great multitude, threatening the other tribe "to beat a Roldan," and awaiting their chance to attack them. We inquiring again regarding the country, they told us that in this region they had murdered the Spaniards, surrounding them with fire and burning them all, and that they had with them one who had escaped, injured by the fire. Counsel and opinion being taken as to what must be done in a matter of such importance, it was decided to seize some Indians, both to take with us as guides and also to verify the statements of their enemies, and it was a fortunate coincidence that their chief, or captain, whom they call Catarax, was there at the time. It was remarkable to note how they obeyed him and served him, like a people more united, peaceful, and settled. As evidence of this it is enough to say that while they might with justice have become aroused because of his arrest, they did not do so, merely because he signalled to them that they should withdraw.

We took him with us, treating him well, as was proper, and in order to carry out our plans we crossed the river, at a very good ford. Having travelled half a league we came to a settlement containing more than twelve hundred houses, all established along the bank of another good-sized river which flowed into the large one. They were all round, built of forked poles and bound with rods, and on the outside covered to the ground with dry grass. Within, on the sides, they had frameworks or platforms which served them as beds on which they slept. Most of them were large enough to hold eight or ten persons. They were two lance-lengths high and all had granaries or platforms, an *estado* high, which they must have used in summer, and which would hold three or four persons, being most appropriate for enjoying the fresh air. They entered them through a small grass door. They ascended to this platform by means of a movable wooden ladder. Not a house lacked these platforms. We found the pueblo entirely deserted but not lacking maize, of which there was much and of good quality. For this reason the enemy wished to sack it; but in no manner were they permitted to do so, nor to do any damage except to take away a little maize. Thereupon the governor dismissed them and gave them express commands to go to their ranchería, which they did.

We remained here for one day in this pleasant spot surrounded on all sides by fields of maize and crops of the Indians. The stalks of the maize were as high as that of New Spain and in many places even higher. The land was so rich that, having harvested the maize, a new growth of a span in height had sprung up over a large portion of the same ground, without any cultivation or labor other than the removal of the weeds and the making of holes where they planted the maize.

There were many beans, some gourds, and, between the fields, some plum trees. The crops were not irrigated but dependent on the rains, which, as we noted, must be very regular in that land, because in the month of October it rained as it does in August in New Spain. It was thought certain that it had a warm climate, for the people we saw went about naked, although they wore skins. Like the other settled Indians they utilize cattle in large numbers. It is incredible how many there are in that land.

Here we took new information from the Indian, who appeared to be one of the *caciques* or lords of the land, regarding what there was further ahead, and he informed us that up the river were settled people like these in large numbers, and that at one side was another large river which divided into six or seven branches, on all of which there were many people, and that the people whom Umaña had brought had been killed eighteen days' journey from here. We compared the statements of these Indians with those of Indians of the ranchería who had remained in our company, and without discrepancy in any point they said the same, adding that down the river also, going due east, it was all settled by people. They accordingly persuaded us that under no circumstances should we proceed, saying that the people who had withdrawn from this settlement had done so in order on the third day to assemble their friends, who were so numerous that in the course of a whole day they would not be able to pass by their houses, and that undoubtedly, our number being so small, they would soon put an end to us, not a single persons escaping.

Although this spurred us on to go ahead, on the following day, having travelled three leagues, all the way through a populated district, and seeing that the houses continued beyond, and having positive knowledge of the large assemblage of people which was awaiting us, it was necessary to take counsel as to what should be done. And seeing that the horses and mules were tired out and exhausted, because of the many leagues travelled, and that the chief purpose of our journey had been achieved, and that his Majesty would be better served by learning the wonders of this land, that he might issue the orders most necessary to the royal service and to the acceleration of the salvation of these souls, and seeing that it would be foolhardy for our small number to proceed where more than three hundred persons were necessary, it was unanimously agreed to present a petition to the governor and adelantado, representing to him the combination of just reasons for not proceeding, making known to him how much greater service would be rendered to his Majesty by informing him of the fertility of the soil, of its many people, of the wealth of the innumerable cattle, so beyond number that they alone would suffice to enrich thousands of men with suet, tallow, and hides; of the suitableness of the land for founding many important settlements, fortunately possessing all materials necessary for the purpose; and above all, of how important it was that the King our Lord should speedily learn what all the world had so much desired to know, so that his Majesty's orders might be carried out; and although it was a hard blow to the governor's courage and bravery, and though he was very sorry to curtail his journey, upon realizing the justness of the petition made in his Majesty's name, he granted it.

Having travelled up to this point more than two hundred and twenty leagues, matters were rearranged so as to return as speedily as possible. On reaching the place whence we had set out the previous day, which was that of the first settlement, unsuspecting any treason, we found therein the Indians who at first had pretended to be friends, now converted into cruel enemies, and entrenched within the same houses, ready to carry out their evil intent. This being so contrary to our intent, the *maese de campo* had gone forward half a league with a dozen companions, without taking any military precautions, to explore the land. When he reached the point where the people were they failed to come out with signs of peace, but on the run began to surround him and his companions, with bows and arrows in their hands; but he, like a good soldier, did not give them a chance to do so, for, retreating in good order, he emerged from among them with no more damage than the loss of a horse or a couple of arrow wounds.

Seeing the treason and that it was necessary to pass where they were, or very near to them, the governor ordered that all the men should provide themselves with armored horses, which they always had with them, and, the *maese de campo* telling them what they should do, the whole camp marched forward with express orders that all

should enter in peace, since they had not come to injure anybody; but although they did all this, and entered with the signal which the Indians used, which was to raise their hands as a token of peace, those who most desired war began it with very great fury, presenting in their first stand more than fifteen hundred persons, who, placed in order in a semicircle, attacked with great valor and force.

The governor, noting that they did not cease their attack, that the shower of arrows was great, and that they made no sign [of peace], gave the signal to his people to defend themselves; and, the battle thickening on both sides, it pleased God our Lord to take our part, for without this aid it would have been almost impossible, as their people were multiplying. The brave soldiers showed an excess of courage and spirit, and in a short while repelled the attack of the people, killing and wounding many of a group who were stationed at an *arroyo*, whereas only two of our soldiers were wounded. But the battle continued and the Indians became more furious than at the beginning, keeping it up for more than two hours with the greatest of courage, although at their own cost, for they proved the valor of the Spanish nation. At the end of this time, the greater part of our men being wounded, though not dangerously in any case, the adelantado and governor, seeing the great barbarity of our enemies, and that many of them were dead, and that they were not to be frightened and would not turn their backs, ordered his men to retreat; and, freeing some women whom the soldiers had captured, he would not consent that they be further injured, although they took some boys upon the request of the religious, in order to instruct them in the matters of our holy Catholic faith, and an Indian who could furnish information of all this land.

Thereupon we returned to the camp to sleep, and, the wounded having recovered, on the following day we set out, travelling with our usual care, and in fifty-nine days we reached this camp of San Gabriel, having spent in the entire journey the time from the 23d of June until the 24th of November.

The carts went over the country to the settlements very nicely, and so far as the nature of the land was concerned they could have gone as far as the North Sea, which could not have been very far, because some of the Indians wore shells from it on their foreheads. May God our Lord be forever praised, and may He be pleased to hasten the salvation of so many souls, and may He have pity on this land, so that in it His holy gospel may be preached and many poor souls be saved, for, judging from what we have seen, it must in time become their place of refuge and bring wealth to many.

845. 1605. A letter on Oñate's discoveries in the west.

This was the first news of Oñate's discoveries to reach England. Richard Hakluyt had become acquainted with Lucas Tribaldos de Toledo when he was secretary of a Spanish mission in London and began a correspondence with him which produced this letter after he had returned to Spain. It was not printed until it appeared, in translation from the Latin, in S. Purchas, Pilgrimes, *IV (1625), 1625–1627 (XVIII [1906], 76–80).*

A Letter written from Vallodolid by Ludovicus Tribaldus Toletus to Master Richard Hakluyt, translated out of Latin, touching Ivan de Onate his Discoveries in New Mexico, five hundred leagues to the North from the old Mexico.

When you shall see the English returned home out of our Spaine, and can finde no Letters sent unto you from us, perhaps, and that worthily you will accuse us of breach of our friendship, and also as little mindfull of our promise. Yet we as free from this fault salute you most willingly. For it is not long since we arrived here, that is to say in this Court, a little after the departure of your Countrimen into England. Yet we made our journie by Sea and by Land indifferent pleasantly and according to our desire. After we had rested our selves a small while, we desired nothing more then to visit Andrew Garsia Cespedes, a man for many respects linked unto us in most straight bands of friendship. He greatly rejoyced of your goodwill toward him: And shewed me a certaine briefe yet very perspicuous Relation of things atchieved by Don Juan de Onate, among the Indians of New Mexico.

For therein is written, that he departed from old Mexico in the yeere 1599. with an Armie and carriages of five thousand men [*sic* for 500], in which number boyes, women, young men and Souldiers are included. He carried also great store of victuals with him, flockes of Sheepe and Goates, Herds of Oxen, and all things necessarie for life, also Horses and Armour, and other things which in these kind of Expeditions ought to be provided. Therefore having travelled through divers Countries five hundred leagues, hee found divers Nations by the way, noble for their builded Townes and reasonable civill manners. All which he received into the friendship of the King of Spaine, and they openly testified the same by publike instruments, and giving of their faith. And when with his company he came unto a Towne very strong by situation of the place, built upon a most high and mightie Rocke, and was freely received by the Inhabitants, giving their right hands to each other, they courteously supplied them with all things necessarie for their reliefe, and promised within a while after that they would furnish them with more, sufficient to make a very long journie. When Onate had waited for this thing, at the day appointed hee sent his Nephew by his sister with a few Souldiers, who entring the Towne, came into the Market place, where almost all the multitude of the Townesmen were assembled together. Now while hee with his company was busie in buying of things, suddenly the Traitours from all parts rushed upon him and his fellowes unawares, and by most wicked treason cut off the Captaines head and six others; the rest being wounded hardly escaped by flight from so great a multitude that assaulted them, yet some of the enemies were slaine and thrust through. When speedily the same hereof came to Onate, taking with him a choice number of Souldiers, in a great furie he came unto the Towne, besieged it, and after a long fight by maine force he tooke the same, slue most part, tooke the rest, burnt the Towne and razed it to the ground, that no tokens might remaine of so great a wickednesse committed against him. The Townes name was Acoma: and none of our men was slaine in the siege thereof.

After this he easily proceeded forward on his journie as he did before, till he came to a mightie great Citie: he inforced this City with the villages adjoyning to sweare obedience to the King of Spaine, not altogether unwilling, yet feared by the example and ruine of the towne that was destroyed. From hence he came to a greater Citie, which likewise after hee had obtained it by great friendship he sent certain men from thence to search out the oxen of Cibola, long since known by the report of one, (to wit of Vasquez de Coronado) whether they were such indeed or no. Who when they had found a great multitude of these oxen, and would compasse them about, and force them into certaine inclosures or toiles, their enterprize prevailed but a little: they are so wild and so swift. Yet after they had killed many of them, bringing store of them with them, as though they had bin Deere, returning to their company and General, to the great admiration of all men, they declared the wildnesse and innumerable number of these Oxen.

Afterward employing of themselves to keepe those things which they had gotten, they builded a Towne, which they called Saint Johns Towne, and entring into very great friendship with the people which they had lately discovered, after they had found certaine very rich Mynes of gold and silver, being laden with store of other riches, they determined to live pleasantly and quietly, and to end their travels, with singular profit of the Inhabitants in the Christian Religion, and abjuring of their Idols, which in former time they worshipped most religiously.

At length within these two yeeres, leaving his fellowes there, Onate undertooke a new Discoverie toward that most famous River of the North, which at length he discovered, being everywhere courteously entertained by the Inhabitants. At last he came to the Lake whereof long since, have gone many reports. This is the Lake of Conibas, on the brinke whereof hee beheld a farre off a Citie seven leagues long, and above two leagues broad. The houses of this Citie were separated the one from the other, and trimly and artificially builded, adorned with many trees and most goodly Gardens; and often divided with streames running betweene them. Yet none of the Inhabitants did appeare. Therefore being not furnished with a sufficient Armie, he kept his Souldiers about him in a strong place, yet he sent certaine Horsemen into the Towne to view it: who after they had ridden by a certaine space through certaine exceeding faire streets of the Citie, and could see none of the Citizens, at length came to an exceeding great Market place, which was filled with an exceeding great company of men, fortified with Rampiers and other fortifications in manner of a Fortresse. Therefore perceiving themselves to be unequall to so infinite a number, they retired backe to their fellowes without attempting any thing, and so returned home to their owne houses under the conduct of Onate, defferring the assaulting of so great a Towne untill a more convenient time: and now they keepe those places diligently, which they have alreadie found, and doing violence to none of the Inhabitants, they live in all happinesse and prosperitie.

Moreover, other newes is brought from New Spaine, to wit, that by the commandement of the Vice-roy, the Coasts of the South Sea toward Cape Mendoçino are discovered, and that exceeding faire and large Havens are found neere the Californias, which hitherto no man knew, and that Castles are there to be builded and fortified, fit to withstand the force of the enemie: which I saw painted with the precise longitudes and latitudes, annexed unto them.

There is no newes come of the Voyage to the Iland lately found out toward Nova Guinea. If any newes come, I will carefully advertise you thereof.

It remaineth, that I speake somewhat of the instruction which I promised you, and now send unto you: to wit, that the same was sent to the West Indies, and that according to the precepts therein contained, all things are observed very exactly, and written to the Councell of the Indies: and that Cespedes our friend having diligently read over these Writings, hath written an excellent Volume; but he hath not obtained leave to publish the same: for they will not have all these things particularly to come to light.

And these be the things which I now thought good to write unto you, my Hakluyt, meaning to have written more, if there had beene any fresher things to have written of. Neither have I yet sought out all those that might informe me of these new Discoveries: for I could not yet doe it by reason of the shortnesse of the time. I hope hereafter I shall have leisure: and I know you will commmend mee for my friendship towards you. Farewell from Valladolid the Nones of July 1605.

846. March 31, 1605. The viceroy, the Marquis de Montescláros, writes to Philip III about Oñate.

The letter represents very well the position of the Mexican viceroy concerning New Mexico. Oñate has been charged with various misdemeanors and has not yet been cleared. Even if he is, there remains considerable doubt as to whether on economic grounds New Mexico is worth retaining. A formal inquiry on the spot might provide a solution.

A.G.I., Mexico 26; translated in G. B. Hammond and A. Rey, Oñate, II, 1001–1005, from which it is taken.

By your majesty's letter of May 26 of the past year, 1603, you ordered me to encourage the expedition to New Mexico, in case it should be continued, and to favor Don Juan de Oñate, who is in charge of it. As some of the charges filed against him with the royal Council have not been verified and your majesty ordered me to investigate them, I, to comply with this order, examined the documents, reports, and proceedings bearing on this matter which Don Juan de Oñate had sent. Likewise I examined those relating to the case which the Count, my predecessor, had compiled. As they seemed important and most of them related to cases of justice brought by interested people who were pressing for a decision, I determined not to entrust the matter solely to my own judgment, but called a secret meeting of three judges of the audiencia, those most detached in family and friends, and the fiscal, to study the proceedings relating to the criminal charges. The findings of this committee may be seen in a summary report which accompanies the opinion.

In regard to the quality of the land, basing my judgment on the very conflicting reports that all furnish in regard to it, I understand that the slight evidence of wealth noted thus far and the humble and poor clothes of the natives are strong witnesses in support of those who speak ill of the success of the expedition.

Just lately letters have come from Don Juan de Oñate, together with samples of ores obtained from the mines that have been discovered. These I had assayed here, and thus far the richest ore produced one-eighth part copper, without any trace of silver. With this letter I am sending your majesty samples of these metals and a detailed report of what each one produced, in order that you may have them assayed if you desire. All other communications from there express nothing but hopes, which, even if not realized, always leave the possibility that they may turn into realities.

All these conjectures, Sir, are arguments that lead nowhere, and in some cases their outcome is doubtful. This is especially true in this particular instance, which may produce such opposite results of benefit or harm. It would be a rash individual who would give your majesty a definite recommendation.

The light that we have thus far gathered on this expedition reveals that the people are rustic, wretched in clothes and spirit, that they do not possess silver or gold, dwell in straw and grass houses, and live on native fruits such as maize and vegetables, which they say are grown twice a year in places. Instead of cotton, I have been assured that they weave dog hair.

That this should suffice to induce a private individual to enter the country on such slight assurances and to risk losing more than he will find, I do not consider a novelty, particularly in the Indies. Whether this enterprise could be taken over by such a great and mighty king, without any obligation on the royal conscience, is a responsibility that you must judge. To the best of my understanding, the most riches hoped for from the present state of affairs by those who started on this expedition lie in its continuation, and to attain this end the best means would be to induce your majesty to contribute something from your royal treasury, whereupon this worthless land, the object of such ill-advised expenditures, would be transformed into an object of pride, and the costs to maintain it, now considered excessive, and that could be avoided, would become necessary and light.

This increases my confusion, so I cannot take further steps in this matter without instructions from your majesty. Don Juan de Oñate's offer that he and his relatives would pay the expenses of one-fourth of these people, the cost of the others to be met by the royal treasury, so that four hundred in all would be recruited, is not being carried out. On the contrary, I believe that they are uncertain of their ability to do it, for they are again asking that we loan them from the royal treasury what they offered originally and that we accept as security the guarantors they want. Once this lending door is opened, there is no doubt but that they will agree to anything that is required of them because they will realize that they have but little responsibility in case they cannot meet their obligations and that their safeguard rests on this very impossibility.

Finally, Sir, after explaining to your majesty the difficulties that I encounter and which serve to increase the doubt as to whether this conquest should be continued, I feel quite sure that both the time and expenditure put into it will be wasted, or that at the best it is a gamble, as its success rests on flimsy and doubtful information. In either case of loss or speculation, your majesty, as the final authority, should make the decision without my doing anything except to point out the inconveniences that are likely to ensue.

Should your majesty and the Council find stronger reasons for expecting ultimate benefit and expansion of the royal crown and decide to continue what has been initiated, there is one point of doubt which I wish to emphasize, namely, that the documents concerning the charges against Don Juan de Oñate do not at present justify any penalty on him personally and he should not be punished until he has been heard, but from what we know already in regard to these excesses, there is sufficient reason why your majesty should not entrust the continuation of the expedition to him.

Moreover, if an announcement should be made right away of the sending of a visitador, the governor's reputation, which may be unsullied, would suffer, and he might even be driven to some rash action, frightened by the clamor that such things cause; and so, since the land is so far away, it might be well for your majesty to use as a pretext the divergent reports about the nature of the land and your wish to be informed by one of your own agents who has seen it and appraised the value of the mines discovered there, and to send someone from this audiencia, either an oidor or alcalde, with the necessary escort for safety, who, after seeing it, could render a detailed report of it all. The one chosen might go under this pretext and at the same time carry a commission and secret instructions to investigate this charge and, if desirable, he might be authorized to arrest

Don Juan and his guilty relatives, leaving the land in charge of some competent person of his own choice and instructing him not to undertake any entrada but to hold what has been conquered and to defend and protect the friars who might be there and ministering to the baptized Indians. For, although the insecurity of the settlements and the uncertainty of preserving the land have been responsible for the number of baptized being very small, nonetheless, if there should be one lone Christian, your majesty would be obligated through justice, conscience, and prestige to preserve him, even at great cost to the royal treasury. Therefore, a presidio must be established there by all means, for defense and protection, not only in order that the Indians may receive no harm, but that those who wish to submit peacefully may be kindly treated and won over. Perhaps this will prove to be a more effective means of finding the treasures which they have possibly concealed, though some have thought of no more effective way of subduing them than to burn them alive in their houses, not to mention numerous other cruelties.

In case Don Juan de Oñate should not be found guilty in the investigation conducted by the judge sent there, greater prestige and credit for the expedition would result and your majesty might employ Don Juan de Oñate either in the prosecution of the conquest or the preservation of what has been won.

If the sending of a visitador of the ability I suggest should seem fitting—there must be but very few men qualified for this task and it is very important to select the right person—I should like to nominate Doctor Morga, alcalde of this audiencia, who, I feel sure, would discharge this commission most satisfactorily. Another choice might be Licentiate Morquecho, oidor of this audiencia, for, although the name Oñate in his wife's name and the Oñates in this kingdom may induce some to believe that they are related, I do not believe that this would be an obstacle to his doing his duty in this matter. If either of them or someone else goes, it would not be desirable that he return to the audiencia, because he would incur the enmity of most of the people in the kingdom with whom others of this name are related. While I am not yet sure of some members of the audiencia, I doubt whether the one who may go would dare to risk administering justice with complete impartiality unless he felt sure of his reward. May your majesty order what you please in all of this. God preserve you, as Christendom needs. Mexico, March [31]. 1605. Marquis of Montesclaros.

847. October, 1604 to April, 1605. Expedition by Juan de Oñate westward from New Mexico and down the Colorado River to the Gulf of California.

When Fray Francisco de Escobar, commissary of the Franciscan friars in New Mexico, arrived at the city of Mexico with certain soldiers from New Mexico in October, 1605, the viceroy, the Marquis de Montesclaros, saw that their story of Oñate's expedition was designed to rehabilitate him with the authorities, who had decided in principle to recall him. The soldiers were, therefore, very carefully examined on what had happened on the journey. Their reports of this interesting journey did not lead to any reendorsement of the governor, who gave up his command in 1607.

A.G.I., Seville, Mexico 20; translated in G. B. Hammond and A. Rey, Oñate, II, 1011–1131, from which it is taken.

This is a faithful and accurate copy of a Relation which Fray Francisco de Escobar, of the order of Saint Francis, who is said to be commissary general of the provinces of New Mexico, seems to have given to his excellency, the Marquis of Montesclaros, viceroy of New Spain, of a particular exploration and of certain declarations made by the said Fray Francisco, the tenor of which is as follows:

Three hundred and sixty leagues from the city of Mexico toward the north pole, on the banks of a large river named the Río del Norte (because it flows toward the south), there are seven or eight provinces and nations of peoples, all of different languages. The Spaniards generally call these provinces New Mexico. They must contain thirty thousand souls or more. The country is very poor and cold, and has much snow, but is quite habitable for a Spanish colony of moderate size, pro-

vided the people have clothing to wear and that they will bring cattle from New Spain to provide food and to till the soil, for none of these are produced there, and although the cattle brought multiply readily, the land is too limited in resources to raise large numbers of them.

The people of these provinces are very affable and docile. They all live in pueblos, which, for Indian dwellings, are very well arranged. In each pueblo there are many good estufas, where, with little fire, they keep warm and wherein they spend the cold weather and snows of winter. Their clothes consist of cotton blankets, woven in their pueblos, and of very well-dressed white buckskins, of which, for their way of living, they have sufficient, for they are satisfied with little, but they do not have enough of them with which to pay tribute to the Spaniards. They are in great need and find this burden hard to bear, so that many abandon their pueblos at the time when the tribute is gathered. The amount collected is now very small and a considerable obstacle to their conversion. If they were relieved of this payment and if they were sent interpreters to preach to them and teach them our holy faith, I believe that most of them would embrace it readily. This will be quite difficult if we persist in collecting tribute, which is so burdensome to them and of so little benefit to the Spaniards that, although it is gathered every year, the Spaniards are destitute. Moreover, those who are to live in these provinces are in no way able to protect the ministers of the gospel unless they get the necessary succor in clothes with which to dress and keep warm, and cattle for food and for tilling and cultivating their farms and fields.

The Indians in this land raise maize, which constitutes their main food, and beans and calabashes. In the winter they wear skins or hides of the buffalo which are tanned and very well dressed, have very soft hair, and which are brought to these provinces to trade for corn flour and cotton blankets by the Indians who live among the cattle and who commonly live in tents or movable houses made of these same hides. Their ordinary pack animals are dogs, which they take along, loaded, on their travels.

The governor and adelantado, Don Juan de Oñate, set out from these provinces of New Mexico on October 7, 1604, with thirty soldiers for the discovery of the South sea or gulf of California. I went with this party as commissary of the friars in these provinces. After traveling for fifty leagues almost directly west, we came to the province of Quini [Zuñi], which has six pueblos, four of them almost completely in ruins, although all inhabited. The largest and the head town of these was called Scíbola by the Spaniards, and the Indians recognize it by this name, although in their own language it is called Hauico.

I surmise that the pueblos all together comprise three hundred inhabited houses. The people are very hospitable and tractable. They welcome to their homes the Spaniards who come through this province, and serve and provide them joyfully and courteously with the food they have. This consists of maize, beans, hares, and rabbits, in which the country is rich. They dress or cover themselves with buckskin, and in the winter with skins of the buffalo, which are brought there from the provinces where the Spaniards are now, but what they most commonly use are blankets which they make from a small palm, soaked, like iztle in New Spain, or hemp in Spain, but not so strong. Their houses, for Indian houses, are very good, all built of stone, with very good estufas in each pueblo for the cold of winter, which is intense.

After traveling about twenty leagues almost to the northwest, we arrived at the province of Moqui, a land as poor and cold as the provinces of Zuñi and those of New Mexico. It has only five pueblos, four of them half in ruins and destroyed, containing not more than five hundred occupied houses. The people are very friendly to the Spaniards, whom they lodge in their houses when they travel through this province, serving and feeding them joyfully and courteously.

From what could be gathered from the Indians in the pueblos, they plant and harvest an abundant supply of maize, having more of it than the natives in the province of Zuñi. They grow also beans, calabashes, and cotton. From the latter they make blankets, rather heavy ones, the best in this land, and they color them better than do the Indians in the other provinces. This is the type of clothing which they use to dress or cover themselves, as well as very well-dressed buckskin, and in the winter buffalo hides. There is very little firewood and still less water. Everywhere in this province there are excellent estufas in each pueblo, so that with a small amount of wood they keep very warm the whole winter. The houses are not as good as those in the province of Zuñi, but they are not very bad for their manner of living.

Not only in this province, but in the others as well, they have no temples for their worship, although some of the houses in which they live, it was noticed, were devoted to their ceremonies and worship and had some small stone or wooden idols, and some rustic, small animals, poorly shaped. I do not think these houses are often visited, and not by all the people, but, from what I could gather, only by the leading and oldest Indians.

Ten leagues from this province to the west we came to a river which we named Saint Joseph because we spent that feast day by it. At this place it flows southeast-northwest. It is a river with many trees, although with little water, except at the season when the snow melts, which is from March until June or July. During this season, it seems to me, one could transport by way of this river to the gulf of California and to the port or bay of Conversion much lumber and timbers from the great pine forests which are not far from this river. There must be more than one hundred and twenty leagues, more or less, from these forests to the sea. I am certain that this river empties into another large stream which disembogues in the harbor of Conversion, which I shall discuss later on.

Seventeen leagues from this river to the west we came to another stream named San Antonio. It flowed from north to south among great mountains. From this river on, the country is more temperate and not quite so cold, and has better pastures and water. The river does not carry much water, although it has some throughout the year. It has abundant fine fish.

Five leagues from this river to the west we saw another one just as large and with as many fish. It is called the Sacramento. It flowed northwest-southeast along the slopes of a high range from which the Spaniards have obtained many copper ores from some mines that had been discovered by Antonio de Espejo.

In this country there are Indians whom the Spaniards called Cruzados on account of some crosses which most of them wear on the forehead. Most of these crosses were made of reeds. The origin of this custom is not known, but it is believed that they acquired it from Christians, for when there are Spaniards in their land they wear them more regularly. As a rule they are very friendly to the Spaniards.

They do not grow or harvest maize or beans, but subsist on venison and wild sheep; the latter have skins like deer and head and horns like sheep, although their horns are very unequal in length. There are many wild sheep and deer in this land, from whose skins they make buckskin, with which both men and women clothe themselves. This is the common type of clothing which they wear. They also eat maguey, prickly pears, mesquite, and some small fruit produced by the juniper, of which there are great forests.

We went ten or twelve leagues along the banks of this river to its source. After traveling from here sixteen leagues almost due west, we came to another river which we named San Andrés, because it was discovered on his feast day. It flows to the west, among high and rough mountain ranges, which are bare and without grass, being mostly all bare rock. This may be due also to the summer heat, as the land indicates that it must be intense. The river ordinarily carries no water, except for short distances, where it issues or gushes forth from the sand, although there were signs of high floods. From this river onward the country has a different climate, for it does not snow nor is it at all cold. We did not feel any, even though it was in the midst of winter, it being in the month of December.

Following this river, most of the time in its bed, for its banks consisted mostly of rocky cliffs, we arrived, after going twenty leagues, at another river, as large as the Duero in Spain. We named it Buena Esperanza, because of reaching it on the day of the Expectation or Hope of the most blessed delivery of the Virgin Mary, our Lady. At the place where it joins the San Andrés river it flows northwest-southeast and from here turns northeast-southwest until it reaches the sea or the gulf of California. It is bordered on both sides by high ranges, between which it forms a very wide meadow, all densely settled with people, who are found on both banks as far as the sea, which, it seemed to me, must have been fifty leagues away, a few more or less. The river appeared to be navigable throughout this distance, according to men who understand navigation, and as was inferred from its very slow current.

The first nation of people whom we met at this river was called Amauaca. We found them to be very friendly. They furnished us with maize, beans, and calabashes, which constitute the ordinary food of all the people along this river and which they grow throughout this river valley. However, I did not think that they had a great abundance of maize and I attribute this to their indolence, for the spacious meadows seemed ample to plant much more, to establish farms, and to settle Spaniards, although there is but little grass for cattle, since all the ranges and hills are barren and it is found only in the river valley, and even then not everywhere. The Indians derive much food also from mesquite, which is plentiful throughout the valley, and they gather many grass seeds, which would indicate that there is not a great surplus of maize. Although we saw many extensive cornfields, they were not adequate for the great number of people living there.

Adjoining this nation on this same river there is another called Bahacecha. They speak a somewhat different language, although, as the difference is small, it is not a hindrance to commerce and communication among them, for it is as if they were all of one language. The people are courteous and tractable like those of Amacaba, or even more so. They received us in a most friendly manner and with much rejoicing, giving us of their scanty supply of food in all the rancherías through which we passed. Eager to see their strange guests, a large multitude of Indian men, women, and children accompanied us on our way, for the rancherías of the same nation were not very far apart.

The people of these two nations and of all this river are very friendly and of good disposition, tall of stature and well proportioned. The custom in regard to dress is not to wear any, but to go naked from the sole of the foot to the head, which is the general practice among all the people who live along this river. Only the women cover merely their privy parts with two bunches of grass or fibre, which at least cover them, but they do not try to cover any other portion of the body. They all wore their hair loose, reaching only to the shoulders. The nature of the land permits them to go about in this scanty attire, as it is not cold, nor were we cold in all the time we were there, which was in the heart of winter.

Their language seemed to me easy, free from difficulties in pronunciation. An Indian chieftain from this nation of Bahaçecha, for he who is most important among them is very unimportant and his standing among them no different from the rest, told us, and after him many others at this river, we having shown him a coral, that they procured this substance not far from there, toward the south, and that the Indians dug it from the sand at low tide. The governor found some corals among the Indians of this river, and even more in the province of Zuñi on our way back. This is because the Indians who live in the direction of the coral coast trade more with the people of this province than with the people at the river of Buena Esperanza. The corals are not fine. I do not know the reason, whether there are no better ones at this sea or whether the ones brought by the Indians are cut by the continuous motion of the waves. The Indians maintain that they get them out of the sand, broken, as they are cast up by the sea.

From this Indian we learned also, and from many others, by showing them silver or steel buttons, that not far from this gulf toward the west, five of their day's travel, which are only five or six leagues each, this metal was to be found. They said the same when we showed them a silver spoon, and they maintained that they made large bowls of this metal in which they cooked their meat over the fire, both over flames and coals. They did this with a silver plate, which we showed them, and they affirmed that the bowls were like it in shape, but much larger and deeper, that they sounded like the above plate, that they did not break when dropped on the ground, nor were they made of pottery like the bowls and ollas from which they eat. They gave us to understand that they dug this metal from a sierra located on the opposite shore of the sea, across from an island, which they pointed out was five days' journey toward the west from where we were and to which they cross in some canoes or pirogues, whose form and shape they drew on the ground. They explained that the hollow of the bowls was made by digging out the piece of metal and not by beating it, which made me fear that the metal of which they made these bowls was tin, because their way of cutting and making them indicates, in my opinion, the softness of the metal and its abundance. There was even an Indian who told

me that the metates on that island were made of this same metal, or that he had seen in it some of this same metal, even though not all were like it. This was an indication that this metal was very plentiful, and that one may suspect it to be tin. Nevertheless, all the Indians of this Bahaçecha nation maintained that it was like the silver plates, that it sounded like it, and that they put them over the fire to cook their meat in them. All of this leaves me perplexed as to whether it is tin or silver. Only an examination of the metal, in case it exists, as so many Indians affirm, will dispel my doubts. They called this metal *ñaño querroo*.

We learned also from the same Indian chieftain who told us about this, and whose name was Otata, that near here, nine or ten days' travel, there was a lake on whose shores lived people who wore on their wrists bands or bracelets of a yellow metal, which they explained by pointing to gold and brass *punzones* which we showed them. Putting them on and wearing them on their wrists or arms, they said that they were like the metal which those Indians wore on their wrists, and afterwards two old Indians said the same. When shown a small plate of brass, they said that the other metal was darker and that they called it *anopacha*. This same name was given to it later by other Indians who were three, four, or even more leagues distant from those who had seen the little brass watch that I carried, this without my asking them any questions at the time about the matter. From this one may clearly infer that there is a yellow metal in this land. In fact, there is a common name in the entire province for it, but it was reported only by the Indians of Bahacehe and Amacaba. When I asked about it of other Indians whom we met on the same river closer toward the sea, they could not give me any information about the matter, either because they did not understand me or because they did not know about it. However, there were so many at Bahaçecha and Amacaua who told about it that they almost convinced me beyond all doubt that there were both yellow and white metals in the land, though there is no proof that the yellow metal is gold or that the white is silver, for of this my doubts are still very great.

After leaving this Bahaçecha nation, whose ranchería extends seven or eight leagues along the valley on both sides of the river, we came to another large river, which, though much smaller than the Buena Esperanza, reached to the pack saddles of the horses. It was called Nombre de Jesús. This river empties into the Buena Esperanza from the southeast to the north twenty leagues before reaching the sea. Above the junction, the Buena Esperanza river makes a bend of four or five leagues from north to south on account of a mountain range that it cuts through.

By this river there were four or five rancherías (as the houses all along this river are huts [ranchos], I call their settlements rancherías), whose people speak a different language. From them I learned that the Nombre de Jesús river is inhabited by one group who raised maize, beans, and calabashes, like the people of Amacaua and Bahaçecha, and wove cotton blankets, some of which I saw and which are coarse like those from the province of New Mexico. The people or nation of this Nombre de Jesús river are called Oseca, and from some words that I learned from them I suspect that they are Tepiguanes, although I do not definitely so state as these words were only a few, for once, on seeing in the town of Sombrerete a friar versed in the Tepeguana language, I learned that the mode of dress of the Tepeguanans was the same as that of the people of Osera, and I observed also that they used the same two or three words which I remembered, and, having found those Indians less friendly, more annoying, and less tractable than any of those who lived along the Buena Esperanza river, I learned fewer words of their language than of the Amacaua.

The women of this Ocara nation dress in the same manner as the other women met before. The mode of dress of the men differed only as to the hair, as the people here wear it very long, tied with a maguey cord, and wound around the head. Otherwise they go about naked like all the others.

Near the rancherías of these people we left twenty or more horses, as there was good grazing, in order to restore them from the lack of fodder which they had suffered, and so that they might be in condition to make the return trip to the provinces of New Mexico. When we returned from the sea we found that the Indians had killed and eaten thirteen of them. We were almost positive that these natives and no others had done it, although they denied it in great fear, casting the blame on others. We had to stand the loss patiently, since we had given them occasion to inflict it, for in our presence no one misbehaved, nor was it ever necessary for us to watch our horses at night. This we were spared from the time we left the provinces of New Mexico until we returned, such was the friendliness of the Indians.

From the river Nombre de Jesús to the sea, which, as I have said, was twenty leagues, the valley seemed still wider, the mesquite more dense, and the people more numerous than up to that place. They belonged, however, to the same nation, and some to a different one, although they differed very little in their method of trade and communication, in their clothes, friendliness, good disposition, and pleasing ways, which were the same as those of the people at Amacaua and Bahaçecha. Like the people met before, they grow maize, calabashes, and beans, and they also gather much mesquite. The valley is good and seemed ample for Spanish farming. The land seemed fertile, but lacked grass, and the hills and mountains were so bare that we could not learn whether there were rains in the land for the crops. We saw many cornfields, but they were not irrigated. There were some branches which extended out from the river and carried water all the year round, and from which, in case of lack of rain, some ditches could be made.

The first settlement that we found beyond the Nombre de Jesús river was called Alebdoma. I learned from an Indian that it had eight rancherías, but we could not see them all, although they were all in the river valley. The first and largest of these eight rancherías had one hundred and sixty huts. It was thought that it contained two thousand people and that the entire settlement with its eight rancherías had four or five thousand.

Near this settlement there was another one called Coguana, which comprised nine rancherías, all within a short distance. We saw some of them, and although we did not visit all the rancherías we saw many people from all of them, as they came to see us. This settlement had another five thousand souls.

Close to this one there is another settlement called Agalle, which has five rancherías. Close by there was another one called Agalec-qua-maya, with its rancherías. These two settlements had another four or five thousand souls.

Two leagues farther on we came to another settlement called Cocapa. It extends to the sea, or to the point reached by the salt water, which goes up the river a distance of four or five leagues. This settlement has nine rancherías and seemed to me to be the largest of all. We visited only two of the rancherías, one of which had about one thousand souls and the other less than five hundred. I reckoned that the entire population of Cocapa might be five or six thousand, because, while we were there, so many Indians gathered to see us that everyone judged that they must have numbered at least three thousand souls, nor did it seem to me that there were even sixty women among them, and very few children, while from the previous settlements there were only seven Indians who had accompanied us as guides. They did not dare to go on as they were two or three leagues away from the people farther back, and they feared enemy Indians, for all on the opposite bank of the river were hostile and used to sally forth to kill them at that uninhabited forest. So the natives of the rancherías farther back did not dare to go on with us as they had done until then, for there were days when we had been accompanied on our way by more than three hundred persons.

I thought that the settlements and rancherías of people which we found on the Buena Esperanza river comprised more than thirty thousand souls, not including those on the opposite bank of the river who were their enemies. In view of this fact, they did not cross to visit us. We were told that they were numerous. The Indians of the Osera river told me about eighteen or twenty rancherías, all named. They are the ones who live near the coral coast and who profit by the corals.

After crossing all these nations, settlements, and rancherías, where we were very cordially and joyfully received and where they gave us everywhere maize, beans, and calabashes (not much in quantity, nor according to the large number of people, nor to our needs, until we returned to the province of Moqui, and we were forced to eat seven or eight horses before we arrived there when we came back), on the day of the conversion of the glorious apostle, Saint Paul, with much rejoicing, we reached the sea or gulf of California. Here, according to experienced seamen, we saw the most famous bay or harbor (it goes by both names), that any of them had ever seen. We named it port of the Conversion, because it was discovered on that day.

The bay is formed by the Buena Esperanza river, where it empties into the sea, its mouth being three or four leagues across, as was affirmed by seamen who saw it with me. The mouth of the river is divided into two parts by a small island which rises in the middle. This island is about one and a half or two leagues long. It extends from southeast to northwest and makes a splendid protection for the bay, leaving each mouth of the river one and a half or two leagues wide. This little island seemed to be formed of clay, as is also the beach or shore of the bay. There were not found in it any pebbles, sand, reefs, or any sign of them. The bay seemed of good depth, even close to the shore.

The Buena Esperanza river enters the sea from west to east at the foot of a mountain range which extends toward the sea almost from north to south, or from north-northwest to south-east. A spur of this range extends about six leagues into the bay. It ends in three low, round peaks, the farthest one higher than the other two. Beyond these, toward the land side, there is a higher point where this range forms a spur that extends more than twenty leagues from north-northwest to south-southeast, from which alone one may infer how this range enters the sea. The latter runs east and west along this coast, making a turn back of the mountain range, according to the Indians, tending always north and northwest, but none of them knew where the sea ended.

Among the Indians of this coast there were found many shells, some white and others green, of various shades. On being questioned about them, some Indians maintained that they obtained very large pearls from these shells, but we could not find a single one among the Indians, even though the governor did his best.

When we returned from the sea and reached the Vacecha nation, where the chieftain, called Otata, had told us of the little island containing the silver or tin, of which the bowls are made which he said they had, and of the yellow metal of which the Indians at the lake made the bracelets that they wore, he and many others again told us the same things that they had said before, without contradicting themselves in any detail, even though more than forty days had passed since they had furnished us this information. Many other Indians corroborated these reports; some of them were from near the island and had come to see us. It is evident that they were of different language and dress and that they were friends of the people of Bahacecha and knew their language.

This Indian Otata also told us about all the people who live on the Buena Esperanza river, up to its source, indicating that this was near the sea, to the northwest, and many others confirmed this, all agreeing with him that the gulf of California makes this complete turn. He told also of the people who live on the Buena Esperanza river and the sea, making a sketch of the land on a piece of paper, in which he indicated many nations of people so strange that only at great risk of not being believed do I venture to report these things, since I have not seen them, nor could they be visited because of the few people and horses and scanty provisions which the governor had, and also because the land promised little or no grass for the horses. For horses so extremely thin and exhausted as were most of those we had left, the enterprise seemed impossible; even to cherish the hope that we might succeed with such lack of the necessary means seemed of no small temerity. Although some may reprove my boldness in narrating such monstrous things which have never been seen in our times nor in the past (nevertheless, even if one should tell them as things actually seen, the persons who might vouch for them are so far away that there always remains room for doubt and each one may believe what he wishes), accordingly, I dare to tell what I heard a multitude of Indians report in my presence, for I must uphold the truth of what I saw with my own eyes, and I shall do so.

The Indian Otata told us in the presence of many others, who supported his story, of a nation of people with so large and long ears that they dragged on the ground, and that five or six persons could stand under each one. This nation was called Esmalca Tatanacha in their own language. Esmalca in the language of the Bahacecha nation means "ear," so the etymology of this word explains the characteristic of the nation.

Not far from this nation there was another one, he told us, whose men had virile members so long that they wound them four times around the waist, and in the act of copulation the man and woman were far apart. This nation was called Medará Quachoquata.

From this Indian and the others we learned also that near this nation there was another whose people had only one foot. These people were called Niequetata.

They told us of other people, not far from the latter, who dwelt on the shore of a lake, and that at night they all slept under the water. They said that these were the people who wore bands or bracelets of yellow metal, which they called anpacha, and so they were called the same, though with more propriety we might have named them Hamaca Cosmacha fish.

From all these Indians we learned that near this nation there was another whose people slept always in trees. We could not learn whether this was because of fear of wild beasts or reptiles, or because it was their natural characteristic or habit. This nation was called Ahalcos Macha.

The monstrosities did not end here, for they claimed that there was another nation near the last one, whose people sustained themselves solely on the odor of their food. They prepared it only for this purpose, not eating anything at all because they lacked the natural means of discharging excrement from the body. This nation was called Xamoco Huicha.

They told us of another nation of people not far away who never laid down to sleep but who always slept on their feet with some burden on the head. They called this nation Tascaná Paycosmacha.

At this place we learned from all these Indians what we had already learned long before from many others, great and small, that the chief person obeyed by the Indians who lived on the island was a woman called Ciñaca Cohotá. This signifies "principal woman" or "chieftainess." We heard from all of these Indians that she was a giant, that she lived alone with a sister on the island, and that there was no one left of her generation, which must have ended with them.

From many of these Indians we learned that most of the men who lived on this island were completely bald-headed.

Here ended the monstrosities. However, doubt as to the existence of such portentous things in such a short distance and so near to us need not be permanent, for the Indians affirmed that they were all on one river, which it was necessary to cross to reach the island and which was only five days' travel away. This might have been twenty-five or thirty leagues. But, whatever doubt there may arise in regard to these matters, it seemed to me that I would be wrong in not telling of things which, if discovered, would, I believe, redound to the glory of God and the service of the king our lord.

For even though those things may be so strange in themselves and may never have been seen before, whoever reflects on the marvels that God continuously performs in this world will not find it hard to believe that since He is able to create them, He may have done so, and that since such a variety and multitude of peoples, some more than two hundred leagues away, have corroborated them, there must be some basis for these stories. Furthermore, these Indians were not the first inventors of such news, for there are many books which treat of them and of even greater monstrosities, things of great amazement.

And even if our stories should cause wonder, I do not think that the way to verify them or the other reports of riches and the communication between these seas, if such a communication should exist, is wholly barred. With the favor of heaven, the truth about this whole matter could be established with less than one hundred men, including the existence of silver or tin, or whatever metal there may be on this island; of gold, copper, or bronze, of which the Indians from the lake wear bracelets or bands; of corals and pearls, which the Indians maintain were obtained from the shells that we saw and some of which the governor brought and which so many soldiers affirm were found in the gulf of California; also in regard to the bend which the Indians say the gulf makes to the north and northeast, for we did not find anyone who knew its end; and the existence of these monstrous nations which so many Indians reported, some maintaining that they had seen them, and others that they had heard about them. In both cases, there were Indians from ten different nations, some from more than two hundred leagues away.

We learned also from the Indian Otata and many others that at the source of this Buena Esperanza river and six days' journey before reaching it there were many buffalo, and very large deer that roam around with them. From its source to where the river ends in the sea or port of Conversion, they said it was thirty days' travel, all through settlements of people who grow maize like those of Amauaca. If this is true, as the Indians insisted, then there can be no shortage of grass where the buffalo graze and the country must of necessity be colder. This proves it. So it seems to me that, if no more appropriate suggestion is made, one could better make an exploration, both by land and sea, from the source of the Buena Esperanza river, for since the Indians affirm that there are a great many buffalo, there must be grass for our cattle and for the horses. The Indians suggested that the land was even better for farming, saying that the maize grew taller and the calabashes larger. The same facilities would be found for making the exploration by water, for the Indians maintain that the river has its source near the sea, though there is no more reason to believe this than the other things which they told us. Yet it might happen that there would be better facilities to build boats or some sort of brigantine, since there is no timber at the port of Conversion, unless it is taken from the pine forests near the San Joseph river, whence I believe it could be brought down the river to the sea, although I do not affirm this, as I have not seen what obstacles there may be.

After we had left the Buena Esperanza river and entered the land of the Cruzado Indians, of the few that we saw there on our return, some gave us information, when we asked them, about all these nations of monstrous peoples. At the province of Moqui, three other Indians of this same nation of the Cruzados who were there gave us the same report, saying that they had heard it from people of their own nation who had come from the sea. Another Indian from a nation called Tacabuy, which is situated at the San Joseph river, gave this report, stating, on being asked, that he knew about it beforehand. Some Indians of the provinces of Moqui and Zuñi, and of many other provinces of New Mexico, when we asked them through the interpreter, on our return, affirmed that they had heard about some of these strange nations long before the Spaniards came to their land. Two Indian chiefs of the Tegua nation declared also that they had heard and seen in the provinces of New Mexico savage Indians whose body, arms, and legs were entirely covered with hair, that they had come from the west, bearing numerous shells like those that we now brought from there. Some soldiers told me that when we were at the Buena Esperanza river they had heard about these savage Indians and that they lived between the Buena Esperanza river and the sea, but as I had not been able to make proper inquiries, and as the Indian chief Otata had not told me about them, I paid no attention to this report.

These are the events of our journey and what we saw and heard from the Indians at the Buena Esperanza river and the seacoast on the trip. May the majesty of our mighty God be pleased with the many hardships that we endured on this expedition, suffering hunger, cold, snow, and a thousand other misfortunes, borne through His divine love and through zeal for the conversion of souls, and that these tribulations may not be lost but be of some value. All this was done to serve His divine majesty, to extend His faith, and to make known to these many people, blind and ignorant of the road to heaven and of salvation, the way, and that the royal crown of the king our lord may be extended and increased.

On our return from the expedition, the governor found among the Indians, on reaching the province of Moqui, which is seventy leagues from the present headquarters of the Spaniards, some stones which seemed to be mineral and which revealed different colors when viewed from different angles. Generally they disclose two different colors, some stones showing it better than others. These colors are garnet red and emerald green, but red seems to be the natural color. The stones in themselves do not appear to be of any value, as they are small, and to all indications are not worth much. Nevertheless, as the mines or mine from which they are obtained might be valuable, some samples were brought along in order that a stone expert might examine them. Not knowing whether they were valuable, the governor did not make an effort to discover them, although a mine was found at a pueblo where the Spaniards now live which seemed to contain these stones. There were found also some grains, or small stones, three of which, the largest ones, were the size of chick peas, and brighter and of more intense color than garnet. They were thought to come from the same mine from which the other stones were obtained, but it could not be ascertained as the Indians would not disclose the fact and the mine was not found. Fray Francisco de Escobar, commissary.

In the city of Mexico, October 25, 1605, Father Fray Francisco de Escobar appeared before his excellency, the Marquis of Montesclaros, viceroy of New Spain, and stated that he gave his excellency this memorial and report, which was shown to him, that the signature which reads, "Fray Francisco de Escobar, commissary," is his, that he wrote it and acknowledges it as his. Further, he swore *in verbo sacerdotis*, placing his hand on his breast, that what he has recorded in this memorial is the truth and is what took place on the expedition, and what he thinks of it, and he signed his name to it. Witnesses, the secretary, Pedro Díaz de Villegas, and Martín de Santa Yusti, residents of this city. Marquis of Montesclaros. Fray Francisco de Escobar. Before me, Martín López de Gauna.

Immediately after this, on the said day, October 25, 1605, his excellency ordered four men to appear before him who gave their names as Captain Francisco Rascón, Captain Juan Velarde Colodro, Alférez Pedro Sánchez Monrroy, and Sergeant Francisco Vido. By order of his excellency, I, the present secretary of government, was instructed to swear in the aforesaid witnesses and to have them identify this memorial and report of the father commissary, Fray Francisco de Escobar. They swore in the name of God, holy Mary, and by the sign of the cross in due legal manner and promised to tell the truth. Having been shown the memorial and report by Father Fray Francisco de Escobar, and his signature, and the whole document having been read to them paragraph by paragraph, they declared that everything contained therein was true, that they knew it to be so, because they had visited those places and regions in company with Don Juan de Oñate, governor of New Mexico, and the father commissary, and that this was the truth under the oath they had taken. They ratified and signed this statement with their names, except Pedro Sánchez Monrroy, who said that he did not know how to write. Marquis of Montesclaros. Francisco Rascón. Juan Velarde. Francisco Vido. Before me, Martín López de Gauna.

Thereupon his excellency asked them how many people they had left at the Spanish headquarters, and each one answered individually that there must have been fifty or fifty-three persons of all ages. Asked how many Indians had been baptized, they replied that since the establishment of the headquarters at the villa called San Gabriel, more than nine years earlier, they believe that five or six hundred persons must have been baptized, including young and old, but they do not know how many of them are still living, although they believe that some of these persons have died. The small number of people baptized is not to be blamed on the Indians, but is due to the fact that the friars are slow in baptizing them because they do not know the language.

Asked whether, on reaching the mouth of the river, or the sea, which they saw to the south, they sounded the mouth of the river to find out how deep it was, they replied that they did not sound it because they did not have the equipment to do so. All they knew was that the mouth seemed fairly deep. A soldier named Juan Ruiz dived into the water and said that it was quite deep.

Asked whether anyone climbed some peak or high hill and scanned the sea in order to learn if land could be sighted anywhere beyond the coast where they were, they replied that it was not done because the land was level.

Asked whether the shells and stones shown them were those that were obtained on the expedition, they replied that they were, and that they identified them as such. They added that the Indians of that province gave them some pieces of metal, which the party brought along back, and that these were the samples shown them. All of this they declared under the oath they had taken, that everything stated was the truth, and they signed it with their names. Marquis of Montescláros. Francisco Rascón. Juan Velarde. Francisco Vido. Before me, Martín López de Gauna.

848. August 24, 1607. Juan de Oñate to the viceroy surrendering his post in New Mexico.

Faced with the gradual attrition of his resources and the failure of any decision to be made on New Mexico, Oñate felt nothing remained but for him to leave New Mexico (where he had now been for nine years) and hope that he might be reinstated on his own terms, or at least that a decision would be made about the future of the colony. The letter is a dignified one and expresses his regret, though not his bitterness, at the lack of support he had had.

A.G.I., Seville, Mexico 27; translated in G. B. Hammond and A. Rey, Oñate, II, 1042–1045, from which it is taken.

The arrival of the friars and the maese de campo with so few people caused such discouragement among those who were at this camp that it required no little ingenuity and effort to maintain them this year, but it has served no good purpose, considering the many good men and abundant succor you promised, and therefore I am awaiting the answer from Spain which your excellency promised in your first letter to me. Although I do not tire of waiting or of enduring the hardships that one encounters here, the soldiers are so worn out by seeing themselves put off for so long with mere hopes that they do not wish nor are they able to wait any longer. Nor do I find myself able to restrain them, for they are as exhausted, hard pressed, and in need of help as I am helpless to furnish it.

Furthermore, the friars do not care to proceed with the baptizing of the natives until they know that the affairs of this land are settled, nor am I sure that they are inclined to remain here, as one may judge from a petition of the father commissary, which I beg your excellency to read. Finding myself helpless in every respect, because I have used up on this expedition my estate and the resources of my relatives and friends, amounting to more than six hundred thousand pesos, and anxious that the fruits of so many expenditures and of more than eleven years of labor should not be lost, and especially because I am eager that our holy Catholic faith should be spread in these lands and that the king our lord should increase his dominions by the addition of great and rich provinces, which, according to our information, are at our threshold, I find no other means to attain all of this than to renounce my office, which resignation I am sending your excellency. I am doing this in order that his majesty, since he has failed to support this undertaking as its importance demands, may appoint for this post a person who may be able to carry on the service I have started. To effect this change it was necessary to reach an agreement with the soldiers in the name of his majesty, whereby they will await an answer from your excellency until the end of June of next year. From that date on, I granted them permission to leave at will. Therefore, I beg your excellency to send word within this short period, since I had to promise them that failure to obtain an answer would permit them to leave, and they will not want to remain a moment beyond that date, nor could I force them to stay. This is in accordance with the opinion of the friars who put this matter upon my conscience. They have fulfilled their obligations for so many years, always with great fidelity and perseverance, without ever receiving any support from his majesty or his ministers. Nor have they ever been encouraged by good words, faring equally in this respect with the soldiers and the governor.

As far as I am concerned, matters have moved in such a way that my feelings have been greatly hurt, in view of the fact that those who fled from this camp have gone entirely unpunished. Through extensive testimonies and falsehoods they tried to justify their treason, and they have remained free and my honor has been placed in doubt by those who do not want to see that my perseverance in this land rests solely on my desire to work for the cause of God and the service of his majesty and not for selfish interests, for what we have thus far discovered is nothing but poverty. Nor have I been moved either by rewards received, for my compensation, or lack of it thus far, has been the occasion for my present feeling. Of course, as the devil is so interested in this matter, he will try by all ways and means to hinder this enterprise, and he has brought things to such a state that, unable to overcome my zeal and good purpose, he has exhausted my resources and I find myself unable to explore any further at a moment when the reports are most promising and encouraging, for last year the reports of riches and greatness in the interior of the land were verified, as your excellency may see by a report which I am enclosing.

Therefore, in order that my limited means should not be a hindrance to the work of baptism and the extension of the royal crown, I decided, for the unburdening of my conscience, to resign my office, which I cannot maintain without more help, assured that in doing this I am rendering a most important service to his majesty. Even if I had not incurred so many expenses and endured so many hardships by my many past services, I trust that his majesty will honor and reward me, even if he should not wish to use me in the prosecution of this undertaking.

I wish to point out that if what has been built here should be destroyed, as will be the case unless your excellency sends succor by the time I have stated, many grave inconveniences will result. This must be given serious consideration, for should his majesty wish to make this expedition later, more than six hundred thousand pesos will not suffice to bring matters to the state in which they now are. If we should all leave the land, it will be necessary to take along more than six hundred Christian Indians. The result of this will be not only that holy baptism will be refused in these lands at all times, but the natives will not even dare to welcome the Spaniards in future years if their children, brothers, and relatives are taken away. They are incapable of understanding the reason for our leaving, no matter how much it is explained to them. This will no doubt give rise to many difficulties and dangers, for, at the time of their removal, the land will rise and take up arms to prevent it. This can be taken for granted, considering the nature of these Indians, for even though they may not be naturally warlike, they would become bold on seeing how few of us are left for this task. Were they not to be taken away but to be left here to revert to idolatry, no lesser difficulty would ensue. It would be less harmful to cease making more Christians than to allow those who have already been converted to be lost.

May your excellency be pleased to weigh prudently the gravity of this affair, keeping in mind the Christian zeal that his majesty feels for the preservation of souls, which is the main object that he urges in these discoveries.

The maese de campo is going back to intercede for this cause. He leaves me comforted and even encouraged to hope for an entirely successful arrangement since it will come from the hands of your excellency, to whom his majesty so wisely entrusted the government of New Spain. In this good fortune, I hope that a solution will be found for a province as important as this one, and I believe that I am providing the necessary remedy by withdrawing and placing this government in the hands of your excellency.

849. July 2, 1608. The Council of the Indies advises Philip III to abandon New Mexico.

The new viceroy, Luis de Velasco, who had held the post earlier, recommended that the New Mexico commitment be abandoned. The Council of the Indies agreed. The decision was endorsed to the effect that the viceroy should be written to on behalf of the king to give effect to this decision.
A.G.I., Seville 22; translated in G. B. Hammond and A. Rey, Oñate, *II, 1061–1064, from which it is taken.*

Since your majesty realizes how unfruitful it would be to continue the discovery and pacification of New Mexico (which was granted under contract to Don Juan de Oñate) because all of that land is of little value, and because the aim of Don Juan and of those who joined him in the enterprise was its prolongation for their private aims, your majesty therefore ordered the Marquis of Montesclaros, by a cedula of June 17, 1606, to halt that discovery as soon as he received the message and not to proceed any farther, to recall Don Juan de Oñate with skill and tact under some plausible pretext, and after his return to detain him in Mexico and disband the people who had taken part in the discovery. After this, he was to appoint a suitable governor, a prudent and Christian man, who should govern the land that had been discovered and try to maintain it in justice and peace, protecting and treating the native Indians well, and furnishing them with friars to teach them. And if any of the friars, moved by Christian zeal, should want to go inland to preach, he should allow them to do so in order to obtain greater fruits and in this way to obtain reliable information of provinces not yet discovered, but without the use of arms.

Now Don Luis de Velasco writes to your majesty in a letter of March 7 of this year saying that before the Marquis of Montesclaros left for Peru he learned from him of the situation of the discovery of New Mexico, and also from the above cedula. Moreover, at this time there arrived in Mexico a Franciscan friar, Fray Lázaro Ximénez, who had been sent by his order, by Governor Don Juan de Oñate, and by the residents and soldiers there to ask the viceroy in the name of all for permission to leave the land or that they be provided with adequate support, both of soldiers and provisions, to enable them to remain there. And as it seemed to the viceroy that this friar was an intelligent person, well acquainted with the nature of the land, the spirit and aims of the friars and the Spaniards, and even of the natives, the viceroy questioned him at length and learned of the small number of souls that had been saved thus far and the meager hopes for the future since not only had the natives shown little inclination for the law of the gospel but the friars had no more desire to learn the numerous languages that were used among so few people; he learned also of the difficulty or even impossibility of maintaining any expansion and the great cost it would require because of the poor quality and poverty of the land, its great distance from Mexico (from which supplies would have to come)—it must be some six hundred leagues to the interior of the land, without any gold or silver mines or anything else to attract Spanish settlers.

Furthermore, if the colony should be maintained it would be difficult and expensive to support it because of the enormous distance and because the reinforcements must come through hostile territory and at definite seasons, for the road cannot be traveled at all times. The soldiers who remain to protect the friars and defend the friendly Indians would not cost less than from four hundred and fifty to five hundred pesos each per year, and even then would not remain voluntarily owing to the poverty of the land and the little promise it holds for those who settle there permanently.

In view of these and many other reasons, it seemed to the viceroy and to some of the judges of the audiencia with whom he discussed the matter in a special meeting that the New Mexico expedition should be abandoned and that the Indians who had been baptized, who would not number more than four hundred, be removed from the land. This number is very meager, indeed, for ten or eleven years of labor and expense. This action will put an end to the great costs to the royal treasury, both now and later, costs which will always increase.

The judges, however, could not decide on what to do until his majesty had been notified of the whole matter, but in the meantime they urged the acceptance of Don Juan de Oñate's resignation of his post, since he had not been sent any aid. The viceroy thus decided to appoint someone to replace him, which he did, a suitable person to take charge of the undertaking, and he ordered Don Juan not to leave New Mexico until he received further instructions. Fearing that the governor, friars, and soldiers would abandon the colony without any permission or authorization (because they had so little attachment for the land), with great danger to the newly baptized and to their own lives, the viceroy promised them that by the end of December, 1609, or sooner if possible, he would send them his majesty's decision as to what they should do, and, failing in this, they could abandon the land, removing the church and the Christians to safe and peaceful territory. Don Luis de Velasco begs your majesty to have this decision forwarded without delay.

After studying the matter in the Council with the consideration that it demands, it was agreed that an answer should be sent to the viceroy to the effect that inasmuch as he has this affair before him and is acquainted with the situation in the land, he should stop the expedition and discovery; and in case the settlement is to be completely abandoned, he should discuss the ways and means with learned and conscientious persons, including jurists from the audiencia and the University of Mexico and theologians from the university and the religious orders, consulting with them regarding the justification for taking this step with respect to the Indians there who have embraced the faith. These advisers should consider whether it would be better to leave the Christian Indians in the land, if some friars and laymen should be willing to remain among them voluntarily to preserve them in their new faith, but if volunteers are not found and the natives are to be removed, they should be given every facility and lands from the crown on which they might settle, and they should be exempt from payment of tribute for twenty years.

In case there are neither friars nor laymen who will remain voluntarily in the land, and the Indians refuse to leave of their own accord, but will have to be taken out by force, the viceroy should consult with the said persons as to whether it would be better to leave the natives in their land, the Spaniards urging them when they leave to live and die in the faith that they have embraced, or whether it would be more desirable to take them away even if by force so that they would not run the risk of losing their faith. This business is left in the viceroy's hands in order that after he has studied it and conferred with the said persons, he may do what he considers best for the service of God and your majesty. Finally, let him inform us of the measures he takes. Madrid, July 2, 1608.

[Endorsed by or for Philip III:] Write in accordance with the opinion and urge the viceroy to relieve and satisfy the royal conscience in whatever he does.

850. January 29, 1609. The viceroy, Luis de Velasco, decides that New Mexico should be retained.

In the end the viceroy was left to decide. The pressure on him from the friars not to abandon their alleged 7,000 converts proved decisive, and he went back to an earlier instruction that permitted him to maintain the colony for missionary purposes. This decision was to be final and Peralta was shortly to be dispatched with his fifty soldiers to begin the permanent occupation of the province.

A.G.I., Seville, Mexico 27; translated in G. B. Hammond and A. Rey, Oñate, II, 1076–1077, from which this is taken.

In the city of Mexico, January 29, 1609, his excellency, Don Luis de Velasco, knight of the order of Santiago, viceroy, . . . having consulted with Licentiates Don Pedro de Otalora, Diego Núñez Morquecho, and Doctor Juan Quesada de Figueroa, judges of this royal audiencia, about matters in connection with the expedition to New Mexico, and having examined the letters, reports, and accounts brought recently from there by Fray Isidro Ordóñez, of the order of Saint Francis, Captain Gerónimo Márquez, and Juan Gutiérrez Bocanegra, its procurator general, these judges decided that in consideration of the present state of affairs in that land and of the people there who have been converted to the faith, and in keeping with his majesty's royal cedula dated at Madrid on June 17, 1606, providing that the settlement there must be maintained in its present state without undertaking any further expeditions until his majesty has been informed and he has ordered what should be done for the preservation and expansion of the land and for the protection of the friars that may engage in the conversion of the natives and the preservation of those already converted, there should be a governor and fifty settlers, equipped with the necessary arms for defense, each one of whom should be compensated in accordance with his quality and services; that the Indians who may be allotted in accordance with the instructions which the governor has for this purpose should be assigned without injury to those given in encomienda by Governor Don Juan de Oñate by virtue of his contract; and since, according to the information available about the settlers in that land, who number about sixty persons, only thirty are capable of bearing arms, the judges decided, in order that the number of fifty soldiers may be complete, to recruit twelve soldiers, two more or less, as his excellency may determine, with the usual salary, paid for one year.

Further, they decided to furnish the necessary arms to equip ten additional soldiers, chosen from among the residents most suitable for the purpose, all at the expense of the royal treasury. And, in order to carry out the royal cedula for the conversion and preservation of the natives, six friar-priests and two lay brothers should be chosen, and they should be equipped with everything necessary for the trip at the expense of the royal treasury. As for decisions in other urgent matters, it is left to his excellency to take whatever measures he deems suitable, as the occasion demands. They so ordered and decreed. Don Luis de Velasco. Licentiate Don Pedro de Otalora. Licentiate Diego Núñez Morquecho. Doctor Juan Quesada de Figueroa.

851. [*Circa 1612–1615*]. Gaspar de Villagra gives details of his services.

Among the rarities in the John Carter Brown Library are two pamphlets, without printer or place of publication, which evidently formed part of the campaign of Gaspar de Villagra (circa 1612–1615) to get some recognition at Court of his services in the Oñate venture (on which it throws some light) and elsewhere. A translation has been made of part of one of them, El Capitan Gaspar de Villagra para justificacion de las muertes, justicas, y castigos que el Adelantado don Juan de Oñate dizen que hizo en la Nueva Mexico. *Whether his method was original, or whether Philip III took any notice of it, does not appear to be known.*

Services done for His Majesty by Captain Gaspar de Villagra, so that Your Majesty should reward him.

Firstly he states that, by a commission of the 23rd July of the year '96, when Don Juan de Oñate, Governor, Adelantado and Captain General of New Mexico, was about to undertake his journey inland, at the request of the whole armed forces they named the said Captain Villagra as Procurator General of the Army, since he was an able and suitable person, respected and trusted, charging him six thousand ducats for accepting it: and he accepted it, having spent a great deal of money in leading and raising his company, as he honourably admits, and the General says. As well as this he also graciously served His Majesty with six coats of mail, six armoured thigh-plates, and six visors, six arquebuses with six covers, and six large and small water containers, some of the arquebuses being engraved and gilded, and six decorated leather jackets, some with gold stripes, and in addition six imitation leather hides of buckskin, for six sets of horses' armour, breasts, sides and heads, six mules, harnessed, and a saddle with a bridle, six warhorses, which was all shared out among soldiers who needed it, who went to serve His Majesty.

Also on the 23rd July of the year [15]96 the General named him as Captain of the men who were going on the second expedition, giving an account of how he had served His Majesty on many occasions before that year of [15]96, both in peace and war, with his arms and horse at his own expense and suggestion.

He was also twice appointed as Comissar of these forces, to go out and collect men who had been scattered, in peace and war, and punish rebels after the manner of war.

Also Friar Alonso Martínez, Comissar, and Apostolic Delegate of the provinces of New Mexico named him as his colleague and advisory judge, and assistant in running the church, saying in this commission a clause as follows: 'In view and consideration of the many talents and merits combined in your person, Christianity, prudence, fear of God, abhorrence of greed, knowledge, experience, bravery, age, white hair, etc.'

Also the same general appointed him as one of his council of war in this army.

And by his appointment he was also appointed as agent of the Royal Exchequer for the first treasury to be appointed in this Kingdom.

He was also appointed by this general as Captain and leader of all the civilians and soldiers of this army, who came to ask for help the first time, in whose instructions there appears a clause as follows: 'And since Captain and Procurator General Gaspar de Villagra is well deserving, and one of those who has best served His Majesty on this expedition, as he was in its preparation. He served the King Our Lord on many journeys he made, going from the Valley of St Bartholomew and the mines of Casco, to the cities of Mexico, Zacatecas, and many other different places, with the greatest efficiency and care, journeying by night and day, with the result that His Majesty's Army set out sooner than it would have done without his efficiency and care; also on the journey he made for the Franciscans, he took them and together they reached the camp at the river of St Peter, escorting them on several occasions. He also brought help to the Sergeant Major and twelve soldiers that he had taken to find the Río del Norte, who had only had roots to eat for several days: he found them in such a state that if he had not found them that day they were in great danger of their lives. On another journey that he undertook with the same Sergeant Major to discover a way by which the wagons and the whole Royal road could pass, he went through mountain ranges and banks of sand, and eventually, with his great efficiency, they discovered a way where

it was possible to pass through quite easily. And he also crossed this Río del Norte many times by swimming, looking for a good place where the army and the wagons could pass, in several places, and sometimes he did this at great risk to himself, since this river is very full. At this river, and in all its surrounding areas and mountains, when he was there with this Sergeant Major and only four others, a large number of native Indians came down in peace, those who live there, with the result that since then they have been peaceful and it is safe to travel along this road. Also on the journey he made with me to the settlements and provinces where they gave their allegiance, and more than sixty thousand people with their houses came under the Royal Crown, he explained to them how it was to their advantage to give this allegiance and vassalage. Also on the journey he made with the same Sergeant Major and fourteen companions looking for salt mines, and such was their skill that they found them, as large and productive as there are in all Christendom, of white salt with a good savour and taste. And going on one journey which he did under my commission in pursuit of five soldiers who had run away from this camp, he went after them with four others, travelling night and day for just under two hundred leagues: he caught two of them and had them executed, in accordance with my orders; and finding himself without provisions, and near to the mines of Todos Santos, he went there: from there he wrote to the Viceroy of New Spain about what had happened there and the journey: he did this in sixteen days, travelling among a large number of native Indians, and he gave then what he was carrying, even the clothes he wore, which left them contented and peaceful. And on the way back from this expedition, after going into the settlements, he received the news that I was travelling away from the camp, and very distant, procuring the allegiance of certain provinces to His Majesty, and to tell me what he had done, he came after me alone. He came to the fortified town of Acoma, saw that the Indians did not receive him favourably, and gave him no provisions; on his way from there he came to a large hole, which these Indians had already made, covered and disguised, so that the Spaniards should fall in it, and they should kill them, and he fell into it on his horse: this horse died there, and he got out of it with great difficulty, and continued his journey for four more days on foot, without food or drink; he escaped with his life because of a clever trick, by turning his shoes back to front: after four days, being almost on the point of death from hunger, thirst and tiredness, he was found by some soldiers who were off in search of horses, having carried as usual all the arms on his person, night and day, even though he was in a very bad state, as soldiers should. And he journeyed on land in the course of a year over one thousand five hundred leagues, eight hundred of them through lands at war, and in winter weather, with snow and rain, frost, hunger and hardship: in all of which he has done great service to His Majesty, and greatly helped everyone in the Royal camp. And most recently in the expedition to conquer the town and fortress of Acoma, where he was found as a valiant Captain in the forefront of the battle, fighting, encouraging the soldiers, and giving help in the places where it was most necessary, with the result of achieving one of the most one-sided and successful battles there has been, because seventy Spaniards conquered, killed and captured more than one thousand five hundred people, when the enemy had such a great advantage in their position, in the fort where they were. For all these reasons I choose, name and appoint him as Captain and Leader of all men of peace and war, etc.'

This account of his services is confirmed by Juan Guerra de Resa, Lieutenant to the Governor and Captain General, saying in one clause: 'Since the said Captain Gaspar de Villagra, in addition to the services which he has done to His Majesty, has also done others here in New Spain, among which one was very important: a number of Guachichil Indians had installed themselves in the Mountain Range in this kingdom that they call Hermosillo, and they used to come out from there to raid the Royal Silver Road that leads from the mines of Sombrerete to the city of Zacatecas and Mexico: here they killed a number of Spaniards and Indians, and as a result the road was closed, because it was only possible to go along it with great risk to life. I had some Indian spies, to give warning if these Guachichil Indians were setting off for the road, and at two in the afternoon one day these Indian spies came and said that these Indians were carrying a large quantity of stolen clothes, mules and horses; and the Captain set off with them at my orders, and wounded and killed a number of these Indians, with the result that the land became peaceful and that the Indians still have not returned to this road; etc.'

Also the Count of Monterrey, who was Viceroy of New Spain appointed him as captain of the horses, mentioning and approving in his order all the services and duties mentioned above without exception, with great distinction and clarity.

Also the Council, Magistrates and Councillors, and the whole army of New Mexico, appointed him for a second time Procurator of the Kingdom, honouring him in writing, and with the power entrusted to him in words and assurances of their great respect.

Also the same General declared that this Captain had complied with all his obligations, and that since this was the case he ought to enjoy all the privileges of a knight hidalgo. Speaking of this Captain Villagra, there is a clause as follows: 'In consideration of how often and how well you have served the King our Lord, and the shining virtues of your mind, and the rewards they deserve, your well-known good habits, the integrity of your life, your wide experience, your good judgement, hard work and skill, your experience and knowledge of warfare, all of which I know to be gifts of yours, being certain of them from having seen and noticed them on many occasions, both in peace and in war.'

Also in the deposition of the Commander Vicente de Zaldibar, there appears a clause as follows (speaking of this Captain Villagra): 'He has always been esteemed and respected in the Army by the Governor Don Juan de Oñate, and as such was always at his table and at mine; and since I had come to know him well, both in peace and war, I always took him in my company and had him sleep in my tent, taking him as my companion and comrade. And since this Captain was such a person, after serving His Majesty very well on the first expedition, he came for help from New Mexico to New Spain, and took inland to Santa Barbara one of the most distinguished companies that has assembled in Peru or New Spain, being composed entirely of Captains and officers who arranged it themselves and asked this Captain Gaspar de Villagra to enlist them under his standard and give orders to them as their Captain, since they were completely satisfied in him: and I also saw with my own eyes how in matters of work, in suffering hunger, thirst and hardship, in risking his life, in bringing help to soldiers, and to myself when I was suffering hunger, in loyalty, in calming and resolving arguments among soldiers, in being generally respected and courteous, and in times of war and battles where his hands were very much needed, there was noone in the army who was superior to him: and because of the many good services he has given, he now serves His Majesty at his own cost and suggestion both in these and in other matters of great importance, and money which he has spent from the start of this expedition (which is getting on for seven years), in which time his house has always been a resting place and refuge for soldiers, Captains and officers who have been his guests there, and he has offered them his table with great generosity and openness, etc.'

Also in the deposition of Don Cristóbal de Oñate, Lieutenant to the General, there appears a clause as follows: 'I certify that Captain Gaspar de Villagra has served His Majesty at his own cost and suggestion, without having received in approximately thirteen years any help in expenses, assistance or perks, neither from His Majesty nor from the Governor Don Juan de Oñate my brother, as have been given to many other Captains, officers and soldiers; but in addition to this he gave a loan of seven thousand five hundred pesos, at eight reales per peso, for the preparation of this expedition, etc.'

Also in the deposition of Don Rodrigo de Vivero, Governor and Captain General of the kingdom of Vizcaya, there appears a clause as follows: 'I certify that Captain Gaspar de Villagra served His Majesty in this reign as chief magistrate, and captain of the men of Tepeguana: I gave him this post because of the trust I placed in him,

being the most important post in that kingdom; since many years back His Majesty spent a lot of money there on clothes-stores and soldiers' garrisons that were there because that is where the frontier was, and which was incurring expense, according to the reports that came to the Count of Monterrey, Viceroy here of New Spain, until at my orders this Captain Gaspar de Villagra went to serve in this garrison, and after a few days (being a good captain) he told the truth to the Viceroy and to me, that these expenses on the stores and garrisons were unnecessary: so we were relieved of all the expense and cost incurred on these stores and soldiers, and the area stayed and still stays peaceful. For this, and the good period of office he served as chief magistrate, this captain deserves that His Majesty should be pleased with him and reward him in matters of importance; etc.'

All the above is confirmed in provisions, depositions, warrants and instructions, which have been presented to this Captain Villagra by his Generals, Commanders, the Audiencia of Guadalajara and the Viceroy of New Spain.

Therefore he begs Your Majesty that in respect of Your justice you consider just two things: firstly, that these services have been carried out at his own expense and suggestion, and that the expenses he has incurred must be many thousand ducats, in duties that are exceptionally difficult and dangerous; and secondly, that you should realize that it is one thing to read about these hardships, and quite another to have suffered and endured them for so many years.

There is official information, and the view of the Royal Audiencia of Guadalajara, which recounts and confirms all these services.

NOTES ON THE MAPS

128. 1597. Cornelis Wytfliet's Map of Florida and Apalache.

The map of Florida and Apalache which Cornelis Wytfliet included in his *Descriptionis Ptolemaicae augmentum* (Louvain, 1597) was based ultimately on Spanish sources, but was modelled on one published by Ortelius in 1584 (W. P. Cumming, *The Southeast in Early Maps* [Princeton, 1958], Plate 9). It would not have proved at all informative on the progress of the Spanish colony in Florida since 1565. The Mississippi appears as R. de S. Spirito, but the river system associated with it is almost wholly imaginary.

129. 1597. Cornelis Wytfliet's Map of New France and Canada.

In his map of New France and Canada, Cornelis Wytfliet, *Descriptionis Ptolemaicae augmentum* (Louvain, 1597), incorporated much of the material deriving from the Cartier-Roberval voyages of 1534–1543, but little else except some changes of nomenclature. Basically, he uses the Mercator world map of 1569. His depiction of Newfoundland as an archipelago was by this time considerably out of date, since most maps of the 1580s were showing it as a single island, or at most two. The exaggeration of the Saguenay River, not named as such, would continue to arouse interest in this region, to which French and Spanish Basque ships were going each year for furs. The Ottawa River is also exaggerated, and the St. Lawrence River continued its course unchecked by falls to the southern limit of the map.

130. 1597. Cornelis Wytfliet's Map of Labrador, Davis Strait, and Greenland.

The map of Labrador, Davis Strait, and Greenland by Cornelis Wytfliet, *Descriptionis Ptolemaicae augmentum* (Louvain, 1597), is based mainly on that of Mercator in his world map of 1569, which in turn incorporated much of the mythical material in the Zeno map of 1558. But, largely from English sources, those of the Frobisher and Davis voyages of the years 1576 to 1587, he is able to assimilate much of the material on Greenland, Baffin Island, and Labrador produced by these voyages. Here he makes a valuable attempt at a synthesis of what was known or surmised at the time he made his map. One of the more valuable aspects of it is that it does not make any specific claim that a Northwest Passage had been discovered, though the open sea shown north of Davis Strait (now so named) would point to the probability of an open passage northwards over the Pole.

131. 1597. Cornelis Wytfliet's Map of the East Coast of North America.

In his map of the East Coast from Cape Fear to Cape Breton, Cornelis Wytfliet, *Descriptionis Ptolemaicae augmentum* (Louvain, 1597), uses the map of the Cape Fear-Chesapeake segment of the East Coast published by Theodor de Bry, *America*, part i (Frankfurt-am-Main, 1590), after John White. But he conflates it with a totally distorted impression of the Spanish profile, standard since the expedition of Estevão Gomes in 1525, of the area farther north. What was our Cape Cod on the Spanish profile now becomes Cape Henry, and the latter is placed at 42° N., six degrees too high, and, indeed, in a higher latitude than Cape Cod itself. The White map (which covers approximately 34° to 37° N.) is made to extend from 37° to 43°. The whole of the coast of Norumberga is thus distorted: the area between the Chesapeake and "R. grande" (the Penobscot) being foreshortened, and the shore from the Penobscot to Cape Breton vastly extended. It is a characteristic example of bad cartography by a professional engraver who knew little of the territory with which he was concerned, but drew incorrectly from what were sometimes quite good authorities.

132. 1597. Cornelis Wytfliet's Map of Anian and Quivira.

The map of the Kingdom of Anian and of the Kingdom of Quivira given by Cornelis Wytfliet, *Descriptionis Ptolemaicae augmentum* (Louvain, 1597), is entirely imaginary. As the only exploration of the West Coast which had carried Spanish ships any substantial distance northward went back to the early 1540s, mapmakers had to base their maps on myth, together with garbled accounts of the inland explorations of Coronado long before. Wytfliet is not much worse than his many predecessors in this field of fancy. According to R. A. Skelton, in his introduction to the facsimile in *Theatrum Orbis Terrarum*, series 1, vol. V (Amsterdam, 1964), p. VIII, he followed Mercator's world map of 1569, as revised by Petrus Plancius's printed world map of 1592.

133. 1597. Cornelis Wytfliet's Map of New Granada and California.

The map of New Granada and California, which Cornelis Wytfliet printed in his *Descriptionis Ptolomaicae augmentum* (Louvain, 1597), included in the former province the country of The Seven Cities, as well as the whole of the territory bordering the Gulf of California on the east. The peninsula of California is shown in a somewhat exaggerated form, largely derived from Mercator's world map of 1569. According to R. A. Skelton, in the facsimile in *Theatrum Orbis Terrarum* series 1, vol V (Amsterdam, 1964), p. VIII, he also used part of the nomenclature of the 1564 map by Ortelius.

134. 1597. Cornelis Wytfliet's Map of Conibas.
In his map of the mythical region of Conibas, Cornelis Wytfliet, *Descriptionis Ptolemaicae augmentum* (Louvain, 1597), made the first separate map of north-central North America. He thus tries to show how the discoveries of the Spaniards in the West and South link up with those of the French in the East and North. His map is made up almost wholly from elements in Mercator's printed world map of 1569, together with interpretations of the published account of the expedition of Antonio de Espejo, 1583, though his New Mexico is not specifically included in the map.

135. 1597. Cornelis Wytfliet's Map of New Spain.
In his map of New Spain, Cornelis Wytfliet, *Descriptionis Ptolomaicae augmentum* (Louvain, 1597), included a substantial part of the Gulf of Mexico and part of what he styled Florida, north of the R. de Palmas, but absurdly placed S. Juan de Ulua to the north of Pánuco, as well as S. Jan de Liza south of Vera Cruz. There is no indication of the mouth of the Mississippi.

136. 1608. Robert Tindall's Chart of the Lower Chesapeake Area.
London, British Library, Cotton MS, Augustus I. ii. 66.
Robert Tindall's chart (oriented to the south) is the earliest map to survive from the Jamestown colony. It shows the entrance to Chesapeake Bay and then details the course both of the James and the York rivers, so far as they were known at the time of compilation. Tindall was able to make use of Newport's exploration of the James River in 1607 and 1608 (and includes the Chickahominy) and of the first stage of John Smith's exploration, covering the York, as well as the Pamunkey and Mattaponi Rivers into which it divides. Considerable detail is given of shoals in the bay and rivers, and the location of Jamestown on its peninsula is accurately set out, while a number of Indian villages are precisely indicated. Tindall was a gunner by profession and apparently sent this chart to Prince Henry who was his patron.

137. 1608. English Map of Virginia Sent to Spain by Pedro de Zúñiga.
Archivo General de Simancas, M.P.D. IV-66, XIX-163. Courtesy of New York Public Library.
This map, obtained in London by the Spanish ambassador, Pedro de Zúñiga, and sent to Philip III, has been fully described and reproduced by Philip Barbour, *The Jamestown Voyages*, I, 238–240. It is the work, or is based on the work, of John Smith in Virginia, down to at least June, 1608. It contains the names of 66 villages in the regions he explored by June 2, with much additional information and notes. Its size and the difficulty of accurate reproduction make Dr. Barbour's description essential.

138. 1608. The Kraus Virginia Map.
Austin Humanities Research Center Library, University of Texas (first published in H. P. Kraus, *Acta Cartographica*, catalogue 28, page 43 [pl. p. 45]).
This crude map was unknown until 1970, but there is no need to doubt its authenticity. It postdates Smith's surveys in 1608 but need not be later than late 1608 or early 1609. One object was to indicate the disposition of Indian villages on the rivers by crude half-circles. Only "Werowamacomaco," Powhatan's seat until late 1608 or early 1609, is named, the first villages of the Monacan Indians up the James River being characterized as "Mónacon enemyis to powaton." Cape Henry is named and to the south of it, rivers, with Indian sites in what Smith was later to call "Old Virginia," are given, but little can be made of them in detail (Smith's emissaries had been in this area in 1608). The final objective was to indicate a range of mountains to the west of the rivers running into the Chesapeake and to suggest that they acted as a watershed for further rivers flowing (?) to the Pacific, which was to be a long-held illusion of Virginia promoters. This rough sketch, therefore, is the record of an attempt to make sense of the area within reach of Jamestown in terms of rivers and of Indian occupation. In most respects Smith's own map, published in 1612, was infinitely more effective, even if, topographically, it did not range so far afield.

139. 1610. English Chart of the North Atlantic ("The Virginia Company Chart"), Including North America.
New York Public Library, I. N. Phelps Stokes Collection.
This chart gives a good impression of the state of knowledge in England of the North Atlantic about 1610. I. N. Phelps Stokes, into whose possession this chart came, labelled it "The Virginia Company Chart, 1606–

1610." It has no known connection with the Virginia Company, though it could have been useful to its directors in planning expeditions to either North or South Virginia. The chart contains a reasonable amount of information, rather formally displayed, on the English delineation of "North Virginia" between 1602 and 1608, and some rather generalized information on "South Virginia," giving a non-specific picture of Chesapeake Bay. Its most striking feature is the depiction of the Hudson River, and this means that it cannot be earlier than the end of 1609 and is most probably 1610 or even a little later. It has no information whatever from the Champlain voyages of 1603–1607. It is very much in the style of the early professional cartographers of the Thames School, and represents for North America the kind of information which a reasonably well-informed cartographer, in touch with members of the Virginia Company and possibly with Hudson himself, could have acquired. It shows nothing of the sophisticated expertise of the Velasco map.

140. 1610 or 1611. English Map of Eastern North America Sent to Spain by Pedro de Velasco.
Archivo General de Simancas, M.P.y.D. I-1 Estado 2588-25. See also Vol. V, Plates 108 and 111.
This is the most valuable single cartographic record we have of the English, French, and Dutch discoveries of the period from 1602 to 1609. It was made in England by an unknown cartographer who was capable of very high quality work. How he obtained his information is unknown. He assimilates in it information about Virginia from 1607 to 1609, based on John Smith's still unpublished map. He has knowledge of Henry Hudson's discovery of the Hudson River in 1609. He has collected information on lost English maps and charts of the New England area for 1602–1608 and has had access to unpublished material of Champlain's for the New England-Acadia coast for 1604–1607, and also of Champlain's activities on the St. Lawrence River, 1608–1609. It deserves much further study. It was sent by Alonso de Velasco to Philip III on March 22, 1611. No copy has so far been found in English sources. The note on it in Cumming, Skelton and Quinn, *The Discovery of North America* (1971), p. 264, is of value as also is its treatment by Philip L. Barbour, *The Jamestown Voyages*, II (1969), 336.

141. 1612. John Smith's Map of Virginia.
John Smith, *A Map of Virginia* (Oxford, 1612).
This is the baseline map for all the studies of Virginia. Smith's explorations, the limits of which are marked by Maltese crosses, and the additional information on the interior he obtained from the Indians was a great tribute to his energy and his accuracy so far as the river banks were concerned. He is less happy in his depiction of the Chesapeake Bay itself and of the Eastern Shore, as he remained ignorant of its outer coast.

142. 1624. Map from John Smith's *Generall historie of Virginia* (London, 1624), Showing "Old Virginia" (Ralegh's Virginia).
While he was in Virginia from 1607 to 1609, John Smith made various attempts to have the area affected by the Roanoke Voyages of 1584–1590 re-explored and to find some traces of the Lost Colony of 1587. He obtained some data on the country but never visited it himself. In 1624, on the strength of the maps of the earlier period, he renamed many of the islands and provided new and old adventurers with records of their activities or investments. He retained a number of the 1590 Indian village names (which may not then have borne any relation to their location in 1624). He embellished the map with scenes of his adventures between 1607–1609 in Virginia itself, which had only a few touches of authenticity.

143. 1566. Zaltieri's Map of North America, Showing the Western "Strait of Anian."
London, Map Library, British Library. Published by Bolognino Zaltieri, Venice, 1566.
This gives a good idea of the general impression cartographers had of North America in this period. It is important for showing (for the first time so far as is known) a strait, "The Strait of Anian," between western America and Asia. See Cumming, Skelton and Quinn, *Discovery of North America* (1971), p. 103.

144. 1592. North America in Christian Sgrooten's Map Showing an Exaggerated California.
Madrid, Biblioteca Nacional. fol. 2 (B. 1); manuscript atlas of 1592.
This portion of a world map indicates how the concept of an enormous California peninsula and of a wide Strait of Anian developed in the later sixteenth century.

145. *Circa* 1612. English Manuscript World Chart, Showing the Eastern and Western Sides of North America.
Collection of the Duke of Northumberland, Alnwick Castle, Northumberland.
This chart shows some knowledge of post-1606 discoveries in Virginia and also indicates the Hudson (which runs through to the St. Lawrence). It represents the type of information which would be available to

professional map and chartmakers of the Thames School of about this period. Its depiction of western North America shows some originality, and the presence of the name "New Albion" indicates continued English interest in that region.

146. 1625. Henry Brigg's Conception of California as an Island.

Map by Henry Briggs in Samuel Purchas, *Pilgrimes* (London, 1625).

The gradual exaggeration of the California peninsula by the late sixteenth-century cartographers led in the end to its detachment as an island. This map is later than our period but gives a good representation of this myth which developed after some reports of the Vizcaino expedition of 1602 suggested that this might be so.

147. 1611. World Map by Jodocus Hondius.

Map of the World by Jodocus Hondius, 1611, ed. E. L. Stevenson (New York, 1907). Courtesy of Library of Congress, Division of Geography and Maps.

This large, folding, printed map of the world in two hemispheres by Jodocus Hondius, *Novissima ac exactissima totius Orbis Terrarum descriptio* (Amsterdam, 1611) gives a good impression of the Americas and their place on the world map at the end of the period covered by this collection.

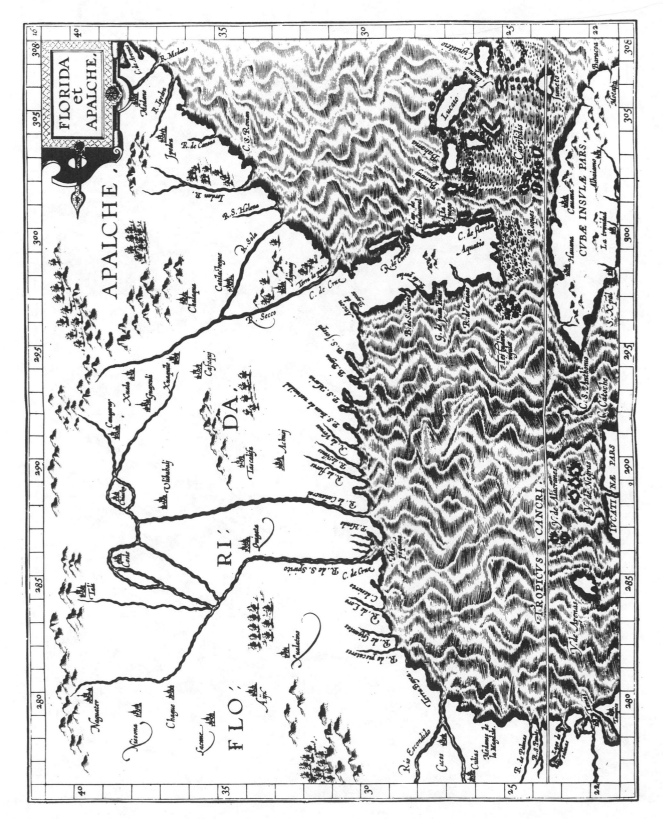

128. 1597. Cornelis Wytfliet's Map of Florida and Apalache.

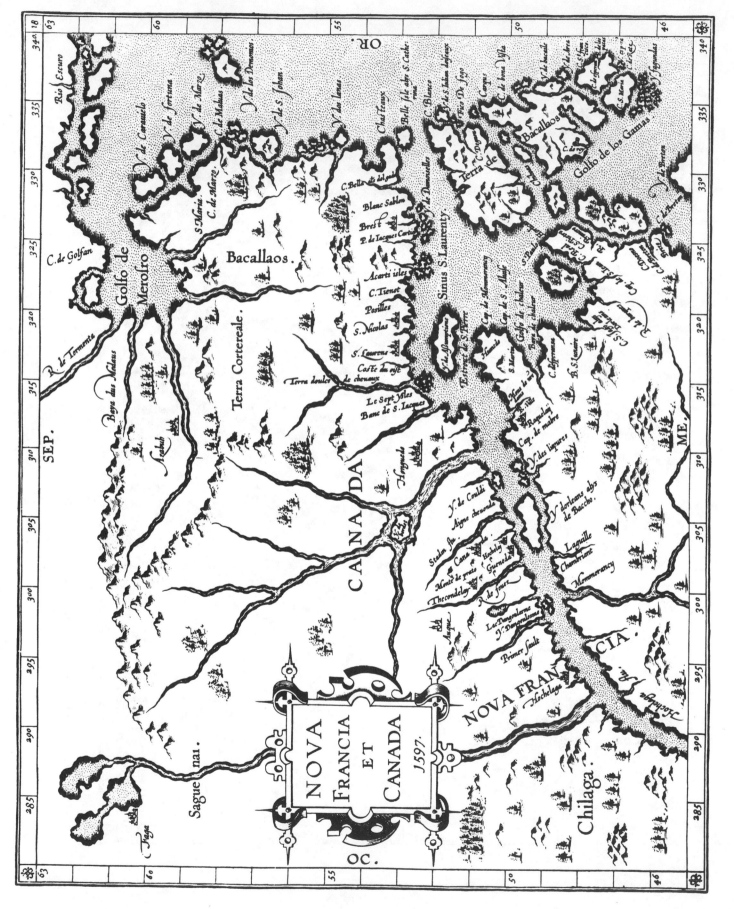

129. 1597. Cornelis Wytfliet's Map of New France and Canada.

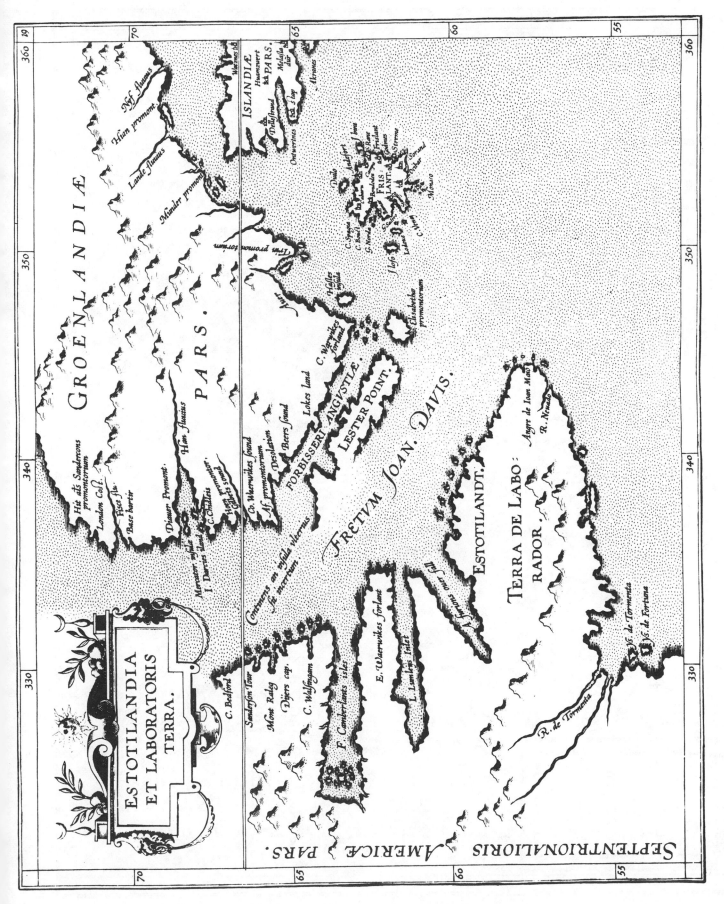

130. 1597. Cornelis Wytfliet's Map of Labrador, Davis Strait, and Greenland.

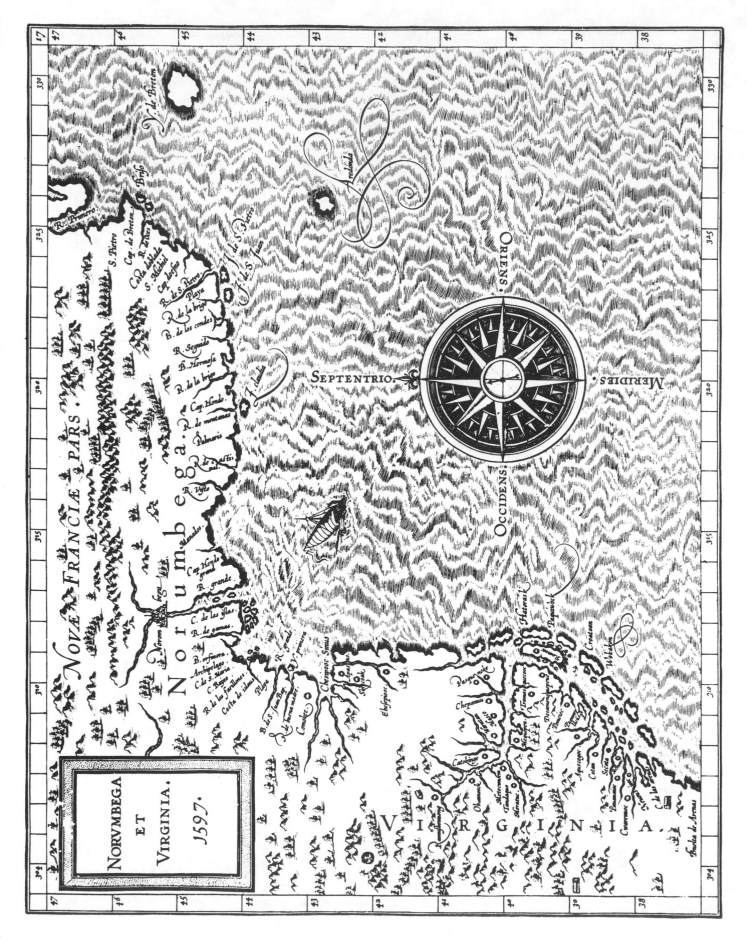

131. 1597. Cornelis Wytfliet's Map of the East Coast of North America.

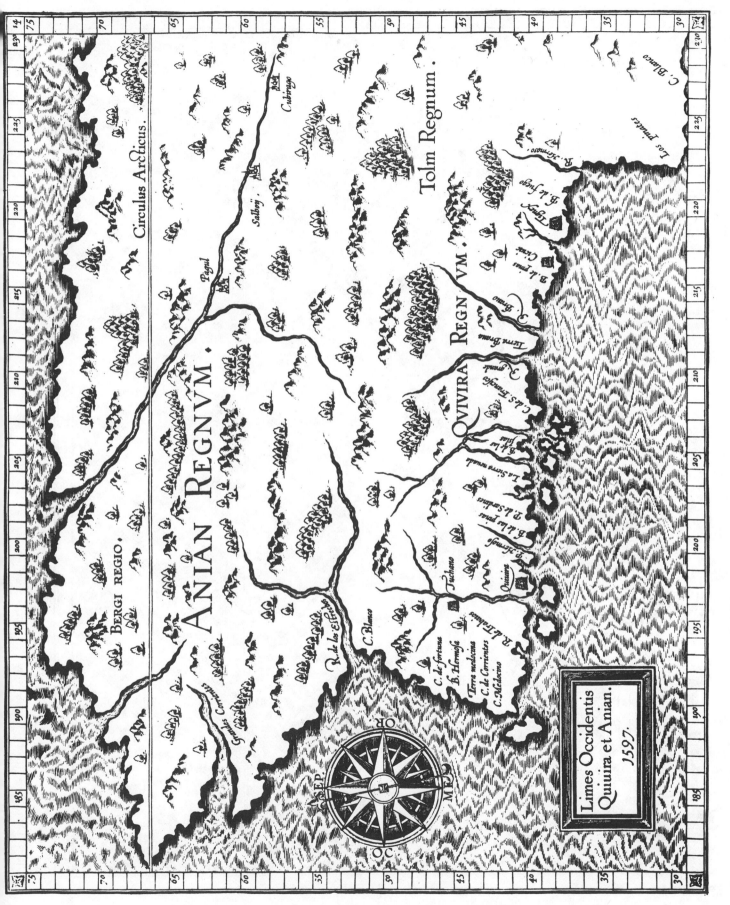

132. 1597. Cornelis Wytfliet's Map of Anian and Quivira.

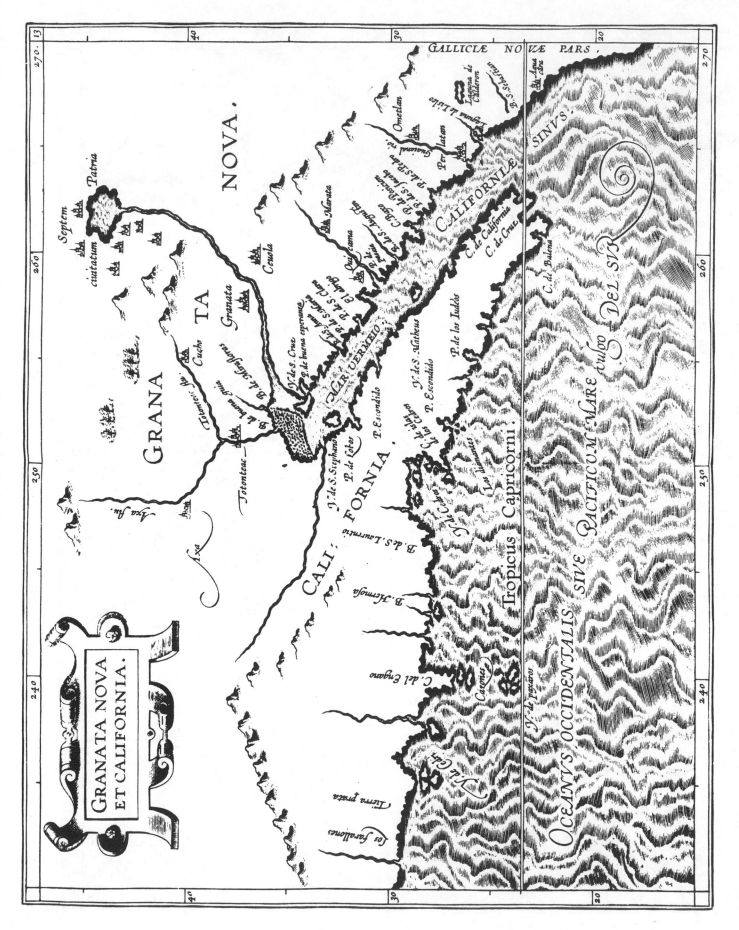

133. 1597. Cornelis Wytfliet's Map of New Granada and California.

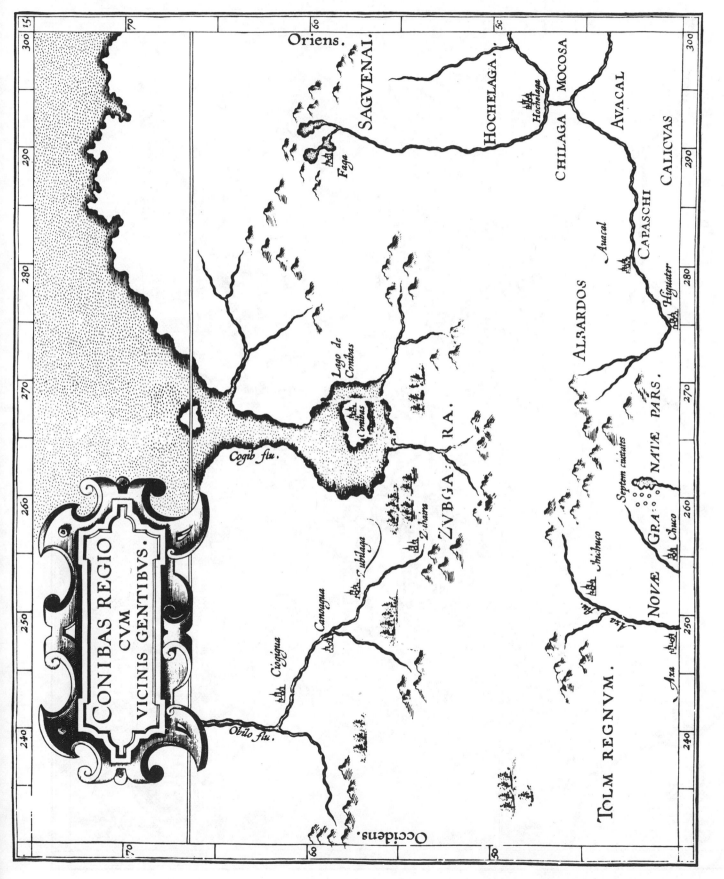

134. 1597. Cornelis Wytfliet's Map of Conibas.

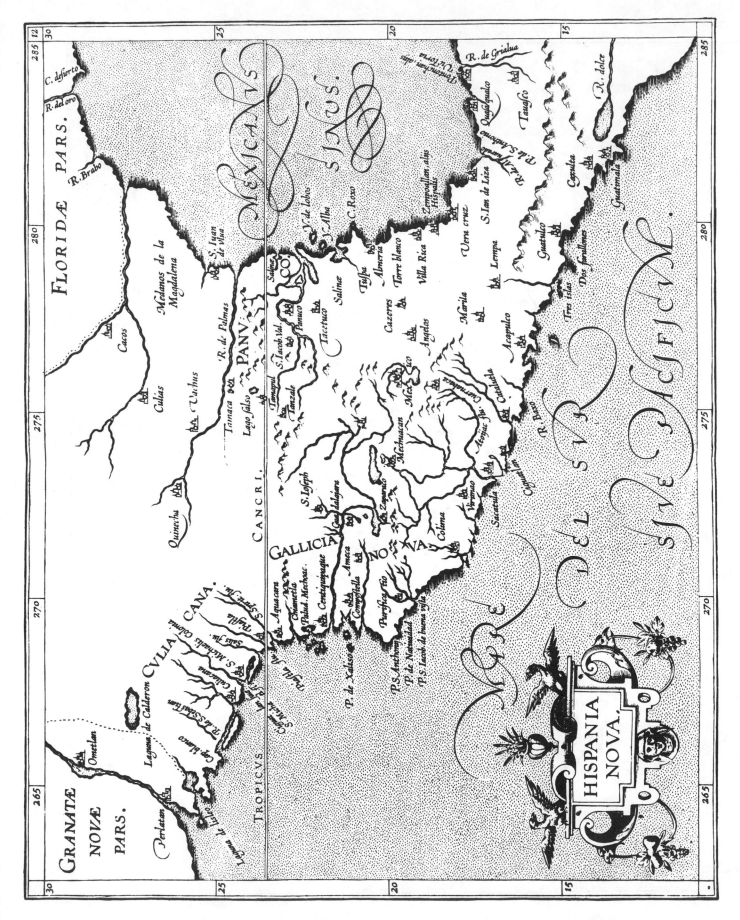

135. 1597. Cornelis Wytfliet's Map of New Spain.

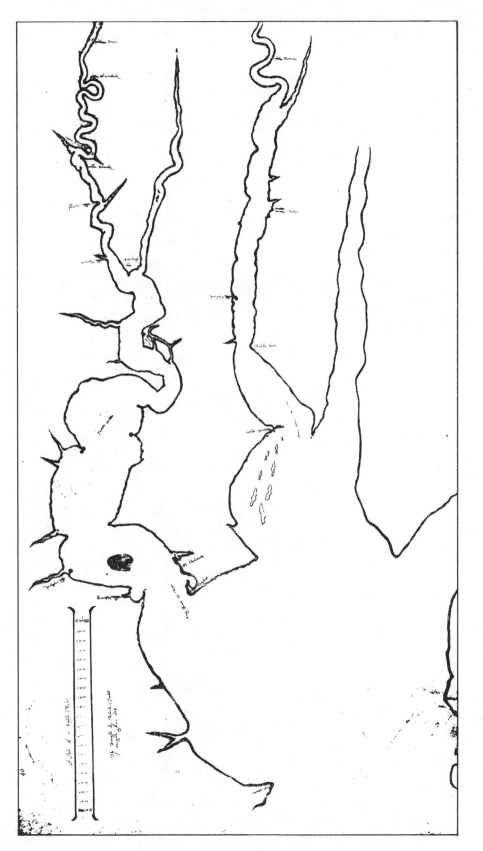

136. 1608. Robert Tindall's Chart of the Lower Chesapeake Area.

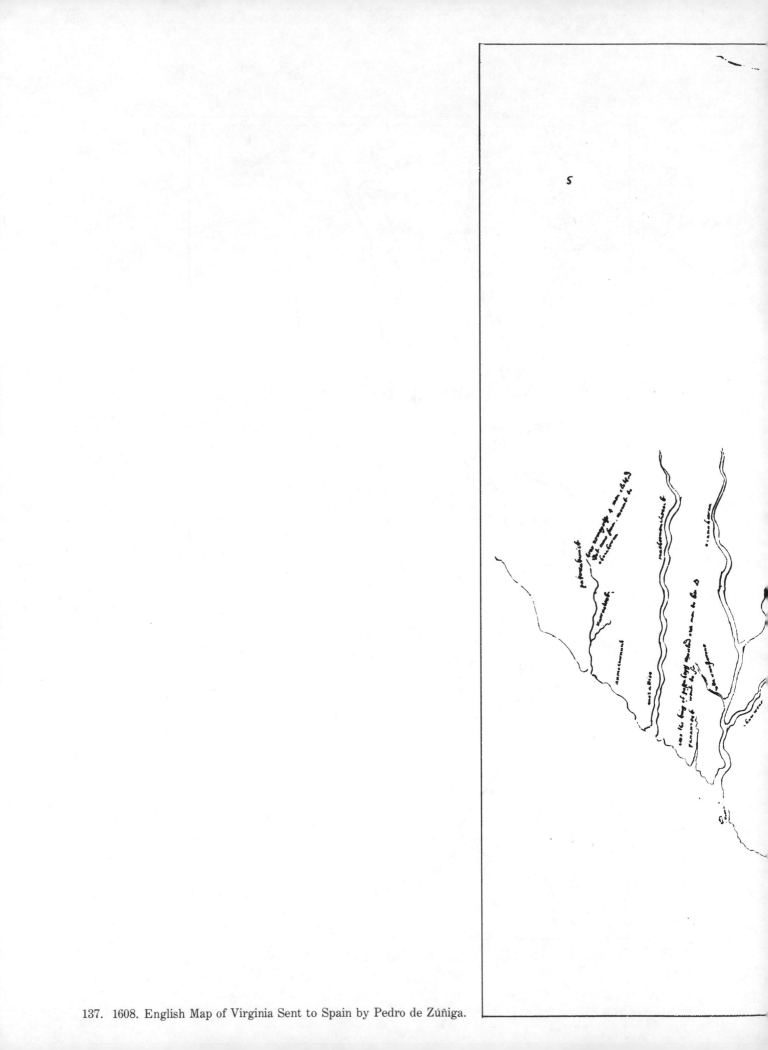

137. 1608. English Map of Virginia Sent to Spain by Pedro de Zúñiga.

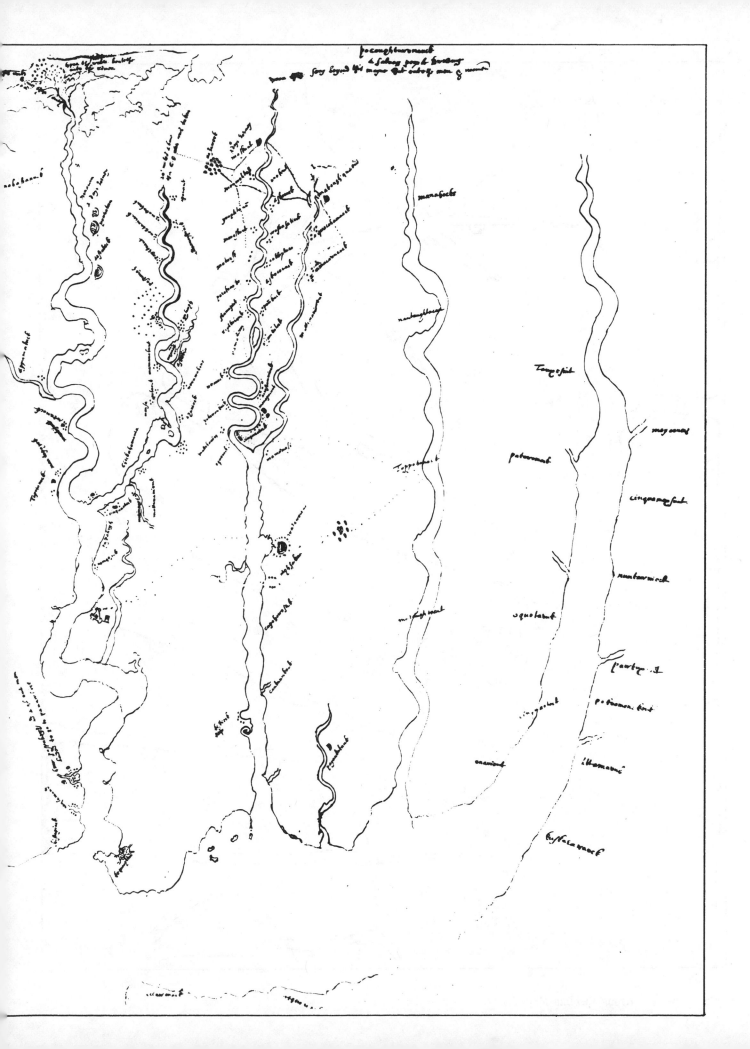

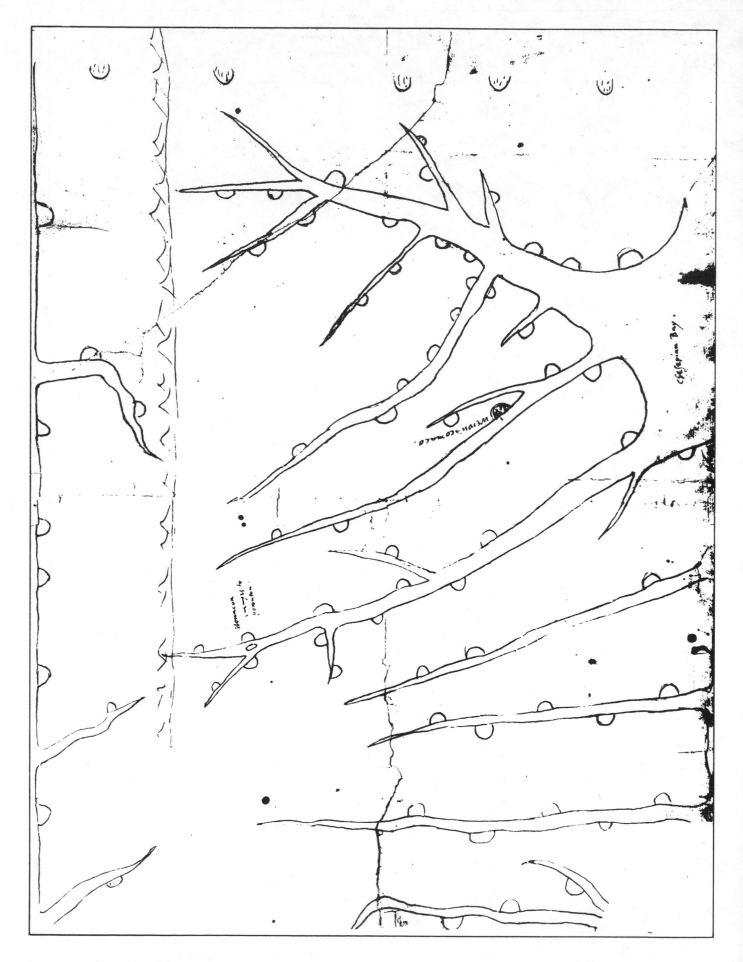

138. 1608. The Kraus Virginia Map.

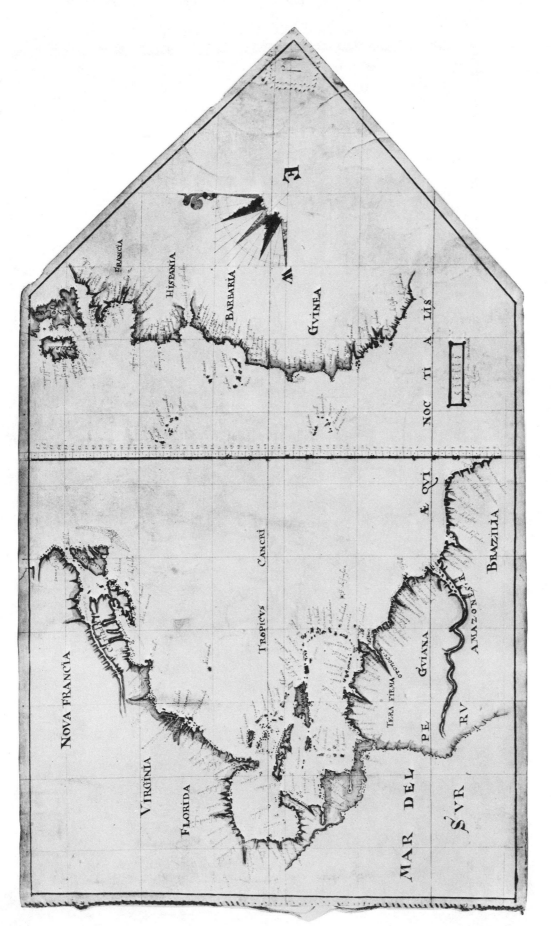

139. 1610. English Chart of the North Atlantic ("The Virginia Company Chart"), Including North America.

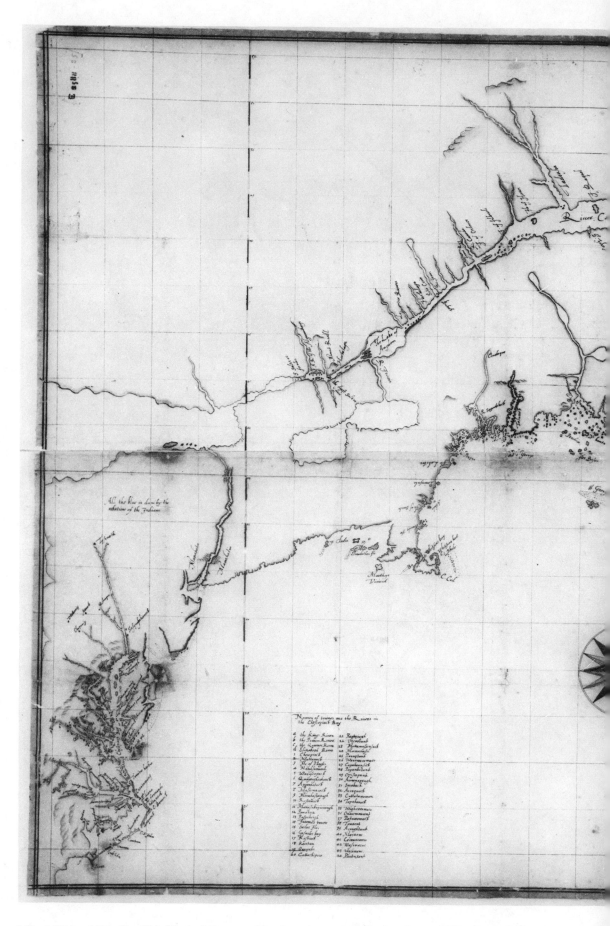

140. 1610 or 1611. English Map of Eastern North America Sent to Spain by Pedro de Velasco.

The Bay of S.t Lawrene

Newfound
Land

Bay Chalene

Bay franc9

The Baße

The Jle of John Lewis

Leages 20 in a degre

MP y D
J - 1

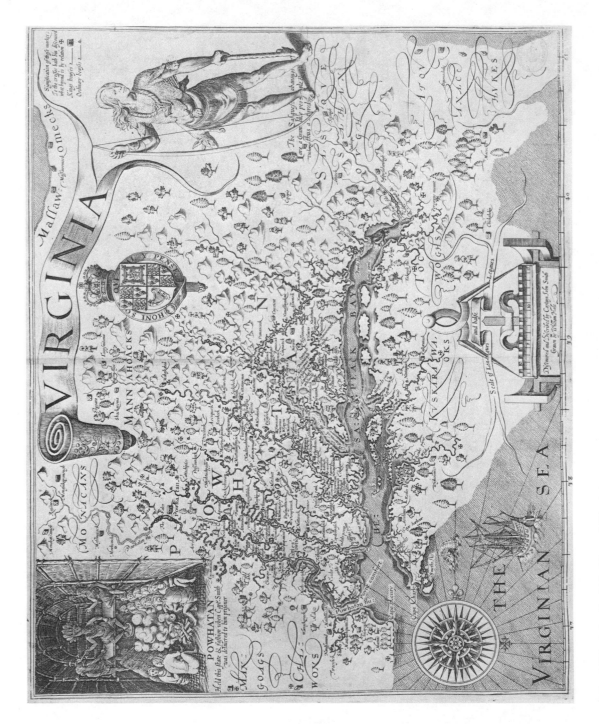

141. 1612. John Smith's Map of Virginia.

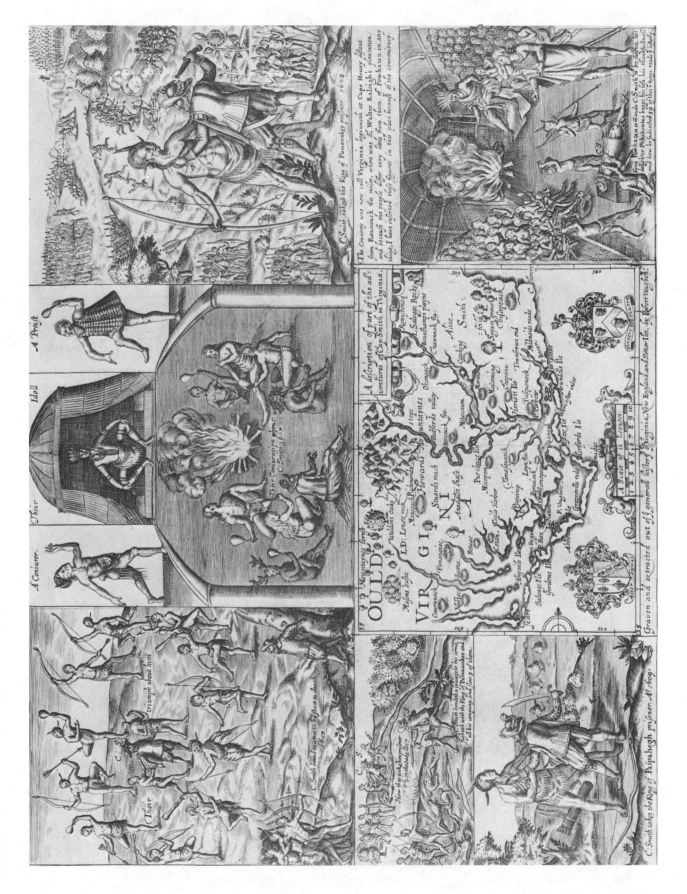

142. 1624. Map from John Smith's *Generall historie of Virginia* (London, 1624), Showing "Old Virginia" (Ralegh's Virginia).

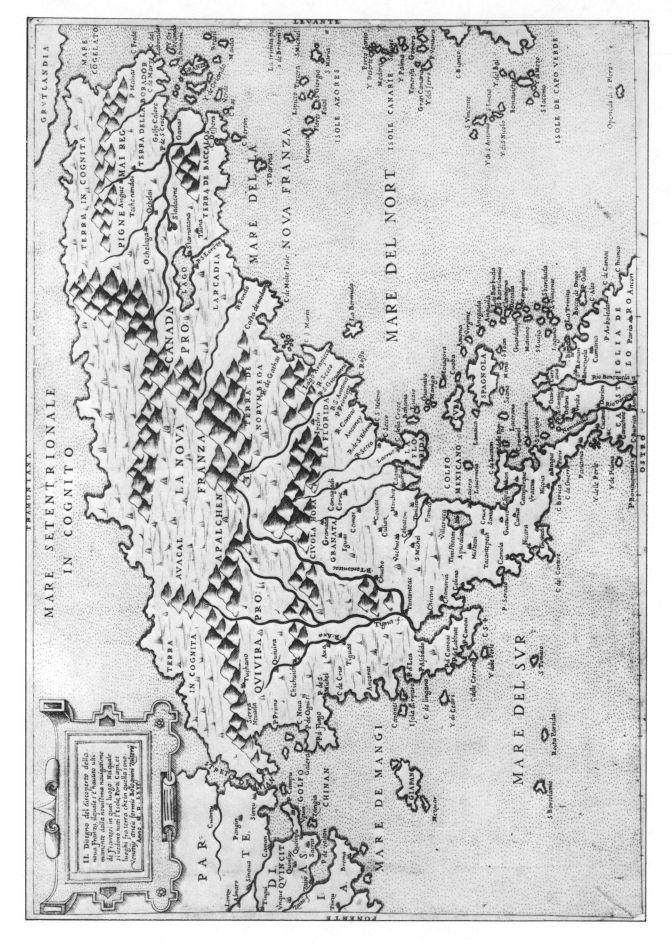

143. 1566. Zaltieri's Map of North America, Showing the Western "Strait of Anian."

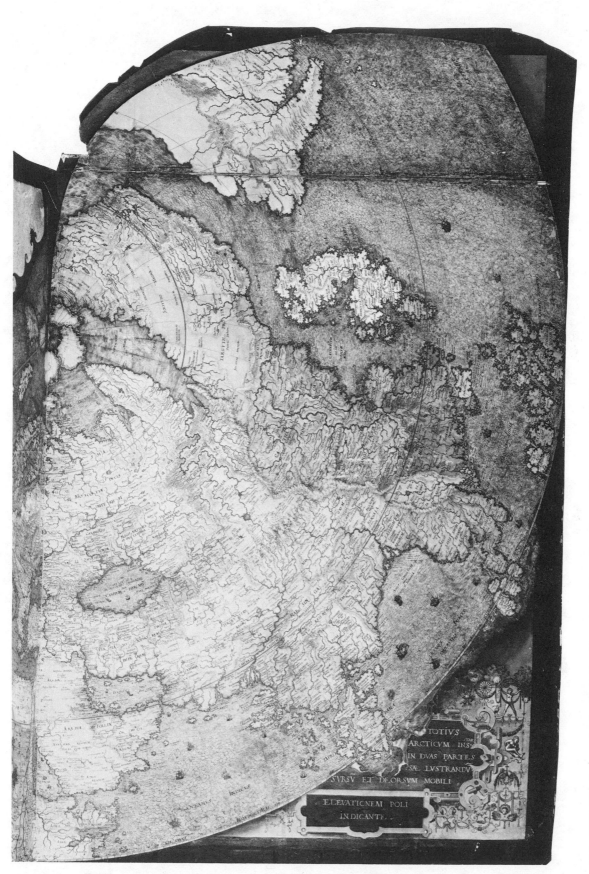

144. 1592. North America in Christian Sgrooten's Map, Showing an Exaggerated California.

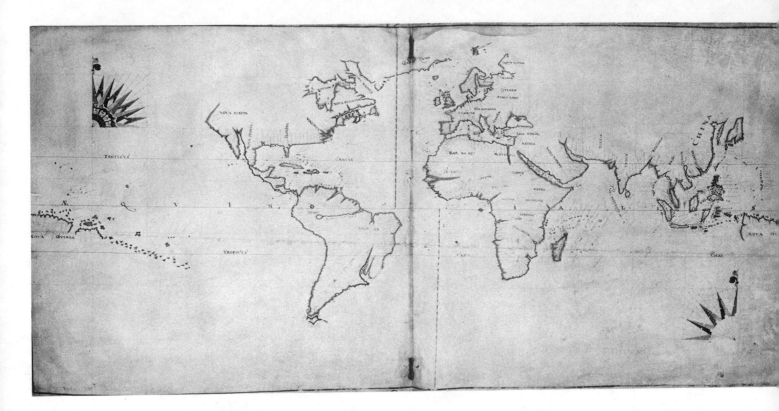

145. *Circa* 1612. English Manuscript World Chart, Showing the Eastern and Western Sides of North America.

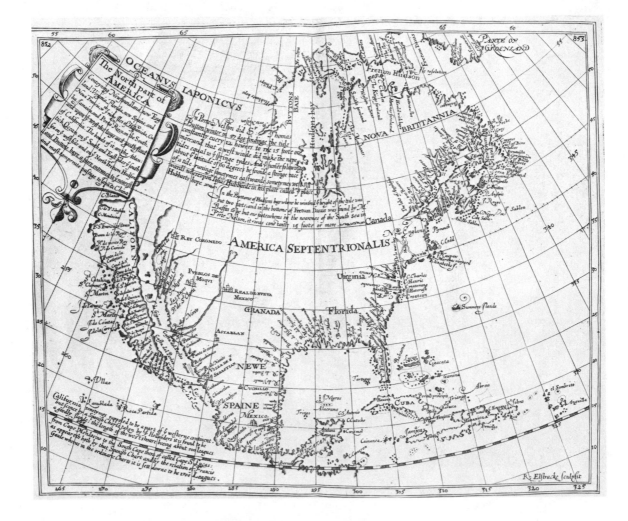

146. 1625. Henry Brigg's Conception of California as an Island.

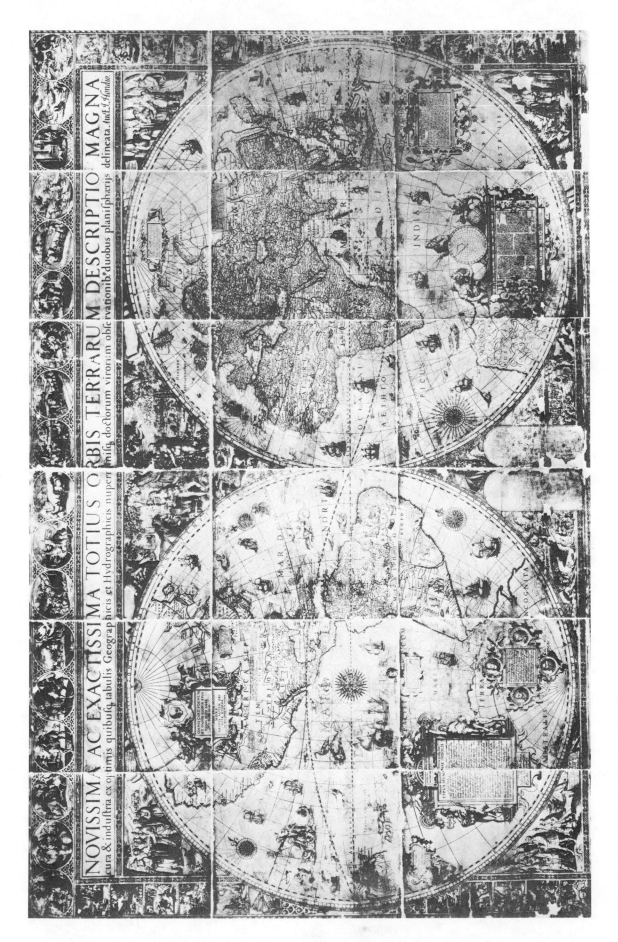

147. 1611. World Map by Jodocus Hondius.

BIBLIOGRAPHY

MANUSCRIPTS
(Numbers in brackets after MS references are item numbers)

UNITED STATES

Library of Congress. Spanish Transcripts.
  A.G.I., Seville, Patronato: 2-1-2/26, May 20, 1529 (234); 54/5/9, October 4, 1597 and October 7, 1598 (translations from Lowery Collection by J. T. Connor), May 19, 1606 (751, 752, 769); 54/5/14, August 3, 1598 (754); 54/5/16, February 19 and 20, 1600 (758, 759); 54/5/17, May 5, 1609, October 13, 1612, October 16, 1612 (772, 774, 775); 140/7/33, June 4, 1580 (724); 145/3/1, April 12, 1604 (762); 145/5/16, February 27, 1606, January 16, 1607 (765, 768); 145/7/9, 1566 (328); 153/1/18, August 18, 1568 (341); location unnoted, May 5, 1569 (346)
Georgetown University Library. John Gilmary Shea MSS, papers dated June 26, 1523, April 8, 1524, November 21, 1605 (183, 767)
New York Historical Society.
  Buckingham Smith Papers, Testimonio é informacion que dieron ciertos soldados (294, 295)
J. Pierpont Morgan Library, New York.
  Diego Guzman de Silva MSS, Entry Book of Letters, March 2, 1566 (322)
John Carter Brown Library, Providence, Rhode Island.
  Reales Cédulas Codex Sp 8, fols. 86–89v., 141v.–142, December 18, 1553, June 1, 1574 (245, 354)
Huntington Library, San Marino, California.
  Ellesmere MS 1683, November 26, 1608 (814)
Princeton University Library.
  André de Coppet Collection, November, 1565, January 20, 1566, March 17, 1566 and 1566–1567 (318, 320, 323, 324)
University of North Carolina Library.
  North Carolina (Ralegh) Collection, Chapel Hill, Talbot MS, October 15, 1585 (443)
University of Virginia (Alderman) Library.
  Tracy McGregor Library, Manchester (Rich) Papers, MS9202AN5, October 30, 1605 (466)
Research Library, Colonial Williamsburg Inc., Williamsburg, Virginia.
  Virginia Colonial Record Project, Survey Report no. 3993, 1608 (502)

CANADA

Public Archives of Canada, Ottawa.
  Transcripts MG 18, fol. 84, January 12, 1598 (693); MG 18. B2, fol. 212, 1598 (687)

ENGLAND

Public Record Office, London.
  PC2/22, p. 167, March 25, 1597 (565)
  SP12/118, 40, I, November 8, 1577 (660); SP12/151, 36, 1582 (528); SP12/153, 14, April 19, 1582 (393); SP12/173, 13, 1585 (542); SP12/177, 58, fols. 153–153v., 1584 or 1585 (540); SP12/179, 21–22, 1585 (541); SP12/185, fol. 133, 1586 (547); SP12/246, 46, 1597 (564); SP63/118, 73, 1584 (603); SP63/223, 64, April 5, 1608 (472); SP94/4, fol. 65v., 1591 (557); SP94/4, fols. 9–10, 1595 (561); SP94/4, 14, May 24, 1607 (482)
  CO1/1, 9, 1592–1600 (367);
  C2/James I/G1/26, May 22, 1608–October 2, 1615 (511); C24/150, February 3–July 10, 1580 (386)
  E122/20, 12, April 1504 (82); E164/35, fols. 9–26, 1576 (657); E356/24, m. 2, December 12, 1504–September 29, 1505 (86); E356/24, m. 3v., September 29, 1508–September 29, 1509 (90); E356/24, m. 3v., September 29, 1508–September 20, 1509 (90); E368/276, 18 Henry VII, m. 11d., 1501–1502 (75); E368/278, Trinity Term, 20 Henry VII, m. 2 (84); E368/279, 1504 (85,b); E368/283, Hilary Term, 1 Henry VIII (89); E368/283, May 7,

1509 (91); E404/84, 1, December 6, 1503 (81); E414, 6, August 10–11, 1497 (55); E414, 16, January–April, 1498 (64); E415, 3, September, 1502 (77); E415, 3, January 2–7, 1502 (72)

HCA1/47, fols. 217v.–218, July 22, 1611 (819); HCA1/47, fol. 298, 1610–1611 (821); HCA1/48, fols. 120–121v., February 7, 1617 (676); HCA1/48, fols. 130–130v., May 13, 1617 (677); HCA3/ Book of Acts, 1608–1610, fols. 56, 59v., 79 (502); HCA13/3, fols. 61–63, 100–101, 147–147v., March 17–March 29, 1537 (151); HCA13/23, fols. 315–316v., May, 1579 (385); HCA13/25, January 26, 1585 (602); HCA13/25, April 25, 1583 (530–531); HCA13/25, April 27, 1583 (532); HCA13/25, October 16, 1583 (583); HCA13/32, January 17, 1596 (612); HCA13/32, December 30, 1597 (615); HCA13/38, February 16, 1607 (477); HCA13/38, November 15–17, 1606 (788–792, 794–796); HCA13/39, June 10–23, 1608 (505–509); HCA13/39, September 3, 1607 (471); HCA13/91, November 7, 1597 (568); HCA13/96, August 20, 1591 (610); HCA13/91, June 7, 1608 (503); HCA14/24, 1588 (607); HCA14/24, 31, January 25, 1588 (605); HCA14/38, 118, February 16–19, 1607 (476); HCA/14, 39, 239, August 14, 1606 (470); HCA23/6, part I, fols. 314–318, December, 1606 (787, 793); HCA24/2, 13, 1536 (149); HCA24/3, 14, 1536 (152); HCA24/3, 15, 1536 (150); HCA24/34, 289, April 13, 1562 (584); HCA24/63, 23, 1594–1595 (613); HCA24/66, 51, 1596 (550); HCA24/72, 97, September, 1607 (471); HCA24/73, 449, June 8, 1608 (504)

British Library, Reference Division (formerly British Museum Library), Department of Manuscripts.
Cotton MS, Otho E.VIII, fol. 9, 1577 (266)
Additional: MS 11405, fols. 304–305, 1584 (539); MS 12505, fols. 447–478v., 1567 (569); MS 33983, fol. 328v., March 28, 1568 (649); MS 38823, fols. 1–8, 1582 (401)
Harleian MS 598, fol. 18v., 1591 (556b)
Lansdowne: MS 37, May 10, 1586 (362); MS 100, fols. 363–364, January 10, 1586 (363–364); MS 67, fols. 146, 190, 1591 (556a); MS 144, fol. 384, December, 1579 (556c); MS 160, fols. 356–357 (786)
College of Arms, London.
Talbot MS G, fol. 255, July 20, 1584 (601)
Fishmongers' Company, Fishmongers' Hall, London.
Ledger I (1592–1610), fol. 547, March 20, 1609 (806a)
Grocers' Company, Grocers' Hall, London.
Orders of the Court of Assistants of the Grocers' Company, 1591–1616, pp. 528, 582 (806b and 806c)
Wardens' Accounts, 1601–1611, fol. 356v., April 25, 1610 (806d)
Guildhall Library, London.
MS 5570/1 (Fishmongers' Company Ledger I, deposited) (806a)
MS11588/2 (Grocers' Company, Orders of the Courts of Assistants, deposited) (806b and 806c)
MS 11571/9 (Grocers' Company, Wardens' Accounts, 1601–1611, deposited) (806d)
Lambeth Palace Library, London.
Lambeth MS 250, fols. 406–412, October 7–November 25, 1612 (641)
Trinity House, London.
Transactions, 1609–1625: fol. 1–1v., February 9 and 24, 1610 (628–629); fols. 11v.–12, October 24, 1611 (675)
Hatfield House, Hatfield, Hertfordshire.
Cecil Papers: 94/160, August 21, 1602 (458); 116/123, June 28, 1606 (468); 192/96, 123, June 19, 1606 (467)
Petitions 1055, 1594 or later (462)
Bristol City Record Department.
BRO 13748 (4), William Addams, "A Summarie or pettie Chronicle" (53)
St. Stephen's Parish Register, 1559–1663, November 1577, deposited (661)
Cambridge University Library.
MS Dd3.85, no. 4, 1592 or 1593 (366)
Chester City Record Office.
Chester Assembly Book, 1539–1624, February 18–April 7, 1584 AB/1, fols. 194–194v. (425)
Exeter Public Library.
MS ECM 58/7/5/1. Act Book of the Merchant Adventurers of Exeter, 1558–1603, December, 1583–January 1584 (423)
Exeter Chamber Act Book, 1601–1611, March 27, 1607 (493)
Will, August 23, 1602 (617)

Nottingham University Library.

Middleton Manuscripts (deposited by Lord Middleton): MS Mi x 1/1, May 1610 (631–633); MS Mi x 1/1, fols. 16v.–17, April 3, 1613 (627); MS Mi x 1/2, August 9, 1610 and October 6, 1610 (634–635); MS Mi x 1/4, February 14, 1612 (636); MS Mi x 1/7, June 17, 1612 (637); MS Mi x 1/12, August 18, 1612 (639); MS Mi x 1/14, August 23, 1612 (640); MS Mi x 1/66, fols. 2–28, September 1, 1612–April 1, 1613 (642)

Plymouth Public Library.

Plymouth City Archives. Devon Record Office (West Devon Area); W.360/18, June 11, 1606 (495); W.359/54, February 17, 1609 (520); Serjeant Hele's "Precedent Book," W.50 (620–623)

Guildhall, Shrewsbury, Shropshire.

Shrewsbury Assembly Book, 1553–1584, February 5, 1584 (424)

Southampton City Record Office.

SC 2/6/5. Book of Instruments, 1575–1587, April 1583 (624a)

SC 2/6/6. Book of Instruments, 1597–1689; fol. 66v., February, 1601 (624b); fol. 51v., March 31, 1600 (624c); fol. 111, January 10, 1603 (624d); fol. 123v., March 28, 1604 (624f); fol. 201, January 2, 1606–1607 (624g)

SC 2/8. Star Chamber Miscellanea, Box 1, 1616–1617, *Eliot v. Bedford* (625)

Library of Stonyhurst College, Lancashire.

MS Anglia III, no. 53 (463)

Weymouth and Portland Museum of Local History.

Records of the Borough of Weymouth and Melcombe Regis. Item S.145 (751)

SPAIN

Archivo de Indias, Seville.

Patronato 2-1-2/26, May 20, 1529 (234)

Audiencia de Santo Domingo 224: October 4, 1597 (751); October 7, 1597–January 12, 1598 (752); September 22, 1602 (760); March 15, 1604 (763); November 21, 1605 (767); May 19, 1606 (769); Santo Domingo 229: August 3, 1598 (754); Santo Domingo 231: February 19, 1600 (758); February 20, 1600 (759); Santo Domingo 232: May 5, 1609 (772); October 13, 1612 (775)

Indiferente General 541, fol. 7v., November 27, 1586 (742); Indiferente General 739, June 4, 1580 (724); Indiferente General 1420, April 12, 1604 (762); Indiferente General 1530, 1536 (328); Indiferente General 1867, January 16, 1607 (765); February 27, 1606 (768); Indiferente General 2673, August, 1568 (341)

Archivo General, Simancas.

Estado 2024, April, 1606 (764)

Estado Francia: B.57, nos. 100–168 [K.1564] (446); B.89, fols. 1–17, April, 1605 (766)

Estado Inglaterra, E 1139 (455)

Museo Naval, Madrid.

Colección Navarrete, XIV (309-315, 748)

Archivo Histórico de Protocolos de Guipúzcoa, Oñate.

Partido de Vergara, no. 2574, part i, fols. 18v.–19, 1547 (581)

Partido de San Sebastian (Fuenterrabia): no. 327, fols. 6–7, 1541 (580); no. 373, fols. 86–86v., September 5, 1567 (585); no. 335, fol. 11, 1574 (589)

Partido de Azpeitia (Deva), no. 1913, fols. 79–80, April 7, 1571 (588)

Archivo Histórico Provincial de Guipúzcoa, Tolosa.

Seccion II, no. 12, legajo no. 16, March 22, 1587 (604)

Archivo del Consulado, Burgos.

Legajo 43, fol. 514v., May 23, 1572 (587); Legajo 99, 1563 (586)

BOOKS

Abstracts of English Records. p.p., Boston, 1929.

Abulfeda. *La géographie d'Aboulféda.* Ed. & trans. Stanislas Guyard and M. Reinard. 2 vols. Paris, 1848.

Acts of the Privy Council, 1578–1580. London, 1895; *1580–1582.* 1896; *1597.* 1903.

Adam of Bremen (Adamus Bremensis). *History of the Archbishops of Hamburg-Bremen.* Trans. Francis J. Tschan. New York, 1959.

────── *Quellen des 9. und 11. Jahrhunderts zur Geschischte de Hamburgischen Kirche.* Ed. Werner Trillmich. Berlin, 1961.

Ailly, Pierre d'. *Ymago mundi.* Ed. & trans. Edmond Buron. 3 vols. Paris, 1930.

Al-Masudi. *Meadows of Gold and Mines of Gems.* Trans. Aloys Sprenger, I. London, 1841.

────── *Les prairies d'or.* Trans. Barbier de Meynard and Pavet de Courteille. 2 vols. Paris, 1962–1965.

Andrade, Charles W. *Florida on Trial, 1593–1602.* Coral Gables, 1959.

Andrews, Kenneth R. *English Privateering Voyages to the West Indies 1588–95.* Cambridge, Eng., Hakluyt Soc., 1959.

Anghiera, Pietro Martiro d'; Angleria, Pedro Martino; Anglerius, Petrus Martyr. See Martyr, Peter; Eden, Richard.

Apian, Peter. *Cosmographicus liber.* Landshut, 1524.

Aristotle. *De Coelo.* Trans. W. K. C. Guthrie. Cambridge, Mass., Loeb Classics, 1939.

Arruda, Manuel Moneiro Velho. *Coleccão de documentos relativos ao descrobimento e pouoamente dos Acôres.* Ponta Delgado, 1932.

Asher, G. M., ed. *Henry Hudson the Navigator.* London, Hakluyt Soc., 1860.

Atkinson, Geoffroy. *La Littérature géographique française de la Renaissance.* 2 parts. Paris, 1927–1936.

Bacchiani, Alessandro. "Giovanni Da Verrazzano e le sue scoperta nell' America Setentrionale," *Bolletino della Società Geografica Italiana,* XI (1909), 1272–1323.

Bacon, Roger. *Opus majus.* Ed. & trans. Robert B. Burke. Philadelphia, 1928.

Ballard, Edward, ed. *Popham Memorial Volume.* Portland, Me., 1863.

Bandelier, A. F. and F. R. Bandelier, eds. *Historical Documents Relating to New Mexico, Nueva Vizcaya and Approaches Thereto.* 3 vols. Albuquerque, 1923.

Banks, C. E. "New documents, relating to the Popham expedition, 1607." *Proceedings of the American Antiquarian Society,* XXXIX (1929), 307–333.

Baptista de Lima, Manuel C. "Uma tentiva açoriana de colonazação da ilha denominada 'Barcellona' no século XVI." Congresso Internacional de História des Descobrimentos, *Actas.* 6 vols. Lisbon, 1960–1961.

────── "A ilha Terceira e a colonização do Nordeste do Continent Americano no século XVI." *Boletim do Instituto Histórico da Ilha Terceira,* XVIII (1963), 5–37.

Barbour, Philip L., ed. *The Jamestown Voyages under the First Charter.* 2 vols. Cambridge, Eng., Hakluyt Soc., 1969.

Barcia, A. G. de. *Ensayo cronológico de la Florida.* Madrid, 1723.

────── *Barcia's Chronological History of Florida.* Trans. Anthony Kerrigan. Gainesville, Fla., 1951.

Barkham, Selma. "The Spanish province of Terra Nova." *Canadian Archivist* (November, 1974).

Barlowe, Roger. *A Briefe Summe of Geographie.* Ed. E. G. R. Taylor. London, Hakluyt Soc., 1932.

Barrientos, Bartolomé. *Pedro Menéndez de Avilés, Founder of Florida.* Trans. Anthony Kerrigan. Gainesville, Fla., 1965.

Basas Fernández, Manuel. *El seguro marítimo en España del siglo XVI.* Bilbao, 1963.

Baxter, James P. *Sir Ferdinando Gorges and his Province of Maine.* 3 vols. Boston, Prince Soc., 1890.

Bembo, Pietro. *Della istoria Viniziana.* 2 vols. Milan, 1809.

Bemiss, Samuel H., ed. *The Three Charters of the Virginia Company.* Williamsburg, 1957.

Bennett, Charles E. *Laudonnière and Fort Caroline.* Gainesville, Fla., 1964.

────── *Settlement of Florida.* Gainesville, Fla., 1968.

Bernard, Charles. *Navires et gens de mer à Bordeaux.* 3 vols. Paris, 1968.

Best, George. *A true discourse of the late voyages of discoverie, for the finding of a passage to Cathaya, by the Northwest, under the conduct of Martin Frobisher.* London, 1578.

Biggar, H. P., ed. *Precursors of Jacques Cartier 1496–1534.* Ottawa, Public Archives of Canada, 1911.

────── "Jean Ribault's Discoverye of Terra Florida," *English Historical Review,* XXXIII (1917), 263–270.

────── ed. *The Voyages of Jacques Cartier.* Ottawa, Public Archives of Canada, 1924.

———— See also Champlain, Samuel de.

Bigges, Walter [and others]. *A summarie and true discourse of Sir Frances Drakes West Indian voyage.* London, 1589. *Expeditio Francisci Draki equitis Angli in Indias occidentales A. M. D. LXXXV.* Leiden, 1588.

Bolton, Herbert E., ed. *Spanish Explorations in the Southwest 1542–1706.* New York, 1908.

Bourne, Edward G., ed. *Narratives of the Career of Hernando de Soto.* 2 vols. New York, 1904.

Bourne, William. *A Regiment for the Sea.* Ed. E. G. R. Taylor. Cambridge, Eng., Hakluyt Soc. 1963.

Bordone, Benedetto. *Libro di Benedetto Bordone.* Venice, 1528.

Brandt (Brant), Sebastian. *Narrenschiff.* [1494, etc.].

  Trans. Alexander Barclay, *The ship of folys.* London, Rycharde Pynson, 1509.

  Trans. Henry Watson, *The shyppe of fooles.* London, Wynkyn de Worde, 1517.

Brendan, Saint. *Here begynneth the lyfe of saynt Brandon.* London, [c. 1520].

————*Navigatio Sancti Brandani abbati.* Ed. Carl Selmer. Notre Dame, Indiana, 1959.

  Trans. Denis O'Donoghue, in *Brendaniana* (Dublin, 1893).

Brereton, John. *A briefe and true relation of the discoverie of the north part of Virginia . . . made this present yeere 1602.* London, 1602.

Brooks, Abbie M. and Annie Averette. *The Unwritten History of Old St. Augustine.* Saint Augustine, 1909.

Brown, Alexander. *The Genesis of the United States.* 2 vols. Boston, 1890.

———— *The First Republic in America.* New York, 1898.

Bry, Theodor de. *America* part i, 1590; part ii, 1591. Frankfurt-am-Main.

Burrage, Henry. *English and French Voyages, 1534–1608.* New York, 1906.

Cabeza de Vaca. See Nuñez Cabeza de Vaca, Alvar.

[Cabot, Sebastian]. *Declaratio chartae novae navigatoriae almirantis.* [1544].

Cabreiro Blanco, Luis, ed. *Colección de diarios y relaciones para la historia de los viajes y descubrimientos.* 5 vols. Madrid, 1943.

Calendar of Letters and Papers, Foreign and Domestic, Henry VIII. IV, pt.i. London, 1870; XVI. 1898.

Calendar of State Papers, Foreign, January–July 1589. London, 1950.

Calendar of State Papers, Spanish, 1550–1552. London, 1914; *1553.* 1916; *1559–1567.* 1892; *1568–1579.* 1894; *1587–1603.* 1899.

Calendar of State Papers, Milan. vol. I. London, 1913.

Calendar of State Papers, Venetian, 1520–1526. London, 1869.

Calendar of Cecil [Hatfield] Manuscripts. See Historical Manuscripts Commission.

Camden, William, *Annales.* London, 1615.

———— *The history of . . . Princess Elizabeth.* London, 1688.

Campeau, Lucien. *Lettres du Bas-Canada,* VIII (Montreal, 1954).

———— ed. *Monumenta Novae Franciae I. La Première mission d'Acadie (1602–1616).* Rome and Québec, 1967.

Carayon, Auguste, ed. *La première mission des Jésuites au Canada.* Paris, 1864.

Carleill, Christopher. *A breef and sommarie discourse . . . written by Captaine Carleill in Aprill 1583.* London, 1583.

———— *A discourse upon the intended voyage to the hethermost partes of America written by Captain Carleill.* [London, 1583.]

Carr, C. T., ed. *Select Charters of Trading Companies A.D. 1530–1707.* London, Selden Society, 1913.

Cartier, Jacques. *Brief récit de la navigation faicte es isles de Canada.* Paris, 1545.

———— *A short and brief narration of the two navigations and discoveries to the northweast partes called Newe France.* Trans. John Florio. London, 1580.

Carus-Wilson, E. M., ed. *The Overseas Trade of Bristol in the Later Middle Ages.* Bristol Record Society, VII, Bristol, 1937.

Casas, Bartolomé de las. See Las Casas, Bartolomé de.

Castillo, Bernal Diaz del. *The True History of New Spain.* Trans. A. P. Maudsley. 5 vols. London, Hakluyt Soc., 1908–1916.

Caxton, William, trans. *Legenda aurea.* Westminster, [1483]. See Jacobus de Varagine.

Cell, Gillian T. *English Enterprise in Newfoundland, 1577–1660.* Toronto, 1969.

Champlain, Samuel de. *Oeuvres de Champlain*. Ed. C. H. Lavadière. 3 vols. Université Laval, Québec, 1870.

────── *The Works of Samuel de Champlain*. Ed. H. P. Biggar. 7 vols. Toronto, Champlain Soc., 1922–1936; reprinted 1971.

────── *Des Sauvages, ou voyage de Samuel Champlain, de Brouage, fait en la France l'an mil six cents trois*. Paris, 1604.

────── *Les voyages du sieur de Champlain*. Paris, 1613.

────── *Les voyages de la Nouvelle France occidentale, dicte Canada, faits par Sieur de Champlain*. Paris, 1632.

Chiapelli, Fredi, ed. *The First Images of America*. 2 vols. Los Angeles, 1976.

Churchyard, Thomas. *A discourse . . . whereunto is adjoyned a commendation of Sir Humfrey Gilberts ventrous journey*. London, 1578.

Coignet, Michel. *Instruction nouvelle des poincts plus excellent necessaire touchant l'art de naviguer*. Antwerp, 1581.

Collección de documentos inéditos de Indias. See Pacheco, Joaquin F.

Collins, Arthur, ed. *Letters and Memorials of State Written and Collected by Sir Henry Sidney* [and others]. 2 vols. London, 1746.

Collinson, Richard, ed. *The Three Voyages of Martin Frobisher*. London, Hakluyt Soc., 1867.

Colón, Fernando. *Le historie di Cristoforo Colombo*. Venice, 1571.

────── *The Life of the Admiral Christopher Columbus*. Trans. Benjamin Keen. New Brunswick, N.J., 1959.

Columbus, Christopher. *The Journal of Christopher Columbus*. Ed. Cecil Jane and L. A. Vigneras. London, 1960; New York, 1961.

Connor, Jeanette Thurber, ed. *Colonial Records of Spanish Florida, 1570–1580*. 2 vols. Deland, Florida State Historical Soc., 1925–1930.

Coppie d'un lettre venant de la Floride, envoyée à Rouen et depuis au seigneur d'Everon. Paris, 1565.

Corbett, Sir Julian, ed. *The Spanish war 1585–87*. London, Navy Records Soc., 1898.

Cortés, Hernando. *Praeclara*. Nürnburg, 1524.

────── *Historia de Nueva Espagna*. Mexico, 1770.

Cortés, Martín. *Breve compendio de la spera y de la arte de navegar*. Seville, 1551.

Cortesão, Armando. *History of Portuguese Cartography*. 2 vols. Lisbon, 1968.

Cortesão, A. and A. Teixeira da Mota, eds. *Portugaliae Monumenta Cartographica*. 6 vols. Lisbon, 1960.

Craigie, W. G., ed. *The Maitland Manuscript*. 2 vols. Edinburgh, Scottish Text Soc., 1919–1927.

Crashaw, William, *A sermon preached in London before the Right Honorable the Lord Lawarre, lord governour and captaine generall of Virginia*. London, 1610.

Craven, Wesley Frank. *The Southern Colonies in the Seventeenth Century*. Baton Rouge, La., 1949.

Crinò, S. *Come fu scoperta l'America*. Milan, 1943.

Croft, Pauline, ed. *The Spanish Company*. London, London Record Soc., 1973.

Cumming, William P. *The Southeast in Early Maps*. Princeton, 1958.

────── "The Parreus Map (1562) of French Florida." *Imago Mundi*, XVII (1963), 27–40.

Cumming, W. P., R. A. Skelton and D. B. Quinn. *The Discovery of North America*. London, 1971, New York, 1972.

Cutter, Donald C., ed. *The California Coast. Documents from the Sutro Collection*. Norman, 1969.

Davenport, Harbert, trans. "The Expedition of Panfilo de Narvaez." *The Southwestern History Quarterly*, XXVII (1923–1924). 120–139, 217–241, 276–304; XXVIII (1924–1925), 56–74, 122–163.

Davidson, George C. *An Examination of Some of the Early Voyages of Discovery and Exploration in the Northwest Coast of America from 1539 to 1603*. Washington, D.C., 1886.

────── *Pacific Coast Pilot of California, Oregon and Washington Territory*. 4th edition. U.S. Coast and Geodetic Survey, Washington, D.C., 1889.

────── "Francis Drake on the Northwest Coast of America in the year 1579", *Transactions and Proceedings of the Geographical Society of the Pacific*, 2nd series, V (1908).

Davila Padilla, Agustín. *Historia de la fundación y discurso de la provincia de Santiago de Mexico de la Orden de Predicatores*. Madrid, 1596.

────── *Historia . . . de la Orden de Predicatores*. Brussels, 1625.

Davis, John. *The Voyages and Works of John Davis*. Ed. A. H. Markham. London, Hakluyt Soc., 1880.

———— *The worldes hydrographical discription*. London, 1595.

Davis, T. F., trans. "History of Juan Ponce de Leon's voyages to Florida, source records," *Florida Historical Quarterly*, XIV (1935).

De La Warr, Lord. See West, Thomas.

D'Ewes, Simonds. *The Journals of all the parliaments during the reign of Queen Elizabeth*. London, 1682.

Douais, Célestin, ed. *Dépêches de M. de Fourquevaux*. 3 vols. Paris, 1896–1904.

———— ed. *Lettres de Charles IX à M. de Fourquevaux 1565–1572*. Paris, 1897.

Drake, Sir Francis. "The Francis Drake Controversy," *California Historical Quarterly*, LIII (1974), 197–292.

Drake, Sir Francis, Bart., ed. *The world encompassed by Sir Francis Drake . . . Carefully collected out of the notes of Master Francis Fletcher, Preacher in this employment, and divers others his followers in the same*. London, 1628 and 1635.

———— *The world encompassed*. Ed. W. S. W. Vaux. London, Hakluyt Soc., 1854.

Ducéré, Edmond. *Les corsaires sous l'ancien régime*. Bayonne, 1895.

Eden, Richard. *Treatyse of the newe India*. London, 1553.

———— *The Decades of the newe world or West India*. London, 1555.

————*Art of navigation*. London, 1561.

Edwards, Edward. *The Life of Sir Walter Ralegh, with his Letters*. 2 vols. London, 1866.

Ellis, Thomas. *A true report of the third voyage by Frobisher*. London, 1578.

Elvas, Gentleman of. *Relaçām verdadeira dos trabalhos que ho governador dom Fernando do souto & certos fidalgos portugueses passarom no descobrimento da provincia da Frolida*. Evora, André de Burgos, 10 February, 1557.

———— *Virginia richly valued*. Trans. Richard Hakluyt. London, 1609.

———— *The worthye and famous history of . . . Terra Florida*. Trans. Richard Hakluyt, London, 1611.

———— *The Discovery and Conquest of Terra Florida by Don Fernando de Soto*. Ed. W. B. Rye. London, Hakluyt Soc., 1851.

———— *True Relation of the Hardship Suffered by Governor Fernando de Soto . . . During the Discovery of the Province of Florida*. Ed. James A. Robertson. Deland, Florida Historical Soc., 1933.

———— *Verdadeira relacão*. Ed. F. G. Perey Vidal. Lisbon, 1940.

Enciso. See Fernández de Enciso, Martín.

Escalante Fontaneda, Hernando de. *Memoir of D^e d'Escalante Fontaneda*. Ed. David O. True. Coral Gables, 1945.

Espejo, Antonio de. *El viaje que hizo Antonio de Espejo*. Paris, 1586.

———— *Histoire des terres nouvellement descouvertes*. Paris, 1586.

———— *New Mexico*. Trans. A. F. London, 1587.

Eusebius of Caesarea. *Chronicon. Nova additio*. Ed. Henri Estienne. Paris, 1512.

Fernández de Enciso, Martin. *Suma de geographia*. Seville, 1519.

———— *A briefe description of the portes, creeks, bayes and havens of the Weast India*. Trans. John Frampton. London, 1578.

Fernández de Oviedo, Gonzalo. *Sumario de las natural y general istoria de las Indias*. Toledo, 1526.

———— *La historia general y natural de las Indias*. Seville, 1535; Salamanca, 1547; Valladolid, 1557.

———— *Historia general y natural de las Indias*. 4 vols. Madrid, 1851.

———— *Historia general y natural de las Indias*. Ed. Juan Perez de Tudela Bueso. 5 vols. Madrid, 1959.

———— See also Davenport, Harbert.

Fischer, Joseph and Franz von Weiser, eds. *The Oldest Map with the Name America of the Year 1507*. Innsbruck and London, 1903; reprinted Amsterdam, 1968.

Folmer, Henry. *Franco-Spanish Rivalry in North America, 1524–1723*. Glendale, Calif., 1932.

Fontaneda. See Escalante Fontaneda, Hernando de.

Force, Peter, ed. *Tracts and Other Papers*. 4 vols. Washington, D.C., 1836–1846.

Fourquevaux, M. de. See Douais, Célestin.

French, B. F., ed. *Historical Collections of Louisiana*. 1st series. 5 vols. New York, 1846–1853.

———— ed. *Historical Collections of Louisiana and Florida*. 2nd series. I. New York, 1871.

Gaffarel, Paul. *La Floride française.* Paris, 1875.

Galvão (Galvano), Antonio. *Tratado . . . de todos os descobrimentos.* Lisbon, 1563.

—————*The discoveries of the world unto the yeere 1555.* Trans. Richard Hakluyt. London, 1601.

————— *The Discoveries of the World.* Trans. Richard Hakluyt. Ed. C. R. D. Bethune. London, Hakluyt Soc., 1862.

————— *Tradado dos descobrimentos.* Oporto, 1944.

Ganong, W. F. *Crucial Maps in the Early Cartography and Place-nomenclature of the Atlantic Coast of Canada.* Toronto, 1964.

García, Genero, ed. *Dos antiquos relaciones de la Florida.* Mexico City, 1902.

Garcilaso de la Vega, el Inca. *La Florida de la Inca.* Lisbon, 1605.

————— *The Florida of the Inca.* Trans. J. G. Varner and J. J. Varner. Austin, Texas, 1951.

Geraldini, Alessandro. *Itinerarium.* Rome, 1631.

Gerónimo de Oré, Luis. *Relacion de los martires que a avido en las provincias de la Florida.* No place, date, or printer.

————— *Relación historico de la Florida en el siglo XVII.* Ed. Atanasio López. 2 vols. Madrid, 1931–1933.

————— *The martyrs of Florida, 1513–1616.* Trans. Maynard Geiger. Franciscan Studies no. 18. New York, 1936.

Gerritz, Hessel. *Descriptio et deliniatio geographica detectionis freti ab H. Hudson inventi.* Amsterdam, 1612.

Gilbert, Sir Humphrey. *A discourse of a discoverie for a new passage to Cataia.* London, 1576.

Goís, Damião de. *Cronico do felicissimo rei D. Manuel.* 4 parts. Lisbon, 1566–1567.

————— *Cronico de felicissimo rei D. Manuel.* Ed. D. Lopes. 4 parts. Coimbra, 1949.

Gomera. See López de Gomera, Francisco.

González de Mendoza, Juan. *Historia . . . de la China.* Madrid, 1585 [etc.].

Gookin, Warner F. and Barbour, P. L. *Bartholomew Gosnold.* Hamden, Conn., 1965.

[Gourgues, Dominique de]. *Histoire memorable de Dominique de Gourgues de la reprinse de l'isle de la Florida, faict par François.* [1568].

Grafton, Richard. *A cronicle at large . . . of the affayres of England.* London, 1568.

Gravit, Francis W. "Un document inédit sur le Canada." *Revue de l'Université Laval,* I (Québec, 1946), 282.

Gray, Robert. *A good speed to Virginia.* London, 1609.

Grynaeus, Simon. *Nova, et integre universi orbis descriptio.* Paris, 1532.

Hackett, C. W., ed. *Historical Documents Relating to New Mexico.* 2 vols. Washington, D.C., 1923–1937.

Hakluyt, Richard. *Discourse concerning Western Planting* ["A particuler discourse"]. Ed. Charles Deane. Cambridge, Mass., 1877. Also in Maine Historical Society. *Documentary History of Maine,* II (1877).

————— "Discourse of Western Planting," in E. G. R. Taylor, ed. *Original Writings and Correspondence of the Two Richard Hakluyts.* II. London, Hakluyt Soc., 1935.

————— *Divers voyages touching the discoverie of America.* London, 1582.

————— *Divers voyages.* Facsimile in *Richard Hakluyt, Editor.* Ed. D. B. Quinn. II. Amsterdam, 1967.

————— *Principall navigations.* London, 1589.

————— *Principall navigations (1589).* Facsimile, eds. D. B. Quinn and R. A. Skelton. 2 vols. Cambridge, Eng., and Salem, Mass. 1965.

————— *Principal navigations.* 3 vols. London, 1598–1600.

————— *Principal Navigations.* 12 vols. Glasgow, 1903–1905.

Hall, Edward. *The union of the two noble and illustre families of Lancaster & Yorke.* London, 1550.

Hall, Edward Hagemann, trans. "Giovanni da Verrazzano and his discoveries in North America," *Fifteenth Annual Report of the American Scenic and Preservation Society* (Albany, 1910), pp. 179–226.

Hammond, George P. and Agapito Rey, eds. *Narratives of the Coronado Expedition.* Albuquerque, 1940.

————— *Oñate, Colonizer of New Mexico.* 2 vols. Albuquerque, 1953.

————— *Rediscovery of New Mexico 1580–1594.* Albuquerque, 1966.

Hampden, John, ed. *Francis Drake, Privateer.* London, 1972.

Harriot, Thomas. *A briefe and true report of the new found land of Virginia.* London, 1588.

Harrisse, Henry. *Les Corte-Reals.* Paris, 1883.

————— *Découverte et évolution cartographique de Terre-Neuve.* Paris and London, 1900.

Harrison, W. E. C. "An early voyage of discovery." *The Mariner's Mirror,* XVI (1930), 198–199.

BIBLIOGRAPHY 521

Hening, William. *The Statutes at Large, being a Collection of All the Laws of Virginia from the First Session of the Legislature in the Year 1619.* I. Richmond, 1823.

Hermannsson, Halldór, ed. *The Book of the Icelanders.* (*Islandica*, XX [1930].)

——— ed. *The Vinland Sagas.* Ithaca, N.Y., 1944.

Hermannsson, Hermann. "The Problem of Wineland," *Icelandica*, XV (1936), 64.

Herrera, Antonio de. *Historia general de los hechos de los Castellanos.* 8 vols. Madrid, 1601–1615.

——— *Historia general de los hechos de los Castellanos.* Ed. J. Nátalicio González. 10 vols. Ascunción, Paraguay, 1944–1947.

Historical Manuscripts Commission. *Calendar of Cecil [Hatfield] Manuscripts.* IV (London, 1892); V (1894); VI (1895); XIV (1923); XVIII (1940).

——— *Calendar of De L'Isle and Dudley Manuscripts.* II (London, 1933).

Hitchcock, Robert. *A pollitique platt, for the honour of the prince.* London, 1580.

Hodge, Frederick W., ed. *Spanish Explorers in the Southern United States, 1528–1543.* New York, 1907.

——— ed. *Journey of Francisco Vásquez de Coronado.* Los Angeles, 1933.

Hoffman, Bernard G. *Cabot to Cartier.* Toronto, 1961.

Holinshed, Raphael. *Chronicles.* 3 vols. London, 1587.

Hondius, Jodocus. *Vera totius expeditionis nautica descriptio D. Franc. Draci ex Anglia solvens anno 1577 in Angliam rediit 1580. Addita est etiam viva delineatio navigationis Thomae Caundish 1586 . . . 1588.* [London, 1595?]

Hoyarsabal, Martin de. *Les voyages avantureux du Capitaine Martin de Hoyarsabel.* Bordeaux, 1579 and 1633.

Hulton, Paul. *The Work of Jacques Le Moyne de Morgues.* London, 1977.

Hulton, Paul and D. B. Quinn. *The American Drawings of John White.* 2 vols. London and Chapel Hill, 1964.

Hudūd al 'Ālam. *The regions of the world. A Persian Geography 372 A.H.–482 A.H.* Trans. V. Minorsky. 1937.

Ibn-Khaldūn. *The Muqaddimah.* Trans. Franz Rosenthal. 3 vols. Princeton, 1967.

Idrisi, Kitab al-Riyari el. *Géographie d'Edrisi.* Trans. P. Amédée Jaubert. 2 vols. Paris, 1836.

——— *Charta Rogeriana.* Trans. in Youssouf Kamal, *Monumenta Cartographica*, III. Cairo, 1935.

Íman, Âfeta. *The Life and Works of the Turkish Admiral Pirî Reis.* Ankara, 1954.

Ingstad, Anne Stine. "The Norse Settlement at L'Anse aux Meadows." *Acta Archaeologica*, XLI (1970), 109–154.

Ingstad, Helge. *Westward to Vinland.* New York and London, 1969.

Innis, Harold A. *The Cod Fisheries.* New Haven, 1940.

Jacobus de Varagine. *Legenda aurea.* Trans. William Caxton. Westminster [1483].

Jameson, J. F., ed. *Narratives of the New Netherlands 1609–1664.* New York, 1909.

——— "Notes and Queries." *Virginia Magazine*, XIX (1911), 195–196.

Jane, Cecil, ed. *The Voyages of Christopher Columbus.* 2 vols. London, Hakluyt Soc., 1930.

Jode, Gérard de and Cornelis de. *Speculum orbis terrae.* Antwerp, 1593.

John Carter Brown Library. *The Italians and the Creation of America.* Providence, R. I., 1976.

Johnson, A. H. *The History of the Worshipfull Company of the Drapers of London.* 3 vols. Oxford, 1915.

Johnson, George. *A discourse of some trouble and excommunications in the banished English church at Amsterdam.* [Amsterdam, 1603].

Johnson, Robert. *Nova Britaania: offring most excellent fruites by planting in Virginia. Exciting all such as are well affected to further the same.* London, Samuel Macham, 1609.

Jones, Gwyn, ed. and trans. *The Norse Atlantic Saga.* Oxford, 1964.

Julien, Charles-André, ed. *Les Francais en Amérique pendant la première moitié du XVIe siècle.* Paris, 1946.

——— *Les voyages de découverte et les premiers établissements.* Paris, 1948.

Keeler, Mary F., ed. *Sir Francis Drake's West Indian Voyage.* London, Hakluyt Soc., 1978.

Kingsbury, Susan M., ed. *The Records of the Virginia Company of London.* 4 vols. Washington, D.C., 1906–1935.

Kiralfy, A. K. R. *A Source Book of English Law.* London, 1957.

Kirkpatrick, F. A. "The first recorded English voyage to the West Indies". *English Historical Review.* XX (1905), 115–124.

Kraus, H. P. *Acta cartographica.* New York, 1970.

Kretschmer, Konrad. *Die entdeckung Amerika's.* Berlin, 1892.

Kunstmann, F. *Atlas zur Entdeckungsgeschichte Amerikas.* Munich, 1859.

Laet, Johann de. *Nieuwe Wereldt.* Leiden, 1625.

La Ferrière-Percy, Hector de, ed. *Lettres de Catherine de Médicis.* II. Paris, 1885.

Lanctot, Gustave. *Réalisations françaises de Cartier à Montcalm.* Montreal, 1951.

La Morandière, Charles de. *Histoire de la pêche française de la morue dans l'Amérique septentrionale.* 3 vols. Paris, 1962–1966.

La Roncière, Charles de. *Histoire de la marine française.* 7 vols. Paris, 1923.

———— *La carte de Cristophe Colomb.* Paris, 1924.

Las Casas, Bartolomé de. *Historia de las Indias.* 4 vols. Madrid, 1875.

———— *Obras escogidas.* Ed. Juan Perez de Tudela Bueso. 4 vols. Madrid, 1965.

Latham, Agnes M. C. "A birth-date for Sir Walter Ralegh." *Êtudes anglaises,* IX (1956), 243–245.

Laudonnière, René de. *L'histoire notable de la Florida.* Ed. Martin Basanier. Paris, 1586.

———— *A notable historie containing foure voyages made by certaine French captaines unto Florida.* Trans. Richard Hakluyt. London, 1587.

———— *A Notable Historie (1587).* Facsimile with preface by Thomas R. Adams. Farnham, Surrey, Eng., 1964.

Layng, T. E. *Sixteenth Century Maps of Canada.* Ottawa, 1957.

Le Blanc, Robert and René Baudry, eds. *Nouveaux documents sur Champlain et son époque.* I. Ottawa, Public Archives of Canada, 1967.

Le Challeux, Nicolas. *Discours de l'histoire de la Florida, contenant le cruauté des Espanols contre les subjets du Roy, en l'an mil cinq cens soixante cinq.* Dieppe, 1566.

———— *A true and perfect description, of the last voyage attempted by Capitaine John Rybaut, into Terra Florida this last year past 1565.* London, 1566.

Lescarbot, Marc. *Histoire de la Nouvelle France.* Paris, 1609.

———— *Nova Francia.* Trans. Pierre Erondelle. London, 1609.

———— *Histoire de la Nouvelle France.* Ed. H. P. Biggar and W. L. Grant. 3 vols. Toronto, Champlain Soc., 1908–1912.

———— *La conversion des sauvages qui ont esté baptizés en La Nouvelle France cette année 1610.* Paris, 1610.

———— *Relation dernière qui s'est passé au voyage de sieur de Poutreincourt en La Nouvelle France.* Paris, 1612.

Letts, Malcolm. *Sir John Mandeville, the Man and his Book.* London, 1949.

———— *Mandeville's Travels, Texts and Translations.* 2 vols. Hakluyt Soc. London, 1953.

Levermore, Charles H., ed. *Forerunners and Competitors of the Pilgrims.* 2 vols. Brooklyn, N.Y., 1912.

Lewis, Clifford M. and Albert J. Loomie. *The Spanish Jesuit Mission in Virginia, 1570–1572.* Chapel Hill, 1953.

Lollis, Cesare de, ed. *Raccolta di documentie e studi publicati della r. commissione Columbiana.* Vol. i, part ii. Rome, 1894.

———— ed. *Scritti di Cristoforo Columbo.* 2 vols. Rome, 1894.

López de Gomara, Francisco. *Historia general de las Indias y conquista de Mexico.* Sargossa, 1552. *Mexico,* part ii. Antwerp, 1554.

López de Velasco, Juan. *Geografía universal de las Indias (1571–1574).* Madrid, 1894.

———— *Historia general de las Indias.* 2 vols. Madrid, 1932.

Lowery, Woodbury. *The Spanish Settlements within the Present Limits of the United States, 1513–1574.* 2 vols. New York, 1901 and 1905.

Lussagnet, Susanne, ed. *Les Français en Amérique dans la deuxième partie du XVIᵉ siècle.* Part ii, La Floride française. Paris, 1959.

Lyell, Laetitia, ed. *Acts of Court of the Mercers' Company, 1453–1526. Cambridge, Eng., 1936.*

Mackenzie, William Mackay, ed. *The Poems of William Dunbar.* Edinburgh, 1932.

Magnusson, Magnus and Hermann Pálsson, trans. *The Vinland Sagas. The Norse Discovery of America.* Harmondsworth, Middlesex, Eng., 1965.

Manucy, Albert C. *The History of Castillo de San Marcos & Fort Matanzas.* Washington, D.C., National Park Service, 1955.

Markham, Sir Clements, ed. *Book of the Knowledge of All the Kingdoms, Lands, and Lordships that are in the World.* London, Hakluyt Soc., 1912.

Martyr, Peter. *De orbe novo decades*. Alcalá, 1516.

———— *De orbe novo decades octo*. Alcalá, 1530.

———— *Summario della generale istoria dell' Indie Occidentali. Libro primo della Historia dell' Indie Occidentali.* Venice, 1534.

———— *De orbe novo decades octo*. Ed. Richard Hakluyt. Paris, 1587.

———— *De novo orbe or the historie of the West Indies*. Trans. Michael Lok. London, 1612.

———— *De Orbe Novo*. Ed. and trans. F. A. MacNutt. 2 vols. New York, 1912.

———— *Opus epistolarum*. Alcalá, 1530.

———— *Fuentes historicas sobre Colón y América*. Ed. Joaquin Torres Asensio. 4 vols. Madrid, 1892.

———— See also Eden, Richard.

Mathes, W. Michael, ed. *Californiana. Documentos para la historia de la demarcación comercial de California, 1580–1630*. 2 vols. Madrid, 1965.

———— *Vizcaino and Spanish Expansion on the Pacific Ocean, 1580–1630*. Los Angeles, 1972.

Mendoza. See González de Mendoza, Juan.

Mercator, Gerard. *Gerard Mercator's Map of the World 1569*. Ed. V. van't Hoff. s'Gravenhage, 1961.

Meteren, Emanuel van. *Commentarien ofte Memorien Van-de Nederlandtschen Staet Handel Oorlogher ende Gheschiedenissen van-Onsen tyden etc.*. Leiden, 1611.

Mollat, Michel. "Choix de documents realtifs a la Normandie pour servir a l'histoire du commerce maritime (xv–xvie siècles)." Société de l'histoire de Normandie, *Mélanges*, 6e ser. (Rouen and Paris, 1958).

Monardes, Nicolás Bautista. *Segunda parte del libro de las cosas que se traen de nuestras Indias Occidentales que sirven al uso de medicina*. Seville, 1571.

———— *Primera y segunda y tercera partes de la historia medicinal de las cosas que se traen de nuestras Indias Occidentales*. Seville, 1574.

———— *Joyfull newes out of the newe founde worlde*. Trans. John Frampton. London, 1577, enlarged 1580 and 1596.

———— *Joyfull newes out of the newe founde worlde*. Ed. Stephen Gaselee. 2 vols. London, 1925.

Montalboddo, Fracan da. *Paesi novamente retrovati*. 1507.

Morgan, Edmund E. *American Slavery, American Freedom: The Ordeal of Colonial Virginia*. New York, 1975.

Morison, Samuel Eliot, ed. *Journals and other Documents on the Life and Voyages of Christopher Columbus*. New York, 1963.

———— *The European Discovery of America: The Northern Voyages*. Boston, 1971.

———— *The European Discovery of America: The Southern Voyages*. Boston, 1974.

Morse, Henry Inglis. *Acadiensia Nova*. 2 vols. London, 1929.

Murga Sanz, Vicente. *Juan Ponce de León*. San Juan, P. R., 1959.

Murphy, Henry C. *Hudson in Holland*. The Hague, 1909.

Mustawfi, Hamd-Allah. *The Geographical part of the Nuzhatual-Qulub*. Ed. and trans. Guy Le Strange. Leiden, 1919.

Nansen, Fridtjof. *In Northern Mists*. 2 vols. London, 1911.

Navarrete, Martín Fernández de. *Obras*. 3 vols. Madrid, 1954–1964.

———— *Colección de documentos y manuscritos compilados para Fernández de Navarrete*. 32 vols. Nendeln, Lichtenstein, 1971.

New England, Council of. *A briefe relation of the discovery and plantation of New England. Published by the presedent and council*. London, 1622.

Newton, A. P., "An Early Grant to Sebastian Cabot." *English Historical Review*, XXXVII (1922), 564–565.

Nordenskiold, A. E. *Facsimile Atlas*. Stockholm, 1899.

Nuñez Cabeza de Vaca, Alvar. *La relacion que dio Alvar Nuñez Cabeza de Vaca*. Zamora, Augustín de Paz and Juan Picardo for Juan Pedro Musetti, 1542.

———— *Commentarios*. Valladolid, 1555.

———— *The Journey of Cabeza de Vaca*. Trans. T. Buckingham Smith. Washington, D.C., 1851.

———— *Relación de los naufragios y comentarios de Alvar Nuñez Cabeza de Vaca*. Ed. M. Serrano y Sanz. 2 vols. Madrid, 1906.

———— *The Narrative of Alvar Nuñez Cabeza de Vaca*. Barre, Mass., 1972.

Nuttall, Zelia, ed. *New Light on Drake*. London, Hakluyt Soc., 1914.

O'Donoghue, Denis. *Brendaniana*. Dublin, 1893.

Oré. See Geronimo de Oré, Luis.

Oresme, Nicole. *Le livre du ciel et du monde*. Ed. and trans. Albert D. Menut and Alexander J. Denomy. Madison, 1968.

Ortelius, Abraham. *Theatrum orbis terrarum*. Antwerp, 1570.

——*Theatrum Orbis Terrarum*, facsimile, with introduction by R. A. Skelton. Amsterdam, 1964.

Oviedo. See Fernández de Oviedo, Gonzalo.

Pacheco, Joaquin F., Francisco de Cárdenas and Louis Torres de Mendoza, eds. *Colección de documentos inéditos relativos al descubrimientos, conquista y colonización de las posesiones Españoles en América y Oceanía*. 1st series. 42 vols. Madrid, 1864–1889.

Parker, John. *Books to Build an Empire*. Amsterdam, 1965.

Parkman, Francis. *Pioneers of France in the New World*. Revised edition. New York, 1885.

Parks, G. B. "New material on the third voyage of Martin Frobisher." *Huntington Library Quarterly*, II, 59–65.

Pasqualigo, Pietro in *Paesi novamente retrovati*. Venice, 1507.

—— *Paesi novamente retrovati* [*1508*]. Princeton, Vespucci Reprints, 1916.

Peckham, Sir George. *A true reporte of the late discoveries and possession, taken in the right of the Crown of Englande, of the Newfound Landes: by that valiant and worthy gentleman, Sir Humphrey Gilbert knight*. London, 1583.

Pelham, Edward. *God's power and providence*. London, 1631.

Percy, George. *Observations Gathered out of "A Discourse of the Southern Colony in Virginia by the English,"* *1606*. Ed. D. B. Quinn. Charlottesville, 1967.

Piccolomini, Aeneas Silvius. *Historia rerum unique questarum*. Basel, 1471.

Pliny (Caius Plinius Secundus). *Naturalis historia*. Trans. H. Rackham. Cambridge, Mass., Loeb Classics, 1938.

Polo, Marco. *The Book of Ser Marco Polo*. Ed. Sir Henry Yule and Henri Cordier. 3 vols. London, 1903–1920.

Powell, David, ed. *The historie of Cambria*. London, 1584.

Priestley, Herbert I., ed. and trans. *The Luna Papers, 1559–1561*. 2 vols. Deland, Fla., 1928, reprinted New York, 1971.

Proclus, Diadochus. *De Sphaera*. Trans. Thomas Linacre. Vienna, 1500.

—— *The descripcion of the sphere or the frame of the worlde*. Trans. Wyllyam Salysbury. London, 1550.

Prowse, J. W. *History of Newfoundland*. London, 1895: 2nd edition, 1896.

Ptolemy, Claudius. *Geographia*. Ulm, 1482; Rome, 1490; Rome 1507; Venice, 1511; Strassburg, 1513; Venice, 1548; Venice, 1561.

——*Geography of Claudius Ptolemy*. Ed and trans. Edward Luther Stevenson. New York, New York Public Library, 1932.

Purchas, Samuel. *Pilgrimage*. 1st edition, London, 1613; 2nd ed., London, 1614; 3rd ed., London, 1617; 4th ed., London, 1626.

—— *Hakluytus posthumus or Purchas his pilgrimes*. 4 vols. London, 1625.

—— *Hakluytus posthumus or Purchas his pilgrimes*. 20 vols. Glasgow, 1905–1907.

Quattlebaum, Paul. *The Land called Chicora*. Gainesville, 1956.

Quinn, D. B. "An Anglo-French 'Voyage of Discovery' to North America in 1604–5, and its sequel." *Miscellania Charles Verlinden* (Gent 1974), 513–534.

—— "Edward IV and exploration." *The Mariner's Mirror*, XXI (1935), 275–284.

—— *England and the Discovery of America*. New York and London, 1974.

—— ed. *The Hakluyt Handbook*. 2 vols. Cambridge, Eng., Hakluyt Soc., 1974.

—— "James I and the beginnings of empire in America." *Journal of British Commonwealth History*, II (1974), 1–19.

—— "John Cabot's *Matthew*." *The Times Literary Supplement* (8 June 1967), p. 517.

—— "New geographical horizons: literature," in Fredi Chiapelli, ed. *First Images of America*, II (1976), 635–658.

—— *North America from Earliest Discovery to First Settlements*. New York, 1977.

—— "Renaissance influences in English colonization," *Transactions of the Royal Historical Society*, 5th series, XXVI (1976), 73–93.

—— *Richard Hakluyt, Editor*. [Introductory volume to facsimile edition of R. Hakluyt, *Divers Voyages (1582)*. 2 vols. Amsterdam, 1967.]

—— ed. *The Roanoke Voyages, 1584–1590*. 2 vols. Cambridge, Eng., Hakluyt Soc., 1955.

—— "Thomas Harriot and the New World," in John W. Shirley, *Thomas Harriot, Renaissance Scientist*, (Oxford, 1975), pp. 36–53.

—— "The voyage of Étienne Bellenger to the Maritimes in 1583: a new document." *Canadian Historical Review*, LXIII (1962), 328–343.

—— "The voyage of *Triall*, 1606–1607." *American Neptune*, XXXI (1971), 85–103.

—— ed. *The Voyages and Colonising Enterprises of Sir Humphrey Gilbert*. 2 vols. London, Hakluyt Soc., 1940.

Quinn, D. B. and N. M. Cheshire. *The New Found Land of Stephen Parmenius*. Toronto, 1972.

Ramos-Coelho, José, ed. *Alguns documentos do Archívo Nacional da Torre do Tombe*. Lisbon, 1891.

Ramusio, Giovanni Battista. *Summario de la generale historia de l'Indie Occidentali*. Venice, 1534.

—— *Navigationi et viaggi*. 3 vols. Venice, 1550–1559.

Rastell, John. *A new interlude and a mery of the nature of the .iiij. elements*. London [c. 1519].

—— *The Four Elements*. Ed. Roger Coleman. Cambridge, Eng., 1971.

Reed, A. W. "John Rastell's voyage in 1517." *The Mariner's Mirror*, IX (1923), 137–147.

Reisch, Gregor. *Margarita philosophica*. Strassburg, 1513.

Ribault, Jean. *The whole and true discoverye of Terra Florida*. London, T. Hacket, 1563.

—— *The Whole and True Discoverye of Terra Florida*. Ed. Jeanette T. Connor. Deland, Fla., 1928; reprinted Gainesville, Fla., 1966.

Rich, Richard. *Newes from Virginia*. London, 1610.

Roberts, Henry. *News from the Levane seas*. London, 1594.

Rogers, John D. *The Historical Geography of Newfoundland*. Oxford, 1911.

Rosier, James. *A true relation of the most prosperous voyage made in this present yeere 1605, by Captaine George Waymouth*. London, 1605.

Ruddock, Alwyn A. "Columbus and Iceland." *Geographical Journal*, CXXXVI (1970).

—— "John Day of Bristol and the English voyages across the Atlantic before 1497." *Geographical Journal*, CXXXII (1966), 225–233.

—— "The reputation of Sebastian Cabot." *Bulletin of the Institute of Historical Research*, XLVII (1974), 94–98.

Ruídiaz y Caravia, Eugenio. *La Florida*. 2 vols. Madrid, 1893.

Sabin, Joseph [and others]. *Biblioteca Americana*. 29 vols. New York, 1868–1936.

Sacrobosco, Johannes de. *The Sphere of Sacrobosco and its Commentators*. Ed. and trans. Lynn Thorndike. Chicago, 1949.

Salysburye, Wyllyam. *The descripcion of the sphere or the frame of the worlde*. London, 1550. See Proclus.

Santa Cruz, Alonso de. *Islario general de todas las islas del mundo*. Ed. Antonio Blásquez. 2 vols. Madrid, 1918.

Sanz, Carlos. *Diario de Colón*. 2 vols. Madrid, 1962.

Schroder, Albert H. and Dan S. Matson. *A Colony on the Move. Gaspar Castaña de Sosa's Journal 1590–1591*. Santa Fe, 1965.

Scott, E. and A. E. Hudd, ed. and trans. *The Cabot Roll*. Bristol, 1897.

Seary, E. R. *Place Names of the Avalon Peninsula of the Island of Newfoundland*. St. John's and Toronto, 1971.

Seneca, Lucius Annaeus. *Seneca his tenne tragedies*. Trans. John Heywood and others. London, 1581.

—— *Quaestiones naturales*. Trans. John Clarke, in *Physical Science in the Time of Nero*. London, 1910.

Serrano y Sanz, Manuel. *Documentos históricos de la Florida y la Luisiana, siglos XVI al XVII*. Madrid, 1913.

Settle, Dionyse. *A true reporte of Capteine Frobisher his last voyage into the West and Northwest regions this present yere 1577*. London, 1577.

Shea, John Gilmary. *The Church in the Colonies, 1531–1763*. New York, 1886.

Shirley, John W., ed. *Thomas Harriot. Renaissance Scientist*. Oxford. 1974.

Slafter, Carlos, ed. *Sir Humfrey Gylberte*. Boston, Prince Soc., 1903.

Smith, John. *A true relation of such occurances and accidents of noate as hath hapned in Virginia since the first planting of that colony*. London, 1608.

———— *A map of Virginia.... Written by captaine Smith. Whereunto is annexed the proceedings of those colonies*. Oxford, Joseph Barnes, 1612.

———— *Description of New England*. London, 1616.

———— *The generall historie of Virginia*. London, 1624.

———— *Works*. Ed. E. Arber. Birmingham, 1884; reprinted 2 vols., with introduction by A. G. Bradley, London, 1910.

Smith, T. Buckingham. *Colección de varios documentos para la historia de la Florida*. I. London, 1857.

———— Trans. *A Letter of Hernando de Soto and Memoir of Hernando de Escalante Fontaneda*. Washington, D.C., 1854.

Solinus, Caius Julius. *The worthie worke of Julius Solinus polyhistor. Contayning many noble actions of humaine creatures*. Trans. Arthur Golding. London, 1587. In *The rare and singuler worke of Pomponius Mela*. London, T. Hacket, 1590.

Solís de Merás, Gonzalo. *Pedro Menéndez de Avilés. Memorial by Gonzalo Solís de Merás*. Trans. and ed. Jeanette T. Connor. Deland, Fla., 1923; reprinted Gainesville, Fla., 1965.

Soto, Hernando de. *Narratives of the Career of Hernando de Soto*. Ed. and trans. T. Buckingham Smith. New York, 1866.

———— *Narratives of the Career of Hernando de Soto*. Ed. E. G. Bourne. 2 vols. New York, 1904.

———— See also T. B. Smith above.

Spedding, J. *Letters and life of Francis Bacon*. 7 vols. London, 1868.

Stefani, F., ed. *I diarii di Marino Sanuto*. IV. Venice, 1880.

Stefansson, V. and E. McCaskill, eds. *The Three Voyages of Martin Frobisher*. 2 vols. London, 1938.

Stevenson, F. L., ed. *Marine World Chart 1502 (circa) by Nicolo de Canerio*. New York, 1907.

Stith, William. *The History of the First Discovery and Settlement of Virginia*. Williamsburg, 1747.

Stobnicza, Jan de. *Introductio in Ptholomei cosmographiam*. Cracow, 1512.

Storm, Gustav. *Islandske Annaler indtil 1578*. Christiana, 1888.

Strabo. *Geography*. Trans. Howard Leonard Jones. Cambridge, Mass., Loeb Classics, 1917.

Strachey, William. *For the colony in Virginea Britannia. Lawes divine morall and martial*. Ed. D. Flaherty. Charlottesville, 1969.

———— *The Historie of Travaile into Virginia Britannia*. Ed. R. H. Major. London, Hakluyt Soc., 1849.

———— *The Historie of Travell into Virginia Britania*. Ed. Louis B. Wright and Virginia Freund. London, Hakluyt Soc., 1953.

Swanton, John R. *Early History of the Creek Indians and their Neighbors*. (Smithsonian Institution, Bureau of American Ethnology, *Bulletin* 73. [1922].)

Taylor, Eva G. R. "Instructions to a colonial surveyor in 1582." *The Mariner's Mirror*, XXXVII (1951), 48–62.

———— "The missing draft project of Drake's voyage of 1577–80." *Geographical Journal*, LXXV (1930), 44–47.

———— ed. *The Original Writings and Correspondence of the two Richard Hakluyts*. 2 vols. London, Hakluyt Soc., 1935.

———— *Tudor Geography*. London, 1930.

Ternaux-Compans, Henri, ed. *Voyages, relations et mémoires originaux pour servir a l'histoire de la découverte de l'Amérique*. 20 vols. Paris, 1837–1840. Vol. XX. *Receuil des pièces sur la Floride*.

Thayer, Henry, ed. *The Sagadahoc Colony*. Portland, Me., Gorges Soc., 1892.

Thevet, André. *Les singularitez de la France Antarctique*. Paris, 1558.

———— *Cosmographie universelle*. Paris, 1573.

Thomas, A. H., and I. D. Thornley, eds. *The Great Chronicle of London*. London, 1938.

Thomson, J. Oliver. *History of Ancient Geography*. Cambridge, Eng., 1948.

Thwaites, Reuben G., ed. *Jesuit Relations and Allied Documents*. 73 vols. Cleveland, 1895–1901; reissued in 29 vols., New York, 1963.

Toribio Medina, J. *El veneciano Sebastián Caboto al servicio de España*. 2 vols. Santiago, Chile, 1908.

———— *Esteban Gómez, piloto portuguese en el servicio de España*. Santiago, Chile, 1908.

Torquemada, Juan de. *Monarquia Indiana*. Seville, 1615.

———— *Primera parte de los viente i un libros spirituales i monarchia Indiana, con el origen i guerras de los Indios Ocidentales, de sus poblaciones, descubrimientos, conquesta, conversión i otras marveillosas de la mesma tierra*. Brussels, 1723.

Trillmich, Werner, ed. *Quellen des 9. und 11. Jahrhunderts zur Geschischte de Hamburgischen Kirche*. Berlin, 1961.

Trudel, Marcel. *Histoire de la Nouvelle France*. I. Les Vaines Tentatives, 1624–1603. Montreal, 1959; II. Le Comptoir, 1603–1627. Montreal, 1965.

———— *The Beginnings of New France, 1524–1663*. Montreal, 1974.

A true and sincere declaration of the state of Virginia. See Virginia Company.

A true declaration of the estate of the colonie in Virginia. See Virginia Company.

Tyler, Victor. "A Spanish expedition to Chesapeake Bay in 1609." *American Neptune*, XVII (1957), 181–194.

United States De Soto Expedition Committee. *Final Report*. Washington, D.C., 1939.

Varagine. See Jacobus de Varagine.

Vigneras, Louis-André. "The cartographer Diogo Ribeiro." *Imago Mundi*, XVI (1962), 76–83.

———— "A Spanish discovery of North Carolina in 1566." *North Carolina Historical Review*, XLVI (1969), 398–415.

———— "El viaje de Estéban Gómez a Norte America." *Revista de Indias*, XVII (1957), supplement.

———— "The voyage of Estéban Gómez from Florida to the Baccalos." *Terrae Incognitae*, II (1970), 25–28.

———— "The voyages of Diogo and Manoel de Barcelos to Canada in the sixteenth century." *Terrae Incognitae*, V (1973), 61–64.

———— *The Discovery of South America and the Andalusian Voyages*. Chicago, 1976.

See also Columbus, Christopher.

Villegra, Gaspar Perez de. *El Capitan Gaspar de Vilagra para justificacion de las muertes, justicias, y castigos que el Adelantado don Juan de Oñate dizen que hizo en La Nueva Mexico*. [n.d., n.p., unique copy in John Carter Brown Library.]

———— *Servicios que a su Magestad la hecho el Capitán Gaspar de Villegra para que V.M. le haga merced*. [n.d., n.p., unique copy in John Carter Brown Library.]

———— *Historia de la Nueva Mexico*. Alcalá, 1610.

———— *The History of New Mexico*. Trans. Gilbert Espinosa. Los Angeles, 1933; reissued Chicago, 1962.

Virginia Company of London. *A true and sincere declaration of the purpose and ends of the plantation begun in Virginia. Sett forth by the authority of the governors and councellors established for that plantation*. London, 1609.

———— *A true declaration of the estate of the colonie in Virginia, with a confutation of such scandalous reports as have tended to the disgrace of so worthy an enterprise. Published by advise and direction of the councell of Virginia*. London, 1610.

Voisin, Lancelot, Seigneur de la Popellinière. *Les trois mondes*. Paris, 1582.

Wagner, Henry R. *Spanish Voyages to the North West Coast of America in the Sixteenth Century*. San Francisco, 1920; reissued Amsterdam, 1966.

Waldseemüller, Martin. *Cosmographiae introductio*. St-Dié, 1507–1508.

Ware, Henry, trans. "Letters of Pedro Menéndez de Avilés." *Massachusetts Historical Society Proceedings*, second series, VIII (1894), 416–468.

Waters, David W. *The Art of Navigation in England in Elizabethan and Early Stuart Times*. London, and New Haven, 1958.

Wenhold, Lucy L., trans. "Manrique de Rojas's report on French settlements in Florida, 1564." *Florida Historical Quarterly*, XXXVIII (1959), 45–62.

West, Thomas, Lord De La Warr. *The relation of the most honourable the Lord De-la-Warre, lord governour of the colonie, planted in Virginia*. London, 1611.

Weston, P. C. G. *Documents Connected with the History of South Carolina*. p.p., 1856.

Wheeler, G. M. *Report Upon the United States Geographical Surveys West of the One Hundredth Meridian*. VII. Washington, D.C., 1879.

Whitbourne, Richard. *A discourse and discovery of New-found-land*. London, 1620.

Williams, Roger. *A briefe discourse of warre.* London, 1590.

Williamson, James Alexander. *The Voyages of the Cabots and the Discovery of North America.* London, 1929.

—— *The Cabot Voyages and Bristol Discovery under Henry VII.* Cambridge, Eng., Hakluyt Soc., 1962.

Willys, Richard. *The history of travayle in the West and East Indies.* London, 1577.

Winsor, Justin. *Narrative and Critical History of America.* 8 vols. Cambridge, Mass., 1886–1889.

Winship, George P. "The Coronado expedition, 1540–1542." Smithsonian Institution, Bureau of American Ethnology, *Fourteenth Report,* pp. 329–637. Washington, D.C., 1896.

—— ed. *The Journey of Coronado.* New York, 1904.

Wolfenbüttel, Herzog August Bibliothek. *The New World in the Treasures of an old European Library.* Wolfenbüttel, 1976.

Worcestre, William. *Itineraries.* Ed. J. H. Harvey. Oxford, 1969.

Wright, Irene A., ed. *Documents Concerning English Voyages to the Spanish Main, 1569–1580.* London, Hakluyt Soc., 1932.

—— *The Early History of Cuba.* Havana, 1916.

—— ed. *Further English Voyages to Spanish America, 1583–1594.* London, Hakluyt Soc., 1951.

—— ed. *Spanish Documents Concerning English Voyages to the Caribbean, 1527–1568.* London, Hakluyt Soc., 1927.

—— "Spanish policy toward Virginia, 1606–1612." *American Historical Review.* XXV (1920).

Wroth, Lawrence C. *The Voyages of Giovanni da Verrazzano.* New Haven, 1970.

Wytfliet, Cornelis. *Descriptionis Ptolemaicae augmentum.* Louvain, 1597.

Zeno, Nicolò. *De i commentarii del viaggio in Persia di M. Caterino Zeno... Et dello scoprimento dell' Isole Frislanda, Eslanda, Engronelanda, Estotilanda, et Icaria, fatto... da due fratelli Zeni, M. Nicolò... e M. Antonio.* Venice, 1558.

Zubillaga, Félix. *La Florida. La misión Jesuitica 1560–1572 y la colonización Española.* Rome, 1941.

—— ed. *Monumenta antiquae Floridae, 1566–1572.* Rome, 1956.

PERMISSIONS

Acknowledgment of author and title for all extracts quoted from published works is given in the text and headnotes. However, the publishers would like to acknowledge permission in particular for the following (Numbers within parentheses refer to document numbers):

(806a) Fishmongers' Company, London; (806b,c) Grocers' Company, London; (631–633), (627), 634–635), (636), (637), (639), (640), (642), Middleton Manuscripts, Nottingham University Library; (458), (467), (468), (462), Hatfield House, Hatfield; (751), (752), (760), (763), (767), (769), (754), (758), (759), (772), (775), Audiencia de Santo Domingo, Archivo de Indias, Seville; (742), (724), (762), (328), (765), (768), (341), Indiferente General, Archivo de Indias, Seville (reproductions of many of the originals from the Manuscript Division, The Library of Congress); (764), (446), (766), (455), Archivo General, Simancas; (266) Cotton, (539), (569), (649), (401) Additional, (556b) Harleian, (362), (363), (364), (556a&c), (786), Lansdowne, British Library, Reference Division, London; extracts (342–344) University of North Carolina Press, Chapel Hill; extracts from the Hakluyt Society publications are used by permission of the Society; (565), (660), (528), (393), (542), (540), (541), (547), (564), (603), (472), (557), (561), (482), (367), (511), (386), (82), (657), (86), (90), (75), (84), (85b), (89), (91), (81), (55), (64), (77), (72), (819), (821), (676), (677), (502), (151), (385), (602), (530–531), (532), (583), (612), (615), (788–792), (794–796), (505–509), (471), (568), (610), (503), (607), (476), (470), (787), (793), (152), (150), (584), (613), (550), (471), (504), Public Record Office, London; extract (108) from *The Life of Admiral Christopher Columbus by his Son Ferdinand*, tr. and ed. by Benjamin Keen, Rutgers University Press; (643–646) "A Spanish Discovery of North Carolina in 1566", *North Carolina Historical Review*; (814) The Huntington Library, San Marino, California; (443) University of North Carolina Library, Chapel Hill; (322) The Pierpont Morgan Library, New York; (235, 246, 354, 851) John Carter Brown Library, Providence; (641) Lambeth Palace Library, London; (423), (493), (617) Exeter Public Library, Exeter; (693), (687) Public Archives of Canada, Ottawa; (502) Research Library, Colonial Williamsburg; (201) in L. C. Wroth, *The Voyages of Giovanni da Verrazzano*, tr. by Susan Tarrow; (294), (295) Buckingham Smith Papers, New York Historical Society, New York; (13) Le Strange, E. J. Brill, Leiden; (11) Princeton University Press; (19) Columbia University Press, New York; (16) University of Wisconsin, Madison; (403—411) Toronto University Press; (301) *Florida Historical Quarterly*, Gainesville; (236) courtesy of Gerald Theisen; (183), (317), (326) The University Presses of Florida, Gainesville; (318), (320), (323), (324) Princeton University Library; (242, 674–677) University of Texas Press, Austin; (1), (2), (4) Harvard University Press, Cambridge; (135) Cambridge University Press, New York; (5) New York Public Library; extracts from H. P. Biggar and W. L. Grant, eds., *The History of New France* by Marc Lescarbot, and H. P. Biggar, ed., *The Works of Champlain*, by permission of The Champlain Society, Toronto; extracts from G. P. Hammond and A. Rey, *Rediscovery of New Mexico* and *Oñate: Colonizer of New Mexico*, University of New Mexico Press, Albuquerque; (495), (520), (620–623) Devon Record Office, (West Devon Area), Plymouth City Archives, Plymouth, England; extracts (22–23) from Gwyn Jones, ed., *The Norse Atlantic Saga*, Oxford University Press, Oxford, England; (14) The University of Chicago Press; (597) Sweet & Maxwell Ltd., London; (624a), (624b), (624c), (624d), (624f), (624g), (625) Southampton City Record Office, Southampton, England; (15) The University of Pennsylvania Press, Philadelphia; (366) Cambridge University Library, Cambridge, England; (425) Chester City Record Office, Chester, England; (357) Westminster Abbey Library, London; (751) Weymouth and Portland Museum of Local History, Weymouth, England; (601) The College of Arms, London; (618) London Record Society, London; (12) the Gibb Memorial Trust, Cambridge, England; (108) Clarkson N. Potter, Inc., New York; (466) Tracy McGregor Library, University of Virginia, Charlottesville (761) University of Miami, Coral Gables.

The editor and publisher thank the following institutions for permission to reproduce the maps in these volumes. Maps are listed by plate number. Bibliothèque Nationale, Paris: 1, 13, 21, 56, 85; James Ford Bell Library, University of Minnesota, Minneapolis: 5, 28; Biblioteca Marciana, Venice: 6, 10; British Library, London: 2, 8, 26, 53, 54, 76, 89, 106, 124, 136, 143; British Museum, London: 66, 67, 94, 96; Biblioteca Nazionale Centrale, Florence: 9, 12; Beinecke Library, Yale University, New Haven: 14; Rand McNally Company, New York: 16; Museo Naval, Madrid: 18, 79; Biblioteca Estense, Modena: 19, 20; Library of Congress, Washington: 25, 30, 36, 88 (Lessing Rosenwald Collection), 91, 106, 147; Bayerische Staatsbibliothek, Munich: 24; Biblioteca e Musei Oliveriani, Pesaro: 23; Huntington Library, San Marino, California: 22, 57; Wolfegg Castle, Germany: 29; Herzog August Bibliothek, Wolfenbüttel: 37; Academia das Cienzias, Lisbon: 39, 77; Archivo General de Indias, Seville: 40, 71; The Hispanic Society of America, New York: 42; Bibliotheca Apostolica Vaticana, Rome: 44, 47; Archivo Marchesi

Castiglioni, Mantua: 45; Biblioteca Mediceo-Laurenziana, Florence: 46; Biblioteca Nacional, Madrid: 49, 50, 122, 144; John Rylands University Library, Manchester: 55, 113; The Pierpont Morgan Library, New York: 58, National Maritime Museum, London: 60; Ministère des Armées, Paris: 61, 75; Newberry Library, Chicago: 62; John Carter Brown Library, Brown University, Providence: 72, 73; Archivo Histórico Nacional, Madrid: 84; The Free Library of Philadelphia, William M Elkins Collection: 90; Public Record Office, London: 93; Paul Mellon Collection, Upperville, Virginia: 97; Archivo General de Simancas: 107, 108, 137, 140; Maritiem Museum 'Prins Hendrick,' Rotterdam: 112; Österreichische Nationalbibliothek, Vienna: 115; Humanities Research Center Library, University of Texas, Austin: 138; New York Public Library, I. N. Phelps Stokes Collection, New York: 139; Collection of the Duke of Northumberland, Alnwick Castle, Northumberland: 145; Alegemeen Rijksarchief, The Hague: 110, 111.

INDEX

Plate numbers (pl.) follow page numbers and refer to both plates and map notes.

Seloy, Fla., blockhouse, II: 532

Selva di Lauri, Atlantic coast, I: 282

Sellman, Edward, IV: 182

Seneca (Lucius Annaeus), I: 6, 8; *Medea*, I: 8; *Quaestiones naturales*, I: 8, 23, 24, 28, 77

Senissas I., Calif., V: 427

Sequanus, Johannes Metellus, III: 94–5

Sequotan (Secoton), Indian settlement, N.C., III: 280, 286, 295, 317, 318

Serrano y Sanz, Manuel, II: 16

Settle, Dionyse, IV: 180, 182; *True report... of Frobisher* (1577), I: lxxii; IV: 182, 207–16

Seven Cities, country of the, IV: pl. *133*

Seven Cities (Antilia), Island of the, I: lv, lxxxi, 3, 74, 83, 84, 86, 96, 101, pl. *13;* alleged discovery, I: 74, 75, 77, 78, 132, 145

Seville, Spain, I: 162, 179, 231, 254, 355; Archivo de Indias, I: lvii, lxi–lxii, lxiii; V: xviii; 438; Archivo de Protocolos, I: lix; *Perularia*, I: 162; pilots' school, III: 99; *see also* Casa de Contratación

Seymour, Edward, III: 455, 462

Seymour, Peter, with Drake (1585), III: 308

Setola, II: 592

Sgrooten, Christian, map (1592), IV: pl. *122;* V: pl. 144

Shawakatoc River, Me., III: 421, 423–4

Shea, John Gilmary, I: 254; II: 201; III: 364

Sheep, Island of, Atlantic Oc., I: 16, 56, 57

Shelley, William, III: 216, 217

Sheyfue, Johan, I: 219–20

Ships: equipment, fittings, IV: 193–200; navigation instruments, IV: 197; ordnance, I: 192, 196, 197, 199, 203, 205, 281; IV: 194–5; trade goods, I: 192, 194, 201; victualing, I: 162, 163, 192, 256, 281; IV: 195–6; *see also* Navigation

Aid (1577), IV: 208

Amitie (1590), III: 339

Anne Ager (Aucher) (1578), III: 190, 211

Anne Francis (1578), IV: 222

Anne Stucley (1563), II: 285

Archangel (1584), IV: 109–11

Archangel (1605), III: 363

Armenell (1578), IV: 223

Asunción (1605), V: 108, 112

Asunción (1609), V: 142

A Vera Cruz (1568), IV: 183, 184

Barbara (1517), I: 161, 162, 164, 166, 167, 168

Barke Bonner (1585), III: 305

Bark Dennye (1587), III: 190, 191, 199

Barke Dionyse (1578), IV: 221, 224

Bark Ralegh (1583), III: 182, 276; IV: 23, 29

Bark Talbot (1584), IV: 113

Bark Young (1590), IV: 53, 54

Beare (1578), IV: 208

Blessing (1609), V: 252, 286

Bonaventure (1591), IV: 56, 58, 60–1

Bonaventure (1597), IV: 120

Brave (1588), III: 323

Bravosa de isla de Ré (La Brave de l'Ile de Ré) (1555), IV: 96

Bravosa de San Pau de Leon (La Brave de Saint-Pol de Léon) (1555), IV: 96

Breton (1565), II: 344

Bretona (1526), I: 260

Bretona (1555), IV: 96

Buen Jesus (1590), III: 331

Busse (1578), IV: 222, 224

Capitanía (flagship) (1565), II: 410, 422

Castor and Pollux (1605), I: lviii; V: 103, 108–27, 161; inventory, V: 124–6

ships (cont.)

Catalina (1597), IV: 78

Catherine de St. Vincent (1591), IV: 56, 61

Chancewell (1597), IV: 67, 68

Charles (1591), IV: 58

Chorruca (1526), I: 260, 263

Christophe (1533), IV: 91

Clemence (1603), IV: 125

Conclude (1590), III: 331

Concord (1602), III: 345–6, 348

Concord (1611), V: 302

Consent (1611), IV: 147

Consolación (1513), I: 233

Cuba de Bayona (1555), IV: 97

Dainty (1590), III: 339

Dauphin (1524), I: 281–9

David (1595), IV: 119

Delight (1583), III: 40–1, 182, 246; IV: 23, 29, 35; wrecked, IV: 37–8, 42–4

Deliverance (1610), V: 293

Diamond (1609), V: 286

Discoverer (1603), III: 359

Discovery (1602), IV: 255, 256

Discovery (1610), III: 469; IV: xxii, 254, 277, 293; V: 188, 197, 293, 296, 307–8, 349

Dominus Vobiscum (recte *William*) (1527), I: 191

Dorothy (1585), III: 276, 283

Eagle (1590), III: 339

Edward Bonaventure (1554), I: 225–6

Edward Bonaventure (1590), III: 339

Elephant (1578), III: 190, 191, 203–4

Elizabeth (1585), III: 283

Elizabeth (1587), IV: 247

Elizabeth (1603), V: 161, 163

Elizabeth Bonaventure (1585), III: 306

Epaule de Mouton (1564), II: 380

Esperanza (1565), II: 429

Espíritu Santo (1565), II: 429

Falcon (1578), III: 181, 190, 199, 204, 209–10

Falcon (1609), V: 252, 286

Faulcon (1564), II: 361

Foresight (1590), III: 339

Fortune Stuckley (1563), II: 285

Francis (1585), III: 305

Francis of Foy (1578), IV: 222, 223

Gabriel (1576), IV: 201, 208, 222, 224, 226; fitting out of, IV: 193–200

Gabriell (1502), I: 109, 100, 117

Galiote (1565), II: 344

Gallion (1578), III: 191

George (1481), I: 92

George (1600), IV: 124

Gift of God (1607), III: 425, 427, 429, 432, 442, 445–54, 455

Godspeed (1602), IV: 255, 256

Godspeed (1606), V: 197

Golden Hind (1579), I: 462, 477; V: 360

Golden Hind (1583—Hayes), III: 34, 40–1, 182; IV: 23, 29, 35, 38

Golden Lion (1585), IV: 47

Golden Royal (1585), IV: 47, 49–50

Good Companion (1585), IV: 47

Grace (1594), IV: 64–5

Grace de Dieu (1611), IV: 387

Gran Fatasia de San Brin (La Grande-Fantaisie de Saint-Brieuc) (1555), IV: 97

Gran Francesa de San Malo (La Grande-Françoise de Saint-Malo) (1555), IV: 97

Grande Gatera (1555), IV: 98

66 711